World History
JOURNEY ACROSS TIME

Jackson J. Spielvogel, Ph.D.

NATIONAL
GEOGRAPHIC

 Glencoe

New York, New York   Columbus, Ohio   Chicago, Illinois   Peoria, Illinois   Woodland Hills, California

Authors

Jackson J. Spielvogel is associate professor emeritus of history at the Pennsylvania State University. He received his Ph.D. from The Ohio State University, where he specialized in Reformation history under Harold J. Grimm. His articles and reviews have been published in several scholarly publications. He is co-author (with William Duiker) of *World History,* published in 1994 (4th edition, 2003). Professor Spielvogel has won five major university-wide awards, and in 1997, he became the first winner of the Schreyer Institute's Student Choice Award for innovative and inspiring teaching.

The National Geographic Society, founded in 1888 for the increase and diffusion of geographic knowledge, is the world's largest nonprofit scientific and educational organization. Since its earliest days, the Society has used sophisticated communication technologies, from color photography to holography, to convey geographic knowledge to a worldwide membership. The Education Products Division supports the Society's mission by developing innovative educational programs—ranging from traditional print materials to multimedia programs including CD-ROMs, videodiscs, and software.

Contributing Authors

Stephen F. Cunha, Ph.D.
Professor of Geography
Director, California Geographic Alliance
Humboldt State University
Arcata, California

Douglas Fisher, Ph.D.
Professor
San Diego State University
San Diego, California

Nancy Frey, Ph.D.
Assistant Professor
San Diego State University
San Diego, California

Robin C. Scarcella, Ph.D.
Professor and Director
Academic English/ESL
University of California, Irvine
Irvine, California

Emily M. Schell, Ed.D.
Visiting Professor, San Diego State University
Social Studies Education Director
SDSU City Heights Educational Collaborative
San Diego, California

David Vigilante
Associate Director
National Center for History in the Schools
San Diego, California

About the cover: Throughout history, people around the world have channeled, spanned, and sailed upon one of Earth's greatest resources—its water reserves. Top: the great Pont du Gard aqueduct built in France by ancient Romans; middle right, the Tower Bridge, London, spanning the Thames; bottom left, a Chinese junk sailing in Hong Kong Harbor.

 **Glencoe**

The McGraw-Hill Companies

Send all inquiries to:
Glencoe/McGraw-Hill
8787 Orion Place
Columbus, OH 43240-4027

ISBN: 0-07-868873-6

Printed in the United States of America.

4 5 6 7 8 9 10   071/055   09 08 07 06 05

Consultants & Reviewers

Academic Consultants

Winthrop Lindsay Adams
Associate Professor of History
University of Utah
Salt Lake City, Utah

Sari J. Bennett
Director, Center for Geographic Education
University of Maryland Baltimore County
Baltimore, Maryland

Richard G. Boehm
Jesse H. Jones Distinguished Chair in
   Geographic Education
Texas State University
San Marcos, Texas

Sheilah Clarke-Ekong
Associate Professor of Anthropology and
   Interim Dean
Evening College
University of Missouri, St. Louis
St. Louis, Missouri

Timothy E. Gregory
Professor of History
The Ohio State University
Columbus, Ohio

Robert E. Herzstein
Department of History
University of South Carolina
Columbia, South Carolina

Kenji Oshiro
Professor of Geography
Wright State University
Dayton, Ohio

Joseph R. Rosenbloom
Adjunct Professor, Jewish and Near
   Eastern Studies
Washington University
St. Louis, Missouri

FOLDABLES **Dinah Zike**
Educational Consultant
Dinah-Might Activities, Inc.
San Antonio, Texas

Reading Consultants

Maureen D. Danner
Project CRISS
National Training Consultant
Kalispell, Montana

ReLeah Cossett Lent
Florida Literacy and Reading Excellence
   Project Coordinator
University of Central Florida
Orlando, Florida

Steve Qunell
Social Studies Instructor
Montana Academy
Kalispell, Montana

Carol M. Santa Ph.D.
CRISS: Project Developer
Director of Education
Montana Academy
Kalispell, Montana

Bonnie Valdes
Master CRISS Trainer
Project CRISS
Largo, Florida

Teacher Reviewers

Destin L. Haas
Social Studies Teacher
Benton Central Junior-Senior High School
Oxford, Indiana

Anna Marie Lawrence
Social Studies Teacher
Snellville Middle School
Snellville, Georgia

Richard Meegan
Social Studies Department Chair
Masconomet Regional School District
Topsfield, Massachusetts

J. Keith Miller
Social Studies Teacher
Bragg Middle School
Gardendale, Alabama

Beth Neighbors
Social Studies Teacher
Pizitz Middle School
Vestavia Hills, Alabama

Virgina Parra
Social Studies Teacher
Osceola Middle School
Ocala, Florida

Susan Pearson
Social Studies Teacher
The Academy for Science and
   Foreign Languages
Huntsville, Alabama

Nancy Perkins
Social Studies Implementer 1–12
Bonny Eagle Middle School
Buxton, Maine

Beverly Prestage
Social Studies Program Supervisor
Cranston High School West
Cranston, Rhode Island

Julie A. Scott
Social Studies Teacher
East Valley Middle School
Spokane, Washington

Larry W. Smith
Heritage Education Teacher
Massie Heritage Interpretation Center
Savannah, Georgia

Jerry A. Taylor
Social Studies Teacher
Towns County Comprehensive School
Hiawassee, Georgia

Contents

▼ Ancient Assyrian soldiers

◀ Ancient Egyptian artwork of a funeral boat

The Ancient World 108

Early Civilizations 1

Contents

Tang dynasty bottle ▶

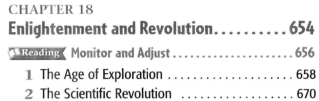

◄ Anasazi jewelry

Unit 5

A Changing World 564

Figure of Mayan ► leader

◄ The Alhambra

Contents

▲ Stalin, Roosevelt, and Churchill at the Tehran Conference

Features

Primary Source

Features

Biography

◀ Albert Einstein

Queen Elizabeth I ▶

Features

Linking Past & Present

SkillBuilder Handbook

NATIONAL GEOGRAPHIC HISTORY MAKERS

You Decide . . .

Primary Source Quotes

Ed. = Editor	Tr. = Translator	V = Volume

Primary Source Quotes

Primary Source Quotes

Maps, Charts, Graphs, and Diagrams

National Geographic Maps

NATIONAL GEOGRAPHIC Reference Atlas

NATIONAL GEOGRAPHIC Geography Handbook GH1

Unit 1

Unit 2

Unit 3

Unit 4

Maps, Charts, Graphs, and Diagrams

Unit 5

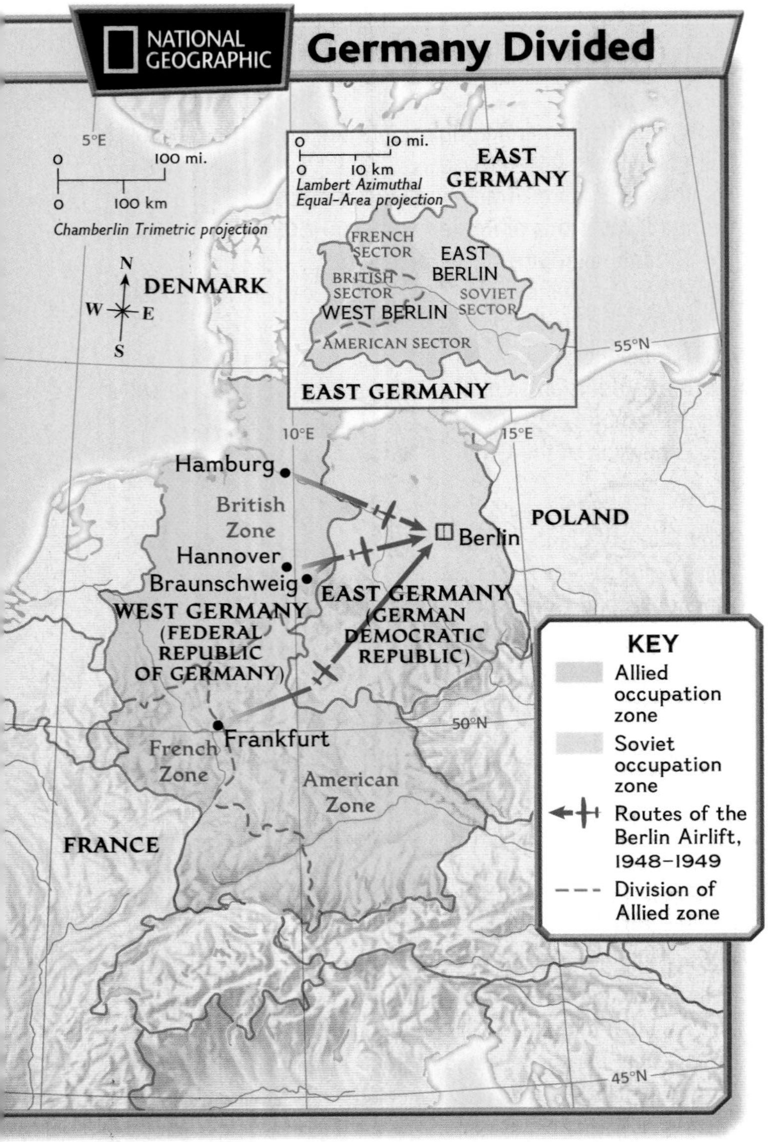

NATIONAL GEOGRAPHIC
Germany Divided
5°E
0 100 mi.
0 100 km
Chamberlin Trimetric projection
N
W E
S
DENMARK
0 10 mi.
0 10 km
Lambert Azimuthal Equal-Area projection
EAST GERMANY
FRENCH SECTOR
EAST BERLIN
BRITISH SECTOR
SOVIET SECTOR
WEST BERLIN
AMERICAN SECTOR
EAST GERMANY
55°N
10°E
15°E
Hamburg
British Zone
Hannover
Braunschweig
Berlin
POLAND
WEST GERMANY (FEDERAL REPUBLIC OF GERMANY)
EAST GERMANY (GERMAN DEMOCRATIC REPUBLIC)
Frankfurt
50°N
French Zone
American Zone
FRANCE
45°N
KEY
Allied occupation zone
Soviet occupation zone
Routes of the Berlin Airlift, 1948–1949
Division of Allied zone

Unit 6

Charts and Graphs

Diagrams

Be an Active Reader

Think about your textbook as a tool that helps you learn more about the world around you. It is an example of nonfiction writing—it describes real-life events, people, ideas, and places. Here is a menu of reading strategies that will help you become a better textbook reader. As you come to passages in your textbook that you do not understand, refer to these reading strategies for help.

1 Before You Read

Set a Purpose
- Why are you reading the textbook?
- How does the subject relate to your life?
- How might you be able to use what you learn in your own life?

Preview
- Read the chapter title to find what the topic will be.
- Read the subtitles to see what you will learn about the topic.
- Skim the photos, charts, graphs, or maps. How do they support the topic?
- Look for vocabulary words that are boldfaced. How are they defined?

Draw From Your Own Background
- What have you read or heard concerning new information on the topic?
- How is the new information different from what you already know?
- How will the information that you already know help you understand the new information?

2 As You Read

Question

- What is the main idea?
- How do the photos, charts, graphs, and maps support the main idea?

Connect

- Think about people, places, and events in your own life. Are there any similarities with those in your textbook?
- Can you relate the textbook information to other areas of your life?

Predict

- Predict events or outcomes by using clues and information that you already know.
- Change your predictions as you read and gather new information.

Visualize

- Pay careful attention to details and descriptions.
- Create graphic organizers to show relationships that you find in the information.

Look for Clues As You Read

Comparison and Contrast Sentences

- Look for clue words and phrases that signal comparison, such as *similarly, just as, both, in common, also,* and *too.*
- Look for clue words and phrases that signal contrast, such as *on the other hand, in contrast to, however, different, instead of, rather than, but,* and *unlike.*

Cause-and-Effect Sentences

- Look for clue words and phrases such as *because, as a result, therefore, that is why, since, so, for this reason,* and *consequently.*

Chronological Sentences

- Look for clue words and phrases such as *after, before, first, next, last, during, finally, earlier, later, since,* and *then.*

3 After You Read

Summarize

- Describe the main idea and how the details support it.
- Use your own words to explain what you have read.

Assess

- What was the main idea?
- Did the text clearly support the main idea?
- Did you learn anything new from the material?
- Can you use this new information in other school subjects or at home?
- What other sources could you use to find more information about the topic?

Previewing Your Textbook

Follow the reading road map through the next few pages to learn about using your textbook. Knowing how your text is organized will help you discover interesting events, fascinating people, and faraway places.

Units

Your textbook is divided into units. Each unit begins with four pages of information to help you begin your study of the topics.

WHY IT'S IMPORTANT

Each unit begins with a **preview** of important events and *Why It's Important* to read about them.

TIME LINE

A time line shows you **when** the events in this unit happened. It also compares events and people from different places.

MAP

This map shows you where the events in this unit happened.

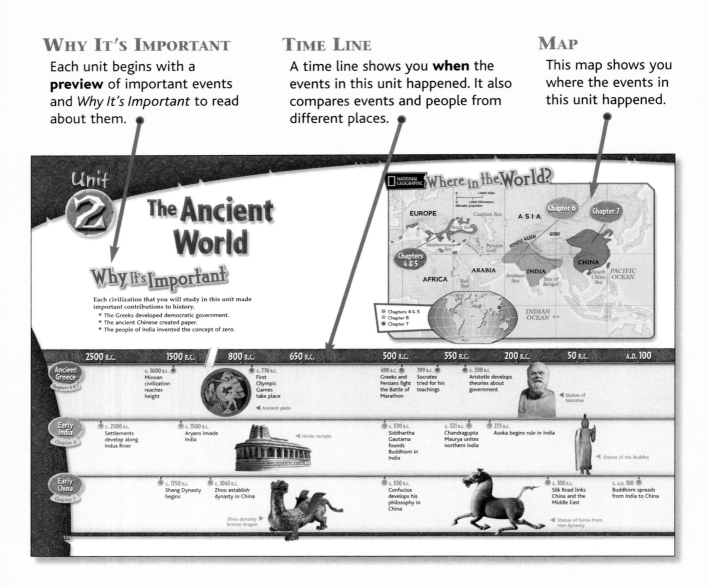

Chapters

Each unit of *Journey Across Time* is divided into chapters. Each chapter starts by giving you some background information about what you will be reading.

CHAPTER TITLE

The chapter title tells you the **main topic** you will be reading about.

CHAPTER PREVIEW

The **preview** describes what you will be reading about in this chapter.

HISTORY ONLINE

This tells you where you can go **online** for more information.

WHEN AND WHERE?

Here you can see **when** and **where** events in this chapter happened.

SUMMARIES

Summary statements give you the **main idea** in each section.

FOLDABLES™

Use the *Foldables* to **take notes** as you read.

Previewing Your Textbook

Chapter Reading Skill

Because reading about Social Studies is different than reading a novel or magazine, every chapter offers help with reading skills.

READING STRATEGY

This shows you what *Reading Skill* you will be learning about—**making connections.**

PRACTICE IT!

Next comes an easy-to-follow **practice** activity.

WRITING

Writing about what you read will help you remember the event.

Chapter 4 Reading Social Studies

Reading Skill
Making Connections

1 Learn It!
Use What You Know

Unlock meaning by making a connection between what you read and what you already know. Your own experiences can help you understand words or ideas that are unfamiliar. Read the paragraph below. Make a connection between a Greek **agora** and a place that is familiar to you.

Do you know what an **agora** looks like?

> Below the acropolis was an open area called an agora (A·guh·ruh). This space had two functions: it was both a **market** and a place where people could meet and debate issues.
>
> — *from page 122*

You know what a *market* looks like. Can you also visualize *a place where people could meet*? If so, then you have a good idea of what an agora might look like.

Reading Tip

Try to create a picture in your mind as you read. Imagine a mini-movie as you "see" what the author is describing.

114

2 Practice It!
Making the Connection

Read the following paragraph from Chapter 4. What ideas can you connect to your own experiences? Use the questions below to help you begin a class discussion about things in your life that relate to life in ancient Greece.

> At age 20, Spartan men entered the regular army. The men remained in military barracks for 10 more years. They ate all their meals in dining halls with other soldiers. A typical meal was a vile-tasting dish called black broth—pork boiled in animal blood, salt, and vinegar.
>
> Spartans returned home at age 30 but stayed in the army until age 60. They continued to train for combat. They expected to either win on the battlefield or die, but never to surrender. One Spartan mother ordered her son to "Come home carrying your shield or being carried on it."
>
> — *from pages 126–127*

Read to Write
Choose one of the connections from your discussion. Write a paragraph to explain why you made such a connection. Use vivid details.

- Do you have any family members or friends who are 20 years old? What would they say if they were required to serve in the army for 40 years?
- Have you ever seen or tasted food that looks like "black broth"?

3 Apply It!
As you read the chapter, choose five words or phrases that make a connection to something you already know.

115

READING TIP

This **Reading Tip** tells you more about making connections.

APPLY IT!

Here is an opportunity to **apply** what you have learned.

Sections

A Section is a division, or part, of the chapter. The first page of the Section, the Section Opener, helps you set a purpose for reading.

GET READY TO READ!

Read the **connection** between what you already know and what you are about to read.

MAPS

Maps help you learn how **geography** and history are related.

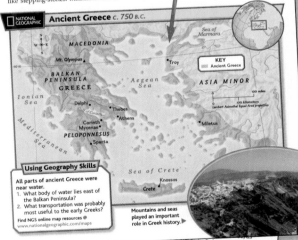

Section 1

The Early Greeks

Get Ready to Read!

What's the Connection?
In Chapters 1 and 2, you learned about Mesopotamia and Egypt. These civilizations grew up in great river valleys with rich soil. Greece had no great river valleys. Instead, it had mountains, rocky soil, and many miles of seacoasts.

Focusing on the Main Ideas
- The geography of Greece influenced where people settled and what they did. *(page 117)*
- The Minoans earned their living by building ships and trading. *(page 118)*
- Mycenaeans built the first Greek kingdoms and spread their power across the Mediterranean region. *(page 119)*
- Colonies and trade spread Greek culture and spurred industry. *(page 121)*
- The idea of citizenship developed in Greek city-states. *(page 122)*

Locating Places
Crete (KREET)
Mycenae (my•SEE•nee)
Peloponnesus (PEH•luh•puh•NEE•suhs)

Meeting People
Agamemnon (A•guh•MEHM•nahn)

Building Your Vocabulary
peninsula (puh•NIHN•suh•luh)
colony (KAH•luh•nee)
polis (PAH•luhs)
agora (A•guh•ruh)

Reading Strategy
Finding Details Draw a diagram like the one below. In each oval write one detail about a polis.

polis

NATIONAL GEOGRAPHIC When & Where?

GREECE
Mycenae
Crete — Knossos

2000 B.C.	1250 B.C.	500 B.C.
c. 2000 B.C. Minoans control eastern Mediterranean	c. 1200 B.C. Mycenaean civilization declines	c. 750 B.C. Greece's Dark Age comes to an end

116   CHAPTER 4   The Ancient Greeks

The Geography of Greece

Main Idea The geography of Greece influenced where people settled and what they did.

Reading Focus Do you rake leaves in the fall? Do you walk uphill to school? Your answers explain how geography shapes your life. Read to learn how geography shaped life in early Greece.

If you fly over Greece today, you will see a mountainous land framed by sparkling blue water. To the west is the Ionian (eye•OH•nee•uhn) Sea, to the south is the Mediterranean Sea, and to the east is the Aegean (ih•JEE•uhn) Sea. Hundreds of islands lie offshore, stretching across to Asia like stepping-stones. Mainland Greece is a

peninsula (puh•NIHN•suh•luh)—a body of land with water on three sides.

Many ancient Greeks made a living from the sea. They became fishers, sailors, and traders. Others settled in farming communities. Greece's mountains and rocky soil were not ideal for growing crops. However, the climate was mild, and in some places people could grow wheat, barley, olives, and grapes. They also raised sheep and goats.

Ancient Greeks felt deep ties to the land, but the mountains and seas divided them from one another. As a result, early Greek communities grew up fiercely independent.

Reading Check Cause and Effect How did geography discourage Greek unity?

NATIONAL GEOGRAPHIC
Ancient Greece c. 750 B.C.

MACEDONIA
Mt. Olympus
BALKAN PENINSULA
GREECE
Ionian Sea
Delphi
Gulf of Corinth
Corinth
Mycenae
Thebes
Athens
Sparta
PELOPONNESUS
Mediterranean Sea
Aegean Sea
Troy
ASIA MINOR
Miletus
Sea of Marmara
Sea of Crete
Knossos
Crete
KEY
Ancient Greece

Using Geography Skills
All parts of ancient Greece were near water.
1. What body of water lies east of the Balkan Peninsula?
2. What transportation was probably most useful to the early Greeks?
Find NGS online map resources @ www.nationalgeographic.com/maps

Mountains and seas played an important role in Greek history.

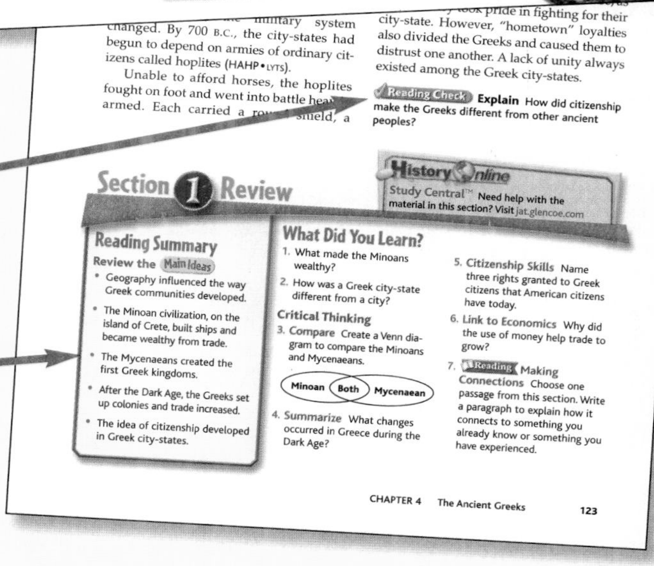

...changed. By 700 B.C., the city-states had begun to depend on armies of ordinary citizens called hoplites (HAHP•LYTS).

Unable to afford horses, the hoplites fought on foot and went into battle heavily armed. Each carried a round shield, a...

...took pride in fighting for their city-state. However, "hometown" loyalties also divided the Greeks and caused them to distrust one another. A lack of unity always existed among the Greek city-states.

Reading Check Explain How did citizenship make the Greeks different from other ancient peoples?

Section 1 Review

Reading Summary
Review the Main Ideas
- Geography influenced the way Greek communities developed.
- The Minoan civilization, on the island of Crete, built ships and became wealthy from trade.
- The Mycenaeans created the first Greek kingdoms.
- After the Dark Age, the Greeks set up colonies and trade increased.
- The idea of citizenship developed in Greek city-states.

What Did You Learn?
1. What made the Minoans wealthy?
2. How was a Greek city-state different from a city?

Critical Thinking
3. Compare Create a Venn diagram to compare the Minoans and Mycenaeans.

Minoan — Both — Mycenaean

4. Summarize What changes occurred in Greece during the Dark Age?

5. Citizenship Skills Name three rights granted to Greek citizens that American citizens have today.
6. Link to Economics Why did the use of money help trade to grow?
7. Reading Making Connections Choose one passage from this section. Write a paragraph to explain how it connects to something you already know or something you have experienced.

History Online
Study Central™ Need help with the material in this section? Visit jat.glencoe.com

CHAPTER 4   The Ancient Greeks   123

MAIN IDEAS

Preview the **main ideas** in each section.

READING CHECK

This is a **self-check** to see if you understand the main ideas.

SECTION REVIEW

Review the main ideas and answer the questions.

Previewing Your Textbook

Special Features

Look for special features that help history come alive.

YOU DECIDE . . .
Imagine you were there and could give your **opinion.**

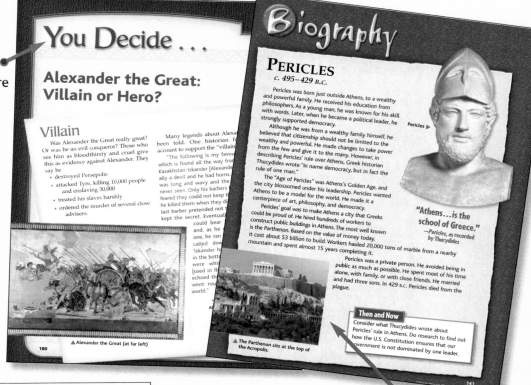

You Decide . . .

Alexander the Great: Villain or Hero?

Villain

Was Alexander the Great really great? Or was he an evil conqueror? Those who see him as bloodthirsty and cruel give this as evidence against Alexander. They say he

- destroyed Persepolis
- attacked Tyre, killing 10,000 people and enslaving 30,000
- treated his slaves harshly
- ordered the murder of several close advisers.

Many legends about Alexa... been told. One historian f... account to support the "villain...

"The following is my favou... which is found all the way fro... Kazakhstan: Iskander [Alexande... ally a devil and he had horns... was long and wavy and the... never seen. Only his barbers... feared they could not keep th... he killed them when they di... last barber pretended not t... kept the secret. Eventuall... could bear... and, as he... one, he ran... called dow... 'Iskander h... in the bott... were whi... [used in fl... echoed th... went rou... world."

▲ Alexander the Great (at far left)

180

Biography

PERICLES
c. 495–429 B.C.

Pericles was born just outside Athens, to a wealthy and powerful family. He received his education from philosophers. As a young man, he was known for his skill with words. Later, when he became a political leader, he strongly supported democracy.

Although he was from a wealthy family himself, he believed that citizenship should not be limited to the wealthy and powerful. He made changes to take power from the few and give it to the many. However, in describing Pericles' rule over Athens, Greek historian Thucydides wrote "In name democracy, but in fact the rule of one man."

The "Age of Pericles" was Athens's Golden Age, and the city blossomed under his leadership. Pericles wanted Athens to be a model for the world. He made it a centerpiece of art, philosophy, and democracy.

Pericles' goal was to make Athens a city that Greeks could be proud of. He hired hundreds of workers to construct public buildings in Athens. The most well known is the Parthenon. Based on the value of money today, it cost about $3 billion to build. Workers hauled 20,000 tons of marble from a nearby mountain and spent almost 15 years completing it.

Pericles was a private person. He avoided being in public as much as possible. He spent most of his time alone, with family, or with close friends. He married and had three sons. In 429 B.C. Pericles died from the plague.

Pericles ▶

"Athens…is the school of Greece."
—Pericles, as recorded by Thucydides

Then and Now
Consider what Thucydides wrote about Pericles' rule in Athens. Do research to find out how the U.S. Constitution ensures that our government is not dominated by one leader.

▲ The Parthenon sits at the top of the Acropolis.

141

BIOGRAPHY
Read more about famous **people.**

Greek Drama

Main Idea Greek drama still shapes entertainment today.

Reading Focus Think about your favorite movie. How would you describe it? Is it a tragedy? Is it a comedy? Read to find out how Greek plays still influence our entertainment.

What is **drama** (DRAH•muh)? Drama is a story told by actors who pretend to be characters in the story. In a drama, actors speak, show emotion, and imitate the actions of the characters they represent.

Today's movies, plays, and television shows are all examples of drama.

Tragedies and Comedies The Greeks performed plays in outdoor theaters as part of their religious festivals. They developed two kinds of dramas—comedies and tragedies.

In a **tragedy** (TRA•juh•dee), a person struggles to overcome difficulties but fails. As a result, the story has an unhappy ending. Early Greek tragedies presented people in a struggle against their fate. Later Greek tragedies showed how a person's character flaws caused him or her to fail.

Linking Past & Present
The Theater

THEN Tragedies and comedies were staged at a theater on the slopes of the Acropolis in Athens. The plays included music and dance. Greek actors wore costumes and held large masks. The masks told the audience who the actor was supposed to be—a king, a soldier, or a god. All the actors were men, even those playing female parts.

▼ A modern-day play

NOW Actors today include both men and women—and even children and animals. Special effects and makeup have replaced handheld masks. Music in modern theater is sometimes just as important as the actors' words. *If you watched a Greek play, what might it tell you about life in ancient Greece?*

▲ Ruins of a Greek theater

160   CHAPTER 5 Greek Civilization

The Way It Was
Focus on Everyday Life

Women's Duties In ancient Athens, a woman's place was in the home. Her two main responsibilities were caring for the household and raising children. The Greek writer Xenophon (ZEH•nuh•fuhn) recorded a man's explanation of women's duties.

"Your duty will be to remain indoors and send out those servants whose work is outside, and supervise those who are to work indoors … and take care that the sum laid by for a year be not spent in a month. And when wool is brought to you, you must see that cloaks are made for those who want them. You must see that the dry corn is in good condition for making food."

—Xenophon, Memorabilia and Oeconomicus

...each home was the women's quarters. An Athenian woman lived there with her children. She was expected to keep her children well and happy. She encouraged them to learn sports and play with toys, and taught them how to interact with friends and family members. Although boys left home at age seven to attend school, girls stayed with their mothers, learning how to care for a house and children.

▲ Greek woman and servant

Connecting to the Past
1. Why do you think women and children lived on the second floor of the home?
2. Over what areas of life did an Athenian woman have authority?

CONNECTING PAST & PRESENT
See the connections between the **past** and the **present.**

xxvi

Scavenger Hunt

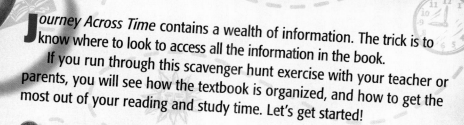

Journey Across Time contains a wealth of information. The trick is to know where to look to access all the information in the book. If you run through this scavenger hunt exercise with your teacher or parents, you will see how the textbook is organized, and how to get the most out of your reading and study time. Let's get started!

1. What civilizations are discussed in Unit 3?

2. What is the topic of Chapter 10?

3. Who is the topic of the *Biography* on page 272?

4. What *Reading Skill* will you be learning about on pages 340–341?

5. What does the *Foldables™ Study Organizer* on page 369 ask you to do?

6. How are the key terms in Chapter 9, Section 2, *plague* and *inflation*, highlighted in the text?

7. There are four types of Web site boxes in Chapter 11. One box previews the chapter, one suggests a Web activity, and one provides help with homework. What does the fourth box provide help with?

8. What do you find on page 365?

9. What is the topic of *The Way It Was* feature on page 389?

10. What is the topic of the map on page 269?

REFERENCE ATLAS

 NATIONAL GEOGRAPHIC

ATLAS KEY

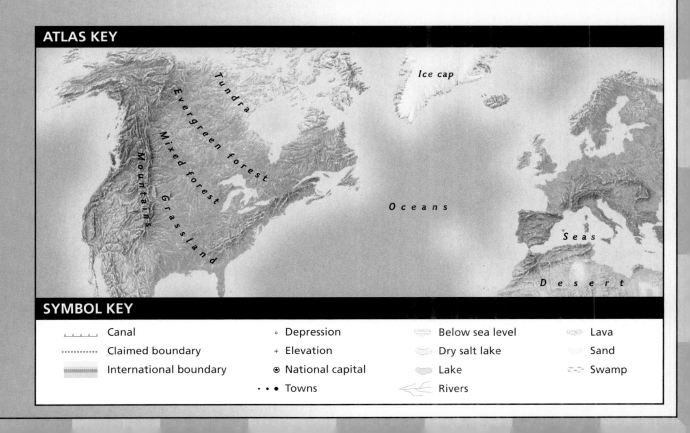

SYMBOL KEY

⊥⊥⊥⊥ Canal	∘ Depression	Below sea level	Lava
·········· Claimed boundary	+ Elevation	Dry salt lake	Sand
International boundary	⊛ National capital	Lake	Swamp
	· · ● Towns	Rivers	

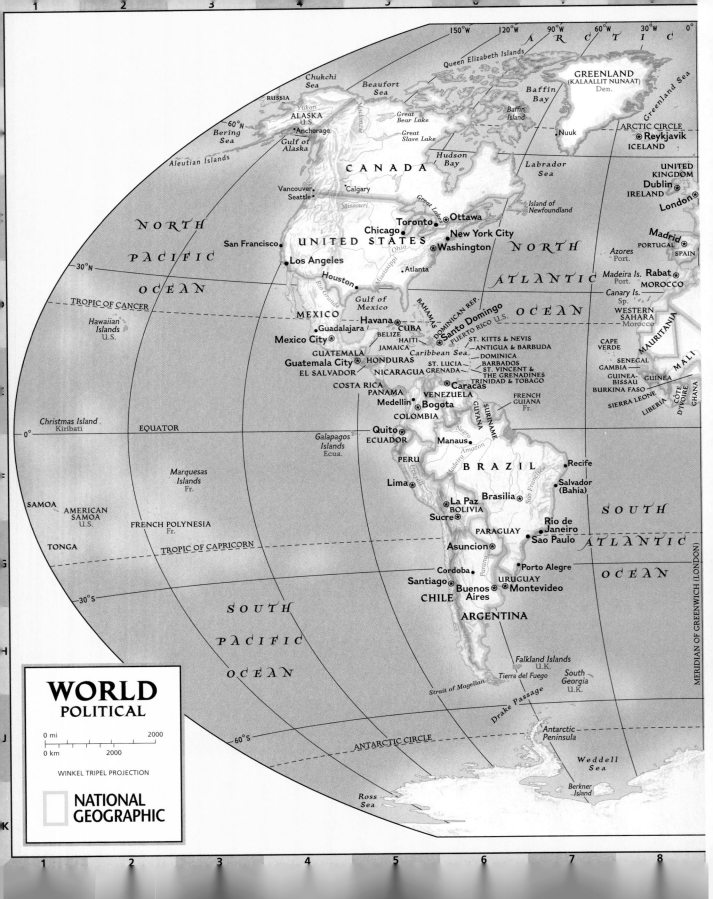

WORLD
POLITICAL

0 mi — 2000
0 km — 2000

WINKEL TRIPEL PROJECTION

NATIONAL GEOGRAPHIC

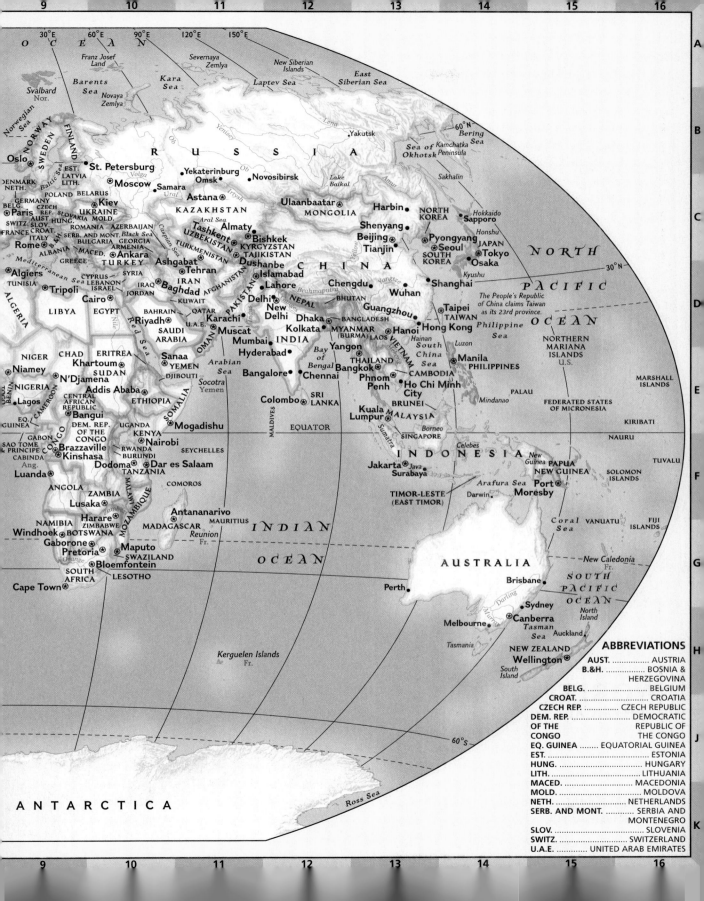

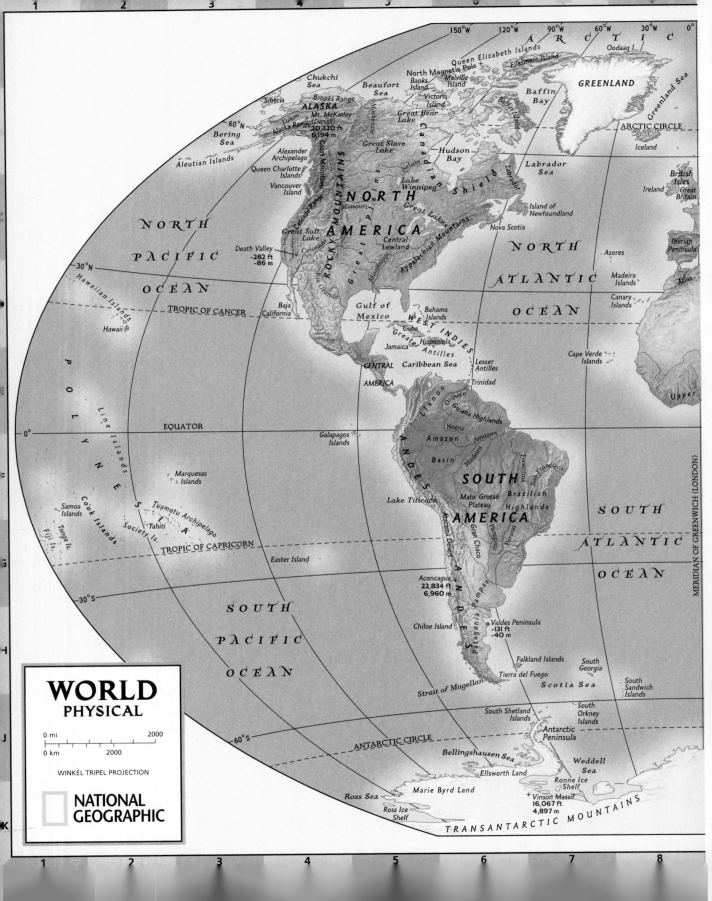

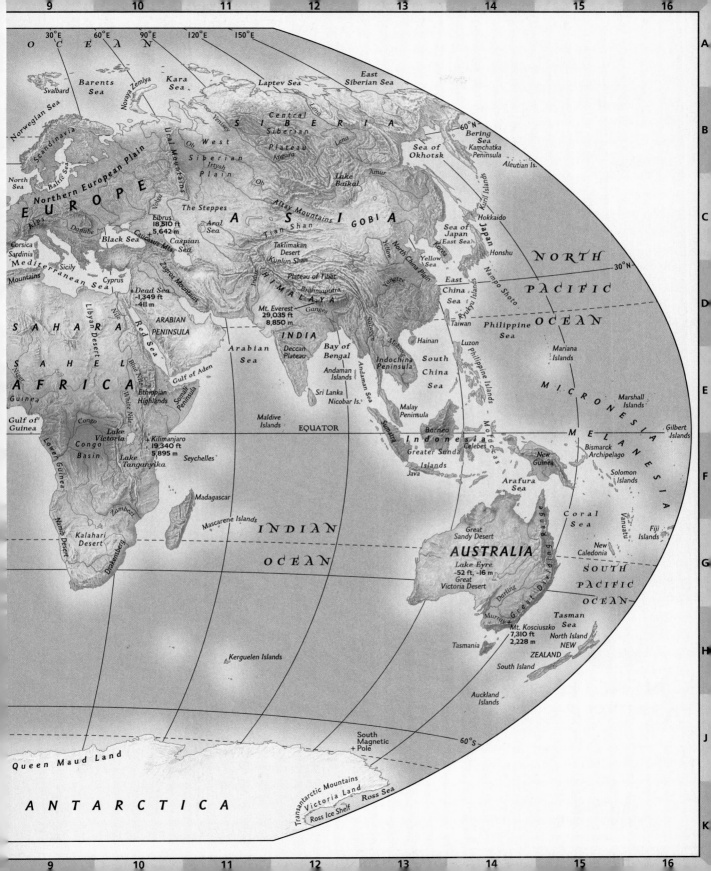

NORTH AMERICA
POLITICAL

0 mi 1000
0 km 1000

AZIMUTHAL EQUIDISTANT PROJECTION

NATIONAL GEOGRAPHIC

1. BAJA CALIFORNIA
2. BAJA CALIFORNIA SUR
3. SONORA
4. CHIHUAHUA
5. SINALOA
6. DURANGO
7. COAHUILA
8. NUEVO LEON
9. ZACATECAS
10. TAMAULIPAS
11. NAYARIT
12. AGUASCALIENTES
13. SAN LUIS POTOSI
14. JALISCO
15. GUANAJUATO
16. QUERETARO
17. HIDALGO
18. COLIMA
19. MICHOACAN
20. MEXICO
21. DISTRITO FEDERAL
22. TLAXCALA
23. MORELOS
24. PUEBLA
25. VERACRUZ
26. GUERRERO
27. OAXACA
28. TABASCO
29. CHIAPAS
30. CAMPECHE
31. QUINTANA ROO
32. YUCATAN

NORTH AMERICA
PHYSICAL

0 mi   1000
0 km   1000

AZIMUTHAL EQUIDISTANT PROJECTION

NATIONAL GEOGRAPHIC

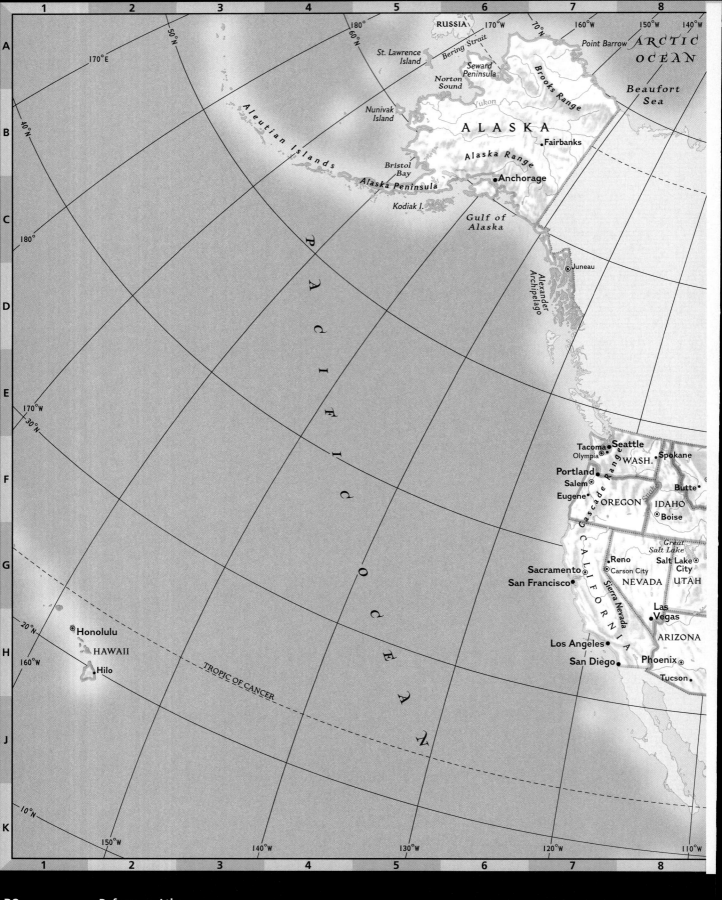

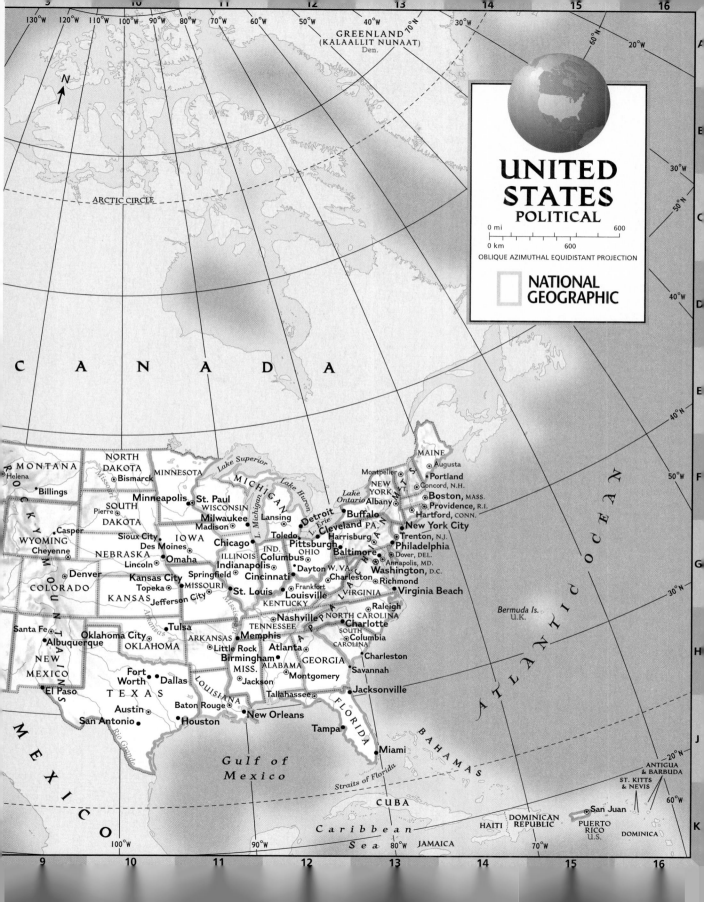

UNITED STATES POLITICAL

0 mi — 600
0 km — 600

OBLIQUE AZIMUTHAL EQUIDISTANT PROJECTION

NATIONAL GEOGRAPHIC

GREENLAND
(KALAALLIT NUNAAT)
Den.

ARCTIC CIRCLE

C A N A D A

MONTANA
•Helena
•Billings

NORTH
DAKOTA
•Bismarck

MINNESOTA
Lake Superior

MICHIGAN
Lake Huron

MAINE
•Augusta
Montpelier•
•Portland
Concord, N.H.
NEW YORK
Albany•
•Boston, MASS.
•Providence, R.I.
•Hartford, CONN.

SOUTH
DAKOTA
Pierre•

Minneapolis• •St. Paul
WISCONSIN
Milwaukee• Lansing• Madison•
L. Michigan

Detroit• •Buffalo
Cleveland PA.
L. Erie

•New York City

WYOMING
•Casper
Cheyenne•

Sioux City•
IOWA
Des Moines•

Chicago•
ILLINOIS
IND.
Columbus•
OHIO

Toledo•
Pittsburgh•
Harrisburg•
•Philadelphia
Trenton, N.J.
•Dover, DEL.

NEBRASKA
Lincoln•
Omaha•

Indianapolis•
Springfield•
Cincinnati•
Dayton•
W. VA.
•Annapolis, MD.
•Washington, D.C.

COLORADO
•Denver

Topeka•
Kansas City•
MISSOURI
St. Louis•
Frankfort•
Louisville•
KENTUCKY
Charleston•
•Richmond
VIRGINIA
•Virginia Beach

Santa Fe•
•Albuquerque

KANSAS
Jefferson City•

Tulsa•
Nashville•
TENNESSEE
Memphis•
Raleigh•
NORTH CAROLINA
•Charlotte
SOUTH
CAROLINA
Columbia•

Oklahoma City•
OKLAHOMA
ARKANSAS
•Little Rock
Atlanta•
•Charleston

NEW
MEXICO
•El Paso

Fort
Worth•
•Dallas
MISS.
•Jackson
Birmingham•
ALABAMA
GEORGIA
Montgomery•
•Savannah

T E X A S
LOUISIANA
Baton Rouge•
Tallahassee•
•Jacksonville

Austin•
San Antonio•
•Houston
•New Orleans
FLORIDA
Tampa•

M E X I C O
Rio Grande

G u l f o f
M e x i c o

•Miami

BAHAMAS

ROCKY   MOUNTAINS

APPALACHIAN   MTS.

A t l a n t i c   O c e a n

Bermuda Is.
U.K.

Straits of Florida
CUBA

C a r i b b e a n
S e a
JAMAICA

DOMINICAN
REPUBLIC
HAITI
•San Juan
PUERTO
RICO
U.S.

ANTIGUA
& BARBUDA
ST. KITTS
& NEVIS
DOMINICA

130°W 120°W 110°W 100°W 90°W 80°W 70°W 60°W 50°W 40°W 30°W 20°W
60°N
50°N
40°N
30°N
20°N
60°W
50°W
40°W
30°W
20°W

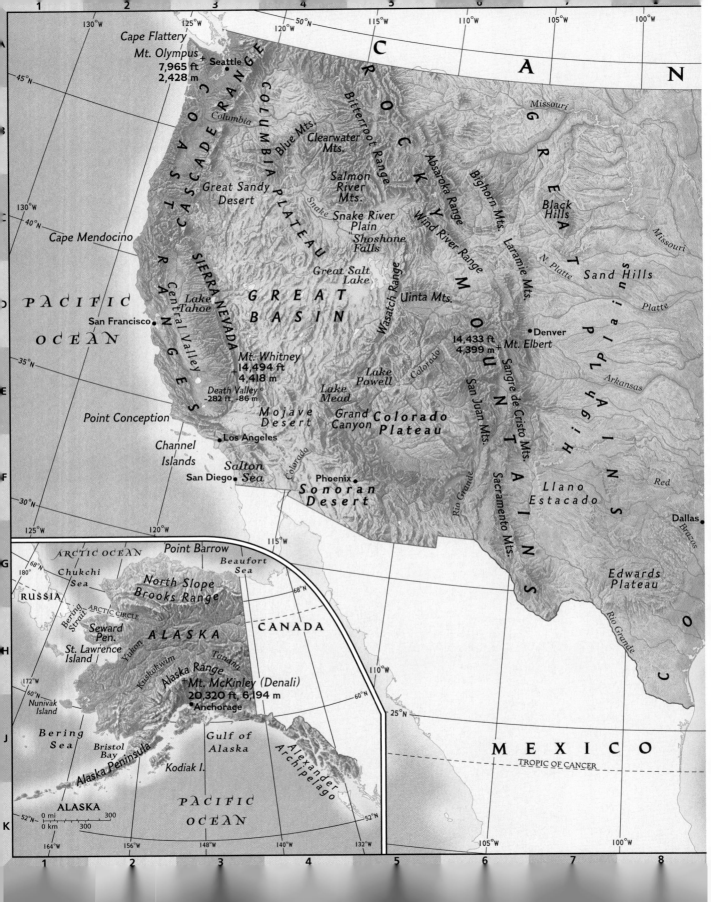

1 · **2** · **3** · **4** · **5** · **6** · **7** · **8**

C A N

ROCKY

A — 130°W — 125°W — 120°W — 50°N — 115°W — 110°W — 105°W — 100°W

Cape Flattery
Mt. Olympus
7,965 ft
2,428 m · Seattle

45°N

Columbia

C A S C A D E   R A N G E

COLUMBIA PLATEAU

Blue Mts.
Clearwater Mts.

Bitterroot Range

Salmon River Mts.

Missouri

B

Great Sandy Desert

Snake

Snake River Plain
Shoshone Falls

Absaroka Range

Bighorn Mts.

Black Hills

G R E A T

130°W — 40°N
Cape Mendocino

C

S I E R R A   N E V A D A

Great Salt Lake

Wind River Range

Laramie Mts.

N. Platte

Sand Hills

Missouri

D

P A C I F I C

O C E A N

Lake Tahoe

Central Valley

San Francisco

GREAT BASIN

Wasatch Range

Uinta Mts.

Colorado

14,433 ft
4,399 m · Mt. Elbert · Denver

P l a i n s

Platte

35°N

Mt. Whitney
14,494 ft
4,418 m

Death Valley °
-282 ft, -86 m

Lake Mead

Lake Powell

San Juan Mts.

Sangre de Cristo Mts.

M O U N T A I N S

Arkansas

H i g h

E

Point Conception

Mojave Desert

Grand Canyon

Colorado Plateau

Colorado

Los Angeles

Channel Islands

Salton Sea

San Diego

Phoenix

Sonoran Desert

Rio Grande

Sacramento Mts.

Llano Estacado

Red

Dallas
Brazos

F

30°N

125°W — 120°W — 115°W

G

ARCTIC OCEAN
Point Barrow
Beaufort Sea

68°N

68°N

CANADA

60°N

Edwards Plateau

Rio Grande

25°N

C O

Chukchi Sea

RUSSIA

Bering Strait   ARCTIC CIRCLE

North Slope
Brooks Range

Seward Pen.
St. Lawrence Island

ALASKA

Yukon

Kuskokwim

Alaska Range
+Mt. McKinley (Denali)
20,320 ft, 6,194 m
· Anchorage

Tanana

H

172°W

60°N
Nunivak Island

J

Bering Sea

Bristol Bay

Alaska Peninsula

Gulf of Alaska

Kodiak I.

Alexander Archipelago

M E X I C O

TROPIC OF CANCER

52°N — 164°W

ALASKA

0 mi   300
0 km   300

156°W

P A C I F I C

O C E A N

148°W   140°W   132°W   52°N

105°W   100°W

K

1 · **2** · **3** · **4** · **5** · **6** · **7** · **8**

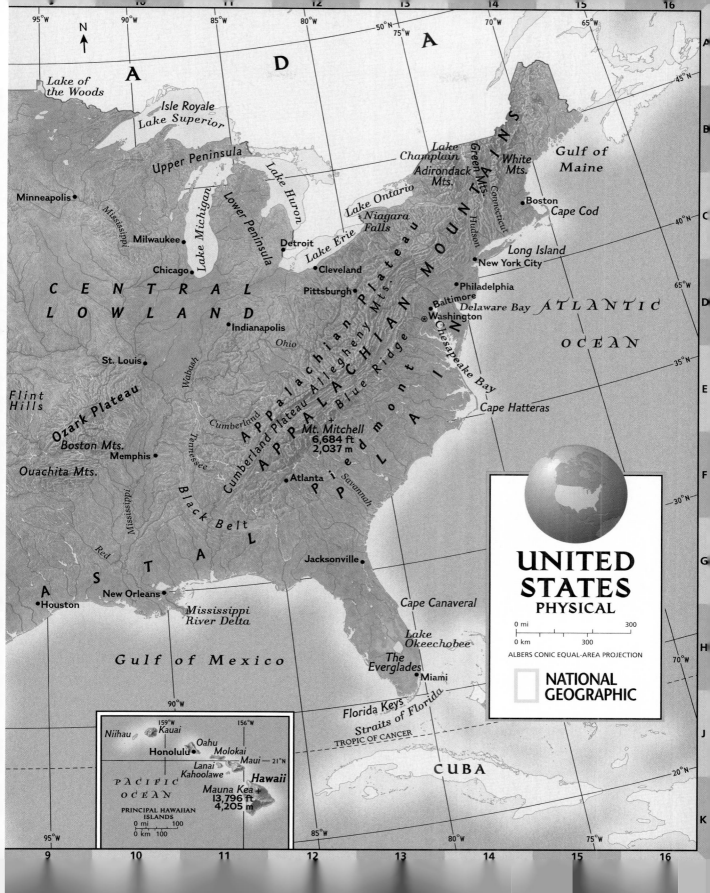

N

C A N A D A

Lake of
the Woods

Isle Royale
Lake Superior

Upper Peninsula

Gulf of
Maine

Lake
Champlain

Adirondack
Mts.

Green Mts.

White
Mts.

Minneapolis

Lake Huron

Lower
Peninsula

Lake Michigan

Lake Ontario

Niagara
Falls

Boston
Cape Cod

Connecticut

Hudson

Milwaukee

Detroit

Lake Erie

Cleveland

Long Island

New York City

C E N T R A L

Chicago

Pittsburgh

Philadelphia

65°W

Appalachian Plateau

Allegheny Mts.

Baltimore

Delaware Bay

A T L A N T I C

L O W L A N D

Indianapolis

Ohio

Washington

Chesapeake Bay

O C E A N

St. Louis

Wabash

Flint
Hills

Ozark Plateau

Cumberland

Cumberland Plateau

A P P A L A C H I A N

Blue Ridge

Piedmont

Cape Hatteras

Boston Mts.

Tennessee

Mt. Mitchell
6,684 ft
2,037 m

Memphis

Ouachita Mts.

Atlanta

Savannah

Black Belt

Mississippi

Red

Jacksonville

C O A S T A L

Houston

New Orleans

Cape Canaveral

Mississippi
River Delta

UNITED
STATES
PHYSICAL

Lake
Okeechobee

0 mi   300

0 km   300

ALBERS CONIC EQUAL-AREA PROJECTION

Gulf of Mexico

The
Everglades

Miami

NATIONAL
GEOGRAPHIC

Florida Keys

Straits of Florida

TROPIC OF CANCER

159°W

Kauai

156°W

Niihau

Oahu

Molokai

Honolulu

Lanai   Maui — 21°N

Kahoolawe

P A C I F I C

O C E A N

Hawaii

Mauna Kea +
13,796 ft
4,205 m

PRINCIPAL HAWAIIAN
ISLANDS

0 mi   100

0 km   100

C U B A

95°W

90°W

85°W

80°W

75°W

9

10

11

12

13

14

15

16

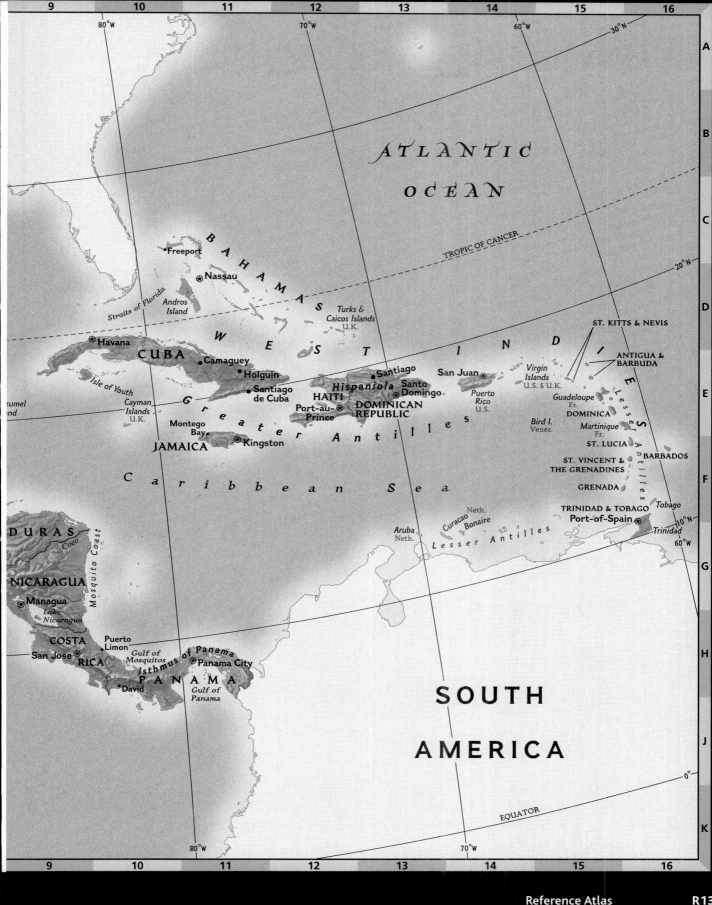

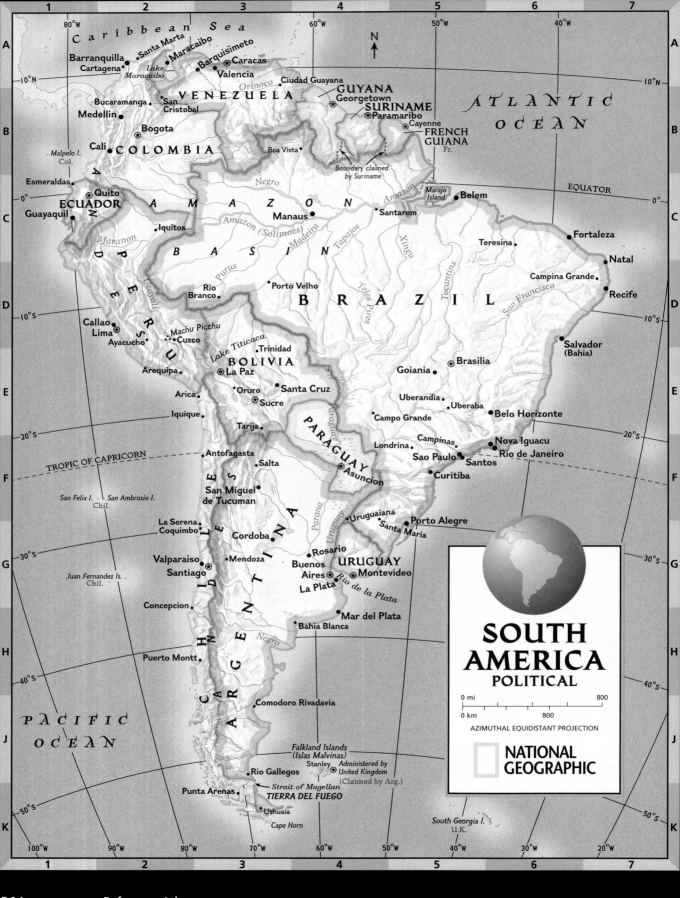

SOUTH AMERICA POLITICAL

0 mi — 800
0 km — 800

AZIMUTHAL EQUIDISTANT PROJECTION

NATIONAL GEOGRAPHIC

SOUTH AMERICA
PHYSICAL

0 mi   800

0 km   800

AZIMUTHAL EQUIDISTANT PROJECTION

NATIONAL GEOGRAPHIC

EUROPE
POLITICAL

0 mi   400
0 km   400

AZIMUTHAL EQUIDISTANT PROJECTION

NATIONAL
GEOGRAPHIC

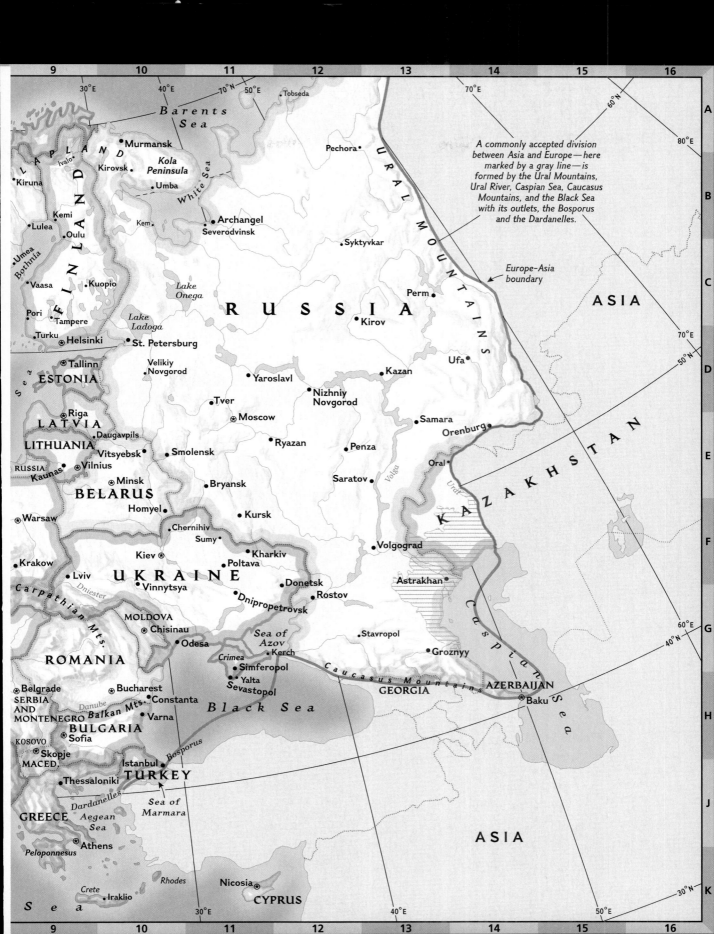

A
B
C
D
E
F
G
H
J
K

30°E 40°E 70°N 50°E 70°E 60°N 80°E

70°N

50°N

70°E

60°N

40°N

30°N

Barents Sea

•Tobseda

•Murmansk

Pechora•

•Kirovsk   **Kola Peninsula**

•Kiruna

•Umba

•Kemi

•Lulea

White Sea

•Syktyvkar

•Archangel
Severodvinsk

•Kem

FINLAND

LAPLAND

Ivalo•

•Vaasa   •Kuopio

Lake Onega

RUSSIA

•Pori   •Tampere

Lake Ladoga

Perm•

•Turku   ⊛Helsinki

•Kirov

Velikiy Novgorod

⊛Tallinn   •St. Petersburg

•Yaroslavl

Kazan•

ESTONIA

•Tver

•Nizhniy Novgorod

Ufa•

⊛Riga

⊛Moscow

LATVIA

•Daugavpils

•Ryazan

Samara•

LITHUANIA

•Vitsyebsk   •Smolensk

•Penza

Orenburg•

RUSSIA

Kaunas•   ⊛Vilnius

Oral•

⊛Minsk

•Bryansk

Saratov•

Volga

BELARUS

•Homyel

•Kursk

KAZAKHSTAN

⊛Warsaw

•Chernihiv

Sumy•

•Volgograd

•Kharkiv

•Krakow

Kiev⊛   •Poltava

•Lviv   **UKRAINE**

Ural

•Vinnytsya

•Donetsk

Astrakhan•

Carpathian Mts.

•Dnipropetrovsk

•Rostov

Dniester

MOLDOVA

⊛Chisinau

•Stavropol

Sea of Azov

Caspian Sea

•Odesa

•Kerch

•Groznyy

ROMANIA

Crimea

•Simferopol

Caucasus Mountains

•Yalta
Sevastopol

⊛Belgrade

⊛Bucharest   **GEORGIA**   **AZERBAIJAN**

SERBIA AND MONTENEGRO

•Constanta

Danube   **Balkan Mts.**

•Baku

•Varna

Black Sea

BULGARIA

KOSOVO   ⊛Sofia

⊛Skopje

Bosporus

MACED.

•Thessaloniki   Istanbul•   **TURKEY**

Dardanelles

GREECE   **Sea of Marmara**

Aegean Sea

⊛Athens

Peloponnesus

Crete   Rhodes

•Iraklio   Nicosia⊛

Sea   **CYPRUS**

ASIA

A commonly accepted division between Asia and Europe—here marked by a gray line—is formed by the Ural Mountains, Ural River, Caspian Sea, Caucasus Mountains, and the Black Sea with its outlets, the Bosporus and the Dardanelles.

Europe-Asia boundary

ASIA

URAL MOUNTAINS

30°E 40°E 50°E

Reference Atlas

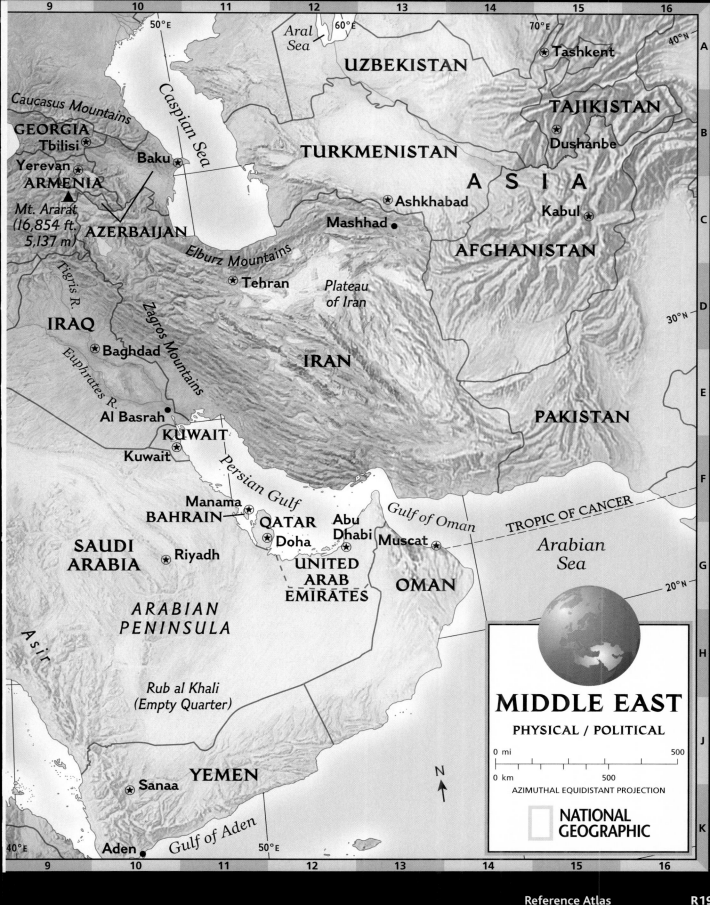

MIDDLE EAST

PHYSICAL / POLITICAL

0 mi   500

0 km   500

AZIMUTHAL EQUIDISTANT PROJECTION

NATIONAL GEOGRAPHIC

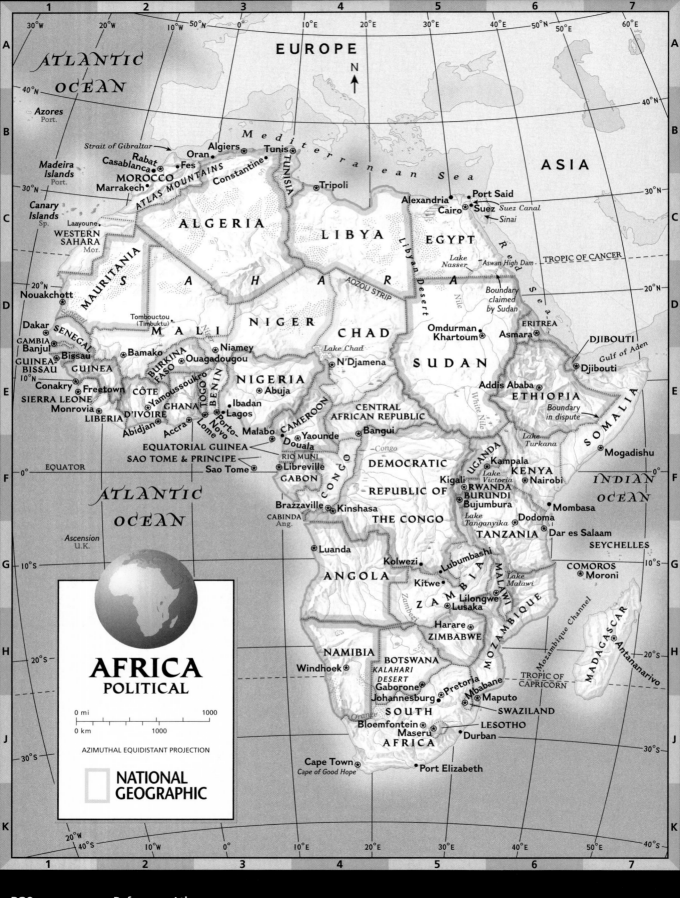

AFRICA
POLITICAL

0 mi   1000
0 km   1000

AZIMUTHAL EQUIDISTANT PROJECTION

NATIONAL GEOGRAPHIC

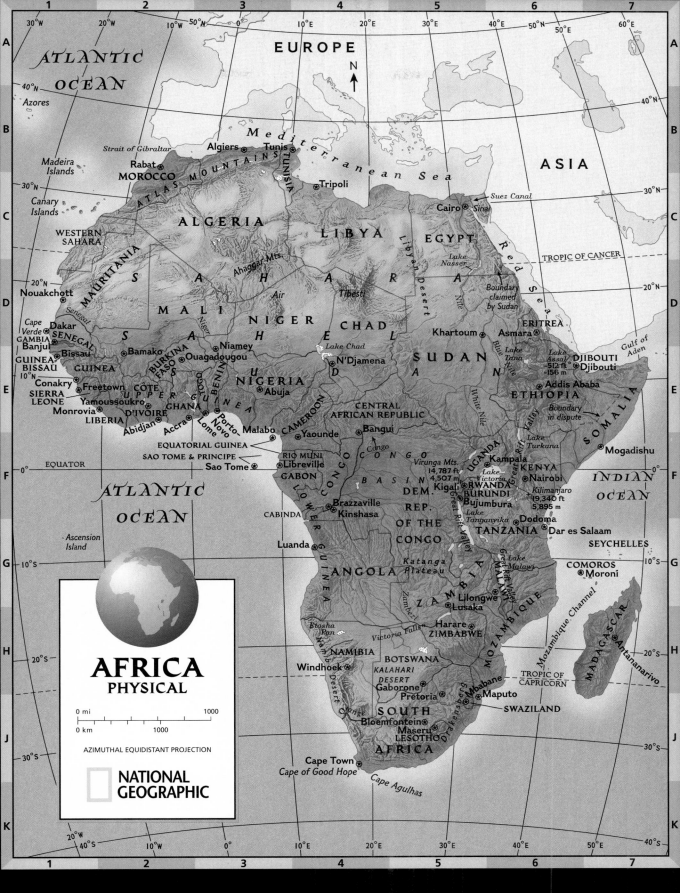

AFRICA
PHYSICAL

0 mi 1000
0 km 1000

AZIMUTHAL EQUIDISTANT PROJECTION

NATIONAL GEOGRAPHIC

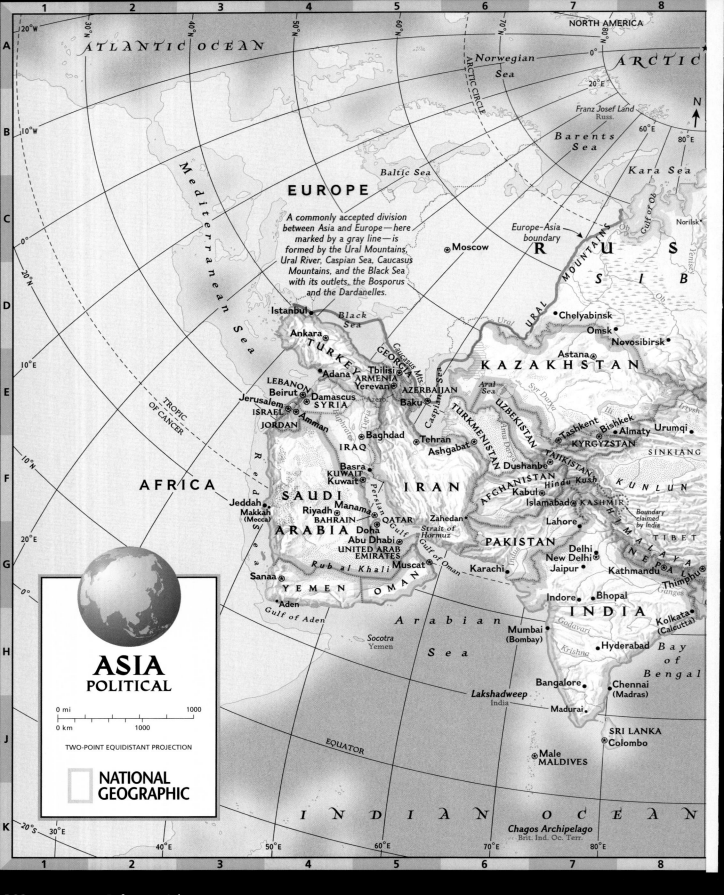

ATLANTIC OCEAN

ARCTIC

NORTH AMERICA

Norwegian
Sea

Franz Josef Land
Russ.

Barents
Sea

Kara Sea

EUROPE

Baltic Sea

Gulf of Ob

Norilsk

A commonly accepted division
between Asia and Europe—here
marked by a gray line—is
formed by the Ural Mountains,
Ural River, Caspian Sea, Caucasus
Mountains, and the Black Sea
with its outlets, the Bosporus
and the Dardanelles.

Moscow

Europe-Asia
boundary

R   U   S

Chelyabinsk
Omsk
Novosibirsk

S   I   B

Mediterranean Sea

Istanbul

Black
Sea

Ankara

TURKEY

Caucasus Mts.

GEORGIA
Tbilisi
ARMENIA
Yerevan
AZERBAIJAN
Baku

Azerb.

Caspian Sea

Astana

KAZAKHSTAN

Aral
Sea

Syr Darya

UZBEKISTAN

Ili

Irtysh

Tashkent
Bishkek
Almaty   Urumqi

KYRGYZSTAN

SINKIANG

Adana

LEBANON
Beirut
Jerusalem
ISRAEL
JORDAN

Damascus
SYRIA
Amman

TROPIC
OF CANCER

Euphrates

Tigris

Baghdad

IRAQ

Tehran

Ashgabat

TURKMENISTAN

Amu Darya

TAJIKISTAN

Dushanbe

AFGHANISTAN

Hindu Kush

KUNLUN

10°E

Basra
KUWAIT
Kuwait

IRAN

Kabul
Islamabad

KASHMIR

HIMALAYA

TIBET

AFRICA

Red Sea

SAUDI

Manama
Riyadh
BAHRAIN
ARABIA   Doha
Abu Dhabi
UNITED ARAB
EMIRATES

Persian Gulf

QATAR

Zahedan

Strait of
Hormuz

PAKISTAN

Lahore

Boundary
claimed
by India

NEPAL

Jeddah
Makkah
(Mecca)

Gulf of Oman

Karachi

Indus

Delhi
New Delhi
Jaipur

Kathmandu
Thimphu

Rub al Khali

Muscat

OMAN

Ganges

Sanaa
YEMEN

Aden

Gulf of Aden

Socotra
Yemen

Arabian

Sea

Muscat

Indore
Bhopal

INDIA

Godavari

Mumbai
(Bombay)

Krishna

Hyderabad

Bay
of
Bengal

Kolkata
(Calcutta)

ASIA
POLITICAL

0 mi   1000

0 km
        1000

TWO-POINT EQUIDISTANT PROJECTION

NATIONAL
GEOGRAPHIC

Bangalore

Lakshadweep
India

Madurai

Chennai
(Madras)

SRI LANKA
Colombo

EQUATOR

Male
MALDIVES

INDIAN   OCEAN

Chagos Archipelago
Brit. Ind. Oc. Terr.

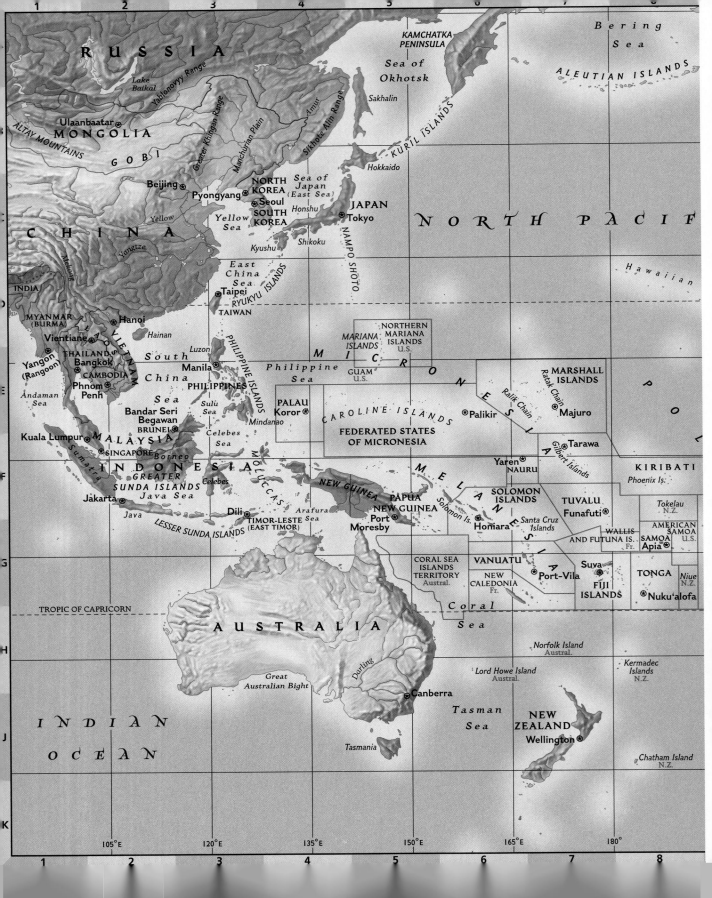

| | 9 | 10 | 11 | 12 | 13 | 14 | 15 | 16 |

A

Gulf of Alaska

Kodiak I.

Alexander Archipelago

Queen Charlotte Islands

Vancouver Island

Coast Mountains

ROCKY MOUNTAINS

CANADA

Hudson Bay

B

45°N

Cascade Range

GREAT PLAINS

Missouri

Great Lakes

Ottawa ⊗

APPALACHIAN MTS.

CANADIAN SHIELD

C

IC OCEAN

30°N

UNITED STATES

CENTRAL LOWLAND

Mississippi

COASTAL PLAIN

Washington ⊗

ATLANTIC OCEAN

Baja California

Sierra Madre Occidental

Gulf of California

MEXICO

Sierra Madre Oriental

D

TROPIC OF CANCER

Gulf of Mexico

Nassau ⊗

BAHAMAS

Havana ⊗

CUBA

DOMINICAN REPUBLIC

JAMAICA HAITI

Santo Domingo

Islands

HAWAII U.S.

Mexico City ⊗

BELIZE

HONDURAS

Caribbean Sea

E

15°N

GUATEMALA

Guatemala City ⊗

San Salvador ⊗

EL SALVADOR

Tegucigalpa ⊗

NICARAGUA

Managua ⊗

Panama City ⊗

Caracas ⊗

Line Islands

Kiritimati

San Jose ⊗

COSTA RICA

PANAMA

LLANOS

VENEZ.

Bogota ⊗

COLOMBIA

F

EQUATOR

0°

Galapagos Islands Ecua.

Quito ⊗

ECUADOR

ANDES

AMAZON BASIN

BRAZIL

P O L Y N E S I A

Marquesas Is.

PERU

Lima ⊗

G

15°S

Tuamotu Archipelago

COOK ISLANDS N.Z.

Society Is.

FRENCH POLYNESIA Fr.

La Paz ⊗

BOLIVIA

Austral Is.

Pitcairn Island U.K.

H

30°S

SOUTH

Santiago ⊗

CORDILLERA DE LOS ANDES

ARGENTINA

PATAGONIA

J

PACIFIC

OCEAN

45°S

Chiloe Island

K

| | 9 | 10 | 11 | 12 | 13 | 14 | 15 | 16 |

165°W 150°W 135°W 120°W 105°W 90°W 75°W

PACIFIC RIM
PHYSICAL/POLITICAL

0 mi — 1500

0 km — 1500

MILLER CYLINDRICAL PROJECTION

NATIONAL GEOGRAPHIC

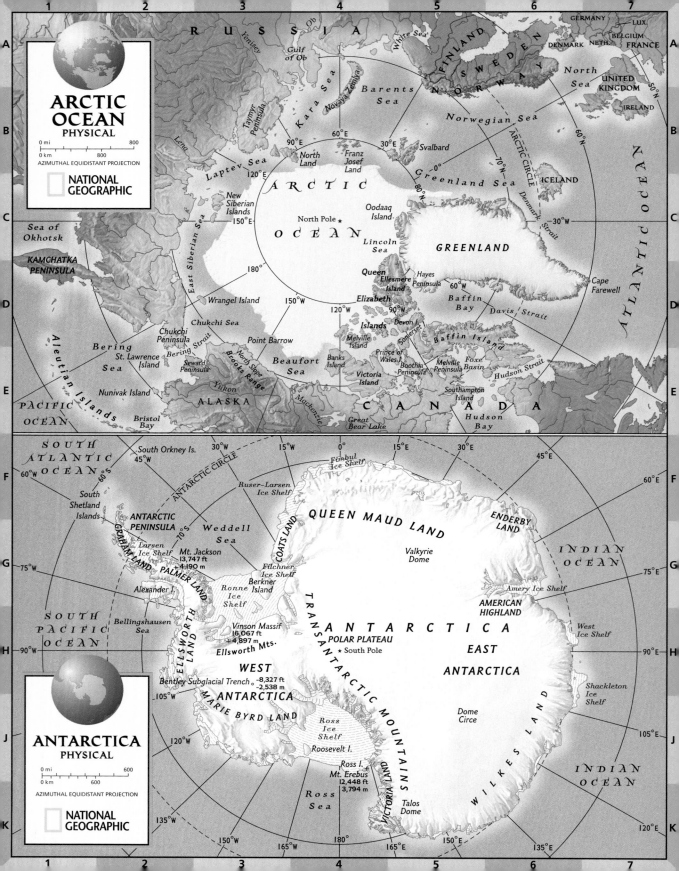

ARCTIC OCEAN
PHYSICAL

0 mi 800
0 km 800
AZIMUTHAL EQUIDISTANT PROJECTION

NATIONAL GEOGRAPHIC

Arctic Ocean map labels:

RUSSIA
Ob
Yenisey
Gulf of Ob
White Sea
FINLAND
SWEDEN
GERMANY
LUX.
DENMARK
NETH.
BELGIUM
FRANCE
Taymyr Peninsula
Kara Sea
Novaya Zemlya
Barents Sea
NORWAY
Norwegian Sea
North Sea
UNITED KINGDOM
IRELAND
Lena
North Land
Franz Josef Land
Svalbard
90°E
60°E
30°E
0°
ARCTIC CIRCLE
60°N
50°N
70°W
Laptev Sea
120°E
ARCTIC
Greenland Sea
80°W
ICELAND
ATLANTIC OCEAN
New Siberian Islands
150°E
OCEAN
North Pole ★
Oodaaq Island
Lincoln Sea
GREENLAND
30°W
Sea of Okhotsk
Queen
Ellesmere Island
Hayes Peninsula
60°W
KAMCHATKA PENINSULA
180°
Elizabeth
90°W
Baffin Bay
Davis Strait
Cape Farewell
150°W
Wrangel Island
Islands
Devon I.
East Siberian Sea
Chukchi Sea
120°W
Melville Island
Somerset I.
Baffin Island
Chukchi Peninsula
Point Barrow
Banks Island
Prince of Wales I.
Boothia Peninsula
Melville Peninsula
Foxe Basin
Bering Strait
Beaufort Sea
Victoria Island
Hudson Strait
Bering Sea
St. Lawrence Island
North Slope
Brooks Range
Southampton Island
Aleutian Islands
Seward Peninsula
Nunivak Island
Yukon
ALASKA
Mackenzie
CANADA
Hudson Bay
PACIFIC OCEAN
Bristol Bay
Great Bear Lake

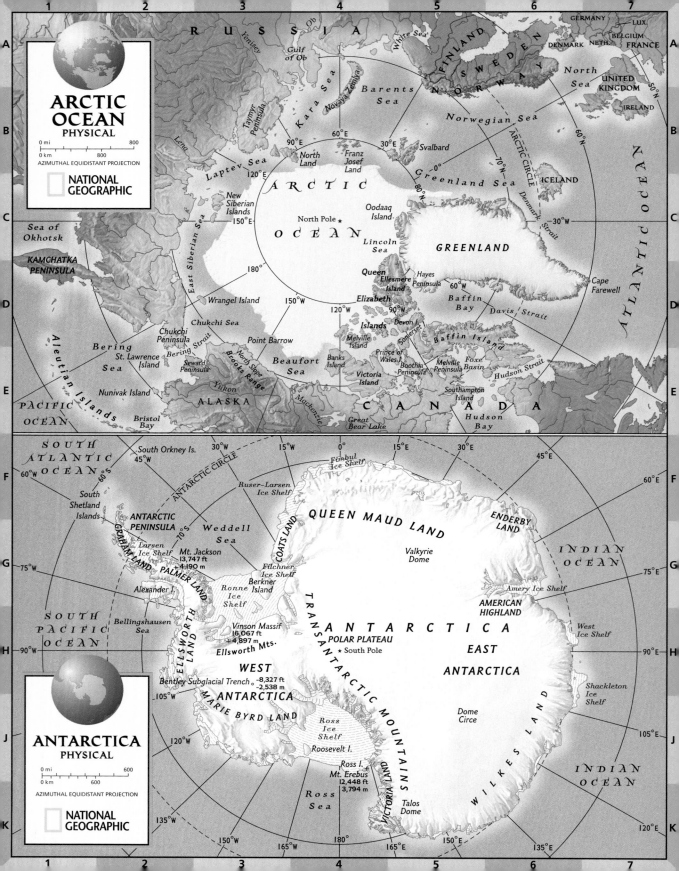

ANTARCTICA
PHYSICAL

0 mi 600
0 km 600
AZIMUTHAL EQUIDISTANT PROJECTION

NATIONAL GEOGRAPHIC

Antarctica map labels:

SOUTH ATLANTIC OCEAN
South Orkney Is.
30°W
15°W
0°
15°E
30°E
45°E
60°W
60°S
45°W
ANTARCTIC CIRCLE
Fimbul Ice Shelf
60°E
South Shetland Islands
South Sandwich
Ruser-Larsen Ice Shelf
QUEEN MAUD LAND
ENDERBY LAND
INDIAN OCEAN
ANTARCTIC PENINSULA
Weddell Sea
COATS LAND
75°E
GRAHAM LAND
70°S
Larsen Ice Shelf
Mt. Jackson 13,747 ft 4,190 m
Filchner Ice Shelf
Valkyrie Dome
PALMER LAND
Berkner Island
AMERICAN HIGHLAND
Amery Ice Shelf
Alexander I.
Ronne Ice Shelf
West Ice Shelf
90°E
SOUTH PACIFIC OCEAN
Bellingshausen Sea
Vinson Massif 16,067 ft 4,897 m
ANTARCTICA
EAST ANTARCTICA
ELLSWORTH MTS.
POLAR PLATEAU
★ South Pole
Ellsworth Mts.
WEST
TRANSANTARCTIC MOUNTAINS
Shackleton Ice Shelf
105°W
Bentley Subglacial Trench -8,327 ft -2,538 m
ANTARCTICA
105°E
MARIE BYRD LAND
Dome Circe
WILKES LAND
120°W
Ross Ice Shelf
Roosevelt I.
VICTORIA LAND
Talos Dome
INDIAN OCEAN
135°W
Ross I.
Mt. Erebus 12,448 ft 3,794 m
120°E
Ross Sea
150°W
165°W
180°
165°E
150°E
135°E

NATIONAL GEOGRAPHIC

Geography Handbook

The story of the world begins with geography—the study of the earth in all of its variety. Geography describes the earth's land, water, and plant and animal life. It is the study of places and the complex relationships between people and their environment.

The resources in this handbook will help you get the most out of your textbook—and provide you with skills you will use for the rest of your life.

▼ The Gui River, Guilin, China

▲ Saharan sand dunes, Morocco

The Amazon, Brazil ▶

How Do I Study Geography?

To understand how our world is connected, some geographers have broken down the study of geography into five themes. The **Five Themes of Geography** are (1) location, (2) place, (3) human/environment interaction, (4) movement, and (5) regions. You will see these themes highlighted in the Chapter Assessment Geography Skills of *Journey Across Time.*

• Six Essential Elements

Recently, geographers have begun to look at geography in a different way. They break down the study of geography into **Six Essential Elements.** Being aware of these elements will help you sort out what you are learning about geography.

Element 2

Places and Regions

Place has a special meaning in geography. It means more than where a place is. It also describes what a place is like. It might describe physical characteristics such as landforms, climate, and plant or animal life. Or it might describe human characteristics, including language and way of life.

To help organize their study, geographers often group places into regions. **Regions** are united by one or more common characteristics.

Element 1

The World in Spatial Terms

Geographers first take a look at where a place is located. **Location** serves as a starting point by asking "Where is it?" Knowing the location of places helps you develop an awareness of the world around you.

Element 3

Physical Systems

When studying places and regions, geographers analyze how **physical systems**—such as hurricanes, volcanoes, and glaciers—shape the earth's surface. They also look at communities of plants and animals that depend upon one another and their surroundings for survival.

Element 4

Human Systems

Geographers also examine **human systems,** or how people have shaped our world. They look at how boundary lines are determined and analyze why people settle in certain places and not in others. A key theme in geography is the continual **movement** of people, ideas, and goods.

Element 5

Environment and Society

How does the relationship between people and their natural surroundings influence the way people live? This is one of the questions that the theme of **human/environment interaction** investigates. It also shows how people use the environment and how their actions affect the environment.

Element 6

The Uses of Geography

Knowledge of geography helps us understand the relationships among people, places, and environments over time. Understanding geography and knowing how to use the tools and technology available to study it prepares you for life in our modern society.

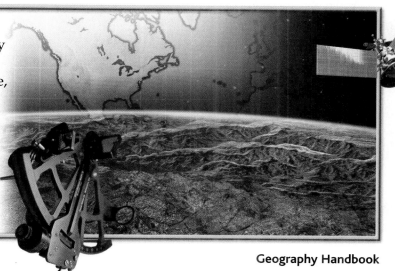

How Do I Use Maps and Globes?

Hemispheres

To locate a place on the earth, geographers use a system of imaginary lines that crisscross the globe. One of these lines, the **Equator,** circles the middle of the earth like a belt. It divides the earth into "half spheres," or **hemispheres.** Everything north of the Equator is in the Northern Hemisphere. Everything south of the Equator is in the Southern Hemisphere.

Another imaginary line runs from north to south. It helps divide the earth into half spheres in the other direction. Find this line—called the **Prime Meridian** on a globe. Everything east of the Prime Meridian for 180 degrees is in the Eastern Hemisphere. Everything west of the Prime Meridian for 180 degrees is in the Western Hemisphere.

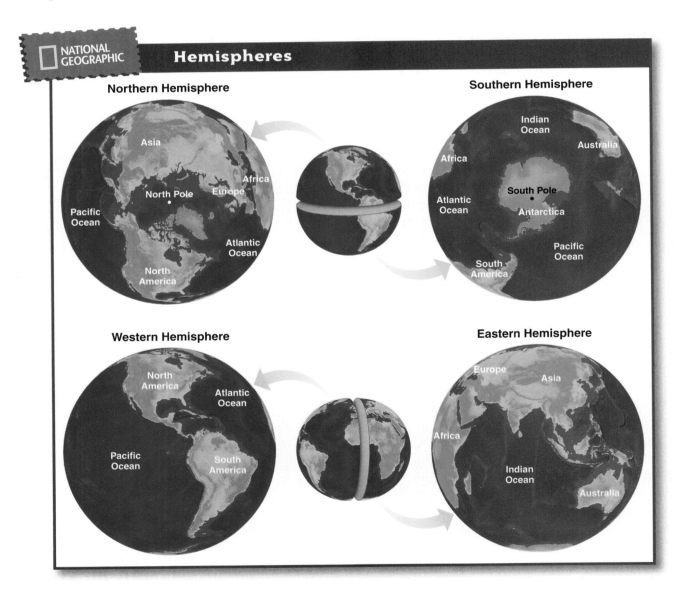

NATIONAL GEOGRAPHIC

Hemispheres

Northern Hemisphere

Asia
Africa
Europe
North Pole
Pacific Ocean
Atlantic Ocean
North America

Southern Hemisphere

Indian Ocean
Australia
Africa
South Pole
Atlantic Ocean
Antarctica
Pacific Ocean
South America

Western Hemisphere

North America
Atlantic Ocean
Pacific Ocean
South America

Eastern Hemisphere

Europe
Asia
Africa
Indian Ocean
Australia

Understanding Latitude and Longitude

Lines on globes and maps provide information that can help you easily locate places on the earth. These lines—called **latitude** and **longitude**—cross one another, forming a pattern called a grid system.

Latitude

Lines of latitude, or **parallels,** circle the earth parallel to the **Equator** and measure the distance north or south of the Equator in degrees. The Equator is at 0° latitude, while the North Pole lies at latitude 90°N (north).

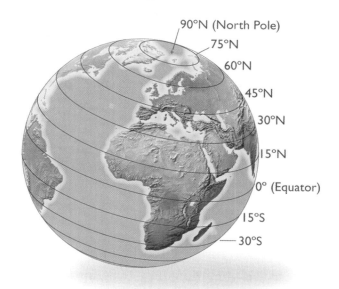

Longitude

Lines of longitude, or **meridians,** circle the earth from Pole to Pole. These lines measure distances east or west of the starting line, which is at 0° longitude and is called the **Prime Meridian.** The Prime Meridian runs through the Royal Observatory in Greenwich, England.

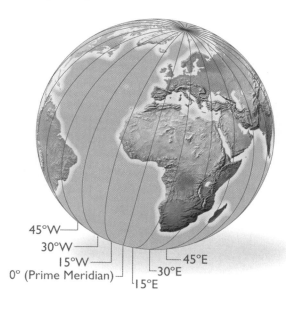

Absolute Location

The grid system formed by lines of latitude and longitude makes it possible to find the absolute location of a place. Only one place can be found at the point where a specific line of latitude crosses a specific line of longitude. By using degrees (°) and minutes (') (points between degrees), people can pinpoint the precise spot where one line of latitude crosses one line of longitude—an **absolute location.**

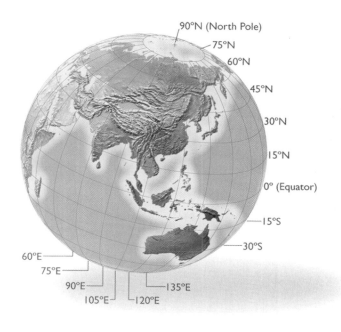

From Globes to Maps

The most accurate way to depict the earth is as a **globe,** a round scale model of the earth. A globe gives a true picture of the relative sizes of continents and the shapes of landmasses and bodies of water. Globes accurately represent distance and direction.

A **map** is a flat drawing of all or part of the surface of the earth. Unlike globes, maps can show small areas in great detail. Maps can also display political boundaries, population densities, or even voting results.

From Globes to Maps

Maps, however, do have their limitations. As you can imagine, drawing a round object on a flat surface is very difficult. **Cartographers,** or mapmakers, use mathematical formulas to transfer information from the round globe to a flat map. However, when the curves of a globe become straight lines on a map, the size, shape, distance, or area can change or be distorted.

Great Circle Routes

Mapmakers have solved some problems of going from a globe to a map. A **great circle** is an imaginary line that follows the curve of the earth. Traveling along a great circle is called following a **great circle route.** Airplane pilots use great circle routes because they are the shortest routes.

The idea of a great circle shows one important difference between a globe and a map. Because a globe is round, it accurately shows great circles. On a flat map, however, the great circle route between two points may not appear to be the shortest distance. Compare Maps A and B on the right.

Mapmaking With Technology

Technology has changed the way maps are made. Most cartographers use software programs called **geographic information systems (GIS).** This software layers map data from satellite images, printed text, and statistics. A **Global Positioning System (GPS)** helps consumers and mapmakers locate places based on coordinates broadcast by satellites.

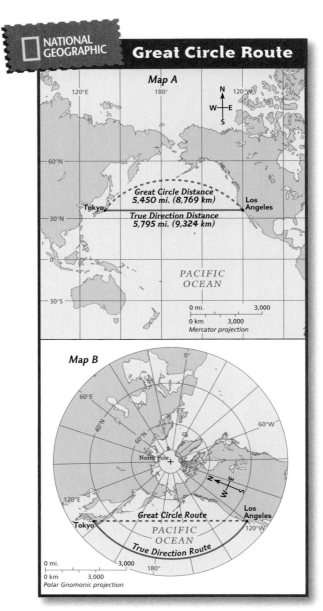

Great Circle Route

Map A

Great Circle Distance 5,450 mi. (8,769 km)
True Direction Distance 5,795 mi. (9,324 km)

Tokyo — Los Angeles

PACIFIC OCEAN

0 mi. 3,000
0 km 3,000
Mercator projection

Map B

North Pole

Great Circle Route
Los Angeles
Tokyo
PACIFIC OCEAN
True Direction Route

0 mi. 3,000
0 km 3,000
Polar Gnomonic projection

Common Map Projections

Imagine taking the whole peel from an orange and trying to flatten it on a table. You would either have to cut it or stretch parts of it. Mapmakers face a similar problem in showing the surface of the round earth on a flat map. When the surface of the earth is flattened, big gaps open up. To fill in the gaps, mapmakers stretch parts of the earth. They choose to show either the correct shapes of places or their correct sizes. It is impossible to show both. As a result, mapmakers have developed different **projections,** or ways of showing the earth on a flat piece of paper.

Goode's Interrupted Equal-Area Projection

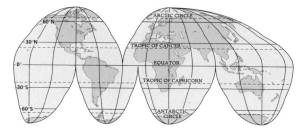

▲ Take a second look at your peeled, flattened orange. You might have something that looks like a map based on **Goode's Interrupted Equal-Area** projection. A map with this projection shows continents close to their true shapes and sizes. This projection is helpful to compare land areas among continents.

Robinson Projection

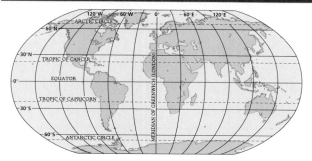

▲ A map using the **Robinson** projection has minor distortions. Land on the western and eastern sides of the Robinson map appears much as it does on a globe. The areas most distorted on this projection are near the North and South Poles.

Winkel Tripel Projection

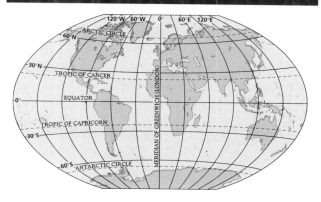

▲ The **Winkel Tripel** projection gives a good overall view of the continents' shapes and sizes. Land areas in a Winkel Tripel projection are not as distorted near the Poles as they are in the Robinson projection.

Mercator Projection

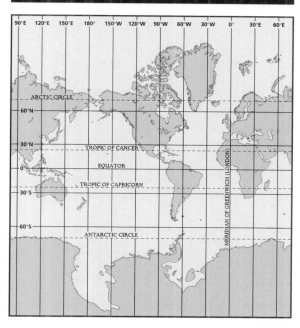

▲ The **Mercator** projection shows true direction and land shapes fairly accurately, but not size or distance. Areas that are located far from the Equator are quite distorted on this projection. Alaska, for example, appears much larger on a Mercator map than it does on a globe.

Parts of Maps

Map Key An important first step in reading a map is to note the map key. The **map key** explains the lines, symbols, and colors used on a map. For example, the map on this page shows the various climate regions of the United States and the different colors representing them. Cities are usually symbolized by a solid circle (•) and capitals by a (✪). On this map, you can see the capital of Texas and the cities of Los Angeles, Seattle, New Orleans, and Chicago.

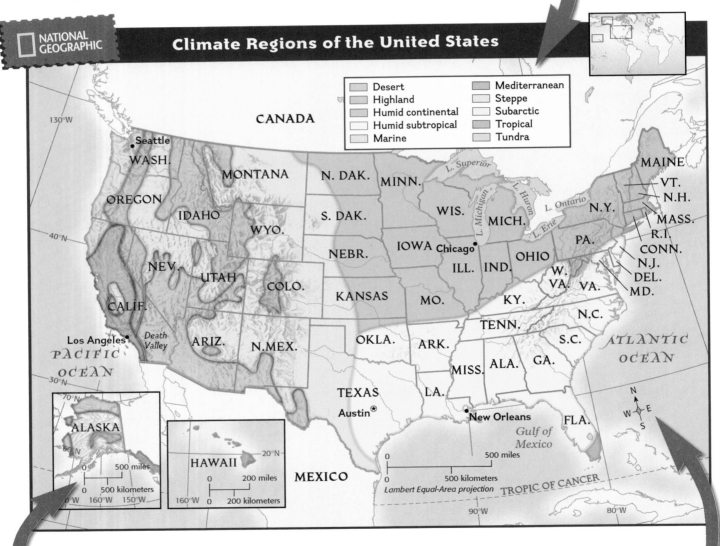

Climate Regions of the United States

NATIONAL GEOGRAPHIC

Key:
- Desert
- Highland
- Humid continental
- Humid subtropical
- Marine
- Mediterranean
- Steppe
- Subarctic
- Tropical
- Tundra

Lambert Equal-Area projection

Scale A measuring line, often called a **scale bar,** helps you figure distance on the map. The map scale tells you what distance on the earth is represented by the measurement on the scale bar.

Compass Rose A map has a symbol that tells you where the **cardinal directions**—north, south, east, and west—are positioned.

Types of Maps

General Purpose Maps

Maps are amazingly useful tools. Geographers use many different types of maps. Maps that show a wide range of general information about an area are called **general purpose maps.** Two of the most common general purpose maps are physical and political maps.

Physical Maps

Physical maps call out landforms and water features. The physical map of Sri Lanka (below) shows rivers and mountains. The colors used on physical maps include brown or green for land and blue for water. In addition, physical maps may use colors to show **elevation**—the height of an area above sea level. A key explains what each color and symbol stands for.

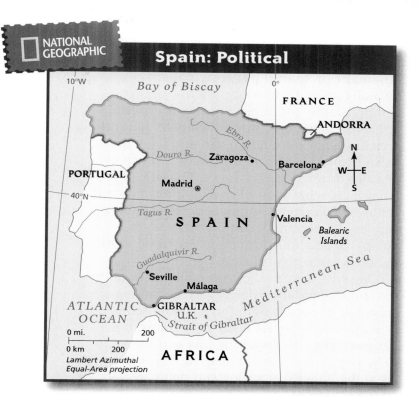

Spain: Political

Political Maps

Political maps show the names and boundaries of countries, the location of cities and other human-made features of a place, and often identify major physical features. The political map of Spain (above), for example, shows the boundaries between Spain and other countries. It also shows cities and rivers within Spain and bodies of water surrounding Spain.

Sri Lanka: Physical

Special Purpose Maps

Some maps are made to present specific kinds of information. These are called **thematic** or **special purpose maps.** They usually show themes or patterns, often emphasizing one subject or theme. Special purpose maps may present climate, natural resources, or population density. They may also display historical information, such as battles or territorial changes. The title of a map tells what kind of special information it shows. Colors and symbols in the map key are especially important on these types of maps. Special purpose maps are often found in books of maps called atlases.

One type of special purpose map uses colors to show population density, or the average number of people living in a square mile or square kilometer. As with other maps, it is important to first read the title and the key. The population density map of Egypt shows that the Nile River valley and delta are very densely populated.

Some other special purpose maps such as the one of China's Defenses are not presented in color. They print in black and white. This is an example of a map you might find on a standardized test or in a newspaper.

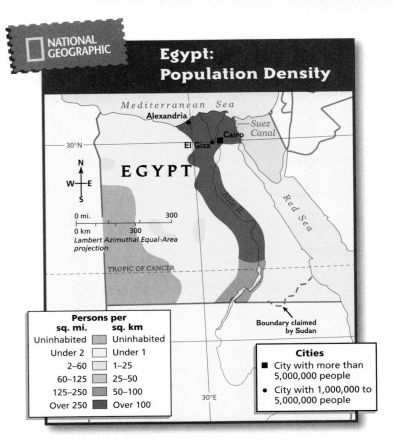

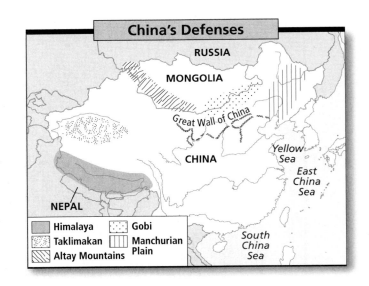

Using Graphs, Charts, and Diagrams

Bar, Line, and Circle Graphs

A graph is a way of summarizing and presenting information visually. Each part of a graph gives useful information. First read the title of the graph to find out its subject. Then read the labels along the **axes** of the graph—the vertical line along the left side of the graph and the horizontal line along the bottom. One axis will tell you what is being measured. The other axis tells what units of measurement are being used.

Graphs that use bars or wide lines to compare data visually are called **bar graphs.** Look carefully at the bar graph (right) which compares world languages. The vertical axis lists the languages. The horizontal axis gives speakers of the language in millions. By comparing the lengths of the bars, you can quickly tell which language is spoken by the most people. Bar graphs are especially useful for comparing quantities.

Bar graph

A **line graph** is a useful tool for showing changes over a period of time. The amounts being measured are plotted on the grid above each year and then are connected by a line. Line graphs sometimes have two or more lines plotted on them. The line graph (below) shows that the number of farms in the United States has decreased since 1940.

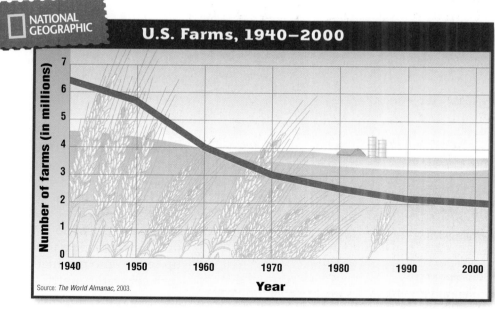

Line graph

You can use **circle graphs** when you want to show how the whole of something is divided into its parts. Because of their shape, circle graphs are often called pie graphs. Each "slice" represents a part or percentage of the whole "pie." On the circle graph at right, the whole circle (100 percent) represents the world's population in 2002. The slices show how this population is divided among some of the most heavily populated areas of the world.

Charts

Charts present facts and numbers in an organized way. They arrange data, especially numbers, in rows and columns for easy reference. To interpret the chart, first read the title. Look at the chart on page 91. It tells you what information the chart contains. Next, read the labels at the top of each column and on the left side of the chart. They explain what the numbers or data on the chart are measuring.

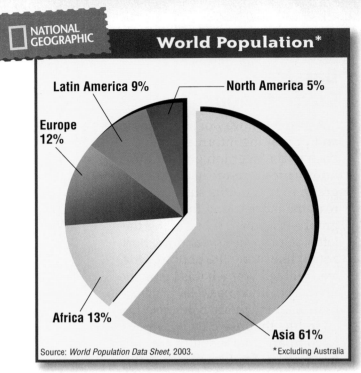

NATIONAL GEOGRAPHIC

World Population*

Latin America 9%
North America 5%
Europe 12%
Africa 13%
Asia 61%

Source: *World Population Data Sheet*, 2003.
*Excluding Australia

Circle graph

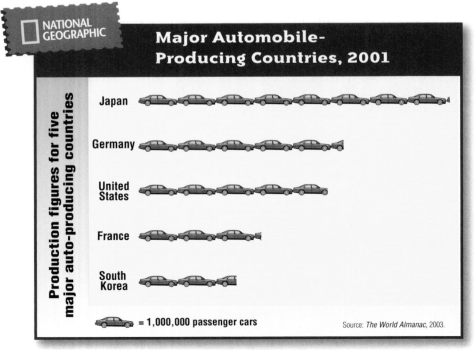

NATIONAL GEOGRAPHIC

Major Automobile-Producing Countries, 2001

Production figures for five major auto-producing countries

Japan
Germany
United States
France
South Korea

= 1,000,000 passenger cars

Source: *The World Almanac*, 2003.

Pictograph

Pictographs

Like bar and circle graphs, pictographs are good for making comparisons. **Pictographs** use rows of small pictures or symbols, with each picture or symbol representing an amount. Look at the pictograph (left) showing the number of automobiles produced in the world's five major automobile-producing countries. The key tells you that one car symbol stands for 1 million automobiles. The total number of car symbols in a row adds up to the auto production in each selected country.

Climographs

A **climograph,** or climate graph, combines a line graph and a bar graph. It gives an overall picture of the long-term weather patterns in a specific place. Climographs include several kinds of information. The green vertical bars on the climograph of Moscow (right) show average monthly amounts of precipitation (rain, snow, and sleet). These bars are measured against the axis on the right side of the graph. The red line plotted above the bars represents changes in the average monthly temperature. You measure this line against the axis on the left side.

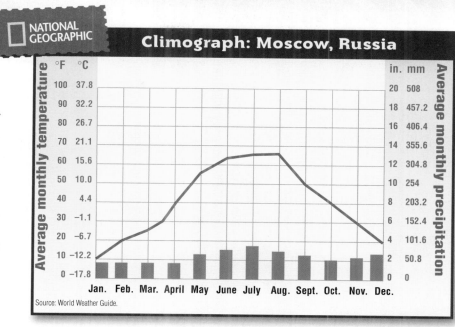

Climograph: Moscow, Russia

Source: World Weather Guide.

Climograph

Diagrams

Diagrams are drawings that show steps in a process, point out the parts of an object, or explain how something works. An **elevation profile** is a type of diagram that can be helpful when comparing the elevations—or height—of an area. It shows an exaggerated side view of the land as if it were sliced and you were viewing it from the side. The elevation profile of Africa (below) clearly shows sea level, low areas, and mountains.

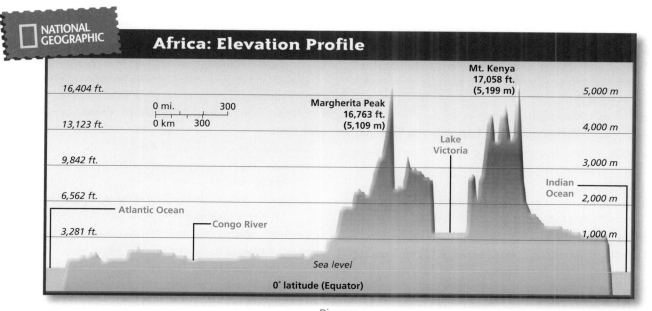

Africa: Elevation Profile

Diagram

NATIONAL GEOGRAPHIC
Geographic Dictionary

Volcano

Mountain peak

Strait

Sound

Valley

Island

Cape

Ocean

Cliff

Isthmus

Bay

Harbor

As you read about world history, you will encounter the terms listed below. Many of the terms are pictured in the diagram.

Gulf

Delta

Peninsula

Seacoast

absolute location exact location of a place on the earth described by global coordinates

basin area of land drained by a given river and its branches; area of land surrounded by lands of higher elevation

bay part of a large body of water that extends into a shoreline, generally smaller than a gulf

canyon deep and narrow valley with steep walls

cape point of land that extends into a river, lake, or ocean

channel wide strait or waterway between two landmasses that lie close to each other; deep part of a river or other waterway

cliff steep, high wall of rock, earth, or ice

continent one of the seven large landmasses on the earth

cultural feature characteristic that humans have created in a place, such as language, religion, housing, or settlement pattern

delta flat, low-lying land built up from soil carried downstream by a river and deposited at its mouth

divide stretch of high land that separates river systems

downstream direction in which a river or stream flows from its source to its mouth

elevation height of land above sea level

Equator imaginary line that runs around the earth halfway between the North and South Poles; used as the starting point to measure degrees of north and south latitude

glacier large, thick body of slowly moving ice

gulf part of a large body of water that extends into a shoreline, generally larger and more deeply indented than a bay

harbor a sheltered place along a shoreline where ships can anchor safely

highland elevated land area such as a hill, mountain, or plateau

hill elevated land with sloping sides and rounded summit; generally smaller than a mountain

island land area, smaller than a continent, completely surrounded by water

isthmus narrow stretch of land connecting two larger land areas

lake a sizable inland body of water

latitude distance north or south of the Equator, measured in degrees

longitude distance east or west of the Prime Meridian, measured in degrees

lowland land, usually level, at a low elevation

map drawing of the earth shown on a flat surface

meridian one of many lines on the global grid running from the North Pole to the South Pole; used to measure degrees of longitude

mesa broad, flat-topped landform with steep sides; smaller than a plateau

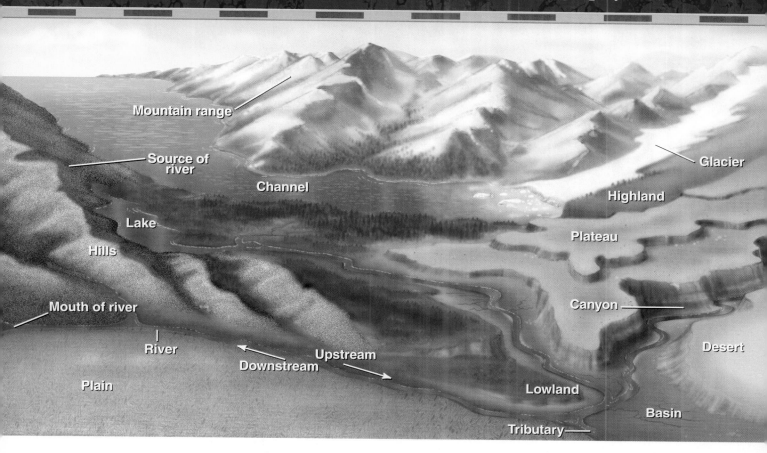

mountain land with steep sides that rises sharply (1,000 feet [305 m] or more) from surrounding land; generally larger and more rugged than a hill

mountain peak pointed top of a mountain

mountain range a series of connected mountains

mouth (of a river) place where a stream or river flows into a larger body of water

ocean one of the four major bodies of salt water that surround the continents

ocean current stream of either cold or warm water that moves in a definite direction through an ocean

parallel one of many lines on the global grid that circle the earth north or south of the Equator; used to measure degrees of latitude

peninsula body of land jutting into a lake or ocean, surrounded on three sides by water

physical feature characteristic of a place occurring naturally, such as a landform, body of water, climate pattern, or resource

plain area of level land, usually at a low elevation and often covered with grasses

plateau area of flat or rolling land at a high elevation, about 300–3,000 feet (91–914 m) high

Prime Meridian line of the global grid running from the North Pole to the South Pole through Greenwich, England; starting point for measuring degrees of east and west longitude

relief changes in elevation over a given area of land

river large natural stream of water that runs through the land

sea large body of water completely or partly surrounded by land

seacoast land lying next to a sea or ocean

sea level position on land level with surface of nearby ocean or sea

sound body of water between a coastline and one or more islands off the coast

source (of a river) place where a river or stream begins, often in highlands

strait narrow stretch of water joining two larger bodies of water

tributary small river or stream that flows into a larger river or stream; a branch of the river

upstream direction opposite the flow of a river; toward the source of a river or stream

valley area of low land between hills or mountains

volcano mountain created as liquid rock or ash erupts from inside the earth

Tools of the Historian

A historian is a person who studies and writes about the people and events of the past. Historians find out how people lived, what happened to them, and what happened around them. Historians look for the reasons behind events. They also study the effects of events.

Have you ever wondered if you could be a historian? To answer that question, you will need to find out how history is researched and written. Historians use a number of tools to research and organize information. You can learn about these tools in the next few pages. As you study this textbook, you will see that these tools will help you understand world history.

Archaeologists ► are scientists who unearth the remains of the past. Historians depend on their work.

Digging Up the Past

What Do Archaeologists Study?
- Human and animal bones, seeds, trees
- Pottery, tools, weapons
- Mounds, pits, canals

▲ Prehistoric pottery

How Do They Gather Data?
- Surveys on foot
- Photographs taken from airplanes or satellites
- Ground-penetrating radar
- Locations plotted on maps
- Evidence gathered with tools from heavy equipment to shovels
- Sonar scanning to find underwater objects

How Do They Interpret Findings?
- Organize artifacts into groups based on similarities
- Compare objects in relation to other objects
- Look for evidence of changes over a period of time
- Date once-living objects by measuring carbon-14 levels
- Use microscopic and biological tests to date objects

Carbon-14 dating ►

Do Your Own Digging

Research the library and Internet to find information on two archaeological diggings, one past and the other, very recent. Compare and contrast the methods used in each digging. What changes do you notice in tools archaeologists have used over time?

Measuring Time

Main Idea

Historians rely on calendars and the dating of events to measure time.

Reading Focus Have you ever thought about traveling back in time to a place long ago? Historians do just that. Read to see how historians keep track of past events.

Calendars Historians rely on *calendars*, or dating systems, to measure time. Cultures throughout the world have developed different calendars based on important events in their history. Western nations begin their calendar on the year in which Jesus was thought to have been born. The Jewish calendar begins about 3,760 years before the Christian calendar. This is the time when Jewish tradition says the world was created. Muslims date their calendar from the time their first leader, Muhammad, left the city of Makkah for Madinah. This was a.d. 622 in the Christian calendar.

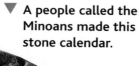

▼ **A people called the Minoans made this stone calendar.**

The dates in this book are based on the Western calendar. In the Western calendar, the years before the birth of Jesus are known as "B.C.," or "before Christ." The years after are called "A.D.," or *anno domini*. This phrase comes from the Latin language and means "in the year of the Lord."

▲ **About A.D. 500, a Christian monk, or religious person, developed the Western way of dating events.**

Dating Events To date events *before* the birth of Christ, or "B.C.," historians count backwards from A.D. 1. There is no year "0." The year before A.D. 1 is 1 B.C. (Notice that "A.D." is written before the date, while "B.C." is written following the date.) Therefore, a date in the 100 years before the birth of Christ lies between 100 B.C. and A.D. 1.

To date events after the birth of Christ, or "A.D.," historians count forward, starting at A.D. 1. A date in the first 100 years after the birth of Christ is between A.D. 1 and A.D. 100.

Thinking Like a Historian

1. **Identify** What do "B.C." and "A.D." mean? How are they used?

2. **Dating Events** What year came *after* 184 B.C.?

3. **Comparing and Contrasting** As you read, use the Internet to find out the current year in the calendars mentioned in your text. Why are calendars different from culture to culture?

Organizing Time

◀ Tools made by prehistoric people

Main Idea

Historians organize history by dividing it into blocks of time.

Reading Focus Have you ever thought about the names given to a block of events, such as "summer vacation" or "the baseball season?" Read to see how historians use names to describe different stretches of time in history.

Periods of History Historians divide history into blocks of time known as *periods*, or *eras*. For example, a period of 10 years is called a *decade*. A period of 100 years is known as a *century*. Centuries are grouped into even longer time periods, which are given names.

The first of these long periods is called *Prehistory*. Prehistory refers to the time before people developed writing, about 5,500 years ago. This is followed by the period known as *Ancient History*, ending c. A.D. 500. (c., or *circa*, means "about"). Historians call the next thousand years the *Middle Ages*, or the medieval period. From c. 1500, *Modern History* begins

▲ A young couple of ancient Rome

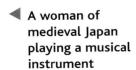

◀ A woman of medieval Japan playing a musical instrument

◀ Educated Europeans of the early modern period discussing new ideas

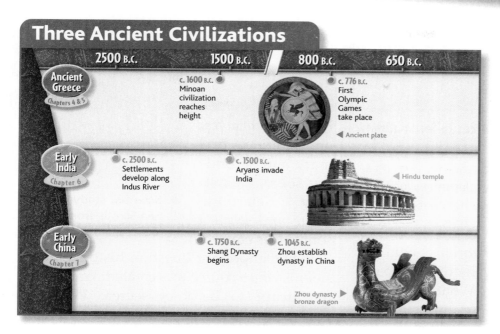

Three Ancient Civilizations

	2500 B.C.	1500 B.C.	800 B.C.	650 B.C.

Ancient Greece Chapters 4 & 5

c. 1600 B.C. Minoan civilization reaches height

c. 776 B.C. First Olympic Games take place

◄ Ancient plate

Early India Chapter 6

c. 2500 B.C. Settlements develop along Indus River

c. 1500 B.C. Aryans invade India

◄ Hindu temple

Early China Chapter 7

c. 1750 B.C. Shang Dynasty begins

c. 1045 B.C. Zhou establish dynasty in China

Zhou dynasty ► bronze dragon

and continues to the present day. In this book, you will study the history of the world from prehistory to the beginning of the modern period.

What Is a Time Line? Which came first: the American Civil War or World War II? Did the train come before or after the invention of the airplane? In studying the past, historians focus on *chronology,* or the order of dates in which events happened.

You might be wondering how to make sense of the flow of dates and events. An easy way is to use or make a time line. A *time line* is a diagram that shows the order of events within a period of time.

Most time lines are divided into sections in which the years are evenly spaced. In some cases, however, a spread of time may be too long to show all of the years in even spaces. To save space, a period of time may be omitted from the time line. Where this happens, a slanted or jagged line appears on the time line to show a break in the even spacing of events. For example, the time line above shows a break between 1500 B.C. and 800 B.C.

A time line also labels events. Each event on the time line appears beside the date when the event took place. Sometimes events and their dates are shown on a single time line. In other cases, two or more time lines are stacked one on top of the other. These are called multilevel time lines. They help you to compare events in different places at certain periods of time. For example, the multilevel time line above shows events in three ancient civilizations from 2500 B.C. to 650 B.C. The skill "Reading a Time Line" on page 905 will help you learn to work with time lines.

Thinking Like a Historian

1. **Reading a Time Line** Look over the time line above to get an idea of what a time line shows. What is the title? When does it begin and end? What two features make this time line different from many other time lines? Why are they used?

2. **Understanding a Time Line** Why do you think the dates on the time line are marked with a "c."?

3. **Making a Time Line** Create a time line using the terms B.M.B. (before my birth) and A.M.B. (after my birth). Fill in the time line with five key events that happened before and after you were born. Illustrate the time line with copies of photos from your family album.

How Does a Historian Work?

Historians study a variety of sources to learn about the past.

Reading Focus Have you ever searched for clues on a treasure hunt? Read to find out how historians look for clues to create a written record about the past.

....

Where Is the Evidence? Historians begin by asking questions, such as: Why did two particular countries go to war? What effect did their fighting have on the lives of their people? How does the conflict influence our world today? Such questions help historians identify and focus on historical problems.

Historians generally find evidence in primary sources and secondary sources. *Primary sources* are firsthand pieces of evidence from people who saw or experienced an event. They include written documents, such as letters, diaries, and official records. They also include spoken interviews as well as objects, such as photos, paintings, clothing, and tools. The skill "Analyzing Primary Source Documents" on page 910 will give you a chance to work with written primary sources.

Secondary sources, on the other hand, are created *after* the events by people who played no part in them. Secondary sources can be partially based on primary sources. They include biographies, encyclopedias, and history books—even this textbook.

Historians study secondary sources for background information and for a larger view of an event. However, to get new evidence that advances knowledge, historians must turn to the firsthand information found only in primary sources.

Examining Sources
Historians *analyze*, or examine, primary and secondary sources. First, they determine *where* and *when* a source was created.

▲ Scientist studying Dead Sea Scrolls from southwest Asia

Another important question historians consider is *why* a source was created. Was it a letter meant to be kept secret? Was it a government document published for all citizens to read?

Can the Sources Be Trusted? Historians examine sources for *credibility,* or truthfulness. This is because each source reflects a *point of view,* or a general attitude about people and life. The creator of a source uses his or her point of view to decide what events were important, which people were key players, and what details were worth recording. Sometimes point of view is expressed as a *bias,* or an unreasoned, emotional judgment about people and events.

Historians try to be aware of point of view and bias both in their sources and in themselves. Therefore, they check new

▲ Ruins of Mayan temple in Central America

The Decline of Rome

Weak Roman Government
• Dishonest government officials provide poor leadership.

Social Problems
• Famine and disease spread throughout the empire.

Declining Economy
• Income and wages fall.
• Wealthy fail to pay taxes.

Reform Fails and Rome Divides in Two
• Government fails to keep order.
• Violence and tension increase.
• Diocletian divides the empire.

Eastern Roman Empire
• Constantinople becomes the new capital.
• The empire survives attacks and prospers.

Western Roman Empire
• Numerous attacks threaten the empire.
• Territory is slowly lost to invaders.

Byzantine Empire
• This empire is created from the Eastern Roman Empire and lasts nearly 1,000 years.

Rome Falls
• The city of Rome falls in A.D. 476.
• The Western Roman Empire is divided into Germanic kingdoms by A.D. 550.

sources and their own ideas against sources already known to be trustworthy. They also examine many sources that express different points of view about an event. In this way, historians try to get a clear, well-rounded view of what happened.

Historians piece together the credible evidence and draw conclusions. In drawing conclusions, they use their own thinking and knowledge of the past to *interpret*, or explain, the meaning of the events.

Cause and Effect

Historical events are linked by cause and effect. A *cause* is what makes an event happen. The event that happens as a result of the cause is known as an *effect*. Historians look for cause-and-effect links to explain *why* events happen.

Usually, one event is produced by many causes. Similarly, one event often produces several different effects. These cause-and-effect links form what is called a *cause-and-effect chain*. Because so many historical events are related, cause-and-effect chains can become very long and can include events that occur over a long period of time. The chart above shows such a chain of events.

Thinking Like a Historian

1. **Understanding Evidence** Suppose a friend wanted to write a history of your life so far. What primary sources might he or she use to find evidence of your daily activities?

2. **Analyzing Sources** Find two written accounts of a recent event in your town. Which of the two accounts do you think is the most credible? Why?

3. **Recognizing Cause and Effect** Study the cause-and-effect chart on this page. What were three major causes of Rome's decline? What were two important effects of Rome's decline upon history?

History and Geography

Historians try to understand how climate, landforms, and human activities have shaped past events.

Reading Focus Have you ever had a party or sports event cancelled because of bad weather? Read to find out how historians study the effects of the natural world on history.

▲ Growing rice in China

Geography is the study of the earth's physical and human features. In this text, you will discover how geography has shaped the course of events in world history. Sometimes the study of geography is broken down into five themes. *The Five Themes of Geography* are:

- **location** (Where is it?)
- **place** (What is it like?)
- **human/environment interaction** (What is the relationship between people and their surroundings?)
- **movement** (How do people in one area relate to people in other areas?)
- **region** (What common features bring geographical areas together?)

The Acropolis, Athens, Greece ▶

Location

"Where is it?" In using geography, historians first look at where a place is located. Every place has an absolute location and a relative location. *Absolute location* refers to the exact spot of a place on the earth's surface. For example, the city of Atlanta, Georgia, is located at one place and one place only. No other place on Earth has exactly the same location. *Relative location* tells where a place is, compared with one or more other places. Atlanta is northwest of Miami, Florida, and southwest of New York City.

Place

"What is it like?" *Place* describes all of the characteristics that give an area its own special quality. These can be physical features, such as mountains, waterways, climate, and plant or animal life. Places can also be described by human characteristics, such as language, religion, and architecture.

Human/Environment Interaction

"What is the relationship between people and their surroundings?" Landforms, waterways, climate, and natural resources all have helped or hindered human activities. People in turn have responded to their environment, or natural surroundings, in different ways. Sometimes they have adjusted to it. At other times, people have changed their environment to meet their needs.

▲ Camel caravan in North Africa

◀ Settlement in Mongolia

▲ Wall painting showing life in ancient Egypt

Movement

"How do people in one area relate to people in other areas?" Historians answer this question within the theme of *movement.* Throughout history, people, ideas, goods, and information have moved from place to place. Movement has brought the world's people closer together. Transportation—the movement of people and goods—has increased the exchange of ideas and cultures. Communication—the movement of ideas and information—has allowed people to find out what is happening in other parts of the world.

Region

"What common features bring geographical areas together?" To make sense of all the complex things in the world, historians often view places or areas as regions. A *region* is an area that is defined by common features. Regions can be defined by physical features, such mountains and rivers, or by human features, such as religion, language, or livelihood.

Six Essential Elements

Recently the study of geography has been broken down into *Six Essential Elements:*
- The World in Spatial Terms
- Places and Regions
- Physical Systems
- Human Systems
- Environment and Society
- The Uses of Geography

You can learn about the Six Essential Elements in the Geography Handbook on pages GH2–GH3. Knowing these elements will help you in your study of history.

Thinking Like a Historian

1. **Identify** How are absolute location and relative location different?

2. **Analyzing Themes** What characteristics do geographers use to describe a place?

3. **Linking History and Geography** Make a list of the Five Themes of Geography. Under each theme, explain how you think geography has shaped the history of your community.

What Is a Historical Atlas?

Main Idea

Maps give information about areas of the world at different periods of history.

Reading Focus Have you used a map to go from one place to another? Read to find out how you can rely on maps for clues about the past.

Historical Maps An *atlas* is a book of maps showing different parts of the world. A *historical atlas* has maps showing different parts of the world at different periods of history. Maps that show political events, such as invasions, battles, and boundary changes, are called *historical maps.*

Some historical maps show how territories in a certain part of the world changed over time. Below are two maps. One map shows the areas of Europe, Asia, and Africa that were ruled by Alexander the Great in 323 B.C. The other map shows the same region as it looks today. Placed next to each other, the maps help you compare historical changes in the region from ancient times to today.

In the larger map, Alexander's empire stretches from the Mediterranean Sea in the west to the Indus River in the east. There are no political borders. Instead, other things are shown. For example, the arrows on the map represent the movement of Alexander's armies as they conquered new lands. On the smaller map, lines show modern political boundaries in the region today.

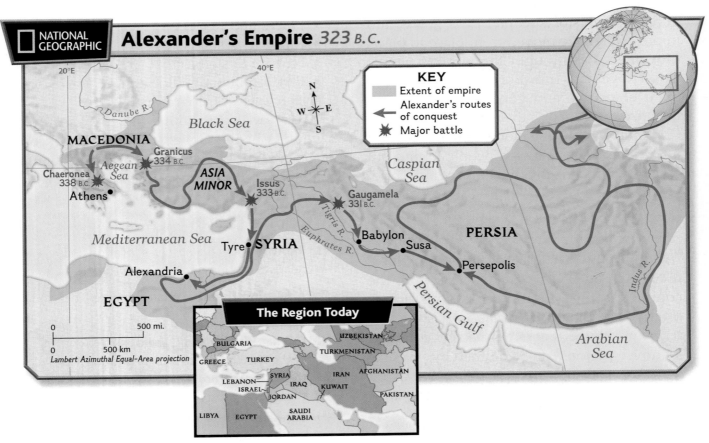

NATIONAL GEOGRAPHIC

Alexander's Empire 323 B.C.

KEY
- Extent of empire
- ← Alexander's routes of conquest
- ✳ Major battle

20°E · Danube R. · Black Sea · 40°E · N W E S · Caspian Sea

MACEDONIA · Granicus 334 B.C. · Aegean Sea · ASIA MINOR · Issus 333 B.C.

Chaeronea 338 B.C. · Athens · Gaugamela 331 B.C. · Tigris R. · Babylon · Susa · PERSIA

Mediterranean Sea · Tyre · SYRIA · Euphrates R. · Persepolis

Alexandria · EGYPT · Persian Gulf · Indus R. · Arabian Sea

0   500 mi.
0   500 km
Lambert Azimuthal Equal-Area projection

The Region Today

BULGARIA · UZBEKISTAN · GREECE · TURKEY · TURKMENISTAN · LEBANON · SYRIA · IRAN · AFGHANISTAN · ISRAEL · IRAQ · KUWAIT · JORDAN · PAKISTAN · LIBYA · EGYPT · SAUDI ARABIA

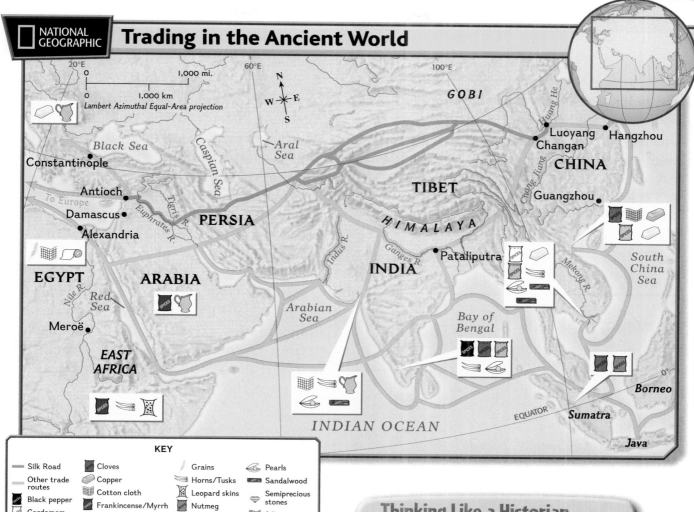

Trading in the Ancient World

NATIONAL GEOGRAPHIC

KEY

- ━━ Silk Road
- ━━ Other trade routes
- Black pepper
- Cardamom
- Cinnamon
- Cloves
- Copper
- Cotton cloth
- Frankincense/Myrrh
- Gold
- Ginger
- Grains
- Horns/Tusks
- Leopard skins
- Nutmeg
- Oils
- Papyrus
- Pearls
- Sandalwood
- Semiprecious stones
- Silk
- Teakwood

Historical Routes On some maps, lines may show *historical routes.* These are roads or courses over which people or goods have traveled all through history. Such routes are often colored. On the map above, the purple line shows the Silk Road, the ancient trading route between Asia and Europe.

On maps of historical routes, the key gives clues to what is shown on the maps. This map key shows the different goods traded throughout the ancient world.

Thinking Like a Historian

1. **Comparing Maps** Alexander's empire included many different territories. In what territory was the city of Persepolis located? What present-day country covers this area today?

2. **Reading a Map Legend** Look at the map of ancient trade routes. What goods came from southern India? How were goods carried from place to place in ancient times?

3. **Analyzing Maps** Select any chapter in your textbook. List the titles of the maps found in that chapter. Beside each map title, state what kind of symbols are used in each map key and what they represent.

Links Across Time

....

The people and events of the past have left their mark on our world today.

Reading Focus How have older family members shaped your life today? In the same way, many things link past to present in world history. Read about examples of past-and-present links for each of the six units you will be studying in your text.

....

▲ Fighting today between Palestinians and Israelis

Unit 1 Early Civilizations

Civilizations arose at different times in different parts of the world. Many civilizations grew out of farming settlements in river valleys. Southeast Asia was an early center of civilized life. For centuries, people in southwest Asia have fought over scarce land and water. Religious and ethnic differences also have led to wars.

Today, one of the fiercest and longest conflicts has been between Palestinian Arabs and Israelis. Although many Arabs and Israelis support peace efforts, hatred and fear run deep on both sides.

▼ Ancient warriors attack walled city

People in ancient civilizations admired the deeds of their heroes. The ancient Greeks held the first Olympic games about 776 B.C. Athletes came from all over the Greek-speaking world to compete in the games. Today the modern Olympics draw athletes from all over the world.

▼ **Ancient Greek athletes**

▲ **Racers in modern Olympics**

▲ **Roman Senate**

Unit 3 New Empires and New Faiths

After 500 B.C., strong governments and new religions arose in many parts of the world. The Romans created a common culture among the many different peoples living in the Mediterranean world. The Roman system of laws was a lasting achievement. The Romans believed that laws apply equally to all citizens. Today, the U.S. Congress is the part of our national government that makes laws. Its upper body—the U.S. Senate—is named after the Senate of ancient Rome.

◀ **U.S. Congress**

Links Across Time

Unit 4 The Middle Ages

The period from about A.D. 500 to A.D. 1500 is known as the Middle Ages. During this time, trade routes expanded, and ideas and goods spread. Sometimes, these contacts led to wars that lasted for years. In other cases, ideas and practices were peacefully adopted.

In medieval China, the Grand Canal increased trade and prosperity. Today, modern China is building the Three Gorges Dam to provide electric power for its growing cities.

▲ Grand Canal

▶ Three Gorges Dam

Unit 5 A Changing World

Beginning about A.D. 1500, thinkers developed new ideas about government. An age of exploration led to global trade and the conquest of empires. Meanwhile, people began to use scientific ideas to explore nature. One discovery or invention led to another, creating an explosion of knowledge. Advances in science continue today.

▲ Early telescope, A.D. 1600s

◀ Modern Space Station

Unit 6 Modern Times

Modern times refers to the period from the late 1700s to the present. During this era of momentous change, uprisings led to the overthrow of vast empires and the rise of new nations. Dictators ruled in some countries, but democracy and respect for human rights became widely accepted. New inventions and discoveries raised standards of living and brought the world's cultures closer together. However, access to new weapons threatened world peace. Nations began to work together to find answers to common problems.

▼ Students using computers to access the Internet

▼ Building collapses in London during World War II

Thinking Like a Historian

As you read *Journey Across Time*, notice how the past affects the present. When you begin each unit, collect newspaper or magazine articles about a current event from the area you are studying. Then, after completing each unit, write down how you think a past event in that region is related to the current event.

Early Civilizations

Why It's Important

Each civilization that you will study in this unit made important contributions to history.

- The Mesopotamians developed writing.
- The Egyptians created papyrus.
- The Israelites' scripture influenced the religions of Europe.

8000 B.C.   5000 B.C.   2000 B.C.

First Civilizations
Chapter 1

c. 8000 B.C.
Farming begins in southwest Asia

c. 3200 B.C.
Sumerians in Mesopotamia develop writing

c. 1790 B.C.
Hammurabi introduces code of laws

Hammurabi stands before a god

Ancient Egypt
Chapter 2

c. 5000 B.C.
Hunter-gatherers settle Nile River valley

c. 2540 B.C.
Egyptians complete building of Great Pyramid

c. 1500 B.C.
Queen Hatshepsut becomes pharaoh

Pyramids at Giza, Egypt

Ancient Israelites
Chapter 3

c. 2000 B.C.
Abraham enters Canaan

Abraham leads Israelites to Canaan

Where in the World?

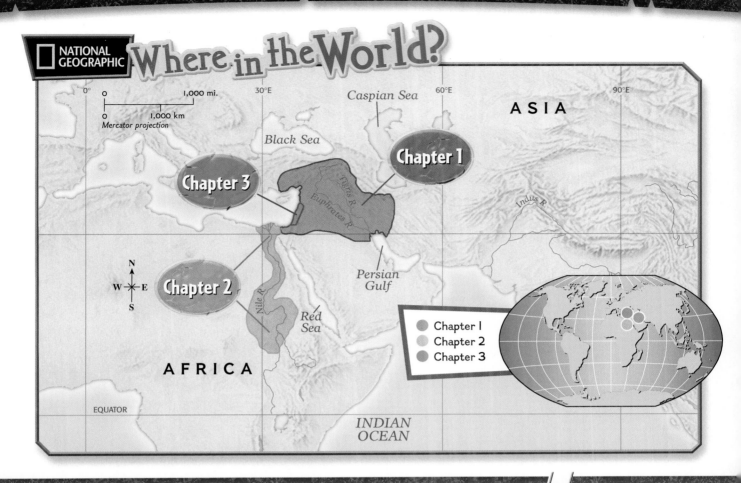

Chapter 3

Chapter 1

Chapter 2

ASIA

AFRICA

Caspian Sea

Black Sea

Tigris R.

Euphrates R.

Indus R.

Nile R.

Persian Gulf

Red Sea

EQUATOR

INDIAN OCEAN

0°   30°E   60°E   90°E

0   1,000 mi.
0   1,000 km
Mercator projection

N
W   E
S

● Chapter 1
● Chapter 2
● Chapter 3

| 1000 B.C. | 750 B.C. | 500 B.C. | 250 B.C. | A.D. 100 |

c. 744 B.C. Assyria expands into Babylon

c. 612 B.C. Chaldeans capture Assyrian capital

Hanging gardens of Babylon ▶

c. 1000 B.C. Kush breaks free of Egypt

728 B.C. Kush conquers Egypt

Kushite king Taharqa ▶

Lion statue honoring ▶ Kushite king Aspalta

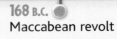

c. 1000 B.C. King David rules Israel

586 B.C. Chaldeans capture Jerusalem

168 B.C. Maccabean revolt

A.D. 70 Romans destroy temple in Jerusalem

◀ Jews led into exile

Ancient Jerusalem ◀

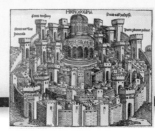

1

Mediterranean Sea

1 Ishtar Gate
See First Civilizations 
Chapter 1

2 Sumerian figures 
See First Civilizations
Chapter 1

5

3

AFRICA

Red Sea

4

People to Meet

Ötzi

c. 3300 B.C.
Iceman found in the Alps
Chapter 1, page 12

Hammurabi

Ruled c. 1792–1750 B.C.
Babylonian king
Chapter 1, page 22

Hatshepsut

Ruled c. 1473–1458 B.C.
Egyptian pharaoh
Chapter 2, page 63

ASIA

Caspian Sea

Persian Gulf

① ②

③ Egyptian sphinx

See Ancient Egypt
Chapter 2

④ Kushite pyramids

See Ancient Egypt
Chapter 2

⑤ Western Wall

See Ancient Israelites
Chapter 3

Ramses II

Ruled 1279–1213 B.C.
Egyptian ruler
Chapter 2, page 66

Ruth and Naomi

c. 1100 B.C.
Israelite women
Chapter 3, page 99

King David

Ruled c. 1000–970 B.C.
King of Israel
Chapter 3, page 88

The First Civilizations

Ruins of a ziggurat in Iraq ▶

NATIONAL GEOGRAPHIC When & Where?

3000 B.C.	2000 B.C.	1000 B.C.
c. 3000 B.C. Bronze Age begins	c. 1792 B.C. Hammurabi rules Mesopotamia	612 B.C. Nineveh captured; Assyrian Empire crumbles

Chapter Preview

Some of the first civilizations arose in southwest Asia. The people of these civilizations gradually learned how to farm and developed systems of government, writing, and religion.

 View the Chapter 1 video in the *World History: Journey Across Time* Video Program.

History Online
Chapter Overview Visit jat.glencoe.com for a preview of Chapter 1.

 ## Early Humans

The earliest humans hunted animals and gathered plants for food. When farming developed, people settled in towns and cities.

 ## Mesopotamian Civilization

In early Mesopotamian civilizations, religion and government were closely linked. Kings created strict laws to govern the people.

 ## The First Empires

New empires arose in Mesopotamia around 900 B.C. These civilizations included the Assyrians and the Chaldeans. They used powerful armies and iron weapons to conquer the region.

 **Study Organizer**

Compare and Contrast *Make this foldable to help you compare and contrast the ancient civilizations of Mesopotamia.*

Step 1 *Fold a sheet of paper in half from side to side.*

Fold it so the left edge lies about $\frac{1}{2}$ inch from the right edge.

Step 2 *Turn the paper and fold it into thirds.*

Step 3 *Unfold and cut the top layer only along both folds.*

This will make three tabs.

Step 4 *Label as shown.*

The First Civilizations
| Early Humans | Mesopo-tamia | Empires |

Reading and Writing *As you read the chapter, write notes under each appropriate tab of your foldable. Keep in mind that you are trying to compare these civilizations.*

Chapter 1

Reading Social Studies

Reading Skill

Previewing

1 Learn It!

Get Ready to Read!

Before you read, take time to preview the chapter. This will give you a head start on what you are about to learn. Follow the steps below to help you quickly read, or skim, Section 1 on page 9.

2–The Main Idea under each main head tells you the "big picture." It summarizes the main point of what you are about to read.

3–The **Reading Focus** helps you to make a connection between what you might already know and what you are about to read.

> **Early Humans**
>
> Main Idea **Paleolithic people adapted to their environment and invented many tools to help them survive.**
>
> **Reading Focus** What do you view as the greatest human achievement? Sending people to the moon, perhaps, or inventing the computer? Read to learn about the accomplishments of people during the Paleolithic Age.
>
> **History is the story of humans . . .**
>
> **Tools of Disovery**

1–Read the main headings in large red type. They show the main topics covered in the section or chapter.

4–Under each main head, read the subheads in blue type. Subheads break down each main topic into smaller topics.

Reading Tip

As you skim, also look at pictures, maps, and charts.

2 Practice It!
Preview by Skimming

Read to Write ┄┄┄┄┄┄
Use each main head, the main ideas, and the subheads in Section 2 of this chapter to create a study outline.

Section 3 The First Empires

Skim all of the main heads and main ideas in Section 3 starting on page 26. Then, in small groups, discuss the answers to these questions.

- Which part of this section do you think will be most interesting to you?
- What do you think will be covered in Section 3 that was not covered in Section 2?
- Are there any words in the Main Ideas that you do not know how to pronounce?
- Choose one of the Reading Focus questions to discuss in your group.

3 Apply It!

Skim Section 2 on your own. Write one thing in your notebook that you want to learn by reading this chapter.

Early Humans

Get Ready to Read!

What's the Connection?
Today people live in towns and cities of various sizes and make their living in different ways. Read to find out how early humans lived by moving from place to place, forming settlements, and exploring different ways to provide for themselves and their families.

Focusing on the Main Ideas
- Paleolithic people adapted to their environment and invented many tools to help them survive. *(page 9)*
- In the Neolithic Age, people started farming, building communities, producing goods, and trading. *(page 13)*

Locating Places
Jericho (JEHR•ih•KOH)
Çatal Hüyük
(chah•TAHL   hoo•YOOK)

Building Your Vocabulary
historian (hih•STOHR•ee•uhn)
archaeologist
(AHR•kee•AH•luh•jihst)
artifact (AHR•tih•FAKT)
fossil (FAH•suhl)
anthropologist
(AN•thruh•PAH•luh•jihst)
nomad (NOH•MAD)
technology (tehk•NAH•luh•jee)
domesticate (duh•MEHS•tih•KAYT)
specialization
(SPEH•shuh•luh•ZAY•shuhn)

Reading Strategy
Determine Cause and Effect Draw a diagram like the one below. Use it to explain how early humans adapted to their environment.

Cause:	→	Effect:
Cause:	→	Effect:
Cause:	→	Effect:

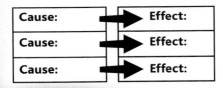

NATIONAL GEOGRAPHIC When & Where?

Çatal Hüyük

Jericho

| 8000 B.C. | 6000 B.C. | 4000 B.C. | 2000 B.C. |

c. 8000 B.C.
Jericho founded

c. 6700 B.C.
Çatal Hüyük settled

c. 3000 B.C.
Bronze Age begins

Early Humans

Main Idea Paleolithic people adapted to their environment and invented many tools to help them survive.

Reading Focus What do you view as the greatest human achievement? Sending people to the moon, perhaps, or inventing the computer? Read to learn about the accomplishments of people during the Paleolithic Age.

History is the story of humans in the past. It tells what they did and what happened to them. **Historians** (hih•STOHR•ee•uhns) are people who study and write about the human past. They tell us that history began about 5,500 years ago, when people first began to write. But the story of people really begins in prehistory—the time *before* people developed writing.

Tools of Discovery What we know about the earliest people comes from the things they left behind. Scientists have worked to uncover clues about early human life. **Archaeologists** (AHR•kee•AH•luh•jihsts) hunt for evidence buried in the ground where settlements might once have been. They dig up and study **artifacts** (AHR•tih•FAKTS)—weapons, tools, and other things made by humans. They also look for **fossils** (FAH•suhls)—traces of plants or animals that have been preserved in rock. **Anthropologists** (AN•thruh•PAH•luh•jihsts) focus on human society. They study how humans developed and how they related to one another.

Historians call the early period of human history the Stone Age. The name comes from the fact that people during this time used stone to make tools and weapons.

Archaeological Dig

Archaeologists use special techniques and tools when carrying out a dig. Artifacts are photographed or sketched and their locations are mapped and noted. Soil is passed through a mesh screen to collect small fragments of tools or bone. *What types of artifacts do archaeologists look for?*

BELOW THE SURFACE
Layers of soil are deposited one on top of another. In general, the farther the layer is below the surface, the older its soil and artifacts are.

PRESERVING
Archaeologists may use plaster to make a form or an imprint of something they have found.

LOOKING FOR FRAGMENTS
This scientist uses a wire mesh screen to sift the soil to discover small fragments of artifacts.

GRIDS
Grids like these help archaeologists record and map any artifacts found.

CLEANING
Artifacts must be handled and cleaned carefully, often with soft brushes or other instruments.

Paleolithic Cave Paintings

The oldest examples of Paleolithic art are cave paintings found in Spain and France. Most of the paintings are of animals. The paintings show that Paleolithic artists often used several colors and techniques. They sometimes used the uneven surface of the rock to create a three-dimensional effect.

▲ **Painting of bison in Spanish cave**

DBQ Document-Based Question

What does this cave painting tell us about life in the Paleolithic Age?

The earliest part of the period is the Paleolithic or Old Stone Age. *Paleolithic* means "old stone" in the Greek language. Paleolithic times began roughly 2.5 million years ago and lasted until around 8000 B.C.

Who Were the Hunter-Gatherers?
Try to imagine the world during the Stone Age, long before any roadways, farms, or villages existed. Early humans spent most of their time searching for food. They hunted animals, caught fish, ate insects, and gathered nuts, berries, fruits, grains, and plants.

Because they hunted and gathered, Paleolithic people were always on the move. They were **nomads** (NOH•MADS), or people who regularly move from place to place. They traveled in bands of 30 or so members because it was safer and made the search for food easier.

Men and women did different tasks within the group. Women stayed close to the campsite, which was typically near a stream or other water source. They looked after the children and searched nearby woods and meadows for berries, nuts, and grains.

Men hunted animals—an activity that sometimes took them far from camp. They had to learn the habits of animals and make tools for the kill. At first, they used clubs or drove the animals off cliffs. Over time, Paleolithic people invented spears, traps, and bows and arrows.

Adapting to the Environment
The way that Paleolithic people lived depended on where they lived. Those in warm climates needed little clothing or shelter. People in cold climates sought protection from the weather in caves. Over time, Paleolithic people created new kinds of shelter. The most common was probably made of animal hides held up by wooden poles.

Paleolithic people made a life-changing discovery when they learned to tame fire. Fire gave warmth to those gathered around it. It lit the darkness and scared away wild animals. Food cooked over the fire tasted better and was easier to digest. In addition, smoked meat could be kept longer.

Archaeologists believe that early humans started fires by rubbing two pieces of wood together. Paleolithic people later made drill-like wooden tools to start fires.

What Were the Ice Ages?
Fire was a key to the survival of Paleolithic people during the Ice Ages. These were long periods of extreme cold. The last Ice Age began about 100,000 B.C. From then until about 8000 B.C.,

thick ice sheets covered parts of Europe, Asia, and North America.

The Ice Age was a threat to human life. People risked death from the cold and also from hunger. Early humans had to adapt by changing their diet, building sturdier shelters, and using animal furs to make warm clothing. The mastery of fire helped people live in this environment.

Language, Art, and Religion

Another advance in Paleolithic times was the development of spoken language. Language made it far easier for people to work together and to pass on knowledge.

Early people expressed themselves not only in words but in art. They crushed yellow, black, and red rocks to make powders for paint. Then they dabbed this on cave walls, creating scenes of lions, oxen, panthers, and other animals.

Historians are not sure why these cave paintings were created. They may have had religious meaning. Early people also might have thought that painting an animal would bring good luck in the hunt.

The Invention of Tools

Paleolithic people were the first to use **technology** (tehk•NAH•luh•jee)—tools and methods to help humans perform tasks. People often used a hard stone called flint to make tools. By hitting flint with a hard stone, they could make it flake into pieces with very sharp edges. To make hand axes or hunting spears, they tied wooden poles to pieces of flint that were the right shape for the tool.

Over time, early people grew more skilled at making tools. They crafted smaller and sharper tools, such as fishhooks and needles made from animal bones. They used needles to make nets and baskets and to sew hides together for clothing.

✓ **Reading Check** **Contrast** How are fossils and artifacts different?

The Way It Was

Science and Inventions

Tools One of the most important advances of prehistoric people was the creation of stone tools. Tools made hunting, gathering, building shelter, and making clothing much easier.

The first tools were made of stones. Early humans quickly learned that grinding, breaking, and shaping the stones to create sharp edges made them more useful.

As technology advanced, people began making specific tools such as food choppers, meat scrapers, and spear points. In time, people learned that hitting a stone in a particular way would produce a flake—a long, sharp chip. Flakes were similar to knives in the way they were used.

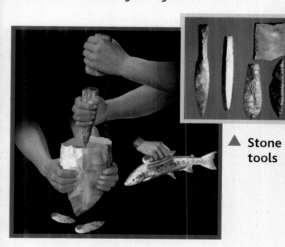

▲ Stone tools

▲ Flaking tools from a larger stone

Connecting to the Past

1. Why do you think early people chose stones to make their first tools?
2. How were flakes created?

Biography

ÖTZI THE ICEMAN

c. 3300 B.C.

In A.D. 1991 two hikers near the border between Austria and Italy discovered the frozen body of a man. The man was called "Ötzi" after the Ötztal Alps, the mountains where he was found. Scientists studied Ötzi's body, his clothes, and the items found with him to uncover clues about his life and death. One of the first amazing facts scientists learned was that Ötzi lived 5,300 years ago, during the Neolithic Age.

▲ Scientists created this reproduction to show what Ötzi may have looked like.

Ötzi was dressed warmly because of the cold climate. He was wearing a fur hat and a long grass cloak. Under the cloak was a leather jacket that was well-made but had been repaired several times. To keep his feet warm, he had stuffed grass in the bottom of his leather shoes. Scientists studied the tools and supplies Ötzi was carrying and decided that he planned to be away from home for many months. A bow and arrows, copper ax, and backpack were among the supplies found near Ötzi's body. Experts believe Ötzi was a shepherd who traveled with his herd. Ötzi probably returned to his village only twice a year.

From recent tests, scientists have learned more about the last hours of Ötzi's life. Shortly before he died, Ötzi ate a type of flat bread that is similar to a cracker, an herb or other green plant, and meat. Pollen found in Ötzi's stomach showed that he ate his last meal in the valley, south of where he was found. When Ötzi finished eating, he headed up into the mountains. Eight hours later, he died. Scientists believe that Ötzi's last hours were violent ones. When found, he clutched a knife in his right hand. Wounds on his right hand suggest that he tried to fight off an attacker. His left shoulder had been deeply pierced by an arrow. Some scientists think Ötzi may have wandered into another tribe's territory. Ötzi is now displayed at the South Tyrol Museum of Archaeology in Bolzano, Italy.

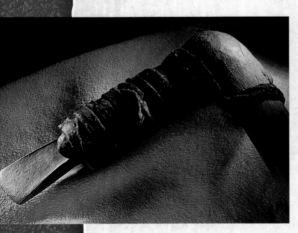

▲ This copper ax, along with the bow and arrows that you can see above, were Ötzi's main weapons.

Then and Now

If scientists 5,300 years from now discovered the remains of someone from our time, what might they conclude about our society?

Neolithic Times

Main Idea In the Neolithic Age, people started farming, building communities, producing goods, and trading.

Reading Focus Did you know that, today, more than a third of the world's people work in agriculture? Read to learn how farming began and how it changed the world.

After the last Ice Age ended, people began to change their way of life. They began to **domesticate** (duh•MEHS•tih•KAYT), or tame animals and plants for human use. Animals provided meat, milk, and wool. They also carried goods and pulled carts.

In addition, people also learned how to grow food. For the first time, people could stay in one place to grow grains and vegetables. Gradually, farming replaced hunting and gathering.

This change in the way people lived marked the beginning of the Neolithic Age, or New Stone Age, which began about 8000 B.C. and lasted until about 4000 B.C.

Why Was Farming Important?
Historians call the changes in the Neolithic Age the farming revolution. The word *revolution* refers to changes that greatly affect many areas of life. Some historians consider the farming revolution the most important event in human history.

Farming did not begin in one region and spread. People in different parts of the world discovered how to grow crops at about the same time. In Asia, people grew wheat, barley, rice, soybeans, and a grain called millet. In Mexico, farmers grew corn, squash, and potatoes. In Africa, they grew millet and a grain called sorghum.

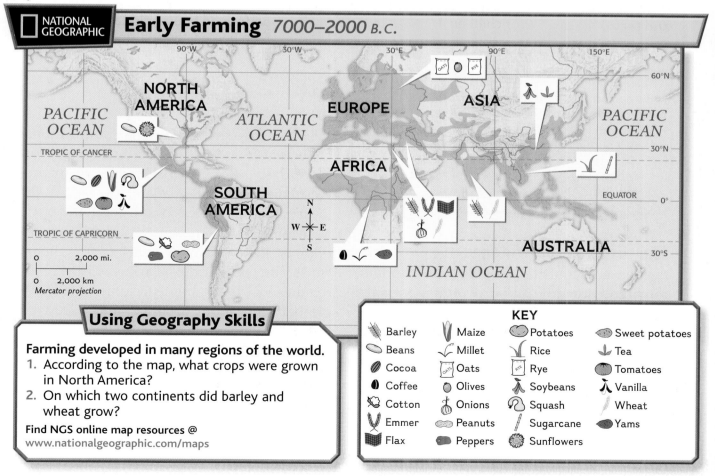

NATIONAL GEOGRAPHIC **Early Farming** *7000–2000 B.C.*

Using Geography Skills

Farming developed in many regions of the world.
1. According to the map, what crops were grown in North America?
2. On which two continents did barley and wheat grow?

Find NGS online map resources @
www.nationalgeographic.com/maps

KEY

Barley	Maize	Potatoes	Sweet potatoes
Beans	Millet	Rice	Tea
Cocoa	Oats	Rye	Tomatoes
Coffee	Olives	Soybeans	Vanilla
Cotton	Onions	Squash	Wheat
Emmer	Peanuts	Sugarcane	Yams
Flax	Peppers	Sunflowers	

Comparing the Neolithic and Paleolithic Ages

	Paleolithic Age	Neolithic Age

Description of Art and Crafts	Paleolithic people painted cave walls. They usually painted animals.	Neolithic people made pottery and carved objects out of wood. They also built shelters and tombs.
How Humans Obtained Food	People hunted animals and gathered nuts, berries, and grains.	People began to farm in permanent villages. They continued to raise and herd animals.
How Humans Adapted	People learned to make fire, created a language, and made simple tools and shelters.	People built mud-brick houses and places of worship. They specialized in certain jobs and used copper and bronze to create more useful tools.
Work of Women and Men	Women gathered food and cared for children. Men hunted.	Women cared for children and performed household tasks. Men herded, farmed, and protected the village.

Understanding Charts

Humans made great advances from the Paleolithic Age to the Neolithic Age.
1. How did the work of men change from the Paleolithic Age to the Neolithic Age?
2. **Describe** What advances were made in toolmaking between the Paleolithic and Neolithic Ages?

The Growth of Villages People who farmed could settle in one place. Herders remained nomadic and drove their animals wherever they could find grazing land. Farmers, however, had to stay close to their fields to water the plants, keep hungry animals away, and harvest their crops. They began to live in villages, where they built permanent homes.

During the Neolithic Age, villages were started in Europe, India, Egypt, China, and Mexico. The earliest known communities have been found in the Middle East. One of the oldest is **Jericho** (JEHR•ih•KOH) in the West Bank between what are now Israel and Jordan. This city dates back to about 8000 B.C.

Another well-known Neolithic community is **Çatal Hüyük** (chah•TAHL hoo•YOOK) in present-day Turkey. Little of it remains, but it was home to some 6,000 people between about 6700 B.C. and 5700 B.C. They lived in simple mud-brick houses that were packed tightly together and decorated inside with wall paintings. They used other buildings as places of worship. Along with farming, the people hunted, raised sheep and goats, and ate fish and bird eggs from nearby marshes.

The Benefits of a Settled Life The shift to settled life brought Neolithic people greater security than they had ever known. Steady food supplies meant healthy, growing populations. With a bigger population, there were more workers to produce a bigger crop.

Because villagers produced more than enough to eat, they began to trade their extra foodstuffs. They traded with people in their own communities and also with people who lived in other areas.

People began to practice **specialization** (SPEH•shuh•luh•ZAY•shuhn), or the development of different kinds of jobs. Because not everyone was needed for farming, some people had the time to develop other types of skills. They made pottery from clay to store their grain and other foods. They used plant fibers to make mats and to weave cloth. These craftspeople, like farmers, also took part in trade. They exchanged the things they made for goods they did not have.

In late Neolithic times, people continued to make advances. Toolmakers created better farming tools, such as the sickle for cutting grain. In some places, people began to work with metals. At first they used copper. They heated rocks to melt the copper inside and then poured it into molds for tools and weapons.

After 4000 B.C., craftspeople in western Asia mixed copper and tin to form bronze. Bronze was harder and longer lasting than copper. It became widely used between 3000 B.C. and 1200 B.C., the period known as the Bronze Age.

✓ **Reading Check** **Compare** How did the Paleolithic and Neolithic Ages differ?

Study Central™ Need help with the material in this section? Visit jat.glencoe.com

Section 1 Review

Reading Summary
Review the Main Ideas

- Early humans were nomads who moved around to hunt animals and gather food. They built shelters and used fire to survive. In time, they developed language and art.

- During the farming revolution, people began to grow crops and domesticate animals, which allowed them to settle in villages.

What Did You Learn?

1. Who are archaeologists and what do they study?

2. How did domesticating animals help the Neolithic people?

Critical Thinking

3. **Determine Cause and Effect** Draw a diagram like the one below. List some of the effects that farming had on people's lives.

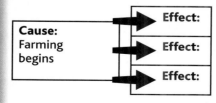

4. **Explain** Why were Paleolithic people nomads?

5. **Compare** Compare the technology of the Paleolithic Age with that of the Neolithic Age.

6. **Analyze** Why was the ability to make a fire so important?

7. **Reading** Previewing Create a three-column chart. In the first column, write what you knew about early humans before you read this section. In the second column, write what you learned after reading. In the third, write what you still would like to know.

Mesopotamian Civilization

Get Ready to Read!

What's the Connection?

In Section 1, you learned about early humans settling in towns. Some settled in Mesopotamia, an area called the "cradle of civilization."

Focusing on the Main Ideas

- Civilization in Mesopotamia began in the valleys of the Tigris and Euphrates Rivers. *(page 17)*

- Sumerians invented writing and made other important contributions to later peoples. *(page 20)*

- Sumerian city-states lost power when they were conquered by outsiders. *(page 23)*

Locating Places

Tigris River (TY•gruhs)
Euphrates River (yu•FRAY•teez)
Mesopotamia (MEH•suh•puh•TAY•mee•uh)
Sumer (SOO•muhr)
Babylon (BA•buh•luhn)

Meeting People

Sargon (SAHR•GAHN)
Hammurabi (HA•muh•RAH•bee)

Building Your Vocabulary

civilization (SIH•vuh•luh•ZAY•shuhn)
irrigation (IHR•uh•GAY•shuhn)
city-state
artisan (AHR•tuh•zuhn)
cuneiform (kyoo•NEE•uh•FAWRM)
scribe (SKRYB)
empire (EHM•PYR)

Reading Strategy

Sequencing Information Use a diagram to show how the first empire in Mesopotamia came about.

city-states formed
↓
↓

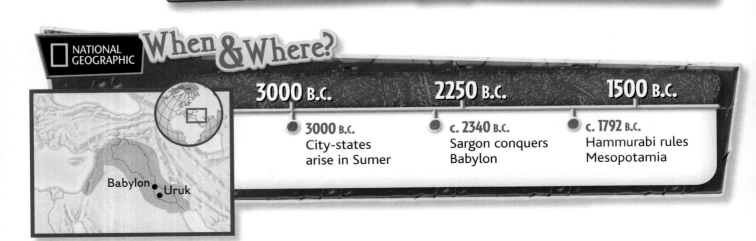

NATIONAL GEOGRAPHIC When & Where?

3000 B.C.

2250 B.C.

1500 B.C.

3000 B.C.
City-states arise in Sumer

c. 2340 B.C.
Sargon conquers Babylon

c. 1792 B.C.
Hammurabi rules Mesopotamia

Babylon • Uruk

Mesopotamia's Civilization

Main Idea Civilization in Mesopotamia began in the valleys of the Tigris and Euphrates Rivers.

Reading Focus Do you live in a region that receives plenty of rain or in a region that is dry? Think about how that affects you as you read how the Sumerians' environment affected them.

Over thousands of years, some of the early farming villages developed into civilizations. **Civilizations** (SIH•vuh•luh•ZAY•shuhns) are complex societies. They have cities, organized governments, art, religion, class divisions, and a writing system.

Why Were River Valleys Important? The first civilizations arose in river valleys because good farming conditions made it easy to feed large numbers of people. The rivers also made it easy to get from one place to another and to trade. Trade provided a way for goods and ideas to move from place to place. It was no accident, then, that cities grew up in these valleys and became the centers of civilizations.

As cities took shape, so did the need for organization. Someone had to make plans and decisions about matters of common concern. People formed governments to do just that. Their leaders took charge of food supplies and building projects. They made laws to keep order and assembled armies to fend off enemies.

With fewer worries about meeting their basic needs, people in the river valleys had more time to think about other things. They developed religions and the arts. To pass on

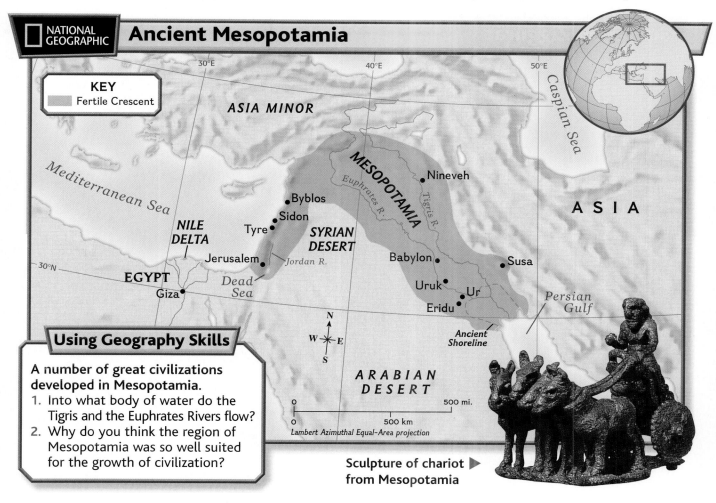

NATIONAL GEOGRAPHIC
Ancient Mesopotamia

KEY
Fertile Crescent

ASIA MINOR

Mediterranean Sea

NILE DELTA

EGYPT
Giza

Byblos
Sidon
Tyre

Jerusalem
Jordan R.
Dead Sea

SYRIAN DESERT

Euphrates R.

MESOPOTAMIA

Tigris R.

Nineveh

Babylon

Uruk
Ur
Eridu

Susa

ASIA

Caspian Sea

Persian Gulf

Ancient Shoreline

ARABIAN DESERT

N W E S

0   500 mi.
0   500 km
Lambert Azimuthal Equal-Area projection

30°E   40°E   50°E
30°N

Using Geography Skills

A number of great civilizations developed in Mesopotamia.

1. Into what body of water do the Tigris and the Euphrates Rivers flow?
2. Why do you think the region of Mesopotamia was so well suited for the growth of civilization?

Sculpture of chariot ▶ from Mesopotamia

information, they invented ways of writing. They also created calendars to tell time.

Early civilizations shared another feature—they had a class structure. That is, people held different places in society depending on what work they did and how much wealth or power they had.

The Rise of Sumer

The earliest-known civilization arose in what is now southern Iraq, on a flat plain bounded by the **Tigris River** (TY•gruhs) and the **Euphrates River** (yu•FRAY•teez). This area was called **Mesopotamia** (MEH•suh•puh•TAY•mee•uh), which is Greek for "the land between the rivers." Mesopotamia lay in the eastern part of the Fertile Crescent, a curving strip of land that extends from the Mediterranean Sea to the Persian Gulf.

Mesopotamia had a hot, dry climate. In the spring, the rivers often flooded, leaving behind rich soil for farming. The problem was that the flooding was very unpredictable. It might flood one year, but not the next. Every year, farmers worried about their crops. They came to believe they needed their gods to bless their efforts.

Over time, the farmers learned to build dams and channels to control the seasonal floods. They also built walls, waterways, and ditches to bring water to their fields. This way of watering crops is called **irrigation** (IHR•uh•GAY•shuhn). Irrigation allowed the farmers to grow plenty of food and support a large population. By 3000 B.C., many cities had formed in southern Mesopotamia in a region known as **Sumer** (SOO•muhr).

Sumerian Ziggurat

The top of the ziggurat was considered to be a holy place, and the area around the ziggurat contained palaces and royal storehouses. The surrounding walls had only one entrance because the ziggurat also served as the city's treasury. *How did people reach the upper levels of the ziggurat?*

▲ Statues of Sumerians praying

What Were City-States? Sumerian cities were isolated from each other by geography. Beyond the areas of settlement lay mudflats and patches of scorching desert. This terrain made travel and communication difficult. Each Sumerian city and the land around it became a separate **city-state.** It had its own government and was not part of any larger unit.

Sumerian city-states often went to war with one another. They fought to gain glory and to control more territory. For protection, each city-state surrounded itself with a wall. Because stone and wood were in short supply, the Sumerians used river mud as their main building material. They mixed the mud with crushed reeds, formed bricks, and left them in the sun to dry. The hard waterproof bricks were used for walls, as well as homes, temples, and other buildings.

Gods and Rulers
The Sumerians believed in many gods. Each was thought to have power over a natural force or a human activity—flooding, for example, or basket weaving. The Sumerians tried hard to please the gods. They built a grand temple called a ziggurat (ZIH•guh•RAT) to the chief god. The word *ziggurat* means "mountain of god" or "hill of heaven."

With tiers like a giant square wedding cake, the ziggurat dominated the city. At the top was a shrine, or special place of worship that only priests and priestesses could enter. The priests and priestesses were powerful and controlled much of the land. They may even have ruled at one time.

▲ A portion of the Royal Standard of Ur, a decorated box that shows scenes of Sumerian life

◀ These ruins are from the Sumerian city-state of Uruk. *What was a city-state?*

Later, kings ran the government. They led armies and organized building projects. The first kings were probably war heroes. Their position became hereditary. That is, after a king died, his son took over.

What Was Life Like in Sumer?
While Sumerian kings lived in large palaces, ordinary people lived in small mud-brick houses. Most people in Sumer farmed. Some, however, were **artisans** (AHR•tuh•zuhns), or skilled workers who made metal products, cloth, or pottery. Other people in Sumer worked as merchants or traders. They traveled to other cities and towns and traded tools, wheat, and barley for copper, tin, and timber—things that Sumer did not have.

People in Sumer were divided into three social classes. The upper class included kings, priests, and government officials. In the middle class were artisans, merchants, farmers, and fishers. These people made up the largest group. The lower class were enslaved people who worked on farms or in the temples.

Enslaved people were forced to serve others. Slaveholders thought of them as property. Some slaves were prisoners of war. Others were criminals. Still others were enslaved because they had to pay off their debts.

In Sumer, women and men had separate roles. Men headed the households. Only males could go to school. Women, however, did have rights. They could buy and sell property and run businesses.

▲ Sumerian cuneiform

Reading Check **Explain** How did Mesopotamians control the flow of the Tigris and Euphrates Rivers?

A Skilled People

Main Idea Sumerians invented writing and made other important contributions to later peoples.

Reading Focus Do you like to read? If so, you owe a debt to the Sumerians, because they were the first to invent writing. Read about this achievement and others.

The Sumerians left a lasting mark on world history. Their ideas and inventions were copied and improved upon by other peoples. As a result, Mesopotamia has been called the "cradle of civilization."

Why Was Writing Important?
The people of Sumer created many things that still affect our lives today. Probably their greatest invention was writing. Writing is important because it helps people keep records and pass on their ideas to others.

People in Sumer developed writing to keep track of business deals and other events. Their writing was called **cuneiform** (kyoo•NEE•uh•FAWRM). It consisted of hundreds of wedge-shaped marks cut into damp clay tablets with a sharp-ended reed. Archaeologists have found thousands of these cuneiform tablets, telling us much about Mesopotamian life.

Only a few people—mostly boys from wealthy families—learned how to write. After years of training, they became **scribes** (SKRYBS), or record keepers. Scribes held honored positions in society, often going on to become judges and political leaders.

Sumerian Literature
The Sumerians also produced works of literature. The world's oldest known story comes from Sumer. It is called the *Epic of Gilgamesh* (GIHL•guh•MEHSH). An epic is a long poem that tells the story of a hero. The hero Gilgamesh is a king who travels around the world with a friend and performs great deeds. When his

friend dies, Gilgamesh searches for a way to live forever. He learns that this is possible only for the gods.

Advances in Science and Math The Mesopotamians' creativity extended to technology too. You read earlier about Sumerian irrigation systems. Sumerians also invented the wagon wheel to help carry people and goods from place to place. Another breakthrough was the plow, which made farming easier. Still another invention was the sailboat, which replaced muscle power with wind power.

Sumerians developed many mathematical ideas. They used geometry to measure fields and put up buildings. They also created a number system based on 60. We have them to thank for our 60-minute hour, 60-second minute, and 360-degree circle.

In addition, Sumerian people watched the skies to learn the best times to plant crops and to hold religious festivals. They recorded the positions of the planets and stars and developed a 12-month calendar based on the cycles of the moon.

✓ **Reading Check** **Identify** What kind of written language did the Sumerians use?

Linking Past & Present

Education

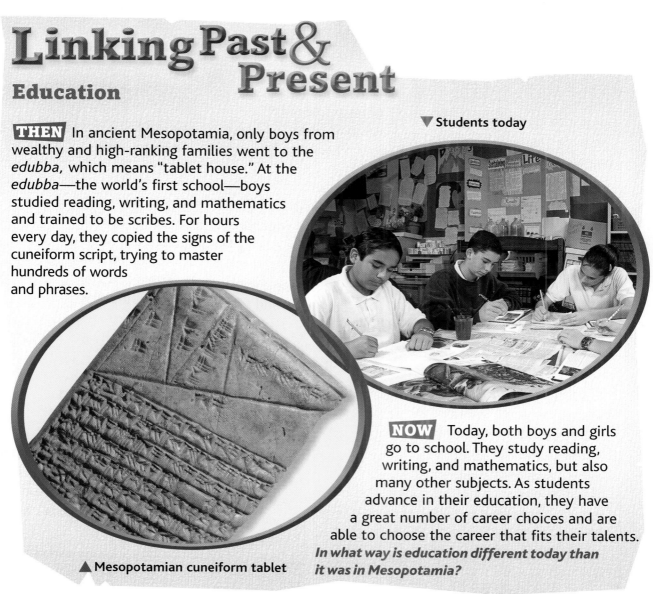

THEN In ancient Mesopotamia, only boys from wealthy and high-ranking families went to the *edubba*, which means "tablet house." At the *edubba*—the world's first school—boys studied reading, writing, and mathematics and trained to be scribes. For hours every day, they copied the signs of the cuneiform script, trying to master hundreds of words and phrases.

▼ **Students today**

NOW Today, both boys and girls go to school. They study reading, writing, and mathematics, but also many other subjects. As students advance in their education, they have a great number of career choices and are able to choose the career that fits their talents.

In what way is education different today than it was in Mesopotamia?

▲ **Mesopotamian cuneiform tablet**

Biography

HAMMURABI
Reigned c. 1792–1750 B.C.

▲ **Hammurabi**

Hammurabi was a young man when he succeeded his father, Sinmuballit, as king of Babylon. When Hammurabi became king, Babylon was already a major power in Mesopotamia. During his reign, however, Hammurabi transformed Babylon from a small city-state into a large, powerful state. He also united Mesopotamia under one rule. Hammurabi called himself "Strong King of Babel."

Hammurabi was directly involved in the ruling of his kingdom. He personally directed projects, such as building city walls, restoring temples, and digging and cleaning irrigation canals. A great deal of planning went into his projects. City streets, for example, were arranged in straight lines and intersected at right angles, much like the way our cities are planned today.

One of Hammurabi's goals was to control the Euphrates River because it provided water for Babylon's farms and trade routes for cargo ships. However, other kings also wanted control of the river. One of Hammurabi's rivals in the battle for the Euphrates was Rim-Sin of Larsa. During Hammurabi's last 14 years as king, he and his soldiers fought against Rim-Sin and other enemies. Hammurabi actually used water to defeat Rim-Sin and his people. He sometimes did this by damming the water and releasing a sudden flood, and sometimes by withholding water needed for drinking and for crops.

After defeating his enemies, Hammurabi ruled briefly over a unified Mesopotamia. Hammurabi soon became ill, and his son, Samsuiluna, took over his duties and was crowned king after his death. Because of Hammurabi's great efforts, however, the center of power in Mesopotamia shifted from the south to Babylon in the north, where it remained for the next 1,000 years.

Then and Now

Do any nations currently have law codes that resemble Hammurabi's? Use the Internet and your local library to identify countries with law codes that you think are somewhat fair but somewhat cruel.

Sargon and Hammurabi

Main Idea Sumerian city-states lost power when they were conquered by outsiders.

Reading Focus Have you heard of the Roman Empire, the Aztec Empire, or the British Empire? The rise and fall of empires is an important part of history. Read on to learn about the first empires in the world.

Over time, conflicts weakened Sumer's city-states. They became vulnerable to attacks by outside groups such as the Akkadians (uh•KAY•dee•uhnz) of northern Mesopotamia.

The king of the Akkadians was named **Sargon** (SAHR•GAHN). In about 2340 B.C., Sargon conquered all of Mesopotamia. He set up the world's first empire. An **empire** (EHM•PYR) is a group of many different lands under one ruler. Sargon's empire lasted for more than 200 years before falling to invaders.

In the 1800s B.C., a new group of people became powerful in Mesopotamia. They built the city of **Babylon** (BA•buh•luhn) by the Euphrates River. It quickly became a center of trade. Beginning in 1792 B.C., the Babylonian king, **Hammurabi** (HA•muh•RAH•bee), began conquering cities to the north and south and created the Babylonian Empire.

Hammurabi is best known for his law code, or collection of laws. (See pages 24 and 25.) He took what he believed were the best laws from each city-state and put them in one code. The code covered crimes, farming and business activities, and marriage and the family—almost every area of life. Although many punishments in the Code of Hammurabi were cruel, his laws mark an important step toward a fair system of justice.

Reading Check **Explain** Why was Sargon's empire important?

Section 2 Review

Study Central™ Need help with the material in this section? Visit jat.glencoe.com

Reading Summary

Review the Main Ideas

- In time, farming villages developed into civilizations with governments, art, religion, writing, and social class divisions. The first city-states developed in Mesopotamia.

- Many important ideas and inventions, including writing, the wheel, the plow, and a number system based on 60, were developed in the region of Mesopotamia.

- Several empires, including the Babylonian Empire, took control of Mesopotamia.

What Did You Learn?

1. What is a civilization?

2. What was the Code of Hammurabi?

Critical Thinking

3. **Summarize Information** Draw a chart like the one below. Use it to list the achievements of Mesopotamian civilization.

Achievements of Mesopotamian Civilization

4. **Geography Skills** How was the geography of Mesopotamia suited for the growth of population and creation of a civilization?

5. **Science Link** Why did the Sumerians record the positions of stars and planets and develop a calendar?

6. **Persuasive Writing** Imagine you are living in a city-state in ancient Sumer. Write a letter to a friend describing which Mesopotamian idea or invention you believe will be the most important to humanity.

You Decide . . .

Hammurabi's Laws: Fair or Cruel?

Fair

Around 1750 B.C., King Hammurabi wrote 282 laws to govern the people of Babylon. Historians and scholars agree that these ancient laws were the first to cover all aspects of society. However, historians and scholars do not agree whether Hammurabi's laws were fair or cruel.

Those who see the laws as just and fair give the following reasons. They say the laws

- stated what all people needed to know about the rules of their society
- brought order and justice to society
- regulated many different activities, from business contracts to crime.

King Hammurabi wrote an introduction to his list of laws. In that introduction, he says that the laws were written to be fair. His intention was "to bring about the rule of righteousness in the land, to destroy the wicked and evil-doers, so that the strong should not harm the weak. . . ."

Some of the laws reflect that fairness.

- Law 5: If a judge makes an error through his own fault when trying a case, he must pay a fine, be removed from the judge's bench, and never judge another case.

- Law 122: If someone gives something to someone else for safekeeping, the transaction should be witnessed and a contract made between the two parties.

- Law 233: If a contractor builds a house for someone and the walls start to fall, then the builder must use his own money and labor to make the walls secure.

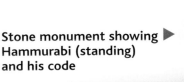

Stone monument showing ▶
Hammurabi (standing)
and his code

▲ Cuneiform tablet with the text of the introduction to the Code of Hammurabi

Cruel

Some historians and scholars think Hammurabi's laws were cruel and unjust. They say the laws
- called for violent punishments, often death, for nonviolent crimes
- required different punishments for accused persons of different social classes
- allowed no explanation from an accused person.

Some of the laws reflect this cruelty.
- Law 3: If someone falsely accuses someone else of certain crimes, then he shall be put to death.
- Law 22: If someone is caught in the act of robbery, then he shall be put to death.
- Law 195: If a son strikes his father, the son's hands shall be cut off.
- Law 202: If someone strikes a man of higher rank, then he shall be whipped 60 times in public.

You Be the Historian

Checking for Understanding
1. Why do some people think Hammurabi's laws were fair?
2. Why do others think the laws were cruel?
3. Were the laws fair or cruel? Take the role of a historian. Write a brief essay that explains how you view Hammurabi's laws. Be sure to use facts to support your position. You can compare Hammurabi's laws to our modern laws to support your argument.

The First Empires

Get Ready to Read!

What's the Connection?

In Section 2, you learned about the empires of Sargon and Hammurabi. Later empires—those of the Assyrians and the Chaldeans—used their military power in new ways.

Focusing on the Main Ideas

- Assyria's military power and well-organized government helped it build a vast empire in Mesopotamia by 650 B.C. *(page 27)*

- The Chaldean Empire built important landmarks in Babylon and developed the first calendar with a seven-day week. *(page 29)*

Locating Places

Assyria (uh•SIHR•ee•uh)
Persian Gulf (PUHR•zhuhn)
Nineveh (NIH•nuh•vuh)
Hanging Gardens

Meeting People

Nebuchadnezzar
  (NEH•byuh•kuhd•NEH•zuhr)

Building Your Vocabulary

province (PRAH•vuhns)
caravan (KAR•uh•VAN)
astronomer
  (uh•STRAH•nuh•muhr)

Reading Strategy

Compare and Contrast Complete a Venn diagram like the one below listing the similarities and differences between the Assyrian Empire and the Chaldean Empire.

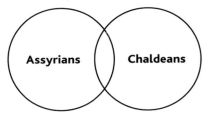

Assyrians — Chaldeans

NATIONAL GEOGRAPHIC When & Where?

900 B.C.

c. 900 B.C.
Assyrians control Mesopotamia

700 B.C.

612 B.C.
Nineveh captured; Assyrian Empire crumbles

500 B.C.

539 B.C.
Persians conquer Chaldeans

Nineveh
Babylon

The Assyrians

Main Idea Assyria's military power and well-organized government helped it build a vast empire in Mesopotamia by 650 B.C.

Reading Focus Today, many countries have armed forces to protect their interests. Read to find out how the Assyrians built an army strong enough to conquer all of Mesopotamia.

About 1,000 years after Hammurabi, a new empire arose in Mesopotamia. It was founded by a people called the Assyrians (uh•SIHR•ee•uhns), who lived in the north near the Tigris River. **Assyria** (uh•SIHR•ee•uh) had fertile valleys that attracted outside invaders. To defend their land, the Assyrians built a large army. Around 900 B.C., they began taking over the rest of Mesopotamia.

Why Were the Assyrians So Strong? The Assyrian army was well organized. At its core were groups of foot soldiers armed with spears and daggers. Other soldiers were experts at using bows and arrows. The army also had chariot riders and soldiers who fought on horseback.

This fearsome and mighty force was the first large army to use iron weapons. For centuries, iron had been used for tools, but it was too soft to serve as a material for weapons. Then a people called the Hittites (HIH•TYTZ), who lived northwest of Assyria, developed a way of making iron stronger. They heated iron ore, hammered it, and rapidly cooled it. The Assyrians learned this technique from the Hittites. They produced iron weapons that were stronger than those made of copper or tin.

The Assyrians at War

When attacking a walled city, the Assyrians used massive war machines. The wheeled battering ram was powered by soldiers. It was covered to protect the soldiers inside, but it had slits so they could shoot arrows out.
What other methods did Assyrian soldiers use to attack cities?

Assyrian Empire

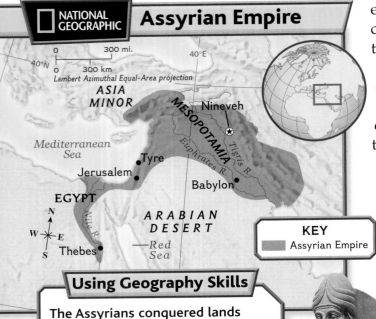

ASIA MINOR

MESOPOTAMIA

Nineveh

Mediterranean Sea

Tyre

Jerusalem

EGYPT

Babylon

Euphrates R.

Tigris R.

ARABIAN DESERT

Thebes

Nile R.

Red Sea

N W E S

KEY
Assyrian Empire

Using Geography Skills

The Assyrians conquered lands from Mesopotamia to Egypt.

1. What major rivers were part of the Assyrian Empire?
2. What geographical features may have kept the Assyrians from expanding their empire to the north and south?

The Assyrians were ferocious warriors. To attack cities, they tunneled under walls or climbed over them on ladders. They loaded tree trunks onto movable platforms and used them as battering rams to knock down city gates. Once a city was captured, the Assyrians set fire to its buildings. They also carried away its people and goods.

Anyone who resisted Assyrian rule was punished. The Assyrians drove people from their lands and moved them into foreign territory. Then they brought in new settlers and forced them to pay heavy taxes.

A Well-Organized Government

Assyrian kings had to be strong to rule their large empire. By about 650 B.C., the empire stretched from the **Persian Gulf** (PUHR•zhuhn) in the

▲ Assyrian winged bull

east to Egypt's Nile River in the west. The capital was at **Nineveh** (NIH•nuh•vuh) on the Tigris River.

Assyrian kings divided the empire into **provinces** (PRAH•vuhn•suhs), or political districts. They chose officials to govern each province. These officials collected taxes and enforced the king's laws.

Assyrian kings built roads to join all parts of their empire. Government soldiers were posted at stations along the way to protect traders from bandits. Messengers on government business used the stations to rest and change horses.

Life in Assyria The Assyrians lived much like other Mesopotamians. Their writing was based on Babylonian writing, and they worshiped many of the same gods. Their laws were similar, but lawbreakers often faced more brutal and cruel punishments in Assyria.

As builders, the Assyrians showed great skill. They erected large temples and palaces that they filled with wall carvings and statues. The Assyrians also produced and collected literature. One of the world's first libraries was in Nineveh. It held 25,000 tablets of stories and songs to the gods. Modern historians have learned much about ancient civilizations from this library.

Assyria's cruel treatment of people led to many rebellions. About 650 B.C., the Assyrians began fighting each other over who would be their next king. A group of people called the Chaldeans (kahl•DEE•uhns) seized the opportunity to rebel. They captured Nineveh in 612 B.C., and the Assyrian Empire soon crumbled.

Reading Check Explain Why were the Assyrian soldiers considered brutal and cruel?

The Chaldeans

Main Idea The Chaldean Empire built important landmarks in Babylon and developed the first calendar with a seven-day week.

Reading Focus What landmarks exist in your town or the nearest city? Read to learn some of the special landmarks that made the Chaldean capital of Babylon famous.

The Chaldeans wanted to build an empire. Led by King **Nebuchadnezzar** (NEH•byuh•kuhd•NEH•zuhr), they controlled all of Mesopotamia from 605 B.C. to 562 B.C.

The City of Babylon Most of the Chaldeans were descendants of the Babylonian people who made up Hammurabi's empire about 1,200 years earlier. They rebuilt the city of Babylon as the glorious center of their empire.

Babylon quickly became the world's largest and richest city. It was surrounded by a brick wall so wide that two chariots could pass on the road on top. Built into the wall at 100-yard (91.4-m) intervals were towers where soldiers kept watch.

Large palaces and temples stood in the city's center. A huge ziggurat reached more than 300 feet (91.4 m) into the sky. Another marvel, visible from any point in Babylon, was an immense staircase of greenery: the **Hanging Gardens** at the king's palace.

These terraced gardens showcased large trees, masses of flowering vines, and other beautiful plants. A pump brought in water from a nearby river. Nebuchadnezzar built the gardens to please his wife, who missed the mountains and plants of her homeland in the northwest.

History Online

Web Activity Visit jat.glencoe.com and click on *Chapter 1—Student Web Activity* to learn more about the first civilizations.

Hanging Gardens

The Hanging Gardens of Babylon were considered one of the Seven Wonders of the Ancient World. A complex irrigation system brought water from the Euphrates River to the top of the gardens. From there, the water flowed down to each of the lower levels of the gardens. *What other sights made Babylon a grand city?*

▲ Ruins of the Hanging Gardens

▲ The Ishtar Gate was at the main entrance to ancient Babylon. *Describe the wall that surrounded Babylon.*

One Greek historian in the 400s B.C. described the beauty of Babylon. He wrote, "In magnificence, there is no other city that approaches it." Outside the center of Babylon stood houses and marketplaces. There, artisans made pottery, cloth, baskets, and jewelry. They sold their wares to passing **caravans** (KAR•uh•VANZ), or groups of traveling merchants. Because Babylon was located on the major trade route between the Persian Gulf and the Mediterranean Sea, it became rich from trade.

Babylon was also a center of science. Like earlier people in Mesopotamia, the Chaldeans believed that changes in the sky revealed the plans of the gods. Their **astronomers** (uh•STRAH•nuh•muhrs)—people who study the heavenly bodies—mapped the stars, the planets, and the phases of the moon. The Chaldeans made one of the first sundials and were the first to have a seven-day week.

Why Did the Empire Fall? As time passed, the Chaldeans began to lose their power. They found it hard to control the peoples they had conquered. In 539 B.C. Persians from the mountains to the northeast captured Babylon. Mesopotamia became part of the new Persian Empire.

 **Reading Check** **Identify** What were the Hanging Gardens of Babylon?

Section ③ Review

History Online

Study Central™ Need help with the material in this section? Visit jat.glencoe.com

Reading Summary
Review the Main Ideas

- Using cavalry and foot soldiers armed with iron weapons, the Assyrians created a large empire that included all of Mesopotamia and extended into Egypt.

- The Chaldeans built a large empire that included Babylon, the largest and richest city in the world at that time.

What Did You Learn?

1. Why was the Assyrian army a powerful fighting force?

2. What were some of the accomplishments of Chaldean astronomers?

Critical Thinking

3. **Summarize Information** Draw a chart like the one below. Use it to describe the city of Babylon under the Chaldeans.

Babylon under Chaldeans

4. **Analyze** How did the Assyrians set up a well-organized government?

5. **Conclude** Why do you think the Assyrians took conquered peoples from their lands and moved them to other places?

6. **Science Link** What different types of knowledge and skills would the Babylonians need to build the Hanging Gardens?

7. **Descriptive Writing** Write a paragraph that might be found in a travel brochure describing the beauty of ancient Babylon.

Chapter 1 Reading Review

Section 1 Early Humans

Vocabulary
historian
archaeologist
artifact
fossil
anthropologist
nomad
technology
domesticate
specialization

Focusing on the Main Ideas

- Paleolithic people adapted to their environment and invented many tools to help them survive. *(page 9)*
- In the Neolithic Age, people started farming, building communities, producing goods, and trading. *(page 13)*

Section 2 Mesopotamian Civilization

Vocabulary
civilization
irrigation
city-state
artisan
cuneiform
scribe
empire

Focusing on the Main Ideas

- Civilization in Mesopotamia began in the valleys of the Tigris and Euphrates Rivers. *(page 17)*
- Sumerians invented writing and made other important contributions to later peoples. *(page 20)*
- Sumerian city-states lost power when they were conquered by outsiders. *(page 23)*

Sumerian figurines ▶

Section 3 The First Empires

Vocabulary
province
caravan
astronomer

Focusing on the Main Ideas

- Assyria's military power and well-organized government helped it build a vast empire in Mesopotamia by 650 B.C. *(page 27)*
- The Chaldean Empire built important landmarks in Babylon and developed the first calendar with a seven-day week. *(page 29)*

Review Vocabulary

1. Write a brief paragraph that describes and compares the following terms.

historian   archaeologist   artifact

fossil   anthropologist

Indicate which of the following statements are true. Replace the word in italics to make false statements true.

___ 2. An *artisan* kept records in cuneiform.

___ 3. Assyrian kings divided their empire into political districts called *provinces*.

___ 4. A *civilization* is a group of many different lands under one ruler.

Review Main Ideas

Section 1 • Early Humans

5. How did Paleolithic people adapt to their environment?

6. What were the major differences between people who lived in the Paleolithic period and those who lived in the Neolithic period?

Section 2 • Mesopotamian Civilization

7. Where were the first civilizations in Mesopotamia?

8. How did Sumerian city-states lose power?

Section 3 • The First Empires

9. What helped Assyria build an empire in Mesopotamia?

10. What scientific advancement did the Chaldeans make?

Critical Thinking

11. **Explain** Why do you think Mesopotamia is sometimes called the "cradle of civilization"?

12. **Analyze** Why was the switch from hunting and gathering to farming important enough to be called the farming revolution?

13. **Describe** What rights did women have in the city-states of Sumer?

14. **Predict** How successful do you think the Assyrian army would have been if it had not learned how to strengthen iron?

Review

Reading Skill ▸ Previewing

Get Ready to Read!

Choose the best answer.

15. In this textbook, to make a connection between what you know and what you are about to read, you should look at the ___.

    a. Reading Tip

    b. Reading Focus

    c. main head

    d. subhead

16. What is the purpose of a subhead?

    a. to break down a large topic into smaller topics

    b. to show the main topic covered in a section

    c. to summarize the "big picture"

    d. to help you study for a test

To review this skill, see pages 6–7.

Geography Skills

Study the map below and answer the following questions.

17. **Location** On what continent was the earliest fossil evidence of humans found?
18. **Movement** Based on fossil evidence, where did early humans go first, Europe or Australia?
19. **Analyze** Which three continents are not shown on this map? How do you think early humans reached those continents?

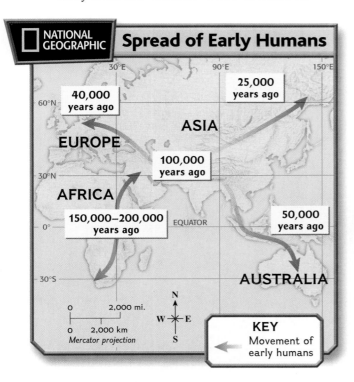

NATIONAL GEOGRAPHIC **Spread of Early Humans**

40,000 years ago
25,000 years ago
ASIA
EUROPE
100,000 years ago
AFRICA
150,000–200,000 years ago   EQUATOR
50,000 years ago
AUSTRALIA

0   2,000 mi.
0   2,000 km
Mercator projection

KEY
Movement of early humans

Read to Write

20. **Persuasive Writing** Suppose you are a merchant in Çatal Hüyük. A new group of people wants to trade with you and the other merchants in the village. You think trading with them is a good idea, but other merchants are not so sure. Write a short speech you could give to convince them.

21. **Using Your FOLDABLES** Use your Chapter 1 foldable to create an illustrated time line. Your time line should extend from the date Jericho was founded to the fall of the Chaldean Empire. Create drawings or photocopy maps, artifacts, or architecture to illustrate your time line. Use your time line as a study tool for the Chapter Test.

History **O**nline
Self-Check Quiz To help you prepare for the Chapter Test, visit jat.glencoe.com

Using Technology

22. **Using the Internet** Use the Internet to locate a university archaeology department Web site. Use the information on the site to create a summary that describes current research. Include location of archaeological sites and relevant discoveries.

Linking Past and Present

23. **Analyzing Information** Imagine you are a nomad who travels from place to place to hunt and gather food. What things would you carry with you to help you survive? Make a list of items to share and discuss with your classmates.

Primary Source Analyze

The following passage is from a poem called "The Mesopotamian View of Death" that was written by an unknown Mesopotamian mother.

Hark the piping!
My heart is piping in the wilderness
    where the young man once went free.
He is a prisoner now in death's kingdom,
    lies bound where once he lived.
The ewe gives up her lamb
    and the nanny-goat her kid.
My heart is piping in the wilderness
    an instrument of grief.

—"The Mesopotamian View of Death," *Poems of Heaven and Hell from Ancient Mesopotamia*, N.K. Sanders, trans.

DBQ Document-Based Questions

24. To what does the mother compare death's kingdom?
25. What is the "instrument of grief"?

Ancient Egypt

▼ Sphinx and pyramid in Giza, Egypt

NATIONAL GEOGRAPHIC **When & Where?**

3500 B.C.	2500 B.C.	1500 B.C.	500 B.C.
c. 3100 B.C. Narmer unites Egypt	c. 2540 B.C. Great Pyramid at Giza built	c. 1500 B.C. Queen Hatshepsut reigns	728 B.C. Piye of Kush defeats Egyptians

Chapter Preview

While the people of Mesopotamia fought wars, people along Africa's Nile River formed rich and powerful civilizations. Read this chapter to learn how the people of Egypt and Kush built large monuments that still stand today.

 View the Chapter 2 video in the *World History: Journey Across Time* Video Program.

 ## The Nile Valley

The fertile land along the great Nile River supported the Egyptian civilization.

 ## Egypt's Old Kingdom

During the Old Kingdom period, Egyptians built cities, great pyramids, and a strong kingdom.

 ## The Egyptian Empire

Many changes occurred during Egypt's Middle and New Kingdoms. It expanded into a great empire as art, literature, and architecture blossomed.

 ## The Civilization of Kush

South of Egypt a new civilization arose called Kush. Kushites adopted Egyptian ways and eventually conquered Egypt itself.

FOLDABLES™
Study Organizer

Organizing Information *Make this foldable to help you organize the key events and ideas from ancient Egypt and Kush.*

Step 1 *Stack two sheets of paper so that the front sheet is one inch higher than the back sheet.*

Step 2 *Fold down the top edges of the paper to form four tabs. Align the edges so that all of the layers or tabs are the same distance apart.*

This makes all the tabs the same size.

Step 3 *Crease the paper to hold the tabs in place, then staple them together. Cut the top three thicknesses to create a layered book.*

 *Staple together along the fold.*

Step 4 *Label the booklet as shown and take notes on the inside.*

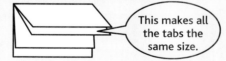

Egypt	Kush
where?	where?
when?	when?
what?	what?

Reading and Writing
As you read the chapter, take notes under the appropriate tabs. Write main ideas and key terms under the "what" tab.

Reading Social Studies

Reading Skill

Predicting

1 Learn It!

What Do You Predict?

A *prediction* is a guess based on what you already know. Making predictions before you read can help you understand and remember what you read.

How do you make predictions? Read the Main Ideas below. They were taken from the opening page of Section 2 on page 47. Use these main ideas to make predictions about what you will read in this chapter.

Predict what the term "all-powerful" means.

What does "life after death" mean?

Can you predict what tools the Egyptians used to build the pyramids?

Main Ideas

- Egypt was ruled by **all-powerful** pharaohs.

- The Egyptians believed in many gods and goddesses and in **life after death** for the pharaohs.

- The Egyptians of the Old Kingdom built **huge stone pyramids as tombs** for their pharaohs.

—*from page 47*

Reading Tip

As you read, check your predictions to see if they were correct.

2 Practice It!
Making Predictions

Read the Main Ideas below from Section 1 of this chapter.

Read to Write ········
Select one blue sub-head in this chapter. Without reading the text under that subhead, write a paragraph that you think might appear there. Check the facts in your paragraph to see if they are correct.

Main Ideas

- The Egyptian civilization began in the fertile Nile River valley, where natural barriers discouraged invasions.
- The Egyptians depended on the Nile's floods to grow their crops.
- Around 3100 B.C., Egypt's two major kingdoms, Upper Egypt and Lower Egypt, were combined into one.
- Egyptian society was divided into social groups based on wealth and power.

—*from page 38*

Make at least one prediction about each of the main ideas. Write down each prediction. Then, as you read this section, decide if your predictions were correct.

3 Apply It!

Before you read the chapter, skim the questions on pages 74–75 in the Chapter Assessment and Activities. Choose three questions and predict what the answers will be.

The Nile Valley

Get Ready to Read!

What's the Connection?

In Chapter 1, you learned about the early civilization in Mesopotamia. At about the same time, another civilization was forming near the Nile River. We call this civilization ancient Egypt.

Focusing on the Main Ideas

- The Egyptian civilization began in the fertile Nile River valley, where natural barriers discouraged invasions. *(page 39)*

- The Egyptians depended on the Nile's floods to grow their crops. *(page 41)*

- Around 3100 B.C., Egypt's two major kingdoms, Upper Egypt and Lower Egypt, were combined into one. *(page 43)*

- Egyptian society was divided into social groups based on wealth and power. *(page 45)*

Locating Places

Egypt (EE•jihpt)
Nile River (NYL)
Sahara (suh•HAR•uh)

Meeting People

Narmer (NAR•muhr)

Building Your Vocabulary

cataract (KA•tuh•RAKT)
delta (DEHL•tuh)
papyrus (puh•PY•ruhs)
hieroglyphics (HY•ruh•GLIH•fihks)
dynasty (DY•nuh•stee)

Reading Strategy

Organizing Information Create a diagram to describe Egyptians' irrigation systems.

Irrigation

NATIONAL GEOGRAPHIC When & Where?

Memphis

Nile R.

5000 B.C.

4000 B.C.

3000 B.C.

c. 5000 B.C. Agriculture begins along Nile River

c. 4000 B.C. Egypt is made up of two kingdoms

c. 3100 B.C. Narmer unites Egypt

Settling the Nile

Main Idea The Egyptian civilization began in the fertile Nile River valley, where natural barriers discouraged invasions.

Reading Focus Did you know that the Nile River is longer than the Amazon, the Mississippi, and every other river in the world? Read on to find out when ancient peoples first moved to its fertile banks.

Between 6000 B.C. and 5000 B.C., hunters and food gatherers moved into the green Nile River valley from less fertile areas of Africa and southwest Asia. They settled down, farmed the land, and created several dozen villages along the riverbanks. These people became the earliest Egyptians.

A Mighty River

Although **Egypt** (EE•jihpt) was warm and sunny, the land received little rainfall. For water, the Egyptians had to rely on the **Nile River** (NYL). They drank from it, bathed in it, and used it for farming, cooking, and cleaning. The river provided fish and supported plants and animals. To the Egyptians, then, the Nile was a precious gift. They praised it in a song: "Hail O Nile, who comes from the earth, who comes to give life to the people of Egypt."

Even today, the Nile inspires awe. It is the world's longest river, flowing north from the heart of Africa to the Mediterranean Sea. This is a distance of some 4,000 miles (6,437 km). Traveling the length of the Nile would be like going from Atlanta, Georgia, to San Francisco, California, and then back again.

The Nile begins as two separate rivers. One river, the Blue Nile, has its source in the mountains of eastern Africa. The other, the White Nile, starts in marshes in central Africa. The two rivers meet and form the Nile just south of Egypt. There, narrow cliffs and boulders in the Nile form wild rapids called **cataracts** (KA•tuh•RAKTS). Because of the cataracts, large ships can use the Nile only for its last 650 miles (1,046 km), where it flows through Egypt.

A Sheltered Land

In Egypt, the Nile runs through a narrow, green valley. Look at the map below. You can see that the Nile looks like the long stem of a flower. Shortly before the Nile reaches the Mediterranean Sea, it divides into different branches that look like the flower's blossom. These branches fan out over an area of fertile soil called a **delta** (DEHL•tuh).

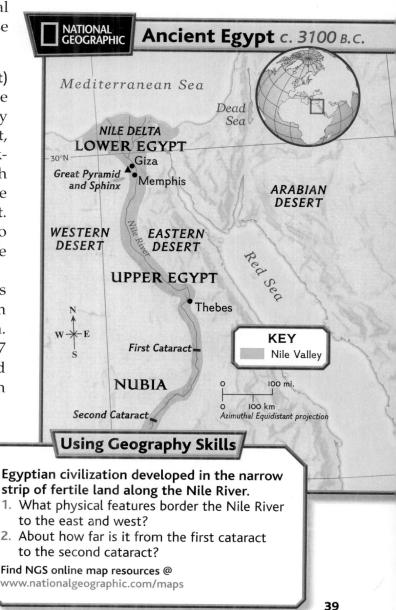

NATIONAL GEOGRAPHIC

Ancient Egypt c. 3100 B.C.

Mediterranean Sea

Dead Sea

NILE DELTA
LOWER EGYPT
30°N
Giza
Great Pyramid and Sphinx
Memphis

ARABIAN DESERT

WESTERN DESERT

Nile River

EASTERN DESERT

Red Sea

UPPER EGYPT

Thebes

KEY
Nile Valley

First Cataract

NUBIA

Second Cataract

0   100 mi.
0   100 km
Azimuthal Equidistant projection

N W E S

Using Geography Skills

Egyptian civilization developed in the narrow strip of fertile land along the Nile River.
1. What physical features border the Nile River to the east and west?
2. About how far is it from the first cataract to the second cataract?

Find NGS online map resources @
www.nationalgeographic.com/maps

▲ Today, the Nile River valley makes up only about 3 percent of Egypt's land, yet most Egyptians live and work in the area. *How did the deserts surrounding the Nile Valley help protect Egypt?*

On both sides of the Nile Valley and its delta, deserts unfold as far as the eye can see. To the west is a vast desert that forms part of the **Sahara** (suh•HAR•uh), the largest desert in the world. To the east, stretching to the Red Sea, is the Eastern Desert. In some places, the change from green land to barren sand is so abrupt that a person can stand with one foot in each.

The ancient Egyptians called the deserts "the Red Land" because of their burning heat. Although these vast expanses could not support farming or human life, they did serve a useful purpose: they kept outside armies away from Egypt's territory.

Other geographic features also protected the Egyptians. To the far south, the Nile's dangerous cataracts blocked enemy boats from reaching Egypt. In the north, the delta marshes offered no harbors for invaders approaching from the sea. In this regard, the Egyptians were luckier than the people of Mesopotamia. In that region, few natural barriers protected the cities. The Mesopotamians constantly had to fight off attackers, but Egypt rarely faced threats. As a result, Egyptian civilization was able to grow and prosper.

Despite their isolation, the Egyptians were not completely closed to the outside world. The Mediterranean Sea bordered Egypt to the north, and the Red Sea lay beyond the desert to the east. These bodies of water gave the Egyptians a way to trade with people outside Egypt.

Within Egypt, people used the Nile for trade and transportation. Winds from the north pushed sailboats south. The flow of the Nile carried them north. Egyptian villages thus had frequent, friendly contact with one another, unlike the hostile relations between the Mesopotamian city-states.

✓ **Reading Check** **Summarize** What was Egypt's physical setting like?

The River People

Main Idea The Egyptians depended on the Nile's floods to grow their crops.

Reading Focus When you hear about floods, do you picture terrible damage and loss of life? Read on to learn why the Egyptians welcomed, rather than feared, the flooding of the Nile.

In Chapter 1, you learned that the people of Mesopotamia had to tame the floods of the Tigris and Euphrates Rivers in order to farm. They learned to do so, but the unpredictable rivers loomed as a constant threat.

Regular Flooding Like the Mesopotamians, the Egyptians also had to cope with river floods. However, the Nile floods were much more dependable and gentle than those of the Tigris and the Euphrates. As a result, the Egyptians were able to farm and live securely. They did not worry that sudden, heavy overflows would destroy their homes and crops, or that too little flooding would leave their fields parched.

Every spring, heavy rains from central Africa and melting snows from the highlands of east Africa added to the waters of the Nile as it flowed north. From July to October, the Nile spilled over its banks. When the waters went down, they left behind a layer of dark, fertile mud. Because of these deposits, the Egyptians called their land *Kemet* (KEH•meht), "the Black Land."

How Did the Egyptians Use the Nile? The Egyptians took advantage of the Nile's floods to become successful farmers. They planted wheat, barley, and flax seeds in the wet, rich soil. Over time, they grew more than enough food to feed themselves and the animals they raised.

One reason for their success was the wise use of irrigation. Egyptian farmers first dug basins, or bowl-shaped holes, in the earth to trap the floodwaters. The farmers then dug canals to carry water from the basins to fields beyond the river's reach. The Egyptians also built dikes, or earthen banks, to strengthen the basin walls.

In time, Egyptian farmers developed other technology to help them in their work. For example, they used a shadoof (shuh•DOOF), a bucket attached to a long pole, to lift water from the Nile to the basins. Many Egyptian farmers still use this device today.

Primary Source — Hymn to the Nile

This passage is part of a hymn written around 2100 B.C. It shows how important the Nile River was to the people of ancient Egypt.

"You create the grain, you bring forth the barley, assuring perpetuity [survival] to the temples. If you cease your toil and your work, then all that exists is in anguish."

—author unknown, "Hymn to the Nile"

▲ A shadoof

DBQ Document-Based Question

How does this hymn show that the ancient Egyptians thought of the Nile as a god?

Early Egyptians also developed geometry to survey, or measure, land. When floods washed away boundary markers dividing one field from the next, the Egyptians surveyed the fields again to see where one began and the other ended.

Papyrus (puh•PY•ruhs), a reed plant that grew along the shores of the Nile, became a useful resource. At first the Egyptians harvested papyrus to make baskets, sandals, and river rafts. Later, they used papyrus for papermaking. The first step was to cut the stalks of the plant into narrow strips. Then the Egyptians soaked the strips and pounded them flat. Left in the air to dry, the strips became stiff. They could then be joined to form a roll of paper.

What Were Hieroglyphics? The Egyptians used their papyrus rolls as writing paper. Like the people of Mesopotamia, the Egyptians developed their own system of writing. Called **hieroglyphics** (HY•ruh•GLIH•fihks), it was made up of hundreds of picture symbols. Some symbols stood for objects and ideas. To communicate the idea of a boat, for example, a scribe would draw a boat. Other symbols stood for sounds, just as the letters of our alphabet do.

Scribes painstakingly carved hieroglyphics onto stone walls and monuments. For everyday purposes, scribes invented a simpler script and wrote on papyrus.

In ancient Egypt, few people could read and write. Some Egyptian men, however, went to special schools located at Egyptian temples to study reading and writing and learn to become scribes. Scribes kept records and worked for the rulers, priests, and traders.

✓ **Reading Check** **Identify** What crops did the ancient Egyptians grow?

The Way It Was

Focus on Everyday Life

From Farming to Food Harvesting wheat and turning it into bread was vital to the ancient Egyptians. Some people were full-time farmers, but many others were drafted by the government to help during busy seasons.

The process began as men cut the wheat with

▲ Tomb painting showing wheat being harvested

wooden sickles and women gathered it into bundles. Animals trampled the wheat to separate the kernels from the husks. The grain was then thrown into the air so the wind would carry away the lightweight seed coverings. Finally, the grain was stored in silos for later use.

▲ Tomb painting showing Egyptian man and woman plowing and planting

A United Egypt

Main Idea Around 3100 B.C., Egypt's two major kingdoms, Upper Egypt and Lower Egypt, were combined into one.

Reading Focus What types of services does your local government provide? Read on to find out about the government in ancient Egypt.

In Egypt, as in Mesopotamia, skillful farming led to surpluses—extra amounts—of food. This freed some people to work as artisans instead of farmers. They wove cloth, made pottery, carved statues, or shaped copper into weapons and tools.

As more goods became available, Egyptians traded with each other. Before long, Egyptian traders were carrying goods beyond Egypt's borders to Mesopotamia. There they may have picked up ideas about writing and government.

The Rise of Government The advances in farming, crafts, and trade created a need for government in Egypt. Irrigation systems had to be built and maintained, and surplus grain had to be stored and passed out in times of need. In addition, disputes over land ownership had to be settled. Gradually, government emerged to plan and to direct such activities.

The earliest rulers were village chiefs. Over time, a few strong chiefs united groups of villages into small kingdoms. The strongest of these kingdoms eventually overpowered the weaker ones. By 4000 B.C., Egypt was made up of two large kingdoms. In the Nile delta was Lower Egypt. To the south, upriver, lay Upper Egypt.

Egypt's Ruling Families About 3100 B.C., the two kingdoms became one. Credit for this goes to **Narmer** (NAR•muhr), also known

Baking bread in pots ▶

◀ Wheat being harvested today

Turning grain into bread was a long process. Women ground the grain into flour, then men pounded it until it became very fine. For the wealthy, seeds, honey, fruit, nuts, and herbs were added to the dough for flavor. Unfortunately, it was almost impossible to keep small stones and sand out of the flour. As a result, many Egyptians developed tooth decay as these particles wore down their tooth enamel.

▲ A replica of an ancient Egyptian bakery

Connecting to the Past

1. How did the government ensure that enough people were available to harvest the wheat?

2. Why do you think seeds, fruit, and other additives were reserved for the wealthy?

Comparing Mesopotamia to Egypt

	Mesopotamia	Egypt
Natural Defenses	Flat mud plains; few natural defenses	Many defenses: Nile delta, Sahara, Eastern Desert, and cataracts
Rivers	Tigris and Euphrates Rivers	Nile River
Floods	Unpredictable, and a constant threat to the people	Dependable and regular; not feared
Economy	Farming and trade	Farming and trade
Government	City-state led by kings and priests; eventually empires formed	Villages led by chiefs, then united into kingdoms; kingdoms later united and ruled by pharaohs
Work of Artisans	Metal products, pottery, cloth	Metal products, pottery, cloth
Advances	• Cuneiform writing • Number system based on 60 • 12-month calendar • Wagon wheel, plow, sailboat	• Hieroglyphic writing • 365-day calendar • Number system based on 10, and fractions • Medicine and first medical books

Understanding Charts

The civilizations of both Mesopotamia and Egypt depended on rivers for fertile lands and irrigation.
1. Which civilization had greater natural defenses? Explain.
2. Compare Use the chart to compare the governments of the two civilizations.

as Menes (MEE•neez). As king of Upper Egypt, he led his armies north and took control of Lower Egypt.

Narmer ruled from Memphis, a city he built on the border between the two kingdoms. To symbolize the kingdom's unity, Narmer wore a double crown: the helmet-like white crown represented Upper Egypt, and the open red crown represented Lower Egypt.

Narmer's united kingdom held together long after his death. Members of his family passed the ruling power from father to son to grandson. Such a line of rulers from one family is called a **dynasty** (DY•nuh•stee). When one dynasty died out, another took its place.

Over time, ancient Egypt would be ruled by 31 dynasties, which together lasted about 2,800 years. Historians group Egypt's dynasties into three main time periods called kingdoms. The earliest period, the Old Kingdom, was followed by the Middle Kingdom and then the New Kingdom. Each marked a long period of strong leadership and stability.

✓ **Reading Check** **Define** What is a dynasty?

Early Egyptian Life

Main Idea Egyptian society was divided into social groups based on wealth and power.

Reading Focus Did you play with dolls or balls when you were young? Egyptian children did too. Keep reading for more details about the Egyptians' daily life.

If you made a diagram of the different social groups in ancient Egypt, you would find that they make a pyramid shape. At the top was the king and his family. Beneath that level was a small upper class of priests, army commanders, and nobles. Next came a larger base of skilled middle-class people, such as traders, artisans, and shopkeepers. At the bottom was the largest group—unskilled workers and farmers.

Egypt's Social Classes Egypt's upper class was made up of nobles, priests, and other wealthy Egyptians who worked as the government officials. They lived in cities and on large estates along the Nile River. They had elegant homes made of wood and mud bricks, with beautiful gardens and pools filled with fish and water lilies. Wealthy families had servants to wait on them and to perform household tasks. The men and women dressed in white linen clothes and wore heavy eye makeup and jewelry.

Egypt's middle class included people who ran businesses or produced goods. They lived in much smaller homes and dressed more simply. Artisans formed an important group within the middle class. They produced linen cloth, jewelry, pottery, and metal goods.

Ancient Egyptian society was ▶ highly structured. At the top was the pharaoh and his family. At the bottom was the group with the least wealth—unskilled workers. *What group was just below the pharaoh in Egyptian society?*

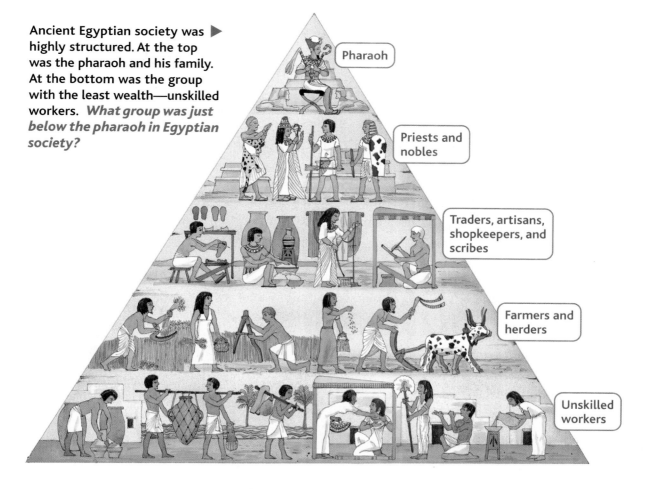

Pharaoh

Priests and nobles

Traders, artisans, shopkeepers, and scribes

Farmers and herders

Unskilled workers

Farmers made up the largest group of early Egyptians. Some rented their land from their ruler, paying him with a hefty portion of their crops. Most, however, worked the land of wealthy nobles. They lived in villages along the Nile, in one-room huts with roofs made of palm leaves. They had a simple diet of bread, beer, vegetables, and fruit.

Many of Egypt's city dwellers were unskilled workers who did physical labor. Some unloaded cargo from boats and carried it to markets. Others made and stacked mud bricks for buildings. Workers lived in crowded city neighborhoods. They had small mud-brick homes with hard-packed dirt floors and a courtyard for the family's animals. On the flat rooftops, families talked, played games, and slept. Women worked on the rooftops, drying fruit, making bread, and weaving cloth.

Family Life In ancient Egypt, the father headed the family. However, Egyptian women had more rights than females in most other early civilizations. In Egypt, women could own and pass on property. They could buy and sell goods, make wills, and obtain divorces. Upper-class women were in charge of temples and could perform religious ceremonies.

Few Egyptians sent their children to school. Mothers taught their daughters to sew, cook, and run a household. Boys learned farming or skilled trades from their fathers. Egyptian children had time for fun, as well. They played with board games, dolls, spinning tops, and stuffed leather balls.

✓ **Reading Check** **Identify** Who made up the largest group in Egyptian society?

History Online

Study Central™ **Need help with the material in this section? Visit** jat.glencoe.com

Section 1 Review

Reading Summary

Review the Main Ideas

- The deserts on either side of the Nile Valley, along with the Nile cataracts and delta marshes, protected Egypt from invaders.

- The Egyptians became successful farmers using the Nile River's floods and irrigation.

- About 3100 B.C., Narmer united Lower Egypt and Upper Egypt.

- Egypt's society was divided into upper-class priests and nobles, middle-class artisans and merchants, and lower-class workers and farmers.

What Did You Learn?

1. What is papyrus and how did the Egyptians use it?

2. What rights did women have in ancient Egypt?

Critical Thinking

3. **Cause and Effect** Draw a diagram to show three things that led to the growth of government in ancient Egypt.

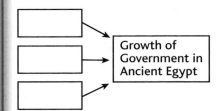

Growth of Government in Ancient Egypt

4. **Geography Skills** How did the geography of the Nile River valley lead to the growth of a civilization there?

5. **Describe** Describe the Egyptian writing system.

6. **Analyze** What was the significance of Narmer's double crown?

7. **Reading** **Predicting** Use what you have learned in this section to write a paragraph predicting what life might have been like on an ancient Egyptian farm.

Egypt's Old Kingdom

Get Ready to Read!

What's the Connection?

In Section 1, you learned that Egyptian dynasties are divided into the Old Kingdom, Middle Kingdom, and New Kingdom. In Section 2, you will learn about the Egyptians' leaders, religion, and way of life in the Old Kingdom.

Focusing on the Main Ideas

- Egypt was ruled by all-powerful pharaohs. *(page 48)*

- The Egyptians believed in many gods and goddesses and in life after death for the pharaohs. *(page 49)*

- The Egyptians of the Old Kingdom built huge stone pyramids as tombs for their pharaohs. *(page 50)*

Locating Places

Giza (GEE•zuh)

Meeting People

King Khufu (KOO•foo)

Building Your Vocabulary

pharaoh (FEHR•oh)
deity (DEE•uh•tee)
embalming (ihm•BAHM•ihng)
mummy (MUH•mee)
pyramid (PIHR•uh•MIHD)

Reading Strategy

Organizing Information Use a graphic organizer like the one below to identify the different beliefs in Egypt's religion.

Egyptian beliefs

NATIONAL GEOGRAPHIC **When & Where?**

Giza
Memphis
Nile R.

2600 B.C.   **2400 B.C.**   **2200 B.C.**

c. 2600 B.C.
Old Kingdom period begins

c. 2540 B.C.
Great Pyramid at Giza built

c. 2300 B.C.
Old Kingdom declines

Old Kingdom Rulers

Main Idea Egypt was ruled by all-powerful pharaohs.

Reading Focus Would you want your student body president or your sports team captain to have unlimited authority? Think what it would be like to have such a leader as you read about the rulers of ancient Egypt.

Around 2600 B.C., the period known as the Old Kingdom began in Egypt. The Old Kingdom lasted until about 2300 B.C. During those years, Egypt grew and prospered. The Egyptians built cities and expanded trade, and their kings set up a strong government.

The Egyptian kings, or **pharaohs** (FEHR•ohs) as they were called, lived with their families in grand palaces. In fact, the word *pharaoh* originally meant "great house." The pharaoh was an all-powerful ruler who guided Egypt's every activity. His word was law, and it had to be obeyed without question.

Pharaohs appointed many officials to carry out their wishes. These officials saw to it that irrigation canals and grain storehouses were built and repaired. They made sure that crops were planted as the pharaoh directed. They also controlled trade and collected tax payments of grain from farmers.

Why did Egyptians willingly serve the pharaoh? One reason was that they believed the unity of the kingdom depended on a strong leader. Another was that they considered the pharaoh to be the son of Re (RAY), the Egyptian sun god. As a result, his subjects paid him the greatest respect. Whenever he appeared in public, people played music on flutes and cymbals. Bystanders along the road had to bow down and "smell the earth," or touch their heads to the ground.

The Egyptians thought their pharaoh was a god on earth who controlled Egypt's welfare. He carried out certain rituals that were thought to benefit the kingdom. For example, he drove a sacred bull around Memphis, the capital city. The Egyptians believed this ceremony would keep the soil rich and ensure good crops. The pharaoh was also the first to cut ripe grain. Egyptians believed this would bring a good harvest.

✓ **Reading Check** **Analyze** Why did the pharaohs hold so much power?

◄ The Great Sphinx, a huge statue with the head of a man (perhaps a pharaoh) and the body of a lion, stands guard outside the tomb of a pharaoh. *What did the word pharaoh mean, and why was it used for Egypt's rulers?*

Egypt's Religion

Main Idea The Egyptians believed in many gods and goddesses and in life after death for the pharaohs.

Reading Focus Have you seen mummies in horror movies? Maybe you've even wrapped yourself in strips of cloth to be a mummy for a costume party. Keep reading to find out how the ancient Egyptians made mummies, and why.

Religion was deeply woven into Egyptian culture. Like the people of Mesopotamia, the ancient Egyptians worshiped many **deities** (DEE•uh•teez), or gods and goddesses. The Egyptians believed these deities controlled the forces of nature and human activities.

The main Egyptian god was the sun god Re. This was probably because of Egypt's hot, sunny climate and the importance of the sun for good harvests. Another major god was Hapi (HAH•pee), who ruled the Nile River. The most important goddess was Isis (EYE•suhs). She represented the loyal wife and mother, and she ruled over the dead with her husband Osiris (oh•SY•ruhs).

Life After Death

Unlike the Mesopotamians, who imagined a gloomy life after death, the Egyptians took a hopeful view. They believed that life in the next world would be even better than life on Earth. Following a long journey, the dead would reach a place of peace and plenty.

One of the most important manuscripts written in ancient Egypt was the *Book of the Dead*. This was a collection of spells and prayers that Egyptians studied to obtain life after death. They believed that the god Osiris would meet newcomers at the entrance to the next world. If they had led good lives and knew the magic spells, Osiris would grant them life after death.

▲ During the embalming process, the pharaoh's body was placed on a special table. The chief embalmer was dressed as Anubis, the god of mummification. *Why did the Egyptians embalm the pharaoh's body?*

For centuries, Egyptians believed that only the pharaohs and an elite few could enjoy the afterlife. They also believed that the pharaoh's spirit needed a body to make the journey to the afterlife. If the pharaoh's body decayed after death, his spirit would be forced to wander forever. It was vital that a pharaoh's spirit reach the next world. There, the pharaoh would continue to care for Egypt.

To protect the pharaoh's body, the Egyptians developed a process called **embalming** (ihm•BAHM•ihng). First, priests removed the body's organs. A special kind of salt was then applied to the body, and it was stored for a number of days to dry. After this, the body was filled with spices and perfumes, then stitched closed. Next, it was cleaned with oils and tightly wrapped with long strips of linen. The wrapped body was known as a **mummy** (MUH•mee). It was put in several wooden coffins, one fitting inside the other. The pharaoh was then ready for burial in a tomb.

Egyptian Medicine

In the course of embalming the dead, the Egyptians learned much about the human body. Egyptian doctors used herbs and drugs to treat many different illnesses. They grew skilled at sewing up cuts and setting broken bones.

Some doctors focused on treating particular parts of the body, becoming the first specialists in medicine. Egyptians also wrote the world's first medical books on scrolls of papyrus.

✓ **Reading Check** **Identify** Who were some of the Egyptians' main gods and goddesses?

The Pyramids

Main Idea The Egyptians of the Old Kingdom built huge stone pyramids as tombs for their pharaohs.

Reading Focus Do you think the Statue of Liberty or the White House will still be here in 4,000 years? The giant pyramids of Egypt have stood for about that long. Read to find out how and why they were built.

No ordinary tomb would do for a pharaoh of Egypt. Instead, the Egyptians built mountainlike **pyramids** (PIHR•uh•MIHDS) entirely of stone. These gigantic structures, the size of several city blocks, protected the bodies of dead pharaohs from floods, wild animals, and grave robbers. The pyramids also held supplies that the pharaoh might need in the spirit world, including clothing, furniture, jewelry, and food.

Egypt's Religion

▼ Osiris

▲ In this painting, the god Osiris (seated at right) watches as other animal-headed gods weigh a dead man's soul and record the results. The scales have balanced, so the dead man may enter the underworld. *What was the Book of the Dead?*

How Was a Pyramid Built? It took thousands of people and years of backbreaking labor to build a pyramid. Most of the work was done by farmers during the Nile floods, when they could not tend their fields. In addition, surveyors, engineers, carpenters, and stonecutters lent their skills.

Each pyramid sat on a square base, with the entrance facing north. To determine true north, the Egyptians studied the heavens and developed principles of astronomy. With this knowledge, they invented a 365-day calendar with 12 months grouped into 3 seasons. This calendar became the basis for our modern calendar.

To determine the amount of stone needed for a pyramid, as well as the angles necessary for the walls, the Egyptians made advances in mathematics. They invented a system of written numbers based on 10. They also created fractions, using them with whole numbers to add, subtract, and divide.

After the pyramid site was chosen, workers went wherever they could find stone—sometimes hundreds of miles away. Skilled artisans used copper tools to cut the stone into huge blocks. Other workers tied the blocks to wooden sleds and pulled them to the Nile over a path "paved" with logs. Next, they loaded the stones onto barges that were floated to the building site. There, workers unloaded the blocks and dragged or pushed them up ramps to be set in place.

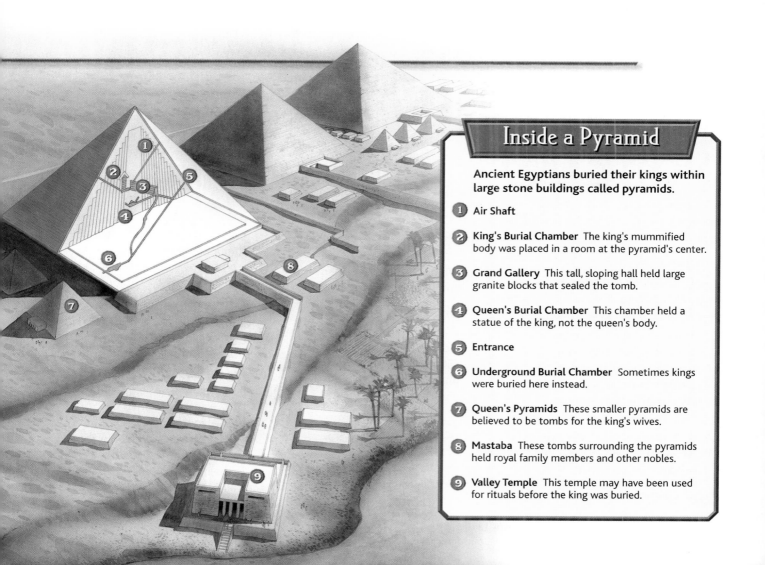

Inside a Pyramid

Ancient Egyptians buried their kings within large stone buildings called pyramids.

1. **Air Shaft**

2. **King's Burial Chamber** The king's mummified body was placed in a room at the pyramid's center.

3. **Grand Gallery** This tall, sloping hall held large granite blocks that sealed the tomb.

4. **Queen's Burial Chamber** This chamber held a statue of the king, not the queen's body.

5. **Entrance**

6. **Underground Burial Chamber** Sometimes kings were buried here instead.

7. **Queen's Pyramids** These smaller pyramids are believed to be tombs for the king's wives.

8. **Mastaba** These tombs surrounding the pyramids held royal family members and other nobles.

9. **Valley Temple** This temple may have been used for rituals before the king was buried.

▲ The pyramid shown above is that of King Khafre, son of Khufu. Although smaller than the Great Pyramid, Khafre's pyramid was built on higher ground so as to appear taller. *About how tall is the Great Pyramid?*

The Great Pyramid About 2540 B.C., the Egyptians built the largest and grandest of the pyramids known as the Great Pyramid. It is located about 10 miles from the modern city of Cairo. This pyramid, built for **King Khufu** (KOO•foo), is one of three still standing in **Giza** on the west bank of the Nile. It rises nearly 500 feet (153 m) above the desert, covers an area about the size of nine football fields, and contains more than 2 million stone blocks. Each block weighs an average of 2.5 tons.

The Great Pyramid was the tallest structure in the world for more than 4,000 years. It is equal to the size of a 48-story building and is the largest of about 80 pyramids found in Egypt. The Great Pyramid is truly a marvel because the Egyptians built it without using beasts of burden, special tools, or even the wheel.

✓ **Reading Check** **Explain** What was the purpose of pyramids?

History Online
Study Central™ Need help with the material in this section? Visit jat.glencoe.com

Section ② Review

Reading Summary
Review the (Main Ideas)
- The all-powerful rulers of Egypt, called pharaohs, were believed to be related to Egypt's main god.
- The Egyptians believed in many gods and goddesses. They also believed in life after death for the pharaoh, whose body would be mummified before burial.
- The pyramids, built as huge stone tombs for the pharaohs, required many years and thousands of workers to construct.

What Did You Learn?
1. How was stone for a pyramid transported to the building site?
2. What did Egyptians learn from embalming bodies?

Critical Thinking
3. **Organize Information** Draw a diagram like the one below. Fill in details about the pharaohs of the Old Kingdom and their duties.

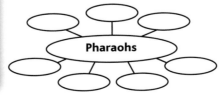

4. **Math/Science Link** How did the building of the pyramids lead to advances in science and mathematics?

5. **Compare and Contrast** How did the Egyptians' religious beliefs compare to those of the Mesopotamians?

6. **Persuasive Writing** Suppose you are an Egyptian pharaoh who wants a pyramid built to house your tomb. Write a letter to the farmers and workers in your kingdom explaining why it is their duty to build the pyramid for you.

WORLD LITERATURE

THE PRINCE WHO KNEW HIS FATE

Translated by Lise Manniche

Before You Read

The Scene: This story takes place in ancient times in Egypt and in an area that is now Iraq.

The Characters: The first characters introduced are the king of Egypt, his son, and the seven Hathor goddesses, who predict the prince's death. When the prince travels, he meets Chief of Naharín and his daughter.

The Plot: For many years, the king of Egypt protects his son from the death that was predicted for him. The prince convinces his father to let him travel. He meets a princess, and together they try to prevent his fate.

Vocabulary Preview

destiny: an already-determined course of events

ferried: carried by boat

enchant: to cast a spell on something

fugitive: a person who runs away or escapes

folly: a foolish action

vessel: a container

exalting: praising

In this story, a prince must avoid three types of animals because it was predicted that one of them would kill him. The people who love him try to prevent him from coming into contact with the animals, but the prince does not want to live in fear.

As You Read

This is one of the world's oldest known fairy tales. It was written in hieroglyphics more than 3,000 years ago. The places in the tale are real, and the prince and princess may have been based on real people, as well. The ancient Egyptians often made important people the main characters in their stories.

There once was a king of Egypt who had no sons at all. So the king asked the gods of his time for a son and they decided that he should have one. . . .

The seven Hathor goddesses[1] came to decide the boy's fate and they declared, "He is destined to be killed by a crocodile or a snake or a dog."

The people who were at the boy's side heard this. They reported it to the king and his heart grew sad.

The king had a house of stone built for the boy at the edge of the desert, supplied with servants and with all sorts of good things from the palace, for the child was not to go outside. There the boy grew up.

One day he climbed up to the roof of the house and saw a dog following a man, who was walking along the road.

"What is that?" he asked his servant.

---

[1]**seven Hathor goddesses:** goddesses who visited newborn children to discover their fates

"It's a dog," the servant replied.

"Let me have a dog like that," the boy said.

The servant reported this to the king and the king said, "His heart is sad. Let him have a bounding little puppy."

So they gave the boy a dog.

In time, the young prince grew restless and he sent a message to his father, saying, "Why should I stay here doing nothing? After all, my destiny has been determined. Allow me to do as I wish until I meet my fate."

The king replied saying "Let a chariot[2] be prepared for him, equipped with all sorts of weapons, and assign a servant to accompany him."

So they did as the king commanded and gave him all that he needed. Then they ferried him across the Nile to the east bank and said to him, "Now go as you wish."

And the dog was with him.

The prince traveled as he pleased northwards across the desert, living on the best of all desert game.

Thus he came to the realm of the Chief of Naharín,[3] who had no children—except one daughter. He had built a house for her with a window seventy cubits[4] from the ground.

The Chief of Naharín then sent for all the sons of all the chiefs of Kharu,[5] saying, "He who can jump up to the window of my daughter shall have her for his wife."

The sons of all the chiefs had been trying to reach the window each day for many days when the prince passed by them.

They took the prince to their house, and they bathed him, they rubbed him with oil, and they bandaged his feet. They gave fodder[6] to his horses and food to his servant. They did everything for the young man.

And to start a conversation, they said, "Where do you come from, you handsome youth?"

"I am the son of a chariot officer from Egypt. My mother died and my father took another wife. My stepmother grew to hate me and I have fled her."

They welcomed him and kissed him.

---

[6]**fodder:** food for cattle, horses, and sheep

---

[2]**chariot:** a two-wheeled, horse-drawn car
[3]**Naharín:** an area east of the Euphrates River in present-day Iraq
[4]**cubits:** units of length based on the length of the arm from the elbow to the fingertips
[5]**Kharu:** an area in present-day Syria

Several days later the prince asked the youths, "What are you doing here in Naharín?"

"The past three months we have spent each day jumping, for the Chief of Naharín will give his daughter to the one who reaches her window," they said.

"Oh, if only I could enchant my feet, I would jump with you," said the prince.

The youths went off to jump, as it was their daily custom, while the prince stood at a distance, watching.

From her window the daughter of the Chief of Naharín gazed at him.

At last, when many days had passed, the prince joined the sons of the chiefs.

He jumped and he reached the window of the daughter of the Chief of Naharín.

She embraced him and she kissed him.

A messenger went to inform her father.

"One of the young men has reached the window of your daughter," the messenger said.

"Whose son is it?" the Chief of Naharín inquired.

"He is the son of a chariot officer from Egypt. He has fled from his stepmother."

The Chief of Naharín grew very angry. "Am I to give my daughter to a fugitive from Egypt? Send him home!"

"You must go back where you came from," the messenger said to the prince.

But the princess clung to the prince, and she swore, "As Re lives, if they take him from me, I will not eat, I will not drink, I will die within the hour!"

When the messenger had reported everything she had said to her father, her father sent men to kill the prince then and there.

Again the princess swore, "As Re lives, if they kill him, I shall die before sunset. I will not live an hour more than he!"

They repeated this to her father, and the Chief of Naharín had the prince and his daughter brought before him.

The young man impressed the Chief, who welcomed him and kissed him and said, "Now you are like my own son. Tell me about yourself."

"I am the child of a chariot officer from Egypt," said the young man, "My mother died and father took another wife. She grew to hate me, and I have fled from her."

The Chief of Naharín gave his daughter to the prince, and he gave him a house and fields and herds and everything they needed.

When they had lived together for some time, the young man told his wife, "I know my fate. I shall be killed by one of three: a crocodile or a snake or a dog."

"Then," she said, "the dog that follows you everywhere must be killed."

"That would be folly," he replied. "I will not have the dog killed for I have had it ever since it was a puppy."

So his wife began to watch over him closely, and she did not allow him to go out alone.

It so happened that on the very day the prince had arrived in Naharín, the crocodile, his fate, began to follow him. It caught up with him in the town where the prince lived with his wife.

But there in the lake was a giant who would not let the crocodile out, and so the crocodile refused to let the giant out. For three whole months they had been fighting all day long, beginning each day at sunrise.

The prince spent many pleasant days in his house, and in the evenings when the breeze died down, he went to bed. One evening when sleep had overcome him, his wife filled a vessel with wine and another with beer. Then she sat down beside him, but she did not sleep.

A snake came out of its hole intending to bite the prince, but the vessels tempted it and the snake drank from them, got drunk and rolled over on its back to sleep.

His wife chopped the snake in three pieces with her axe. Then she roused her husband and said to him, "See, your god has placed one of your fates in your hands. He is protecting you."

The prince made offerings to his god Re, adoring him and exalting his power each day that passed.

After some time, the prince went for a stroll around his estate. His wife stayed at home, but his dog followed him.

Suddenly the dog turned on him and the prince fled from it.

He ran to the edge of the lake and jumped into water to escape the dog, but there the crocodile seized him and dragged him off to find the giant.

"I am pursuing you, for I am your fate," said the crocodile. "Listen, for three whole months I have been fighting with the giant. I will let you go now if you will take my side and kill the giant when he returns to fight."

So the prince waited by the water all that night, and when dawn broke and a second day began, the giant returned.

The giant began to fight the crocodile at once, but the prince stepped forward with his scimitar[7] in his hand. He cut out the heart of the giant and the giant died.

At that very moment the dog sneaked up behind the prince. It attacked him and tore him to bits and spread the pieces all about.

When the prince failed to return, his wife set out to look for him. After seven days and seven nights in search for him, she came upon his remains.

She collected all the pieces of her husband's body and put them back together again—except for his heart. That she placed in a lotus flower which was blooming on the water.

Lo and behold, the prince reappeared as he had been before.

From that day on the prince and princess lived together happily until they crossed over to the fields of the blessed.

---

[7]**scimitar** (SIH•muh•tuhr): a long sword with a curved blade

Responding to the Reading

1. How did the prince's father and wife try to protect him?

2. How would this story be different if it were told from the point of view of the prince?

3. **Evaluating Information** Do you think the prince paid enough attention to the goddesses' warning? Why or why not? Support your opinion with examples.

4. **Drawing Conclusions** Why do you think the prince lied to the Chief of Naharín about his parents?

5. **Reading** **Read to Write** Suppose you are the prince, captive in the stone house, or the princess, captive in the tower. Write three diary entries about your daily life, your feelings about being kept away from society, and your hopes for the future.

Section 3

The Egyptian Empire

Get Ready to Read!

What's the Connection?
During the Old Kingdom, Egyptians established their civilization. During the Middle Kingdom and the New Kingdom, Egypt's powerful pharaohs expanded the empire by conquering other lands.

Focusing on the Main Ideas
- The Middle Kingdom was a golden age of peace, prosperity, and advances in the arts and architecture. *(page 60)*

- During the New Kingdom, Egypt acquired new territory and reached the height of its power. *(page 61)*

- Akhenaton tried to change Egypt's religion, while Tutankhamen is famous for the treasures found in his tomb. *(page 64)*

- Under Ramses II, Egypt regained territory and built great temples, but the empire fell by 1150 B.C. *(page 65)*

Locating Places
Thebes (THEEBZ)

Meeting People
Ahmose (AHM•OHS)
Hatshepsut (hat•SHEHP•soot)
Thutmose III (thoot•MOH•suh)
Akhenaton (AHK•NAH•tuhn)
Tutankhamen
  (TOO•TANG•KAH•muhn)
Ramses II (RAM•SEEZ)

Building Your Vocabulary
tribute (TRIH•byoot)
incense (IHN•SEHNS)

Reading Strategy
Categorizing Information Create a diagram to show the major accomplishments of Ramses II.

```
        Ramses
      /   |   \
    ( )  ( )  ( )
```

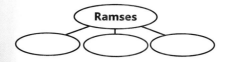

NATIONAL GEOGRAPHIC When & Where?

Memphis
Thebes
Nile R.

2400 B.C.　　　　1600 B.C.　　　　800 B.C.

c. 2050 B.C.
Middle Kingdom begins

c. 1500 B.C.
Queen Hatshepsut reigns

c. 1279 B.C.
Ramses II takes the throne

The Middle Kingdom

(Main Idea) **The Middle Kingdom was a golden age of peace, prosperity, and advances in the arts and architecture.**

Reading Focus Have you heard older people talk about enjoying their "golden years"? Countries can also experience such happy, productive times. In the following paragraphs, you'll learn why the Middle Kingdom was a golden age for Egypt.

About 2300 B.C., the pharaohs lost control of Egypt as nobles battled one another for power. Almost 200 years of confusion followed. Finally, a new dynasty of pharaohs came to power. They moved their capital south from Memphis to a city called **Thebes** (THEEBZ). There they restored order and stability, ushering in a new period called the Middle Kingdom.

The Middle Kingdom lasted from about 2050 B.C. to 1670 B.C. During this time, Egyptians enjoyed a golden age of stability, prosperity, and achievement.

The Drive for More Land

During the Middle Kingdom, Egypt took control of new lands. Soldiers captured Nubia to the south and attacked what is now Syria. The conquered peoples sent **tribute** (TRIH•byoot), or forced payments, to the Egyptian pharaoh, enriching the kingdom. Within Egypt, the pharaohs added more waterways and dams. They increased the amount of land being farmed and built a canal between the Nile River and the Red Sea.

The Arts Blossom

During the Middle Kingdom, arts, literature, and architecture thrived. Painters covered the walls of tombs and temples with colorful scenes of the deities and daily life. Sculptors created large wall carvings and statues of the pharaohs, showing them as ordinary people rather

▲ This artwork with gold inlay from the Middle Kingdom period shows a funeral boat. *How did architecture change during the Middle Kingdom?*

than godlike figures. Poets wrote love songs and tributes to the pharaohs.

A new form of architecture was also created. Instead of building pyramids, pharaohs had their tombs cut into cliffs west of the Nile River. This area became known as the Valley of the Kings.

Who Were the Hyksos?

The Middle Kingdom came to an end in 1670 B.C. Nobles were again plotting to take power from the pharaohs. This time, however, Egypt also faced a serious threat from outside. A people known as the Hyksos (HIHK•SAHS), from western Asia, attacked Egypt.

History Online

Web Activity Visit jat.glencoe.com and click on *Chapter 2—Student Web Activity* to learn more about ancient Egypt.

The Hyksos were mighty warriors. They crossed the desert in horse-drawn chariots and used weapons made of bronze and iron. Egyptians had always fought on foot with copper and stone weapons. They were no match for the invaders.

The Hyksos ruled Egypt for about 150 years. Then, around 1550 B.C., an Egyptian prince named **Ahmose** (AHM•OHS) led an uprising that drove the Hyksos out of Egypt.

Reading Check **Identify** Who were the Hyksos?

The New Kingdom

Main Idea During the New Kingdom, Egypt acquired new territory and reached the height of its power.

Reading Focus Do you know the names of any women who hold political office? In ancient civilizations, women rarely held positions of power. Read to learn how a woman became ruler of Egypt.

Ahmose's reign in Egypt began a period known as the New Kingdom. During this time, from about 1550 B.C. to 1080 B.C., Egypt became even richer and more powerful.

Linking Past & Present

Hieroglyphs and Computer Icons

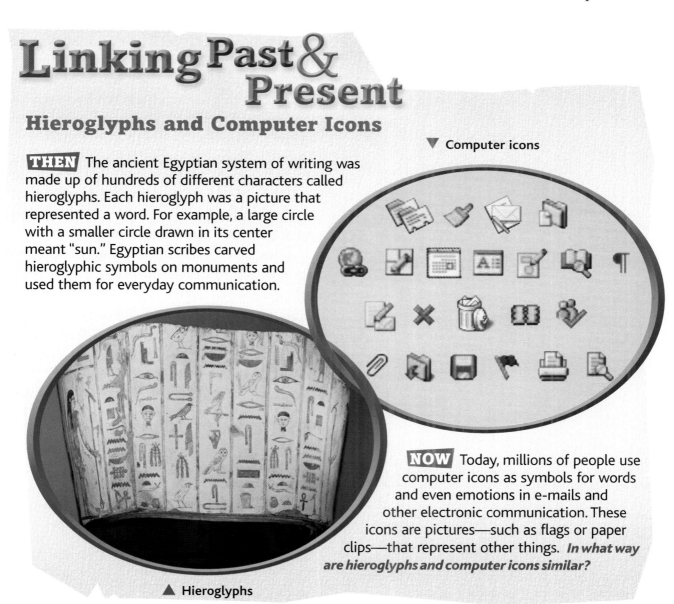

THEN The ancient Egyptian system of writing was made up of hundreds of different characters called hieroglyphs. Each hieroglyph was a picture that represented a word. For example, a large circle with a smaller circle drawn in its center meant "sun." Egyptian scribes carved hieroglyphic symbols on monuments and used them for everyday communication.

▼ Computer icons

NOW Today, millions of people use computer icons as symbols for words and even emotions in e-mails and other electronic communication. These icons are pictures—such as flags or paper clips—that represent other things. *In what way are hieroglyphs and computer icons similar?*

▲ Hieroglyphs

Most pharaohs made empire building a priority. They marched their armies east into western Asia and fought wars to bring other lands under their control. During the New Kingdom, Egypt reached the height of its glory.

A Woman Ruler About 1473 B.C., a queen named **Hatshepsut** (hat•SHEHP•soot) came to power in Egypt. She ruled first with her husband and then, after his death, on behalf of her young nephew. Finally she made herself pharaoh. Hatshepsut became one of the few women to rule Egypt.

Hatshepsut was more interested in trade than conquest. During her reign, Egyptian traders sailed along the coast of East Africa. They exchanged beads, metal tools, and weapons for gold, ivory, ebony, and **incense** (IHN•SEHNS), a material burned for its pleasant smell. These trade journeys brought even greater wealth to Egypt.

Hatshepsut used some of this wealth to build monuments. One of her greatest projects was a great temple and tomb in the limestone cliffs of the Valley of the Kings.

Expanding the Empire When Hatshepsut died, her nephew, **Thutmose III** (thoot•MOH•suh), became pharaoh. Under Thutmose, Egypt began aggressive wars of conquest. Thutmose's armies expanded Egypt's borders north to the Euphrates River in Mesopotamia. His troops also moved south and regained control of Nubia, which had broken free from Egypt earlier. Under Thutmose, Egypt controlled more territory than it ever had.

Thutmose's empire grew rich from trade and tribute. In addition to claiming gold, copper, ivory, and other valuable goods from conquered peoples, Egypt enslaved many prisoners of war. These unlucky captives were put to work rebuilding Thebes. They filled the city with beautiful palaces, temples, and monuments.

Slavery had not been widespread in Egypt before. During the New Kingdom, however, it became common. Enslaved people did have some rights. They could own land, marry, and eventually be granted their freedom.

✓ **Reading Check** **Summarize** Describe Egyptian trade during the rule of Hatshepsut.

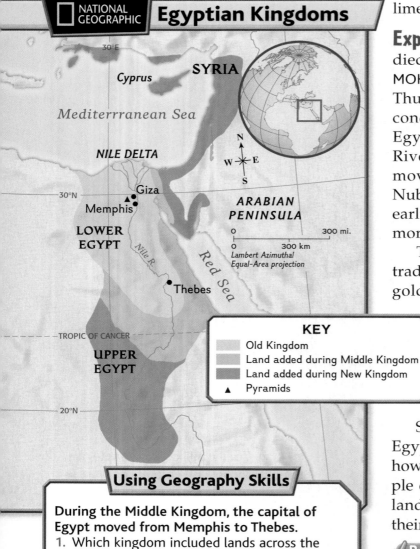

NATIONAL GEOGRAPHIC **Egyptian Kingdoms**

30°E

SYRIA

Cyprus

Mediterrranean Sea

NILE DELTA

N W E S

30°N

Giza

Memphis

ARABIAN PENINSULA

LOWER EGYPT

Nile R.

Red Sea

0 300 mi.
0 300 km
Lambert Azimuthal Equal-Area projection

TROPIC OF CANCER

UPPER EGYPT

Thebes

20°N

KEY
Old Kingdom
Land added during Middle Kingdom
Land added during New Kingdom
▲ Pyramids

Using Geography Skills

During the Middle Kingdom, the capital of Egypt moved from Memphis to Thebes.
1. Which kingdom included lands across the Mediterranean Sea?
2. What physical feature makes up much of the eastern border of the Middle Kingdom?

Biography

HATSHEPSUT
Reigned 1473–1458 B.C.

Hatshepsut ▶

Hatshepsut was the daughter of King Thutmose I and Queen Aahmes. Even as a young princess, she was confident, describing herself as "exceedingly good to look upon . . . a beautiful maiden" who was "serene [peaceful] of nature." During her marriage to King Thutmose II, Hatshepsut influenced her husband's decisions and hoped to someday have more power. She saw an opportunity when Thutmose died and declared herself pharaoh.

Because the position of pharaoh was usually passed from father to son, Hatshepsut had to prove that she was a good leader. She often wore men's clothing to convince the people that she could handle what had always been a man's job. Unlike other pharaohs, Hatshepsut avoided military conquests. She focused her attention instead on expanding Egypt's economy. She restored Egypt's wealth through trade with Africa and Asia. Returning home from trading expeditions, cargo ships were loaded with ebony, gold, ivory, incense, and myrrh. During her reign, Hatshepsut also rebuilt many of Egypt's great temples, including the temple at Karnak. In her temple at Deir el Bahri, the reliefs on the walls recorded the major events of Hatshepsut's reign.

Hatshepsut's 21-year reign was peaceful, but her stepson, Thutmose III, was plotting against her. He overthrew Hatshepsut and her government. It is unknown how Hatshepsut died, but after her death, Thutmose III ordered that the reliefs and statues in Hatshepsut's temple be destroyed.

"A dictator excellent of plans"
—Egyptian scribe quoted in
Barbarian Tides

Then and Now

Make a list of Hatshepsut's strengths as a leader. Then choose a present-day female leader and list her leadership strengths. Write a paragraph comparing their similarities and differences.

The Way It Was

Focus on Everyday Life

Cats in Ancient Egypt In ancient Egypt, cats were loved and even worshiped. Egyptians valued the ability of wild cats to protect villages' grain supplies from mice and rats. Over several hundred years, cats became tame, and their role developed from valued hunter to adored family pet to goddess.

In ancient Egyptian tombs, archaeologists have found many wall paintings, carvings, and statues of cats. Often the statues were adorned with beautiful jewelry, such as silver or gold earrings, nose rings, and collars. When an Egyptian family's cat died, its owners shaved their eyebrows to show their grief and had the cat's body mummified.

▲ Egyptian goddess depicted as a cat

Egyptians worshiped cats because they associated them with the goddess Bastet. She represented motherhood, grace, and beauty, and often appears in paintings and statues as a woman with the head of a cat.

Connecting to the Past

1. Why did ancient Egyptians first value cats?
2. With what goddess did the ancient Egyptians associate cats?

The Legacies of Two Pharaohs

Main Idea Akhenaton tried to change Egypt's religion, while Tutankhamen is famous for the treasures found in his tomb.

Reading Focus If you ask people to name an Egyptian pharaoh, the answer you're likely to get is "King Tut." Read on to find out more about him and his predecessor.

About 1370 B.C., Amenhotep IV (AH•muhn•HOH•TEHP) came to the throne. With the help of his wife, Nefertiti (NEHF•uhr•TEET•ee), Amenhotep tried to lead Egypt in a new direction.

A Religious Reformer Amenhotep realized that Egypt's priests were gaining power at the expense of the pharaohs. In an attempt to maintain his own power, Amenhotep introduced a new religion that swept away the old gods and goddesses. Instead, only one god, called Aton (AH•tuhn), was to be worshiped. When Egypt's priests resisted these changes, Amenhotep removed many from their positions, seized their lands, and closed temples. He then changed his name to **Akhenaton** (AHK•NAH•tuhn), which means "Spirit of Aton." He began ruling Egypt from a new city.

To most Egyptians, Akhenaton's attacks on the gods seemed to be an attack on Egypt itself. They refused to accept Aton as the only god. Meanwhile, Akhenaton became so devoted to his new religion that he neglected his duties as pharaoh. The administrators he appointed were not as experienced as the priests they replaced, and Akhenaton took no action when enemies from what is now Turkey, the Hittites, attacked Egypt. As a result, Egypt lost most of its lands in western Asia, greatly shrinking the empire.

◀ Tutankhamen's gold mask

The Boy King When Akhenaton died, his son-in-law inherited the throne. The new pharaoh, **Tutankhamen** (TOO•TANG•KAH•muhn), was a boy about 10 years old. He relied on help from palace officials and priests, who convinced him to restore the old religion. After ruling for only nine years, Tutankhamen died unexpectedly. He may have suffered a fall or been murdered; no one is sure.

What *is* certain is that "King Tut," as he is nicknamed, played only a small role in Egypt's history. Why, then, is he the most famous of all pharaohs? The boy king captured people's imaginations after a British archaeologist, Howard Carter, found his tomb in A.D. 1922.

The tomb contained the king's mummy and incredible treasures, including a brilliant gold mask of the young pharaoh's face. Carter's find was a thrilling discovery, because most royal tombs in Egypt were looted by robbers long ago.

✓ **Reading Check** **Evaluate** Why is Tutankhamen so famous today?

The End of the New Kingdom

Main Idea Under Ramses II, Egypt regained territory and built great temples, but the empire fell by 1150 B.C.

Reading Focus Egypt remained mighty for thousands of years, but it finally fell to outsiders. Read to learn about Egypt's last great pharaoh and the empire's decline.

During the 1200s B.C., pharaohs worked to make Egypt great again. The most effective of these pharaohs was **Ramses II** (RAM•SEEZ). He reigned for a remarkable 66 years, from 1279 B.C. to 1213 B.C. During this time, Egyptian armies regained lands in western Asia and rebuilt the empire. Ramses also launched an ambitious building program, constructing several major new temples.

▲ Temple of Karnak

Biography

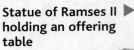

RAMSES II

Reigned 1279–1213 B.C.

Statue of Ramses II ▶
holding an offering
table

Ramses II began his military training at a very young age. Ramses' father, Seti I, allowed his 10-year-old son to serve as a captain in his army. Seti also made his son coruler of Egypt. By the time Ramses was crowned pharaoh of Egypt, he was a great warrior and experienced leader. Nine kings who ruled after Ramses II named themselves in his honor. Many centuries later, archaeologists nicknamed the pharaoh "Ramses the Great" because of his fame on the battlefield, his construction and restoration of buildings and monuments, and his popularity among the Egyptian people. His subjects fondly called him "Sese," an abbreviation of Ramses.

Ramses continued in his father's footsteps by trying to restore Egyptian power in Asia. In the early years of his reign, he defeated forces in southern Syria and continuously battled Egypt's longtime enemy, the Hittites. Details about one costly battle with the Hittites were carved on temple walls, showing the Egyptians succeeding against great odds.

> "They all came bowing down to him, to his palace of life and satisfaction."
>
> –hieroglyphic translation by James B. Pritchard, *Ancient Near Eastern Texts*

During his 66-year reign, Ramses II undertook a large-scale building program. He could afford such an expensive plan because Egypt was very prosperous during his reign. He restored the Sphinx, completed the Temple of Karnak, and built himself a city with four temples as well as beautiful gardens and orchards. He is famous for the temple built at Abu Simbel. It was carved out of a solid rock cliff and featured four huge statues of Ramses II, two on each side of the doorway.

Ramses' first wife, Queen Nefertari, died early in his reign. Like other pharaohs, Ramses had many wives. Ramses II was proud of his large family, which included more than 100 children.

▲ Coffin of Ramses II

Then and Now

Use the Internet and your local library to learn about Mount Rushmore, a monument in South Dakota. Describe Mount Rushmore, and then compare it to Ramses' temple at Abu Simbel.

Why Were Temples Built? Under Ramses II and other New Kingdom rulers, scores of new temples rose throughout Egypt. Many were built by enslaved people captured in war. The most magnificent was Karnak at Thebes. Its huge columned hall decorated with colorful paintings still impresses visitors today.

Unlike modern churches, temples, and mosques, Egyptian temples did not hold regular services. Instead, most Egyptians prayed at home. They considered the temples as houses for the gods and goddesses. Priests and priestesses, however, performed daily temple rituals, washing statues of the deities and bringing them food.

The temples also served as banks. Egyptians used them to store valuable items, such as gold jewelry, sweet-smelling oils, and finely woven cloth.

Egypt's Decline and Fall After Ramses II, Egypt's power began to fade. Later pharaohs had trouble keeping neighboring countries under Egyptian control. Groups from the eastern Mediterranean attacked Egypt by sea, using strong iron weapons. The Egyptians had similar arms, but they paid dearly for them because Egypt lacked iron ore.

By 1150 B.C., the Egyptians had lost their empire and controlled only the Nile delta. Beginning in the 900s B.C., Egypt came under the rule of one outside group after another. The first conquerors were the Libyans from the west. Then in 760 B.C., the people of Kush, a land to the south, seized power and ruled Egypt for the next 70 years. Finally, in 670 B.C., Egypt was taken over by the Assyrians.

✓ **Reading Check** **Identify** What groups conquered Egypt starting in the 900s B.C.?

History Online
Study Central™ Need help with the material in this section? Visit jat.glencoe.com

Section 3 Review

Reading Summary
Review the Main Ideas

- During the Middle Kingdom, Egypt expanded its borders, and the arts flourished.

- Under New Kingdom rulers, Egypt built a strong empire and expanded trade.

- Akhenaton failed in his attempt to create a new religion. Tutankhamen ruled briefly but gained fame because of treasures found buried with him.

- Ramses II was Egypt's last great pharaoh. In the 900s B.C., Egypt lost power to outside invaders.

What Did You Learn?

1. What improvements did the Middle Kingdom rulers make?

2. What purposes did temples serve in Egypt?

Critical Thinking

3. **Organizing Information** Create a chart like the one below. Fill in details about Egypt's Middle Kingdom and New Kingdom.

Middle Kingdom	New Kingdom

4. **Evaluate** What was unusual about the reign of Hatshepsut?

5. **Analyze** How did Akhenaton upset the traditional order?

6. **Compare and Contrast** Describe the similarities and differences between the rule of Hatshepsut and Ramses II.

7. **Expository Writing** Which of the rulers discussed in this section do you think had the greatest effect upon Egyptian history? Write a short essay to explain your answer.

Section 4

The Civilization of Kush

Get Ready to Read!

What's the Connection?
In Sections 1, 2, and 3, you learned about the rise and fall of civilizations in ancient Egypt. Another civilization in early Africa was Kush. It was located near Egypt and was very similar.

Focusing on the Main Ideas
- To the south of Egypt, the Nubians settled in farming villages and became strong warriors. *(page 69)*

- The people of Kush devoted themselves to ironworking and grew wealthy from trade. *(page 70)*

Locating Places
Nubia (NOO•bee•uh)
Kush (KUHSH)
Kerma (KAR•muh)
Napata (NA•puh•tuh)
Meroë (MEHR•oh•ee)

Meeting People
Kashta (KAHSH•tuh)
Piye (PY)

Building Your Vocabulary
savanna (suh•VA•nuh)

Reading Strategy
Compare and Contrast Use a Venn diagram like the one below to show the similarities and differences between Napata and Meroë.

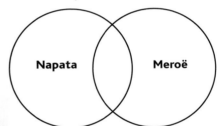

Napata   Meroë

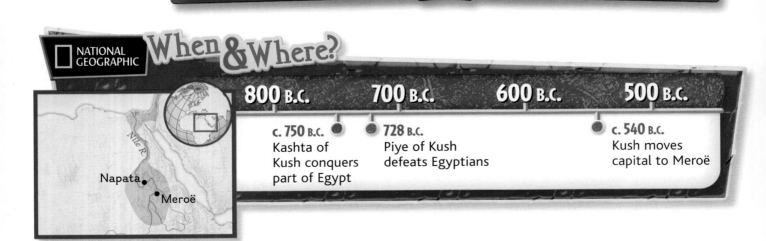

NATIONAL GEOGRAPHIC When & Where?

| 800 B.C. | 700 B.C. | 600 B.C. | 500 B.C. |

c. 750 B.C. Kashta of Kush conquers part of Egypt

728 B.C. Piye of Kush defeats Egyptians

c. 540 B.C. Kush moves capital to Meroë

Napata
Meroë
Nile R.

Nubia

Main Idea To the south of Egypt, the Nubians settled in farming villages and became strong warriors.

Reading Focus Are you on good terms with your neighbors? It's not always easy–for individuals or countries. Read on to find out about the Egyptians' neighbors to the south and the ways the two civilizations mixed.

The Egyptians were not alone in settling along the Nile River. Farther south, in present-day Sudan, another strong civilization arose. This was in a region called **Nubia** (NOO•bee•uh), later known as **Kush** (KUHSH).

Historians do not know exactly when people arrived in Nubia. Evidence suggests that cattle herders arrived in about 2000 B.C. They grazed their herds on the **savannas** (suh•VA•nuhs), or grassy plains, that stretch across Africa south of the Sahara. Later, people settled in farming villages in Nubia. They grew crops, but they were also excellent hunters, skilled at using the bow and arrow. Soon the Nubians began forming armies known for their fighting skills.

The Kingdom of Kerma
The more powerful Nubian villages gradually took over the weaker ones and created the kingdom of **Kerma** (KAR•muh). Kerma developed close ties with Egypt to the north. The Egyptians were happy to trade for Kerma's cattle, gold, ivory, and enslaved people. They also admired Nubian skills in warfare and hired Nubian warriors to fight in their armies.

Kerma became a wealthy kingdom. Its artisans made fine pottery, jewelry, and metal goods. Like Egyptian pharaohs, the kings of Kerma were buried in tombs that held precious stones, gold, jewelry, and pottery. These items were as splendid as those found in Egypt during the same period.

▲ In this wall painting, four Nubian princes offer rings and gold to an Egyptian ruler.
What kingdom was formed when more powerful Nubian villages took over weaker ones?

Why Did Egypt Invade Nubia? As you learned earlier, the Egyptian pharaoh Thutmose III sent his armies into Nubia in the 1400s B.C. After a 50-year war, the kingdom of Kerma collapsed, and the Egyptians took control of much of Nubia. They ruled the Nubians for the next 700 years.

During this time, the people of Nubia adopted many Egyptian ways. They began to worship Egyptian gods and goddesses along with their own. They learned how to work copper and bronze and changed Egyptian hieroglyphs to fit their own language. As people and goods continued to pass between Nubia and Egypt, the two cultures mixed.

✓**Reading Check** **Identify** Where was Kush located?

The Rise of Kush

Main Idea **The people of Kush devoted themselves to ironworking and grew wealthy from trade.**

Reading Focus Do you and your friends ever trade video games or CDs? Trading may be a casual activity for you, but it was very important to ancient peoples. Read to find how Kush took advantage of its location along an important trade route.

As Egypt declined at the end of the New Kingdom, Nubians saw their chance to break away. By 850 B.C., a Nubian group had formed the independent kingdom of Kush. For the next few centuries, powerful Kushite kings ruled from the city of **Napata** (NA•puh•tuh).

Napata was in a favorable location. It stood along the upper Nile where trade caravans crossed the river. Caravans soon carried gold, ivory, valuable woods, and other goods from Kush to Egypt.

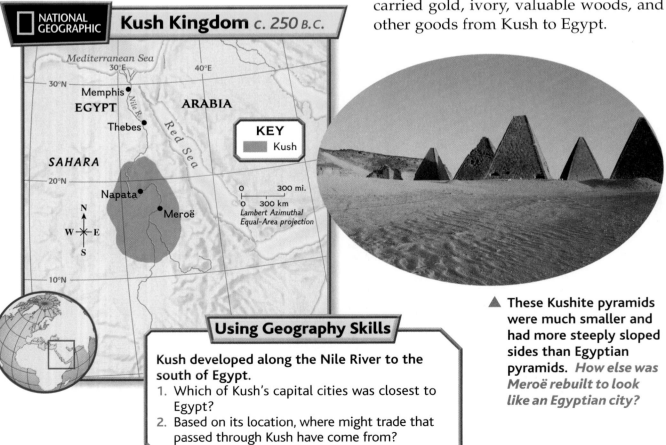

NATIONAL GEOGRAPHIC
Kush Kingdom c. 250 B.C.

Mediterranean Sea
30°E   40°E
30°N
Memphis
EGYPT   ARABIA
Thebes
Nile R.
Red Sea
KEY
Kush
SAHARA
20°N
Napata
300 mi.
Meroë
0   300 km
Lambert Azimuthal
Equal-Area projection
N
W E
S
10°N

Using Geography Skills

Kush developed along the Nile River to the south of Egypt.

1. Which of Kush's capital cities was closest to Egypt?
2. Based on its location, where might trade that passed through Kush have come from?

▲ These Kushite pyramids were much smaller and had more steeply sloped sides than Egyptian pyramids. *How else was Meroë rebuilt to look like an Egyptian city?*

In time, Kush became rich enough and strong enough to take control of Egypt. About 750 B.C., a Kushite king named **Kashta** (KAHSH•tuh) headed north with a powerful army. His soldiers began the conquest of Egypt that his son **Piye** (PY) completed in 728 B.C. Piye founded a dynasty that ruled both Egypt and Kush from Napata.

The kings of Kush greatly admired Egyptian culture. In Napata they built white sandstone temples and monuments similar to those of the Egyptians. The Kushites also built small pyramids in which to bury their kings. The ruins of these pyramids can still be seen today.

The Importance of Iron Kush's rule in Egypt did not last long. During the 600s B.C., the Assyrians invaded Egypt. Armed with iron weapons, they drove the Kushites back to their homeland in the south.

Despite their losses, the Kushites gained something from the Assyrians—the secret of making iron. The Kushites became the first Africans to devote themselves to iron-working. Soon, farmers in Kush were using iron for their hoes and plows instead of copper or stone. With these superior tools, they were able to grow large amounts of grain and other crops.

Kush's warriors also began using iron spears and swords, increasing their military power. Meanwhile, traders from Kush carried iron products and enslaved people as far away as Arabia, India, and China. In return, they brought back cotton, textiles, and other goods.

A New Capital About 540 B.C., Kush's rulers left Napata and moved farther south to be out of the Assyrians' reach. In the city of **Meroë** (MEHR•oh•ee), they set up a royal court. Like Napata, the new capital had

access to the Nile River for trade and transportation. The rocky desert east of Meroë, however, contained rich deposits of iron ore. As a result, Meroë became not only a trading city but also a center for making iron.

With their growing wealth, Kush's kings rebuilt Meroë to look like an Egyptian city. Small pyramids stood in the royal graveyard. A huge temple sat at the end of a grand avenue lined with sculptures of rams. Sandstone palaces and red-brick houses had walls decorated with paintings or blue and yellow tiles.

Building a Profitable Trade Meroë became the center of a huge trading network that stretched north to Egypt's border and south into central Africa. Kush's traders received leopard skins and valuable woods from the interior of Africa. They traded these goods, along with enslaved workers and their own iron products, to people throughout the Mediterranean and the Indian Ocean area.

Kush remained a great trading power for some 600 years. By the A.D. 200s, though, the kingdom began to weaken. As Kush declined, another kingdom rose to take its place. The kingdom is called Axum and was located in what is today the country of Ethiopia. Around A.D. 350, the armies of Axum burned Meroë to the ground. You will read more about the kingdom of Axum when you study Africa.

✔ **Reading Check** **Explain** How did Kush become a wealthy kingdom?

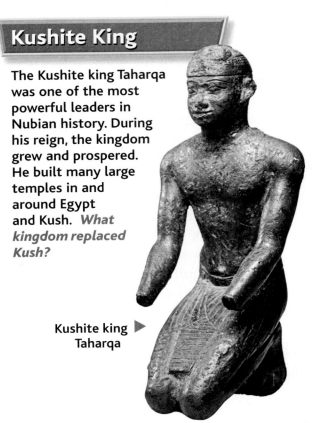

Kushite King

The Kushite king Taharqa was one of the most powerful leaders in Nubian history. During his reign, the kingdom grew and prospered. He built many large temples in and around Egypt and Kush. *What kingdom replaced Kush?*

► Kushite king Taharqa

History Online

Study Central™ Need help with the material in this section? Visit jat.glencoe.com

Section 4 Review

Reading Summary

Review the Main Ideas

• In the Nile Valley to the south of Egypt, the Nubians founded the kingdom of Kerma and traded with the Egyptians.

• The Kushites set up a capital at Meroë that became a center for ironmaking and the base of a huge trading network.

What Did You Learn?

1. Who were the Nubians?

2. What were the Kushites' most important economic activities?

Critical Thinking

3. **Sequencing** Draw a diagram to show events that led up to the Kushite conquest of Egypt.

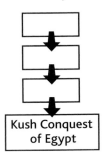

Kush Conquest of Egypt

4. **Geography Skills** Why was Napata's location advantageous?

5. **Analyze** How did the Kushite kings demonstrate their admiration for Egyptian culture?

6. **Compare** Describe the similarities between Kush and Egypt.

7. **Persuasive Writing** Create an advertisement that could have been used in ancient Egypt and Kush to promote the many uses of iron.

Section 1 The Nile Valley

Vocabulary
cataract
delta
papyrus
hieroglyphics
dynasty

Focusing on the Main Ideas
- The Egyptian civilization began in the fertile Nile River valley, where natural barriers discouraged invasions. *(page 39)*
- The Egyptians depended on the Nile's floods to grow their crops. *(page 41)*
- Around 3100 B.C., Egypt's two major kingdoms, Upper Egypt and Lower Egypt, were combined into one. *(page 43)*
- Egyptian society was divided into social groups based on wealth and power. *(page 45)*

Section 2 Egypt's Old Kingdom

Vocabulary
pharaoh
deity
embalming
mummy
pyramid

Focusing on the Main Ideas
- Egypt was ruled by all-powerful pharaohs. *(page 48)*
- The Egyptians believed in many gods and goddesses and in life after death for the pharaohs. *(page 49)*
- The Egyptians of the Old Kingdom built huge stone pyramids as tombs for their pharaohs. *(page 50)*

Section 3 The Egyptian Empire

Vocabulary
tribute
incense

Focusing on the Main Ideas
- The Middle Kingdom was a golden age of peace, prosperity, and advances in the arts and architecture. *(page 60)*
- During the New Kingdom, Egypt acquired new territory and reached the height of its power. *(page 61)*
- Akhenaton tried to change Egypt's religion, while Tutankhamen is famous for the treasures found in his tomb. *(page 64)*
- Under Ramses II, Egypt regained territory and built great temples, but the empire fell by 1150 B.C. *(page 65)*

▲ Tutankhamen's gold mask

Section 4 The Civilization of Kush

Vocabulary
savanna

Focusing on the Main Ideas
- To the south of Egypt, the Nubians settled in farming villages and became strong warriors. *(page 69)*
- The people of Kush devoted themselves to ironworking and grew wealthy from trade. *(page 70)*

73

Assessment and Activities

Review Vocabulary

Match the definitions in the second column to the terms in the first column. Write the letter of each definition.

_____ 1. savanna

_____ 2. tribute

_____ 3. cataract

_____ 4. delta

_____ 5. hieroglyphics

_____ 6. pharaoh

_____ 7. papyrus

a. area of fertile soil at the end of a river

b. reed plant used to make baskets, rafts, and paper

c. grassy plain

d. rapids

e. Egyptian writing system

f. forced payments

g. title for Egyptian leaders

Review Main Ideas

Section 1 • The Nile Valley

8. What natural barriers protected Egypt from invasion?

9. What factors divided Egyptians into social groups?

Section 2 • Egypt's Old Kingdom

10. What were the Egyptians' religious beliefs?

11. Where did Egyptians of the Old Kingdom bury their pharaohs?

Section 3 • The Egyptian Empire

12. Why was the Middle Kingdom called a golden age?

13. Why are Akhenaton and Tutankhamen well-known?

Section 4 • The Civilization of Kush

14. Where did the Nubians live?

15. What made the Kushites wealthy?

Critical Thinking

16. **Describe** Identify the four social groups in ancient Egypt, and explain who belonged to each group.

17. **Synthesize** How do you think religious leaders reacted to Akhenaton's changes?

18. **Analyze** Do you agree that Egyptian civilization can be called "the Gift of the Nile"? Explain.

19. **Compare** In what ways did Meroë look like an Egyptian city?

Review

Reading Skill | Predicting

What Do You Predict?

Read these sentences from page 72.

As Kush declined, another kingdom rose to take its place. The kingdom is called Axum and was located in what is today the country of Ethiopia. Around A.D. 350, the armies of Axum burned Meroë to the ground. You will read more about the kingdom of Axum when you study Africa.

20. Based on what you know about the location of Ethiopia and the culture of Kush and Egypt, predict what the kingdom of Axum might be like. Check your predictions when you read about medieval Africa.

To review this skill, see pages 36–37.

Geography Skills

Study the map below and answer the following questions.

21. **Location** The Nile River delta empties into what body of water?
22. **Movement** Why would ancient Egyptians find it easier to travel north and south than to travel east and west?
23. **Human/Environment Interaction** Why is most farming in ancient Egypt and in present-day Egypt done along the Nile?

NATIONAL GEOGRAPHIC

Ancient Egypt

KEY
Nile Valley

Mediterranean Sea

Dead Sea

30°E

NILE DELTA
LOWER EGYPT
30°N — Giza
Great Pyramid and Sphinx — Memphis

ARABIAN DESERT

WESTERN DESERT

Nile River

EASTERN DESERT

Red Sea

UPPER EGYPT
Thebes

N
W — E
S

0   100 mi.
0   100 km
Azimuthal Equidistant projection

Read to Write

24. **Descriptive Writing** Imagine you are an ancient Egyptian pharaoh. You are making plans that your followers will carry out after your death. Describe the types of items you want buried with you in your pyramid. Then explain what people from later centuries will know about you if they find those items.

25. **Using Your** FOLDABLES Use your foldable to describe one of the civilizations from the chapter, including such things as religious life, family life, and contributions. A classmate should identify which civilization you are describing. Then your classmate will describe a civilization, and you will identify it. When you are finished, discuss similarities and differences among the civilizations.

History Online
Self-Check Quiz To help prepare for the Chapter Test, visit jat.glencoe.com

Using Technology

26. **Developing Multimedia Presentations** Use the Internet and your local library to find out more about the reign of one of the Egyptian pharaohs. Create a computer slide show presentation that includes details about the pharaoh's reign and life. Include an illustrated time line of significant events.

Linking Past and Present

27. **Organizing Information** Use the Internet and atlases to locate present-day countries that rely heavily on a major river. Make a chart listing the country, the river, the river's length and average depth, and how the people of that country use the river.

Primary Source **Analyze**

The Greek historian Herodotus noticed that the Nile was different from other rivers.

"The Nile, when it floods, spreads over not only the Delta but parts of what are called Libya and Arabia for two days' journey in either direction, more or less. . . . This that I have mentioned was the subject of my persistent asking why, and also why it is that it is the only river that has no breezes blowing from it."

—Herodotus, *The History*, 2.19

DBQ **Document-Based Questions**

28. According to Herodotus, how much land does the Nile cover when it floods?
29. What two questions does Herodotus ask about the Nile?

The Ancient Israelites

The wall surrounding the ▼
old city of Jerusalem

NATIONAL GEOGRAPHIC **When & Where?**

2000 B.C.	1300 B.C.	600 B.C.	A.D. 100
c. 1800 B.C. Israelites settle in Canaan	**c. 1290 B.C.** Moses leads Israelites from Egypt	**722 B.C.** Assyrians conquer Israel	**A.D. 66** Jews revolt against Romans

Chapter Preview

Like the Sumerians, the ancient Israelites developed a society based on ideas of justice and strict laws. The Israelites believed that there was only one God.

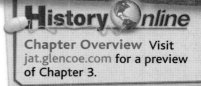
History Online

Chapter Overview Visit jat.glencoe.com for a preview of Chapter 3.

 View the Chapter 3 video in the *World History: Journey Across Time* Video Program.

 ## The First Israelites

Abraham founded the 12 tribes of Israel in the land of Canaan. The Israelites believed in one God.

 ## The Kingdom of Israel

Under David and Solomon, the people of Israel built a powerful kingdom with a new capital in Jerusalem.

 ## The Growth of Judaism

The Jews continued to keep their religion even though other people ruled them. They settled in many places in Asia and Europe.

Summarizing Information *Make this foldable and use it to organize note cards with information about the Israelites.*

Step 1 *Fold a horizontal sheet of paper (11"x17") into thirds.*

Step 2 *Fold the bottom edge up two inches and crease well. Glue the outer edges of the tab to create three pockets.*

Glue here.

Glue here.

Reading and Writing *As you read the chapter, summarize key facts on note cards or on quarter sheets of paper about Israel and the growth and spread of Judaism. Organize your notes by placing them in your pocket foldable inside the appropriate pockets.*

Step 3 *Label the pockets as shown. Use these pockets to hold notes taken on index cards or quarter sheets of paper.*

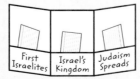

First Israelites | Israel's Kingdom | Judaism Spreads

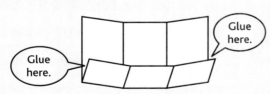

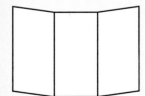

3 Reading Social Studies

Reading Skill

Main Idea

1 Learn It!

Finding the Main Idea

Main ideas are the most important ideas in a paragraph, section, or chapter. Supporting details are facts or examples that explain the main idea. Read the following paragraph from Section 1 and notice how the author explains the main idea. The main idea is identified for you. The supporting details are highlighted in color.

Main idea

> Through trade, the Phoenicians spread ideas and goods. One of their most important ideas was an alphabet, or a group of letters that stood for sounds. The letters could be used to spell out the words in their language.
>
> —*from page 85*

Supporting details

Reading Tip

Often, the first sentence in a paragraph will contain a main idea, and supporting details will come in following sentences. However, main ideas can also appear in the middle or at the end of a paragraph.

2 Practice It!

Create a Graphic Organizer

Read the following paragraph. Draw a graphic organizer like the one shown below. Write the main ideas in a box and supporting details in circles around the box.

Read to Write

Choose one of the **Main Ideas** listed on page 93. Use it as a topic sentence, and add supporting details to create a full paragraph.

While in Babylon, small groups of Jews met on the Sabbath. This was their weekly day of worship and rest. The Jews would pray and discuss their religion and history. These meetings took place at synagogues, or Jewish houses of worship. The synagogue meetings gave the people hope.

—from page 94

▲ Menorah

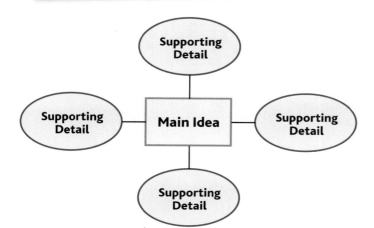

3 Apply It!

As you read Chapter 3, create your own graphic organizer to show the main idea and supporting details from at least one paragraph.

79

The First Israelites

Get Ready to Read!

What's the Connection?

You have read how the Egyptians built a great civilization. At about the same time, another nation was forming. The Egyptians called the people of this nation *habiru*, or foreigners. The people called themselves Israelites or the Children of Israel.

Focusing on the Main Ideas

• The Israelites believed in one God who set down moral laws for his people. They recorded their history in the Bible. *(page 81)*

• The Israelites had to fight the Canaanites to return to their promised land. *(page 84)*

Locating Places

Canaan (KAY•nuhn)
Mount Sinai (SY•NY)

Meeting People

Abraham
Jacob
Moses
Deborah
Phoenician (fih•NEE•shuhn)

Building Your Vocabulary

monotheism
(MAH•nuh•thee•IH•zuhm)
tribe
Torah (TOHR•UH)
covenant (KUHV•nuhnt)
alphabet

Reading Strategy

Sequencing Information Create a sequence chart to help trace the movement of the Israelites.

☐ → ☐ → ☐

When & Where?

NATIONAL GEOGRAPHIC

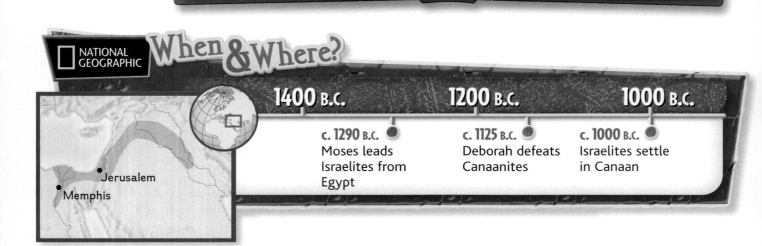

1400 B.C.

1200 B.C.

1000 B.C.

c. 1290 B.C.
Moses leads Israelites from Egypt

c. 1125 B.C.
Deborah defeats Canaanites

c. 1000 B.C.
Israelites settle in Canaan

Jerusalem
Memphis

The Early Israelites

Main Idea The Israelites believed in one God who set down moral laws for his people. They recorded their history in the Bible.

Reading Focus Where do your ideas about right and wrong come from? Read on to find out how the Israelites developed their ideas about right and wrong.

About 1200 B.C., great changes took place around the Mediterranean Sea. Empires fell and new people entered the region. Many set up small kingdoms. Around 1000 B.C., a people called Israelites (IHZ•ruh•LYTS) built a kingdom in **Canaan** (KAY•nuhn). Canaan lies along the Mediterranean Sea in southwest Asia.

Who Were the Israelites? Although the Israelite population was small, the religion they practiced would one day affect most of the world. Most people at this time worshiped many gods and goddesses. The Israelite religion focused on only one God. The belief in one god is called **monotheism** (MAH•nuh•thee•IH•zuhm).

The Israelite faith became the religion known today as Judaism (JOO•dee•IH•zuhm). The followers of Judaism were eventually known as Jews. Judaism influenced Christianity and Islam, and also helped shape the beliefs and practices of societies in Europe and America.

The Israelites spoke a language called Hebrew. They wrote down much of their history and many of their religious beliefs in what later became the Hebrew Bible. Through this book, Jewish values and religion later spread to Europe.

The earliest Israelites were herders and traders. According to the Bible, they came from Mesopotamia and settled in Canaan. Today, Lebanon, Israel, and Jordan occupy the land that was once Canaan.

▲ This painting shows Abraham leading the Israelites from Mesopotamia to Canaan. *Why did the Israelites eventually leave Canaan?*

The Israelites believed they were descended from a man named **Abraham.** In the Bible, it says that God told Abraham and his followers to leave Mesopotamia and go to Canaan. There, they were to worship the one true God. In return, God promised that the land of Canaan would belong to Abraham and his descendants. According to the Bible, this is the reason that the Israelites settled in Canaan.

Abraham had a grandson named **Jacob.** Jacob was also called Israel, which means "one who struggles with God." Later this name was given to Jacob's descendants.

According to the Bible, Jacob raised 12 sons in Canaan. His family was divided into **tribes,** or separate family groups. These groups later became known as the 12 tribes of Israel. The Israelites lived in Canaan for about 100 years. Then a long drought began. Crops withered and livestock died. To survive, the Israelites went to Egypt.

From Slavery to Freedom Life was not good in Egypt. The Egyptian pharaoh needed men to build his pyramids, so he

Moses and the Ten Commandments

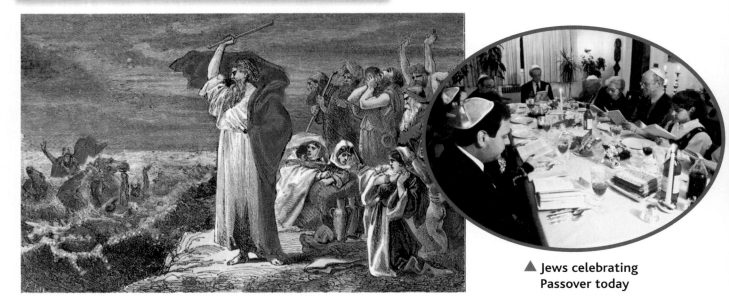

▲ Jews celebrating Passover today

▲ In this painting, Moses watches as the Red Sea closes in on the Egyptian soldiers who were pursuing the Israelites. *What is the Israelites' escape from Egypt called?*

enslaved the Israelites. To prevent a rebellion he ordered all baby boys born to Israelites thrown into the Nile River.

The Bible says that one desperate mother put her baby in a basket and hid it on the riverbank. The pharaoh's daughter found the baby and named him **Moses.**

When Moses grew up, he tended sheep outside Egypt. Around 1290 B.C., he saw a burning bush and heard a voice. He believed that God was telling him to lead the Israelites out of Egypt to freedom.

To get the pharaoh to let the Israelites go, the Bible says that God sent 10 plagues to trouble Egypt. A plague is sometimes a disease, but it can also mean something that causes problems for a lot of people. The last plague God sent killed all first-born children, except for those of Israelites who marked their doorway with lamb's blood. This plague convinced the pharaoh to let the Israelites leave. Jews today celebrate a holiday called Passover to remember

how God "passed over" their homes with the tenth plague and then delivered them from Egypt.

As Israelites headed east out of Egypt, the pharaoh changed his mind and sent his army after the Israelites. According to the Bible, God parted the Red Sea to let his people pass. When the Egyptians followed, the water flowed back and drowned the soldiers. The Israelite escape from Egypt is known as the Exodus.

What Are the Ten Commandments? On

their way back to Canaan, the Israelites had to travel through the Sinai desert. The Bible says that during this journey, Moses went to the top of **Mount Sinai** (SY•NY). There, he received laws from God. These laws were known as the **Torah** (TOHR•uh). They later became the first part of the Hebrew Bible. The Torah described a **covenant** (KUHV•nuhnt), or agreement, with God. In the agreement, God promised to return the Israelites to Canaan if they followed his laws.

▲ **The Ark of the Covenant was a box, which, according to Jewish beliefs, held the Ten Commandments.**
How did the Ten Commandments help shape the basic moral laws of many European nations?

The Torah explained what God considered to be right and wrong. The most important part of the Torah is the Ten Commandments. They are summarized in the feature to the right. The Ten Commandments told the Israelites to be loyal only to God, whose name was never to be spoken. They must never worship any other gods or images. The belief that there should be only one god became the foundation for both Christianity and Islam.

The Ten Commandments helped shape the basic moral laws of many nations. The Ten Commandments told people not to steal, murder, or tell lies about others. They told people to avoid jealousy and to honor their parents. The Ten Commandments also helped develop a belief in the "rule of law." This is the idea that laws should apply to everyone equally.

✓ **Reading Check** **Explain** What covenant was described in the Torah?

Primary Source The Ten Commandments

According to the Bible, Moses received the Ten Commandments and other laws from God on Mount Sinai. Moses and the Israelites promised to follow these laws.

1. Do not worship any god except me.
2. Do not . . . bow down and worship idols.
3. Do not misuse my name.
4. Remember that the Sabbath Day belongs to me.
5. Respect your father and your mother.
6. Do not murder.
7. Be faithful in marriage.
8. Do not steal.
9. Do not tell lies about others.
10. Do not want anything that belongs to someone else.

—Exodus 20:3-17

◄ **Moses with the Ten Commandments**

▲ **Mount Sinai**

DBQ **Document-Based Questions**

1. How many of the commandments tell people how to interact with other people?
2. How many tell them how to worship and show respect for God?

The Promised Land

Main Idea The Israelites had to fight the Canaanites to return to their promised land.

Reading Focus What qualities do you think a good leader should have? Read on to find out about the leaders of the Israelites.

It probably took the Israelites about 40 years to reach Canaan. Moses never lived to see the Promised Land. After Moses died, a leader named Joshua took over and brought the Israelites into Canaan. When they arrived, however, they found other people living there. Most were Canaanites (KAY•nuh•NYTS). The Israelites believed it was God's will that they conquer the Canaanites, so Joshua led them into battle.

The story of the campaign is told in the Bible. Joshua led the Israelites to the city of Jericho and told them to march around the city's walls. For six days, they marched while seven priests blew their trumpets. On the seventh day, the trumpets sounded one last time, and Joshua told the Israelites to raise a great shout. According to the story, the walls of Jericho crumbled, and the Israelites overran the city.

Joshua led the Israelites in three more wars. The land they seized was divided among the 12 tribes.

Who Were the Fighting Judges?

After Joshua died, the Israelites looked to judges for leadership. A judge was usually a military leader. Generally, he or she commanded 1 or 2 tribes, but seldom all 12. The Bible tells about Barak, Gideon, Samuel, Eli, Samson, and others, including a woman judge. Her name was **Deborah.**

Deborah told Barak to attack the army of the Canaanite king Jabin. She went along to the battlefield as an adviser. With Deborah's help, Barak and 10,000 Israelites destroyed King Jabin and his army in about 1125 B.C.

Over time, the Israelites won control of the hilly region in central Canaan. The Canaanites kept the flat, coastal areas. To protect themselves, the Israelites built walled towns. They also created an alphabet and a calendar based on Canaanite ideas.

The Phoenician Alphabet

One group of Canaanites, the **Phoenicians** (fih•NEE•shuhns), lived in cities along the Mediterranean

▲ According to the Bible story, the walls of Jericho came down as the trumpets of the Israelites sounded. *Who led the Israelites in their return to Canaan?*

▲ The town of Jericho today

Sea. The Phoenicians were skilled sailors and traders. Their ships carried goods across the Mediterranean to Greece, Spain, and even western Africa.

Through trade, the Phoenicians spread ideas and goods. One of their most important ideas was an **alphabet,** or a group of letters that stood for sounds. The letters could be used to spell out the words in their language.

The alphabet made writing simpler and helped people keep records. The Phoenicians brought the idea of an alphabet to the Greeks. They, in turn, passed it on to the Romans. Most Western alphabets are based on the Roman alphabet.

✓ **Reading Check** **Identify** Who led the Israelites into Canaan, and what city did they conquer under his leadership?

Alphabets

Modern Characters	Ancient Phoenician	Ancient Hebrew	Ancient Greek	Early Roman
A	⥿ ⥿	⥿	⥿ ⥿ ⥿	⥿⥿⥿
B	⥿ ⥿	⥿ ⥿	⥿ ⥿	B B
G	⥿ ⥿	⥿ ⥿	⥿ ⥿⥿	C C
D	⥿ ⥿	⥿ ⥿	⥿⥿⥿	⥿ D
E	⥿	⥿	⥿⥿⥿	E
F	⥿	⥿	⥿⥿⥿	F
Z	Z		I	Z
TH	⥿		⊙	
I	⥿ ⥿	⥿	⥿ ⥿	I

▲ The Phoenician idea of an alphabet was passed on to the Greeks and then the Romans. It is the basis for the English alphabet today. *Which modern letter most closely resembles its Phoenician character?*

History Online
Study Central™ Need help with the material in this section? Visit jat.glencoe.com

Section ❶ Review

Reading Summary
Review the Main Ideas

• Led by Abraham, the Israelites settled in Canaan. They later moved to Egypt and were enslaved, but then escaped. The Israelites used the Ten Commandments as rules to live by.

• Joshua and the judges, including Deborah, won back territory in central Canaan for the Israelites.

What Did You Learn?

1. Why was the religion of Israel unique in the ancient world?

2. What is the Torah, and how did the Israelites obtain it?

Critical Thinking

3. **Summarizing Information** Use a web diagram like the one below to list the parts of Jewish religion that are still important in our society.

Jewish Ideas

4. **Analyze** What was the importance of the Phoenician alphabet?

5. **Summarize** What problems did the Israelites face when they returned to Canaan?

6. **Expository Writing** Which one of the Ten Commandments do you think is most important today? Write a short essay to explain your selection.

7. **Reading** **Main Idea** Write a paragraph by adding supporting details to this main idea: The Phoenician alphabet had an impact on many civilizations.

Section 2

The Kingdom of Israel

Get Ready to Read!

What's the Connection?

In Section 1, you read about the constant fighting between the Israelites and the Canaanites. The tribes of Israel longed for peace. Many thought the way to peace was to unite as one nation.

Focusing on the Main Ideas

- The Israelites chose a king to unite them against their enemies. *(page 87)*

- King David built an Israelite empire and made Jerusalem his capital city. *(page 89)*

- The Israelites were conquered and forced to leave Israel and Judah. *(page 90)*

Locating Places
Jerusalem (juh•ROO•suh•luhm)
Judah (JOO•duh)

Meeting People
Philistine (FIH•luh•STEEN)
Saul (SAWL)
David
Solomon (SAHL•uh•muhn)
Nebuchadnezzar
  (NEH•byuh•kuhd•NEH•zuhr)

Building Your Vocabulary
prophet (PRAH•fuht)
empire (EHM•PYR)
tribute (TRIH•byoot)
proverb (PRAH•VUHRB)

Reading Strategy
Categorizing Information Complete a chart like the one below identifying characteristics of Israel and Judah.

Location		
Capital City		
Date Conquered		
Conquered By		

NATIONAL GEOGRAPHIC When & Where?

Samaria
Babylon
Jerusalem

1000 B.C.

750 B.C.

500 B.C.

c. 1000 B.C.
David becomes king

722 B.C.
Assyrians conquer Israel

597 B.C.
Nebuchadnezzar captures Jerusalem

The Israelites Choose a King

Main Idea The Israelites chose a king to unite them against their enemies.

Reading Focus What does "united we stand, divided we fall" mean to you? Read on to find out what it meant to the 12 tribes of Israel.

Around 1000 B.C., the strongest people living in Canaan were not the Israelites, but the **Philistines** (FIH•luh•STEENS). The Philistines had strong cities, and they knew how to make iron tools and weapons. Fearing the power of the Philistines, many Israelites copied their ways and worshiped their gods.

In the past, the 12 tribes often quarreled. If they were going to save their religion and way of life, they would have to learn how to work together. They needed a king to unite them against the Philistines.

Web Activity Visit jat.glencoe.com and click on *Chapter 3—Student Web Activity* to learn more about the ancient Israelites.

The Rule of King Saul In 1020 B.C. the Israelites asked Samuel to choose a king. Samuel was a judge and a **prophet** (PRAH• fuht). A prophet is a person who claims to be instructed by God to share God's words. Samuel warned that a king would tax the Israelites and make them slaves. The Israelites still demanded a king, so they chose a warrior-farmer named **Saul** (SAWL).

Samuel anointed Saul as king. In other words, he blessed him with oil to show that God had chosen him. Saul was tall and handsome and had won many battles.

Saul defeated the Israelites' enemies in battle after battle. However, according to the Bible, the king displeased God by disobeying some of his commands. God then chose another king and instructed Samuel to anoint him in secret. The new king was a young shepherd named **David.**

✓ **Reading Check** **Explain** Why did the Israelites want a king?

▼ According to the Bible, David had to be called in from the fields where he was tending his sheep when Samuel arrived to anoint him. *Why did God have Samuel anoint David?*

Biography

DAVID
Reigned c. 1000–970 B.C.

The story of David's life is told in several books of the Old Testament, including Samuel I and II and Psalms. During his youth, David worked as an aide in King Saul's court. While at court, he formed a close friendship with the king's son, Jonathan. David fought courageously against the Philistines as a soldier in Saul's army. He also killed the Philistine giant, Goliath, with only a slingshot and stones. The first book of Samuel tells how David's harp playing pleased King Saul. But the king grew jealous of David's friendship with Jonathan and of David's growing popularity as a brave soldier.

To save his own life, David fled into the desert. During this time, David led a group of other outlaws. David and his band protected people from raiders and returned possessions that had been stolen. By the time David returned to Jerusalem, he was well-known throughout the land.

After the death of King Saul, David became the second king of Israel. David successfully united all the tribes of Israel. He then conquered Jerusalem and made it the kingdom's capital. During his reign, David built Israel into an empire and dominated neighboring kingdoms.

David was not only a brave warrior and successful leader, he was also a talented poet. Many of the hymns in the Old Testament's book of Psalms have been credited to David, including Psalm 23, which begins "The Lord is my shepherd, I shall not want; he makes me lie down in green pastures. He leads me beside still waters; he restores my soul. He leads me in paths of righteousness for his name's sake."

▲ King David

"The sweet psalmist of Israel"
–David, 2 Samuel 23:1

▲ David versus Goliath

Then and Now

In David's time, kings were expected to excel in battle. Conduct research to find at least three U.S. presidents who built their reputations in the military.

David and Solomon

Main Idea King David built an Israelite empire and made Jerusalem his capital city.

Reading Focus What person do you think was most important in the history of the United States? Read to learn why King David is so important to the history of the Jewish people.

David's fame as a warrior spread. The Bible shows his fame by telling this story. Just before a battle against the Philistines, a giant Philistine named Goliath called out in a loud voice. He dared any Israelite to fight him one-on-one. David stepped forward with his shepherd's staff, a slingshot, and five smooth stones.

"Am I a dog that you come against me with a staff?" Goliath roared. He rushed forward with a heavy spear, but David was too quick for him. He hurled one stone straight at the giant's forehead, and Goliath dropped dead on the spot.

Saul put David in charge of the army. As his victories grew, Israelite women sang his praises. "Saul has slain his thousands, and David his ten thousands." Saul grew envious and plotted to kill David.

David hid out in enemy territory until Saul and his three sons were killed in battle. The bitter rivalry was over. David was able to take the throne in about 1000 B.C.

Once in power, David drove the Philistines from the area. He conquered other neighboring nations and created an **empire** (EHM•PYR). An empire is a nation that rules several other nations. Conquered peoples in the area had to pay David and the Israelites **tribute** (TRIH•byoot). Tribute is money or slaves given to a stronger ruler.

David made the Israelites pay heavy taxes. He needed money to expand his new capital of **Jerusalem** (juh•ROO•suh•luhm). He wanted a fine temple there so that

Primary Source

Proverbs

Solomon's proverbs are recorded in the Bible. Read these three, then answer the question.

"What you gain by doing evil won't help you at all, but being good can save you from death.

―――

At harvest season it's smart to work hard, but [unwise] to sleep.

―――

You will be safe, if you always do right, but you will get caught, if you are dishonest."

—Proverbs 10: 2, 5, 9

▲ King Solomon

DBQ Document-Based Question

How would the third proverb above convince people to tell the truth?

sacred religious objects cherished by the Israelites would finally have a permanent home. David died before he built the temple, but for centuries, the Israelites remembered him as their greatest king.

The Rule of King Solomon When David died, his son **Solomon** (SAHL•uh•muhn) became king. It was Solomon who built a splendid stone temple in Jerusalem. It became the symbol and center of the Jewish religion.

In the Bible, Solomon was known for his wise sayings, or **proverbs** (PRAH•VUHRBS), but many Israelites hated his rule. Solomon taxed the people to pay for his great buildings.

The Israelites in the north were especially unhappy with Solomon. To get more money, Solomon had made many of their young men work in the mines of a neighboring country.

When Solomon died, the northerners rebelled and fighting broke out. Ten of the 12 tribes set up their own nation in the north. It was called the kingdom of Israel, and its capital was Samaria. In the south, the other two tribes founded the smaller kingdom of **Judah** (JOO•duh). Its capital was Jerusalem, and its people were called Jews.

✓ **Reading Check** **Explain** Why did Solomon tax the people so heavily?

A Troubled Time

Main Idea **The Israelites were conquered and forced to leave Israel and Judah.**

Reading Focus Have you ever moved and left a home you loved? Read to find out why many Israelites were forced to leave their home.

While the Israelites were dividing their kingdom, the Assyrians and Chaldeans (kal•DEE•uhns) were building empires in southwest Asia. These peoples wanted to control the trade routes that ran through the Israelite kingdoms. Small and weak, the kingdoms of Israel and Judah felt threatened by their powerful neighbors.

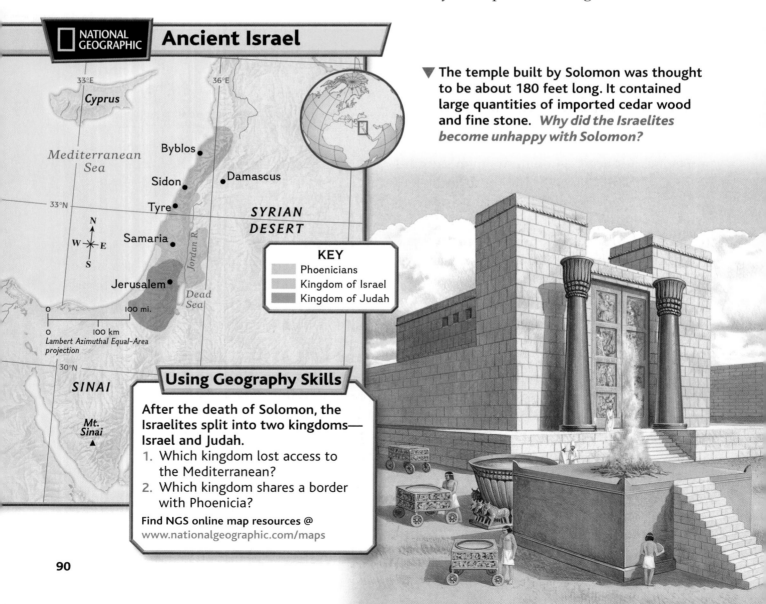

NATIONAL GEOGRAPHIC **Ancient Israel**

33°E
36°E
Cyprus
Mediterranean Sea
Byblos
33°N
Sidon
Damascus
Tyre
SYRIAN DESERT
Samaria
Jordan R.

KEY
Phoenicians
Kingdom of Israel
Kingdom of Judah

Jerusalem
Dead Sea

0   100 mi.
0   100 km
Lambert Azimuthal Equal-Area projection

30°N
SINAI
Mt. Sinai ▲

Using Geography Skills

After the death of Solomon, the Israelites split into two kingdoms—Israel and Judah.
1. Which kingdom lost access to the Mediterranean?
2. Which kingdom shares a border with Phoenicia?

Find NGS online map resources @ www.nationalgeographic.com/maps

▼ The temple built by Solomon was thought to be about 180 feet long. It contained large quantities of imported cedar wood and fine stone. *Why did the Israelites become unhappy with Solomon?*

Major Hebrew Prophets

Name	Time Period	Teachings
Elijah	874–840 B.C.	Only God should be worshiped—not idols or false gods.
Amos	780–740 B.C.	The kingdom of King David will be restored and will prosper.
Hosea	750–722 B.C.	God is loving and forgiving.
Isaiah	738–700 B.C.	God wants us to help others and promote justice.
Micah	735–700 B.C.	Both rich and poor have to do what is right and follow God.
Jeremiah	626–586 B.C.	God is just and kind—he rewards as well as punishes.
Ezekiel	597–571 B.C.	Someone who has done wrong can choose to change.

Understanding Charts

The Israelites believed that God shared his word with them through a series of prophets.
1. Which prophet taught that both the rich and the poor needed to obey God's word?
2. Compare What do the teachings of Isaiah, Micah, and Ezekiel have in common?

Who Were the Prophets? During this troubled time, many Israelites forgot their religion. The rich mistreated the poor, and government officials stole money.

The prophets wanted to bring Israelites back to God's laws. Their special message was that being faithful meant more than going to a temple to worship. It meant working for a just society. The prophet Amos said that justice should "roll down like waters and righteousness as a mighty stream." The goal of a just society became an important part of Christianity and Islam.

What Caused the Fall of Israel? The warlike Assyrians were feared everywhere in the region. When they conquered a nation, the Assyrians destroyed its main buildings and scattered the population. Assyrians then settled in the territory.

In 722 B.C. the Assyrians conquered Israel and scattered the 10 tribes across their empire. Over time, the Israelites who were forced to move lost their religion and way of life. They are often called the "lost tribes of Israel."

The Assyrians settled the area around Samaria and became known as Samaritans. The Assyrian settlers were afraid that Israel's God might punish them for taking the Israelites' land, so they offered sacrifices to Israel's God. They also read the Torah and followed the Israelites' religious laws. After many years, the Samaritans worshiped only the God of Israel.

The people of Judah looked down on the Samaritans. They believed that God accepted only the sacrifices from the temple at Jerusalem. They did not believe that other people were God's people too.

Why Did Judah Fall? Now, only the small kingdom of Judah was left of the once proud empire of David. It did not last long, because the Egyptians conquered it about 620 B.C. The Jews were able to keep their king but paid tribute to Egypt.

However, Egyptian rule was cut short when the Chaldeans conquered Egypt in 605 B.C. The Chaldeans became the new rulers of Judah. At first, the Chaldeans treated the Israelites like the Egyptians had before. They allowed the Jews to keep their king as long as they paid tribute.

Several years later, the Jews united with the Egyptians to rebel against the Chaldeans. Judah held out against the Chaldean invasion until 597 B.C. That year, King

Nebuchadnezzar (NEH•byuh•kuhd•NEH• zuhr) of the Chaldeans captured Jerusalem. He punished the Jews severely. He made 10,000 Jews leave the city and live in Babylon, the Chaldean capital. Then he appointed a new Jewish king.

Soon the new king of Judah was planning a revolt against the Chaldeans. A prophet named Jeremiah warned him that another revolt was dangerous, but the king did not listen. In 586 B.C. he revolted. This time, the Chaldean ruler crushed Jerusalem. He destroyed the temple, bound the king in chains, and took him and thousands of Jews to Babylon. In Jewish history, this time became known as the Babylonian Captivity.

✓ **Reading Check** **Explain** Why did the Assyrians and Chaldeans want to control the land belonging to the Israelites?

History Online
Study Central™ Need help with the material in this section? Visit jat.glencoe.com

Section 2 Review

Reading Summary
Review the Main Ideas

- Saul was the first king of the Israelites. He united the 12 tribes into one kingdom.

- King David built an Israelite empire and made Jerusalem his capital. Solomon built a great temple at Jerusalem, but after he died, the Israelites split into two kingdoms—Israel and Judah.

- The Assyrians and then the Chaldeans conquered Israel and Judah, and forced many Israelites to leave their homeland.

What Did You Learn?

1. Why was David anointed king while Saul was still in charge of the Israelites?

2. Who were the prophets, and why were they important to the Israelites?

Critical Thinking

3. **Compare** Draw a chart like the one below. Use it to compare the accomplishments of King David and King Solomon.

King David	King Solomon

4. **Summarize** What happened to the Israelites after the death of Solomon?

5. **Describe** Who were the Samaritans, and what did the people of Judah think of them?

6. **Infer** Why do you think the Assyrians, and later the Chaldeans, moved Jews away from Israel and Judah after those areas were conquered?

7. **Reading** **Main Idea** Choose one paragraph from the Biography on page 88. Create a graphic organizer to show the main idea and supporting details in that paragraph.

Get Ready to Read!

What's the Connection?
In Section 2, you learned that the Chaldeans forced thousands of Jews to go to Babylon. Life in Babylon was very difficult. Many of Judah's people looked to their religion for hope and strength.

Focusing on the Main Ideas
- The Jews continued their religion during their exile in Babylon. *(page 94)*
- Jews spread their beliefs to the Greek world and regained control of Judah. *(page 95)*
- Religion shaped the Jewish way of life. *(page 97)*
- Under Roman rule, the Jews were divided and rebellious. In response, the Romans destroyed the temple and exiled the Jews. *(page 100)*

Locating Places
Babylon (BA•buh•luhn)

Meeting People
Judas Maccabeus
(JOO•duhs   MAK•uh•BEE•uhs)
Herod (HEHR•uhd)
Zealot (ZEH•luht)
Johanan ben Zakkai
(YOH•kah•nahn   behn•zah•KY)

Building Your Vocabulary
exile (EHG•ZYL)
Sabbath (SA•buhth)
synagogue (SIH•nuh•GAHG)
Diaspora (dy•AS•pruh)
messiah (muh•SY•uh)
rabbi (RA•BY)

Reading Strategy
Summarizing Information Use a diagram like the one below to describe the Maccabees.

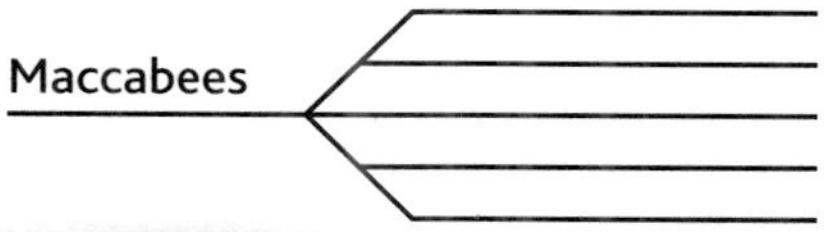

Maccabees

NATIONAL GEOGRAPHIC When & Where?

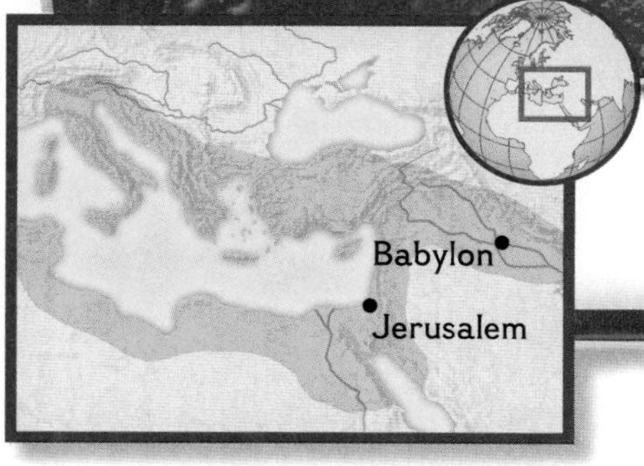

Babylon •
• Jerusalem

600 B.C.

250 B.C.

A.D. 100

538 B.C.
Cyrus allows Jews to return to Judah

168 B.C.
Judas Maccabeus rebels against Antiochus

A.D. 66
Jews revolt against Romans

Exile and Return

Main Idea The Jews continued their religion during their exile in Babylon.

Reading Focus Have you ever learned something important by experiencing a hardship? Read on to find out what lessons the Jews learned from hard times.

The Jews called their time in Babylon an **exile** (EHG•zyl). This means they were forced to live in a foreign land. During their exile, the Israelite religion became what we call Judaism.

While in **Babylon** (BA•buh•luhn), small groups of Jews met on the **Sabbath** (SA•buhth). This was their weekly day of worship and rest. The Jews would pray and discuss their religion and history. These meetings took place at **synagogues** (SIH•nuh•GAHGS), or Jewish houses of worship. The synagogue meetings gave the people hope.

Why Did Jews Return to Judah? During the 500s B.C., a group of people called Persians swept across southwest Asia. The Persians defeated the Chaldeans and took over Babylon. In 538 B.C. the Persian king Cyrus permitted Jews to return to Judah.

Some Jews stayed in Babylon, but many went home. They rebuilt Jerusalem and the temple. Cyrus appointed officials to rule the country and collected taxes from the people. Because Persians controlled their government, the Jews looked to their religion for leadership.

The leaders of the Jews became the temple priests and scribes, or religious scholars and writers. Under a scribe named Ezra, the Jews wrote the five books of the Torah on pieces of parchment. They sewed the pieces together to make long scrolls. The Torah and writings that were added later made up the Hebrew Bible.

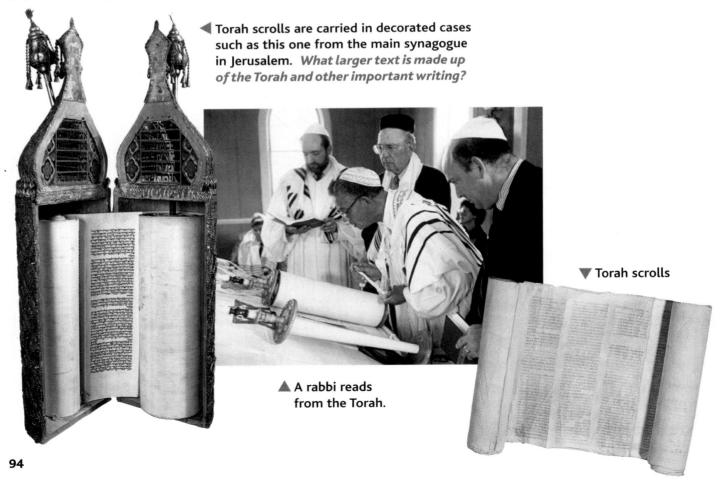

◀ Torah scrolls are carried in decorated cases such as this one from the main synagogue in Jerusalem. *What larger text is made up of the Torah and other important writing?*

▼ Torah scrolls

▲ A rabbi reads from the Torah.

What Is in the Hebrew Bible?

The Hebrew Bible is really a series of books collected together. It includes the five books of the Torah and 34 other books. These books describe events in Jewish history. The Jews believed that God had a special role for them in history and that events had meaning.

For example Genesis, the first book of the Torah, tells how God punished the world for its bad behavior. In Genesis, God tells Noah to build an ark, or large boat. Noah, his family, and two of every animal on Earth boarded the ark. Then a great flood covered the land, and only those on the ark escaped drowning. After the flood, God created a rainbow as a symbol of his promise to never again destroy the world with a flood.

Genesis also explains why the world has languages. It tells how the people of Babel tried to build a tower to heaven. God disapproved and made the people speak in different languages, then scattered them across the earth.

The Jews Look to the Future

Parts of the Bible described God's plan for a peaceful future. The book of Daniel addressed this issue. Daniel lived in Babylon and was a trusted adviser of the king. However, he refused to worship Babylonian gods. The Chaldeans threw Daniel into a lion's den, but God protected Daniel from the lions. The story was meant to remind Jews that God would rescue them.

The Jews believed that evil and suffering would eventually be replaced by goodness. Christians and Muslims share this idea of good triumphing over evil.

Reading Check **Identify** Who allowed the Jews to return to Judah?

The Jews and the Greeks

Main Idea Jews spread their beliefs to the Greek world and regained control of Judah.

Reading Focus How do you show loyalty to friends and family? In the following paragraphs, you'll learn how Jews showed loyalty to their religion and country.

In 334 B.C. a king named Alexander the Great began taking over kingdoms around the Mediterranean. In 331 B.C. his armies defeated the Persians, so Judah came under his control. Fortunately, Alexander allowed the Jews to stay in Judah. However, Alexander, who loved all things Greek, introduced the Greek language and Greek ways to Judah.

What Was the Diaspora?

At the time, Jews were also living in other parts of Alexander's empire. Many still lived in Babylon. Some lived in Egypt and other lands around the Mediterranean Sea. The Jews outside of Judah became known as the

▼ According to the Bible, Daniel is thrown into a lion's den for refusing to worship the Babylonian gods. God, however, kept Daniel safe from the lions. *What lesson did this story present to the Jews?*

Diaspora (dy•AS•pruh). *Diaspora* is a Greek word that means "scattered."

Many Jews of the Diaspora learned the Greek language and Greek ways but remained loyal to Judaism. A group of them copied the Hebrew Bible into Greek. This Greek version helped people who were not Jews to read and understand the Hebrew Bible. As a result, Jewish ideas spread throughout the Mediterranean world.

Who Were the Maccabees?
In 168 B.C. a Greek ruler named Antiochus (an•TY•uh kuhs) controlled Judah. He decided to make the Jews of Judah worship Greek gods and goddesses. A priest named **Judas Maccabeus** (JOO•duhs   MAK•uh•BEE•uhs) and his followers rebelled. They fled to the hills and formed an army known as the Maccabees.

After many battles, the Maccabees drove the Greeks out of Judah. They destroyed all traces of Greek gods and goddesses in their temple and made it a temple for worshiping the God of Israel. Each year Jews recall the cleansing of the temple when they celebrate Hanukkah (HAH•nuh•kuh).

Priests from Judas Maccabeus's family became the new rulers of Judah. Under their leadership, Judah took over land that had been part of the kingdom of Israel.

✓ **Reading Check** **Analyze** How did Alexander the Great affect the Israelites?

Major Jewish Holidays

Name	Time of Year	Length	Reason for the Holiday	Customs
Passover	April	8 days (7 in Israel)	to celebrate God's passing over of the Jews during the final plague in Egypt that enabled the Jews to return to the Promised Land	limited work; some fasts; sell certain foods that cannot be eaten or owned during the holiday; perform rituals
Rosh Hoshana	September or October	2 days	to celebrate the Jewish New Year	plan changes for the new year; no work; synagogue services; a shofar (horn) is blown in synagogues
Yom Kippur	September or October	25 hours	to make amends for sins of the past year	no work; synagogue services; pray; fast; apologize for wrongs during the past year
Hanukkah	December	8 days	to celebrate the Maccabees' victory, and reclaiming of the temple in Jerusalem	light candles each night; eat fried foods; play a game called dreidel; give gifts

◀ Menorah

The Jewish Way of Life

Main Idea Religion shaped the Jewish way of life.

Reading Focus What types of things influence the way you live? Read to find out how religion influenced Jewish life.

Jewish law set out many rules for Jews to follow that affected their daily life. These laws influenced their education, the foods they ate, and even the clothes they wore. The laws emphasized self-control and reminded Jews of their religion. This became important when they no longer had their own land and king.

Family Life The Jews placed great importance on family. Sons were especially valued because they carried on the family name. Upon a father's death, the son became head of the family.

Education was also important. Jewish children's first teachers were their mothers. When sons grew old enough, fathers taught them how to earn a living and to worship God. Later, elders took over the religious education of boys and taught them the Torah. Because reading the Torah was central to Jewish life, religious teachers became important community leaders.

Linking Past & Present

Head Coverings

THEN Under Greek rule, Jewish leaders began covering their heads to distinguish themselves from the Greeks and to remind themselves to think about God. Gradually, all Jewish men started wearing turbans or skull caps. Jewish women always kept their heads covered because a woman's hair was considered very private.

▼ Jews in modern-day head coverings

NOW Jews still wear head coverings, but only the most conservative—Orthodox Jews—wear them at all times. Most Jewish men wear skull caps called yarmulkes. Jewish women wear scarves or skull caps. *Why do you think Jews of the Diaspora are more reluctant to wear head coverings than Jews in Israel?*

▲ Ancient Jewish head covering

The Way It Was

Young People In...

Education in Ancient Israel and Judah

Early Israelites placed a high value on education. Rabbis—Jewish religious teachers—taught their followers, "If you have knowledge, you have everything." Unfortunately, only boys were allowed to go to school.

Fathers taught their young sons the commandments. They also taught them about the meanings of Jewish traditions and holy feasts. At age five, boys went to a school that was connected with the synagogue. There, the hazan, or minister of the synagogue, taught them the Torah. Everything the students learned—from the alphabet to Jewish history—they learned from the Torah.

Jewish laws decided the stages of students' education. Different subjects were introduced at the ages of 5, 10, and 13. Most Jewish boys finished their education at age 13. At that age, boys became adults.

▲ Children studying the Torah today

Connecting to the Past

1. Why was education important to the ancient Israelites?

2. What was a father's role in his son's education?

Mothers educated their daughters at home. The girls learned to be good wives, mothers, and housekeepers. This included learning Jewish laws about food and clothing. They also learned about the courageous women of ancient Israel. One of these women was named Ruth. Her biography appears on the next page. Her courage and devotion to her family provided an example for Jewish girls to follow.

The Jewish Diet Under Jewish law, Jews could eat only certain animals. For example, they could eat beef and lamb but not pork. They could eat scaly fish, like salmon, but not smooth-skinned fish, like eels. Laws about food were known as kashrut, which means "that which is proper."

Today, food that is prepared according to Jewish dietary laws is called kosher. Animals used for kosher meat must be killed in a special way. The meat must be inspected, salted, and soaked. To be kosher, Jews must not cook or eat milk products with meat.

In ancient times, everyday meals were made up of fish, fruit, vegetables, and barley bread. Beverages included mainly milk, water, wine, and beer.

Jewish Clothing Jewish law forbade mixing some fabrics. So women used flax or wool to make cloth but did not combine the two.

Jewish men wore tunics made of linen next to their skin. Some men layered another tunic on top of the first. In cold weather, they added wool or sheepskin cloaks. On their heads, they wore caps or turbans. On their feet, they wore sandals.

Women draped themselves in long, simple dresses. They covered their heads with shawls. Only wealthy women could afford leather shoes. They also wore makeup and jewelry.

✓ **Reading Check** **Analyze** Why were sons especially valued in Jewish society?

RUTH AND NAOMI

To show the importance of family love and devotion, Jewish girls learned about the relationship between Ruth and Naomi. The Book of Ruth in the Hebrew Bible tells about Ruth's life and of her dedication to her mother-in-law, Naomi. Years before, there was so little food in Bethlehem that Naomi, her husband, and their two sons moved to Moab. There, one of their sons married Ruth. Tragically, Naomi's husband and both of her sons died. Naomi wanted to return to Bethlehem, but she urged Ruth to stay in Moab with her parents and friends. Ruth refused to leave Naomi by herself. She insisted on traveling with her to Bethlehem. Ruth said to Naomi, "Wherever you go, I will go; wherever you lodge; I will lodge; your people shall be my people, and your God my God."

Naomi and Ruth arrived in Bethlehem at the beginning of the barley harvest. Because Ruth was from Moab, she was considered an outsider by the Israelites. Furthermore, because Ruth was a widow and did not have children, she did not have any property rights. To survive in Bethlehem, she had to rely upon her mother-in-law's advice and the kindness of a wealthy landowner named Boaz.

During the harvest, Ruth worked in Boaz's fields, gathering grain left behind on the ground by the reapers. It was hard work that began at dawn and ended at dusk, but Ruth never complained. She soon earned the respect and admiration of her new people. In time, Ruth married Boaz. They had a son named Obed. In the Hebrew Bible, at the end of the Book of Ruth, Obed is named as the grandfather of David, the future king of Israel.

▲ Naomi and Ruth

Then and Now

To survive in Bethlehem, Ruth had to rely on Naomi and Boaz. If a present-day woman moved to a new city, what resources would she use to help her find work, shelter, and other necessities?

The Jews and the Romans

Main Idea Under Roman rule, the Jews were divided and rebellious. In response, the Romans destroyed the temple and exiled the Jews.

Reading Focus Do you consider freedom worth fighting for? Read to find out what happened to the Jews after they fought for their freedom.

In 63 B.C. a people known as the Romans conquered Judah. Led by powerful generals, the Romans were intent on expanding their empire. The Roman capital was far to the west in what is today the country of Italy. When the Romans conquered Judah, they renamed it Judaea (joo•DEE•uh). At first, the Romans allowed Jewish rulers to run Judaea.

The Rule of King Herod

The most famous ruler of Judaea during this time was King **Herod** (HEHR•uhd). He was known for his cruelty and his changes to the Jewish temple in Jerusalem. He made the temple one of the most awe-inspiring buildings in the Roman world. Today he is best known as the king who ruled Judaea when Jesus was born.

Shortly after Herod died, the Romans replaced the Jewish king with Roman officials. The Jews were eager to regain control, but because they had splintered into different groups, they did not have as much power.

One group of Jews was known as the Pharisees (FAR•uh•seez). They taught the Torah and how to apply its laws to daily life. In doing so, they helped make Judaism a religion of the home and family. The Pharisees taught in synagogues and were supported by the common people.

The Sadducees (SA•juh•SEEZ) also accepted the Torah. However, they were more concerned about how it applied to the priests in the Temple. This was because most of them were priests and scribes. They did not agree with many of the Pharisees' teachings.

A third group was called Essenes (ih•SEENZ). They were priests who broke away from the Temple in Jerusalem. Many Essenes lived together in the desert. They spent their lives praying and waiting for God to deliver the Jews from the Romans.

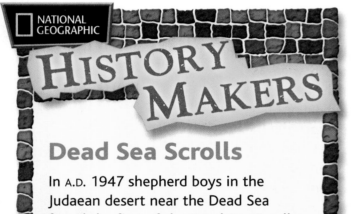

NATIONAL GEOGRAPHIC

HISTORY MAKERS

Dead Sea Scrolls

In A.D. 1947 shepherd boys in the Judaean desert near the Dead Sea found the first of the Dead Sea Scrolls in a cave. The Dead Sea Scrolls are ancient scrolls of leather, papyrus, and copper written between 200 B.C. and A.D. 68. The documents include the oldest complete copy of the book of Isaiah and pieces of many other books of the Hebrew Bible. Most scholars believe that the scrolls were part of a library that belonged to an early Jewish community.

► Restoration of the Dead Sea Scrolls

▲ Today Jews come to the Western Wall, also known as the Wailing Wall, to pray. *What structure is the Western Wall the remains of?*

In A.D. 1947 ancient scrolls were found in the desert near the Dead Sea. They were probably written by Essenes and are called the Dead Sea Scrolls. The scrolls have helped historians understand more about Judaism during Roman times.

Jewish Revolts During the A.D. 60s, Jewish hatred of Roman rule was at its peak. Many Jews were waiting for a **messiah** (muh•SY• uh), or deliverer sent by God. Other Jews known as **Zealots** (ZEH•luhts) wanted to fight the Romans for their freedom.

In A.D. 66 the Zealots revolted against the Romans and drove them out of Jerusalem. Four years later, the Romans retook Jerusalem. They killed thousands of Jews and forced many others to leave. The Romans also destroyed the temple in Jerusalem. The Western Wall is all that remains of it today.

The Jews revolted again in A.D. 132. Three years later, the Romans put down the revolt. This time, the Romans forbade Jews to live in or even visit Jerusalem. They gave Judah the name of Palestine. This name refers to the Philistines, whom the Israelites had conquered centuries before.

Jewish Teachers Despite losing their land, the Jews managed to survive. They no longer had priests. Instead, leaders called **rabbis** (RA•BYZ) became important. Rabbis were teachers of the Torah.

One of the most famous rabbis was **Johanan ben Zakkai** (YOH•kah•nahn behn zah•KY). After the revolt of A.D. 70, he made sure the study of the Torah continued.

He founded a school in northern Palestine that became a center of Torah studies for centuries. Other rabbis founded Torah schools in places as far away as Babylon and Egypt.

The rabbis wanted to save and pass on teachings about the Torah. They combined the teachings in a book called the Talmud. To this day, the Talmud remains an important record of Jewish law.

For 2,000 years, most Jews lived outside of Palestine. They often faced hatred and persecution. In A.D. 1948 Palestine was divided, and a new Jewish nation called Israel was created.

✓ **Reading Check** **Explain** How did the Roman conquest affect the Jews?

Primary Source
The Talmud

Part of the Talmud declares that most types of work and business are not allowed on the Sabbath, or Jewish day of worship. This passage identifies the only times it is okay to break those rules.

"One is permitted to remove debris on the Sabbath in order to save a life or to act for the benefit of the community; and we may assemble in the synagogue on the Sabbath to conduct public business [i.e., matters of community concern]."

—*The Talmud for Today*, Rabbi Alexander Feinsilver, trans. and ed.

▲ **Jews reading the Talmud today**

DBQ **Document-Based Question**

Why do you think these exceptions were made for the benefit of the community?

Section 3 Review

History Online

Study Central™ Need help with the material in this section? Visit jat.glencoe.com

Reading Summary
Review the Main Ideas

• During their exile in Babylon, the Jews developed their religion, which is based upon the stories in the Hebrew Bible.

• Jews spread their ideas to the Greek world. About 168 B.C., they fought the Greeks for control of Judah.

• Religious laws concerning food and clothing affected everyday Jewish life.

• In 63 B.C. Judah was taken over by the Roman Empire.

What Did You Learn?

1. What was the Diaspora?

2. What was education like within a Jewish family?

Critical Thinking

3. **Organizing Information** Draw a table to describe the differences between these three Jewish groups.

Pharisees	Sadducees	Essenes

4. **Summarize** How did the Jews practice their religion during the exile in Babylon?

5. **Identify** Who were the Zealots, and why were they important?

6. **Draw Conclusions** Do you think that Jewish beliefs and values would have spread so widely if the lands of Israel and Judah had not been conquered by other peoples? Explain.

7. **Persuasive Writing** Imagine you are living in Judaea during the Roman conquest. Write a letter to a friend describing how you might have felt about the Romans and what actions you would like to see taken to make Judaea free again.

Section ① The First Israelites

Vocabulary
monotheism
tribe
Torah
covenant
alphabet

Focusing on the Main Ideas
- The Israelites believed in one God who set down moral laws for his people. They recorded their history in the Bible. *(page 81)*
- The Israelites had to fight the Canaanites to return to their promised land. *(page 84)*

Moses with the ▶
Ten Commandments

Section ② The Kingdom of Israel

Vocabulary
prophet
empire
tribute
proverb

Focusing on the Main Ideas
- The Israelites chose a king to unite them against their enemies. *(page 87)*
- King David built an Israelite empire and made Jerusalem his capital city. *(page 89)*
- The Israelites were conquered and forced to leave Israel and Judah. *(page 90)*

Section ③ The Growth of Judaism

Vocabulary
exile
Sabbath
synagogue
Diaspora
messiah
rabbi

Focusing on the Main Ideas
- The Jews continued their religion during their exile in Babylon. *(page 94)*
- Jews spread their beliefs to the Greek world and regained control of Judah. *(page 95)*
- Religion shaped the Jewish way of life. *(page 97)*
- Under Roman rule, the Jews were divided and rebellious. In response, the Romans destroyed the temple and exiled the Jews. *(page 100)*

▲ Torah scrolls

Chapter 3 Assessment and Activities

Review Vocabulary

Match the definitions in the second column to the terms in the first column.

1. tribe
2. prophet
3. synagogue
4. Sabbath
5. messiah
6. monotheism
7. covenant
8. exile

a. Jewish house of worship
b. claims to be inspired by God
c. family group
d. holy day of worship and rest
e. forced absence
f. belief in one god
g. deliverer sent by God
h. agreement

Review Main Ideas

Section 1 • The First Israelites
9. Where did the Israelites record their history and religious beliefs?
10. Why did the Israelites fight the Canaanites?

Section 2 • The Kingdom of Israel
11. Why did the Israelites choose a king?
12. What happened when the Israelites were conquered?

Section 3 • The Growth of Judaism
13. How did Jewish ideas spread throughout the Mediterranean world?
14. How did Romans respond to Jewish rebellions?

Critical Thinking

15. **Contrast** How was the Jewish religion different from religions of other ancient cultures?
16. **Analyze** Why do you think the Israelites felt so strongly about a Promised Land?
17. **Compare and Contrast** How were Saul and David similar, and how were they different?
18. **Explain** How did the Jewish religion survive during the exile of the Jews?
19. **Describe** What is celebrated on the Jewish holiday Hanukkah?

Review Reading Skill / Main Idea — Finding the Main Idea

20. Read the paragraph at the right from page 101. Create a graphic organizer that shows the main idea and supporting details.

In A.D. 1947 ancient scrolls were found in the desert near the Dead Sea. They were probably written by Essenes and are called the Dead Sea Scrolls. The scrolls have helped historians understand more about Judaism during Roman times.

To review this skill, see pages 78–79.

Geography Skills

Study the map below and answer the following questions.

21. **Location** Which kingdom—Israel or Judah—had an advantage when it came to trade? Why?
22. **Identify** What advantage did Judah have over Israel?
23. **Analyze** Why did the Phoenicians focus on trade rather than farming?

NATIONAL GEOGRAPHIC

Israelite Kingdoms

Mediterranean Sea

Byblos

Sidon

Damascus

SYRIAN DESERT

Tyre

Samaria

Jordan R.

Jerusalem

Dead Sea

KEY
- Phoenicians
- Kingdom of Israel
- Kingdom of Judah

N W E S

0   100 mi.
0   100 km
Lambert Azimuthal Equal-Area projection

Read to Write

24. **Descriptive Writing** Imagine you are living in Jerusalem during the time of King Solomon. Write a letter to a friend describing the things Solomon is doing as leader. Be sure to mention which of these things the people like and which they do not like.

25. **Summarize** Choose three events in this chapter that you think were the most important to the history of the Israelites. Write a headline for each that might have appeared in a newspaper of that time.

26. **Using Your FOLDABLES** Use the information you wrote in your three-pocket foldable to create a fill-in-the-blank quiz for a classmate. Write a paragraph about one of the sections, leaving blanks for your classmate to fill in. Leave blanks for vocabulary words or significant places and people.

History Online

Self-Check Quiz To help you prepare for the Chapter Test, visit jat.glencoe.com

Using Technology

27. **Organizing Information** Search the Internet or your local library for information about the early Phoenicians and Philistines. Use the computer to create a chart comparing the two cultures. Include headings such as Location, Time Period, Major Contributions, and Achievements.

Linking Past and Present

28. **Making Comparisons** The Israelites moved from place to place within the same region along the Mediterranean. Trace the route of one of their journeys on a map of ancient times. Then trace the route again on a map showing that region as it is today. Identify the current nations and landmarks in that region.

Primary Source

Analyze

The following passage describes the effects of the attack on Judaea. The passage is written by Josephus, a Jewish historian in the Roman era.

"Throughout the city people were dying of hunger in large numbers. . . . In every house the merest hint of food sparked violence, and close relatives fell to blows. . . . No respect was paid even to the dying; the ruffians searched them, in case they were concealing food somewhere in their clothes."

—Josephus, "The Siege of Jerusalem"

DBQ Document-Based Questions

29. What does Josephus mean when he says "No respect was paid even to the dying"?
30. How might this account have been different if it had been written by a Roman soldier?

Comparing Civilizations

Compare the civilizations that you have read about by reviewing the information below. Can you see how the people of these civilizations helped to build the world we live in today?

Where in the World?
- Chapter 1
- Chapter 2
- Chapter 3

NATIONAL GEOGRAPHIC

	First Civilizations Chapter 1	Ancient Egypt Chapter 2	Ancient Israelites Chapter 3
Where did these civilizations develop?	• Between the Tigris and Euphrates Rivers	• Along the banks of the Nile River 	• In an area called Canaan
Who are some important people in these civilizations?	• Sargon, c. 2340–2279 B.C. • Hammurabi, c. 1792–1750 B.C. • Nebuchadnezzar, c. 605–562 B.C.	• King Khufu, c. 2540 B.C. • Hatshepsut, c. 1470 B.C. • Ramses II, c. 1279–1213 B.C. • Kashta, c. 750 B.C.	• Abraham, c. 1800 B.C. • Moses, c. 1250 B.C. • David, c. 1000–970 B.C. • The Maccabees, 168 B.C.
Where did most of the people live?	• Most people lived on farms near walled cities • The center of the city was the ziggurat	• Some people lived in large cities • Most people lived in villages along the Nile	• Most people lived in small villages or near the city of Jerusalem

	First Civilizations Chapter 1	Ancient Egypt Chapter 2	Ancient Israelites Chapter 3
What were these people's beliefs?	• Worshiped many different gods • The gods appointed the rulers 	• Worshiped gods and goddesses • Believed in life after death	• Worshiped one God • Used the Bible as a record of their history
What was their government like?	• Early Mesopotamians were ruled by priests • Later, kings ruled the people; they believed kings had divine approval	• King was a ruler-priest and a god • Pharaoh owned all land in Egypt	• Early Israelites were led by prophets • Later, they were led by judges, then kings 
What was their language and writing like?	• Early: cuneiform: wedge-shaped characters • Later: a Semitic language	• Hieroglyphics: images that stood for ideas 	• Adapted Phoenician characters to form letters and words
What contributions did they make?	• Developed writing • Created system of mathematics • Studied systems of time and created calendars • Introduced iron weapons	• Built machines to move water to crops • Developed a calendar • Built large temples and pyramids	• Developed ideas of legal system • Passed on ideas of justice, fairness, and compassion in society and government • Believed in one God
How do these contributions affect me? *Can you add any?*	• Similar measurements are still used in building today • Our system of time is based on seconds, minutes, and hours	• Pyramids and other structures still amaze people today	• Many religions today are based on ideas similar to those of the early Israelites 

Unit 2

The Ancient World

Why It's Important

Each civilization that you will study in this unit made important contributions to history.

- The Greeks developed democratic government.
- The ancient Chinese created paper.
- The people of India invented the concept of zero.

2500 B.C.	1500 B.C.	800 B.C.	650 B.C.

Ancient Greece
Chapters 4 & 5

c. 1600 B.C.
Minoan civilization reaches height

c. 776 B.C.
First Olympic Games take place

◀ Ancient plate

Early India
Chapter 6

c. 2500 B.C.
Settlements develop along Indus River

c. 1500 B.C.
Aryans invade India

◀ Hindu temple

Early China
Chapter 7

c. 1750 B.C.
Shang dynasty begins

c. 1045 B.C.
Zhou establish dynasty in China

Zhou dynasty bronze dragon ▶

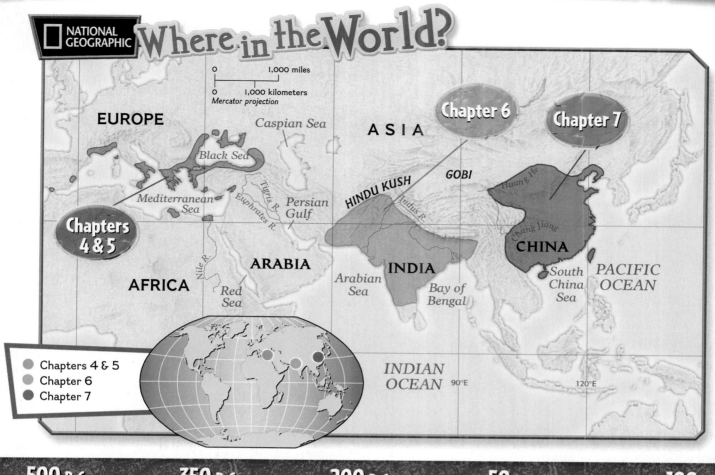

NATIONAL GEOGRAPHIC — Where in the World?

EUROPE

Caspian Sea

Black Sea

Mediterranean Sea

Tigris R.

Euphrates R.

Persian Gulf

ASIA

Chapter 6

Chapter 7

GOBI

HINDU KUSH

Indus R.

Huang He

Chang Jiang

CHINA

Chapters 4 & 5

Nile R.

ARABIA

AFRICA

Red Sea

Arabian Sea

INDIA

Bay of Bengal

South China Sea

PACIFIC OCEAN

1,000 miles
1,000 kilometers
Mercator projection

- Chapters 4 & 5
- Chapter 6
- Chapter 7

INDIAN OCEAN   90°E   120°E

500 B.C.	350 B.C.	200 B.C.	50 B.C.	A.D. 100

490 B.C. Greeks and Persians fight the Battle of Marathon

399 B.C. Socrates tried for his teachings

c. 330 B.C. Aristotle develops theories about government

◀ Statue of Socrates

c. 530 B.C. Siddhartha Gautama founds Buddhism in India

c. 321 B.C. Chandragupta Maurya unites northern India

273 B.C. Asoka begins rule in India

◀ Statue of the Buddha

c. 530 B.C. Confucius develops his philosophy in China

c. 100 B.C. Silk Road links China and the Middle East

c. A.D. 100 Buddhism spreads from India to China

◀ Statue of horse from Han dynasty

EUROPE

AFRICA

1 Greek Parthenon

See Ancient Greece
Chapters 4 & 5

2 Alexandria lighthouse

See Ancient Greece
Chapter 5

① ②

People to Meet

Homer
c. 750 B.C.
**Greek poet, wrote *Iliad*
and *Odyssey***
Chapter 5, page 159

Siddhartha Gautama
c. 563–483 B.C.
Founder of Buddhism
Chapter 6, page 207

Confucius
551–479 B.C.
Chinese philosopher
Chapter 7, page 237

Pericles
c. 495–429 B.C.
**Athenian general and
leading statesman**
Chapter 4, page 141

ASIA

NATIONAL GEOGRAPHIC

3 Harappan priest-king

See Early India
Chapter 6

4 Statue of god Siva

See Early India
Chapter 6

5 Great Wall of China

See Early China
Chapter 7

*Pacific
Ocean*

*Indian
Ocean*

Aristotle

384–322 B.C.
Greek philosopher
Chapter 5, page 172

**Alexander
the Great**

c. 356–323 B.C.
**Macedonian
general and king**
Chapter 5, page 180

Asoka

Ruled c. 273–232 B.C.
Philosopher-king of India
Chapter 6, page 212

**Qin
Shihuangdi**

c. 259–210 B.C.
**Built the first Great
Wall of China**
Chapter 7, page 243

The Ancient Greeks

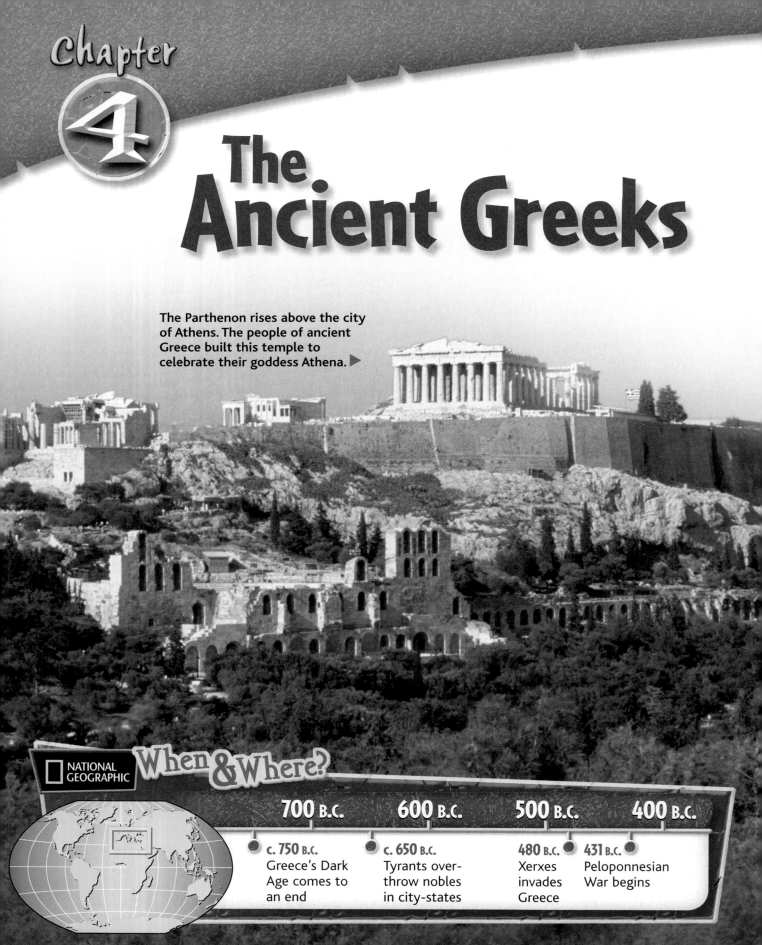

The Parthenon rises above the city of Athens. The people of ancient Greece built this temple to celebrate their goddess Athena. ▶

NATIONAL GEOGRAPHIC **When & Where?**

700 B.C.	600 B.C.	500 B.C.	400 B.C.
c. 750 B.C. Greece's Dark Age comes to an end	**c. 650 B.C.** Tyrants over-throw nobles in city-states	**480 B.C.** Xerxes invades Greece	**431 B.C.** Peloponnesian War begins

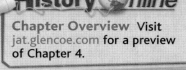
Chapter Preview

Greek civilization began almost 4,000 years ago, but Greek ideas about government, science, and the arts are still important today.

 View the Chapter 4 video in the *World History: Journey Across Time* Video Program.

 ## The Early Greeks

The earliest civilizations in Greece were the Minoans and the Mycenaeans. Greece's mountains, climate, and surrounding seas played a large role in their history.

 ## Sparta and Athens

Athens and Sparta became the two most powerful city-states in ancient Greece. Sparta focused on its military force, while Athens focused on trade, culture, and democracy.

 ## Persia Attacks the Greeks

The Persian Empire gained control of most of southwest Asia. However, when the Persians tried to conquer the Greeks, Athens and Sparta united to defeat them.

 ## The Age of Pericles

Under the leadership of Pericles, Athens became a powerful city-state and culture blossomed.

 **Study Organizer**

Summarizing Information *Make this foldable to help you organize and summarize information about the ancient Greeks.*

Step 1 *Mark the midpoint of a side edge of one sheet of paper. Then fold the outside edges in to touch the midpoint.*

Step 2 *Fold the paper in half again from side to side.*

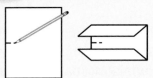

Step 3 *Open the paper and cut along the inside fold lines to form four tabs.*

Cut along the fold lines on both sides.

Step 4 *Label as shown.*

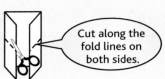

Reading and Writing *As you read the chapter, write information under each appropriate tab. Be sure to summarize the information you find by writing only main ideas and supporting details.*

Reading Social Studies

1 Learn It!

Use What You Know

Unlock meaning by making a connection between what you read and what you already know. Your own experiences can help you understand words or ideas that are unfamiliar. Read the paragraph below. Make a connection between a Greek **agora** and a place that is familiar to you.

> Below the acropolis was an open area called an **agora** (A • guh • ruh). This space had two functions: it was both a **market** and a place where people could meet and debate issues.
>
> — *from page 122*

Do you know what an **agora** looks like?

You know what a *market* looks like. Can you also visualize *a place where people could meet*? If so, then you have a good idea of what an agora might look like.

Reading Tip

Try to create a picture in your mind as you read. Imagine a mini-movie as you "see" what the author is describing.

2 Practice It!

Making the Connection

Read the following paragraph from Chapter 4. What ideas can you connect to your own experiences? Use the questions below to help you begin a class discussion about things in your life that relate to life in ancient Greece.

Read to Write

Choose one of the connections from your discussion. Write a paragraph to explain why you made such a connection. Use vivid details.

At age 20, Spartan men entered the regular army. The men remained in military barracks for 10 more years. They ate all their meals in dining halls with other soldiers. A typical meal was a vile-tasting dish called black broth—pork boiled in animal blood, salt, and vinegar.

Spartans returned home at age 30 but stayed in the army until age 60. They continued to train for combat. They expected to either win on the battlefield or die, but never to surrender. One Spartan mother ordered her son to "Come home carrying your shield or being carried on it."

—*from pages 126–127*

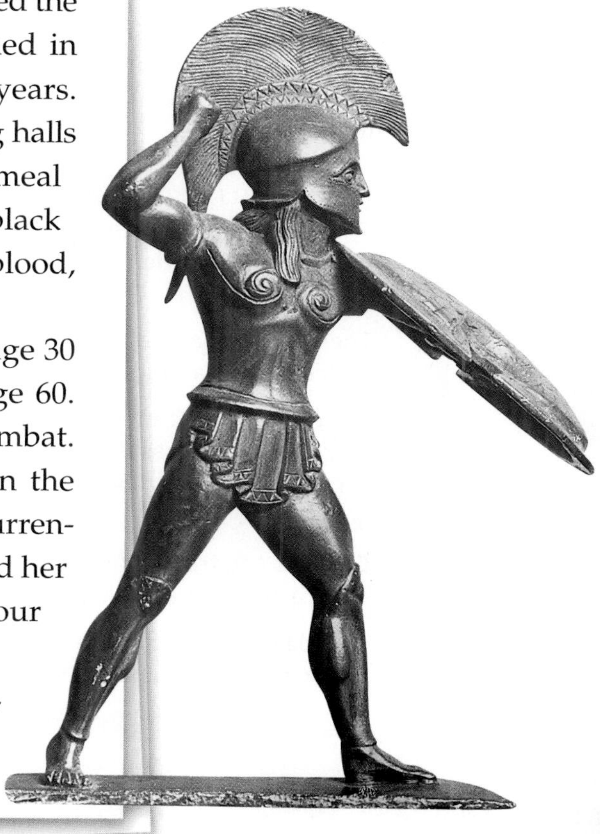

- Do you have any family members or friends who are 20 years old? What would they say if they were required to serve in the army for 40 years?

- Have you ever seen or tasted food that looks like "black broth"?

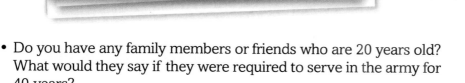

3 Apply It!

As you read the chapter, choose five words or phrases that make a connection to something you already know.

The Early Greeks

Get Ready to Read!

What's the Connection?

In Chapters 1 and 2, you learned about Mesopotamia and Egypt. These civilizations grew up in great river valleys with rich soil. Greece had no great river valleys. Instead, it had mountains, rocky soil, and many miles of seacoasts.

Focusing on the Main Ideas

- The geography of Greece influenced where people settled and what they did. *(page 117)*

- The Minoans earned their living by building ships and trading. *(page 118)*

- Mycenaeans built the first Greek kingdoms and spread their power across the Mediterranean region. *(page 119)*

- Colonies and trade spread Greek culture and spurred industry. *(page 121)*

- The idea of citizenship developed in Greek city-states. *(page 122)*

Locating Places

Crete (KREET)
Mycenae (my•SEE•nee)
Peloponnesus (PEH•luh•puh•NEE•suhs)

Meeting People

Agamemnon (A•guh•MEHM•nahn)

Building Your Vocabulary

peninsula (puh•NIHN•suh•luh)
colony (KAH•luh•nee)
polis (PAH•luhs)
agora (A•guh•ruh)

Reading Strategy

Finding Details Draw a diagram like the one below. In each oval write one detail about a polis.

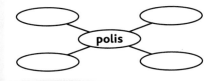

NATIONAL GEOGRAPHIC When & Where?

GREECE
Mycenae
Crete — Knossos

2000 B.C.	1250 B.C.	500 B.C.
c. 2000 B.C. Minoans control eastern Mediterranean	**c. 1200 B.C.** Mycenaean civilization declines	**c. 750 B.C.** Greece's Dark Age comes to an end

The Geography of Greece

Main Idea The geography of Greece influenced where people settled and what they did.

Reading Focus Do you rake leaves in the fall? Do you walk uphill to school? Your answers explain how geography shapes your life. Read to learn how geography shaped life in early Greece.

If you fly over Greece today, you will see a mountainous land framed by sparkling blue water. To the west is the Ionian (eye•OH•nee•uhn) Sea, to the south is the Mediterranean Sea, and to the east is the Aegean (ih•JEE•uhn) Sea. Hundreds of islands lie offshore, stretching across to Asia like stepping-stones. Mainland Greece is a peninsula (puh•NIHN•suh•luh)—a body of land with water on three sides.

Many ancient Greeks made a living from the sea. They became fishers, sailors, and traders. Others settled in farming communities. Greece's mountains and rocky soil were not ideal for growing crops. However, the climate was mild, and in some places people could grow wheat, barley, olives, and grapes. They also raised sheep and goats.

Ancient Greeks felt deep ties to the land, but the mountains and seas divided them from one another. As a result, early Greek communities grew up fiercely independent.

Reading Check **Cause and Effect** How did geography discourage Greek unity?

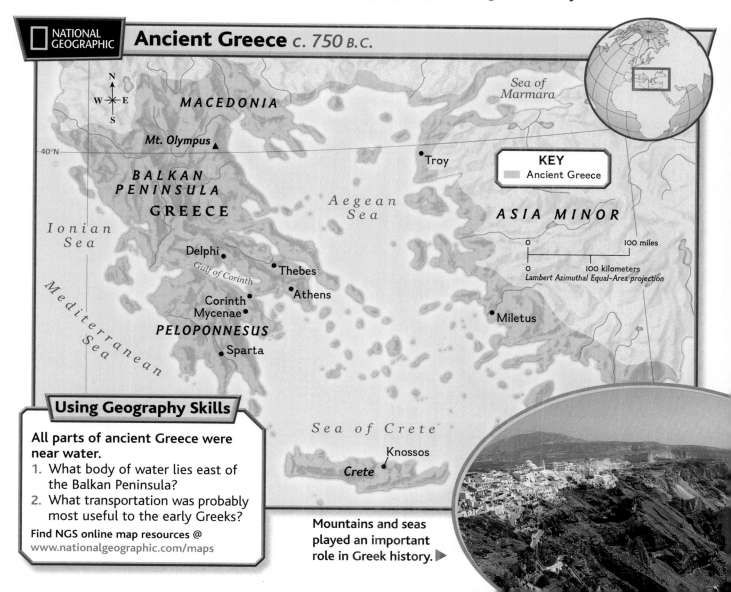

NATIONAL GEOGRAPHIC

Ancient Greece c. 750 B.C.

MACEDONIA

Mt. Olympus ▲

40°N

BALKAN PENINSULA

GREECE

Troy

Sea of Marmara

Aegean Sea

KEY
Ancient Greece

ASIA MINOR

Ionian Sea

Delphi

Gulf of Corinth

Thebes

Athens

0   100 miles

0   100 kilometers
Lambert Azimuthal Equal-Area projection

Corinth

Mycenae

PELOPONNESUS

Sparta

Miletus

Mediterranean Sea

Sea of Crete

Knossos

Crete

Using Geography Skills

All parts of ancient Greece were near water.

1. What body of water lies east of the Balkan Peninsula?
2. What transportation was probably most useful to the early Greeks?

Find NGS online map resources @
www.nationalgeographic.com/maps

Mountains and seas played an important role in Greek history. ▶

The Minoans

Main Idea **The Minoans earned their living by building ships and trading.**

Reading Focus Imagine what it would be like to uncover a building that is more than 5,000 years old. Read to learn how such a discovery unlocked clues to Greece's ancient past.

The island of **Crete** (KREET) lies southeast of the Greek mainland. There, in 1900, an English archaeologist by the name of Arthur Evans made the find of a lifetime. Evans uncovered the ruins of a grand palace that had been the center of Minoan (muh•NOH•uhn) civilization. The Minoans were not Greeks, but their civilization was the first to arise in the region that later became Greece.

The palace at Knossos (NAH•suhs) revealed the riches of an ancient society. Its twisting passageways led to many different rooms: private quarters for the royal family and storerooms packed with oil, wine, and grain. Other spaces were workshops for making jewelry, vases, and small ivory statues. The palace even had bathrooms.

The Minoans made their wealth from trade. They built ships from oak and cedar trees and sailed as far as Egypt and Syria. There they traded pottery and stone vases for ivory and metals. By 2000 B.C., Minoan ships controlled the eastern Mediterranean Sea. They carried goods to foreign ports and kept the sea free of pirates.

About 1450 B.C., the Minoan civilization suddenly collapsed. Some historians think undersea earthquakes caused giant waves that washed away the Minoans' cities. Others think the cities were destroyed by a group of Greeks from the mainland. These invaders were called the Mycenaeans (MY•suh•NEE•uhns).

Reading Check **Explain** How did the Minoans become a trading civilization?

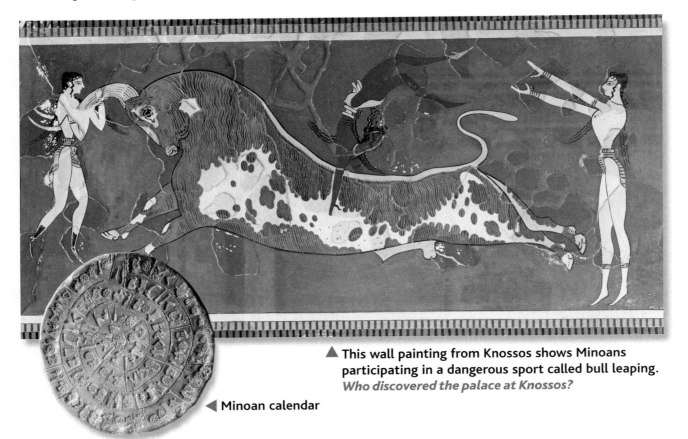

▲ This wall painting from Knossos shows Minoans participating in a dangerous sport called bull leaping. *Who discovered the palace at Knossos?*

◀ Minoan calendar

The First Greek Kingdoms

Main Idea Mycenaeans built the first Greek kingdoms and spread their power across the Mediterranean region.

Reading Focus What is the most important building in the area where you live? Is it a government building, a grocery store, or a hospital? Read to find out what building was most important in the Mycenaean civilization.

The Mycenaeans were originally from central Asia. They invaded the Greek mainland around 1900 B.C. and conquered the people living there. The Mycenaean leaders became the first Greek kings. Their warriors became nobles who ruled the people they had conquered. In the late 1800s, a German named Heinrich Schliemann (HYN•rihk SHLEE•MAHN) discovered one of their walled palaces in **Mycenae** (my•SEE•nee). He named the people of this civilization the Mycenaeans.

What Were Mycenaean Kingdoms Like?

The centerpiece of each Mycenaean kingdom was a fortified palace on a hill. The ruler lived there, surrounded by giant stone walls. Beyond the palace walls lay large farms, or estates, that belonged to the nobles. Slaves and farmers lived on the estates and took shelter inside the fortress in times of danger.

Mycenaean palaces hummed with activity. Artisans tanned leather, sewed clothes, and made jars for wine and olive oil. Other workers made bronze swords and ox-hide shields. Government officials kept track of the wealth of every person in the kingdom. Then they collected wheat, livestock, and honey as taxes and stored them in the palace.

Power From Trade and War

Soon after the Mycenaeans set up their kingdoms, Minoan traders began to visit from Crete.

▲ The ruins at Mycenae included this gate. *What lay outside the walls of a Mycenaean palace?*

Gold mask of Agamemnon ▶

As a result, Mycenaeans learned much about Minoan culture. They copied the ways Minoans worked with bronze and built ships. They learned how the Minoans used the sun and stars to find their way at sea. The Mycenaeans even started worshiping the Earth Mother, the Minoans' chief goddess.

Around 1400 B.C., the Mycenaeans replaced the Minoans as the major power on the Mediterranean. They traded widely, sailing to Egypt and southern Italy. Some

The Greek Alphabet

Greek Letter	Written Name	English Sound
A	alpha	a
B	beta	b
Γ	gamma	g
Δ	delta	d
E	epsilon	e
Z	zeta	z
H	eta	e
Θ	theta	th
I	iota	i
K	kappa	c, k
Λ	lambda	l
M	mu	m
N	nu	n
Ξ	xi	x
O	omicron	o
Π	pi	p
P	rho	r
Σ	sigma	s
T	tau	t
Y	upsilon	y, u
Φ	phi	ph
X	chi	ch
Ψ	psi	ps
Ω	omega	o

▲ **The Greek alphabet was based on the Phoenician alphabet.** *What happened to Greek writing during the Dark Age?*

historians think they conquered Crete and nearby islands.

Although trade made the Mycenaeans wealthy, they were prouder of their deeds in battle. Their most famous victory is probably the Trojan War. In the next chapter, you will learn the legend of how the Mycenaean king **Agamemnon** (A•guh•MEHM•nahn) used trickery to win that war.

What Was the Dark Age?

By 1200 B.C., the Mycenaeans were in trouble. Earthquakes and fighting among the kingdoms had destroyed their hilltop forts. By 1100 B.C., Mycenaean civilization had collapsed.

The years between 1100 B.C. and 750 B.C. were difficult for the Greeks. Overseas trade slowed and poverty took hold. Farmers grew only enough food to meet their own family's needs. People also stopped teaching others how to write or do craftwork. Before long, the Greeks had forgotten their written language and how to make many things. As a result, historians call this time the Dark Age.

The changes that took place in the Dark Age were not all bad, however. One positive development was a huge population shift. Thousands of Greeks left the mainland and settled on islands in the Aegean Sea. Other Greeks moved to the western shores of Asia Minor, to what is now the country of Turkey. This wave of movement expanded the reach of Greek culture.

Meanwhile, a Greek-speaking people known as the Dorians (DOHR•ee•uhns), who lived in Greece's northern mountains, began to move south. Many settled in the **Peloponnesus** (PEH•luh•puh•NEE•suhs). The Dorians brought iron weapons with them, giving Greece more advanced technology. Iron weapons and farm tools were stronger and cheaper than those made of bronze.

Gradually, people began to farm again and to produce surplus food. As a result, trade revived. One benefit of the increased trade was a new way of writing. As you read in Chapter 3, the Greeks picked up the idea of an alphabet from the Phoenicians, one of their trading partners who lived on the coast of the eastern Mediterranean.

The Greek alphabet had 24 letters that stood for different sounds. It made reading and writing Greek much simpler than ever before. Soon people were writing down tales that had been passed down by storytellers for generations.

Reading Check **Identify** What changes occurred during Greece's Dark Age?

A Move to Colonize

Main Idea Colonies and trade spread Greek culture and spurred industry.

Reading Focus If you read labels, you know that your food and clothing come from all over the world. Read to find out where the early Greeks got their goods.

As Greece recovered from its Dark Age, its population rose quickly. By 700 B.C., farmers could no longer grow enough grain to feed everyone. As a result, cities began sending people outside Greece to start **colonies** (KAH•luh•nees). A colony is a settlement in a new territory that keeps close ties to its homeland.

Between 750 B.C. and 550 B.C., adventurous Greeks streamed to the coasts of Italy, France, Spain, North Africa, and western Asia. With each new colony, Greek culture spread farther.

Colonists traded regularly with their "parent" cities, shipping them grains, metals, fish, timber, and enslaved people. In return, the colonists received pottery, wine, and olive oil from the mainland. Overseas trade got an extra boost during the 600s B.C., when the Greeks began to mint coins. Merchants were soon exchanging goods for money rather than for more goods.

The growth of trade led to the growth of industry. As the demand for goods grew, producers had to keep pace. People in different areas began specializing in making certain products. For example, pottery making became popular in places with large amounts of clay.

Reading Check **Cause and Effect** How did new colonies affect industry?

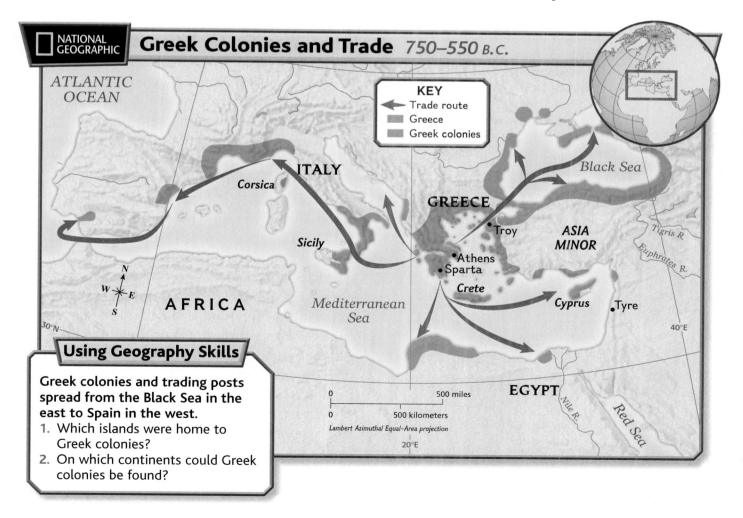

NATIONAL GEOGRAPHIC

Greek Colonies and Trade 750–550 B.C.

KEY
- → Trade route
- Greece
- Greek colonies

ATLANTIC OCEAN

ITALY

Corsica

Sicily

GREECE

Troy

Black Sea

ASIA MINOR

Athens

Sparta

Crete

Cyprus

Tyre

Tigris R.

Euphrates R.

AFRICA

Mediterranean Sea

EGYPT

Nile R.

Red Sea

30°N   40°E

20°E

0   500 miles
0   500 kilometers
Lambert Azimuthal Equal-Area projection

Using Geography Skills

Greek colonies and trading posts spread from the Black Sea in the east to Spain in the west.

1. Which islands were home to Greek colonies?
2. On which continents could Greek colonies be found?

The Polis

Main Idea The idea of citizenship developed in Greek city-states.

Reading Focus Did you know that the word "politics" comes from *polis*, the Greek term for a city-state? Read to find how the Greeks also created the idea of citizenship.

By the end of the Dark Age, many nobles who owned large estates had overthrown the Greek kings. They created city-states. Like the Mesopotamian city-states you read about in Chapter 1, those in Greece were made up of a town or city and the surrounding countryside. Each Greek city-state, known as a **polis** (PAH•luhs), was like a tiny independent country.

The main gathering place in the polis was usually a hill. A fortified area, called an acropolis (uh•KRAH•puh•luhs), stood at the top of the hill. It provided a safe refuge in case of attacks. Sometimes the acropolis also served as a religious center. Temples and altars were built there to honor the many Greek gods and goddesses.

Below the acropolis was an open area called an **agora** (A•guh•ruh). This space had two functions: it was both a market and a place where people could meet and debate issues.

City-states varied in size. Some were a few miles square, while others covered hundreds of square miles. They also varied in population. Nearly 300,000 people lived in Athens by 500 B.C. Most city-states were much smaller, however.

What Was Greek Citizenship? Each Greek city-state was run by its citizens. When we speak of citizens, we mean members of a political community who treat each other as equals and who have rights and responsibilities. This was very different from ancient Mesopotamia or Egypt. There, most people were subjects. They had no rights, no say in government, and no choice but to obey their rulers.

The Greeks were the first people to develop the idea of citizenship. Today, the word applies to almost everyone in a society. However, in most Greek city-states, only free native-born men who owned land could be citizens. From their point of view, the city-state was made up of their lands, and it was their responsibility to run it. They did not think anyone else should be a citizen.

Some city-states, such as Athens, eventually dropped the land-owning requirement. Slaves and foreign-born residents, however,

Primary Source

Athenian Soldier's Oath

In the Greek city of Athens, soldiers took this oath:

"I will not bring dishonor upon my weapons nor desert the comrade by my side. I will strive to hand on my fatherland greater and better than I found it. I will not consent to anyone's disobeying or destroying the constitution but will prevent him, whether I am with others or alone. I will honor the temples and the religion my forefathers established."

—oath of enrollment in Epheboi corps, c. 300s B.C.

◀ Greek soldier

DBQ Document-Based Question

Identify six things each soldier promises to protect in taking the oath.

continued to be excluded. As for women and children, they might qualify for citizenship, but they had none of the rights that went with it.

What exactly were the rights of Greek citizens? They could gather in the agora to choose their officials and pass laws. They had the right to vote, hold office, own property, and defend themselves in court. In return, citizens had a duty to serve in government and to fight for their polis as citizen soldiers.

Citizens as Soldiers In early Greece, wars were waged by nobles riding horses and chariots. As the idea of citizenship developed, however, the military system changed. By 700 B.C., the city-states had begun to depend on armies of ordinary citizens called hoplites (HAHP•LYTS).

Unable to afford horses, the hoplites fought on foot and went into battle heavily armed. Each carried a round shield, a

◄ Greek plate showing soldiers in battle

short sword, and a 9-foot (2.7-m) spear. Row upon row of soldiers marched forward together, shoulder to shoulder. With their shields creating a protective wall, they gave their enemies few openings to defeat them.

Hoplites made good soldiers because, as citizens, they took pride in fighting for their city-state. However, "hometown" loyalties also divided the Greeks and caused them to distrust one another. A lack of unity always existed among the Greek city-states.

✓ **Reading Check** **Explain** How did citizenship make the Greeks different from other ancient peoples?

Section 1 Review

History Online

Study Central™ Need help with the material in this section? Visit jat.glencoe.com

Reading Summary

Review the Main Ideas

- Geography influenced the way Greek communities developed.

- The Minoan civilization, on the island of Crete, built ships and became wealthy from trade.

- The Mycenaeans created the first Greek kingdoms.

- After the Dark Age, the Greeks set up colonies and trade increased.

- The idea of citizenship developed in Greek city-states.

What Did You Learn?

1. What made the Minoans wealthy?

2. How was a Greek city-state different from a city?

Critical Thinking

3. **Compare** Create a Venn diagram to compare the Minoans and Mycenaeans.

Minoan (Both) Mycenaean

4. **Summarize** What changes occurred in Greece during the Dark Age?

5. **Citizenship Skills** Name three rights granted to Greek citizens that American citizens have today.

6. **Link to Economics** Why did the use of money help trade to grow?

7. **Reading** **Making Connections** Choose one passage from this section. Write a paragraph to explain how it connects to something you already know or something you have experienced.

Section 2

Sparta and Athens

Get Ready to Read!

What's the Connection?

Although Greek city-states developed the idea of citizenship, they had many different types of government. This section describes their different governments and compares the best-known city-states, Athens and Sparta.

Focusing on the Main Ideas

- Tyrants were able to seize power from the nobles with the support of Greek farmers, merchants, and artisans. *(page 125)*

- The Spartans focused on military skills to control the people they conquered. *(page 126)*

- Unlike Spartans, Athenians were more interested in building a democracy than building a military force. *(page 128)*

Locating Places
Sparta (SPAHR•tuh)
Athens (A•thuhnz)

Meeting People
Solon (SOH•luhn)
Peisistratus (py•SIHS•truht•uhs)
Cleisthenes (KLYS•thuh•NEEZ)

Building Your Vocabulary
tyrant (TY•ruhnt)
oligarchy (AH•luh•GAHR•kee)
democracy (dih•MAH•kruh•see)
helot (HEH•luht)

Reading Strategy
Compare and Contrast Use a Venn diagram to compare and contrast life in Sparta and Athens.

Sparta — Both — Athens

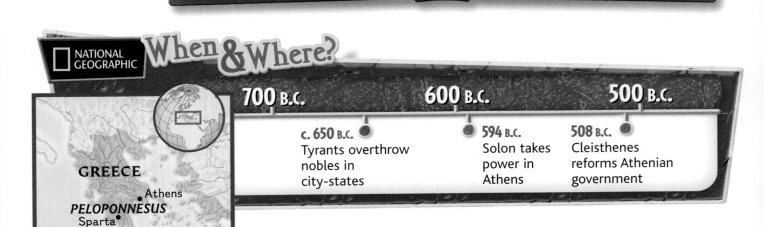

NATIONAL GEOGRAPHIC **When & Where?**

GREECE
PELOPONNESUS
Athens
Sparta

700 B.C.   **600 B.C.**   **500 B.C.**

c. 650 B.C.
Tyrants overthrow nobles in city-states

594 B.C.
Solon takes power in Athens

508 B.C.
Cleisthenes reforms Athenian government

Tyranny in the City-States

Main Idea Tyrants were able to seize power from the nobles with the support of Greek farmers, merchants, and artisans.

Reading Focus How do you feel when someone makes a decision that affects you without asking for your opinion? Read to find out how ancient Greeks who were shut out of governing made their voices heard.

As you read in the last section, kings ruled the first Greek communities. However, by the end of the Dark Age, the nobles who owned large farms had seized power from the kings.

Rule by the nobles would also be short-lived. The first challenge to their rule came from the owners of small farms. These farmers often needed money to live on until they could harvest and sell their crops. Many borrowed money from the nobles, promising to give up their fields if they could not repay the loans. Time and time again, farmers lost their land. Then they had to work for the nobles or become laborers in the city. In desperate cases, they sold themselves into slavery.

By 650 B.C., small farmers began to demand changes in the power structure. Merchants and artisans also wanted to share in governing. Both groups had become very wealthy from the trade between city-states. Because they did not own land, however, they were not citizens and had no say in running the polis.

The growing unhappiness led to the rise of tyrants. A **tyrant** (TY•ruhnt) is someone who takes power by force and rules with

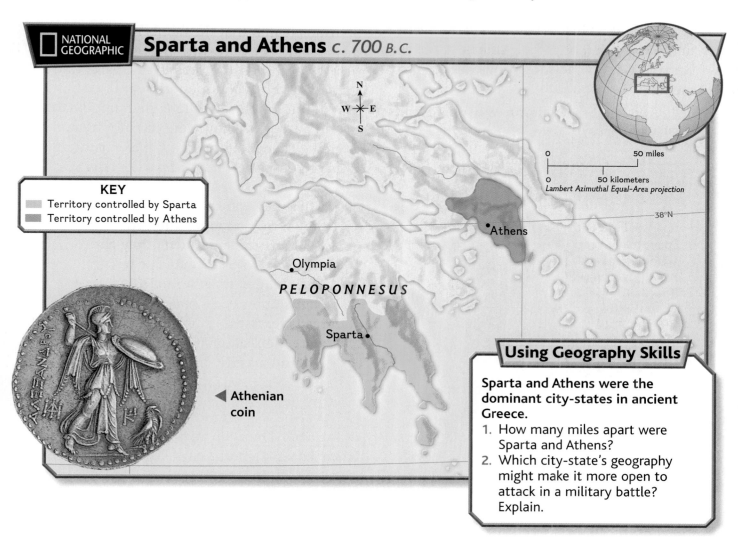

NATIONAL GEOGRAPHIC

Sparta and Athens c. 700 B.C.

KEY
■ Territory controlled by Sparta
■ Territory controlled by Athens

Athens
Olympia
PELOPONNESUS
Sparta

◀ Athenian coin

0 — 50 miles
0 — 50 kilometers
Lambert Azimuthal Equal-Area projection

38°N

Using Geography Skills

Sparta and Athens were the dominant city-states in ancient Greece.
1. How many miles apart were Sparta and Athens?
2. Which city-state's geography might make it more open to attack in a military battle? Explain.

total authority. Today the word describes a harsh, oppressive ruler. Most early Greek tyrants, though, acted wisely and fairly.

During the 600s B.C., tyrants managed to overthrow the nobles because they had the backing of the common people. Key support came from the hoplites in the army, many of whom were also farmers.

Tyrants made themselves popular by building new marketplaces, temples, and walls. However, rule by one person was the opposite of what most Greeks wanted. They longed for rule by law with all citizens participating in the government.

By 500 B.C., tyrants had fallen out of favor in Greece. Most city-states became either oligarchies or democracies. In an **oligarchy** (AH•luh•GAHR•kee), a few people hold power. In a **democracy** (dih•MAH•kruh•see), all citizens share in running the government. The oligarchy of **Sparta** (SPAHR•tuh) and the democracy of **Athens** (A•thuhnz) became two of the most powerful governments of early Greece.

✓ **Reading Check** **Evaluate** Why were tyrants popular in the city-states?

Spartan Warrior

Spartan boys and men spent many years training for war. *At what age did Spartan boys leave their families for the military?*

Sparta

Main Idea The Spartans focused on military skills to control the people they conquered.

Reading Focus What would it be like to leave home when you were only seven? Read to learn how Spartan boys faced this challenge.

As you read in the last section, Sparta was founded by the Dorians—Greeks who invaded the Peloponnesus in the Dark Age. Like other city-states, Sparta needed more land as it grew, but its people did not set up colonies. Instead, they conquered and enslaved their neighbors. The Spartans called their captive workers **helots** (HEH•luhts). This name comes from the Greek word for "capture."

Why Was the Military So Important?

Spartans feared that the helots might someday rebel. As a result, the government firmly controlled the people of Sparta and trained the boys and men for war.

At age seven, boys left their family to live in barracks. They were harshly treated to make them tough. The Greek historian Plutarch describes life for Spartan boys:

❝ After they were twelve years old, they were no longer allowed to wear any undergarment; they had one coat to serve them a year; . . . They lodged together in little bands upon beds made of the reeds [grasses] . . . which they were to break off with their hands without a knife. ❞

—Plutarch, "Spartan Discipline"

At age 20, Spartan men entered the regular army. The men remained in military barracks for 10 more years. They ate all their meals in dining halls with other soldiers.

Spartan girls were trained in sports. ▼

▲ Spartan boys began training for the military at age 7. *Why did the Spartan government want its young people to be physically fit?*

A typical meal was a vile-tasting dish called black broth—pork boiled in animal blood, salt, and vinegar.

Spartans returned home at age 30 but stayed in the army until age 60. They continued to train for combat. They expected to either win on the battlefield or die, but never to surrender. One Spartan mother ordered her son to "Come home carrying your shield or being carried on it."

Girls in Sparta were trained in sports—running, wrestling, and throwing the javelin. They kept fit to become healthy mothers. Wives lived at home while their husbands lived in the barracks. As a result, Spartan women were freer than other Greek women. They could own property and go where they wanted.

What Was Sparta's Government Like?

The Spartan government was an oligarchy. Two kings headed a council of elders. The council, which included 28 citizens over age 60, presented laws to an assembly.

All Spartan men over age 30 belonged to the assembly. They voted on the council's laws and chose five people to be ephors (EH•fuhrs) each year. The ephors enforced the laws and managed tax collection.

To keep anyone from questioning the Spartan system, the government discouraged foreign visitors. It also banned travel abroad for any reason but military ones. It even frowned upon citizens who studied literature or the arts.

The Spartans succeeded in keeping control over the helots for nearly 250 years. However, by focusing on military training, the Spartans fell behind other Greeks in trade. They also knew less about science and other subjects. However, their soldiers were especially strong and swift. The Spartans would play a key role in defending Greece.

Reading Check **Cause and Effect** Why did the Spartans stress military training?

Athens

(Main Idea) Unlike Spartans, Athenians were more interested in building a democracy than building a military force.

Reading Focus When visiting a new city, does everything feel strange to you? Spartans who visited Athens probably felt the same way. Read to find out why.

Athens lay northeast of Sparta, at least a two-day trip away. The two city-states were also miles apart in their values and systems of government.

History Online

Web Activity Visit jat.glencoe.com and click on *Chapter 4—Student Web Activity* to learn more about ancient Greece.

What Was Life in Athens Like? Athenian citizens raised their children very differently from Spartans. In Athenian schools, one teacher taught boys to read, write, and do arithmetic. Another teacher taught them

Linking Past & Present

The Olympics

THEN In ancient Greece, only men could participate in and view the Olympic games. Athletes competed by themselves, not as part of a team. Contests included running, jumping, wrestling, and boxing. Each winning athlete won a crown of olive leaves and brought glory to his city.

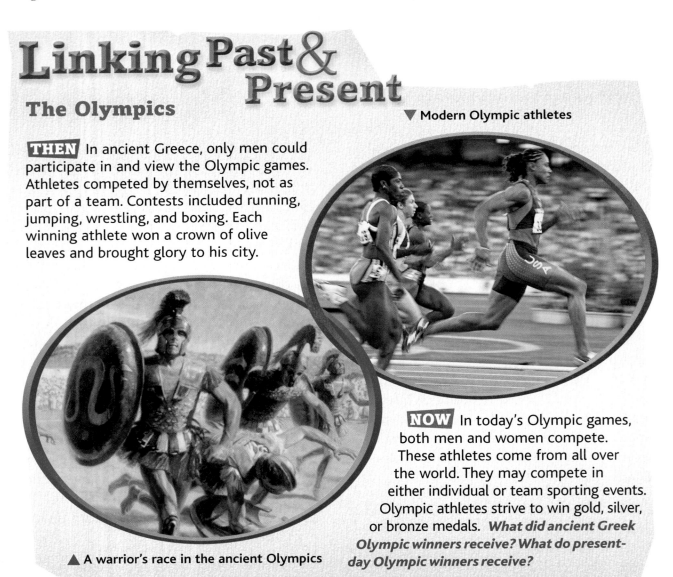

▼ Modern Olympic athletes

▲ A warrior's race in the ancient Olympics

NOW In today's Olympic games, both men and women compete. These athletes come from all over the world. They may compete in either individual or team sporting events. Olympic athletes strive to win gold, silver, or bronze medals. *What did ancient Greek Olympic winners receive? What do present-day Olympic winners receive?*

sports. A third teacher taught them to sing and to play a stringed instrument called the lyre. This kind of education created well-rounded Athenians with good minds and bodies. At age 18, boys finished school and became citizens.

Athenian girls stayed at home. Their mothers taught them spinning, weaving, and other household duties. Only in some wealthy families did girls learn to read, write, and play the lyre. When they married, women stayed home to keep house and to teach their own daughters.

A Budding Democracy Early Athens, like other city-states, was ruled by landowning nobles during the 600s B.C. An assembly of all citizens existed, but it had few powers. Actually, the government was an oligarchy, as in Sparta.

Around 600 B.C., the Athenians began to rebel against the nobles. Most farmers owed the nobles money, and many sold themselves into slavery to pay their debts. Over and over, farmers demanded an end to all debts, along with land for the poor.

In 594 B.C. the nobles turned to the one man both sides trusted: a noble named **Solon** (SOH•luhn). Solon canceled all the farmers' debts and freed those who had become slaves. He also allowed all male citizens to participate in the assembly and law courts. A council of 400 wealthy citizens wrote the laws, but the assembly had to pass them.

Solon's reforms were popular among the common people. However, the farmers

◄ The city of Athens was named for the goddess Athena. *What group ruled Athens during the 600s B.C.?*

continued to press Solon to give away the wealthy nobles' land. This he refused to do.

After Solon, there were 30 years of turmoil. Finally, a tyrant named **Peisistratus** (py•SIHS•truht•uhs) seized power in 560 B.C. He won the support of the poor by dividing large estates among landless farmers. He also loaned money to poor people and gave them jobs building temples and other public works.

▲ Token used to select jurors for Athenian courts.

The most important leader after Peisistratus died was **Cleisthenes** (KLYS•thuh•NEEZ). When he came to power in 508 B.C., he reorganized the assembly to play the central role in governing. As before, all male citizens could belong to the assembly and vote on laws. However, members had new powers. They could debate matters openly, hear court cases, and appoint army generals.

Most importantly, Cleisthenes created a new council of 500 citizens to help the assembly carry out daily business. The council proposed laws, dealt with foreign countries, and oversaw the treasury.

Athenians chose the members of the council each year in a lottery. They believed this system was fairer than an election, which might favor the rich.

Cleisthenes' reforms did not bring all Athenians into the political process.

Stone carving of ▶ **Democracy crowning a figure that symbolizes Athens.** *What leader is credited with making Athens a democracy?*

Non-citizens, which included all women, foreign-born men, and slaves, were still excluded. Nonetheless, Cleisthenes is credited with making the government of Athens a democracy.

✓ **Reading Check** **Explain** How did Cleisthenes build a democracy in Athens?

History Online
Study Central™ Need help with the material in this section? Visit jat.glencoe.com

Section 2 Review

Reading Summary
Review the Main Ideas

- The support of wealthy merchants and artisans helped tyrants seize power from nobles in the city-states.

- Sparta was a powerful city-state. It created a military state to control the people it conquered and to prevent uprisings.

- Athens was a powerful democratic city-state. Athenians were more involved in government, education, and the arts than the Spartans.

What Did You Learn?

1. Who were the helots?
2. Why did tyrants fall out of favor with the Greeks?

Critical Thinking

3. **Classifying Information** Draw a diagram like the one below. In each oval write a fact about the Spartan oligarchy.

Oligarchy

4. **Evaluate** Why did Athenians choose officials by lottery? Would there be drawbacks to this method? Explain.

5. **Explain** How did Greek nobles gain power?

6. **Analyze** Why was Solon popular among some Athenian farmers and unpopular among others?

7. **Civics Link** How did Athenian democracy keep one person from gaining too much power?

8. **Descriptive Writing** Imagine that you are a 28-year-old man living in Sparta in 700 B.C. Write a letter to your 6-year-old nephew telling him what to expect when he leaves home on his next birthday.

Section 3

Persia Attacks the Greeks

Get Ready to Read!

What's the Connection?

Section 2 explained how Greeks built strong but separate city-states. At the same time far to the east, the Persians were building a powerful empire. It was only a matter of time before Persia would try to invade Greece.

Focusing on the Main Ideas

- The Persian Empire united a wide area under a single government. *(page 132)*

- Both Sparta and Athens played roles in defeating the Persians. *(page 134)*

Locating Places

Persia (PUHR•zhuh)
Marathon (MAR•uh•THAHN)
Thermopylae
  (thuhr•MAH•puh•lee)
Salamis (SA•luh•muhs)
Plataea (pluh•TEE•uh)

Meeting People

Cyrus the Great (SY•ruhs)
Darius (duh•RY•uhs)
Xerxes (ZUHRK•SEEZ)
Themistocles
  (thuh•MIHS•tuh•KLEEZ)

Building Your Vocabulary

satrapies (SAY•truh•peez)
satrap (SAY•TRAP)
Zoroastrianism (ZOHR•uh•WAS•tree•uh•NIH•zuhm)

Reading Strategy

Organizing Information Create a chart like the one below to list the accomplishments of Cyrus, Darius, and Xerxes.

Ruler	Accomplishments
Cyrus	
Darius	
Xerxes	

NATIONAL GEOGRAPHIC When & Who?

650 B.C.	550 B.C.	450 B.C.
660 B.C. Zoroaster born	559 B.C. Cyrus becomes ruler of Persia	480 B.C. Xerxes invades Greece

The Persian Empire

Main Idea The Persian Empire united a wide area under a single government.

Reading Focus Have you ever seen soldiers marching through city streets on the news? Imagine the same thing happening in Asia in the 500s B.C. Read to learn what happened as Persian armies marched westward from Asia.

The people of **Persia** (PUHR•zhuh) lived in what is today southwestern Iran. Early Persians were warriors and nomads who herded cattle. For a time, they were dominated by others. Then one remarkable leader, **Cyrus the Great** (SY•ruhs), managed to unite the Persians into a powerful kingdom. Under Cyrus, who ruled from 559 B.C. to 530 B.C., Persia began building an empire larger than any yet seen in the world.

The Rise of the Persian Empire In 539 B.C. Cyrus's armies swept into Mesopotamia and captured Babylon. Then they took over northern Mesopotamia, Asia Minor, Syria, Canaan, and the Phoenician cities. Cyrus treated all his new subjects well. As you read in Chapter 3, he allowed the captive Jews in Babylon to return home. Cyrus's merciful rule helped hold his growing empire together.

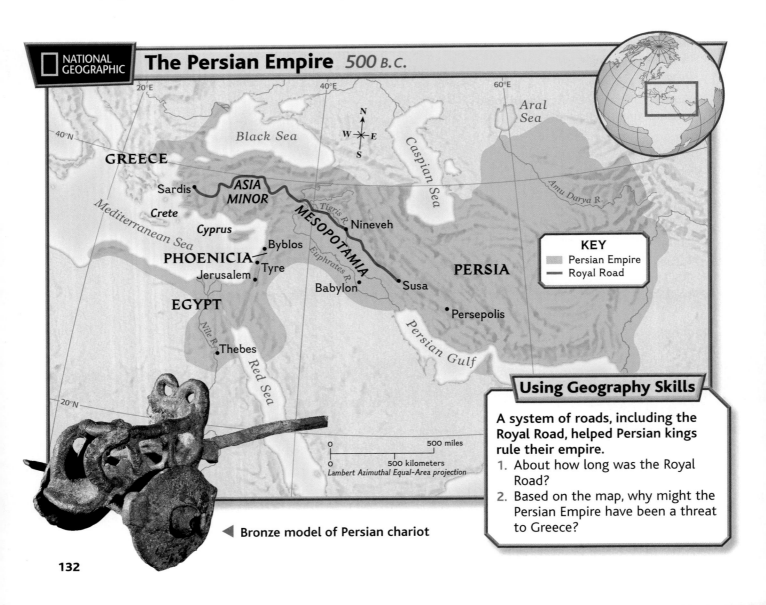

NATIONAL GEOGRAPHIC

The Persian Empire 500 B.C.

KEY
Persian Empire
Royal Road

500 miles

0
0   500 kilometers
Lambert Azimuthal Equal-Area projection

Using Geography Skills

A system of roads, including the Royal Road, helped Persian kings rule their empire.

1. About how long was the Royal Road?
2. Based on the map, why might the Persian Empire have been a threat to Greece?

◀ Bronze model of Persian chariot

The leaders who followed Cyrus continued to add to Persian territory. They conquered Egypt, western India, and Thrace, a region northeast of Greece. From one end to the other, the Persian Empire was about the size of the continental United States today.

To connect their vast holdings, the Persians built miles of roads. The Royal Road stretched from Asia Minor to Susa, the Persian capital. Along the way, the Persians set up roadside stations to supply food, shelter, and fresh horses to the king's messengers.

What Was Persian Government Like? As the Persian Empire grew bigger, it became very difficult to manage. When **Darius** (duh•RY•uhs) came to the throne in 521 B.C., he reorganized the government to make it work better.

Darius divided the empire into 20 provinces called **satrapies** (SAY•truh•peez). Each was ruled by an official with the title of **satrap** (SAY•TRAP), meaning "protector of the kingdom." The satrap acted as tax collector, judge, chief of police, and head recruiter for the Persian army. However, all the satraps answered to the Persian king.

The king's power depended upon his troops. By the time of Darius, Persia had a large army of professional soldiers. Unlike the Greek city-states, where the citizens took up arms in times of war, in Persia the government paid people to be full-time soldiers. Among them were 10,000 specially trained soldiers who guarded the king. They were called the Immortals because when a member died, he was immediately replaced.

The Persian Religion The Persian religion was called **Zoroastrianism** (ZOHR•uh•WAS•tree•uh•NIH•zuhm). Its founder, Zoroaster,

King Darius

Darius helped to organize the Persian government. *What methods did he use?*

was born in 660 B.C. He began preaching after seeing visions as a young man.

Like the Jews, Zoroaster believed in one god. He viewed this supreme being as the creator of all things and a force of goodness. However, Zoroaster recognized evil in the world, too. He taught that humans had the freedom to choose between right and wrong, and that goodness would triumph in the end. The Persians practiced Zoroastrianism for centuries, and it still has a small number of followers today.

✓ **Reading Check** **Explain** Why did Darius create satrapies?

The Persian Wars

Main Idea Both Sparta and Athens played roles in defeating the Persians.

Reading Focus Have you and a rival ever set aside your differences to work for a common cause? This happened in ancient Greece when Sparta and Athens came together to fight the Persians. Read about the outcome.

As the Greeks set up colonies in the Mediterranean area, they often clashed with the Persians. By the mid-500s B.C., Persia already controlled the Greek cities in Asia Minor. In 499 B.C. the Athenian army helped the Greeks in Asia Minor rebel against their Persian rulers. The rebellion failed, but King Darius decided the mainland Greeks had to be stopped from interfering in the Persian Empire.

The Battle of Marathon In 490 B.C. a Persian fleet landed 20,000 soldiers on the plain of **Marathon** (MAR•uh•THAHN), only a short distance from Athens. For several days, the Persians waited there for the Athenians to advance. The Athenians, however, did not take the bait. They had only 10,000 soldiers compared to the Persians' 20,000. They knew that attacking was too dangerous. Instead they held back in the hills overlooking the plain.

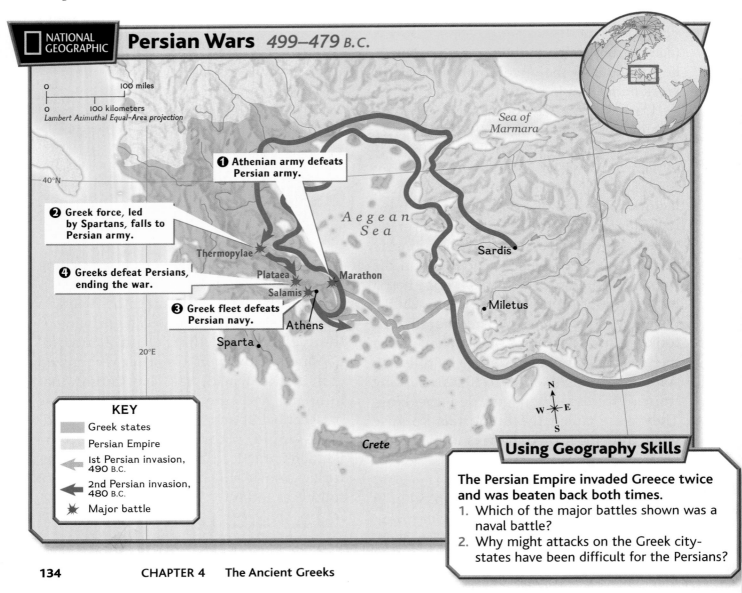

NATIONAL GEOGRAPHIC

Persian Wars 499–479 B.C.

0 — 100 miles
0 — 100 kilometers
Lambert Azimuthal Equal-Area projection

❶ Athenian army defeats Persian army.

❷ Greek force, led by Spartans, falls to Persian army.

❹ Greeks defeat Persians, ending the war.

❸ Greek fleet defeats Persian navy.

Sea of Marmara

Aegean Sea

Thermopylae

Plataea
Salamis
Marathon
Athens
Sparta

Sardis

Miletus

Crete

KEY

- Greek states
- Persian Empire
- 1st Persian invasion, 490 B.C.
- 2nd Persian invasion, 480 B.C.
- ✳ Major battle

Using Geography Skills

The Persian Empire invaded Greece twice and was beaten back both times.
1. Which of the major battles shown was a naval battle?
2. Why might attacks on the Greek city-states have been difficult for the Persians?

Tired of waiting, the Persian commander decided to sail south and attack Athens directly. He ordered his troops back onto the ships, and it was then that he made a big mistake. The first to board, he decided, would be the horsemen in the cavalry, the strongest part of the Persian army.

As soon as the cavalry was out of fighting range, the Greeks charged down from the hills and onto the plain of Marathon. They caught the Persian foot soldiers standing in the water, waiting their turn to board the ships. Unable to defend themselves, the Persians were easily defeated.

According to legend, the Athenians sent a messenger named Pheidippides (fy•DIHP•uh•DEEZ) home with the news. The runner raced nearly 25 miles (40.2 km) from Marathon to Athens. He collapsed from exhaustion and, with his last breath, announced, "Victory." Then he died. Modern marathon races are named for this famous run and are just over 26 miles long.

Another Persian Strike After Darius died in 486 B.C., his son **Xerxes** (ZUHRK•SEEZ) became the Persian king. Xerxes vowed revenge against the Athenians. In 480 B.C. he launched a new invasion of Greece, this time with about 180,000 troops and thousands of warships and supply vessels.

To defend themselves, the Greeks joined forces. Sparta sent the most soldiers, and their king, Leonidas (lee•AH•nuh•duhs), served as commander. Athens provided the navy. An Athenian general, **Themistocles** (thuh•MIHS•tuh•KLEEZ), came up with a plan to fight the Persians.

The Greeks knew that as the huge Persian army marched south, it depended on shipments of food brought in by boat. Themistocles argued that the Greeks' best strategy would be to attack the Persians' ships and cut off food supplies to the army.

Primary Source — Herodotus's History

▲ Herodotus reading to a crowd

The Greek historian Herodotus (hih•RAH•duh•tuhs) wrote *History of the Persian Wars*. This is thought to be the first real history in Western civilization. Herodotus described the conflict between the Greeks and Persians as one between freedom and dictatorship. Here he tells of Xerxes' address to Persian nobles:

"And truly I have pondered upon this, until at last I have found out a way whereby we may at once win glory, and likewise get possession of a land which is as large and as rich as our own . . . while at the same time we obtain satisfaction and revenge . . . My intent is to . . . march an army through Europe against Greece, that thereby I may obtain vengeance from the Athenians for the wrongs committed by them against the Persians and against my father."

—Herodotus, *The Persian Wars*, Book VII

DBQ **Document-Based Question**

What reasons besides revenge does Xerxes have for invading Greece?

To ready their fleet for battle, the Greeks needed to stall the Persian army before it reached Athens. The Greeks decided the best place to block the Persians was at **Thermopylae** (thuhr•MAH•puh•lee). Thermopylae was a narrow pass through the mountains that was easy to defend. About 7,000 Greek soldiers held off the Persians there for two days. The Spartans in the Greek army were especially brave. As one story has it, the Greeks heard that Persian arrows would darken the sky. A Spartan warrior responded, "That is good news. We will fight in the shade!"

Unfortunately for the Greeks, a traitor directed the Persians to a mountain path that led them around the Greeks. As the Persians mounted a rear attack, King Leonidas sent most of his troops to safety. He and several hundred others, however, stayed behind and fought to the death. The Greeks lost the battle at Thermopylae, but their valiant stand gave Athens enough time to assemble 200 ships.

The Greek fleet attacked the Persian fleet in the strait of **Salamis** (SA•luh•muhs), not far from Athens. A strait is a narrow strip of water between two pieces of land. The Greeks expected to have the upper hand in the battle because their ships could maneuver well in tight spaces. Greek ships were smaller, faster, and easier to steer than the big Persian ships, which became easy targets.

The Greek plan worked. After a ferocious battle, the Greeks destroyed almost the entire Persian fleet. Still, the Persian army marched on. When their troops reached Athens, the Greeks had already fled.

The Persians burned the city. This only stiffened the resolve of the Greek city-states.

Battle of Salamis

At the Battle of Salamis, smaller, faster Greek ships defeated the Persian fleet. *Near what Greek city-state was the strait of Salamis located?*

In early 479 B.C., they came together to form the largest Greek army ever assembled. With solid body armor, longer spears, and better training, the Greek army crushed the Persian army at **Plataea** (pluh•TEE•uh), northwest of Athens.

The battle was a turning point for the Greeks, convincing the Persians to retreat to Asia Minor. By working together, the Greek city-states had saved their homeland from invasion.

What Caused the Persian Empire to Fall?

When the Greeks defeated the Persian army, they helped to weaken it. The empire was already facing internal problems. As these problems worsened, the empire would gradually lose its strength.

Persia remained intact for almost 150 more years. However, after Darius and Xerxes, other Persian rulers raised taxes to gain more wealth. They spent the gold and silver that flowed into the treasuries on luxuries for the royal court.

The high taxes angered their subjects and caused many rebellions. At the same time, the Persian royal family fought over who was to be king. Many of the later Persian kings were killed by other family members who wanted the throne.

Persian kings had many wives and children. The sons had little, if any, power so they were constantly plotting to take over the throne. As a result of such plots, six of the nine rulers after Darius were murdered.

All of these problems made Persia vulnerable to attack. By the time a young Greek conqueror named Alexander invaded the empire in 334 B.C., the Persians were no match for his troops.

By 330 B.C., the last Persian king was dead and Alexander ruled over all his lands. You will learn more about Alexander the Great and his many achievements in Chapter 5.

Reading Check **Cause and Effect** What led to the Persian Wars?

History Online

Study Central™ Need help with the material in this section? Visit jat.glencoe.com

Section 3 Review

Reading Summary

Review the Main Ideas

• The Persian Empire united its many lands under a single government.

• The Persian Empire attacked Greece several times. Despite their rivalry, Athens and Sparta joined forces to defeat the Persians.

What Did You Learn?

1. Why was Cyrus considered a fair ruler?

2. What was the Royal Road?

Critical Thinking

3. **Summarize** Draw a table like the one below. Then summarize what happened at each battle in the Persian Wars.

Battle	Action
Marathon Thermopylae Salamis Plataea	

4. **Persuasive Writing** Imagine you are an adviser to Xerxes and are alarmed about his plan for revenge on Greece. Compose a letter to him outlining reasons why he should cancel his invasion of Greece.

5. **Reading** **Making Connections** The Persians wanted revenge against the Greeks. Describe an event in your own life or on the news where revenge was involved. What was the outcome?

Section 4

The Age of Pericles

Get-Ready to Read!

What's the Connection?

In Section 3, you learned how the Greeks defeated the Persians at Plataea. One lesson the Greeks drew from the war was that they needed each other for security. Athens and several other city-states soon banded together in a league for the common defense.

Focusing on the Main Ideas

- Under Pericles, Athens became very powerful and more democratic. *(page 139)*

- Athenian men and women had very different roles. *(page 142)*

- Sparta and Athens went to war for control of Greece. *(page 144)*

Locating Places

Delos (DEE•LAHS)

Meeting People

Pericles (PEHR•uh•KLEEZ)
Aspasia (as•PAY•zhuh)

Building Your Vocabulary

direct democracy
    (dih•MAH•kruh•see)
representative democracy
    (REH•prih•ZEHN•tuh•tihv)
philosopher (fuh•LAH•suh•fuhr)

Reading Strategy

Organizing Information Create a circle graph to show how many citizens, foreigners, and enslaved people lived in Athens in the 400s B.C.

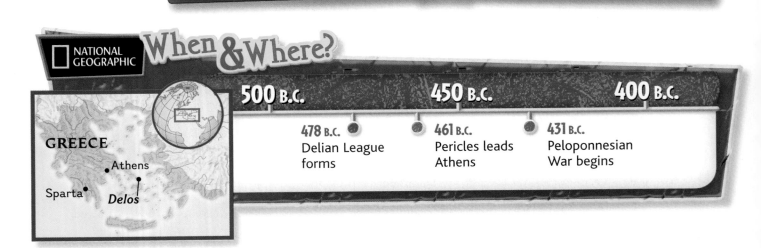

NATIONAL GEOGRAPHIC When & Where?

GREECE

• Athens
Sparta • • Delos

500 B.C.   **450 B.C.**   **400 B.C.**

478 B.C.
Delian League forms

461 B.C.
Pericles leads Athens

431 B.C.
Peloponnesian War begins

The Athenian Empire

Main Idea Under Pericles, Athens became very powerful and more democratic.

Reading Focus Do you vote in school elections? Why do you choose one classmate over another? Read to learn why Athenians kept electing Pericles.

As you read in Section 3, the Battle of Plataea in 479 B.C. put an end to the Persians' invasion of Greece. Although the Persians retreated, they still remained a threat. In 478 B.C. Athens joined with other city-states—but not Sparta—to form the Delian League.

The Delian League promised to defend its members against the Persians. It also worked to drive Persia out of Greek territories in Asia Minor. Eventually, the league freed almost all of the Greek cities under Persia's control.

At its start, the Delian League had headquarters on the island of **Delos** (DEE•LAHS). However, its chief officials—the treasurers in charge of its money and the commanders in charge of its fleet—were from Athens, as were most of the troops. Little by little, Athens gained control over the other city-states in the alliance. Soon the league was no longer a partnership to fight Persia but an Athenian empire.

In 454 B.C. the Athenians moved the Delian League's treasury from Delos to Athens. The Athenians also began sending troops to other Greek city-states, to help the common people rebel against the nobles in power.

Democracy in Athens
Athenians had a strong faith in their democratic system. We call their system **direct democracy** (dih•MAH•kruh•see). In a direct democracy, people gather at mass meetings to decide on government matters. Every citizen can vote firsthand on laws and policies.

▲ These ruins are of the agora—an ancient marketplace in Athens where the assembly met. *What type of democracy did Athens have?*

Can you imagine such a system in the United States? A mass meeting of our millions of citizens would be impossible! Instead, in the United States we have a **representative democracy** (REH•prih•ZEHN•tuh•tihv). Under this type of democracy, citizens choose a smaller group to make laws and governmental decisions on their behalf. This is a much more practical system when the population is large.

What made direct democracy workable in ancient Athens was the relatively small number of citizens. In the mid-400s B.C., about 43,000 male citizens over 18 years old made up the assembly. Usually fewer than 6,000 attended the meetings, which were held every 10 days. The assembly passed all laws, elected officials, and made decisions on war and foreign affairs. Ten officials known as generals carried out the assembly's laws and policies.

Comparing Governments

	Athenian Democracy	American Democracy
Type of Democracy	Direct	Representative
Right to Vote	Only adult males born in Athens	All citizens, male and female age 18 or over
Laws	Proposed by the council and approved by a majority in the assembly	Approved by both houses of Congress and signed by the president
Citizen Involvement	Citizens with voting rights can vote for or against any law	Citizens with voting rights can vote for or against the officials who make the laws

Understanding Charts

The small number of citizens made a direct democracy possible in Athens.

1. In Athens, how was a law approved?
2. **Compare** Which government granted the right to vote to more of its population?

The Achievements of Pericles Athenians reelected their favorite generals again and again. After the Persian Wars, the leading figure in Athenian politics was a general named **Pericles** (PEHR•uh•KLEEZ). This great statesman guided Athens for more than 30 years, from 461 B.C., when he was first elected, until 429 B.C., shortly before his death.

Pericles helped Athens dominate the Delian League. He treated the other city-states like subjects, demanding strict loyalty and steady payments from them. He even insisted that they use Athenian coins and measures.

At the same time, Pericles made Athens more democratic at home. He believed that people's talents were more important than their social standing. For this reason, Pericles included more Athenians than ever before in government. He allowed lower-class male citizens to run for public office, and he also paid officeholders. As a result, even poor citizens could, for the first time, be part of the inner circle running the government.

Culture also blossomed under the rule of Pericles. The Age of Pericles was a period of tremendous creativity and learning that peaked in the mid-400s B.C. The Persians had destroyed much of the city during the Persian Wars. So Pericles started a major rebuilding program. He had new temples and statues built across the city.

Pericles supported artists, architects, writers, and **philosophers** (fuh•LAH•suh•fuhrs). Philosophers are thinkers who ponder questions about life. In Chapter 5, you will read more about the Greeks' achievements and understand why Pericles called Athens "the school of Greece."

Reading Check **Identify** What is the difference between a direct democracy and a representative democracy?

Biography

PERICLES
c. 495–429 B.C.

Pericles was born just outside Athens, to a wealthy and powerful family. He received his education from philosophers. As a young man, he was known for his skill with words. Later, when he became a political leader, he strongly supported democracy.

Although he was from a wealthy family himself, he believed that citizenship should not be limited to the wealthy and powerful. He made changes to take power from the few and give it to the many. However, in describing Pericles' rule over Athens, Greek historian Thucydides wrote "In name democracy, but in fact the rule of one man."

The "Age of Pericles" was Athens's Golden Age, and the city blossomed under his leadership. Pericles wanted Athens to be a model for the world. He made it a centerpiece of art, philosophy, and democracy.

Pericles' goal was to make Athens a city that Greeks could be proud of. He hired hundreds of workers to construct public buildings in Athens. The most well known is the Parthenon. Based on the value of money today, it cost about $3 billion to build. Workers hauled 20,000 tons of marble from a nearby mountain and spent almost 15 years completing it.

◀ Pericles

> "Athens...is the school of Greece."
> —*Pericles*, as recorded by Thucydides

Pericles was a private person. He avoided being in public as much as possible. He spent most of his time alone, with family, or with close friends. He married and had three sons. In 429 B.C. Pericles died from the plague.

Then and Now

Consider what Thucydides wrote about Pericles' rule in Athens. Do research to find out how the U.S. Constitution ensures that our government is not dominated by one leader.

▲ The Parthenon sits at the top of the Acropolis.

Daily Life in Athens

Main Idea Athenian men and women had very different roles.

Reading Focus School may be difficult at times, but how would you feel if you could not go to school? Read on to learn about the limits placed on some Athenians.

In the 400s B.C., more people lived in Athens than in any other Greek city-state. Athens had about 285,000 residents in all. Some 150,000 were citizens, although only 43,000 of these were men with political rights. Foreigners in Athens numbered about 35,000. The population also included about 100,000 enslaved people.

Slavery was common in the ancient world. There was at least one enslaved person in most Athenian homes, and wealthy Athenian households often had many. Some worked as household servants—cooks, maids, or tutors. Others toiled in the fields, in industry, and in artisans' shops. Without their labor, Athens could not have supported its bustling economy.

Athenian Homes

Many wealthy Athenians had large homes made of mud bricks and tiled roofs. They had many small windows to let light and air in the house. *Where are religious influences seen in the house?*

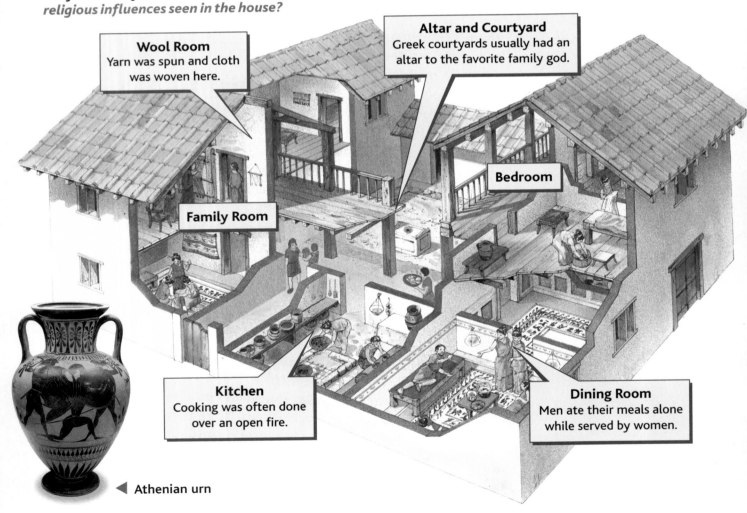

Wool Room
Yarn was spun and cloth was woven here.

Altar and Courtyard
Greek courtyards usually had an altar to the favorite family god.

Bedroom

Family Room

Kitchen
Cooking was often done over an open fire.

Dining Room
Men ate their meals alone while served by women.

◄ Athenian urn

What Drove the Athenian Economy?

Many Athenians depended on farming for a living. Herders raised sheep and goats for wool, milk, and cheese. Some farmers grew grains, vegetables, and fruit for local use. Others grew grapes and olives to make wine and olive oil to sell abroad.

Athens did not have enough farmland to grow crops for all its people. As a result, the city had to import grain from other places. During the 400s B.C., Athens became the trading center of the Greek world. Merchants and artisans grew wealthy by making and selling pottery, jewelry, leather goods, and other products.

Roles of Men and Women

Athenian men usually worked in the morning and then exercised or attended meetings of the assembly. In the evenings, upper-class men enjoyed all-male gatherings where they drank, dined, and discussed politics and philosophy.

For Athenian women, life revolved around home and family. Girls married early—at 14 or 15—and were expected to have children and take care of household duties. Poor women might also work with their husbands in the fields or sell goods in the agora. Respectable upper-class women, however, stayed at home. They supervised the household servants and worked wool into cloth—spinning, dyeing, and weaving it. They rarely went out, except to funerals or festivals. Even then, they could leave the house only if a male relative went with them.

Although Athenian women could not attend school, many learned to read and to play music. Still, even educated women were not considered the equals of men. They had no political rights and could not own property. Fathers took charge of unmarried daughters. Husbands looked after their wives. Sons or other male relatives looked after widows.

NATIONAL GEOGRAPHIC

The Way It Was

Focus on Everyday Life

Women's Duties In ancient Athens, a woman's place was in the home. Her two main responsibilities were caring for the household and raising children. The Greek writer Xenophon (ZEH•nuh•fuhn) recorded a man's explanation of women's duties.

"Thus your duty will be to remain indoors and send out those servants whose work is outside, and superintend those who are to work indoors . . . and take care that the sum laid by for a year be not spent in a month. And when wool is brought to you, you must see that cloaks are made for those that want them. You must see too that the dry corn is in good condition for making food."

—Xenophon, *Memorabilia and Oeconomicus*

The second floor of each home was the women's quarters. An Athenian woman lived there with her children. She was expected to keep her children well and happy. She encouraged them to learn sports and play with toys, and taught them how to interact with friends and family members. Although boys left home at age seven to attend school, girls stayed with their mothers, learning how to care for a house and children.

▲ Greek woman and servant

Connecting to the Past

1. Why do you think women and children lived on the second floor of the home?
2. Over what areas of life did an Athenian woman have authority?

A few women did move more freely in public life. **Aspasia** (as•PAY•zhuh) is perhaps the most famous example. Aspasia was not a native Athenian. This gave her special status. She was well-educated and taught public speaking to many Athenians. Her writings have not survived, but Plato, the famous Greek philosopher, said her work helped shape his ideas. Pericles often consulted Aspasia, as did many other Athenian leaders. In this way, she became influential in politics even though she was not allowed to vote or hold office.

✓ **Reading Check** **Describe** How did Athenian men and women spend their time?

The Peloponnesian War

Main Idea Sparta and Athens went to war for control of Greece.

Reading Focus Have you ever tried to get people to work together and been frustrated when they will not cooperate? Read to find out how the Greek city-states' refusal to cooperate nearly led to their destruction.

As the Athenian empire became rich and powerful, other city-states grew suspicious of its aims. Led by Sparta, they joined forces against Athens. Sparta and Athens had built two very different kinds of societies, and neither state understood or trusted the other. The two groups clashed several times over

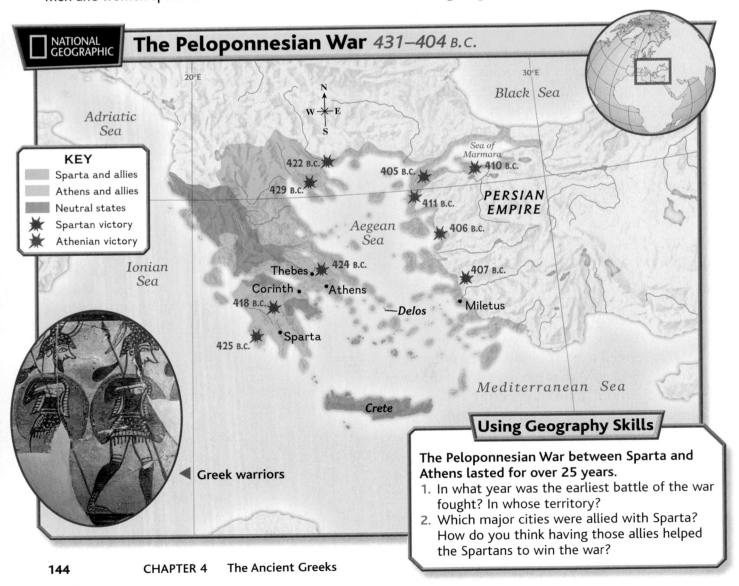

NATIONAL GEOGRAPHIC

The Peloponnesian War *431–404 B.C.*

KEY
- Sparta and allies
- Athens and allies
- Neutral states
- ✴ Spartan victory
- ✴ Athenian victory

Greek warriors

Using Geography Skills

The Peloponnesian War between Sparta and Athens lasted for over 25 years.
1. In what year was the earliest battle of the war fought? In whose territory?
2. Which major cities were allied with Sparta? How do you think having those allies helped the Spartans to win the war?

what Sparta and its allies saw as Athenian aggression. Finally, war broke out in 431 B.C. It would drag on until 404 B.C. and shatter any possibility of future cooperation among the Greeks. Historians call this conflict the Peloponnesian War because Sparta was located in the Peloponnesus.

Pericles' Funeral Oration

In the first winter of the war, the Athenians held a public funeral. Its purpose was to honor those who had died in battle. The relatives of the dead wept for their loved ones. The rest of the citizens joined in a procession.

As was the custom, a leading Athenian addressed the crowd. On this day, Pericles spoke. He talked about the greatness of Athens and reminded the people that they made their government strong.

In this famous speech, called the Funeral Oration, Pericles pointed out that Athenians were part of a community. As citizens, they agreed to obey the rules in their constitution—their framework of government. They accepted certain duties, such as paying taxes and defending the city. They also gained certain rights, such as the ability to vote and run for office.

Pericles' speech reminded Athenians of the power of democracy and gave them the courage to keep fighting. Its ideas are still important for people living in democratic nations today.

Why Was Athens Defeated?

At the beginning of the Peloponnesian War, both Sparta and Athens thought they knew how to win. The Spartans and their allies surrounded Athens. They hoped that the Athenians would send out an army to fight. However, Pericles knew that Spartan forces could beat the Athenians in open battles. Believing his people would be safe behind the city walls, he urged farmers and others on the outskirts to move inside the city. There

Primary Source — Pericles' Funeral Oration

Pericles was a dominant figure in Athenian politics between 461 B.C. and 429 B.C., a period historians call the Age of Pericles. In his Funeral Oration, given during the Peloponnesian War, Pericles described democracy, the importance of the individual, and citizenship.

▲ Pericles

"Our constitution is called a democracy because power is in the hands not of a minority but of the whole people. When it is a question of settling private disputes, everyone is equal before the law; when it is a question of putting one person before another in positions of public responsibility, what counts is not membership of a particular class, but the actual ability which the man possesses. No one . . . is kept [out of government] because of poverty. And, just as our political life is free and open, so is our day-to-day life in our relations with each other."

—Pericles, as recorded by Thucydides, *History of the Peloponnesian War*

DBQ Document-Based Question

When Pericles said "everyone is equal before the law," what did he mean?

Athenians stayed put and had the navy deliver supplies from their colonies and allies. Because Sparta did not have a navy, it could not attack the Athenian ships.

Athens escaped serious harm for some time. Then, in the second year of the war, a deadly disease spread through the overcrowded city. It killed more than a third of the people, including Pericles himself in 429 B.C. Despite these terrible losses, the

Athenians fought on. The standoff continued for another 25 years.

The historian Thucydides recorded what he saw:

> **❝ This, then, was the calamity which fell upon Athens, and the times were hard indeed, with men dying inside the city and the land outside being laid waste. ❞**
>
> —Thucydides,
> *History of the Peloponnesian War*

Finally, desperate to win, the Spartans made a deal with the Persian Empire. In exchange for enough money to build a navy, they gave the Persians some Greek territory in Asia Minor.

In 405 B.C. Sparta's new navy destroyed the Athenian fleet. The next year, after losing more battles on land, Athens surrendered. The Spartans and their allies then tore down the city walls and broke up the Athenian empire. The war was over at last.

The Peloponnesian War weakened all of the major Greek city-states, both the winners and the losers. Many people died in the fighting, and many farms were destroyed. Thousands of people were left without jobs. The war also made it impossible for the Greeks to unite and work together again.

After defeating Athens, Sparta tried to rule all of Greece. Within 30 years, however, the city-states rebelled, and a new war began. While they were fighting amongst themselves, the Greeks failed to notice that to their north, the kingdom of Macedonia was growing in power. This would eventually cost them their freedom.

✓ **Reading Check** **Cause and Effect** What effects did the Peloponnesian War have on Greece?

History Online

Study Central™ Need help with the material in this section? Visit jat.glencoe.com

Section 4 Review

Reading Summary

Review the Main Ideas

- Democracy and culture in Athens flourished under the leadership of Pericles.

- Athenian men worked as farmers, artisans, and merchants, while most women stayed secluded at home.

- Athens and Sparta fought each other in the Peloponnesian War. The fighting led to the defeat of Athens and the weakening of all the Greek states.

What Did You Learn?

1. What caused the Peloponnesian War?

2. According to Pericles, what duties did Athenian citizens have?

Critical Thinking

3. **Summarize** Use a chart like the one below to summarize what Athens was like in the Age of Pericles.

Government	
Economy	
Culture	
Wars	

4. **Analyze** What caused the lack of trust between Sparta and Athens?

5. **Interpreting Visuals** Examine the drawing of the Athenian home on page 142. What does it show about the role of women in Athens?

6. **Civics Link** How did the direct democracy of Athens differ from the democracy we have in the United States?

7. **Expository Writing** Describe the role of the Delian League in the creation of the Athenian empire.

Chapter 4 Reading Review

Section 1 The Early Greeks

Vocabulary
peninsula
colony
polis
agora

Focusing on the Main Ideas
- The geography of Greece influenced where people settled and what they did. *(page 117)*
- The Minoans earned their living by building ships and trading. *(page 118)*
- Mycenaeans built the first Greek kingdoms and spread their power across the Mediterranean region. *(page 119)*
- Colonies and trade spread Greek culture and spurred industry. *(page 121)*
- The idea of citizenship developed in Greek city-states. *(page 122)*

▲ Minoan calendar

Section 2 Sparta and Athens

Vocabulary
tyrant
oligarchy
democracy
helot

Focusing on the Main Ideas
- Tyrants were able to seize power from the nobles with the support of Greek farmers, merchants, and artisans. *(page 125)*
- The Spartans focused on military skills to control the people they conquered. *(page 126)*
- Unlike Spartans, Athenians were more interested in building a democracy than building a military force. *(page 128)*

Section 3 Persia Attacks the Greeks

Vocabulary
satrapies
satrap
Zoroastrianism

Focusing on the Main Ideas
- The Persian Empire united a wide area under a single government. *(page 132)*
- Both Sparta and Athens played roles in defeating the Persians. *(page 134)*

Section 4 The Age of Pericles

Vocabulary
direct democracy
representative democracy
philosopher

Focusing on the Main Ideas
- Under Pericles, Athens became very powerful and more democratic. *(page 139)*
- Athenian men and women had very different roles. *(page 142)*
- Sparta and Athens went to war for control of Greece. *(page 144)*

Review Vocabulary

Write the vocabulary word that completes each sentence. Write a sentence for each word not used.

   a. satrap   d. direct democracy

   b. agora   e. oligarchy

   c. democracy   f. peninsula

1. In a(n) ___, a few wealthy people hold power.
2. The Greek mainland is a(n) ___, a body of land with water on three sides.
3. In a(n) ___, people at mass meetings make decisions for the government.
4. A(n) ___ acted as tax collector, judge, chief of police, and army recruiter.

Review Main Ideas

Section 1 • The Early Greeks

5. How did the geography of Greece influence where people settled and how they made a living?
6. How did the Greek colonies help industry to grow?

Section 2 • Sparta and Athens

7. Why were tyrants able to seize control from Greek nobles?
8. Describe the differences between Athens and Sparta.

Section 3 • Persia Attacks the Greeks

9. What system did Darius use to unite his large empire under one government?
10. Why did Sparta and Athens unite during the Persian Wars?

Section 4 • The Age of Pericles

11. How was democracy expanded during the Age of Pericles?
12. What was the result of the Peloponnesian War?

Critical Thinking

13. **Cause and Effect** How did the geography of Greece help to encourage trade?
14. **Conclude** Did the people of ancient Athens have a full democracy? Explain.
15. **Explain** Do you think people would enjoy more freedom in an oligarchy or a tyranny? Explain.

Review Reading Skill — Making Connections

Use What You Know

16. Which of these experiences would help you to better understand the meaning of *democracy*?

  ___ a. running for class president

  ___ b. trading CDs with your friend

  ___ c. picking up litter in your neighborhood

  ___ d. checking out a book at a library

17. The lives of Athenian girls were very different than the lives of girls today. Write a paragraph that explains the differences. As examples, use your own experiences or the experiences of someone you know.

To review this skill, see pages 114–115.

Geography Skills

Study the map below and answer the following questions.

18. **Place** What sea lies along the west coast of Greece?
19. **Location** Where was Knossos?
20. **Movement** If you traveled from Athens to Troy, in what direction would you be going?

NATIONAL GEOGRAPHIC
Ancient Greece

Read to Write

21. **Paraphrasing** Select a quotation or primary source from one of the sections in this chapter. Reread it and then paraphrase what you have read. Remember that when you paraphrase, you restate in your own words all of the words in the passage, not just the main ideas.

22. **Descriptive Writing** Work in a small group to create a script for a play about an Athenian citizen who visits Sparta for the first time. Perform your play for the class.

23. **Using Your FOLDABLES** Use the information from your completed chapter opener foldables to create a brief study guide for the chapter. Your study guide should include at least five questions for each section. Questions should focus on the main ideas. Exchange your study guide with a partner and answer each of the questions.

Linking Past and Present

24. **Making Comparisons** Choose a person mentioned in Chapter 4. Write a description of someone in the news today who has similar ideas or has acted in similar ways. Give examples of their similarities.

Building Citizenship Skills

25. **Analyze** Democracy is not easy to achieve or maintain. Make a chart like the one below to identify things that challenged or threatened democracy in Athens.

Democratic Idea	Challenges

Primary Source Analyze

Study the following quote, then answer the questions that follow.

"Our constitution does not copy the laws of neighbouring states; we are rather a pattern to others than imitators ourselves. Its administration favours the many instead of the few; this is why it is called a democracy. . . . The freedom which we enjoy in our government extends also to our ordinary life. . . . Further, we provide plenty of means for the mind to refresh itself from business. We celebrate games and sacrifices all the year round."

—Pericles, as recorded by Thucydides, *The Peloponnesian War*

DBQ Document-Based Questions

26. According to Pericles, why is Athens considered a democracy?
27. What does Pericles mean when he says, "we provide plenty of means for the mind to refresh itself from business"?

Greek Civilization

The temple of Delphi was very important to ancient Greeks. Many people believed the priestess here could foretell the future. ▶

NATIONAL GEOGRAPHIC **When & Where?**

400 B.C.	300 B.C.	200 B.C.
399 B.C. Socrates sentenced to death	**330 B.C.** Alexander the Great conquers Persian Empire	**c. 287 B.C.** Mathematician and inventor Archimedes is born

Chapter Preview

Many Greeks studied science, philosophy, mathematics, and the arts. When Alexander the Great conquered the Persian Empire, he spread Greek culture and ideas throughout southwest Asia and the Mediterranean world.

History Online
Chapter Overview Visit jat.glencoe.com for a preview of Chapter 5.

 View the Chapter 5 video in the *World History: Journey Across Time* Video Program.

Section 1 The Culture of Ancient Greece

The Greeks made great strides in the arts. Greek poetry, art, and drama are still part of our world today.

Section 2 Greek Philosophy and History

The Greeks' love of wisdom led to the study of history, politics, biology, and logic.

Section 3 Alexander the Great

Alexander the Great was only 25 years old when he conquered the Persian Empire. As a result of his conquests, Greek art, ideas, language, and architecture spread throughout southwest Asia and North Africa.

Section 4 The Spread of Greek Culture

Greek cities became centers of learning and culture. Greek scientists developed advanced ideas about astronomy and mathematics.

FOLDABLES™ Study Organizer

Organizing Information *Make the following foldable to help you organize information about Greek culture and philosophy.*

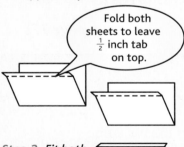

Step 1 *Fold two sheets of paper in half from top to bottom.*

Fold both sheets to leave $\frac{1}{2}$ inch tab on top.

Step 3 *Fit both sheets of paper together to make a cube as shown.*

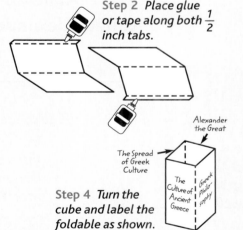

Step 2 *Place glue or tape along both $\frac{1}{2}$ inch tabs.*

Step 4 *Turn the cube and label the foldable as shown.*

Alexander the Great
The Spread of Greek Culture
The Culture of Ancient Greece
Greek Philosophy

Reading and Writing *As you read the chapter, list the developments that occurred in ancient Greece. Write the developments under the correct foldable category.*

Chapter 5

Reading Social Studies

Reading Skill

Context

1 Learn It!

Using Context Clues

When you have trouble understanding the words in a passage, it is very difficult to get the author's message. You may know part of a word's definition or even how to pronounce it, but you still may not understand its full meaning.

Look at the word *inspiration* in the following paragraph. Use the highlighted words to help you understand its meaning.

The key to Alexander's courage may have been his childhood education. Alexander kept a copy of the *Iliad* under his pillow. Most likely his inspiration was Homer's warrior-hero Achilles. In the end, Alexander's reputation outstripped even Achilles', and today he is called Alexander the Great.

—from page 177

Look at phrases around the word to find clues to its meaning.

In this paragraph, the word *inspiration* means something that influences or has an effect on someone.

Reading Tip

When you don't understand a word or a concept, reread the sentence or paragraph. Find other words that will give you clues to its meaning.

2 Practice It!

What Does It Mean?

Read the following paragraph about Aesop. Write down all the words or phrases that help you fully understand the meaning of the word *fable*.

About 550 B.C., a Greek slave named Aesop (EE•SAHP) made up his now famous fables. A fable (FAY•buhl) is a short tale that teaches a lesson. In most of Aesop's fables, animals talk and act like people. These often funny stories point out human flaws as well as strengths. Each fable ends with a message, or moral.

—*from page 158*

—*from page 158*

Read to Write

Turn to any page in this chapter. Close your eyes and point to a word. It can be any word, even "a" or "the." Now write a paragraph explaining how the rest of the words in the sentence or paragraph where that word appears helped you to determine its meaning.

Aesop ▶

3 Apply It!

As you read the chapter, create five word webs. Put an important word or idea in a center circle. Surround it with circles containing words from the text that help explain it.

153

The Culture of Ancient Greece

Get Ready to Read!

What's the Connection?

You have read that under Pericles, Athens became a center of beauty and culture. During this Golden Age, Greek thinkers, writers, and artists contributed many new ideas to the world.

Focusing on the Main Ideas

- The Greeks believed that gods and goddesses controlled nature and shaped their lives. *(page 155)*

- Greek poetry and fables taught Greek values. *(page 157)*

- Greek drama still shapes entertainment today. *(page 160)*

- Greek art and architecture expressed Greek ideas of beauty and harmony. *(page 162)*

Locating Places

Mount Olympus (uh•LIHM•puhs)
Delphi (DEHL•FY)

Meeting People

Homer (HOH•muhr)
Aesop (EE•SAHP)
Sophocles (SAH•fuh•KLEEZ)
Euripides (yu•RIH•puh•DEEZ)

Building Your Vocabulary

myth (MIHTH)
oracle (AWR•uh•kuhl)
epic (EH•pihk)
fable (FAY•buhl)
drama (DRAH•muh)
tragedy (TRA•juh•dee)
comedy (KAH•muh•dee)

Reading Strategy

Compare and Contrast Create a Venn diagram showing similarities and differences between an epic and a fable.

Epic — Both — Fable

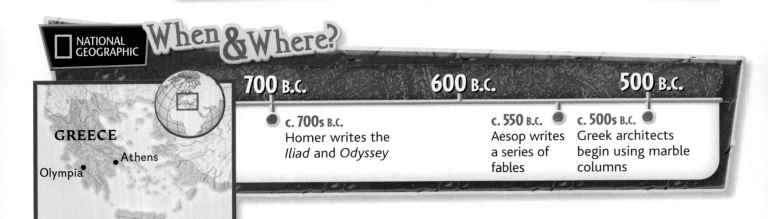

When & Where?

NATIONAL GEOGRAPHIC

GREECE
Olympia • Athens

700 B.C.   **600** B.C.   **500** B.C.

c. 700s B.C.
Homer writes the *Iliad* and *Odyssey*

c. 550 B.C.
Aesop writes a series of fables

c. 500s B.C.
Greek architects begin using marble columns

Greek Mythology

Main Idea The Greeks believed that gods and goddesses controlled nature and shaped their lives.

Reading Focus Have you ever wondered why crops grow or why the sun rises and sets? To get the answer, you would read a science book. Read to learn how the Greeks used religion to explain nature.

Myths (MIHTHS) are traditional stories about gods and heroes. Greek mythology expressed the Greek people's religious beliefs. The Greeks believed in many gods and goddesses. They believed gods and goddesses affected people's lives and shaped events. That is why the most impressive buildings in Greek cities were religious temples.

Greek Gods and Goddesses The Greeks believed that the gods and goddesses controlled nature. According to Greek myth, the god Zeus ruled the sky and threw lightning bolts, the goddess Demeter made the crops grow, and the god Poseidon caused earthquakes.

The 12 most important gods and goddesses lived on **Mount Olympus** (uh•LIHM•puhs), the highest mountain in Greece. Among the 12 were Zeus, who was the chief god; Athena, the goddess of wisdom and crafts; Apollo, the god of the sun and poetry; Ares, the god of war; Aphrodite, the goddess of love; and Poseidon, the god of the seas and earthquakes.

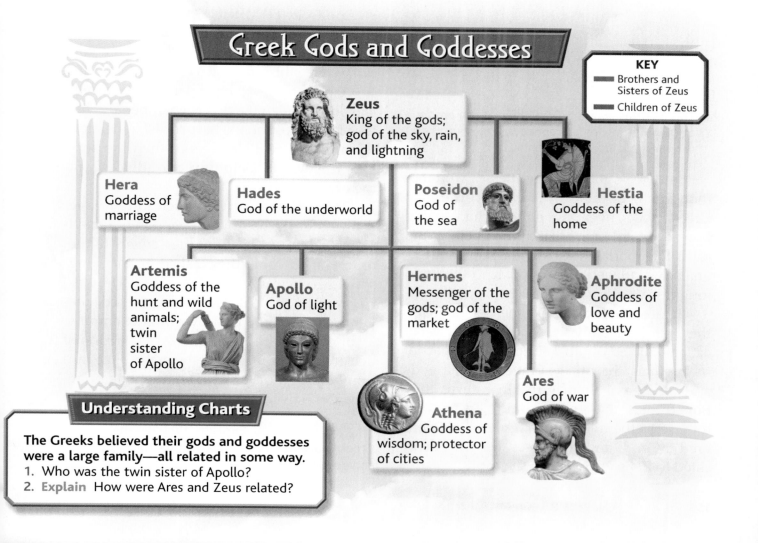

Greek Gods and Goddesses

KEY
▬ Brothers and Sisters of Zeus
▬ Children of Zeus

Zeus King of the gods; god of the sky, rain, and lightning

Hera Goddess of marriage

Hades God of the underworld

Poseidon God of the sea

Hestia Goddess of the home

Artemis Goddess of the hunt and wild animals; twin sister of Apollo

Apollo God of light

Hermes Messenger of the gods; god of the market

Aphrodite Goddess of love and beauty

Athena Goddess of wisdom; protector of cities

Ares God of war

Understanding Charts

The Greeks believed their gods and goddesses were a large family—all related in some way.
1. Who was the twin sister of Apollo?
2. **Explain** How were Ares and Zeus related?

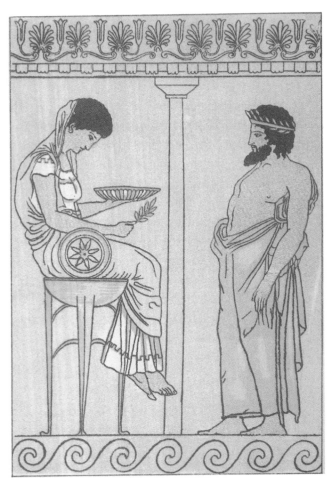

▲ This painting shows a Greek man at the oracle at Delphi receiving a prophecy. *Why were these prophecies often confusing?*

But Greek gods and goddesses were not thought to be all-powerful. According to Greek myths, even though gods had special powers, they looked like human beings and acted like them. They married, had children, quarreled, played tricks on each other, and fought wars.

Because Greeks sought their gods' favor, they followed many rituals. A ritual is a set of actions carried out in a fixed way. As part of their rituals, the Greeks prayed to their gods and also gave them gifts. In return, they hoped that the gods would grant good fortune to them. Many Greek festivals honored the gods and goddesses. Festivals dedicated to Zeus were held at Olympia.

The Greeks also believed in an afterlife. When people died, the Greeks believed their spirits went to a gloomy world beneath the earth ruled by a god named Hades.

What Was a Greek Oracle? The Greeks believed that each person had a fate or destiny. They believed that certain events were going to happen no matter what they did. They also believed in prophecy. A prophecy is a prediction about the future. The Greeks believed that the gods gave prophecies to people to warn them about the future in time to change it.

To find out about the future, many Greeks visited an **oracle** (AWR•uh•kuhl). This was a sacred shrine where a priest or priestess spoke for a god or goddess. The most famous was the oracle at the Temple of Apollo at **Delphi** (DEHL•FY). The oracle chamber was deep inside the temple. The room had an opening in the floor where volcanic smoke hissed from a crack in the earth.

A priestess sat on a tripod—a three-legged stool—in the oracle chamber and listened to questions. The priests translated her answers. State leaders or their messengers traveled to Delphi to ask advice from the oracle of Apollo.

The priestess in the oracle often gave answers in riddles. When one king, named Croesus (KREE•suhs), sent messengers to the oracle at Delphi, they asked if the king should go to war with the Persians. The oracle replied that if Croesus attacked the Persians, he would destroy a mighty empire. Overjoyed to hear these words, Croesus declared war on the Persians. The Persian army crushed his army. The mighty empire King Croesus had destroyed was his own!

✔ **Reading Check** **Explain** Why did the Greeks have rituals and festivals for their gods and goddesses?

Greek Poetry and Fables

Main Idea Greek poetry and fables taught Greek values.

Reading Focus Do you have favorite stories? Are the characters in the stories brave and clever? Read about the characters of the best-loved stories in early Greece.

Greek poems and stories are the oldest in the Western world. For hundreds of years, Europeans and Americans have used these early works as models for their own poems and stories. Shakespeare, for example, borrowed many Greek plots and settings.

The earliest Greek stories were **epics** (EH•pihks). These long poems told about heroic deeds. The first great epics of early Greece were the *Iliad* and the *Odyssey*. The poet **Homer** (HOH•muhr) wrote these epics during the 700s B.C. He based them on stories of a war between Greece and the city of Troy, which once existed in what is today northwestern Turkey.

In the *Iliad*, a prince of Troy kidnaps the wife of the king of Sparta. The kidnapping outrages the Greeks. The king of Mycenae and the brother of the king of Sparta lead the Greeks in an attack on Troy.

The battle for Troy drags on for 10 years. Finally, the Greeks come up with a plan to take the city. They build a huge, hollow, wooden horse. The best Mycenaean warriors hide inside the horse.

The Trojan Horse

After building the Trojan horse, the Greeks returned to their ships and pretended to retreat. Despite warnings, the Trojans brought the horse within their city as a war trophy. The Greeks inside the horse opened the city gates for their fellow soldiers and captured the city. *What epic included the story of the Trojan horse?*

▲ Clay carving of the Trojan horse

The Greek soldiers hid in the belly of the horse.

Troops left the horse through a trapdoor.

The wooden horse was placed on a platform with wheels.

The Trojans, thinking the horse was a gift from the Greeks, celebrate and roll the giant horse into the city. That night, the Greek warriors quietly climb from the horse and capture the city.

The *Odyssey* tells the story of Odysseus, another Greek hero. It describes his journey home from the Trojan War. Odysseus faces storms, witches, and giants before returning to his wife. Because it took Odysseus 10 years to get home, we use the word *odyssey* today to mean a long journey with many adventures.

Greeks believed the *Iliad* and the *Odyssey* were more than stories. They looked on the epics as real history. These poems gave the Greeks an ideal past with a cast of heroes. Generations of Greeks read Homer's works. One Athenian wrote, "My father was anxious to see me develop into a good man . . . [so] he compelled me to memorize all of Homer."

Homer's stories taught courage and honor. They also taught that it was important to be loyal to your friends and to value the relationship between husband and wife. The stories showed heroes striving to be the best they could be. Heroes fought to protect their own honor and their family's honor. Homer's heroes became role models for Greek boys.

Who Was Aesop?
About 550 B.C., a Greek slave named **Aesop** (EE•SAHP) made up his now famous fables. A **fable** (FAY•buhl) is a short tale that teaches a lesson. In most of Aesop's fables, animals talk and act like people. These often funny stories point out human flaws as well as strengths. Each fable ends with a message, or moral.

One of the best-known fables is "The Tortoise and the Hare." In this fable, a tortoise and a hare decide to race. More than

Aesop

According to legend, Aesop was freed from slavery and became an adviser to Greek rulers. *What is a fable?*

halfway into the race, the hare is way ahead. He stops to rest and falls asleep. Meanwhile, the tortoise keeps going at a slow but steady pace and finally wins the race.

The moral of the story is "slow and steady wins the race." Some of the phrases we hear today came from Aesop's fables. "Sour grapes," "a wolf in sheep's clothing," and "appearances often are deceiving" are examples.

For about 200 years, Aesop's fables were a part of Greece's oral tradition. This means they were passed from person to person by word of mouth long before they were ever written down. Since then, countless writers have retold the stories in many different languages.

✓ **Reading Check** **Describe** What are the characteristics of a fable?

Biography

HOMER
c. 750 B.C.

Homer ▶

Homer's epic poems—the *Iliad* and the *Odyssey*—are famous, but until the 1900s, historians believed that Homer never existed. Historians now know Homer was a real person, but they still debate whether he wrote his poems alone or with the help of other poets.

Many historians have speculated, or made educated guesses, about Homer's personal life. Some say that Homer came from Ionia and seven cities claim to be his birthplace. Some believe that he was blind. Others believe that he wandered from town to town.

Legends tell of Homer's strong influence on his readers. For example, as a young child, Alexander the Great is said to have slept with a copy of the *Iliad* under his pillow.

Homer used the term *aoidos* for a poet. This word means "singer," which tells us that the poetry created during Homer's time was memorized and recited, not written down. Usually, short, simple poems that were easy to remember were told to an audience as entertainment.

Homer created a different style of poetry that influenced all Western literature that followed. His epics are long and involve complex characters, dramatic action, and interesting events. Because each section of the *Iliad* and the *Odyssey* has these characteristics, most historians today think that only one poet could have created both epics. Whoever Homer was, his two epics have influenced readers for more than 3,000 years.

> **"I hate as I hate [Hades'] own gate that man who hides one thought within him while he speaks another."**
> —Homer, the *Iliad*

Then and Now

Review the characteristics of an epic. Then do research to identify a modern epic.

Greek Drama

Main Idea **Greek drama still shapes entertainment today.**

Reading Focus Think about your favorite movie. How would you describe it? Is it a tragedy? Is it a comedy? Read to find out how Greek plays still influence our entertainment.

What is **drama** (DRAH•muh)? Drama is a story told by actors who pretend to be characters in the story. In a drama, actors speak, show emotion, and imitate the actions of the characters they represent.

Today's movies, plays, and television shows are all examples of drama.

Tragedies and Comedies The Greeks performed plays in outdoor theaters as part of their religious festivals. They developed two kinds of dramas—comedies and tragedies.

In a **tragedy** (TRA•juh•dee), a person struggles to overcome difficulties but fails. As a result, the story has an unhappy ending. Early Greek tragedies presented people in a struggle against their fate. Later Greek tragedies showed how a person's character flaws caused him or her to fail.

Linking Past & Present

The Theater

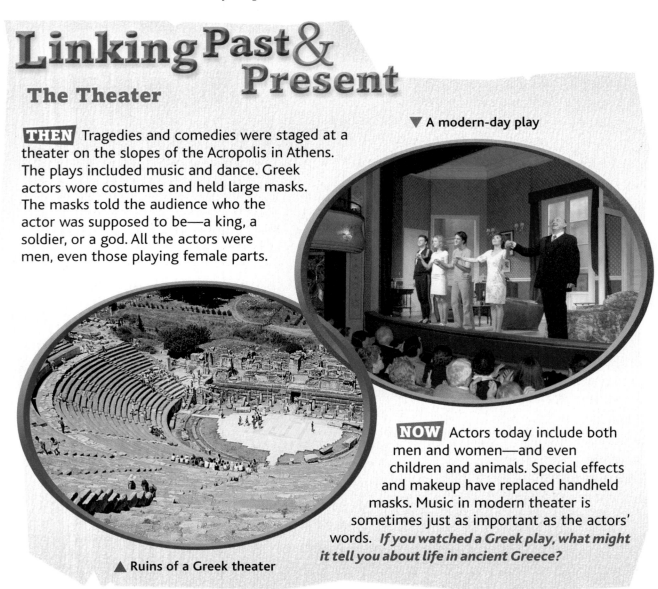

THEN Tragedies and comedies were staged at a theater on the slopes of the Acropolis in Athens. The plays included music and dance. Greek actors wore costumes and held large masks. The masks told the audience who the actor was supposed to be—a king, a soldier, or a god. All the actors were men, even those playing female parts.

▼ A modern-day play

NOW Actors today include both men and women—and even children and animals. Special effects and makeup have replaced handheld masks. Music in modern theater is sometimes just as important as the actors' words. *If you watched a Greek play, what might it tell you about life in ancient Greece?*

▲ Ruins of a Greek theater

In a **comedy** (KAH•muh•dee), the story ends happily. Today we use the word *comedy* to mean a story filled with humor. The word actually means any drama that has a happy ending.

Greek stories dealt with big questions, such as:

- What is the nature of good and evil?
- What rights should people have?
- What role do gods play in our lives?

The three best-known writers of Greek tragedies were Aeschylus (EHS•kuh•luhs), **Sophocles** (SAH•fuh•KLEEZ), and **Euripides** (yu•RIH•puh•DEEZ). The best-known writer of Greek comedies was Aristophanes (ar•uh•STAH•fuh•NEEZ).

Early Greek tragedies had only one actor who gave speeches and a chorus that sang songs describing the events. Aeschylus was the first to introduce the idea of having two actors. This let the writer tell a story involving conflict between the two people. Aeschylus also introduced costumes, props, and stage decorations—all ideas we still use today.

One of Aeschylus's best-known plays is a group of three plays called the *Oresteia* (ohr•eh•STY•uh). Aeschylus wrote the plays in 458 B.C. They describe what happens when the king of Mycenae returns home from the Trojan War. The *Oresteia* teaches that evil acts cause more evil acts and suffering. In the end, however, reason triumphs over evil. The moral of these plays is that people should not seek revenge.

Sophocles, a general and a writer of plays, developed drama even further. He used three actors in his stories instead of one or two. He also placed painted scenes behind the stage as a backdrop to the action. Two of Sophocles' most famous plays are *Oedipus Rex* (EH•duh•puhs REHKS) and *Antigone* (an•TIH•guh•nee) In *Antigone*, Sophocles

▲ This artwork shows actors preparing for a play. *When and where were Greek plays performed?*

◀ Comedy and tragedy masks

asks the question "Is it better to follow orders or to do what is right?"

Euripides, a later playwright, tried to take Greek drama beyond heroes and gods. His characters were more down-to-earth. Euripides' plots show a great interest in real-life situations. He questioned traditional thinking, especially about war. He showed war as cruel and women and children as its victims.

The works of Aristophanes are good examples of comedies. They make fun of leading politicians and scholars. They encourage the audience to think as well as to laugh. Many of Aristophanes' plays included jokes, just like popular television comedies do today.

Reading Check **Summarize** What two types of drama did the Greeks create?

Greek Art and Architecture

Main Idea Greek art and architecture expressed Greek ideas of beauty and harmony.

Reading Focus Do you consider any building in your neighborhood a work of art? Read on to find out about buildings that people have admired as art for centuries.

Artists in ancient Greece believed in certain ideas and tried to show those ideas in their work. These ideas have never gone out of style. Greek artists wanted people to see reason, moderation, balance, and harmony in their work. They hoped their art would inspire people to base their lives on these same ideas.

We know that the Greeks painted murals, but none of them have survived. However, we can still see examples of Greek painting on Greek pottery. The pictures on most Greek pottery are either red on a black background or black on a red background. Large vases often had scenes from Greek myths. Small drinking cups showed scenes from everyday life.

The Parthenon

Standing at almost 230 feet long and 100 feet wide, the Parthenon was the glory of ancient Athens. It was built between 447 and 432 B.C. *What was the purpose of the Parthenon?*

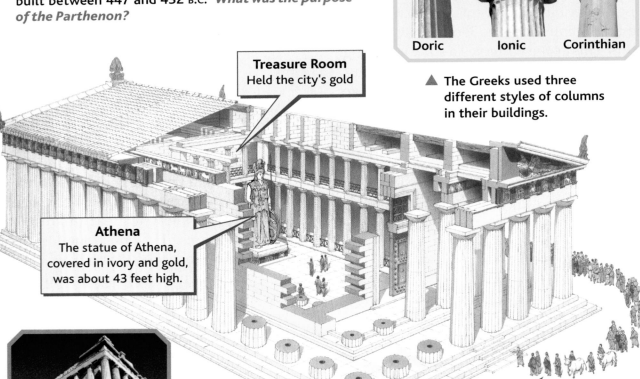

Doric   Ionic   Corinthian

▲ The Greeks used three different styles of columns in their buildings.

Treasure Room
Held the city's gold

Athena
The statue of Athena, covered in ivory and gold, was about 43 feet high.

Festival
Athenians came to honor Athena every four years.

▲ Today the Parthenon still rises above Athens.

In addition to making pottery, the Greeks were skilled architects. Architecture is the art of designing and building structures. In Greece, the most important architecture was the temple dedicated to a god or goddess. The best-known example is the Parthenon. Temples, such as the Parthenon, had a walled room in their centers. Statues of gods and goddesses and the gifts offered to them were kept in these central rooms.

Large columns supported many Greek buildings. The first Greek columns were carved from wood. Then, in 500 B.C., the Greeks began to use marble. Marble columns were built in sections. Large blocks of marble were chiseled from stone quarries and brought by oxen-drawn wagon to the building site. The sections were stacked on top of each other. To keep them from toppling, the column's sections were joined with wooden pegs. Today, marble columns are common features of churches and government buildings. Some of the best-known buildings in our nation's capital, such as the White House and the Capitol, have columns similar to Greek columns.

Many Greek temples were decorated with sculpture. Greek sculpture, like Greek architecture, was used to express Greek ideas. The favorite subject of Greek artists was the human body. Greek sculptors did not copy their subjects exactly, flaws and all. Instead, they tried to show their ideal version of perfection and beauty.

✓ **Reading Check** **Identify** What was the most important type of building in ancient Greece?

History Online

Study Central™ Need help with the material in this section? Visit jat.glencoe.com

Section ① Review

Reading Summary

Review the (Main Ideas)

- The Greeks believed gods and goddesses influenced their lives. They believed oracles spoke for the gods and goddesses.

- The Greeks wrote long poems, called epics, and short tales, called fables, to pass on Greek values.

- The Greeks created the ideas of tragedy and comedy that are still used in drama today.

- Greek art forms, such as painting, architecture, and sculpture, expressed Greek ideas of beauty, harmony, and moderation.

What Did You Learn?

1. How and why did the Greeks honor their gods?

2. What values did the epic poems of Homer teach Greeks?

Critical Thinking

3. **Contrast** How do Greek tragedies and comedies differ?

4. **Summarizing Information** Draw a table to describe the characteristics of Greek architecture and pottery.

Greek Architecture	
Greek Pottery	

5. **Evaluate** Do you think the themes of Euripides' plays would be popular today?

6. **Make Generalizations** Why did Greek artists include the ideas of reason, moderation, balance, and harmony in their works?

7. **Expository Writing** Greek literature tells us what the Greeks thought was important. Choose a modern book, movie, or television show. Write a paragraph to explain what it would tell others about our society.

8. **Reading** Context Clues Explain how the words in the following sentence would help you find the meaning of the word *moral*.
"The moral of the story is 'slow and steady wins the race.'"

ICARUS AND DAEDALUS

Retold by Josephine Preston Peabody

Before You Read

The Scene: This story takes place on the Greek island of Crete in the legendary time when both humans and gods lived in ancient Greece.

The Characters: Daedalus is the master architect for King Minos of Crete. Icarus is the son of Daedalus.

The Plot: King Minos once liked and trusted his servant, the architect Daedalus. The king's favor, though, soon runs out and he locks Daedalus and his son, Icarus, in a high tower. Daedalus secretly plans to escape.

Vocabulary Preview

mortal: human

veer: to shift or change direction

waver: to become unsteady

rash: done without thought or preparation

reel: to turn or seem to turn around and around

quench: to satisfy or put an end to a need or desire

vainly: without success

Have you ever known someone who ignored warnings and did something dangerous? This is the story of a young boy who does not listen to his father and suffers the consequences.

As You Read

Keep in mind that a myth is a special kind of story, usually involving gods or goddesses. Greek myths, like this one, were told and retold over many hundreds of years. Try to figure out why the Greeks told this story. What lesson does it teach?

Among all those mortals who grew so wise that they learned the secrets of the gods, none was more cunning than Daedalus.[1]

He once built, for King Minos of Crete, a wonderful Labyrinth of winding ways so cunningly tangled up and twisted around that, once inside, you could never find your way out again without a magic clue. But the king's favor veered with the wind, and one day he had his master architect imprisoned in a tower. Daedalus managed to escape from his cell; but it seemed impossible to leave the island, since every ship that came or went was well guarded by order of the king.

At length, watching the sea-gulls in the air—the only creatures that were sure of liberty,—he thought of a plan for himself and his young son Icarus,[2] who was captive with him.

Little by little, he gathered a store of feathers great and small. He fastened these together with thread, moulded them in with wax, and so fashioned two great wings like those of a bird. When they were done, Daedalus fitted them to his own shoulders, and after one or two efforts, he found that by waving his arms he could winnow the air and cleave[3] it, as a swimmer does the sea. He held himself aloft, wavered this way and that with the wind, and at last, like a great fledgling,[4] he learned to fly.

---

[1]**Daedalus** (DEH • duhl • uhs): architect for King Minos
[2]**Icarus** (IH • kuh • ruhs): son of Daedalus
[3]**winnow . . . and cleave:** here, both mean "to separate or divide"
[4]**fledgling:** a young bird without feathers that cannot yet fly

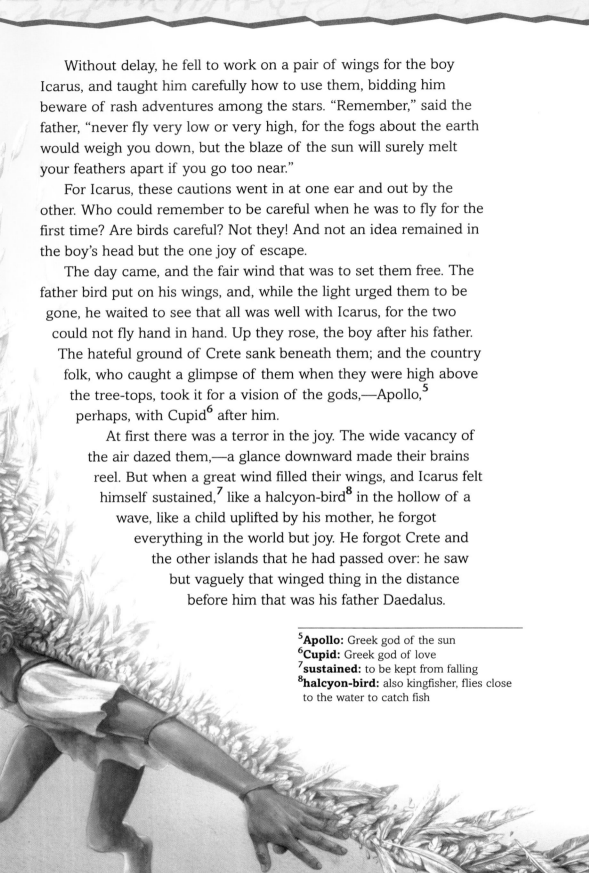

Without delay, he fell to work on a pair of wings for the boy Icarus, and taught him carefully how to use them, bidding him beware of rash adventures among the stars. "Remember," said the father, "never fly very low or very high, for the fogs about the earth would weigh you down, but the blaze of the sun will surely melt your feathers apart if you go too near."

For Icarus, these cautions went in at one ear and out by the other. Who could remember to be careful when he was to fly for the first time? Are birds careful? Not they! And not an idea remained in the boy's head but the one joy of escape.

The day came, and the fair wind that was to set them free. The father bird put on his wings, and, while the light urged them to be gone, he waited to see that all was well with Icarus, for the two could not fly hand in hand. Up they rose, the boy after his father. The hateful ground of Crete sank beneath them; and the country folk, who caught a glimpse of them when they were high above the tree-tops, took it for a vision of the gods,—Apollo,[5] perhaps, with Cupid[6] after him.

At first there was a terror in the joy. The wide vacancy of the air dazed them,—a glance downward made their brains reel. But when a great wind filled their wings, and Icarus felt himself sustained,[7] like a halcyon-bird[8] in the hollow of a wave, like a child uplifted by his mother, he forgot everything in the world but joy. He forgot Crete and the other islands that he had passed over: he saw but vaguely that winged thing in the distance before him that was his father Daedalus.

[5]**Apollo:** Greek god of the sun
[6]**Cupid:** Greek god of love
[7]**sustained:** to be kept from falling
[8]**halcyon-bird:** also kingfisher, flies close to the water to catch fish

He longed for one draught[9] of flight to quench the thirst of his captivity: he stretched out his arms to the sky and made toward the highest heavens.

Alas for him! Warmer and warmer grew the air. Those arms, that had seemed to uphold him, relaxed. His wings wavered, drooped. He fluttered his young hands vainly,—he was falling,—and in that terror he remembered. The heat of the sun had melted the wax from his wings; the feathers were falling, one by one, like snowflakes; and there was none to help.

He fell like a leaf tossed down the wind, down, down, with one cry that overtook Daedalus far away. When he returned, and sought high and low for the poor boy, he saw nothing but the bird-like feathers afloat on the water, and he knew that Icarus was drowned.

The nearest island he named Icaria, in memory of the child; but he, in heavy grief, went to the temple of Apollo in Sicily, and there hung up his wings as an offering. Never again did he attempt to fly.

9**draught:** here, means "a taste"

Responding to the Reading

1. What does King Minos do to keep Daedalus and Icarus from escaping from Crete?

2. How does the setting of the story influence the plot? Support your ideas with details from the story.

3. **Drawing Conclusions** Do you think Daedalus is a concerned father? Why or why not? Support your opinion with examples.

4. **Evaluating Information** Why does Icarus disobey his father's words of caution?

5. **Reading Read to Write** Imagine you are Icarus. Would you listen to your father's advice? Write one or two paragraphs explaining what you would have done and why.

Greek Philosophy and History

Get Ready to Read!

What's the Connection?
Section 1 discussed early Greek artists and writers. Many of them made the years between 500 and 350 B.C. the Golden Age for Greece. Greek thinkers and historians also produced works that shape people's views of the world today.

Focusing on the Main Ideas
- Greek philosophers developed ideas that are still used today. *(page 169)*
- Greeks wrote the first real histories in Western civilization. *(page 173)*

Meeting People
Pythagoras (puh•THA•guh•ruhs)
Socrates (SAH•kruh•TEEZ)
Plato (PLAY•TOH)
Aristotle (AR•uh•STAH•tuhl)
Herodotus (hih•RAH•duh•tuhs)
Thucydides (thoo•SIH•duh•DEEZ)

Building Your Vocabulary
philosophy (fuh•LAH•suh•fee)
philosopher (fuh•LAH•suh•fuhr)
Sophist (SAH•fihst)
Socratic method (suh•KRA•tihk)

Reading Strategy
Categorizing Information Use diagrams like the one below to show the basic philosophies of Socrates, Plato, and Aristotle.

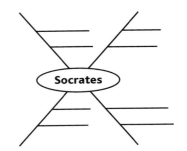

Socrates

NATIONAL GEOGRAPHIC When & Who?

500 B.C.   400 B.C.   300 B.C.

435 B.C. Herodotus writes history of Persian Wars

399 B.C. Socrates sentenced to death

335 B.C. Aristotle opens the Lyceum in Athens

Greek Philosophers

Main Idea Greek philosophers developed ideas that are still used today.

Reading Focus Who are you? Why are you here? Read to learn how the ancient Greeks tried to answer similar "big" questions.

The word **philosophy** (fuh•LAH•suh•fee) comes from the Greek word for "love of wisdom." Greek philosophy led to the study of history, political science, science, and mathematics. Greek thinkers who believed the human mind could understand everything were called **philosophers** (fuh•LAH•suh•fuhrs).

Many philosophers were teachers. One Greek philosopher, **Pythagoras** (puh•THA•guh•ruhs), taught his pupils that the universe followed the same laws that governed music and numbers. He believed that all relationships in the world could be expressed in numbers. As a result, he developed many new ideas about mathematics. Most people know his name because of the Pythagorean theorem that is still used in geometry. It is a way to determine the length of the sides of a triangle.

Who Were the Sophists? The **Sophists** (SAH•fihsts) were professional teachers in ancient Greece. They traveled from city to

▲ This artwork shows Greek philosophers involved in a discussion. *Where does the word* philosophy *come from?*

Greek Philosophers

Thinker Or Group	Sophists	Socrates	Plato	Aristotle
Main Idea	Sophists like Libanius (above) thought that people should use knowledge to improve themselves. They believed that there is no absolute right or wrong.	He was a critic of the Sophists. Socrates believed that there was an absolute right and wrong.	He rejected the idea of democracy as a form of government. Plato believed that philosopher-kings should rule society.	Aristotle taught the idea of the "golden mean." He believed observation and comparison were necessary to gain knowledge.
Important Contribution	They developed the art of public speaking and debate.	He created the Socratic method of teaching.	He described his vision of the ideal government in his work the *Republic*.	He wrote over 200 books on philosophy and science. He divided all governments into three basic types.
Influence on Today	The importance of public speaking can be seen in political debates between candidates.	His methods influenced the way teachers interact with their students.	He introduced the idea that government should be fair and just.	His political ideas still shape political ideas today.

city and made a living by teaching others. They believed students should use their time to improve themselves. Many taught their students how to win an argument and make good political speeches.

Sophists did not believe that gods and goddesses influenced people. They also rejected the idea of absolute right or wrong. They believed that what was right for one person might be wrong for another.

The Ideas of Socrates One critic of the Sophists was **Socrates** (SAH•kruh•TEEZ). Socrates was an Athenian sculptor whose true love was philosophy. Socrates left no writings behind. What we know about him we have learned from the writings of his students.

Socrates believed that an absolute truth existed and that all real knowledge was within each person. He invented the **Socratic method** (suh•KRA•tihk) of teaching still used today. He asked pointed questions to force his pupils to use their reason and to see things for themselves.

Some Athenian leaders considered the Socratic method a threat to their power. At one time, Athens had a tradition of questioning leaders and speaking freely. However, their defeat in the Peloponnesian War changed the Athenians. They no longer trusted open debate. In 399 B.C. the leaders accused Socrates of teaching young Athenians to rebel against the state. A jury found Socrates guilty and sentenced him to death. Socrates could have fled the city, but he chose to remain. He argued that he had lived under the city's laws, so he had to obey them. He then drank poison to carry out the jury's sentence.

The Ideas of Plato One of Socrates' students was **Plato** (PLAY•toh). Unlike Socrates, we are able to learn a lot about Plato from his writings. One work Plato wrote is called the *Republic*. It explains his ideas about government. Based on life in Athens, Plato decided that democracy was not a good system of government. He did not think that rule by the people produced fair or sensible policies. To him, people could not live good lives unless they had a just and reasonable government.

In the *Republic*, Plato described his ideal government. He divided people into three basic groups. At the top were philosopher-kings, who ruled using logic and wisdom. Warriors made up the second group. They defended the state from attack.

The third group included the rest of the people. They were driven by desire, not by wisdom like the first group or courage like the second. These people produced the state's food, clothing, and shelter. Plato also believed that men and women should have the same education and an equal chance to have the same jobs.

Who Was Aristotle? Plato established a school in Athens known as the Academy. His best student was **Aristotle** (AR•uh•STAH•tuhl). Aristotle wrote more than 200 books on topics ranging from government to the planets and stars.

In 335 B.C. Aristotle opened his own school called the Lyceum. At the Lyceum, Aristotle taught his pupils the "golden mean." This idea holds that a person should do nothing in excess. For example, a person should not eat too little or too much but just enough to stay well.

Aristotle also helped to advance science. He urged people to use their senses to make observations, just as scientists today make observations. Aristotle was the first person to group observations according to their similarities and differences. Then he made generalizations based on the groups of facts.

Like Plato, Aristotle wrote about government. He studied and compared the governments of 158 different places to find the best form of government. In his book *Politics*, Aristotle divided the governments into three types:

- Government by one person, such as a monarch (king or queen) or a tyrant
- Government by a few people, which might be an aristocracy or an oligarchy
- Government by many people, as in a democracy

Aristotle noticed that governments run by a few people were usually run by the rich. He noticed that most democracies were run by the poor. He thought the best government was a mixture of the two.

Aristotle's ideas shaped the way Europeans and Americans thought about government. The founders of the United States Constitution tried to create a mixed government that balanced the different types Aristotle had identified.

✓ **Reading Check** **Contrast** How did Aristotle's idea of government differ from Plato's?

History Online

Web Activity Visit jat.glencoe.com and click on *Chapter 5—Student Web Activity* to learn more about ancient Greece.

Biography

PLATO AND ARISTOTLE
Plato c. 428–347 B.C.
Aristotle 384–322 B.C.

Plato was from a noble Greek family and had planned a career in politics. However, he was so horrified by the death of his teacher, Socrates, that he left politics and spent many years traveling and writing. When Plato returned to Athens in 387 B.C., he founded an academy, where he taught using Socrates' method of questioning. His academy drew bright young students from Athens and other Greek city-states. Plato looked for truth beyond the appearances of everyday objects and reflected this philosophy in his writing and teaching. He believed the human soul was the connection between the appearance of things and ideas.

Plato ▲

Plato and Aristotle—two of the greatest ancient Greek philosophers—met as teacher and student at Plato's Academy in Athens. Aristotle left his home in Stagira and arrived on the Academy's doorstep when he was eighteen years old. He remained at Plato's Academy for 20 years, until the death of his teacher. Unlike Plato, Aristotle did not come from a noble family. His father was the court physician to the king of Macedonia. At an early age, Aristotle's father introduced him to the topics of medicine and biology, and these became his main interests of study. Aristotle sought truth through a systematic, scientific approach. He liked to jot down notes and details about different topics—from weather to human behavior—and arrange them in categories. He did not trust the senses' ability to understand the universe.

After Plato's death, Aristotle traveled for about 12 years. He also tutored the future Alexander the Great. Later in his life, he returned to Athens and opened his own school, the Lyceum. He made his school the center for research in every area of knowledge known to the Greeks.

▲ **Aristotle**

Then and Now

Aristotle spent 20 years at Plato's Academy. What present-day careers or subjects of study require lifelong learning?

Greek Historians

Main Idea Greeks wrote the first real histories in Western civilization.

Reading Focus Why is history important? Read on to find out what Greek historians thought was important.

In most places in the ancient world, people did not write history. Legends and myths explained their past. Some civilizations kept long lists of rulers and the dates they were in power, but no one tried to explain the past by studying events. Then, in 435 B.C., a Greek named **Herodotus** (hih•RAH•duh•tuhs) wrote the history of the Persian Wars.

In his book, Herodotus tried to separate fact from legend. He asked questions, recorded answers, and checked the truthfulness of his sources. Although his history includes some errors and uses gods and goddesses to explain some events, Western historians consider him the "father of history."

Many historians consider **Thucydides** (thoo•SIH•duh•DEEZ) the greatest historian of the ancient world. Thucydides fought in the Peloponnesian War. After he lost a battle, he was sent into exile. There he wrote his *History of the Peloponnesian War.*

Unlike Herodotus, Thucydides saw war and politics as the activities of human beings, not gods. He also stressed the importance of having accurate facts:

> **Either I was present myself at the events which I have described or else I heard of them from eyewitnesses whose reports I have checked with as much thoroughness as possible.**
>
> —Thucydides, *History of the Peloponnesian War*

Reading Check **Identify** How did Thucydides view war and politics?

Study Central™ Need help with the material in this section? Visit jat.glencoe.com

What Did You Learn?

1. Who were the Sophists and what were their beliefs?

2. Before Herodotus, how did Greeks explain the past?

Critical Thinking

3. **Organizing Information** Draw a diagram like the one below. Use the diagram to organize Plato's ideas about an ideal government.

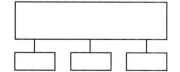

4. **Science Link** How are Aristotle's teachings related to the scientific method used by scientists today?

5. **Contrast** What is different about the works of Herodotus and Thucydides?

6. **Summarize** Describe Aristotle's contributions to government.

7. **Persuasive Writing** Do you agree with Plato's vision of the ideal state in the *Republic?* Write an editorial expressing your viewpoint.

Reading Summary

Review the **Main Ideas**

- The ideas of Greek philosophers, including Socrates, Plato, and Aristotle, still affect modern thinking about education, government, and science.

- Herodotus and Thucydides are considered western civilization's first historians. They believed that people could understand the present by studying the past.

Section 3

Alexander the Great

Get Ready to Read!

What's the Connection?
In Section 2, you learned that the Greek philosopher Aristotle was also a teacher. The king of Macedonia admired Greek culture and hired Aristotle to tutor his son, Alexander. Years later, his son would take control of the Greek world.

Focusing on the Main Ideas
- Philip II of Macedonia united the Greek states. *(page 175)*

- Alexander the Great conquered the Persian Empire and spread Greek culture throughout southwest Asia. *(page 176)*

Locating Places
Macedonia (MA•suh•DOH•nee•uh)
Chaeronea (KEHR•uh•NEE•uh)
Syria (SIHR•ee•uh)
Alexandria (A•lihg•ZAN•dree•uh)

Meeting People
Philip II
Alexander the Great

Building Your Vocabulary
legacy (LEH•guh•see)
Hellenistic Era (HEH•luh•NIHS•tihk)

Reading Strategy
Sequencing Create a diagram like the one below to track the achievements of Alexander the Great.

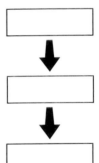

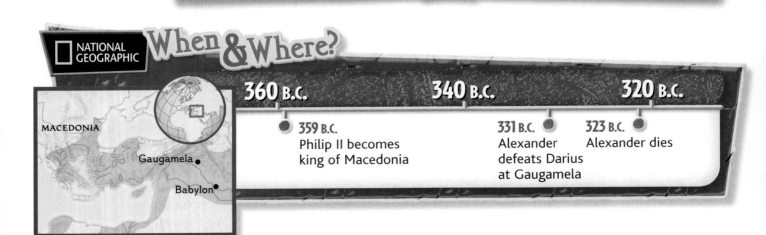

National Geographic When & Where?

360 B.C. **340 B.C.** **320 B.C.**

359 B.C.
Philip II becomes king of Macedonia

331 B.C.
Alexander defeats Darius at Gaugamela

323 B.C.
Alexander dies

MACEDONIA
Gaugamela
Babylon

Macedonia Attacks Greece

Main Idea Philip II of Macedonia united the Greek states.

Reading Focus Have you ever wanted something because your neighbor had it? Read to find what the king of Macedonia wanted from his neighbors, the Greeks.

Macedonia (MA•suh•DOH•nee•uh) lay north of Greece. The Macedonians raised sheep and horses and grew crops in their river valleys. They were a warrior people who fought on horseback. The Greeks looked down on them, but by 400 B.C., Macedonia had become a powerful kingdom.

A Plan to Win Greece
In 359 B.C. **Philip II** rose to the throne in Macedonia. Philip had lived in Greece as a young man. He admired everything about the Greeks—their art, their ideas, and their armies. Although Macedonia was influenced by Greek ideas, Philip wanted to make his kingdom strong enough to defeat the mighty Persian Empire. In order to achieve this goal, Philip needed to unite the Greek city-states with his own kingdom.

Philip trained a vast army of foot soldiers to fight like the Greeks. He took over the city-states one by one. He took some city-states by force and bribed the leaders of others to surrender. Some united with his kingdom voluntarily.

Demosthenes (dih•MAHS•thuh•NEEZ) was a lawyer and one of Athens's great public speakers. He gave several powerful speeches warning Athenians that Philip was a threat to Greek freedom. He urged Athens and other city-states to join together to fight the Macedonians.

Primary Source

Demosthenes' Warning

As King Philip II of Macedonia became more powerful, he began to take part in the affairs of Greece. Demosthenes realized that Macedonia's powerful army would eventually be a threat to Greece. He tried to warn the Greeks to take action.

"Remember only that Philip is our enemy, that he has long been robbing and insulting us, that wherever we have expected aid from others we have found hostility, that the future depends on ourselves, and that unless we are willing to fight him there we shall perhaps be forced to fight here. . . . You need not speculate [guess] about the future except to assure yourselves that it will be disastrous unless you face the facts and are willing to do your duty."

—Demosthenes, *"The First Philippic"* in *Orations of Demosthenes*

▼ Demosthenes

DBQ Document-Based Question

Which line of Demosthenes' speech tells what he thinks will happen if the Greeks ignore Philip?

However, by the time the Greeks saw the danger, it was too late. The Peloponnesian War had left the Greeks weak and divided. In many Greek city-states, the population had declined after the Peloponnesian War. Fighting had destroyed many farms and left people with no way to earn a living. As a result, thousands of young Greeks left Greece to join the Persian army. Many who stayed behind began fighting among themselves. The city-states grew weaker.

Although the Athenians joined some other Greek states to fight Philip's army, they could not stop the invasion. In 338 B.C. the Macedonians crushed the Greek allies at the Battle of **Chaeronea** (KEHR•uh•NEE•uh) near Thebes. Philip now controlled most of Greece.

✓ **Reading Check** **Summarize** Why did Philip II invade Greece?

Alexander Builds an Empire

Main Idea Alexander the Great conquered the Persian Empire and spread Greek culture throughout southwest Asia.

Reading Focus What will you be doing at age 20? Read to learn what Philip's son Alexander achieved.

Philip planned to conquer the Persian Empire with the Greeks' help. Before Philip could carry out his plan, however, he was murdered. As a result, the invasion of Asia fell to his son.

Alexander was only 20 when he became king of Macedonia. Philip had carefully trained his son for leadership. While still a boy, Alexander often went with his father to the battlefront. At age 16 he rose to commander in the Macedonian army. After his

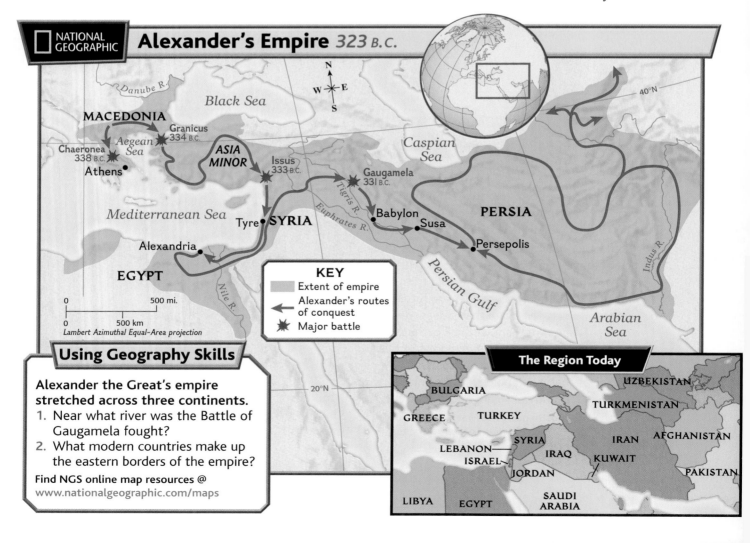

NATIONAL GEOGRAPHIC
Alexander's Empire 323 B.C.

KEY
- Extent of empire
- ← Alexander's routes of conquest
- ✳ Major battle

0 — 500 mi.
0 — 500 km
Lambert Azimuthal Equal-Area projection

Using Geography Skills

Alexander the Great's empire stretched across three continents.
1. Near what river was the Battle of Gaugamela fought?
2. What modern countries make up the eastern borders of the empire?

Find NGS online map resources @
www.nationalgeographic.com/maps

The Region Today

father's death, Alexander was ready to fulfill his father's dream—the invasion of the Persian Empire.

Alexander's Conquests In the spring of 334 B.C., Alexander invaded Asia Minor with about 37,000 Macedonian and Greek foot soldiers. He also took along 5,000 mounted warriors. With Alexander at their head, the cavalry destroyed the forces of the local Persian satraps at the Battle of Granicus.

By the next year, Alexander had freed the Greek cities in Asia Minor from Persian rule and defeated a large Persian army at Issus. He then turned south. By the winter of 332 B.C., he had captured **Syria** (SIHR•ee•uh) and Egypt. Then he built the city of **Alexandria** (A•lihg•ZAN•dree•uh) as a center of business and trade. The city became one of the most important cities in the ancient world.

In 331 B.C. Alexander headed east and defeated the Persians at Gaugamela, near Babylon. After this victory, his army easily overran the rest of the Persian Empire. However, Alexander did not stop at Persia. Over the next three years, he marched east as far as modern Pakistan. In 326 B.C. he crossed the Indus River and entered India. There he fought a number of bloody battles. Weary of continuous war, his soldiers refused to go farther. Alexander agreed to lead them home.

On the return march, the troops crossed a desert in what is now southern Iran. Heat and thirst killed thousands of soldiers. At one point, a group of soldiers found a little water and scooped it up in a helmet. Then they offered the water to Alexander. According to a Greek historian, Alexander, "in full view of his troops, poured the water on the ground. So extraordinary was the effect of this action that the water wasted by

Alexander the Great

▲ This carving of Alexander the Great on his horse decorated the side of a tomb. *Was Alexander able to fulfill his plans of conquest? Explain.*

Alexander was as good as a drink for every man in the army."

In 323 B.C. Alexander returned to Babylon. He wanted to plan an invasion of southern Arabia but was very tired and weak from wounds. He came down with a bad fever. Ten days later he was dead at age 32.

Alexander's Legacy Alexander was a great military leader. He was brave and even reckless. He often rode into battle ahead of his men and risked his own life. He inspired his armies to march into unknown lands and risk their lives in difficult situations.

The key to Alexander's courage may have been his childhood education. Alexander kept a copy of the *Iliad* under his pillow. Most likely his inspiration was Homer's warrior-hero Achilles. In the end, Alexander's reputation outstripped even Achilles', and today he is called **Alexander the Great.**

A **legacy** (LEH•guh•see) is what a person leaves behind when he or she dies. Alexander's skill and daring created his legacy. He helped extend Greek and Macedonian rule over a vast area. At the same time, he and his armies spread Greek art, ideas, language, and architecture wherever they went in southwest Asia and northern Africa. Greeks, in turn, brought new ideas back from Asia and Africa.

Alexander's conquests marked the beginning of the **Hellenistic Era** (HEH•luh•NIHS•tihk). The word *Hellenistic* comes from a Greek word meaning "like the Greeks." It refers to a time when the Greek language and Greek ideas spread to the non-Greek people of southwest Asia.

The Empire Breaks Apart Alexander the Great planned to unite Macedonians, Greeks, and Persians in his new empire. He used Persians as officials and encouraged his soldiers to marry Asian women. After Alexander died, however, his generals fought one another for power. As a result, the empire that Alexander had created fell apart. Four kingdoms took its place: Macedonia, Pergamum (PUHR•guh•muhm), Egypt, and the Seleucid Empire (suh•LOO•suhd). Look at the map on page 179 to see where these kingdoms were located.

All government business in the Hellenistic kingdoms was conducted in the Greek language. Only those Asians and Egyptians who spoke Greek could apply

Alexandria, Egypt

Alexandria

▼ Modern Alexandria

◀ The lighthouse of Alexandria was one of the Seven Wonders of the Ancient World. A fire in its tall tower guided ships into harbor. *What was special about Alexandria in 100 B.C.?*

for government posts. The kings preferred to give the jobs to Greeks and Macedonians. In this way, Greeks managed to stay in control of the governments.

By 100 B.C., the largest city in the Mediterranean world was Alexandria, which Alexander had founded in Egypt. In addition, the Hellenistic kings created many new cities and military settlements.

These new Greek cities needed architects, engineers, philosophers, artisans, and artists. For this reason, Hellenistic rulers encouraged Greeks and Macedonians to settle in south-west Asia. These colonists provided new recruits for the army and a pool of government officials and workers. They helped spread Greek culture into Egypt and as far east as modern-day Afghanistan and India.

✔ Reading Check **Explain** What was Alexander's legacy?

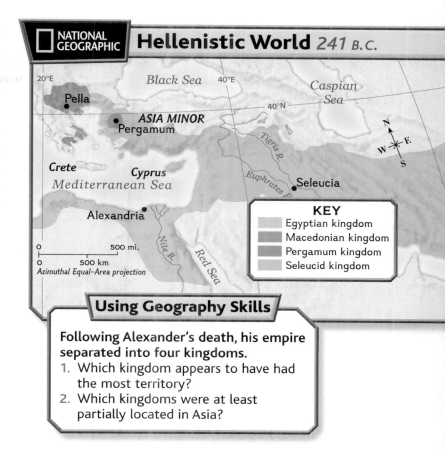

NATIONAL GEOGRAPHIC **Hellenistic World** *241* B.C.

KEY
- Egyptian kingdom
- Macedonian kingdom
- Pergamum kingdom
- Seleucid kingdom

Using Geography Skills

Following Alexander's death, his empire separated into four kingdoms.
1. Which kingdom appears to have had the most territory?
2. Which kingdoms were at least partially located in Asia?

History Online

Study Central™ Need help with the material in this section? Visit jat.glencoe.com

Section ③ Review

Reading Summary

Review the Main Ideas

- Following the Battle of Chaeronea in 338 B.C., King Philip of Macedonia ruled all of Greece.

- Alexander the Great, King Philip's son, conquered an empire that stretched to Africa in the south and India in the east. After Alexander's death, his empire split into several kingdoms.

What Did You Learn?

1. How did Philip II of Macedonia feel about the Greeks?

2. What ended Alexander's conquest of India?

Critical Thinking

3. **Analyze** Why was Alexander a good leader?

4. **Summarize** Draw a table to summarize what you know about each topic.

Philip of Macedonia	Alexander the Great	Alexander's Empire After His Death

5. **Predict** How might history have been different if Alexander had lived longer?

6. **Geography Skills** How many continents did Alexander's empire reach?

7. **Reading** Context Clues What do you think the word *assure* means in this passage?

". . . assure yourselves that it will be disastrous unless you face the facts and are willing to do your duty."

What words give clues to its meaning?

You Decide . . .

Alexander the Great: Villain or Hero?

Villain

Was Alexander the Great really great? Or was he an evil conqueror? Those who see him as bloodthirsty and cruel give this as evidence against Alexander. They say he

- destroyed Persepolis
- attacked Tyre, killing 10,000 people and enslaving 30,000
- treated his slaves harshly
- ordered the murder of several close advisers.

Many legends about Alexander have been told. One historian found this account to support the "villain theory."

"The following is my favourite [story] which is found all the way from Turkey to Kazakhstan: Iskander [Alexander] was actually a devil and he had horns. But his hair was long and wavy and the horns were never seen. Only his barbers knew. But he feared they could not keep the secret. So, he killed them when they discovered. His last barber pretended not to notice and kept the secret. Eventually though he could bear it no longer and, as he could tell no one, he ran to a well and called down the well: 'Iskander has horns!' But in the bottom of the well were whispering reeds [used in flutes] and they echoed the story until it went round the whole world."

—Michael Wood,
"In the Footsteps of
Alexander the Great"

▲ Alexander the Great (at far left)

Arrian, a Greek historian who lived in the A.D. 100s, wrote about Alexander this way:

"For my own part, I think there was at that time no race of men, no city, nor even a single individual to whom Alexander's name and fame had not penetrated. For this reason it seems to me that a hero totally unlike any other human being could not have been born without the agency [help] of the deity [gods]."

—Arrian, *The Anabasis of Alexander*

On two points all historians agree: Alexander was a brilliant general and he was a brave fighter. He once boasted to his men:

"For there is no part of my body, in front at any rate, remaining free from wounds; nor is there any kind of weapon used either for close combat or for hurling at the enemy, the traces of which I do not bear on my person. For I have been wounded with the sword in close fight, I have been shot with arrows, and I have been struck with missiles projected from engines of war; and though oftentimes I have been hit with stones and bolts of wood for the sake of your lives, your glory, and your wealth, I am still leading you as conquerors over all the land and sea, all rivers, mountains, and plains. I have celebrated your weddings with my own, and the children of many of you will be akin to my children."

—Arrian, *The Anabasis of Alexander*

▲ Alexander the Great

Hero

Other historians consider Alexander the Great to be a hero. They claim he brought progress, order, and culture to each new land he conquered. In support of him, they say Alexander

- tried to promote learning
- visited all of his wounded men after each battle
- spared the lives of the queen and princess of Persia
- built new cities where others had been destroyed.

You Be the Historian

Checking for Understanding
1. Why do some people view Alexander the Great as a villain?
2. Why do others view him as a hero?
3. Was Alexander wicked or heroic? Take the role of a historian. Write a brief essay or persuasive speech that explains how you see Alexander the Great. Be sure to use facts to support your position. You can compare him to other famous rulers to strengthen your argument.

Section 4

The Spread of Greek Culture

Get Ready to Read!

What's the Connection?

In Section 3, you read that Alexander's conquests helped to spread Greek culture. The kings who came after Alexander also tried to attract the best and brightest Greeks to Asia and Egypt. They hoped to re-create the glory of Greece's Golden Age in their own kingdoms.

Focusing on the Main Ideas

- Hellenistic cities became centers of learning and culture. *(page 183)*

- Epicurus and Zeno showed the world different ways to look at happiness. *(page 184)*

- Hellenistic scientists made major discoveries in math and astronomy. *(page 185)*

Locating Places

Rhodes (ROHDZ)
Syracuse (SIHR•uh•KYOOS)

Meeting People

Theocritus (thee•AH•kruh•tuhs)
Aristarchus (AR•uh•STAHR•kuhs)
Eratosthenes (EHR•uh•TAHS•thuh•NEEZ)
Euclid (YOO•kluhd)
Archimedes (AHR•kuh•MEE•deez)

Building Your Vocabulary

Epicureanism (EH•pih•kyu•REE•uh•NIH•zuhm)
Stoicism (STOH•uh•SIH•zuhm)
astronomer (uh•STRAH•nuh•muhr)
plane geometry (jee•AH•muh•tree)
solid geometry (jee•AH•muh•tree)

Reading Strategy

Summarizing Information Create a diagram to show the major Greek contributions to Western civilization.

Contributions

When & Where?

| 350 B.C. | | 275 B.C. | | 200 B.C. |

c. 300 B.C.
King Ptolemy I invites Euclid to Alexandria

291 B.C.
Menander, the playwright, dies

212 B.C.
Archimedes killed by Romans

Greek Culture Spreads

Main Idea Hellenistic cities became centers of learning and culture.

Reading Focus Imagine you are a leading citizen in a new city. How would you make it the best city possible? Read to find out how leaders in the Hellenistic Era improved their cities.

During the Hellenistic Era, philosophers, scientists, poets, and writers flocked to the new Greek cities in southwest Asia and Egypt, especially Alexandria. Many came to take advantage of Alexandria's library. Its more than 500,000 scrolls were useful to students of literature and language. Alexandria also had a museum where researchers went to do their work.

Architecture and Sculpture

The Hellenistic kingdoms were lands of opportunity for Greek architects. New cities were being founded, and old ones were being rebuilt. The Hellenistic kings wanted to make these cities like the cultural centers of Greece. They paid handsome fees to line the streets with baths, theaters, and temples.

Hellenistic kings and other wealthy citizens hired Greek sculptors to fill their towns and cities with thousands of statues. These statues showed the same level of workmanship as the statues from Greece's Golden Age.

Literature and Theater

Hellenistic leaders also admired talented writers. Kings and leading citizens spent generous sums of money supporting writers' work. As a result, the Hellenistic Age produced a large body of literature. Sadly, very little of this writing has survived.

One of the works we know about is an epic poem by Appolonius (A•puh•LOH•nee•uhs) of **Rhodes** (ROHDZ). Called *Argonautica*, it tells the legend of Jason and his band of heroes. They sail the seas in search of a ram

Primary Source: The Poetry of Theocritus

Theocritus is considered the creator of pastoral poetry. Pastoral poetry deals with rural life, especially the lives of shepherds. It often compares rural and city life. In this selection, he talks about shepherding as a way of life.

"Shepherd, your song is sweeter than the water

that tumbles and splashes down from the rocks.

If the Muses get the ewe for their prize,

you'll win the [baby] lamb. But if they choose

the lamb, you'll carry away the ewe."

—Theocritus, "First Idyll"

▲ Sculpture of shepherd

DBQ Document-Based Question

How does Theocritus describe the song of the shepherd?

with golden fleece. Another poet, **Theocritus** (thee•AH•kruh•tuhs), wrote short poems about the beauty of nature.

Athens remained the center of Greek theater. Playwrights in Athens created a new kind of comedy. The stories had happy endings and still make people laugh. However, unlike the comedies of Greece's Golden Age, they did not poke fun at political leaders. Instead the plays told stories about love and relationships. One of the best known of the new playwrights was Menander (muh•NAN•duhr), who lived from 343 B.C. to 291 B.C.

✓ **Reading Check** **Explain** How did the Hellenistic kingdoms spread Greek culture?

Science and Inventions

Greek Medicine The ancient Greeks believed that their gods had the power to cure them of illnesses and injuries. Greek temples were places of healing as well as places of worship. In temples, priests treated patients with herbs, prayed, and made sacrifices to the gods as part of the healing process.

In the 400s B.C., the practice of medicine began to change. Hippocrates (hih • PAH • kruh • TEEZ), a doctor and pioneer of medical science, began to separate medicine from religion. He stressed that it was important to examine the body and look at a patient's symptoms to find out why someone was ill. He also taught that it was important to have a healthy diet.

Hippocrates is well known for the oath, or pledge, that he asked his medical students to recite. His students had to promise never to harm and always to care for their patients. New doctors still take a version of the Hippocratic Oath when they graduate from medical school.

▲ Greek doctor treating patients

Connecting to the Past

1. How were illnesses and injuries treated before Hippocrates?
2. How did Hippocrates change the way medicine was practiced in ancient Greece?

Philosophy

Main Idea Epicurus and Zeno showed the world different ways to look at happiness.

Reading Focus What makes you happy? Read on to learn about different Greek ideas about happiness.

During the Hellenistic Era, Athens continued to attract the most famous philosophers in the Greek world. The two most important philosophers were Epicurus and Zeno.

Epicureans Epicurus founded a philosophy we now know as **Epicureanism** (EH • pih • kyu • REE • uh • NIH • zuhm). He taught his students that happiness was the goal of life. He believed that the way to be happy was to seek out pleasure.

Today the word *epicurean* means the love of physical pleasure, such as good food or comfortable surroundings. However, to Epicurus, pleasure meant spending time with friends and learning not to worry about things. Epicureans avoided worry by staying out of politics and public service.

Who Were the Stoics? A Phoenician named Zeno developed **Stoicism** (STOH • uh • SIH • zuhm). It became a very popular philosophy in the Hellenistic world. When Zeno came to Athens, he could not afford to rent a lecture hall. So he taught at a building known as the "painted porch" near the city market. "Stoicism" comes from *stoa,* the Greek word for "porch."

For Stoics, happiness came from following reason, not emotions, and doing your duty. Today the word *stoic* is used to describe someone who is not affected by joy or grief. Unlike Epicureans, Stoics thought people had a duty to serve their city.

☑ **Reading Check** **Contrast** What were the differences between Epicureanism and Stoicism?

Greek Science and Math

Main Idea Hellenistic scientists made major discoveries in math and astronomy.

Reading Focus Do you know how to find the area of a square? If so, you are doing geometry. Read on to find out about the person who created geometry and other scientists from the Hellenistic Era.

Scientists, especially mathematicians and astronomers, made major contributions during the Hellenistic Era. **Astronomers** (uh•STRAH•nuh•muhrs) study stars, planets, and other heavenly bodies. **Aristarchus** (AR•uh•STAHR•kuhs), an astronomer from Samos, claimed that the sun was at the center of the universe and that Earth circled the sun. At the time, other astronomers rejected Aristarchus's ideas. They thought that Earth was the center of the universe.

Another astronomer, **Eratosthenes** (EHR•uh•TAHS•thuh•NEEZ), was in charge of the library at Alexandria. Eratosthenes concluded that Earth is round. He then used his knowledge of geometry and astronomy to measure Earth's circumference—the distance around Earth.

Eratosthenes put two sticks in the ground far apart from each other. When the sun was directly over one stick, the shadow was shorter than the shadow at the other stick. By measuring the shadows, he was able to calculate the curve of Earth's surface.

Using his measurements, Eratosthenes estimated that the distance around Earth equaled 24,675 miles (39,702 km). Amazingly, his estimate was within 185 miles (298 km) of the actual distance. Using similar methods, he measured the distance to the sun and to the moon. His measurements were quite accurate.

Euclid (YOO•kluhd) is probably the most famous Greek mathematician. His best-known book *Elements* describes plane geometry. **Plane geometry** (jee•AH•muh•tree) is the branch of mathematics that shows

Greek Scientists and Their Contributions

Scientist	Scientific "Firsts"
Archimedes	Established the science of physics Explained the lever and compound pulley
Aristarchus	Established that Earth revolves around the sun
Eratosthenes	Figured out that Earth is round
Euclid	Wrote a book that organized information about geometry
Hipparchus	Created a system to explain how planets and stars move
Hippocrates	Known as the "Father of Medicine" First to write a medical code of good behavior
Hypatia	Expanded knowledge of mathematics and astronomy
Pythagoras	First to establish the principles of geometry

Archimedes ▶

Understanding Charts

The ancient Greeks made advances in science.
1. What were Archimedes' achievements?
2. **Identify** Who wrote a code of behavior that doctors still follow today?

▲ Euclid

how points, lines, angles, and surfaces relate to one another. Around 300 B.C., King Ptolemy I (TAH•luh•mee) of Egypt asked Euclid if he knew an easier way to learn geometry than by reading *Elements.* Euclid answered that "there is no royal way" to learn geometry.

The most famous scientist of the Hellenistic Era was **Archimedes** (AHR•kuh•MEE•deez) of **Syracuse** (SIHR•uh•KYOOS). He worked on **solid geometry** (jee•AH•muh•tree)—the study of ball-like shapes called spheres and tubelike shapes called cylinders. He also figured out the value of *pi*. This number is used to measure the area of circles and is usually represented by the symbol π.

Archimedes was also an inventor. One story about Archimedes tells how he invented weapons. "Give me a lever and a place to stand on," Archimedes said to the king of Syracuse, "and I will move the earth."

The king of Syracuse was impressed. He asked Archimedes to use his levers to defend the city. So Archimedes designed catapults—machines that hurled arrows, spears, and rocks. When Romans attacked Syracuse in 212 B.C., Archimedes' catapults drove them back. It took the Romans three years to capture Syracuse. During the massacre that followed, Archimedes was killed.

✓ **Reading Check** **Explain** Who was the most famous scientist of the Hellenistic Era? What did he contribute?

History Online
Study Central™ Need help with the material in this section? Visit jat.glencoe.com

Section 4 Review

Reading Summary
Review the Main Ideas

• Hellenistic cities, such as Alexandria, attracted some of the Greek world's best architects, sculptors, and writers.

• During the Hellenistic Era, new philosophies, such as Stoicism and Epicureanism, developed.

• Hellenistic scientists, including Aristarchus, Eratosthenes, Euclid, and Archimedes, made important advances in the fields of astronomy and mathematics.

What Did You Learn?

1. Why did the city of Alexandria attract scholars?

2. Describe the form of philosophy developed by Zeno.

Critical Thinking

3. **Summarize** Draw a table like the one below. Write several facts about each scientist in the correct column.

Aristarchus	
Eratosthenes	
Euclid	
Archimedes	

4. **Compare and Contrast** How were the comedies of the Hellenistic Era and those of Greece's Golden Age similar and different?

5. **Analyze** How would knowledge of geometry be helpful to the Greeks?

6. **Identify** What did the Epicureans believe about happiness?

7. **Reading** Context Clues Name two words in this sentence that help define the word *playwright.* "Playwrights in Athens created a new kind of comedy."

Chapter 5 Reading Review

Section 1 The Culture of Ancient Greece

Vocabulary
myth
oracle
epic
fable
drama
tragedy
comedy

Focusing on the Main Ideas
- The Greeks believed that gods and goddesses controlled nature and shaped their lives. *(page 155)*
- Greek poetry and fables taught Greek values. *(page 157)*
- Greek drama still shapes entertainment today. *(page 160)*
- Greek art and architecture expressed Greek ideas of beauty and harmony. *(page 162)*

Section 2 Greek Philosophy and History

Vocabulary
philosophy
philosopher
Sophist
Socratic method

Focusing on the Main Ideas
- Greek philosophers developed ideas that are still used today. *(page 169)*
- Greeks wrote the first real histories in Western civilization. *(page 173)*

Section 3 Alexander the Great

Vocabulary
legacy
Hellenistic Era

Focusing on the Main Ideas
- Philip II of Macedonia united the Greek states. *(page 175)*
- Alexander the Great conquered the Persian Empire and spread Greek culture throughout southwest Asia. *(page 176)*

▲ Alexander the Great

Section 4 The Spread of Greek Culture

Vocabulary
Epicureanism
Stoicism
astronomer
plane geometry
solid geometry

Focusing on the Main Ideas
- Hellenistic cities became centers of learning and culture. *(page 183)*
- Epicurus and Zeno showed the world different ways to look at happiness. *(page 184)*
- Hellenistic scientists made major discoveries in math and astronomy. *(page 185)*

Chapter 5 Assessment and Activities

Review Vocabulary

1. Write a brief paragraph that defines and compares the following terms.

    epic   fable   myth

Decide if each statement is *True* or *False*.

____ 2. An oracle was a shrine Greeks visited to receive prophecies.

____ 3. Sophists were professional teachers.

____ 4. The death of Socrates marks the beginning of the Hellenistic Era.

____ 5. Astronomers study stars, planets, and other heavenly bodies.

____ 6. Euclid developed plane geometry.

Review Main Ideas

Section 1 • The Culture of Ancient Greece

7. What did the Greeks believe about their gods and goddesses?

8. What did Greek art and architecture express?

Section 2 • Greek Philosophy and History

9. How long did the ideas of Greek philosophers last?

10. Why are Greek historians so important?

Section 3 • Alexander the Great

11. Which leader united the Greek states?

12. What are the two main accomplishments of Alexander the Great?

Section 4 • The Spread of Greek Culture

13. Why were Hellenistic cities important?

14. In what fields did Hellenistic scientists make advances?

Critical Thinking

15. **Understanding Cause and Effect** How did the Peloponnesian War weaken the Greek states?

16. **Analyze** Why would knowing the circumference of Earth have been helpful to the Greeks?

17. **Compare** How was religion in ancient Greece similar to religion in ancient Egypt?

18. **Analyze** Why do you think the development of written history is important?

Review Reading Skill — Context

Words in Context

Read this passage from page 158.

"My father was anxious to see me develop into a good man . . . [so] he compelled me to memorize all of Homer."

19. Based on how *compelled* is used in this sentence, what do you think it means?

____ a. asked

____ b. taught

____ c. forced

____ d. dared

To review this skill, see pages 152–153.

Geography Skills

Study the map below and answer the following questions.

20. **Location** Analyze the location of the Hellenistic kingdoms. What present-day countries control territory that was controlled by the Seleucid empire?

21. **Human/Environment Interaction** Which kingdom do you think was the most difficult to govern based on its geography?

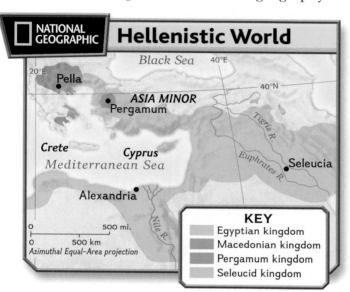

NATIONAL GEOGRAPHIC

Hellenistic World

Black Sea

40°E

20°E

Pella

40°N

ASIA MINOR
Pergamum

Tigris R.

Crete

Cyprus

Mediterranean Sea

Euphrates R.

Seleucia

Alexandria

Nile R.

0   500 mi.
0   500 km
Azimuthal Equal-Area projection

KEY
Egyptian kingdom
Macedonian kingdom
Pergamum kingdom
Seleucid kingdom

Read to Write

22. **Descriptive Writing** Imagine you are a journalist living in Alexandria, Egypt, during the Hellenistic Era. Write an article describing life in the city.

23. **Using Your FOLDABLES** Review the developments in early Greece that you listed on your foldable. Using numbers, rank each development from the most valuable to the least valuable. Explain the reason for your highest and lowest ranking.

Linking Past and Present

24. **Expository Writing** The Nobel prize is awarded yearly to people who have made great achievements. Do research to find out more about the award. Then choose one Greek philosopher, writer, scientist, or leader who you think deserves the Nobel prize. Write a short speech to explain why. Present your speech to the class.

Using Technology

25. **Creating a Multimedia Presentation** Use the Internet and print resources, such as newspapers and magazines, to research Greek architecture. Then use the computer or posterboard to design and construct your own building using Greek designs. The Greeks dedicated some of their buildings to gods and goddesses. Dedicate your building to someone in history and design it with that person in mind. Share your research and design with the class.

Primary Source Analyze

In this account, Thucydides describes the masses of people who entered Athens around 430 B.C. seeking relief from the plague.

"There were no houses for them, and, living as they did during the hot season in badly ventilated huts, they died like flies. . . . For the catastrophe was so overwhelming that men, not knowing what would happen next to them, became indifferent to every rule of religion or law. All the funeral ceremonies which used to be observed were now disorganized, and they buried the dead as best they could."

—Thucydides, *History of the Peloponnesian War*

DBQ Document-Based Questions

26. What hardships did newcomers to Athens face during the time of the plague?
27. What does Thucydides mean when he says that men "became indifferent to every rule of religion or law"?

Early India

The Hindu temple of Devi Jagadambi in Khajuraho, India ▼

NATIONAL GEOGRAPHIC **When & Where?**

2500 B.C.	1500 B.C.	500 B.C.	A.D. 500
c. 3000 B.C. India's first civilization begins	c. 1500 B.C. The Aryans arrive in India	563 B.C. The Buddha is born	A.D. 320 The Gupta empire begins

Chapter Preview

Like ancient Greece, early India was a land of warriors, thinkers, and scientists. Read this chapter to find out how ideas from India affect how you do math today.

 View the Chapter 6 video in the *World History: Journey Across Time* Video Program.

History Online

Chapter Overview Visit jat.glencoe.com for a preview of Chapter 6.

 ## India's First Civilizations

The earliest Indian civilization developed on the Indus River. Later, the Aryans arrived in northern India. They changed the government and created a new social system.

 ## Hinduism and Buddhism

India's two main religions were Hinduism and Buddhism. These two religions affected every aspect of people's lives.

 ## India's First Empires

India had two great empires: the Maurya and the Gupta. The Mauryans helped spread Buddhism throughout Asia. Art and learning flourished during the Gupta empire.

FOLDABLES™ Study Organizer

Identifying *Make this foldable to help you identify and learn key terms.*

Step 1 *Stack four sheets of paper, one on top of the other. On the top sheet of paper, draw a large circle.*

Step 2 *With the papers still stacked, cut out all four circles at the same time.*

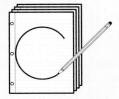

Reading and Writing *As you read the chapter, write the terms from Building Your Vocabulary in your foldable. Write a definition for each term. Then turn your foldable over (upside down) to write a short sentence using each term.*

Step 3 *Staple the paper circles together at one point around the edge.*

Staple here.

This makes a circular booklet.

Step 4 *Label the front circle as shown and take notes on the pages that open to the right.*

Chapter 6 Key Terms

Reading Social Studies

1 Learn It!

Building Your Vocabulary

What do you do when you are reading and come to a word you do not know? Here are some hints:

1. Use clues in the sentence (called context clues) to help you define it.
2. Look for prefixes, suffixes, or root words that you already know.
3. Look it up in the glossary or a dictionary.
4. Write it down and ask for help with the meaning.
5. Guess at its meaning.

Look at the word *Untouchables* in the following paragraph.

> **Context** If you know what a *varna* is, it will help you figure out the meaning of *Untouchables*.

> **Context** The "Untouchables" were a "group."

> There was one group that did not belong to any *varna*. Its members were called Pariahs, or the Untouchables. They performed work other Indians thought was too dirty, such as collecting trash, skinning animals, or handling dead bodies.
>
> —*from page 200*

Reading Tip

Read the paragraphs that appear before and after the word to help you understand its meaning.

Prefixes and Suffixes You might know that the prefix **un-** means "not" and the suffix **-able** means "to be able to." You might guess that the meaning of *Untouchable* is an Indian who was not to be touched by others.

Context The fact that they performed the "dirty" work indicates how they were viewed by others in Indian society.

192

2 Practice It!
Defining Words

What are three things you could do to help you understand the meaning of the word *subcontinent* in this paragraph?

Look at the map below. India looks like a diamond hanging from the bottom of Asia. India is a **subcontinent** (SUHB • KAHN • tuhn • uhnt) because even though it is part of Asia, huge mountains make a barrier between India and the rest of Asia. These mountains are the **Himalaya** (HIH • muh • LAY • uh), the highest mountains in the world.

—*from page 195*

Read to Write

Take one word from the vocabulary bookmark that you make in the **Apply It!** activity. Find its definition. Then create a cartoon strip. Have one of the characters in your cartoon strip use the word correctly.

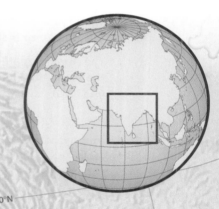

KARAKORAM RANGE

Indus R.

H I M A L A Y A

Mt. Everest
29,035 ft.
(8,850 m)

30°N

Ganges R.

I N D I A

Bay of
Bengal

Arabian
Sea

3 Apply It!

Make a vocabulary bookmark using a 2-inch-wide strip of paper. As you read the chapter, write down words you do not know or want to find out more about.

India's First Civilizations

Get Ready to Read!

What's the Connection?

In India, just as in Egypt and Mesopotamia, the first civilizations developed in fertile river valleys.

Focusing on the Main Ideas

• Climate and geography influenced the rise of India's first civilization. *(page 195)*

• The Aryans introduced new ideas and technology to India. *(page 198)*

• The Aryans created a caste system that separated Indians into groups. *(page 199)*

Locating Places

Himalaya (HIH•muh•LAY•uh)
Ganges River (GAN•JEEZ)
Indus River (IHN•duhs)
Harappa (huh•RA•puh)
Mohenjo-Daro (moh•HEHN•joh   DAHR•oh)

Meeting People

Aryans (AR•ee•uhnz)
Brahmans (BRAH•muhns)

Building Your Vocabulary

subcontinent (SUHB•KAHN•tuhn•uhnt)
monsoon (mahn•SOON)
Sanskrit (SAN•SKRIHT)
raja (RAH•juh)
caste (KAST)
guru (GUR•oo)

Reading Strategy

Organizing Information Complete a diagram like the one below showing how the Aryans changed India.

Major Ways Aryans Changed India
↓   ↓   ↓   ↓

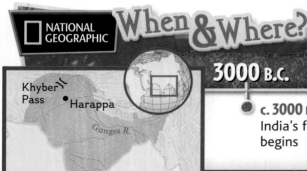

NATIONAL GEOGRAPHIC When & Where?

Khyber Pass • Harappa
Ganges R.

3000 B.C.

2000 B.C.

1000 B.C.

c. 3000 B.C.
India's first civilization begins

c. 1500 B.C.
Aryans invade India

c. 1000 B.C.
Aryans control northern India

The Land of India

Main Idea Climate and geography influenced the rise of India's first civilization.

Reading Focus Do you have tornadoes or hurricanes where you live? Read to find out how geography and weather affected India's first civilization.

Look at the map below. India looks like a diamond hanging from the bottom of Asia. India is a **subcontinent** (SUHB•KAHN•tuhn•uhnt) because even though it is part of Asia, huge mountains make a barrier between India and the rest of Asia. These mountains are the **Himalaya** (HIH•muh•LAY•uh), the highest mountains in the world.

Today, there are five nations that occupy the Indian subcontinent: India, Pakistan in the northwest, Nepal, Bhutan, and Bangladesh in the northeast.

India has two very fertile river valleys. Both are fed by the mountains in the north. When the snow in the Himalaya melts, water flows into the **Ganges River** (GAN•JEEZ) and the **Indus River** (IHN•duhs). If the water is controlled, the land near these rivers can be used for farming.

The Ganges River runs south of the Himalaya and flows into the Indian Ocean. The Indus River empties into the Arabian Sea. The area around the Indus is called the Indus River valley.

South of the river valleys is the dry and hilly Deccan Plateau. The eastern and western coasts of India are lush, fertile plains.

Monsoons (mahn•SOONZ) are an important part of the Indian climate. A monsoon is a strong wind that blows one direction in winter and the opposite direction in summer. The winter monsoon brings the cold, dry air of the mountains. The summer monsoon brings warm, wet air from the Arabian Sea, which produces drenching rains.

When the monsoon rains begin, many farmers celebrate. If the rains come on time and the rainy season lasts long enough, the crop will be good. If the rains are delayed, a drought will occur. This extended period

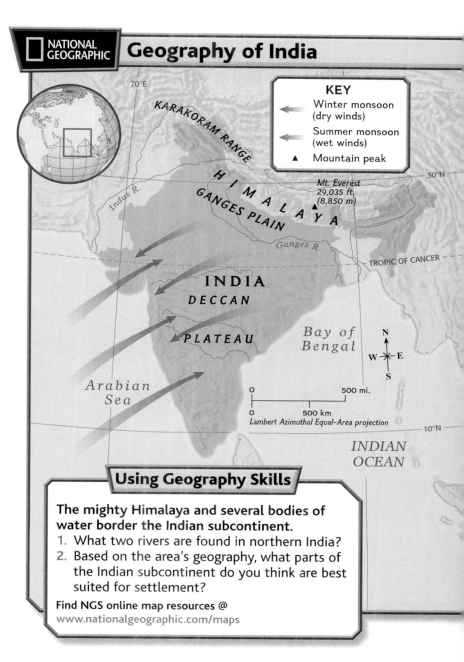

NATIONAL GEOGRAPHIC

Geography of India

KEY

Winter monsoon (dry winds)

Summer monsoon (wet winds)

▲ Mountain peak

70°E

KARAKORAM RANGE

HIMALAYA

GANGES PLAIN

Indus R.

Mt. Everest 29,035 ft. (8,850 m) ▲

30°N

Ganges R.

TROPIC OF CANCER

INDIA

DECCAN

PLATEAU

Bay of Bengal

Arabian Sea

N
W—E
S

0   500 mi.

0   500 km
Lambert Azimuthal Equal-Area projection

10°N

INDIAN OCEAN

Using Geography Skills

The mighty Himalaya and several bodies of water border the Indian subcontinent.

1. What two rivers are found in northern India?
2. Based on the area's geography, what parts of the Indian subcontinent do you think are best suited for settlement?

Find NGS online map resources @ www.nationalgeographic.com/maps

without rain can be disastrous for farmers. Few crops will be harvested and many people will starve.

India's First Civilization

In earlier chapters, you learned about civilizations that began in river valleys. Indian civilization also began in a river valley.

India's first civilization grew up near the Indus River. When the summer monsoon began, the river rose higher and higher. When the river flooded nearby land, it left behind rich, fertile soil.

Farmers used the rich soil to grow crops to feed their families. Because people had a plentiful supply of food, they could spend time doing other things, such as making tools or building houses. As people began to trade their extra food and goods with other people, their wealth grew. This allowed them to build larger and larger cities.

India's first civilization in the Indus River valley began about 3000 B.C. and lasted until 1500 B.C. More than a thousand villages and towns were part of this civilization, which stretched from the Himalaya to the Arabian Sea. We know something about the way these people lived from studying the ruins of two major cities, **Harappa** (huh•RA•puh) and **Mohenjo-Daro** (moh•HEHN•joh DAHR•oh). The civilization of this time is called the Harappan or Indus civilization.

Harappa and Mohenjo-Daro

Harappa and Mohenjo-Daro were large cities for their time. The well-planned cities had as many as 35,000 people. A fortress was built on a brick platform to keep guard over the residents. There were wide main streets and smaller side streets. A wall surrounded each neighborhood, and narrow lanes separated the houses.

Early Indian Civilization

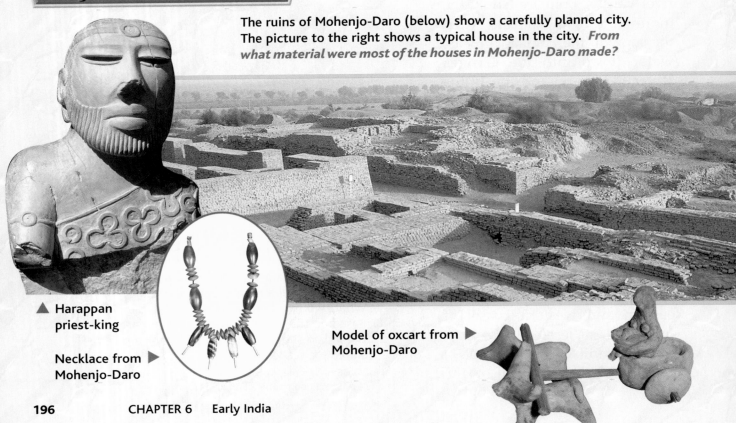

The ruins of Mohenjo-Daro (below) show a carefully planned city. The picture to the right shows a typical house in the city. *From what material were most of the houses in Mohenjo-Daro made?*

▲ Harappan priest-king

Necklace from ▶ Mohenjo-Daro

Model of oxcart from ▶ Mohenjo-Daro

Most houses had flat roofs and were built with mud bricks that were baked in ovens. Some houses were larger than others, but they all had a similar layout. There was a courtyard in the middle and smaller rooms around it.

These ancient city dwellers had some surprising conveniences. Wells supplied water, and residents even had indoor bathrooms. Wastewater flowed to drains under the streets, running through pipes to pits outside the city walls. Houses also had garbage chutes connected to a bin in the street. It is likely the city government was well organized to be able to provide so many services.

Harappan Society Because the Harappans left no written records, we do not know much about their society or government. From the ruins, though, we can tell that the royal palace and the temple were both enclosed in the fortress. This reveals that religion and politics were closely connected.

Most Harappans were farmers. They grew rice, wheat, barley, peas, and cotton. City dwellers made copper and bronze tools, clay pottery, and cotton cloth, as well as jewelry from gold, shells, and ivory. Archaeologists have also found many toys among the ruins, such as small monkeys that could be made to climb up a string.

It is likely that the Harappans began trading with the Mesopotamians about 2300 B.C. Some Harappan sailors followed the coastline and crossed the Arabian Sea, and others traveled overland.

One item rarely found in the ruins of Harappan cities was weapons. This suggests that the Harappans were not only prosperous but also peaceful.

Reading Check **Explain** How is India separated from the rest of Asia?

Roofs were used to dry crops in the sun. The dried crops were then placed in cool storage rooms in the house.

Outer walls of buildings had no windows. This helped prevent the hot summer sun from heating the insides of the house.

Bathrooms had an advanced drainage system. Drains started from houses and joined the main sewer, which carried the water out of town.

Almost every building had its own well. Cool water was pulled up when needed.

The Aryans

Main Idea The Aryans introduced new ideas and technology to India.

Reading Focus What would your life be like without cars or computers? Read to find out how new ideas and technology affected the Indians.

The Harappan civilization collapsed about 1500 B.C. Historians think that several earthquakes and floods damaged the cities. Then the Indus River changed its course, killing many people and forcing others to flee the area. In the years that followed, a group of people called the **Aryans** (AR•ee•uhnz) began settling in the region. Soon a new civilization emerged.

Who Were the Aryans? The Aryans lived in central Asia where they raised and herded animals. The Aryans were not a race or ethnic group. They were part of a larger group of people historians refer to as Indo-Europeans. The Indo-Europeans all spoke similar languages. Some migrated south to India and Iran. Others went west to Europe.

Cattle were a prized possession because they provided meat, milk, and butter. Cattle were so important that the Aryans even used them as money. Individual wealth was measured by the number of cattle a person owned.

The Aryans were good warriors. They were expert horse riders and hunters. They had metal-tipped spears and wooden chariots, which they sometimes used to invade nearby villages for food.

After 2000 B.C., the Aryans began leaving their home territory. They moved in waves, and some groups crossed through the mountain passes in the Himalaya. They entered the Indus River valley around 1500 B.C.

Around 1000 B.C., the Aryans began expanding across the Punjab and Ganges Plains and south into the Deccan Plateau. Their civilization spread to all of India except the southern tip.

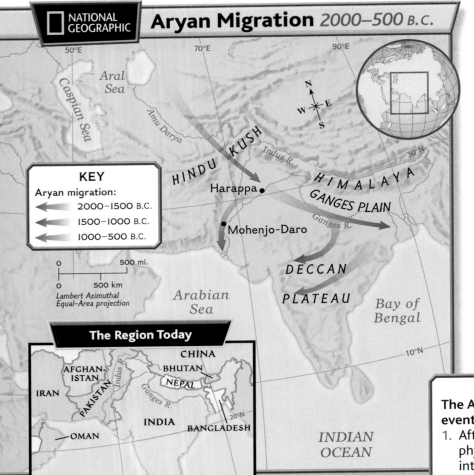

NATIONAL GEOGRAPHIC

Aryan Migration 2000–500 B.C.

KEY
Aryan migration:
- 2000–1500 B.C.
- 1500–1000 B.C.
- 1000–500 B.C.

0   500 mi.
0   500 km
Lambert Azimuthal Equal-Area projection

The Region Today

IRAN, AFGHANISTAN, PAKISTAN, CHINA, BHUTAN, NEPAL, INDIA, BANGLADESH, OMAN, SRI LANKA

Using Geography Skills

The Aryans were nomadic herders who eventually controlled much of India.
1. After crossing the mountains, what physical feature did the Aryans follow into India?
2. Into what area of southern India did the Aryans travel?

The Aryans Bring Change When the Aryans arrived in India, they no longer lived as nomads. They became farmers but continued to raise cattle. Eventually, the Aryans would declare that cattle were sacred and forbid them to be used as food.

Because Aryans were skilled ironworkers, they improved farming in India. They invented an iron plow to help clear India's many jungles and built canals to irrigate. They slowly turned the Ganges River valley into good farmland.

India's varied climate supported many types of crops. In the north, farmers grew grains such as wheat, barley, and millet. Rice was grown in the river valleys. In the south, there was a mix of crops, including spices such as pepper, ginger, and cinnamon.

The Aryans also brought a new language to India. As nomads, they had no written language, but in India they developed a written language called **Sanskrit** (SAN•SKRIHT). Now the songs, stories, poems, and prayers that Aryans had known for many centuries could be written down.

The Aryans were organized into tribes. Each tribe was led by a **raja** (RAH•juh), or prince. The rajas ran their own small kingdoms, which often fought among themselves. Rajas fought over cattle and treasure and over women kidnapped from other states. These small rival kingdoms existed in India for about a thousand years, from 1500 B.C. to 400 B.C.

Reading Check Analyze Why do you think nomads like the Aryans were great warriors?

Web Activity Visit jat.glencoe.com and click on *Chapter 6—Student Web Activity* to learn more about India.

Society in Ancient India

Main Idea The Aryans created a caste system that separated Indians into groups.

Reading Focus Have you ever wondered why some people seem to be treated differently than other people? As you read, try to find out why this idea was accepted in India.

One of the results of the Aryan arrival in India was the development of a caste system. A **caste** (KAST) is a social group that someone is born into and cannot change.

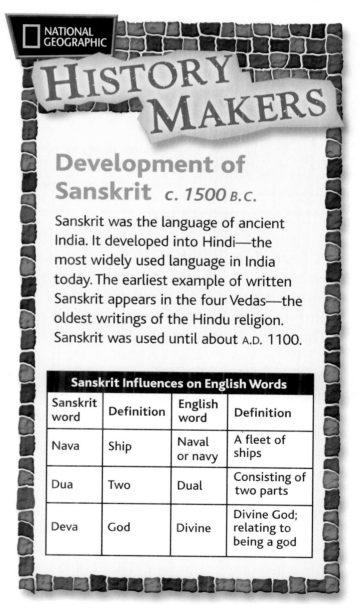

NATIONAL GEOGRAPHIC

HISTORY MAKERS

Development of Sanskrit c. 1500 B.C.

Sanskrit was the language of ancient India. It developed into Hindi—the most widely used language in India today. The earliest example of written Sanskrit appears in the four Vedas—the oldest writings of the Hindu religion. Sanskrit was used until about A.D. 1100.

Sanskrit Influences on English Words			
Sanskrit word	Definition	English word	Definition
Nava	Ship	Naval or navy	A fleet of ships
Dua	Two	Dual	Consisting of two parts
Deva	God	Divine	Divine God; relating to being a god

A Brahman ▶

Today, Untouchables refer to ▶ themselves as *Dalit*, which means "oppressed." *Why did the Aryans create the caste system?*

Early India's Social System

Brahmans Priests
Kshatriyas Warriors, rulers
Vaisyas Common people
Sudras Unskilled laborers, servants
Pariahs Untouchables

A caste dictates what job you will have, whom you can marry, and with whom you can socialize. In India, the word for caste (a term used by Portuguese merchants) is *jati*. Thousands of *jati* exist in India.

Why was a caste system created? No one is sure, but ideas about skin color were probably part of it. The Aryans were a light-skinned people. They thought they were better than the dark-skinned people they had encountered in India. This idea was wrong, but the Aryans believed it.

Another reason the Aryans might have created the caste system was because the people they encountered in India outnumbered them. The caste system set the rules for everyone's behavior. This helped the Aryans stay in control.

Social Classes of Indian Society The thousands of different *jati* in Indian society were grouped together into four classes called *varnas*. The top two varnas were **Brahmans** (BRAH•muhns) and Kshatriyas (KSHA•tree•uhs). Brahmans were the priests—the only people who could perform religious ceremonies. The Kshatriyas were warriors who ran the government and army.

On the next level down were the Vaisyas (VYSH•yuhs), or commoners. Vaisyas were usually farmers and merchants. Below the Vaisyas came the Sudras (SOO•druhs). Sudras were manual laborers and servants and had few rights. Most Indians belonged to the Sudra caste.

There was one group that did not belong to any *varna*. Its members were called Pariahs, or the Untouchables. They performed work other Indians thought was too dirty, such as collecting trash, skinning animals, or handling dead bodies.

Life for an Untouchable was very hard. Most Indians believed that being near an Untouchable was harmful, so they forced them to live apart from others. When Untouchables traveled, they had to tap two sticks together so that everyone would hear them coming and have time to move away.

The Role of Men and Women In ancient India, the family was the center of life. Grandparents, parents, and children all lived together in an extended family. The oldest man in the family was in charge.

Men had many more rights than women. Unless there were no sons in a family, only a man could inherit property. Only men could go to school or become priests.

In families at the top of Indian society, a boy had a **guru** (GUR•oo), or teacher, until he went to the city for more education. Young men from these families could marry only when they had finished 12 years of schooling.

In India, parents arranged marriages for their children. Even today, parents arrange the majority of marriages in India. Boys and girls often married in their teens. Some were as young as 13. Divorce was almost never allowed, but if a couple could not have children, the husband could marry a second wife.

One custom shows how the lives of Indian men were considered more important than the lives of Indian women. In India, people were cremated, or burned, when they died. When a man from a prominent family died, his wife was expected to leap into the flames. This practice was called suttee (suh•TEE). If the wife resisted and did not kill herself, it was a great shame. Everyone would avoid the woman from then on.

✓ **Reading Check** **Identify** What were the five major groups in Indian society?

History Online
Study Central™ Need help with the material in this section? Visit jat.glencoe.com

Section ① Review

Reading Summary
Review the Main Ideas

• India's first civilization, including the cities of Harappa and Mohenjo-Daro, developed in the fertile Indus River valley.

• The Aryans, a group of nomadic herders, migrated into the northern part of India by about 1000 B.C. They brought the iron plow and the Sanskrit language to India.

• India's caste system divided people into rigid social and economic classes. Ancient Indian society favored men over women.

What Did You Learn?

1. Describe the cities of Harappa and Mohenjo-Daro.

2. Why are monsoons important to Indian farmers?

Critical Thinking

3. **Cause and Effect** What caused the collapse of Harappan civilization?

4. **Cause and Effect** Draw a diagram to show how the Aryans changed the lifestyle of the Indians.

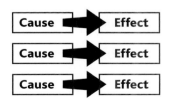

5. **Contrast** How did the Aryan and Harappan lifestyles differ?

6. **Explain** How did India's social classes, or varnas, shape India's society?

7. **Descriptive Writing** Write a description of the city of Harappa or Mohenjo-Daro that could have been used to attract residents to that city in ancient India.

8. **Reading** **Vocabulary** Explain how the suffix in the word *plentiful* can help you determine its meaning.

Hinduism and Buddhism

Get-Ready to Read!

What's the Connection?

Much of Indian civilization is based on Aryan ideas and culture, which you learned about in the last section. One of the most important and long-lasting contributions of the Aryans is the main religion of India, Hinduism.

Focusing on the Main Ideas

- Hinduism grew out of the ancient beliefs of the Aryans. *(page 203)*

- A new religion, Buddhism, appealed to many people in India and other parts of Asia. *(page 205)*

Locating Places
Nepal (nuh•PAWL)
Tibet (tuh•BEHT)

Meeting People
Siddhartha Gautama (sih•DAHR• tuh GOW•tuh•muh)
Dalai Lama (DAH•LY LAH•muh)

Building Your Vocabulary
Hinduism (HIHN•doo•IH•zuhm)
Brahman (BRAH•muhn)
reincarnation
   (REE•ihn•kahr•NAY•shuhn)
dharma (DAHR•muh)
karma (KAHR•muh)
Buddhism (BOO•DIH•zuhm)
nirvana (nihr•VAH•nuh)
theocracy (thee•AH•kruh•see)

Reading Strategy
Summarizing Information Create a web diagram like the one below. In the ovals, identify major beliefs of Hinduism.

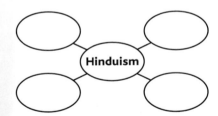

Hinduism

NATIONAL GEOGRAPHIC When & Where?

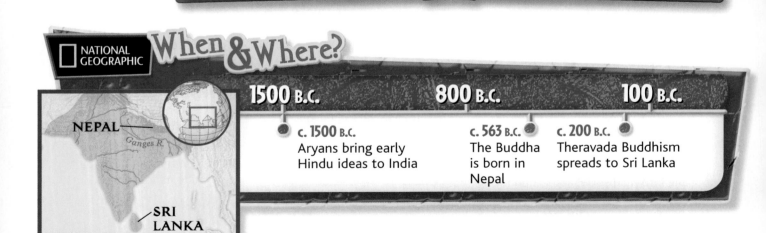

NEPAL
Ganges R.

SRI LANKA

1500 B.C.

800 B.C.

100 B.C.

c. 1500 B.C.
Aryans bring early Hindu ideas to India

c. 563 B.C.
The Buddha is born in Nepal

c. 200 B.C.
Theravada Buddhism spreads to Sri Lanka

Hinduism

Main Idea Hinduism grew out of the ancient beliefs of the Aryans.

Reading Focus Have you ever wondered why most people try to behave properly or do good deeds? As you read this section, find out how a Hindu would answer this question.

Hinduism (HIHN•doo•IH•zuhm) is one of the oldest religions in the world, and today it is the third largest. It began with the religion of the Aryans, who arrived in India about 1500 B.C. The Aryans believed in many gods and goddesses who controlled the forces of nature. We know about Aryan religion from their ancient hymns and poetry, especially their epics, or long poems.

For centuries, the priests, or Brahmans, recited these works, and much later they were written down in Sanskrit. Over the centuries, Aryan religion changed. It borrowed some religious ideas from the people the Aryans conquered in India. This mix of beliefs eventually became Hinduism.

Early Hinduism Hinduism grew out of the religious customs of many people over thousands of years. This might explain why Hinduism has thousands of gods and goddesses. Hindus tend to think of all gods and goddesses as different parts of one universal spirit. This universal spirit is called **Brahman** (BRAH•muhn).

The search for a universal spirit is described in the ancient religious writings known as the Upanishads (oo•PAH•nih•SHADZ). Those writings say that every living being has a soul that wants to be reunited with Brahman and that this happens when a person dies.

The Upanishads describe how a person unites with Brahman: A soul that becomes one with Brahman is like a lump of salt thrown into water. The lump of salt is gone, but the water tastes salty. The salt has become part of the water.

What Is Karma? Hindus believe that a soul is not joined to the Brahman immediately after a person dies. Instead, a person must pass through many lives to be united

◀ **Hindu temple**

▲ **Hindus meet to discuss holy writings.**
What ancient religious writings describe the search for a universal spirit?

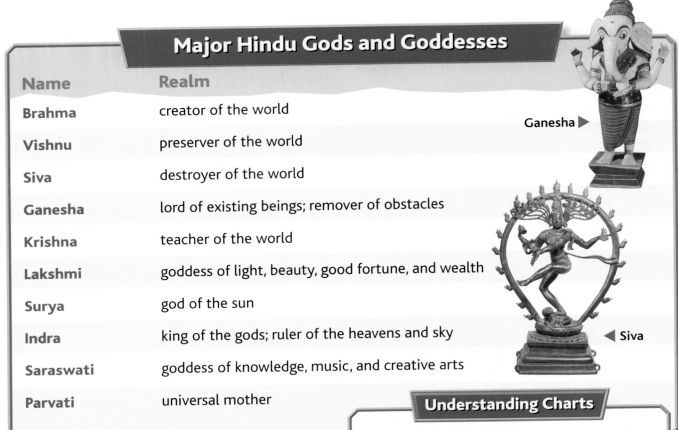

Major Hindu Gods and Goddesses

Name	Realm
Brahma	creator of the world
Vishnu	preserver of the world
Siva	destroyer of the world
Ganesha	lord of existing beings; remover of obstacles
Krishna	teacher of the world
Lakshmi	goddess of light, beauty, good fortune, and wealth
Surya	god of the sun
Indra	king of the gods; ruler of the heavens and sky
Saraswati	goddess of knowledge, music, and creative arts
Parvati	universal mother

Ganesha ▶

◀ Siva

Understanding Charts

Brahma, Vishnu, and Siva are considered the three main Hindu gods.
1. Which god is known as the "teacher of the world"?
2. **Conclude** Why does Hinduism have so many gods?

with Brahman. On its journey, a soul might be reborn into a higher *varna* or *jati*. If a person lived a bad life, he or she might be reborn into a lower *varna* or *jati*.

This idea of passing through many lives to reach the Brahman is called **reincarnation** (REE•ihn•kahr•NAY•shuhn). It is very important in Hinduism and it influences how Hindus live their daily lives. It even affects how they treat animals because they consider all life sacred.

To earn the reward of a better life in their next life, Hindus believe they must perform their duty. **Dharma** (DAHR•muh) is the divine law. It requires people to perform the duties of their *jati*. A farmer has different duties than a priest and men have different duties than women.

The consequences of how a person lives are known as **karma** (KAHR•muh). If Hindus

do their duty and live a good life, they will have good karma. This will move them closer to the Brahman in their next life.

How did the belief in reincarnation affect Indians? For one thing, it made them more accepting of the *varna* and *jati* system. People believed they had to be happy with their role in life. A dedicated Hindu believes that the people in a higher *varna* are superior and that they are supposed to be on top. The belief in reincarnation gave hope to everyone, even servants. If servants did their duty, they might be reborn into a higher social class in their next life.

✓ **Reading Check** **Explain** How is karma related to reincarnation?

Buddhism

Main Idea A new religion, Buddhism, appealed to many people in India and other parts of Asia.

Reading Focus What do you think makes a person free and happy? Find out how the Buddha answered this important question as you read this section.

By 600 B.C., many Indians began to question Hindu ideas. The Brahman priests seemed to care only about their temple ceremonies and not about the needs of the people. Ordinary Hindus wanted a simpler, more spiritual religion. Many would find what they needed in **Buddhism** (BOO•DIH•zuhm), a new religion founded by **Siddhartha Gautama** (sih•DAHR•tuh GOW•tuh•muh).

Who Is the Buddha?

Prince Siddhartha Gautama was born around 563 B.C. in a small kingdom near the Himalaya. Today, this area is in southern **Nepal** (nuh•PAWL).

Siddhartha seemed to have it all. He was wealthy and handsome, happily married, and had a fine new son. Then one day he decided to explore the kingdom beyond the palace walls. As he traveled, he became very upset. He saw beggars, people who were ill, and people broken down by age with no home and nowhere to go. For the first time, he was truly aware of suffering.

Then and there, Siddhartha decided to seek an answer to this great riddle: Why did people suffer and how could their suffering be cured? He left his family and riches and began his search. At first he lived like a hermit, fasting and sleeping on the hard ground. Siddhartha nearly starved, but he still had no answer to his questions.

Then he decided to meditate for as long as it took to get the answer. Legend tells us that Siddhartha sat under a tree to meditate, and after 49 days, he finally understood. It was as if he had seen a great light.

▲ **This shrine in northern India marks the location where it is believed the Buddha delivered his first sermon.** *With what groups of Indians did the Buddha's message become popular?*

Siddhartha spent the rest of his life wandering the countryside and telling people what he had discovered. His lessons about life and the nature of suffering became known as Buddhism. To his followers, he became known as the Buddha, or "Enlightened One."

What Is Buddhism?

To understand the Buddha's ideas, one first has to see the world as he did. Like any good Hindu, Siddhartha did not think that the normal, everyday world was real. Trees, houses, animals, the sky, and the oceans were just illusions. So were poverty and sickness, pain and sorrow.

Siddhartha believed that the only way to find the truth about the world was to give up all desires. By giving up the desire for fame, the desire for money, and the desire for all worldly things, pain and sorrow would vanish.

If a person gave up all desires, he or she would reach **nirvana** (nihr•VAH•nuh). Nirvana is not a place but a state of wisdom. The word *nirvana* came from the Sanskrit word for blowing out a candle flame.

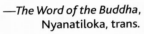

Primary Source — Morality in the Eightfold Path

This passage describes the way a person should act according to the Eightfold Path.

"He avoids the killing of living beings. . . . He avoids stealing, and abstains from [avoids] taking what is not given to him. Only what is given to him he takes, waiting till it is given; and he lives with a heart honest and pure. . . . He avoids lying. . . . He speaks the truth, is devoted to the truth, reliable, worthy of confidence, no deceiver of men."

—*The Word of the Buddha*, Nyanatiloka, trans.

▲ The Buddha

DBQ Document-Based Question

According to the passage, what is the correct way to accept something?

The heart of the Buddha's teachings is contained in the Four Noble Truths. The Four Noble Truths are:

1. *Life is full of suffering.*
2. *People suffer because they desire worldly things and self-satisfaction.*
3. *The way to end suffering is to stop desiring things.*
4. *The only way to stop desiring things is to follow the Eightfold Path.*

The Buddha's fourth truth says people should follow eight steps to eliminate suffering. The Buddha's Eightfold Path was this:

1. *Know and understand the Four Noble Truths.*

2. *Give up worldly things and don't harm others.*
3. *Tell the truth, don't gossip, and don't speak badly of others.*
4. *Don't commit evil acts, like killing, stealing, or living an unclean life.*
5. *Do rewarding work.*
6. *Work for good and oppose evil.*
7. *Make sure your mind keeps your senses under control.*
8. *Practice meditation as a way of understanding reality.*

One reason the Buddha's ideas became popular was that he did not accept the *varna* and *jati* systems. A person's place in life depended on the person, he thought. The Buddha did believe in reincarnation, but with a difference. If people wanted to stop being reborn into new lives, the Buddha said, they would only have to follow his Eightfold Path.

Many people liked the Buddha's message, especially Untouchables and lower-class Indians. For the first time, these groups heard that they, too, could reach enlightenment.

Buddhism in Southeast Asia For more than 40 years, the Buddha preached his ideas. Disciples gathered around him, and after his death, they spread his message all over Asia.

As more and more people practiced Buddhism, disagreements arose about the Buddha's ideas. Finally, Buddhists split into two groups. The first was Theravada Buddhism. *Theravada* means "teachings of the elders." It sees the Buddha as a great teacher, not a god.

Buddhist teachers and merchants spread the ideas of Theravada to the south and east. It was adopted in Ceylon in the 200s B.C. Ceylon, an island located near the southern tip of India, is now called Sri Lanka. Theravada Buddhism also became popular in Myanmar, Thailand, Cambodia, and Laos.

Biography

THE BUDDHA
C. 563–483 B.C.

The Buddha ▶

Siddhartha Gautama—the thinker and teacher who would later be called the Buddha—was born in what is now Nepal. According to legend, his mother had a dream shortly before his birth that was interpreted to mean that her son would become a great leader.

The Gautama family belonged to the warrior caste. Siddhartha's father, Suddhodana, ruled a group called the Shakyas. His mother, Maya, died shortly after his birth.

Siddhartha was very intelligent. According to legend, the young man knew 64 languages and mastered all his studies without needing instruction. At age 29, Siddhartha realized that he wanted to search for truth, enlightenment, and a way to rise above suffering. He left his wife, Yasodhara, and son, Rahula, to study with priests.

At age 35, Siddhartha is said to have reached full enlightenment while sitting beneath a tree. The Buddha began traveling to teach others about his discoveries and about the nature of life and suffering.

"Our life is shaped by our mind; we become what we think."

–The Buddha

◀ Sculpture of the Buddha sitting on a cobra

Then and Now
What types of present-day occupations often involve traveling to teach others?

207

Mahayana Buddhism

The second kind of Buddhism is called Mahayana Buddhism. It teaches that the Buddha is a god who came to save people. Mahayana Buddhists believe that following the Eightfold Path is too hard for most people in this world. They believe that by worshiping the Buddha instead, people will go to a heaven after they die. There, they can follow the Eightfold Path and reach nirvana.

Mahayana Buddhists also have special affection for the bodhisattvas (BOH•dih•SUHT•vuhz). Bodhisattvas are the enlightened people who postpone going to heaven. Instead, bodhisattvas have decided to stay on Earth to help others and do good deeds.

▲ A Tibetan monk today

Mahayana Buddhism spread northward into China and from there to Korea and Japan.

A special kind of Mahayana Buddhism developed in central Asia in the country of **Tibet** (tuh•BEHT). There it mixed with Tibet's traditional religion and with Hinduism.

In Tibet, the Buddhist leaders, called lamas, also led the government. When religious leaders head a government, it is called a **theocracy** (thee•AH•kruh•see). The **Dalai Lama** (DAH•ly LAH•muh) was the lama who headed the government, and the Panchen Lama was the lama who led the religion. Both were considered reincarnations of the Buddha.

Today, many Buddhists live in countries like Thailand, Cambodia, and Sri Lanka, but few live in India where the Buddha first preached.

✓**Reading Check** **Identify** How could a Buddhist reach nirvana?

History Online

Study Central™ Need help with the material in this section? Visit jat.glencoe.com

Section 2 Review

Reading Summary

Review the Main Ideas

- Hinduism is an old religion with many gods. Hindus believe in reincarnation and that a person's place in life is determined by his or her karma.

- In the 500s B.C., Siddhartha Gautama founded the religion of Buddhism in northern India. According to Buddhism, a person who follows the Four Noble Truths and the Eightfold Path can achieve nirvana.

What Did You Learn?

1. What are the Upanishads?

2. What is reincarnation?

Critical Thinking

3. **Compare and Contrast** Draw a chart like the one below. Then add details to compare the two main branches of Buddhism.

Branches of Buddhism	
Theravada Buddhism	Mahayana Buddhism

4. **Describe** Explain the concept of karma.

5. **Explain** What is the importance of the Four Noble Truths and the Eightfold Path?

6. **Analyze** How did the belief in reincarnation both strengthen the divisions in Indian society and provide hope for the lower classes?

7. **Expository Writing** Write a short essay describing Siddhartha Gautama's journey to enlightenment.

India's First Empires

Get Ready to Read!

What's the Connection?
In the last section, you learned about Hinduism and Buddhism. Both religions developed when India was a land of small kingdoms. These rival kingdoms would be forced to unite, however, when foreigners invaded.

Focusing on the Main Ideas
• The Mauryan dynasty built India's first great empire. *(page 210)*

• The Gupta empire reunited much of northern India and became wealthy through trade. *(page 213)*

• The Mauryan and Gupta empires made important contributions in literature, mathematics, and science. *(page 214)*

Locating Places
Pataliputra
(PAH•tuh•lih•POO•truh)

Meeting People
Chandragupta Maurya (CHUHN• druh•GUP•tuh   MAH•oor•yuh)
Asoka (uh•SOH•kuh)
Kalidasa (KAH•lih•DAH•suh)

Building Your Vocabulary
dynasty (DY•nuh•stee)
stupa (STOO•puh)
pilgrim (PIHL•gruhm)

Reading Strategy
Categorizing Information Complete a chart like the one below, identifying the important dates, capital city, and government of the Mauryan empire.

	Mauryan Empire
Dates	
Capital City	
Government	

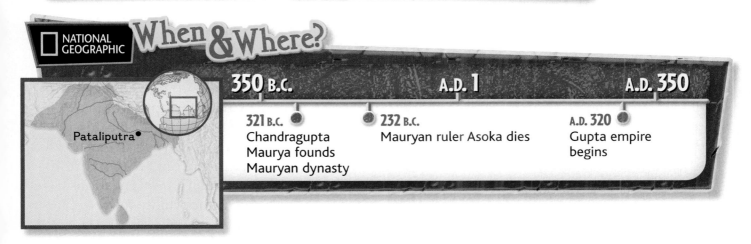

NATIONAL GEOGRAPHIC
When & Where?

Pataliputra•

350 B.C.	A.D. 1	A.D. 350

321 B.C.
Chandragupta Maurya founds Mauryan dynasty

232 B.C.
Mauryan ruler Asoka dies

A.D. 320
Gupta empire begins

The Mauryan Dynasty

Main Idea The Mauryan dynasty built India's first great empire.

Reading Focus Do you think political leaders should promote religion? How might religion help a king hold his country together? Read to learn why one Indian emperor decided to support Buddhism.

India's princes fought over their small kingdoms for centuries. Then two big invasions taught the Indians a lesson. First, the Persians invaded the Indus Valley in the 500s B.C. and made it part of the great Persian Empire. Then, as you have already read, Alexander the Great invaded India in 327 B.C.

Although Alexander's troops conquered northern India, he did not stay long. His soldiers were homesick and tired and threatened to rebel unless he turned back. The invasion did have one important effect, however. It led to the first great Indian empire.

Who Built India's First Empire? India's first empire was founded by **Chandragupta Maurya** (CHUHN•druh•GUP•tuh MAH•oor•yuh). Chandragupta was an Indian prince who conquered a large area in the Ganges River valley soon after Alexander invaded western India. Alexander's invasion weakened many of India's kingdoms. After Alexander left, Chandragupta seized the opportunity to conquer and unite almost all of northern India.

He founded the Mauryan dynasty in 321 B.C. A **dynasty** (DY•nuh•stee) is a series of rulers from the same family. To run his empire, Chandragupta set up a centralized government. In a centralized government, rulers run everything from a capital city. To control everything from his capital, **Pataliputra** (PAH•tuh•lih•POO•truh), Chandragupta had to have a strong army. He also needed a good spy system to make sure no one was planning to rebel. Communications were also important, so he set up a postal system.

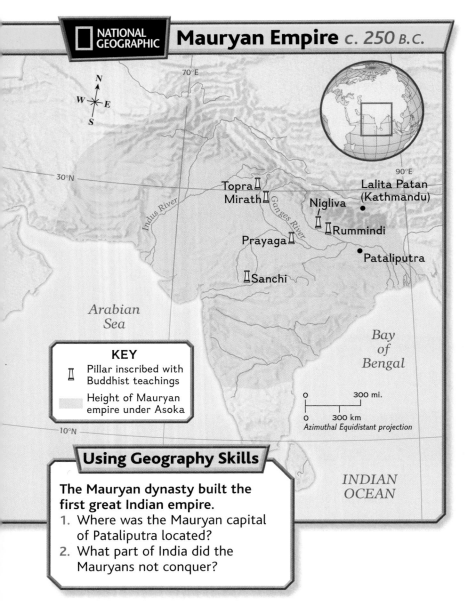

NATIONAL GEOGRAPHIC

Mauryan Empire c. 250 B.C.

70°E
30°N
Indus River
Topra
Mirath
Ganges River
Nigliva
Lalita Patan
(Kathmandu)
90°E
Rummindi
Prayaga
Pataliputra
Sanchi
Arabian Sea
Bay of Bengal
INDIAN OCEAN

KEY
Ⅱ Pillar inscribed with Buddhist teachings

Height of Mauryan empire under Asoka

10°N

0   300 mi.
0   300 km
Azimuthal Equidistant projection

Using Geography Skills

The Mauryan dynasty built the first great Indian empire.
1. Where was the Mauryan capital of Pataliputra located?
2. What part of India did the Mauryans not conquer?

▲ This stupa from central India is one of the best-preserved shrines from the 200s B.C. *What other type of structure did Indians create to honor the Buddha?*

The Buddha ▶

Emperor Asoka's Reign Chandragupta founded the Mauryan dynasty, but many historians think the empire's greatest king was **Asoka** (uh•SOH•kuh). Asoka ruled from about 273 B.C. to 232 B.C.

Asoka was an unusual ruler. Like many kings, he was a strong military leader, but he came to hate bloodshed. After one bloody fight, he walked over the battlefield. When he saw the dead and wounded, he was horrified and made a vow. He would dedicate his life to peace and follow the teachings of the Buddha.

Asoka was history's first great Buddhist king. He built hospitals for people and for animals, too. He built new roads so it was easier to trade and put shelters and shade trees along the roads where travelers could rest.

Asoka sent many Buddhist teachers throughout India and the rest of Asia. They carried the religion to new believers. In India, laborers carved the Buddha's teachings on stone pillars for people to read. Asoka also had laborers build thousands of **stupas** (STOO•puhs). Stupas are Buddhist shrines that have the shape of a dome or mound.

Although he was a Buddhist, Asoka allowed his Hindu subjects to practice their religion. His tolerance was unusual for the time.

With a good road system and a strong ruler, the empire prospered. India became the center of a huge trade network that stretched to the Mediterranean Sea.

The Fall of the Mauryan Empire Asoka died in 232 B.C. Unfortunately, the kings who followed him were not very good leaders, and the empire grew weak.

These kings made bad decisions that turned the people against them. They forced merchants to pay heavy taxes and seized peasants' crops for themselves. Things were so bad that in 183 B.C., the last Mauryan ruler was killed by one of his own generals.

Reading Check **Summarize** Why was Asoka an important ruler?

Biography

EMPEROR ASOKA
Reigned c. 273–232 B.C.

Emperor Asoka vowed to relieve suffering wherever he found it. He discovered that Buddhism reflected his new beliefs, so he became a Buddhist.

Emperor Asoka had a strong, energetic personality. He began preaching the Buddhist ideas that people should be honest, truthful, and nonviolent. He preached that people should live with compassion toward all humans and animals. Asoka taught by example and tried to live his life with "little sin and many good deeds." He ordered his government officials to adopt those virtues for their own lives. He also ordered his officials to keep him informed of the needs of the people in his empire.

Emperor Asoka regularly visited people in the rural areas of his kingdom and found practical ways to improve their lives. He founded hospitals and supplied medicine. He ordered wells to be dug and trees to be planted along the roads.

▼ Asoka

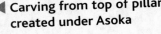

◄ Carving from top of pillar created under Asoka

Then and Now

Asoka combined religion and government. Do you think that the two should be combined or kept separate? Explain, providing examples to support your answer.

The Gupta Empire

Main Idea The Gupta empire reunited much of northern India and became wealthy through trade.

Reading Focus What types of products does the United States trade with other countries? Read to learn how the Gupta empire built its wealth on trade.

For 500 years, India had no strong ruler. Once again, small kingdoms fought with one another and made life miserable for their subjects. Then, in A.D. 320, one prince in the Ganges River valley grew more powerful than the others. Like an earlier ruler, his name was Chandragupta. This Chandragupta chose to rule from the old capital of the Mauryan empire—Pataliputra.

Chandragupta founded the Gupta dynasty. When he died, his son, Samudragupta, took over the throne and expanded the Gupta empire in northern India. Soon, the new kingdom dominated almost all of northern India. The Guptas ruled for about 200 years. Gupta rulers had one advantage over the earlier Mauryan kings. The empire was smaller and that made it easier to manage.

The Gupta empire grew wealthy from trade. Salt, cloth, and iron were common goods traded in India. Indian merchants also traded with China and with kingdoms in southeast Asia and the Mediterranean. The Gupta rulers controlled much of the trade and became very wealthy. They owned silver and gold mines and large estates.

Trade created jobs for people in India and made many people and cities prosperous. Cities grew up along the trade routes, and many people traveled. Some people, called **pilgrims** (PIHL•gruhms), often used the trade routes to travel to a religious shrine or site. Just as cities today make money from tourism, Indian cities that were famous for their temples became wealthy from visiting pilgrims.

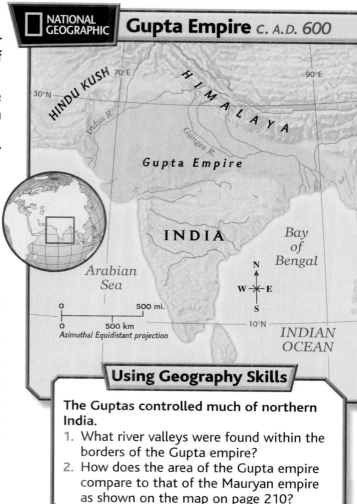

NATIONAL GEOGRAPHIC **Gupta Empire** C. A.D. 600

Using Geography Skills

The Guptas controlled much of northern India.

1. What river valleys were found within the borders of the Gupta empire?
2. How does the area of the Gupta empire compare to that of the Mauryan empire as shown on the map on page 210?

Asoka had converted to Buddhism, but the Guptas were Hindus like many of their subjects. They made Hinduism the official religion and gave money to support Hindu scholars and Hindu shrines. The shrines they built to Hindu gods and goddesses inspired Hindus. They often had brightly painted sculptures of images from the Upanishads and other sacred writings.

During the Gupta empire, art and science also began to develop. Earlier, you learned that Greece had a golden age of art and learning. India also had a golden age of art and learning during the Gupta empire.

Reading Check **Explain** How did the Gupta empire become wealthy?

Indian Literature and Science

Main Idea The Mauryan and Gupta empires made important contributions in literature, mathematics, and science.

Reading Focus What do you think modern movies, books, and television reveal about our values? As you read, try to see if Indian poetry tells a story about values during the Gupta period.

Artists, builders, scientists, and writers produced many works while the Mauryan and Gupta kings ruled.

India's Most Famous Poems

The Vedas of India are ancient hymns and prayers for religious ceremonies. No one is certain how old they are because for a long time they were only recited, not written down. Once Aryan people came to India and developed Sanskrit, then the Vedas could be recorded.

Later, other kinds of literature were also written down. Two epics are very famous in India, and Indians today still love to read them. The first is the *Mahabharata* (muh•HAH•BAH•ruh•tuh), and the second is the *Ramayana* (rah•mah•YAH•nah). Both of these long poems tell about brave warriors and their heroic deeds.

The *Mahabharata* is the longest poem in any written language—about 88,000 verses. Historians think several different authors wrote it and that it was written down around 100 B.C. It describes a great war for control of an Indian kingdom about 1,000 years earlier.

The best-known section is the Bhagavad Gita (BAH•guh•VAHD GEE•tuh), or "Song of the Lord." It is very important in Hindu writings. In it, the god Krishna preaches a sermon before a battle. He tells his listeners how noble it is to do one's duty even when it is difficult and painful.

Primary Source

The Bhagavad Gita

In the Bhagavad Gita, Arjuna prepares to go into battle. He asks the god Krishna questions about war and death. The following passage is part of Krishna's answer.

"Thou grievest where no grief should be! . . .

. . . .

All, that doth live, lives always! . . .

. . . .

The soul that with a strong and constant calm
Takes sorrow and takes joy indifferently,
Lives in the life undying!

—*Bhagavadgita*, Sir Edwin Arnold, trans.

DBQ **Document-Based Question**

What does Krishna believe about life after death?

▼ Painting titled *Krishna and Maidens*

The *Ramayana* is another long poem. It was written at about the same time as the *Mahabharata*. It tells of the great king Rama and his queen Sita (SEE•tuh). Rama's enemies have him banished from the kingdom. He is forced to live as a hermit in the forest. Later, he fights and defeats the demon Ravana, who had kidnapped Sita. As in many Indian epics, they live happily ever after.

Like the *Mahabharata,* the *Ramayana* contains many religious and moral lessons. Rama is the perfect hero, king, and son. Sita is the perfect, faithful wife. However, people enjoyed the epics for other reasons as well. Like adventure movies of today, these poems told thrilling stories about great heroes.

Other writings from ancient India have also survived. These are quite different from the *Mahabharata* and *Ramayana*. One of India's best-known authors was **Kalidasa** (KAH•lih•DAH•suh). He lived during the Gupta dynasty. Kalidasa wrote plays, poems, love stories, and comedies. His poem *The Cloud Messenger* is one of the most popular Sanskrit poems. It is a love story that also contains beautiful descriptions of the mountains, forests, and rivers of northern India. A completely different work is the *Panchantantra*. It is similar to Aesop's fables. In these tales, talking animal characters present lessons about life. Most Indian literature stresses the importance of dharma. Each person, regardless of social status, must do his or her duty.

Indian Math and Science
Indian mathematicians, especially in the Gupta period, made important contributions. Aryabhata (AHR•yuh•BUHT•uh) was the leading mathematician of the Gupta empire. He was

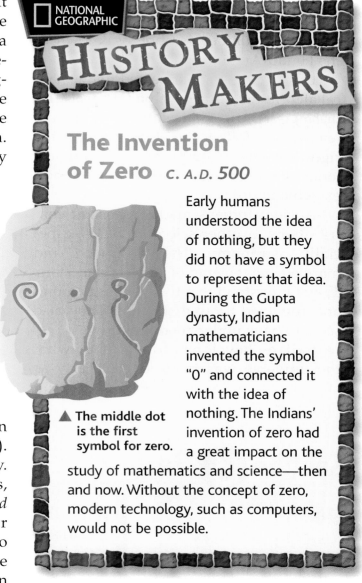

NATIONAL GEOGRAPHIC

HISTORY MAKERS

The Invention of Zero C. A.D. 500

▲ The middle dot is the first symbol for zero.

Early humans understood the idea of nothing, but they did not have a symbol to represent that idea. During the Gupta dynasty, Indian mathematicians invented the symbol "0" and connected it with the idea of nothing. The Indians' invention of zero had a great impact on the study of mathematics and science—then and now. Without the concept of zero, modern technology, such as computers, would not be possible.

one of the first scientists known to have used algebra. Indian mathematicians developed the idea of zero and a symbol to represent it. They also explained the concept of infinity—something without an end.

Gupta mathematicians created the symbols for the numbers 1 to 9 that we use today. These number symbols, or numerals, were adopted by Arab traders in the A.D. 700s. European traders borrowed them from the Arabs. Use of these numbers spread through Europe in the A.D. 1200s, replacing Roman numerals. Today, this system of number symbols is known as the Hindu-Arabic numerical system.

Early Indians also invented mathematical algorithms. An algorithm (AHL•gohr•ih•thuhm) is a series of steps that solve a problem. If you follow the steps, you get the right answer. Computer programmers today often use algorithms to tell computers what to do.

Ancient Indians made important contributions in other scientific fields, especially astronomy. They followed and mapped movements of planets and stars. They understood that the Earth was round and revolved around the sun. They also seem to have understood gravity.

Indians developed ideas about what the universe was made of. As early as the 500s B.C., Indian thinkers believed that the universe was made up of many very tiny particles. They came up with ideas of atoms before the Greeks in the West did.

In the field of medicine, Gupta doctors were advanced for their time. They could set broken bones and perform operations. They also invented many medical tools.

An Indian doctor named Shushruta (shoosh•ROO•tah) carried out an early form of plastic surgery. He worked to restore damaged noses. Indian doctors used herbs in treating illnesses.They also believed it was important to remove the causes of a disease and not just cure the disease itself.

✓ **Reading Check** **Summarize** In what branches of science did ancient Indians make advances?

History **O**nline

Study Central™ Need help with the material in this section? Visit jat.glencoe.com

Section 3 Review

Reading Summary
Review the Main Ideas

• The Mauryan empire, under leaders such as Chandragupta Maurya and Asoka, united most of India for over a hundred years.

• The Gupta dynasty reunited northern India and grew wealthy from trade.

• During the Mauryan and Gupta empires, the arts and sciences flourished in India. Several great works of literature, including the *Mahabharata* and the *Ramayana*, came from this period.

What Did You Learn?

1. Describe trade during the Gupta empire.

2. What is the message of the Bhagavad Gita?

Critical Thinking

3. **Organizing Information** Draw a diagram to show the contributions of Indian mathematicians during the Mauryan and Gupta empires.

Contributions

4. **Analyze** How were Asoka's Buddhist beliefs reflected in his accomplishments as king?

5. **Expository Writing** Which of the Indian emperors described in this section do you think was the greatest ruler? Write a short essay explaining your choice.

6. **Math Link** Why would the development of a number system be important in a civilization that depended on trade?

7. **Reading** **Vocabulary** Explain how you could use context to determine the meaning of the word *prospered* in this sentence.

"With a good road system and a strong ruler, the empire prospered."

Section 1 India's First Civilizations

Vocabulary

subcontinent
monsoon
Sanskrit
raja
caste
guru

Focusing on the Main Ideas

- Climate and geography influenced the rise of India's first civilization. *(page 195)*
- The Aryans conquered India and introduced new ideas and technology. *(page 198)*
- The Aryans created a caste system that separated Indians into groups. *(page 199)*

Section 2 Hinduism and Buddhism

Vocabulary

Hinduism
Brahman
reincarnation
dharma
karma
Buddhism
nirvana
theocracy

Focusing on the Main Ideas

- Hinduism grew out of the ancient beliefs of the Aryans. *(page 203)*
- A new religion, Buddhism, appealed to many people in India and other parts of Asia. *(page 205)*

Ganesha ▶

Section 3 India's First Empires

Vocabulary

dynasty
stupa
pilgrim

Focusing on the Main Ideas

- The Mauryan dynasty built India's first great empire. *(page 210)*
- The Gupta empire reunited much of northern India and became wealthy through trade. *(page 213)*
- The Mauryan and Gupta empires made important contributions in literature, mathematics, and science. *(page 214)*

Review Vocabulary

1. Write a paragraph about the basic beliefs of Buddhism using the following words.

   reincarnation   karma   dharma

   Write the vocabulary word that best completes each sentence. Then write a sentence for each term not chosen.

   a. stupa   e. pilgrim
   b. guru   f. theocracy
   c. *varna*   g. monsoon
   d. raja   h. dynasty

2. Each Aryan tribe was led by a ___.
3. In a ___, government is led by religious leaders.
4. A ___ is a line of rulers who belong to the same family.
5. A ___ travels to religious places.

Review Main Ideas

Section 1 • India's First Civilizations

6. What influenced the rise of India's first civilizations?
7. What was the purpose of the *varna* system?

Section 2 • Hinduism and Buddhism

8. From what did Hinduism form?
9. Which religion appealed to people in India and other parts of Asia?

Section 3 • India's First Empires

10. Which dynasty built India's first great empire?
11. Why was the Gupta empire important?

Critical Thinking

12. **Compare** How do you think the Eightfold Path is similar to the Ten Commandments of Judaism?

13. **Analyze** How does the *Mahabharata* reflect the ideals of ancient India?

14. **Explain** How did the monsoons affect the development of India's first civilizations?

15. **Predict** What do you think might have happened if Asoka had approved of the slaughter on the battlefield during his wars of conquest?

Review
Reading Skill Vocabulary Building Your Vocabulary

16. Read the following excerpt from page 205. Then explain how context clues can help you determine the meaning of the word *hermit*.

He left his family and riches and began his search. At first he lived like a hermit, fasting and sleeping on the hard ground. Siddhartha nearly starved, but he still had no answer to his questions.

To review this skill, see pages 192–193.

Geography Skills

Study the map below and answer the following questions.

17. **Human/Environment Interaction** Why did Harappa and Mohenjo-Daro develop so near the Indus River?

18. **Place** The winter monsoon winds come from the northeast. What makes the winds from that monsoon cold?

19. **Location** Name at least two natural features that protected Harappa and Mohenjo-Daro from invaders.

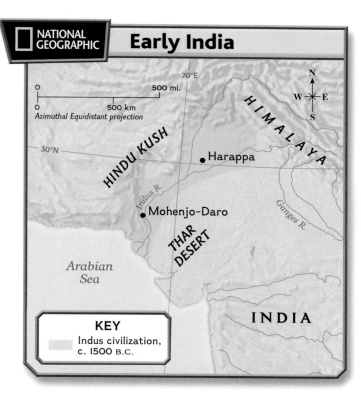

NATIONAL GEOGRAPHIC

Early India

70°E

500 mi.

500 km

Azimuthal Equidistant projection

N W E S

30°N

HINDU KUSH

HIMALAYA

Harappa

Indus R.

Mohenjo-Daro

Ganges R.

THAR DESERT

Arabian Sea

INDIA

KEY
Indus civilization, c. 1500 B.C.

Read to Write

20. **Persuasive Writing** In the *Mahabharata,* the god Krishna advises Arjuna, "Get ready for battle without thought of . . . gain and loss, victory and defeat." Write a paragraph in which you agree or disagree with that advice.

21. **Using Your** **FOLDABLES** Use the information you recorded in your foldable to create a fill-in-the-blank quiz for a classmate. Write a paragraph about one of the sections, leaving blanks for your classmates to fill in. Also write an answer key.

History Online
Self-Check Quiz To help you prepare for the Chapter Test, visit jat.glencoe.com

Using Technology

22. **Researching** Use the Internet and your local library to find information about the *varnas* and *jati* in India today. You may wish to investigate where the systems are still practiced and how they affect modern society. You may also wish to research attempts at reforming the system and how the system is affected by national law. Prepare a report to share with the class.

Building Citizenship Skills

23. **Analyzing Information** Dharma is the Hindu idea of duty. Is it important for people in a society to do their duty? Make a list of duties Americans have today. Then write a paragraph explaining why those duties are important.

Primary Source **Analyze**

Read the excerpt from the Buddha's Farewell Address. Then answer the questions.

"'Hold fast to the truth as a lamp. Seek salvation alone in the truth. Do not look for assistance to anyone besides yourselves. . . .

Those who, either now or after I am dead, shall be lamps unto themselves . . . holding fast to the truth as their lamp, and seeking their salvation in the truth alone . . . it is they . . . who shall reach the very topmost height! But they must be anxious to learn.'"

—*The Teachings of Buddha,* The Buddha's Farewell Address, compiled by Paul Carus

DBQ Document-Based Questions

24. Why does the Buddha compare the truth to a lamp?

25. What quality must people have if they want to reach the topmost height?

Chapter 7

Early China

The first Great Wall of China was built more than 2,000 years ago to keep out invaders. The current wall, which is about 4,000 miles long, was built about 500 years ago. ▼

NATIONAL GEOGRAPHIC When & Where?

1800 B.C.   **1150** B.C.   **500** B.C.   **A.D. 150**

c. **1750** B.C.
Shang dynasty begins

1045 B.C.
Wu Wang creates Zhou dynasty

551 B.C.
Confucius is born

c. **A.D. 100**
Silk Road established

Chapter Preview

The ancient Chinese, like the Egyptians, established long-ruling dynasties. The Chinese valued three great philosophies: Confucianism, Daoism, and Legalism.

 View the Chapter 7 video in the *World History: Journey Across Time* Video Program.

 Section **1** **China's First Civilizations**

Chinese civilization was shaped by geography such as mountains and large rivers. Long-lasting dynasties gained power through strong armies.

 Section **2** **Life in Ancient China**

Early Chinese society had three main social classes: aristocrats, farmers, and merchants. During periods of unrest, ideas such as Confucianism and Daoism developed.

 Section **3** **The Qin and Han Dynasties**

Both the Qin and Han dynasties created strong central governments. New inventions developed during the Han dynasty helped to improve the lives of Chinese people.

 **Study Organizer**

Organizing Information *Make this foldable to help you organize information about the important people in the early history of China.*

Step 1 *Fold a sheet of paper in half from side to side.*

Fold it so the left edge lies about $\frac{1}{2}$ inch from the right edge.

Step 2 *Turn the paper and fold it into thirds.*

Step 3 *Unfold and cut the top layer only along both folds.*

This will make three tabs.

Step 4 *Turn the paper and label it as shown.*

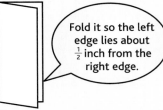

China's First Civilizations

Chinese Philosophers

Qin and Han

Reading and Writing *As you read the chapter, list important people and what they did or taught during these periods in Chinese history.*

Reading Social Studies

1 Learn It!

Headings and Punctuation

As you read this chapter, pay attention to bold headings and punctuation. They are used by authors to help you better understand what you are reading. Look at the heading on page 235, **Chinese Thinkers.** By putting these words in red, the author lets you know, even before you begin reading, that this part of the chapter is about famous thinkers in Chinese history. Paying attention to punctuation marks also can help you understand the text. Look at the punctuation marks in the paragraph below.

Words are indented to show where a new paragraph and a new idea begin.

> **To Confucius, the best way to behave was similar to an idea known as the Golden Rule: "Do unto others as you would have others do unto you."**
>
> *—from page 236*

A colon (:) tells you that the words that follow are an illustration or an explanation of the first part of the sentence.

Quotation marks have several uses. Here they are used to set off words taken from another source.

Reading Tip

Read a section out loud. Say the names of the punctuation marks as you read. This will help you remember why certain punctuation marks are used.

222

2 Practice It!
Punctuation Clues

Look at the heading and punctuation in the following paragraph and answer the questions that follow.

The Zhou Empire Falls Over time, the local rulers of the Zhou territories became powerful. They stopped obeying the Zhou kings and set up their own states. In 403 B.C. fighting broke out. For almost 200 years, the states battled each other. Historians call this time the "Period of the Warring States."

—*from page 231*

1. Based on the heading, what do you think this section will be about?

2. Why do you think the phrase "Period of the Warring States" is in quotation marks?

3. How will you know when a new paragraph begins?

▲ Winged dragon from Zhou dynasty

3 Apply It!

As you read the chapter, jot down punctuation or section headings that you do not understand. Write them in your notebook to discuss later.

China's First Civilizations

Get Ready to Read!

What's the Connection?

In earlier chapters, you learned that many civilizations developed in river valleys. The civilizations of China also began in river valleys. However, other features of the land, such as mountains and deserts, affected China's history as well.

Focusing on the Main Ideas

- Rivers, mountains, and deserts helped shape China's civilization. *(page 225)*

- Rulers known as the Shang became powerful because they controlled land and had strong armies. *(page 226)*

- Chinese rulers claimed that the Mandate of Heaven gave them the right to rule. *(page 229)*

Locating Places

Huang He (HWAHNG HUH)
Chang Jiang (CHAHNG JYAHNG)
Anyang (AHN•YAHNG)

Meeting People

Wu Wang (WOO WAHNG)

Building Your Vocabulary

dynasty (DY•nuh•stee)
aristocrat (uh•RIHS•tuh•KRAT)
pictograph (PIHK•tuh•GRAF)
ideograph (IH•dee•uh•GRAF)
bureaucracy (byu•RAH•kruh•see)
mandate (MAN•DAYT)
Dao (DOW)

Reading Strategy

Summarizing Information Complete a chart like the one below describing the characteristics of the Shang and Zhou dynasties.

	Shang Dynasty	Zhou Dynasty
Dates		
Leadership		
Accomplishments		

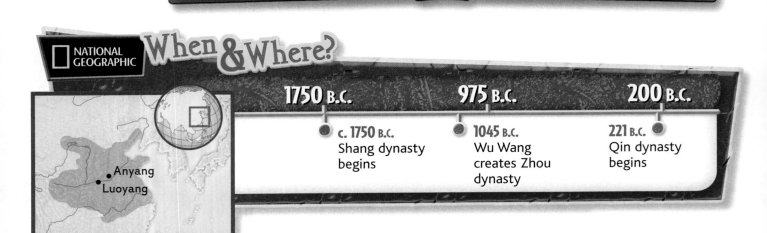

NATIONAL GEOGRAPHIC When & Where?

Anyang
Luoyang

1750 B.C.

c. 1750 B.C.
Shang dynasty
begins

975 B.C.

1045 B.C.
Wu Wang
creates Zhou
dynasty

200 B.C.

221 B.C.
Qin dynasty
begins

China's Geography

Main Idea Rivers, mountains, and deserts helped shape China's civilization.

Reading Focus Why do you think so many cities and towns were built beside rivers? Read to learn why rivers were important to the development of China.

The **Huang He** (HWAHNG HUH), or Yellow River, flows across China for more than 2,900 miles (4,666 km). It gets its name from the rich yellow soil it carries from Mongolia to the Pacific Ocean.

Like rivers in early Mesopotamia and Egypt, China's Huang He flooded the land. The flooding was good and bad for the Chinese. When the river overflowed, many people drowned and many homes were destroyed. As a result, the Chinese called the Huang He "China's sorrow."

The river, however, also brought a gift. When the river flooded, it left behind rich topsoil in the Huang He valley. As a result, farmers could grow large amounts of food on very small farms.

China also has another great river, called the **Chang Jiang** (CHAHNG JYAHNG), or the Yangtze River. The Chang Jiang is even longer than the Huang He. It flows for about 3,400 miles (5,471 km) east across central China where it empties into the Yellow Sea. Like the Huang He valley, the valley of the Chang Jiang also has rich soil for farming.

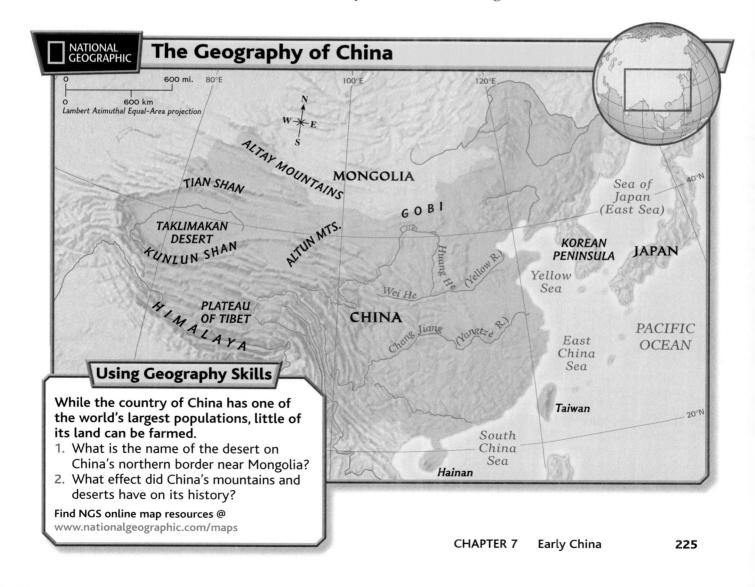

NATIONAL GEOGRAPHIC **The Geography of China**

600 mi.
600 km
Lambert Azimuthal Equal-Area projection

ALTAY MOUNTAINS
TIAN SHAN
MONGOLIA
GOBI
TAKLIMAKAN DESERT
KUNLUN SHAN
ALTUN MTS.
Huang He (Yellow R.)
Wei He
PLATEAU OF TIBET
HIMALAYA
CHINA
Chang Jiang (Yangtze R.)
Sea of Japan (East Sea)
KOREAN PENINSULA
JAPAN
Yellow Sea
East China Sea
PACIFIC OCEAN
South China Sea
Taiwan
Hainan

Using Geography Skills

While the country of China has one of the world's largest populations, little of its land can be farmed.

1. What is the name of the desert on China's northern border near Mongolia?
2. What effect did China's mountains and deserts have on its history?

Find NGS online map resources @ www.nationalgeographic.com/maps

Even though China has rich soil along its rivers, only a little more than one-tenth of its land can be farmed. That is because mountains and deserts cover most of the land. The towering Himalaya close off China to the southwest. The Kunlun Shan and Tian Shan are mountain ranges on China's western border. The Gobi, a vast, cold, rocky desert, spreads east from the mountains. These mountains and deserts shaped much of Chinese history. They were like a wall around the Chinese, separating them from most other peoples.

Over time, the Chinese people united to form one kingdom. They called their homeland "the Middle Kingdom." To them, it was the world's center and its leading civilization. The Chinese developed a way of life that lasted into modern times.

✓**Reading Check** **Identify** Name two rivers important to early Chinese civilizations.

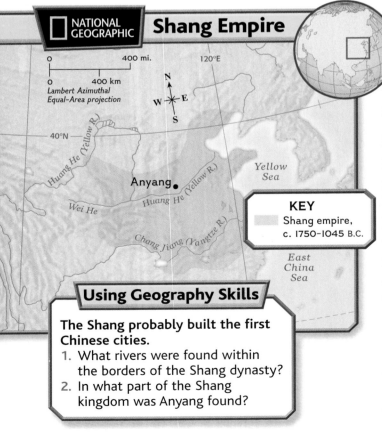

Using Geography Skills

The Shang probably built the first Chinese cities.
1. What rivers were found within the borders of the Shang dynasty?
2. In what part of the Shang kingdom was Anyang found?

The Shang Dynasty

Main Idea Rulers known as the Shang became powerful because they controlled land and had strong armies.

Reading Focus Who are the leaders in your community? What gives them their power? Read to learn why some people in early China had more power than others.

Little is known about how Chinese civilization began. Archaeologists, however, have found pottery in the Huang He valley dating back thousands of years. These artifacts show that the Huang He valley was the first center of Chinese civilization. Archaeologists think that people stayed in the valley and farmed the land because of rich soil. As their numbers rose, they began building towns, and soon after, the first Chinese civilization began.

China's first rulers were probably part of the Xia (SYAH) dynasty. A **dynasty** (DY• nuh•stee) is a line of rulers who belong to the same family. Little is known about the Xia. We know more about the next dynasty, the Shang. The Shang kings ruled from about 1750 B.C. to 1045 B.C.

Who Were the Shang? Archaeologists have found huge walls, royal palaces, and royal tombs from the time of the Shang. These remains show that the Shang may have built the first Chinese cities. One of these cities was **Anyang** (AHN•YAHNG) in northern China. Anyang was China's first capital. From there, the Shang kings ruled the early Chinese people.

The people of the Shang dynasty were divided into groups. The most powerful group was the king and his family. The first Shang king ruled over a small area in northern China. His armies used chariots and bronze weapons to take over nearby areas.

In time, the Shang kings ruled over most of the Huang He valley.

Later, Shang kings chose warlords to govern the kingdom's territories. Warlords are military leaders who command their own armies. However, the king controlled even larger armies who defended the kingdom's borders. The king's armies helped him stay in power.

Under the king, the warlords and other royal officials made up the upper class. They were **aristocrats** (uh•RIHS•tuh•KRATS), nobles whose wealth came from the land they owned. Aristocrats passed their land and their power from one generation to the next.

In Shang China, a few people were traders and artisans. Most Chinese, however, were farmers. They worked the land that belonged to the aristocrats. They grew grains, such as millet, wheat, and rice, and raised cattle, sheep, and chickens. A small number of enslaved people captured in war also lived in Shang China.

Spirits and Ancestors
People in Shang China worshiped gods and spirits. Spirits were believed to live in mountains, rivers, and seas. The people believed that they had to keep the gods and spirits happy by making offerings of food and other goods. They believed that the gods and spirits would be angry if they were not treated well. Angry gods and spirits might cause farmers to have a poor harvest or armies to lose a battle.

People also honored their ancestors, or departed family members. Offerings were made in the hope that ancestors would help in times of need and bring good luck. To this day, many Chinese still remember their ancestors by going to temples and burning small paper copies of food and clothing.

NATIONAL GEOGRAPHIC

The Way It Was

Focus on Everyday Life

The Role of Women Zheng Zhenxiang was China's first female archaeologist. In 1976 she found the tomb of Fu Hao, China's first female general. In the tomb were more than 2,000 artifacts from the Shang dynasty, including weapons, bronze vessels, jade objects, and bones with Chinese characters carved on them.

▲ Bronze vessel

Fu Hao, the wife of King Wu Ding, was given a royal burial. She was famous for her strength, martial arts skills, and military strategies. She often helped her husband defeat their enemies on the battlefield. Fu Hao was the first female in China's history to receive the highest military rank.

Her tomb and its artifacts reveal the grand civilization of China's Shang dynasty. During this period, the Chinese developed writing, a calendar, and musical instruments.

Jade sculpture of a ▶ seated human figure

Connecting to the Past
1. What was Fu Hao famous for during her life?
2. Describe what the artifacts found in Fu Hao's tomb might reveal about life during that time.

These copies represent things that their departed relatives need in the afterlife.

Telling the Future Shang kings believed that they received power and wisdom from the gods, the spirits, and their ancestors.

HISTORY MAKERS

Chinese Writing

The Chinese writing system was created nearly 3,500 years ago during the Shang dynasty. The earliest examples of Chinese writing have been found on animal bones. The carvings on these bones show that Chinese writing has always used symbols to represent words. Some of the carvings are pictures. For example, the verb *to go* was represented by a picture of a foot. The characters were carved in vertical columns and read from top to bottom, like modern Chinese writing. The writing on the bones recorded the Shang kings' questions about a wide range of topics—from the weather to good fortune. Chinese writing has changed in many ways, but it still reflects its ancient roots in pictures and symbols.

Oracle bone ▶

Shang religion and government were closely linked, just as they were in ancient Mesopotamia and Egypt. An important duty of Shang kings was to contact the gods, the spirits, and ancestors before making important decisions.

The kings asked for the gods' help by using oracle (AWR•uh•kuhl) bones. They had priests scratch questions on the bones, such as "Will I win the battle?" and "Will I recover from my illness?" Then the priests placed hot metal rods inside the bones, causing them to crack. They believed that the pattern of the cracks formed answers from the gods. The priests interpreted the answers and wrote them down for the kings. Scratches on oracle bones are the earliest known examples of Chinese writing.

The Chinese Language The scratches on oracle bones show how today's Chinese writing began. However, the modern Chinese language is much more complex.

Like many other ancient languages, early Chinese writing used pictographs and ideographs. **Pictographs** (PIHK•tuh•GRAFS) are characters that stand for objects. For example, the Chinese characters for a mountain, the sun, and the moon are pictographs. **Ideographs** (IH•dee•uh•GRAFS) are another kind of character used in Chinese writing. They join two or more pictographs to represent an idea. For example, the ideograph for "east" relates to the idea of the sun rising in the east. It is a combination of pictographs that show the sun coming up behind trees.

Unlike Chinese, English and many other languages have writing systems based on an alphabet. An alphabet uses characters that stand for sounds. The Chinese use some characters to stand for sounds, but most characters still represent whole words.

Shang Artists The people in Shang China developed many skills. Farmers produced silk, which weavers used to make colorful clothes. Artisans made vases and dishes from fine white clay. They also carved statues from ivory and a green stone called jade.

The Shang are best known for their works of bronze. To make bronze objects, artisans made clay molds in several sections. Next, they carved detailed designs into the clay. Then, they fit the pieces of the mold tightly together and poured in melted bronze. When the bronze cooled, the mold was removed. A beautifully decorated work of art remained.

Shang bronze objects included sculptures, vases, drinking cups, and containers called urns. The Shang used bronze urns to prepare and serve food for rituals honoring ancestors.

Reading Check **Explain** What was the role of Shang warlords?

The Zhou Dynasty

Main Idea Chinese rulers claimed that the Mandate of Heaven gave them the right to rule.

Reading Focus Who gives you permission to do the things you do? Your mother? Your teacher? Read to find out how the rulers of the Zhou dynasty turned to the heavens for permission to rule.

During the rule of the Shang, a great gap existed between the rich and the poor. Shang kings lived in luxury and began to treat people cruelly. As a result, they lost the support of the people in their kingdom. In 1045 B.C. an aristocrat named **Wu Wang** (WOO WAHNG) led a rebellion against the Shang. After defeating the Shang, Wu began a new dynasty called the Zhou (JOH).

The Zhou Government The Zhou dynasty ruled for more than 800 years—longer than any other dynasty in Chinese history.

Zhou kings ruled much like Shang rulers. The Zhou king was at the head of the government. Under him was a large **bureaucracy** (byu•RAH•kruh•see). A bureaucracy is made up of appointed officials who are responsible for different areas of government. Like the Shang rulers, the Zhou king was in charge of defending the kingdom.

◄ Buffalo-shaped bronze vessel from the Shang dynasty

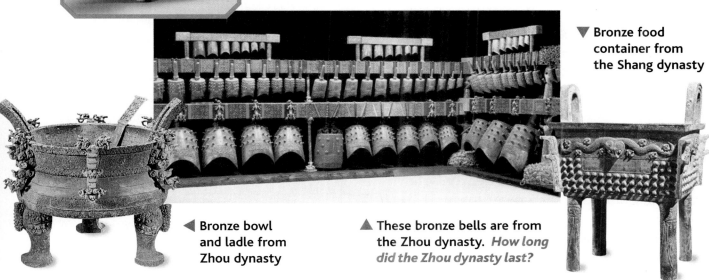

▼ Bronze food container from the Shang dynasty

◄ Bronze bowl and ladle from Zhou dynasty

▲ These bronze bells are from the Zhou dynasty. *How long did the Zhou dynasty last?*

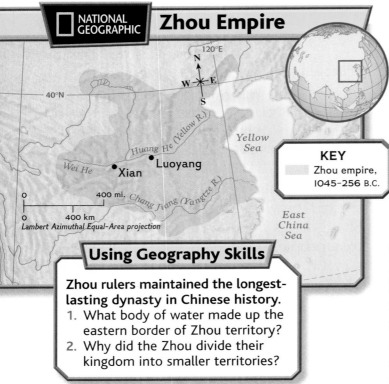

NATIONAL GEOGRAPHIC

Zhou Empire

KEY
Zhou empire, 1045–256 B.C.

Using Geography Skills

Zhou rulers maintained the longest-lasting dynasty in Chinese history.
1. What body of water made up the eastern border of Zhou territory?
2. Why did the Zhou divide their kingdom into smaller territories?

The Zhou kings copied the Shang system of dividing the kingdom into smaller territories. The kings put aristocrats they trusted in charge of each territory. The positions the aristocrats held were hereditary. That meant that when an aristocrat died, his son or another relative would take over as ruler of the territory.

The Chinese considered the king their link between heaven and earth. His chief duty was to carry out religious rituals. The Chinese believed these rituals strengthened the link between them and the gods. This belief paved the way for a new idea that the Zhou kings introduced to government. They claimed that kings ruled China because they had the Mandate of Heaven.

What Was the Mandate of Heaven?

According to Zhou rulers, a heavenly law gave the Zhou king the power to rule. This **mandate** (MAN•DAYT), or formal order, was called the Mandate of Heaven. Based on the mandate, the king was chosen by heavenly order because of his talent and virtue. Therefore, he would rule the people with goodness and wisdom.

The Mandate of Heaven worked in two ways. First, the people expected the king to rule according to the proper "Way," called the **Dao** (DOW). His duty was to keep the gods happy. A natural disaster or a bad harvest was a sign that he had failed in his duty. People then had the right to overthrow and replace the king.

The Mandate of Heaven also worked another way. It gave the people, as well as the king, important rights. For example, people had the right to overthrow a dishonest or evil ruler. It also made clear that the king was not a god himself. Of course, each new dynasty claimed it had the Mandate of Heaven. The only way people could question the claim was by overthrowing the dynasty.

New Tools and Trade For thousands of years, Chinese farmers depended on rain to water their crops. During the Zhou dynasty, the Chinese developed irrigation and flood-control systems. As a result, farmers could grow more crops than ever before.

Improvements in farming tools also helped farmers produce more crops. By 550 B.C., the Chinese were using iron plows. These sturdy plows broke up land that had been too hard to farm with wooden plows. As a result, the Chinese could plow more and produce more crops. Because more food could support more people, the population increased. During the late Zhou dynasty, China had a population of about 50 million people.

History Online

Web Activity Visit jat.glencoe.com and click on *Chapter 7—Student Web Activity* to learn more about ancient China.

Trade and manufacturing grew along with farming. An important trade item during the Zhou dynasty was silk. Pieces of Chinese silk have been found throughout central Asia and as far away as Greece. This suggests that the Chinese traded far and wide.

◄ **This statue of a winged dragon is from the Zhou dynasty.** *From what metal did the Chinese make plows and weapons during the Zhou dynasty?*

The Zhou Empire Falls Over time, the local rulers of the Zhou territories became powerful. They stopped obeying the Zhou kings and set up their own states. In 403 B.C. fighting broke out. For almost 200 years, the states battled each other. Historians call this time the "Period of the Warring States."

Instead of nobles driving chariots, the warring states used large armies of foot soldiers. To get enough soldiers, they issued laws forcing peasants to serve in the army. The armies fought with swords, spears, and crossbows. A crossbow uses a crank to pull the string and shoots arrows with great force.

As the fighting went on, the Chinese invented the saddle and stirrup. These let soldiers ride horses and use spears and crossbows while riding. In 221 B.C. the ruler of Qin (CHIHN), one of the warring states, used a large cavalry force to defeat the other states and set up a new dynasty.

✓ **Reading Check** **Identify** What was the chief duty of Chinese kings?

History Online

Study Central™ Need help with the material in this section? Visit jat.glencoe.com

Section ❶ Review

Reading Summary

Review the Main Ideas

- China's first civilizations formed in river valleys. The Chinese were isolated from other people by mountains and deserts.

- The rulers of the Shang dynasty controlled the area around the Huang He valley.

- The Zhou dynasty replaced the Shang and claimed to rule with the Mandate of Heaven. During the Zhou dynasty, farming methods improved and trade increased.

What Did You Learn?

1. What is a dynasty?

2. What were oracle bones and how were they used?

Critical Thinking

3. **Analyze** How did the Mandate of Heaven allow for the overthrow of kings in ancient China?

4. **Summarizing Information** Draw a diagram like the one below. Add details that describe the members of Shang society.

Shang Society

5. **Evaluate** What were some important technological changes during the Zhou dynasty, and how did they lead to a larger population?

6. **Explain** How did ancient Chinese kings maintain control of their dynasties?

7. **Reading** Text Structure Explain why parentheses are used in the following sentence. "The Huang He (HWAHNG HUH), or Yellow River, flows across China for more than 2,900 miles (4,666 km)."

Life in Ancient China

Get Ready to Read!

What's the Connection?

In Section 1, you learned about the Chinese government under the Zhou dynasty. This section describes what life was like during the Zhou dynasty.

Focusing on the Main Ideas

• Chinese society had three main social classes: landowning aristocrats, farmers, and merchants. *(page 233)*

• Three Chinese philosophies, Confucianism, Daoism, and Legalism, grew out of a need for order. *(page 235)*

Meeting People

Confucius (kuhn•FYOO•shuhs)
Laozi (LOWD•ZOO)
Hanfeizi (HAN•fay•DZOO)

Building Your Vocabulary

social class
filial piety
    (FIH•lee•uhl   PY•uh•tee)
Confucianism
    (kuhn•FYOO•shuh•NIH•zuhm)
Daoism (DOW•IH•zuhm)
Legalism (LEE•guh•LIH•zuhm)

Reading Strategy

Organizing Information Create a pyramid diagram like the one below showing the social classes in ancient China from most important (top) to least important (bottom).

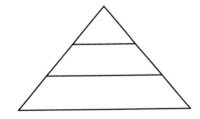

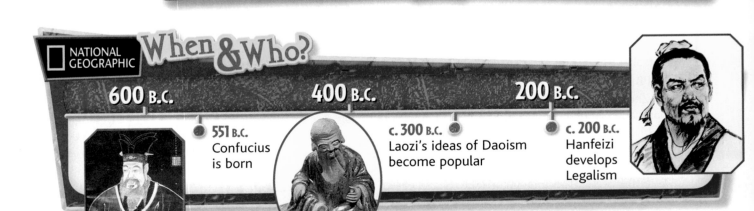

NATIONAL GEOGRAPHIC When & Who?

600 B.C.   **400** B.C.   **200** B.C.

551 B.C.
Confucius is born

c. 300 B.C.
Laozi's ideas of Daoism become popular

c. 200 B.C.
Hanfeizi develops Legalism

Life in Ancient China

Main Idea Chinese society had three main social classes: landowning aristocrats, farmers, and merchants.

Reading Focus Have you heard the terms *high society* and *working class?* They describe social classes in America. Read on to find out about social classes in early China.

A **social class** includes people who share a similar position in society. Early Chinese society had three main social classes:

- landowning aristocrats
- peasant farmers
- merchants

Classes in Chinese Society

China's aristocratic families owned large estates in early China. They lived in large houses with tile roofs, courtyards, and gardens. Fine furniture and silk hangings filled their rooms, and their houses were surrounded by walls to keep out bandits.

The aristocratic families did not own large estates for long. Each aristocrat divided his land among his sons. As a result, sons and grandsons owned much less property than their fathers and grandfathers had owned.

Aristocrats relied on farmers to grow the crops that made them rich. About nine out of ten Chinese were farmers. They lived in simple houses inside village walls. The aristocrats owned the fields outside the village walls. In these fields, farmers in northern China grew wheat and a grain called millet. In the south, where the climate was warmer and wetter, they were able to grow rice.

Chinese Village

Chinese farmers lived in small villages made up of several families. They farmed fields outside the village walls.
How did farmers pay for the use of the land they farmed?

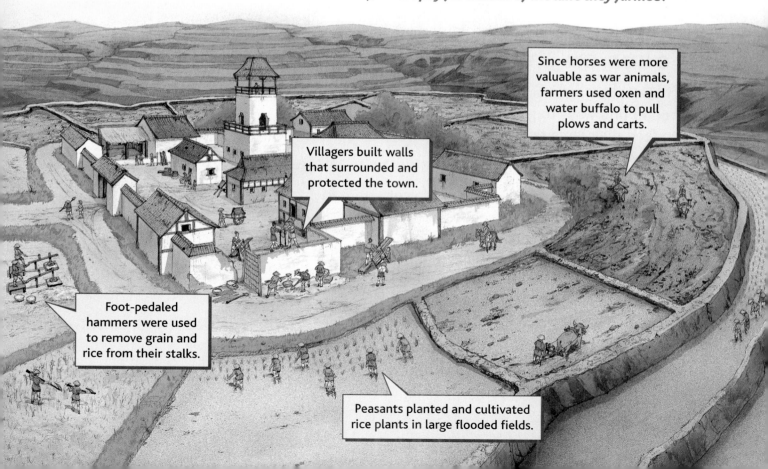

Since horses were more valuable as war animals, farmers used oxen and water buffalo to pull plows and carts.

Villagers built walls that surrounded and protected the town.

Foot-pedaled hammers were used to remove grain and rice from their stalks.

Peasants planted and cultivated rice plants in large flooded fields.

To pay for the use of the land, the farmers gave part of their crop to the landowners.

Most farmers also owned a small piece of land where they grew food for their family. A typical family ate fish, turnips, beans, wheat or rice, and millet. The farmers had to pay taxes and work one month each year building roads and helping on other big government projects. In wartime, the farmers also served as soldiers.

In Chinese society, farmers ranked above merchants. The merchant social class included shopkeepers, traders, and bankers. The merchants lived in towns and provided goods and services to the landowners.

Many merchants became quite rich, but landowners and farmers still looked down on them. Chinese leaders believed that government officials should not be concerned with money. As a result, merchants were not allowed to have government jobs.

What Was Life Like in a Chinese Family?

The family was the basic building block of Chinese society. Because farming in ancient China required many workers, people had big families to help them produce more and become wealthier. Even the young children of a family worked in the fields. Older sons raised their own crops and provided food for their parents. Chinese families also took care of people in need—the aged, the young, and the sick.

Chinese families practiced **filial piety** (FIH•lee•uhl PY•uh•tee). This meant that children had to respect their parents and older relatives. Family members placed the needs and desires of the head of the family before their own. The head of the family was the oldest male, usually the father. However, a son could take on this role, and then even his mother had to obey him.

NATIONAL GEOGRAPHIC **The Way It Was**

Focus on Everyday Life

Chinese Farming Farmers in ancient China had to find ways to grow enough food to feed their large population. It was often difficult because of the dry, mountainous land.

Over centuries, farmers learned to cut terraces—flat areas, like a series of deep steps—into the mountain slopes. Terraces made more land available for farming and kept the soil from eroding, or wearing away. Early farmers also used the terraces as a way to irrigate their crops. As rain fell, it flowed down from one terrace to the

▲ Terrace farming in China

Men and women had very different roles in early China. Men were respected because they grew the crops. They went to school, ran the government, and fought wars. The Chinese considered these jobs more important than the work that women did. Most women raised children and managed the household.

Chinese women could not hold government posts. However, women in the royal court could influence government decisions. Wives of rulers or women in the royal family often convinced men in power to see things their way.

▲ Chinese female figurine

✓ **Reading Check** **Explain** Why did the amount of land owned by each aristocrat decrease over time?

Chinese Thinkers

Main Idea **Three Chinese philosophies, Confucianism, Daoism, and Legalism, grew out of a need for order.**

Reading Focus If people around you were arguing and fighting, what would you do? Read to learn about early Chinese ideas for restoring order.

As the Zhou kingdom weakened in the 500s B.C., violence became common. During the Period of the Warring States, rulers sent armies to destroy enemy states. Whole villages of men, women, and children were beheaded. Many Chinese began looking for ways to restore order to society.

Between 500 B.C. and 200 B.C., Chinese thinkers developed three major theories about how to create a peaceful society. These theories are called Confucianism, Daoism, and Legalism.

next, watering the crops. This method of farming, called terrace farming, is still used in China today.

Farmers in ancient China were the first to use insects to protect their crops from damage by other insects. As early as A.D. 304, Chinese farmers used ants to prevent other insects from damaging their citrus fruit trees. They also used frogs and birds for pest control.

The ancient Chinese used bronze and ▶ iron tools like those on the right, to farm their land and harvest crops.

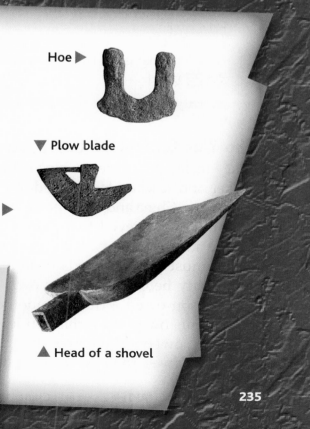

Hoe ▶

▼ Plow blade

▲ Head of a shovel

Connecting to the Past
1. How did farmers in ancient China increase the amount of productive farmland?
2. What three farming methods helped farmers in ancient China grow more food?

Chinese Numbering System

Chinese Number	English Number	Chinese Number	English Number
零	0	七	7
一	1	八	8
二	2	九	9
三	3	十	10
四	4	百	100
五	5	千	1,000
六	6	万	10,000

Examples:

二十	(2 × 10)
二百	(2 × 100)
三千	(3 × 1,000)
四百五十六	[(4 × 100) + (5 × 10) + (6)]

Understanding Charts

The Chinese system of numbering is based on units of 10. It uses characters to represent 0 through 9 and the powers of 10 (10, 100, 1,000, and so forth).

1. How would you write the number 328 using the Chinese numbering system?
2. **Analyze** What is the English number for 六百四十一?

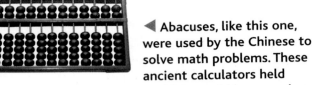

◀ Abacuses, like this one, were used by the Chinese to solve math problems. These ancient calculators held stones on wooden pegs, which would be moved up and down to add, subtract, multiply, and divide.

wives owed their husbands obedience. Above all, rulers had to set good examples. If a king ruled for the common good, his subjects would respect him and society would prosper.

Confucius believed that if each person did his or her duty, society as a whole would do well. He also urged people to be good and to seek knowledge:

❝ There are those who act without knowing; I will have none of this. To hear a lot, choose the good, and follow it, to see a lot and learn to recognize it: this is next to knowledge. ❞

—Confucius, *Analects*

To Confucius, the best way to behave was similar to an idea known as the Golden Rule: "Do unto others as you would have others do unto you." Confucius urged people to "measure the feelings of others by one's own," for "within the four seas all men are brothers."

Confucius traveled through China trying to persuade government leaders to follow his ideas. **Confucianism** (kuhn•FYOO•shuh•NIH•zuhm) taught that all men with a talent for governing should take part in government. Of course, this idea was not popular with aristocrats, and few leaders listened.

Over time, Confucius won many followers who honored him as a great teacher. They wrote down his sayings and carried his message. After Confucius died in 479 B.C., his sayings spread throughout China.

Who Was Confucius?

Confucius (kuhn•FYOO•shuhs) was ancient China's first great thinker and teacher. He wanted to end the problems in China and bring peace to society.

Confucius believed that people needed to have a sense of duty. Duty meant that a person must put the needs of family and community before his or her own needs. Each person owed a duty to another person. Parents owed their children love, and children owed their parents honor. Husbands owed their wives support, and

Biography

CONFUCIUS

551–479 B.C.

Confucius ▶

Historians believe that the great thinker and teacher Confucius was born in the small state of Lu and named Kong Qui. His parents were poor, although his family had probably been wealthy at one time. One record says that Confucius was only three years old when his father died. His mother may have also died when he was young, because another record describes Confucius as an orphan.

Even as a teenager, Confucius was a talented scholar with strong, fixed beliefs. He devoted himself to learning and mastered literature, history, music, and arithmetic. He served as an apprentice to a bookkeeper and a stable manager but really wanted to obtain a government position. When he was 19, Confucius married and soon had a son and a daughter.

Confucius finally obtained a government job and wanted to use his position to improve society. He wanted everyone to return to the beliefs and rituals of their ancestors, because he felt that would teach them how to live together peacefully. Government officials in Lu were not interested in his ideas, so at age 30 Confucius left politics and began his teaching career. He devoted the rest of his life to improving society through learning and teaching. Confucius did not write down any of his ideas, but his followers put together a book of his sayings called the *Lun Yü* (Analects).

"What you do not want done to yourself, do not do to others."
—Confucius

Then and Now

Give an example of how the above quote from Confucius might help society today.

Chinese Philosophers

	Confucianism	Daoism	Legalism
Founder	Confucius 	Laozi 	Hanfeizi 
Main Ideas	People should put the needs of their family and community first.	People should give up worldly desires in favor of nature and the Dao.	Society needs a system of harsh laws and strict punishment.
Influence on Modern Life	Many Chinese today accept his idea of duty to family. His ideas helped open up government jobs to people with talent.	Daoism teaches the importance of nature and encourages people to treat nature with respect and reverence.	Legalists developed laws that became an important part of Chinese history.

Understanding Charts

Three philosophies developed in early China.
1. Which philosophy encourages followers to concentrate on duty and humanity?
2. **Conclude** Which of these philosophies do you think would be most popular in the world today? Explain.

▲ Some legends state that Laozi rode his water buffalo westward into a great desert and disappeared after writing *Dao De Jing*. *When did the ideas of Daoism become popular?*

What Is Daoism? Daoism (DOW•IH•zuhm) is another Chinese philosophy that promotes a peaceful society. Daoism (also called Taoism) is based on the teachings of **Laozi** (LOWD•ZOO). Laozi, or the Old Master, lived around the same time as Confucius. Scholars do not know if Laozi was a real person. However, the ideas credited to him became popular between 500 B.C. and 300 B.C.

The ideas of Daoism are written in *Dao De Jing* (The Way of the Dao). Like Confucianism, Daoism tells people how to behave. Daoists believed that people should give up worldly desires. They should turn to nature and the Dao—the force that guides all things. To show how to follow the Dao, Daoists used examples from nature:

> ❝Higher good is like water:
> the good in water benefits all,
> and does so without contention.
> It rests where people dislike to be,
> so it is close to the Way.
> Where it dwells becomes
> good ground;
> profound is the good in its heart,
> Benevolent the good it bestows.❞
>
> —Laozi, *Tao Te Ching*

In some ways, Daoism is the opposite of Confucianism. Followers of Confucius taught that people should work hard to improve the world. Daoism called on people to give up their concerns about the world. It said they should seek inner peace and live in harmony with nature. Many Chinese followed both Confucianism and Daoism.

What Is Legalism? A third group of thinkers disagreed with the idea that honorable men in government could bring peace to society. Instead, they argued for a system of laws. People called their thinking **Legalism** (LEE•guh•LIH•zuhm), or the "School of Law."

A scholar named **Hanfeizi** (HAN•fay•DZOO) developed the teachings of Legalism during the 200s B.C. Unlike Confucius or Laozi, Hanfeizi taught that humans were naturally evil. He believed that they needed harsh laws and stiff punishments to force them to do their duty. His followers believed that a strong ruler was needed to keep order in society.

Many aristocrats liked Legalism because it favored force and power, and did not require rulers to show kindness or understanding. Its ideas led to the cruel laws and punishments often used to control Chinese farmers.

 **Reading Check** **Explain** Why did Hanfeizi believe that people needed laws and punishments?

Section 2 Review

History Online

Study Central™ Need help with the material in this section? Visit jat.glencoe.com

Reading Summary
Review the Main Ideas

- Early Chinese society had three main social classes: aristocrats, farmers, and merchants. The family was the basis of Chinese society.

- During a time of disorder, three new philosophies developed in China: Confucianism, Daoism, and Legalism.

What Did You Learn?

1. Describe the concept of filial piety.

2. Why did many aristocrats favor the philosophy of Legalism?

Critical Thinking

3. **Compare** Draw a table to compare the three main classes of ancient Chinese society.

Chinese Society		
Aristocrats	Farmers	Merchants

4. **Contrast** How did Daoism differ from Confucianism?

5. **Writing Questions** Suppose you could interview Confucius about his concept of duty. Write five questions you might ask him about the subject. Include possible responses.

6. **Expository Writing** Do you think any of the Chinese philosophies studied in this section are reflected in our society today? Write an essay explaining your answer.

The Qin and Han Dynasties

Get Ready to Read!

What's the Connection?
Each of China's early dynasties was led by rulers who were very different. In this section, you will see how the Qin and Han dynasties differed because of their rulers.

Focusing on the Main Ideas
- Qin Shihuangdi used harsh methods to unify and defend China. *(page 241)*
- Developments during the Han dynasty improved life for all Chinese. *(page 244)*
- The Silk Road carried Chinese goods as far as Greece and Rome. *(page 246)*
- Unrest in China helped Buddhism to spread. *(page 248)*

Locating Places
Guangzhou (GWAHNG•JOH)
Silk Road
Luoyang (loo•WOH•YAHNG)

Meeting People
Qin Shihuangdi (CHIHN   SHEE• hwahng•dee)
Liu Bang (lee•OO   BAHNG)
Han Wudi (HAHN   WOO•DEE)

Building Your Vocabulary
acupuncture (A•kyuh•PUHNGK• chuhr)

Reading Strategy
Determining Cause and Effect Complete a diagram like the one below showing the inventions of the Han dynasty and the resulting impact on society.

Invention		Effect
	→	
	→	
	→	

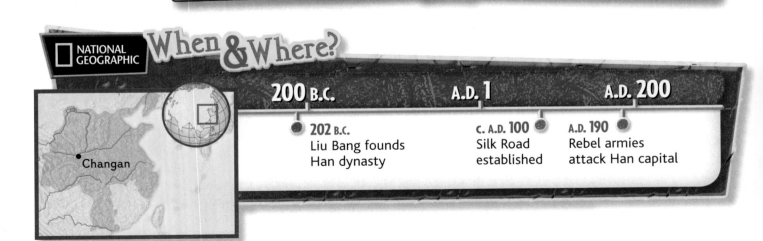

When & Where?

NATIONAL GEOGRAPHIC

200 B.C.   A.D. 1   A.D. 200

202 B.C. Liu Bang founds Han dynasty

C. A.D. 100 Silk Road established

A.D. 190 Rebel armies attack Han capital

Changan

Emperor Qin Shihuangdi

Main Idea Qin Shihuangdi used harsh methods to unify and defend China.

Reading Focus Imagine your city or state without any roads. How would people get from one place to another? Read to find out how a Chinese ruler used roads and canals to unite China.

You have read about the problems in China from about 400 B.C. to 200 B.C. The rulers of powerful local states fought one another and ignored the Zhou kings. One of these states was called Qin. Its ruler took over neighboring states one by one. In 221 B.C. the Qin ruler declared himself **Qin Shihuangdi** (CHIHN SHEE•hwahng•dee),

which means "the First Qin Emperor." The Qin ruler made changes in China's government that would last for 2,000 years.

A Powerful Ruler Qin based his rule on the ideas of Legalism. He had everyone who opposed him punished or killed. Books opposing his views were publicly burned. Qin made the central government stronger than ever before. He appointed government officials, called censors, to make sure government officials did their jobs.

Second in power to the central government were provinces and counties. Under Zhou kings, officials who ran these areas passed on their posts to sons or relatives. Under Qin, only he could fill these posts.

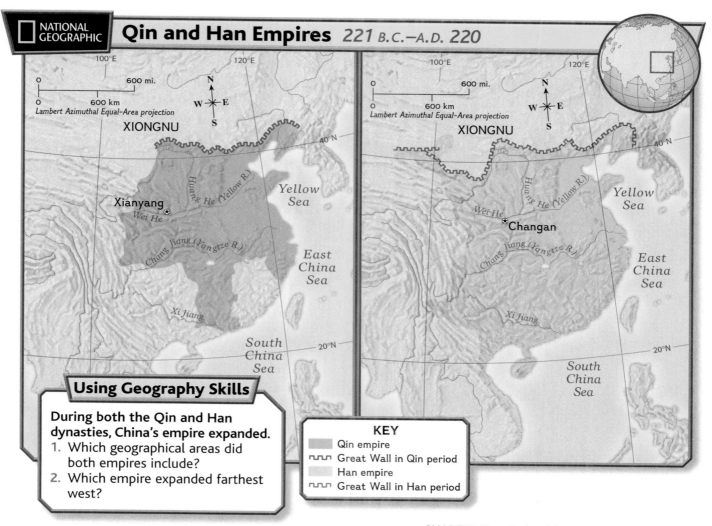

NATIONAL GEOGRAPHIC

Qin and Han Empires 221 B.C.–A.D. 220

Using Geography Skills

During both the Qin and Han dynasties, China's empire expanded.
1. Which geographical areas did both empires include?
2. Which empire expanded farthest west?

KEY
- Qin empire
- Great Wall in Qin period
- Han empire
- Great Wall in Han period

Qin Shihuangdi unified China. He created one currency, or type of money, to be used throughout the empire. He also ordered the building of roads and a huge canal. The canal connected the Chang Jiang in central China to what is today the city of **Guangzhou** (GWAHNG•JOH) in southern China. He used the canal to ship supplies to his troops in far-off territories.

The Great Wall Northern China was bordered by the vast Gobi. Nomads, people who move from place to place with herds of animals, lived in the Gobi. The Chinese knew them as the Xiongnu (SYEHN•NOO). The Xiongnu were masters at fighting on horseback. They often attacked Chinese farms and villages. Several Chinese rulers in the north built walls to keep out the Xiongnu.

Qin Shihuangdi forced farmers to leave their fields and work on connecting and strengthening the walls. The result was the Great Wall of China, built with stone, sand, and piled rubble. However, Qin did not build the wall that we know today. It was built 1,500 years later.

Why Did People Rebel? Many Chinese viewed Qin Shihuangdi as a cruel leader. Aristocrats were angry because he reduced their power. Scholars hated him for burning their writings. Farmers hated him for forcing them to build roads and the Great Wall. Four years after the emperor died in 210 B.C., the people overthrew his dynasty. Civil war followed, and a new dynasty soon arose.

Reading Check **Explain** Why did Qin face little opposition during most of his reign?

◀ This artwork shows the Great Wall many years after the reign of Qin Shihuangdi. Most of the wall built by Qin was made of stone and rubble, and was located north of the Great Wall we see today. Little remains of Qin's wall. *Who was the wall meant to keep out?*

Biography

QIN SHIHUANGDI
c. 259–210 B.C.

At the age 13, Ying Zheng became the leader of the Chinese state of Qin. The state was already very powerful because of Zheng's father, the previous ruler. Its government and military were well organized. With the help of his generals, young Zheng defeated Qin's six rival states. By 221 B.C., he had united all of the Chinese states under his rule. To mark a new beginning for China and to show his supremacy, Zheng gave himself the title Qin Shihuangdi—"The First Qin Emperor."

Qin Shihuangdi energetically went to work organizing his country. He divided the land into 36 districts, each with its own governor and a representative who reported directly to him. He made laws and taxes uniform throughout the country. He also standardized weights and measurements. Throughout China, the emperor had his achievements inscribed on stone tablets.

Qin Shihuangdi did strengthen and organize China, but many people disliked him because of his harsh laws and punishments. Many people also disliked how he spent lavish amounts of money to build palaces and a gigantic tomb for himself. He had an entire lifelike army—over 6,000 soldiers and horses—built of clay and placed in the tomb.

Three attempts to kill the emperor were made during the last years of his life. Qin Shihuangdi grew fearful and searched for a magic potion that would give him everlasting life. He died while on a trip in eastern China.

▲ Qin Shihuangdi

"I have brought order to the mass of beings."
—Qin Shihuangdi

▲ Part of the terra-cotta army found in Qin Shihuangdi's tomb

Then and Now

Why do you think modern historians disagree in their evaluation of Qin Shihuangdi's leadership?

The Han Dynasty

Main Idea Developments during the Han dynasty improved life for all Chinese.

Reading Focus How much time do you spend studying for tests? Find out why some Chinese people spent years studying for one special test.

In 202 B.C. **Liu Bang** (lee•OO BAHNG) founded the Han dynasty. Liu Bang, who was once a peasant, became a military leader and defeated his rivals. He declared himself Han Gaozu—"Exalted Emperor of Han." Although Han Gaozu threw out the harsh policies of the Qin dynasty, he continued to use censors and also divided the empire into provinces and counties.

What Was the Civil Service? The Han reached its peak under the leadership of **Han Wudi** (HAHN WOO•DEE), which means "Martial Emperor of Han." He ruled from

141 B.C. to 87 B.C. Because Wudi wanted talented people to fill government posts, job seekers had to take long, difficult tests to qualify for openings in the bureaucracy. Those with the highest scores got the jobs.

In time, Wudi's tests became the civil service examinations. This system for choosing officials remained part of Chinese civilization for 2,000 years. The system was supposed to help anyone with the right skills get a job with the government. However, it actually favored the rich. Only wealthy families could afford to educate their sons for the difficult exams.

Students preparing for these tests learned law, history, and the teachings of Confucius. They began to memorize the works of Confucius at age seven. Students were not allowed to do physical labor or to play most sports. They could go fishing, however, because it was considered the sport of scholars. After many years of schooling, the students took their civil service examinations. Only one in five passed. Those who failed taught school, took jobs as assistants to officials, or were supported by their families.

The Chinese Empire Grows A large bureaucracy was needed to rule the rapidly growing empire. The population had grown from about 20 million under Han Gaozu to more than 60 million under Han Wudi.

Because farmers had to divide their lands among more and more sons, the average farmer owned only about one acre of land. With so little land, farm families could not raise enough to live. As a result, many sold their land to aristocrats and became tenant farmers. Tenant farmers work on land that is owned

▲ This painting shows students taking a civil service examination. *Why did the civil service system favor rich job seekers?*

Linking Past & Present

Papermaking

THEN The Chinese were the first people to make paper. The oldest piece of paper found in China dates from the first century B.C. Papermakers soaked tree bark, hemp, and rags in water and pounded it into pulp. They lowered a bamboo screen into a vat of the pulp and then lifted it out. It held a thin sheet of pulp which dried into a single sheet of paper.

▼ Modern papermaking

▲ A modern artist demonstrates an ancient way of making paper.

NOW Papermaking today is a huge international industry. Most paper is made in paper mills by machines, but the basic process is the same. Instead of tree bark, rags, and hemp, most paper today is made from wood pulp. *Why do you think some modern artists continue to make paper using pulp and a frame?*

---

by someone else and pay rent in crops. The aristocrats now owned thousands of acres. They hired armies to force more farmers into selling their land and working as tenants.

China's empire grew in size as well as in population. Han armies added lands to the south and pushed Chinese borders westward. The Han dynasty also made the country more secure. Wudi's armies drove back the Xiongnu—the nomads to the north. After Wudi's death, the Chinese lived in peace for almost 150 years.

An Era of Inventions New inventions during the Han dynasty helped Chinese workers produce more than ever. Millers used newly invented waterwheels to grind more grain, and miners used new iron drill bits to mine more salt. Ironworkers invented steel. Paper, another Han invention, was used by government officials to record a growing amount of information.

Chinese medicine also improved under the Han. Doctors discovered that certain foods prevented disease. They used herbs to cure illnesses and eased pain by sticking thin needles into patients' skin. This treatment is known as **acupuncture** (A•kyuh•PUHNGK•chuhr).

The Chinese also invented the rudder and a new way to move the sails of ships. These changes allowed ships to sail into the wind for the first time. Chinese merchant ships could now travel to the islands of Southeast Asia and into the Indian Ocean. As a result, China established trade as far away as India and the Mediterranean Sea.

✓ Reading Check **Explain** How did China's empire increase in size during the Han dynasty?

The Silk Road

Main Idea The Silk Road carried Chinese goods as far as Greece and Rome.

Reading Focus Many of the things we buy today are made in China. How do these goods get to the United States? Read to learn how goods made in China long ago made it all the way to Europe.

Chinese merchants made a lot of money by shipping expensive goods to other countries. Silk was the most valuable trade product. Some of it went by ship to Southeast

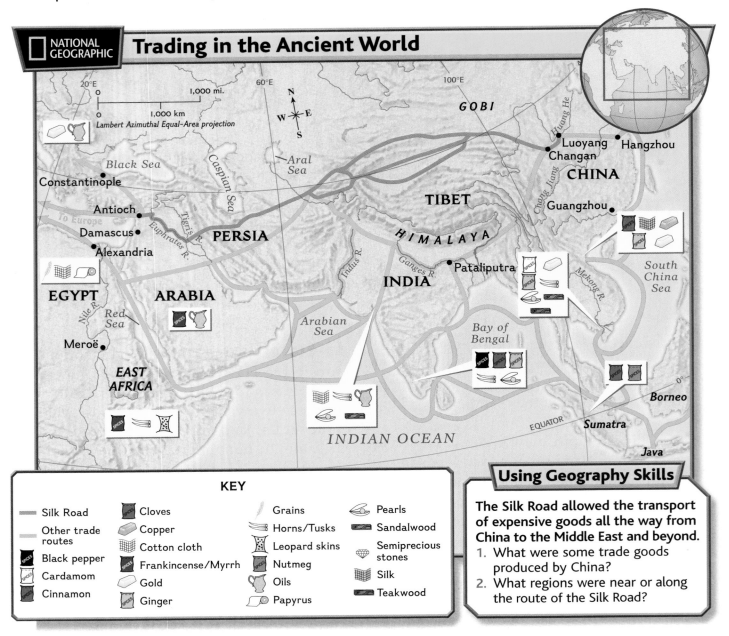

NATIONAL GEOGRAPHIC

Trading in the Ancient World

KEY

- — Silk Road
- — Other trade routes
- Black pepper
- Cardamom
- Cinnamon
- Cloves
- Copper
- Cotton cloth
- Frankincense/Myrrh
- Gold
- Ginger
- Grains
- Horns/Tusks
- Leopard skins
- Nutmeg
- Oils
- Papyrus
- Pearls
- Sandalwood
- Semiprecious stones
- Silk
- Teakwood

Using Geography Skills

The Silk Road allowed the transport of expensive goods all the way from China to the Middle East and beyond.

1. What were some trade goods produced by China?
2. What regions were near or along the route of the Silk Road?

Four Chinese Dynasties

	SHANG	ZHOU	QIN	HAN
When	1750–1045 B.C.	1045–256 B.C.	221–206 B.C.	202 B.C.–A.D. 220
Important Leaders	Numerous kings with large armies and control over the land; ruled from capital city of Anyang	Wu	Qin Shihuangdi	Liu Bang
Main Ideas and Accomplishments	Developed social classes that included farmers, merchants, aristocrats, and royal family	Longest-lasting dynasty in Chinese history; established Mandate of Heaven	Strengthened central government; created single monetary system	Population and landmass grew under Han; opened China to trade and commerce by building Silk Road
Influences on Chinese Culture	Influenced Chinese religion and culture; created Chinese written language	Developed irrigation and flood-control systems to help farmers grow more crops	Introduced use of censors to check on government officials; Qin built the first Great Wall to keep out invaders	Created government's civil service examination; major inventions: steel, paper, acupuncture, advanced sea travel

Understanding Charts

The four dynasties of early China were separated by brief periods of unrest.
1. Under which dynasty was a single monetary system put in place?
2. **Evaluate** Which dynasty do you think contributed the most to Chinese culture? Why?

Asia. However, most went overland on the **Silk Road.** This large network of trade routes stretched 4,000 miles (6,436 km) from western China to southwest Asia.

Merchants began using the Silk Road between 200 B.C. and A.D. 100. Han Wudi sent out a general named Zhang Qian (JAHNG CHYEHN) to explore areas west of China. After 13 years, Zhang returned to China with amazing stories.

He told of a mighty empire to the west with large cities full of people "who cut their hair short, wear embroidered clothes, and ride in very small chariots." Zhang was describing the Roman Empire. His stories sparked China's interest in the West and trade on the Silk Road increased. Merchants used camels to carry their goods across deserts and mountains to central Asia. From there Arabs carried the goods to the Mediterranean Sea.

The trip over the Silk Road was expensive because it was difficult and dangerous. Merchants had to pay taxes to many kingdoms as they moved the goods east and west. For this reason, they carried only high-priced goods such as silk, spices, tea, and porcelain.

✓ **Reading Check** **Conclude** Why were only expensive goods carried on the Silk Road?

Major Changes in China

Main Idea Unrest in China helped Buddhism to spread.

Reading Focus What do you do when you feel frightened or unsafe? Read to find out how those feelings triggered the spread of Buddhism from India to China.

As you read in Chapter 6, Buddhism began in India, but it soon spread to other countries as well. Merchants and teachers from India brought Buddhism to China during the A.D. 100s. At first, only a few merchants and scholars were interested in the new religion. In time, however, Buddhism became very popular. One of the most important reasons that the Chinese people began to believe in Buddhism was the fall of the Han dynasty.

The Han emperors after Wudi were weak and foolish. As a result, the central government lost respect and power. At the same time, as you read earlier, the aristocrats began grabbing more land and wealth. Dishonest officials and greedy aristocrats caused unrest among the farmers.

Wars, rebellions, and plots against the emperor put an end to the Han dynasty. In A.D. 190 a rebel army attacked the Han capital, **Luoyang** (loo•WOH•YAHNG). By A.D. 220, China had plunged into civil war. To make the situation worse, the northern nomads invaded the country.

The collapse of the government and the beginning of the civil war frightened many Chinese. They felt unsafe. Buddhist ideas helped people cope with the stress and their fear. Even the followers of other religions found Buddhism attractive. Followers of Confucius and Daoists admired Buddhist ideas. By the 400s, Buddhism had become popular in China.

✓ Reading Check **Identify** What groups in China were the first to adopt Buddhism?

History Online

Study Central™ Need help with the material in this section? Visit jat.glencoe.com

Section 3 Review

Reading Summary

Review the Main Ideas

- The short-lived Qin dynasty helped to unify China.
- During the Han dynasty, people began taking tests for government jobs. New inventions, such as the waterwheel and paper, were created.
- The Silk Road was an important trade route that linked China to the West.
- As the Han dynasty lost power, many Chinese became followers of Buddhism.

What Did You Learn?

1. Why did Qin Shihuangdi have the Great Wall built?

2. What were civil service examinations and why were they created?

Critical Thinking

3. **Cause and Effect** Draw a diagram to show the factors that caused the Han dynasty to fall.

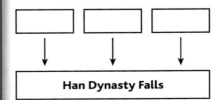

Han Dynasty Falls

4. **Geography Skills** What barriers did merchants who used the Silk Road have to cross?

5. **Explain** How did Qin Shihuangdi make China's central government stronger?

6. **Analyze** Why did the Qin dynasty fall?

7. **Descriptive Writing** Zhang Qian wrote that Romans had short hair, wore embroidered clothes, and rode in chariots. Name three things that he might have written about people in the United States after seeing them for the first time.

Section 1 China's First Civilizations

Vocabulary
dynasty
aristocrat
pictograph
ideograph
bureaucracy
mandate
Dao

Focusing on the Main Ideas
- Rivers, mountains, and deserts helped shape China's civilization. *(page 225)*
- Rulers known as the Shang became powerful because they controlled land and had strong armies. *(page 226)*
- Chinese rulers claimed that the Mandate of Heaven gave them the right to rule. *(page 229)*

Bronze bowl and ladle ▶
from Zhou dynasty

Section 2 Life in Ancient China

Vocabulary
social class
filial piety
Confucianism
Daoism
Legalism

Focusing on the Main Ideas
- Chinese society had three main social classes: landowning aristocrats, farmers, and merchants. *(page 233)*
- Three Chinese philosophies, Confucianism, Daoism, and Legalism, grew out of a need for order. *(page 235)*

Laozi ▶

Section 3 The Qin and Han Dynasties

Vocabulary
acupuncture

Focusing on the Main Ideas
- Qin Shihuangdi used harsh methods to unify and defend China. *(page 241)*
- Developments during the Han dynasty improved life for all Chinese. *(page 244)*
- The Silk Road carried Chinese goods as far as Greece and Rome. *(page 246)*
- Unrest in China helped Buddhism to spread. *(page 248)*

Chapter 7 Assessment and Activities

Review Vocabulary

Match the words with the definitions below.

___ 1. dynasty
___ 2. aristocrat
___ 3. bureaucracy
___ 4. mandate
___ 5. social class
___ 6. filial piety
___ 7. acupuncture
___ 8. Daoism
___ 9. Confucianism

a. right to command
b. line of rulers in the same family
c. upper class whose wealth is based on land
d. The ideas of ___ included a duty to participate in government.
e. appointed government officials
f. head of family honored by other members
g. medical treatment using thin needles
h. people with a similar position in society
i. The teachings of Laozi are the basis of ___.

Review Main Ideas

Section 1 • China's First Civilizations
10. What geographical features shaped China's civilizations?
11. Why did the Shang rulers become powerful?

Section 2 • Life in Ancient China
12. What were the three main classes in Chinese society?
13. Identify three Chinese philosophies and the reason they emerged.

Section 3 • The Qin and Han Dynasties
14. How did developments during the Han dynasty affect the Chinese people?
15. What was the purpose of the Silk Road?

Critical Thinking

16. **Contrast** How is the ancient Chinese writing system different from cuneiform and hieroglyphic writing?
17. **Describe** How did Shang artisans create bronze urns?
18. **Analyze** How is Daoism the opposite of Confucianism in some ways?

Review

Reading Skill | Text Structure | Headings and Punctuation

19. Read each of the headings below. Three could be subheads in a chapter about ancient China. Which one would most likely be the main head?
   a. The Ideas of Confucius
   b. Daoist Beliefs
   c. Chinese Philosophy
   d. Hanfeizi

20. What would be a good main head for these subheads: Papermaking, Civil Service Examinations, Acupuncture?
   e. The Rise of the Zhou Dynasty
   f. Inventions of the Qin Dynasty
   g. Developments of the Han Dynasty
   h. Life in the Shang Dynasty

To review this skill, see pages 222–223.

Geography Skills

Study the map below and answer the following questions.

21. **Human/Environment Interaction** Which dynasty controlled the most land?
22. **Location** In what direction did the Qin dynasty expand the most?
23. **Analyze** How do you think the East China Sea affected expansion?

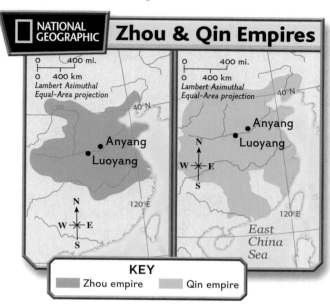

NATIONAL GEOGRAPHIC
Zhou & Qin Empires

0 400 mi.
0 400 km
Lambert Azimuthal Equal-Area projection
40°N
• Anyang
Luoyang
N W E S
120°E

0 400 mi.
0 400 km
Lambert Azimuthal Equal-Area projection
40°N
• Anyang
Luoyang
N W E S
120°E
East China Sea

KEY
Zhou empire   Qin empire

Read to Write

24. **Expository Writing** Imagine you are planning a trip on the Silk Road and you need someone to go with you. Write a want ad describing the type of person you need. Explain what will be expected of that person on the trip.

25. **Using Your FOLDABLES** Choose one person that you included in your foldable. Write a list of 10 questions that you would ask that person in an interview. Exchange lists with a partner and play the role of the person being interviewed.

Using Technology

26. **Internet Research** The Chinese built the Great Wall of China to protect themselves. Use the Internet and your local library to research ways other countries have protected themselves from enemies. Describe at least two examples to your classmates.

Building Citizenship Skills

27. **Plan a Debate** With your class, plan and participate in a three-way debate. Divide into three teams. One team will represent the Legalists, one will represent followers of Confucius, and one will represent Daoists. As a team, research each philosophy. Record key points on note cards for easy reference. Begin the debate by asking the question "Which philosophy is best reflected in a democratic society such as that of the United States?"

Primary Source Analyze

The main ideas of Daoism are explained in a book titled *Dao De Jing* (The Way of the Dao). This passage describes the Daoist position against violence.

"When leading by the way of the Tao [Dao], abominate [hate] the use of force, for it causes resistance, and loss of strength. . . .

Achieve results but not through violence, for it is against the natural way, and damages both others' and one's own true self. . . .

The wise leader achieves results, but does not glory in them . . . and does not boast of them.

He knows that boasting is not the natural way, and that he who goes against that way, will fail in his endeavours."

—"A Caveat Against Violence,"
The Tao Te Ching, Stan Rosenthal, trans.

DBQ Document-Based Questions

28. According to Daoist thought, what is the result of using force or violence?
29. What do you think the following statement means?
"The wise leader achieves results, but does not glory in them."

Comparing Civilizations

Compare the civilizations that you have read about by reviewing the information below. Can you see how the people of these civilizations helped to build the world we live in today?

Where in the World?

- Chapters 4 & 5
- Chapter 6
- Chapter 7

NATIONAL GEOGRAPHIC

	Ancient Greece Chapters 4 & 5	Early India Chapter 6	Early China Chapter 7
Where did these civilizations develop?	• On Mediterranean islands and the Balkan Peninsula	• In the Indus River valley	• In the Huang He valley
Who were some important people in these civilizations?	• Homer, c. 750 B.C. • Pericles, c. 495–429 B.C. • Socrates, c. 470–399 B.C. • Alexander the Great, c. 356–323 B.C.	• Siddhartha Gautama, c. 563–483 B.C. • Chandragupta Maurya, ruled c. 321–298 B.C. • Asoka, ruled c. 273–232 B.C.	• Wu Wang, ruled c. 1045–1043 B.C. • Confucius, 551–479 B.C. • Qin Shihuangdi, ruled 221–210 B.C. • Liu Bang, ruled 202–195 B.C.
Where did most of the people live?	• Early Greeks lived on estates near walled palaces • Later Greeks lived in a polis and in nearby farms and villages	• Many lived in farming villages and towns near major rivers • Some lived in very large cities	• Landowning aristocrats lived in large houses with gardens and courtyards • Most people were farmers living in simple houses in villages or cities

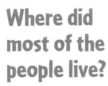

	Ancient Greece Chapters 4 & 5	**Early India** Chapter 6	**Early China** Chapter 7
What were these people's beliefs?	• Greeks worshiped many gods and goddesses and believed in fate	• Hinduism: complex religion with many gods representing an eternal spirit • Buddhism: enlightenment available to anyone	• Confucianism: duty directs your life • Daoism: people should try to be in harmony with nature • Legalism: people need harsh laws to be good • Worship of ancestors
What was their government like?	• Early Greeks were ruled by kings • Later, some Greeks developed governments run by citizens	• The warrior class ran the government, usually ruled by a king	• A king or emperor ruled the country • Aristocrats ran the provinces
What was their language and writing like?	• Greek: used characters to form letters and words	• Sanskrit: used characters to form letters and words	• Chinese: symbols that represent objects were combined to represent ideas
What contributions did they make?	• Introduced democracy • Architecture was copied by others • Developed the idea of theater and drama	• Made advances in medicine, mathematics, science, and literature • Developed two major religions	• Invented paper and gunpowder • Cultivated silk
How do these contributions affect me? *Can you add any?*	• We have a democratic government in the United States • Modern plays, movies, and television shows have their roots in Greek theater	• "0" is now a part of our number system • Many people still practice Buddhism and Hinduism	• The papermaking process allows us to create books, newspapers, and other paper products • Gunpowder and silk are still in use

Unit 3

New Empires and New Faiths

Why It's Important

Each civilization that you will study in this unit made important contributions to history.

- The Romans invented concrete and used the arch in building.
- The Christians helped shape the West's religious beliefs.
- The Muslims spread the religion of Islam and invented algebra.

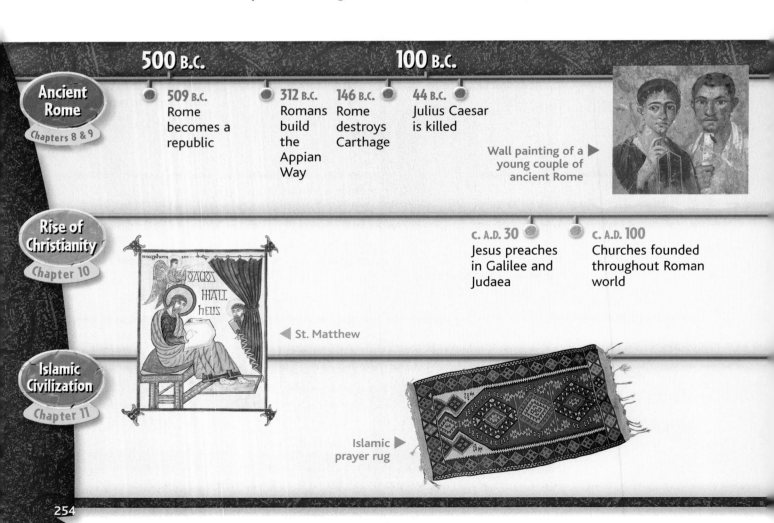

500 B.C.

100 B.C.

Ancient Rome
Chapters 8 & 9

509 B.C.
Rome becomes a republic

312 B.C.
Romans build the Appian Way

146 B.C.
Rome destroys Carthage

44 B.C.
Julius Caesar is killed

▶ Wall painting of a young couple of ancient Rome

Rise of Christianity
Chapter 10

c. A.D. 30
Jesus preaches in Galilee and Judaea

c. A.D. 100
Churches founded throughout Roman world

◀ St. Matthew

Islamic Civilization
Chapter 11

Islamic ▶
prayer rug

Where in the World?

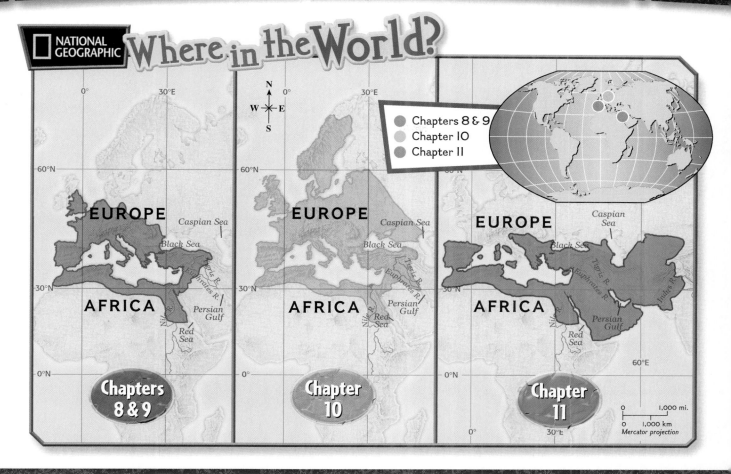

EUROPE

Caspian Sea

Black Sea

Tigris R.
Euphrates R.

Persian Gulf

Red Sea

Chapters 8 & 9

EUROPE

Caspian Sea

Black Sea

Nile R.
Red Sea

Tigris R.
Euphrates R.

Persian Gulf

AFRICA

Chapter 10

EUROPE

Caspian Sea

Black Sea

Tigris R.
Euphrates R.

Indus R.

AFRICA

Persian Gulf

Red Sea

60°E

Chapter 11

- Chapters 8 & 9
- Chapter 10
- Chapter 11

N W E S

0 1,000 mi.
0 1,000 km
Mercator projection

A.D. 300

A.D. 700

A.D. 1100

A.D. 476
Western Roman Empire ends

A.D. 534
Justinian reforms Roman law

◄ Gladiators in battle

A.D. 392
Christianity becomes Rome's official religion

◄ Church of Hagia Sophia ("Holy Wisdom")

A.D. 1054
Eastern Orthodox and Roman Catholic Churches separate

◄ Mosque in Baghdad

A.D. 624
Muhammad founds Islamic state in Arabia

C. A.D. 830
Baghdad reaches its height as center of Islamic learning

C. A.D. 1200
Muslim rule reaches to northern India

Unit 3

Places to Locate

EUROPE

Mediterranean Sea

AFRICA

Roman aqueduct
See Ancient Rome
Chapters 8 & 9

Roman Pantheon
See Ancient Rome
Chapters 8 & 9

People to Meet

Augustus
63 B.C.–A.D. 14
Roman emperor
Chapter 8, page 289

Jesus
C. 6 B.C. –A.D. 30
Crucifixion led to rise of Christianity
Chapter 10, page 346

Paul
C. A.D. 10–65
Christian thinker
Chapter 10, page 349

Constantine
C. A.D. 280–337
Roman emperor
Chapter 9, page 321

ASIA

3 Hagia Sophia

See Ancient Rome
Chapters 8 & 9

4 Mount of the Beatitudes

See Rise of Christianity
Chapter 10

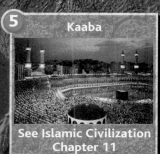

5 Kaaba

See Islamic Civilization
Chapter 11

5

*Arabian
Sea*

Augustine

A.D. 354–430
**Christian
philosopher**
Chapter 10, page 357

Theodora

C. A.D. 500–548
Byzantine empress
Chapter 9, page 331

Muhammad

C. A.D. 570–632
**Muslims believe Allah
dictated the Quran to
Muhammad**
Chapter 11, page 376

Omar Khayyam

A.D. 1048–1131
**Islamic poet
and philosopher**
Chapter 11, page 392

The Rise of Rome

◀ Ruins of the Forum in Rome, Italy

NATIONAL GEOGRAPHIC When & Where?

500 B.C.	300 B.C.	100 B.C.	A.D. 100
451 B.C. Romans adopt the Twelve Tables	**267 B.C.** Rome controls most of Italy	**27 B.C.** Octavian becomes Rome's first emperor	**A.D. 96** Rule of the Good Emperors begins

Chapter Preview

While the Chinese civilization arose in East Asia, the Romans created an empire that covered much of the Mediterranean world. Read this chapter to discover how the Romans were able to win control of such a large area.

 View the Chapter 8 video in the *World History: Journey Across Time* Video Program.

Chapter Overview Visit jat.glencoe.com for a preview of Chapter 8.

Rome's Beginnings

The civilization of Rome began in Italy. Rome grew from a small city into an economic and military power.

The Roman Republic

Rome was a republic for almost 500 years. During this time, it gradually expanded the right to vote. After many years of war and following the destruction of the Carthaginian Empire, Rome took control of the Mediterranean region.

The Fall of the Republic

As Rome's territory grew, the army gained political power. The Roman Republic, weakened by civil wars, gave way to the Roman Empire.

The Early Empire

Augustus and many of his successors governed well. Rome's empire grew larger and wealthier.

Know-Want-Learn *Make this foldable to help you organize what you know, what you want to know, and what you learn about the rise of Rome.*

Step 1 *Fold four sheets of paper in half from top to bottom.*

Step 2 *On each folded paper, make a cut 1 inch from the side on the top flap.*

Cut 1 inch from the edge through the top flap only.

Step 3 *Place the folded papers one on top of the other. Staple the four sections together and label the top four tabs: Rome's Beginnings, The Roman Republic, The Fall of the Republic, and The Early Empire.*

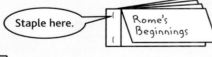

Staple here.

Rome's Beginnings

Reading and Writing *Before reading the chapter, write what you already know about the beginning of Rome, the rise and fall of its republic, and the early Roman Empire under the tabs of your foldable. Also write one question you have on each tab. As you read, summarize what you learn under each tab.*

8 Reading Social Studies

1 Learn It!

Note Taking

Did you know that when you take notes, you remember more than three-fourths of the information you recorded? That is why it is important to learn to take careful notes as you are reading.

Read this paragraph from Section 3.

Trouble in the Republic

Rome's armies were victorious wherever they went. Yet problems were building at home. Dishonest officials stole money, and the gap between rich and poor was growing. Thousands of farmers faced ruin, and the cities were becoming overcrowded and dangerous.

—from page 278

Here is one method of note taking for the above paragraph.

Reading Tip

Authors of textbooks help with note taking by giving you headings and subheadings. If you are not sure of the main topic, it is a safe bet that headings in bold are important.

Main Topic	Important Details
Republic's Problems	1. dishonest officials 2. gap between rich and poor 3. farmers faced ruin 4. cities overcrowded

Practice It!

Make a T-Chart

Read the first few pages of Section 2 and use this T-chart as a guide to help you practice taking notes.

Read to Write ⋯⋯⋯

On page 273, read about Rome's first code of laws, the Twelve Tables. Come up with your own 12 Tables of School Law, and explain why each one should be used to govern the students in your school.

Main Topic	Important Details
Rome's government	1.
	2.
Social groups in Rome	1.
	2.
Roman law	1.
	2.

3 **Apply It!**

As you read Section 1, write the names of important people or places on the left column of your note-taking paper. On the right side, list details from your reading.

Rome's Beginnings

Get Ready to Read!

What's the Connection?

In previous chapters, you learned about the civilization of ancient Greece. Greek ways did not die with the end of Greece's freedom. They were adopted and spread widely by another civilization, Rome.

Focusing on the Main Ideas

• Geography played an important role in the rise of Roman civilization. **(page 263)**

• The Romans created a republic and conquered Italy. By treating people fairly, they built Rome from a small city into a great power. **(page 265)**

Locating Places

Sicily (SIH•suh•lee)
Apennines (A•puh•NYNZ)
Latium (LAY•shee•uhm)
Tiber River (TY•buhr)
Etruria (ih•TRUR•ee•uh)

Meeting People

Romulus (RAHM•yuh•luhs)
and Remus (REE•muhs)
Aeneas (ih•NEE•uhs)
Latins (LA•tuhnz)
Etruscans (ih•TRUHS•kuhnz)
Tarquins (TAHR•kwihnz)

Building Your Vocabulary

republic (rih•PUH•blihk)
legion (LEE•juhn)

Reading Strategy

Summarizing Information Use a diagram like the one below to show how the Etruscans affected the development of Rome.

Etruscans	

NATIONAL GEOGRAPHIC **When & Where?**

ITALY
• Rome

Sicily

AFRICA

650 B.C.

450 B.C.

250 B.C.

c. 650 B.C.
Etruscans rule Rome

509 B.C.
Rome becomes a republic

267 B.C.
Rome controls most of Italy

The Origins of Rome

Main Idea Geography played an important role in the rise of Roman civilization.

Reading Focus If you were founding a new city, what natural features would influence your choice of a building site? As you read this section, think about the choices that the early Romans made.

Italy is in an important location in the middle of the Mediterranean region. It is a long, narrow peninsula with a distinctive shape: it looks like a high-heeled boot jutting into the sea. The heel points toward Greece and the toe toward the island of **Sicily** (SIH•suh•lee). Across the top of the boot are the Alps, craggy mountains that separate Italy from European lands to the north. Another mountain range, the **Apennines** (A•puh•NYNZ), runs all the way down the boot from north to south.

The landscape of Italy is similar to that of Greece, but the Apennines are not as rugged as Greece's mountains. They can be crossed much more easily. As a result, the people who settled in Italy were not split up into small, isolated communities as the Greeks were. In addition, Italy had better farmland than Greece. Its mountain slopes level off to large flat plains that are ideal for growing crops. With more capacity to produce food, Italy could support more people than Greece could.

Historians know little about the first people to live in Italy. There is evidence, however, that groups from the north slipped through Italy's mountain passes between about 1500 B.C. and 1000 B.C. Attracted by the mild climate and rich soil, a small but steady stream of newcomers settled in the hills and on the plains. Among these peoples were a Latin-speaking people who built the city of Rome on the plain of **Latium** (LAY•shee•uhm) in central Italy.

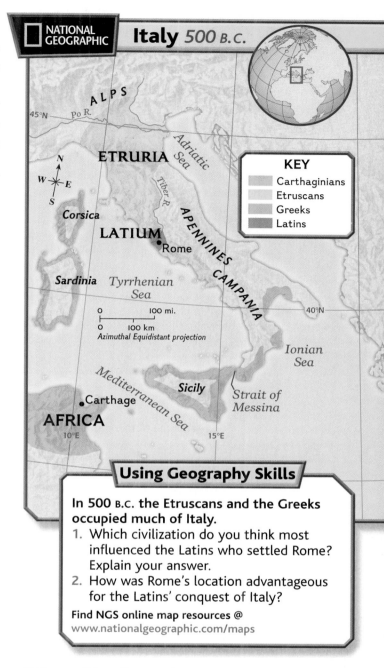

NATIONAL GEOGRAPHIC

Italy 500 B.C.

KEY
- Carthaginians
- Etruscans
- Greeks
- Latins

0   100 mi.
0   100 km
Azimuthal Equidistant projection

Using Geography Skills

In 500 B.C. the Etruscans and the Greeks occupied much of Italy.
1. Which civilization do you think most influenced the Latins who settled Rome? Explain your answer.
2. How was Rome's location advantageous for the Latins' conquest of Italy?

Find NGS online map resources @
www.nationalgeographic.com/maps

Where Was Rome Located? Geography played a major part in the location of Rome. The site chosen for Rome was about 15 miles (24 km) up the **Tiber River** (TY•buhr) from the Mediterranean Sea. The Tiber River gave the Romans a source of water and a way to the rest of the Mediterranean world. At the same time, Rome was far enough from the sea to escape raids by pirates.

The *Aeneid*

Two legends describe the beginning of Rome. One says that after Troy was destroyed, Aeneas and the other Trojans went in search of another place to live.

"Weeping, I drew away from our old country. . . . I took to the open sea, borne outward into exile with my people, my son, my hearth gods, and the greater gods. . . . Now making landfall under the southwind there, I plotted out on that curved shore the walls of a colony—though fate opposed it—and I devised the name Aeneadae for the people, from my own."

▲ Virgil

—adapted from Virgil, *Aeneid*

DBQ Document-Based Question

What type of person do you think Aeneas was to build a new city after having the first one destroyed?

In addition, Rome was built on seven hills. The Romans did this on purpose. The hills were very steep, making it easy to defend the city against enemy attack. Rome was also located at a place where people could easily cross the Tiber River. As a result, Rome became a stopping place for people traveling north and south in western Italy and for merchant ships sailing in the western Mediterranean.

How Did Rome Begin? Two different legends describe how Rome began. The traditional story is that twin brothers named **Romulus** (RAHM•yuh•luhs) and **Remus** (REE•muhs) founded the city. As babies, the boys were abandoned near the Tiber River. Rescued by a wolf and raised by a shepherd, they decided to build a city in 753 B.C. The twins quarreled, however, and Remus made fun of the wall his brother was building. In a fury, Romulus lashed out at Remus and killed him. Romulus went on to become the first king of Rome, the new city he named after himself.

The seeds of Rome are traced even farther back in the *Aeneid*, a famous epic by the Roman poet Virgil. The *Aeneid* is the story of the Trojan hero **Aeneas** (ih•NEE•uhs). He and a band of followers are said to have sailed the Mediterranean Sea after the Greeks captured Troy. After many adventures, the Trojans landed at the mouth of the Tiber. Through warfare and then marriage to the local king's daughter, Aeneas united the Trojans and some of the **Latins** (LA•tuhnz), the local people. He thus became the "father" of the Romans.

Historians are not sure how Rome began. They think that Latins lived in the area of Rome as early as 1000 B.C. They built huts on Rome's hills, tended herds, and grew crops. Sometime between 800 B.C. and 700 B.C., they decided to band together for protection. It was this community that became known as Rome.

Early Influences After about 800 B.C., other groups joined the Romans in Italy. Two of these groups, the Greeks and the **Etruscans** (ih•TRUHS•kuhnz), played a major role in shaping Roman civilization.

Many Greeks came to southern Italy and Sicily between 750 B.C. and 550 B.C., when Greece was busily building overseas colonies. From the Greeks, Romans learned to grow olives and grapes. They also adopted the Greek alphabet, and they

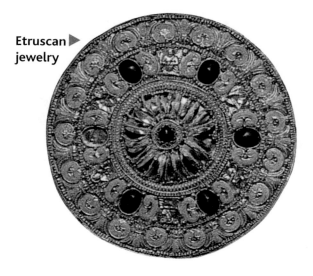

◀ Etruscan jewelry

would eventually model their architecture, sculpture, and literature after the Greeks.

Rome's early growth was influenced most, however, by the Etruscans. The Etruscans lived north of Rome in **Etruria** (ih•TRUR•ee•uh). After 650 B.C., they moved south and took control of Rome and most of Latium.

The Etruscans were skilled metalworkers who became rich from mining and trade. They forced enslaved people to do the heaviest work and made their own lives comfortable. Their tomb paintings show men and women feasting, dancing, and playing music and sports. Some murals also show bloody battle scenes, revealing the Etruscans' pride in their military.

The Etruscans changed Rome from a village of straw-roofed huts into a city of wood and brick buildings. They laid out streets, temples, and public buildings around a central square. Etruscans also taught Romans a new style of dress, featuring short cloaks and togas—loose garments draped over one shoulder. More importantly, the Etruscan army would serve as a model for the mighty army the Romans eventually assembled.

✔ Reading Check **Explain** How did geography help the Romans prosper?

The Birth of a Republic

Main Idea The Romans created a republic and conquered Italy. By treating people fairly, they built Rome from a small city into a great power.

Reading Focus Have you heard the phrase "winning hearts and minds"? It means convincing people to support you rather than just forcing them to obey. Read on to learn how the Romans not only conquered other people in Italy but also won their hearts and minds.

The Etruscans ruled Rome for more than 100 years. Under the Etruscans, Rome became wealthy and powerful. However, the ruling family, called the **Tarquins** (TAHR•kwihnz), grew more and more cruel.

Finally, in 509 B.C., the Romans rebelled. They overthrew the Tarquins and set up a **republic** (rih•PUH•blihk). A republic is a form of government in which the leader is not a king or queen but someone put in office by citizens with the right to vote. In a republic, the citizens have the power. The rise of the Roman Republic marked the beginning of a new chapter in Rome's history.

▲ Etruscan murals often showed lively scenes of daily life, such as religious ceremonies or people enjoying music and feasts. *How did the Etruscans become wealthy?*

At the time Rome became a republic, it was still a small city, surrounded by enemies. Over the next 200 years, the Romans fought war after war against their neighbors. In 338 B.C. they finally defeated the other Latins living nearby. Next they attacked the Etruscans and defeated them in 284 B.C. By 267 B.C., the Romans had also conquered the Greeks in southern Italy. With this victory, the Romans became the masters of almost all of Italy.

Roman Legionary

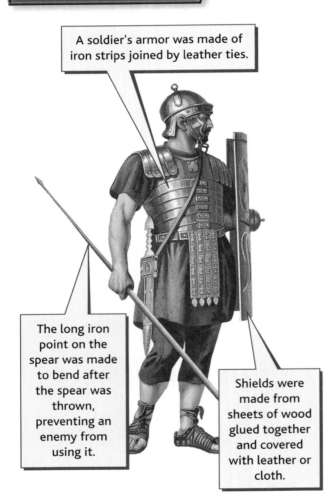

A soldier's armor was made of iron strips joined by leather ties.

The long iron point on the spear was made to bend after the spear was thrown, preventing an enemy from using it.

Shields were made from sheets of wood glued together and covered with leather or cloth.

At first, the Roman army was made up of ordinary citizens. Later the army contained well-trained professional soldiers and was one of the best fighting forces in the world. *What was a standard, and why did the army carry them?*

Why Was Rome So Strong? Rome was able to conquer Italy because the Romans were excellent soldiers. In the republic's early days, every male citizen who owned land had to serve in the army. Discipline was harsh, and deserters were punished by death. The tough discipline helped mold Roman soldiers into fighters who did not give up easily. In addition, they were practical problem solvers.

For example, Roman armies at first fought like Greek armies. Row upon row of soldiers marched shoulder to shoulder, keeping their shields together and holding long spears. Roman generals soon realized that this way of fighting was slow and hard to control. They reorganized their soldiers into smaller groups called **legions** (LEE•juhnz). Each legion had about 6,000 men and was further divided into groups of 60 to 120 soldiers. These small groups could quickly cut through enemy lines.

Roman soldiers, or legionaries, were armed with a short sword called a *gladius* and a spear called a *pilum.* Each unit also carried its own standard—a tall pole topped with a symbol. In battle, standards helped keep units together because the soldiers could see them above the action.

Shrewd Rulers The Romans were not only good fighters but also smart planners. As they expanded throughout Italy, they built permanent military settlements in the areas they conquered. Then they built roads between these towns. These roads allowed troops to travel swiftly to any place in their growing territory.

To rule their new conquests, the Romans created the Roman Confederation. Under this system, Romans gave full citizenship to some peoples, especially other Latins. They could vote and serve in the government, and they were treated the same as other citizens under the law. The Romans granted other peoples the status of allies.

Allies were free to run their own local affairs, but they had to pay taxes to the republic and provide soldiers for the army. The Romans made it clear that loyal allies could improve their position and even become Roman citizens.

With these policies, the Romans proved themselves clever rulers. They knew that conquered peoples would be more loyal to the government if they were well treated. Rome's generosity paid off. As a result, the republic grew stronger and more unified.

All the same, Rome was not afraid to use force if necessary. If conquered peoples revolted against Roman rule, their resistance was swiftly put down.

Reading Check **Describe** How did Rome rule its new conquests?

▲ This mosaic, or picture made from bits of stone, shows a group of Roman legionaries. *How many soldiers made up a legion?*

Study Central™ Need help with the material in this section? Visit jat.glencoe.com

Section 1 Review

Reading Summary

Review the **Main Ideas**

- The Romans, a Latin-speaking people, settled the region of Rome on the west side of Italy. The region's geography, as well as Etruscan and Greek ideas, helped Rome grow.

- In 509 B.C. the Romans overthrew Etruscan rule and established a republic. By about 275 B.C., Roman legions had conquered most of Italy.

What Did You Learn?

1. Where did the Greeks live in Italy, and how did they influence Roman civilization?

2. Describe the two legends that tell of the founding of Rome. Then describe how and when Rome was actually founded.

Critical Thinking

3. **Geography Skills** Draw a diagram like the one below. List examples of how geography determined Rome's location.

The Location of Rome

4. **Summarize** Describe the Roman conquest of Italy.

5. **Compare and Contrast** How did geography affect the development of civilization in Greece and Italy?

6. **Expository Writing** Write a short essay discussing the reasons Rome was so successful in its conquest of Italy.

7. **Reading** **Taking Notes** Use the blue subheads in Section 1 to create notes about Rome's beginnings. List each subhead on the left of a T-chart and details on the right.

Section 2

The Roman Republic

Get Ready to Read!

What's the Connection?
Romans had suffered under cruel Etruscan kings. When they had the chance to create their own government, they chose something very different.

Focusing on the (Main Ideas)
- Rome's republic was shaped by a struggle between wealthy landowners and regular citizens as it gradually expanded the right to vote. *(page 269)*

- Rome slowly destroyed the Carthaginian Empire and took control of the entire Mediterranean region. *(page 274)*

Locating Places
Carthage (KAHR•thihj)
Cannae (KA•nee)
Zama (ZAY•muh)

Meeting People
Cincinnatus (SIHN•suh•NA•tuhs)
Hannibal (HA•nuh•buhl)
Scipio (SIH•pee•OH)

Building Your Vocabulary
patrician (puh•TRIH•shuhn)
plebeian (plih•BEE•uhn)
consul (KAHN•suhl)
veto (VEE•toh)
praetor (PREE•tuhr)
dictator (DIHK•TAY•tuhr)

Reading Strategy
Categorizing Information Complete a chart like the one below listing the government officials and legislative bodies of the Roman Republic.

Officials	Legislative Bodies

NATIONAL GEOGRAPHIC When & Where?

450 B.C.

300 B.C.

150 B.C.

451 B.C. Romans adopt the Twelve Tables

264 B.C. Punic Wars begin

146 B.C. Rome destroys Carthage

SPAIN

ITALY
• Rome

Carthage •

GREECE

Rome's Government

Main Idea Rome's republic was shaped by a struggle between wealthy landowners and regular citizens as it gradually expanded the right to vote.

Reading Focus Do you know where our word *republic* comes from? It is made up of two Latin words meaning "thing of the people." Read on to learn about the republican government that early Romans created.

Early Romans were divided into two classes: patricians and plebeians. The **patricians** (puh•TRIH•shuhnz) were wealthy landowners. These nobles made up Rome's ruling class. Most of Rome's people, however, were **plebeians** (plih•BEE•uhnz). This group included artisans, shopkeepers, and owners of small farms.

Both patrician and plebeian men were Roman citizens. They had the right to vote and the responsibility to pay taxes and serve in the army. However, plebeians had less social status. Marriage between members of the two classes was forbidden. Plebeians also lacked an important political right: they could not hold public office. Only patricians could serve in the government.

How Did Rome's Government Work? In the Roman Republic, the top government officials were the **consuls** (KAHN•suhlz). Two consuls—both patricians—were chosen every year. They headed the army and ran the government. Because they served such short terms, there was little risk that they would abuse their power. The consuls also

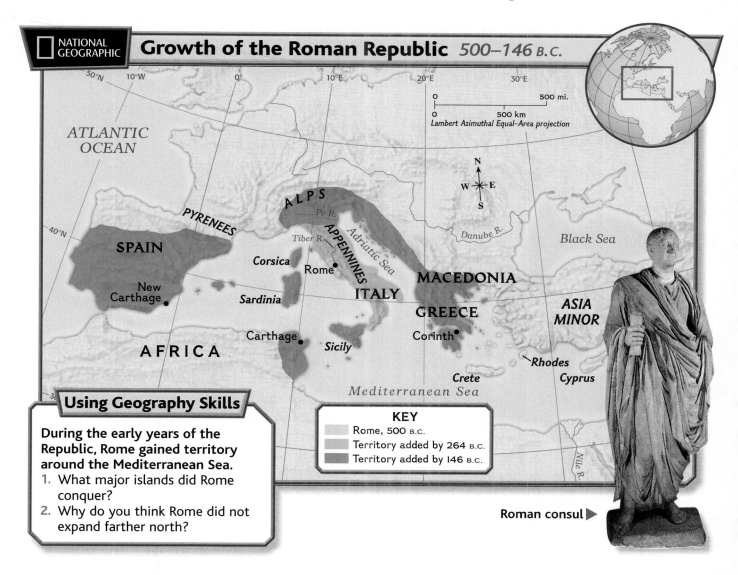

NATIONAL GEOGRAPHIC

Growth of the Roman Republic 500–146 B.C.

ATLANTIC OCEAN

PYRENEES

ALPS

Po R.

SPAIN

Tiber R.

APPENNINES

Adriatic Sea

Danube R.

Black Sea

New Carthage

Corsica

Rome

ITALY

MACEDONIA

ASIA MINOR

Sardinia

GREECE

Carthage

Sicily

Corinth

AFRICA

Crete

Rhodes

Cyprus

Mediterranean Sea

Nile R.

500 mi.

500 km

Lambert Azimuthal Equal-Area projection

KEY

	Rome, 500 B.C.
	Territory added by 264 B.C.
	Territory added by 146 B.C.

Using Geography Skills

During the early years of the Republic, Rome gained territory around the Mediterranean Sea.

1. What major islands did Rome conquer?
2. Why do you think Rome did not expand farther north?

Roman consul ▶

A Roman Triumph

Sometimes military leaders returning to Rome after a victory took part in a great parade called a triumph.

"Thus arrayed [decoratively dressed], they entered the city, having at the head of the procession the spoils and trophies and figures representing the captured forts, cities, mountains, rivers, lakes, and seas— everything, in fact, that they had taken. . . . [When] . . . the victorious general arrived at the Roman Forum . . . he rode up to the Capitol. There he performed certain rites and made offerings."

▲ Roman soldiers

—Zonaras, "A Roman Triumph"

DBQ Document-Based Question

Why do you think the military leaders and their troops were dressed decoratively before the triumph?

kept each other in line because each could **veto** (VEE•toh), or reject, the other's decision. The word *veto* is Latin for "I forbid."

Rome had other important officials called **praetors** (PREE•tuhrz). Their main job was to interpret the law and act as judges in court cases. Various other officials performed specialized duties—keeping tax records, handling public finances, supervising public festivals, and so forth.

Rome's most important legislative, or lawmaking, body was the Senate. This was a select group of 300 patrician men who served for life. In the beginning, the Senate only gave advice to the consuls. Over time, the power of the Senate grew. By the 200s B.C., it could also propose laws, hold debates on important issues, and approve building programs.

Another legislative body was the Assembly of Centuries. It elected important officials, such as consuls and praetors, and passed laws. Like the Senate, the Assembly of Centuries was under the control of the patricians.

Plebeians Against Patricians As you might expect, plebeians complained about having so little power in the Roman Republic. After all, they fought alongside patricians in the army, and their tax payments helped the republic thrive. It seemed reasonable that they should have equal rights.

Eventually, the plebeians took action to bring about change. In 494 B.C. many plebeians went on strike. They refused to serve in the army. They also left the city to set up a republic of their own. These moves frightened the patricians into agreeing to share power.

In 471 B.C. the plebeians were allowed to set up their own body of representatives, called the Council of the Plebs. The assembly elected tribunes who brought plebeian concerns to the government's attention. The tribunes also won the right to veto government decisions. In 455 B.C. plebeians and patricians were allowed to marry, and in the 300s B.C., plebeians were allowed to become consuls.

The most far-reaching political reform came in 287 B.C. In that year, the Council of the Plebs finally gained the power to pass laws for all Romans. Now all male citizens had equal political standing, at least in theory. In practice, a few wealthy patrician families still held most of the power, and women remained without a voice in government. The Roman Republic had become more representative, but it was far from a full-fledged democracy.

Who Was Cincinnatus?

An unusual feature of the Roman Republic was the office of **dictator** (DIHK•tay•tuhr). We define a dictator today as an oppressive ruler with complete control over the state. Roman dictators also had complete control, but they served the people and ruled on a temporary basis during emergencies. The Senate would appoint a dictator in times of great danger. As soon as the danger was past, Roman dictators gave up their power.

The best-known early Roman dictator is **Cincinnatus** (SIHN•suh•NA•tuhs). About 460 B.C., a powerful enemy had surrounded a Roman army. Officials decided that the crisis called for a dictator and that Cincinnatus was the man for the job. The officials found Cincinnatus plowing his fields. A loyal and devoted citizen, Cincinnatus left his farm and gathered an army. He defeated the enemy in short order and returned to Rome in triumph. Although he probably could have continued ruling, Cincinnatus did not want power. Having done his duty, he returned to his farm a mere 15 or 16 days after becoming dictator.

Cincinnatus was widely admired in his own time and in later ages. George Washington, for one, took inspiration from his example. Like Cincinnatus, Washington was a farmer when he was asked to head an army: the Continental Army in the American War for Independence. After leading the Americans to victory, Washington returned to his plantation home. Only later, and with some reluctance, did he agree to become the first president of the United States.

The Way It Was

Focus on Everyday Life

Roman Dinner Parties Before Rome became a powerful empire, Romans ate simple meals of porridge, dried vegetables, and greens. People rarely ate meat or seafood. After Rome's conquests, the dining habits of wealthy Romans changed. Newly rich Romans showed off their wealth with expensive feasts that included exotic foods and lively entertainment for their guests.

At Roman dinner parties, guests reclined on couches. The enslaved servants served the food, which would be carried into the banquet room on great silver platters. Roman dishes might include boiled stingray garnished with hot raisins; boiled crane with turnips; or roast flamingo cooked with dates, onions, honey, and wine.

▼ A wealthy Roman woman reclining on a couch

Connecting to the Past

1. Whose eating habits changed after Rome became wealthy and powerful?
2. Describe how their eating habits changed.

Biography

LUCIUS QUINCTIUS CINCINNATUS

c. 519–438 B.C.

The loyal devotion of Cincinnatus greatly impressed the Roman historian Livy. In his *History of Rome,* Livy advised his readers to listen to the worthwhile story of Cincinnatus, whose virtue rose high above any rewards that wealth could bring.

According to Livy, Cincinnatus lived in Rome but owned and worked a four-acre field on the other side of the Tiber River. On the day that the officials looked for Cincinnatus, they found him hard at work in his field, covered with dirt and sweat. Cincinnatus was surprised when the officials asked him to put on his toga and listen as they explained the wishes of the Roman Senate. Cincinnatus must not have been aware of the danger the Roman army faced, because he asked the officials if everything was all right before calling to his wife, Racilia, and asking her to bring him his toga quickly.

The officials explained the emergency situation to Cincinnatus. He agreed to the Senate's request that he become a dictator. Cincinnatus and the officials crossed the Tiber River to Rome and were greeted by his three sons, other relatives and friends, and members of the Senate. Later they escorted Cincinnatus safely to his home. The next morning, before daylight, Cincinnatus went to the Forum and gathered his forces to attack the enemy.

▲ Cincinnatus is asked to lead Rome.

"The city was in the grip of fear."
–Livy, *The Rise of Rome*

Then and Now

Name a modern-day leader that you think historians will write about with great admiration. Explain why.

Roman Law One of Rome's chief gifts to the world was its system of law. The legal system of the United States owes much to the Roman system.

Rome's first code of laws was the Twelve Tables, adopted about 451 B.C. Before this time, Rome's laws were not written down. As a result, plebeians claimed that patrician judges often favored their own class. They demanded that the laws be put in writing for everyone to see.

The patricians finally agreed. They had the laws carved on bronze tablets that were placed in Rome's marketplace, or the Forum (FOHR•uhm). The Twelve Tables became the basis for all future Roman laws. They established the principle that all free citizens had the right to be treated equally by the legal system.

The Twelve Tables, however, applied only to Roman citizens. As the Romans took over more lands, they realized that new rules were needed to solve legal disputes between citizens and noncitizens. They created a collection of laws called the Law of Nations. It stated principles of justice that applied to all people everywhere.

These standards of justice included ideas that we still accept today. A person was seen as innocent until proven guilty. People accused of crimes could defend themselves before a judge. A judge had to look at the evidence carefully before making a decision.

The idea that the law should apply to everyone equally and that all people should be treated the same way by the legal system

NATIONAL GEOGRAPHIC

HISTORY MAKERS

Twelve Tables c. 451 B.C.

The Twelve Tables were laws written on tablets that described the rights of each person in the Roman Republic. The laws were the first set of rules to govern Rome. Writing the laws down and putting them on public display ensured that everyone knew the laws and that judges did not apply the laws differently to different people.

The laws on the Twelve Tables explained a person's rights concerning property, wills, public behavior, family law, and court actions. The Twelve Tables were the first step toward equal rights for citizens of all classes in ancient Rome. They were also a first step toward the idea of the rule of law that we still uphold today.

▲ These bundles of rods and axes, called fasces, symbolized the legal authority of Roman leaders.

is called the "rule of law." In the age of Rome, the rule of law was still a new idea. In many lands, people at the top of society often had special privileges and did not have to obey the same laws or use the same courts as people lower down. In some places, people at the bottom of society did not have any legal rights at all. The rule of law is one of the key ideas that the Romans gave to the world. It is still the basis of our legal system today.

✓ **Reading Check** **Contrast** Before 471 B.C., what right did patricians have that plebeians did not?

Rome Expands

Main Idea Rome slowly destroyed the Carthaginian Empire and took control of the entire Mediterranean region.

Reading Focus When you achieve a victory—whether it is in academics, sports, or some other field—do you then strive for more success? That may have been how the Romans felt once they had taken over Italy. Read on to learn how they continued to expand their power.

While Rome developed its government, it also faced challenges abroad. The Romans had completed their conquest of Italy. However, they now faced a powerful rival in the Mediterranean area. This enemy was the state of **Carthage** (KAHR•thihj) on the coast of North Africa. It had been founded around 800 B.C. by the Phoenicians. As you learned earlier, the Phoenicians were sea traders from the Middle East.

Carthage ruled a great trading empire that included parts of northern Africa and southern Europe. By controlling the movement of goods in this region, Carthage made itself the largest and richest city in the western Mediterranean.

The First Punic War Both Carthage and Rome wanted to control the island of Sicily. In 264 B.C. the dispute brought the two powers to blows. The war that began in 264 B.C. is called the First Punic War. *Punicus* is the Latin word for "Phoenician." The war started when the Romans sent an army to Sicily to prevent a Carthaginian

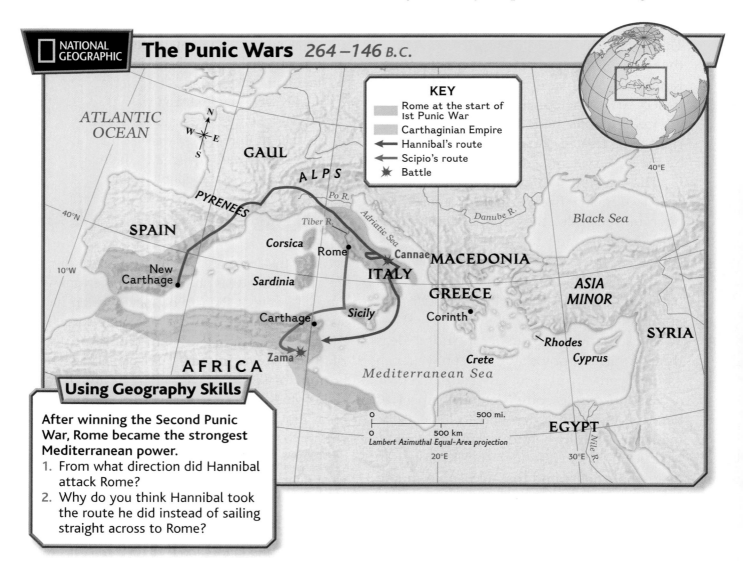

NATIONAL GEOGRAPHIC

The Punic Wars *264–146 B.C.*

KEY
- Rome at the start of 1st Punic War
- Carthaginian Empire
- Hannibal's route
- Scipio's route
- Battle

Using Geography Skills

After winning the Second Punic War, Rome became the strongest Mediterranean power.

1. From what direction did Hannibal attack Rome?
2. Why do you think Hannibal took the route he did instead of sailing straight across to Rome?

Lambert Azimuthal Equal-Area projection

takeover. The Carthaginians, who already had colonies on the island, were determined to stop this invasion.

Up until then, the Romans had fought their wars on land. However, they soon realized they could not defeat a sea power like Carthage without a navy. They quickly built a large fleet of ships and confronted their enemy at sea. The war dragged on for more than 20 years. Finally, in 241 B.C., Rome crushed Carthage's navy off the coast of Sicily. Carthage was forced to leave Sicily and pay a huge fine to the Romans. The island then came under Roman rule.

The Second Punic War

To make up for its loss of Sicily, Carthage expanded its empire into southern Spain. Roman leaders were not happy about Carthage gaining land near Rome's northern border. They helped the people living in Spain rebel against Carthage. Of course, Carthaginians were angry. To punish Rome, Carthage sent its greatest general, **Hannibal** (HA•nuh•buhl), to attack Rome in 218 B.C. This started the Second Punic War.

Hannibal's strategy was to take the fighting into Italy itself. To do this, Hannibal gathered an army of about 46,000 men, many horses, and 37 elephants. He landed his forces in Spain and then marched east to attack Italy.

Even before reaching Italy, Hannibal's forces suffered severe losses crossing the steep, snowy Alps into Italy. The brutal cold, gnawing hunger, and attacks by

▼ In December 218 B.C., Hannibal's forces and the Roman army met in battle near the Trebbia River in northern Italy. In a well-planned attack, the Carthaginian forces badly defeated the Romans. Hannibal made good use of his elephants in the attack, but most died following the battle. *At what other battle in Italy were the Romans defeated by Hannibal?*

275

mountain tribes killed almost half of the soldiers and most of the elephants. The remaining army, however, was still a powerful fighting force when it reached Italy.

The Romans suffered a severe loss in 216 B.C. at the Battle of **Cannae** (KA•nee) in southern Italy. Even though Hannibal's army was outnumbered, it overpowered the Roman force and began raiding much of Italy.

The Romans, however, raised another army. In 202 B.C. a Roman force led by a general named **Scipio** (SIH•pee•OH) invaded Carthage. Hannibal, who was waging a war in Italy, had no choice but to return home to defend his people.

At the Battle of **Zama** (ZAY•muh), Scipio's troops defeated the Carthaginians. Carthage gave up Spain to Rome. It also had to give up its navy and pay a large fine. Rome now ruled the western Mediterranean.

More Conquests While Carthage was no longer a military power, it remained a trading center. In 146 B.C. Rome finally destroyed its great rival in the Third Punic War. Roman soldiers burned Carthage and enslaved 50,000 men, women, and children. Legend says that the Romans even spread salt on the earth so no crops would grow. Carthage became a Roman province, or regional district.

During the Punic Wars, Rome successfully battled states in the eastern Mediterranean. In 148 B.C. Macedonia came under Roman rule. Two years later, the rest of Greece became Roman. In 129 B.C. Rome gained its first province in Asia. It was no wonder that the Romans began to call the Mediterranean *mare nostrum*—"our sea."

✓ **Reading Check** **Describe** How did Rome punish Carthage at the end of the Third Punic War?

History Online
Study Central™ Need help with the material in this section? Visit jat.glencoe.com

Section ② Review

Reading Summary

Review the Main Ideas

- During the Roman Republic, the government changed as the plebeians, or lower classes, and the patricians, or ruling class, struggled for power.

- Beginning in 264 B.C., Rome fought and won a series of wars with Carthage and other powers and gained control of the Mediterranean region.

What Did You Learn?

1. Who were the top government officials in the Roman Republic, and what were their duties?

2. What does *mare nostrum* mean, and why did the Romans use the term?

Critical Thinking

3. **Sequencing Information** Draw a diagram to describe the sequence of events from the start of the First Punic War to the start of the Second Punic War.

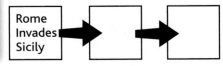

4. **Geography Skills** Where was Carthage located, and why did it compete with Rome?

5. **Summarize** What other conquests did Rome carry out during the period of the Punic Wars?

6. **Evaluate** Why do you think the legacy of Roman law is considered so important?

7. **Persuasive Writing** Write a speech demanding equal rights for plebeians in the early republic.

The Fall of the Republic

Get Ready to Read!

What's the Connection?

By the end of the Third Punic War, Rome ruled the Mediterranean world. All was not well, however. Closer to home, the republic faced increasing dangers that would soon lead to its end.

Focusing on the Main Ideas

- The use of enslaved labor hurt farmers, increased poverty and corruption, and brought the army into politics. *(page 278)*

- Military hero Julius Caesar seized power and made reforms. *(page 280)*

- The Roman Republic, weakened by civil wars, became an empire under Augustus. *(page 282)*

Locating Places

Rubicon (ROO•bih•KAHN)
Actium (AK•shee•uhm)

Meeting People

Julius Caesar
(jool•yuhs   SEE•zuhr)
Octavian (ahk•TAY•vee•uhn)
Antony (AN•tuh•nee)
Cicero (SIH•suh•ROH)
Augustus (aw•GUHS•tuhs)

Building Your Vocabulary

latifundia (LA•tuh•FUHN•dee•uh)
triumvirate (try•UHM•vuh•ruht)

Reading Strategy

Finding the Main Idea Use a chart like the one below to identify the main ideas of Section 3 and supporting details.

Main Idea		
Supporting Detail	Supporting Detail	Supporting Detail
Supporting Detail	Supporting Detail	Supporting Detail

NATIONAL GEOGRAPHIC When & Where?

GAUL
SPAIN
ITALY
Rome
ASIA MINOR
GREECE

100 B.C.   60 B.C.   20 B.C.

82 B.C.
Sulla becomes dictator of Rome

44 B.C.
Group of senators murder Julius Caesar

27 B.C.
Octavian becomes Rome's first emperor

Trouble in the Republic

Main Idea The use of enslaved labor hurt farmers, increased poverty and corruption, and brought the army into politics.

Reading Focus Poverty, corruption, unemployment, crime, and violence are problems we hear about today. Read on to learn how the Romans struggled with these same issues 2,000 years ago.

Rome's armies were victorious wherever they went. Yet problems were building at home. Dishonest officials stole money, and the gap between rich and poor was growing. Thousands of farmers faced ruin, and the cities were becoming overcrowded and dangerous.

Rich Versus Poor As you read in Section 2, most of the people who ruled Rome were patricians—rich people who owned large farms. These rich landowners ran the Senate and held the most powerful government jobs. They handled Rome's finances and directed its wars. Despite some gains for the plebeians, many people became very unhappy about this situation.

Rome had few privileged citizens compared with the many Romans who farmed small plots of land. In the 100s B.C., however, these farmers were sinking into poverty and debt. Why? Many of them had been unable to farm because they were fighting in Rome's wars. Others had suffered damage to their farms during Hannibal's invasion of Italy.

Moreover, small farmers could not compete with wealthy Romans who were buying up land to create **latifundia** (LA•tuh•FUHN•dee•uh), or large farming estates. These rich landowners used a new source of labor—the thousands of prisoners brought to Italy during the wars. By using these enslaved people to tend their crops, wealthy Romans could force owners of small farms out of business.

Faced with debts they could not pay off, many farmers sold their land and headed to the cities, desperate for work. However, jobs were hard to find. Enslaved people did most of the work. If free men were lucky enough to be hired, they earned low wages. These conditions created widespread anger.

▲ **This image shows Romans farming their land.** *Why were Roman farmers becoming poor in the 100s B.C.?*

Roman politicians were worried about riots breaking out, but they quickly turned the situation to their advantage. To win the votes of the poor, they began providing cheap food and entertainment. This policy of "bread and circuses" helped many dishonest rulers come to power.

Why Did Reform Fail?

Not all wealthy people ignored the problems facing the Roman Republic. Two prominent officials who worked for reforms were Tiberius and Gaius Gracchus (GRA•kuhs). These brothers thought that many of Rome's problems were caused by the loss of small farms. They asked the Senate to take back public land from the rich and divide it among landless Romans.

Many senators, however, were among those who had claimed parcels of public land. Putting their own interests above the general welfare, they fought the Gracchus brothers' proposals. A band of senators even went so far as to kill Tiberius in 133 B.C. Twelve years later, Gaius met the same fate. These were dark days for the Roman Republic, when the people charged with making and upholding the laws could so shockingly violate them.

The Army Enters Politics

Matters only worsened as the Roman army took on a new role. Until now, the army had mostly stayed out of government affairs. Things changed when a military leader named Marius became consul in 107 B.C. Previously, most soldiers were owners of small farms. Now because this type of farmer was disappearing, Marius began to recruit soldiers from the

Tiberius Gracchus (left) and his brother Gaius believed that moving poor Romans from the city to farms would help solve the republic's problems. *What happened to the Gracchus brothers?*

poor. In return for their service, he paid them wages and promised them the one thing they desperately wanted—land.

Marius changed the Roman army from citizen volunteers to paid professional soldiers. The new troops, however, were motivated by material rewards rather than a sense of duty. They felt loyal to their general, not to the Roman Republic. This gave individual generals a great deal of influence and good reason to become involved in politics. They needed to get laws passed that would provide the land they had promised their soldiers.

Marius's new military system led to new power struggles. It was not long before Marius faced a challenge from a rival general with his own army, a man named Sulla. In 82 B.C. Sulla drove his enemies out of Rome and made himself dictator.

Over the next three years, Sulla changed the government. He weakened the Council of the Plebs and strengthened the Senate. Then he stepped down from office. He hoped that the Roman Republic could heal its wounds and recapture its glory. Instead, Rome plunged into an era of civil wars for the next 50 years. Ambitious men saw how Sulla used an army to seize power. They decided to follow the same path.

✓ **Reading Check** **Explain** What change did Marius make to the Roman army?

History Online

Web Activity Visit jat.glencoe.com and click on *Chapter 8—Student Web Activity* to learn more about the rise of Rome.

Julius Caesar

Main Idea Military hero Julius Caesar seized power and made reforms.

Reading Focus Did you know that George Washington, Andrew Jackson, William H. Harrison, Zachary Taylor, Ulysses S. Grant, and Dwight D. Eisenhower all commanded armies before becoming president? Read to learn about a famous Roman who made a similar jump from military leader to political leader.

After Sulla left office, different Roman leaders battled for power, supported by their loyal armies. In 60 B.C. three men were on top: Crassus, Pompey, and **Julius Caesar** (jool•yuhs SEE•zuhr). Crassus was a military leader and one of the richest men in Rome. Pompey and Caesar were not as rich, but both were successful military men. Drawing on their wealth and power, they formed the First Triumvirate to rule Rome. A **triumvirate** (try•UHM•vuh•ruht) is a political alliance of three people.

Caesar's Military Campaigns The members of the Triumvirate each had a military command in a remote area of the republic. Pompey was in Spain, Crassus in Syria, and Caesar in Gaul (modern France). While in Gaul, Caesar battled foreign tribes and invaded Britain. He became a hero to Rome's lower classes. Senators and others back home in Rome feared that Caesar was becoming too popular and might seize power like Sulla.

After Crassus was killed in battle in 53 B.C., the Senate decided that Pompey should return to Italy and rule alone. In 49 B.C. the Senate ordered Caesar to give up his army and come home. Caesar faced a difficult choice. He could obey the Senate and perhaps face prison or death at the hands of his rivals, or he could march on Rome with his army and risk a civil war.

Caesar decided to hold on to his 5,000 loyal soldiers. He marched into Italy by crossing the **Rubicon** (ROO•bih•KAHN), a

Caesar's Rise to Power

Caesar was part of the First Triumvirate, whose members are shown below.

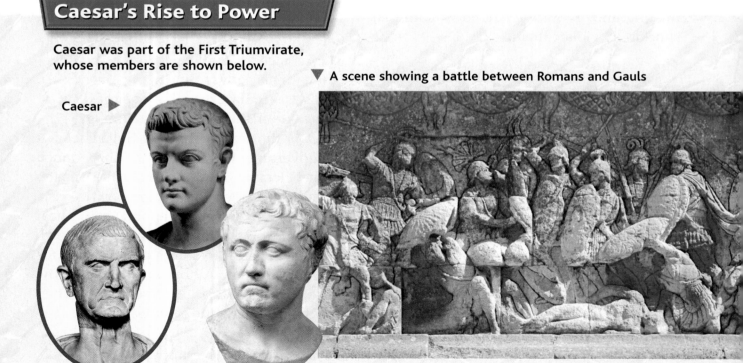

▼ A scene showing a battle between Romans and Gauls

Caesar ▶

▲ Crassus

▲ Pompey

small river at the southern boundary of his command area. By doing so, Caesar knew that he was starting a civil war and that there was no turning back. The phrase "crossing the Rubicon" is used today to mean making a decision that you cannot take back.

Pompey tried to stop Caesar, but Caesar was the better general. He drove Pompey's forces from Italy and then destroyed Pompey's army in Greece in 48 B.C.

Caesar's Rise to Power In 44 B.C. Caesar had himself declared dictator of Rome for life. This broke with the Roman tradition that allowed dictators to hold power for only short periods of time. To strengthen his hold on power, Caesar filled the Senate with new members who were loyal to him.

At the same time, Caesar knew that reforms were needed. He granted citizenship to people living in Rome's territories outside the Italian peninsula. He started new colonies to provide land for the landless and created work for Rome's jobless people. He ordered landowners using slave labor to hire more free workers. These measures made Caesar popular with Rome's poor.

Caesar also created a new calendar with 12 months, 365 days, and a leap year. The Julian calendar, as it was called, was used throughout Europe until A.D. 1582. That year it was modified slightly to become the Gregorian calendar. This calendar, based on the birth of Christ, has been used in the United States since its beginning and is used by most countries in the world today.

While many Romans supported Caesar, others did not. His supporters believed he was a strong leader who brought peace and order to Rome. His enemies, however, feared that Caesar wanted to be king. These opponents, led by the senators Brutus and Cassius, plotted to kill him. Caesar ignored a famous warning to "beware the Ides of March" (March 15). On that date in 44 B.C., Caesar's enemies surrounded him and stabbed him to death.

Reading Check **Explain** Why did Brutus, Cassius, and others kill Caesar?

▼ **Caesar crossing the Rubicon**

Brutus (left) was one of the senators who killed Caesar. Antony (above) supported Caesar and his nephew Octavian and fought against Caesar's assassins.

Rome Becomes an Empire

Main Idea The Roman Republic, weakened by civil wars, became an empire under Augustus.

Reading Focus Have you ever been in a traffic jam and wished that a police officer would show up to get things moving? Read on to learn how Romans welcomed the arrival of a strong new ruler.

Caesar's death plunged Rome into another civil war. On one side were forces led by the men who had killed Caesar. On the other side was Caesar's grandnephew **Octavian** (ahk•TAY•vee•uhn), who had inherited Caesar's wealth, and two of Caesar's top generals, **Antony** (AN•tuh•nee) and Lepidus. After defeating Caesar's assassins, these three men created the Second Triumvirate in 43 B.C.

The Second Triumvirate The members of the Second Triumvirate began quarreling almost at once. Octavian soon forced Lepidus to retire from politics. Then the two remaining leaders divided the Roman world between themselves. Octavian took the west; Antony took the east.

In short order, though, Octavian and Antony came into conflict. Antony fell in love with the Egyptian queen Cleopatra VII and formed an alliance with her. Octavian told the Romans that Antony, with Cleopatra's help, planned to make himself the sole ruler of the republic. This alarmed many Romans and enabled Octavian to declare war on Antony.

In 31 B.C., at the Battle of **Actium** (AK•shee•uhm) off the west coast of Greece, Octavian crushed the army and navy of Antony and Cleopatra. The couple then fled to Egypt. A year later, as Octavian closed in, they killed themselves. Octavian, at the age of 32, now stood alone at the top of the Roman world. The period of civil wars was

Primary Source

Cicero Calls for War

This excerpt is from Cicero's sixth speech about the struggle between Octavian and Antony (Marcus Antonius):

"Therefore, when I saw that a nefarious [evil] war was waged against the republic, I thought that no delay ought to be interposed to our pursuit of Marcus Antonius; and I gave my vote that we ought to pursue with war that most audacious [bold] man, who . . . was at this moment attacking a general of the Roman people. . . . I said further, that . . . the garb of war should be assumed by the citizens, in order that all men might apply themselves with more activity and energy to avenging the injuries of the republic."

▲ Cicero

—Cicero, "The Sixth Oration of M.T. Cicero Against Marcus Antonius"

DBQ **Document-Based Question**

Why did Cicero want Rome to fight Antony?

over, but so was the republic. Octavian would lay the foundation for a new system of government—the Roman Empire.

Who Was Augustus? Octavian could have made himself dictator for life, like Julius Caesar did. He knew, though, that many people favored a republican form of government. One such person was

Cicero (SIH•suh•ROH), a political leader, writer, and Rome's greatest public speaker. Cicero had argued against dictators and called for a representative government with limited powers.

Cicero's speeches and books swayed many Romans. Centuries later, his ideas would also influence the writers of the United States Constitution.

Although Cicero did not live to see Octavian rule, he had supported him, hoping he would restore the republic. In 27 B.C. Octavian announced that he was doing just that.

He knew the Senate wanted this form of government. However, Octavian also knew that the republic had been too weak to solve Rome's problems. Although he gave some power to the Senate, he really put himself in charge. His title, *imperator,* translates to "commander in chief," but it came to mean

▲ At the Battle of Actium, Octavian's forces defeated those of Antony after Cleopatra's ships retreated. *How did the Battle of Actium affect the history of Rome?*

"emperor." Octavian also took the title of **Augustus** (aw•GUHS•tuhs)—"the revered or majestic one." From this point on, he was known by this name.

✓ **Reading Check** **Explain** How did Octavian's government reflect the ideas of Cicero?

History Online

Study Central™ Need help with the material in this section? Visit jat.glencoe.com

Section 3 Review

Reading Summary
Review the Main Ideas

- As the gap between the ruling class and the poor in Rome increased, a number of reforms failed, and generals began to gather power.

- Julius Caesar became dictator and carried out reforms to aid Rome's poor. Later he was assassinated by members of the Senate.

- Caesar's grandnephew Octavian defeated Antony and Cleopatra and became Augustus, the first Roman emperor.

What Did You Learn?

1. What is a triumvirate?

2. Who was Cicero, and how did he influence the writers of the United States Constitution?

Critical Thinking

3. **Understanding Cause and Effect** Draw a diagram like the one below. Fill in the chain of effects that was caused by the thousands of enslaved prisoners that were brought to Italy from Rome's many wars.

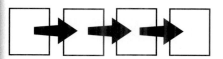

4. **Summarize** What reforms did the Gracchus brothers suggest?

5. **Analyze** What was the "bread and circuses" policy, and how did Roman politicians benefit from it?

6. **Analyze** What reforms did Julius Caesar put in place that increased his popularity with poor and working-class Romans?

7. **Persuasive Writing** Imagine you are a Roman citizen. Decide whether you would have been for or against Julius Caesar's rise to power and his reforms. Then write a newspaper editorial explaining your views. Be sure to include facts to support your opinions.

You Decide . . .

Was Caesar a Reformer or a Dictator?

Great Reformer

During his life, Julius Caesar was greatly admired by many people. He was also hated and feared by many others. Some believed he was too ambitious—exceptionally eager for fame and power—and that his ambition would keep him from acting in Rome's best interest.

Was Caesar a great reformer or an ambitious dictator? Those who saw him as a great leader and reformer said that he

- won the support of his soldiers through his military leadership and strategy
- treated many of his defeated enemies generously and appointed some of them—including Brutus—to government positions
- ended the rule of corrupt Roman nobles
- brought order and peace to Rome
- restored cities that had been destroyed by the republic
- strengthened and expanded the state of Rome
- started public jobs programs to aid the poor
- granted Roman citizenship to people from foreign countries or states.

▲ The assassination of Julius Caesar

Ambitious Dictator

Caesar also had many enemies, including some who had been his friends. They saw Caesar as a dangerous dictator and thought he was taking advantage of his growing power.

They said that he

- became an enemy when he refused to follow the Senate's order to return to Rome
- started a civil war that led to the destruction of the republic
- increased the number of senators to add to his number of supporters
- treated his defeated enemies with cruelty
- punished those who wanted to uphold the traditions and laws of the republic
- weakened the Senate to gain absolute power over Rome
- kept hidden any facts that did not make him look brave and intelligent
- sought glory for himself at the expense of the republic.

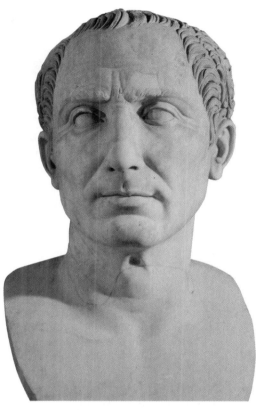

▲ Julius Caesar

You Be the Historian

Checking for Understanding

1. Define *ambition*. Identify some ways ambition can be a positive characteristic and some ways it can be a negative characteristic.
2. What could Caesar have done to show his enemies that he was not abusing his power?
3. Do you think Caesar was a great leader and reformer or an ambitious dictator? Write a brief essay that explains how you view Caesar. Use facts to support your position.

Section 4

The Early Empire

Get Ready to Read!

What's the Connection?

You learned in Section 3 that when Octavian became Augustus, the Roman world began to change. The republic gave way to an empire, and peace and prosperity spread throughout the Mediterranean.

Focusing on the Main Ideas

• By expanding the empire and reorganizing the military and government, Augustus created a new era of prosperity. *(page 287)*

• Rome's system of roads, aqueducts, ports, and common currency made the empire rich and prosperous. *(page 290)*

Locating Places

Rhine River (RYN)
Danube River (DAN•YOOB)
Puteoli (pyu•TEE•uh•LY)
Ostia (AHS•tee•uh)

Meeting People

Caligula (kuh•LIH•gyuh•luh)
Nero (NEE•roh)
Hadrian (HAY•dree•uhn)

Building Your Vocabulary

Pax Romana
  (pahks   roh•MAH•nah)
aqueduct (A•kwuh•DUHKT)
currency (KUHR•uhn•see)

Reading Strategy

Cause and Effect Use a chart like the one below to show the changes Augustus made in the Roman Empire and the effect of each change.

Causes		Effects
	→	
	→	
	→	
	→	

NATIONAL GEOGRAPHIC When & Where?

BRITAIN
GAUL
ITALY GREECE
SPAIN Rome
PALESTINE
EGYPT

A.D. 10

A.D. 14
Augustus dies

A.D. 110

A.D. 96
Rule of the Good Emperors begins

A.D. 210

A.D. 180
Pax Romana ends

The Emperor Augustus

Main Idea By expanding the empire and reorganizing the military and government, Augustus created a new era of prosperity.

Reading Focus What makes a good or bad leader? Think about this question as you read about Augustus and other Roman emperors.

Augustus paved the way for 200 years of peace and prosperity in Rome. The emperors who followed him were not all good rulers, but they helped the Roman Empire reach its peak. For centuries, the Mediterranean region had been filled with conflict. Under Augustus and his successors, the region was under the control of one empire. A long era of peace began with Augustus and lasted until A.D. 180. It was called the *Pax Romana* (pahks roh•MAH•nah), or "Roman Peace."

What Did Augustus Achieve?
Upon becoming emperor in 27 B.C., Augustus set out to make the empire strong and safe. To provide security, he built a permanent, professional army of about 150,000 men—all Roman citizens. Augustus also created a special unit called the Praetorian Guard.

This force consisted of about 9,000 men in charge of guarding the emperor. The Praetorian Guard later became very influential in Roman politics.

Augustus's legions conquered new territories and added vast stretches of northern Europe to the empire. All of Spain and Gaul came under Roman rule, as did land in what is today Austria, Hungary, Romania, and Bulgaria.

Meanwhile, Augustus rebuilt Rome with stately palaces, fountains, and splendid public buildings. "I found Rome a city of brick," he boasted, "and left it a city of marble." The arts flourished as never before, and Augustus also imported grain from Africa to feed the poor. He knew that a well-fed population would be less likely to cause trouble.

Augustus devoted much of his energy to improving Rome's government. During his reign, more than 50 million people lived in the Roman Empire. To rule this huge population, Augustus appointed a proconsul, or governor, for each of Rome's provinces. These new officials replaced the politicians who had been chosen by the Senate. Augustus often traveled to the provinces to see how the governors were doing.

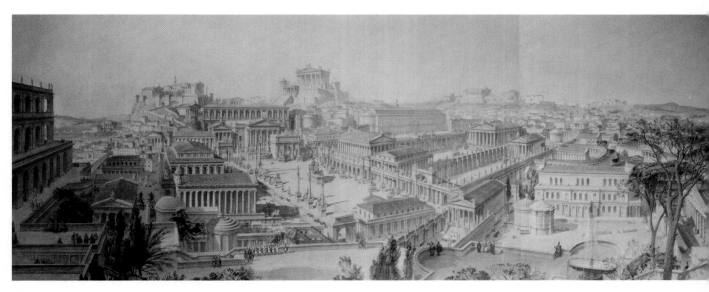

▲ The city of Rome at the height of the Roman Empire

The Julio-Claudian Emperors

Emperor	Accomplishments
Tiberius	14–37 A.D. Great military leader; regulated business to prevent fraud; kept Rome's economy stable
Caligula	37–41 A.D. Abolished sales tax; allowed people in exile to return; increased court system's power
Claudius	41–54 A.D. Built new harbor at Ostia and new aqueduct for Rome; conquered most of Britain
Nero	54–68 A.D. Constructed many new buildings; gave slaves the right to file complaints; assisted cities suffering from disasters

Understanding Charts

The four emperors who followed Augustus were all relatives of Augustus.
1. Under which emperor was Britain conquered?
2. Conclude Why do you think the Roman Empire remained at peace even with weak emperors such as Caligula and Nero?

Augustus also reformed the Roman tax system. Previously, individual tax collectors paid the government for the right to do the job. To make their investment worthwhile, tax collectors were allowed to keep some of the money they gathered. Many of them, however, were dishonest and took too much. Augustus solved this problem by making tax collectors permanent government workers. This change made the tax system fairer.

Augustus also reformed the legal system. He created a set of laws for people in the provinces who were not citizens. As time passed, however, most of these people gained citizenship. The laws of Rome then applied to everyone, although the legal system generally stressed the authority of the government over the rights of the individual.

Who Came After Augustus?

After ruling for almost 40 years, Augustus died in A.D. 14. No law stated how the next emperor was to be chosen. Augustus, however, had trained a relative, Tiberius, to follow him. The next three emperors—**Caligula** (kuh•LIH•gyuh•luh), Claudius, and **Nero** (NEE•roh)—also came from Augustus's family. They are called the Julio-Claudian emperors. Unfortunately, they were not all fit to lead. Tiberius and Claudius ruled capably. Caligula and Nero, however, proved to be cruel leaders.

Mental illness caused Caligula to act strangely and to treat people cruelly. He had many people murdered, wasted a lot of money, and even gave his favorite horse the position of consul. Eventually, the Praetorian Guard killed him and put Claudius on the throne.

Nero was also a vicious man. Among those he had killed were his mother and two wives. He is best remembered for having "fiddled while Rome burned." According to legend, he was playing music miles from Rome when a fire destroyed much of the city in A.D. 64. Eventually, he committed suicide.

Reading Check Explain What did Augustus do to make the empire safer and stronger?

Biography

AUGUSTUS
63 B.C.–A.D. 14

Octavian was born to a wealthy family in a small Italian town southeast of Rome. During his youth, Octavian suffered a number of illnesses. He refused to let his illnesses interfere with his life, however, showing the determination that would later make him Rome's first emperor.

Octavian's father was a Roman senator, but it was Octavian's great-uncle—Julius Caesar—who first introduced Octavian to public life in Rome. In his late teens, Octavian joined Caesar in Africa and then the following year in Spain. At the age of 18, while Octavian was studying at school, he learned that his great-uncle had been murdered. In his will, Caesar had adopted Octavian as his son. Caesar had also made Octavian his heir—a position that Antony had assumed would be his. Against his family's advice, Octavian went to Rome to claim his inheritance. By the time he reached Rome, however, Antony had seized Caesar's papers and money and refused to give them to Octavian. With remarkable political savvy for someone so young, Octavian turned the situation around in his favor. He won the hearts of Caesar's soldiers and the people of Rome by celebrating the public games that Caesar had started.

In his rise to power and during his reign as Emperor Augustus, Octavian pushed himself and his loyal followers with relentless energy. In his private life, however, he lived simply and quietly and shunned personal luxury. He was devoted to his wife, Livia Drusilla, and spent his spare time with her at their home on the outskirts of Rome.

Augustus ▶

"I extended the frontiers of all the provinces of the Roman people."

—Augustus, "Res Gestae: The Accomplishments of Augustus"

Then and Now

Augustus overcame the obstacles of illness and political enemies to become a great emperor. Can you think of any present-day individuals who overcame obstacles to excel at something?

Unity and Prosperity

Main Idea Rome's system of roads, aqueducts, ports, and common currency made the empire rich and prosperous.

Reading Focus Do you find that you are more productive when you are not worried about conflicts at home or school? Read to learn how the Roman Empire prospered during its time of peace.

After Nero committed suicide, Rome passed through a period of disorder until Vespasian, a general and one of Nero's proconsuls, took the throne. Vespasian restored peace and order. He put down several rebellions in the empire, including the Jewish rebellion in Palestine. Troops commanded by his son Titus defeated the Jews and destroyed the Jewish temple in Jerusalem in A.D. 70.

During his reign, Vespasian began construction of the Colosseum—a huge amphitheatre—in central Rome. His son Titus, then his other son Domitian, ruled Rome after he died. Both sons oversaw an era of growth and prosperity in Rome. During Titus's reign, two disasters struck the empire. The volcano Mount Vesuvius erupted, destroying the city of Pompeii, and a great fire badly damaged Rome.

Linking Past & Present

Living in the Shadow of Mt. Vesuvius

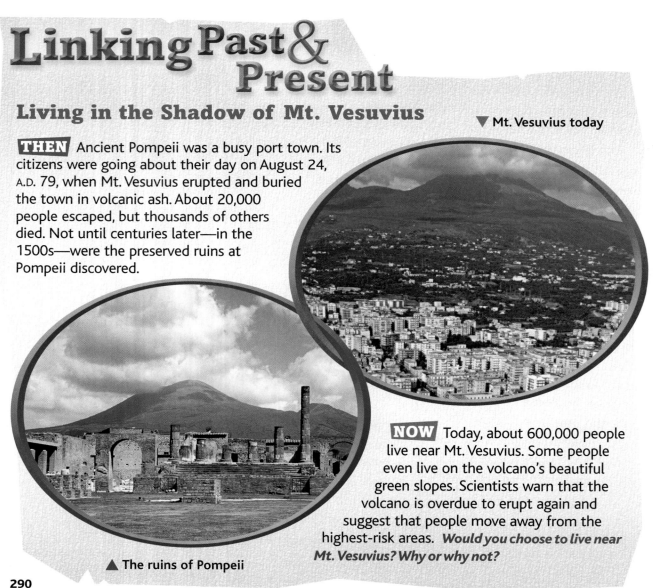

▼ Mt. Vesuvius today

THEN Ancient Pompeii was a busy port town. Its citizens were going about their day on August 24, A.D. 79, when Mt. Vesuvius erupted and buried the town in volcanic ash. About 20,000 people escaped, but thousands of others died. Not until centuries later—in the 1500s—were the preserved ruins at Pompeii discovered.

NOW Today, about 600,000 people live near Mt. Vesuvius. Some people even live on the volcano's beautiful green slopes. Scientists warn that the volcano is overdue to erupt again and suggest that people move away from the highest-risk areas. *Would you choose to live near Mt. Vesuvius? Why or why not?*

▲ The ruins of Pompeii

The "Good Emperors" At the beginning of the A.D. 100s, a series of rulers who were not related to Augustus or Vespasian came to power. These five emperors—Nerva, Trajan, **Hadrian** (HAY•dree•uhn), Antoninus Pius, and Marcus Aurelius—are known as the "good emperors." They presided over nearly a century of prosperity, from A.D. 96 to A.D. 180. Agriculture flourished, trade increased, and the standard of living rose.

During this time, the emperor came to overshadow the Senate more than ever before. The five "good emperors" did not abuse their power, however. They were among the most devoted and capable rulers in Rome's history. They improved Roman life in many ways, naming trained officials to carry out their orders.

Among the achievements of these emperors were programs to help ordinary people. Trajan gave money to help poor parents raise and educate their children. Hadrian made Roman law easier to understand and apply. Antoninus Pius passed laws to help orphans. All the emperors supported public building projects. They built arches and monuments, bridges and roads, and harbors and aqueducts. An **aqueduct** (A•kwuh•DUHKT) is a human-made channel for carrying water long distances.

A Unified Empire Later emperors continued to conquer new territory for Rome. The empire reached its largest size under Trajan. It spread well beyond the Mediterranean, including Britain in the north and part of Mesopotamia in the east.

Trajan's successors, however, realized that the empire had grown too big to rule effectively. Hadrian began to pull back. He removed troops from most of Mesopotamia.

NATIONAL GEOGRAPHIC

The Way It Was

Science and Inventions

Roman Aqueducts Transporting water is a complex problem. Roman engineers solved it by building aqueducts. Roman aqueducts carried water across a valley or hillside using gravity, aboveground stone arches, and underground pipes made of stone or clay. Between 312 B.C. and A.D. 226, 11 aqueducts were built to bring water to Rome from as far away as 57 miles. Once the water made it to Rome, it was held in collecting tanks. Most people gathered water from these public tanks. Only the rich and high-ranking officials had private water tanks in their homes.

Many Roman aqueducts still stand and are used today. Engineers in ancient Persia, India, and Egypt built similar water systems hundreds of years before the Romans. However, historians agree that the Romans were the greatest aqueduct builders of the ancient world.

◀ **Roman aqueduct**

Connecting to the Past
1. How did the Romans transport water to the city of Rome?
2. Why do you think that only the rich and powerful had private water supplies?

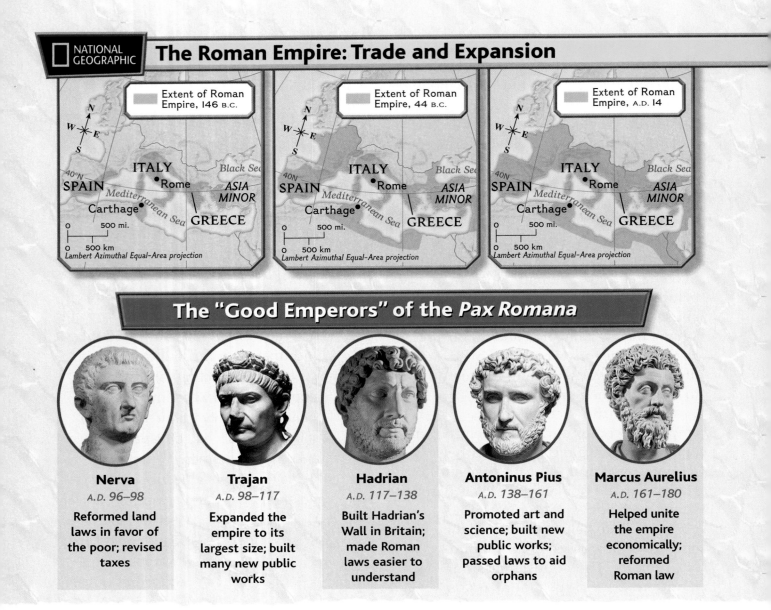

The Roman Empire: Trade and Expansion

Extent of Roman Empire, 146 B.C.

Extent of Roman Empire, 44 B.C.

Extent of Roman Empire, A.D. 14

ITALY · Rome · SPAIN · Black Sea · ASIA MINOR · Mediterranean Sea · Carthage · GREECE · 40°N · 500 mi. · 500 km · Lambert Azimuthal Equal-Area projection

The "Good Emperors" of the *Pax Romana*

Nerva
A.D. 96–98
Reformed land laws in favor of the poor; revised taxes

Trajan
A.D. 98–117
Expanded the empire to its largest size; built many new public works

Hadrian
A.D. 117–138
Built Hadrian's Wall in Britain; made Roman laws easier to understand

Antoninus Pius
A.D. 138–161
Promoted art and science; built new public works; passed laws to aid orphans

Marcus Aurelius
A.D. 161–180
Helped unite the empire economically; reformed Roman law

In Europe, he set the empire's northern boundaries at the **Rhine River** (RYN) and **Danube River** (DAN•YOOB). He also built Hadrian's Wall across northern Britain to keep out the Picts and Scots—two warlike people who lived in northern Britain.

In the A.D. 100s, the Roman Empire was one of the greatest empires in history. It included about 3.5 million square miles (9.1 million square km). Its people spoke different languages—mostly Latin in the west and Greek in the east. They also practiced different local customs. What unified the empire, though, were Roman law, Roman rule, and a shared identity as Romans.

Roman culture had been carried into every province by the soldiers who protected the empire and by the officials sent to govern. The Romans were generous in granting citizenship. In A.D. 212 every free person was made a Roman citizen.

A Booming Economy Most people in the Roman Empire made a living from the land. Small farms dotted northern Italy. In

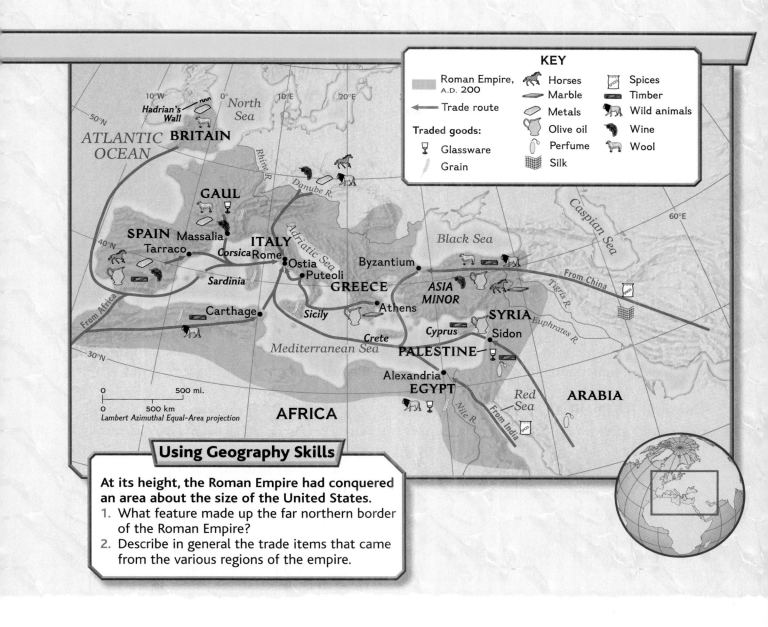

KEY

Roman Empire, A.D. 200

← Trade route

Traded goods:

- Glassware
- Grain
- Horses
- Marble
- Metals
- Olive oil
- Perfume
- Silk
- Spices
- Timber
- Wild animals
- Wine
- Wool

Using Geography Skills

At its height, the Roman Empire had conquered an area about the size of the United States.

1. What feature made up the far northern border of the Roman Empire?
2. Describe in general the trade items that came from the various regions of the empire.

southern and central Italy, latifundia, or large estates worked by enslaved people, were common. On these estates and in the provinces of Gaul and Spain, farmers produced grapes and olives. The making of wine and olive oil became big business. In Britain and Egypt, the chief crops were grains. Bountiful harvests from these regions kept Rome's people well fed.

Agriculture was the most important part of the economy, but industry was important too. Potters, weavers, and jewelers produced goods and cities became centers for making glass, bronze, and brass.

Traders came from all over the empire—and beyond—to ports in Italy. Two of the largest port cities were **Puteoli** (pyu•TEE•uh•ly) on the Bay of Naples and **Ostia** (AHS•tee•uh) at the mouth of the Tiber. The docks were lively places. Luxury items, including silk goods from China and spices from India, poured in to satisfy the rich. Raw materials, such as British tin, Spanish lead, and iron from Gaul, went to the workshops of Roman cities.

Roads and Money A good transportation network was vital to the empire's trade. During the *Pax Romana,* Rome's system of roads reached a total length of 50,000 miles (80,000 km). On the seas, the Roman navy helped to rid the Mediterranean of pirates. Goods could be shipped more safely to and from Rome's ports.

Rome's trade was helped by a common **currency** (KUHR•uhn•see), or system of money. Roman coins were accepted throughout the Mediterranean region by A.D. 100. Merchants could use the same money in Gaul or Greece as they did in Italy. The Romans also created a standard system of weights and measures. This made it easier for people to price goods, trade, and ship products.

Ongoing Inequality The Roman Empire's prosperity did not reach all of its people.

▲ Roman coins could be used throughout most of the empire, making trade much easier. *How else did Rome improve trade during the empire?*

Shopkeepers, merchants, and skilled workers benefited from the empire's trade. Rich Romans built great fortunes and lived in luxury. However, most city dwellers and farmers remained poor, and many remained enslaved.

Reading Check **Identify** Who were the "Good Emperors," and what did they accomplish?

History Online
Study Central™ Need help with the material in this section? Visit jat.glencoe.com

Section 4 Review

Reading Summary

Review the Main Ideas

- Augustus conquered new lands and created a professional military and a system of proconsuls. He improved the tax system and the legal system, ushering in the *Pax Romana.*

- Under Vespasian, his sons, and the five good emperors, Romans continued to be prosperous. They built an elaborate system of roads and developed a common currency that promoted trade and economic growth.

What Did You Learn?

1. What was the *Pax Romana?*

2. What products came from the farms of Italy, Gaul, and Spain?

Critical Thinking

3. **Organizing Information** Draw a diagram like the one below. Add details about the improvements and changes Augustus made to the Roman Empire during his reign.

Changes Under Augustus

4. **Sequencing Information** Describe the sequence of emperors who ruled Rome, from Augustus through the "Good Emperors."

5. **Analyze** Why was Rome's creation of a common currency important?

6. **Evaluate** Who do you think was a more important leader, Julius Caesar or Augustus? Explain.

7. **Creative Writing** Write a short play in which several Roman citizens discuss one of the emperors mentioned in this section and his accomplishments.

Chapter 8 Reading Review

Section ① Rome's Beginnings

Vocabulary
republic
legion

Focusing on the Main Ideas
- Geography played an important role in the rise of Roman civilization. *(page 263)*
- The Romans created a republic and conquered Italy. By treating people fairly, they built Rome from a small city into a great power. *(page 265)*

Section ② The Roman Republic

Vocabulary
patrician
plebeian
consul
veto
praetor
dictator

Focusing on the Main Ideas
- Rome's republic was shaped by a struggle between wealthy landowners and regular citizens as it gradually expanded the right to vote. *(page 269)*
- Rome slowly destroyed the Carthaginian Empire and took control of the entire Mediterranean region. *(page 274)*

Roman consul ▶

Section ③ The Fall of the Republic

Vocabulary
latifundia
triumvirate

Focusing on the Main Ideas
- The use of enslaved labor hurt farmers, increased poverty and corruption, and brought the army into politics. *(page 278)*
- Military hero Julius Caesar seized power and made reforms. *(page 280)*
- The Roman Republic, weakened by civil wars, became an empire under Augustus. *(page 282)*

Section ④ The Early Empire

Vocabulary
Pax Romana
aqueduct
currency

Focusing on the Main Ideas
- By expanding the empire and reorganizing the military and government, Augustus created a new era of prosperity. *(page 287)*
- Rome's system of roads, aqueducts, ports, and common currency made the empire rich and prosperous. *(page 290)*

Assessment and Activities

Review Vocabulary

Each of the following statements is false. Replace each word in italics with a word that makes the statement true. Write the correct words on a separate sheet of paper.

____ 1. A *legion* is a form of government in which the citizens choose their leader.

____ 2. *Patricians* included artisans and shopkeepers.

____ 3. The judge in a Roman court case was a *consul*.

____ 4. In early Rome, the role of *praetor* lasted only until a crisis had passed.

____ 5. Large farming estates that used enslaved people to tend crops were called *aqueducts*.

____ 6. A *veto* was a human-made channel for carrying water.

Review Main Ideas

Section 1 • Rome's Beginnings

7. Describe the role geography played in the rise of Roman civilization.

8. How did treating people fairly help Rome to increase its power?

Section 2 • The Roman Republic

9. How did the roles of patricians and plebeians differ in Roman society?

10. Explain how Rome gradually defeated the Carthaginians.

Section 3 • The Fall of the Republic

11. How did slavery weaken the Roman Republic?

12. How did Augustus change the Roman Republic?

Section 4 • The Early Empire

13. Was Augustus a successful ruler? Explain your answer.

14. How did the Roman Empire change during the *Pax Romana?*

Critical Thinking

15. **Compare** In the chapter, Cincinnatus is compared to George Washington. Think of another person or character who is similar to Cincinnatus. Explain how they are similar.

16. **Explain** Why did Caesar fight Pompey?

17. **Predict** What do you think would have happened if Hadrian had tried to further expand the Roman Empire?

Review
Reading Skill — Taking Notes — Note Taking

18. Read the following paragraph from page 269. Take notes on the information by making a T-chart.

> Early Romans were divided into two classes: patricians and plebeians. The patricians were wealthy landowners. These nobles made up Rome's ruling class. Most of Rome's people, however, were plebeians. This group included artisans, shopkeepers, and owners of small farms.

To review this skill, see pages 260–261.

Geography Skills

Study the map below and answer the following questions.

19. **Place** Which areas did Rome control after the Punic Wars?

20. **Human/Environment Interaction** What does the building of Hadrian's Wall say about the Picts and Scots?

21. **Region** Why was it important to the Romans to control Mediterranean lands?

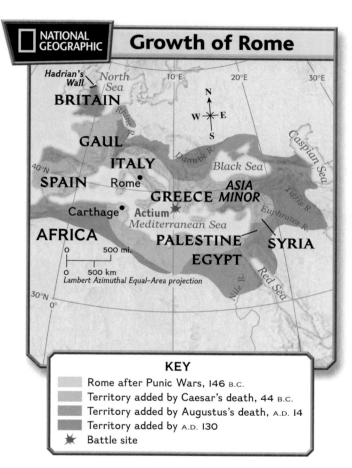

NATIONAL GEOGRAPHIC
Growth of Rome

KEY
Rome after Punic Wars, 146 B.C.
Territory added by Caesar's death, 44 B.C.
Territory added by Augustus's death, A.D. 14
Territory added by A.D. 130
✳ Battle site

Read to Write

22. **Persuasive Writing** Suppose you were working with Tiberius and Gaius to reform Rome. Write a letter or speech that explains why reform is needed and what types of reforms should occur.

23. **Using Your FOLDABLES** Use your foldable to write a series of questions about the chapter. With a partner, take turns asking and answering questions until you have reviewed the entire chapter.

History Online
Self-Check Quiz To help prepare for the Chapter Test, visit jat.glencoe.com

Building Citizenship

24. **Making Connections** Use the Internet and your local library to research the Twelve Tables. Work with your classmates to design a similar series of laws, and record them, using modern language. How is your law code similar to and different from the Twelve Tables?

Using Technology

25. **Creating Promotional Materials** Use the Internet to find at least five places related to ancient Rome that can be visited by tourists. Create a guidebook or brochure on the computer advertising these links to the past and persuading people to visit that area. Share your final product in a report to the class.

Primary Source Analyze

Augustus wrote a historical document describing his accomplishments. This passage is about his military leadership.

"About 500,000 Roman citizens were under military oath to me. Of these, when their terms of service were ended, I settled in colonies or sent back to their own municipalities a little more than 300,000, and to all these I allotted lands or granted money as rewards for military service."

—Augustus, "Res Gestae: The Accomplishments of Augustus"

DBQ Document-Based Questions

26. Why did Augustus give money to his retired soldiers?
27. Why do you think Augustus did not explain the reasons for his actions?

Roman Civilization

▼ The Colosseum in Rome, Italy

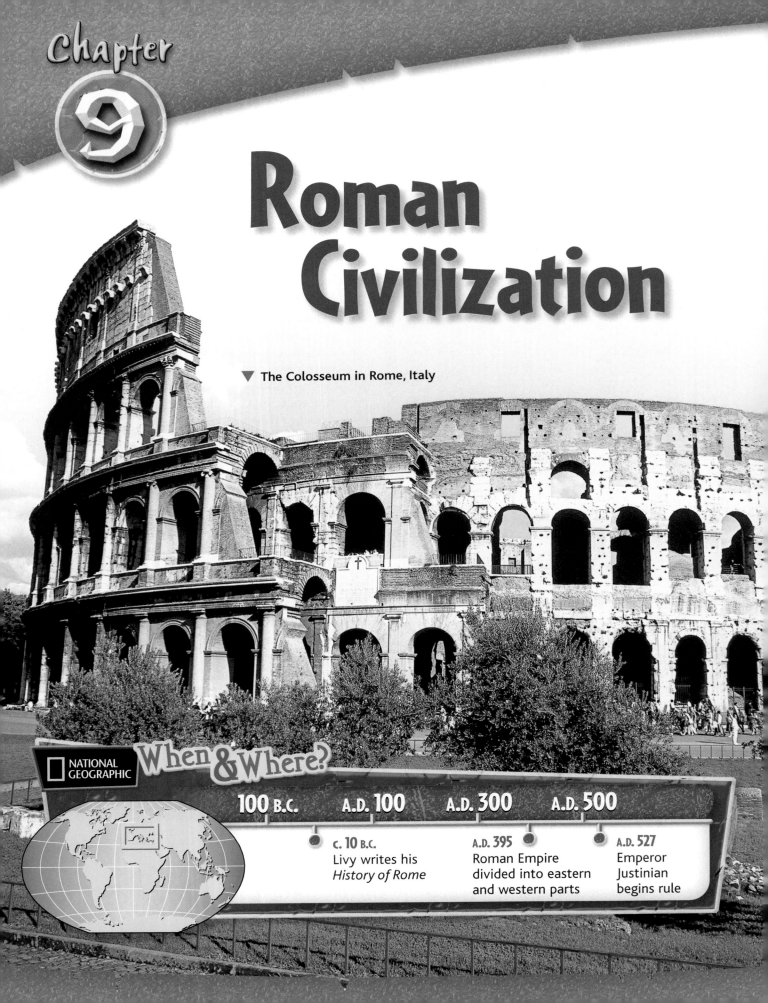

NATIONAL GEOGRAPHIC When & Where?

100 B.C.	A.D. 100	A.D. 300	A.D. 500
	c. 10 B.C. Livy writes his *History of Rome*	A.D. 395 Roman Empire divided into eastern and western parts	A.D. 527 Emperor Justinian begins rule

Chapter Preview

The Romans developed a civilization as well as an empire. Read this chapter to find out about Roman achievements that still influence your life today.

 History Online
Chapter Overview Visit jat.glencoe.com **for a preview of Chapter 9.**

 View the Chapter 9 video in the *World History: Journey Across Time* Video Program.

Section 1 — Life in Ancient Rome

The Romans learned from the Greeks but changed what they borrowed to suit their own needs. The lives of rich and poor Romans were very different.

Section 2 — The Fall of Rome

Rome finally fell when Germanic invaders swept through the empire in the A.D. 400s. Roman achievements in government, law, language, and the arts are still important today.

Section 3 — The Byzantine Empire

As the Western Roman Empire fell, the Eastern Roman, or Byzantine, Empire grew rich and powerful. The Byzantines developed a culture based on Roman, Greek, and Christian ideas.

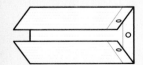 **FOLDABLES™ Study Organizer**

Organizing Information *Make this foldable to help you organize and analyze information by asking yourself questions about Roman civilization.*

Step 1 *Fold a sheet of paper into thirds from top to bottom.*

Step 2 *Turn the paper horizontally, unfold, and label the three columns as shown.*

Life in Ancient Rome | The Fall of Rome | The Byzantine Empire

Reading and Writing *As you read the chapter, write the main ideas for each section in the appropriate columns of your foldable. Then write one statement that summarizes the main ideas in each column.*

Chapter 9 Reading Social Studies

Reading Skill

Responding & Reflecting

1 Learn It!

Your Point of View

An important part of reading involves thinking about and responding to the text from your own point of view.

Read the following paragraph about daily life in Rome and look at how one student reflects as she reads.

> **The city of Rome was crowded, noisy, and dirty. People tossed garbage into the streets from their apartments, and thieves prowled the streets at night. Most people in Rome were poor. They lived in apartment buildings made of stone and wood. High rent forced families to live in one room.**
>
> *—from page 306*

"Reminds me of a city I visited once"

"What would that look like? What would it smell like?"

"Were they like apartment buildings today?"

"Sounds like it would be very uncomfortable and crowded!"

Reading Tip

While you do not want to daydream as you are reading, you do want to think about the text. Good readers' minds are busy, almost "talking back" to the text as they read.

2 Practice It!

Reflect and Respond

Read the following paragraph. Take a few minutes to reflect on what you have read and then respond by exchanging thoughts with a partner. Some suggested topics are listed below.

Read to Write ·······

In Section 2, you will read why historians believe the Roman Empire fell. Choose one of the reasons and respond to it, explaining why you think this is the most likely reason for the decline of the Roman Empire.

Between the ages of 14 and 16, a Roman boy celebrated becoming a man. He would burn his toys as offerings to the household gods. Then he would put on a toga, a loose-fitting robe that Roman men wore. Once he came of age, a man might join his family's business, become a soldier, or begin a career in the government. Roman women did not become adults until they married. A woman usually wore a long flowing robe with a cloak called a *palla*.

—*from pages 307–308*

- Do boys do anything today to show that they have become men?
- What does a toga look like? What does a *palla* look like?
- Why did a woman have to wait until she married to become an adult?
- Why were boys and girls treated so differently?

3 Apply It!

As you read, keep a reader's notebook. Record responses to facts or ideas that you find interesting.

Section 1

Life in Ancient Rome

Get Ready to Read!

What's the Connection?

You have already learned about Rome's rise to power. Life in Rome was not easy, but as the empire grew, its people accomplished many things in art, science, and engineering.

Focusing on the Main Ideas

- In addition to their own developments in science and engineering, Roman artists and writers borrowed many ideas from the Greeks. *(page 303)*

- The rich and poor had very different lives in the Roman Empire, as did men and women. *(page 306)*

Meeting People
Virgil (VUHR•juhl)
Horace (HAWR•uhs)
Galen (GAY•luhn)
Ptolemy (TAH•luh•mee)
Spartacus (SPAHR•tuh•kuhs)

Building Your Vocabulary
vault (VAWLT)
satire (SA•TYR)
ode (OHD)
anatomy (uh•NA•tuh•mee)
Forum (FOHR•uhm)
gladiator (GLA•dee•AY•tuhr)
paterfamilias
   (PA•tuhr•fuh•MIH•lee•uhs)
rhetoric (REH•tuh•rihk)

Reading Strategy
Compare and Contrast Use a Venn diagram like the one below to show similarities and differences between the rich and the poor in Rome.

Roman Rich   Roman Poor

NATIONAL GEOGRAPHIC When & Where?

BRITAIN
GAUL   GREECE
SPAIN ITALY
   Rome•   •Constantinople
   PALESTINE—
      EGYPT

100 B.C.

73 B.C.
Spartacus leads revolt of enslaved people

A.D. 1

c. 10 B.C.
Livy writes his *History of Rome*

A.D. 100

c. A.D. 80
Colosseum completed

Roman Culture

Main Idea In addition to their own developments in science and engineering, Roman artists and writers borrowed many ideas from the Greeks.

Reading Focus Are there people in your life that you admire? What have you learned from them? Read to find out what the Romans learned from the Greeks.

The Romans admired and studied Greek statues, buildings, and ideas. They copied the Greeks in many ways. However, they changed what they borrowed to suit their own needs. In one important way, the Romans were very different from the Greeks. The Greeks loved to talk about ideas. To the Romans, ideas were only important if they could solve everyday problems.

What Was Roman Art Like? The Romans admired Greek art and architecture. They placed Greek-style statues in their homes and public buildings. Roman artists, however, carved statues that looked different from those of the Greeks. Greek statues were made to look perfect. People were shown young, healthy, and with beautiful bodies. Roman statues were more realistic and included wrinkles, warts, and other less attractive features.

In building, the Romans also turned to the Greeks for ideas. They used Greek-style porches and rows of columns called colonnades. But they also added their own features, such as arches and domes. Roman builders were the first to make full use of the arch. Arches supported bridges, aqueducts, and buildings. Rows of arches were often built against one another to form a **vault** (VAWLT), or curved ceiling. Using this technique, the Romans were able to build domes from many rings of shaped stone.

The Romans were the first people to invent and use concrete, a mixture of volcanic ash, lime, and water. When it dried, this mix was as hard as rock. Concrete made buildings sturdier and allowed them to be built taller.

Rome's concrete buildings were so well built that many still stand today. One of the most famous is the Colosseum, completed about A.D. 80. It was a huge arena that could seat about 60,000 people. Another famous building is the Pantheon, a temple built to honor Rome's gods. The Pantheon's domed roof was the largest of its time.

▼ **This Roman bridge still stands in Spain.** *In what other structures were arches used?*

The Book of Epodes

In this poem excerpt, Horace praises the lifestyle of those who farm their family's land.

"Happy the man who, far from business and affairs

Like mortals of the early times,

May work his father's fields with oxen of his own,

Exempt [free] from profit, loss, and fee,

Not like the soldier roused by savage trumpet's blare,

Not terrified by seas in rage,

Avoiding busy forums and the haughty doors

Of influential citizens."

—Horace, *The Book of Epodes*

▲ Horace

DBQ Document-Based Question

According to Horace, what kinds of things does the farmer avoid?

Roman Literature Roman authors based much of their writing on Greek works. For example, the Roman writer **Virgil** (VUHR•juhl) drew some of his ideas from Homer's *Odyssey*. Virgil's epic poem, the *Aeneid* (uh•NEE•uhd), describes the adventures of the Trojan prince Aeneas and how he came to Italy. Virgil presents Aeneas as the ideal Roman—brave, self-controlled, and loyal to the gods.

Rome's other famous writers also looked to the Greeks for inspiration. Using Greek models, the poet **Horace** (HAWR•uhs) wrote **satires** (SA•TYRZ). These works poked fun at human weaknesses. Horace also composed **odes** (OHDZ), or poems that express strong emotions about life. The

Roman writer Ovid wrote works that were based on the Greek myths. The poet Catullus also admired Greek writings. He wrote short poems about love, sadness, and envy.

Like the Greeks, Rome's historians recorded the events of their civilization. One of Rome's most famous historians was Livy. He wrote his *History of Rome* about 10 B.C. In this book, Livy describes Rome's rise to power. Livy greatly admired the deeds of the early Romans, and he believed that history had important moral lessons to teach people.

Livy celebrated Rome's greatness, but the Roman historian Tacitus took a darker view. He believed that Rome's emperors had taken people's freedom. Tacitus also thought Romans were losing the values that made them strong. He accused them of wasting time on sports and other pleasures.

Also like the Greeks, the Romans enjoyed plays. Roman plays were often based on Greek tragedies and comedies. Playwrights such as the tragedy writer Seneca and the comedy writers Plautus and Terence wrote plays for religious festivals. Romans especially liked plays with humor.

Roman authors influenced later writers in Europe and America, but the language of the Romans, Latin, had an even bigger impact on future generations. Latin became Europe's language for government, trade, and learning until about A.D. 1500. Latin became the basis of many modern European languages, such as Italian, French, and Spanish, and shaped many others. Many of the English words we use today come from Latin as well.

Roman Science and Engineering

The Romans also learned from Greek science. A Greek doctor named **Galen** (GAY•luhn)

brought many medical ideas to Rome. For example, he emphasized the importance of **anatomy** (uh•NA•tuh•mee), the study of body structure. To learn about inner organs, Galen cut open dead animals and recorded his findings. Doctors in the West studied Galen's books and drawings for more than 1,500 years.

Another important scientist of the Roman Empire was **Ptolemy** (TAH•luh•mee). Ptolemy lived in Alexandria, in Egypt. He studied the sky and carefully mapped over 1,000 different stars. He also studied the motion of planets and stars and created rules explaining their movements. Even though Ptolemy incorrectly placed Earth at the center of the universe, educated people in Europe accepted his ideas for centuries.

While Roman scientists tried to understand how the world worked, Roman engineers built an astonishing system of roads and bridges to connect the empire. Have you ever heard the saying "All roads lead to Rome"? Roman engineers built roads from Rome to every part of the empire. These roads were well built, and some have survived to this day.

The Romans also used advanced engineering to supply their cities with freshwater. Engineers built aqueducts to bring water from the hills into the cities. Aqueducts were long troughs supported by rows of arches. They carried water over long distances. At one time, 11 great aqueducts fed Rome's homes, bathhouses, fountains, and public bathrooms. Roman cities also had sewers to remove waste.

Reading Check **Explain** How was the character Aeneas an ideal Roman?

The Roman Colosseum

The Colosseum in Rome could hold some 60,000 people. The arena even had a removable canvas awning to protect spectators from the hot Roman sun.
What was concrete made from?

A system of cages, ropes, and pulleys brought wild animals up to the Colosseum floor from rooms underground. ▼

The Way It Was

Sports & Contests

Ancient Roman Sports Sports were important to the Romans. Paintings on vases, frescoes [moist plaster], and stone show Romans playing ball, including a version of soccer. Roman girls are shown exercising with handheld weights and throwing an egg-shaped ball. Balls were made of different materials such as wool, hair, linen, sponges, and pig bladders wrapped in string.

Some Roman sporting events took place in the Colosseum, amphitheaters, and the Circus Maximus. Wild beast fights, battles between ships, and gladiator contests attracted Roman spectators by the thousands. Chariot racing was held in the Circus Maximus, and the drivers wore team colors of red, white, green, and blue.

▲ Scene showing gladiators in battle

Connecting to the Past

1. How do we know sports were important to the Romans?
2. How are today's sports different from Roman sports? How are they similar?

Daily Life in Rome

Main Idea The rich and poor had very different lives in Rome, as did men and women.

Reading Focus Do you think there is a big difference in the lives of boys and girls you know today? Why or why not? Read to learn how the lives of Roman boys and girls were very different from each other.

What was it like to live in Rome over 2,000 years ago? Rome was one of the largest cities in the ancient world. By the time of Augustus, over a million people lived there. Rome was carefully planned, as were many Roman cities. It was laid out in a square with the main roads crossing at right angles. At its center was the **Forum** (FOHR•um). This was an open space that served as a marketplace and public square. Temples and public buildings were built around it.

Wealthy Romans lived in large, comfortable houses. Each home had large rooms, fine furniture, and beautiful gardens. In the center was an inner court called an atrium. Wealthy Romans also had homes called villas on their country estates.

The city of Rome was crowded, noisy, and dirty. People tossed garbage into the streets from their apartments, and thieves prowled the streets at night. Most people in Rome were poor. They lived in apartment buildings made of stone and wood. High rent forced families to live in one room.

Roman apartments were up to six stories high. They often collapsed because they were so poorly built. Fire was a constant danger because people used torches and lamps for lighting and cooked with oil. Once started, a fire could destroy entire blocks of apartments.

To keep the people from rioting, the Roman government provided "bread and circuses," or free grain and shows. Romans of all classes flocked to the chariot races and gladiator contests. **Gladiators** (GLA•dee•AY•tuhrz)

▲ Chariot races were held in an arena called the Circus Maximus, one of the largest arenas ever made. *Besides chariot races, what other types of shows attracted Romans?*

fought animals and each other. Most gladiators were enslaved people, criminals, or poor people. Gladiators were admired, much like sports heroes are today.

What Was Family Life Like?
Family life was important to the Romans. Their families were large. They included not only parents and young children but also married children and their families, other relatives, and enslaved servants. The father was the head of the household. Called the **paterfamilias** (PA•tuhr•fuh•MIH•lee•uhs), or "father of the family," he had complete control over family members. For example, he punished children severely if they disobeyed. He also arranged their marriages.

In some cases, the paterfamilias made sure his children were educated. Poor Romans could not afford to send their children to school. Wealthy Romans, however, hired tutors to teach their young children at home. Some older boys did go to schools, where they learned reading, writing, and **rhetoric** (REH•tuh•rihk), or public speaking.

Older girls did not go to school. Instead, they studied reading and writing at home. They also learned household duties.

Between the ages of 14 and 16, a Roman boy celebrated becoming a man. He would burn his toys as offerings to the household gods. Then he would put on a toga, a loose-fitting robe that Roman men wore. Once he came of age, a man might join his family's business, become a soldier, or begin a career

▼ A Roman teacher and student

in the government. Roman women did not become adults until they married. A woman usually wore a long flowing robe with a cloak called a *palla*.

Women in Rome Women in early Rome had some rights, but they were not full citizens. The paterfamilias looked after his wife and controlled her affairs. However, he often sought her advice in private. Women had a strong influence on their families, and some wives of famous men, including emperors, became well-known themselves. For example, the empress Livia (LIHV•ee•uh), wife of Augustus, had a say in Rome's politics. She was later honored as a goddess.

The freedoms a Roman woman enjoyed depended on her husband's wealth and standing. Wealthy women had a great deal of independence. They could own land, run businesses, and sell property. They managed the household and had enslaved people do the housework. This left the women free to study literature, art, and fashion. Outside the home, they could go to the theater or the amphitheater, but in both places they had to sit in areas separate from men.

Women with less money had less freedom. They spent most of their time working in their houses or helping their husbands in family-run shops. They were allowed to leave home to shop, visit friends, worship at temples, or go to the baths. A few women did work independently outside the home. Some served as priestesses, while others worked as hairdressers and even doctors.

A Roman House

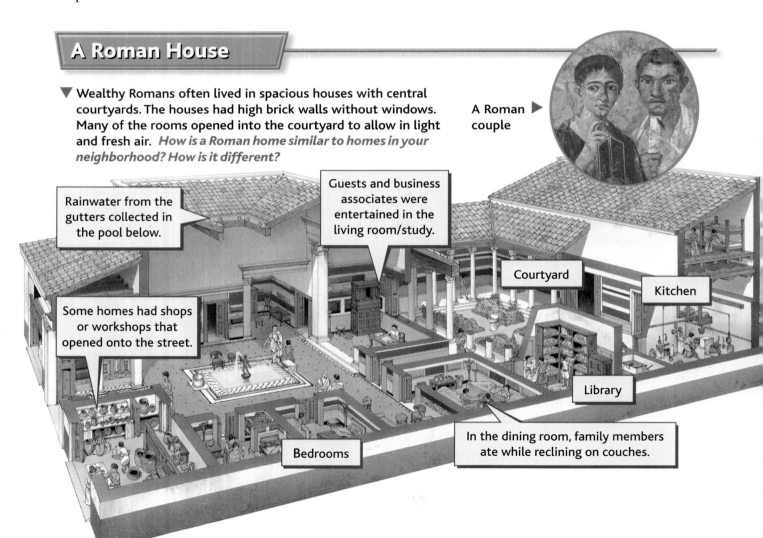

▼ Wealthy Romans often lived in spacious houses with central courtyards. The houses had high brick walls without windows. Many of the rooms opened into the courtyard to allow in light and fresh air. *How is a Roman home similar to homes in your neighborhood? How is it different?*

A Roman ▶ couple

Rainwater from the gutters collected in the pool below.

Guests and business associates were entertained in the living room/study.

Courtyard

Kitchen

Some homes had shops or workshops that opened onto the street.

Library

Bedrooms

In the dining room, family members ate while reclining on couches.

These apartments were built of brick and stone for wealthy Romans. *What sort of buildings did poor Romans live in?*

▼ A Roman family at the dinner table

How Did Romans Treat Enslaved People?

Slavery was a part of Roman life from early times. But the use of slave labor grew as Rome took over more territory. Thousands of prisoners from conquered lands were brought to Italy. Most spent their lives performing slave labor. By 100 B.C., about 40 percent of the people in Italy were enslaved.

Enslaved people did many different jobs. They worked in homes, fields, mines, and workshops. They helped build roads, bridges, and aqueducts. Many enslaved Greeks were well educated. They served as teachers, doctors, and artisans. Enslaved people who earned wages usually were able to buy their freedom.

For most enslaved people, life was miserable. They were punished severely for poor work or for running away. To escape their hardships, enslaved people often rebelled.

In 73 B.C. a slave revolt broke out in Italy. It was led by a gladiator named **Spartacus** (SPAHR•tuh•kuhs). Under Spartacus, a force of 70,000 enslaved people defeated several

Roman armies. The revolt was finally crushed two years later. Spartacus and 6,000 of his followers were crucified, or put to death by nailing on a cross.

Roman Religion The ancient Romans worshiped many gods and goddesses. They also believed that spirits lived in natural things, such as trees and rivers. Greek gods and goddesses were popular in Rome, although they were given Roman names. For example, Zeus became Jupiter, the sky god, and Aphrodite became Venus, the goddess of love and beauty. Roman emperors also were worshiped. This practice strengthened support for the government.

Romans honored their gods and goddesses by praying and offering food. Every Roman home had an altar for their household gods. At these altars, the head of the family carried out rituals. Government officials made offerings in temples. There the important gods and goddesses of Rome were honored. Some Roman priests looked for messages from the gods. They studied

Greek and Roman Gods

Greek God	Roman God	Role
Ares	Mars	god of war
Zeus	Jupiter	chief god
Hera	Juno	wife of chief god
Aphrodite	Venus	goddess of love
Artemis	Diana	goddess of the hunt
Athena	Minerva	goddess of wisdom
Hermes	Mercury	messenger god
Hades	Pluto	god of the underworld
Poseidon	Neptune	god of the sea
Hephaestus	Vulcan	god of fire

Minerva, goddess of wisdom ▶

the insides of dead animals or watched the flight of birds, looking for meaning.

As the empire grew larger, Romans came into contact with other religions. These religions were allowed, as long as they did not threaten the government.

Those that did faced severe hardships. You will read about one of these religions—Christianity—in the next chapter.

Reading Check **Contrast** Describe the freedoms of upper-class women that were not available to women of other classes.

History Online

Study Central™ Need help with the material in this section? Visit jat.glencoe.com

Section 1 Review

Reading Summary
Review the Main Ideas

• Roman art, literature, and science borrowed much from the Greeks. Roman engineers made advances, including the development of cement, the arch, aqueducts, and domes.

• Religion and family were important parts of Roman life. Enslaved people carried out many different tasks in Roman society.

What Did You Learn?

1. What were some of Ptolemy's scientific achievements?

2. How were the Roman and Greek religions similar?

Critical Thinking

3. **Compare and Contrast** Draw a chart like the one below. Fill in details to compare and contrast Roman and Greek art and architecture.

Greek Art	Roman Art

Greek Architecture	Roman Architecture

4. **Analyze** Explain the importance of the language of the Romans.

5. **Describe** Describe the education of Roman children.

6. **Conclude** The Romans borrowed ideas from other peoples. Do you think our culture today borrows ideas from other peoples? Explain your answer.

7. **Reading** Responding and Reflecting Look at the art showing the Roman house on page 308. Write five things that come to mind as you view this picture.

A WILD-GOOSE CHASE
THE STORY OF PHILEMON AND BAUCIS

Retold by Geraldine McCaughrean

Before You Read

The Scene: This story takes place in ancient Rome in the legendary time when gods visited Earth to interact with humans in person.

The Characters: Philemon and Baucis are the man and woman who welcome guests to their home. Clio is their goose. Jupiter and Mercury are two ancient Roman gods.

The Plot: A husband and wife welcome two guests into their cottage. They have no food for the guests, but they do have a pet goose. As the pair try to provide their guests with food, the guests reveal their identities and reward the host and hostess for their generosity.

Vocabulary Preview

fowl: bird

wielding: controlling

gaped: hung open

quills: feathers

hospitality: friendliness and generosity toward guests

ramshackle: falling apart

disintegrated: broke into small pieces

gilded: decorated with gold

preening: grooming and making pretty

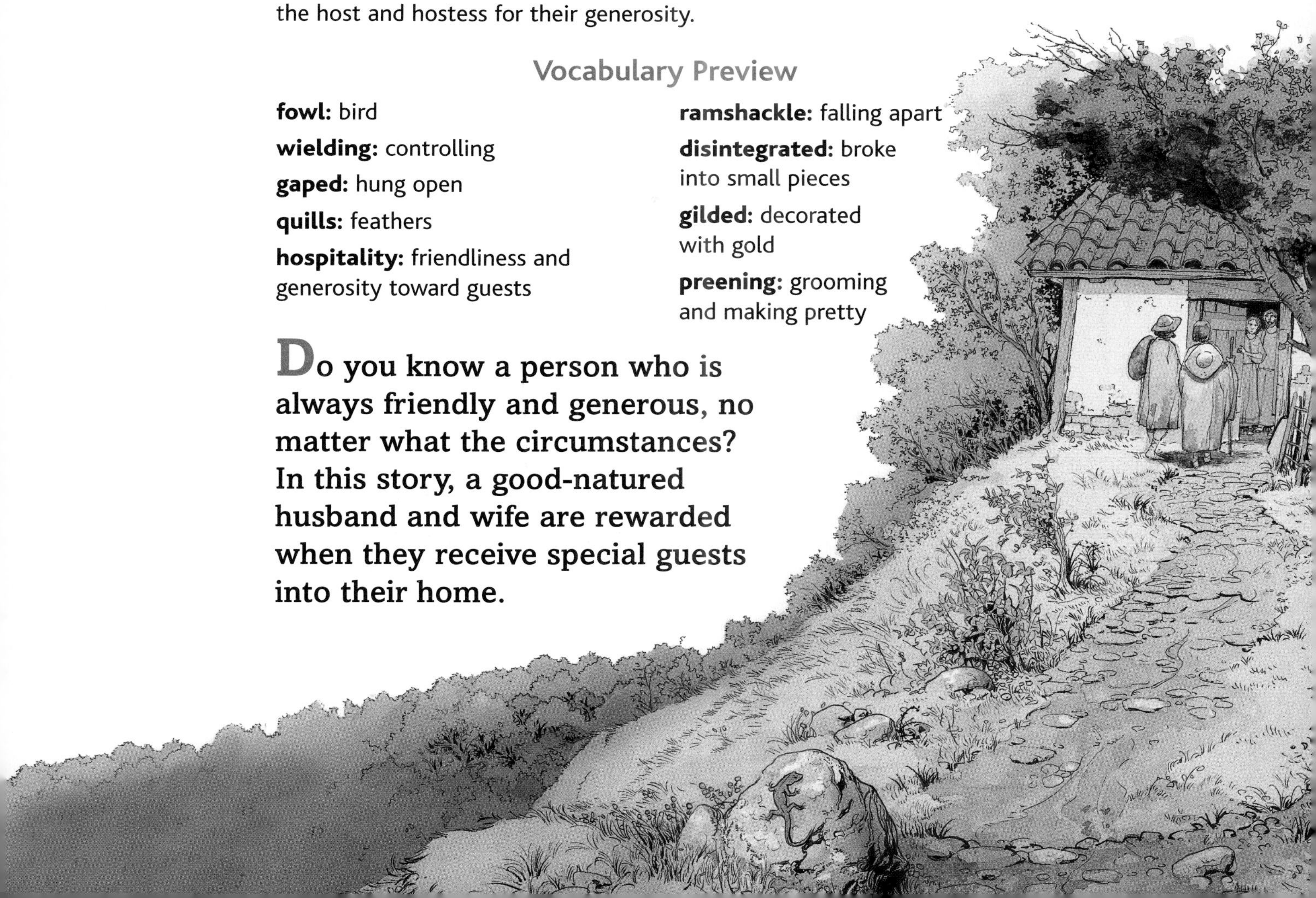

Do you know a person who is always friendly and generous, no matter what the circumstances? In this story, a good-natured husband and wife are rewarded when they receive special guests into their home.

WORLD LITERATURE

As You Read

Keep in mind that this story is a myth. Like the Greeks, Romans passed myths from one generation to the next to explain some aspect of the world. Often, the stories involved gods and goddesses as well as humans.

A knock at the door. A pair of passing strangers. Philemon and Baucis did not know the two men on their doorstep, but they had never yet failed to offer a warm welcome to anyone who called at their little cottage.

"Come in! Sit down! My wife will cook you supper!" said Philemon.

His wife tugged at his sleeve. She did not need to say more. Both of them knew there was no food in the house. Not a bite. Baucis and Philemon themselves had been living on eggs and olives for days. There was not even any bread.

Philemon smiled sadly at Baucis, and she smiled sadly back. "It's the goose, is it?" he said.

"The goose it is," she replied.

Clio was all they had left. She was more like a pet than a farmyard fowl. And yet, guests are a blessing sent by the gods, and guests must be fed. So Philemon fetched his sharp ax and Baucis began to chase the goose, trying to drive it into the cottage.

Jupiter sat back in his chair and waited patiently for dinner. "Do you think we should help?" he said to Mercury, hearing the commotion in the yard.

"I know we shall have a wait," replied Mercury.

"Here—you try," said Baucis, passing the ax to Philemon.

The goose was squawking, Baucis was yelping, and Philemon was coughing as he ran

about wielding the ax. He struck at Clio, but the goose moved, and he demolished a bush. He swung again and hit the wooden pail. The goose shrieked with outrage, then with terror, and slapped about on her big, triangular feet—plat, plat, plat—skidding into their homemade altar piled high with flowers, into the fish-drying rack,[1] into the washing on the tree.[2] Olives rained down on the roof of the shack.

"Do you think we should go?" said Jupiter, as he and Mercury listened to the wild-goose chase and their hungry stomachs growled quietly.

At last Philemon and Baucis cornered the goose against the cottage door. Her orange beak gaped. Philemon raised the ax . . . and Clio bolted backward into the shack, running around the room like a black-footed pillow fight until she caught sight of Jupiter.

Now, animals are not so easily fooled by disguises, and although Jupiter and Mercury were dressed as peasants, in woolen tunics and straw hats, she instantly recognized the King of the gods and threw herself on his mercy. Neck outstretched, eyes bulging, she ran straight between his knees and into his lap. He was overrun with goose.

"A thousand pardons, friend," gasped Baucis, crawling in at the door, her hair stuck with goose quills. "Won't you take an olive while you wait?"

Jupiter stroked the goose, which stood paddling[3] on his thighs, and spat out a few feathers. "Shield me! Save me! Protect me!" said the goose, in the language of geese.

---

[1]**fish-drying rack:** large wooden structure on which fish are hung to dry
[2]**washing on the tree:** laundry hung on the tree branches to dry
[3]**paddling:** moving its feet

Jupiter tickled it under the beak. "Your hospitality is a marvel, dear Philemon, gentle Baucis. In all my long travels over the face of the world, I have never met such unselfish hosts. Here is your only goose, and you were ready to cook it for us! Your generosity surpasses that of the gods themselves!"

"Now, sir," said Baucis sternly. "You may be a guest, but I'll have no ill spoken of the gods in this house. Though we have little to offer, the gods have been good to us, have they not, my love?"

"They have, they have," said Philemon. Mercury concealed a grin.

"And they shall be good to you ever after!" declared Jupiter, rising to his feet. He rose and rose, 'til his head touched the rafters, and his face brightened 'til the room was light as day. His disguise fell away and Mercury folded it small and smaller 'til it fit inside one fist and was gone.

"As you see, I am Jupiter, King of the gods, and this is my messenger, Mercury. We like to travel the world and visit the people whose sacrificial smoke perfumes the halls of Heaven. But travel where we may and stay where we might, we never met with such hospitality as yours! Name any favor and it shall be your reward. A small kingdom, perhaps? A palace? A chest of sea treasure from the vaults of Poseidon?[4] Wings to fly or the gift of prophecy? Name it!"

Mercury looked uneasy. He had seen the greed and ambition of mortals all too often. This mild-looking couple would probably demand to be gods and to dine at the table of the gods; would ask for immortality or a banner of stars wide as the Milky Way, spelling out "Philemon the Philanthropist,"[5] "Baucis the Beautiful."

Baucis looked at Philemon, and Philemon smiled back and wrung his hat shyly between his hands.

"Almighty Jupiter, you have done our little house such an honor today that we have

---

[4]**Poseidon:** Roman god of the sea
[5]**philanthropist:** someone who is charitable

hardly breath enough to speak our thanks. Our greatest joy in life has always been to worship at our humble little altar—out there in the yard. What more could we ask than to go on doing that—oh, and both to die at the same hour, so that we may never be parted. My Baucis and I."

Jupiter complained of a speck of dust in his eye and went outside. He could be heard blowing his nose loudly. When he ducked back through the door, his eyes were quite red-rimmed. "Come, priest and priestess of my shrine! Your temple awaits you!"

All of a sudden, the drafty, ramshackle little hut disintegrated, like a raft of leaves on a river. Around and above it rose the pillars of a mighty temple. The simple cairn[6] of stones that had served for an altar still stood there, piled with firewood and swagged with flowers, but now it stood on a marble floor, and from that floor rose forty marble pillars cloaked with beaten gold, supporting a roof gilded with stars. The living quarters for priest and priestess were piled with feather mattresses and silken pillows, and priestly robes of soft cotton hung waiting about the shoulders of Carrara[7] statues.

---

[6]**cairn:** mound
[7]**Carrara:** an Italian city known for its white marble
quarries and statues

W🌐RLD LITERATURE

Already, from all corners of the landscape, pilgrims were setting out at a run to visit the marvelous new temple of Jupiter, whose red roof signaled to them across miles of open countryside. Philemon and Baucis would be kept busy receiving their sacrifices, tending the sacrificial flame, sweeping up the ashes.

But they thrived on the hard work, just as they had always done. The worshipers brought not only flowers for the altar but baskets of delicious food for the priest and priestess whose fame spread far and wide. Tirelessly they worked until, being mortal, even Baucis and Philemon became exhausted. Watching from the terraces of Heaven, Jupiter saw them pause now, each time they passed one another, and lean one against the other for a moment's rest, Baucis laying her head on Philemon's shoulder.

"They are weary," said Mercury.

"You are right," said Jupiter. "It is time for them to rest."

So instead of breathing in the fragrance from the altar below, he breathed out—a breath that wafted away the white robes of priest and priestess and left behind two noble trees at the very door of the temple. One was an oak, the other a linden tree, and they leaned one toward another, their branches intertwined, casting welcome shade over the threshold.

Clio the goose liked to rest there at noon, preening her . . . feathers and singing.

Responding to the Reading

1. Why do Philemon and Baucis fail to recognize their guests? Which character does recognize them?
2. Jupiter said that he and Mercury like to "visit the people whose sacrificial smoke perfumes the halls of Heaven." Who does he mean?
3. **Cause and Effect** What is the result of Jupiter's gift to Philemon and Baucis?
4. **Analyze** Why do Philemon and Baucis not ask the gods for fame and power?
5. **Reading** **Read to Write** Imagine that friends who live in another town visit you. What would you provide for them? Would it be different from the things you provide for yourself? Imagine you are Philemon or Baucis, and write one or two paragraphs explaining how you would have treated their guests.

Section 2

The Fall of Rome

Get Ready to Read!

What's the Connection?

In Section 1, you learned about Roman life and achievements when the empire was at its height. Over time, however, the Roman Empire began to have problems, and it gradually grew weaker. Eventually, Rome fell to outside invaders.

Focusing on the Main Ideas

- Poor leadership, a declining economy, and attacks by Germanic tribes weakened the Roman Empire. *(page 318)*

- Rome finally fell when invaders swept through the empire during the A.D. 400s. *(page 322)*

- Rome passed on many achievements in government, law, language, and the arts. *(page 325)*

Locating Places

Constantinople
(KAHN•STAN•tuhn•OH•puhl)

Meeting People

Diocletian (DY•uh•KLEE•shuhn)
Constantine (KAHN•stuhn•TEEN)
Theodosius
 (THEE•uh•DOH•shuhs)
Alaric (A•luh•rihk)
Odoacer (OH•duh•WAY•suhr)

Building Your Vocabulary

plague (PLAYG)
inflation (ihn•FLAY•shuhn)
barter (BAHR•tuhr)
reform (rih•FAWRM)

Reading Strategy

Sequencing Information Create a diagram to show the events that led up to the fall of the Western Roman Empire.

```
[ ] ➡ [ ] ➡ [ Fall of the Roman Empire ]
```

NATIONAL GEOGRAPHIC When & Where?

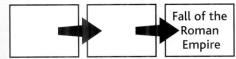

BRITAIN
GAUL
SPAIN   ITALY
      Rome
            Constantinople
   GREECE
      EGYPT

A.D. 250	A.D. 350	A.D. 450
A.D. 284 Diocletian tries to reform empire	**A.D. 395** Roman Empire divided into eastern and western parts	**A.D. 476** Rome's last emperor overthrown

The Decline of Rome

Main Idea Poor leadership, a declining economy, and attacks by Germanic tribes weakened the Roman Empire.

Reading Focus What do you do when you face a difficult problem? Do you try to solve it yourself? Do you ask other people for help? Read to learn about the problems the Roman Empire faced and how its leaders responded.

In A.D. 180 Marcus Aurelius died. His son, Commodus (KAH•muh•duhs), became emperor. Commodus was cruel and wasted money. Instead of ruling Rome, Commodus spent much of his time fighting as a gladiator. In A.D. 192 the emperor's bodyguard killed him. Nearly a century of confusion and fighting followed.

After Commodus, emperors called the Severans ruled Rome. Much of their time was spent putting down revolts and protecting Rome's borders. The Severans stayed in power by paying the army well, but they ignored the growing problems of crime and poverty.

Political and Social Problems When the last Severan ruler died in A.D. 235, Rome's government became very weak. For almost 50 years, army leaders fought each other for the throne. During this time, Rome had 22 different emperors.

Poor leadership was not Rome's only difficulty. Fewer Romans honored the old ideals of duty, courage, and honesty. Many government officials took bribes. As problems

The Decline of Rome

Weak Roman Government
- Dishonest government officials provide poor leadership.

Social Problems
- Famine and disease spread throughout the empire.

Declining Economy
- Income and wages fall.
- Wealthy fail to pay taxes.

Reform Fails and Rome Divides in Two
- Government fails to keep order.
- Violence and tension increase.
- Diocletian divides the empire.

Eastern Roman Empire
- Constantinople becomes the new capital.
- The empire survives attacks and prospers.

Western Roman Empire
- Numerous attacks threaten the empire.
- Territory is slowly lost to invaders.

Byzantine Empire
- This empire is created from the Eastern Roman Empire and lasts nearly 1,000 years.

Rome Falls
- The city of Rome falls in A.D. 476.
- The Western Roman Empire is divided into Germanic kingdoms by A.D. 550.

Understanding Charts

Many issues, including a weak government, lack of food, and fewer jobs, led to Rome's decline.
1. According to the flow chart, what occurs after reform fails?
2. **Cause and Effect** What were the final effects of the Roman Empire being split in two?

increased, talented people often refused to serve in government. Many wealthy citizens even stopped paying taxes. Fewer people attended schools, and a large number of the empire's people were now enslaved. Wealthy Romans supported slavery because it was a cheap way to get work done.

Economic and Military Problems

During the A.D. 200s, Rome's economy began to fall apart. As government weakened, law and order broke down. Roman soldiers and invaders seized crops and destroyed fields. Farmers grew less food, and hunger began to spread.

As the economy worsened, people bought fewer goods. Artisans produced less, and shopkeepers lost money. Many businesses closed, and the number of workers dropped sharply. Many workers had to leave jobs and serve in the army. A **plague** (PLAYG), or a disease that spreads widely, also took its toll. It killed one out of every ten people in the empire.

Rome also began to suffer from **inflation** (ihn•FLAY•shuhn), or rapidly increasing prices. Inflation happens when money loses its value. How did this happen? The weak economy meant fewer taxes were paid. With less money coming in, the Roman government could not afford to defend its territories and had to find a way to pay its soldiers and officials. One way for the government to get the money it needed was to put less gold in its coins.

By putting less gold in each coin, the government could make extra coins and pay for more things. People soon learned that the coins did not have as much gold in them, and the coins began losing value. Prices went up, and many people stopped using money altogether. They began to **barter** (BAHR•tuhr), or exchange goods without using money.

The Way It Was

Focus on Everyday Life

Slavery in the Roman Empire Public and private slavery were common in Roman society. Public slaves were owned by the state. They took care of important buildings and served government officials. Educated public slaves were used to help organize the governments of conquered areas.

Private slaves were owned by individuals. They were often forced to work long hours and could be sold at any time. Wealthy Romans had hundreds or even thousands of enslaved people. Most enslaved people worked on farms.

Most enslaved people were men. This was probably because their work required great strength. Some enslaved men also became gladiators. Enslaved women made clothing and cooked for their owner's family.

▼ Roman slaves at work

Connecting to the Past

1. What was the main difference between public and private enslavement?
2. Which jobs were probably considered the most desirable by enslaved people?

Distrust of Money

As the Roman Empire declined, people refused to trust the value of money issued by each emperor.

"Whereas [because] the public officials have assembled and have accused the bankers of the exchange banks of having closed them because of their unwillingness to accept the divine coin of the emperors, it has become necessary to issue an order to all owners of the banks to open them and to accept and exchange all coin except the absolutely spurious [false] and counterfeit—and not alone to them but to those who engage in business transactions of any kind."

—"Distrust of Imperial Coinage," *Oxyrhynchus Papyrus*, no. 1411, Vol. 2, A.S. Hunt, trans.

▲ Roman coins

DBQ Document-Based Question

What do you think was happening to the economy of the empire as people stopped using the official money?

Meanwhile, invaders swept into the empire. In the west, Germanic tribes raided Roman farms and towns. In the east, armies from Persia pushed into the empire's territory. As fighting increased, the government could no longer enlist and pay Romans as soldiers. It began using Germanic warriors in the army. However, these Germanic soldiers were not loyal to Rome.

What Were Diocletian's Reforms? In A.D. 284 a general named **Diocletian** (DY•uh•KLEE•shuhn) became emperor. To stop the empire's decline, he introduced **reforms** (rih•FAWRMZ), or political changes to make things better. Because the empire was too large for one person to rule, Diocletian divided it into four parts. He named officials to rule these areas but kept authority over all.

Diocletian also worked to boost the economy. To slow inflation, he issued rules that set the prices of goods and the wages to be paid to workers. To make sure more goods were produced, he ordered workers to remain at the same jobs until they died. Diocletian's reforms failed. The people ignored the new rules, and Diocletian did not have enough power to make them obey.

Who Was Constantine? In A.D. 305 Diocletian retired from office. After a period of conflict, another general named **Constantine** (KAHN•stuhn•TEEN) became emperor in A.D. 312. To aid the economy, Constantine issued several orders. The sons of workers had to follow their fathers' trades, the sons of farmers had to work the land their fathers worked, and the sons of soldiers had to serve in the army.

Constantine's changes did not halt the empire's decline in the west. As a result, Constantine moved the capital from dying Rome to a new city in the east. He chose the site of the Greek city of Byzantium (buh•ZAN•tee•uhm). There he built a forum, an amphitheater called the Hippodrome, and many palaces. The city became known as **Constantinople** (KAHN•STAN•tuhn•OH•puhl). Today, Constantinople is called Istanbul.

☑ **Reading Check** **Explain** How did Diocletian try to reverse the decline of Rome?

Biography

CONSTANTINE THE GREAT

c. A.D. 280–337

First Christian Roman Emperor

Constantine was the first Roman Emperor to become a Christian, although he was not baptized until near his death in A.D. 337. He first came to believe in Christianity many years earlier, when he was a military leader. Constantine believed he had seen a flaming cross in the sky that said, "By this sign thou shall conquer." The next day his army was victorious in an important battle. He believed that the cross was a call to the Christian God.

During his reign, Constantine granted new opportunities to Christians and helped advance the power of the early Catholic Church. At the Council of Nicea in A.D. 325, he encouraged discussion about the acceptance of the Trinity (Father, Son, and Holy Spirit). He also boosted the political positions and power of bishops within the Roman government.

Even though Constantine had many political and religious successes, his life was filled with controversy and tragedy. Constantine married a woman named Fausta. His eldest son from a previous marriage was named Crispus. Fausta accused Crispus of crimes and claimed that he was planning to seize the throne. Constantine was so shocked that he had his son killed. Constantine later discovered that Fausta had lied because she wanted her own son to be in line for the throne. He then had Fausta killed.

▲ Constantine

▲ Modern-day Constantinople

Then and Now

Constantine believed freedom of religion was important for the success of his empire and made sure that Christians could no longer be persecuted. What part of the U.S. Constitution protects freedom of religion?

Rome Falls

Main Idea Rome finally fell when invaders swept through the empire during the A.D. 400s.

Reading Focus How would you feel if a favorite place—a shop, park, or recreation center—was closed after being open for many years? Read to learn how the Romans had to face an even greater loss when their city and empire fell.

Both Diocletian and Constantine failed to save the Roman Empire. When Constantine died in A.D. 337, fighting broke out again. A new emperor called

Rome Is Attacked

In this excerpt from one of his letters, the Christian leader Jerome describes attacks on the Roman provinces.

▲ Saint Jerome

"Who would believe that Rome, victor over all the world, would fall, that she would be to her people both the womb and the tomb. . . . Where we cannot help we mourn and mingle with theirs our tears. . . . There is not an hour, not even a moment, when we are not occupied with crowds of refugees, when the peace of the monastery is not invaded by a horde of guests so that we shall either have to shut the gates or neglect the Scriptures for which the gates were opened."

—Jerome, "News of the Attacks"

DBQ Document-Based Question

Does Jerome think the gates of the monastery should be shut? Explain.

Theodosius (THEE•uh•DOH•shuhs) finally gained control and ended the fighting.

Ruling the empire proved to be difficult. Theodosius decided to divide the empire after his death. In A.D. 395, the Roman Empire split into two separate empires. One was the Western Roman Empire, with its capital at Rome. The other was the Eastern Roman Empire, with its capital at Constantinople.

Rome Is Invaded As Rome declined, it was no longer able to hold back the Germanic tribes on its borders. Many different Germanic groups existed—Ostrogoths, Visigoths, Franks, Vandals, Angles, and Saxons. They came from the forests and marshes of northern Europe.

These Germanic groups were in search of warmer climates and better grazing land for their cattle. They also were drawn by Rome's wealth and culture. In addition, many were fleeing the Huns, fierce warriors from Mongolia in Asia.

In the late A.D. 300s, the Huns entered Eastern Europe and defeated the Ostrogoths (AHS•truh•GAHTHS). The Visigoths, fearing they would be next, asked the Eastern Roman emperor for protection. He let them settle just inside the empire's border. In return they promised to be loyal to Rome.

Before long, trouble broke out between the Visigoths and Romans. The empire forced the Visigoths to buy food at very high prices. The Romans also kidnapped and enslaved many Visigoths.

History Online

Web Activity Visit jat.glencoe.com and click on *Chapter 9—Student Web Activity* to learn more about Roman civilization.

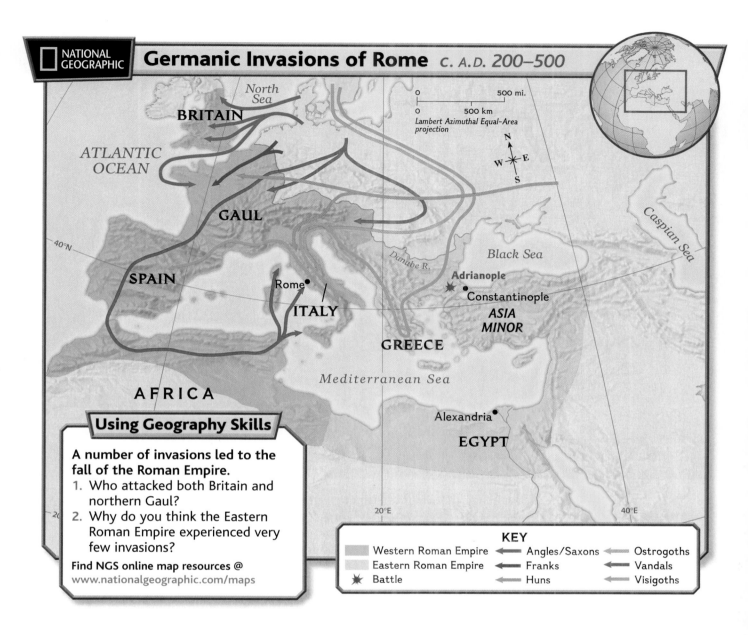

Germanic Invasions of Rome c. A.D. 200–500

NATIONAL GEOGRAPHIC

North Sea

BRITAIN

ATLANTIC OCEAN

GAUL

SPAIN

Rome

ITALY

AFRICA

40°N

Danube R.

Black Sea

Adrianople

Constantinople

ASIA MINOR

GREECE

Mediterranean Sea

Alexandria

EGYPT

Caspian Sea

20°E

40°E

0   500 mi.
0   500 km
Lambert Azimuthal Equal-Area projection

Using Geography Skills

A number of invasions led to the fall of the Roman Empire.

1. Who attacked both Britain and northern Gaul?
2. Why do you think the Eastern Roman Empire experienced very few invasions?

Find NGS online map resources @
www.nationalgeographic.com/maps

KEY

Western Roman Empire	← Angles/Saxons	← Ostrogoths
Eastern Roman Empire	← Franks	← Vandals
✳ Battle	← Huns	← Visigoths

Finally, the Visigoths rebelled against the Romans. In A.D. 378 they defeated Roman legions at the Battle of Adrianople (AY•dree•uh•NOH•puhl). After that defeat, Rome was forced to surrender land to the Visigoths.

The Germanic tribes now knew that Rome could no longer defend itself. More and more Germanic warriors crossed the borders in search of land. In the winter of A.D. 406, the Rhine River in Western Europe froze. Germanic groups crossed the frozen river and entered Gaul, which is today

France. The Romans were too weak to force them back across the border.

In A.D. 410 the Visigoth leader **Alaric** (A•luh•rihk) and his soldiers captured Rome itself. They burned records and looted the treasury. Rome's capture by Alaric was a great shock to the empire's people. It was the first time Rome had been conquered in 800 years.

Another Germanic group known as the Vandals overran Spain and northern Africa. They enslaved some Roman landowners and drove others away. Then the Vandals

▲ **An image showing the Visigoths invading Rome.** *What leader did the Visigoths overthrow to take control of Rome?*

sailed to Italy. In A.D. 455 they entered Rome. They spent 12 days stripping buildings of everything valuable and burning them. From these attacks came the English word *vandalism,* which means "the willful destruction of property."

Rome Falls By the mid-A.D. 400s, several Germanic leaders held high posts in Rome's government and army. In A.D. 476 a Germanic general named **Odoacer** (OH•duh•WAY•suhr) took control, overthrowing the western emperor, a 14-year-old boy named Romulus Augustulus (RAHM•yuh•luhs aw•GUHS•chah•luhs). After Romulus Augustulus, no emperor ever again ruled from Rome. Historians often use this event to mark the end of the Western Roman Empire.

Odoacer controlled Rome for almost 15 years. Then a group of Visigoths seized the city and killed Odoacer. They set up a kingdom in Italy under their leader, Theodoric (thee•AH•duh•rihk). Elsewhere in Europe, other Germanic kingdoms arose.

By A.D. 550, the Western Roman Empire had faded away. Many Roman beliefs and practices remained in use, however. For example, Europe's new Germanic rulers adopted the Latin language, Roman laws, and Christianity. Although the Western Roman Empire fell to Germanic invaders, the Eastern Roman Empire prospered. It became known as the Byzantine Empire and lasted nearly 1,000 more years.

✓ **Reading Check** **Identify** Which event usually marks the fall of the Western Roman Empire?

The Legacy of Rome

Main Idea Rome passed on many achievements in government, law, language, and the arts.

Reading Focus Do you know where the words "doctor," "animal," "circus," and "family" come from? These words come from the Latin language spoken by the Romans. Read to discover other things we have borrowed from the Romans.

Our world would be very different if the Roman Empire had never existed. Many words in the English language and many of our ideas about government come from the Romans. The same is true for our system of laws and our knowledge about building. As you will read in the next chapter, the peace and order brought by Roman rule also allowed the Christian religion to spread.

Roman Ideas and Government Today

Roman ideas about law, as first written in the Twelve Tables, are with us today. We, like the Romans, believe that all people are equal under the law. We expect our judges to decide cases fairly, and we consider a person innocent until proven guilty.

Linking Past & Present

Roman and Modern Architecture

THEN Early Romans borrowed architectural ideas from the Greeks, but they also developed their own style. Roman designs often included vaults, columns, domes, and arches. New architectural ideas meant that buildings could be constructed in new ways. Because of concrete and a new design, Roman theaters did not have to be built on natural slopes to have tiered seating.

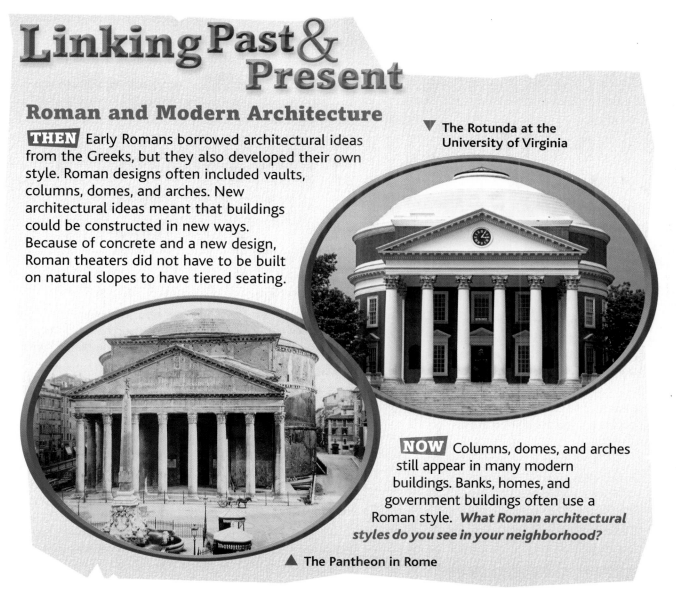

▼ The Rotunda at the University of Virginia

NOW Columns, domes, and arches still appear in many modern buildings. Banks, homes, and government buildings often use a Roman style. *What Roman architectural styles do you see in your neighborhood?*

▲ The Pantheon in Rome

Roman ideas about government and citizenship are also important today. Like the early Romans, Americans believe that a republic made up of equal citizens is the best form of government. We also believe that a republic works best if citizens do their duty, participate in government, and work to make their society better.

Roman Influence on Culture Today the alphabet of the Latin language, which expanded from 22 to 26 letters, is used throughout the Western world. Latin shaped the languages of Italy, France, Spain, Portugal, and Romania. Many English words also come from Latin. Scientists, doctors, and lawyers still use Latin phrases. Every known species of plant and animal has a Latin name. Today, we also still admire the works of great Roman writers such as Virgil, Horace, Livy, and Tacitus.

Ancient Rome also left a lasting mark on building in the Western world. We still use concrete today for much of our construction, and Roman architectural styles are still seen in public buildings today. When you visit Washington, D.C., or the capital city of any state, you will see capitol buildings with domes and arches inspired by Roman architecture.

Christianity As you probably know, Christianity is one of the major religions in the world today. Christianity began in the Roman Empire. When Rome's government adopted Christianity in the A.D. 300s, it helped the new religion to grow and spread. After Rome's fall, many Roman ideas blended with those of Christianity.

 **Reading Check** **Compare** Which aspects of the Roman Empire are reflected in present-day cultures?

History Online
Study Central™ Need help with the material in this section? Visit jat.glencoe.com

 Section ❷ Review

Reading Summary
Review the Main Ideas

- A series of weak emperors, invasions by outsiders, disease, and a number of other factors led to a greatly weakened Roman Empire.

- Numerous invasions by Germanic peoples led to the fall of Rome in A.D. 476.

- Roman ideas about government and Roman architecture are just some of the legacies of ancient Rome.

What Did You Learn?

1. What social problems helped cause the empire's decline?

2. Why did the Roman government use Germanic warriors in its army?

Critical Thinking

3. **Summarizing Information** Draw a diagram like the one below. Fill in details about Rome's legacies in the areas of government, law, and citizenship.

Roman Legacies

4. **Cause and Effect** How did inflation affect Rome?

5. **Describe** Who were the Visigoths, and how did they contribute to the fall of Rome?

6. **Identify** Give examples of Roman ideas in language and architecture that exist today.

7. **Persuasive Writing** Imagine you are living in Rome around the time of the fall of the empire. Write an editorial for a newspaper identifying what you think is the main reason for the decline and fall of the empire, and what might have been done to prevent it.

Section 3

The Byzantine Empire

Get Ready to Read!

What's the Connection?

In the last section, you learned that even though the Roman Empire in the West fell, the Eastern Roman Empire survived and prospered. It became known as the Byzantine Empire. The Byzantines developed a new civilization based on Greek, Roman, and Christian ideas.

Focusing on the Main Ideas

• The Eastern Roman Empire grew rich and powerful as the Western Roman Empire fell. *(page 328)*

• The policies and reforms of Emperor Justinian and Empress Theodora helped make the Byzantine Empire strong. *(page 329)*

• The Byzantines developed a rich culture based on Roman, Greek, and Christian ideas. *(page 332)*

Locating Places
Black Sea
Aegean Sea (ih•JEE•uhn)

Meeting People
Justinian (juh•STIH•nee•uhn)
Theodora (THEE•uh•DOHR•uh)
Belisarius (BEH•luh•SAR•ee•uhs)
Tribonian (truh•BOH•nee•uhn)

Building Your Vocabulary
mosaic (moh•ZAY•ihk)
saint (SAYNT)
regent (REE•juhnt)

Reading Strategy
Cause and Effect Complete a chart to show the causes and effects of Justinian's new law code.

```
Causes
   ↓
New Code of Laws
   ↓
Effects
```

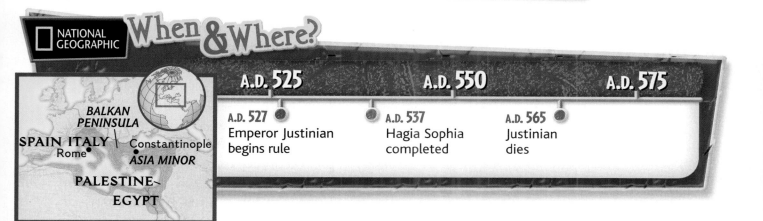

When & Where?

A.D. 525 — A.D. 550 — A.D. 575

A.D. 527 Emperor Justinian begins rule

A.D. 537 Hagia Sophia completed

A.D. 565 Justinian dies

BALKAN PENINSULA
SPAIN ITALY
Rome
Constantinople
ASIA MINOR
PALESTINE
EGYPT

The Rise of the Byzantines

Main Idea The Eastern Roman Empire grew rich and powerful as the Western Roman Empire fell.

Reading Focus Think of your own community. How have groups of people from different backgrounds contributed to its character? What would your town or city be like without these contributions from all the different groups? Read to learn about the different groups that made up the Byzantine Empire.

The Eastern Roman, or Byzantine, Empire reached a high point in the A.D. 500s. At this time, the empire stretched west to Italy, south to Egypt, and east to the border with Arabia. Greeks made up the empire's largest group, but many other peoples were found within the empire. They included Egyptians, Syrians, Arabs, Armenians, Jews, Persians, Slavs, and Turks.

▲ The ancient walled city of Constantinople

Why Is Constantinople Important? In the last section, you learned that Emperor Constantine moved the capital of the Roman Empire from Rome to a new city called Constantinople. Constantine's city became the capital of the Byzantine Empire. By the A.D. 500s, Constantinople was thriving and had become one of the world's great cities.

One reason for Constantinople's success was its location. It lay on the waterways between the **Black Sea** and the **Aegean Sea** (ih•JEE•uhn). Its harbors offered a safe shelter for fishing boats, trading ships, and warships. Constantinople also sat at the crossroads of trade routes between Europe and Asia. The trade that passed through made the city extremely wealthy.

Constantinople had a secure land location. Lying on a peninsula, Constantinople was easily defended. Seas protected it on three sides, and on the fourth side, a huge wall guarded the city. Later a huge chain was even strung across the city's north harbor for greater protection. Invaders could not easily take Constantinople.

Influence of Greek Culture The Byzantines at first followed Roman ways. Constantinople was known as the "New Rome." Its public buildings and palaces were built in the Roman style. The city even had an oval arena called the Hippodrome, where chariot races and other events were held.

Byzantine political and social life also were based on that of Rome. Emperors spoke Latin and enforced Roman laws. The empire's poor people received free bread and shows. Wealthy people lived in town or on large farming estates. In fact, many of them had once lived in Rome.

As time passed, the Byzantine Empire became less Roman and more Greek. Most Byzantines spoke Greek and honored their Greek past. Byzantine emperors and officials began to speak Greek too. The ideas of non-Greek peoples, like the Egyptians and the Slavs, also shaped Byzantine life. Still other customs came from Persia to the east. All of these cultures blended together to form the Byzantine civilization. Between A.D. 500 and A.D. 1200, the Byzantines had one of the world's richest and most-advanced empires.

Reading Check **Explain** Why did the Byzantine Empire have such a blending of cultures?

Emperor Justinian

Main Idea The policies and reforms of Emperor Justinian and Empress Theodora helped make the Byzantine Empire strong.

Reading Focus Do you sometimes rewrite reports to make them easier to understand? Read to learn how Justinian rewrote and reorganized the Byzantine law code.

Justinian (juh•STIH•nee•uhn) became emperor of the Byzantine Empire in A.D. 527 and ruled until A.D. 565. Justinian was a strong leader. He controlled the military, made laws, and was supreme judge. His order could not be questioned.

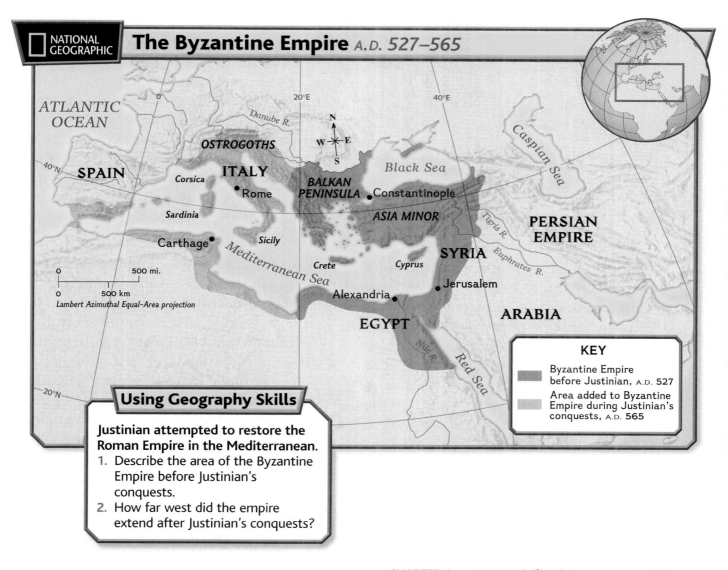

NATIONAL GEOGRAPHIC

The Byzantine Empire A.D. 527–565

Using Geography Skills

Justinian attempted to restore the Roman Empire in the Mediterranean.

1. Describe the area of the Byzantine Empire before Justinian's conquests.
2. How far west did the empire extend after Justinian's conquests?

KEY

Byzantine Empire before Justinian, A.D. 527

Area added to Byzantine Empire during Justinian's conquests, A.D. 565

Primary Source

Theodora Refuses to Flee

Justinian's court historian recorded Theodora's opinion about whether to escape or fight during the A.D. 532 revolt.

"My opinion then is that the present time . . . is inopportune [not a good time] for flight, even though it brings safety. . . . For one who has been an emperor, it is unendurable to be a fugitive. . . . May I not live that day on which those who meet me shall not address me as empress. If, now, it is your wish to save yourself, O Emperor, there is no difficulty."

—Procopius, "The Nika Riot"

Theodora ▶

DBQ Document-Based Question

Why did the empress not wish to escape?

Justinian's wife, the empress **Theodora** (THEE•uh•DOHR•uh), helped him run the empire. Theodora, a former actress, was intelligent and strong-willed, and she helped Justinian choose government officials. Theodora also convinced him to give women more rights. For the first time, a Byzantine wife could own land. If she became a widow, she now had the income to take care of her children.

In A.D. 532 Theodora helped save Justinian's throne. Angry taxpayers threatened to overthrow Justinian and stormed the palace. Justinian's advisers urged him to leave Constantinople. Theodora, however, told him to stay and fight. Justinian took Theodora's advice. He stayed in the city and crushed the uprising.

Justinian's Conquests Justinian wanted to reunite the Roman Empire and bring back Rome's glory. To do this, he had to conquer Western Europe and northern Africa. He ordered a general named **Belisarius** (BEH•luh•SAR•ee•uhs) to strengthen and lead the Byzantine army.

When Belisarius took command, he reorganized the Byzantine army. Instead of foot soldiers, the Byzantine army came to rely on cavalry—soldiers mounted on horses. Byzantine cavalry wore armor and carried bows and lances, which were long spears.

During Justinian's reign, the Byzantine military conquered most of Italy and northern Africa and defeated the Persians in the east. However, Justinian conquered too much too quickly. After he died, the empire did not have the money to maintain an army large enough to hold the territory in the west.

Justinian's Law Code Justinian decided that the empire's laws were disorganized and too difficult to understand. He ordered a group of legal scholars headed by **Tribonian** (truh•BOH•nee•uhn) to reform the law code.

The group's new simplified code became known as the Justinian Code. Officials, businesspeople, and individuals could now more easily understand the empire's laws. Over the years, the Justinian Code has had a great influence on the laws of almost every country in Europe.

✔ **Reading Check** **Explain** What did Justinian accomplish during his reign?

Biography

EMPRESS THEODORA

c A.D. 500–548

Theodora began life in the lower class of Byzantine society but rose to the rank of empress. The historian Procopius recorded the events of her early life. According to Procopius, Theodora's father worked as a bear keeper at the Hippodrome. After his death, Theodora followed her mother's advice and became an actress. A career in acting was not as glamorous then as it is now. It was a job of the lower class, like wool spinning, which was Theodora's other job.

Even though Theodora was of the lower class, she began dating Justinian. Justinian was attracted to Theodora's beauty and intelligence. Because Justinian wanted to marry Theodora, his uncle, the emperor, changed the law that prevented upper-class nobles from marrying actresses. The two were married in A.D. 525.

Justinian considered Theodora his intellectual equal. In his writings, Justinian said he asked for Theodora's advice on laws and policies. At Theodora's urging, he granted more rights to women. Some historians believe Theodora had great power within the royal court, perhaps more than Justinian. For example, nearly all the laws passed during Theodora's reign as empress mention her name. Theodora and Justinian had no children together. When Theodora died from cancer in A.D. 548, Justinian was overcome with grief. He had her portrait incorporated into many works of art, including numerous Byzantine mosaics.

▲ Empress Theodora advises Emperor Justinian.

"She was extremely clever and had a biting wit."
—Procopius, *The Secret History*

Then and Now

Name a modern-day female political leader that you think has great influence in making and changing laws. Explain your choice.

Byzantine Civilization

Main Idea The Byzantines developed a rich culture based on Roman, Greek, and Christian ideas.

Reading Focus Do you think a multicultural population adds to a country's interest and success? Read to learn how the diverse groups of the Byzantine Empire contributed to its culture.

The Byzantine Empire lasted approximately 1,000 years. For much of that time, Constantinople was the largest and richest city in Europe. The Byzantines were highly educated and creative. They preserved and passed on Greek culture and Roman law to other peoples. They gave the world new methods in the arts. As you will learn, they also spread Christianity to people in Eastern Europe.

The Importance of Trade From the A.D. 500s to the A.D. 1100s, the Byzantine Empire was the center of trade between Europe and Asia. Trade goods from present-day Russia in the north, Mediterranean lands in the south, Latin Europe in the west, and Persia and China in the east passed through the empire. From Asia, ships and caravans brought luxury goods—spices, gems, metals, and cloth—to Constantinople. For these items, Byzantine merchants traded farm goods as well as furs, honey, and enslaved people from northern Europe.

This enormous trade made the Byzantine Empire very rich. However, most Byzantines were not merchants. Instead they were farmers, herders, laborers, and artisans. One of the major Byzantine industries was weaving silk. It developed around

◀ Sculpture showing chariot racing at the Hippodrome

▲ Byzantine jewelry

▲ The style of the Hagia Sophia, shown here, and other Byzantine churches influenced the architecture of churches throughout Russia and Eastern Europe. *What does the name "Hagia Sophia" mean?*

A.D. 550. At that time, Byzantine travelers smuggled silkworm eggs out of China. Brought to Constantinople, the silkworms fed on mulberry leaves and produced silk threads. Weavers then used the threads to make the silk cloth that brought wealth to the empire.

Byzantine Art and Architecture

Justinian and other Byzantine emperors supported artists and architects. They ordered the building of churches, forts, and public buildings throughout the empire. Constantinople was known for its hundreds of churches and palaces. One of Justinian's greatest achievements was building the huge church called Hagia Sophia (HAH•jee•uh soh•FEE•uh), or "Holy Wisdom." It was completed in A.D. 537 and became the religious center of the Byzantine Empire. It still stands today in Istanbul.

Inside Hagia Sophia, worshipers could see walls of beautiful marble and mosaics. **Mosaics** (moh•ZAY•ihks) are pictures made from many bits of colored glass or stone. They were an important type of art in the Byzantine Empire. Mosaics mainly showed figures of **saints** (SAYNTS), or Christian holy people.

Byzantine Women

The family was the center of social life for most Byzantines. Religion and the government stressed the importance of marriage and family life. Divorces were rare and difficult to get.

Byzantine women were not encouraged to lead independent lives. They were expected to stay home and take care of their families. However, women did gain some important rights, thanks to Empress Theodora. Like Theodora herself, some Byzantine women became well educated and involved in politics. Several

The Way It Was

Focus on Everyday Life

Byzantine Mosaics Imagine taking bits of glass and turning them into beautiful masterpieces. Byzantine artists did just that starting around A.D. 330. Roman mosaics were made of natural-colored marble pieces and decorated villas and buildings. Byzantine mosaics were different. They were made of richly colored, irregular pieces of glass and decorated the ceilings, domes, and floors of Byzantine churches.

Byzantine mosaics were created to honor religious or political leaders. The centers of domes—because they were the highest points of the churches—were commonly reserved for images of Jesus. Mosaics were expensive. They were ordered and paid for by emperors, state officials, or church leaders. Many mosaics are still intact and can be seen today inside churches, monasteries, and museums.

◀ **Mosaic from the Byzantine Empire**

Connecting to the Past

1. Why do you think the name of the person who paid for the mosaic—rather than the name of the person who made the mosaic—was often recorded in the inscription?

2. What types of art do present-day artists make with glass?

royal women served as regents. A **regent** (REE•juhnt) is a person who stands in for a ruler who is too young or too ill to govern. A few ruled the empire in their own right.

Byzantine Education Learning was highly respected in Byzantine culture. The government supported the training of scholars and government officials. In Byzantine schools, boys studied religion, medicine, law, arithmetic, grammar, and other subjects. Wealthy Byzantines sometimes hired tutors to teach their children. Girls usually did not attend schools and were taught at home.

Most Byzantine authors wrote about religion. They stressed the need to obey God and save one's soul. To strengthen faith, they wrote about the lives of saints. Byzantine writers gave an important gift to the world. They copied and passed on the

▲ This Byzantine religious text is beautifully illustrated. *What did Byzantine boys study at school?*

writings of the ancient Greeks and Romans. Without Byzantine copies, many important works from the ancient world would have disappeared forever.

✓ **Reading Check** **Identify** What church is one of Justinian's greatest achievements?

History Online

Study Central™ Need help with the material in this section? Visit jat.glencoe.com

Section 3 Review

Reading Summary

Review the Main Ideas

- With its capital at Constantinople and strong Greek influences, the Byzantine Empire grew powerful and wealthy.

- The Byzantine emperor, Justinian, reconquered much of the land that had been held by the old Roman Empire in the Mediterranean. It also issued a new law code known as the Justinian Code.

- As the Byzantine Empire grew wealthy from trade, art, architecture, and education flourished.

What Did You Learn?

1. What is a mosaic, and where were mosaics found in the Byzantine Empire?

2. How did silk weaving develop in the Byzantine Empire?

Critical Thinking

3. **Organizing Information** Draw a diagram like the one below. Fill in details about Constantinople's location.

4. **Describe** What were some of the trade items that were exchanged between merchants in Constantinople?

5. **Explain** Why were divorces difficult to get in the Byzantine Empire?

6. **Analyze** What important service did Byzantine writers provide to the rest of the world? Explain its significance.

7. **Persuasive Writing** Which civilization do you think was the most advanced—that of the Greeks, the Romans, or the Byzantines? Write a speech explaining your answer.

Section 1 Life in Ancient Rome

Vocabulary
vault
satire
ode
anatomy
Forum
gladiator
paterfamilias
rhetoric

Focusing on the Main Ideas
- In addition to their own developments in science and engineering, Roman artists and writers borrowed many ideas from the Greeks. *(page 303)*
- The rich and poor had very different lives in the Roman Empire, as did men and women. *(page 306)*

A Roman family at ▶ the dinner table

Section 2 The Fall of Rome

Vocabulary
plague
inflation
barter
reform

Focusing on the Main Ideas
- Poor leadership, a declining economy, and attacks by Germanic tribes weakened the Roman Empire. *(page 318)*
- Rome finally fell when invaders swept through the empire during the A.D. 400s. *(page 322)*
- Rome passed on many achievements in government, law, language, and the arts. *(page 325)*

Section 3 The Byzantine Empire

Vocabulary
mosaic
saint
regent

Focusing on the Main Ideas
- The Eastern Roman Empire grew rich and powerful as the Western Roman Empire fell. *(page 328)*
- The policies and reforms of Emperor Justinian and Empress Theodora helped make the Byzantine Empire strong. *(page 329)*
- The Byzantines developed a rich culture based on Roman, Greek, and Christian ideas. *(page 332)*

Review Vocabulary

Match the definitions in the second column to the terms in the first column.

___ 1. plague   **a.** pictures made of many bits of colored glass or stone

___ 2. anatomy   **b.** rapidly increasing prices

___ 3. inflation   **c.** father of a family

___ 4. gladiator   **d.** emotional poem about life's ups and downs

___ 5. regent   **e.** study of the body's structure

___ 6. mosaic   **f.** a disease that spreads widely

___ 7. paterfamilias   **g.** a person who stands in for a ruler who cannot govern

___ 8. ode   **h.** a warrior who fought animals and people in public arenas

Review Main Ideas

Section 1 • Life in Ancient Rome

9. What did the Romans borrow from the Greeks? What did they develop on their own?

10. What were the lives of the rich and poor like in Rome?

Section 2 • The Fall of Rome

11. What weakened the Roman Empire?

12. What caused the fall of Rome in the A.D. 400s?

Section 3 • The Byzantine Empire

13. What policies and reforms helped make the Byzantine Empire strong?

14. What different groups of people contributed to the Byzantine culture?

Critical Thinking

15. **Cause and Effect** Why did Alaric's capture of Rome shock the Roman people?

16. **Predict** What do you think would have happened if Theodosius had not divided the Roman Empire?

Review

Reading Skill   Responding and Reflecting   **Your Point of View**

17. Read the following paragraph from page 330. Write at least five things you might reflect on as you read this information.

> In A.D. 532 Theodora helped save Justinian's throne. Angry taxpayers threatened to overthrow Justinian and stormed the palace. Justinian's advisers urged him to leave Constantinople. Theodora, however, told him to stay and fight. Justinian took Theodora's advice. He stayed in the city and crushed the uprising.

To review this skill, see pages 300–301.

Geography Skills

Study the map below and answer the following questions.

18. **Place** Which areas were conquered by Justinian's military?

19. **Human/Environment Interaction** Why do you think Justinian decided to conquer lands to the west of his empire?

20. **Movement** What made it difficult for the Byzantine Empire to hold on to Justinian's conquests?

NATIONAL GEOGRAPHIC

Byzantine Empire

ATLANTIC OCEAN

SPAIN

ITALY

Corsica

Rome

Constantinople

Sardinia

Carthage

Sicily

Crete

Mediterranean Sea

Danube R.

0°   10°E   20°E

40°N

30°N

0   500 mi.

0   500 km

Lambert Azimuthal Equal-Area projection

KEY

Byzantine Empire before Justinian, A.D. **527**

Byzantine Empire after Justinian's conquests, A.D. **565**

N W E S

Read to Write

21. **Descriptive Writing** Suppose you are a newspaper reporter living in the time of the Roman Empire. Write a front-page article about the slave revolt in 73 B.C., the content of Theodosius's will, or the removal of Romulus Augustulus. Remember to include a headline.

22. **Using Your FOLDABLES** Use the information you wrote in your foldable to create a brief study guide for the chapter. For each section, your study guide should include at least five questions that focus on the main ideas.

History Online

Self-Check Quiz To help you prepare for the Chapter Test, visit jat.glencoe.com

Linking Past and Present

23. **Analyzing** In the chapter, you learned that the culture of the Byzantine Empire was greatly influenced by the Romans and Greeks, as well as the Egyptian, Slavic, and Persian cultures. Think about the culture of the United States, in which many cultures have blended. Work with a classmate to identify aspects of the U.S. culture that were originally part of other cultures.

Building Citizenship Skills

24. **Analyzing** Growing political and social problems helped set the stage for Rome's final fall. Traditional Roman ideas of duty, courage, and honesty lost their importance. Why do you think duty, courage, and honesty are important in keeping a society and political system strong?

Primary Source Analyze

The Roman Empire did have some laws to prevent the extreme abuse of slaves.

"At the present time neither Roman citizens nor any other persons who are under the rule of the Roman people are permitted to treat their slaves with excessive and baseless [reasonless] cruelty. . . . A man who kills his own slave without cause is ordered to be held just as liable as one who kills another's slave."

—Gaius, "Legislation Against the Abuse of Slaves"

DBQ Document-Based Questions

25. How does this law pertain to people passing through the empire?

26. How does this statement leave a loophole in the regulation of abuse against slaves?

The Rise of Christianity

▼ Mount of the Beatitudes on the Sea of Galilee in Israel

When & Where?

A.D. 50	A.D. 400	A.D. 750	A.D. 1100
A.D. 30 Jesus preaches in Galilee and Judaea	**A.D. 312** Constantine accepts Christianity	**A.D. 726** Emperor Leo III removes icons from churches	**A.D. 1054** Orthodox and Catholic Churches separate

Chapter Preview

While the Romans built their empire, a group called the Christians spread a new religion called Christianity. Read this chapter to find out how Christianity grew to become one of the major influences on European civilization.

 View the Chapter 10 video in the *World History: Journey Across Time* Video Program.

History Online

Chapter Overview Visit jat.glencoe.com **for a preview of Chapter 10.**

Section 1 The First Christians

After the Romans conquered Judah, some Jews opposed Rome peacefully, while others rebelled. During that period, Jesus of Nazareth began preaching a message of love and forgiveness. His life and teachings led to the rise of Christianity.

Section 2 The Christian Church

In time, Christianity became the Roman Empire's official religion. Early Christians organized the church and collected the New Testament of the Bible.

Section 3 The Spread of Christian Ideas

Church and government worked closely together in the Byzantine Empire. Christians founded new communities and spread their faith through Europe.

FOLDABLES™
Study Organizer

Sequencing Information *Make this foldable to help you sequence information about the rise of Christianity.*

Step 1 *Fold a piece of paper from top to bottom.*

Step 2 *Then fold back each half to make quarter folds.*

This makes an accordian shape.

Step 3 *Unfold and label the time line as shown.*

The Rise of Christianity

Step 4 *Fill in important dates as you read like those shown.*

A.D. 30	The Rise of Christianity	Jesus begins to preach
A.D. 64		Romans persecute Christians
A.D. 312		Constantine's conversion
A.D. 726		Emperor Leo III removes icons

Reading and Writing *As you read the chapter, write the important events that occurred in the rise of Christianity.*

Chapter 10

Reading Social Studies

Reading Skill

Sequence Clues

1 Learn It!

Looking for Sequence Clues

When we speak, read, or write, we automatically use clues to tell us what happened when. These clues are called sequence words, and they show us the order in which events occur.

Read the following passage about the spread of Christianity. Notice the highlighted sequence words or phrases.

> **After the fall of Rome, the people of Western Europe faced confusion and conflict. As a result, people were looking for order and unity. Christianity helped to meet this need. It spread rapidly into lands that had once been part of the Roman Empire.**
>
> *—from page 361*

Reading Tip

When you have trouble understanding the order in which things occur, create a rough time line to help you keep track of events as you read.

Now read the paragraph again and leave out the highlighted sequence words. Do you see how important they are in helping you understand what you are reading?

2 Practice It!
Finding Clue Words

Read this passage and write down any word or phrase that helps you recognize the sequence of events.

Read to Write
Look at the time line that appears at the bottom of page 342. Write a paragraph that uses sequence clues to describe when these events occurred.

Even with all of the hardships, Christianity spread. Over time it even began to draw people from all classes. After A.D. 250, many Romans grew tired of war and feared the end of the empire. They began to admire the faith and courage of the Christians. At the same time, many Christians started to accept the empire.

—*from pages 353–354*

The apostle Peter preaching ▼

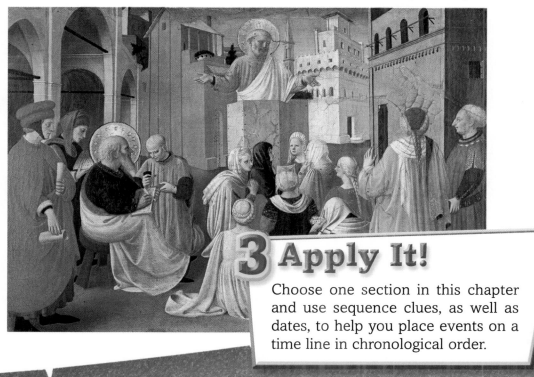

3 Apply It!

Choose one section in this chapter and use sequence clues, as well as dates, to help you place events on a time line in chronological order.

The First Christians

Get Ready to Read!

What's the Connection?
You learned that the Romans ruled many areas of the Mediterranean. In one of these areas, Judaea, a new religion, Christianity, began.

Focusing on the Main Ideas
- Roman rule of Judaea led some Jews to oppose Rome peacefully, while others rebelled. *(page 343)*

- Jesus of Nazareth preached of God's love and forgiveness. He was eventually crucified and then reported to have risen from the dead. *(page 344)*

- Jesus' life and a belief in his resurrection led to a new religion called Christianity. *(page 348)*

Locating Places
Jerusalem (juh•ROO•suh•luhm)
Judaea (ju•DEE•uh)
Nazareth (NA•zuh•ruhth)
Galilee (GA•luh•LEE)

Meeting People
Jesus (JEE•zuhs)
Peter
Paul

Building Your Vocabulary
messiah (muh•SY•uh)
disciple (dih•SY•puhl)
parable (PAR•uh•buhl)
resurrection (REH•zuh•REHK•shuhn)
apostle (uh•PAH•suhl)
salvation (sal•VAY•shuhn)

Reading Strategy
Summarizing Information Complete a diagram like the one below showing the purposes of early Christian churches.

Purposes of Churches

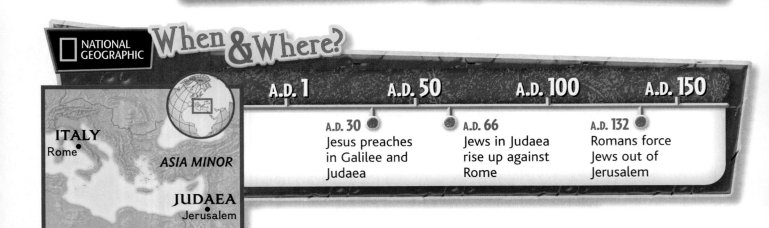

NATIONAL GEOGRAPHIC When & Where?

ITALY
Rome

ASIA MINOR

JUDAEA
Jerusalem

A.D. 1   A.D. 50   A.D. 100   A.D. 150

A.D. 30
Jesus preaches in Galilee and Judaea

A.D. 66
Jews in Judaea rise up against Rome

A.D. 132
Romans force Jews out of Jerusalem

The Jews and the Romans

Main Idea Roman rule of Judaea led some Jews to oppose Rome peacefully, while others rebelled.

Reading Focus Suppose you were separated from your home and could not easily return to it. What effect might this have on you? Read to learn how the Jews were forced to leave their capital city.

As you learned earlier, during the 900s B.C., two great kings, David and Solomon, united the Israelites and created the kingdom of Israel. Its capital was **Jerusalem** (juh•ROO•suh•luhm). This unity did not last long, however. Israel divided into two kingdoms: Israel and Judah. These small kingdoms were later taken over by more powerful neighbors. Israel was destroyed, and its people scattered. But the Jews, the people of Judah, survived.

Roman Rule

In 63 B.C. the Romans took over Judah. At first, they ruled through Jewish kings. Then, in A.D. 6, Emperor Augustus turned Judah into a Roman province called **Judaea** (ju•DEE•uh). Instead of a king, a Roman governor called a procurator (PRAH•kyuh•RAY•tuhr) ruled the new province.

The Jews argued among themselves over what to do about the Romans. Some favored working with the Romans. Others opposed Roman rule by closely following Jewish traditions. Still others turned their backs on the Romans. They settled in isolated areas and shared their belongings.

The Jews Rebel

Some Jews believed that they should fight the Romans and take back control of their kingdom. These people, called Zealots, convinced many Jews to take up arms against the Romans in A.D. 66. The rebellion was brutally crushed. The Romans destroyed the temple and killed thousands of Jews. A Jewish general named Josephus (joh•SEE•fuhs) fought in the war but later sided with the Romans. He wrote about the horrors of Jerusalem's fall in his work *History of the Jewish War.*

The Jews rebelled again in A.D. 132 and were again defeated. This time the Romans forced all Jews to leave Jerusalem and banned them from ever returning to the city. Saddened by the loss of Jerusalem, many Jews found new homes elsewhere.

By A.D. 700, the Jews had set up communities as far west as Spain and as far east as central Asia. In later centuries, they settled throughout Europe and the Americas. In their scattered communities, the Jews kept their faith alive by studying and following their religious laws.

Reading Check **Explain** Why did many Jews leave Judaea after the A.D. 132 revolt?

These ruins are of the mountaintop Jewish fortress at Masada in Israel. Jewish rebels were defeated by Roman troops here in A.D. 73. *What were the Jewish rebels called?*

The Life of Jesus

Main Idea **Jesus of Nazareth preached of God's love and forgiveness. He was eventually crucified and then reported to have risen from the dead.**

Reading Focus If you could give someone advice on how to behave, what would you tell them? Why? Read to learn how Jesus thought people should behave.

During Roman times, many Jews hoped that God would send a **messiah** (muh•SY•uh), or deliverer. This leader would help them win back their freedom. The Israelite prophets had long ago predicted that a messiah would come. Many Jews expected the messiah to be a great king, like David. They thought the messiah would restore the past glories of the Israelite kingdom.

A few decades before the first Jewish revolt against Rome, a Jew named **Jesus** (JEE•zuhs) left his home in **Nazareth** (NA•zuh•ruhth) and began preaching. From about A.D. 30 to A.D. 33, Jesus traveled throughout Judaea and **Galilee** (GA•luh•LEE), the region just north of Judaea, preaching his ideas. Crowds gathered to hear him preach. He soon assembled a small band of 12 close followers called **disciples** (dih•SY•puhlz).

What Did Jesus Teach? According to the Christian Bible, Jesus preached that God was coming soon to rule the world. He urged people to turn from their sins. He also told them that following Jewish religious laws was not as important as having a relationship with God, whom Jesus referred to as his Father.

The main points of Jesus' message are given in a group of sayings known as the Sermon on the Mount. In them, Jesus made it clear that a person had to love and forgive

The Teachings of Jesus

▼ Jesus traveled throughout the regions of Judaea and Galilee, preaching to all who would listen to his religious message. In the Sermon on the Mount, illustrated below, Jesus described God's love and how to be a good person. At right, Jesus is shown as the Good Shepherd, a popular image in early Christian art. *What did Jesus teach about Jewish religious laws?*

from the heart and not just go through the motions of following religious laws. Among Jesus' sayings were "Blessed are the merciful, for they will obtain mercy" and "Blessed are the peacemakers, for they will be called the children of God."

Jesus told his listeners to love and forgive each other because God loves and forgives people. According to Jesus, God's command was simple. He repeated the age-old Jewish teaching: "Love the Lord your God with all your heart and with all your soul and with all your mind and with all your strength." Jesus also stressed another teaching: "Love your neighbor as yourself." Jesus' message of love and forgiveness helped shape the values many people in Europe and America hold today.

To present his message, Jesus often used **parables** (PAR•uh•buhlz). These were stories that used events from everyday life to express spiritual ideas. In the story of the Prodigal (wasteful) Son, Jesus told how a father welcomed back his reckless son with open arms. He forgave his son's mistakes. In another parable, he told of a shepherd who left his flock unguarded to go after one lost sheep. Both stories taught that God forgives mistakes and wants all people to turn away from bad deeds and be saved.

The parable of the Good Samaritan is one of the best known. In this story, a man is beaten by robbers. A priest and another religious leader refuse to help the injured man. However, a Samaritan, a member of a group looked down upon by Jesus' listeners, stops to help the victim. He treats the man's wounds and pays for his stay at an inn. Jesus asked his followers, "Which man do you think truly showed love to his neighbor?"

▼ Jesus used stories, called parables, to describe correct behaviors to his followers. The parables of the Prodigal Son (below) and the Good Samaritan (right) are shown here. *What lesson was taught by the parable of the Prodigal Son?*

Biography

JESUS OF NAZARETH
c. 6 B.C.–A.D. 30

▲ Jesus entering Jerusalem

Much of what we know about Jesus, whose life and teachings established the Christian religion, is based on accounts found in the Bible. According to the Bible, Jesus' birth was guided by God. An angel visited Mary, Jesus' mother, to tell her she was going to have a baby. The angel told Mary her baby would be the Son of God. An angel also visited Joseph, Mary's fiancé, and instructed him to marry her.

Jesus was humbly born in a stable, beside barn animals, in the town of Bethlehem. Mary and Joseph had traveled there to take part in a census ordered by the Romans. Shepherds and wise men, possibly princes from neighboring kingdoms, followed a brightly shining star to honor Jesus in the stable. Christmas is a celebration of Jesus' birth.

> **"I am the light that has come into the world."**
> –Jesus of Nazareth, John 12:46

The Bible tells very little about the middle years of Jesus' life. He grew up in Nazareth, a small town in Galilee, where he learned the carpenter's trade from Joseph. Later in life, Jesus set out to share his religious teachings. At this point, the Bible provides many stories of Jesus' travels and the miracles he performed. The accounts of Jesus' miracles, such as giving a blind man sight, raising a man from the dead, and calming a storm at sea, brought many followers to his teachings. When Jesus entered Jerusalem the week before his death, he was greeted by cheering crowds. One of Jesus' closest followers, however, betrayed him and turned him over to Roman authorities. Jesus was questioned by Jewish and Roman officials and sentenced to death. Soon afterwards, reports that he had risen from the dead would lead to a new religion—Christianity.

◀ An early depiction of Jesus on his throne

Then and Now

What event does Christmas celebrate? What aspects of Christmas today are not related to its traditional meaning?

What Is the Crucifixion? Jesus and his message drew strong responses from people. His followers called attention to instances in which they believed he healed the sick and performed other miracles. They said he was the long-awaited messiah. Other Jews disagreed and said he was a deceiver. Above all, Judaea's Roman rulers feared the effects of Jesus' preaching. A person who could spark such strong reactions might threaten law and order.

About A.D. 33, Jesus went to Jerusalem to celebrate Passover, an important Jewish holiday. There he was greeted by large, cheering crowds. In an event known as the Last Supper, Jesus celebrated the holiday with his 12 disciples. Fearing trouble, leaders in Jerusalem arrested Jesus. Jesus was charged with treason, or disloyalty to the government. As punishment, Jesus was crucified, or hung from a cross until dead. This was Rome's way of punishing political rebels and lower-class criminals.

After Jesus' death, his followers made a startling claim. They announced that Jesus had risen from the dead. Christian tradition states that Mary Magdalene, one of Jesus' followers, was the first to see Jesus alive again. Others, including Jesus' disciples, reported seeing him as well. The disciples also pointed to his empty tomb as proof that Jesus was the messiah. These reports of Jesus' **resurrection** (REH•zuh•REHK•shuhn), or rising from the dead, led to a new religion called Christianity.

✓ **Reading Check** **Describing** What were the main ideas Jesus taught during his life?

▲ According to the Bible, just before his death, Jesus gathered his disciples together for a meal known as the Last Supper. *Why did the Romans fear Jesus?*

The First Christians

Main Idea Jesus' life and a belief in his resurrection led to a new religion called Christianity.

Reading Focus Have you ever read news stories about people sacrificing their lives to help others? Read to learn about the sacrifice Christians believe Jesus made for everyone.

Jesus' disciples began to spread the message of Jesus and his resurrection. Small groups in the Greek-speaking cities of the eastern Mediterranean accepted this message. Some were Jews, but others were not.

Primary Source

Sermon on the Mount

Jesus encouraged his disciples with the Sermon on the Mount.

"Happy are you when men insult you and persecute you and tell all kinds of evil lies against you because you are my followers. Be happy and glad, for a great reward is kept for you in heaven. This is how the prophets who lived before you were persecuted."

—Matthew 5:11–12

▲ Jesus and his followers

DBQ Document-Based Question

Why does Jesus tell his followers to ignore—even rejoice in—persecution?

Those who accepted Jesus Christ and his teachings became known as Christians. The word *Christ* comes from *Christos,* the Greek word for "messiah."

The early Christians formed churches, or communities for worship and teaching. They met in people's houses, many of which were owned by women. At these gatherings, Christians prayed and studied the Hebrew Bible. They also shared in a ritual meal like the Last Supper to remember Jesus' death and resurrection.

Who Were Peter and Paul? Apostles

(uh•PAH•suhlz), or early Christian leaders who helped set up churches and spread the message of Jesus, played an important role in the growth of Christianity. Perhaps the two most important were **Peter** and **Paul.**

Simon Peter was a Jewish fisher. He had known Jesus while he was alive and had been one of the original 12 people Jesus had called to preach his message. Christian tradition states that he went to Rome after the death of Jesus and helped set up a church there. Today, the leader of Catholic Christians resides in Rome.

Paul of Tarsus was another important Christian leader. He was a well-educated Jew and a Roman citizen. Paul at first hated Christianity and persecuted Christians in Jerusalem. The chief Jewish priest in Jerusalem then sent him to Damascus (duh•MAS•kuhs), a city in Syria, to stop Christians in the city from spreading their ideas.

While on the road to Damascus, Paul had an unusual experience. According to Christian belief, he saw a great light and heard Jesus' voice. Paul became a Christian on the spot. He spent the rest of his life spreading Jesus' message. Paul traveled widely. He founded churches throughout the eastern Mediterranean.

Biography

PAUL OF TARSUS
c. A.D. 10–65

▲ Paul of Tarsus

Without the apostle Paul, Christianity might not have become one of the world's most widely accepted religions. It was Paul who spread the word about Jesus to the Gentiles, or non-Jews, and helped Jesus gain acceptance as the messiah.

Paul was a Jew from Tarsus, a major city in Asia Minor. His father was a Roman citizen, and his family followed the laws and rules of the Pharisees—a Jewish group that stressed the need to follow Jewish laws. His parents named their son Saul after the first king of the Jews. The first trade Saul learned was tent making. Around age 10, he was sent to Jerusalem to attend a school under the direction of the famed Pharisee teacher Gamaliel. Saul received a well-rounded education. He learned the language and history of the Romans, Jews, and Greeks.

When Saul was in his twenties, he opposed and persecuted Christians and their newly formed church in Jerusalem. He was on his way to Damascus in Syria to find and arrest Christians there when a vision of Jesus led him to accept Christianity.

Saul began using the Latin name Paul after his conversion to Christianity. He traveled extensively, preaching and writing to Gentiles. He also wrote many important letters, known as epistles, to churches in Rome, Greece, and Asia Minor. These letters are included in the Christian Bible.

Paul convinced many people that if they died as Christians, they would have eternal life. Even though Paul's only meeting with Jesus was supposedly in his vision, Paul visited more places and preached to more people than most of the apostles who had known Jesus in person. Paul worked as a missionary for around 35 years. He was probably killed when the Roman emperor Nero ordered that Christians in Rome be arrested and put to death.

> **"I showed how you should work to help everyone."**
> —Paul, Acts 20:35

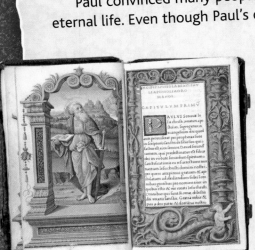
▲ A book containing the teachings of Paul

Then and Now

Can you think of any groups of people in today's world who are persecuted for their beliefs?

▲ This painting shows the apostle Peter preaching to followers. *What was the role of apostles in the spread of Christianity?*

What Do Christians Believe?
From the beginning, Christians taught that Jesus was the Son of God and had come to save people. By accepting Jesus and his teachings, people could gain **salvation** (sal•VAY•shuhn), or be saved from sin and allowed to enter heaven. Like Jesus, after death they would be resurrected and join God in everlasting life.

Because of their faith in Jesus, Christians began to understand God in a new way. Like the Jews, Christians believed in the God of Israel and studied the Hebrew Bible. However, most Christians came to believe that the one God existed in three persons: Father, Son, and Holy Spirit. This idea became known as the Trinity, which comes from a word meaning "three."

✓ **Reading Check** **Identify** Who were Peter and Paul, and why were they important?

Study Central™ Need help with the material in this section? Visit jat.glencoe.com

Section 1 Review

Reading Summary
Review the Main Ideas

• While some Jews opposed Roman rule peacefully, others revolted, leading the Romans to banish Jews from Jerusalem.

• Jesus preached of God's love and forgiveness and gained many followers. After his crucifixion, his followers claimed that he rose from the dead.

• A new religion, Christianity, based on the teachings of Jesus and a belief in his resurrection, spread in the Mediterranean region.

What Did You Learn?

1. What are parables, and why did Jesus use them?

2. What do Christians believe they will gain by accepting Jesus and his teachings?

Critical Thinking

3. **Summarize Information** Draw a diagram like the one below. Add details to identify some of the Christian beliefs taught by Jesus.

Christian Beliefs

4. **Analyze** Why were the Jews looking for a messiah? Did Jesus fulfill most Jews' expectations for a messiah? Explain.

5. **Explain** Why was Jesus put to death?

6. **Expository Writing** Write an essay comparing Christianity to one or more religions that you have already learned about.

7. **Reading** Sequence Clues List five words in this section that serve as sequence clues. Explain how each word provided clues as to when an event occurred.

Section

2

The Christian Church

Get Ready to Read!

What's the Connection?

In the last section, you read about the origins of Christianity. In this section, you will discover how Christianity grew and was organized.

Focusing on the **Main Ideas**

• Christianity won many followers and eventually became the official religion of the Roman Empire. **(page 352)**

• Early Christians set up a church organization and explained their beliefs. **(page 355)**

Locating Places
Rome

Meeting People
Constantine (KAHN•stuhn•TEEN)
Helena (HEHL•uh•nuh)
Theodosius (THEE•uh•DOH•shuhs)

Building Your Vocabulary
persecute (PURH•sih•KYOOT)
martyr (MAHR•tuhr)
hierarchy (HY•uhr•AHR•kee)
clergy (KLUHR•jee)
laity (LAY•uh•tee)
doctrine (DAHK•truhn)
gospel (GAHS•puhl)
pope

Reading Strategy
Organizing Information Complete a diagram like the one below showing reasons for the growth of Christianity.

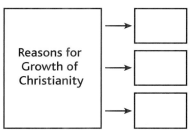

Reasons for Growth of Christianity →

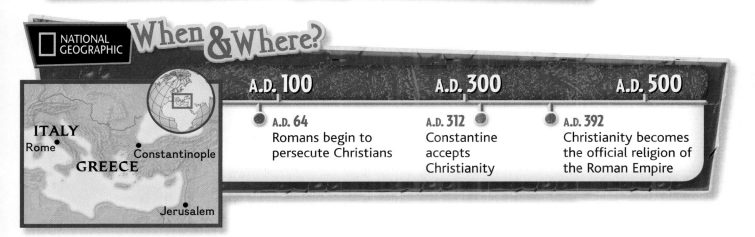

NATIONAL GEOGRAPHIC **When & Where?**

ITALY
Rome
GREECE
Constantinople
Jerusalem

A.D. 100 — A.D. 300 — A.D. 500

A.D. 64 Romans begin to persecute Christians

A.D. 312 Constantine accepts Christianity

A.D. 392 Christianity becomes the official religion of the Roman Empire

A Growing Faith

Main Idea Christianity won many followers and eventually became the official religion of the Roman Empire.

Reading Focus Why do you think people like to belong to a community? Read to learn about early Christian communities.

During the 100 years after Jesus' death, Christianity won followers throughout the Roman world. The empire itself helped spread Christian ideas. The peace and order established by **Rome** allowed people to travel in safety. Christians used well-paved Roman roads to carry their message from place to place. Since most of the empire's people spoke either Latin or Greek, Christians could talk with them directly.

Why did Christianity attract followers? First, the Christian message gave meaning to people's lives. Rome's official religion urged people to honor the state and the emperor. Christianity instead reached out to the poor and the powerless who led very hard lives. It offered hope and comfort.

Second, the ideas of Christianity were familiar to many Romans. They already knew about other eastern Mediterranean religions. Like these faiths, Christianity

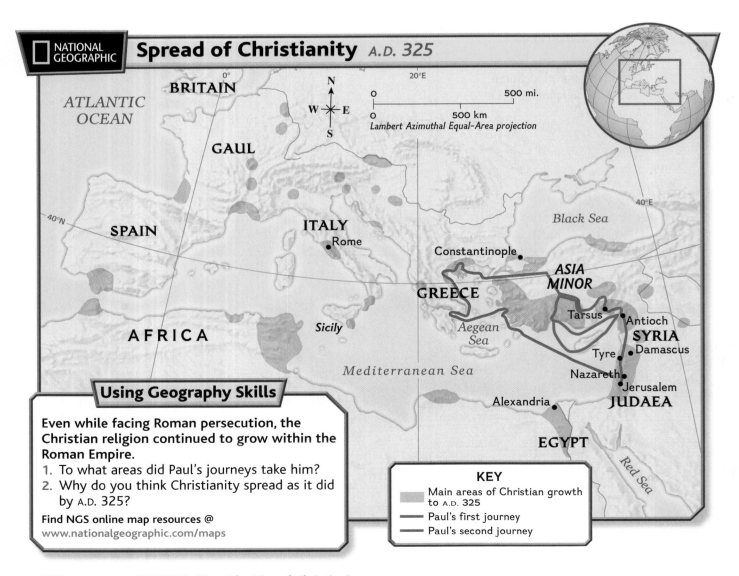

NATIONAL GEOGRAPHIC

Spread of Christianity A.D. 325

Lambert Azimuthal Equal-Area projection

Using Geography Skills

Even while facing Roman persecution, the Christian religion continued to grow within the Roman Empire.

1. To what areas did Paul's journeys take him?
2. Why do you think Christianity spread as it did by A.D. 325?

Find NGS online map resources @
www.nationalgeographic.com/maps

KEY

- Main areas of Christian growth to A.D. 325
- Paul's first journey
- Paul's second journey

appealed to the emotions and promised happiness after death.

Finally, Christianity gave people the chance to be part of a caring group. Within their churches, Christians not only worshiped together but helped each other. They took care of the sick, the elderly, widows, and orphans. Many women found that Christianity offered them new roles. They ran churches from their homes, spread Jesus' message, and helped care for those in need.

How Did the Romans Treat Christians?
Over time, Roman officials began to see the Christians as a threat to the government. All people in the empire were usually allowed to worship freely, but the Romans expected everyone to honor the emperor as a god. Christians, like the Jews, refused to do this. They claimed that only God could be worshiped. Christians also refused to serve in the army or hold public office. They criticized Roman festivals and games. As a result, the Romans saw the Christians as traitors who should be punished.

In A.D. 64 the Roman government began to **persecute** (PURH•sih•KYOOT), or mistreat, Christians. At this time, the emperor Nero accused Christians of starting a terrible fire that burned much of Rome. Christianity was made illegal, and many Christians were killed.

Other persecutions followed. During these difficult times, many Christians became **martyrs** (MAHR•tuhrz), people willing to die rather than give up their beliefs. In Rome, because of their beliefs, Christians were forced to bury their dead in catacombs, or underground burial places.

Even with all of the hardships, Christianity spread. Over time it even began to draw people from all classes. After A.D. 250, many Romans grew tired of war

The Way It Was

Focus on Everyday Life

Christian Catacombs Christians believed in resurrection, the idea that the body would one day reunite with the soul. For this reason, they would not allow their dead bodies to be burned, which was the Roman custom. Also, Roman law did not allow bodies to be buried aboveground. Therefore, starting in the A.D. 100s, Christians buried their dead beneath the city of Rome in a series of dark, cold, stench-filled tunnels called catacombs.

Each tunnel was about 8 feet (2.4 m) high and less than 3 feet (1 m) wide. Bodies were stacked in slots along the sides of the tunnels. The catacomb walls were painted with images from the Bible or from Greek or Roman mythology.

More than five million bodies were buried under Roman streets and buildings. Many of the Christians buried there were martyrs who had been killed for their beliefs.

◄ Christian catacombs in Rome

Connecting to the Past
1. Why did Christians bury their dead in catacombs?
2. What skills do you think would be necessary to dig and plan catacombs?

and feared the end of the empire. They began to admire the faith and courage of the Christians. At the same time, many Christians started to accept the empire.

Rome Adopts Christianity In the early A.D. 300s the emperor Diocletian carried out the last great persecution of Christians. Diocletian failed, and Roman officials began to realize that Christianity had grown too strong to be destroyed by force.

Then, in A.D. 312, the Roman emperor **Constantine** (KAHN•stuhn•TEEN) accepted Christianity. According to tradition, Constantine saw a flaming cross in the sky as he was about to go into battle. Written beneath the cross were the Latin words that meant "In this sign you will conquer."

Constantine won the battle and believed that the Christian God had helped him.

In A.D. 313 Constantine issued an order called the Edict of Milan. It gave religious freedom to all people and made Christianity legal. Constantine began giving government support to Christianity. With the help of his mother, **Helena** (HEHL•uh•nuh), he built churches in Rome and Jerusalem. He also let church officials serve in government and excused them from paying taxes.

Constantine's successor, the emperor **Theodosius** (THEE•uh•DOH•shuhs), made Christianity Rome's official religion in A.D. 392. At the same time, he outlawed other religions.

✓ **Reading Check** **Explain** Why did the Romans see the Christians as traitors?

Constantine's Conversion

▼Constantine led his troops to victory at the Battle of the Milvian Bridge after his conversion to Christianity. Constantine's enemies were defeated as a bridge made of boats collapsed under their weight. The *X* and *P* symbols on the shields represented the first two letters of the Greek word for *Christ*. *How did Constantine's Edict of Milan support Christianity?*

The Early Church

Main Idea **Early Christians set up a church organization and explained their beliefs.**

Reading Focus How can good organization make the difference between whether a plan or project fails or succeeds? Read how early Christians organized their churches and chose what to include in the Bible.

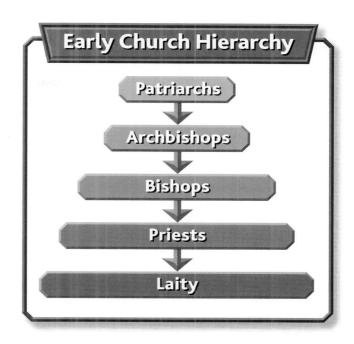

Early Church Hierarchy

Patriarchs → Archbishops → Bishops → Priests → Laity

In its early years, Christianity was loosely organized. Leaders like Paul traveled from one Christian community to another. They tried to unify the scattered groups. In their teaching, they emphasized that all the individual groups of Christians were part of one body called the church. Early Christians, however, faced a challenge. How were they to unite?

Organizing the Church The early Christians turned to a surprising model to organize the church—the Roman Empire itself. Like the Roman Empire, the church came to be ruled by a **hierarchy** (HY•uhr•AHR•kee). A hierarchy is an organization with different levels of authority.

The **clergy** (KLUHR•jee) were the leaders of the church. They had different roles from the **laity** (LAY•uh•tee), or regular church members. As the church's organization grew, women were not permitted to serve in the clergy. However, as members of the laity, they continued to care for the sick and needy.

By around A.D. 300, local churches were led by clergy called priests. Several churches formed a diocese (DY•uh•suhs), led by a bishop. A bishop in charge of a city diocese was sometimes also put in charge of an entire region. This made him an archbishop. The five leading archbishops became known as patriarchs (PAY•tree•AHRKS). They led churches in large cities and were in charge of large areas of territory.

The bishops explained Christian beliefs. They also took care of church business. From time to time, bishops met to discuss questions about Christian faith. Decisions they reached at these meetings came to be accepted as **doctrine** (DAHK•truhn), or official church teaching.

What Is the New Testament? Along with explaining Christian ideas, church leaders preserved a written record of the life of Jesus and put together a group of writings to help guide Christians. Jesus himself left no writings. His followers, however, passed on what they knew about him. By A.D. 300, four accounts of Jesus' life, teachings, and resurrection had become well-known. Christians believed these accounts were written by early followers of Jesus named Matthew, Mark, Luke, and John.

Each work was called a **gospel** (GAHS•puhl), which means "good news." Christians later combined the four gospels with the writings of Paul and other early Christian leaders. Together, these works form the New Testament of the Bible.

◀ Saint Matthew wrote one of the four gospels in the New Testament of the Bible. *What is the subject of the gospels of Matthew, Mark, Luke, and John?*

Other important writings also influenced early Christians. Scholars known as the Church Fathers wrote books to explain church teachings. One leading Church Father was a bishop in North Africa named Augustine. In his writings, Augustine defended Christianity against its opponents. He wrote *The City of God*—one of the first history books written from a Christian viewpoint. He also wrote a work called *Confessions*. It was an account of his personal journey to the Christian faith.

Who Is the Pope? As the church grew, the bishop of Rome, who was also the patriarch of the West, began to claim power over the other bishops. He believed that he had the authority of Peter, Jesus' leading disciple. Also, his diocese was in Rome, the capital of the empire.

By A.D. 600, the bishop of Rome had gained a special title—**pope**. The title comes from a Latin word meaning "father." Latin-speaking Christians accepted the pope as head of the church. Their churches became known as the Roman Catholic Church. Greek-speaking Christians would not accept the pope's authority over them. You will read in the next section about Christians in the Eastern Roman Empire and their form of Christianity.

✓ **Reading Check** **Identify** What are the gospels, and why are they significant?

History Online

Study Central™ Need help with the material in this section? Visit jat.glencoe.com

Section ❷ Review

Reading Summary
Review the Main Ideas

• After its followers suffered Roman persecution for several hundred years, Christianity became the official religion of the Roman Empire under Emperor Theodosius.

• As Christianity grew, the church became more united under a hierarchy of leaders. Christian writings were gathered into the New Testament of the Bible.

What Did You Learn?

1. What is a martyr?

2. What writings are included in the New Testament of the Bible?

Critical Thinking

3. **Organizing Information** Draw a chart like the one below. Fill in details on the effects each of the emperors listed had on the acceptance and growth of Christianity.

Roman Emperors		
Diocletian	Constantine	Theodosius

4. **Analyze** Following Jesus' death, why was Christianity able to attract followers?

5. **Analyze** Why do you think the Christian church came to be ruled by a hierarchy?

6. **Conclude** Do you think the Christian religion would have spread so quickly if it had developed in a time other than that of the Roman Empire?

7. **Writing Questions** Write five questions that a reporter who lived at the same time as Constantine might have asked him about Christianity.

Biography

SAINT AUGUSTINE
A.D. 354–430

▲ St. Augustine

Augustine was born in North Africa, in what is today the country of Algeria, to upper-class parents. His mother was Christian, but his father was not. His father sent him to the North African city of Carthage to attend good schools. Although he appeared to be an outstanding student, Augustine later said that he made many poor choices during his time at school.

When Augustine finished his education, he returned home to teach grammar. His mother again tried to convince him of the truth of Christianity, but he had joined a group of people who were critical of Christians. According to Augustine's writings, his mother was saddened until a vision promised her that her son would eventually accept Christianity.

Augustine moved to several cities, often teaching rhetoric (the art of speaking). He ended up in Milan, Italy. There he listened to Milan's bishop Ambrose preaching, not because he liked his messages but because he admired the way Ambrose spoke. Slowly, Augustine began to think about the messages of Ambrose's sermons. One day in A.D. 386, Augustine heard a child's voice say to him, "Take up and read." Nearby was a friend's copy of Paul's letters. He began to read the letters and decided that he believed the messages of Christianity. Augustine was soon baptized and founded a monastery—probably the first monastery in his area of North Africa. Later Augustine became a bishop. He recorded his life in A.D. 401 in the book *Confessions*.

> ### "Even when sad, I remember my times of joy."
> —Saint Augustine, *Confessions*

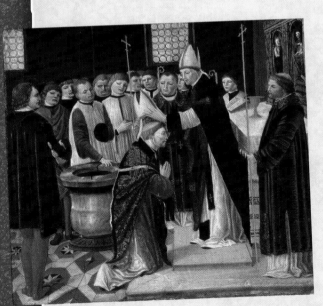

▲ St. Augustine being blessed by the pope

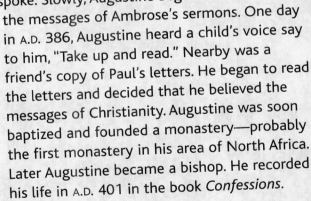

Then and Now

Do research to find out how Christianity has influenced the development of the United States. Provide examples of how it has affected government, society, and the economy.

The Spread of Christian Ideas

Get Ready to Read!

What's the Connection?

In the last section, you read about the growth of the Christian church. In this section, you will learn how the church underwent a great division and how Christians spread their faith to new lands.

Focusing on the Main Ideas

- Church and government worked closely together in the Byzantine Empire. *(page 359)*

- Christians founded new communities and spread their faith to various parts of Europe. *(page 361)*

Locating Places

Byzantine Empire
(BIH•zuhn•TEEN   EHM•PYR)
Britain (BRIH•tuhn)
Ireland (EYER•luhnd)

Meeting People

Charlemagne (SHAHR•luh•MAYN)
Basil (BAY•zuhl)
Benedict (BEH•nuh•DIHKT)
Cyril (SIHR•uhl)
Patrick

Building Your Vocabulary

icon (EYE•KAHN)
iconoclast (eye•KAH•nuh•KLAST)
excommunicate
(EHK•skuh•MYOO•nuh•KAYT)
schism (SIH•zuhm)
monastery (MAH•nuh•STEHR•ee)
missionary (MIH•shuh•NEHR•ee)

Reading Strategy

Organizing Information Create a diagram to show the reach of Christian missionaries.

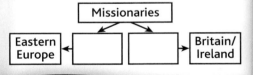

When & Where?

NATIONAL GEOGRAPHIC

IRELAND
BRITAIN
GAUL
SPAIN   ITALY   Constantinople
Rome•   •ASIA MINOR
GREECE
AFRICA   Jerusalem•

A.D. 400

c. A.D. 450
Patrick preaches Christianity in Ireland

A.D. 800

A.D. 726
Emperor Leo III removes icons from churches

A.D. 1200

A.D. 1054
Eastern Orthodox and Roman Catholic Churches separate

The Byzantine Church

Main Idea Church and government worked closely together in the Byzantine Empire.

Reading Focus In our country, religion and government are separated. Read to learn about the relationship between religion and government in the Byzantine Empire.

As you learned earlier, the church of Rome survived the fall of the Western Roman Empire. Its head, the pope, became the strongest leader in Western Europe. Under the pope, the Latin churches of the region became known as the Roman Catholic Church. In the East, however, the Roman Empire continued. It developed into the **Byzantine Empire** (BIH•zuhn•TEEN EHM•PYR). Like Roman Catholics in the West, the Byzantines developed their own form of Christianity. It was based on their Greek heritage and was known as the Eastern Orthodox Church.

Church and State
Church and government worked closely together in the Byzantine Empire. The Byzantines believed their emperor represented Jesus Christ on Earth. The emperor was crowned in a religious ceremony.

The emperor also chose the patriarch of Constantinople, the leading Church official in the Byzantine Empire. In this way, the emperor controlled the Church as well as the government. Byzantines believed that God wanted them to preserve and spread Christianity. All Church and government officials were united in this goal.

History Online
Web Activity Visit jat.glencoe.com and click on *Chapter 10—Student Web Activity* to learn more about the rise of Christianity.

Religious Arguments
Byzantines, from the emperor down to the poorest farmer, were very interested in religious matters. In homes and shops, they argued about religious questions. For example, Byzantines loved to discuss the exact relationship between Jesus and God.

In the A.D. 700s, a major dispute divided the Church in the Byzantine Empire. The argument was over the use of **icons** (EYE•KAHNZ). Icons are pictures or images of Jesus, Mary (the mother of Jesus), and the saints, or Christian holy people. Many Byzantines honored icons. They covered the walls of their churches with them. A few important icons were even believed to work miracles.

Some Byzantines, however, wanted an end to the use of icons. They thought that honoring them was a form of idol worship forbidden by God. Supporters of icons,

▼ This gold Byzantine incense burner is in the shape of a church. *What was the Christian church that developed in the Byzantine Empire called?*

▲ This icon on wood shows the archangel Gabriel, who served as a messenger for God according to the Bible. *What reasons were given to support the use of icons?*

Byzantine cross ▶

however, claimed that icons were symbols of God's presence in daily life. These images, they also said, helped explain Christianity to people.

Emperor Leo III did not approve of icons. In A.D. 726 he ordered all icons removed from the churches. Government officials who carried out his orders were known as **iconoclasts** (eye•KAH•nuh•KLASTS), or image breakers. We use this word today to mean someone who attacks traditional beliefs or institutions.

Most Byzantines, many church leaders, and even the pope in Rome opposed the emperor's order. In fact, the dispute over icons damaged ties between the churches of Rome and Constantinople. Over the next 100 years, the argument cooled, and the use of icons became accepted once again. They are still an important part of Eastern Orthodox religious practice.

Conflicts Between Churches Icons were not the only issue that caused bitterness between the churches of Constantinople and Rome. The most serious argument was about how churches were to be run. The pope claimed that he was the head of all Christian churches. The Byzantines did not accept the pope's claim. They believed the patriarch of Constantinople and other bishops were equal to the pope.

Making matters worse was the fact that each church sometimes refused to help the other when outsiders attacked. In the late A.D. 700s, the Byzantine emperor refused to help the pope when Italy was invaded. The pope turned instead to a Germanic people called the Franks for help. The Franks were Roman Catholics and loyal to the pope.

The pope was grateful to the Franks for stopping the invasion. In A.D. 800 he gave the Frankish king, **Charlemagne** (SHAHR•luh•MAYN), the title of emperor. This angered the Byzantines. They believed the leader of the Byzantines was the only true emperor.

This conflict pointed out the differences in how each church felt about relations with the government. In the Byzantine Empire, the emperor was in control, with church leaders respecting his wishes. In the West, however, the pope claimed both spiritual and political power. He often quarreled with kings over church and government affairs.

Finally, after centuries of tension, the pope and the patriarch of Constantinople took a drastic step in their ongoing feud. In A.D. 1054 they **excommunicated** (EHK•skuh•MYOO•nuh•KAY•tuhd) each other. Excommunication means to declare that a person or group no longer belongs to the church. This began a **schism** (SIH•zuhm), or separation, of the two most important branches of Christianity. The split between the Roman Catholic and Eastern Orthodox Churches has lasted to this day.

✓ **Reading Check** **Describe** How did church and government work together in the Byzantine Empire?

Christian Ideas Spread

Main Idea Christians founded new communities and spread their faith to various parts of Europe.

Reading Focus Have you ever tried to get someone to believe something you believe? Read to learn how Christians spread their faith across Europe.

After the fall of Rome, the people of Western Europe faced confusion and conflict. As a result, people were looking for order and unity. Christianity helped to meet this need. It spread rapidly into lands that had once been part of the Roman Empire. It

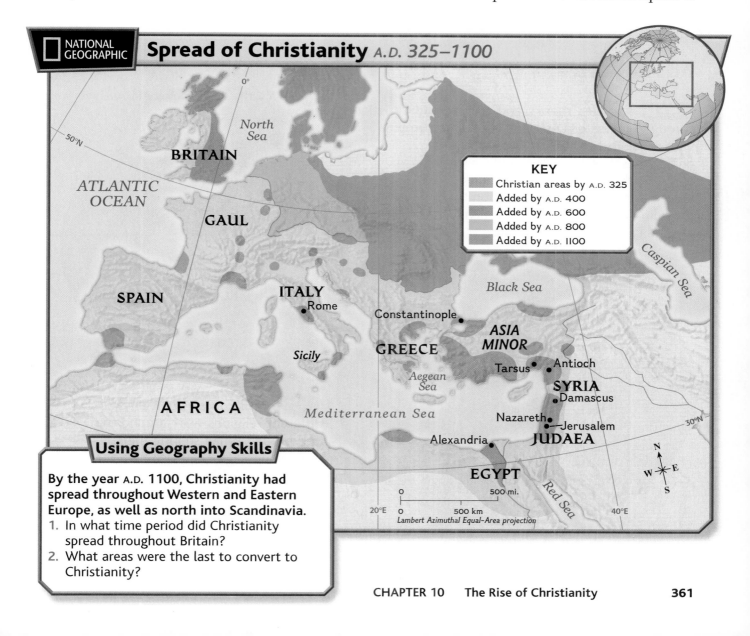

NATIONAL GEOGRAPHIC
Spread of Christianity A.D. 325–1100

KEY
- Christian areas by A.D. 325
- Added by A.D. 400
- Added by A.D. 600
- Added by A.D. 800
- Added by A.D. 1100

BRITAIN
North Sea
ATLANTIC OCEAN
GAUL
SPAIN
ITALY
Rome
Sicily
AFRICA
Mediterranean Sea
Constantinople
Black Sea
GREECE
Aegean Sea
ASIA MINOR
Tarsus
Antioch
SYRIA
Damascus
Nazareth
Jerusalem
JUDAEA
Alexandria
EGYPT
Red Sea
Caspian Sea
0°
50°N
30°N
20°E
40°E

0   500 mi.
0   500 km
Lambert Azimuthal Equal-Area projection

Using Geography Skills

By the year A.D. 1100, Christianity had spread throughout Western and Eastern Europe, as well as north into Scandinavia.
1. In what time period did Christianity spread throughout Britain?
2. What areas were the last to convert to Christianity?

also brought new ways of thinking and living to these areas.

What Are Monasteries? During the A.D. 300s, a new kind of religious group was born in the Eastern Roman Empire. Men called monks banded together in religious communities called **monasteries** (MAH•nuh• STEHR•eez). Some monasteries were built near cities, while others arose in isolated areas.

One of the earliest monks was Anthony, who founded a monastery in the deserts of Egypt. Monks tried to live a spiritual life apart from the temptations of the world. Many also tried to do good deeds and be examples of Christian living. Women soon followed the monks' example and formed communities of their own. These women were called nuns, and they lived in convents.

In the early A.D. 400s, Paula, a Roman widow, gave up her wealth and went to Palestine. There she built churches, a hospital, and a convent. Well-educated, Paula helped a scholar named Jerome translate the Bible from Hebrew and Greek into Latin.

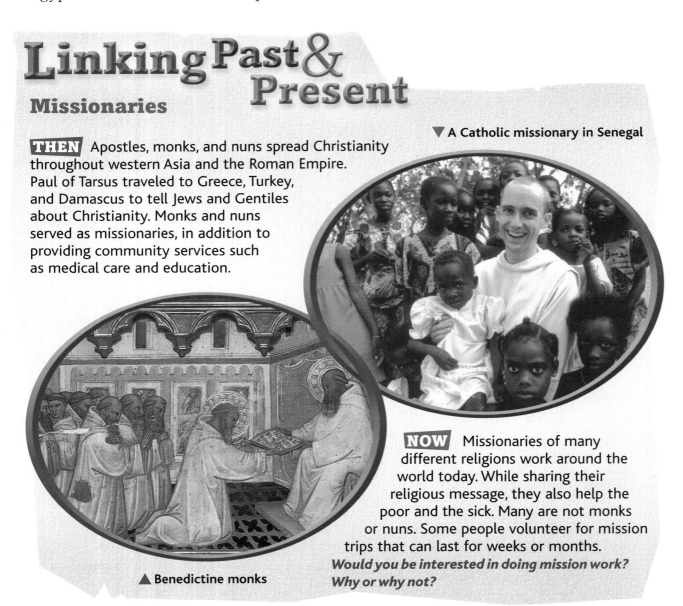

Linking Past & Present

Missionaries

THEN Apostles, monks, and nuns spread Christianity throughout western Asia and the Roman Empire. Paul of Tarsus traveled to Greece, Turkey, and Damascus to tell Jews and Gentiles about Christianity. Monks and nuns served as missionaries, in addition to providing community services such as medical care and education.

▼ **A Catholic missionary in Senegal**

NOW Missionaries of many different religions work around the world today. While sharing their religious message, they also help the poor and the sick. Many are not monks or nuns. Some people volunteer for mission trips that can last for weeks or months.
Would you be interested in doing mission work? Why or why not?

▲ **Benedictine monks**

A bishop called **Basil** (BAY•zuhl) drew up a list of rules for monks and nuns to follow. This list, called the Basilian (buh•ZIH•lee•uhn) Rule, became the model for Eastern Orthodox religious life.

In the West, another set of rules was followed. It was written by an Italian monk named **Benedict** (BEH•nuh•DIHKT). Monks who followed the Benedictine Rule gave up their belongings, lived simply, and spent their time in work and prayer. Like Basil's rule in the East, Benedict's rule became the model for monasteries and convents in the West. Basilian and Benedictine communities still exist today.

Monks and nuns began to play important roles in Roman Catholic and Eastern Orthodox life. They ran hospitals and schools and aided the poor. They also helped preserve Greek and Roman writings. One important duty was to serve as **missionaries** (MIH•shuh•NEHR•eez). Missionaries teach their religion to those who do not believe.

Christianity Spreads North
Among the most successful Byzantine missionaries were two brothers, **Cyril** (SIHR•uhl) and Methodius. They carried the Christian message to the Slavs, a people of Eastern Europe.

About A.D. 863, Cyril invented a new alphabet. He wanted to present the Christian message in the Slavic languages. He believed that people would be more interested in Christianity if they could worship and read the Bible in their own languages. The Cyrillic (suh•RIH•lihk) alphabet was based on Greek letters. It is still used today by Russians, Ukrainians, Serbs, and Bulgarians.

Eastern Orthodox missionaries traveled in northern lands that bordered the Byzantine Empire. At the same time, other missionaries from Rome were also busy.

The Cyrillic Alphabet

Cyrillic Letter	Written Name	English Sound
Б	beh	B
Г	gey	G
Ж	zheh	ZH
М	em	M
П	pey	P
С	ess	S
Ф	ef	F
Ч	cheh	CH

Cyril, a Byzantine missionary, developed the Cyrillic alphabet, part of which is shown above. *What peoples still use the Cyrillic alphabet today?*

Christianity Spreads West
In the West, Christian missionaries looked to the islands of **Britain** (BRIH•tuhn) and **Ireland** (EYER•luhnd). In the A.D. 300s, Roman soldiers in Britain were called home to defend the empire against Germanic invaders. When the Romans left, Britain was opened to attack by others.

Starting in the A.D. 400s, tribes from what are today Germany and Denmark invaded Britain. These people were the Angles and the Saxons. These groups united to become the Anglo-Saxons. They built settlements and set up several small kingdoms. The southern part of Britain soon became known as Angleland, or England.

While invading Britain, the Angles and Saxons pushed aside the people already living there. These people were called the Celts (KEHLTS). Some Celts fled to the mountainous regions of Britain. Others went to Ireland.

In the A.D. 400s, a priest named **Patrick** brought Christianity to Ireland. He set up a number of monasteries and churches. Over

the next centuries, Irish monks played an important role in preserving Christian and Roman learning.

The Anglo-Saxon kingdoms of Britain were slower than Ireland to accept the new religion. In A.D. 597 Pope Gregory I sent about 40 monks from Rome to take Christianity to England.

The missionaries converted Ethelbert, the ruler of the English kingdom of Kent. Ethelbert allowed the missionaries to build a church in his capital city of Canterbury. In about 100 years, most of England was Christian. Today, Canterbury is still an important center of Christianity in England.

✓ Reading Check **Analyze** Why were Basil and Benedict important?

◀ Gregory was a monk before he became Pope Gregory I in the late 500s. *How did Gregory impact Christianity in England?*

History Online
Study Central™ Need help with the material in this section? Visit jat.glencoe.com

Section ③ Review

Reading Summary
Review the Main Ideas

• In the Byzantine Empire, Christianity developed into the Eastern Orthodox Church, which in time split with the Roman Catholic Church in the West.

• Eastern Orthodox and Catholic missionaries helped spread Christianity to areas such as Eastern Europe, Ireland, and Britain.

What Did You Learn?

1. What are icons, and why was their use controversial?

2. What roles did monks and nuns play in Roman Catholic and Eastern Orthodox life?

Critical Thinking

3. **Cause and Effect** Draw a diagram to show the causes that led to the schism between the Roman Catholic and Eastern Orthodox Churches.

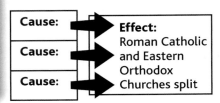

4. **Describe** How did Cyril make the Christian message available to the Slavs?

5. **Explain** What role did the Frankish king Charlemagne play in the schism between the Roman Catholic and Eastern Orthodox Churches?

6. **Analyze** Why do you think the Basilian and Benedictine Rules were put in place for monks?

7. **Expository Writing** Write a newspaper article that describes the spread of Christianity to Ireland and Britain.

Section 1 The First Christians

Vocabulary
messiah
disciple
parable
resurrection
apostle
salvation

Focusing on the Main Ideas
- Roman rule of Judaea led some Jews to oppose Rome peacefully, while others rebelled. *(page 343)*
- Jesus of Nazareth preached of God's love and forgiveness. He was eventually crucified and then reported to have risen from the dead. *(page 344)*
- Jesus' life and a belief in his resurrection led to a new religion called Christianity. *(page 348)*

Section 2 The Christian Church

Vocabulary
persecute
martyr
hierarchy
clergy
laity
doctrine
gospel
pope

Focusing on the Main Ideas
- Christianity won many followers and eventually became the official religion of the Roman Empire. *(page 352)*
- Early Christians set up a church organization and explained their beliefs. *(page 355)*

Saint Matthew ▶

Section 3 The Spread of Christian Ideas

Vocabulary
icon
iconoclast
excommunicate
schism
monastery
missionary

Focusing on the Main Ideas
- Church and government worked closely together in the Byzantine Empire. *(page 359)*
- Christians founded new communities and spread their faith to various parts of Europe. *(page 361)*

Review Vocabulary

1. Write a paragraph about the basic beliefs of Christianity using the following words.

   messiah   **salvation**

   resurrection   **gospel**

Write the vocabulary word that completes each sentence. Then write a sentence for each word not chosen.

   a. laity   e. parables

   b. missionaries   f. schism

   c. martyrs   g. apostle

   d. iconoclasts   h. pope

2. Jesus told symbolic stories called ___.

3. The bishop of Rome was called the ___.

4. The ___ in the Christian churches happened in A.D. 1054.

5. Christians who died for their faith were ___.

Review Main Ideas

Section 1 • The First Christians

6. How did Jews react to the Roman rule of Judaea?

7. On what is Christianity based?

Section 2 • The Christian Church

8. How did the Roman Empire eventually recognize Christianity?

9. What did early Christians do to organize their religion?

Section 3 • The Spread of Christian Ideas

10. What was the relationship between the church and the government in the Byzantine Empire?

11. How and where did the Christian religion spread?

Critical Thinking

12. **Analyze** Why do you think Jesus' followers remembered his teachings more when he used parables?

13. **Contrast** How did Jews and Christians differ in their belief about Jesus and his message?

14. **Predict** How would the growth of Christianity have been affected if the emperor Constantine had not become a Christian?

Review Reading Skill | Sequence Clues | Looking for Sequence Clues

Find the words in each of these sentences that help you identify the order in which events occur.

15. At the same time, many Christians started to accept the empire.

16. While on the road to Damascus, Paul had an unusual experience.

17. It is still used today by Russians, Ukrainians, Serbs, and Bulgarians.

18. The southern part of Britain soon became known as Angleland, or England.

19. After Jesus' death, his followers made a startling claim.

20. At first, they ruled through Jewish kings.

To review this skill, see pages 340–341.

Geography Skills

Study the map below and answer the following questions.

21. **Human/Environment Interaction** What geographical feature do you think most helped the spread of Christianity?

22. **Location** By A.D. 325, Christianity had spread to which continents?

23. **Region** Why do you think the cities of Judaea were all important centers of Christianity?

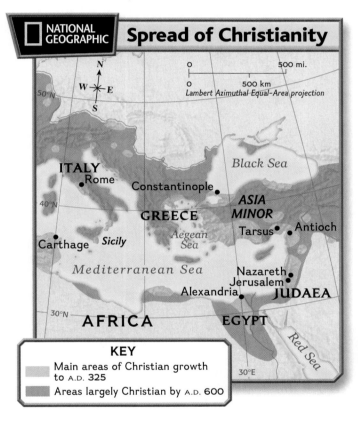

NATIONAL GEOGRAPHIC

Spread of Christianity

Lambert Azimuthal Equal-Area projection

500 mi.
500 km

ITALY
Rome
Constantinople
Black Sea
ASIA MINOR
GREECE
Tarsus
Antioch
Carthage Sicily
Aegean Sea
Mediterranean Sea
Nazareth
Jerusalem
Alexandria JUDAEA
AFRICA EGYPT
Red Sea

KEY
Main areas of Christian growth to A.D. 325
Areas largely Christian by A.D. 600

Read to Write

24. **Creative Writing** Rewrite the parable of the Good Samaritan as if the events took place in the present day. Read your parable to your classmates, and explain any changes in the meaning that occurred as you modernized it.

25. **Using Your** FOLDABLES Use your foldable to write three sentences that summarize the main ideas of this chapter. Share your sentences with the class, and listen to their sentences. Then vote for the one you think best summarizes the chapter.

Using Technology

26. **Reviewing Media** Use a video or DVD player to view one of the many films made about the life of Jesus or the impact of Christianity on the people of the Roman Empire. Some examples are *Ben Hur, The Robe, The Silver Chalice,* and *The Greatest Story Ever Told.* After you watch the movie, write a review of it. Based on what you have learned about the Roman Empire and Christianity, how accurate is the movie? How does it present Jesus, his early followers, the different Jewish groups in Judaea, and the Romans? Share your review with your classmates.

Linking Past and Present

27. **Recognizing Patterns** Conduct research to find out the number of people worldwide who are Christian, Jewish, Buddhist, Hindu, and Muslim. Also record the countries where people of each religion live. What do you notice about religions in different regions of the world?

Primary Source **Analyze**

Benedict wrote of the importance of keeping busy.

"Idleness [inactivity] is the enemy of the soul. Therefore should the brethren be occupied at stated times in manual labour, and at other fixed hours in sacred reading."

—Benedict, *The Rule*, "Of the Daily Manual Labour"

DBQ **Document-Based Questions**

28. What does Benedict mean when he says inactivity is "the enemy of the soul"?

29. What do you think probably follows these lines?

Islamic Civilization

Muyims gather around the Kaaba ▼
at the Great Mosque in Makkah.

**Muslims gather around the Kaaba ▼
at the Great Mosque in Makkah.**

NATIONAL GEOGRAPHIC **When & Who?**

A.D. 600	A.D. 900	1200	1500

c. A.D. 610
Muhammad receives prophetic call

A.D. 750
Abbasids overthrow Umayyads

c. 1100
Omar Khayyam writes the *Rubaiyat*

1258
Mongols burn Baghdad

c. 1375
Ibn Khaldun writes histories

Chapter Preview

A few hundred years after the beginnings of Christianity, another important religion arose in the Middle East: Islam. Followers of Islam conquered much of the Middle East, northern Africa, and part of Europe. They also made great cultural contributions to the world.

History Online

Chapter Overview Visit jat.glencoe.com **for a preview of Chapter 11.**

 View the Chapter 11 video in the *World History: Journey Across Time* Video Program.

 ## The Rise of Islam

The religion of Islam originated in Arabia. It was based on the teachings of Muhammad.

 ## Islamic Empires

Followers of Islam, called Muslims, conquered or converted people as they spread their faith throughout the Middle East and the Mediterranean.

 ## Muslim Ways of Life

Muslims were skilled traders and builders. They established large cities and made many advances in mathematics, science, and the arts.

Categorizing Information *Make the following foldable to organize information about the people and places of Islamic civilization.*

Step 1 *Collect two sheets of paper and place them about 1 inch apart.*

Keep the edges straight.

Step 2 *Fold down the top edges of the paper to form four tabs.*

This makes all the tabs the same size.

Step 3 *When all the tabs are the same size, crease the paper to hold the tabs in place and staple the sheets together. Turn the paper and label each tab as shown.*

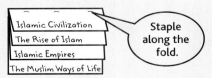

Islamic Civilization
The Rise of Islam
Islamic Empires
The Muslim Ways of Life

Staple along the fold.

Reading and Writing *As you read, use your foldable to write down what you learn about Islamic civilization. Write facts under each appropriate tab.*

Reading Skill

Main Idea

1 Learn It!

Main Ideas and Details

Main ideas are the most important ideas in a paragraph, section, or chapter. Supporting details are facts or examples that explain the main idea. Read the following paragraph from Section 3 and notice how the author explains the main idea.

> Several things explain the success of Muslim trade. When Muslim empires expanded, they spread the Arabic language. As a result, Arabic became the language of trade. Muslim rulers also made trade easier by providing merchants with coins.
>
> —*from page 388*

Reading Tip

Often, the first sentence in a paragraph will contain a main idea. Supporting details will come in following sentences.

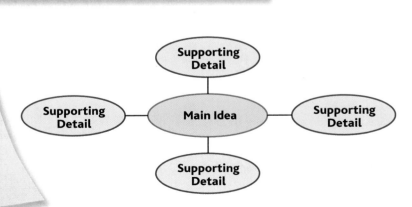

2 Practice It!

Using a Graphic Organizer

Read the following paragraph, and find the main idea and supporting details. Create a graphic organizer like the one that appears at the bottom of page 370.

Read to Write

"The famous Mogul ruler Akbar could not read, yet he set up a large library because he valued education, books, and art." Write a letter to Akbar telling him about your favorite book and why it should be included in his library.

Times were good in India under Akbar. Farmers and artisans produced more food and goods than the Indians needed. As a result, trade increased. Muslim merchants brought paper, gunpowder, and fine porcelain from China to India. In addition, Muslim architects introduced new building styles, such as the arch and dome, to India.

—*from page 386*

3 Apply It!

As you read Chapter 11, create your own graphic organizer to show the main idea and supporting details from at least one paragraph.

The Rise of Islam

Get Ready to Read!

What's the Connection?

Previously, you learned about early empires in southwest Asia. During the A.D. 600s, people called Arabs began a new empire in the region. The driving force behind their empire building was the religion of Islam.

Focus on the (Main Ideas)

• The deserts, coastline, and oases of Arabia helped shape the Arab way of life. *(page 373)*

• The prophet Muhammad brought the message of Islam to the people of Arabia. *(page 374)*

• The Quran provided guidelines for Muslims' lives and the governments of Muslim states. *(page 377)*

Locating Places
Makkah (MAH•kuh)
Kaaba (KAH•buh)
Madinah (mah•DEE•nah)

Meeting People
Bedouin (BEH•duh•wuhn)
Muhammad (moh•HAH•muhd)

Building Your Vocabulary
oasis (oh•AY•suhs)
sheikh (SHAYK)
caravan (KAR•uh•VAN)
Quran (koh•RAHN)

Reading Strategy
Organizing Information Use a diagram like the one below to identify the Five Pillars of faith.

Five Pillars

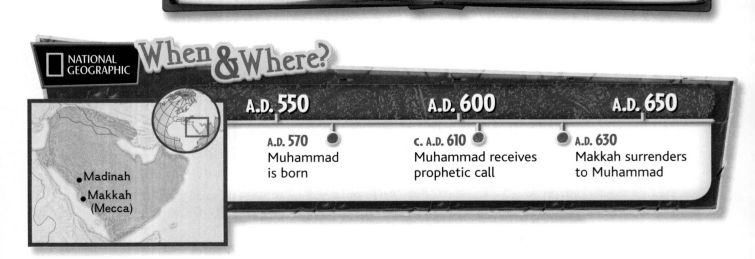

NATIONAL GEOGRAPHIC When & Where?

• Madinah
• Makkah (Mecca)

A.D. 550   A.D. 600   A.D. 650

A.D. 570
Muhammad is born

C. A.D. 610
Muhammad receives prophetic call

A.D. 630
Makkah surrenders to Muhammad

Daily Life in Early Arabia

Main Idea The deserts, coastline, and oases of Arabia helped shape the Arab way of life.

Reading Focus Do you ever think about how rainfall shapes your life? Read on to find out how lack of rain helped shape the Arabs' way of life.

Desert stretches over most of the Arabian peninsula. The heat is intense, and a sandstorm can blind any traveler. Water is found only at **oases** (oh AY seez), green areas fed by underground water. Not all of Arabia is dry, however. In the mountains of the southwest, enough rain falls to support plants such as juniper and olive trees.

To survive, early Arabs organized into tribes who were very loyal to one another. The head of the tribe was called a **sheikh** (SHAYK).

Who Are the Bedouins?

Some Arabs were desert herders. To water and graze their camels, goats, and sheep, they went from oasis to oasis. They were called **Bedouins** (BEH•duh•wuhnz).

Bedouins lived in tents and ate dried fruits and nuts. They drank the milk of their animals. Only rarely would they eat meat. Their animals were much too valuable to be used as food.

Trade and Towns

Many Arabs lived in villages where they farmed or raised animals. These villages were near oases or in the mountain valleys.

Some of the villagers were merchants who transported goods across the desert. To fend off attacks by Bedouins, many traveled in a **caravan** (KAR•uh•VAN), or group of traveling merchants and animals.

By about A.D. 500, Arabian merchants handled most trade between India and the Mediterranean Sea. As their trade grew, Arab merchants founded towns along the trade routes in Arabia. **Makkah** (MAH•kuh), also known as Mecca, became the largest and richest of them all. It was a crossroads for merchants, and it was also an important religious site. The holiest place in Arabia was in this city.

▼ Today, many Bedouins still roam the desert and live in tents. *Where did Bedouins graze their animals in the desert?*

▲ Bedouin woman making bread

The Middle East, C.A.D. 600

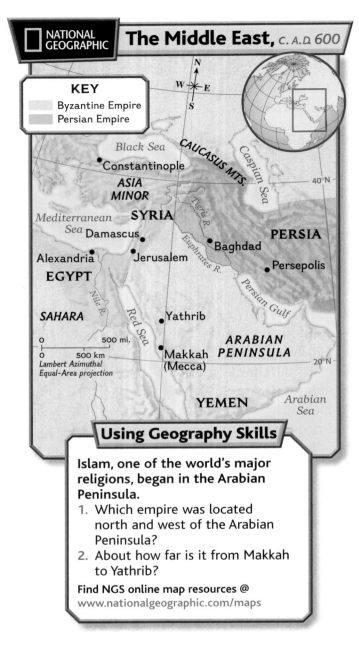

KEY
Byzantine Empire
Persian Empire

Black Sea
Constantinople
ASIA MINOR
CAUCASUS MTS.
Caspian Sea
40°N
SYRIA
Mediterranean Sea
Damascus
Tigris R.
Baghdad
PERSIA
Alexandria
Jerusalem
Euphrates R.
Persepolis
EGYPT
Nile R.
Persian Gulf
SAHARA
Red Sea
Yathrib
ARABIAN PENINSULA
0   500 mi.
0   500 km
Lambert Azimuthal Equal-Area projection
Makkah (Mecca)
20°N
YEMEN
Arabian Sea

Using Geography Skills

Islam, one of the world's major religions, began in the Arabian Peninsula.

1. Which empire was located north and west of the Arabian Peninsula?
2. About how far is it from Makkah to Yathrib?

Find NGS online map resources @ www.nationalgeographic.com/maps

In the middle of Makkah was the **Kaaba** (KAH buh), a low square building surrounded by statues of gods and goddesses. Arabs believed that the great stone inside the Kaaba was from heaven. Pilgrims, people who travel to a holy place, flocked to Makkah. Arabians worshiped many gods, but the most important was Allah. Allah was considered to be the creator.

Reading Check **Analyze** How did geography shape life in Arabia?

Muhammad: Islam's Prophet

Main Idea The prophet Muhammad brought the message of Islam to the people of Arabia.

Reading Focus Have you ever heard someone speak and been moved to tears? The following paragraphs tell about a prophet who moved the Arab people with his words.

Muhammad's Message In A.D. 570 a man named **Muhammad** (moh•HAH•muhd) was born in Makkah. An orphan, he was raised by an uncle. As a teenager, he worked in the trusted job of caravan leader and eventually became a successful merchant. He married and had children.

Despite his success, Muhammad was dissatisfied. He felt that the wealthy town leaders should return to the old ways. He thought they should honor their families, be fair in business, and help the poor.

Muhammad went into the hills to pray. In about A.D. 610, he said he was visited by an angel and told to preach Islam. *Islam* means "surrendering to the will of Allah." *Allah* is the Arabic word for "God."

Inspired, Muhammad returned to Makkah. Everywhere he went, he told people to destroy statues of false gods and to worship only Allah, the one true God.

Muhammad also preached that all people were equal and that the rich should share their goods. In Makkah, where most people lived humbly, this vision of a just society was very powerful. Muhammad was saying that wealth was not as important as leading a good life. When the Day of Judgment arrived, he said God would reward the good people and punish the evildoers.

Opposition to Islam Slowly Muhammad convinced people that his message was true. At first, only his family became

Muslims, or followers of Islam. Soon, however, many of the poor were attracted to his message that goods should be shared.

Wealthy merchants and religious leaders did not like Muhammad's message. They thought he was trying to take away their power. They made his life difficult and beat and tortured his followers.

In A.D. 622 Muhammad and his followers left Makkah. They moved north to a town called Yathrib (YA•thruhb). The journey of Muhammad and his followers to Yathrib became known as the Hijrah (HIH•jruh). The word comes from Arabic and means "breaking off relationships." Later Muslims made the year A.D. 622 the first year of a new Muslim calendar. Yathrib welcomed Muhammad and his followers. Their city was renamed **Madinah** (mah•DEE•nah), which means "the city of the prophet."

Muhammad's Government The people of Madinah accepted Muhammad as God's prophet and their ruler. Muhammad proved to be an able leader. He applied the laws he believed God had given him to all areas of life. He used these laws to settle disputes among the people. Muhammad created an Islamic state—a government that uses its political power to uphold Islam. He required all Muslims to place loyalty to the Islamic state above loyalty to their tribe.

To defend his new government, Muhammad built an army. His soldiers conquered Makkah in A.D. 630, and Muhammad then made it a holy city of Islam. Two years later, Muhammad died. By this time, Islam was spreading to all of Arabia.

Reading Check **Explain** Why did Muhammad's message appeal to the poor?

A pilgrimage to Makkah ▶

A Holy Journey

A pilgrimage to the holy city of Makkah often involved a long, difficult journey across deserts and other rough country. Muslim travelers carried palm leaves to show that they were on a pilgrimage. *Where was Muhammad born?*

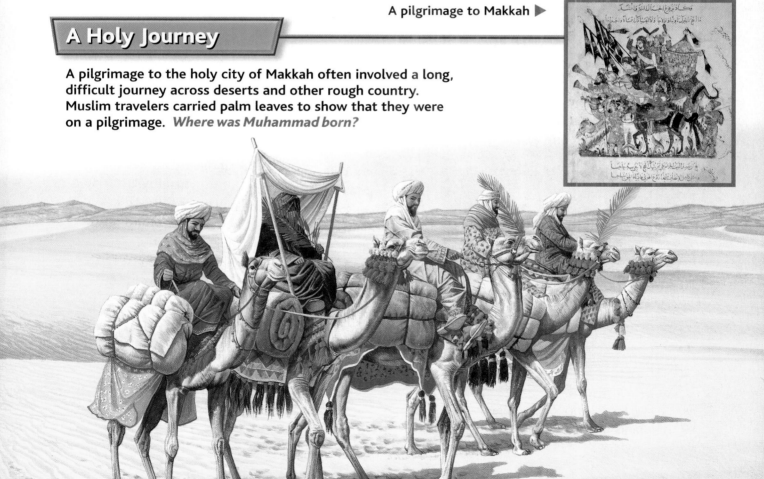

Biography

MUHAMMAD
A.D. 570–632

Muhammad experienced great poverty and many hardships early in his life. His father, Abd Allah, died before he was born. His grandfather, Abd al-Muttalib, took care of Muhammad in Makkah for a short time. Abd al-Muttalib felt that Makkah was an unhealthy place to raise a baby, but he could not leave because he was a political leader in the city. So he entrusted Muhammad to a tribe of nomads. They took the baby Muhammad to their home, the desert. When Muhammad was six years old, his mother died. Two years later, when Muhammad was eight, his grandfather also died. Arab custom did not allow minors to inherit anything, so the property and money from Muhammad's father and grandfather could not be passed down to him. To survive, Muhammad needed the protection of Abu Talib, his uncle who now headed the family.

▲ The Mosque of the Prophet in Madinah contains Muhammad's tomb.

Under the care of Abu Talib, Muhammad traveled by camel on trading journeys to Syria. On one of these trips, when he was about twenty-five years old, Muhammad met a wealthy woman named Khadijah. She and Muhammad married and had four daughters. They also had at least two sons who did not live past childhood. Muhammad's marriage to Khadijah made him a wealthy man and a member of Makkah's prosperous merchant class.

However, Muhammad could not forget his early experiences. His childhood had deeply influenced Muhammad and made him a thoughtful person. He often would go up into the hills near Makkah and spend nights in a cave. Alone there, he would reflect on the problems he saw in Makkah and the growing tension between the few people with great wealth and the many people with nothing. It was in these hills that Muhammad claimed an angel told him, "You are the Messenger of God."

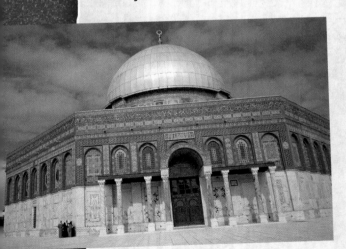

▲ The Dome of the Rock in Jerusalem marks the place where Muhammad is believed to have ascended to heaven.

Then and Now

Are any of the problems Muhammad saw in Makkah similar to problems in society we see today? Explain.

Islam's Teachings

Main Idea The Quran provided guidelines for Muslims' lives and the governments of Muslim states.

Reading Focus Do you ever wonder how you should act in certain situations? In the following paragraphs, you will learn where Muslims looked for guidance.

Islam, Judaism, and Christianity have some beliefs in common. Like Jews and Christians, Muslims believe in one God. Muslims believe this one God holds all power and created the universe. They also believe that God determines right and wrong. People are expected to obey God's laws if they want to be blessed in the afterlife.

Jews, Christians, and Muslims also believe that God spoke to people through prophets. For Muslims, early prophets were Abraham, Moses, Jesus, and finally Muhammad. For Christians, Jesus was more than a prophet. He was the son of God and therefore divine. In Islam, Muhammad is seen as a prophet and a very good person but not as divine.

What Is the Quran? Muslims wrote down the messages that Muhammad said he received from Allah. These writings became the **Quran** (koh•RAHN), or holy book of Islam. For Muslims, the Quran is God's written word. For this reason, Muslims strive to follow the Quran.

The Quran instructs Muslims about how they should live. Many of its moral teachings are like those of the Bible. For example, Muslims are told to be honest and to treat others fairly. They are to honor their parents, show kindness to their neighbors, and give generously to the poor. Murder, lying, and stealing are forbidden.

▲ A child studies the Quran

▲ **Muslim pilgrims surround the Kaaba in Makkah.** *When did Muhammad's soldiers capture the city of Makkah?*

The Five Pillars of Islam

Belief	Muslims must declare that there is no god but Allah and that Muhammad is his prophet.
Prayer	Muslims must pray five times per day facing toward Makkah.
Charity	Muslims must give to the poor.
Fasting	Muslims must not eat from dawn to dusk during the sacred holiday of Ramadan.
Pilgrimage	Muslims must visit Makkah once in their life.

▲ The Five Pillars are acts of worship that all Muslims must carry out. *How many times should Muslims pray each day?*

Many rules in the Quran apply to Muslims' daily life. According to these rules, Muslims should not eat pork, drink liquor, or gamble. The Quran also has rules about marriage, divorce, family life, property rights, and business practices.

Muslims are expected to fulfill the Five Pillars of Islam, or acts of worship. These are shown in the chart at the left.

Scholars of Islam also created a law code that explains how society should be run. This code is taken from the Quran and the Sunna (SUH•nuh). The Sunna is the name given to customs based on Muhammad's words and deeds. Islam's law code covers all areas of daily life. It applies the teachings of the Quran to family life, business, and government.

 **Reading Check** **Evaluate** What role do the Quran and Sunna play in Muslim daily life?

History Online

Study Central™ Need help with the material in this section? Visit jat.glencoe.com

Section 1 Review

Reading Summary

Review the Main Ideas

- In the desert of the Arabian Peninsula, the Arab people were mostly herders and traders.

- In the town of Makkah, Muhammad began to preach a new religion, Islam, which soon spread to all of Arabia.

- Muslims believe that Muhammad was Allah's final prophet and that their holy book, the Quran, is Allah's written word.

What Did You Learn?

1. What are oases, and why were they important to Arabs?

2. Name some activities the Quran prohibits.

Critical Thinking

3. **Compare and Contrast** Draw a Venn diagram to compare and contrast Islam, Judaism, and Christianity.

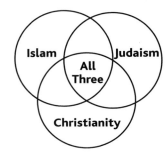

Islam — Judaism — All Three — Christianity

4. **Conclude** Why do you think Muhammad's teachings were popular with poorer people?

5. **Analyze** How did Muhammad link religion and government?

6. **Expository Writing** Suppose you are living in Makkah at the time Muhammad began preaching. Write a short newspaper article that describes Muhammad's teachings and the reactions of people in the city to those teachings.

7. **Reading** **Main Idea** Draw a graphic organizer to show the supporting details for this main idea: *Geography shaped the way that the early Arabs lived.*

Section 2

Islamic Empires

Get Ready to Read!

What's the Connection?

In Section 1, you learned how Islam spread from Madinah to Makkah. In time, Islam's followers brought their beliefs to all of Southwest Asia and parts of Southeast Asia, Africa, and Europe.

Focus on the Main Ideas

• Arabs spread Islam through preaching, conquest, and trade. *(page 380)*

• While Muslims split into two groups, the Arab Empire reached new heights. *(page 382)*

• Turks and Moguls built Muslim empires in Asia, Africa, and Europe. *(page 384)*

Locating Places

Damascus (duh•MAS•kuhs)
Indonesia (IHN•duh•NEE•zhuh)
Timbuktu (TIHM•BUHK•TOO)
Baghdad (BAG•dad)
Delhi (DEH•lee)

Meeting People

Umayyad (oo•MY•uhd)
Sufi (SOO•fee)
Abbasid (uh•BA•suhd)
Suleiman I (SOO•lay•MAHN)
Mogul (MOH•guhl)
Akbar (AK•buhr)

Building Your Vocabulary

caliph (KAY•luhf)
Shiite (SHEE•eyet)
Sunni (SU•nee)
sultan (SUHL•tuhn)

Reading Strategy

Cause and Effect Create a diagram to show why the Arabs were successful conquerors.

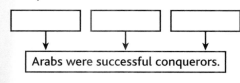

Arabs were successful conquerors.

NATIONAL GEOGRAPHIC

When & Where?

Córdoba
Constantinople
Baghdad
Delhi

A.D. **500**   **1100**   **1700**

A.D. **750**
Abbasids overthrow Umayyads

1258
Mongols burn Baghdad

1526
Moguls rule India from Delhi

The Spread of Islam

Main Idea Arabs spread Islam through preaching, conquest, and trade.

Reading Focus When you come up with a new idea, how do you let others know about it? Read on to find out how Arabs spread Islam.

When Muhammad died, his followers chose his successor. He was called a **caliph** (KAY•luhf), which meant successor to the Messenger of God.

The first caliph was Muhammad's father-in-law, Abu Bakr. The first four caliphs ruled from Madinah and were called the Rightly Guided Caliphs. That is because they tried to follow in Muhammad's footsteps. They lived simply, treated others fairly, and also fought hard for Islam. They wanted to spread Allah's message to everyone. Under their rule, the empire expanded to include all of southwest Asia.

Expansion continued under the **Umayyad** (oo•MY•uhd) caliphs, who ruled from A.D. 661 to A.D. 750. They made their capital the city of **Damascus** (duh•MAS•kuhs) in Syria. Now the Arab Empire included North Africa, Spain, and some of India.

The Muslims Build an Empire Just 100 years after Muhammad's death, the Islamic state became a great empire. Why were the Arabs so successful?

Arabs had always been good on horseback and good with the sword, but as Muslims, they also were inspired by their religion. They were fighting to spread

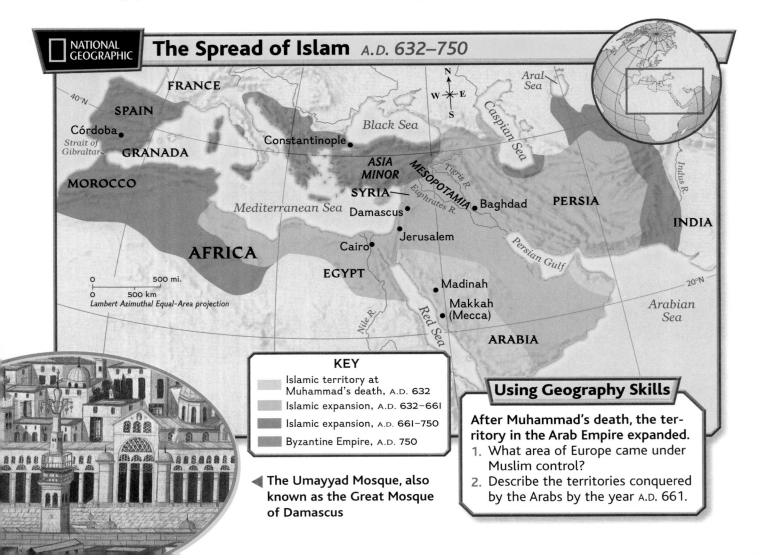

NATIONAL GEOGRAPHIC — The Spread of Islam A.D. 632–750

FRANCE · SPAIN · Córdoba · Strait of Gibraltar · GRANADA · MOROCCO · Constantinople · Black Sea · Aral Sea · Caspian Sea · ASIA MINOR · MESOPOTAMIA · Tigris R. · Euphrates R. · Baghdad · PERSIA · Indus R. · INDIA · SYRIA · Damascus · Mediterranean Sea · Cairo · Jerusalem · Persian Gulf · AFRICA · EGYPT · Nile R. · Red Sea · Madinah · Makkah (Mecca) · ARABIA · Arabian Sea

0 500 mi.
0 500 km
Lambert Azimuthal Equal-Area projection

KEY
- Islamic territory at Muhammad's death, A.D. 632
- Islamic expansion, A.D. 632–661
- Islamic expansion, A.D. 661–750
- Byzantine Empire, A.D. 750

◀ The Umayyad Mosque, also known as the Great Mosque of Damascus

Using Geography Skills

After Muhammad's death, the territory in the Arab Empire expanded.
1. What area of Europe came under Muslim control?
2. Describe the territories conquered by the Arabs by the year A.D. 661.

The Rightly Guided Caliphs

	Abu Bakr	Umar	Uthman	Ali
Relationship to Muhammad	father-in-law	friend	son-in-law, member of the Umayyad family	first cousin, son-in-law
Career	merchant	merchant	merchant	soldier, writer
Caliphate	A.D. 632–634	A.D. 634–644	A.D. 644–656	A.D. 656–661
Achievements as Caliph	spread Islam to all of Arabia; restored peace after death of Muhammad; created code of conduct in war; compiled Quran verses	spread Islam to Syria, Egypt, and Persia; redesigned government; paid soldiers; held a census; made taxes more fair; built roads and canals; aided poor	spread Islam into Afghanistan and eastern Mediterranean; organized a navy; improved the government; built more roads, bridges, and canals; distributed text of the Quran	reformed tax collection and other government systems; spent most of caliphate battling Muawiya, the governor of Syria

◀ Islamic glass horse

Understanding Charts

Under the caliphs, Islam spread through the Middle East and into North Africa.
1. Which caliph organized a navy?
2. **Compare** What achievements did Umar and Ali have in common?

Islam. Muslims believed anyone who died in battle for Islam would go to paradise.

The Arabs were also successful because they let conquered peoples practice their own religion. They called Christians and Jews "People of the Book," meaning that these people, too, believed in one God and had holy writings. Muslims did not treat everyone equally, though. Non-Muslims had to pay a special tax.

When a people are conquered, they tend to adopt the religion and customs of their new rulers. In the Arab Empire, many people became Muslims and learned Arabic. The customs of the conquered countries also influenced the Arabic rulers. Eventually, the term *Arab* meant only that a person spoke Arabic, not that he or she was from Arabia.

Preaching and Trading Muslims also spread Islam by preaching. A group called **Sufis** (SOO•feez) spent their time praying and teaching Islam. They won many followers throughout the Arab Empire.

Arab merchants also helped to spread Islam. They set up trading posts throughout southeast Asia and taught Islam to the people there. Today, the country of **Indonesia** (IHN•duh•NEE•zhuh) includes more Muslims than any other nation in the world.

Some Arab merchants crossed the Sahara to trade with kingdoms in West Africa. In the 1300s, the west African city of **Timbuktu** (TIHM•BUHK•TOO) became a leading center of Muslim learning.

✓ **Reading Check** **Explain** How did Arabs spread the religion of Islam through trade?

Struggles Within Islam

Main Idea While Muslims split into two groups, the Arab Empire reached new heights.

Reading Focus Have you ever belonged to a club whose members could not agree on a leader? Read to find out what happened when Muslims disagreed about who should lead them.

From the moment Muhammad died, Muslims began arguing about who had the right to be caliph. The quarrel over who should succeed Muhammad split the Muslim world into two groups, the Sunnis and the Shiites. This division has remained to the present day. Today most Muslims are Sunnis. Iran and Iraq have the largest populations of Shiites.

How Did Islam Split?

Shiites (SHEE•eyets) believed that Ali, Muhammad's son-in-law, should succeed him and that all future caliphs should be Ali's descendants. According to the Shiites, the Umayyad caliphs in Damascus had no right to rule.

Sunnis (SU•nees), who outnumbered Shiites, accepted the Umayyad dynasty as rightful caliphs, though they did not always agree with their policies. Over time, the Shiites and Sunnis developed different religious practices and customs.

Who Were the Abbasids?

The Abbasids (uh•BA•suhds) were the dynasty that came after the Umayyads. The Umayyads lost power in A.D. 750 because they angered many Muslims, especially in Persia. Persian Muslims felt that Arab Muslims got special treatment. They got the best jobs and paid fewer taxes.

When these Muslims rebelled, people all over the empire joined them. They overthrew the Umayyads, and a new dynasty began. The new caliph was a descendant of Muhammad's uncle. His name was Abu al-Abbas. The new Abbasid dynasty lasted until 1258.

The Abbasids devoted their energies to trade, scholarship, and the arts. They also built a new capital, **Baghdad** (BAG•dad).

Baghdad prospered because it was beside the Tigris River and near the Euphrates River. It was a good location to trade since many people used the rivers to ship goods north and south. As a result, the Arab Empire grew even wealthier.

The Abbasid dynasty is also known for bringing Persian influence into the empire.

Primary Source

Royal Caliphs

Ibn Khaldun recorded historical events and his interpretation of them.

"When one considers what God meant the caliphate to be, nothing more needs [to be said] about it. God made the caliph his substitute to handle the affairs of His servants. He is to make them do the things that are good for them and forbid them to do those that are harmful. He has been directly told so. A person who lacks the power to do a thing is never told to do it."

—Ibn Khaldun,
"The Muqaddimah"

▲ The Great Mosque of Damascus built by the Umayyad caliphs.

DBQ Document-Based Question

According to Khaldun, what is the relationship between God and the caliph?

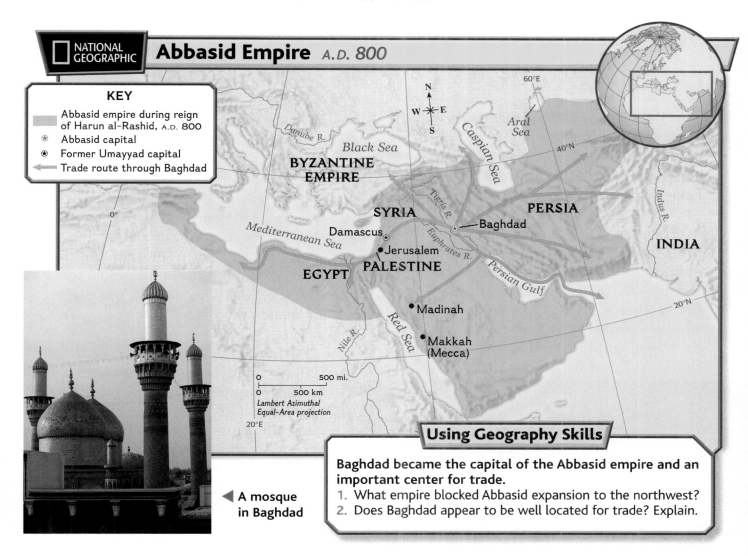

Abbasid Empire A.D. 800

KEY

Abbasid empire during reign of Harun al-Rashid, A.D. 800

⊛ Abbasid capital

⊛ Former Umayyad capital

← Trade route through Baghdad

BYZANTINE EMPIRE

SYRIA

Damascus ⊛

Jerusalem

EGYPT

PALESTINE

Madinah

Makkah (Mecca)

Black Sea

Aral Sea

Caspian Sea

PERSIA

Baghdad

INDIA

Mediterranean Sea

Persian Gulf

Tigris R.

Euphrates R.

Indus R.

Nile R.

Red Sea

Danube R.

0°   20°E   60°E   40°N   20°N

0   500 mi.
0   500 km
Lambert Azimuthal
Equal-Area projection

N W E S

A mosque in Baghdad

Using Geography Skills

Baghdad became the capital of the Abbasid empire and an important center for trade.

1. What empire blocked Abbasid expansion to the northwest?
2. Does Baghdad appear to be well located for trade? Explain.

Baghdad was very close to Persia, and the Abbasid rulers came to know and love the art and literature of Persia.

The Seljuk Turks Time brought many changes in the 500 years of Abbasid rule. In Egypt and Spain, the Muslims wanted their own caliphs. About the same time, a new people, the Seljuk Turks of central Asia, began moving south into the Arab Empire. The Abbasids were losing control.

The Seljuk Turks were nomads and great warriors. When they first moved into the empire, the Abbasids hired them as soldiers. Soon, however, the Seljuk Turks saw how weak the Abbasids were. They decided to take power for themselves.

First, the Seljuks took over much of what is now Iran and Turkey. Then, in 1055, they boldly took Baghdad itself. The Seljuks were satisfied to rule only the government and army. They let the Abbasid caliph remain as the religious leader. The Seljuk ruler called himself **sultan** (SUHL•tuhn), or "holder of power."

For 200 more years, the empire continued in this way. The Seljuks ruled, but it was still the Abbasid dynasty. Then, in the 1200s, another people swept into the empire. These were the fierce Mongols of central Asia. The Mongols were building their own empire and destroying many of the civilizations they conquered. In 1258 they stormed into Baghdad and burned it to the ground. The Arab Empire had ended.

✓ **Reading Check** **Contrast** What is the difference between Shiite and Sunni Muslims?

Later Muslim Empires

Main Idea Turks and Moguls built Muslim empires in Asia, Africa, and Europe.

Reading Focus How do you react when someone treats you unfairly? Read on to find out how Muslims in Turkey and India treated the people they conquered.

The Arabs built—and lost—the first Muslim empire. Later on, other Muslim groups created empires in Asia, Africa, and Europe. One of the largest and most powerful of these empires was the Ottoman empire that began in Turkey. Another was the Mogul empire in India.

Who Were the Ottomans? In the late 1200s, a group of Turks in the northwest corner of Asia Minor began to build a new empire. The ruler of these Turks was named Osman, and as a result, these Turks became known as the Ottoman Turks.

The Ottomans quickly conquered most of the land that today makes up the country of Turkey. They attacked the Byzantine Empire and pushed north into Europe. In 1453 they seized Constantinople, the Byzantine capital. They changed the city's name to Istanbul and made it the center of their empire.

Ottoman armies also marched south, conquering Syria, Palestine, Egypt, Mesopotamia, and parts of Arabia and North Africa. They used guns and cannons to fight their battles and built a large navy to control the Mediterranean Sea.

Like the Seljuks, the Ottomans called their leader a sultan. The most famous sultan was **Suleiman I** (SOO•lay•MAHN), who ruled in the 1500s. Suleiman was a man of many talents. He was enthusiastic about architecture and built many schools and mosques.

Suleiman was also a brilliant general, who brought Ottoman armies north into Europe. He even threatened the great European capital of Vienna. For all these reasons, Ottomans called him Suleiman the Magnificent.

After his rule, the Ottoman empire began to weaken. Little by little, they lost territory. The empire finally collapsed at the end of World War I.

◀ Muslims pray beneath the large decorated dome of Selimiye Mosque in Edirne, Turkey. Suleiman built this beautiful mosque for his son Selim II. *What were some of the reasons that Suleiman was called "the Magnificent"?*

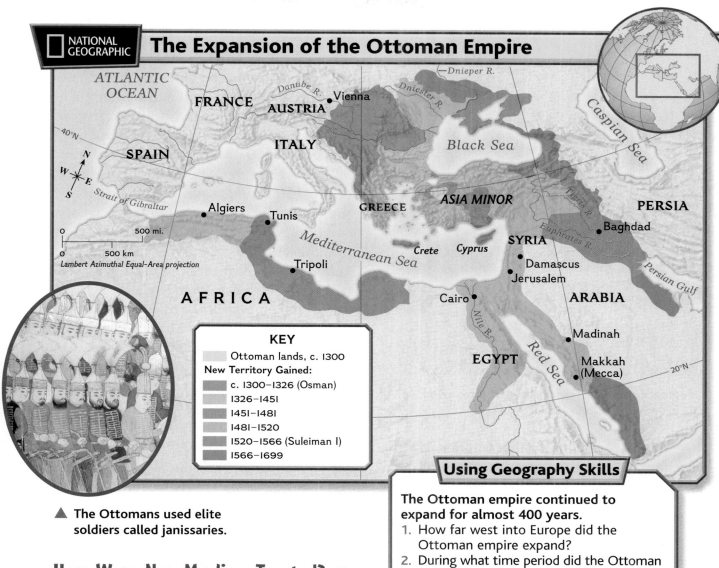

The Expansion of the Ottoman Empire

NATIONAL GEOGRAPHIC

KEY

Ottoman lands, c. 1300
New Territory Gained:
c. 1300–1326 (Osman)
1326–1451
1451–1481
1481–1520
1520–1566 (Suleiman I)
1566–1699

▲ The Ottomans used elite soldiers called janissaries.

Using Geography Skills

The Ottoman empire continued to expand for almost 400 years.
1. How far west into Europe did the Ottoman empire expand?
2. During what time period did the Ottoman empire expand to the Persian Gulf?

How Were Non-Muslims Treated? The Ottoman empire had many different people, including Turks, Arabs, Greeks, Albanians, Armenians, and Slavs. These groups practiced several religions. While many were Muslims, others were Christians or Jews.

The government made different laws for non-Muslims. They had to pay a special tax, and in return, they were free to practice their religion. They also could run their own affairs. These groups chose leaders to present their views to the sultan.

However, the sultan made some demands on the conquered people. For example, Christian families in Eastern Europe had to send their sons to Istanbul. There the boys became Muslims and trained as soldiers for the sultan.

Who Were the Moguls? During the 1500s, the **Moguls** (MOH•guhlz) created another Muslim empire in India. These Muslim warriors came from the mountains north of India. The Moguls used guns, cannons, elephants, and horses to conquer territory. In 1526 they made the city of **Delhi** (DEH•lee) the center of their empire.

The greatest Mogul ruler was **Akbar** (AK•buhr). He brought peace and order to the part of India he ruled by treating all his subjects fairly. Most of India's people were Hindu. He allowed them to practice their religion. Both Hindus and Muslims served in Akbar's government.

▲ Mogul emperor Akbar passing the crown to his grandson Shah Jahan

Times were good in India under Akbar. Farmers and artisans produced more food and goods than the Indians needed. As a result, trade increased. Muslim merchants brought paper, gunpowder, and fine porcelain from China to India. In addition, Muslim architects introduced new building styles, such as the arch and dome, to India.

After Akbar, the Mogul empire began to decline. Later rulers spent too much money trying to expand the empire and imposed heavy taxes on the people. Others tried to force the Hindus to convert to Islam and banned the building of Hindu temples. These policies led to many rebellions, and parts of the empire broke away.

At the same time the Moguls began losing power over their subjects, they had to deal with European merchants. The merchants came to India to trade but used their military power to take over Mogul territory. Eventually, the Mogul empire collapsed, and Great Britain took control of most of India.

✓ **Reading Check** **Describe** How did Constantinople change in 1453?

History Online

Study Central™ Need help with the material in this section? Visit jat.glencoe.com

Section 2 Review

Reading Summary

Review the Main Ideas

- Arab armies spread Islam as far west as Spain and as far east as India. Muslim traders helped spread the religion to southeast Asia and west Africa.

- Despite splitting into two groups, the Sunni and the Shiite, Muslim power reached its greatest height under the Abbasids.

- In the 1400s and 1500s, two great Muslim empires, the Ottoman and the Mogul, arose.

What Did You Learn?

1. How did the Muslims treat conquered peoples?

2. How far did the Arab Empire spread under the Umayyads?

Critical Thinking

3. **Organizing Information** Draw a chart to organize information about the Ottoman and Mogul empires.

Ottoman Empire	Mogul Empire

4. **Contrast** Describe the differences between the Shiite and Sunni Muslims.

5. **Summarize** Besides conquests by Arab armies, how was Islam spread?

6. **Evaluate** Why was Akbar considered a great ruler?

7. **Persuasive Writing** Which Muslim empire—the Umayyads, the Ottomans, or the Moguls—treated its non-Muslim subjects the most fairly? The least fairly? Write a paragraph to defend your answer.

Section 3

Muslim Ways of Life

Get Ready to Read!

What's the Connection?

In Section 2, you learned that many Muslim rulers brought peace and order to their empires. Peace and order helped trade to increase. Trade, in turn, brought great wealth to the Muslim empires.

Focus on the Main Ideas

- While Muslim traders enjoyed great success and cities grew, most Muslims lived in villages in the country. *(page 388)*

- Muslims made valuable contributions in math, science, and the arts. *(page 390)*

Locating Places

Granada (gruh•NAH•duh)
Agra (AH•gruh)

Meeting People

Mamun (mah•MOON)
al-Razi (ahl•RAH•zee)
Ibn Sina (IH•buhn SEE•nuh)
Omar Khayyam
  (OH•MAHR KY•YAHM)
Ibn Khaldun (IH•buhn KAL•DOON)

Building Your Vocabulary

mosque (MAHSK)
bazaar (buh•ZAHR)
minaret (MIH•nuh•REHT]
crier (KRY•uhr)

Reading Strategy

Organizing Information Create a pyramid to show the social classes in the early Muslim world.

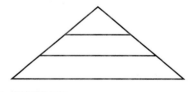

A.D. 800   1100   1400

c. A.D. 900
Al-Razi writes medical texts

c. 1100
Omar Khayyam writes the *Rubaiyat*

c. 1375
Ibn Khaldun writes histories

Trade and Everyday Life

Main Idea While Muslim traders enjoyed great success and cities grew, most Muslims lived in villages in the country.

Reading Focus Have you ever visited a mall or a farm market? These are both places where people gather to sell goods. Read to learn about Muslim traders and their marketplaces.

History Online

Web Activity Visit jat.glencoe.com and click on *Chapter 11—Student Web Activities* to learn more about Islamic civilization.

Muslims were the leading merchants in the Middle East and northern Africa until the 1400s. Their caravans traveled overland from Baghdad to China. Their ships crossed the Indian Ocean to India and Southeast Asia. They carried spices, cloth, glass, and carpets. On their return, they brought rubies, silk, ivory, gold, and slaves.

The Success of Muslim Traders

Several things explain the success of Muslim trade. When Muslim empires expanded, they spread the Arabic language. As a result, Arabic became the language of trade. Muslim rulers also made trade easier by providing merchants with coins.

Muslim merchants kept detailed records of their business deals and the money they made. In time, these practices developed into a new business—banking. Muslims respected traders for their skills and the wealth they created.

What Were Muslim Cities Like?

Trade helped the leading Muslim cities grow. Baghdad, Cairo, and Damascus were located on trade routes that ran from the Mediterranean Sea to central Asia. However, Muslim cities were not only places of trade.

▼ **Muslims shop at a textile market.**
What was a bazaar in a Muslim city?

They also became important centers of government, learning, and the arts.

Muslim cities looked very similar. The major buildings were palaces and mosques. **Mosques** (mahsks) are Muslim houses of worship. They also serve as schools, courts, and centers of learning.

Another important part of every Muslim city was the **bazaar** (buh•ZAHR), or marketplace. Stalls and shops made up the bazaars. Sellers in the stalls and shops sold goods from Asia. Buyers from all over, including Europe, went from stall to stall to find goods to take home and sell.

Although cities were important, most Muslims lived in villages and farmed the land. Because water was scarce, Muslim farmers used irrigation to bring water to their crops. They grew wheat, rice, beans, and melons in the fields. They raised almonds, blackberries, apricots, figs, and olives in their orchards. Some farmers also raised flowers for use in perfume.

At first, Muslim villagers owned small farms. Later, wealthy landowners took over some of these farms and formed large estates. Farmers and enslaved people worked for the landowners.

Muslim Society
The Muslim people fell into social groups based on power and wealth. At the top were government leaders, landowners, and traders. Below them were artisans, farmers, and workers. The lowest group was made up of enslaved people.

As in other civilizations, slavery was widespread. Because Muslims could not be enslaved, traders brought enslaved people

▲ A Muslim woman weaving a rug

The Way It Was

Focus on Everyday Life

Muslim Carpets and Weavings

Carpets were woven in the Middle East long before the coming of Islam. They became popular in the Islamic world because Muslims used them in their daily worship.

Carpets were often made of sheep's wool or goat hair. Shepherds might knot them by hand, or the carpets might be made on portable looms. Flowers and geometric shapes were popular designs.

The carpets used for the Muslim's daily prayers are called prayer rugs. No matter where Muslims live, they pray five times daily. They kneel down on their prayer rug and pray facing toward Makkah. Prayer rugs are small and can be folded and carried from place to place.

Fine carpets of silk and wool are often hung on the walls of mosques and public buildings. They are considered fine art.

Muslim carpet ▶

Connecting to the Past
1. What animals were needed to make carpets?
2. What is the main reason Muslim carpets have continually been in demand?

from non-Muslim areas. Many of these people were prisoners of war. They often served as servants or soldiers and could buy back their freedom.

Men and women played different roles in the Muslim world. As in other parts of the world, men ran government, society, and business. Women, on the other hand, helped run Muslim families. They also could inherit wealth and own property. Many places had laws requiring women to cover their faces and to wear long robes in public.

Reading Check **Explain** How did Muslim rulers give their merchants an advantage?

Muslim Achievements

Main Idea Muslims made valuable contributions in math, science, and the arts.

Reading Focus Did you know that the numbers you use are called Arabic numerals? Read on to find out what other contributions Muslims made.

Arabic was the common language of the Muslim empires. You have already read how Arabic language encouraged trade. It also helped different people in the empires to share knowledge. For example, in A.D. 830 the Abbasid caliph **Mamun** (mah•MOON)

Linking Past & Present

Hijab

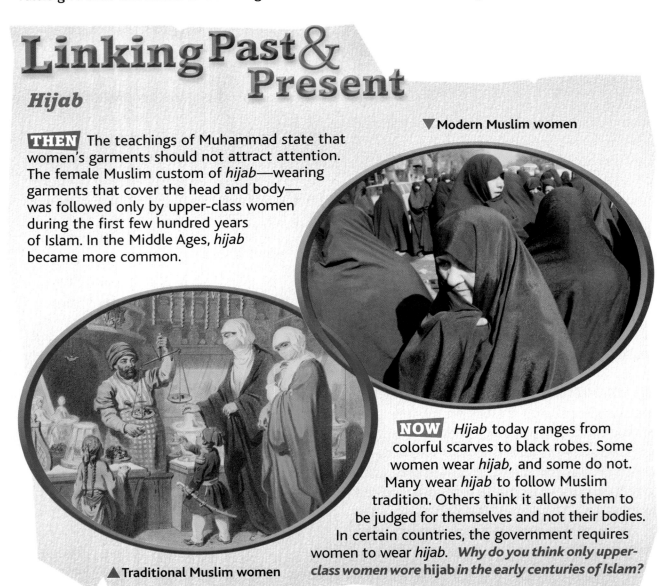

THEN The teachings of Muhammad state that women's garments should not attract attention. The female Muslim custom of *hijab*—wearing garments that cover the head and body—was followed only by upper-class women during the first few hundred years of Islam. In the Middle Ages, *hijab* became more common.

▼ **Modern Muslim women**

NOW *Hijab* today ranges from colorful scarves to black robes. Some women wear *hijab*, and some do not. Many wear *hijab* to follow Muslim tradition. Others think it allows them to be judged for themselves and not their bodies. In certain countries, the government requires women to wear *hijab*. *Why do you think only upper-class women wore* hijab *in the early centuries of Islam?*

▲ **Traditional Muslim women**

founded the House of Wisdom in Baghdad. Mamun staffed his center with Christian, Jewish, and Muslim scholars. These scholars exchanged ideas and rewrote Greek, Persian, and Indian works in Arabic.

Scholars in Muslim lands saved much of the learning of the ancient world. Europeans in the West had lost this knowledge after the Western Roman Empire fell. Through Muslim scholars, western Europeans found out about Aristotle and other ancient Greek thinkers.

Mathematics and Science

Muslims made important advances in mathematics. Later, they passed on these discoveries to Europeans. For example, Muslims invented algebra, a type of mathematics still taught in schools today. The Arabs also borrowed the symbols 0 through 9 from Hindu scholars in India. These numbers were later used by Europeans. Today, they are known as "Arabic numerals."

Muslims also made progress in science. Muslim scientists who studied the heavens perfected the Greek astrolabe. Sailors used this tool to study the stars and then determine their location at sea. Muslim scientists used the astrolabe to measure the size and distance around the earth. Based on their measurements, they realized that the earth is round.

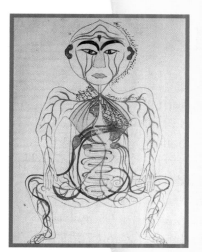

▲ Muslim medical drawing

◀ Muslim astrolabe

Primary Source: The Mystery of Smallpox

The Muslim scientist al-Razi urged scientists and doctors to search for the causes of disease, rather than just treatments.

"Although [scholars] have certainly made some mention of the treatment of the Small-Pox . . . there is not one of them who has mentioned the cause of the existence of the disease, and how it comes to pass that hardly any one escapes it . . ."

—Al-Razi, "On the Causes of Small-Pox"

Al-Razi's own theory about the cause of smallpox was incorrect. His efforts to find the cause, however, helped change how doctors and scientists investigated diseases.

DBQ Document-Based Question

Why was al-Razi concerned about previous scholars' studies of smallpox?

Other Muslim scientists experimented with metals and kept records of their work. As a result, the Arabs are considered the founders of chemistry. One of the best-known Muslim chemists was **al-Razi** (ahl•RAH•zee), who lived from A.D. 865 to A.D. 925. Al-Razi developed a system for categorizing substances as animal, mineral, or vegetable. He also wrote books for doctors that helped them to identify diseases.

Arab doctors were the first to discover that blood circulates, or moves to and from the heart. The Persian doctor **Ibn Sina** (IH•buhn SEE•nuh) showed how diseases spread from person to person. As they worked, Muslim doctors published their findings.

Biography

OMAR KHAYYAM
1048–1131
and IBN KHALDUN
1332–1406

Omar Khayyam—who was born in Persia—was a mathematician, astronomer, and philosopher, but he is best known as a poet. Scholars believe that Khayyam wrote only parts of his most famous poem, the *Rubaiyat*, but they are certain that at least 120 verses and the main concepts are his. Stanza XII reads:

> "A Book of Verses underneath the Bough,
> A Jug of Wine, a Loaf of Bread—and Thou
> Beside me singing the Wilderness—
> Oh, Wilderness were Paradise enow [enough]!"
>
> —Omar Khayyam, *Rubaiyat*

▲ Omar Khayyam

Khayyam wrote books on algebra and music before he was 25 years old. He led an observatory for 18 years and developed a more accurate calendar.

Ibn Khaldun is one of the most famous Arab scholars. He was a historian, geographer, sociologist, and politician. He was born in Tunisia and worked for the rulers of Tunis and Morocco. He also served as ambassador to one of the Spanish kingdoms and as a judge in Cairo, Egypt. He wrote much about social and political change. His best-known work is *Muqaddimah* (Introduction), written in 1375. It is the first volume of his book *Kitab al-Ibar* (universal history). In this book, he tried to develop a scientific way to analyze historical events. He is one of the first historians who studied how geography, economics, and culture affect history.

▲ Ibn Khaldun

Then and Now

The *Rubaiyat* is a collection of 4-line verses called quatrains. Find a modern poem that is made up of quatrains.

Muslim Writing The Quran is probably the most famous collection of writings in the Muslim world, but Muslims produced other famous works, as well. One of the most well known is *The Thousand and One Nights,* also called *The Arabian Nights*. It includes tales from India, Persia, and Arabia. One of the stories tells about Aladdin and his magic lamp.

Another Muslim, the Persian poet **Omar Khayyam** (OH•MAHR KY•YAHM), wrote the *Rubaiyat* (ROO•bee•AHT) around 1100. Many consider it one of the finest poems ever written.

In addition to stories and poems, Muslims wrote history. The great Muslim historian **Ibn Khaldun** (IH•buhn KAL•DOON)

wrote in 1375 that all civilizations rise, grow, and then fall. He also was one of the first historians to study the effect of geography and climate on people.

Art and Buildings Muslims developed their own form of art based on Islam. Muslims are not allowed to show images of Muhammad or the events of his life in art. They believe that such images might cause people to worship Muhammad instead of Allah. Instead, designs entwined with flowers, leaves, and stars make up most Muslim art. Muslims use these designs to decorate walls, books, rugs, and buildings.

Muslims were known for their beautiful buildings. Mosques filled Muslim cities like Baghdad, Damascus, Cairo, and Istanbul.

Islamic Mosque

In Islamic cities and towns, mosques were centers of religious and daily life. Besides being places of worship, mosques also served as meeting places, schools, and courts. *What was the most striking architectural feature of a mosque?*

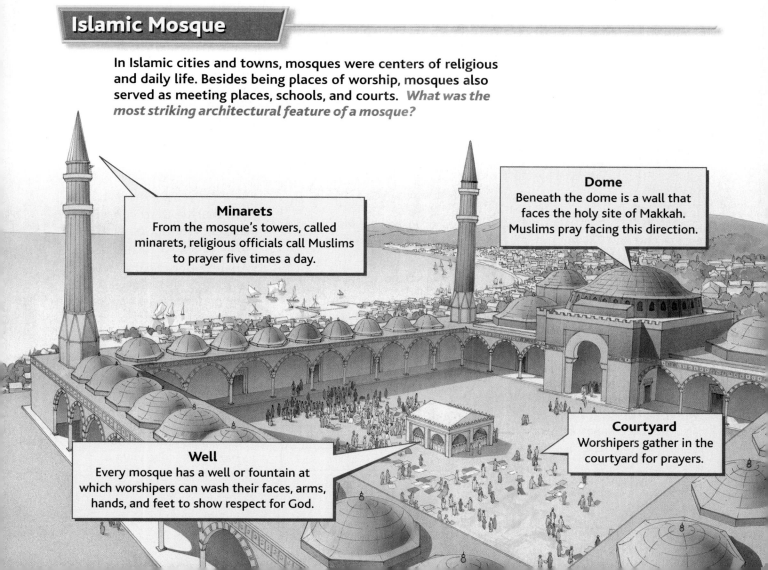

Minarets
From the mosque's towers, called minarets, religious officials call Muslims to prayer five times a day.

Dome
Beneath the dome is a wall that faces the holy site of Makkah. Muslims pray facing this direction.

Well
Every mosque has a well or fountain at which worshipers can wash their faces, arms, hands, and feet to show respect for God.

Courtyard
Worshipers gather in the courtyard for prayers.

▲ The Taj Mahal took more than 20 years to build. *Where is the Taj Mahal located?*

Domes top many of the mosques, but a mosque's most striking feature is its **minarets** (MIH•nuh•REHTS). These are towers from which a **crier** (KRY•uhr), or announcer, calls believers to prayer five times a day.

Islamic rulers lived in large brick palaces. These palaces often had courtyards at their center. To cool the courtyards, palace builders added porches, fountains, and pools. To provide protection, they surrounded the palaces with walls. The most famous example of a Muslim palace is the Alhambra (al•HAM•bruh) in **Granada** (gruh•NAH•duh), Spain. It was built in the 1300s.

Another famous Muslim building is the Taj Mahal in **Agra** (AH•gruh), India. The Mogul ruler Shah Jahan built it as a tomb for his wife after she died in 1629. Made of marble and precious stones, the Taj Mahal is one of the world's most beautiful buildings.

Today, the Muslim empires are gone. However, Islam is still a major world religion. About one out of every six persons in the world is a Muslim.

✓ **Reading Check** **Identify** What contributions did Muslims make in math and science?

Section 3 Review

History Online
Study Central™ Need help with the material in this section? Visit jat.glencoe.com

Reading Summary
Review the Main Ideas

- There were many Muslim cities such as Baghdad, Cairo, and Damascus, but most Muslims remained farmers in small villages.

- Muslim scholars made important discoveries in fields such as algebra and chemistry, and Muslim writers, artists, and architects also produced important works.

What Did You Learn?

1. Describe the three Muslim social groups.

2. What contributions did Muslims make in the field of medicine?

Critical Thinking

3. **Organizing Information** Draw a chart like the one below. Fill in details about Muslim contributions in the areas of math, science, and the arts.

Math	Science	Arts

4. **Summarize** Describe several factors that made Muslim trade strong.

5. **Analyze** How did the Arabic language and Muslim leaders help preserve and advance the world's knowledge?

6. **Evaluate** Which Muslim contribution do you think had the greatest effect on later civilizations?

7. **Descriptive Writing** Imagine you are living in a Muslim city. Write to a friend describing a bazaar. Describe what a bazaar is and some of the items you might find there.

Section 1 The Rise of Islam

Vocabulary
oasis
sheikh
caravan
Quran

Focusing on the Main Ideas

- The deserts, coastline, and oases of Arabia helped shape the Arab way of life. *(page 373)*
- The prophet Muhammad brought the message of Islam to the people of Arabia. *(page 374)*
- The Quran provided guidelines for Muslims' lives and the governments of Muslim states. *(page 377)*

A child studies ▶ the Quran

Section 2 Islamic Empires

Vocabulary
caliph
Shiite
Sunni
sultan

Focusing on the Main Ideas

- Arabs spread Islam through preaching, conquest, and trade. *(page 380)*
- While Muslims split into two groups, the Arab Empire reached new heights. *(page 382)*
- Turks and Moguls built Muslim empires in Asia, Africa, and Europe. *(page 384)*

Section 3 Muslim Ways of Life

Vocabulary
mosque
bazaar
minaret
crier

Focusing on the Main Ideas

- While Muslim traders enjoyed great success and cities grew, most Muslims lived in villages in the country. *(page 388)*
- Muslims made valuable contributions in math, science, and the arts. *(page 390)*

Chapter 11 Assessment and Activities

Review Vocabulary

Write the key term that completes each sentence.

a. caravan
b. caliph
c. sultan
d. mosque
e. Quran
f. minaret
g. sheikh
h. bazaar
i. Sunnis
j. Shiites

1. A crier called Muslims to prayer from the ___ of a mosque.
2. After Muhammad died, his followers chose a ___ to lead them.
3. The most famous ___ was Suleiman.
4. In each Muslim city, a ___ sold goods to local and out-of-town merchants.
5. Arab merchants traveling in a ___ used camels to carry goods across the desert.
6. The Muslim holy book is called the ___.
7. Each tribe of early Arabs was led by a ___.
8. Each ___ was a house of worship and a school.
9. The ___ believed that Muhammad's son-in-law should succeed him.
10. According to the ___, the Umayyad dynasty were rightful caliphs.

Review Main Ideas

Section 1 • The Rise of Islam
11. How did geography affect the early Arabs' way of life?
12. What guidelines did the Quran provide for the governments of Muslim states?

Section 2 • Islamic Empires
13. How did the Arabs spread Islam?
14. Why did the Muslims split into two groups?

Section 3 • Muslim Ways of Life
15. What scientific advances were made by early Muslims?
16. What is significant about Ibn Khaldun's recording of history?

Critical Thinking

17. **Compare** How are Islam, Judaism, and Christianity similar?
18. **Evaluate** Do you think a government that allows people to practice any religion they choose will be stronger than one that does not? Explain.

Review Reading Skill | Main Idea — Main Ideas and Details

19. Read the paragraph below. Create a graphic organizer to show the main idea and supporting details.

> The Muslim people fell into social groups based on power and wealth. At the top were government leaders, landowners, and traders. Below them were artisans, farmers, and workers. The lowest group was made up of enslaved people.

To review this skill, see pages 370–371.

Geography Skills

Study the map below and answer the following questions.

20. **Movement** Why was the Abbasid empire unable to expand to the Black Sea?

21. **Region** What bodies of water could Abbasid merchants use to trade with the outside world?

22. **Place** You learned that the Abbasids changed the capital city from Damascus to Baghdad. Look at the locations of those cities. Which do you think would have been the best location for a capital city? Why?

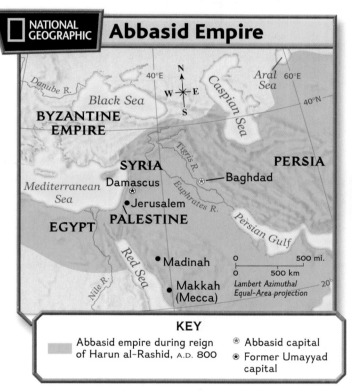

NATIONAL GEOGRAPHIC **Abbasid Empire**

KEY

Abbasid empire during reign of Harun al-Rashid, A.D. 800

⊛ Abbasid capital

⊛ Former Umayyad capital

Read to Write

23. **Descriptive Writing** Suppose you are an Arab merchant traveling in the desert with a caravan. Write three diary entries, each describing the events of your day. Each day you choose to describe should focus on a different aspect of the life of a merchant. Share your entries with the class.

24. **Using Your** FOLDABLES Write a poem or short story using the facts from your completed foldable.

History Online

Self-Check Quiz To help you prepare for the Chapter Test, visit jat.glencoe.com

Using Technology

25. **Exploring Language** Use the Internet and your local library to find English words that have their origins in the Arabic language. Create a chart using your computer showing English words and their Arabic roots.

Linking Past and Present

26. **Evaluating Impact** Which Islamic invention or development do you think has the greatest effect on the world today? Explain your choice.

Building Citizenship Skills

27. **Analyzing Documents** Do research to find out how the United States Constitution protects religious freedoms. Do you think the way Muslim empires treated religion would be allowed under the U.S. Constitution? Explain.

Primary Source **Analyze**

In the first stanza of the *Rubaiyat,* Omar Khayyam welcomes the morning.

"Wake! for the sun, the shepherd of the sky,
Has penned [confined] the stars within their fold on high,
And, shaking darkness from his mighty limbs,
Scatters the daylight from his burning eye."

—*Rubáiyát of Omar Khayyám:
A Paraphrase From
Several Literal Translations,*
by Richard Le Gallienne

DBQ **Document-Based Questions**

28. What has been penned up by the sun?

29. *Personification* is when a writer gives human qualities to something that is not human. How does Khayyam personify the sun in this stanza?

Comparing New Empires and Faiths

Compare ancient Rome, early Christianity, and early Islam by reviewing the information below. Can you see how the peoples of these civilizations had lives that were very much like yours?

Where in the World?

● Chapters 8 & 9
● Chapter 10
● Chapter 11

NATIONAL GEOGRAPHIC

	Ancient Rome Chapters 8 & 9	Rise of Christianity Chapter 10	Islamic Civilization Chapter 11
Where did these civilizations develop?	• Began on Italian peninsula • Won control of Mediterranean world	• Began in Palestine • Spread throughout the Roman Empire	• Began in Arabia • Arab Empire stretched from North Africa to central Asia
Who were some important people in these civilizations?	• Cincinnatus c. 519–438 B.C. • Augustus, ruled 27 B.C.–A.D. 14 • Theodora c. A.D. 500–548	• Jesus c. 6 B.C.–A.D. 30 • Helena c. A.D. 248–328 • Augustine A.D. 354–430	• Muhammad A.D. 570–632 • Omar Khayyam A.D. 1048–1131 • Suleiman I, ruled A.D. 1520–1566
Where did most of the people live?	• Farming villages • Major cities included Rome and Alexandria	• Ports and cities of Mediterranean area	• Desert oases • Farming villages • Major cities included Makkah and Baghdad

	Ancient Rome Chapters 8 & 9	Rise of Christianity Chapter 10	Islamic Civilization Chapter 11
What were these people's beliefs?	• Belief in many gods and goddesses • Emperors honored as gods • Many local religions	• Belief in one God and Jesus as Son of God and the Savior • Major groups: Eastern Orthodox and Roman Catholic	• Belief in one God (Allah) • Muhammad is final prophet • Major groups: Sunni and Shiite 
What was their government like?	• Rome developed from a republic into an empire • An emperor was the chief leader • Army played role in government 	• Ranked order of priests, bishops, and archbishops • Bishop of Rome became head of the Roman Catholic Church	• Muhammad founds Islamic state • After Muhammad, leaders called caliphs held religious and political power
What was their language and writing like?	• Latin was official language; Greek spoken in empire's eastern part • Many local languages	• New Testament of Bible written in Greek • Latin became language of Roman Catholic Church	• Quran written in Arabic • Arabic was Arab Empire's official language • Persian and Turkish also spoken
What contributions did they make?	• Introduced ideas about law and government • Developed new styles of building 	• Christianity became a world religion • Shaped beliefs and values of Western civilization	• Islam became a world religion • Developed ideas in medicine and mathematics 
How do these changes affect me? *Can you add any?*	• Latin contributed many words to English language • Rome's idea of a republic followed by governments today	• Christianity is major religion of the West today • Birth date of Jesus is starting date for Western calendar	• Islam is a major religion today • Developed algebra • Developed game of chess

The Middle Ages

Why It's Important

Each civilization that you will study in this unit made important contributions to history.

- The Chinese first produced gunpowder, the compass, and printed books.
- Africans south of the Sahara developed new forms of music and dance.
- The Japanese developed martial arts, such as judo and karate.
- The Europeans took the first steps toward representative government.

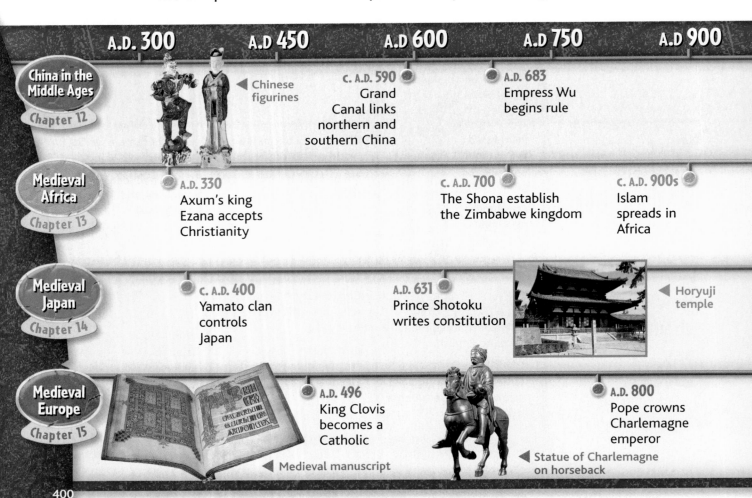

| A.D. 300 | A.D. 450 | A.D 600 | A.D 750 | A.D 900 |

China in the Middle Ages
Chapter 12

◄ Chinese figurines

c. A.D. 590
Grand Canal links northern and southern China

A.D. 683
Empress Wu begins rule

Medieval Africa
Chapter 13

A.D. 330
Axum's king Ezana accepts Christianity

c. A.D. 700
The Shona establish the Zimbabwe kingdom

c. A.D. 900s
Islam spreads in Africa

Medieval Japan
Chapter 14

c. A.D. 400
Yamato clan controls Japan

A.D. 631
Prince Shotoku writes constitution

◄ Horyuji temple

Medieval Europe
Chapter 15

A.D. 496
King Clovis becomes a Catholic

A.D. 800
Pope crowns Charlemagne emperor

◄ Medieval manuscript

◄ Statue of Charlemagne on horseback

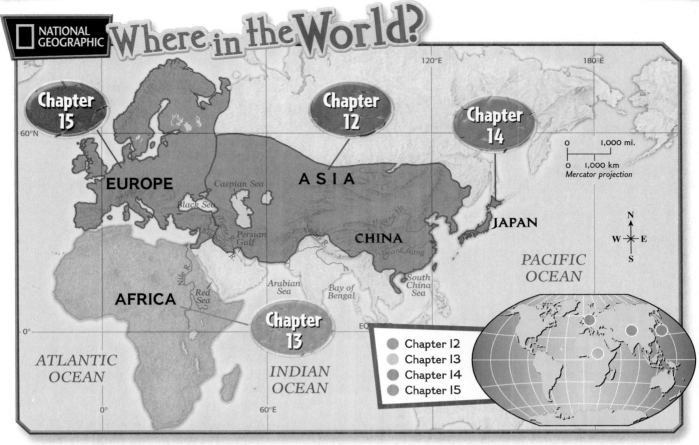

NATIONAL GEOGRAPHIC
Where in the World?

Chapter 15

Chapter 12

Chapter 14

60°N

EUROPE

Caspian Sea

Black Sea

ASIA

120°E

180°E

0   1,000 mi.
0   1,000 km
Mercator projection

Tigris R.

Euphrates R.

Persian Gulf

CHINA

Huang He

JAPAN

N
W — E
S

AFRICA

Nile R.

Red Sea

Arabian Sea

Bay of Bengal

Chang Jiang

South China Sea

PACIFIC OCEAN

0°

EQ

Chapter 13

ATLANTIC OCEAN

INDIAN OCEAN

Chapter 12
Chapter 13
Chapter 14
Chapter 15

0°

60°E

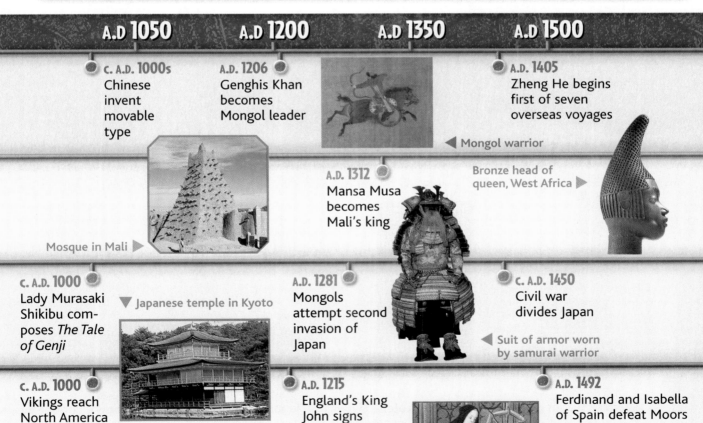

A.D 1050   **A.D 1200**   **A.D 1350**   **A.D 1500**

C. A.D. 1000s
Chinese invent movable type

A.D. 1206
Genghis Khan becomes Mongol leader

A.D. 1405
Zheng He begins first of seven overseas voyages

◄ Mongol warrior

A.D. 1312
Mansa Musa becomes Mali's king

Bronze head of queen, West Africa ▶

► Mosque in Mali

C. A.D. 1000
Lady Murasaki Shikibu composes *The Tale of Genji*

▼ Japanese temple in Kyoto

A.D. 1281
Mongols attempt second invasion of Japan

C. A.D. 1450
Civil war divides Japan

◄ Suit of armor worn by samurai warrior

C. A.D. 1000
Vikings reach North America

A.D. 1215
England's King John signs Magna Carta

A.D. 1492
Ferdinand and Isabella of Spain defeat Moors

◄ Medieval woman spinning wool

Places to Locate

1 Buddha statue

See China in the Middle Ages
Chapter 12

2 Djenne mosque

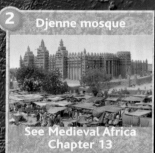

See Medieval Africa
Chapter 13

4 **5** EUROPE

2

AFRICA

Atlantic Ocean

People to Meet

Prince Shotoku

A.D. 573–621
Japanese leader
Chapter 14, p. 489

Charlemagne

A.D. 742–814
Frankish ruler
Chapter 15, p. 517

Murasaki Shikibu

C. A.D. 973–1025
Japanese writer
Chapter 14, p. 502

Genghis Khan

C. A.D. 1167–1227
Mongol conqueror
Chapter 12, p. 427

NATIONAL GEOGRAPHIC

ASIA

Pacific Ocean

3 Todaiji temple

See Medieval Japan
Chapter 14

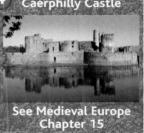

4 Caerphilly Castle

See Medieval Europe
Chapter 15

5 Mont St. Michel

See Medieval Europe
Chapter 15

①

③

Thomas Aquinas

A.D. 1225–1274
Christian thinker
Chapter 15, p. 551

Mansa Musa

Ruled A.D. 1312–1337
King of Mali
Chapter 13, p. 466

Zheng He

A.D. 1371–1433
Chinese admiral
Chapter 12, p. 434

Joan Of Arc

A.D. 1412–1431
French heroine
Chapter 15, p. 556

403

China in the Middle Ages

▼ Imperial Palace at the Forbidden City

NATIONAL GEOGRAPHIC **When & Who?**

A.D. 600	A.D. 900	1200	1500
A.D. 581 Wendi founds Sui dynasty	**A.D. 868** Chinese print world's first book	**1206** Genghis Khan unites the Mongols	**1405** Zheng He begins overseas voyage

Chapter Preview

Like the Arabs, the Chinese were interested in science and technology. Read this chapter to learn about Chinese inventions and how they influence your life today.

 View the Chapter 12 video in the *World History: Journey Across Time* Video Program.

 Section 1 ## China Reunites

During the Middle Ages, Chinese rulers brought peace, order, and growth to China. Buddhism became a major religion in China, but the Chinese government supported Confucian ideas.

 Section 2 ## Chinese Society

Farming and trade brought wealth to China. The Chinese developed new technology and enjoyed a golden age of art and writing.

 Section 3 ## The Mongols in China

Led by Genghis Khan, the Mongols built a vast empire. Under his son, Kublai Khan, they went on to conquer China as well.

 Section 4 ## The Ming Dynasty

China's Ming rulers strengthened government and brought peace and prosperity. They supported trading voyages to other parts of Asia and to East Africa.

Categorizing Information *Make this foldable to help you organize your notes about China in the Middle Ages.*

Step 1 *Fold a sheet of paper in half from side to side, leaving $\frac{1}{2}$ inch tab along the side.*

Leave $\frac{1}{2}$ inch tab here.

Step 2 *Turn the paper and fold it into fourths.*

Fold in half, then fold in half again.

Reading and Writing
As you read the chapter, identify the main ideas in the chapter. Write these under the appropriate tab.

Step 3 *Unfold and cut along the top three fold lines.*

This makes four tabs.

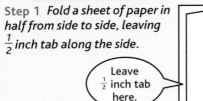
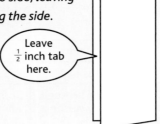

Step 4 *Label as shown.*

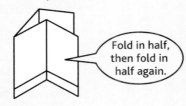

| China Reunites | Chinese Society | The Mongols in China | The Ming Dynasty |

China in the Middle Ages

Reading Social Studies

1 Learn It!

Reading Between the Lines

To infer means to evaluate information and arrive at a conclusion. When you make inferences, you "read between the lines," or draw conclusions that are not stated directly in the text. We naturally make inferences about things we read, see, and hear every day.

Read this paragraph from Section 3.

> **Genghis Khan gathered an army of more than 100,000 warriors. He placed his soldiers into well-trained groups. Commanding them were officers chosen for their abilities, not for their family ties. These changes made the Mongols the most skilled fighting force in the world at that time.**
>
> —*from page 425*

Reading Tip

Sometimes you make inferences by asking yourself questions or making predictions about what is going to come next.

Use this Think-Through chart to help you make inferences.

Text	Question	Inference
Genghis Khan	Who was he?	A powerful leader?
The army had 100,000 warriors	Why did he need so many warriors?	To take over another country or to defend his own?
Officers not chosen for family ties	Why did Genghis Khan want officers without strong family ties?	So they would not worry about their families to better concentrate on battle?
Mongols	Who were they?	Genghis Khan's countrymen? People from Mongolia?

2 Practice It!
Making Inferences

Read the next paragraph, also about Genghis Khan's warriors, and pay attention to highlighted words as you make inferences.

> Genghis Khan began building his empire by conquering other people on the steppes. These victories brought him wealth and new soldiers to fill the army. Soon the Mongols were strong enough to attack major civilizations. In 1211 Mongol forces turned east and invaded China. Within three years, they had taken all of northern China. They then moved west and struck at the cities and kingdoms that controlled parts of the Silk Road.
>
> —*from pages 425–426*

Create your own Think-Through Chart to help you make further inferences about Genghis Khan's army. You might want to use the highlighted words in your first column and label it **Text.** Your second and third columns can be labeled **Questions** and **Inference.** Read the rest of page 426 to see if your inferences were correct.

Read to Write

Read the text under the heading **Scholar-Officials** in Section 1, page 414. Pay attention to the paragraph about how important it was for students to pass tests. Write about any experiences with tests you have had to help you understand the fears and hopes of Chinese students during the Middle Ages.

3 Apply It!

We also make inferences about other types of text, such as poetry. Read the poems on pages 420–421, and create a Think-Through chart to help understand the poems.

China Reunites

Get Ready to Read!

What's the Connection?

Earlier you read that the Han dynasty of China collapsed and China plunged into civil war. As you will read, China eventually reunited. The new dynasties took Chinese civilization to even higher levels.

Focusing on the Main Ideas

• The Sui and Tang dynasties reunited and rebuilt China after years of war. **(page 409)**

• Buddhism became popular in China and spread to Korea and Japan. **(page 412)**

• The Tang dynasty returned to the ideas of Confucius and created a new class of scholar-officials. **(page 413)**

Locating Places

Korea (kuh•REE•uh)
Japan (juh•PAN)

Meeting People

Wendi (WHEHN•DEE)
Empress Wu (WOO)

Building Your Vocabulary

warlord
economy (ih•KAH•nuh•mee)
reform
monastery (MAH•nuh•STEHR•ee)

Reading Strategy

Categorizing Information Complete a table like the one below to show the time periods, the most important rulers, and the reasons for the decline of the Sui and Tang dynasties.

	Sui	Tang
Time Period		
Important Rulers		
Reasons for Decline		

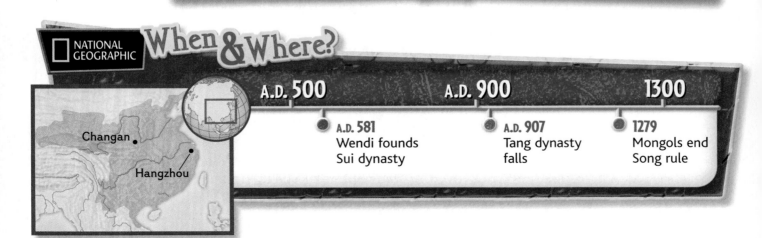

NATIONAL GEOGRAPHIC When & Where?

Changan
Hangzhou

A.D. 500   **A.D. 900**   **1300**

A.D. 581 Wendi founds Sui dynasty

A.D. 907 Tang dynasty falls

1279 Mongols end Song rule

Rebuilding China's Empire

Main Idea The Sui and Tang dynasties reunited and rebuilt China after years of war.

Reading Focus Have you ever thought about how the economy in your town or city works? How do goods get to your local stores? Who makes sure roads are paved? Read to learn how China dealt with these issues.

Earlier you read that China's Han empire ended in A.D. 220. For the next 300 years, China had no central government. It broke into 17 kingdoms. War and poverty were everywhere. Chinese **warlords**—military leaders who run a government—fought with each other while nomads conquered parts of northern China.

While China was absorbed in its own problems, it lost control of some of the groups it had conquered. One of these groups was the people of **Korea** (kuh•REE•uh). They lived on the Korean Peninsula to the northeast of China. The Koreans decided to end Chinese rule of their country. They broke away and built their own separate civilization.

The Sui Dynasty Reunites China China finally reunited in A.D. 581. In that year, a general who called himself **Wendi** (WHEHN•DEE) declared himself emperor. Wendi won battle after battle and finally reunited China. He then founded a new dynasty called the Sui (SWEE).

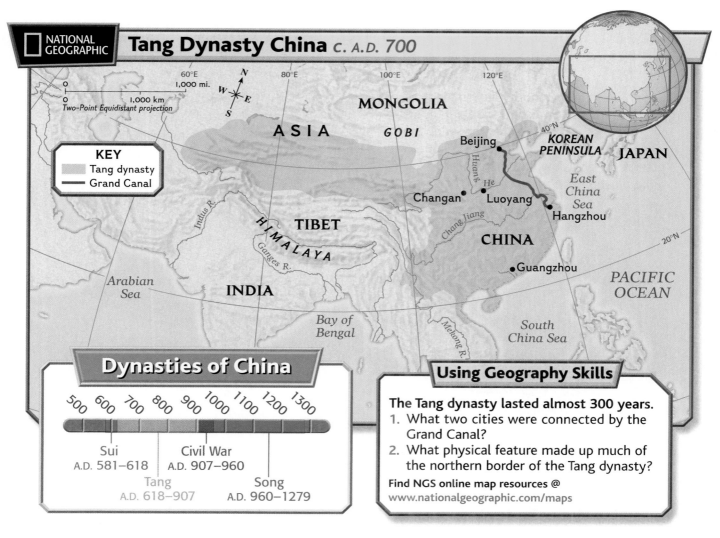

NATIONAL GEOGRAPHIC
Tang Dynasty China c. A.D. 700

KEY
Tang dynasty
Grand Canal

MONGOLIA
ASIA
GOBI
Beijing
KOREAN PENINSULA
JAPAN
Changan • Luoyang
East China Sea
Hangzhou
TIBET
HIMALAYA
Indus R.
Ganges R.
CHINA
Chang Jiang
Hwang He
Arabian Sea
INDIA
Guangzhou
PACIFIC OCEAN
Bay of Bengal
Mekong R.
South China Sea

1,000 mi.
1,000 km
Two-Point Equidistant projection

Dynasties of China

500 600 700 800 900 1000 1100 1200 1300

Sui
A.D. 581–618

Civil War
A.D. 907–960

Tang
A.D. 618–907

Song
A.D. 960–1279

Using Geography Skills

The Tang dynasty lasted almost 300 years.
1. What two cities were connected by the Grand Canal?
2. What physical feature made up much of the northern border of the Tang dynasty?

Find NGS online map resources @ www.nationalgeographic.com/maps

After Wendi died, his son Yangdi (YAHNG•DEE) took the Chinese throne. Yangdi wanted to expand China's territory. He sent an army to fight the neighboring Koreans, but the Chinese were badly defeated. At home, Yangdi took on many ambitious building projects. For example, the Great Wall had fallen into ruins, and Yangdi had it rebuilt.

Yangdi's greatest effort went into building the Grand Canal. This system of waterways linked the Chang Jiang (Yangtze River) and Huang He (Yellow River). The Grand

History Online

Web Activity Visit jat.glencoe.com and click on *Chapter 12—Student Web Activity* to learn more about China.

Canal became an important route for shipping products between northern and southern China. It helped unite China's economy. An **economy** (ih•KAH•nuh•mee) is an organized way in which people produce, sell, and buy things.

Linking Past & Present

Grand Canal and Three Gorges Dam Project

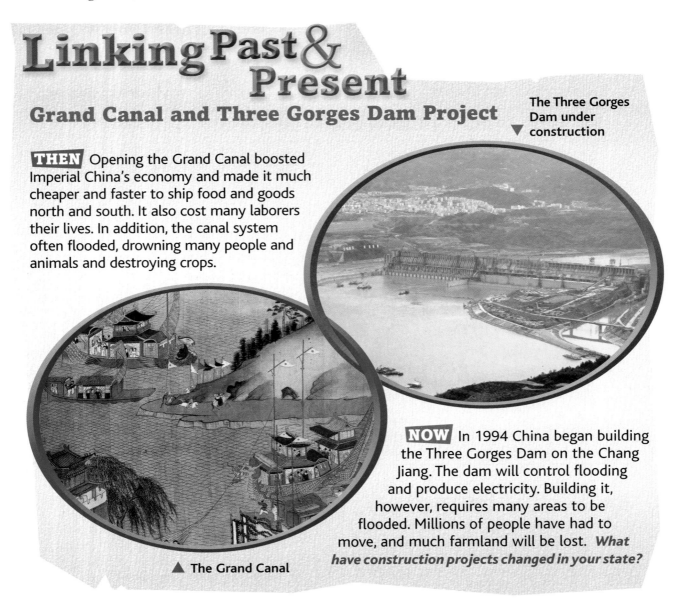

The Three Gorges Dam under construction ▼

THEN Opening the Grand Canal boosted Imperial China's economy and made it much cheaper and faster to ship food and goods north and south. It also cost many laborers their lives. In addition, the canal system often flooded, drowning many people and animals and destroying crops.

▲ The Grand Canal

NOW In 1994 China began building the Three Gorges Dam on the Chang Jiang. The dam will control flooding and produce electricity. Building it, however, requires many areas to be flooded. Millions of people have had to move, and much farmland will be lost. *What have construction projects changed in your state?*

Yangdi rebuilt China, but he did it by placing hardships on the Chinese people. Farmers were forced to work on the Great Wall and the Grand Canal. They also had to pay high taxes to the government for these projects. Finally, the farmers became so angry that they revolted. The army took control and killed Yangdi. With Yangdi gone, the Sui dynasty came to an end.

The Tang Dynasty
In A.D. 618 one of Yangdi's generals took over China. He made himself emperor and set up a new dynasty called the Tang (TAHNG). Unlike the short-lived Sui, the Tang dynasty was in power for about 300 years—from A.D. 618 to A.D. 907. The Tang capital at Changan became a magnificent city, with about one million people living there.

Tang rulers worked to strengthen China's government. They carried out a number of **reforms,** or changes that brought improvements. The most powerful Tang emperor was named Taizong (TY•ZAWNG). He restored the civil service exam system. Government officials were once again hired based on how well they did on exams rather than on their family connections. Taizong also gave land to farmers and brought order to the countryside.

During the late A.D. 600s, a woman named Wu ruled China as empress. She was the only woman in Chinese history to rule the country on her own. A forceful leader, **Empress Wu** (WOO) added more officials to the government. She also strengthened China's military forces.

Under the Tang, China regained much of its power in Asia and expanded the areas under its control. Tang armies pushed west into central Asia, invaded Tibet, and took control of the Silk Road. They marched into Korea and forced the Korean kingdoms to

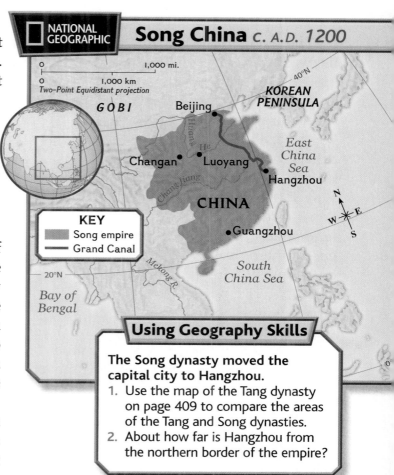

NATIONAL GEOGRAPHIC

Song China c. A.D. 1200

KEY
- Song empire
- Grand Canal

Using Geography Skills

The Song dynasty moved the capital city to Hangzhou.
1. Use the map of the Tang dynasty on page 409 to compare the areas of the Tang and Song dynasties.
2. About how far is Hangzhou from the northern border of the empire?

pay tribute, a special kind of tax that one country pays to another to be left alone. The Tang also moved south and took control of northern Vietnam.

By the mid-A.D. 700s, however, the Tang dynasty began to have problems. A new group of nomads—the Turks that you read about earlier—drove the Tang armies out of central Asia and took control of the Silk Road. This damaged China's economy. Revolts in Tibet and among Chinese farmers at home further weakened the Tang. In A.D. 907 all of this disorder brought down the Tang dynasty.

The Song Dynasty
For about 50 years after the fall of the Tang, military leaders ruled China. Then, in A.D. 960, one of the generals declared himself emperor and set up the Song (SOONG) dynasty.

The Song dynasty ruled from A.D. 960 to 1279. This period was a time of prosperity and cultural achievement for China. From the start, however, the Song faced problems that threatened their hold on China. Song rulers did not have enough soldiers to control their large empire. Tibet broke away, and nomads took over much of northern China. For safety, the Song moved their capital farther south to the city of Hangzhou (HAHNG•JOH). Hangzhou was on the coast near the Chang Jiang delta.

✓ **Reading Check** **Explain** How did Wendi unite China?

▲ Statue of the Buddha, carved about A.D. 460 in the Yun-Kang caves in China.

Buddhism Spreads to China

Main Idea Buddhism became popular in China and spread to Korea and Japan.

Reading Focus Where do you turn when you are having problems? Read to learn why many Chinese turned to Buddhism when China was in trouble.

Earlier you learned that traders and missionaries from India brought Buddhism to China in about A.D. 150. At the time, the Han dynasty was already weak. Soon afterward, China collapsed into civil war. People everywhere were dying from war and a lack of food and shelter. It was a time of great suffering. Because Buddhism taught that people could escape their suffering, many Chinese seeking peace and comfort became Buddhists.

Chinese Buddhism Early Tang rulers were not Buddhists, but they allowed Buddhism to be practiced in China. They even

City Life in Tang China

Under the Tang, China grew and was prosperous. Tang cities could be large, with many activities occurring within the city's walls. A city contained many shops and temples. The homes of rich families often had two or three floors. *When did the Tang rule China?*

Musicians and dancers

Farmers selling goods

Civil service examinations

Print shop

Making pottery

supported the building of Buddhist temples. Many Chinese Buddhists became monks and nuns. They lived in places called **monasteries** (MAH•nuh•STEHR•eez), where they meditated and worshiped.

Buddhist temples and monasteries provided services for people. They ran schools and provided rooms and food for travelers. Buddhist monks served as bankers and provided medical care.

Not all Chinese people liked Buddhism, however. Many thought that it was wrong for the Buddhist temples and monasteries to accept donations. Others believed that monks and nuns weakened respect for family life because they were not allowed to marry.

In the early A.D. 800s, Tang officials feared Buddhism's growing power. They saw Buddhism as an enemy of China's traditions. In A.D. 845 the Tang had many Buddhist monasteries and temples destroyed. Buddhism in China never fully recovered.

Chinese Buddhism Spreads East As you read earlier, Korea broke free of China when the Han dynasty fell in A.D. 220. For several hundred years after, Korea was divided into three independent kingdoms.

In the A.D. 300s, Chinese Buddhists brought their religion to Korea. About A.D. 660, the Koreans united to form one country. After that, with government support, Buddhism grew even stronger in Korea.

Buddhism later spread to the nearby islands of **Japan** (juh•PAN). According to legend, one of Korea's kings wrote to Japan's emperor. The letter contained a statue of the Buddha and Buddhist writings. "This religion is the most excellent of all teachings," the king wrote. As time passed, Buddhism won many followers in Japan as well.

✓ **Reading Check** **Explain** Why did some Chinese people dislike Buddhism?

New Confucian Ideas

Main Idea The Tang dynasty returned to the ideas of Confucius and created a new class of scholar-officials.

Reading Focus Have you ever seen someone get a reward that he or she did not earn? Read to learn how China's rulers tried to avoid this problem when hiring government officials.

You have already read about Confucius and his teachings. Confucius and his followers believed that a good government depended on having wise leaders. The civil service examinations introduced by Han

Primary Source — Defending Confucianism

Han Yü (A.D. 768 to A.D. 824) encouraged the Chinese people to remain faithful to Confucianism.

"What were the teachings of our ancient kings? Universal love is called humanity. To practice this in the proper manner is called righteousness. To proceed according to these is called the Way.... They offered sacrifices to Heaven and the gods came to receive them.... What Way is this? I say: This is what I call the Way, and not what the Taoists [Daoists] and the Buddhists called the Way...."

—Han Yü, "An Inquiry on The Way" (Tao)

▲ Han Yü

DBQ **Document-Based Question**

Why does Han Yü think Confucianism should be followed?

Focus on Everyday Life

Civil Service Exams Proficiency tests and final exams today take a lot of preparation, but they are not as difficult as China's civil service examinations given during the Tang dynasty. Men of almost all ranks tried to pass the exams so they could hold government jobs and become wealthy. Thousands attempted the tests, but only a few hundred people qualified for the important positions.

Chinese boys began preparing for the exams in primary school. After many years of learning to read and write more than 400,000 words and sayings, the boys—now men in their twenties or early thirties—would take the first of three levels of exams. Students traveled to huge testing sites to take the tests. Food and beds were not provided, so they had to bring their own. Many men became sick or insane because of the stress of the tests and the poor conditions under which they were tested.

▲ Students taking civil service exams

Connecting to the Past

1. How old were the Chinese when they took the tests?
2. Why do you think taking the tests was so stressful for these men?

rulers were a product of Confucian ideas. They were supposed to recruit talented government officials.

After the fall of the Han dynasty, no national government existed to give civil service examinations. Confucianism lost much support, and Buddhism with its spiritual message won many followers. Tang and Song rulers, however, brought Confucianism back into favor.

What Is Neo-Confucianism? The Tang dynasty gave its support to a new kind of Confucianism called neo-Confucianism. This new Confucianism was created, in part, to reduce Buddhism's popularity. It taught that life in this world was just as important as the afterlife. Followers were expected to take part in life and help others.

Although it criticized Buddhist ideas, this new form of Confucianism also picked up some Buddhist and Daoist beliefs. For many Chinese, Confucianism became more than a system of rules for being good. It became a religion with beliefs about the spiritual world. Confucian thinkers taught that if people followed Confucius's teachings, they would find peace of mind and live in harmony with nature.

The Song dynasty, which followed the Tang, also supported neo-Confucianism. The Song even adopted it as their official philosophy, or belief system.

Scholar-Officials Neo-Confucianism also became a way to strengthen the government. Both Tang and Song rulers used civil service examinations to hire officials. In doing so, they based the bureaucracy on a merit system. Under a merit system, people are accepted for what they can do and not on their riches or personal contacts.

The examinations tested job seekers on their knowledge of Confucian writings. To pass, it was necessary to write with style as well as understanding. The tests were supposed to be fair, but only men were allowed to take the tests. Also, only rich people had the money that was needed to help their sons study for the tests.

Passing the tests was very difficult. However, parents did all they could to prepare their sons. At the age of four, boys started learning to write the characters of the Chinese language. Later, students had to memorize all of Confucius's writings. If a student recited the passages poorly, he could expect to be hit by his teacher.

After many years of study, the boys took their examinations. Despite all the preparation, only one in five passed. Those who failed usually found jobs helping officials or teaching others. However, they would never be given a government job.

▲ Chinese scholar-officials on horseback

Over the years, the examination system created a new wealthy class in China. This group was made up of scholar-officials. Strict rules set the scholar-officials apart from society. One rule was that they could not do physical work. Students preparing for the tests were taught never to use their hands except for painting or writing.

Reading Check **Describe** How did Confucianism change in China?

History Online

Study Central™ Need help with the material in this section? Visit jat.glencoe.com

Section 1 Review

Reading Summary

Review the Main Ideas

- While the Sui dynasty was short-lived, the Tang and Song dynasties lasted for hundreds of years and returned power and prosperity to China.

- Buddhism became popular in China and also spread to Korea and Japan.

- A new kind of Confucianism developed in China during the Tang and Song dynasties, and the government used civil service tests to improve itself.

What Did You Learn?

1. What made Buddhism so popular in China?

2. How was neo-Confucianism a response to Buddhism's popularity, and what did it teach?

Critical Thinking

3. **Compare and Contrast** Create a diagram to show how the reigns of Wendi and Yangdi were similar and how they were different.

Wendi   Yangdi

4. **Cause and Effect** What events led to the fall of the Tang dynasty?

5. **Sequencing Information** Describe the history of Buddhism during the Tang dynasty.

6. **Analyze** Why had Confucianism fallen out of favor in China before the Tang and Song dynasties?

7. **Drawing Conclusions** Do you think China's civil service system truly brought the most talented individuals into the government? How would you make the system fairer?

Section 2

Chinese Society

Get Ready to Read!

What's the Connection?

In the last section, you learned about the rise and fall of the Sui, Tang, and Song dynasties. During those dynasties, China's economy began to grow again. Chinese inventors developed many new technologies, and Chinese artists and writers produced new works that are still admired today.

Focusing on the Main Ideas

• The Tang dynasty strengthened China's economy by supporting farming and trade. *(page 417)*

• The Chinese developed new technologies, such as steelmaking and printing. *(page 418)*

• During the Tang and the Song dynasties, China enjoyed a golden age of art and literature. *(page 420)*

Locating Places
Changan (CHAHNG•AHN)

Meeting People
Li Bo (LEE   BOH)
Duo Fu (DWAW   FOO)

Building Your Vocabulary
porcelain (POHR•suh•luhn)
calligraphy (kuh•LIH•gruh•fee)

Reading Strategy
Organizing Information Complete a chart like the one below describing the new technologies developed in China during the Middle Ages.

New Technologies

NATIONAL GEOGRAPHIC When & Where?		
A.D. 600	A.D. 900	1200
A.D. 618 Tang dynasty takes power	A.D. 868 Chinese print world's first complete book	c. 1150 Chinese sailors are the first to use compass

Changan

Hangzhou

A Growing Economy

Main Idea **The Tang dynasty strengthened China's economy by supporting farming and trade.**

Reading Focus Do you know anyone who drinks tea or wears silk clothing? Both of these goods were first produced in China. Read to learn how farming changed under the Tang dynasty.

When the Han dynasty in China collapsed in the A.D. 200s, it was a disaster for China's economy. As fighting began, cities were damaged and farms were burned. Artisans made fewer goods, farmers grew fewer crops, and merchants had less to trade. Under the Tang dynasty, these problems were solved.

Why Did Farming Improve?
When the Tang rulers took power in A.D. 618, they brought peace to the countryside and gave more land to farmers. As a result, farmers were able to make many advances. They improved irrigation and introduced new ways of growing their crops. Farmers also developed new kinds of rice, which grew well in poor soil, produced more per acre, grew faster, and were resistant to disease.

These changes helped farmers grow more and more rice. China's farmers also began to grow tea, which became a popular drink. They made improvements in other crops as well. With more food available, the number of people in China greatly increased. At the same time, more people moved southward, where rice grew abundantly in the Chang Jiang valley.

China's Trade Grows
Tang rulers also had roads and waterways built. These changes made travel within and outside of China much easier. Chinese merchants were able to increase trade with people in other parts of Asia. The Silk Road, now under Tang control, once again bustled with activity.

▲ A worker holds a tray of silkworms eating mulberry leaves. Eventually the worms will spin cocoons. Workers then collect and unravel the cocoons to make silk thread. *Why do you think silk is still expensive today?*

▼ Silk, shown here being harvested, remained an important trade item for the Chinese. *How did Tang rulers help increase trade?*

One of the items traded by the Chinese was silk fabric. This product gave the road its name and was popular in markets to the west of China. In addition, China traded tea, steel, paper, and porcelain. **Porcelain** (POHR•suh•luhn) is made of fine clay and baked at high temperatures. In return, other countries sent China products such as gold, silver, precious stones, and fine woods.

Other trade routes were also established. Roads linked China to central Asia, India, and southwest Asia. In addition, the Tang opened new ports along China's coast to boost trade.

√ Reading Check **Cause and Effect** How did the new kinds of rice developed in China help its population grow?

New Technology

Main Idea **The Chinese developed new technologies, such as steelmaking and printing.**

Reading Focus This book is made of paper with letters printed on the paper by a machine. Read to learn how printing was first invented in China during the Tang dynasty.

During the Tang and Song dynasties, new inventions changed China's society. In time, these discoveries spread to other parts of the world.

China Discovers Coal and Steel For most of China's history, people burned wood to heat their homes and cook their food. By

Changan's Royal Palace

The Tang capital city of Changan may have had a population of one million people at its peak. The city had large blocks that included houses, businesses, and temples set along straight streets. Its layout inspired the design of many later cities. The area containing the royal palace, shown below, was bordered by parklands. *What improvements to agriculture allowed China's population to grow during the Tang dynasty?*

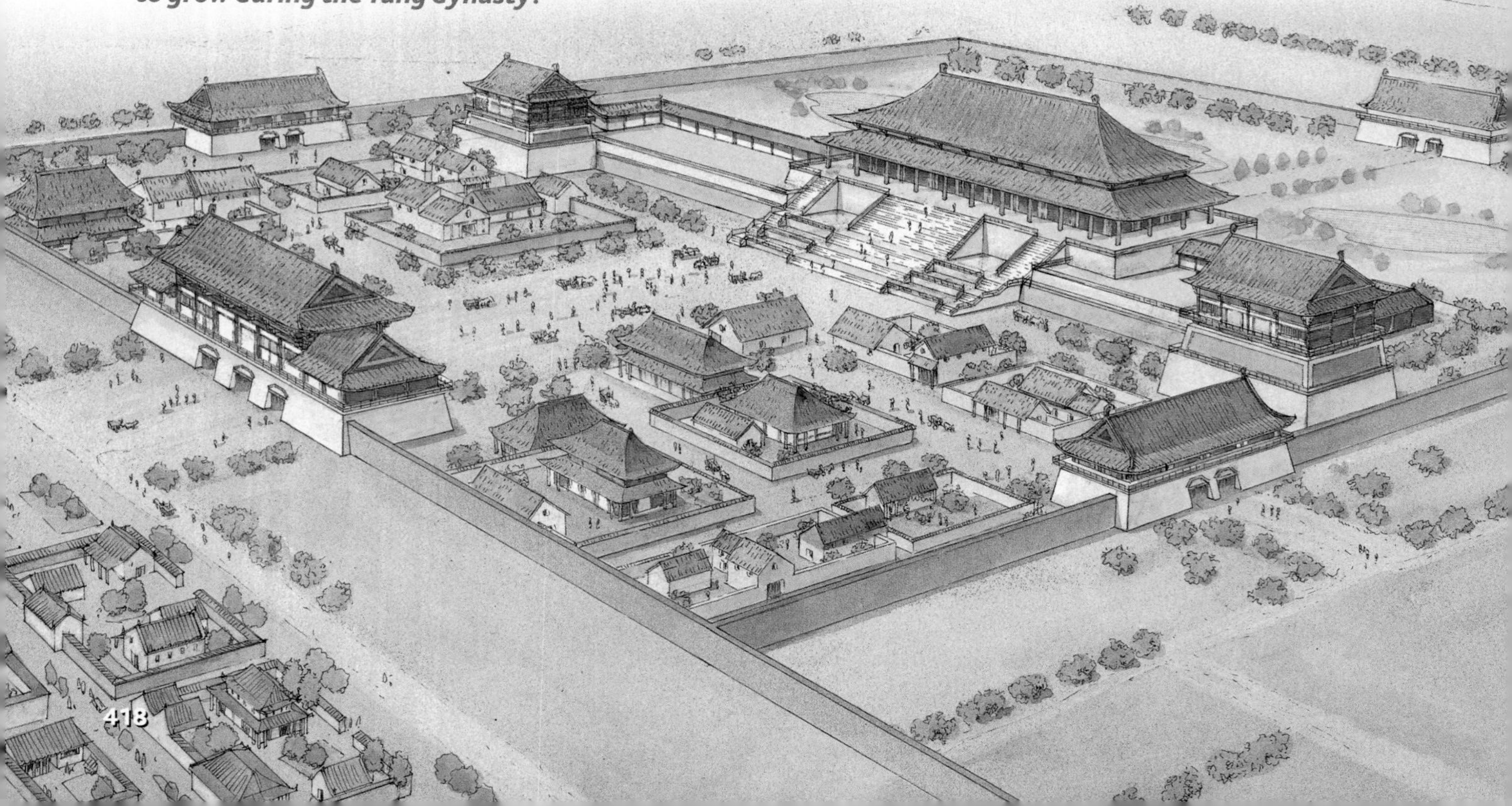

the time of the Tang dynasty, wood was becoming scarce in China. However, the Chinese had discovered that coal could be used to heat things, and soon a coal-mining industry developed.

The Chinese used coal to heat furnaces to high temperatures, which led to another discovery. When iron was produced in hot furnaces heated by coal, the molten iron mixed with carbon from the coal. This created a new, stronger metal known today as steel.

The Chinese used steel to make many things. They made armor, swords, and helmets for their army, but they also made stoves, farm tools, drills, steel chain, and even steel nails and sewing needles.

The Printing Process

Another Chinese invention was a method for printing books. Before printing, books had to be copied by hand. As a result, few books were made, and they were very expensive. The Chinese began printing in the A.D. 600s. They used blocks of wood on which they cut the characters of an entire page. Ink was placed over the wooden block. Then paper was laid on the block to make a print. Cutting the block took a long time. When they were completed, however, the woodblocks could be used again and again to make many copies.

The Chinese soon began printing books. The earliest known printed book dates from about A.D. 868. It is a Buddhist book called the *Diamond Sutra*. The invention of printing was very important. It helped to spread ideas more rapidly.

In the A.D. 1000s, a Chinese printer named Pi Sheng (BEE SHUHNG) invented movable type for printing. With movable type, each character is a separate piece. The pieces can be moved around to make sentences and used again and again. Pi Sheng made his pieces from clay and put them together to produce book pages. However,

---

Science and Inventions

Printing When the Chinese invented movable type, they improved the art of printing. A Chinese author described the work of Pi Sheng:

"He took sticky clay and cut in it characters as thin as the edge of a copper coin. Each character formed as it were a single type. He baked them in the fire to make them hard. He had previously prepared an iron plate and he had covered this plate with a mixture of pine resin, wax, and paper ashes. When he wished to print, he took an iron frame and set it on the iron plate. In this he placed the type, set close together. When the frame was full, the whole made one solid block of type."

—Shên Kua, *Dream Pool Jottings*

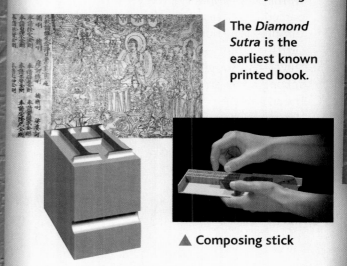

◀ The *Diamond Sutra* is the earliest known printed book.

▲ Composing stick

▲ Movable type block

Connecting to the Past

1. Why do you think Pi Sheng used clay to make his characters?
2. In what instance would woodblock printing have been a better method to use than movable type?

because written Chinese has so many characters, woodblock printing was easier and quicker than using movable type.

Other Chinese Inventions The Chinese made gunpowder for use in explosives. One weapon was the fire lance, an ancestor of the gun. It used gunpowder and helped make the Chinese army a strong force. The Chinese also used gunpowder to make fireworks.

The Chinese also built large ships with rudders and sails. About 1150, Chinese sailors began using the compass to help them find their way. This let ships sail farther from land.

✓ **Reading Check** **Analyze** Why was the invention of printing so important?

Primary Source

Li Bo

In the following poem, Li Bo writes about parting from a friend.

"Green hills sloping from the northern wall, white water rounding the eastern city: once parted from this place the lone weed tumbles ten thousand miles.

Drifting clouds—a traveler's thoughts; setting sun—an old friend's heart. Wave hands and let us take leave now, *hsiao-hsiao* our hesitant horses neighing."

—Li Bo, "Seeing a Friend Off"

▲ Li Bo

DBQ Document-Based Question

How are drifting clouds like a traveler's thoughts?

Art and Literature

Main Idea During the Tang and the Song dynasties, China enjoyed a golden age of art and literature.

Reading Focus If you were to choose one poem to read to the class, which poem would it be? Below, you will read a poem that is a Chinese favorite.

The Tang and Song eras were a golden age for Chinese culture. The invention of printing helped to spread Chinese ideas and artwork. Chinese rulers actively supported art and literature, and invited artists and poets to live and work in the capital city of **Changan** (CHAHNG•AHN).

What Was Tang Poetry Like? Chinese writers best expressed themselves in poems. In fact, the Tang dynasty is viewed as the great age of poetry in China. Some Tang poems celebrated the beauty of nature, the thrill of seasons changing, and the joy of having a good friend. Other Tang poems expressed sadness for the shortness of life and mourned the cruelty of friends parting.

Li Bo (LEE BOH) was one of the most popular poets of the Tang era. His poems often centered on nature. The poem below by Li Bo is probably the best-known poem in China. For centuries, Chinese schoolchildren have had to memorize it. Its title is "Still Night Thoughts."

❝ Moonlight in front of my bed—
I took it for frost on the ground!
I lift my eyes to watch the
    mountain moon,
lower them and dream of home. ❞

—Li Bo,
"Still Night Thoughts"

Another favorite poet of that time was **Duo Fu** (DWAW FOO). He was a poor civil servant who had a hard life. Civil war swept

▲ This Chinese landscape was painted in the 1100s. *How were Daoist beliefs depicted in landscapes painted during the Song dynasty?*

▼ Chinese calligraphy

▲ Ink and watercolor drawing on silk

China, and food was hard to find. Duo Fu nearly died of starvation. His problems opened his eyes to the sufferings of the common people.

As a result, Duo Fu's poems often were very serious. They frequently dealt with issues such as social injustice and the problems of the poor. Duo Fu wrote the poem below after a rebellion left the capital city in ruins. It is called "Spring Landscape."

> 66 Rivers and mountains survive
>   broken countries.
> Spring returns. The city grows
>   lush again.
> Blossoms scatter tears thinking of
>   us, and this
> Separation in a bird's cry startles
>   the heart.
>
> Beacon-fires have burned
>   through three months.
> By now, letters are worth ten
>   thousand in gold.
>
> 99
>
> —Duo Fu,
>   "Spring Landscape"

Painting in Song China

The painting of landscapes became widespread during the Song dynasty. However, Chinese artists did not try to make exact pictures of the landscapes they were painting. Instead, they wished to portray the "idea" of the mountains, lakes, and other features of their landscapes. Also, empty spaces were left in the paintings on purpose. This is because of the Daoist belief that a person cannot know the whole truth about something.

Daoist beliefs also can be seen in the way people are portrayed. They are tiny figures, fishing in small boats or wandering up a hillside trail. In other words, the people are living in, but not controlling, nature. They are only a part of the harmony of the natural setting.

Chinese painters often wrote poetry on their works. They used a brush and ink to write beautiful characters called **calligraphy** (kuh•LIH•gruh•fee).

Chinese Porcelain

During the Tang period, Chinese artisans perfected the making of porcelain. Because porcelain later came from

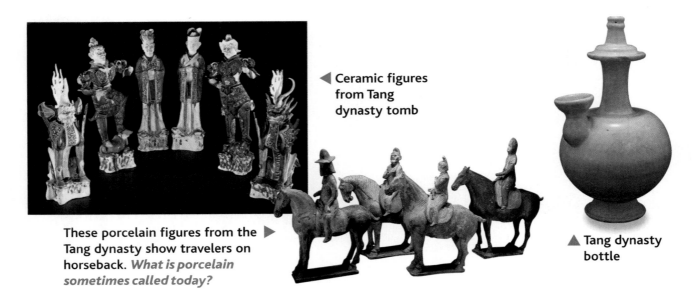

◀ Ceramic figures from Tang dynasty tomb

These porcelain figures from the ▶ Tang dynasty show travelers on horseback. *What is porcelain sometimes called today?*

▲ Tang dynasty bottle

China to the West, people today sometimes call porcelain by the name "china."

Porcelain can be made into plates, cups, figurines, and vases. In A.D. 851 an Arab traveler described the quality of Tang porcelain: "There is in China a very fine clay from which are made vases. . . . Water in these vases is visible through them, and yet they are made of clay."

The technology for making porcelain spread to other parts of the world. It finally reached Europe in the 1700s.

✓ **Reading Check** **Identify** What did Duo Fu often write about?

History **O**nline

Study Central™ Need help with the material in this section? Visit jat.glencoe.com

Section 2 Review

Reading Summary
Review the Main Ideas

- During the Tang dynasty, both farming and trade flourished, and the empire grew much larger than ever before.

- Many important inventions were developed in China during the Tang and Song dynasties, including steel, printing, and gunpowder.

- Chinese literature and arts, including poetry, landscape painting, and porcelain making, reached new heights during the Tang and Song dynasties.

What Did You Learn?

1. What products were traded by China along the Silk Road?

2. What were some of the subjects of Tang poetry?

Critical Thinking

3. **Organizing Information** Draw a chart to describe the new technologies developed in China.

Metalworking	
Printing	
Weapons	
Sailing	

4. **Summarize** Describe the changes to Chinese agriculture during the Tang dynasty.

5. **Contrast** How do the two forms of printing invented by the Chinese differ?

6. **Evaluate** Which invention of the Tang and Song dynasties do you think has been most important? Explain.

7. **Creative Writing** Read the poem "Still Night Thoughts" by Li Bo again. Then write a short, four-stanza poem similar to Li Bo's about the view from your bedroom or kitchen window.

The Mongols in China

Get Ready to Read!

What's the Connection?

As a complex culture developed in China, a northern enemy waited to attack.

Focusing on the Main Ideas

- Genghis Khan and his sons built the Mongol Empire, which stretched from the Pacific Ocean to Eastern Europe. *(page 424)*

- The Mongols conquered China and created a new dynasty that tried to conquer Japan and began trading with the rest of Asia. *(page 428)*

Locating Places

Mongolia (mahn•GOH•lee•uh)
Gobi (GOH•bee)
Karakorum (KAHR•uh•KOHR•uhm)
Khanbaliq (KAHN•buh•LEEK)
Beijing (BAY•JIHNG)

Meeting People

Genghis Khan
(GEHNG•guhs KAHN)
Kublai Khan (KOO•BLUH KAHN)
Marco Polo
(MAHR•koh POH•loh)

Building Your Vocabulary

tribe
steppe (STEHP)
terror (TEHR•uhr)

Reading Strategy

Organizing Information Use a diagram like the one below to show the accomplishments of Genghis Khan's reign.

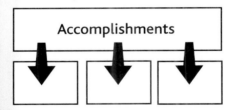

Accomplishments

When & Where?

1206
Genghis Khan unites Mongols

1271
Kublai Khan becomes China's emperor

1368
Yuan (Mongol) dynasty falls

Karakorum
Baghdad
Khanbaliq (Beijing)

The Mongols

Main Idea Genghis Khan and his sons built the Mongol Empire, which stretched from the Pacific Ocean to Eastern Europe.

Reading Focus Have you ever had the chance to ride a horse? For thousands of years, the horse was the most important form of transportation in the world. Read to learn how one people used their skills as horse riders to build a vast empire.

The Mongols lived in an area north of China called **Mongolia** (mahn•GOH•lee•uh). They were made up of **tribes,** or groups of related families, loosely joined together. The Mongols raised cattle, goats, sheep, and horses. They followed their herds as the animals grazed Mongolia's great **steppes** (STEHPS). Steppes are wide rolling grassy plains that stretch from the Black Sea to northern China.

From an early period in their history, the Mongols were known for two things. One was their ability to ride horses well. Mongols practically lived on horseback, learning to ride at age four or five.

The other skill for which the Mongols were known was the ability to wage war. They could fire arrows at enemies from a distance while charging at them. Then they would attack with spears and swords.

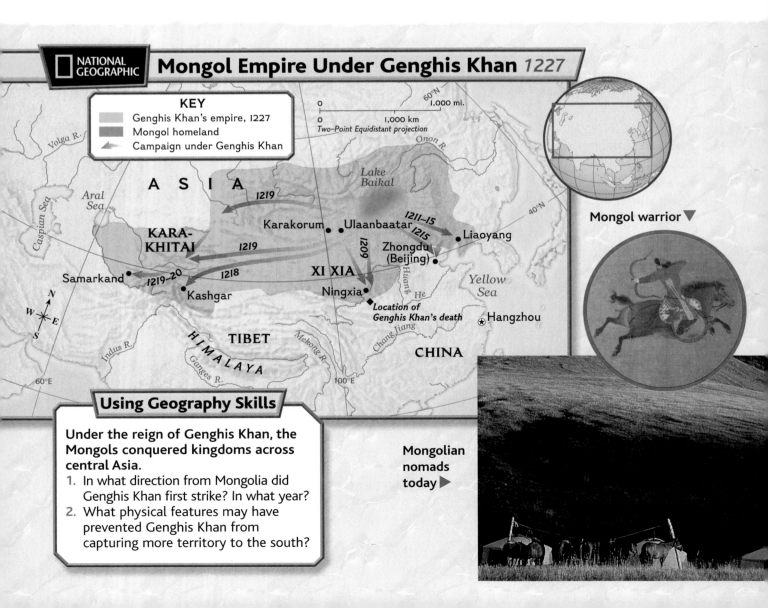

NATIONAL GEOGRAPHIC

Mongol Empire Under Genghis Khan *1227*

KEY
- Genghis Khan's empire, 1227
- Mongol homeland
- Campaign under Genghis Khan

0   1,000 mi.
0   1,000 km
Two–Point Equidistant projection

Volga R.

ASIA

Aral Sea

Caspian Sea

Lake Baikal

Onon R.

60°N

40°N

KARA-KHITAI

1219

1219

Karakorum · Ulaanbaatar

1211–15

1215

Liaoyang

1209

Zhongdu (Beijing)

Samarkand ·

1219–20

1218

Kashgar

XI XIA

Ningxia

Huang He

Yellow Sea

Location of Genghis Khan's death

Hangzhou

N W E S

Indus R.

HIMALAYA

Ganges R.

TIBET

Mekong R.

Chang Jiang

CHINA

60°E

100°E

Mongol warrior ▼

Using Geography Skills

Under the reign of Genghis Khan, the Mongols conquered kingdoms across central Asia.

1. In what direction from Mongolia did Genghis Khan first strike? In what year?
2. What physical features may have prevented Genghis Khan from capturing more territory to the south?

Mongolian nomads today ▶

Who Was Genghis Khan? The man who would unite the Mongols was born in the 1160s. He was named Temujin (teh•MOO•juhn), which means "blacksmith." Temujin showed his leadership skills early. He was still a young man when he began to unite the Mongol tribes.

In 1206 a meeting of Mongol leaders took place somewhere in the **Gobi** (GOH•bee), a vast desert that covers parts of Mongolia and China. At that meeting, Temujin was elected **Genghis Khan** (GEHNG•guhs KAHN), which means "strong ruler." Genghis Khan brought together Mongol laws in a new code. He also created a group of tribal chiefs to help him plan military campaigns. From the time of his election until the end of his life, Genghis Khan fought to conquer the lands beyond Mongolia.

Genghis Khan gathered an army of more than 100,000 warriors. He placed his soldiers into well-trained groups. Commanding them were officers chosen for their abilities, not for their family ties. These changes made the Mongols the most skilled fighting force in the world at that time.

Genghis Khan began building his empire by conquering other people on the steppes. These victories brought him wealth and new soldiers to fill the army.

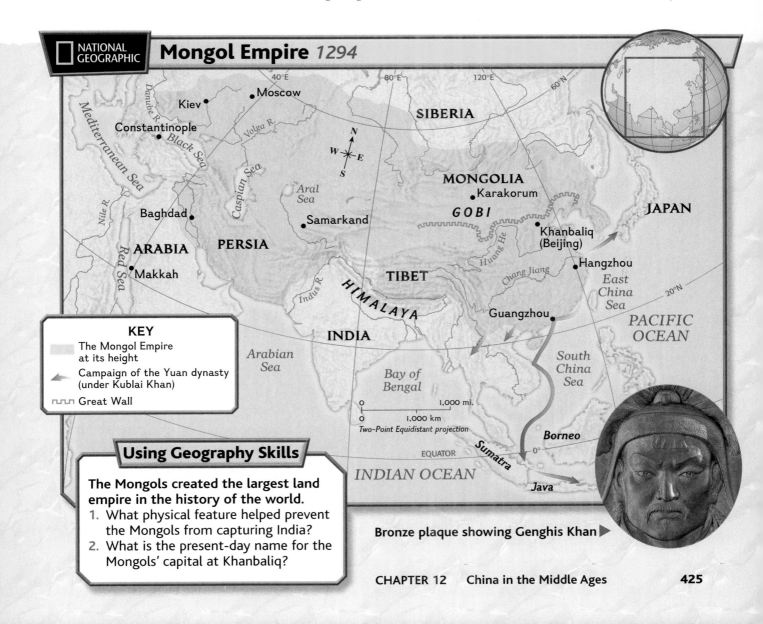

NATIONAL GEOGRAPHIC
Mongol Empire 1294

KEY
- The Mongol Empire at its height
- Campaign of the Yuan dynasty (under Kublai Khan)
- Great Wall

1,000 mi.
1,000 km
Two-Point Equidistant projection

Using Geography Skills

The Mongols created the largest land empire in the history of the world.
1. What physical feature helped prevent the Mongols from capturing India?
2. What is the present-day name for the Mongols' capital at Khanbaliq?

Bronze plaque showing Genghis Khan ▶

▲ In the battle scene shown here, Mongol troops storm across the Chang Jiang on a bridge made of boats. *After conquering northern China, what areas did the Mongols attack?*

Soon the Mongols were strong enough to attack major civilizations. In 1211 Mongol forces turned east and invaded China. Within three years, they had taken all of northern China. They then moved west and struck at the cities and kingdoms that controlled parts of the Silk Road.

Genghis Khan and his Mongol warriors became known for their cruelty and use of **terror** (TEHR•uhr). Terror refers to violent actions that are meant to scare people into surrendering, or giving up. Mongol warriors attacked, robbed, and burned cities. Within a short time, the Mongols became known for their fierce ways, and many people surrendered to them without fighting.

The Mongol Empire Genghis Khan died in 1227. His large empire was divided among his four sons. Under their leadership, the empire continued to expand. The Mongols swept into parts of eastern and central Europe. They also conquered much of southwest Asia. In 1258 the famous Muslim city of Baghdad fell to the Mongols. Mongol armies then pushed through Syria and Palestine to Egypt. They were finally stopped by the Muslim rulers of Egypt in 1260.

The Mongols united all of these different territories under their rule. Their empire reached from the Pacific Ocean in the east to Eastern Europe in the west and from Siberia in the north to the Himalaya in the south. It was the largest land empire the world had ever known.

Despite widespread destruction, the Mongols eventually brought peace to the lands they ruled. Peace encouraged trade, which helped the Mongols. Many of Asia's trade routes now lay in Mongol hands. The Mongols taxed the products traded over these roads and, as a result, grew wealthy.

The Mongols felt great respect for the advanced cultures they conquered. Sometimes they even adopted some of the beliefs and customs they encountered. For example, the Mongols in southwest Asia accepted Islam and adopted Arab, Persian, and Turkish ways.

The Mongols also learned many things from the Chinese. As they battled Chinese troops, they learned about gunpowder and its use as an explosive. They also saw the Chinese use the fire lance, a weapon that used gunpowder. Quickly, the Mongols adopted both gunpowder and the fire lance for use in battle. These new weapons made Mongol armies even more frightening to their enemies.

✓ **Reading Check** **Analyze** What military and economic reasons explain why the Mongols were able to build an empire so quickly?

Biography

GENGHIS KHAN
c. A.D. 1167–1227

Mongol Leader

Was Genghis Khan a ruthless warrior who enjoyed causing death and destruction, or was he a skilled leader who improved the lives of those in his empire, or both? Genghis Khan built a huge empire across Asia using loyal, strong, and well-trained warriors. His men killed hundreds of thousands on the quest. Although the wars he and his sons fought were brutal and bloody, they eventually brought peace and prosperity to most of Asia.

Genghis Khan was named Temujin by his father, the Mongol chief Yisugei. Folklore says Temujin had a large blood clot in his right hand, which meant he was destined to become a great warrior. Temujin grew up in his father's camp along the Onon River in Mongolia.

Temujin's father arranged a marriage for his nine-year-old son. His wife came from another tribe, and the marriage helped bring wealth to his family. Borte, his wife at age ten, was beautiful. Temujin and Borte, had four sons when they both became older.

Years later, when his father was killed by the Tartars and his loyal warriors left the tribe, Temujin lost his wealth. His poverty and the disloyalty of his father's soldiers angered him so much that he decided to become a great warrior. Over time, Temujin became Ghengis Khan. When he died after falling from a horse, his son Ogodei was picked to succeed him.

▲ Genghis Khan

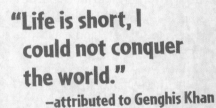

"Life is short, I could not conquer the world."
—attributed to Genghis Khan

▲ Genghis Khan's camp

Then and Now

In Mongolia today, Genghis Khan is considered a national hero. What do you think? Was Genghis Khan a villain or a hero?

Mongol Rule in China

Main Idea The Mongols conquered China and created a new dynasty that tried to conquer Japan and began trading with the rest of Asia.

Reading Focus What does it mean to be tolerant? Read to find out how the Mongols used tolerance to rule the Chinese.

In 1260 the Mongols named Genghis Khan's grandson, Kublai, to be the new khan, or ruler. **Kublai Khan** (KOO•BLUH KAHN) continued the Mongol conquest of China that his father had begun. In 1264 Kublai moved his capital from **Karakorum** in Mongolia to **Khanbaliq** in northern China. Today the modern city of **Beijing** (BAY•JIHNG) stands on the site of the Mongols' Chinese capital.

Primary Source: Kublai Khan's Park

Marco Polo recorded a description of the luxury in which Kublai Khan lived.

"[The palace wall] encloses and encircles fully sixteen miles of parkland well watered with springs and streams . . . Into this park there is no entry except by way of the palace. Here the Great Khan keeps game animals of all sorts . . . to provide food for the gerfalcons [large, arctic falcons] and other falcons which he has in here in mew [an enclosure]."

—Marco Polo, "Kublai Khan's Park, c. 1275"

▲ Kublai Khan presents golden tablets to Marco Polo

DBQ Document-Based Question

Why did Kublai Khan keep game animals—ones hunted for sport or food—in his park?

What Did the Mongols Do in China?

In 1271 Kublai Khan decided to become China's next emperor. Within 10 years, the Mongols had conquered southern China and put an end to the Song dynasty. Kublai Khan started the Yuan (YOO•AHN) dynasty. *Yuan* means "beginning," and its name showed that the Mongols wanted to rule China for a long time. But the Yuan dynasty would last only about 100 years. Kublai would rule for 30 of those years.

Kublai Khan gave Mongol leaders the top jobs in China's government, but he knew he needed Chinese scholar-officials to run the government. So he let many of the Chinese keep their government jobs.

The Mongols were different from the Chinese in many ways. They had their own language, laws, and customs. This kept them separate from Chinese society. The Mongols were rulers at the top of Chinese society, but they did not mix with the Chinese people.

Like many Chinese, the Mongols were Buddhists. They were tolerant, however, of other religions. For example, Kublai Khan invited Christians, Muslims, and Hindus from outside China to practice their faiths and to win converts.

Under Mongol rule, China reached the height of its wealth and power. Its splendor drew foreigners who came to China over the Silk Road. Khanbaliq, the capital, became known for its wide streets, beautiful palaces, and fine homes.

One of the most famous European travelers to reach China was **Marco Polo** (MAHR•koh POH•loh). He came from the city of Venice in Italy. Kublai Khan was fascinated by Marco Polo's stories about his travels. For about 16 years, Kublai sent Polo on many fact-finding trips. When Polo finally returned to Europe, he wrote a book about his adventures. His accounts of the wonders of China amazed Europeans.

Trade and Conquest The Mongols ruled a large empire that stretched from China to eastern Europe. As a result, China prospered from increased trade with other areas. Goods such as silver, spices, carpets, and cotton flowed in from Europe and other parts of Asia. In return, China shipped out tea, silk, and porcelain. Europeans and Muslims also brought Chinese discoveries, such as steel, gunpowder, and the compass, back to their homelands.

The Mongols enlarged China's empire and conquered Vietnam and northern Korea. The rulers of Korea, called the Koryo, remained in power because they accepted

▲ This drawing from a historic map shows Marco Polo's journey along the Silk Road. *From what European city did Marco Polo travel?*

Mongol control. The Mongols forced thousands of Koreans to build warships. These ships were used by the Mongols to invade Japan. You will read about the Mongol invasions of Japan in a later chapter.

Reading Check **Identify** Who founded the Yuan dynasty?

Section 3 Review

History Online

Study Central™ Need help with the material in this section? Visit jat.glencoe.com

Reading Summary

Review the Main Ideas

- Under leaders such as Genghis Khan and his sons, the Mongol Empire expanded until it stretched from the Pacific Ocean to Eastern Europe, and from Siberia south to the Himalaya.

- Kublai Khan conquered China, which led to increased trade between China and other parts of the world.

What Did You Learn?

1. Who was Marco Polo?

2. What areas did the Mongols conquer?

Critical Thinking

3. **Sequencing Information** Draw a time line like the one below. Fill in details to show the Mongols' rise to power in China.

```
|——+——+——+——+——|
1160s          1281
Temujin        Mongols
born           conquer
               China
```

4. **Analyze** How did the Mongols use terror in their conquests?

5. **Summarize** How did the Mongols benefit from their contact with the Chinese?

6. **Descriptive Writing** Imagine you are Marco Polo visiting Kublai Khan in Khanbaliq. Write a journal entry describing some of the things you are learning about the Mongol Empire under Kublai Khan.

The Ming Dynasty

Get Ready to Read!

What's the Connection?

In Section 3, you read about the Mongol conquest. Eventually, the Chinese drove the Mongols out, and a new dynasty arose.

Focusing on the Main Ideas

• Ming rulers strengthened China's government and brought back peace and prosperity. *(page 431)*

• During the Ming dynasty, China sent a fleet to explore Asia and East Africa. *(page 433)*

Locating Places

Nanjing (NAHN•JIHNG)
Portugal (POHR•chih•guhl)

Meeting People

Zhu Yuanzhang
 (JOO   YOO•AHN•JAHNG)
Yong Le (YUNG   LEE)
Zheng He (JUNG   HUH)

Building Your Vocabulary

treason (TREE•zuhn)
census (SEHN•suhs)
novel (NAH•vuhl)
barbarian (bahr•BEHR•ee•uhn)

Reading Strategy

Cause and Effect Use a chart like the one below to show cause-and-effect links in China's early trade voyages.

Cause
Zheng He traveled to parts of Asia and Africa.

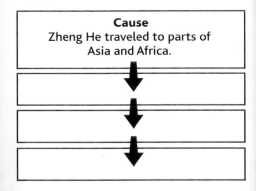

NATIONAL GEOGRAPHIC   When & Where?

Beijing

Nanjing

Macao

1400

1500

1600

1405
Zheng He begins first overseas voyage

1514
Portuguese ships arrive in China

1644
Ming dynasty falls

The Rise of the Ming

Main Idea **Ming rulers strengthened China's government and brought back peace and prosperity.**

Reading Focus Think about all the different things the government does for people. Imagine if you were running the government and had to rebuild the country after a war. What would you do? Read to learn how the Ming rulers in China rebuilt their country after the Mongols left.

Kublai Khan died in 1294. A series of weak rulers followed him, and Mongol power began to decline. During the 1300s, problems mounted for the Yuan dynasty. Mongol groups in Mongolia to the north broke away. At the same time, many Chinese resented Mongol controls and wanted their own dynasty.

How Did the Ming Dynasty Begin? A series of rebellions finally drove out the Mongols. In 1368 a rebel leader named **Zhu Yuanzhang** (JOO YOO•AHN•JAHNG) became emperor. Zhu reunited the country and set up his capital at **Nanjing** (NAHN• JIHNG) in southern China. There, he founded the Ming, or "Brilliant," dynasty.

As emperor, Zhu took the name Hong Wu, or the "Military Emperor." He brought back order, but he also proved to be a cruel leader. Hong Wu trusted no one and killed officials he suspected of **treason** (TREE• zuhn), or disloyalty to the government. Hong Wu ruled China for 30 years. When he died in 1398, his son became emperor and took the name of **Yong Le** (YUNG LEE).

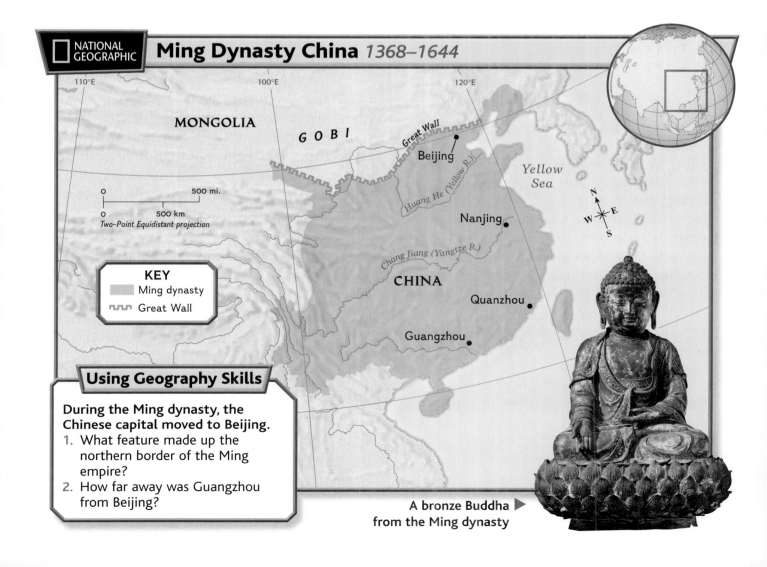

NATIONAL GEOGRAPHIC
Ming Dynasty China 1368–1644

MONGOLIA

GOBI

Great Wall

Beijing

Huang He (Yellow R.)

Yellow Sea

Nanjing

Chang Jiang (Yangtze R.)

CHINA

Quanzhou

Guangzhou

0   500 mi.
0   500 km
Two-Point Equidistant projection

KEY
Ming dynasty
Great Wall

Using Geography Skills

During the Ming dynasty, the Chinese capital moved to Beijing.
1. What feature made up the northern border of the Ming empire?
2. How far away was Guangzhou from Beijing?

▶ A bronze Buddha from the Ming dynasty

▲ This image, from a Ming dynasty vase, shows Chinese farmworkers collecting tea.

Yong Le worked hard to show that he was a powerful emperor. In 1421 he moved the capital north to Beijing. There, he built a large area of palaces and government buildings known as the Imperial City. The very center of the Imperial City was known as the Forbidden City. Only top officials could enter the Forbidden City because it was home to China's emperors.

The Forbidden City had beautiful gardens and many palaces with thousands of rooms. The emperor and his court lived there in luxury for more than 500 years. The buildings of the Forbidden City still exist. You can visit them if you travel to China.

How Did the Ming Reform China? Ming

emperors made all the decisions, but they still needed officials to carry out their orders. They restored the civil service examinations and made the tests even harder. From time to time, Ming officials carried out a **census** (SEHN•suhs), or a count of the number of people. This helped them collect taxes more accurately.

With the strong government of the early Ming emperors providing peace and security, China's economy began to grow. Hong Wu ordered many of the canals and farms destroyed by the Mongols to be rebuilt and ordered people to move to the new farms. He also ordered new forests to be planted and new roads to be paved.

Agriculture thrived as farmers worked on the new lands and grew more crops. Ming rulers repaired and expanded the Grand Canal so that rice and other goods could again be shipped from southern to northern China. They imported new types of rice from southeast Asia that grew faster. This helped feed the growing number of people living in cities. The Ming also supported the silk industry and encouraged farmers to start growing cotton and weaving cloth. For the first time, cotton became the cloth worn by most Chinese.

Chinese Culture Chinese culture also advanced under the Ming. As merchants and artisans grew wealthier, they wanted to learn more and be entertained. During the Ming period, Chinese writers produced many **novels** (NAH•vuhls), or long fictional stories. The Chinese also enjoyed seeing dramas on stage. These works combined spoken words and songs with dances, costumes, and symbolic gestures.

✓ Reading Check **Identify** What was the Forbidden City?

China Explores the World

Main Idea During the Ming dynasty, China sent a fleet to explore Asia and East Africa.

Reading Focus You probably have heard of Christopher Columbus and his trip to America. Imagine if China had sent ships to America first. Read to learn about Chinese explorations of Asia and East Africa.

Early Ming emperors were curious about the world outside of China. They also wanted to increase China's influence abroad. To reach these goals, Ming emperors built a large fleet of ships. The new ships usually traveled along China's coast. However, they could also sail in the open sea.

Who Was Zheng He? From 1405 to 1431, Emperor Yong Le sent the fleet on seven overseas voyages. The emperor wanted to trade with other kingdoms, show off China's power, and demand that weaker kingdoms pay tribute to China.

The leader of these journeys was a Chinese Muslim and court official named **Zheng He** (JUNG HUH). Zheng He's voyages were quite impressive. His first fleet had 62 large ships, 250 smaller ships, and almost 28,000 men. The largest ship was over 440 feet (134 m) long. That made it more than *five times* as long as the *Santa María* that Christopher Columbus sailed almost 90 years later!

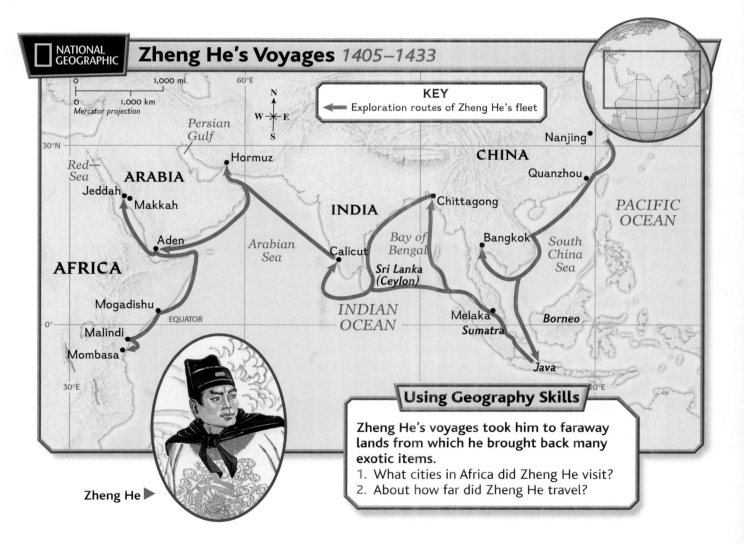

NATIONAL GEOGRAPHIC

Zheng He's Voyages *1405–1433*

KEY
Exploration routes of Zheng He's fleet

1,000 mi.
1,000 km
Mercator projection

Persian Gulf
Red Sea
ARABIA
Jeddah
Makkah
Aden
AFRICA
Mogadishu
Malindi
Mombasa
Hormuz
Arabian Sea
INDIA
Calicut
INDIAN OCEAN
Chittagong
Bay of Bengal
Sri Lanka (Ceylon)
CHINA
Nanjing
Quanzhou
Bangkok
Melaka
Sumatra
Java
Borneo
South China Sea
PACIFIC OCEAN
EQUATOR
30°N
0°
30°E
60°E
120°E

Zheng He ▶

Using Geography Skills

Zheng He's voyages took him to faraway lands from which he brought back many exotic items.
1. What cities in Africa did Zheng He visit?
2. About how far did Zheng He travel?

Biography

ZHENG HE
1371–1433

Zheng He ▶

Chinese Navigator

The famous Chinese navigator Zheng He was born in Kunyang in southwest China in 1371. His birth name was Ma He, and he was from a poor Chinese Muslim family. Scholars say that his father and grandfather were honored hajjis—people who successfully made the pilgrimage to Makkah in Arabia. Little did Ma He know that his life would also involve travel. His seven missions across the oceans earned him heroic honors.

His father died when Ma He was little. As a child, Ma He was taken prisoner by the Chinese army. To overcome his sad life, Ma He turned to education. He learned different languages, including Arabic, and studied philosophy and geography. With his language skills and knowledge of the outside world, 10-year-old Ma He became a valuable imperial aide to Chinese officials.

By age 12, he was an assistant to a young prince named Zhu Di. Ma He accompanied the prince on several military missions. The prince, who later became the Emperor Yong Le, became a friend of Ma He. The emperor changed Ma He's name to the honored surname Zheng. Soon after, Zheng He was assigned to lead a fleet of Chinese ships across the Indian Ocean, beginning the career that would make him famous. He's voyages to new lands opened the door for trade among China, India, and Africa. Many of the Chinese moved abroad to sell Chinese goods. Those who learned and spoke more than one language, like Zheng He, prospered.

> **"We have set eyes on barbarian regions far away."**
>
> –Zheng He, as quoted in *Chinese Portraits*

Then and Now

What "Made in China" products do you use on a daily basis? Do research to find out what percentage of goods imported to the United States are from China.

Where Did Zheng He Travel?

Zheng He took his first fleet to southeast Asia. In later voyages, he reached India, sailed up the Persian Gulf to Arabia, and even landed in East Africa. In these areas, Zheng He traded Chinese goods, such as silk, paper, and porcelain. He brought back silver, spices, wood, and other goods. From Africa, Zheng He returned home with giraffes and other animals for the emperor's zoo.

As a result of Zheng He's voyages, Chinese merchants settled in Southeast Asia and India. There, they not only traded goods but also spread Chinese culture. Chinese merchants at home and abroad grew rich from the trade of the voyages and added to China's wealth.

Despite these benefits, Chinese officials complained that the trips cost too much. They also said that trips were bad for China's way of life because they brought in new ideas from the outside world and helped merchants become rich.

Confucius had taught that people should place loyalty to society ahead of their own desires. To the officials, China's merchants were disobeying this teaching by working to gain money for themselves.

After Zheng He's death, the Confucian officials persuaded the emperor to stop the voyages. The boats were dismantled, and no more ships capable of long distance ocean travel were allowed to be built. As a result, China's trade with other countries sharply declined. Within 50 years, the ship-building technology was forgotten.

The Europeans Arrive in China

Chinese officials were not able to cut off all of China's contacts with the outside world. In 1514 a fleet from the European country of **Portugal** (POHR•chih•guhl) arrived off the coast of China. It was the first time Europeans had ever sailed to China and the first direct

▲ Italian missionary Matteo Ricci (left) was one of the most famous Europeans to visit China. He helped in the development of math and science in China during the late 1500s.

contact between China and Europe since the journeys of Marco Polo.

The Portuguese wanted China to trade with their country. They also wanted to convince the Chinese to become Christians. At the time, the Ming government was not impressed by the Portuguese. China was at the height of its power and did not feel threatened by outsiders. The Chinese thought the Europeans were **barbarians** (bahr•BEHR•ee•uhns), or uncivilized people.

At first, the Chinese refused to trade with the Portuguese, but by 1600, they had allowed Portugal to set up a trading post at the port of Macao (muh•KOW) in southern China. Goods were carried on European ships between Macao and Japan. Still, trade between China and Europe remained limited.

Despite restrictions, ideas from Europe did reach China. Christian missionaries traveled to China on European ships. Many of these missionaries were Jesuits, a special group of Roman Catholic priests. They

▲ This porcelain bowl is from the Ming dynasty. *Where in China did the Portuguese set up a trading post?*

were highly educated, and their scientific knowledge impressed the Chinese. To get China to accept European ideas, the Jesuits brought with them clocks, eyeglasses, and scientific instruments. Although they tried, the Jesuits did not convince many Chinese to become Christians.

Why Did the Ming Dynasty Fall? After a long era of prosperity and growth, the Ming dynasty began to decline. Ming emperors had gathered too much power into their own hands. With the emperor having so much control, officials had little desire to make improvements. As time passed, Ming rulers themselves became weak. Greedy officials who lived in luxury took over the country. They placed heavy taxes on the peasants, who began to revolt.

As law and order disappeared, a people called the Manchus attacked China's northern border. The Manchus lived to the northeast of the Great Wall in an area known today as Manchuria. The Manchus defeated Chinese armies and captured Beijing. In 1644 they set up a new dynasty.

✓ **Reading Check** **Cause and Effect** What caused the Ming dynasty to decline and fall?

History Online

Study Central™ Need help with the material in this section? Visit jat.glencoe.com

Section 4 Review

Reading Summary

Review the Main Ideas

- The Ming dynasty rebuilt and reformed China after the Mongols were driven out. Their dynasty restored peace and prosperity to China.

- During the Ming dynasty, China's contacts with the outside world increased as Zheng He led fleets to faraway lands and European ships began arriving in China.

What Did You Learn?

1. What was the purpose of the Forbidden City and where was it located?

2. How did the Chinese react to the arrival of Portuguese traders in 1514?

Critical Thinking

3. **Organizing Information** Draw a diagram like the one below. Fill in details about the achievements of the Ming dynasty.

Ming Dynasty Achievements

4. **Cause and Effect** Why did Ming rulers repair and expand the Grand Canal?

5. **Summarize** Why did the Emperor Yong Le send Zheng He on his voyages? How did Zheng He's voyages benefit China?

6. **Persuasive Writing** Imagine you are living in China at the time of Zheng He's voyages. Write a newspaper editorial either for or against the voyages. Describe why you think the voyages are aiding or hurting the country as a whole.

7. **Predict** What do you think happened after China tried to limit trade?

Section 1 China Reunites

Vocabulary
warlord
economy
reform
monastery

Focusing on the Main Ideas
- The Sui and Tang dynasties reunited and rebuilt China after years of war. *(page 409)*
- Buddhism became popular in China and spread to Korea and Japan. *(page 412)*
- The Tang dynasty returned to the ideas of Confucius and created a new class of scholar-officials. *(page 413)*

Section 2 Chinese Society

Vocabulary
porcelain
calligraphy

Focusing on the Main Ideas
- The Tang dynasty strengthened China's economy by supporting farming and trade. *(page 417)*
- The Chinese developed new technologies, such as steelmaking and printing. *(page 418)*
- During the Tang and the Song dynasties, China enjoyed a golden age of art and literature. *(page 420)*

▲ Porcelain figures from the Tang dynasty

Section 3 The Mongols in China

Vocabulary
tribe
steppe
terror

Focusing on the Main Ideas
- Genghis Khan and his sons built the Mongol Empire, which stretched from the Pacific Ocean to Eastern Europe. *(page 424)*
- The Mongols conquered China and created a new dynasty that tried to conquer Japan and began trading with the rest of Asia. *(page 428)*

Section 4 The Ming Dynasty

Vocabulary
treason
census
novel
barbarian

Focusing on the Main Ideas
- Ming rulers strengthened China's government and brought back peace and prosperity. *(page 431)*
- During the Ming dynasty, China sent a fleet to explore Asia and East Africa. *(page 433)*

Review Vocabulary

Match the word in the first column with its definition in the second column.

____ 1. treason

____ 2. warlord

____ 3. terror

____ 4. economy

____ 5. reform

____ 6. steppe

____ 7. tribe

____ 8. census

a. groups of related families loosely joined together

b. change that brings improvement

c. disloyalty to the government

d. military leader who also runs a government

e. a count of the number of people

f. violent actions meant to scare others

g. organized way to buy, sell, and produce

h. wide grassy plain

Review Main Ideas

Section 1 • China Reunites

9. What did the Sui and Tang dynasties do to improve China?

10. How did the Tang rulers change China?

Section 2 • Chinese Society

11. How did Tang rulers strengthen China's economy?

12. What kind of technologies did the Chinese develop?

Section 3 • The Mongols in China

13. Why were the Mongols able to build a huge empire?

14. How did the Mongols rule China?

Section 4 • The Ming Dynasty

15. How did the Ming rulers affect China?

16. Why did the Portuguese want to explore Africa and Asia?

Critical Thinking

17. **Analyze** How did civil service exams help China develop a strong government?

18. **Explain** How did Confucianism change during the Tang dynasty?

19. **Predict** How do you think China would be different today if Tang rulers had not cracked down on Buddhism in A.D. 845?

20. **Hypothesize** The Mongols conquered a vast amount of land, but their Yuan dynasty lasted only about 100 years. Create a hypothesis that might explain this situation.

Review
Reading Skill Inferences

Reading Between the Lines

21. Poet Duo Fu's poem "Spring Landscape," on page 421, described what it was like in the capital after a rebellion left the city in ruins. One of the lines from his poem appears here. What can you infer from this line of poetry?

"By now, letters are worth ten thousand in gold."

To review this skill, see pages 406–407.

Geography Skills

Study the map below and answer the following questions.

22. **Location** What was the length of the Grand Canal?

23. **Human/Environment Interaction** What part of Asia did the Tang control that helped China's trade?

24. **Region** What geographic features do you think helped the Tang dynasty expand?

NATIONAL GEOGRAPHIC

Tang China

MONGOLIA

Two-Point Equidistant projection

ASIA

GOBI

Beijing

KOREAN PENINSULA

Huang He

Changan

Luoyang

East China Sea

Hangzhou

Chang Jiang

TIBET

CHINA

HIMALAYA

Guangzhou

Mekong R.

Bay of Bengal

South China Sea

KEY

Tang dynasty

Grand Canal

Read to Write

25. **Persuasive Writing** Imagine you are a Portuguese merchant. You have just traveled to China to persuade the Chinese people to trade with your country. Work with a small group to create a script detailing the dialogue that would take place between the Portuguese merchant and a representative of the Chinese government. (Suppose someone is acting as a translator, but do not incorporate the translator into your dialogue.)

26. **Using Your** **FOLDABLES** On your foldable, add details to the main headings in Section 2. Think about how the changes and arts described there might have had an impact on people's lives. Then write three journal entries that tell how these things have affected your family's life in China in the Middle Ages. Illustrate your entries.

Using Technology

27. **Building a Database** Use the Internet to gather more information about Genghis Khan. Use the information to create a database for your classmates. Include text, images, and perhaps a time line. Your database should contain information about Genghis Khan as a person and as a ruler.

Linking Past and Present

28. **Expository Writing** Write a short report that describes similarities and differences between the Imperial City of the Ming dynasty and the United States capital, Washington, D.C.

Primary Source

Analyze

John of Plano Carpini, a friar, explained why the Mongols were such skilled warriors.

"Their children begin as soon as they are two or three years old to ride and manage horses and to gallop on them, and they are given bows to suit their stature [size] and are taught to shoot; they are extremely agile [move quickly and easily] and also intrepid [fearless]."

—John of Plano Carpini, *History of the Mongols*

DBQ **Document-Based Questions**

29. Why did each Mongol warrior shoot so well with a bow and arrows?

30. What other qualities made the Mongols excellent warriors?

Medieval Africa

Islamic mosque and marketplace in Djenne, Mali ▼

NATIONAL GEOGRAPHIC — When & Where?

A.D. 300	A.D. 700	1100	1500
c. A.D. 300 Axum conquers Kush	c. A.D. 750 Arab Muslim traders settle in East Africa	1324 Mansa Musa travels to Makkah	c. 1441 First enslaved Africans arrive in Europe

Chapter Preview

While China enjoyed an artistic golden age, kingdoms in Africa grew rich from trading salt and gold. This chapter will tell you about an African ruler who led a great caravan on a long journey from North Africa to the Arabian Peninsula.

 View the Chapter 13 video in the *World History: Journey Across Time* Video Program.

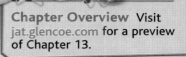
Chapter Overview Visit jat.glencoe.com for a preview of Chapter 13.

 ## The Rise of African Civilizations

Africa's geography influenced the rise of its civilizations. The growth of trade led to the exchange of goods and ideas.

 ## Africa's Government and Religion

African rulers developed different forms of government. Traditional religions, Christianity, and Islam shaped early African culture.

 ## African Society and Culture

The family was the foundation of African society. A growing slave trade, however, would disrupt African society.

FOLDABLES™
Study Organizer

Categorizing Information *Make this foldable to help you organize your notes about medieval Africa.*

Step 1 *Draw a map of Africa on one side of a sheet of paper.*

Step 2 *Fold the sheet of paper into thirds from top to bottom.*

Step 3 *Unfold, turn the paper over (to the clean side), and label as shown.*

The Rise of African Civilizations

Africa's Government and Religion

African Society and Culture

Reading and Writing *As you read about the civilizations of Africa, write down three main questions under each heading. Then write an answer to each question.*

Chapter 13

Reading Social Studies

Reading Skill

Compare and Contrast

1 Learn It!

Making Comparisons

One way authors help you to understand information is by organizing material so that you can see how people, places, things, or events compare (are alike) or contrast (are different). Read the following passage:

The contrasts (differences) are highlighted in blue.

First, look at what is being compared or contrasted. In this case, it is the religions of two groups of people from Africa, highlighted in pink.

Some groups, like the Nanti in East Africa, thought people could talk directly with their god. Others, like the Igbo, thought their creator could only be spoken to through less powerful gods and goddesses who worked for him.

Even though Africans practiced their religion differently in different places, their beliefs served similar purposes. They provided rules for living and helped people stay in touch with their history.

—*from page 463*

The comparisons (similarities) are highlighted in green.

Reading Tip

As you read, look for words that signal the use of comparisons, such as like, similar, or different.

2 Practice It!

Create a Venn Diagram

A Venn diagram can help you to compare and contrast information. Differences are listed in the outside parts of each circle. Similarities are listed in the portion of the two circles that overlap. Read the paragraphs below. Then create a Venn diagram to compare and contrast the roles of European and African women as stated in the paragraphs.

Differences | Similarities | Differences

Read to Write

You will read about the rise and fall of many wealthy kingdoms in Africa during the Middle Ages. Choose one of the kingdoms and do research to find out what modern African nation occupies that same area today. Write a report to compare and contrast the modern nation and the early African kingdom.

As in most medieval societies, women in Africa acted mostly as wives and mothers. Men had more rights and controlled much of what women did. Visitors to Africa, however, saw exceptions. European explorers were amazed to learn that women served as soldiers in some African kingdoms.

African women also won fame as rulers. In the A.D. 600s, Queen Dahia al-Kahina led the fight against the Muslim invasion of her kingdom, which was located about where Mauritania is today. Another woman ruler was Queen Nzinga, who ruled lands in what are now Angola and Congo. She spent almost 40 years battling Portuguese slave traders.

—from page 470

3 Apply It!

As you read each section, make Venn diagrams to help you compare and contrast important details.

The Rise of African Civilizations

Get Ready to Read!

What's the Connection?

Egypt and Kush were Africa's first great civilizations. In this section, you will learn about African civilizations that developed later.

Focusing on the Main Ideas

• Africa has a vast and varied landscape. *(page 445)*

• West African empires grew rich from trade. *(page 447)*

• Africa's rain forests blocked invaders and provided resources. *(page 450)*

• East African kingdoms and states became centers for trade and new ideas. *(page 451)*

Locating Places

Ghana (GAH•nuh)
Mali (MAH•lee)
Timbuktu (TIHM•BUHK•TOO)
Songhai (SAWNG•HY)
Axum (AHK•SOOM)

Meeting People

Sundiata Keita
   (sun•dee•AH•tuh   KY•tuh)
Mansa Musa
   (MAHN•sah   moo•SAH)
Sunni Ali (sun•EE ah•LEE)

Building Your Vocabulary

plateau (pla•TOH)
griot (GREE•OH)
dhow (DOW)

Reading Strategy

Summarizing Information
Create diagrams describing the accomplishments of each medieval African civilization.

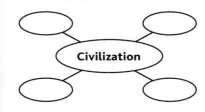

Civilization

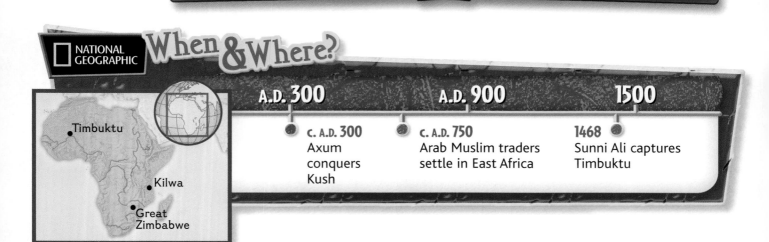

NATIONAL GEOGRAPHIC

When & Where?

A.D. 300	A.D. 900	1500
c. A.D. 300 Axum conquers Kush	c. A.D. 750 Arab Muslim traders settle in East Africa	1468 Sunni Ali captures Timbuktu

Timbuktu
Kilwa
Great Zimbabwe

Africa's Geography

Main Idea Africa has a vast and varied landscape.

Reading Focus How can geography discourage people from exploring another place? Read to learn about the geographic features that made it difficult for people to travel across parts of Africa.

In 1906 a teacher named Hans Vischer explored what he called the "death road," a trade route connecting western Africa to the coast of the Mediterranean Sea. No European or American had ever risked the journey before. The "death road" crossed more than 1,500 miles (2,414 km) of the Sahara, the world's largest desert. To get lost meant certain death.

Only nomads living in the region knew the way, but Vischer hoped to map the route. Like the desert nomads, his life depended upon finding oases. Upon his return, Vischer amazed people with stories of the Sahara. He told of swirling winds and shifting sand dunes.

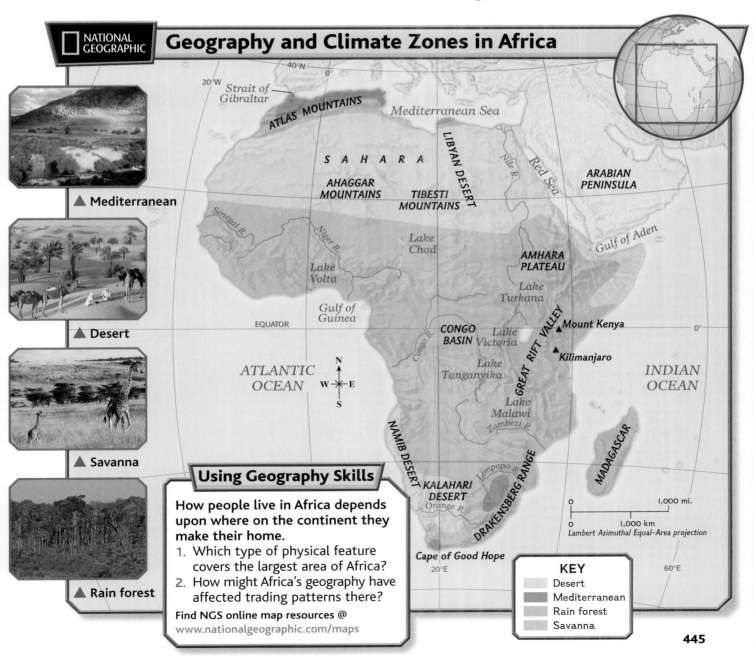

NATIONAL GEOGRAPHIC

Geography and Climate Zones in Africa

▲ Mediterranean

▲ Desert

▲ Savanna

▲ Rain forest

Using Geography Skills

How people live in Africa depends upon where on the continent they make their home.

1. Which type of physical feature covers the largest area of Africa?
2. How might Africa's geography have affected trading patterns there?

Find NGS online map resources @
www.nationalgeographic.com/maps

KEY
- Desert
- Mediterranean
- Rain forest
- Savanna

Map labels: Strait of Gibraltar, ATLAS MOUNTAINS, Mediterranean Sea, SAHARA, LIBYAN DESERT, Nile R., Red Sea, ARABIAN PENINSULA, AHAGGAR MOUNTAINS, TIBESTI MOUNTAINS, Senegal R., Niger R., Lake Chad, Gulf of Aden, AMHARA PLATEAU, Lake Volta, Lake Turkana, Gulf of Guinea, EQUATOR, CONGO BASIN, Lake Victoria, Mount Kenya, GREAT RIFT VALLEY, ATLANTIC OCEAN, Congo R., Lake Tanganyika, Kilimanjaro, INDIAN OCEAN, Lake Malawi, Zambezi R., NAMIB DESERT, MADAGASCAR, KALAHARI DESERT, Limpopo R., DRAKENSBERG RANGE, Orange R., Cape of Good Hope

1,000 mi.
1,000 km
Lambert Azimuthal Equal-Area projection

A Vast and Diverse Continent Africa is the world's second-largest continent. The United States fits into Africa three times, with room to spare. The Equator slices through the middle of the continent. Hot, steamy rain forests stretch along each side of it. Yet the rain forests cover only 10 percent of the land.

Most of Africa lies in the tropics. Here dry, sweeping grasslands reach for thousands of miles. Most of the tropical grasslands, known as savannas, have high temperatures and uneven rains. These wide-open grasslands are perfect for raising herds of animals. For much of Africa's history, the people of the savanna were hunters and herders.

North and south of the savannas are the deserts—the Sahara to the north and the Kalahari to the southwest. For many years, these unmapped seas of sand blocked travel. People had to follow the coastline if they wanted to get past the deserts. Areas of mild climate, good for growing crops, are found along the Mediterranean Sea in northwest Africa and in the south.

The African Plateau Almost all of Africa, except the coastal plains, rests on a **plateau** (pla•TOH)—an area of high flat land. Rivers spill off the plateau in crashing waterfalls and rapids, cutting off inland water routes. Although the Nile River is Africa's longest river, the Congo River winds 2,700 miles (4,345 km) through Africa, near the Equator.

In the east, movements of the earth's crust millions of years ago cracked the continent, and parts of the plateau's surface dropped. This formed the Great Rift Valley, where some of the earliest human fossils have been unearthed. The valley extends through eastern Africa from present-day Mozambique to the Red Sea.

✓ **Reading Check** **Cause and Effect** What caused the Great Rift Valley?

UNITED STATES

AFRICA

Comparing Africa to the U.S.

	Africa	United States
Size	11,667,159 square miles (30,217,894 sq. km)	3,794,085 square miles (9,826,680 sq. km)
Population Today	about 891 million people	about 291 million people
Longest River	Nile River 4,160 miles (6,693 km)	Missouri River 2,565 miles (4,130 km)
Largest Desert	Sahara 3,500,000 square miles (9,065,000 sq. km)	Mojave 15,000 square miles (38,850 sq. km)

Sources: *The World Almanac and Book of Facts*, 2004; *World Population Data Sheet*, 2003; *The New Encyclopaedia Britannica*, 1990

Understanding Charts

Africa has a land area roughly three times that of the United States.
1. How does the size of the Sahara compare to the size of the United States?
2. How does the population of Africa compare to that of the United States?

West African Empires

Main Idea West African empires grew rich from trade.

Reading Focus What would you rather have—a pound of gold or a pound of salt? Both of these goods were important to West Africans and helped them build large trading empires.

Stories of golden lands south of the Sahara seemed hard to believe. There's a country, claimed one story, "where gold grows like plants in the same way as carrots do, and is plucked at sunset."

The Berbers who told the tales had seen the gold with their own eyes. The Berbers, the first known people to settle in North Africa, crossed the Sahara to trade with people in western Africa. They began making the trip about 400 B.C.

For hundreds of years, Berber traders carried goods on horses and donkeys, which often died in the hot Sahara. When the Romans conquered North Africa, they introduced camels from central Asia. Camels, nicknamed "ships of the desert," revolutionized trade. Their broad feet did not sink in the sand, and their humps stored fat for food. In addition, they could travel many days without water.

Traders grouped hundreds, maybe even thousands, of camels together to form caravans. They traded salt and cloth from North Africa and the Sahara for gold and ivory from western Africa. The trade led to the growth of cities in western Africa. Eventually, rulers of these cities began to build a series of empires. During the Middle Ages, these African empires were bigger than most European kingdoms in wealth and size. The first empire to develop was Ghana.

▲ While many of the caravans that crossed the desert going to and from West Africa included about 1,000 camels, some caravans may have had as many as 12,000 camels. *What were some of the items traded by caravans?*

Rise of Ghana Ghana (GAH•nuh) rose to power in the A.D. 400s. It was a "crossroads of trade," a place where trade routes come together. Trade routes reached across the Sahara into North Africa and down the Niger River (NY•juhr) to kingdoms in the rain forest. Some extended all the way to Africa's northeastern coast.

For traders to meet, they had to pass through Ghana. Passage came at a price—a tax paid to Ghana's rulers. These taxes made Ghana rich. Why did traders pay the taxes? First, Ghana knew how to make iron weapons. Like ancient Kush, it used these weapons to conquer its neighbors. Although Ghana owned no gold mines, it controlled the people who did. Second, Ghana built a huge army. "When the king of Ghana calls up his army," said one trader, "he can put 200,000 men in the field."

Third, people wanted the trade items, especially salt and gold, at almost any price. West Africans needed salt to flavor and preserve food, and their bodies needed salt to stay healthy. They paid taxes to get salt from Berber mines in the Sahara. In turn, the Berbers paid taxes to get gold to sell at a huge profit in Europe.

Rise of Mali Ghana did not last forever, however. The discovery of new gold mines outside Ghana's control reduced the taxes it collected. In addition, heavy farming robbed the soil of minerals and made it harder to grow enough crops to feed people. Constant fighting also hurt Ghana. Ghana's rulers had accepted the religion of Islam, but they fought with North African Muslims who wanted to build empires of their own.

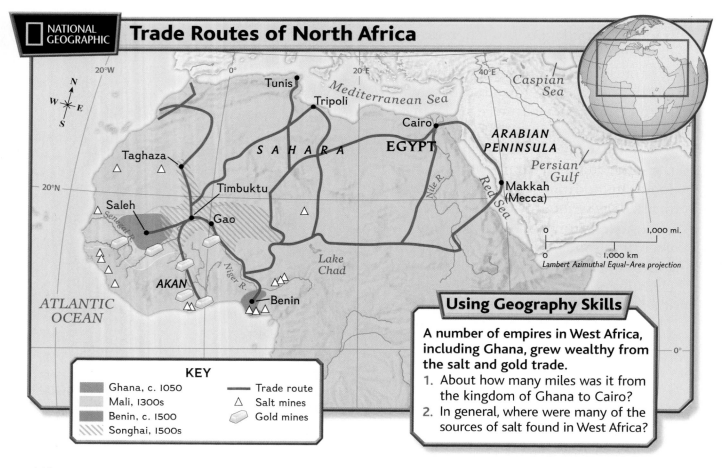

NATIONAL GEOGRAPHIC
Trade Routes of North Africa

KEY
- Ghana, c. 1050
- Mali, 1300s
- Benin, c. 1500
- Songhai, 1500s
- Trade route
- △ Salt mines
- Gold mines

Using Geography Skills

A number of empires in West Africa, including Ghana, grew wealthy from the salt and gold trade.

1. About how many miles was it from the kingdom of Ghana to Cairo?
2. In general, where were many of the sources of salt found in West Africa?

After Ghana fell in the 1200s, the kingdom of **Mali** (MAH•lee) replaced it. West African **griots** (GREE•ohz), or storytellers, give credit to a great warrior-king named **Sundiata Keita** (sun•dee•AH•tuh KY•tuh)—the "Lion Prince." Sundiata, who ruled from 1230 to 1255, seized the capital of Ghana in 1240. He then won control of lands from the Atlantic coast to the trading city of **Timbuktu** (TIHM•BUHK•TOO) and beyond. His conquests put Mali in control of the gold-mining areas, allowing him to rebuild the gold and salt trade.

Rise of Songhai Mali began a slow decline after the death of its last strong king, **Mansa Musa** (MAHN•sah moo•SAH), in 1337. The kings who followed failed to stop Berber conquerors, who for a time even ruled Timbuktu.

In 1468 **Sunni Ali** (sun•EE ah•LEE), the leader of **Songhai** (SAWNG•HY), stormed into Timbuktu and drove out the Berbers. He then began a campaign of conquest. Sunni Ali used Songhai's location along the Niger River to his advantage. He ordered a fleet of war canoes to seize control of the river trade. His armies then swept westward into the Sahara, where they took over Berber salt mines. By the time of his death in 1492, Sunni Ali had built the largest empire in West Africa.

The empire lasted almost 100 more years. In 1591, however, a small army from the Arab kingdom of Morocco crossed the Sahara. Soldiers with cannons, guns, and gunpowder easily cut down Songhai soldiers armed with swords, spears, and bows and arrows. Within months, Songhai's empire was gone.

✓ Reading Check Analyze Why did West Africa become the center of three large trade empires?

The Way It Was

Focus on Everyday Life

Africa's Salt Mines Salt mining began in the Sahara in the Middle Ages. Ancient miners worked underground and in sand dunes to extract solid blocks of salt. The salt trade became a successful business for the African people. In ancient times, salt was so desirable that it was traded ounce for ounce for gold.

There are many salt deposits in western Africa because part of the desert was once a shallow sea made up of salt water. When the sea dried up, salt was left behind.

People need a small amount of salt to stay healthy. It is lost when people and animals sweat, so people need some in their food. In ancient times, before refrigerators or canned foods were invented, salt was used to keep foods from going bad. It also was used to add flavor to food.

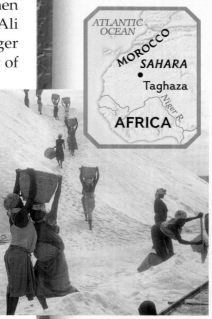

◄ African salt mine today

Connecting to the Past
1. How do salt deposits form?
2. Why do you think salt was so valuable that it was traded ounce for ounce for gold?

Kingdoms of the Rain Forest

Main Idea Africa's rain forests blocked invaders and provided resources.

Reading Focus What does your state make that people in other places want to buy? Africa's rain forest kingdoms had something the savanna kingdoms wanted. It was not gold or salt, but something just as valuable—food.

Ghana, Mali, and Songhai ruled the wide-open savannas. However, the dense rain forests along the Equator kept them from expanding to the southern coast. People living in the rain forests built their own kingdoms and empires. They included Benin, which arose in the Niger delta, and Kongo, which formed in the Congo River basin.

Griots who live in the Niger delta still tell stories about King Ewuare (eh•WOO•ah•ray), who founded the empire of Benin around 1440. In describing his ancestor's accomplishments, one storyteller boasted:

> 66 He fought against and captured 201 towns and villages. . . . He took their . . . rulers captive and caused the people to pay tribute to him. 99
>
> —J.V. Egharevba,
> *A Short History of Benin*

Farmers in the rain forest kingdoms enjoyed many natural advantages, including farmable soil and a warm, wet climate. In cleared-out areas of the forest, they often produced a surplus, or extra supply, of foods like bananas, yams, or rice.

The Kingdom of Benin

◄ Bronze statue of queen from Benin

Statue of horn player ► from Benin

▲ This bronze casting honored the king of Benin. *Around when was the kingdom of Benin founded?*

Food surpluses supported rulers and a class of artisans. Kongo weavers, for example, wove fabrics from bark and plant fibers that looked to Europeans like velvet. In Benin, artists excelled at sculpting and carving metal, wood, and ivory.

Rain forest kingdoms that bordered on the dry savannas traded surplus food and crafts for copper, salt, and leather goods from the savannas. Later, when the Europeans arrived, traders from Benin and Kongo met ships along the coast. They traded, among other things, captives taken in war.

✓ **Reading Check** **Describe** What advantages did farmers in the rain forests have over farmers in other parts of Africa?

East Africa

Main Idea East African kingdoms and states became centers for trade and new ideas.

Reading Focus Have you ever met someone who used to live somewhere far away? Did their ideas help you to think about the world differently? Read to learn how new ideas arrived along the coast of East Africa.

People today in the East African country of Ethiopia trace their history back to 1005 B.C. In that year, Queen Makeda rose to the throne of a great empire called Saba or Sheba. According to the *Glory of Kings*, Ethiopia's oldest written history, Makeda traveled to meet with King Solomon, ruler

African Trading Empires A.D. 100–1600

	Axum	Ghana	Mali	Songhai	Zimbabwe
Location	East Africa	West Africa	West Africa	West Africa	SE Africa
	AXUM Adulis	GHANA Saleh	MALI Timbuktu	SONGHAI Gao	ZIMBABWE Great Zimbabwe
Time Period	c. 100–1400	c. 400–1200	c. 1200–1450	c. 1000–1600	c. 700–1450
Goods Traded	ivory, frankincense, myrrh, slaves	iron products, animal products, salt, gold	salt, gold	salt, gold	gold, copper, ivory
Key Facts	King Ezana converted to Christianity; made it the official religion.	Taxes from traders passing through made Ghana rich.	King Mansa Musa built mosques and libraries.	Songhai gained control of West African trade by conquering Timbuktu and mastering trade by river.	Kings Mutota and Matope built the region's biggest empire.

Understanding Charts

Large trading kingdoms developed in several areas of Africa.
1. Which kingdom developed earliest?
2. **Generalize** What were some of the common trade items of the West African empires?

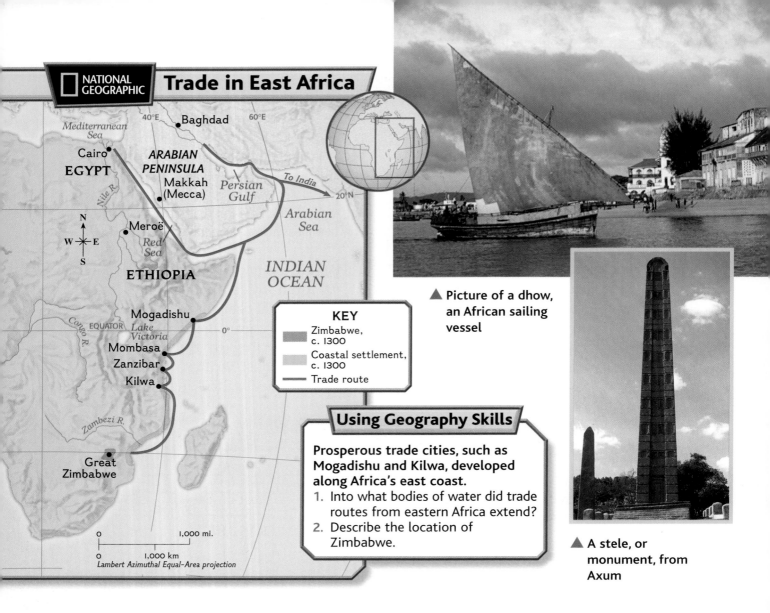

Trade in East Africa
NATIONAL GEOGRAPHIC

▲ Picture of a dhow, an African sailing vessel

KEY
- Zimbabwe, c. 1300
- Coastal settlement, c. 1300
- Trade route

Using Geography Skills

Prosperous trade cities, such as Mogadishu and Kilwa, developed along Africa's east coast.
1. Into what bodies of water did trade routes from eastern Africa extend?
2. Describe the location of Zimbabwe.

▲ A stele, or monument, from Axum

---

of the Israelites. On her return, Makeda introduced ancient Israel's religion to her empire. Over time, eastern Africa would feel the impact of two other religions—Christianity and Islam.

The Rise of Axum Like other empires, Saba declined. However, Ethiopia, known in ancient times as Abyssinia, did not. Its power was centered in a city-state called **Axum** (AHK•soom). Axum owed its strength to its location on the Red Sea. Goods from Africa flowed into Axum, which served as a trading center for the ancient Mediterranean and East Asian worlds.

Axum fought neighboring Kush for control of trade routes to inland Africa. Around

A.D. 300, King Ezana of Axum sent his armies against Kush and defeated it. A few years later, Ezana helped to bring a new religion to Africa when he converted to Christianity. In A.D. 334 he made it the official religion of Axum. Within a few hundred years, another religion—Islam—brought many changes to Axum and other trading states along Africa's eastern coast.

Coastal City-States Arab traders from the Arabian Peninsula had been coming to eastern Africa long before the rise of Islam in the early A.D. 600s. They invented a wind-catching, triangular sail that let them sail to Africa. The sails powered sailboats called **dhows** (DOWZ).

In the A.D. 700s, many Arab Muslim traders settled in East African city-states. Here Africans and Arab Muslims shared goods and ideas. By the 1300s, a string of trading ports extended down the East African coast. They included Mogadishu (MAH•guh•DIH•shoo), Kilwa, Mombasa, and Zanzibar. These ports became major links in an Indian Ocean trading network. They traded with places as far away as China.

Great Zimbabwe Another great trading center known as Zimbabwe (zihm•BAH•bway) arose inland in southeastern Africa. Founded around A.D. 700 by the Shona people, Zimbabwe supplied gold, copper, and ivory to the East African coast. From there, African goods were shipped to Arabia, Persia, India, and China.

▲ Some of the walls of Great Zimbabwe still exist. *What trade goods from the interior of Africa passed through Zimbabwe?*

During the 1400s, two kings—Mutota and his son Matope—made Zimbabwe into a large empire. It stretched from south of the Zambezi River to the Indian Ocean. Evidence of Zimbabwe's power can still be seen at Great Zimbabwe, the empire's capital. Here more than 300 huge stone buildings stand—silent reminders of Zimbabwe's past greatness.

✓ **Reading Check** **Explain** How did new technology help East Africa's trade?

History Online

Study Central™ Need help with the material in this section? Visit jat.glencoe.com

Section 1 Review

Reading Summary

Review the Main Ideas

- The continent of Africa has varied landscapes, including rain forests, grasslands, and deserts.

- Beginning in about A.D. 300, a succession of kingdoms, including Ghana, Mali, and Songhai, arose in West Africa.

- Rain forest kingdoms, including Benin and Kongo, traded with the surrounding savanna kingdoms.

- In East Africa, trade with the Arab world helped kingdoms and port cities grow.

What Did You Learn?

1. What items were traded in the kingdoms of West Africa?

Critical Thinking

2. **Organizing Information** Draw a chart like the one below. For each region, write names of the kingdoms and/or city-states that developed there.

West Africa	African Rain Forests	East Africa

3. **Analyze** What city-states grew as trading ports in East Africa, and why were they successful?

4. **Compare and Contrast** Which African kingdoms developed away from the coast? How did their economies compare to other African kingdoms?

5. **Reading** **Compare and Contrast** Create a Venn diagram that shows the similarities and differences of two African kingdoms.

SUNDIATA
THE HUNGERING LION

Retold by Kenny Mann

Before You Read

The Scene: This story takes place in Mali on the continent of Africa in the 1100s.

The Characters: Balla Fasseke is the griot who tells the story of Sundiata. Sundiata is the Lion King of Mali. Sogolon and Maghan Kon Fatta are Sundiata's parents. Sassouma is the first wife of Maghan Kon Fatta. Sumanguru is a rival king.

The Plot: The Lion King of Mali, Sundiata, is denied the throne. Sundiata has to prove that he is the rightful king.

Vocabulary Preview

guardian: one who takes care of another person

infirmity: weakness

brewed: prepared by boiling

smiths: metalworkers

multitude: a great number of people

exile: period of time away from one's country

lance: a steel-tipped spear

Have you ever known someone who overcame obstacles to achieve great things? In this story, a young leader must learn to speak and walk in order to take control of his kingdom.

As You Read

Keep in mind that this story is a mixture of fact and legend. However, a king named Sundiata did conquer new lands and expand trade while he ruled the kingdom of Mali.

O people, hear my story! I am Balla Fasseke (bah•lah   fah•SEE•kay) of Mali. I am a *griot*.[1] I am the guardian of the word. In my mind rest the stories of my people and the history of our land. O hear me and remember, for I speak the truth.

Long, long ago, the last king of Ghana fell to the sword of Sumanguru, the Sosso king; Sumanguru, the cruel warrior and mighty sorcerer; Sumanguru, who was to meet his fate at the hands of Sundiata, the Lion King of Mali.

I am Sundiata's *griot*. O hear me, for I speak the truth!

Sundiata was born of Sogolon, who married Maghan Kon Fatta, the ruler of Mali, whose totem[2] was the lion. Sogolon was brought to the king as a maiden, disfigured by a hunchback and ill looks. But she was said to possess the mighty spirit of a buffalo, strong and courageous. Her coming had been foretold to the king, and he took Sogolon as his wife and came to love her.

When Sundiata was born, the king rejoiced. The great royal drums carried the news all over the kingdom. But his first wife, Sassouma, was jealous. Her son should inherit the throne! What need had her husband of another son? She vowed that Sundiata would never become king.

---

[1]**griot:** storyteller
[2]**totem:** animal or plant serving as the symbol of a family or clan

In time, Sassouma saw that she had nothing to fear, for Sundiata was stricken by a strange infirmity. He could neither speak nor walk! How great was Sogolon's sorrow! For seven long years, she tried to cure her son. She consulted with all the wise men of the kingdom and brewed herbs and potions, but to no avail.[3] And Sundiata's father, King Maghan Kon Fatta, despaired. But his *griot,* who was my father, advised the king. "The young seed must endure the storm," he said. "And from this small seed shall spring a great tree."

One day, when the king felt death approach, he called the child to him. "I shall give you the gift each king gives to his heir," he said. And on that day, my people, the king gave me—Balla Fasseke—to Sundiata to be his *griot,* as my father had been the king's *griot,* and his father before that. And on that day, for the first time in his life, Sundiata spoke. "Balla, you shall be my *griot,*" he said. And the king knew that his son—the son of the lion and the buffalo—was worthy to be king.

But when Maghan Kon Fatta died, the councilors ignored his wishes. It was the son of Sassouma who ascended the throne, and not Sundiata, the rightful heir. And Sassouma persecuted Sogolon and her son with evil hatred and banished them to a dark corner of the palace. Oh, how Sogolon's tears flowed in her unhappiness! When Sundiata saw his mother's despair, he looked at her calmly and said, "Today I will walk." Then he sent me, Balla Fasseke, to the royal forges.[4] "Tell the smiths to make me the sturdiest iron rod possible," he ordered.

---

[3]**avail:** benefit
[4]**forges:** furnaces where metal is heated and shaped

Six men were needed to carry the iron rod to Sogolon's house. They threw it on the ground before Sundiata. A huge multitude of people had gathered to see if Sundiata would walk. "Arise, young lion!" I commanded. "Roar, and may the land know that from henceforth, it has a master!"

Sundiata gripped the rod with his two hands and held it upright in the ground. Beads of sweat poured from his face. A deathly silence gripped the people. All at once, with a mighty thrust, Sundiata stood upright. The crowd gasped. The iron rod was bent like a bow. And Sogolon, who had been dumb with amazement, suddenly burst into song:

> *Oh day, oh beautiful day,*
> *Oh day, day of joy,*
> *Allah Almighty, this is the finest*
> *day you have created,*
> *My son is going to walk!*
> *Hear me, people, for I speak the truth!*

Sundiata threw away the rod, and his first steps were those of a giant.

From that day on, Sundiata grew in strength. He became a fine hunter and was much loved by all the people. But Sassouma, whose son was now king, feared Sundiata's growing power. Her plots to kill him failed. And she knew that I would perform any deed to bring Sundiata to the throne. So, to separate us, Sassouma sent me far away to the court of the demon king, Sumanguru. And there I remained for several years. I pretended allegiance to Sumanguru, but always I waited for the day when I would sing the praises of Sundiata once more.

Sogolon fled the palace and took Sundiata far from Sassouma's hatred. For seven years they lived in exile, finding food and shelter wherever they could. At last, they came to the city of Mema. Here they met with good luck, for the king of Mema took a liking to Sundiata and treated him like a son. He admired Sundiata's courage and leadership. This king decided to make the young boy his heir and teach him the arts of government and war. And thus, Sundiata grew to manhood.

One day, messengers came running to Sundiata. "Sumanguru has invaded Mali!" they cried. "The king and his mother, Sassouma, have fled. Only you can save our people. Return, young lion, and reclaim your throne!"

This, O people, was the moment of Sundiata's destiny. The king of Mema gave him half his forces. And as Sundiata rode at their head, more and more men joined him until a great army thundered across the plains. And from far-distant Mali, Sumanguru, too, raced to meet his destiny. And I, O my people, I followed, for I knew that soon I would be reunited with Sundiata, my Lion King.

And so it was. Sundiata led his army from Mema, and Sumanguru came from Mali. The two great armies met in battle on the plains of Kirina. I took my chance and escaped at last from Sumanguru. Through the thick clouds of dust and the battle cries of the warriors, I galloped to Sundiata's side. Oh, how great was our joy!

My years with Sumanguru had not been in vain, O my people, for I had learned that Sumanguru feared the magic power of a white rooster. He believed that one touch of the rooster's spur[5] would defeat him forever. And this very spur I had fastened to an arrow, which I gave to my lord, Sundiata.

---

[5]**spur:** a sharp spine on the leg of some birds, especially roosters

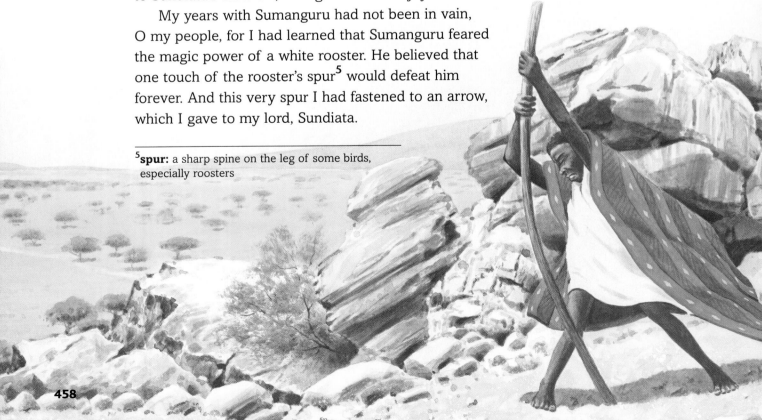

With deadly aim, Sundiata sent the arrow speeding across the battlefield toward Sumanguru. True as a hawk in flight, it met its mark, grazing the sorcerer's shoulder. With a great scream of fear, Sumanguru turned on his horse and fled.

Far away he rode, to the caves of Mount Koulikoro. There we saw Sumanguru, the demon king, fall to his knees and turn to stone. His soldiers, discouraged by his flight, ceased to fight and were defeated.

And so Sundiata returned to Mali to reclaim his throne, and I, Balla Fasseke, went with him to sing of his glory. There waited the twelve kings who had helped Sundiata in exile. Each thrust his lance into the earth before Sundiata. "We shall be united!" they proclaimed. "You have restored peace to our lands. We give you our kingdoms to rule in your great wisdom!" The drums beat out the news. The warriors danced in a joyous frenzy. And the crowd sent a mighty cry to the heavens: "Wassa, Wassa, Ayé!"

And thus did I bear witness to the birth of the great kingdom of Mali. And thus did I see Sundiata become its first emperor.

So listen, O my people, and remember, for I speak the truth. May you live to tell this story to your children, that the name of Sundiata—the Lion King—shall live forever.

Responding to the Reading

1. Why did the king give Sundiata a griot?
2. Foreshadowing is when a storyteller gives you hints of something to come later. This story contains many suggestions that foreshadow Sundiata's successful reign as king. Identify three such hints in the first six paragraphs.
3. **Predict** How might the story be different if Balla Fasseke had not been sent to the court of Sumanguru?
4. **Analyze** Why do you think Sundiata did not walk after receiving his mother's treatments but *did* walk when his half-brother was made king?
5. **Reading** **Read to Write** Suppose you are Sundiata's father. Write a brief speech stating your reasons for choosing Sundiata to be the next king.

Section 2

Africa's Government and Religion

Get Ready to Read!

What's the Connection?

In Section 1, you read about some of the kingdoms and empires that developed in Africa. To hold their kingdoms and empires together, Africans had to create their own governments. One unifying force was the religion of Islam, but many Africans continued to practice their traditional religious beliefs as well.

Focusing on the Main Ideas

- The growth of West African empires led to the growth of centralized governments ruled by kings. *(page 461)*

- Traditional African religions shared certain beliefs and provided a guide for living together. *(page 463)*

- Islam played an important role in medieval Africa, but long-held African beliefs and customs still remained strong. *(page 464)*

Locating Places
Makkah (MAH•kuh)

Meeting People
Olaudah Equiano (oh•LOW•duh EHK•wee•AHN•oh)
Ibn Battuta (IH•buhn bat•TOO•tah)
Askia Muhammad (ahs•KEE•uh moh•HAH•muhd)

Building Your Vocabulary
clan (KLAN)
sultan (SUHL•tuhn)
Swahili (swah•HEE•lee)

Reading Strategy
Organizing Information Use a diagram to show the components of Swahili culture and language.

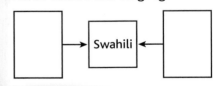

NATIONAL GEOGRAPHIC When & Where?

- Timbuktu
- Mogadishu

1300 — **1400** — **1500**

1324 Mansa Musa travels to Makkah

1352 Ibn Battuta arrives in West Africa

1492 Sunni Ali dies

Government and Society

Main Idea The growth of West African empires led to the growth of centralized governments ruled by kings.

Reading Focus What makes a system of government effective? Read to learn how African rulers governed their empires.

The loud thumping of drums called the citizens of Ghana to a meeting with the king. Anybody with a complaint could speak. In the royal courtyard, the king sat in an open silk tent. He wore a cap of gold and a jewel-covered robe. Royal officials surrounded him. Guard dogs with gold and silver collars stood watch. Before talking to the king, subjects poured dust over their heads or fell to the ground. Bowing, they stated their business and waited for the king's reply.

Ruler and Subject This, said Arab travelers, was how government worked in West Africa. Kings settled arguments, managed trade, and protected the empire. But they expected complete obedience in return.

With the growth of empires, Africans invented new ways to govern themselves. The most successful states, like Ghana, formed some type of central authority. Power usually rested with a king—or, in a few cases, a queen.

Both rulers and people benefited. Merchants received favors from the kings, and the kings received taxes from the merchants. Local rulers kept some power, and the kings in turn received their loyalty. This allowed kingdoms to grow richer and to extend their control over a larger area. The system also helped keep the peace.

Ghana's Government The kings of Ghana relied on help from a council of ministers, or group of close advisers. As the empire

▼ The carving below shows a king of Benin on his throne. The ivory armband (lower left) was worn by the king during ceremonies. *Why did African kings allow local rulers to keep some power?*

grew, rulers divided it into provinces. Lesser kings, often conquered leaders, governed each of these areas. Beneath them, district chiefs oversaw smaller districts. Each district usually included a chief's **clan** (KLAN)—a group of people descended from the same ancestor.

Kings held tightly to their power. They insisted that local rulers send their sons to the royal court. They rode through the countryside seeking reports of injustice or rebellion. Most important, they controlled trade.

Nobody could trade without the king's permission. Also, nobody could own gold nuggets except the king. People traded only in gold dust. "If kings did otherwise," said one Arab traveler, "gold would become so abundant as practically to lose its value."

Ghana Profits From Trade

Al Bekri described the way Ghana taxed merchants to increase its own wealth.

"The king [of Ghana] exacts the right of one *dinar* of gold on each donkey-load of salt that enters his country, and two *dinars* of gold on each load of salt that goes out. A load of copper carries a duty of five *mitqals* and a load of merchandise ten *mitqals*. The best gold in the country comes from Ghiaru, a town situated eighteen days' journey from the capital [Kumbi]."

— Abdullah Abu-Ubayd al Bekri, "Ghana in 1067"

▲ Ghana's wealth came from trade caravans.

DBQ Document-Based Question

Which do you think has more worth, a dinar or a mitqal? Why?

One thing about Ghana's government, however, confused outsiders. "It is their custom," exclaimed an Arab writer, "that the kingdom is inherited only by the son of the king's sister." In Arab states, property passed through a man's sons, not the sons of his sister. In Ghana, the throne went to the king's nephew.

Mali's Government

Mali followed the example of Ghana, but on a larger scale. It had more territory, more people, and more trade, so royal officials had more responsibilites. One supervised fishing on the Niger. Another looked after the empire's forests. A third oversaw farming, and a fourth managed money.

Kings divided the empire into provinces, like Ghana. However, Sundiata, the founder of Mali, put his generals in charge of them. People accepted it because the generals protected them from invaders. Also, the generals often came from the provinces they ruled.

Mali's other great king, Mansa Musa, rewarded citizens with gold, land, and horses to keep them loyal. He granted military heroes the "National Honor of the Trousers." As one Arab said:

66 **Whenever a hero adds to the lists of his exploits, the king gives him a pair of wide trousers. . . . [T]he greater the number of the knight's [soldier's] exploits, the bigger the size of his trousers.** 99

—Al-Dukhari, as quoted in *Topics in West African History*

Because only the king and royal family could wear sewn clothes, this was a big honor indeed. Most people wore only wrapped clothes.

Songhai's Government

Songhai built on the traditions of Ghana and Mali. Its founder, Sunni Ali, divided his empire into provinces. However, he never finished setting up his empire. Sunni continually moved, fighting one battle or another.

In 1492 Sunni Ali died mysteriously on a return trip home. Some say he drowned while crossing a stream. Others say his enemies killed him. The next year, a Songhai general named Muhammad Ture seized control of the government. Unlike Sunni Ali, Muhammad Ture was a loyal Muslim. His religious ideas affected Songhai's government.

✓ Reading Check **Contrast** How was Mali ruled differently from Ghana?

Traditional African Religions

Main Idea Traditional African religions shared certain beliefs and provided a guide for living together.

Reading Focus What questions do most religions try to answer? As you read this section, look for questions answered by traditional African religions.

For centuries, Europeans believed Africans did not have a religion. **Olaudah Equiano** (oh•LOW•duh EHK•wee•AHN•oh), a member of the Igbo, disagreed. The Igbo, he wrote, "believe that there is one Creator of all things, and that he . . . governs events, especially our deaths and captivity."

Most African groups shared the Igbo belief in one supreme god. They understood the Christian and Muslim idea of a single god, but many wanted to continue their own religious practices.

These practices varied from place to place. Some groups, like the Nanti in East Africa, thought people could talk directly with their god. Others, like the Igbo, thought their creator could only be spoken to through less powerful gods and goddesses who worked for him.

Even though Africans practiced their religion differently in different places, their beliefs served similar purposes. They provided rules for living and helped people stay in touch with their history.

When relatives died, many Africans believed their spirits stayed with the community. They believed these spirits could talk to the supreme god or help solve problems. As a result, many Africans honored their ancestors.

Reading Check **Explain** What was the role of ancestors in African religion?

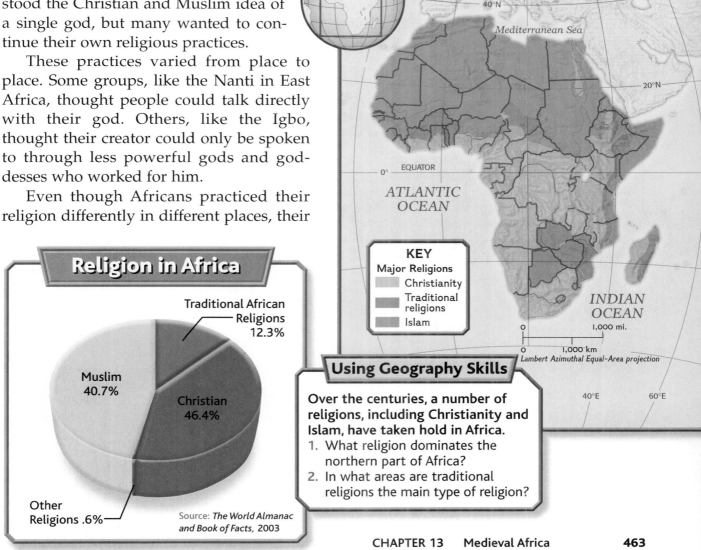

Religion in Africa

- Traditional African Religions 12.3%
- Muslim 40.7%
- Christian 46.4%
- Other Religions .6%

Source: *The World Almanac and Book of Facts*, 2003

African Religions Today

NATIONAL GEOGRAPHIC

Mediterranean Sea

40°N

20°N

EQUATOR 0°

ATLANTIC OCEAN

INDIAN OCEAN

40°E 60°E

KEY
Major Religions
- Christianity
- Traditional religions
- Islam

0 1,000 mi.
0 1,000 km
Lambert Azimuthal Equal-Area projection

Using Geography Skills

Over the centuries, a number of religions, including Christianity and Islam, have taken hold in Africa.
1. What religion dominates the northern part of Africa?
2. In what areas are traditional religions the main type of religion?

Islam in Africa

Main Idea Islam played an important role in medieval Africa, but long-held African beliefs and customs still remained strong.

Reading Focus Have you ever changed your ideas because someone you respect has different ideas than you do? Learn how African rulers helped spread Islam and how Arabs and Africans influenced each other.

Ibn Battuta (IH•buhn bat•TOO•tah), a young Arab lawyer from Morocco, set out in 1325 to see the Muslim world. Since the A.D. 600s, the religion of Islam had spread from the Arabian Peninsula to Africa and elsewhere.

Ibn Battuta traveled throughout the lands of Islam for almost 30 years. He covered a distance of more than 73,000 miles (117,482 km). When Ibn Battuta arrived in West Africa in 1352, Islam had been practiced there for hundreds of years. Yet he soon realized that not all people in West Africa accepted Islam. Many people in the countryside still followed traditional African religions. Islam was popular in the cities where rulers and traders accepted it by choice or because it helped them trade with Muslim Arabs.

Some Muslims complained that Sundiata Keita and Sunni Ali—western Africa's two great empire builders—did not do enough to win people over to Islam. The two leaders were more concerned about stopping rebellions than spreading religion.

Ibn Battuta found things in West Africa that surprised him. He was amazed that women did not cover their faces with a veil,

The City of Djenne

Like Timbuktu, the city of Djenne became a center for both trade and Islam. Traders from the deserts to the north and the rain forests to the south met at Djenne, located on the Bani River. The first Great Mosque at Djenne was probably built in the 1200s.
Did all of the people in West Africa accept Islam? Explain.

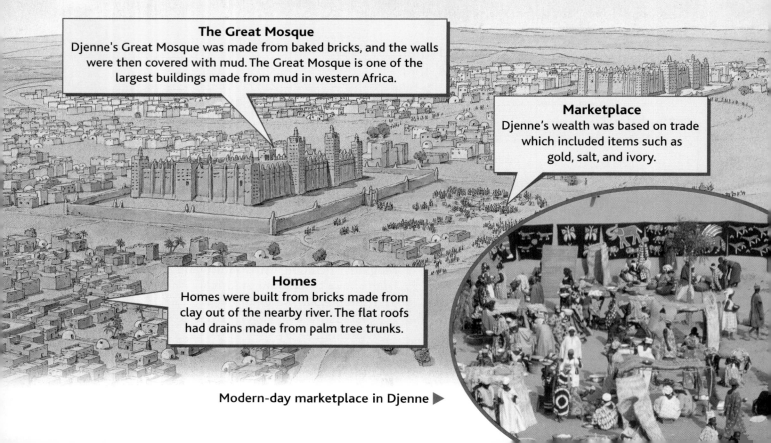

The Great Mosque
Djenne's Great Mosque was made from baked bricks, and the walls were then covered with mud. The Great Mosque is one of the largest buildings made from mud in western Africa.

Marketplace
Djenne's wealth was based on trade which included items such as gold, salt, and ivory.

Homes
Homes were built from bricks made from clay out of the nearby river. The flat roofs had drains made from palm tree trunks.

Modern-day marketplace in Djenne ▶

as was the Muslim custom. However, he did find that West Africans studied the Quran, the Muslim holy book. "They zealously [eagerly] learn the Quran by heart," he wrote.

Mali and Mansa Musa Much of what pleased Ibn Battuta was the work of Mansa Musa. Mansa Musa had allowed different religions but had worked to make Islam stronger. He used the wealth of Mali to build more mosques, or Muslim places of worship. He also set up libraries at Timbuktu, which collected books from all over the Muslim world.

In 1324 Mansa Musa made Mali known to other parts of the world when he set out on a long journey to the city of **Makkah** (MAH•kuh), also known as Mecca. As you read in the chapter on Islam, all Muslims are supposed to make a pilgrimage to the Muslim holy city of Makkah. When Mansa Musa set out on his trip, however, he made sure everybody knew he was the leader of a great empire.

Mansa Musa's caravan had thousands of people, including enslaved people, and 100 pack camels. Each camel carried gold. While in Makkah, Mansa Musa convinced some of Islam's finest architects, teachers, and writers to return with him to Mali. There they helped spread Islam in West Africa.

Songhai and Askia Muhammad Sunni Ali practiced the traditional religion of the Songhai people. However, he declared himself a Muslim to keep the support of townspeople. After Sunni Ali died, his son refused to follow his father's example.

As you read earlier, Muhammad Ture, one of Sunni Ali's generals, saw a chance to take over the government. With the support of Muslim townspeople, he declared himself king. In a bloody war, he drove Sunni Ali's family from Songhai. He then took the name Askia, a rank in the Songhai army.

Primary Source — The Sultan of Mali

The sultan in this passage is Mansa Musa. He is described by an Arab scholar named Ibn Fadl Allah al Omari.

"The sultan of this kingdom presides in his palace on a great balcony called *bembe* where he has a great seat of ebony that is like a throne fit for a large and tall person: on either side it is flanked by elephant tusks turned towards each other. His arms [weapons] stand near him, being all of gold, saber, lance, quiver, bow and arrows. He wears wide trousers made of about twenty pieces [of stuff] of a kind which he alone may wear."

▲ Mansa Musa

—Ibn Fadl Allah al Omari, "Mali in the Fourteenth Century"

DBQ Document-Based Questions

What impression did Mansa Musa want to make on newcomers to his kingdom? How do you know?

Under **Askia Muhammad** (ahs•KEE•uh moh•HAH•muhd), Songhai built the largest empire in medieval West Africa. He kept local courts in place but told them to honor Muslim laws. He also made Timbuktu an important center of Islamic culture and set up some 150 schools to teach the Quran.

History Online

Web Activity Visit jat.glencoe.com and click on *Chapter 13—Student Web Activity* to learn more about medieval Africa.

Biography

MANSA MUSA
Ruled 1312–1337

Mansa Musa ruled the West African empire of Mali with great skill and organization. Under Mansa Musa's guidance, Mali became a great center of education, commerce, and the arts. Mali was one of the largest empires in the world at the time. In fact, the kingdom was so vast that Mansa Musa once bragged it would take a year to travel from the northern border to the southern border.

Despite Mali's enormous size and wealth, the kingdom was not well-known outside the continent of Africa. Mansa Musa's pilgrimage to Makkah in 1324, however, announced Mali's riches and achievements to the world. Traveling on horseback, Mansa Musa was joined by many people, including 8,000 enslaved people, 100 camels to carry baggage, and 24,000 pounds of gold. Each person carried a staff of gold. According to Egyptian historians and the accounts of observers, Mansa Musa spent so much gold in Cairo, Egypt, that the value of gold dropped in Cairo and did not recover for more than 12 years.

Mansa Musa's famous pilgrimage to Makkah brought attention to his kingdom. Mali was included on world maps as early as 1339. Many European nations and kingdoms in North Africa and the Middle East wished to establish trade connections with Mali and gain some of its wealth. Mali's territory and trade connections expanded even further with the capture of the cities Gao and Timbuktu, which also flourished under Mansa Musa's rule.

▲ Mansa Musa

▲ A village in Mali today

Then and Now

Mali was unnoticed by the rest of the world until Mansa Musa's pilgrimage. Is it possible for a present-day country to go unnoticed? Why or why not?

The empire survived family disputes. But, as you have read, it did not survive the guns of Moroccan invaders. The invasion in 1591 shattered the empire.

Islam in East Africa In 1331 Ibn Battuta visited Mogadishu, a trading port on the East African coast. Its **sultan** (SUHL•tuhn), or leader, said in perfect Arabic, "You have honored our country by coming." A moment later, Ibn Battuta heard the sultan speak in **Swahili** (swah•HEE•lee).

The word *Swahili* comes from an Arabic word meaning "people of the coast." By 1331, however, it had come to mean two things: the unique culture of East Africa's coast and the language spoken there.

The Swahili culture and language, which exist in East Africa today, are a blend of African and Muslim influences. African influences came from the cultures of Africa's interior. Muslim influences came from Arab and Persian settlers.

When Europeans from Portugal arrived on the coast in the early 1500s, they tried to destroy the Swahili culture. The Swahili responded by halting inland trade. In the end, the Swahili culture outlived European rule.

Islam's Impact on Africa Islam had a far-reaching impact on northern and eastern Africa. Africans who accepted Islam also adopted Islamic laws and ideas about right and wrong. Sometimes these changes were opposed by people who favored traditional African ways.

Islam also advanced learning. Muslim schools drew students from many parts of Africa and introduced the Arabic language to many Africans. Islam also influenced African art and buildings. Muslim architects built beautiful mosques and palaces in Timbuktu and other cities.

✓ **Reading Check** **Explain** How did Askia Muhammad gain control of Songhai?

History Online

Study Central™ Need help with the material in this section? Visit jat.glencoe.com

Section ② Review

Reading Summary

Review the Main Ideas

- The empires of West Africa were ruled by kings, who closely controlled trade and divided their lands among lesser chiefs to aid in governing.

- Many African religions believed in a single creator and honored the spirits of ancestors.

- Islam became the dominant religion in the kingdoms of West and East Africa.

What Did You Learn?

1. How did the kings of Ghana hold tightly to their power?

2. How did Mansa Musa attempt to strengthen Islam in Mali?

Critical Thinking

3. **Cause and Effect** Draw a diagram to show the effects of Islam on West and East Africa.

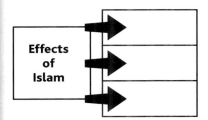

4. **Analyze** How did having the central authority rest with a single person benefit the king, individuals, and the kingdom? How is this model of a government reflected in modern government?

5. **Expository Writing** Imagine you were a witness to Mansa Musa's pilgrimage to Makkah. Write a newspaper article describing the pilgrimage.

6. **Reading** Compare and Contrast Draw a Venn diagram to compare the leadership of Mansa Musa and Askia Muhammad.

African Society and Culture

Get Ready to Read!

What's the Connection?

By the time Europeans came to Africa, people all over the continent had developed complex cultures. For most Africans, life centered on farming villages, like the ones you will read about in this section. Here the family formed the basis of society.

Focusing on the Main Ideas

- The Bantu migrations helped shape many cultures in Africa south of the Sahara. *(page 469)*

- The African slave trade changed greatly when Muslims and Europeans began taking captives from the continent. *(page 472)*

- Enslaved Africans developed rich cultures that influenced many other cultures, including our own. *(page 474)*

Locating Places

Benue River (BAYN•way)

Meeting People

Dahia al-Kahina
(dah•HEE•ah ahl•kah•HEE•nah)
Nzinga (ehn•ZIHN•gah)

Building Your Vocabulary

extended family
matrilineal (MA•truh•LIH•nee•uhl)
oral history

Reading Strategy

Compare and Contrast Create a Venn diagram like the one below showing the similarities and differences between the enslavement of Africans in Africa and the enslavement of Africans in Europe.

Enslavement in Africa   Enslavement in Europe

NATIONAL GEOGRAPHIC When & Where?

3000 B.C.	A.D. 1000	1500
c. 3000 B.C. Bantu begin migration across Africa	**c. A.D. 650** Queen Dahia al-Kahina fights Muslims	**c. 1441** First enslaved Africans arrive in Europe

- Timbuktu
- Kilwa
- Great Zimbabwe

Life in Medieval Africa

Main Idea The Bantu migrations helped shape many cultures in Africa south of the Sahara.

Reading Focus Have you ever noticed that even though people are different, they all have some things in common? Read to learn why people in different regions of Africa have similar traditions and cultures.

Around 3000 B.C., fishing groups along the **Benue River** (BAYN•way) in present day eastern Nigeria packed belongings in their canoes and moved south and west. The wanderers called themselves *Bantu,* meaning "the people."

The Bantu traveled slowly and by different routes. At least some paddled up the Congo River—a waterway twisting 2,700 miles (4,345 km) through the rain forests. Many settled, for a time, in the grasslands of central Africa. From there, they fanned out over much of the land south of the Sahara. By A.D. 400, Bantu peoples had settled much of Africa.

Historians are not sure why the Bantu left their homeland. Perhaps the land became too crowded. Maybe farmers wore out the soil. Or the Bantu may have just drifted, the way pioneers sometimes do.

Wherever they went, the Bantu took their culture with them. They spread skills such as pottery making, mining, and ironworking. They also spread their language. Today more than 120 million Africans speak hundreds of Bantu languages, including Swahili.

The Bantu migrations, or movements of a large number of people, are the reason people all across Africa share some common ideas and traditions. The Bantu, for example, believed in one supreme creator and a spirit world where ancestors live. As you read in the last section, this was a common belief in many places in Africa.

Importance of Family The family formed the basis of African society. People often lived in **extended families,** or families made up of several generations. They included anywhere from ten to hundreds of members.

Many villages, especially Bantu villages, were **matrilineal** (MA•truh•LIH•nee•uhl). They traced their descent through mothers rather than fathers. When a woman married, however, she joined her husband's family. To make up for the loss, her family received gifts—cloth, metal tools, cattle, or goats—from the husband's family.

All families valued children greatly. They saw them as a link between the past and the future. Some people, like the Yoruba of what is today Nigeria, believed

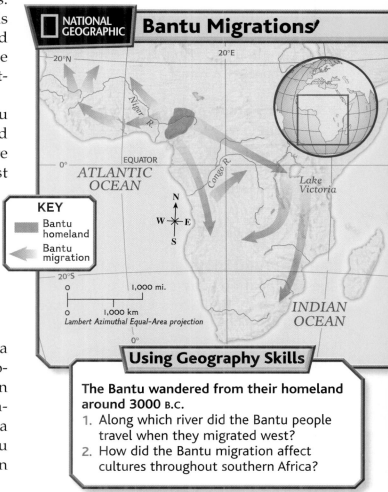

NATIONAL GEOGRAPHIC **Bantu Migrations**

KEY

Bantu homeland

Bantu migration

ATLANTIC OCEAN

INDIAN OCEAN

Lake Victoria

EQUATOR

Niger R.

Congo R.

1,000 mi.

1,000 km

Lambert Azimuthal Equal-Area projection

Using Geography Skills

The Bantu wandered from their homeland around 3000 B.C.
1. Along which river did the Bantu people travel when they migrated west?
2. How did the Bantu migration affect cultures throughout southern Africa?

▲ **This panel shows a family from the Congo at work.**
What was an extended family in Bantu society?

an ancestor might be reborn in a child. They also knew children guaranteed that the family would live on. In praising the family, one Yoruba poet wrote:

> 66 When a group of boys, girls,
>   men, or wives,
>   Go together in a happy company,
>   Dignity attends them in
>   every step.
> · · · · · · · · · · · · · · · · 99
>   —Yoruba, "Dignity"

Education and Community In Africa's villages, education was carried out by the family and other villagers. Children learned the history of their people and the skills needed as adults.

In West Africa, griots, or storytellers, helped in schooling. They kept alive an **oral history**—the stories passed down from generation to generation. Many stories included a lesson about living. Lessons also were given through short proverbs.

One Bantu proverb stated: "A good deed will make a good neighbor." Grandparents and other older people also kept oral histories alive.

Role of Women As in most medieval societies, women in Africa acted mostly as wives and mothers. Men had more rights and controlled much of what women did. Visitors to Africa, however, saw exceptions. European explorers were amazed to learn that women served as soldiers in some African kingdoms.

African women also won fame as rulers. In the A.D. 600s, Queen **Dahia al-Kahina** (dah•HEE•uh ahl•kah•HEE•nah) led the fight against the Muslim invasion of her kingdom, which was located about where Mauritania is today. Another woman ruler was Queen **Nzinga** (ehn•ZIHN•gah), who ruled lands in what are now Angola and Congo. She spent almost 40 years battling Portuguese slave traders.

✓ **Reading Check** **Explain** How were Bantu families organized?

Biography

QUEEN NZINGA
c. 1582–1663

Angolan Warrior-Leader

It was rare in the 1600s for women to take active roles in politics and war, but one African woman—Queen Nzinga of Matamba—was known for her military leadership and political skills. Nzinga was the daughter of the king of the Ndongo people. The Ndongo lived in southwest Africa in what is today called Angola. Nzinga quickly learned archery and hunting. She was intelligent and a natural athlete. Nzinga's father failed to notice his daughter. He was too busy defending the kingdom from the Portuguese, who wanted to buy enslaved Africans and ship them overseas.

Even though she was female, Nzinga knew she could be a strong leader. She did not want to learn the enemy's language, but she soon realized that it could benefit her. She asked a captured priest to teach her Portuguese.

In 1623 Nzinga became queen. She declared all of her territory to be free territory and promised that all enslaved Africans who made it to the kingdom would be free. For nearly 30 years, she led her people in battles against the Portuguese. She allied with other African kingdoms to seal the trade routes used to ship enslaved Africans out of the country. In 1662 she negotiated a peace agreement with the Portuguese. She died the next year at age 81.

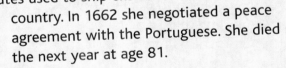

▲ Enslaved Africans in a ship's hold being taken to America.

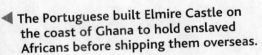

◄ The Portuguese built Elmire Castle on the coast of Ghana to hold enslaved Africans before shipping them overseas.

Then and Now

Do research to find the name of a modern female leader. Compare her leadership skills to those of Queen Nzinga.

471

Slavery

Main Idea The African slave trade changed greatly when Muslims and Europeans began taking captives from the continent.

Reading Focus You know that there was a time in American history when people of African ancestry were enslaved. Read to learn about slavery in African society and the beginning of the European slave trade.

In 1441 a Portuguese sea captain sailed down Africa's western coast. His goal was to bring the first African captives back to Portugal. During the voyage, the captain and his nine sailors seized 12 Africans—men, women, and boys. The ship then sailed back to Portugal. These captives represented only a small portion of a slave trade that would grow into the millions.

Slavery Within Africa
Europeans did not invent slavery. For a long time, it had existed throughout the world. In Africa, Bantu chiefs raided nearby villages for captives. These captives became laborers or were freed for a payment.

Africans also enslaved criminals or enemies taken in war. These enslaved Africans became part of the Saharan trade. However, as long as Africans stayed in Africa, hope of escape still existed. Enslaved Africans might also win their freedom through hard work or by marrying a free person.

The trade in humans also grew as the trade with Muslim merchants increased. The Quran forbade enslavement of Muslims. Muslims, however, could enslave non-Muslims. Arab traders, therefore, began to trade horses, cotton, and other goods for enslaved, non-Muslim Africans.

When Europeans arrived in West Africa, a new market for enslaved Africans opened. Africans armed with European guns began raiding villages to seize captives to sell.

▲ On a slave ship, enslaved people were transported in the dark, crowded spaces of the ship's cargo deck. *Why were enslaved Africans used on Portuguese plantations?*

The European Slave Trade
In 1444 a Portuguese ship docked at a port in Portugal. Sailors unloaded the cargo—235 enslaved Africans. Tears ran down the faces of some. Others cried for help. A Portuguese official described the scene:

❝ **But to increase their sufferings still more, . . . was it needful to part fathers from sons, husbands from wives, brothers from brothers.** ❞

—Gomes Eannes de Zurara, as quoted in *The Slave Trade*

Barely three years had passed since the arrival of the first African captives in Portugal. Some merchants who had hoped to sell gold brought from Africa now sold humans instead. At first, most enslaved Africans stayed in Portugal, working as laborers. This changed when the Portuguese settled the Atlantic islands of Madeira, the Azores, and Cape Verde. There the climate was perfect for growing cotton, grapes, and sugarcane on plantations, or huge farms.

Harvesting sugarcane was hard labor. Planters could not pay high wages to get workers, so they used enslaved Africans instead. Many Africans had farming skills and the ability to make tools. Enslaved people were not paid and could be fed and kept cheaply. By 1500, Portugal was the world's leading supplier of sugar.

The rest of Europe followed Portugal's example. In the late 1400s, Europeans arrived in the Americas. They set up sugar plantations and brought enslaved Africans across the Atlantic Ocean to work the fields. They also used enslaved people to grow tobacco, rice, and cotton.

✓ **Reading Check** **Analyze** How did exploration change the African slave trade?

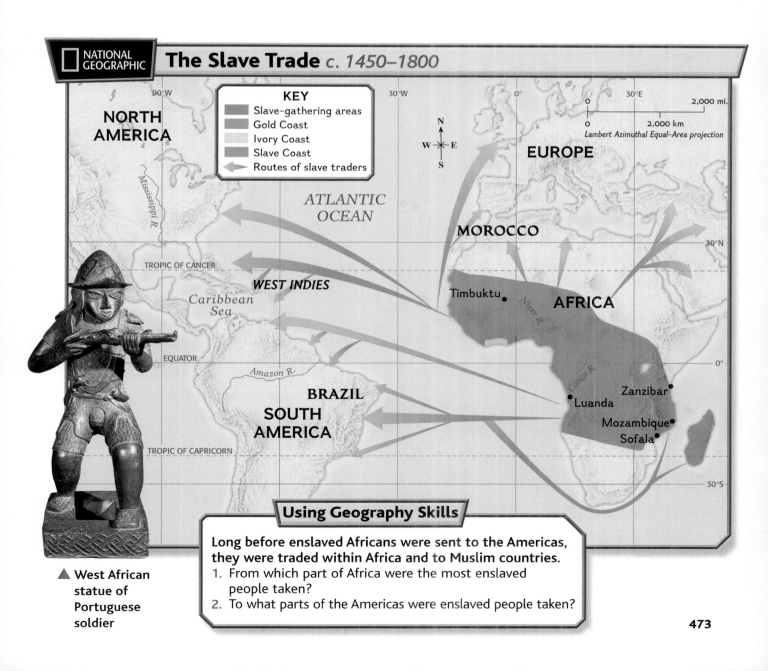

The Slave Trade c. 1450–1800

NATIONAL GEOGRAPHIC

KEY
- Slave-gathering areas
- Gold Coast
- Ivory Coast
- Slave Coast
- → Routes of slave traders

2,000 mi.
2,000 km
Lambert Azimuthal Equal-Area projection

NORTH AMERICA
ATLANTIC OCEAN
EUROPE
MOROCCO
WEST INDIES
Caribbean Sea
Timbuktu
AFRICA
Niger R.
BRAZIL
SOUTH AMERICA
Amazon R.
Congo R.
Zanzibar
Luanda
Mozambique
Sofala
Mississippi R.

TROPIC OF CANCER
EQUATOR
TROPIC OF CAPRICORN

90°W 30°W 0° 30°E 30°N 0° 30°S

▲ West African statue of Portuguese soldier

Using Geography Skills

Long before enslaved Africans were sent to the Americas, they were traded within Africa and to Muslim countries.
1. From which part of Africa were the most enslaved people taken?
2. To what parts of the Americas were enslaved people taken?

473

Focus on Everyday Life

Kente Cloth *Kente* is the name of a colorful woven cloth. Its name comes from a word that means "basket." The first weavers were mostly men. They used fibers to make cloth that looked like the patterns in baskets. Strips were sewn together to make colorful patterns. *Kente* was worn by tribal chiefs and is still popular today. This African folktale about *kente* cloth has been handed down for generations:

One day two friends walked through a rain forest and saw a spider creating designs in its web. They took the spider web to show their friends and family. They were greatly upset when the web fell apart in their hands. They returned the next day to watch and learn as the spider did a weaving dance and spun another web. The friends took their newfound skills to their looms and made colorful cloth they called *kente*.

African women ▶ wearing *kente* cloth

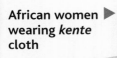

Connecting to the Past

1. Why does the legend suggest that Africans learned to weave *kente* cloth from a spider?
2. Why do you think the first *kente* cloth weavers were mostly men?

African Culture

Main Idea Enslaved Africans developed rich cultures that influenced many other cultures, including our own.

Reading Focus Do you have any traditions that have been in your family for a long time? Read to learn how Africans took their culture with them when they were enslaved and sent overseas.

"We are almost a nation of dancers, musicians, and poets," declared Olaudah Equiano in describing the Igbo people of West Africa. He might have added artists, weavers, woodcarvers, and metalworkers too. African peoples like the Igbo excelled in many art forms.

When slave traders seized Africans like Equiano from their homelands, they also uprooted their cultures. Africans carried these cultures with them in what has become known as the African Diaspora—the spreading of African people and culture around the world.

People of African descent held on to memories of their cultures and passed them down from generation to generation. The heritage of Africa can be seen and heard in the United States today—not just in the faces and voices of African descendants but in their gifts to our culture.

African Art Cave paintings are the earliest form of African art we know about. They show people hunting animals, dancing, and doing everyday chores. As in other parts of the world, African art and religion developed hand in hand. Early African cave paintings, as well as later art, almost always had some religious meaning or use. Woodcarvers made masks and statues, for example, to celebrate African religious beliefs. Each carved piece of wood captured some part of the spiritual world.

African works of art also told stories and served practical purposes. Artists working in wood, ivory, or bronze showed the faces of important leaders, everyday people, and, later, European explorers and traders. Weavers designed cloth similar to cloth still worn today. You may have seen the brightly colored kente cloth of West Africa. Many people wear it today.

Music and Dance Music played a part in almost all aspects of African life. People used it to express their religious feelings or to get through an everyday task, like planting a field.

In many African songs, a singer calls out a line, then other singers repeat it back. Musical instruments, such as drums, whistles, horns, flutes, or banjos, were used to keep the beat.

Africans believed dance allowed the spirits to express themselves. So they used it to celebrate important events such as birth and death. Nearly everybody danced. Lines of men and women swayed and clapped their hands. Individual dancers

Linking Past & Present

African Music

THEN Traditional African music comes from many different sounds and rhythms. Every culture in Africa contributed to its development. Some used drums. Others used wind and string instruments. Many imitated nature through voice and dance. African music was handed down from one generation to another.

▼ **Modern-day musicians**

NOW Traditional African music influences rap, hip-hop, pop, and rock music. The use of drums and a steady beat comes from African tribal music. *Can you name current groups or artists who have been impacted by the African musical style?*

▲ **Traditional African musicians**

◄ Griots still share the stories and lessons of their ancestors. *What were traditional African stories often about?*

leaped and twirled. In the background, drummers sounded out the rhythm.

Enslaved Africans sometimes relied on music to remind them of their homeland. Songs of hardship eventually developed into a type of music that we know today as the blues. Songs of religious faith and hopes for freedom grew into spirituals or gospel songs. Over time, other forms of African-based music developed, such as ragtime, jazz, rock and roll, and, more recently, rap.

Storytelling Africans also kept alive their storytelling tradition. A few enslaved Africans escaped and were able to record their stories. Others retold their stories aloud. Those who heard the stories repeated them. They also retold tales taught by griots in the African homeland. Popular stories often told how small animals, such as turtles and rabbits, outsmarted larger ones.

In more recent times, some African Americans have renewed ties with their past by taking African names or giving them to their children. This also helps keep alive African history and culture.

 **Reading Check** **Explain** Why did Africans use dance to celebrate important events?

History Online

Study Central™ Need help with the material in this section? Visit jat.glencoe.com

Section 3 Review

Reading Summary
Review the Main Ideas

- Many Africans south of the Sahara lived in small villages. Family was very important, and women had fewer rights than men.

- Africans had kept slaves long before they began to trade enslaved persons to Muslims and Europeans.

- As enslaved Africans were taken to new areas, African culture, including art, music, and story-telling, spread around the world.

What Did You Learn?

1. What was the African Diaspora?

2. What is the earliest form of African art known? Describe some of the subjects portrayed in the art.

Critical Thinking

3. **Organizing Information** Draw a diagram like the one below. Fill in details about African music and dance.

African Music and Dance

4. **Compare** How were African art and religion related?

5. **Identify** What was Queen Dahia al-Kahina's greatest accomplishment?

6. **Infer** Why do you think some Africans liked tales in which small animals outsmarted larger animals?

7. **Persuasive Writing** Portuguese plantation owners relied on slave labor to help them grow sugarcane. Suppose you had a family member who was enslaved on a plantation. Write a letter to the plantation owner explaining why this practice is unacceptable.

Chapter 13 Reading Review

Section 1 The Rise of African Civilizations

Vocabulary
plateau
griot
dhow

Focusing on the Main Ideas
- Africa has a vast and varied landscape. *(page 445)*
- West African empires grew rich from trade. *(page 447)*
- Africa's rain forests blocked invaders and provided resources. *(page 450)*
- East African kingdoms and states became centers for trade and new ideas. *(page 451)*

Section 2 Africa's Government and Religion

Vocabulary
clan
sultan
Swahili

Focusing on the Main Ideas
- The growth of West African empires led to the growth of centralized governments ruled by kings. *(page 461)*
- Traditional African religions shared certain beliefs and provided a guide for living together. *(page 463)*
- Islam played an important role in medieval Africa, but long-held African beliefs and customs still remained strong. *(page 464)*

Section 3 African Society and Culture

Vocabulary
extended family
matrilineal
oral history

Focusing on the Main Ideas
- The Bantu migrations helped shape many cultures in Africa south of the Sahara. *(page 469)*
- The African slave trade changed greatly when Muslims and Europeans began taking captives from the continent. *(page 472)*
- Enslaved Africans developed rich cultures that influenced many other cultures, including our own. *(page 474)*

▲ Family life in the Congo

Review Vocabulary

Write *True* for each true statement. Replace the word in italics to make false statements true.

_____ 1. Wooden boats known as *griots* were powered by triangular sails.

_____ 2. An area of high, flat land is a *plateau*.

_____ 3. Each district in Ghana usually included a chief's *clan*.

_____ 4. African *dhows* are storytellers.

_____ 5. *Matrilineal* societies trace their descent through mothers.

_____ 6. *Swahili* culture and language exist in Africa today.

Review Main Ideas

Section 1 • The Rise of African Civilizations

7. What were the advantages of living in Africa's rain forests?

8. Why were East African kingdoms and states important?

Section 2 • Africa's Government and Religion

9. How were West African empires governed?

10. Describe the religious beliefs of medieval Africans.

Section 3 • African Society and Culture

11. What was the result of the Bantu migrations?

12. How did slavery in medieval Africa change?

Critical Thinking

13. **Predict** What do you think would have happened in Ghana if the people had been allowed to trade with gold nuggets instead of gold dust?

14. **Explain** What caused the decline of Ghana and Songhai?

15. **Analyze** Why do you think the Bantu language changed as people moved into different parts of Africa?

Review

Reading Skill Compare and Contrast

Making Comparisons

16. Read the paragraph below, then create a Venn diagram that shows similarities and differences between the continents of Africa and North America.

Africa is the world's second-largest continent. The United States fits into Africa three times, with room to spare. The Equator slices through the middle of the continent. Hot, steamy rain forests stretch along each side of it. Yet the rain forests cover only 10 percent of the land.

To review this skill, see pages 442–443.

Geography Skills

Study the map below and answer the following questions.

17. **Human/Environment Interaction** What obstacle did the empires in western Africa have to overcome in order to trade with cities in northern Africa?

18. **Location** In which parts of Africa do you think people had the best opportunities to trade by sea?

19. **Movement** How do you think more inland water routes would have changed the cultures of Africa?

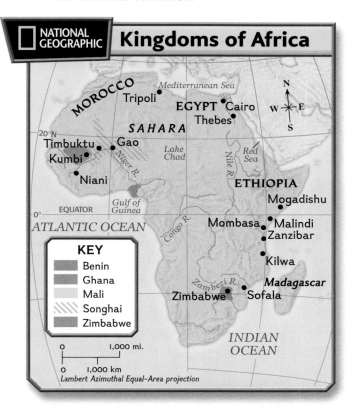

NATIONAL GEOGRAPHIC **Kingdoms of Africa**

MOROCCO
Tripoli
Mediterranean Sea
EGYPT • Cairo
Thebes•
SAHARA
20°N
Timbuktu • • Gao
Kumbi•
Niger R.
Lake Chad
Red Sea
Nile R.
• Niani
ETHIOPIA
Mogadishu
EQUATOR
Gulf of Guinea
0°
ATLANTIC OCEAN
Congo R.
Mombasa • • Malindi
Zanzibar
• Kilwa
Zambezi R.
Madagascar
Zimbabwe • • Sofala
INDIAN OCEAN

KEY
- Benin
- Ghana
- Mali
- Songhai
- Zimbabwe

0   1,000 mi.
0   1,000 km
Lambert Azimuthal Equal-Area projection

Read to Write

20. **Descriptive Writing** Write an essay describing evidence of the African Diaspora in your community, city, or state. Make note of music, dance, literature, art, and other aspects of culture.

21. **Using Your FOLDABLES** Use the answers in your foldable to create a poster that shows what Africa was like in the past. Draw sketches, create maps, find pictures of artifacts, and so on to visually describe the cultures.

History Online
Self-Check Quiz To help you prepare for the Chapter Test, visit jat.glencoe.com

Using Technology

22. **Multimedia Presentation** Choose a present-day African country to research. Use the Internet to find information on that country from its early history to the present. Then create a multimedia presentation about that country, including images and a time line of important events in the country's history. Be sure to include aspects of culture, natural resources, and government.

Linking Past and Present

23. **Narrative Writing** Even though people record many things on paper or on a computer, they often tell stories about their lives as oral histories. Ask a family member, neighbor, teacher, or other adult to tell a story that has been passed down in his or her family. Record that oral history in narrative form.

Primary Source **Analyze**

This report was written by the first engineer ever to see the ruins of Great Zimbabwe.

"The ruins are . . . terraces, which rise up continually from the base to the apex [highest point] of all the hills. . . . The way that the ancients seem to have levelled off the contours of the various hills . . . is very astonishing, as they seem to have been levelled with as much exactitude as we can accomplish with our best mathematical instruments."

—Telford Edwards, as quoted in
The Mystery of the Great Zimbabwe

DBQ Document-Based Questions

24. What in particular amazes the engineer about Great Zimbabwe?
25. How do you think the people of Great Zimbabwe accomplished such precision?

Medieval Japan

Kingaku Temple in Kyoto, Japan ▼

NATIONAL GEOGRAPHIC **When & Where?**

A.D. 300	A.D. 700	1100	1500
c. A.D. 300 Yayoi people organize into clans	**A.D. 646** Taika reforms strengthen emperor's powers	**1192** Rule by shoguns begins	**c. 1300s** Noh plays first performed

Chapter Preview

Warriors in Japan, like those in Africa, were known for their fighting skills. Japanese warriors trained their minds and bodies for battle. Read this chapter to find out about their training methods and how they are used today.

 View the Chapter 14 video in the *World History: Journey Across Time* Video Program.

History Online

Chapter Overview Visit jat.glencoe.com **for a preview of Chapter 14.**

 ## Section 1 — Early Japan

Japan's islands and mountains have shaped its history. The Japanese developed their own unique culture but looked to China as a model.

 ## Section 2 — Shoguns and Samurai

Japan's emperors lost power to military leaders. Warrior families and their followers fought each other for control of Japan.

 ## Section 3 — Life in Medieval Japan

The religions of Shinto and Buddhism shaped Japan's culture. Farmers, artisans, and merchants brought wealth to Japan.

FOLDABLES™ Study Organizer

Categorizing Information *Make this foldable to help you organize information about the history and culture of medieval Japan.*

Step 1 *Mark the midpoint of the side edge of a sheet of paper.*

Draw a mark at the midpoint

Step 2 *Turn the paper and fold in each outside edge to touch at the midpoint. Label as shown.*

Japan

Step 3 *Open and label your foldable as shown.*

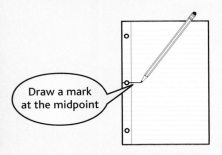

Early Japan | Shoguns and Samurai | Life in Medieval Japan

Reading and Writing *As you read the chapter, organize your notes by writing the main ideas with supporting details under the appropriate tab.*

Reading Social Studies

1 Learn It!

Identifying Cause and Effect

Learning to identify causes (reasons) and effects (results) will help you understand how and why things happen in history. Read the following passage and think about the result (effect) of Japan having mountains. Then see how the information can be pulled out and placed into a graphic organizer.

Cause

> **Because of Japan's mountains, only about 20 percent of its land can be farmed. Throughout Japan's history, local armies often fought over the few patches of fertile farmland. Just as in ancient Greece, the ragged terrain forced many Japanese to turn to the sea for a living.**
>
> —*from page 485*

Effects

Reading Tip

Find different ways to organize information as you read. Create graphic organizers that suit your own learning style to help you make sense of what you are reading.

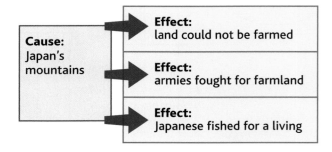

Cause: Japan's mountains

→ **Effect:** land could not be farmed

→ **Effect:** armies fought for farmland

→ **Effect:** Japanese fished for a living

2 Practice It!
Using Graphic Organizers

Read the following paragraph and either use the graphic organizer below or create your own to show the effects of Yoritomo's ruthless rule.

Read to Write ·······
After reading Section 2, write a paragraph that summarizes the reasons why the power of Japan's emperor declined during the A.D. 800s.

Yoritomo proved to be a ruthless ruler. He killed most of his relatives, fearing that they would try to take power from him. Yoritomo and the shoguns after him appointed high-ranking samurai to serve as advisers and to run the provinces. Bound by an oath of loyalty, these samurai lords ruled Japan's villages, kept the peace, and gathered taxes. They became the leading group in Japanese society.

—*from page 495*

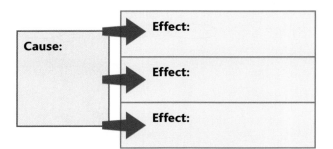

Cause:

Effect:

Effect:

Effect:

3 Apply It!

As you read Chapter 14, be aware of causes and effects in Japanese history. Find at least five causes and their effects, and create graphic organizers to record them.

Section 1

Early Japan

Get Ready to Read!

What's the Connection?

During the Middle Ages, another civilization developed in East Asia. It arose on the islands of Japan off the coast of the Korean Peninsula.

Focusing on the Main Ideas

- Japan's mountains and islands isolated Japan and shaped its society. *(page 485)*

- Japan was settled by people who came from northeast Asia. They were organized into clans and ruled by warriors. *(page 486)*

- Prince Shotoku created Japan's first constitution and borrowed many ideas from China. *(page 488)*

- The Japanese religion called Shinto was based on nature spirits. *(page 490)*

Locating Places

Japan (juh•PAN)
Hokkaido (hah•KY•doh)
Honshu (HAHN•shoo)
Shikoku (shih•KOH•koo)
Kyushu (kee•OO•shoo)

Meeting People

Jomon (JOH•mohn)
Yayoi (YAH•yoy)
Jimmu (jeem•mu)
Shotoku (shoh•TOH•koo)

Building Your Vocabulary

clan (KLAN)
constitution (KAHN•stuh•TOO•shuhn)
animism (A•nuh•MIH•zuhm)
shrine (SHRYN)

Reading Strategy

Organizing Information Create a diagram to show the basics of the Shinto religion.

Shinto Religion

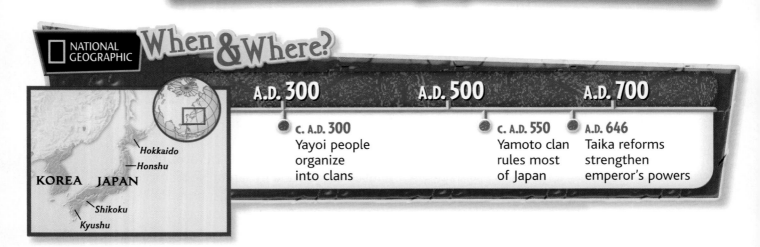

NATIONAL GEOGRAPHIC When & Where?

KOREA JAPAN
Hokkaido
Honshu
Shikoku
Kyushu

A.D. 300

c. A.D. 300
Yayoi people organize into clans

A.D. 500

c. A.D. 550
Yamoto clan rules most of Japan

A.D. 646
Taika reforms strengthen emperor's powers

A.D. 700

Japan's Geography

Main Idea Japan's mountains and islands isolated Japan and shaped its society.

Reading Focus Have you ever been in a place with no television, radio, or telephone? How would you feel if you did not know what was going on outside your home? Read to learn how Japan's geography isolated the Japanese and shaped their society.

Japan (juh•PAN) is a chain of islands that stretches north to south in the northern Pacific Ocean. Japan's islands number more than 3,000, and many of them are tiny. For centuries, most Japanese have lived on the four largest islands: **Hokkaido** (hah•KY•doh), **Honshu** (HAHN•shoo), **Shikoku** (shih•KOH•koo), and **Kyushu** (kee•OO•shoo).

Like China, much of Japan is covered by mountains. In fact, the islands of Japan are actually the tops of mountains that rise from the floor of the ocean. About 188 of Japan's mountains are volcanoes. Many earthquakes occur in Japan because the islands lie in an area where parts of the earth's surface often shift.

Because of Japan's mountains, only about 20 percent of its land can be farmed. Throughout Japan's history, local armies often fought over the few patches of fertile

▼ Mount Fuji is an important national symbol.
How did the region's mountains affect early settlement in Japan?

farmland. Just as in ancient Greece, the rugged terrain forced many Japanese to turn to the sea for a living. Early on, they settled in villages along the coast and fished for food. Fish and seafood are still important in the Japanese diet.

The sea surrounding Japan's islands made it easy for people in ships to travel along the coast and from island to island. It encouraged people to become merchants, traveling from village to village with goods to trade. The vast ocean around Japan's islands, however, kept the Japanese people isolated, or separate, from the rest of Asia. As a result, Japan developed its own fiercely independent society with its own religion, art, literature, and government.

Reading Check **Describe** How did Japan's geography shape its society?

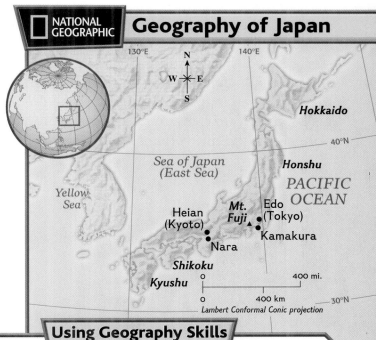

NATIONAL GEOGRAPHIC **Geography of Japan**

Using Geography Skills

Japan's geography isolated the country and helped form a unique culture.
1. List, from north to south, the four major islands that make up Japan.
2. What body of water separates Japan from mainland Asia?

Find NGS online map resources @ www.nationalgeographic.com/maps

The First Settlers

Main Idea Japan was settled by people who came from northeast Asia. They were organized into clans and ruled by warriors.

Reading Focus Do you have many relatives? Do your relatives all come together to do things? Read to learn how the early Japanese people were organized into groups made up of people who were all related to each other.

Japan's earliest people probably came from northeast Asia between 30,000 and 10,000 B.C. At that time, Japan was joined to the Asian continent by land. These early people hunted animals and gathered wild plants. They used fire and stone tools, and they lived in pits dug into the ground.

Who Were the Jomon?
In about 5000 B.C., these wandering groups began to develop a culture. They made clay pottery, using knotted cords to make designs on the clay's surface. Today, this culture is called **Jomon** (JOH•mohn), which means "cord marks" in the Japanese language. Modern archaeologists have found many pieces of Jomon pottery throughout Japan. Over time, the Jomon people settled in fishing villages along the coast. Fishing became their way of life.

Why Are the Yayoi Important?
The Jomon culture lasted until about 300 B.C. At that time, a new group of people appeared in Japan. Modern archaeologists have named this culture **Yayoi** (YAH•yoy), after the place in Japan where they first dug up its artifacts.

The Yayoi were the ancestors of the Japanese people. They introduced farming to Japan and practiced a number of skills that they may have learned from the Chinese and Koreans. They made pottery on a potter's wheel and grew rice in paddies. A paddy is a rice field that is flooded when rice is planted and drained for the harvest.

The Yayoi also were skilled in metalworking. They made axes, knives, and hoes from iron, and swords, spears, and bells from bronze. Bells were used in religious rituals—a practice that is still common in Japan today.

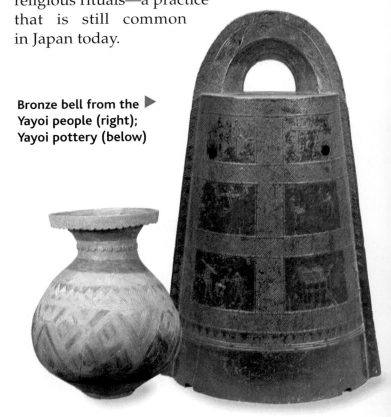

◄ Female figurine from the Jomon culture (left); Jomon vase (below)

Bronze bell from the ► Yayoi people (right); Yayoi pottery (below)

By A.D. 300, the Yayoi, or the early Japanese, had organized themselves into **clans** (KLANZ). A clan is a group of families related by blood or marriage. Yayoi clans were headed by a small group of warriors. Under the warriors were the rest of the people—farmers, artisans, and servants of the warriors. The clan's warrior chiefs protected the people in return for a share of the rice harvest each year.

The Yayoi buried their chiefs in large mounds known as *kofun*. Made of dirt, these tombs were carefully shaped and surrounded by ditches. They were filled with personal belongings, such as pottery, tools, weapons, and armor. Many of the tombs were as big as Egypt's pyramids. The largest tomb still stands today. It is longer than five football fields and at least eight stories high.

Who Are the Yamato?

Like many other people whose society began in ancient times, the Japanese have myths, or stories that tell how things began. The most important myth explained the creation of Japan. It says that centuries ago, two gods dipped a spear into the sea. When they pulled it out, drops of salty water fell on the water's surface and formed the islands of Japan. The two gods then created the sun goddess, Amaterasu, to rule over Earth. They also created the storm god, Susanowo, as her companion.

Susanowo was sent to Earth. There, his children became the first people of Japan. Amaterasu, however, sent her grandson Ninigi to rule over them. To make sure that everyone would accept his power, she gave Ninigi her mirror, her jewel, and a great sword. These objects became the sacred symbols of leadership in early Japan.

Historians today are not sure of the actual events on which this myth is based. However, they do know that during the

▲ The sun goddess, Amaterasu, emerges from her cave, bringing light into the world. *Which group claimed that they came from Amaterasu?*

A.D. 500s, a clan called the Yamato became strong enough to bring most of Japan under its rule. The other clans still held their lands, but they had to give their loyalty to the Yamato chief.

Yamato chiefs claimed that they came from the sun goddess and, therefore, had a right to rule Japan. Japanese legend states that a Yamato leader named **Jimmu** (jeem• mu) took the title "emperor of heaven." He founded a line of rulers in Japan that has never been broken. Akihito (AH•kee•HEE• toh), who is Japan's emperor today, is one of his descendants.

Reading Check Identify What do historians know for sure about the rise of the Yamato?

Prince Shotoku's Reforms

Main Idea Prince Shotoku created Japan's first constitution and borrowed many ideas from China.

Reading Focus When you try something new, are you tempted to use what someone else has done as a model? Read to find out how Shotoku used China as a model for his reforms in Japan.

About A.D. 600, a Yamato prince named **Shotoku** (shoh•TOH•koo) took charge of Japan on behalf of his aunt, the empress Suiko (swee•koh). He wanted to create a strong government, and he looked to China as an example of what to do. You remember that in China, a powerful emperor ruled with the help of trained officials chosen for their abilities.

To reach this goal for Japan, Shotoku created a **constitution** (KAHN•stuh•TOO•shuhn), or a plan of government. Shotoku's constitution gave all power to the emperor, who had to be obeyed by the Japanese people. He also created a bureaucracy and gave the emperor the power to appoint all the officials. The constitution listed rules for working in the government. The rules were taken from the ideas of Confucius.

Shotoku also wanted Japan to learn from China's brilliant civilization. He sent officials and students to China to study. The Japanese not only learned about Buddhist teachings but also absorbed a great deal about Chinese art, medicine, and philosophy.

Shotoku ordered Buddhist temples and monasteries to be built throughout Japan. One of them, called Horyuji (HOHR•yoo•JEE), still stands. It is Japan's oldest temple and the world's oldest surviving wooden building.

After Shotoku, other officials continued to make Japan's government look like China's. In A.D. 646 the Yamato began the Taika, or Great Change. They divided Japan into provinces, or regional districts, all run by officials who reported to the emperor. In addition, all land in Japan came under the emperor's control.

Clan leaders could direct the farmers working the land, but they could not collect taxes anymore. Instead, government officials were to gather part of the farmers' harvest in taxes for the emperor. Together with Shotoku's reforms, this plan created Japan's first strong central government.

Reading Check **Identify** What happened during the Great Change?

Primary Source — Japan's New Constitution

This is part of the constitution created by Shotoku.

"Harmony is to be cherished, and opposition for opposition's sake must be avoided as a matter of principle. . . .

When an imperial command is given, obey it with reverence. The sovereign is likened to heaven, and his subjects are likened to earth. With heaven providing the cover and earth supporting it, the four seasons proceed in orderly fashion, giving sustenance to all that which is in nature. If earth attempts to overtake the functions of heaven, it destroys everything.

Cast away your ravenous desire for food and abandon your covetousness [envy] for material possessions. If a suit is brought before you, render a clear-cut judgement. . . .

Punish that which is evil and encourage that which is good."

—Prince Shotoku,
"The Seventeen Article Constitution"

DBQ Document-Based Question

To what are the emperor and his subjects compared?

Biography

PRINCE SHOTOKU
A.D. 573–621

▲ Statue believed to be of Prince Shotoku

Prince Shotoku was born into the powerful Soga family, as the second son of Emperor Yomei. Shotoku's real name is Umayado, which means "the prince of the stable door." According to legend, Shotoku's mother gave birth to him while she was inspecting the emperor's stables. During Shotoku's childhood, Japan was a society of clans, or large extended families. There was fighting between Shotoku's own Soga family and their rival, the Mononobe family. The Soga and Mononobe clans were Japan's two most powerful families, and each wanted to rule Japan.

Shotoku was a very bright, articulate child. He learned about Buddhism from one of his great uncles. He then studied with two Buddhist priests and became devoted to Buddhism.

At the age of 20, Shotoku became Japan's crown prince. The early teachings of Buddhism strongly influenced his leadership. He introduced political and religious reforms that helped build a strong central government in Japan modeled after China. At the request of his aunt, the empress, Shotoku often spoke about Buddhism and the process of enlightenment. He also wrote the first book of Japanese history.

When Prince Shotoku died, the elderly people of the empire mourned as if they had lost a dear child of their own. A written account describes their words of grief: "The sun and moon have lost their brightness; heaven and earth have crumbled to ruin: henceforward, in whom shall we put our trust?"

▲ The Horyuji temple, built by Prince Shotoku

Then and Now

Think of a recent leader or other public figure whose death caused people to mourn as if they knew that person well. Who is it? Why do you think people identified with that person? Why did the Japanese identify so closely with Shotoku?

What Is Shinto?

◀ Shinto priests

Main Idea The Japanese religion, called Shinto, was based on nature spirits.

Reading Focus Today we know the importance of protecting the environment. Why is nature important to us? Read to learn why the early Japanese thought nature was important.

Like many ancient peoples, the early Japanese believed that all natural things are alive, even the winds, the mountains, and the rivers. They believed that all of these things have their own spirits. This idea is called **animism** (A•nuh•MIH•zuhm). When people needed help, they asked the nature spirits, whom they called *kami,* to help them.

To honor the *kami,* the Japanese worshiped at **shrines** (SHRYNZ), or holy places. There, priests, musicians, and dancers performed rituals for people who asked the gods for a good harvest, a wife or a child, or some other favor.

These early Japanese beliefs developed into the religion of Shinto. The word *Shinto* means "way of the spirits," and many Japanese still follow Shinto today. Followers believe the *kami* will help only if a person is pure. Many things, such as illness, cause spiritual stains that must be cleansed by bathing and other rituals before praying.

✓ **Reading Check** Explain How did the Japanese honor the *kami*?

History Online
Study Central™ Need help with the material in this section? Visit jat.glencoe.com

Section 1 Review

Reading Summary

Review the Main Ideas

- Japan's mountainous islands contain little land for farming, leading many people to turn to the sea for a living.

- Japan was settled by people from northeast Asia, organized into clans and ruled by warriors.

- While ruling Japan, Prince Shotoku made the emperor a strong ruler and set up a government similar to China's.

- Japan's first religion, Shinto, was based on the idea of nature spirits called *kami.*

What Did You Learn?

1. What skills did the Yayoi practice that they may have learned from the Chinese and Koreans?

2. In the Shinto religion, what do people worship? How are they worshiped?

Critical Thinking

3. **Sequencing Information** Draw a time line like the one below. Fill in dates and information related to events in Japanese history from the Jomon to Shotoku.

5000 B.C.   A.D. 646

4. **Summarize** Describe Japanese society under the Yayoi around A.D. 300.

5. **Analyze** In what ways did Shotoku look to China to improve Japan?

6. **Expository Writing** Imagine you are visiting Japan sometime in the A.D. 300s. Write a letter to a friend describing what you have observed and learned about the Shinto religion.

7. **Reading** Cause and Effect Create a cause-and-effect graphic organizer that shows how geography affected the early development of Japan.

Section 2

Shoguns and Samurai

Get Ready to Read!

What's the Connection?

In the last section, you learned how Japan's leaders looked to China as a model of government. As you have learned, warlords sometimes took over parts of China. As you will read, Japan had similar problems.

Focusing on the Main Ideas

- During the A.D. 700s, Japan built a strong national government at Nara, and Buddhism became a popular religion. *(page 492)*

- Japan's civilian government and the emperor came to be dominated by military rulers known as shoguns. *(page 493)*

- As the shogun's power weakened, Japan broke into warring kingdoms run by rulers known as daimyo. *(page 496)*

Locating Places
Heian (HAY•ahn)
Kamakura (kah•MAH•kuh•RAH)

Meeting People
Minamoto Yoritomo (mee•nah• moh•toh   yoh•ree•toh•moh)
Ashikaga Takauji (ah•shee•kah• gah   tah•kow•jee)

Building Your Vocabulary
samurai (SA•muh•RY)
shogun (SHOH•guhn)
daimyo (DY•mee•OH)
vassal (VA•suhl)
feudalism (FYOO•duhl•IH•zuhm)

Reading Strategy
Showing Relationships Create a diagram to show the relationship between daimyo and samurai.

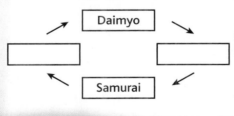

Daimyo

Samurai

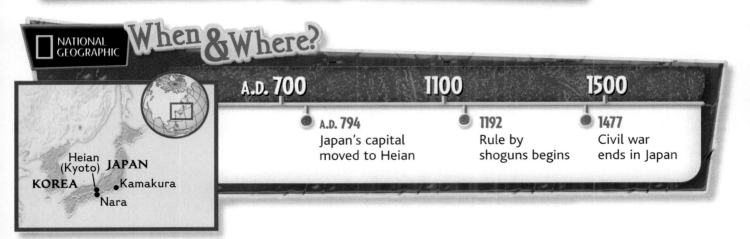

NATIONAL GEOGRAPHIC **When & Where?**

A.D. 700	1100	1500
A.D. 794 Japan's capital moved to Heian	1192 Rule by shoguns begins	1477 Civil war ends in Japan

Heian (Kyoto) JAPAN
KOREA   Kamakura
Nara

Nara Japan

Main Idea During the A.D. 700s, Japan built a strong national government at Nara, and Buddhism became a popular religion.

Reading Focus Do you know anyone who was hired for a job because they were friends with the boss or because the boss knew their family? Read to learn how Japan's emperor chose people for government jobs.

In the early A.D. 700s, Japan's emperors built a new capital city called Nara. For the next 100 years, Nara was the center of government and religion in Japan. Because of Nara's importance, the history of Japan during the A.D. 700s is called the Nara Period.

The city of Nara looked much like China's capital of Changan, only smaller. It had broad streets, large public squares, government offices, Buddhist temples, and Shinto shrines. Nobles and their families lived in large, Chinese-style homes. The typical home of a noble had wooden walls,

▲ Built in the early A.D. 600s, the Horyuji temple in Nara, Japan, is the oldest wooden building in the world.

a heavy tile roof, and polished wooden floors. It also included an inner garden.

The Emperor's Government At Nara, Japanese emperors added to the changes begun by Prince Shotoku. They organized government officials into ranks, or levels of importance from top to bottom. However, unlike China, Japan did not use examinations to hire officials. Instead, the emperor gave the jobs to nobles from powerful families. Once a person was appointed to a job, he could pass on his office to his son or other relatives. For their services, top government officials received estates, or large farms. They also were given farmers to work the land.

The emperor's power came from his control of the land and its crops. To measure Japan's wealth, the government carried out a census. It counted all the people in the country. The census also listed the lands on which people lived and worked. Based on the census results, all people who held land from the emperor had to pay taxes in rice or silk cloth. The men counted in the census had to serve in the army.

Buddhism Spreads in Japan At the same time that the emperor's government was growing strong, Buddhism became popular in Japan. Buddhism came to Japan from Korea in the A.D. 500s. Japanese government officials and nobles were the first to accept the new religion. Then, during the A.D. 600s and A.D. 700s, Buddhism spread rapidly among the common people. It soon became a major religion in Japan and had an important role in government and society.

As Buddhism became more powerful, nobles who were not Buddhists began to oppose the religion. Soon, those who backed Buddhism and those who opposed it were fighting for control of the government.

Inside the ▶
Todaji temple is
Japan's largest
statue of the
Buddha. It is
made of copper
and gold, weighs
250 tons, and is
nearly 50 feet tall.

▲ The Todaji temple was first built in A.D. 752
to serve as the head temple for Buddhism in
Japan. It is the world's largest wooden structure.
This reconstruction was built in 1692.

In A.D. 770 a Buddhist monk who served in
the government tried to seize the throne
and become emperor. He was stopped by
the emperor's family and leading nobles.

Frightened by this event, the emperor
and his family briefly turned away from
Buddhism. Remember how the government in China attacked Buddhist monasteries when they became strong? In Japan,
instead of attacking the Buddhists, the
emperor simply decided to leave Nara and
its many Buddhist monks.

Reading Check Contrast How was the
Japanese system of hiring officials different from
the Chinese system?

The Rise of the Shogun

Main Idea Japan's civilian government and the
emperor came to be dominated by military rulers
known as shoguns.

Reading Focus Every leader promises certain things
to the people in return for their support. In the United
States, what promises do politicians make to win votes?
Read to learn how Japan's nobles increased their power
by giving land in return for people's support.

In A.D. 794, Emperor Kammu of Japan
began building a new capital city called
Heian (HAY•ahn). This city later became
known as Kyoto (kee•OH•toh). Like Nara,
Heian was modeled on the Chinese city of
Changan. It remained the official capital of
Japan for more than 1,000 years.

The Government Weakens During the
A.D. 800s, the emperor's power declined.
Why did this happen? After a time of strong
emperors, a number of weak emperors
came to the throne. Many of these emperors
were still only children, and court officials
known as regents had to govern for them. A
regent is a person who rules for an emperor
who is too young or too sick to rule. When
the emperors grew up, however, the regents
refused to give up their power.

Most regents came from a clan called
the Fujiwara. Under the Fujiwara, Japan's
emperors were honored, but they no longer
had real power. Instead of ruling, these
emperors spent time studying Buddhism or
writing poetry in their palace at Heian.

History Online

Web Activity Visit jat.glencoe.com and click
on *Chapter 14—Student Web Activity* to learn
more about medieval Japan.

As the Fujiwara grew wealthy and powerful in Heian, other powerful nobles gained control of much of the land in the provinces of Japan. This happened because the government gave the nobles lands as a way to pay them for their work. At the same time, new lands were settled as Japan's empire expanded. The nobles who settled farmers on these lands were allowed to keep the lands.

To keep the nobles happy, the government let them stop paying taxes, but it put them in charge of governing the lands under their control. In order to govern their lands, the nobles began collecting more taxes from the peasants working the land.

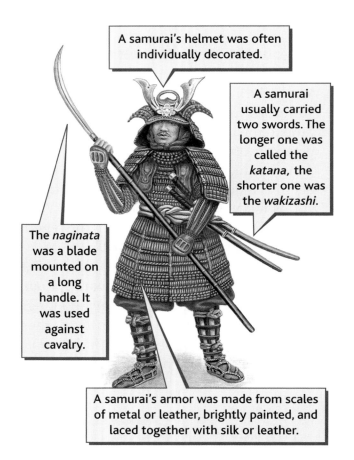

A samurai's helmet was often individually decorated.

A samurai usually carried two swords. The longer one was called the *katana*, the shorter one was the *wakizashi*.

The *naginata* was a blade mounted on a long handle. It was used against cavalry.

A samurai's armor was made from scales of metal or leather, brightly painted, and laced together with silk or leather.

▲ At first, most samurai fought on horseback. Later samurai were foot soldiers who fought with a variety of weapons. *What was the samurai code of conduct called?*

Who Were the Samurai? To protect their lands and enforce the law, nobles formed private armies. To create their armies, they gave land to warriors who agreed to fight for them. These warriors became known as **samurai** (SA•muh•RY).

In battle, samurai fought on horseback with swords, daggers, and bows and arrows. They wore armor made of leather or steel scales laced together with silk cords. Their helmets had horns or crests, and they wore masks designed to be terrifying.

The word *samurai* means "one who serves." The samurai lived by a strict code of conduct. It was called Bushido, or "the way of the warrior." This code demanded that a samurai be loyal to his master as well as courageous, brave, and honorable. Samurai were not supposed to care for wealth. They regarded merchants as lacking in honor.

Pledged to these principles, a samurai would rather die in battle than betray his lord. He also did not want to suffer the disgrace of being captured in battle. The sense of loyalty that set apart the samurai continued into modern times. During World War II, many Japanese soldiers fought to the death rather than accept defeat or capture. Since that conflict, the Japanese have turned away from the military beliefs of the samurai.

What Is a Shogun? By the early 1100s, the most powerful Japanese families had begun fighting each other using their samurai armies. They fought over land and to gain control over the emperor and his government. In 1180 the Gempei War began. The Gempei War was a civil war between the two most powerful clans: the Taira family and the Minamoto family. In 1185 the Minamoto forces defeated the Taira in a sea battle near the island of Shikoku.

The leader of the Minamoto was a man named **Minamoto Yoritomo** (mee•nah• moh•toh yoh•ree•toh•moh). (In Japanese a person's family name comes first, followed by the personal name.) Yoritomo was the commander of the Minamoto armies. After Yoritomo won the Gempei War, the emperor worried that the Minamoto family would try to replace the Yamato family as the rulers of Japan. He decided it would be better to reward Yoritomo to keep him loyal.

In 1192 the emperor gave Yoritomo the title of **shogun** (SHOH•guhn)—commander of all of the emperor's military forces. This decision created two governments in Japan. The emperor stayed in his palace at Heian with his bureaucracy. He was still officially the head of the country, but he had no power. Meanwhile the shogun set up his own government at his headquarters in **Kamakura** (kah•MAH•kuh• RAH), a small seaside town. This military government was known as a shogunate. Japan's government was run by a series of shoguns for the next 700 years.

Yoritomo proved to be a ruthless ruler. He killed most of his relatives, fearing that they would try to take power from him. Yoritomo and the shoguns after him appointed high-ranking samurai to serve as advisers and to run the provinces. Bound by an oath of loyalty, these samurai lords ruled Japan's villages, kept the peace, and gathered taxes. They became the leading group in Japanese society.

The Mongols Attack

In the late 1200s, the Kamakura shogunate faced its greatest test. In 1274 and again in 1281, China's Mongol emperor Kublai Khan sent out ships and

Primary Source

Bushido Code

This passage describes the samurai's Bushido.

"It is further good fortune if . . . [a servant] had wisdom and talent and can use them appropriately. But even a person who is good for nothing . . . will be a reliable retainer [servant] if only he has the determination to think earnestly of [respect and admire] his master. Having only wisdom and talent is the lowest tier [level] of usefulness."

—Yamamoto Tsunetomo, *Hagakure: The Book of the Samurai*

◀ Samurai armor

DBQ Document-Based Question

How powerful is a samurai's determination to respect and admire his master?

warriors to invade Japan. Both times, the Mongols were defeated because violent Pacific storms smashed many of their ships. The Mongol troops who made it ashore were defeated by the Japanese.

The victorious Japanese named the typhoons *kamikaze* (KAH•mih•KAH•zee), or "divine wind," in honor of the spirits they believed had saved their islands. Much later, during World War II, Japanese pilots deliberately crashed their planes into enemy ships. They were named kamikaze pilots after the typhoons of the 1200s.

✓ **Reading Check** **Identify** Who was the shogun, and why was he important?

The Way It Was

Focus on Everyday Life

Samurai The path to becoming a samurai was difficult and dangerous. Mothers in samurai families began teaching their sons Bushido at a young age. They taught their sons to place bravery, honor, and loyalty above all else. Each young warrior knew and could recite from memory the brave feats of his samurai ancestors.

For centuries, young samurai lived apart from their families in the castle of their lord or in the barracks of their lord's town. Beginning in the 1800s, samurai schools were built, and boys lived there to continue the educations their mothers had started. From the age of 10, they trained in the martial arts and studied other subjects, such as math and astronomy. By the age of 16, some young men were already promising warriors who distinguished themselves in battle.

Painting of a ▶ samurai hero

Connecting to the Past

1. What lessons was the mother of a samurai responsible for teaching her young son?
2. Do you think soldiers today have a code of conduct similar to Bushido? Explain.

The Daimyo Divide Japan

Main Idea As the shogun's power weakened, Japan broke into warring kingdoms run by rulers known as daimyo.

Reading Focus Have you ever been promised something and then been upset when the promise was broken? Read to learn how Japan's shogun lost power because the samurai felt he had broken his promises.

The Kamakura shogunate ruled Japan until 1333. By that time, many samurai had become resentful. Over the years, as samurai divided their lands among their sons, the piece of land each samurai owned became smaller and smaller. By the 1300s, many samurai felt they no longer owed the shogun loyalty because he had not given them enough land.

In 1331 the emperor rebelled, and many samurai came to his aid. The revolt succeeded, but the emperor was not able to gain control of Japan because he too refused to give more land to the samurai. Instead, a general named **Ashikaga Takauji** (ah•shee•kah•gah   tah•kow•jee) turned against the emperor and made himself shogun in 1333. A new government known as the Ashikaga shogunate began.

The Ashikaga shoguns proved to be weak rulers, and revolts broke out across Japan. The country soon divided into a number of small territories. These areas were headed by powerful military lords known as **daimyo** (DY•mee•OH).

The daimyo pledged loyalty to the emperor and the shogun. However, they ruled their lands as if they were independent kingdoms. To protect their lands, the daimyo created their own local armies made up of samurai warriors, just as other nobles had done in the past.

Many samurai became **vassals** (VA•suhlz) of a daimyo. That is, a samurai gave an oath of loyalty to his daimyo and promised to serve him in times of war. In return, each daimyo gave land to his samurai warriors—more land than they had been given by the shogun. This bond of loyalty between a lord and a vassal is known as **feudalism** (FYOO•duhl•ih•zuhm). In the next chapter, you will learn about a similar form of feudalism that arose in Europe during the Middle Ages.

With the breakdown of central government, Japan's warriors fought each other. From 1467 to 1477, the country suffered through the disastrous Onin War. During this conflict, the city of Kyoto (Heian) was almost completely destroyed. Armies passed back and forth through the city, burning temples and palaces.

For 100 years after the Onin War, a series of weak shoguns tried to reunite Japan. Powerful daimyo, however, resisted their

▲ The Takamatsu castle was built in 1590. It sits on the edge of a sea and was once surrounded by moats, gates, and towers for protection.

control. Fighting spread throughout the country. The violence finally brought down the Ashikaga shogunate in 1567. By that time, only a handful of powerful daimyo remained. Each of these daimyo was eager to defeat his rivals and rule all of Japan.

Reading Check **Analyze** Why were shoguns unable to regain control of Japan after the Onin War?

Section 2 Review

History Online
Homework Helper Need help with the material in this section? Visit jat.glencoe.com

Reading Summary

Review the Main Ideas

- During the Nara Period, the emperor's power grew, and Buddhism spread among Japan's common people.

- Over time, the Japanese emperors lost power to nobles and their armies of samurai. Eventually a military ruler, called a shogun, ruled the country.

- In the 1400s and 1500s, the shoguns lost power, and military lords, called daimyo, divided Japan into a number of small territories.

What Did You Learn?

1. What was a shogun? Who was the first shogun, and how did he gain his position of power?

2. What prevented the Mongol conquest of Japan?

Critical Thinking

3. **Organizing Information** Draw a diagram like the one below. Add details about the samurai, such as their weapons, dress, and beliefs.

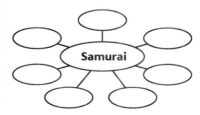

4. **Describe** Describe events related to the growth of Buddhism in Japan.

5. **Explain** Why did the power of the Japanese emperors decline during the A.D. 800s?

6. **Analyze** How did the beliefs of the samurai affect Japanese soldiers in World War II?

7. **Expository Writing** Create a constitution, or plan for government, that describes the relationship between the emperor and shogun, the daimyo, and the samurai.

Section 3

Life in Medieval Japan

Get Ready to Read!

What's the Connection?
In the last section, you learned how warriors known as shoguns and samurai came to rule Japan. During that time, the Japanese suffered from many wars. However, Japan's economy continued to grow, and its people produced beautiful art, architecture, and literature.

Focusing on the Main Ideas
- Buddhism and Shinto shaped much of Japan's culture. These religions affected Japanese art, architecture, novels, and plays. *(page 499)*

- Some Japanese nobles, merchants, and artisans grew wealthy during the shogun period, but the lives of women remained restricted in many areas of life. *(page 503)*

Locating Places
Kyoto (kee•OH•toh)

Meeting People
Murasaki Shikibu (MUR•uh•SAH•kee shee•kee•boo)

Building Your Vocabulary
sect (SEHKT)
martial arts (MAHR•shuhl)
meditation (MEH•duh•TAY•shuhn)
calligraphy (kuh•LIH•gruh•fee)
tanka (TAHNG•kuh)
guild (GIHLD)

Reading Strategy
Summarizing Information Complete a diagram like the one below describing the role of women in the families of medieval Japan.

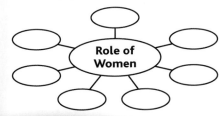

Role of Women

NATIONAL GEOGRAPHIC When & Where?

1000   1200   1400

KOREA
JAPAN
Heian (Kyoto)

c. 1000
Lady Murasaki Shikibu writes *The Tale of Genji*

c. 1100s
Zen Buddhism spreads in Japan

c. 1300s
Noh plays first performed

Japanese Religion and Culture

Main Idea Buddhism and Shinto shaped much of Japan's culture. These religions affected Japanese art, architecture, novels, and plays.

Reading Focus Have you ever seen paintings, sculptures, and works of literature that have religious subjects or messages? In medieval Japan, the religions of Shinto and Buddhism greatly influenced the arts.

During the Middle Ages, religion was a part of everyday life for the Japanese. Most Japanese came to believe in both Buddhism and Shinto, and worshiped at Shinto shrines and Buddhist temples. To them, each religion met different needs. Shinto was concerned with daily life, while Buddhism prepared people for the life to come. During the Middle Ages, Buddhist ideas inspired many Japanese to build temples, produce paintings, and write poems and plays.

Pure Land Buddhism

As you have already learned, Mahayana Buddhism began in India and spread to China and Korea. By the time Buddhism reached Japan, it had developed into many different **sects** (SEHKTS), or smaller religious groups.

One of the most important sects in Japan was Pure Land Buddhism. Pure Land Buddhism was a type of Mahayana Buddhism. It won many followers in Japan because of its message about a happy life after death. Pure Land Buddhists looked to Lord Amida, a buddha of love and mercy. They believed Amida had founded a paradise above the clouds. To get there, all they had to do was have faith in Amida and chant his name.

What Is Zen Buddhism?

Another important Buddhist sect in Japan was Zen. Buddhist monks brought Zen to Japan from China during the 1100s. Zen taught that

▲ A Zen monk sits beside a Japanese rock garden while meditating. *What is the purpose of meditation?*

people could find inner peace through self-control and a simple way of life.

Followers of Zen learned to control their bodies through **martial arts** (MAHR•shuhl), or sports that involved combat and self-defense. This appealed to the samurai, who trained to fight bravely and fearlessly.

Followers of Zen Buddhism also practiced **meditation** (MEH•duh•TAY•shuhn). In meditation, a person sat cross-legged and motionless for hours, with the mind cleared of all thoughts and desires. Meditation helped people to relax and find inner peace.

Art and Architecture

During the Middle Ages, the Japanese borrowed artistic ideas from China and Korea. Then, they went on to develop their own styles. The arts of Japan revealed the Japanese love of beauty and simplicity.

During the Middle Ages, artisans in Japan made wooden statues, furniture, and

Linking Past & Present

Martial Arts

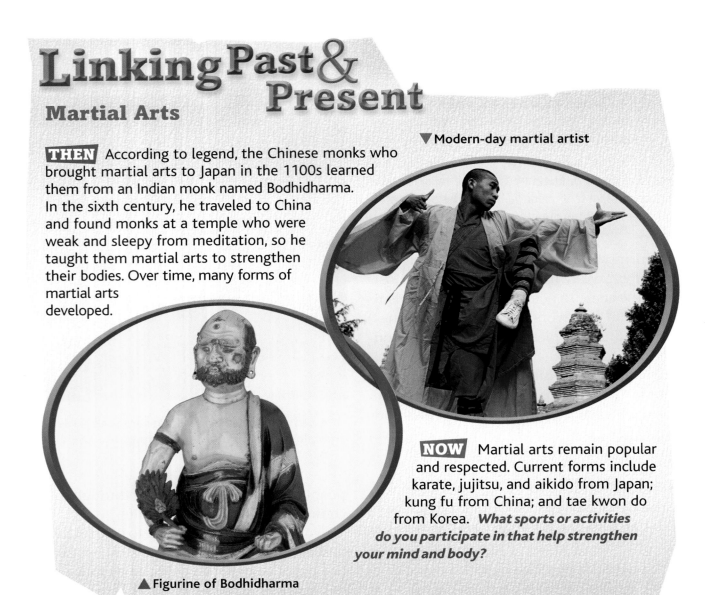

THEN According to legend, the Chinese monks who brought martial arts to Japan in the 1100s learned them from an Indian monk named Bodhidharma. In the sixth century, he traveled to China and found monks at a temple who were weak and sleepy from meditation, so he taught them martial arts to strengthen their bodies. Over time, many forms of martial arts developed.

▼ **Modern-day martial artist**

NOW Martial arts remain popular and respected. Current forms include karate, jujitsu, and aikido from Japan; kung fu from China; and tae kwon do from Korea. *What sports or activities do you participate in that help strengthen your mind and body?*

▲ **Figurine of Bodhidharma**

household items. On many of their works, they used a shiny black and red coating called lacquer. From the Chinese, Japanese artists learned to do landscape painting. Using ink or watercolors, they painted scenes of nature or battles on paper scrolls or on silk. Japanese nobles at the emperor's court learned to fold paper to make decorative objects. This art of folding paper is called origami. They also arranged flowers. Buddhist monks and the samurai turned tea drinking into a beautiful ceremony.

Builders in Japan used Chinese or Japanese styles. Shinto shrines were built in the Japanese style near a sacred rock, tree, or other natural feature that they considered beautiful. Usually a shrine was a wooden building, with a single room and a roof made of rice straw. People entered the shrine through a sacred gate called a torii.

Unlike Shinto shrines, Buddhist temples were built in the Chinese style. They had massive tiled roofs held up by thick, wooden pillars. The temples were richly decorated. They had many statues, paintings, and altars.

Around their buildings, the Japanese created gardens designed to imitate nature in a miniature form. Some of these gardens had carefully placed rocks, raked sand, and a few plants. They were built this way to create a feeling of peace and calmness.

Poems and Plays During the A.D. 500s, the Japanese borrowed China's writing system. They wrote their language in Chinese picture characters that stood for whole words. Because the Japanese and Chinese languages were so different, the Japanese found it difficult to use these characters. Then, in the A.D. 800s, they added symbols that stood for sounds, much like the letters of an alphabet. This addition made reading and writing much easier.

Calligraphy (kuh•LIH•gruh•fee), the art of writing beautifully, was much admired in Japan. Every well-educated person was expected to practice it. A person's handwriting was considered to reveal much about his or her education, social standing, and character.

During the Middle Ages, the Japanese wrote poems, stories, and plays. Japan's oldest form of poetry was the **tanka** (TAHNG•kuh). It was an unrhymed poem of five lines. Tanka poems capture nature's beauty and the joys and sorrows of life. The following tanka was written by an anonymous poet:

> ❝ On autumn nights
> the dew is
> colder than ever—
> in every clump of grasses
> the insects weep ❞
> —author unknown,
> tanka from the *Kokinshū*

Women living in Heian wrote Japan's first great stories around 1000. One woman,

Lady **Murasaki Shikibu** (MUR•uh•SAH•kee shee•kee•boo), wrote *The Tale of Genji*. This work describes the adventures of a Japanese prince. Some people believe the work is the world's first novel, or long fictional story.

About 200 years later, Japan's writers turned out stirring tales about warriors in battle. The greatest collection was *The Tale of Heike*. It describes the fight between the Taira and the Minamoto clans.

The Japanese also created plays. The oldest type of play is called Noh. Created during the 1300s, Noh plays were used to teach Buddhist ideas. Noh plays were performed on a simple, bare stage. The actors wore masks and elaborate robes. They danced, gestured, and chanted poetry to the music of drums and flutes.

✓ **Reading Check** **Analyze** How are martial arts and meditation connected to Zen Buddhism's principle of self-control?

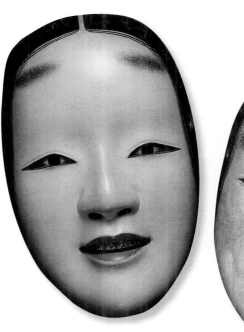
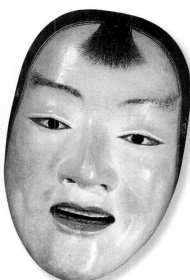

▲ Noh masks like these were often carved from a single piece of wood and were lightweight, so an actor could wear it for several hours. *Why were Noh plays performed?*

Biography

MURASAKI SHIKIBU
c. A.D. 973–1025

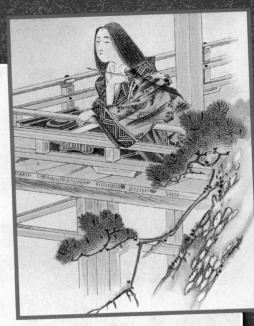

▲ Murasaki Shikibu

Murasaki Shikibu was a great novelist and poet of the Japanese Heian period. She was one of the first modern novelists. Murasaki became famous from writing *The Tale of Genji*, but her work also included a diary and over 120 poems.

Murasaki was born into the Fujiwara clan, a noble family but not a rich family. Her father was a scholar and a governor. In fact, the name Shikibu refers to her father's position at court. Murasaki's mother and older sister died when she was a child. Traditionally, children were raised by the mother and her family, but Murasaki's father decided to raise his daughter himself. He broke another custom by educating his daughter in Chinese language and literature, subjects reserved for boys.

Murasaki married and had a daughter, but her husband died after only a few years of marriage. Around that time, Murasaki began writing *The Tale of Genji* and working as an attendant to Empress Akiko. She based the novel on life at court, which she knew about through her father's job and her own. The last reference to her is in 1014, but many scholars believe that she lived for about a decade after that.

Much about Murasaki's life—and life at the emperor's palace—is revealed in her diary. This excerpt describes the preparations for a celebration honoring the birth of a new prince:

> "Even the sight of the lowest menials [servants], chattering to each other as they walked round lighting the fire baskets under the trees by the lake and arranging the food in the garden, seemed to add to the sense of occasion. Torchbearers stood everywhere at attention and the scene was as bright as day."
>
> —Murasaki Shikibu,
> *The Diary of Lady Murasaki*

▲ Scene from *The Tale of Genji*

Then and Now

Do you keep a diary? What might you and your classmates record in a diary that would be useful to people a few centuries from now?

Economy and Society

Main Idea Some Japanese nobles, merchants, and artisans grew wealthy during the shogun period, but the lives of women remained restricted in many areas of life.

Reading Focus What determines whether a person is wealthy or poor? Read to find what contributed to the growing wealth of Japan.

Under the shoguns, Japan not only developed its arts but also produced more goods and grew richer. However, only a small number of Japanese benefited from this wealth. This group included the emperor, the nobles at his court, and leading military officials. A small but growing class of merchants and traders also began to prosper. Most Japanese, however, were farmers who remained poor.

Farmers and Artisans Much of Japan's wealth came from the hard work of its farmers. Japanese farmers grew rice, wheat, millet, and barley. Some had their own land, but most lived and worked on the daimyo estates. Despite hardships, life did improve for Japan's farmers during the 1100s. They used better irrigation and planted more crops. As a result, they could send more food to the markets that were developing in the towns.

At the same time, the Japanese were producing more goods. Artisans on the daimyo estates began making weapons, armor, and tools. Merchants sold these items in town markets throughout Japan. New roads made travel and trade much easier. As trade increased, each region focused on making goods that it could best produce. These goods included pottery, paper, textiles, and lacquered ware. All of these new products helped Japan's economy grow.

As the capital, **Kyoto** (kee•OH•toh) became a major center of production and trade. Many artisans and merchants settled there. They formed groups called **guilds** (GIHLDZ) (or *za* in Japanese) to protect and increase their profits. The members of these guilds relied on a wealthy daimyo to protect them from rival artisans. They sold the daimyo goods that he could not get from his country estates.

Japan's wealth also came from increased trade with Korea, China, and Southeast Asia. Japanese merchants exchanged lacquered goods, sword blades, and copper for silk, dyes, pepper, books, and porcelain.

◀ This painting shows Japanese farmers working the land. *What were some crops grown by medieval Japanese farmers?*

The Role of Women During the Middle Ages, a Japanese family included grandparents, parents, and children in the same household. A man headed the family and had total control over family members. A woman was expected to obey her father, husband, and son. In wealthy families, parents arranged the marriages of their children to increase the family's wealth.

In early Japan, about the time of Prince Shotoku, wealthy women enjoyed a high position in society. There were several women rulers, and women could own property. When Japan became a warrior society with samurai and daimyo, upper-class women lost these freedoms.

In farming families, women had a greater say in whom they married. However, they worked long hours in the fields planting or harvesting rice. In addition, they cooked, spun and wove cloth, and cared for their children. In the towns, the wives of artisans and merchants helped with family businesses and ran their homes. The wives of merchants were perhaps the best off.

Despite the lack of freedom, some women managed to contribute to Japan's culture. These talented women gained fame as artists, writers, and even warriors. In *The Tale of the Heike*, one female samurai named Tomoe is described this way:

❝ **Tomoe was indescribably beautiful; the fairness of her face and the richness of her hair were startling to behold. Even so, she was a fearless rider and a woman skilled with the bow. Once her sword was drawn, even the gods . . . feared to fight against her. Indeed, she was a match for a thousand.** ❞

—Heike Monogatori,
The Tale of the Heike

✓ **Reading Check** **Identify** Which groups in Japan benefited from the country's wealth?

History Online
Homework Helper Need help with the material in this section? Visit jat.glencoe.com

Section 3 Review

Reading Summary

Review the Main Ideas

• In medieval Japan, several forms of Buddhism, along with Shinto, were practiced, and the arts, architecture, and literature flourished.

• During the time of the shoguns, Japan's economy grew stronger. In the family, women lost some of their freedoms as Japan became a warrior society.

What Did You Learn?

1. How did the Shinto and Buddhist religions meet different needs in Japan?

2. What were Noh plays, and how were they performed?

Critical Thinking

3. **Organizing Information** Draw a table like the one shown. Add details to show the characteristics of Pure Land Buddhism and Zen Buddhism.

Pure Land Buddhism	Zen Buddhism

4. **Describe** How did guilds benefit artisans and daimyos?

5. **Analyze** Why do you think women lost some of their freedoms when Japan became a warrior society?

6. **Descriptive Writing** Write a brief article for a travel magazine describing the architecture of Shinto shrines and Buddhist temples in Japan during the Middle Ages.

Chapter 14 Reading Review

Section 1 Early Japan

Vocabulary
clan
constitution
animism
shrine

Focusing on the Main Ideas
- Japan's mountains and islands isolated Japan and shaped its society. *(page 485)*
- Japan was settled by people who came from northeast Asia. They were organized into clans and ruled by warriors. *(page 486)*
- Prince Shotoku created Japan's first constitution and borrowed many ideas from China. *(page 488)*
- The Japanese religion, called Shinto, was based on nature spirits. *(page 490)*

Section 2 Shoguns and Samurai

Vocabulary
samurai
shogun
daimyo
vassal
feudalism

Focusing on the Main Ideas
- During the A.D. 700s, Japan built a strong national government at Nara, and Buddhism became a popular religion. *(page 492)*
- Japan's civilian government and the emperor came to be dominated by military rulers known as shoguns. *(page 493)*
- As the shogun's power weakened, Japan broke into warring kingdoms run by rulers known as daimyo. *(page 496)*

Section 3 Life in Medieval Japan

Vocabulary
sect
martial arts
meditation
calligraphy
tanka
guild

Focusing on the Main Ideas
- Buddhism and Shinto shaped much of Japan's culture. These religions affected Japanese art, architecture, novels, and plays. *(page 499)*
- Some Japanese nobles, merchants, and artisans grew wealthy during the shogun period, but the lives of women remained restricted in many areas of life. *(page 503)*

Murasaki Shikibu ▶

Review Vocabulary

Write the key term that completes each sentence.

a. tanka
b. daimyo
c. clans
d. sects
e. shogun
f. guilds
g. samurai
h. meditation

1. The ___ was the military leader of Japan.

2. Many artisans and merchants formed ___ for protection and profit.

3. The Yayoi formed ___ that were headed by a small group of warriors.

4. In ___, a person clears the mind of all thoughts and desires.

5. The ___ is an unrhymed poem of five lines.

6. Each vassal gave an oath of loyalty to his ___.

7. The private armies of Japanese nobles were made up of ___.

8. Buddhism was divided into many different ___.

Review Main Ideas

Section 1 • Early Japan

9. How did geography shape Japanese society?

10. How did Shotoku use Chinese government and culture as a model?

Section 2 • Shoguns and Samurai

11. Describe the roles of shoguns.

12. What happened when the shogun's power weakened?

Section 3 • Life in Medieval Japan

13. Which religions shaped much of Japan's culture?

14. How did the shogun period affect different groups of Japanese people?

Critical Thinking

15. **Analyze** Why do you think the early Japanese people were so independent?

16. **Contrast** How were the Yayoi more advanced than the Jomon?

Review Reading Skill · Cause and Effect

Identifying Cause and Effect

17. Read the paragraph below. Create a graphic organizer that shows the cause and effects described in the passage.

The sea surrounding Japan's islands made it easy for people in ships to travel along the coast and from island to island. It encouraged people to become merchants, traveling from village to village with goods to trade. The vast ocean around Japan's islands, however, kept the Japanese people isolated, or separate, from the rest of Asia. As a result, Japan developed its own fiercely independent society with its own religion, art, literature, and government.

To review this skill, see pages 482–483.

Geography Skills

Study the map below and answer the following questions.

18. **Place** Which of the four major Japanese islands has been home to the country's major cities?

19. **Human/Environment Interaction** How do you think Japan's geography and location have helped it become a center of production and trade?

20. **Location** Identify present-day countries, states, or provinces that are made up largely of islands. How are they similar to and different from the Japanese islands?

NATIONAL GEOGRAPHIC Geography of Japan

Read to Write

21. **Creative Writing** Review this chapter and conduct research to gather information about the Mongols' attack on the Kamakura shogunate. Work with a group to write a script for a short play about the events before, during, and after the invasion. Use historical figures as well as fictional characters. Create a mask for each character, similar to the style of early Japanese masks. Present your play to the class.

22. **Using Your** FOLDABLES Write a poem, series of journal entries, or short story using the main ideas and supporting details from your completed foldable.

Using Technology

23. **Designing a City** When Emperor Kammu built Heian, he modeled it on Changan. If you were to design a city, what current cities and towns would inspire you? Use the Internet and your local library to research different features and layouts of cities. Combine the components you like best into a plan for a new city. Use a computer to make a scale drawing of your city. Then list the borrowed components and the current cities from which you borrowed them.

Linking Past and Present

24. **Analyzing Art** Medieval Japanese art, architecture, and literature reflected the Japanese love of beauty and simplicity. What values are reflected in present-day art?

Primary Source Analyze

Seami, a great actor in Noh plays, explained how acting is mastered.

"As long as an actor is trying to imitate his teacher, he is still without mastery.... An actor may be said to be a master when, by means of his artistic powers, he quickly perfects the skills he has won through study and practice, and thus becomes one with the art itself."

—Seami Jūokubushū Hyōshaku, "The Book of the Way of the Highest Flower (*Shikadō-Sho*)"

DBQ Document-Based Questions

25. What is the first step in learning acting?

26. How does an actor "become one with the art itself"?

Medieval Europe

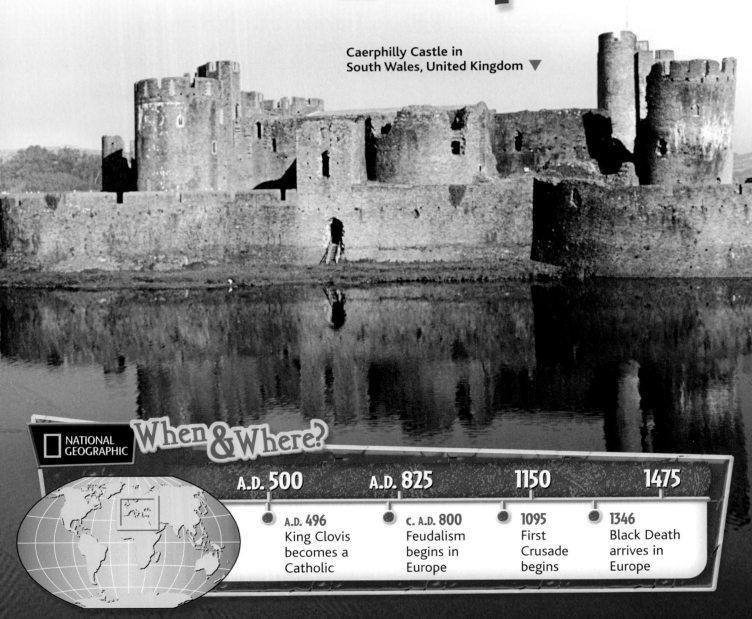

Caerphilly Castle in
South Wales, United Kingdom ▼

NATIONAL GEOGRAPHIC When&Where?

A.D. 500	A.D. 825	1150	1475
A.D. 496 King Clovis becomes a Catholic	C. A.D. 800 Feudalism begins in Europe	1095 First Crusade begins	1346 Black Death arrives in Europe

Chapter Preview

Between A.D. 500 and 1500, Europe was ruled by warriors much like those in early Japan. Despite constant fighting, Europeans made advances in their culture. European ideas about government and religion still shape our lives today.

History **O**nline

Chapter Overview Visit jat.glencoe.com **for a preview of Chapter 15.**

 View the Chapter 15 video in the *World History: Journey Across Time* **Video Program.**

The Early Middle Ages

During the Middle Ages, Western Europe built a new civilization based on Christian, Roman, and Germanic ways.

Feudalism

Government weakness and the need for safety led to the rise of feudalism.

Kingdoms and Crusades

As the kingdoms of England and France established parliaments, Russia's rulers laid the foundations for its government.

The Church and Society

Religion in medieval Europe helped to shape European culture.

The Late Middle Ages

Disease and war took the lives of millions of people in the late Middle Ages.

Sequencing Information *Make this foldable to help you sequence important events that occurred in medieval Europe.*

Step 1 *Fold two sheets of paper in half from top to bottom. Cut each in half.*

Cut along the fold lines.

Step 2 *Turn and fold the four pieces in half from top to bottom.*

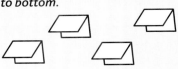

Reading and Writing *As you read the chapter, write the important events and dates that occurred in medieval Europe on each section of your time line.*

Step 3 *Tape the ends of the pieces together (overlapping the edges slightly) to make an accordion time line.*

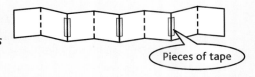

Pieces of tape

Reading Social Studies

1 Learn It!

Just Ask

Answering questions about what you have read is one way to show what you know, but asking thoughtful questions about the topic can often show even greater understanding. How do you learn to ask great questions?

1. Use question starters such as *who, what, when, where, how,* and *why.*
2. Do more than just read the words on the page—think deeply about the concepts. For example, ask questions such as "What would have happened if . . .?"

Read the following passage from Section 5, and look at the questions that follow.

> Charles, the prince who ruled southern France, wanted to take back the north. In 1429 a French peasant girl named Joan was brought to him. She told him that her favorite saints had urged her to free France. Joan's honesty persuaded Charles to let her go with a French army to Orléans. Joan's faith stirred the soldiers, and they took the city.
>
> —*from page 557*

Reading Tip

Make studying like a game. Create questions and then read to find answers to your own questions.

Here are some questions you might ask about the above paragraph:

- What did Joan say to persuade Charles to let her ride with the army?
- How did Joan's faith stir the soldiers?
- Why did Joan believe saints wanted her to free France?
- What happened to Joan after the French took the city?

2 Practice It!
Ask and Answer

Read this passage about the Black Death.

A terrible plague, known as the Black Death, swept across Europe and Asia. A plague is a disease that spreads quickly and kills many people. Most scientists think the Black Death was bubonic plague—a disease caused by a type of bacteria carried by fleas. These fleas infested black rats, and in the Middle Ages, these rats were everywhere.

—*from page 554*

Read to Write ·······

Write a *What If* paragraph based on your reading. For example, *what if* Joan had become Queen of France, or *what if* fleas carried the Black Death today? Add lots of details as if you were answering questions others might ask about your *What If* ideas.

Create three questions based on the above paragraph. Remember that not all questions have answers.

3 Apply It!

As you read the chapter, look for answers to section headings that are in the form of questions. For the other sections, turn the headings into questions that you can answer as you read.

Section 1

The Early Middle Ages

Get Ready to Read!

What's the Connection?
After the fall of Rome came a period called the Middle Ages, or medieval times. It is a fitting name for the period that lies between ancient and modern times.

Focusing on the Main Ideas
- Geography influenced where medieval Europeans settled and what they did. *(page 513)*

- The Franks, Angles, and Saxons of Western Europe built new societies and defended them against Muslims, Magyars, and Vikings. *(page 514)*

- The Catholic Church spread Christianity through Western Europe. *(page 519)*

Locating Places
Aachen (AH•kuhn)
Scandinavia (SKAN•duh•NAY•vee•uh)
Holy Roman Empire

Meeting People
Clovis (KLOH•vuhs)
Charles Martel (mahr•TEHL)
Charlemagne (SHAHR•luh•MAYN)
Otto I (AH•toh)
Gregory the Great

Building Your Vocabulary
fjord (fee•AWRD)
missionary (MIH•shuh•NEHR•ee)
excommunicate (EHK•skuh•MYOO•nuh•KAYT)
concordat (kuhn•KAWR•DAT)

Reading Strategy
Organizing Information Create a table to show the major accomplishments of medieval leaders.

Leader	Major Accomplishments

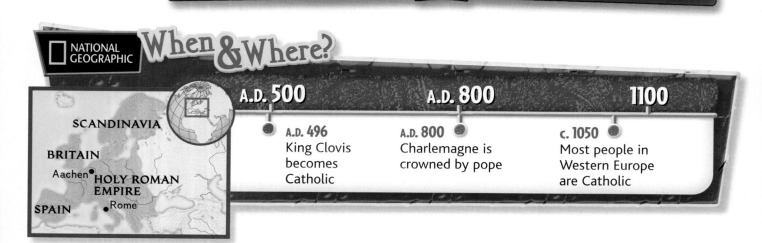

NATIONAL GEOGRAPHIC

When & Where?

SCANDINAVIA
BRITAIN
Aachen• •HOLY ROMAN EMPIRE
SPAIN •Rome

A.D. 500 — **A.D. 800** — **1100**

A.D. 496
King Clovis becomes Catholic

A.D. 800
Charlemagne is crowned by pope

c. 1050
Most people in Western Europe are Catholic

The Geography of Europe

Main Idea Geography influenced where medieval Europeans settled and what they did.

Reading Focus If you wanted to go sledding or swimming, where would you go? Your answer will be based partly on geography. Read to learn how geography shaped life in Europe during the Middle Ages.

The Roman Empire had united all the land surrounding the Mediterranean Sea. When the last Roman emperor in the West fell from power in A.D. 476, that unity was lost. Western Europe was divided into many kingdoms as wave after wave of Germanic invaders swept south and west, conquering large areas of Europe.

Now that Rome no longer united people, Europe's geography began to play a more important role in shaping events. Europe is a continent, but it is also a very large peninsula made up of many smaller peninsulas. As a result, most of Europe lies within 300 miles (483 km) of an ocean or sea. This encouraged trade and fishing and helped Europe's economy to grow.

Rivers also played an important role in Europe. The Rhine, Danube, Vistula, Volga, Seine, and Po Rivers made it easy to travel into the interior of Europe and encouraged people to trade.

The seas and rivers provided safety as well as opportunities for trade. The English Channel, for instance, separated Britain and Ireland from the rest of Europe. As a result,

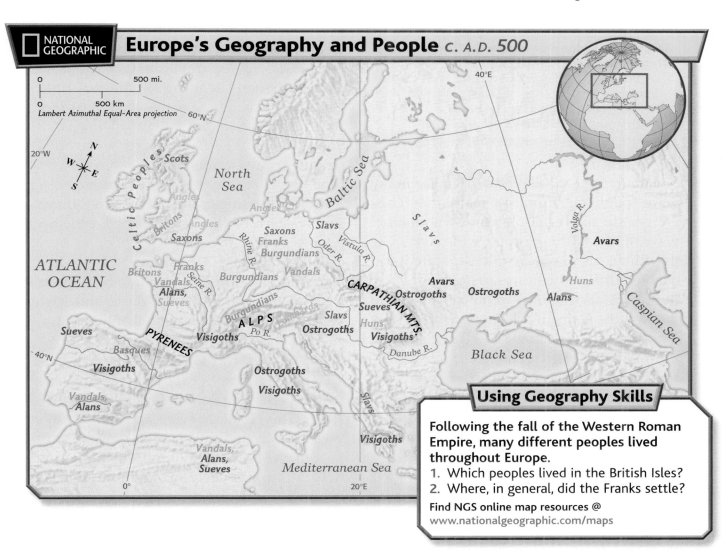

NATIONAL GEOGRAPHIC

Europe's Geography and People c. A.D. 500

Using Geography Skills

Following the fall of the Western Roman Empire, many different peoples lived throughout Europe.
1. Which peoples lived in the British Isles?
2. Where, in general, did the Franks settle?

Find NGS online map resources @ www.nationalgeographic.com/maps

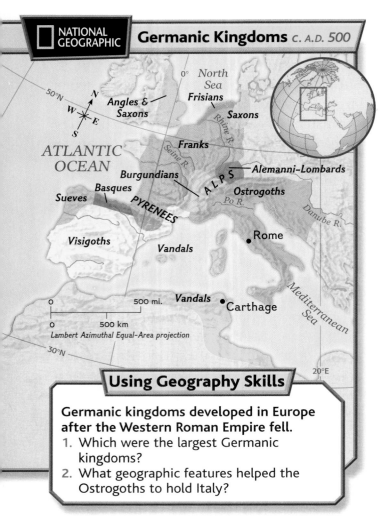

North Sea

Angles & Saxons

Frisians

Saxons

Rhine R.

Franks

Seine R.

ATLANTIC OCEAN

Burgundians

Alemanni–Lombards

Basques

ALPS

Ostrogoths

Sueves

PYRENEES

Po R.

Visigoths

Vandals

Rome

Danube R.

Vandals

Carthage

Mediterranean Sea

500 mi.

500 km

Lambert Azimuthal Equal-Area projection

Using Geography Skills

Germanic kingdoms developed in Europe after the Western Roman Empire fell.

1. Which were the largest Germanic kingdoms?
2. What geographic features helped the Ostrogoths to hold Italy?

people there were sheltered from the many wars fought on Europe's mainland. They were able to develop their own distinct ways of life. Within Europe, wide rivers like the Rhine also kept people separated and enabled different cultures to develop.

Europe also has many mountain ranges. In the east, the Carpathians cut off what is now Ukraine and Russia from southeast Europe. In the middle, the Alps separated Italy from central Europe. To the southwest, the Pyrenees isolated Spain and Portugal. The mountains, like the rivers, made it difficult for one group to rule all of Europe and encouraged the development of independent kingdoms.

Reading Check **Identify** What did Europe's seas and rivers provide for its people?

The Germanic Kingdoms

Main Idea The Franks, Angles, and Saxons of Western Europe built new societies and defended them against Muslims, Magyars, and Vikings.

Reading Focus Have you ever moved to a new place? What adjustments did you have to make? Read to learn how the Germanic peoples who invaded Europe had to adjust to the lands they occupied.

After Rome fell, Western Europe was divided into many kingdoms. These kingdoms developed different societies based on their locations. The Visigoths in Spain and the Ostrogoths in Italy were close to the center of the old Roman Empire. As a result, they adopted many Roman ways. People farther from Rome held on to more of their Germanic traditions.

In Britain as the empire began to weaken, Roman culture declined quickly. In the A.D. 300s, the Roman legions in Britain began heading home to fight Germanic invaders. By the early A.D 400s, the Romans had pulled out of England. Soon the Angles and Saxons invaded Britain from Denmark and Germany. In time, they became the Anglo-Saxons.

When the Angles and Saxons conquered southeastern Britain, they pushed aside the people living there. These people were called the Celts (KEHLTS). Some Celts fled north and west to the mountains. Others went to Ireland. Scottish, Welsh, and Irish people today are descendants of the Celts.

Who Were the Franks? During the A.D. 400s, a Germanic people called the Franks settled the area that is now France. In A.D. 496 King **Clovis** (KLOH•vuhs) of the Franks became a Catholic. This won him the support of the Romans living in his kingdom. Before long, nearly all of the Franks became Catholic.

After Clovis died, his sons divided the kingdom among themselves. Later, their sons divided these kingdoms even further. These kings often fought over land. While they fought, the nobles under them took over many royal duties. The most important of these nobles was called the "mayor of the palace." By A.D. 700, the mayors were giving out land, settling disputes, and fighting their own wars.

Of all the mayors, the most powerful was **Charles Martel** (mahr•TEHL). He wanted to unite all the Frankish nobles under his rule. The Catholic Church wanted to restore the Western Roman Empire and was willing to support rulers who had a chance to reunite Europe. The pope—the head of the Catholic Church—offered his support to Charles Martel.

First, however, Europe had to be kept Christian. In A.D. 711 a Muslim army from North Africa conquered Spain. The Muslim forces wanted to spread Islam across Europe. In A.D. 732 Charles Martel led the Franks against the Muslims. He defeated them at the Battle of Tours. This stopped the Muslim advance into Europe. As a result, Christianity remained Western Europe's major religion.

When Charles Martel died, his son Pepin (PEH•puhn) became mayor of the palace. With the help of the pope and most Frankish nobles, Pepin became the new king of the Franks. When a Germanic group called the Lombards threatened the pope, Pepin took his army into Italy and defeated them. He donated the land he had conquered to the pope. The pope ruled these lands as if he were a king, and they became known as the Papal States.

Who Was Charlemagne?
After Pepin died, his son Charles became king. Like his father, Charles went to the aid of the pope when the Lombards tried to regain their territory. He also invaded Germany and defeated the Saxons living there. He ordered them to convert to Christianity. He then invaded Spain and gained control of the northeastern corner from the Muslims.

By A.D. 800, Charles's kingdom had grown into an empire. It covered much of western and central Europe. Charles's

The Crowning of Charlemagne

In A.D. 800 the pope crowned Charlemagne "Emperor of the Romans," officially creating a new Roman Empire. *How large was Charlemagne's empire in A.D. 800?*

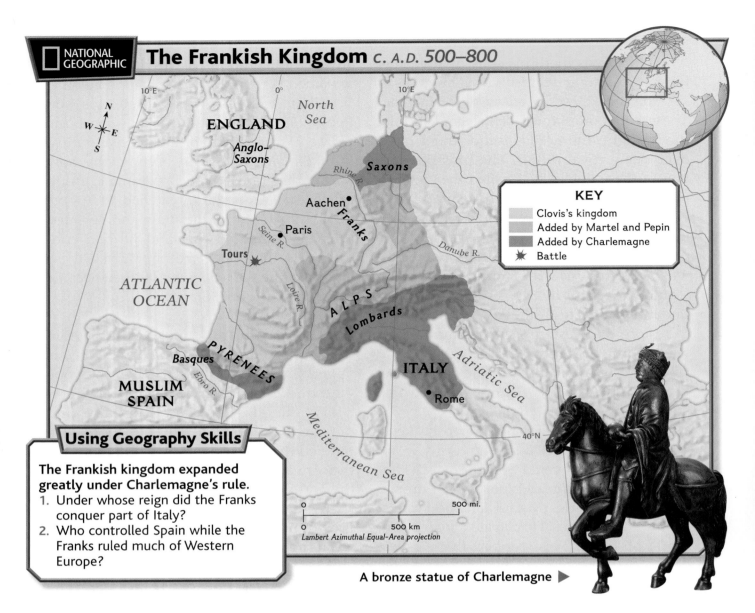

The Frankish Kingdom C. A.D. 500–800

NATIONAL GEOGRAPHIC

ENGLAND

Anglo-Saxons

North Sea

Saxons

Rhine R.

Franks

Aachen

Paris

Seine R.

Tours

ATLANTIC OCEAN

Loire R.

ALPS

Lombards

Danube R.

PYRENEES

Basques

Ebro R.

MUSLIM SPAIN

ITALY

Rome

Adriatic Sea

Mediterranean Sea

40°N

KEY
- Clovis's kingdom
- Added by Martel and Pepin
- Added by Charlemagne
- ✸ Battle

0   500 mi.
0   500 km
Lambert Azimuthal Equal-Area projection

Using Geography Skills

The Frankish kingdom expanded greatly under Charlemagne's rule.
1. Under whose reign did the Franks conquer part of Italy?
2. Who controlled Spain while the Franks ruled much of Western Europe?

A bronze statue of Charlemagne ▶

conquests earned him the name of **Charlemagne** (SHAHR•luh•MAYNE), or Charles the Great.

The pope was impressed with Charlemagne. On Christmas day in A.D. 800, Charlemagne was worshiping at the church of St. Peter in Rome. After the service, the pope placed a crown on Charlemagne's head and declared him the new Roman emperor. Charlemagne was pleased but also concerned. He did not want people to think the pope had the power to choose who was emperor.

Charlemagne made **Aachen** (AH•kuhn) the capital of his empire. To uphold his laws, he set up courts throughout the empire. Nobles called counts ran the courts. To keep the counts under control, Charlemagne sent out inspectors called "the lord's messengers" to make sure the counts were obeying orders.

Unlike other earlier Frankish rulers, Charlemagne believed in education. He had tried late in life to learn to write and wanted his people to be educated too. He asked a scholar named Alcuin (AL•kwuhn) to start a school in one of the royal palaces. Alcuin trained the children of government officials. His students studied religion, Latin, music, literature, and arithmetic.

Biography

CHARLEMAGNE
A.D. 742–814

Charles the Great (Charlemagne) became king of the Franks at age 29. He married and divorced many different women and had at least 18 children.

Charlemagne was an intelligent person. He studied many subjects and especially enjoyed astronomy. He could speak many languages, including German and Latin. He also could read but had trouble writing. Einhard, the king's historian and scribe, wrote that Charlemagne "used to keep tablets under his pillow in order that at leisure hours he might accustom his hand to form the letters; but as he began these efforts so late in life, they met with ill success."

Charlemagne was disappointed to learn that the Franks were not as educated as the people of Britain and Ireland. In A.D. 782 he arranged for several famous scholars to come to his capital in Aachen and create a school in the royal palace. During his reign, schools opened throughout his empire, and many people were educated.

▲ Charlemagne

▼ The Palatine Chapel at Charlemagne's palace in Aachen

"No one shall . . . be kept back from the right path of justice by . . . fear of the powerful."

–Charlemagne, as quoted in "The World of Charlemagne"

Then and Now

Charlemagne realized the importance of education. He arranged reading and writing lessons for his people. What types of school programs does our government fund?

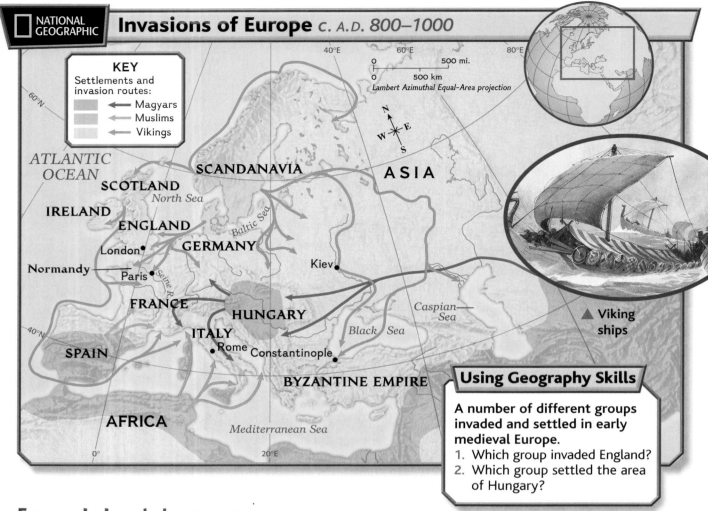

Invasions of Europe C. A.D. 800–1000

KEY
Settlements and
invasion routes:
→ Magyars
← Muslims
← Vikings

ATLANTIC OCEAN

SCANDANAVIA

SCOTLAND
North Sea
IRELAND
ENGLAND
Baltic Sea
London•
GERMANY
Normandy
Paris•
Seine R.
Kiev•
ASIA

FRANCE
HUNGARY
Caspian Sea
ITALY
•Rome
Constantinople•
Black Sea
SPAIN

BYZANTINE EMPIRE

AFRICA
Mediterranean Sea

40°E 60°E 80°E

0 ___ 500 mi.
0 ___ 500 km
Lambert Azimuthal Equal-Area projection

60°N
40°N
0° 20°E

N W E S

▲ Viking ships

Using Geography Skills

A number of different groups invaded and settled in early medieval Europe.
1. Which group invaded England?
2. Which group settled the area of Hungary?

Europe Is Invaded After Charlemagne died in A.D. 814, his empire did not last long. His son Louis was not a strong leader, and after Louis died, Louis's sons divided the empire into three kingdoms.

These three kingdoms were weakened further by a wave of invaders who swept across Europe in the A.D. 800s and A.D. 900s. From the south came Muslims, who raided France and Italy from Spain and North Africa. From the east came the Magyars, a nomadic people who had settled in Hungary. From **Scandinavia** (SKAN•duh•NAY•vee•uh) came the Vikings, whose raids terrified all of Europe.

Scandinavia is in northern Europe. Norway, Sweden, and Denmark are all part of Scandinavia today. Much of Scandinavia

has a long, jagged coastline. It has many **fjords** (fee•AWRDS), or steep-sided valleys that are inlets of the sea. The Viking people lived in villages in the fjords. They were known as the Norsemen, or "north men."

Scandinavia has little farmland. This forced the Vikings to rely on the sea for food and trade. They became skilled sailors and built sturdy boats called longboats. These boats could survive the rough Atlantic and also navigate shallow rivers.

In the A.D. 700s and A.D. 800s, the Vikings began raiding Europe, probably because their population had grown too big to support itself at home. The word *viking* comes from their word for raiding. They robbed villages and churches, carrying off grain, animals, and anything else of value. They even conquered part of western France. This area was named Normandy, after the Norsemen who ruled it.

The Holy Roman Empire
The raids by Muslims, Magyars, and Vikings helped to destroy the Frankish kingdoms. In the A.D. 900s, the eastern Frankish kingdom, which became known as Germany, was divided into many tiny states ruled by counts, dukes, and other nobles. In A.D. 911 a group of these nobles tried to unite Germany by electing a king. The king did not have much power, however, because the nobles wanted to remain independent.

One of the stronger kings of Germany was **Otto I** (AH•toh). He fought the Magyars and sent troops into Italy to protect the pope. To reward Otto for his help, the pope declared him emperor of the Romans in A.D. 962. Otto's territory, which included most of Germany and northern Italy, became known as the **Holy Roman Empire.**

Most of the emperors of the Holy Roman Empire were not very powerful. Two of the strongest ones, Frederick I and Frederick II, tried to unite northern Italy and Germany under a single ruler with a strong central government in the 1100s and 1200s. The popes fought against these plans because they did not want the emperor to control them. They banded together with Italy's cities to resist the emperors' forces. As a result, both Germany and Italy remained divided into small kingdoms until the 1800s.

✓ **Reading Check** Explain Who were the Vikings, and why did they raid Europe?

The Rise of the Catholic Church

Main Idea The Catholic Church spread Christianity through Western Europe.

Reading Focus Do you have a goal you would devote your life to reaching? Read to learn the goals of the Catholic Church in the early Middle Ages.

Both religion and geography played an important role in shaping life in Europe. By the time the Western Roman Empire collapsed, Christianity had become the official religion of Rome. After the Roman government fell apart, the Roman Catholic Church began to play an important role in the growth of a new civilization in Western Europe.

Why Were Monks Important?
At the time Rome fell, much of northwest Europe was not yet Christian. One exception was Ireland. In the A.D. 400s, a priest named Patrick traveled to Ireland, where he spread the Christian message and set up churches and monasteries. For several hundred years,

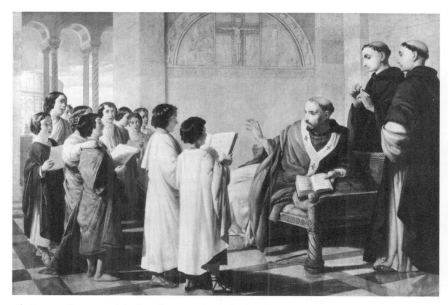

▲ Pope Gregory I helped spread Christianity in a number of ways. Here he is shown teaching boys the songs that became known as Gregorian chants. *Which area of northwest Europe had accepted Christianity before the fall of the Western Roman Empire?*

▲ Monks eating together in a monastery

▲ Illustrated page created by monks

▲ The monastery at Mont St. Michel in France is a beautiful work of architecture that took several hundred years to complete. *How did monasteries help local people in Europe?*

Irish monks played an important role in preserving Roman learning and passing it on to the people of Europe.

Patrick's success inspired others, including Pope Gregory I, or **Gregory the Great.** Gregory I was pope from A.D. 590 to A.D. 604. He wanted all of Europe to become Christian, and he asked monks to become **missionaries** (MIH•shuh•NEHR•eez)—people who are sent out to teach their religion.

In A.D. 597 Gregory sent 40 monks to southern Britain to teach Christianity. The monks converted Ethelbert, ruler of the kingdom of Kent. Ethelbert allowed the missionaries to build a church in his capital city of Canterbury. Meanwhile, Irish monks brought Christianity to northern Britain. By A.D. 800, monks were spreading Christianity throughout Europe. As a result, most people in Western Europe had become Catholics by 1050.

Monasteries played an important role in medieval Europe. Monks schooled people, provided food and rest to travelers, and offered hospital care for the sick. They taught carpentry and weaving and developed better methods of farming. They also helped to preserve knowledge.

Many monasteries had scriptoria, or writing rooms, where monks made copies of important works. The monks copied Christian writings, including the Bible, as well as works of Roman and Greek writers.

Over time, monasteries began to play a role in Europe's politics. Monks took a vow of poverty, wore simple clothes, and ate simple food, but their monasteries could make money. Each monastery produced goods and owned land, and over time many of them became wealthy. The leader of a monastery is called an abbot (A•buht), and many abbots became involved in politics. They served as advisers to kings and acted as rulers of the lands near their monasteries.

Why Is Gregory VII Important? The growing role of abbots and other Church leaders in Europe's politics caused many arguments over who was in charge. Kings wanted Church leaders to obey them, while the pope claimed he could crown kings.

In 1073 Gregory VII was elected pope. He wanted to stop nobles and kings from interfering in Church affairs. He issued a decree, or order, forbidding kings from appointing high-ranking Church officials.

The pope's decree angered Henry IV, the Holy Roman emperor. For many years, the Holy Roman emperor had appointed bishops in Germany. Without them, Henry IV risked losing power to the nobles.

Henry refused to obey Gregory. He declared that Gregory was no longer pope. Gregory then stated that Henry was no longer emperor. He **excommunicated** (EHK•skuh•MYOO•nuh•KAY•tuhd) Henry. This means to exclude a person from church membership. Catholics believed that if they were excommunicated, they could not go to heaven.

When the German nobles defended the pope, Henry backed down. He traveled to Italy and stood barefoot in the snow outside the pope's castle asking to be forgiven. Gregory forgave Henry, but the German nobles still chose a new king. When Gregory accepted the new king as emperor, Henry went to war. He captured Rome and named a new pope. Gregory's allies drove out Henry's forces, but the dispute was not resolved.

In 1122 a new pope and the German king finally agreed that only the pope could choose bishops, but only the emperor could give them jobs in the government. This deal, called the Concordat of Worms, was signed in the city of Worms. A **concordat** (kuhn•KAWR•DAT) is an agreement between the pope and the ruler of a country.

By the time Innocent III became pope in 1198, the Catholic Church was at the height of its power. Innocent was able to control kings. If a ruler did not obey, Innocent would excommunicate him or issue an interdict (IHN•tuhr•DIHKT) against the ruler's people. An interdict forbids priests from providing Christian rituals to a group of people. The pope hoped that by using an interdict, local people would pressure their ruler to obey.

 **Reading Check** **Contrast** How did Gregory VII and Henry IV disagree?

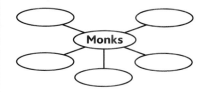

History Online

Homework Helper Need help with the material in this section? Visit jat.glencoe.com

Section 1 Review

Reading Summary

Review the Main Ideas

- During the Middle Ages, Europe's geography affected where people lived, their ways of life, and their relations with other people.

- The Angles and Saxons invaded Britain, the Franks created an empire in Western Europe, and the Saxons created a German kingdom that became the Holy Roman Empire.

- Monks helped spread Christianity throughout Europe, and the Catholic Church became strong in the early Middle Ages.

What Did You Learn?

1. What happened at the Battle of Tours, and why is the battle significant?

2. Why were monasteries important to medieval Europe?

Critical Thinking

3. **Summarizing Information** Draw a diagram like the one below. Use it to describe the role of monks in medieval Europe.

Monks

4. **Analyze** How did Charlemagne demonstrate his support for education?

5. **Describe** Imagine you live in central Europe in medieval times. Prepare a poster that describes the Vikings and the dangers they pose to your town.

6. **Reading** **Asking Questions** Henry IV "stood barefoot in the snow" to gain the pope's forgiveness. If you were asked to interview Henry IV about this experience, what three questions would you ask?

Feudalism

Get Ready to Read!

What's the Connection?

In the last section, you read how the Vikings spread fear and destruction throughout Europe. During the Middle Ages, villagers and townspeople looked to nobles to protect them.

Focusing on the Main Ideas

- Feudalism developed in Europe in the Middle Ages. It was based on landowning, loyalty, and the power of armored knights on horseback. *(page 523)*

- Knights followed a code of chivalry and lived in castles, while peasants lived in simple houses and worked hard all year long. *(page 526)*

- Increased trade led to the growth of towns and cities and the rise of guilds and city governments. *(page 528)*

Locating Places

Venice (VEH•nuhs)
Flanders (FLAN•duhrz)

Building Your Vocabulary

feudalism (FYOO•duhl•IH•zuhm)
vassal (VA•suhl)
fief (FEEF)
knight (NYT)
serf (SUHRF)
guild (GIHLD)

Reading Strategy

Compare and Contrast Complete a Venn diagram like the one below showing the similarities and differences between serfs and slaves.

Serfs   Slaves

NATIONAL GEOGRAPHIC **When & Where?**

A.D. 800   1000   1200

SCANDINAVIA
ENGLAND
Bruges• HOLY ROMAN
FRANCE EMPIRE
SPAIN
•Venice
•Rome
ITALY

c. A.D. 800s
Feudalism
begins in Europe

c. 1100
Flanders and
Italy trade
goods regularly

c. 1200
Guilds are
widespread
in Europe

What Is Feudalism?

Main Idea Feudalism developed in Europe in the Middle Ages. It was based on landowning, loyalty, and the power of armored knights on horseback.

Reading Focus What would it be like to live in a country where the government has fallen apart? Read to learn how the fall of Charlemagne's government changed life for people in the Middle Ages.

When Charlemagne's grandfather, Charles Martel, needed an army to fight the Muslims invading France, he began giving estates—large farms—to nobles willing to fight for him. The nobles used the income from the estates to pay for their horses and weapons. Although Charles Martel did not realize it, he was using a new way of organizing society that would eventually spread across most of Europe.

When Charlemagne's empire collapsed, Western Europe lost its last strong central government. Landowning nobles became more and more powerful. They gained the right to collect taxes and to enforce laws on their estates. When invaders spread ruin throughout Europe, the peasants, or farmers, could not rely on kings. Instead, they looked to nobles for protection.

During the A.D. 800s, this shift of power from kings to nobles led to a new system known as **feudalism** (FYOO•duhl•IH•zuhm). Under feudalism, landowning nobles governed and protected the people in return for services, such as fighting in a noble's army or farming the land. By A.D. 1000, the kingdoms of Europe were divided into thousands of feudal territories. Some of these territories were large, but most were very small, smaller even than the city-states of Greece and Sumeria. At the center of each, however, was not a city but a noble's castle, or fortress.

The Role of Vassals and Knights

Feudalism was based on ties of loyalty and duty among nobles. Nobles were both lords and vassals. A **vassal** (VA•suhl) was a noble who served a lord of higher rank. In return, the lord protected the vassal.

The tie between a lord and his vassal was made known in a public ceremony. The vassal put his hands together and placed them between the hands of his lord. Then the vassal swore "to keep faith and loyalty to you against all others."

▲ Under feudalism each level of society had duties to the groups above and below it. *Which group in the diagram served as vassals to the lords and ladies?*

Kings and queens

Lords and ladies

Knights

Peasants and serfs

A vassal showed his loyalty by serving in his lord's army. In return for the vassal's military service, a lord granted his vassal land and permission to rule the people who lived on it. This grant to a vassal was known as a **fief** (FEEF).

These vassals were **knights** (NYTS), or warriors in armor who fought on horseback. Up until the A.D. 700s, nobles in Western Europe mostly fought on foot. They wore coats of mail—armor made from metal links—and carried swords and shields. In the A.D. 700s, a new invention, the stirrup, made it possible for an armored man to sit on a horse and charge while holding a lance, a long heavy spear. Knights would charge enemies, spearing them with their lances. From the A.D. 700s to the 1200s, armored knights on horseback were the most powerful soldiers in Europe.

Europe was not the only place with a feudal society. As you remember from an earlier chapter, Japan had a similar system between A.D. 800 and 1500. Powerful nobles owed only a loose loyalty to the Japanese emperor. The nobles in turn relied on samurai. Like knights, the samurai owed loyalty to their lords and provided military service for them. Also like knights in Europe, the samurai wore armor and fought on horseback.

What Was the Manorial System?
The lands of the fiefs of the Middle Ages were called manors. The lords ruled the manor, and peasants worked the land. Some peasants were freemen, who paid the noble for the right to farm the land. They had rights under the law and could move whenever and wherever they wished.

Most peasants, however, were **serfs** (SUHRFS). Serfs could not leave the manor, own property, or marry without the lord's approval. Lords even had the right to try

A Medieval Manor

A medieval manor usually consisted of the lord's manor house or castle, the surrounding fields, and a peasant village. While minor knights or nobles would own only one manor, more powerful lords might own several. A powerful lord would spend time at each of his manors during the year. *What duty did lords have to their serfs?*

Fields
In the spring, serfs planted crops such as summer wheat, barley, oats, peas, and beans. Crops planted in the fall included winter wheat and rye. Women often helped in the fields.

serfs in their own court. Serfs were not enslaved, however. Lords could not sell the serfs or take away the land given to serfs to support themselves. Lords also had a duty to protect their serfs, providing them the safety they needed to grow crops.

Serfs worked long hours on the lord's land and performed services for the lord. They spent three days working for the lord and the rest of the week growing food for themselves. They also had to give a portion of their own crops to the lord and pay him for the use of the village's mill, bread oven, and winepress.

It was not easy for serfs to gain their freedom. One way was to run away to the towns. If a serf remained in a town for more than a year, he or she was considered free. By the end of the Middle Ages, serfs in many kingdoms were also allowed to buy their freedom.

How Did Farming Improve? During the Middle Ages, Europeans invented new technology that helped increase the amount of crops they could grow. Perhaps the most important was a heavy wheeled plow with an iron blade. It easily turned over Western Europe's dense clay soils.

Another important invention was the horse collar. The horse collar made it possible for a horse to pull a plow. Horses could pull plows much faster than oxen, allowing peasants to plant more crops and produce more food.

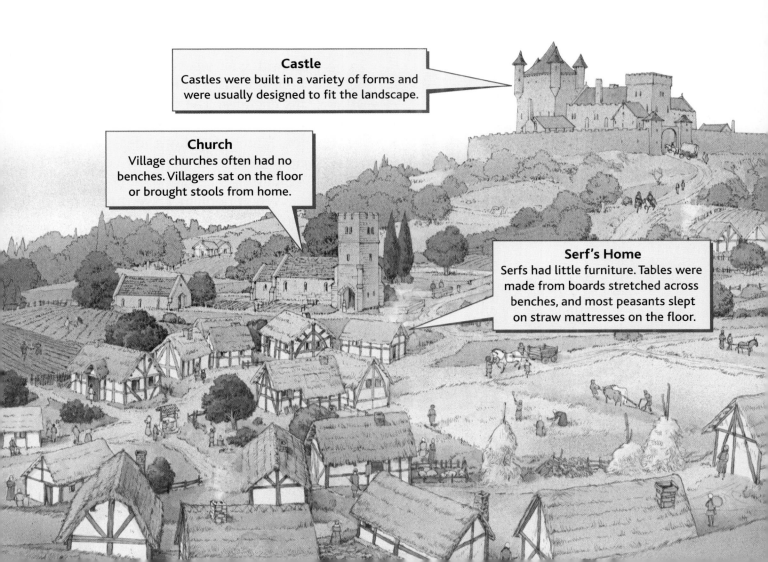

Castle
Castles were built in a variety of forms and were usually designed to fit the landscape.

Church
Village churches often had no benches. Villagers sat on the floor or brought stools from home.

Serf's Home
Serfs had little furniture. Tables were made from boards stretched across benches, and most peasants slept on straw mattresses on the floor.

Europeans also found new ways to harness water and wind power. Europe's many rivers powered water mills that ground grain into flour. Where rivers were not available, windmills were used for grinding grains, pumping water, and cutting wood.

Peasants also learned to grow more food by rotating crops on three fields instead of two. The rotation kept soil fertile. One field was planted in fall and another in spring. The third field was left unplanted. The three-field system meant that only one-third, rather than one-half, of the land was unused at any time. As a result, more crops could be grown.

Reading Check **Explain** How could a noble be both a lord and a vassal?

▲ Nobles celebrated special occasions with large feasts, which included many courses of meats, fruits, and vegetables. *What were the wife's duties when a nobleman went off to war?*

Life in Feudal Europe

Main Idea Knights followed a code of chivalry and lived in castles, while peasants lived in simple houses and worked hard all year long.

Reading Focus Have you heard the phrase "knight in shining armor"? Read to learn why these words apply to how a knight acts as well as how he dresses.

During the Middle Ages, nobles were the most powerful people in Europe. Great lords had much more wealth and land than ordinary knights. However, their belief in the feudal system united lords and knights in defending their society.

How Did Nobles Live? Knights followed certain rules called the code of chivalry (SHIH•vuhl•ree). A knight was expected to obey his lord, to be brave, to show respect to women of noble birth, to honor the church, and to help people. A knight was also expected to be honest and to fight fairly against his enemies. The code of chivalry became the guide to good behavior. Many of today's ideas about manners come from the code of chivalry.

When noblemen went to war, their wives or daughters ran the manors. This was no small job because manors had many officials and servants. Keeping track of the household's accounts took considerable skill. The lady of a manor also had to oversee the storing of food and other supplies needed to run the household.

The center of the manor was a castle. At first, castles were built of wood. Later, they were built of stone. A castle had two basic parts. One was a human-made or

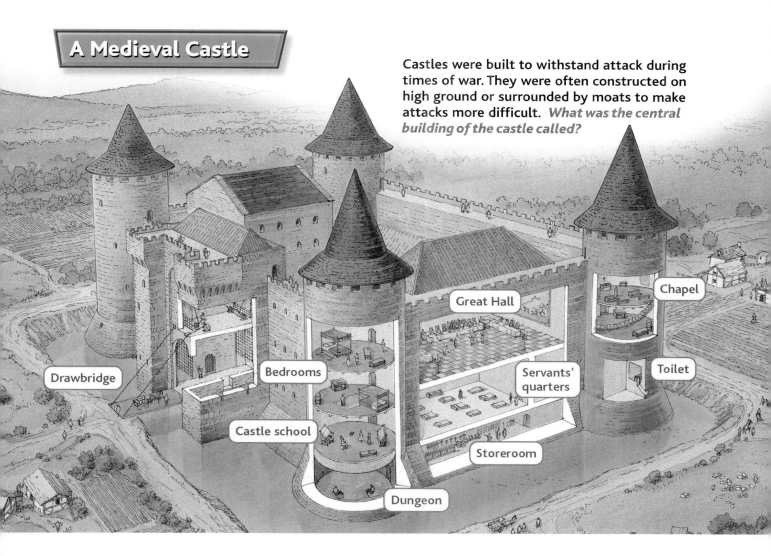

A Medieval Castle

Castles were built to withstand attack during times of war. They were often constructed on high ground or surrounded by moats to make attacks more difficult. *What was the central building of the castle called?*

Drawbridge

Bedrooms

Castle school

Great Hall

Servants' quarters

Chapel

Toilet

Storeroom

Dungeon

naturally steep-sided hill called a motte (MAHT). The bailey was an open space next to the motte. High stone walls encircled the motte and bailey. The keep, or central building of the castle, was built on the motte.

The keep had a number of stories. The basement housed storerooms for tools and food. On the ground floor were kitchens and stables, and above the ground floor was a great hall. Here the people of the household ate and sometimes slept, and the lord of the castle held court and received visitors. Smaller rooms opened off the great hall. They included chapels, toilets, and bedrooms with huge curtained beds.

In the later Middle Ages, nobles owned more jewelry, better clothes, and exotic spices. They also built more elaborate castles with thicker walls, more towers, finer furniture, and richer decoration.

What Was Peasant Life Like? The homes of peasants were much simpler. They lived in wood-frame cottages plastered with clay. Their roofs were thatched with straw. The houses of poorer peasants had a single room. Better cottages had a main room for cooking and eating and another room for sleeping.

Peasants worked year-round. They harvested grain in August and September. In October they prepared the ground for winter crops. In November they slaughtered livestock and salted the meat to keep it for winter. In February and March, they plowed the land for planting oats, barley, peas, and beans. In early summer they weeded the fields, sheared the sheep, and tended small vegetable gardens.

Peasants took a break from work and went to church on Catholic feast days. They celebrated more than 50 feast days each year. The most important were Christmas and Easter. On feast days and at Sunday worship, the village priest taught them the basic beliefs of Christianity.

Peasant women worked in the fields and raised children at the same time. They also gathered and prepared their family's food. Each day they mixed bread dough and baked it in community ovens. Bread was a basic staple of the medieval diet. Peasant bread was dark and heavy. Peasants ate it with vegetables, milk, nuts, and fruits. Sometimes they added eggs or meat, and they often had ale to drink.

✓ **Reading Check** **Identify** What was the code of chivalry?

Trade and Cities

Main Idea Increased trade led to the growth of towns and cities and the rise of guilds and city governments.

Reading Focus What effect would a new shopping mall have on your community? Read to learn how the growth of trade and the rise of cities changed the way people lived and worked in medieval Europe.

When the Roman Empire collapsed, almost all trade in Western Europe came to an end. Bridges and roads fell into disrepair. Law and order vanished. Money was no longer used. Most people spent their entire lives in the tiny villages where they were born and knew almost nothing about the rest of the world.

By 1100, feudalism had made Europe safer, and new technology enabled people to produce more food and goods. Nobles

Medieval City Life

▲ This scene shows a market in a medieval town. *Which area became the center of trade for northern Europe?*

A mayor of London from the early 1200s ▶

repaired bridges and roads, arrested bandits, and enforced the law. As a result, trade resumed.

As trade increased, towns grew larger, and several cities became wealthy from trade. For example, the city of **Venice** (VEH•nuhs) in Italy built a fleet of trading ships. It became a major trading center by A.D. 1000. Venice and other Italian cities began trading with the Byzantine Empire and soon became the center of trade in the Mediterranean.

Meanwhile, towns in **Flanders** (FLAN•duhrz)—which today is part of Belgium—became the center of trade for northern Europe. This area was known for its woolen cloth. Merchants from England, Scandinavia, France, and the Holy Roman Empire met there to trade their goods for wool. Flemish towns such as Bruges and Ghent became centers for making and trading cloth.

By 1100, Flanders and Italy were exchanging goods regularly. To encourage this trade, the counts of Champagne in northern France began holding trade fairs. Northern European merchants exchanged furs, tin, honey, and wool for cloth and swords from northern Italy and silks, sugar, and spices from Asia.

During the early Middle Ages, people bartered, or traded goods for other goods. As trade increased, demand for gold and silver coins rose. Slowly, people began using money again to pay for goods. Merchants set up trading companies and banks to manage the sale of goods and the use of money.

History Online

Web Activity Visit jat.glencoe.com and click on *Chapter 15—Student Web Activity* to learn more about the Middle Ages.

▲ **This illustration from a medieval book shows glassblowers at work.** *What were some of the items exchanged at trade fairs?*

▼ **A stained glass window showing the arms, or symbol, of a blacksmiths' group**

How Were Cities Governed? Towns were often located on land owned by lords. This meant the towns were under their control. However, townspeople needed freedom to trade. They wanted to make their own laws and were willing to pay for the right to make them. In exchange for paying taxes, people in towns were granted certain basic rights by their lords. These included the right to buy and sell property and the freedom from having to serve in the army.

Over time, medieval towns set up their own governments. Only males who had been born in the city or who had lived there for a certain length of time were citizens. In many cities, these citizens elected the members of a city council. The council served as judges, city officials, and lawmakers. Candidates from the wealthiest and most powerful families were usually able to control the elections so that only they were elected.

Crafts and Guilds Trade encouraged manufacturing. People produced cloth, metalwork, shoes, and other goods right in their houses. Over time, these craftspeople organ- ized **guilds** (GIHLDZ), or business groups. By 1200, tanners, carpenters, bakers, and almost every other type of craftspeople had guilds. The rise of towns and guilds created a new middle class in medieval Europe. People in the middle class were not lords, vassals, or serfs. They did not own land, but they did have some wealth and freedom.

Craft guilds set standards for quality in products. They decided how goods were to be made and set the prices at which the finished goods were sold. Guilds also decided who could join a trade and the steps they had to follow to do so.

A person could become an apprentice around the age of 10. An apprentice learned a trade from a master craftsperson who provided room and board but no wages. After five to seven years of service, the apprentice became a journeyman and worked for wages. To become a master, a journeyman had to produce a masterpiece—an outstanding example of the craft.

What Was City Life Like? Medieval cities had narrow, winding streets. Houses were crowded against one another, and the

▲ Medieval streets were narrow and often contained wastewater and garbage. *Why was fire a major threat in medieval cities?*

▼ **A street in France dating back to medieval times**

second and third stories were built out over the streets. Candles and fireplaces were used for light and heat, and the houses were built mostly of wood. As a result, medieval cities could be destroyed rapidly once a fire started.

The cities were often dirty and smelly. Wood fires in people's homes and shops filled the air with ashes and smoke. Brewers, dyers, and poor people who could not afford wood burned cheap coal, polluting the air even more. Butchers and tanners dumped blood and other animal wastes into the rivers. Because of the pollution, cities did not use the rivers for drinking water but used wells instead.

City women ran their households, prepared meals, raised their children, and managed the family's money. Often they

▲ This painting shows a medieval woman spinning wool as her husband warms himself by the fire. *What were some responsibilities of women in medieval cities?*

helped their husbands in their trades. Some women developed their own trades to earn extra money. Sometimes when a master craftsperson died, his widow carried on his trade. As a result, women in medieval towns could lead independent lives. In fact, many women became brewers, weavers, and hatmakers.

✓ **Reading Check** Analyze In what ways do you think the shift from a barter system to a money system changed medieval Europe?

Section 2 Review

History Online

Study Central™ Need help with the material in this section? Visit jat.glencoe.com

Reading Summary

Review the Main Ideas

- Under feudalism, Europe was divided into thousands of territories owned by nobles with the lands worked by serfs.

- During the Middle Ages, nobles lived in large castles, while serfs lived in small wood cottages.

- As medieval trade increased, towns grew and craftspeople organized guilds.

What Did You Learn?

1. What was a vassal?

2. Describe the system of crop rotation used in the later Middle Ages, and explain how it increased the amount of food being grown.

Critical Thinking

3. **Compare and Contrast** Draw a chart to compare the duties and obligations of lords, knights, and serfs.

Lords	Knights	Serfs

4. **Summarize** Explain the shift of power from kings to nobles during the Middle Ages.

5. **Cause and Effect** How did an increase in trade lead to the growth of towns and cities?

6. **Conclude** What were guilds, and why were they important?

7. **Creative Writing** Write a For Sale advertisement for a medieval castle. Describe the castle's rooms and surroundings, including the manor and its residents.

You Decide . . .

Feudalism: Good or Bad?

Feudalism was the major social and political order in medieval Europe. It developed as power passed from kings to local lords.

Good?

Feudalism brought together two powerful groups: lords and vassals. The lords gave vassals land in return for military and other services. Feudalism was a help to Western Europeans for the following reasons:

- Feudalism helped protect communities from the violence and warfare that broke out after the fall of Rome and the collapse of strong central government in Western Europe. Feudalism secured Western Europe's society and kept out powerful invaders.

- Feudalism helped restore trade. Lords repaired bridges and roads. Their knights arrested bandits, enforced the law, and made it safe to travel on roads.

- Feudalism benefited lords, vassals, and peasants. Lords gained a dependable fighting force in their vassals. Vassals received land for their military service. Peasants were protected by their lords. The lord also built mills to grind grain and blacksmith shops and woodworking shops to make tools.

- Feudal ceremonies, oaths, and contracts required lords and vassals to be faithful and to carry out their duties to each other. These kinds of agreements and rituals later helped shape the development of Western governments.

- Feudalism did not allow one person or organization to become too powerful. Power was shared among

◀ **Serfs working the land**

◀ **Landowning nobles often served as knights.**

many people and groups. This was the first step to European ideas about limited government, constitutions, and civil rights.

Bad?

Feudalism did not always work as well in real life as it it did in theory, and it caused many problems for society.

- Feudalism provided some unity and security in local areas, but it often did not have the strength to unite larger regions or countries. Small feudal governments could not afford big projects, such as building aqueducts, sewers, or fleets of ships, that might benefit society.

- Because there was no strong central government to enforce laws fairly, it was easy to use force, violence, and lies to get one's way. This led to many wars among lords. Feudalism protected Western Europe from outside invaders, but it did not bring peace to a region.

- Lords or vassals often placed their personal interests over the interests of the areas they ruled. Feudal lords had complete power in their local areas and could make harsh demands on their vassals and peasants.

- Feudalism did not treat people equally or let them move up in society. A person born a serf was supposed to remain a serf, just as a person born a lord received special treatment without earning it.

- Most peasants were serfs. They were not allowed to leave their lord's lands. Serfs had to work three or four days each week as a payment to the lords or vassals for allowing them to farm for themselves on other days. The serfs were restricted in movement and even daily activities because they could not leave the land without permission.

You Be the Historian

Checking for Understanding

1. Do you think feudalism helped or hurt Western Europe's development?

2. Is there any way feudal lords could have worked their lands without using serfs?

3. Imagine what your life would have been if you were born into a feudal society. Write at least three brief diary entries. Describe your daily life as a lord, vassal, or serf and your relationship with the other two groups. Your entries should show feudalism as either good or bad.

Kingdoms and Crusades

Get Ready to Read!

What's the Connection?

In the last section, you read about how Western Europeans lived during the Middle Ages. This section describes the political changes that took place while people went about their daily lives.

Focusing on the Main Ideas

• England developed a system in which the king's power was shared with Parliament. *(page 535)*

• French kings called the Capetians conquered lands held by the English in western France and set up France's first parliament. *(page 538)*

• After the Mongols destroyed the Kievan state, the rulers of Moscow built a new Russian state headed by a czar. *(page 539)*

• European crusaders captured Jerusalem but were later driven out by the Muslims. *(page 541)*

Locating Places

Normandy (NAWR•muhn•dee)
Kiev (KEE•EHF)
Moscow (MAHS•koh)

Meeting People

William the Conqueror
King John
Philip II (FIH•luhp)
Saladin (SA•luh•DEEN)

Building Your Vocabulary

grand jury
trial jury
clergy (KLUHR•jee)

Reading Strategy

Cause and Effect Complete a diagram to show the causes and effects of the Crusades.

Causes	Effects

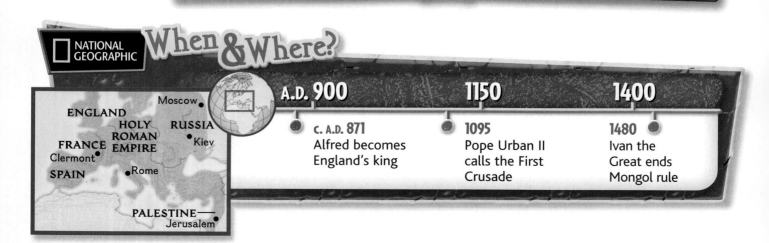

NATIONAL GEOGRAPHIC **When & Where?**

ENGLAND
Moscow
HOLY   RUSSIA
ROMAN
FRANCE EMPIRE Kiev
Clermont
Rome
SPAIN

PALESTINE—
Jerusalem

A.D. 900	1150	1400

C. A.D. 871
Alfred becomes England's king

1095
Pope Urban II calls the First Crusade

1480
Ivan the Great ends Mongol rule

England in the Middle Ages

Main Idea England developed a system in which the king's power was shared with Parliament.

Reading Focus Do you know anyone who has had to go to court or has served on a jury? Read to learn how these institutions began in medieval England.

In section one, you learned that Germanic peoples called the Angles and Saxons invaded Britain in the early A.D. 400s. They took over much of the country from the Celts and set up many small kingdoms. In the late A.D. 800s, Vikings attacked Britain. King Alfred of Wessex, later known as Alfred the Great, united the Anglo-Saxon kingdoms and drove away the Vikings. Alfred's united kingdom became known as "Angleland," or England.

Alfred ruled England from A.D. 871 to A.D. 899. He founded schools and hired scholars to rewrite Latin books in the Anglo-Saxon language. However, the Anglo-Saxon kings who came after him were weak rulers.

Who Was William the Conqueror?
In the A.D. 900s, the Vikings conquered part of western France across the English Channel from England. This region came to be called **Normandy** (NAWR•muhn•dee), after the Vikings, or Norsemen, who ruled it. By the middle of the A.D. 1000s, Normandy was ruled by William, a descendant of the Viking ruler who had conquered Normandy. William was also a cousin of King Edward of England.

When Edward died, a noble named Harold Godwinson claimed England's throne. However, William believed that he, not Harold, should be king of England. In 1066, William and his army of knights landed in England. They defeated Harold and his foot soldiers at the Battle of Hastings. William was then crowned king of England and became known as **William the Conqueror.**

▼ This painting of the Battle of Hastings shows Norman knights on horseback led by William the Conqueror attacking the English foot soldiers. *What area did William rule before he attacked England?*

At first the Anglo-Saxons resisted William's rule. He had to find a way to stop Anglo-Saxon revolts and to control his own soldiers. He did so by giving land to his Norman knights. Then he made them swear loyalty to him as ruler of England.

William wanted to know all about his new kingdom. So he took the first census in Europe since Roman times. This census was known as the Domesday Book. It counted people, manors, and farm animals.

The Normans who ruled England brought Europe's customs to England.

Under William's rule, officials and nobles spoke French. Ordinary Anglo-Saxons still spoke their own language, which later became English. They also learned new skills from Norman weavers and other artisans. The Normans, in turn, kept many of the Anglo-Saxons' government practices. For example, they depended on local officials, called sheriffs, to keep order. As more and more Normans and Anglo-Saxons married, their ways of doing things merged into a new English culture.

Linking Past & Present

The Jury System

THEN The right to a jury trial in England was granted in the Magna Carta, but jury trials began in Europe about 50 years earlier. For each case, 12 jurors were chosen. In some villages, the same jurors were chosen again and again because of their wisdom or status. Jurors were always men. The jury decided whether the accused was guilty or innocent.

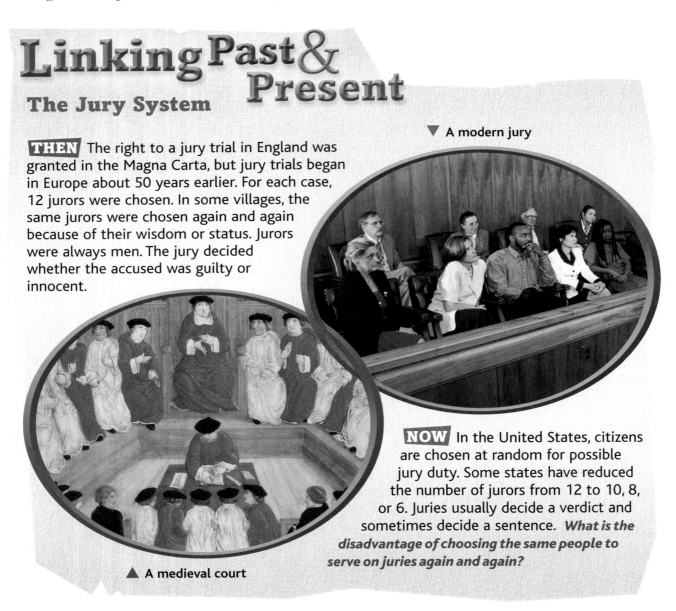

▼ A modern jury

▲ A medieval court

NOW In the United States, citizens are chosen at random for possible jury duty. Some states have reduced the number of jurors from 12 to 10, 8, or 6. Juries usually decide a verdict and sometimes decide a sentence. *What is the disadvantage of choosing the same people to serve on juries again and again?*

Henry II and the Common Law The power of the English king increased under Henry II. Henry ruled England from 1154 to 1189. Henry used the law courts to increase his power. He set up a central court with trained lawyers and judges. Then he appointed circuit judges, who traveled across the country hearing cases. He also established a body of common law, or law that was the same throughout the whole kingdom.

Henry set up juries to handle arguments over land. In time, two kinds of juries developed. The **grand jury** decided whether people should be accused of a crime. The **trial jury** decided whether an accused person was innocent or guilty.

What Was the Magna Carta?

Henry's son John became king of England in 1199. **King John** raised taxes in England and punished his enemies without trials. Many English nobles resented the king's power. They refused to obey him unless he agreed to guarantee certain rights.

The nobles met with King John at a meadow called Runnymede in 1215. There they forced John to sign a document of rights called the Magna Carta, or the Great Charter. The Magna Carta took away some of the king's powers. He could no longer collect taxes unless a group called the Great Council agreed. Freemen accused of crimes had the right to fair trials by their peers, or equals. The Magna Carta also stated that the king and vassals both had certain rights and duties. The Magna Carta was important because it helped to establish the idea that people have rights and that the power of the government should be limited.

In the 1200s, another English king, Edward I, called for a meeting of people from different parts of England. Their

Primary Source

Magna Carta

This excerpt from the Magna Carta describes the right to a trial by jury:

"No free man shall be taken, imprisoned, disseised [seized], outlawed, banished, or in any way destroyed, nor will We proceed against or prosecute him, except by the lawful judgment of his peers and by the law of the land."

—Magna Carta

King John signing the Magna Carta ▲

DBQ Document-Based Question

Why do you think this part of the Magna Carta is important?

job was to advise him and help him make laws. This gathering, called the Parliament, was an important step toward representative government. At first, Parliaments were made up of two knights from every county, two people from every town, and all high-ranking nobles and church officials. Later, Parliament divided into two houses. High-ranking nobles and church officials met as the House of Lords. Knights and townspeople met as the House of Commons.

✓ **Reading Check** **Explain** How did the Magna Carta affect the king's power?

The Kingdom of France

Main Idea French kings called the Capetians conquered lands held by the English in western France and set up France's first parliament.

Reading Focus Has a poll ever been taken in your class? Read to find out how one French king found out what his people were thinking.

In A.D. 843 Charlemagne's empire was divided into three parts. The western part eventually became the kingdom of France. In A.D. 987 Frankish nobles chose Hugh Capet to be their king. Hugh was the first of the Capetian (kuh•PEE•shuhn) kings of France. The Capetians controlled the area around Paris (PAR•uhs), the capital. Many French nobles had more power than the kings did. This began to change when **Philip II** (FIH•luhp) became king of France.

Philip ruled from 1180 to 1223. When he took the throne, England's king ruled parts of western France. Philip went to war against England and conquered most of these territories. As a result, French kings gained more land and became more powerful.

Philip IV, called Philip the Fair, ruled from 1285 to 1314. In 1302 he met with representatives from the three estates, or classes, of French society. The first estate was the **clergy** (KLUHR•jee), or people who had been ordained as priests. Nobles made up the second estate, and townspeople and peasants were the third estate. This meeting began the Estates-General, France's first parliament. It was the first step in France toward representative government.

Reading Check **Describe** How did King Philip II bring power back to French kings?

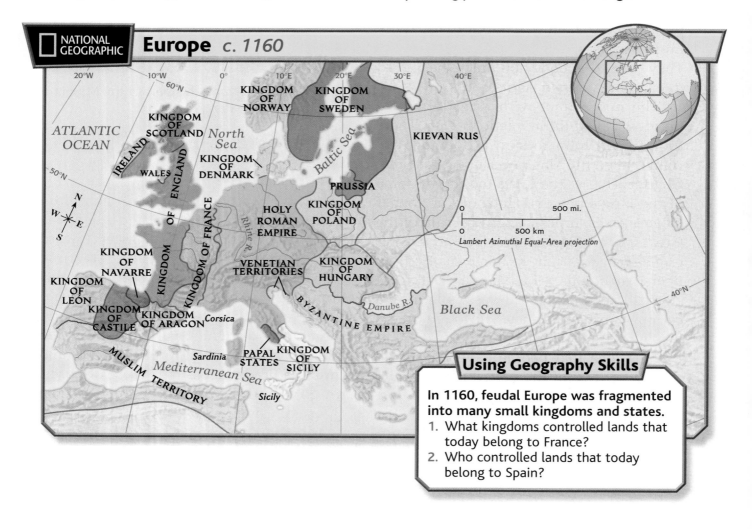

NATIONAL GEOGRAPHIC

Europe c. 1160

Using Geography Skills

In 1160, feudal Europe was fragmented into many small kingdoms and states.
1. What kingdoms controlled lands that today belong to France?
2. Who controlled lands that today belong to Spain?

Eastern Europe and Russia

Main Idea After the Mongols destroyed the Kievan state, the rulers of Moscow built a new Russian state headed by a czar.

Reading Focus Why do you think some of the cities in your state grew large while others stayed small? Read to learn how the cities of Kiev and Moscow grew to become the centers of large Slavic states.

About A.D. 500, a people called the Slavs organized villages in Eastern Europe. Each village was made up of families related to each other. The villagers shared their land, animals, tools, and seeds. Each family built its house partly underground. This kept the family warm during the cold winters.

In time, the Slavs divided into three major groups: the southern, western, and eastern Slavs. The southern Slavs became the Croats, Serbs, and Bulgarians. The western Slavs became the Poles, Czechs, and Slovaks. The eastern Slavs became the Ukrainians (yoo•KRAY•nee•uhnz), Belorussians (BEH•loh•RUH•shuhnz), and Russians (RUH•shuhnz).

By A.D. 600, the eastern Slavs controlled the land between the Carpathian Mountains and the Volga River. In the early Middle Ages, the eastern Slavs created farmland by chopping down the forests and then burning the trees to fertilize the soil. They planted barley, rye, and flax.

What Was the Kievan Rus?

In the late A.D. 700s, Vikings began moving into the Slavs' territory from the north. Over time, the Vikings became rulers of the Slavs. The Slavs called their Viking rulers the Rus. Over time, the Vikings and Slavs intermarried and blended into one people.

Around A.D. 900, a Viking leader named Oleg created a Rus state around the city of **Kiev** (KEE•EHF). Called the Kievan Rus, this state was really a group of small territories.

Primary Source

Ibn Fadlan Describes the Rus

In A.D. 921, the Muslim official Ibn Fadlan encountered the Rus while visiting a settlement on the Volga River.

▲ Statue of a Rus leader

"I have seen the Rūs as they came on their merchant journeys and encamped by the [Volga River]. I have never seen more perfect physical specimens, tall as date palms, blonde and ruddy; they wear neither [coats] nor caftans [long shirts], but the men wear a garment which covers one side of the body and leaves a hand free. . . . They build big houses of wood on the [Volga] shore, each holding ten to twenty persons more or less."

—Ibn Fadlān, *Risāla*

DBQ **Document-Based Question**

Of what occupation are the Rus that Ibn Fadlan describes?

The main ruler was the Grand Duke of Kiev. Local princes, rich merchants, and landowning nobles called boyars (boh•YAHRZ) helped him govern.

The rulers who came after Oleg increased the size of the Kievan Rus. In time, it reached from the Baltic Sea in the north to the Black Sea in the south. It stretched from the Danube River in the west to the Volga River in the east.

The growth of the Kievan Rus attracted missionaries from the Byzantine Empire. One Rus ruler, Vladimir, married the Byzantine emperor's sister. He became an Eastern Orthodox Christian and declared his people Eastern Orthodox.

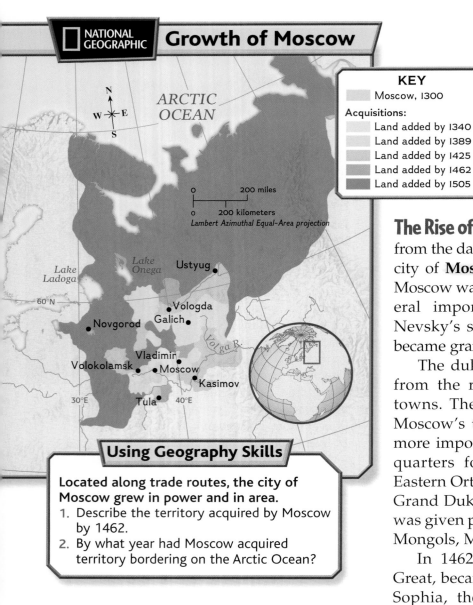

NATIONAL GEOGRAPHIC — Growth of Moscow

KEY
- Moscow, 1300

Acquisitions:
- Land added by 1340
- Land added by 1389
- Land added by 1425
- Land added by 1462
- Land added by 1505

ARCTIC OCEAN

Lambert Azimuthal Equal-Area projection

Lake Ladoga, Lake Onega, Ustyug, Vologda, Galich, Novgorod, Vladimir, Volokolamsk, Moscow, Kasimov, Tula, Volga R.

Using Geography Skills

Located along trade routes, the city of Moscow grew in power and in area.

1. Describe the territory acquired by Moscow by 1462.
2. By what year had Moscow acquired territory bordering on the Arctic Ocean?

Kiev Falls to the Mongols

About 1240, the Mongols swept into the Kievan Rus. The Slavs called the Mongols "Tatars" because one of the Mongol tribes was the Tata people. The Mongols destroyed nearly all the major cities and killed many people.

The only major city of the Kievan Rus that was spared was the northern city of Novgorod. Nonetheless, Novgorod's rulers as well as other Russian rulers, had to pay tribute to the khan, the Mongol leader, and accept the Mongols as their rulers.

Although Novgorod had been spared by the Mongols, it faced attacks from the west by Germans and Swedes. Led by Alexander Nevsky, the Slavs of Novgorod defeated the Swedes and Germans. For his help in defending lands controlled by the Mongols, the Mongol khan rewarded Nevsky with the title of grand duke.

The Rise of Moscow As the Slavs recovered from the damage caused by the Mongols, the city of **Moscow** (MAHS•koh) began to grow. Moscow was located at the crossroads of several important trade routes. Alexander Nevsky's son Daniel and his descendants became grand dukes of Moscow.

The dukes of Moscow married women from the ruling families in other Slavic towns. They also fought wars to expand Moscow's territory. Moscow became even more important when it became the headquarters for the Russian branch of the Eastern Orthodox Church. When Ivan I, the Grand Duke of Moscow from 1328 to 1341, was given permission to collect taxes for the Mongols, Moscow grew even greater.

In 1462 Ivan III, known as Ivan the Great, became the grand duke. He married Sophia, the niece of the last Byzantine emperor. Afterward, Ivan began living in the style of an emperor. He had architects build fine palaces and large cathedrals in the Kremlin—the fortress at the center of Moscow. He even began calling himself czar. Czar was a shortened version of Caesar. In Russian, czar means emperor.

Ivan IV lived up to his title. In 1480 he finally ended Mongol rule over Moscow's territory. Then he expanded his territory to the north and west. When Ivan IV died in 1505, the Russians were well on the way toward building a vast empire.

✓ **Reading Check** Cause and Effect Why was Alexander Nevsky important?

The Crusades

Main Idea European crusaders captured Jerusalem but were later driven out by the Muslims.

Reading Focus Have you ever put all your energy into making something important happen? Read to learn why Europeans thought capturing the city of Jerusalem was important.

During the Middle Ages, the Byzantine Empire in the East came under attack. In 1071 an army of Muslim Turks defeated the Byzantines and seized control of most of the Byzantine lands in Asia Minor.

The Byzantine emperor did not have enough money or troops to drive out the Turks. In desperation, he asked the pope to help him defend his Christian empire against the Muslim invaders.

In 1095 Pope Urban II spoke before a large crowd in eastern France. He asked Europe's lords to launch a crusade, or holy war, against the Muslim Turks. He urged them to capture Jerusalem and free the Holy Land where Jesus had lived from the Muslims. The pope explained why the crusade was needed:

66 Jerusalem is the navel [center] of the world. . . . This is the land which the Redeemer [Jesus] of mankind illuminated by his coming. . . . This royal city, situated in the middle of the world, is now held captive by his enemies. . . . It looks and hopes for freedom; it begs unceasingly that you will come to its aid. 99

—Pope Urban II, as quoted in *The Discoverers*

As the pope spoke, the excited crowd cried out, "It is the will of God, it is the will of God." The Crusades had begun.

Early Victories Several thousand soldiers on horseback and as many as ten thousand on foot headed east. Many of them wore a red cross on their clothes as a sign of their obedience to the pope's call.

In 1098 the First Crusade captured Antioch in Syria. From there, the crusaders entered Palestine, reaching Jerusalem in 1099. After a bloody fight, they stormed the city, killing Muslims, Jews, and Christians alike.

In the painting above, Pope Urban II calls for a crusade against the Muslims. At right, the crusaders attack Jerusalem with siege towers and catapults. *What was the pope's goal for the crusade?*

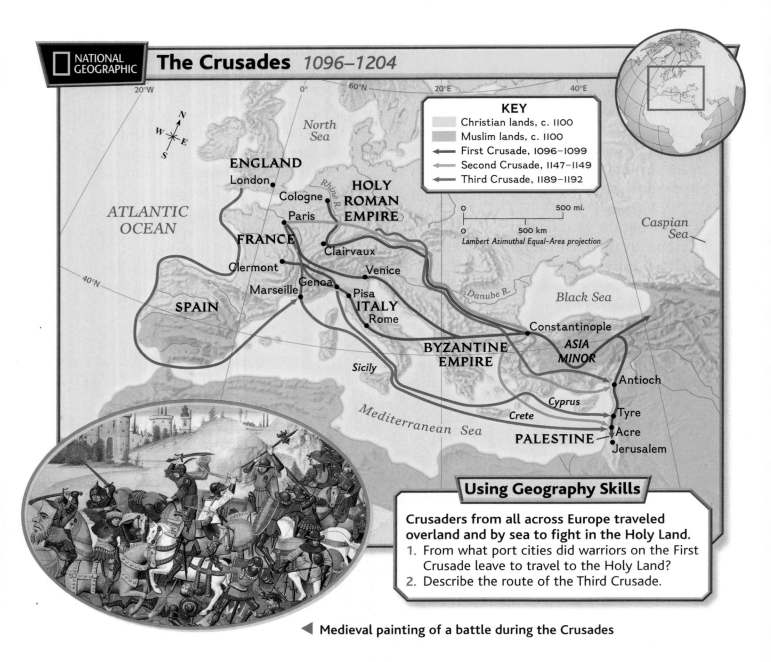

The Crusades 1096–1204

NATIONAL GEOGRAPHIC

KEY
- Christian lands, c. 1100
- Muslim lands, c. 1100
- First Crusade, 1096–1099
- Second Crusade, 1147–1149
- Third Crusade, 1189–1192

500 mi.
500 km
Lambert Azimuthal Equal-Area projection

North Sea
ATLANTIC OCEAN
ENGLAND
London
Cologne
Paris
FRANCE
Clairvaux
Clermont
Venice
Marseille
Genoa
Pisa
ITALY
Rome
SPAIN
HOLY ROMAN EMPIRE
Rhine R.
Danube R.
Caspian Sea
Black Sea
Constantinople
ASIA MINOR
BYZANTINE EMPIRE
Sicily
Antioch
Cyprus
Crete
Tyre
Acre
PALESTINE
Jerusalem
Mediterranean Sea

Using Geography Skills

Crusaders from all across Europe traveled overland and by sea to fight in the Holy Land.
1. From what port cities did warriors on the First Crusade leave to travel to the Holy Land?
2. Describe the route of the Third Crusade.

◀ Medieval painting of a battle during the Crusades

Having driven the Muslims from the region, the crusaders created four states: the Kingdom of Jerusalem in Palestine, the county of Edessa and the principality of Antioch in Asia Minor, and the county of Tripoli where Lebanon is located today. These four states were surrounded by Muslims and depended on the Italian cities of Genoa, Pisa, and Venice for supplies.

The Muslims fought back, however, and in 1144 they captured Edessa. In response, European rulers sent another crusade to

regain the lost lands. This Second Crusade, however, was a total failure.

In 1174 a Muslim named **Saladin** (SA•luh•DEEN) became ruler of Egypt. He united Muslims and declared war against the Christian states the crusaders had built. Saladin proved to be a brilliant commander. He defeated the Christians and captured Jerusalem in 1187.

The fall of Jerusalem led to the Third Crusade. Emperor Frederick of the Holy Roman Empire, King Richard I of England, (known as Richard the Lion-Hearted), and King Philip II of France gathered their armies and headed east to fight Saladin.

The Third Crusade had many problems. Frederick drowned crossing a river. The English and French arrived by sea and captured a coastal city but were unable to push inland. After Philip went home, Richard secured a small territory along the coast. He then agreed to a truce after Saladin promised that Christian pilgrims could travel to Jerusalem in safety.

Around 1200, Pope Innocent III called for a Fourth Crusade. Merchants from Venice used the crusade to weaken their trading rival, the Byzantine Empire. They convinced the crusaders to attack Constantinople, the Byzantine capital. For three days, the crusaders burned and looted the city. The attack shocked Western Europeans and weakened the Byzantines.

Six more crusades were launched over the next 60 years, but they achieved very little. Gradually, the Muslims conquered all of the territory they had lost to the First Crusade. In 1291, a bit more than 200 years after the First Crusade had set out, the last Christian city fell to Muslim forces.

The Crusades affected Europe in two ways. They increased trade between Europe and the Middle East, and they helped break down feudalism. Nobles who joined the Crusades sold their lands and freed their serfs. This reduced their power and helped kings build stronger central governments. Kings also began taxing the new trade with the Middle East. These taxes helped them build stronger kingdoms in Western Europe.

✓ **Reading Check** **Compare and Contrast** What did the First Crusade accomplish? What did the Third Crusade accomplish?

Section 3 Review

History Online
Study Central™ Need help with the material in this section? Visit jat.glencoe.com

Reading Summary

Review the Main Ideas

- The English king granted rights to his people in the Magna Carta and established a parliament.

- French kings regained French territories from the English and, like the English, created a parliament.

- Russia had its beginnings in the territories of the Kievan Rus and Moscow.

- West Europeans launched crusades to capture Jerusalem and Palestine from the Muslims.

What Did You Learn?

1. What is the significance of the Battle of Hastings?

2. What groups developed from the three major divisions of Slavs in Eastern Europe?

Critical Thinking

3. **Organizing Information** Draw a chart to list the kings of England and France and their achievements.

King/Country	Achievements

4. **Evaluate** What was the importance of the Magna Carta?

5. **Summarize** Describe the development of England's Parliament, and discuss its role in changing government.

6. **Explain** Why did cities such as Venice flourish as a result of the Crusades?

7. **Expository Writing** Write an essay describing how the Crusades affected feudalism.

The Church and Society

Get-Ready to Read!

What's the Connection?

Kings and popes had a powerful effect on the lives of medieval people, as did religion. In this section, you will learn how religion in medieval Europe shaped its culture.

Focusing on the Main Ideas

• The Catholic Church played an important role in medieval Europe and used its power to uphold its teachings. *(page 545)*

• Church and government leaders supported learning and the arts in medieval Europe. *(page 549)*

Locating Places
Bologna (buh•LOH•nyuh)

Meeting People
Francis of Assisi
(FRAN•suhs   uhv   uh•SIHS•ee)
Thomas Aquinas
(TAH•muhs   uh•KWY•nuhs)

Building Your Vocabulary
mass
heresy (HEHR•uh•see)
anti-Semitism
(AN•tih•SEH•muh•TIH•zuhm)
theology (thee•AH•luh•jee)
scholasticism
(skuh•LAS•tuh•SIH•zuhm)
vernacular (vuhr•NA•kyuh•luhr)

Reading Strategy
Organizing Information Complete a Venn diagram to show the similarities and differences between Romanesque and Gothic cathedrals.

Romanesque Cathedrals   Gothic Cathedrals

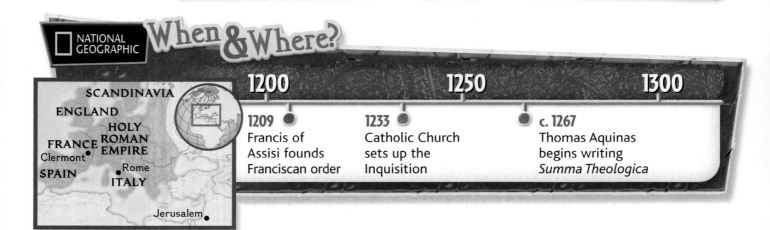

NATIONAL GEOGRAPHIC When & Where?

SCANDINAVIA
ENGLAND
HOLY ROMAN EMPIRE
FRANCE
Clermont
Rome
SPAIN   ITALY
Jerusalem

1200	1250	1300

1209
Francis of Assisi founds Franciscan order

1233
Catholic Church sets up the Inquisition

c. 1267
Thomas Aquinas begins writing *Summa Theologica*

Religion and Society

Main Idea The Catholic Church played an important role in medieval Europe and used its power to uphold its teachings.

Reading Focus Have you ever noticed how many things in society have been influenced by religion? What examples can you give? Read to learn about the important role religion played in the lives of people living in the Middle Ages.

Between 1050 and 1150, a strong wave of religious feeling swept across Western Europe. As a result, more monasteries were built, and new religious orders, or groups of priests, monks, and nuns, were started.

New Religious Orders

The Cistercian (sihs•TUHR•shuhn) order was founded in 1098. Cistercian monks farmed the land as well as worshiped and prayed. They developed many new farming techniques that helped Europeans grow more crops.

The most famous Cistercian monk was Bernard of Clairvaux (klar•VOH). Bernard helped promote the Second Crusade. He also advised the pope and defended the poor against the rich.

Many women entered convents between A.D. 1000 and 1200. Most of them were from noble families. They included widows and women unable or unwilling to marry. Women who were scholars found convents ideal places for study and writing.

Most educated women in medieval Europe were nuns. One famous woman was Hildegard of Bingen (HIHL•duh•GAHRD uhv BIHNG•uhn). She headed a convent in Germany and composed music for the Church. Her work is remarkable because at that time, men wrote most church music.

▲ This religious painting from the wall of a church in Italy depicts the pope and other Christian leaders, a number of saints, and Jesus ruling over all.

How did Cistercian monks aid European society?

The Franciscan Way of Life

Francis of Assisi recorded instructions for living in the Franciscan order. This passage is about the nature of love.

"Blessed that friar who loves his brother as much when he is sick and can be of no use to him as when he is well and can be of use to him. Blessed that friar who loves and respects his brother as much when he is absent as when he is present and who would not say anything behind his back that he could not say charitably [nicely] to his face."

—Francis of Assisi, as quoted in "Admonitions"

Francis of Assisi ▶

DBQ Document-Based Question

Does Francis of Assisi think that love for another person should be constant, or changing? How do you know?

Until the 1200s, most people in religious orders stayed in their monasteries separate from the world. They lived a simple life of prayer and hard work. In the 1200s, several new religious orders were created. The men in these religious orders were called friars. *Friar* comes from a Latin word for "brother."

Friars were different from monks. They did not stay in their monasteries. Instead, they went out into the world to preach. Friars lived by begging. They could not own property or keep any personal wealth.

The first order of friars was founded by **Francis of Assisi** (FRAN•suhs uhv uh•SIHS•ee) in 1209. These friars became known as Franciscans. They lived in towns and taught Christianity to the people. In addition, the Franciscans helped the poor and served as missionaries.

A Spanish priest named Dominic de Guzmán founded another group of friars called the Dominicans. The Domincans' goal was to defend Church teachings. Dominican friars spent years in study so they could preach to well-educated people.

The Role of Religion Throughout medieval Western Europe, daily life revolved around the Catholic Church. Priests ran schools and hospitals. They also recorded births, performed weddings, and conducted burials. On Sundays and holy days, people went to **mass**—or the Catholic worship service.

During mass, medieval Christians took part in Church rituals called sacraments. The most important sacrament was communion, in which people took bread and wine to remind them of Jesus' death on the cross for their sins. Only clergy could give people the sacraments.

Many Christians also prayed to saints. Saints were holy men and women who had died and were believed to be in heaven. Their presence before God enabled the saints to ask favors for people who prayed to them.

Of all the saints, Mary, the mother of Jesus, was the most honored. Many churches were named for her. Several French churches carried the name *Notre Dame,* or "Our Lady," in honor of Mary.

Some people tried to make a connection to the saints by touching relics. Relics were usually bones or personal belongings of saints. People believed that relics had special powers, such as the ability to heal the sick.

Medieval Christians also believed that God blessed pilgrims, or religious travelers who journeyed to holy places. The holiest place was Jerusalem in the Middle East.

What Was the Inquisition?
The Catholic Church was very powerful in medieval society, and most of its leaders wanted everyone to accept the Church's teachings. Church leaders feared that if people stopped believing Church teachings, it would weaken the Church and endanger people's chances of getting into heaven.

Using its power, the Church tried to put an end to **heresy** (HEHR•uh•see), or religious beliefs that conflict with Church teachings. At first, it tried to stop the spread of heresy by sending friars like the Dominicans to preach the Church's message. Then, in 1233, the pope established a court called the Inquisition (IHN•kwuh•ZIH•shuhn), or Church court. To Church leaders, heresy was a crime against God. The Inquisition's job was to try heretics, or people suspected of heresy.

People brought before the Inquisition were urged to confess their heresy and to ask forgiveness. When they confessed, the Inquisition punished them and then allowed them to return to the Church. People who refused to confess could be tortured until they admitted their heresy. Those who did not confess were considered guilty. The Inquisition turned them over to political leaders, who could execute them.

How Were the Jews Treated?
Church leaders persecuted Jews as actively as they punished heretics. Many Europeans hated Jews for refusing to become Christians. Others hated them because many Jews were moneylenders who charged interest. At that time, Christians believed charging interest was a sin.

▲ This painting shows an accused heretic being questioned by the Inquisition. *What happened to people who refused to confess to the Inquisition?*

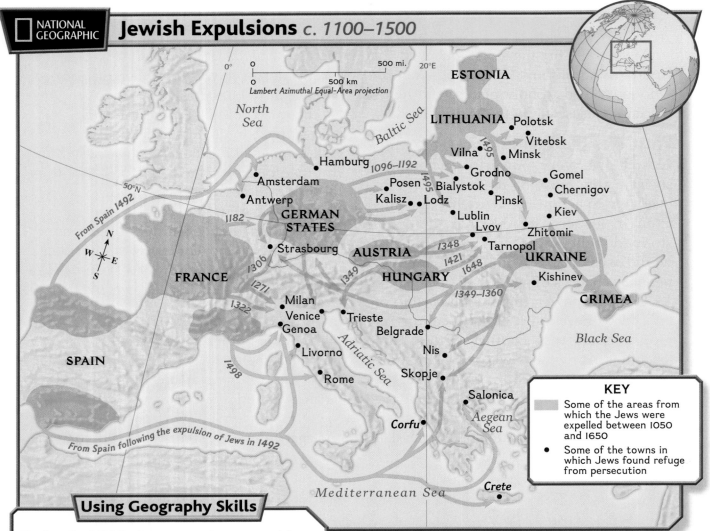

Jewish Expulsions c. 1100–1500

NATIONAL GEOGRAPHIC

KEY

Some of the areas from which the Jews were expelled between 1050 and 1650

• Some of the towns in which Jews found refuge from persecution

Using Geography Skills

During the Middle Ages, many Jews were driven from their homes in Western Europe, sometimes from areas where their families had lived for generations.

1. From where did many of the Jews who moved to Eastern Europe come?
2. Where did many of the Jews expelled from Spain settle?

When disease or economic problems hurt society, people blamed the Jews. Jews became scapegoats—people who are blamed for other people's troubles. Hatred of Jews is known as **anti-Semitism** (AN•tih•SEH•muh•TIH•zuhm).

Anti-Semitism in the Middle Ages took horrible forms. Christian mobs attacked and killed thousands of Jews. Governments made Jews wear special badges or clothing. In some places, Jews had to live in separate communities known as ghettos. Jews also lost the right to own land and to practice certain trades. This was why many of them had to become peddlers and moneylenders, jobs that Christians despised.

Beginning in the 1100s, European rulers began driving out their Jewish subjects. England expelled Jews in 1290. France expelled groups of Jews several times. Some German cities also forced Jews to leave. Many of these Jews settled in Poland and other Eastern European countries. Over the years, the Jews of Eastern Europe established thriving communities based on their religious traditions.

✓ **Reading Check** **Contrast** How did the main goal of the Franciscans differ from the main goal of the Dominicans?

Medieval Culture

Main Idea) **Church and government leaders supported learning and the arts in medieval Europe.**

Reading Focus What are the most important parts of American culture today? Read to learn about the kinds of things that made up the culture of medieval Europe.

As strong governments arose, people in medieval Europe felt safer. As a result, trade, banking, and businesses prospered. A good economy meant more money to support learning and the arts and to pay for new churches and other buildings.

Medieval Art and Architecture Europe experienced a building boom in the A.D. 1000s and 1100s. Architecture is one way a society shows what is important to its culture. In the Middle Ages, religion was an important part of life and society. As a result, Church leaders and wealthy merchants and nobles paid to build large new churches called cathedrals. The new cathedrals were built in either the Romanesque (ROH•muh•NEHSK) style or the Gothic style.

Romanesque churches were rectangular buildings with long, rounded roofs called barrel vaults. These roofs needed huge pillars and thick walls to hold them up. Windows let in little light because they were small and set back in the thick walls.

Gothic cathedrals had ribbed vaults and pointed arches instead of rounded barrel vaults. This allowed Gothic churches to be taller than Romanesque churches. Gothic churches also used flying buttresses. These stone supports were built onto the cathedral's outside walls. They made it possible to build churches with thinner walls and large stained glass windows.

Medieval Church Architecture

Early Christian churches (above) were often rectangular with flat roofs, like some Roman buildings. Romanesque churches (top right) had rounded barrel vault ceilings, eliminating the flat roof. Gothic cathedrals, such as St. Etienne in Bourges (right), used flying buttresses on the exterior to hold up the tall ceiling inside. *Who paid for cathedrals to be built?*

▲ This medieval art shows students in a university classroom. *What were some of the subjects studied in medieval universities?*

Stained glass windows were picture Bibles for Christians who could not read. The pieces of stained glass often formed scenes from Jesus' life and teachings. They also let in sunlight, which came to symbolize the divine light of God.

The First Universities

Two of the first European universities were in **Bologna** (buh•LOH•nyuh), Italy, and Paris, France. Masters, or teachers, were also teaching at Oxford, England by 1096. Oxford University was founded in 1231.

Universities were created to educate and train scholars. They were like the guilds that trained craftspeople. In fact, *university* comes from a Latin word for "guild." In medieval universities, students studied grammar, logic, arithmetic, geometry, music, and astronomy. Students did not have books because books were rare before the European printing press was created in the 1400s.

University students studied their subjects for four to six years. Then a committee of teachers gave them an oral exam. If the students passed, they were given their degree.

After obtaining a basic degree, a student could go on to earn a doctor's degree in law, medicine, or **theology** (thee•AH•luh•jee)—the study of religion and God. Earning a doctor's degree could take 10 years or more.

Who Was Thomas Aquinas?

Beginning in the 1100s, a new way of thinking called **scholasticism** (skuh•LAS•tuh•SIH•zuhm) began to change the study of theology. Followers used reason to explore questions of faith. A Dominican friar and priest named **Thomas Aquinas** (TAH•muhs uh•KWY•nuhs) was scholasticism's greatest champion. He is best known for combining Church teachings with the ideas of Aristotle.

Europeans had forgotten about Aristotle after Rome fell and his works had been lost. In the 1100s, however, Muslim and Jewish scholars reintroduced Aristotle to Europe using copies of his books that had been preserved in Muslim libraries. Aristotle's ideas upset many Christian thinkers because he used reason, not faith, to arrive at his conclusions about the meaning of life.

In the 1200s, Thomas Aquinas wrote several works explaining that Aristotle would have agreed with many Christian teachings. About 1267, Aquinas began writing *Summa Theologica,* or a summary of knowledge on theology. In this book, Aquinas asked hard questions such as "Does God exist?"

Aquinas wrote about government as well as theology, with an emphasis on the idea of natural law. People who believe in natural law think that there are some laws that are part of human nature. These laws do not have to be made by governments.

Aquinas claimed that natural law gave people certain rights that the government should not take away. These included the right to live, to learn, to worship, and to reproduce. Aquinas's writings on natural law have influenced governments to the present day. Our belief that people have rights can partly be traced to the ideas of Thomas Aquinas.

Biography

THOMAS AQUINAS
1225–1274

▲ Thomas Aquinas

Thomas Aquinas was born in 1225 in his family's castle between Rome and Naples, Italy. His parents, Countess Theodora and Count Landulf of Aquino, were from noble families. At age five, Aquinas began school at Monte Cassino, a Benedictine monastery where his uncle was the abbot. Monastic schools required students to learn many subjects, including grammar, speech, mathematics, science, and music. When he was older, Aquinas studied at the University of Naples.

Aquinas joined the Dominican friars around 1244, against the wishes of his family. As a new Dominican, he studied in Paris under Albertus Magnus (Albert the Great). Both Aquinas and Albertus greatly admired the ideas of Aristotle.

Aquinas spent the next few decades studying, teaching, and writing. He lived in Paris, Rome, and other cities in France and Italy and taught theology. He wrote about the Bible, groups within the Church, and the ideas of philosophers. *Summa Theologica* best explains how Aquinas combines Aristotle's ideas with those of the Church. He began writing his *Summa Theologica* around 1267 and worked on it until his death.

"The happy man in this life needs friends."
—St. Thomas Aquinas,
Summa Theologiae

In 1274 the pope asked Aquinas to travel to France to attend the Council of Lyons. Even though he was not in good health, he set out for the French city. He became very sick along the way. Aquinas wanted to live out his last days in a monastery, so he was taken to a Cistercian abbey in the town of Fossanova, where he died on March 7, 1274.

Aquinas's ideas were respected during his lifetime, and as time passed they became even more important. His writings influenced governments and the Roman Catholic Church. He was made a saint in 1323.

▲ Monte Cassino monastery

Then and Now

The writings of Thomas Aquinas influenced governments and religions for a long time after his death. Which present-day writers or leaders do you think have ideas that will influence people for centuries to come?

Medieval Literature During the Middle Ages, educated people throughout Europe generally spoke or wrote in Latin. The Church used Latin in its worship and daily affairs. University teachers taught in Latin, and serious authors wrote in that language.

In addition to Latin, each region had its own local language that people used every day. This everyday language is called the **vernacular** (vuhr•NA•kyuh•luhr). The vernacular included early versions of Spanish, French, English, Italian, and German.

During the 1100s, new literature was written in the vernacular. Educated people enjoyed vernacular literature, especially troubadour (TROO•buh•DOHR) poetry. These poems were about love, often the love of a knight for a lady.

Another type of vernacular literature was the heroic epic. In heroic epics, bold knights fight for kings and lords. Women seldom appear in this literature. An early example of a heroic epic is the *Song of Roland*, written in French about 1100.

In the *Song of Roland*, a brave knight named Roland fights for Charlemagne against the Muslims. Roland sounds his horn for Charlemagne to help him, but it is too late:

> The Count Rollanz [Roland], with sorrow and with pangs,
> And with great pain sounded his olifant [horn]:
> Out of his mouth the clear blood leaped and ran,
> About his brain the very temples cracked.
> Loud is its voice, that horn he holds in hand;
> Charlès [Charlemagne] hath heard, where in the pass he stands,
> And Neimès [a commander] hears, and listen all the Franks.
>
> —*Song of Roland*

 **Reading Check** **Explain** What is natural law?

 **History Online**

Study Central™ Need help with the material in this section? Visit jat.glencoe.com

Section 4 Review

Reading Summary
Review the Main Ideas

• In the Middle Ages, new religious orders developed to spread Christianity. Nonbelievers and people of other faiths were mistreated.

• In medieval Europe, a number of universities opened, large Christian churches known as cathedrals were built, and European languages developed.

What Did You Learn?

1. What is theology?

2. What is vernacular language, and what were common vernacular languages in medieval times?

Critical Thinking

3. **Compare and Contrast** Draw a Venn diagram like the one below. Use it to describe the similarities and differences between Cistercians, Franciscans, and Dominicans.

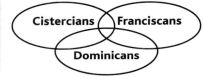
Cistercians Franciscans Dominicans

4. **Summarize** How did the Inquisition treat the people brought before it?

5. **Analyze** How did Christian beliefs result in a resettlement of Jews? Where did many Jews settle in the Middle Ages?

6. **Explain** What were Thomas Aquinas's beliefs related to government?

7. **Persuasive Writing** Write a letter to a medieval university telling them why you would like to become a student there. Be sure to discuss the subjects you would like to study.

Section 5

The Late Middle Ages

Get Ready to Read!

What's the Connection?

In previous sections, you learned about the politics, religion, and culture of much of medieval Europe. In this section, you will find out about the disasters and conflicts of the late Middle Ages.

Focusing on the (Main Ideas)

- A terrible plague, known as the Black Death, swept through Europe in the 1300s, killing millions. *(page 554)*

- Western Europe was devastated by war in the 1300s and 1400s as England and France fought each other, and Spain and Portugal fought against the Muslims. *(page 557)*

Locating Places

Crécy (kray•SEE)
Orléans (AWR•lay•AHN)

Meeting People

Joan of Arc
Isabella of Castile
Ferdinand of Aragon

Building Your Vocabulary

plague (PLAYG)
Reconquista (RAY•kohn•KEES•tuh)

Reading Strategy

Summarizing Information Complete a table like the one below showing the path of the Black Death in Europe and Asia.

Time Period	Affected Areas
1330s	
1340s	
1350s	

NATIONAL GEOGRAPHIC When & Where?

1300

1400

1500

1346 The Black Death arrives in Europe

1429 Joan of Arc inspires the French

1492 The Spanish defeat the Muslims and expel the Jews

- London
- Paris
- Orléans

Granada

SICILY

The Black Death

Main Idea A terrible plague, known as the Black Death, swept through Europe in the 1300s, killing millions.

Reading Focus Have you ever been given a shot to prevent the flu or to protect you from another disease? Read to learn what happened in Europe before modern medicine could control contagious diseases.

The Middle Ages in Europe reached a high point during the 1200s. In the 1300s, however, disaster struck. A terrible **plague** (PLAYG), known as the Black Death, swept across Europe and Asia. A plague is a disease that spreads quickly and kills many people. Most scientists think the Black Death was bubonic plague—a disease caused by a type of bacteria carried by fleas. These fleas infested black rats, and in the Middle Ages, these rats were everywhere.

The Black Death probably began somewhere in the Gobi, a desert in central Asia. It had been around for centuries, but in the 1300s, it began to spread farther and more quickly than ever before. Scientists are still not sure why this happened.

Historians believe the Mongol Empire was partly responsible for the plague spreading so fast. The empire covered all the land from Eastern Europe through central Asia to China. The Mongols opened up trade between China, India, the Middle East, and Europe. They encouraged the use of the Silk Road and other trade routes.

By the early 1300s, more goods were being shipped across central Asia than ever before. This made it possible for the Black Death to spread rapidly, as caravans infested with rats carried it from city to city.

The first outbreak took place in China in 1331. It erupted there again in 1353. The

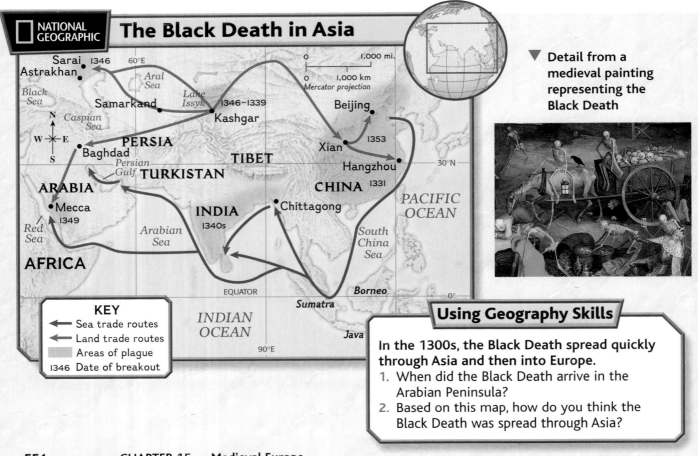

NATIONAL GEOGRAPHIC
The Black Death in Asia

Sarai 1346
Astrakhan
60°E
Black Sea
Aral Sea
Lake Issyk
Samarkand
1346–1339
Kashgar
Beijing
0 1,000 mi.
0 1,000 km
Mercator projection
Caspian Sea
PERSIA
Baghdad
Persian Gulf
TURKISTAN
TIBET
Xian 1353
Hangzhou
30°N
ARABIA
Mecca
1349
Red Sea
INDIA
1340s
Chittagong
CHINA 1331
PACIFIC OCEAN
Arabian Sea
South China Sea
AFRICA
EQUATOR
Sumatra
Borneo
0°
KEY
⬅ Sea trade routes
⬅ Land trade routes
　 Areas of plague
1346 Date of breakout
INDIAN OCEAN
Java
90°E

▼ Detail from a medieval painting representing the Black Death

Using Geography Skills

In the 1300s, the Black Death spread quickly through Asia and then into Europe.
1. When did the Black Death arrive in the Arabian Peninsula?
2. Based on this map, how do you think the Black Death was spread through Asia?

disease killed between 40 and 60 million people, cutting China's population nearly in half. The disease appeared in India in the 1340s and reached Makkah, deep inside Muslim lands, in 1349. In the meantime, it also spread to Europe.

The Black Death appeared in Europe in 1346 at the city of Caffa on the Black Sea. The city had been under attack by Mongols when the plague erupted. The Mongols, with their troops dying, called off the attack. In anger they also threw bodies of infected soldiers into the city.

Caffa was a trade colony controlled by Italian merchants from the city of Genoa. Their ships carried the plague to Sicily in October 1347. From there it spread into Europe. By the end of 1349, it had spread through France and Germany and had arrived in England. By 1351, it had reached Scandinavia, Eastern Europe, and Russia.

As many as 38 million Europeans—nearly one out of every two people—died of the Black Death between 1347 and 1351.

The death of so many people in the 1300s turned Europe's economy upside down. Trade declined and wages rose sharply because workers were few and in demand. At the same time, fewer people meant less demand for food, and food prices fell.

Landlords found they had to pay workers more and charge lower rents. Some peasants bargained with their lords to pay rent instead of owing services. This meant that they were no longer serfs. In this way, the plague, like the Crusades, helped to weaken the feudal system and change European society.

✓ **Reading Check** **Identify** How many Europeans died of the plague between 1347 and 1351?

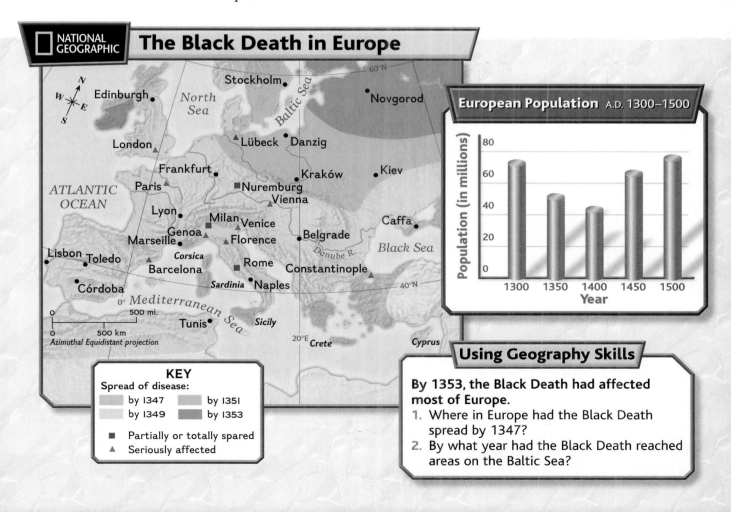

NATIONAL GEOGRAPHIC The Black Death in Europe

European Population A.D. 1300–1500

KEY
Spread of disease:
- by 1347
- by 1351
- by 1349
- by 1353
- ■ Partially or totally spared
- ▲ Seriously affected

Using Geography Skills

By 1353, the Black Death had affected most of Europe.
1. Where in Europe had the Black Death spread by 1347?
2. By what year had the Black Death reached areas on the Baltic Sea?

Biography

JOAN OF ARC

1412–1431

Jeanne d'Arc—better known as Joan of Arc—was born January 6, 1412, in the village of Domremy in eastern France. Joan was the youngest of five children. When she was 13, she began having visions of saints telling her to attend church and to be a good person. As time passed, the voices began telling her to speak with Charles VII about her ability to help France. After three attempts, she was finally allowed to see the leader. Charles spoke with Joan and had her questioned by doctors and priests. All of them believed Joan was a good person and was telling the truth.

Joan was sent with the French army to the city of Orléans, which was surrounded by the English. Everywhere she went, Joan carried a banner with religious pictures on it. Even though she did not have a weapon, she rode at the front of the troops, giving them directions and encouragement. The troops came to believe God was on their side. Inspired by Joan, they fought harder and better than ever before. They defeated the English at Orléans and began driving them out of France.

In 1430 Joan said the saints revealed to her that she would soon be captured. In late May, she was seized by the English and charged with heresy and improper dress—for the soldier's uniform she wore as army commander. Joan was found guilty and told that if she admitted her crimes, she would not be executed. She insisted she had done nothing wrong and was executed on May 30, 1431. Almost two decades later, an investigation into the matter found Joan innocent of all charges. In 1920 she was made a saint by the Roman Catholic Church.

"Courage! Do not fall back."
—Joan of Arc

▲ Joan of Arc on horseback

Then and Now

Joan was tried and found guilty, even though many people felt she was innocent. She was also denied many rights during her trial. What prevents this from happening today in the United States?

A Troubled Continent

Main Idea Western Europe was devastated by war in the 1300s and 1400s as England and France fought each other, and Spain and Portugal fought against the Muslims.

Reading Focus Have you ever had a hero you looked up to? Read to learn what happened when a young peasant girl became a hero to the French people.

The plague was not Europe's only problem in the late Middle Ages. The English and French went to war with each other, while the Spanish and Portuguese fought to drive out the Muslims who had conquered them centuries before.

The Hundred Years' War

In Section 3, you learned that William of Normandy became king of England in 1066, although he still ruled Normandy. French kings wanted to drive the English out of Normandy. English kings claimed a right to the land, and in 1337 the English king Edward III declared himself king of France. This angered the French even more. War began, and it lasted for over 100 years.

The first major battle of the Hundred Years' War took place at **Crécy** (kray•SEE) after Edward invaded France. English archers defeated the French army and forced the French king to give up some of his kingdom.

Under a new king, however, the French slowly won back their land. Then in 1415 Henry V of England went on the attack. England's archers again won the battle and left the English in control of northern France.

Who Was Joan of Arc?

Charles, the prince who ruled southern France, wanted to take back the north. In 1429 a French peasant girl named Joan was brought to him. She told him that her favorite saints had urged her to free France. Joan's honesty persuaded Charles to let her go with a French army to

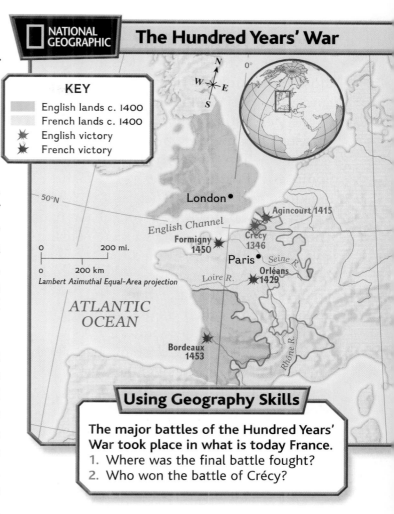

NATIONAL GEOGRAPHIC **The Hundred Years' War**

KEY
- English lands c. 1400
- French lands c. 1400
- ✳ English victory
- ✴ French victory

London

Agincourt 1415

English Channel

Formigny 1450

Crécy 1346

Paris

Seine R.

Orléans 1429

Loire R.

ATLANTIC OCEAN

Bordeaux 1453

Rhone R.

200 mi.

200 km

Lambert Azimuthal Equal-Area projection

Using Geography Skills

The major battles of the Hundred Years' War took place in what is today France.
1. Where was the final battle fought?
2. Who won the battle of Crécy?

Orléans (AWR•lay•AHN). Joan's faith stirred the soldiers, and they took the city.

Shortly after, with Joan at his side, Charles was declared king. A few months later, however, the English captured Joan. They handed her over to the Inquisition, which had her burned at the stake. She later became known as **Joan of Arc.**

The French finally defeated the English in 1453. The king had spent almost all of his money, but the war strengthened French feelings for their country. French kings used that spirit to develop a strong government.

The Hundred Years' War also took a toll on the English and their economy. In addition, a civil war known as the Wars of the Roses, broke out among the nobles over who should be king. The winner, Henry Tudor, became King Henry VII.

Spain and Portugal Fight the Muslims

During the Middle Ages, Muslims ruled most of Spain and Portugal. These two lands make up the Iberian Peninsula. Most of the peninsula's people, however, were Christians. Some were also Jews.

The Muslims developed a rich culture in Spain and Portugal. They built beautiful mosques and palaces, such as the Alhambra in the southern kingdom of Granada. They also founded schools where Muslims, Jews, and Christians studied together. Most Christians, however, opposed Muslim rule. Their struggle to take back the Iberian Peninsula was called the *Reconquista* (RAY•kohn•KEES•tuh), or "reconquest."

By the 1200s, the Christians had set up three kingdoms: Portugal in the west, Castile in the center, and Aragon on the Mediterranean coast. Over the next 200 years, the Muslims slowly lost ground, until all that remained was Granada in the south.

In 1469 Princess **Isabella of Castile** married Prince **Ferdinand of Aragon.** Within 10 years, they became king and queen and joined their lands into one country called Spain. Ferdinand and Isabella wanted all of Spain to be Catholic. They turned first to the Jews. To escape persecution, some Jews became Christians. Ferdinand and Isabella, however, believed many still secretly practiced Judaism. So they set up the Spanish Inquisition.

The Spanish Inquisition tried and tortured thousands of people charged with heresy. In 1492 Ferdinand and Isabella told Jews to convert or leave Spain. Most left the country.

Next the king and queen turned to the Muslims. In 1492 Spain's armies conquered Granada. Ten years later, Muslims had to convert or leave. Most left Spain for North Africa.

✔ **Reading Check** **Cause and Effect** What caused the Hundred Years' War?

Section 5 Review

History Online
Study Central™ Need help with the material in this section? Visit jat.glencoe.com

Reading Summary

Review the Main Ideas

• A plague, known as the Black Death, killed millions of people in Europe and Asia and greatly changed Europe's economy and society.

• Wars between England and France weakened those countries' economies, and Spain became a united Catholic country.

What Did You Learn?

1. How was the Black Death spread?

2. Who was Joan of Arc, and what role did she play in the Hundred Years' War?

Critical Thinking

3. **Understanding Cause and Effect** Draw a diagram like the one below. Fill in some of the effects of the Black Death on Europe.

The Black Death →

4. **Analyze** How did the Hundred Years' War affect the countries involved?

5. **Summarize** Describe the history of Spain and Portugal during the Middle Ages.

6. **Conclude** Do you think the removal of the Jews and Muslims from Spain was a wise policy? Explain your answer.

7. **Reading** **Asking Questions** Write three question that Charles might have asked Joan of Arc to determine if he would support her efforts.

Section 1 The Early Middle Ages

Vocabulary
fjord
missionary
excommunicate
concordat

Focusing on the Main Ideas
- Geography influenced where medieval Europeans settled and what they did. *(page 513)*
- The Franks, Angles, and Saxons of Western Europe built new societies and defended them against Muslims, Magyars, and Vikings. *(page 514)*
- The Catholic Church spread Christianity through Western Europe. *(page 519)*

Section 2 Feudalism

Vocabulary
feudalism
vassal
fief
knight
serf
guild

Focusing on the Main Ideas
- Feudalism developed in Europe in the Middle Ages. It was based on landowning, loyalty, and the power of armored knights on horseback. *(page 523)*
- Knights followed a code of chivalry and lived in castles, while peasants lived in simple houses and worked hard all year long. *(page 526)*
- Increased trade led to the growth of towns and cities and the rise of guilds and city governments. *(page 528)*

Section 3 Kingdoms and Crusades

Vocabulary
grand jury
trial jury
clergy

Focusing on the Main Ideas
- England developed a system in which the king's power was limited by Parliament. *(page 535)*
- French kings called the Capetians conquered lands held by the English in western France and set up France's first parliament. *(page 538)*
- After the Mongols destroyed the Kievan state, the rulers of Moscow built a new Russian state headed by a czar. *(page 539)*
- European crusaders captured Jerusalem but were later driven out by the Muslims. *(page 541)*

Section 4 The Church and Society

Vocabulary
mass
heresy
anti-Semitism
theology
scholasticism
vernacular

Focusing on the Main Ideas
- The Catholic Church played an important role in medieval Europe and used its power to uphold its teachings. *(page 545)*
- Church and government leaders supported learning and the arts in medieval Europe. *(page 549)*

Section 5 The Late Middle Ages

Vocabulary
plague
Reconquista

Focusing on the Main Ideas
- A terrible plague, known as the Black Death, swept through Europe in the 1300s, killing millions. *(page 554)*
- Western Europe was devastated by war in the 1300s and 1400s as England and France fought each other, and Spain and Portugal fought against the Muslims. *(page 557)*

Review Vocabulary

Match the word in the first column with its definition in the second column.

___ 1. fief   **a.** worked their own land and a lord's land

___ 2. serf   **b.** the study of religion and God

___ 3. concordat   **c.** people ordained as priests

___ 4. clergy   **d.** land granted to a vassal

___ 5. heresy   **e.** agreement between the pope and the ruler of a country

___ 6. theology   **f.** a belief different from Church teachings

Review Main Ideas

Section 1 • The Early Middle Ages

7. Which peoples invaded Europe in the Middle Ages?

8. How did the Catholic Church affect medieval Europe?

Section 2 • Feudalism

9. What was the basis for wealth and power in medieval Europe?

10. What was the result of increased trade?

Section 3 • Kingdoms and Crusades

11. What changes in England and France were steps toward representative government?

12. Which groups were at war with each other in the Crusades? For what were they fighting?

Section 4 • The Church and Society

13. How did the Catholic Church use its power to uphold its teachings?

14. Why did learning and the arts flourish in medieval Europe?

Section 5 • The Late Middle Ages

15. What was the Black Death, and how did it change Europe?

16. Which European nations were at war during the 1300s and 1400s?

Critical Thinking

17. **Cause and Effect** What improvements in farming led to an increase in the production of food?

18. **Compare** What did Alfred the Great and William the Conqueror succeed in doing?

Review Reading Skill / Questioning — Just Ask

19. Read the passage from page 525. Write six questions that you might ask about it. Use a different question starter for each question: *who, what, when, where, how,* and *why.*

> During the Middle Ages, Europeans invented new technology that helped increase the amount of crops they could grow. Perhaps the most important was a heavy wheeled plow with an iron blade. It easily turned over Western Europe's dense clay soils.

To review this skill, see pages 510–511.

Geography Skills

Study the map below and answer the following questions.

20. **Place** On which river was the battle of Orléans fought?

21. **Interaction** Which rival do you think had an advantage at the point shown on the map? Consider the battles, amount of land held, natural advantages, and so on.

22. **Location** Why were most battle sites near the English Channel?

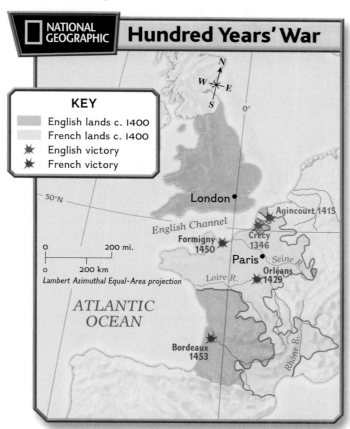

NATIONAL GEOGRAPHIC **Hundred Years' War**

KEY
- English lands c. 1400
- French lands c. 1400
- ✳ English victory
- ✸ French victory

50°N

London

English Channel

Agincourt 1415

Formigny 1450

Crécy 1346

0 — 200 mi.

0 — 200 km

Lambert Azimuthal Equal-Area projection

Paris

Seine R.

Orléans 1429

Loire R.

Rhône R.

ATLANTIC OCEAN

Bordeaux 1453

Read to Write

23. **Script Writing** Suppose you are living in a small medieval town. Suddenly, the people of your town begin dying from the plague. You and your family have to decide whether to stay in the town or leave. Write a dialogue between you, family members, and perhaps some neighbors. The dialogue should give the advantages and disadvantages of both actions and should show the family reaching a decision about what to do.

History Online

Self-Check Quiz To help prepare for the Chapter Test, visit jat.glencoe.com

24. **Using Your FOLDABLES** Discuss as a class why the events of medieval Europe occurred. Then choose one major event from your foldable, and write a paragraph that predicts how history would have been different if that event had not occurred.

Using Technology

25. **Modeling** Do research to find out more about the parts of a manor and its general layout. (For example, you know that the castle of the lord and lady was at the center of the manor.) Then work with your classmates to create a computer drawing or model of a manor.

Linking Past and Present

26. **Comparing** Describe how present-day universities compare to medieval ones, such as those in Bologna, Paris, and Oxford. In your description, explain what it would be like to have to learn without the use of books.

Primary Source Analyze

King Louis IX asked the following of his vassals.

"All vassals of the king are bound to appear before him when he shall summon them, and to serve him at their own expense for forty days and forty nights, with as many knights as each one owes."

—King Louis IX, "Legal Rules for Military Service"

DBQ Document-Based Questions

27. Did knights directly serve the king and appear when he called them?

28. What do you think happened if the king needed the vassals and knights for more than 40 days and nights?

Comparing Medieval Civilizations

Compare civilizations of the Middle Ages by reviewing the information below. Can you see how the peoples of these civilizations had lives that were very much like yours?

Where in the World?

NATIONAL GEOGRAPHIC

● Chapter 12
● Chapter 13
● Chapter 14
● Chapter 15

	China in the Middle Ages — Chapter 12	Medieval Africa — Chapter 13	Medieval Japan — Chapter 14	Medieval Europe — Chapter 15
Where did these civilizations develop?	• Mainland of East Asia	• West Africa; Southern Africa; East Africa	• Islands off coast of East Asia	• Northwestern Europe and Mediterranean area
Who were some important people in these civilizations?	• Taizong, ruled A.D. 627–649 • Empress Wu, ruled A.D. 684–705 • Kublai Khan, ruled A.D. 1271–1294 • Zheng He, A.D. 1371–1433	• Ibn Battuta, A.D. 1307–1377 • Mansa Musa, ruled A.D. 1312–1337 • Sunni Ali, ruled A.D. 1464–1492 • Queen Nzinga, ruled c. A.D. 1623–1663	• Prince Shotoku, A.D. 573–621 • Murasaki Shikibu, c. A.D. 973–1025 • Minamoto Yoritomo, A.D. 1147–1199 • Ashikaga Takauji, A.D. 1305–1358	• Charlemagne, ruled A.D. 768–814 • William the Conqueror, ruled A.D. 1066–1087 • Thomas Aquinas, A.D. 1225–1274 • Joan of Arc, A.D. 1412–1431
Where did most of the people live?	• Farming villages and towns along major rivers	• Farming villages; trading centers, such as Timbuktu and Kilwa	• Fishing and farming villages in coastal plains area	• Farming villages on estates located on plains; trading centers in Italy and Flanders

	China in the Middle Ages Chapter 12	Medieval Africa Chapter 13	Medieval Japan Chapter 14	Medieval Europe Chapter 15
What were these people's beliefs?	• Confucianism, Daoism, Buddhism	• Traditional African religions, Christianity, Islam	• Shintoism, Buddhism	• Roman Catholic with small numbers of Jews and Muslims
What was their government like?	• Emperors ruled with the help of scholar-officials selected by exams	• Ruled by kings, close advisers, and local officials	• Emperors ruled in name but power held by military leaders	• Feudal territories united into kingdoms
What was their language and writing like?	• Chinese: symbols standing for objects are combined to represent ideas	• Many languages and different writing systems, but much knowledge passed on by oral history	• Japanese: Chinese characters standing for ideas as well as symbols representing sounds	• Many languages derived from Latin and Germanic
What contributions did they make?	• Civil service based on merit; invented moveable type, gunpowder, and the compass	• Produced tradition of storytelling, dance, music, and sculpture	• Developed ideas based on harmony with nature; produced martial arts	• Developed universities and representative government
How do these changes affect me? *Can you add any?*	• The Chinese invented fireworks, the compass, and printed books	• Early Africans passed on musical traditions that led to jazz, rap, gospel, reggae	• Japanese warriors developed martial arts, such as judo and karate	• Medieval Europeans passed on Christian ideas and a system of banking

Unit 5

A Changing World

Why It's Important

Each civilization that you will study in this unit made important contributions to history.

- Native Americans built a network of trade routes.
- Renaissance and Reformation Europeans affirmed the importance of the human individual.
- People in early modern Europe and America developed ideas about freedom and democracy.

A.D. 1400	A.D. 1450	A.D. 1500	A.D. 1550

The Americas
Chapter 16

c. A.D. 1400
Aztec Empire reaches its height

Incan gold mask ▶

A.D. 1533
Spanish forces defeat the Inca in Peru

Renaissance and Reformation
Chapter 17

c. A.D. 1440
Johannes Gutenberg uses movable type in printing press

◀ Page from Gutenberg Bible

A.D. 1508
Michelangelo paints Sistine Chapel in Rome

Statue of ▶
David by Michelangelo

A.D. 1555
Peace of Augsburg divides Germany into Catholic and Protestant states

Enlightenment and Revolution
Chapter 18

A.D. 1488
Bartholomeu Dias of Portugal sails around southern tip of Africa

◀ Early compass

A.D. 1518
First enslaved Africans brought to Americas

A.D. 1543
Copernicus presents a new view of the universe

◀ Ferdinand Magellan

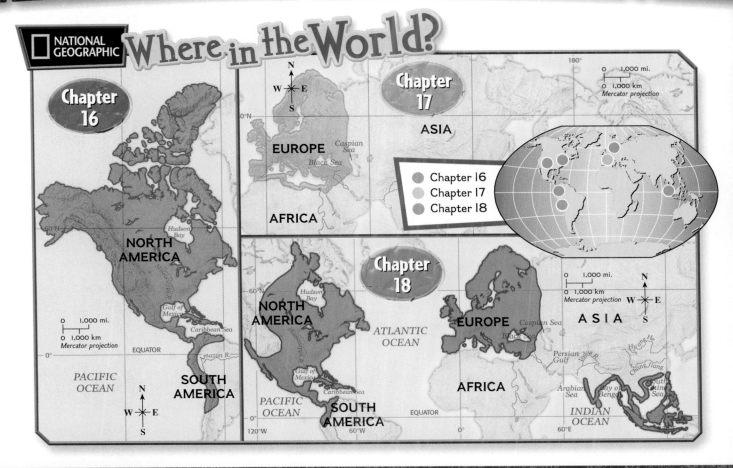

NATIONAL GEOGRAPHIC Where in the World?

Chapter 16

NORTH AMERICA

SOUTH AMERICA

PACIFIC OCEAN

Hudson Bay

Gulf of Mexico

Caribbean Sea

Amazon R.

EQUATOR

0 1,000 mi.
0 1,000 km
Mercator projection

Chapter 17

EUROPE

ASIA

AFRICA

Caspian Sea

Black Sea

0 1,000 mi.
0 1,000 km
Mercator projection

● Chapter 16
● Chapter 17
● Chapter 18

Chapter 18

NORTH AMERICA

SOUTH AMERICA

EUROPE

AFRICA

ASIA

ATLANTIC OCEAN

PACIFIC OCEAN

INDIAN OCEAN

Hudson Bay

Gulf of Mexico

Caribbean Sea

Mississippi R.

Caspian Sea

Black Sea

Persian Gulf

Indus R.

Huang He

Chang Jiang

Arabian Sea

Bay of Bengal

South China Sea

EQUATOR

0 1,000 mi.
0 1,000 km
Mercator projection

120°W

60°W

0°

60°E

180°

A.D. 1600   **A.D. 1650**   **A.D. 1700**   **A.D. 1750**   **A.D. 1800**

● C. A.D. 1570
Eastern Woodland peoples form Iroquois League

● A.D. 1769
Spaniards found mission at San Diego

● A.D. 1839
Scientists uncover Mayan city of Copan

◀ Native American warrior shirt

● A.D. 1598
King Henry IV introduces religious toleration in France

● A.D. 1608
First checks are used to replace cash in the Netherlands

● A.D. 1648
Thirty Years' War ends

◀ Queen Elizabeth I of England

● A.D. 1690
John Locke develops theory of government

● A.D. 1702
First daily newspaper published in London

● A.D. 1776
American Revolution begins

◀ World map, 1630

George Washington ▶

Places to Locate

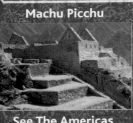

1 Machu Picchu

See The Americas
Chapter 16

2 Tikal

See The Americas
Chapter 16

NORTH
AMERICA

Atlantic
Ocean

Pacific Ocean

SOUTH
AMERICA

People to Meet

Pachacuti

Ruled A.D. 1438–1471
Inca ruler
Chapter 16, page 589

**Leonardo
da Vinci**

A.D. 1452–1519
Italian artist
and scientist
Chapter 17, page 622

**Martin
Luther**

A.D. 1483–1546
German Protestant
leader
Chapter 17, page 638

**Hernán
Cortés**

A.D. 1485–1547
Spanish conqueror
Chapter 16, page 598

ASIA

EUROPE

③

④

⑤

AFRICA

Indian Ocean

③ Sistine Chapel

See Renaissance and Reformation Chapter 17

④ Wittenberg

See Enlightenment and Revolution Chapter 18

⑤ Versailles

See Enlightenment and Revolution Chapter 18

Catherine de' Medici

A.D. 1519–1589
French queen
Chapter 17, page 647

Elizabeth I

Ruled A.D. 1558–1603
English queen
Chapter 18, page 665

John Locke

A.D. 1632–1704
English political thinker
Chapter 18, page 683

Isaac Newton

A.D. 1642–1727
English mathematician
Chapter 18, page 677

The Americas

▼ The ruins of Machu Picchu near Cuzco, Peru

NATIONAL GEOGRAPHIC When & Where?

c. 1500 B.C.　　A.D. 500　　A.D. 1000　　A.D. 1500

c. 1200 B.C.
Olmec build an empire in Mexico

A.D. 500
Mayan cities flourish in Mesoamerica

c. A.D. 1250
Aztec arrive in central Mexico

A.D. 1492
Columbus reaches the Americas

Chapter Preview

During Europe's medieval age, many different peoples were building civilizations in the Americas. Read about how these early Americans grew corn, beans, and other food products that are familiar to you today.

 View the Chapter 16 video in the *World History: Journey Across Time* Video Program.

History Online

Chapter Overview Visit jat.glencoe.com for a preview of Chapter 16.

Section 1 The First Americans

The first people in the Americas arrived thousands of years ago. Farming led to the growth of civilizations in what is now Mexico, Central America, and Peru.

Section 2 Life in the Americas

The Maya, Aztec, and many other Native American cultures developed in North and South America.

Section 3 The Fall of the Aztec and Inca Empires

Spanish explorers and soldiers were drawn to the riches of Native American civilizations. Using horses and guns, they defeated the Aztec and Inca Empires in the early A.D. 1500s.

FOLDABLES™ Study Organizer

Organizing Information *Make this foldable to help you organize information about the history and culture of the Americas.*

Step 1 *Collect two sheets of paper and place them about 1 inch apart.*

Keep the edges straight.

Step 2 *Fold up the bottom edges of the paper to form four tabs.*

This makes all the tabs the same size.

Step 3 *When all the tabs are the same size, crease the paper to hold the tabs in place and staple the sheets together. Label each tab as shown.*

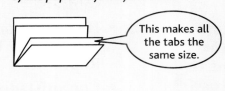

The Americas
The First Americans
Life in the Americas
The Aztec and Inca

Staple along the fold.

Reading and Writing
As you read the chapter, write the main ideas presented in each of the three sections under the tabs of your foldable. Note details that support the main ideas.

Reading Social Studies

Reading Skill

Summarizing

1 Learn It!

Summarizing Information

Summarizing what you have read, either orally or in writing, is a good way to increase your understanding of the text. Read the information about Christopher Columbus on pages 594–595, **Columbus Arrives in America** and **Columbus Returns.** With a partner, summarize the main points. One person should summarize what he or she read while the other listens. Then the second person should resummarize, adding details that the partner may have left out.

When you are finished, look at the following list to see if you included all the important details.

- Columbus first arrived in the Americas in 1492.
- He believed he had reached Asia but actually landed on an island in the Caribbean Sea.
- He took home many exotic treasures to impress the Spanish rulers.
- He returned the next year with soldiers.
- He landed on Hispaniola, which is present-day Haiti and the Dominican Republic.
- Conquistadors conquered the Native Americans.
- Spain gained a foothold in the Americas.

Reading Tip

As you read, place sticky notes at the tops of pages as a reminder to return to sections that you may need to reread.

2 Practice It!

Retelling

Read the description of how **Spain Conquers Mexico** on pages 595–596. Before you begin, read the first paragraph about Cortés aloud:

> The voyages of Christopher Columbus, who sailed to the Americas four times, inspired many poor nobles to go to America to seek their fortunes. Many came from the part of Spain known as the Extremadura. Its poor soil, blistering hot summers, and icy winters held little chance for wealth. One of these nobles was 19-year-old Hernán Cortés.
>
> —*from pages 595–596*

Read to Write

Choose one of the historical figures from Chapter 16 and expand his or her story with details from your own imagination. Add quotes, descriptions, and events that you think might have happened to create a richer, although fictionalized, narrative.

With a partner, summarize the story of Cortés and how he destroyed the Aztec capital. As you are retelling, you may want to refer back to the text, reading aloud words in quotation marks or italics to provide an authentic voice to your story. Listen carefully so that you can add details that your partner may have left out.

3 Apply It!

As you read this chapter, practice summarizing. Stop after each section and write a brief summary of the major points in that section.

The First Americans

Get-Ready to Read!

What's the Connection?

While Western Europe rebuilt itself after the fall of Rome, diverse cultures thrived in the Americas.

Focusing on the Main Ideas

- It is believed that the first people in the Americas came from Asia during the Ice Age. *(page 573)*
- The invention of farming led to the rise of civilizations in the Americas. *(page 574)*
- Early people in the northern part of the Americas built complex cultures based on farming and trade. *(page 578)*

Locating Places

Mesoamerica
(MEH•zoh•uh•MEHR•ih•kuh)
Teotihuacán
(TAY•oh•TEE•wuh•KAHN)
Cuzco (KOOS•koh)
Cahokia (kuh•HOH•kee•uh)

Meeting People

Olmec (OHL•mehk)
Maya (MY•uh)
Toltec (TOHL•TEHK)
Moche (MOH•cheh)
Inca (IHNG•kuh)
Hohokam (HOH•hoh•KAHM)
Anasazi (AH•nuh•SAH•zee)

Building Your Vocabulary

glacier (GLAY•shuhr)
monopoly (muh•NAH•puh•lee)

Reading Strategy

Summarizing Information Create a chart to show the characteristics of the Olmec and Moche.

	Location	Dates	Lifestyle
Olmec			
Moche			

NATIONAL GEOGRAPHIC When & Where?

2000 B.C.	500 B.C.	A.D. 1000

c. 1200 B.C.
Olmec build an empire in Mexico

c. A.D. 500
Mayan cities flourish in Mesoamerica

A.D. 1100
Inca found city of Cuzco

Cahokia
Teotihuacán
Cuzco

Pathway to the Americas

Main Idea It is believed that the first people in the Americas came from Asia during the Ice Age.

Reading Focus When and how did the first people travel to the Americas? Nobody knows for sure. The story of their arrival remains one of history's mysteries.

We know people came to America a long time ago, but how did they get here? Today, America is not connected by land to the rest of the world, but in the past it was. Scientists have studied the earth's geography during the Ice Age—a period when temperatures dropped sharply. At that time, much of the earth's water froze into huge sheets of ice, or **glaciers** (GLAY•shuhrz).

As the ice froze and the seas fell, an area of dry land was exposed between Asia and Alaska. Scientists call this land bridge Beringia (buh•RIHN•jee•uh), after Vitus Bering, a famous European explorer. They think that people in Asia followed the animals they were hunting across this land bridge into the Americas. By testing the age of bones and tools at ancient campsites, scientists estimate that the first people arrived between 15,000 to 40,000 years ago.

When the Ice Age ended about 10,000 years ago, the glaciers melted and released water back into the seas. The land bridge to America disappeared beneath the waves.

Hunting and Gathering Hunters in the Americas were constantly on the move in search of food. They fished and gathered nuts, fruits, or roots. They also hunted massive prey, such as the woolly mammoth, antelope, caribou, and bison.

It took several hunters to kill a woolly mammoth, which could weigh as much as 9 tons. These big animals provided meat, hides for clothing, and bones for tools.

As the Ice Age ended, some animals became extinct, or disappeared from the earth. The warm weather, however, opened new opportunities to early Americans.

✓ **Reading Check** **Explain** Why is there no longer a land bridge between Asia and America?

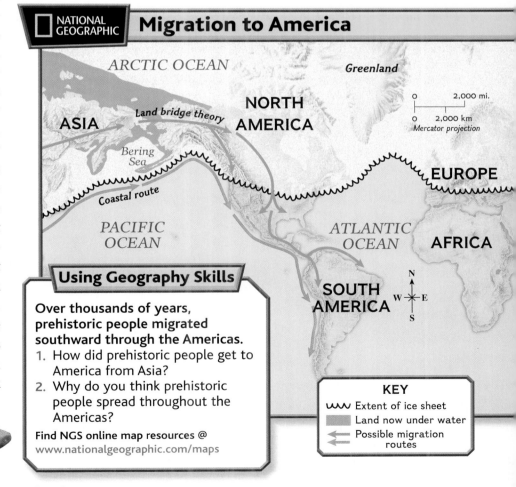

NATIONAL GEOGRAPHIC

Migration to America

ARCTIC OCEAN — Greenland

NORTH AMERICA

ASIA — Land bridge theory

Bering Sea

Coastal route

PACIFIC OCEAN

EUROPE

ATLANTIC OCEAN

AFRICA

SOUTH AMERICA

0 — 2,000 mi.
0 — 2,000 km
Mercator projection

Using Geography Skills

Over thousands of years, prehistoric people migrated southward through the Americas.

1. How did prehistoric people get to America from Asia?
2. Why do you think prehistoric people spread throughout the Americas?

Find NGS online map resources @ www.nationalgeographic.com/maps

KEY
⌇⌇⌇ Extent of ice sheet
▬ Land now under water
← Possible migration routes

◀ Stone arrowhead

CHAPTER 16 The Americas

First American Civilizations

Main Idea The invention of farming led to the rise of civilizations in the Americas.

Reading Focus What would our lives be like if people had never learned to farm? Read to learn how farming made civilization possible in Mexico, Central America, and South America.

The first Americans were hunter-gatherers, but as the Ice Age ended and the climate warmed, people in America made an amazing discovery. They learned that seeds could be planted and they would grow into crops that people could eat.

Farming began in **Mesoamerica** (MEH•zoh•uh•MEHR•ih•kuh) 9,000 to 10,000 years ago. *Meso* comes from the Greek word for "middle." This region includes lands stretching from the Valley of Mexico to Costa Rica in Central America.

The region's geography was ideal for farming. Much of the area had a rich, volcanic soil and a mild climate. Rains fell in the spring, helping seeds to sprout. They decreased in the summer, allowing crops to ripen for harvest. Then, in the autumn, the rains returned, soaking the soil for the next year's crop.

The first crops grown in the Americas included pumpkins, peppers, squash, gourds, and beans. It took longer to develop corn, which grew as a wild grass. Early plants produced a single, one-inch cob. After hundreds of years, the early Americans finally learned how to cross corn

Hunting the Woolly Mammoth

Working in groups, hunters could bring down large prey, such as a woolly mammoth. *Why do you think early hunters preferred to hunt large animals such as mammoths instead of smaller animals?*

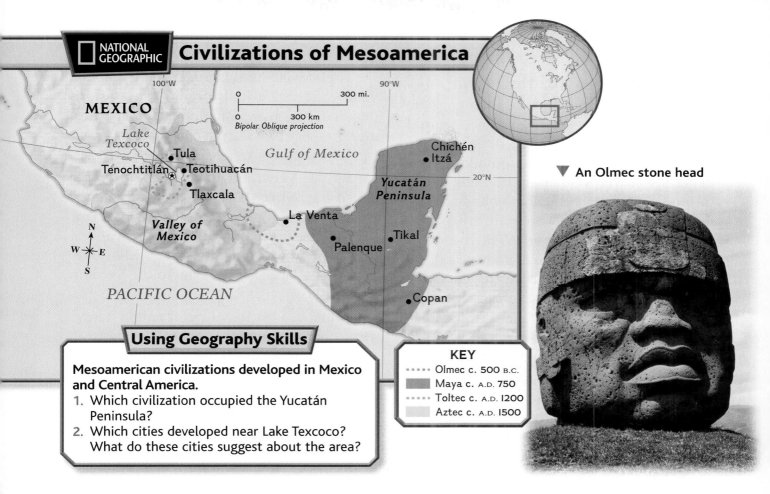

Civilizations of Mesoamerica

MEXICO

Lake Texcoco
Tula
Ténochtitlán ● Teotihuacán
Tlaxcala

100°W

O ____ 300 mi.
O ____ 300 km
Bipolar Oblique projection

Gulf of Mexico

90°W

Chichén Itzá

Yucatán Peninsula

20°N

La Venta
Palenque ● Tikal

Valley of Mexico

N
W ● E
S

PACIFIC OCEAN

● Copan

▼ **An Olmec stone head**

Using Geography Skills

Mesoamerican civilizations developed in Mexico and Central America.
1. Which civilization occupied the Yucatán Peninsula?
2. Which cities developed near Lake Texcoco? What do these cities suggest about the area?

KEY
····· Olmec c. 500 B.C.
▓ Maya c. A.D. 750
····· Toltec c. A.D. 1200
░ Aztec c. A.D. 1500

with other grasses to get bigger cobs and more cobs per plant. With this discovery, corn, also known as maize, became the most important food in the Americas.

Mesoamerican Civilizations Growing corn and other crops allowed the Mesoamericans to stop wandering in search of food. As a result, they formed more complex societies. Starting around 1500 B.C., the first of several ancient civilizations appeared.

Near present-day Vera Cruz, Mexico, a people called the **Olmec** (OHL•mehk) built a far-reaching trading empire. It started around 1200 B.C. and lasted about 800 years.

The Olmec enjoyed rich farming resources, but they lacked other raw materials. They traded salt and beans with inland peoples to get jade for jewelry and obsidian, or volcanic glass, to make sharp-edged knives. They used other trade goods, such as hematite, a shiny volcanic stone, to

make polished mirrors and basalt for carving gigantic stone heads.

The Olmec used the region's many rivers as highways for trade, but eventually, the inland peoples seized control of the trade. One of these groups built the first planned city in the Americas. It became known as **Teotihuacán** (TAY•oh•TEE•wuh•KAHN), or "Place of the Gods." The city reached its height around A.D. 400. It had a population of between 120,000 to 200,000 people.

As Teotihuacán's power spread, a people called the **Maya** (MY•uh) built another civilization in the steamy rain forests of the Yucatán Peninsula (YOO•kuh•TAN). They, too, traded throughout Mesoamerica. The Maya used their central location to reach into what is now southern Mexico and Central America. Mayan traders in sea-going canoes paddled along the coast, perhaps reaching as far as the present-day United States.

What Happened to the Maya? Teotihuacán and Mayan cities hit their peaks in the A.D. 400s and A.D. 500s. Then, around A.D. 600, Teotihuacán started to decline. No one is sure why this happened. Some experts say overpopulation drained the city of food and resources. Others blame a long drought, or period without rain. Still others say that the poor people rebelled against their rich rulers. Whatever the reason, by A.D. 750, the city had been destroyed.

The Mayan civilization lasted about 200 years longer. But it also came to a mysterious end. The Maya abandoned their cities, and by the A.D. 900s, the cities lay deserted, hidden in a thick tangle of vines.

As the Maya left their cities, a people called the **Toltec** (TOHL•TEHK) seized what is now northern Mexico. These warrior nomads built the city of Tula northwest of present-day Mexico City. From Tula, they conquered lands all the way to the Yucatán Peninsula.

Toltec rulers tightly controlled trade. They held a **monopoly** (muh•NAH•puh•lee), or sole right, to the trade in obsidian. As a result, the Toltec kept other people from making weapons to challenge them.

◀ Figure of Mayan leader

▼ This pyramid was in the Mayan city of Tikal, which was located in present-day Guatemala. *What caused the downfall of the Mayan civilization?*

Moche pottery ▶
decorated with
the image of
a face

◀ Moche pottery
in the shape of
a llama

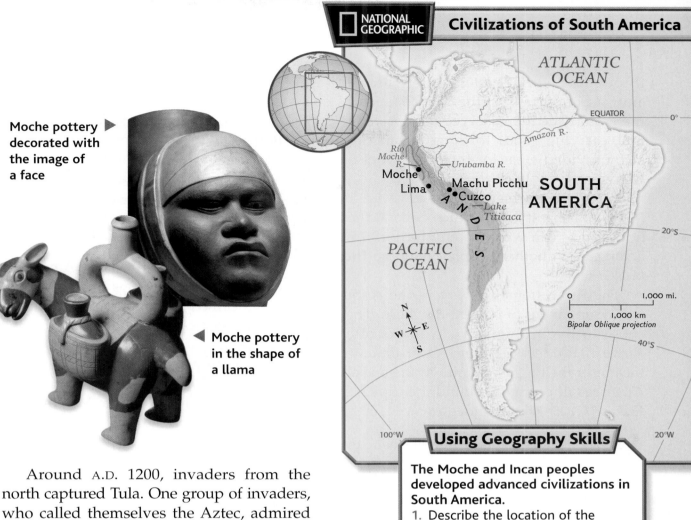

ATLANTIC OCEAN

EQUATOR

Amazon R.

Río Moche R.
Moche•
Urubamba R.
Lima•
Machu Picchu•
•Cuzco
Lake Titicaca

SOUTH AMERICA

PACIFIC OCEAN

A N D E S

0   1,000 mi.
0   1,000 km
Bipolar Oblique projection

100°W   20°W

20°S

40°S

N W E S

Using Geography Skills

The Moche and Incan peoples developed advanced civilizations in South America.
1. Describe the location of the Moche civilization.
2. Estimate in miles the length of the Inca Empire.

Around A.D. 1200, invaders from the north captured Tula. One group of invaders, who called themselves the Aztec, admired the Toltec and copied their ways. Aztec warriors then took control of the region's trade and built a huge empire. When Europeans arrived in the A.D. 1500s, the Aztec ruled about five million people.

The Moche and Inca South of Mesoamerica, other civilizations developed along the west coast of South America. The **Moche** (MOH•cheh) people were located in the dry coastal desert of what is now Peru.

The Moche ruled from about A.D. 100 to A.D. 700. They dug canals that carried water from rivers in the Andes mountain ranges to their desert homeland. Because of this irrigation, the desert bloomed with crops.

The Moche suffered no shortage of food. They ate corn, squash, beans, and peanuts. They also hunted llamas and guinea pigs and fished in the nearby Pacific Ocean.

This wealth of food freed the Moche to do other things. Moche engineers designed huge pyramids, such as the Pyramid of the Sun. Moche traders exchanged goods with people as far away as the rain forests of the Amazon River valley. These goods included pottery, cloth, and jewelry.

The Moche did not have a written language. Instead, their culture's story is told

History Online

Web Activity Visit jat.glencoe.com and click on *Chapter 16—Student Web Activity* to learn more about civilizations in the Americas.

through artwork. Pottery often showed animals important to the Moche, such as the llama. The llama served as a pack animal, carrying goods for long distances. It also provided meat for food and wool for weaving.

For all their achievements, however, the Moche never expanded much beyond their homeland. The work of empire building belonged to another people called the **Inca** (IHNG•kuh).

The Incan homeland lay in the Andes mountain ranges of present-day Peru. They chose to live in high river valleys, often above 10,000 feet (3,048 m). Over time, the Inca built the biggest empire in the ancient Americas. It centered around the capital of **Cuzco** (KOOS•koh), founded in A.D. 1100.

✓ **Reading Check** **Explain** How did the Toltec keep other people from challenging them?

Civilizations in North America

Main Idea Early people in the northern part of the Americas built complex cultures based on farming and trade.

Reading Focus Would you be surprised to learn that early North Americans built large cities? Read to learn about the complex civilizations that developed in the American Southwest, then in the Mississippi River valley.

North of Mesoamerica, Native Americans developed their own ways of living. Still, they had learned something important from their Mesoamerican neighbors. They learned how to farm.

Farming in what would someday be the United States began in the American Southwest. It also spread from Mesoamerica along the coast and up the Mississippi, Missouri, and Ohio Rivers. As farming developed, so did new civilizations.

NATIONAL GEOGRAPHIC **The Way It Was**

Focus on Everyday Life

Anasazi Cliff Dwellings From far away they look like sand castles tightly stacked into the side of a canyon wall. Up close they are life-sized, ancient cliff homes. The two cowboys who discovered them in A.D. 1888 called them the "magnificent city." They found them while crossing a snowy flat-topped mountain in southwestern Colorado. The men had stumbled upon the homes of the Anasazi—an ancient people who once lived in the Southwest.

The Anasazi built nearly 600 cliff dwellings in the area now protected within Mesa Verde National Park. They began building villages under overhanging

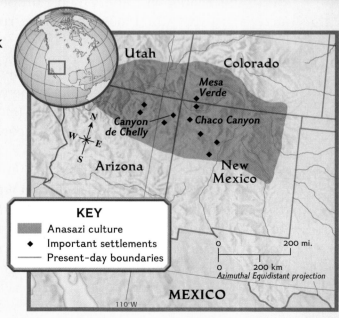

KEY
▨ Anasazi culture
◆ Important settlements
— Present-day boundaries

0   200 mi.
0   200 km
Azimuthal Equidistant projection

The Hohokam and Anasazi News of farming traveled north along with Mesoamerican traders. But it took a long time for nomads in the scorching deserts of the Southwest to try farming.

Finally, around A.D. 300, a people called the **Hohokam** (HOH•hoh•KAHM) planted gardens on lands between the Salt and Gila Rivers. They dug more than 500 miles (805 km) of canals to carry river waters to their fields. They grew corn, cotton, beans, and squash. They also made pottery, turquoise pendants, and the world's first etchings by using cactus juice to eat through the surface of shells.

The Hohokam thrived for about 1,000 years. In the mid-A.D. 1300s, they mysteriously fled. Perhaps a long drought drove them away, or floods from heavy rains destroyed their canals. No one is sure.

Around A.D. 600, as the Hohokam planted fields near rivers, the **Anasazi** (AH•nuh•SAH•zee) moved into the region's canyons and cliffs. They also took up farming. However, they did not rely only on rivers for irrigation. They collected water that ran off cliffs during heavy rains and channeled it to their fields.

Anasazi culture reached its height at Chaco Canyon, an area in present-day New Mexico. The people there controlled the trade in turquoise. They used it like money, to buy goods from many different regions including Mesoamerica.

The Anasazi lived in huge apartment-like houses carved into cliffs. The cliff houses had hundreds of rooms and held thousands of people. Spanish explorers later called these buildings *pueblos*—the Spanish word for "village." The Anasazi

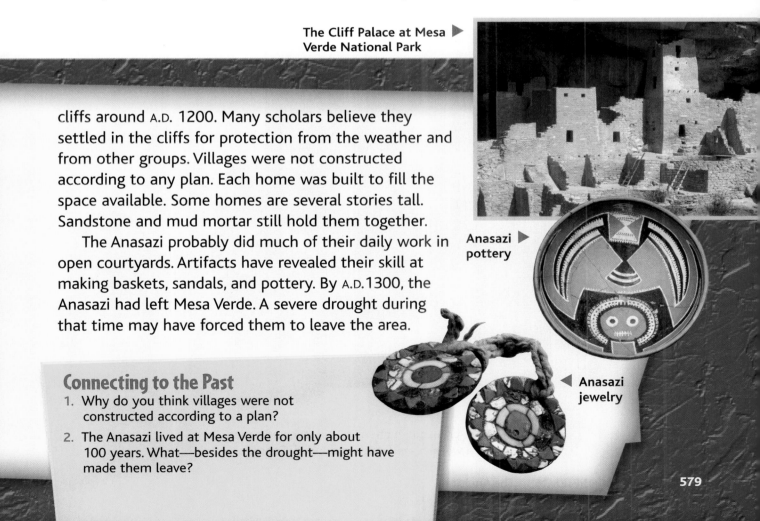

The Cliff Palace at Mesa ▶ Verde National Park

cliffs around A.D. 1200. Many scholars believe they settled in the cliffs for protection from the weather and from other groups. Villages were not constructed according to any plan. Each home was built to fill the space available. Some homes are several stories tall. Sandstone and mud mortar still hold them together.

The Anasazi probably did much of their daily work in open courtyards. Artifacts have revealed their skill at making baskets, sandals, and pottery. By A.D. 1300, the Anasazi had left Mesa Verde. A severe drought during that time may have forced them to leave the area.

Anasazi ▶ pottery

◀ Anasazi jewelry

Connecting to the Past

1. Why do you think villages were not constructed according to a plan?

2. The Anasazi lived at Mesa Verde for only about 100 years. What—besides the drought—might have made them leave?

prospered until a 50-year drought occurred in the early A.D. 1000s. Like the Hohokam, they also drifted away.

Who Were the Mound Builders? Far to the east, across the Mississippi River, another civilization was taking shape. It started around 1000 B.C. and lasted until about A.D. 400. Its founders built huge mounds made of earth, some in the shape of animals. Such earthworks gave these people their name—"Mound Builders."

Two groups formed the mound-building culture—first the Adena, then the Hopewell. Together they settled on lands stretching from the Great Lakes to the Gulf of Mexico.

Although the Mound Builders lived mostly as hunters and gatherers, they experimented with farming. Scientists think they tamed many wild plants, including sunflowers, gourds, and barley. It is likely that women planted the first seeds. Women probably knew the most about plants because they gathered wild foods while the men hunted.

Corn was first brought to the region around A.D. 100, probably carried there by traders. These traders traveled near and far to find raw materials for weapons, jewelry, and fine carvings. Many of these objects were placed in huge burial mounds to honor the dead.

The Mississippians The mound-building culture changed when the Hopewell mysteriously declined and a new people known as the Mississippians emerged. The Mississippians were named for their location in the Mississippi River valley. Their lands reached from present-day Ohio, Indiana, and Illinois, south to the Gulf of Mexico.

◄ **The Great Serpent Mound in southern Ohio is an example of the earthen mounds built by the Adena culture.** *Besides the Adena, what other group made up the mound-building culture?*

**These two-foot-high marble statues of a man ►
and a woman are from a mound in Georgia.**

A Cahokia mound in Illinois ▶

The Mississippians found that plants grew well in the rich floodplains along the river. They harvested enough crops to become full-time farmers. The most common crops included corn, squash, and beans.

As in Mesoamerica, large-scale farming led to the rise of cities. Some contained 10,000 or more people. The largest city, **Cahokia** (kuh•HOH•kee•uh), may have had 30,000 people. The remains of this city can still be seen in southwestern Illinois.

The Mississippians built a different kind of mound. Their mounds were pyramid shaped but with flat tops. The base of the biggest one covered 16 acres (6.5 ha), more than the base of the Great Pyramid of Egypt.

The finished mound, known today as Monks Mound, rose more than 100 feet (30 m) high. From the mound's summit, rulers gazed down at dozens of smaller mounds. The flat tops of the mounds held temples, homes for the rich, and burial places.

In the early A.D. 1300s, the Mississippian civilization collapsed, and the cities were abandoned. Perhaps other Native Americans attacked them, or the city may have become too big to feed itself.

✓ **Reading Check** **Identify** How was turquoise used by the Anasazi of Chaco Canyon?

Section 1 Review

History Online

Study Central™ Need help with the material in this section? Visit jat.glencoe.com

Reading Summary
Review the Main Ideas

- The first Americans were most likely hunter-gatherers who came from Asia across a land bridge.

- A number of civilizations developed in the Americas, including the Olmec, Maya, and Toltec in Central America and Mexico, and the Moche and Inca in South America. All were dependent on farming.

- In North America, farming civilizations arose in the Southwest and then in the Ohio and Mississippi River valleys.

What Did You Learn?

1. Why was Mesoamerica's geography ideal for farming?

2. How did the first Americans develop corn?

Critical Thinking

3. **Summarizing Information** Draw a chart like the one below. Add details about the early peoples of North America.

Native Americans
Southwest
East/Mississippi River Valley

4. **Summarize** How and when did the first people come to the Americas, and how did they live once they were here?

5. **Geography** How did geography shape the development of the Anasazi civilization?

6. **Expository Writing** Write a short essay comparing the civilizations that developed in Mesoamerica to those that developed in South America.

7. **Reading** **Summarizing Information** Write a paragraph that summarizes how farming led to the development of civilizations.

Section 2

Life in the Americas

Get Ready to Read!

What's the Connection?
In Section 1, you read about the rise of the first civilizations in the Americas. The first Americans had to use whatever natural resources the land had to offer. As a result, they developed many different cultures suited to where they lived.

Focusing on the Main Ideas
- The Maya adjusted to life in the tropical rain forest and built a culture based on their religious beliefs. *(page 583)*

- The Aztec moved into the Valley of Mexico, where they created an empire based on conquest and war. *(page 585)*

- To unite their huge empire, Incan rulers set up a highly organized government and society. *(page 588)*

- The geography in lands north of present-day Mexico shaped the developement of many different Native American cultures. *(page 590)*

Locating Places
Petén (peh•TEHN)
Tenochtitlán
   (tay•NAWCH•teet•LAHN)

Meeting People
Pachacuti (PAH•chah•KOO•tee)
Iroquois (IHR•uh•KWOY)

Building Your Vocabulary
quipu (KEE•poo)
igloo
adobe (uh•DOH•bee)
confederation
   (kuhn•FEH•duh•RAY•shuhn)

Reading Strategy
Organizing Information Use a pyramid to show the Inca's social classes.

NATIONAL GEOGRAPHIC When & Where?

| A.D. 1300 | A.D. 1400 | A.D. 1500 |

c. A.D. 1250 Aztec arrive in central Mexico

A.D. 1325 Aztec build Tenochtitlán

c. A.D. 1438 Pachacuti starts to build Inca Empire

Tenochtitlán•
Cuzco•

The Mayan People

Main Idea The Maya adjusted to life in the tropical rain forest and built a culture based on their religious beliefs.

Reading Focus What would it be like to live in a jungle? What resources would be easy to find? Read to learn how the Maya adapted to life in the jungles of Mesoamerica.

In A.D. 1839 an American lawyer named John Lloyd Stevens and an English artist named Frederick Catherwood slashed their way into the tangled Yucatán rain forest. There they made an amazing discovery. They found the vine-covered ruins of an ancient city.

Stevens and Catherwood soon learned that the people who had built the city were called the Maya, and that they were the ancestors of the millions of Maya who still live in present-day Mexico, Guatemala, Honduras, El Salvador, and Belize.

Mayan City-States At first glance, it looked like the Maya had settled in one of the worst spots on Earth. They picked the **Petén** (peh•TEHN), the Mayan word for "flat region." Located in present-day Guatemala, the Petén's dense forests nearly blocked out the sun. Stinging insects filled the air. Poisonous snakes slithered on the ground, and monkeys and parrots screeched in the treetops. Even so, the ancient Maya thrived.

The Maya saw what others missed. Swamps and sinkholes gave them a year-round source of water. The sinkholes—areas where the earth has collapsed—connected the Maya with a huge system of underground rivers and streams. They served as Mayan wells.

Even with a ready water supply, only an organized culture could have succeeded in building cities and fields in the Petén. The effort required cooperation among many people, which could only be accomplished by having an organized government.

▲ This Mayan wall painting shows musicians celebrating a royal birth.
Where did the Maya first settle?

Sports & Contests

Mayan Ball Game Mayan cities had many ball courts. In a Mayan ball game, teams of two or three players tried to drive a hard rubber ball through a decorated stone ring. Players wore helmets, gloves, and knee and hip guards made of animal hide to protect themselves against the hard rubber balls. They were not allowed to use their hands or feet to throw or bat the ball. They had to use their hips to drive the ball through the stone rings.

Because the stone rings were placed 27 feet (8 m) above the ground on a large rectangular field, players had to have incredible skill to score a goal. Making a goal was so rare that when a player scored, crowds rewarded the hero with clothing and jewelry.

Scholars think that a Mayan ball game was more than a sport or contest. It had a religious and symbolic meaning— as well as deadly results. The losing team was sacrificed to the gods in a ceremony after the game.

▲ Mayan ballplayer

Connecting to the Past

1. How did a player score in a Mayan ball game?
2. Why was losing especially painful for a team?

The Maya set up city-states. Within each city-state, rulers supplied the leadership—and military force—for great building projects. Leadership passed from one king to the next, and the city-states often fought with each other.

Life in the Mayan Cities The rulers of Mayan city-states said they were descended from the sun. They claimed the right to rule as god-kings and expected every person to serve them. Service included building huge monuments to honor them.

As god-kings, Mayan rulers taught their subjects how to please the gods. One way was human sacrifice. The Maya believed that the gods gave their life-giving fluid, rain, to keep humans strong. So humans kept the gods strong by giving their own life-giving fluid, blood.

When the Maya marched into battle, they wanted captives more than they wanted land. During times of drought, Mayan priests offered the captives to Chac, the god of rain and sunlight. The Maya believed Chac lived in the waters below the sinkholes. Captives were often thrown into these watery pits to earn the god's favor.

The Maya believed that the gods controlled everything that happened on Earth. As a result, religion was at the core of Mayan life. A huge pyramid with a temple at the top towered over every city. Priests, who claimed to know what the gods wanted, set up a strict class system in which everyone had a place.

Royal Mayan women often married into royal families in distant Mayan city-states. This practice strengthened trade. It also helped form alliances—political agreements between people or states to work together.

▲ Statue of a Mayan god

Women played a large role in the Mayan city-states. In one Mayan carving, a woman wears a war headdress and rides atop a platform carried by soldiers. In the city-state of Calakmul, at least two women served as all-powerful queens. One of them may have helped to found the city.

Mayan Science and Writing Both queens and kings turned to Mayan priests for advice. The priests thought gods revealed their plans through movements of the sun, moon, and stars, so they studied the heavens closely.

The Maya also needed to know when to plant their crops. By watching the sky, the priests learned about astronomy. They developed a 365-day calendar to keep track of heavenly movements. They used it to predict eclipses and to schedule religious festivals, plantings, and harvests. To chart the passage of time, the Maya developed a system of mathematics. They invented a method of counting based on 20.

The Maya also invented a written language to record numbers and dates. Like the Egyptians, the Maya used a system of hieroglyphics. Symbols represented sounds, words, or ideas. Only nobles could read them, however. After the collapse of the Mayan civilization, nobody could read them at all. Only in recent times have scholars begun to unlock the stories told by the hieroglyphics.

Reading Check **Identify** What was the main advantage of living in a tropical rain forest?

The Aztec

Main Idea The Aztec moved into the Valley of Mexico, where they created an empire based on conquest and war.

Reading Focus Why do you think some countries try to conquer other countries? Read to learn why the Aztec people conquered their neighbors and built an empire.

The warlike Aztec nomads who arrived in the Valley of Mexico about A.D. 1250 were anything but welcome. One king was sure he knew a way to get rid of them. He granted the Aztec a patch of snake-filled land. He expected the deadly serpents to destroy them. Instead, the Aztec feasted on roasted snakes and eventually built their own kingdom.

The Aztec Government The Aztec clearly knew how to survive. They had wandered for hundreds of years in search of a home that

An Aztec Warrior

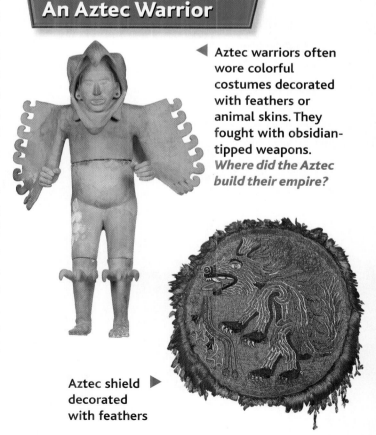

◀ Aztec warriors often wore colorful costumes decorated with feathers or animal skins. They fought with obsidian-tipped weapons. *Where did the Aztec build their empire?*

Aztec shield ▶ decorated with feathers

585

they believed their sun god—the feathered serpent Quetzalcoatl (KWEHT•suhl•kuh•WAH•tuhl)—had promised them. According to legend, the Aztec would know they had found this place when an eagle "screams and spreads its wings, and eats . . . the serpent."

According to Aztec legend, they found their homeland after they sacrificed a local princess to one of their gods. The princess's father vowed to wipe out the Aztec, who only numbered several hundred. The Aztec went on the run. In A.D. 1325, they took shelter on a soggy, swampy island in Lake Texcoco (tehs•KOH•koh). There an eagle greeted them from its perch on a prickly pear cactus. It tore apart a snake dangling from its beak. Then it spread its wings and screamed in triumph. Filled with wonder at this sight, the Aztec believed that they had reached the end of their journey.

Priests, speaking for the gods, told the Aztec what to do next: build a great city. Workers toiled day and night. They dug soil from the lake bottom to build bridges to the mainland. They built floating gardens, piling soil on rafts anchored to the lake bottom.

The Aztec called their new city **Tenochtitlán** (tay•NAWCH•teet•LAHN), which means "place of the prickly pear cactus." As the city rose from the marshes, the Aztec dreamed of conquest and wealth. They wanted to collect tribute, or payment for protection, from conquered peoples.

To fulfill their goal, the Aztec turned to strong kings who claimed descent from the gods. A council of warriors, priests, and nobles picked each king from the royal family. Council members usually chose the last king's son, but not always. They looked for a king who would bring glory to the Aztec. They expected a king to prove himself by leading troops into battle.

Tenochtitlán

At the center of Tenochtitlán was a walled ceremonial area. It contained temples, schools and the priests' houses. *What ceremonial act took place at the top of the Great Temple?*

The founding of ▶ Tenochtitlán

The Great Temple
Atop the Great Temple were two shrines dedicated to the rain god Tlaloc and the sun and war god Huitzilopochtli.

Round Temple
The round temple was dedicated to the Aztec god Quetzalcoatl.

Ball Court
Aztecs played a ritual ball game on courts that were often richly decorated.

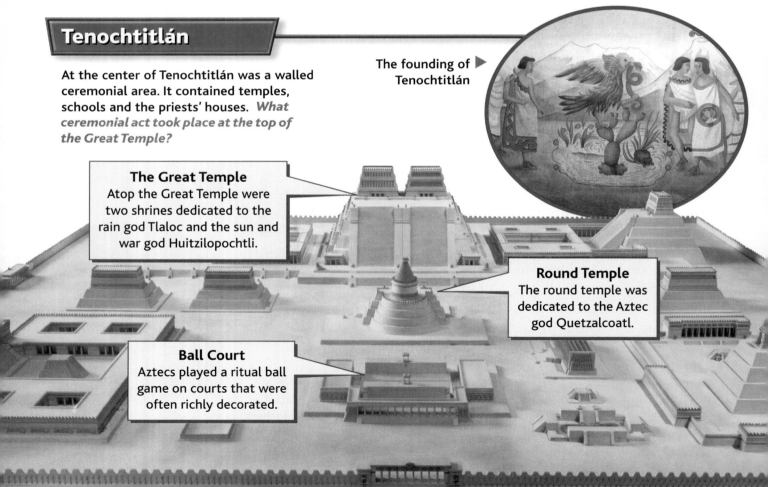

Aztec Daily Life

Aztec homes were simple and built for usefulness rather than beauty. *How do you think the Aztec used each of the household items shown here?*

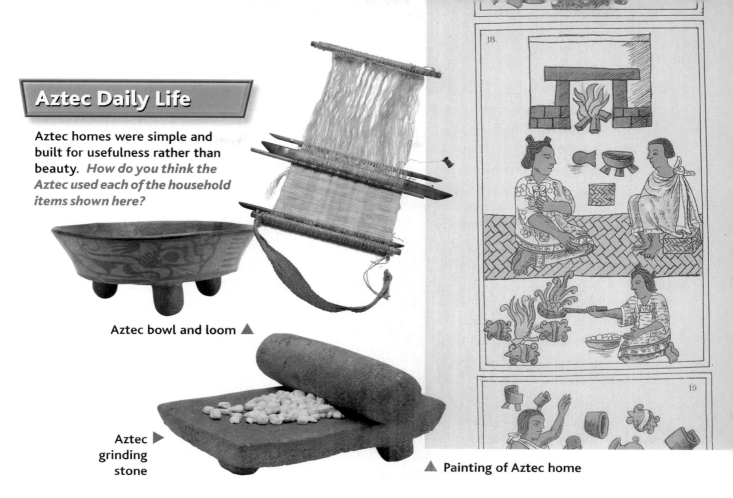

Aztec bowl and loom ▲

Aztec ▶ grinding stone

▲ Painting of Aztec home

Life in the Aztec Empire The king, or emperor, was at the top of Aztec society. The rest of the population fell into four classes: nobles, commoners, unskilled laborers, and enslaved people. Commoners formed the largest group, working as farmers, artisans, or traders. They could join the noble class by performing one act of bravery in war. They, or their children if the soldier died, received land and the rank of noble.

In serving their gods, the Aztec saw death as honorable. Those worthy of an afterlife included soldiers who died in battle, captives who gave their lives in sacrifice, and women who died in childbirth. Others went to the "Land of the Dead," the lowest level in the underworld.

From an early age, children learned about the glories of war and their duties as an Aztec. When a baby boy came into the world, the midwife, or woman who helped with the birth, cried: "You must understand that your home is not here where you have been born, for you are a warrior!"

A baby girl heard different words. As she drew her first breath, the midwife declared: "As the heart stays in the body, so you must stay in the house." Although women stayed at home, those who gave birth were honored as heroes by Aztec society.

Nearly everything the Aztec did grew out of a promise. Speaking through priests, the god Huitzilopochtli (wee•tsee•loh•POHKT•lee) vowed: "We shall conquer all the people in the universe."

This promise inspired the Aztec to honor the god with a huge pyramid in the center of Tenochtitlán. Known as the Great Temple, it rose 135 feet (41 m) high and had more than 100 steps. Thousands of victims were taken to the top, where they were sacrificed to the gods.

Reading Check **Describe** How could commoners move into the noble class?

Life in the Inca Empire

Main Idea To unite their huge empire, Incan rulers set up a highly organized government and society.

Reading Focus Have you ever tried to organize a large number of people? It is not easy to get everyone to work together. Read how the Inca organized their society and developed ways to hold their empire together.

The ancient Inca blamed earthquakes on the god Pachacamac, "Lord of the earth." Whenever Pachacamac lost his temper, the earth shook. Pachacamac was the highest Incan god. It is not surprising that the greatest Incan leader took the name **Pachacuti** (PAH•chah•KOO•tee), which means "Earthshaker."

Pachacuti lived up to his name. Starting around A.D. 1438, Pachacuti and his son, Topa Inca, built the largest ancient empire in the Americas. It stretched north to south about 2,500 miles (4,023 km)—about the distance between present-day Los Angeles and New York.

▲ Incan gold mask

Pachacuti created a plan to hold his empire together. He set up a strong central government but let local rulers stay in power. To ensure their loyalty, he took their sons to Cuzco for training.

Pachacuti united the empire in other ways too. He required people to learn Quechua (KEH•chuh•wuh), the language spoken by the Inca. He also designed a system of roads, which covered about 25,000 miles (40,234 km) when finished.

An Organized Society

The Inca believed the sun god Inti protected Cuzco, the Incan capital. The rulers who lived there called themselves "sons of the sun." As such, rulers and their wives, known as Coyas, were at the top of society.

The head priest and commander of the armies were just below the royal couple. Next came regional army leaders. Below them were temple priests, army commanders, and skilled workers—musicians, artisans, and accountants. The bottom level consisted of farmers, herders, and ordinary soldiers.

The Inca further divided society into 12 job categories. Within these, every man, woman, and child over age five had work to do. Young girls, for example, were baby-sitters, while young boys chased birds from gardens.

What Was Incan Culture Like?

The Inca rarely honored their gods with human sacrifice. They turned to sacrifice only in times of trouble, such as during earthquakes, or on special occasions. Priests most often sacrificed children, whom they thought were more pure than adults. The Inca worshiped the sacrificed children as gods.

To please their gods, the Inca built large works of stone. They had no system of writing, no wheels, and no iron tools. Yet they built places like Machu Picchu (MAH•choo PEE•choo), a retreat for Incan kings.

Building large structures required the Inca to develop a way to do mathematical calculations. The Inca used a **quipu** (KEE•poo), a rope with knotted cords of different lengths and colors. Each knot represented a number or item, which was also a way of keeping records.

The Inca were skilled engineers. Workers fit stones so tightly together that a knife could not slip between them. Because the Inca used no mortar, the stone blocks could slide up and down without collapsing whenever an earthquake rocked the earth.

Reading Check **Explain** How did Pachacuti make sure local leaders would be loyal to him?

Biography

PACHACUTI
Ruled 1438–1471

Pachacuti was the son of the eighth Inca king, Viracocha. In 1438 an enemy from the north attacked the capital city, Cuzco. Viracocha fled, but Pachacuti stayed behind to defend the city and defeat the enemy. Because of his victory, Pachacuti became king.

At first, Pachacuti concentrated on expanding the Inca Empire. When he wanted to conquer a kingdom, he first sent messengers to tell the local rulers all the benefits of being part of the Inca Empire and then asked them to join willingly. If they accepted, they were treated with respect and given some rights. If they refused, the Incas attacked with brutal force.

Pachacuti next turned his attention to rebuilding Cuzco. He was the first to use white granite as a building material. No mortar was needed to hold the granite stones together because the sides of each piece were cut accurately and fit closely together.

Pachacuti built an estate for himself called Machu Picchu. It was made of white granite and was located thousands of feet high in the Andes. Recent research suggests that Machu Picchu was used not only as a home for the royal family, but also as a center for celebrations and ceremonial gatherings.

According to legend translated from a sacred text, Pachacuti became very sick when he was an elderly man. He called all of his relatives to his bedside. He divided his possessions among them and then made a speech with instructions for his burial.

▲ Pachacuti

"I was born as a flower of the field . . ."
–Pachacuti, as quoted in
History of the Incas

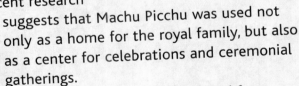
Then and Now

How can a nation today get another nation to do something without threatening war?

▲ Machu Picchu

Life in North America

Main Idea The geography in lands north of present-day Mexico shaped the development of many different Native American cultures.

Reading Focus What would your life have in common with people living in a different place but with the same geography? Read to learn how the geography of North America shaped the life of Native Americans living here.

By A.D. 1500, about two million people lived north of Mesoamerica. They spoke around 300 languages and called themselves by thousands of different names.

These Native Americans had inherited the cultures of their ancestors. As early Americans spread out across North America, they adjusted to the varied environments where they settled. They not only survived—they lived well.

The People of the Far North Scientists think the early people who settled the Arctic regions of present-day Canada and Alaska arrived by boat, perhaps around 3000 B.C. This was long after the Ice Age had ended. These people called themselves the Inuit, which means "the people."

The Inuit, like other early Americans, found ways to live in their harsh environment. They built **igloos,** dome-shaped homes, from blocks of ice and snow. They used dogsleds to travel on land and seal-skin kayaks to travel by sea.

Most peoples of the Far North hunted. They ate seals, walruses, and land animals like caribou and polar bears. They especially prized strips of blubber, or fat, from seals and whales. The fat provided oil for lamps, and it also gave the Inuit valuable calories.

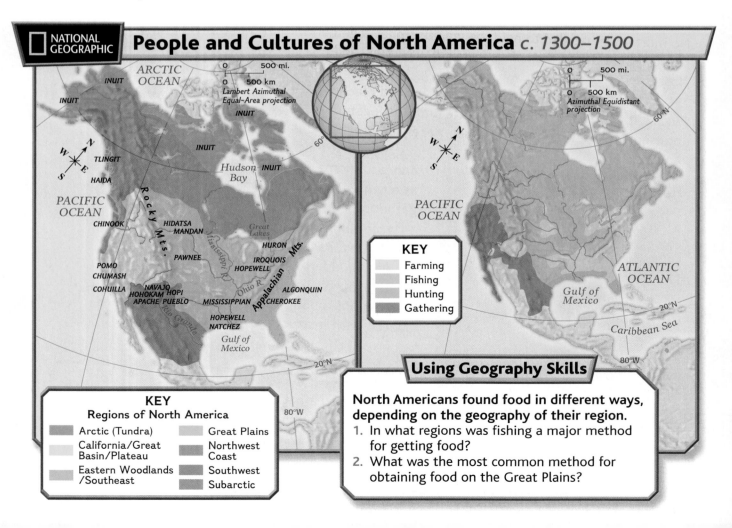

NATIONAL GEOGRAPHIC **People and Cultures of North America** *c. 1300–1500*

KEY
Regions of North America
- Arctic (Tundra)
- California/Great Basin/Plateau
- Eastern Woodlands/Southeast
- Great Plains
- Northwest Coast
- Southwest
- Subarctic

KEY
- Farming
- Fishing
- Hunting
- Gathering

Using Geography Skills

North Americans found food in different ways, depending on the geography of their region.
1. In what regions was fishing a major method for getting food?
2. What was the most common method for obtaining food on the Great Plains?

The carved wooden totem (far right) was made by Native Americans from the Pacific Northwest. The kachina doll (right) was made by the Hopi people of the Southwest. *Why was the Pacific Northwest region heavily populated?*

Life on the West Coast

The groups that settled along North America's Pacific coast enjoyed a milder climate than the Inuit. In the Pacific Northwest, peoples such as the Tlingit (TLIHNG•kuht), Haida, and Chinook used towering cedar trees to build wooden houses and huge oceangoing canoes. They fished the seas for otters, seals, and whales. Each spring, saltwater salmon clogged the rivers as they swam upstream to lay eggs.

Because of rich food resources, the Pacific Northwest was one of the most heavily populated regions north of Mesoamerica. Only the area that is today California supported more people.

Scientists think California was home to about 500 early American cultures. Each culture specialized in using the natural resources found in California's many environments.

Along the northern coast, people like the Chumash fished. In the southern desert, the Cahuilla harvested dates from palm trees and gathered seeds, roots, and pods. In the central valley, the Pomo gathered acorns and pounded them into flour.

Life in the Southwest

People who settled in the dry deserts of the Southwest lacked the abundant resources of the California peoples. However, early Americans like the Hohokam and Anasazi had taught their descendants important lessons. The Hopi, Acoma, Pueblo, and Zuni knew how to farm the dry land. Like their ancestors, they dug irrigation canals. They built apartment-like homes, using a type of sun-dried mud brick called **adobe** (uh•DOH•bee).

In the A.D. 1500s, two groups of hunters—the Apache and the Navajo—moved into the area. The Apache remained hunters, but over time the Navajo started to farm like their neighbors.

Life on the Great Plains

People on the Great Plains farmed, but it was not easy. Seas of grass covered the lands stretching from the Rocky Mountains to the Mississippi River. The dense grass roots made farming difficult, especially without iron tools. Peoples like the Mandan, Hidatsa, and Pawnee grew gardens in the fertile land along the Missouri, Arkansas, and Red Rivers.

While the women tended gardens, the men hunted the huge herds of buffalo that grazed on the grasslands. They hunted on foot, because at that time there were no horses in America. The buffalo gave them meat for food, bones for tools, and skins for clothing and shelter.

Life in the Eastern Woodlands
Unlike the Plains, dense forests covered lands east of the Mississippi River. Here people combined farming with hunting and fishing. Farming was more widespread in the Southeast Woodlands, where a mild climate led to a long growing season. In the cooler Northeast Woodlands, people relied more on hunting.

All over the Woodlands, groups formed governments. Some, such as the Natchez in present-day Mississippi, set up strict social classes. Others, like the Cherokee in Georgia and North Carolina, had formal codes of law.

In a few cases, Native Americans in the Woodlands set up **confederations** (kuhn•FEH•duh•RAY•shuhnz), or governments that link several groups. The most famous was the league formed by the **Iroquois** (IHR•uh•KWOY). The Iroquois League included five groups: Onondaga, Seneca, Mohawk, Oneida, and Cayuga.

The Iroquois formed the league to end the fighting among themselves. A code of laws, known as the Great Peace, governed the league. Women, who controlled Iroquois land, selected male members to sit on a Grand Council. Together council members worked out their differences and made decisions in complete agreement. The Council helped members unite against other Woodland peoples, such as the powerful Algonquian (al•GAHN•kwee•uhn).

✓ **Reading Check** **Describe** How did geography shape the lives of the people north of present-day Mexcio?

History Online

Study Central™ Need help with the material in this section? Visit jat.glencoe.com

Section 2 Review

Reading Summary

Review the Main Ideas

- In the rain forests of Central America, the Maya developed a civilization divided into city-states.

- A fierce warrior people, the Aztec created a strong empire in central Mexico.

- In the Andes, the Inca created the largest empire in the Americas.

- North America's varied geography led to the development of many diverse Native American groups.

What Did You Learn?

1. How did the Incan leader Pachacuti maintain the great empire he built?

2. Who were the people of the Far North, and what sorts of food did they eat?

Critical Thinking

3. **Compare and Contrast** Draw a Venn diagram like the one shown. Add details to compare Aztec and Incan society.

```
   Aztec        Incan
  Society      Society
```

4. **Science Link** How and why did the Maya study astronomy?

5. **Summarize** How did the Aztec find and build their capital city?

6. **Drawing Conclusions** Why do you think the Inca required everyone in their society to do a specific job? Do you think this is a good idea for a society? Explain.

7. **Descriptive Writing** Imagine you are an early European explorer in North America. Write a journal entry describing your encounter with a Native American people in one of the regions described in the section.

Section 3

The Fall of the Aztec and Inca Empires

Get Ready to Read!

What's the Connection?

As the 1400s drew to a close, people in the Americas and Europe knew nothing of each other. This changed when Europeans began exploring the world and searching for trade routes to Asia.

Focusing on the Main Ideas

- Christopher Columbus found the Americas while trying to find a sea route to Asia. *(page 594)*

- Spanish conquerors defeated the Aztec with the help of horses, guns, and European disease. *(page 595)*

- The riches of the Aztec Empire led other Spanish conquerors to seek their fortunes in South America. *(page 599)*

Locating Places
Hispaniola (HIHS•puh•NYOH•luh)
Extremadura
  (EHK•struh•muh•DUR•uh)

Meeting People
Christopher Columbus
Hernán Cortés
  (ehr•NAHN kawr•TEHZ)
Montezuma II (MAHN•tuh•ZOO•muh)
Malintzin (mah•LIHNT•suhn)
Francisco Pizarro
  (fran•SIHS•koh   puh•ZAHR•oh)
Atahualpa (AH•tuh•WAHL•puh)

Building Your Vocabulary
conquistador
  (kahn•KEES•tuh•DAWR)
treason (TREE•zuhn)

Reading Strategy
Cause and Effect Create a diagram to show the reasons Cortés was able to conquer the Aztec.

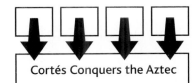

Cortés Conquers the Aztec

NATIONAL GEOGRAPHIC When & Where?

1450

1500

1550

1492
Christopher Columbus reaches the Americas

1521
Cortés defeats Aztec

1533
Francisco Pizarro conquers the Inca

Tenochtitlán
Cuzco

The Spanish Arrive in America

Main Idea Christopher Columbus found the Americas while trying to find a sea route to Asia.

Reading Focus What is the most vivid memory you have of a place you have visited? Read to learn what the Spanish found when they set out to explore the world.

In 1492 the Aztec appeared unbeatable. Around 250,000 people lived in Tenochtitlán, making it the largest city in the Americas—if not the world. In just a few short years, however, people from Europe would destroy their empire.

Columbus Arrives in America
As you learned previously, by the 1400s several strong European kingdoms had developed in Western Europe. Those kingdoms knew that money could be made if they could find a way to trade with the countries of East Asia without having to deal with the Muslim kingdoms in between.

One by one, the people of Western Europe took to the sea to find a route to Asia. The first were the Portuguese, who began mapping Africa's eastern coast, hoping to find a way around Africa.

Next were the Spaniards, who decided to finance a trip by an Italian sea captain named **Christopher Columbus.** Columbus convinced Spain's rulers that he could reach Asia by sailing west across the Atlantic Ocean. He had no idea that two continents blocked his way.

Columbus set sail with three ships in August 1492. In October, he landed on an island in the Caribbean Sea. Columbus believed he had arrived in Asia. He traveled farther into the Caribbean and landed on the island of **Hispaniola** (HIHS•puh•NYOH•luh), which is today Haiti and the Dominican Republic. He then returned home carrying colorful parrots, some gold and spices, and several Native American captives. His success astonished and pleased Spain's rulers and convinced them to pay for another trip.

Columbus Returns
Columbus set out again in 1493. This time, he came to conquer, bringing soldiers to help him. In the spring of 1494, the Spanish landed on Hispaniola.

▲ In the painting above, Christopher Columbus is depicted landing on the island of San Salvador. *Why did Columbus sail west across the Atlantic?*

The Taino who lived there got their first look at the **conquistadors** (kahn•KEES•tuh•DAWRZ), the soldier-explorers sent to the Americas by Spain. What they saw frightened them. Armor-clad men rode on armor-clad horses. Snarling dogs ran by their sides. In a show of power, the soldiers fired guns that spit out flames and lead balls.

Soldiers claimed the island for Spain. Then they enslaved the Taino and forced them to work for the Spanish. Spain now had a foothold in the Americas.

✓ **Reading Check** **Identify** Who were the conquistadors?

Spain Conquers Mexico

Main Idea Spanish conquerors defeated the Aztec with the help of horses, guns, and European disease.

Reading Focus Think of decisions that you have already made today. Read to learn how the decisions made by two people—a Spanish conqueror and an Aztec king—changed the course of history.

The voyages of Christopher Columbus, who sailed to the Americas four times, inspired many poor nobles to go to America to seek their fortunes. Many came from the part of Spain known as the

Linking Past & Present

Chocolate

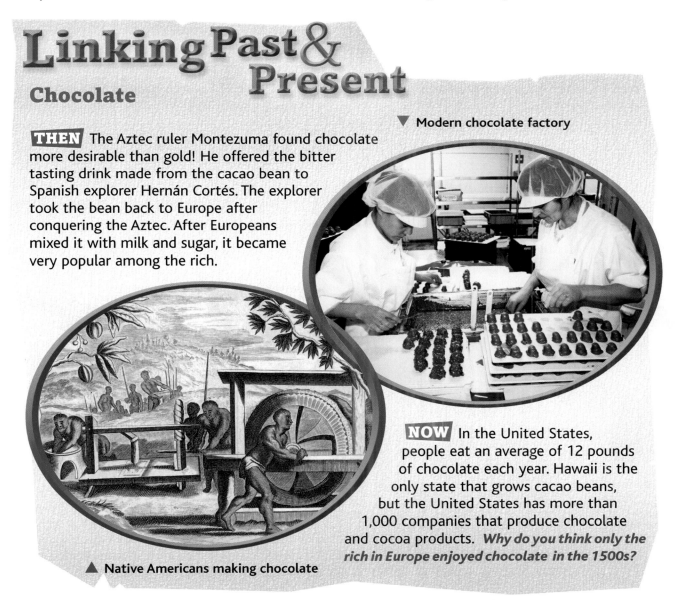

THEN The Aztec ruler Montezuma found chocolate more desirable than gold! He offered the bitter tasting drink made from the cacao bean to Spanish explorer Hernán Cortés. The explorer took the bean back to Europe after conquering the Aztec. After Europeans mixed it with milk and sugar, it became very popular among the rich.

▼ **Modern chocolate factory**

NOW In the United States, people eat an average of 12 pounds of chocolate each year. Hawaii is the only state that grows cacao beans, but the United States has more than 1,000 companies that produce chocolate and cocoa products. *Why do you think only the rich in Europe enjoyed chocolate in the 1500s?*

▲ **Native Americans making chocolate**

Extremadura (EHK•struh•muh•DUR•uh). Its poor soil, blistering hot summers, and icy winters held little chance for wealth. One of these nobles was 19-year-old **Hernán Cortés** (ehr•NAHN kawr•TEHZ).

As a teenager, Cortés had a choice of three jobs: priest, lawyer, or soldier. His parents picked lawyer, but Cortés picked soldier. In 1504 he set out for Hispaniola. In 1511 he took part in the Spanish invasion of Cuba. His courage impressed the Spanish commander, who gave Cortés control over several Native American villages and the goods they produced.

Six years later, smallpox swept across Cuba, killing thousands of Native Americans. The Spanish commander asked Cortés to find new people who could be forced to work for the Spanish. Cortés knew just where to look.

That same year, a ship sent to explore the coast of the Yucatán returned to Cuba. Unlike earlier search parties, the soldiers did not fight with the Maya who lived there. Instead a group of Maya paddled out to greet them. As one soldier recalled:

> 66 They brought gold cast in bars . . . a beautiful gold mask, a figurine [statue] of a man with a half mask of gold, and a crown of gold beads. 99
>
> —Juan Díaz, as quoted in "Conquest and Aftermath"

Cortés needed to hear no more. He made plans to sail. On February 18, 1519, Cortés set sail for Mexico.

Cortés Invades Mexico When Cortés arrived, the Aztec emperor was **Montezuma II** (MAHN•tuh•ZOO•muh), also called Moctezuma. Montezuma expected the invaders. In a dream, he looked into a mirror and saw a huge army headed over the mountains. "What shall I do?" cried the emperor. "Where shall I hide?"

The dreaded invasion began in April 1519 when Cortés stepped onto a beach near present-day Veracruz. He came with 550 soldiers, 16 horses, 14 cannons, and a few dogs. How could such a small force conquer a huge warrior empire?

▲ Aztec war club

◀ The Aztec's simple weapons were no match for the guns and cannons of the Spanish. *Besides weapons and horses, what else did the Spanish bring that would help them defeat the Aztec?*

▲ Spanish armor

▲ Spanish sword

First, Cortés knew how to use Spanish horses and guns to shock Native Americans. In a display of power, he forced thousands of Tabascans (tuh•BAS•kuhnz), a people living in Mesoamerica, to surrender. Second, the Tabascans gave Cortés another weapon—a Mayan woman named **Malintzin** (mah•LIHNT•suhn). She spoke both Mayan and Nahuatl (NAH•WAH•tuhl), the language of the Aztec.

Speaking through a Spaniard who knew Mayan, Malintzin described the Aztec Empire to Cortés. She also told Cortés how subjects of the Aztec resented their rulers and would join with him to fight Montezuma. Acting as a translator, she helped Cortés form alliances.

Finally, Cortés had the help of invisible allies—germs that carried diseases, such as measles and smallpox. These diseases would eventually kill more Aztec than the Spanish swords.

Cortés Defeats the Aztec

The Spaniards traveled 400 miles (644 km) to reach Tenochtitlán, the Aztec capital. Messengers reported their every move to Montezuma. The Aztec believed in a light-skinned god named Quetzalcoatl. This god, who opposed sacrifice, had sailed away long ago, promising to return someday to reclaim his land. Montezuma was afraid Cortés was the god returning home. As a result, he did not want to attack the Spaniards right away.

As Cortés marched closer, Montezuma decided to ambush the Spanish troops. Cortés learned of the plan and attacked first, killing 6,000 people. In November 1519, the Spaniards marched into Tenochtitlán and took control of the city. To prevent the Aztec from rebelling, Cortés took Montezuma hostage. He then ordered the Aztec to stop sacrificing people.

Primary Source

The Aztec Defeat

This excerpt describes the aftermath of Cortés's victory.

▲ Battle scene between Aztec and Spanish soldiers

"Broken spears lie in the roads; we have torn our hair in our grief. The houses are roofless now, and their walls are red with blood. . . . We have pounded our hands in despair against the adobe walls, for our inheritance, our city, is lost and dead. The shields of our warriors were its defense, but they could not save it."

—author unknown, from *The Broken Spears*, *edited* by Miguel Leon-Portilla

DBQ Document-Based Question

The Aztec felt that their lost city was their inheritance. What does that mean?

Cortés's orders angered the Aztec, who planned a rebellion. Fighting erupted, and the Spanish killed thousands of Aztec. Montezuma tried to stop the fighting, but he too was killed. Outnumbered, the Spanish fought their way out of the city and took refuge in the nearby hills with their allies.

While Cortés prepared a second attack, smallpox broke out in Tenochtitlán. Greatly weakened, the Aztec were no match for the Spanish and their allies. In June 1521, the Spanish destroyed the Aztec capital.

Reading Check **Explain** Why did the Aztec think they should welcome Cortés?

Biography

MONTEZUMA II
1480–1520
HERNÁN CORTÉS
1485–1547

Montezuma ▶

Although Montezuma II became known as the emperor who let the Spanish capture the Aztec Empire, most of his years as a ruler had been very successful. Montezuma Xocoyotl was the youngest son of Emperor Axacayatl. Aztec leadership was not hereditary, so after Axacayatl's death a man named Ahuitzotl was selected emperor. Montezuma was in his early twenties when he was chosen emperor. He became a popular leader. He led his armies in battle and won over 40 battles against kingdoms south of the Aztec Empire. His one major mistake was in his dealings with the Spanish conquistadors.

Leading the Spanish march into the Aztec Empire in 1519 was a 34-year-old Spaniard named Hernán Cortés. Cortés was born in the province of Extremadura, Spain. At age 19, Cortés left the university and boarded a ship for the Spanish lands in America. He was determined to make his fortune.

In 1511, Spanish troops led by Diego Velázquez conquered Cuba. Cortés took part in the invasion, and his courage impressed Velázquez. He rewarded Cortés by giving him control of several Native American villages. Six years later, smallpox swept across Cuba, killing thousands of Native Americans. Without Native American workers, the farms and mines the Spanish had built in Cuba could not function. Velázquez asked Cortés to lead an expedition to the Yucatán Peninsula to find new peoples who could be forced to work for the Spanish. He was also asked to investigate reports of a wealthy civilization there. On February 18, 1519, Cortés set sail for Mexico.

▲ Hernán Cortés

Several years later, after conquering the Aztec, Cortés took part in one more expedition to Honduras and then served as Governor General of New Spain. He returned to Spain a very wealthy man and died near the city of Seville in 1547.

Then and Now

Because of their encounter in war, the names of Montezuma and Cortés often appear together in history books. What two leaders today do you think will be paired in future history books? Why?

Pizarro Conquers the Inca

Main Idea The riches of the Aztec Empire led other Spanish conquerors to seek their fortunes in South America.

Reading Focus Have you ever done anything because you have seen other people do it and succeed? Read to learn how another conquistador followed the example of Cortés and conquered the Inca.

In 1513 Vasco Núñez de Balboa (VAHS•koh NOON•yays day bal•BOH•uh) led a band of soldiers across the jungle-covered mountains of present-day Panama. Native Americans said that if Balboa traveled south along a western sea, he would find a great empire filled with gold.

Balboa found the sea, known today as the Pacific Ocean. However, he never found the golden empire. A jealous Spanish official in Panama falsely charged him with **treason** (TREE•zuhn), or disloyalty to the government, and ordered him beheaded.

Francisco Pizarro (fran•SIHS•koh puh•ZAHR•oh), who marched with Balboa, took up the search. Pizarro could not write his name, but he knew how to fight. Like Balboa and Cortés, Pizarro came from the harsh Extremadura. Unlike his neighbors, however, he was not of noble birth.

At age 16, Pizarro fled a job herding pigs to fight in Italy. In 1502 he arrived in the Americas. Helping explore Panama, he became a wealthy landowner. But Pizarro longed to find the golden empire.

Pizarro and the Inca

By the 1530s, the Inca thought they ruled most of the world. Two threats from the north soon proved they did not. The Inca could do nothing to stop the southward spread of smallpox. They also failed to scare away Pizarro, who led 160 adventurers up the mountains to the Incan homeland.

The Inca tried to ignore him, but Pizarro, now in his 50s, would not leave. He raided Incan storehouses and fired guns at villagers. The Incan emperor, **Atahualpa** (AH•tuh•WAHL•puh), thought Pizarro was crazy or a fool. How could this man stand up to an army of 80,000 Incan warriors?

Atahualpa misjudged Pizarro. The Spaniard had an advantage. The Inca knew little about the Europeans, but Pizarro knew a lot about Native Americans. He had spent more than 30 years fighting Native

Primary Source

Incan Record Keeping

A Spanish conquistador wrote about aspects of Incan culture.

"At the beginning of the new year the rulers of each village came to Cuzco, bringing their quipus, which told how many births there had been during the year, and how many deaths. In this way the Inca and the governors knew which of the Indians were poor, the women who had been widowed, whether they were able to pay their taxes, and how many men they could count on in the event of war, and many other things they considered highly important."

—Pedro de Cieza de Léon, *The Second Part of the Chronicle of Peru*

▲ Quipu

DBQ **Document-Based Question**

Quipus were used to calculate records and building plans. How else do you think the Inca might have used quipus?

Americans. Also, his good friend Hernán Cortés gave Pizarro an inside look at the conquest of the Aztec. In late 1532, Pizarro decided on a plan so bold that even Cortés might not have risked it.

Pizarro Defeats the Inca Spanish messengers invited Atahualpa to a meeting. Atahualpa agreed but made the mistake of leaving most of his huge army behind. He believed that his 5,000 bodyguards were enough protection. He also decided, based on Pizarro's small force, that the Inca needed no weapons.

When they met, Pizarro wasted no time in asking the emperor to give up his gods. When Atahualpa laughed at his request, Pizarro ordered an attack. Cannons roared, trumpets blared, and sword-swinging soldiers shrieked battle cries. Pizarro then seized Atahualpa and dragged him off the battlefield.

Atahualpa tried to buy his freedom. He offered to fill his jail cell with gold and a nearby room with silver. Pizarro jumped at the deal. Atahualpa kept his part of the bargain. Pizarro did not. He charged the emperor with many crimes: plotting a rebellion, worshiping false gods, having too many wives, and more. In 1533 a military court found the emperor guilty and sentenced him to death.

To reward Pizarro, the Spanish king made him governor of Peru. Pizarro then chose a new emperor for the Inca, but the emperor had to follow Pizarro's orders. Pizarro's conquest of Peru opened most of South America to Spanish rule. Spain controlled a vast territory covering 375,000 square miles (975,000 sq km) with almost 7 million inhabitants. It was on its way to building the world's first global empire.

✓ **Reading Check** **Explain** How did Pizarro fail to keep his promise to Atahualpa?

History Online
Study Central™ Need help with the material in this section? Visit jat.glencoe.com

Section 3 Review

Reading Summary
Review the Main Ideas
- Searching for a sea route to Asia, Christopher Columbus arrived in the Americas and claimed lands there for Spain.
- With a small army, Spanish conquistador Hernán Cortés conquered Montezuma and the Aztec capital of Tenochtitlán.
- In Peru, a small Spanish force led by Francisco Pizarro captured the Inca Empire.

What Did You Learn?
1. How did Christopher Columbus convince Spanish rulers to pay for a second trip?

2. Why did Cortés sail from Cuba to Mexico in search of the Aztec?

Critical Thinking
3. **Sequencing Information** Draw a time line like the one shown. Fill in events related to Cortés's capture of Tenochtitlán.

├──┼──┼──┼──┼──┤

1517:
Spanish ship brings
back gold from Yucatán

4. **Predict** How might the history of the Aztec people be different without the legend of the Aztec god Quetzalcoatl?

5. **Analyze** Why were the Aztec and the Inca so easily defeated by smaller Spanish forces?

6. **Expository Writing** Imagine you are an Aztec or an Inca seeing a Spanish conquistador for the first time. Write a newspaper article describing what you have observed.

Section ① The First Americans

Vocabulary
glacier
monopoly

Focusing on the Main Ideas

- It is believed that the first people in the Americas came from Asia during the Ice Age. *(page 573)*
- The invention of farming led to the rise of civilizations in the Americas. *(page 574)*
- Early people in the northern part of the Americas built complex cultures based on farming and trade. *(page 578)*

Section ② Life in the Americas

Vocabulary
quipu
igloo
adobe
confederation

Focusing on the Main Ideas

- The Maya adjusted to life in the tropical rain forest and built a culture based on their religious beliefs. *(page 583)*
- The Aztec moved into the Valley of Mexico, where they created an empire based on conquest and war. *(page 585)*
- To unite their huge empire, Incan rulers set up a highly organized government and society. *(page 588)*
- The geography in lands north of present-day Mexico shaped the development of many different Native American cultures. *(page 590)*

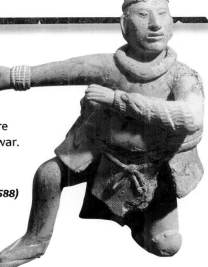

▲ Mayan ballplayer

Section ③ The Fall of the Aztec and Inca Empires

Vocabulary
conquistador
treason

Focusing on the Main Ideas

- Christopher Columbus found the Americas while trying to find a sea route to Asia. *(page 594)*
- Spanish conquerors defeated the Aztec with the help of horses, guns, and European disease. *(page 595)*
- The riches of the Aztec Empire led other Spanish conquerors to seek their fortunes in South America. *(page 599)*

Review Vocabulary

Match the word in the first column with its definition in the second column.

___ 1. conquistador
___ 2. glacier
___ 3. adobe
___ 4. confederation
___ 5. treason

a. disloyalty to the government
b. Spanish soldier-explorer
c. sun-dried mud bricks
d. huge sheet of ice
e. form of government that links several different groups

Review Main Ideas

Section 1 • The First Americans

6. When did the first people arrive in the Americas? On which continent did they live originally?

7. How did farming lead to the rise and development of civilizations in present-day Mexico, Central America, and Peru?

Section 2 • Life in the Americas

8. Explain the differences between the Maya and Aztec civilizations.

9. How did geography shape the development of the Native American cultures north of present-day Mexico?

Section 3 • The Fall of the Aztec and Inca Empires

10. What was the goal of Christopher Columbus's voyage in 1492?

11. What three factors made it possible for the Spanish to conquer the Aztec and the Inca?

Critical Thinking

12. **Analyze** How do the houses of North American peoples reflect the geography of their regions?

13. **Infer** Why do you think the Mayan civilization came to an end?

14. **Predict** What do you think would have happened if the Inca had taken Pizarro's raids more seriously?

Review Reading Skill | Summarizing | Summarizing Information

Read the paragraph below, then choose the statement that best summarizes its content.

The region's geography was ideal for farming. Much of the area had a rich, volcanic soil and a mild climate. Rains fell in the spring, helping seeds to sprout. They decreased in the summer, allowing crops to ripen for harvest.

15. a. The Ice Age ended as the climate warmed.
    b. Rain fell in the spring.
    c. Climate and soil made the region ideal for farming.
    d. Seeds that are planted grow into crops.

To review this skill, see pages 570–571.

Geography Skills

Study the map below and answer the following questions.

16. **Human/Environment Interaction** Why do you think the Inca built stone walls in parts of Cuzco?

17. **Location** What natural defenses existed around Cuzco?

18. **Movement** What do the roads leading out of Cuzco reveal about the contact between the capital city and the rest of the empire?

History Online

Self-Check Quiz To help you prepare for the Chapter Test, visit jat.glencoe.com

Cuzco, Peru c. 1450

Fortress

Huatanay R.

Plaza

Plaza

Temple of the Sun

Tullumayo R.

0   0.25 mi.

0   0.25 km

Lambert Azimuthal Equal-Area projection

KEY
- Cuzco
- Road
- Surviving stone wall
- Assembly hall
- Palace
- Temple
- Ridge

Read to Write

19. **Persuasive Writing** Suppose you are a Native American during the Spanish conquests. Write a letter to the conquistadors to persuade them to trade with your culture rather than conquer it. Your letter should state the ways Europeans and Native Americans can learn from each other.

20. **Using Your FOLDABLES** Create an outline map of the Americas on poster board. It should be big enough for the entire class to work together. Label each country and the location of each civilization from your chapter. Then use your foldables to write facts about each civilization on the map.

Using Technology

21. **Preparing a Report** Use the Internet and your library to gather information about the Mound Builders. Note their reasons for mound building and the shapes of mounds. Then prepare an illustrated report on the computer to compare the mounds to other structures of early civilizations.

Linking Past and Present

22. **Evaluating Information** What impact have Native American ways of the past had on present-day life in the Americas?

23. **Building Citizenship Skills** The Iroquois League was an important confederation of the early Americas. Do confederations exist today? Do they serve the same purpose as the Iroquois League?

Primary Source Analyze

Some Europeans, including this Dominican friar, worked to protect the Native Americans by writing about their cultures.

"They [Native American leaders] issued public edicts and personal commands to all nobles and provincial governors, of whom there were many, that all poor, widows and orphans in each province should be provided for from their own royal rents and riches."

—Bartolomé de las Casas, "Apologetic History of the Indies"

DBQ Document-Based Questions

24. What does this tell you about Native American leaders' attitude toward those in need?

25. Do you think the nobles and provincial governors supported this edict? Why or why not?

Chapter 17

The Renaissance and Reformation

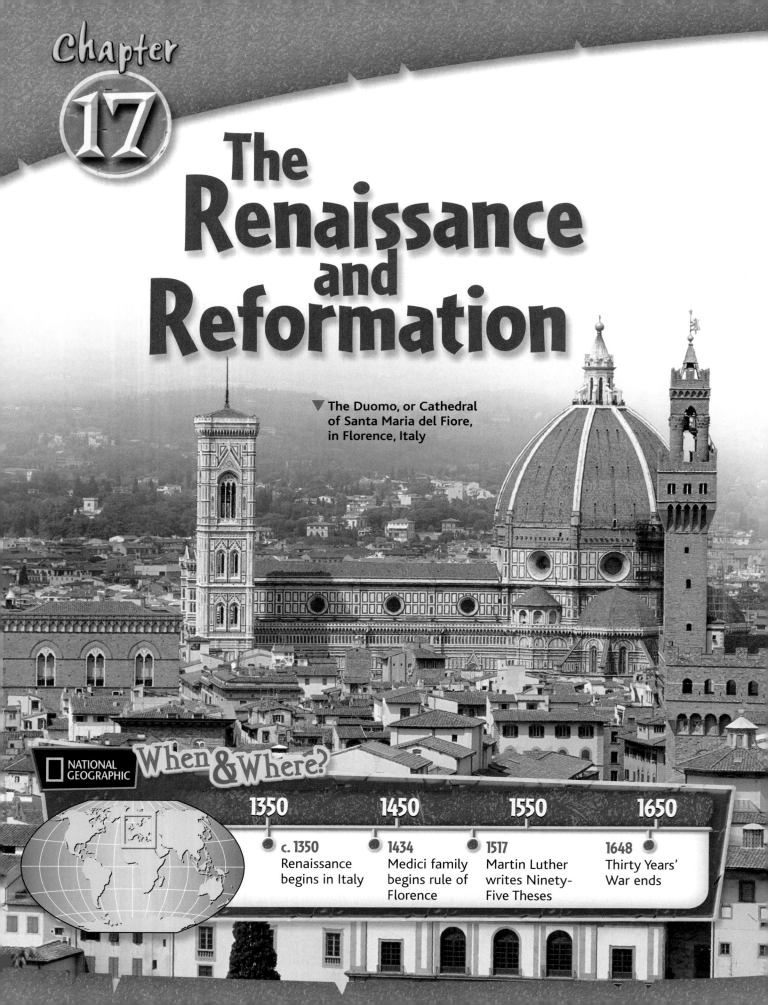

▼ The Duomo, or Cathedral of Santa Maria del Fiore, in Florence, Italy

NATIONAL GEOGRAPHIC **When & Where?**

1350	1450	1550	1650
c. 1350 Renaissance begins in Italy	1434 Medici family begins rule of Florence	1517 Martin Luther writes Ninety-Five Theses	1648 Thirty Years' War ends

Chapter Preview

New ideas brought the Middle Ages to an end. Read this chapter to find out how advances in the arts and learning and dramatic changes to Christianity led to the beginning of modern times in Europe.

 View the Chapter 17 video in the *World History: Journey Across Time* Video Program.

 Section 1 ## The Renaissance Begins

During the Renaissance, new values and new art developed in wealthy Italian city-states.

 Section 2 ## New Ideas and Art

Wealthy leaders in Italian city-states supported talented artists and writers, and Renaissance art and ideas spread from Italy to northern Europe.

 Section 3 ## The Reformation Begins

Martin Luther and other reformers, such as John Calvin, broke from the Catholic Church and began a new Christian movement that came to be called Protestantism.

 Section 4 ## Catholics and Protestants

While the Catholic Church attempted to carry out reforms, Catholics and Protestants fought bloody religious wars across Europe.

 **FOLDABLES™ Study Organizer**

Compare-Contrast *Make this foldable to help you compare and contrast what you learn about the Renaissance and Reformation.*

Step 1 *Fold a sheet of paper in half from side to side.*

Step 2 *Turn the paper and fold it into thirds.*

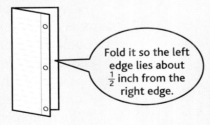 Fold it so the left edge lies about $\frac{1}{2}$ inch from the right edge.

Step 3 *Unfold and cut the top layer only along both folds.*

 This will make three tabs.

Step 4 *Label as shown.*

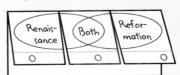 Renaissance   Both   Reformation

Reading and Writing *As you read the sections on the Renaissance and Reformation, record important concepts and events under the appropriate tabs. Then record ideas similar to both under the middle tab.*

Reading Skill

Analyze and Clarify

1 Learn It!

Go Beyond the Words

Analyzing a passage means going beyond the definition of the words. It is a way of reading for deep understanding, not just memorizing or studying to pass a test. Read the following paragraph from Section 2.

> Renaissance painters also used new techniques. The most important was perspective, a method that makes a drawing or painting look three-dimensional. Artists had tried to use perspective before, but Renaissance artists perfected it. Using perspective, objects in a scene appear to be at different distances from the viewer. The result is a more realistic image.
>
> —*from page 623*

How can you analyze this passage? Here are some suggestions:

1. Look at the drawing on page 626. Is the drawing realistic as described by the paragraph?

2. Look at another painting or drawing in this book. Compare the perspective to the drawing on page 626. Which is more realistic? Why?

3. With a partner, sketch a view of your classroom. Exchange sketches and see if you can tell where your partner was standing when he or she made the sketch. Based on your experience, what are some difficulties an artist might encounter in trying to draw a large area realistically?

Reading Tip

When reading, break the text into smaller parts to help you understand the whole.

2 Practice It!

Analyze as You Read

Read this paragraph from Section 2.

> To make their paintings more realistic, Renaissance artists also used a technique called chiaroscuro. Chiaroscuro softened edges by using light and shadows instead of stiff outlines to separate objects. In Italian, *chiaro* means "clear or light," and *oscuro* means "dark." Chiaroscuro created more drama and emotion in a painting.
>
> —*from page 623*

Read to Write ·······

Choose any painting or drawing in this book and analyze, in writing, what is taking place. Use the questions *who, what, when,* or *how* to help you get started.

▲ The *Mona Lisa*

Analyze the above paragraph by doing the following:

1. Look at the painting of Mona Lisa from page 622. Do you see the use of chiaroscuro? If so, in what way does it create drama or emotion?

2. Choose another painting in this or a different text. Look at it carefully to see if the technique of chiaroscuro was used. Describe to a partner the light and dark areas that you see.

3. Try your hand at drawing an object or scene using the technique of chiaroscuro.

3 Apply It!

As you read this chapter, choose at least one section to study and analyze for deeper meaning. Exchange your analysis with a classmate who has analyzed a different passage.

The Renaissance Begins

Get Ready to Read!

What's the Connection?

Previously, you learned about life in medieval Europe. In this section, you will see how Europeans began to look to the ideals of the ancient Greeks and Romans as they left the Middle Ages behind.

Focusing on the Main Ideas

- The wealthy urban society of the Italian city-states brought a rebirth of learning and art to Europe. *(page 609)*

- Italy's location helped its city-states grow wealthy from trade and banking, but many of the cities fell under the control of strong rulers. *(page 611)*

- Unlike medieval nobles, the nobles of the Italian city-states lived in cities and were active in trade, banking, and public life. *(page 614)*

Locating Places
Florence (FLAWR•uhns)
Venice (VEH•nuhs)

Meeting People
Marco Polo (MAHR•koh   POH•loh)
Medici (MEH•duh•chee)
Niccolò Machiavelli (NEE•koh•LOH MA•kee•uh•VEH•lee)

Building Your Vocabulary
Renaissance (REH•nuh•SAHNS)
secular (SEH•kyuh•luhr)
diplomacy (duh•PLOH•muh•see)

Reading Strategy
Summarizing Information Complete a chart like the one below showing the reasons Italian city-states grew wealthy.

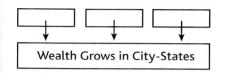

Wealth Grows in City-States

NATIONAL GEOGRAPHIC

When & Where?

1350	1450	1550

Genoa
Venice
Florence
Rome

c. 1350
Renaissance begins in Italy

1434
Medici family begins rule of Florence

1513
Machiavelli writes *The Prince*

The Italian Renaissance

Main Idea The wealthy urban society of the Italian city-states brought a rebirth of learning and art to Europe.

Reading Focus Hollywood makes many of the world's movies. Why is it the center of the movie industry? Read to learn why the city-states of Italy became the center of art during the Renaissance.

Renaissance (REH•nuh•SAHNS) means "rebirth." The years from about 1350 to 1550 in European history are called the Renaissance because there was a rebirth of interest in art and learning.

In some ways the Renaissance was a rebirth of interest in the same subjects the Greeks and Romans had studied. After the horrible years of the Black Death, Europeans began looking to the past when times seemed better. They wanted to learn how to make their own society better.

During the Renaissance, Europeans also began to stress the importance of the individual. They began to believe that people could make a difference and change the world for the better.

People were still very religious during the Renaissance, but they also began to celebrate human achievements. People became more **secular** (SEH•kyuh•luhr). This means they were more interested in this world than in religion and getting to heaven.

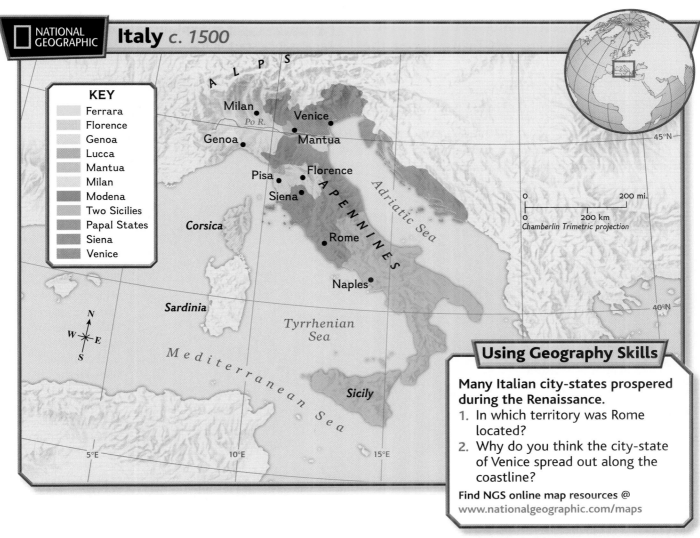

NATIONAL GEOGRAPHIC **Italy** *c. 1500*

KEY
- Ferrara
- Florence
- Genoa
- Lucca
- Mantua
- Milan
- Modena
- Two Sicilies
- Papal States
- Siena
- Venice

ALPS

Milan • *Po R.* Venice •
Genoa • Mantua •
Pisa • Florence •
Siena • A P E N N I N E S
Corsica *Adriatic Sea*
Rome •
Naples •
Sardinia 40°N
Tyrrhenian Sea
45°N
Mediterranean Sea
Sicily

0 ____ 200 mi.
0 ____ 200 km
Chamberlin Trimetric projection

N
W—E
S

5°E 10°E 15°E

Using Geography Skills

Many Italian city-states prospered during the Renaissance.

1. In which territory was Rome located?
2. Why do you think the city-state of Venice spread out along the coastline?

Find NGS online map resources @ www.nationalgeographic.com/maps

Why did the Renaissance begin in Italy? First of all, Italy had been the center of the Roman Empire. Ruins and art surrounded the Italians and reminded them of their past. It was only natural that they became interested in Greek and Roman art and tried to make their own art as good.

Another reason the Renaissance began in Italy was because by the 1300s, Italy's cities had become very wealthy. They could afford to pay painters, sculptors, architects, and other artists to produce new works.

A third reason was because the region was still divided into many small city-states. **Florence** (FLAWR•uhns), **Venice** (VEH•nuhs), Genoa, Milan, and Rome were some of the most important cities of the Renaissance.

The Italian city-states competed with each other. This helped bring about the Renaissance. Wealthy nobles and merchants wanted artists to produce works that increased the fame of their cities.

In most of Europe, the vast majority of people lived in the country, including the knights and nobles who owned estates. In Italy's city-states, the population was becoming more urban. That means more people were living in the city, rather than in the country. So many people living together in a city meant more customers for artists and more money for art.

The large number of people living in cities also led to more discussion and sharing of ideas about art. Just as the city-states of ancient Greece had produced many great works of art and literature, so too did urban society in Italy.

✓ **Reading Check** **Explain** Why did the Renaissance start in Italy?

Florence Cathedral

Florence, Italy, was one of the centers of the Renaissance. The Florence Cathedral became a symbol of the city, as well as one of the finest examples of Renaissance architecture. *What were other important Italian Renaissance cities?*

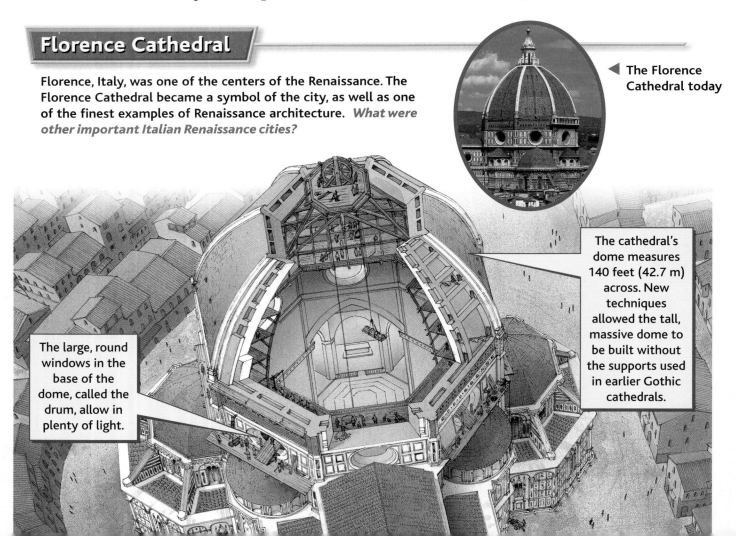

◄ The Florence Cathedral today

The cathedral's dome measures 140 feet (42.7 m) across. New techniques allowed the tall, massive dome to be built without the supports used in earlier Gothic cathedrals.

The large, round windows in the base of the dome, called the drum, allow in plenty of light.

The Rise of Italy's City-States

Main Idea Italy's location helped its city-states grow wealthy from trade and banking, but many of the cities fell under the control of strong rulers.

Reading Focus Do you have a bank account? What are banks for? Read to learn how banking helped to make the Italian city-states wealthy and powerful.

During the Middle Ages, no ruler was able to unite Italy into a single kingdom. There were several reasons for this. First of all, the Roman Catholic Church did everything it could to stop the rise of a powerful kingdom in Italy. Church leaders were afraid that if a strong ruler united Italy, that same ruler would be able to control the pope and the Church.

At the same time, the city-states that developed in Italy were about equal in strength. They fought many wars and often captured territory from each other, but no state was able to defeat all the others.

Probably the most important reason the city-states stayed independent was because they became very wealthy. With their great wealth, they could build large fleets and hire people to fight in their armies. A person who fights in an army for money is called a mercenary. The city-states also loaned money to the kings of Europe. The kings left the city-states alone so they could borrow more money in the future.

Italy's City-States Grow Wealthy

The Italian city-states became wealthy through trade. The geography of the long Italian peninsula meant that most of the city-states had a coastline and ports where merchant ships could dock. They were also perfectly located on the Mediterranean Sea. Spain and France lay to the west, and the Byzantine and Ottoman Empires lay to the east. North Africa was only a short trip to the south.

From the Byzantines, Turks, and Arabs, the Italians bought Chinese silk and Indian spices and sold them to people in Western Europe for very high prices. At the same time, from the Spanish, French, Dutch, and English, they bought goods such as wool, wine, and glass that they could sell in the Middle East. The Italian cities also had many skilled artisans, who could take raw materials the merchants bought and make goods that could be sold for high prices.

Geography was not the only reason for the success of the Italians. Several events led to trade becoming even more important in the city-states. First, the Crusades brought Italian merchants into contact with Arab merchants. Second, the rise of the Mongol Empire united almost all of Asia into one vast trade network.

The Mongols encouraged trade and protected the Silk Road from China to the Middle East. This made it cheaper and easier for caravans to carry goods from China and

▲ This painting shows a wealthy Italian family during the Renaissance. *How did competition between the city-states lead to great works of art?*

India to Muslim and Byzantine cities. As more and more silk and spices were shipped from Asia, the price of these goods fell. More Europeans could afford the luxuries, and demand for the items greatly increased. In turn, business for Italian merchants continued to grow.

Who Was Marco Polo?

Europeans were fascinated with Asia and its goods after reading a book written by **Marco Polo** (MAHR•koh POH•loh), a merchant from the city of Venice. In the 1270s, Marco Polo went on an amazing journey with his father and uncle to China. They set off to meet Kublai Khan, the ruler of the Mongol Empire.

When the Polo family finally made it to the khan's court, the great emperor was impressed with Marco Polo. He sent Marco Polo on business all over China. Marco Polo asked many questions and learned more about Asia than any other European. When he returned to Europe, he published a book about his travels. His stories helped increase interest in China and made many people want to buy China's goods.

The Wealth of Florence

No city was more famous in the Renaissance than Florence. It was the first to grow wealthy, and it produced many famous artists. It sat on the banks of the Arno River surrounded by beautiful hills. It was walled and had many tall towers for defense. Its people were known for their love of elegant clothing.

At first, Florence's wealth came from trading cloth, especially wool. The city's merchants sailed to England to get sheep's wool. Artisans in Florence then wove it into fine fabrics. Florentines also found another way to make money—banking.

With goods pouring into Italy from around the world, merchants needed to know the value of coins from different countries. Florentine bankers became the experts. They used the florin, the gold coin of Florence, to measure the value of other money. Bankers also began lending money and charging interest. Florence's richest

▼ Lorenzo de' Medici

▲ This painting shows bankers in Florence doing business at a counter topped with brightly embroidered cloth. *Why did banking become so important in Florence?*

The Ducal Palace today ▶

▲ This painting from Renaissance Italy shows the busy pier and the Ducal Palace in Venice. *What industry provided some of Venice's wealth?*

family, the **Medici** (MEH•duh•chee), were bankers. They had branch banks as far away as London.

The Rise of Venice

The wealthiest city-state of all was Venice, where Marco Polo was born. Venice is at the northern end of the Adriatic Sea. The Venetians were great sailors and shipbuilders. They built their city on many small, swampy islands just off the coast. Early Venetians learned how to drive long wooden poles into mud to support their buildings.

Instead of paving roads, the Venetians cut canals through their swampy islands and used boats to move about. Even today, many of the streets in the older parts of Venice are canals and waterways. Gondolas—a type of long, narrow boat—still carry people along these canals.

Some of Venice's wealth came from building ships. Artisans worked on ships at a shipyard known as the Arsenal. Teams of workers cut the wood, shaped it into hulls, caulked (or sealed) the wood, and made sails and oars. Sometimes Venetians needed ships quickly. When the Turks tried to take a Venetian colony in the Mediterranean, the Arsenal built 100 ships in only two months to prepare for battle.

✓ **Reading Check** **Describe** How did Florence and the Medici family become so wealthy?

The Urban Noble

Main Idea Unlike medieval nobles, the nobles of the Italian city-states lived in cities and were active in trade, banking, and public life.

Reading Focus How does our society measure wealth? Before the Renaissance, wealth was based on the amount of land a person owned. Read to learn how that changed during the Renaissance.

The wealthy men of the Italian city-states were a new type of leader—the urban noble. Before this time, European nobles got their wealth from land, not trade. In fact, they looked down on trade and believed themselves to be above the town merchants.

In the Italian city-states, old noble families moved to the cities. They mixed with wealthy merchants and decided that money from trade was just as good as money from land.

Meanwhile, wealthy merchants copied the manners and lifestyle of noble families. Soon, the sons and daughters of nobles and rich merchants were marrying each other. Eventually, the old nobles and wealthy merchant families blended together to become the upper class of the city-states.

How Were Italian City-States Run? At first, many of the city-states were republics. A republic is a government controlled by its citizens. Not everyone was a citizen, however, only the artisans and merchants who had membership in the city's guilds.

From your study of the ancient Romans, you might recall that when their cities faced war or rebellion, they gave power to a dictator. The Italian city-states did something similar. In many cases, the cities were ruled by one powerful man who ran the government.

In Venice, the head of state was the duke, or doge (DOHJ). At first, the doge had great power over his council of nobles. Later, he lost power to a small group of nobles.

In Florence, the powerful Medici family gained control of the government in 1434. The Medici ran Florence for many decades. Lorenzo de' Medici ruled the city from 1469 to 1492. Known as "the Magnificent," Lorenzo used his wealth to support artists, architects, and writers. Many of Italy's Renaissance artists owed their success to his support.

Politics in Italy was complicated. Within each city, the rulers had to keep the poor from

Primary Source

The Prince

In Machiavelli's masterpiece, he explains his theories about human nature.

"You should consider then, that there are two ways of fighting, one with laws and the other with force. The first is properly a human method, the second belongs to beasts. But as the first method does not always suffice [meet your needs], you sometimes have to turn to the second. Thus a prince must know how to make good use of both the beast and the man."

—Niccolò Machiavelli,
The Prince

▲ Niccolò Machiavelli

DBQ Document-Based Question

Why must a good leader know more than one way to fight?

rebelling and prevent other wealthy people from seizing power. They had to make deals with merchants, bankers, landlords, church leaders, and mercenaries. At the same time, they had to deal with the leaders of the other city-states.

To deal with the other states around them, the Italians developed **diplomacy** (duh•PLOH•muh•see). Diplomacy is the art of negotiating, or making deals, with other countries. Each city-state sent ambassadors to live in the other city-states and act as representatives for their city. Many of the ideas of modern diplomacy first began in Italy's city-states.

How could a ruler maintain power in the Italian city-states? **Niccolò Machiavelli** (NEE•koh•LOH   MA•kee•uh•VEH•lee),   a diplomat in Florence, tried to answer this question when he wrote *The Prince* in 1513. Machiavelli claimed that people were

▲ This palace served as a government building in Rome for hundreds of years. *What form of government did many of the city-states have at first?*

greedy and self-centered. Rulers should not try to be good, he argued. Rather, they should do whatever is necessary to keep power and protect their city, including killing and lying. Today when we say someone is being Machiavellian, we mean they are being tricky and not thinking about being good.

 **Compare** How were medieval and Renaissance nobles different?

Section 1 Review

History Online

Study Central™ Need help with the material in this section? Visit jat.glencoe.com

Reading Summary

Review the Main Ideas

- A rebirth of learning called the Renaissance began in wealthy Italian city-states in the 1300s.

- Italian city-states, including Florence and Venice, grew wealthy through trade, manufacturing, and banking.

- In the Italian city-states, a noble's wealth was based on trade, rather than the amount of land owned.

What Did You Learn?

1. Why is the era from 1350 to 1550 in Europe called the Renaissance?

2. Why did the Renaissance begin in Italy?

Critical Thinking

3. **Organizing Information** Draw a diagram like the one below. Add details about the characteristics of the Italian Renaissance.

Italian Renaissance

4. **Economics Link** How did Renaissance cities gain their wealth? Give several examples.

5. **Summarize** Describe the governments of Italian city-states during the Renaissance.

6. **Analyze** Who were the Medicis and why were they important?

7. **Persuasive Writing** Write a letter to the editor of a Renaissance newspaper telling whether you agree or disagree with Machiavelli's beliefs about rulers and power during the Renaissance.

You Decide . . .

The Value of City-States

During the Renaissance, Italy was divided into more than 20 city-states. Some people think that the city-state form of government was a good idea. The leaders and wealthy nobles of the city-states encouraged the arts and sciences. This produced masterpieces by Michelangelo, Raphael, Leonardo, and others. Would this rebirth of arts and sciences have happened if Italy's independent city-states had not existed?

Other people, such as Girolamo Savonarola, were against the city-state form of government. After the fall of the Medici family in Florence, Savonarola spoke out in favor of a new type of leadership:

"I tell you that you must select a good form for your new government, and above all no one must think of making himself head if you wish to live in liberty."
— Girolamo Savonarola,
"This Will Be Your Final Destruction"

Examine the advantages and disadvantages of the city-state form of government. Then decide whether you think this system is primarily beneficial or primarily harmful.

Advantages:
- Because of their independent governments, each territory on the Italian peninsula was able to have its own culture.
- Some city-states were led by wealthy families, but most were led by a single leader. Almost all supported cultural and scientific advancement. The competition among city-states also encouraged the development of art and science.
- City-state rulers helped preserve the values and teachings of the ancient Greeks and Romans. They gave their own artists, architects, scholars, and writers opportunities to study classical works and interpret them in their own ways.

▲ A detail from the ceiling of the Sistine Chapel painted by Michelangelo

▲ **Renaissance nobles**

- Many citizens liked their city-state and wanted to help it. This encouraged patriotism.
- Some rulers were generous to the citizens of their city-states. For example, Duke Federigo da Montefeltro (1422–1482), a popular ruler in Urbino, built schools, hospitals, churches, and a library with his own money. He was known for talking to the commoners and helping the poor.
- The city-states helped bring an end to feudalism by making merchants, as well as landowners, wealthy and ending the relationship between lords and vassals.

Disadvantages:

- Many city-states were led by one man. The common people were often mistreated until they revolted and threw out their leaders. This happened to Florence's Medici family in 1527.
- The divided city-states were weaker than a united Italy would have been, so they were often invaded by foreign groups.
- Smaller territories did not always have enough soldiers to defend their cities and land. They hired mercenaries—generals and armies from outside their city—to help them fight. Sometimes mercenaries took over the city-states that had hired them.
- Because many Italians were poor, there were noticeable class differences in the city-states. These differences often led to bloody conflicts between the social classes.
- Wealthy families often battled with each other for control of the city-states.
- Some city-state rulers became even wealthier by overseeing banking and trade. These leaders lived in luxury, while many citizens were very poor.

You Be the Historian

Checking for Understanding

1. Do you think that the art of the Renaissance would have been created if Italy had not been divided into individual city-states? Why or why not?
2. Do you think Italian artists had more artistic freedom under this form of government? Why or why not?
3. Would you have enjoyed living during the Renaissance? Would you have wanted to be a ruler, noble, artist, or commoner? Why?

Section
2

New Ideas and Art

Get Ready to Read!

What's the Connection?

In Section 1, you learned about the growth of Italian city-states. In this section, you will learn how the wealth of the city-states led to an age of artistic achievements.

Focusing on the Main Ideas

• Humanists studied the Greeks and Romans, and the development of the printing press helped spread their ideas. *(page 619)*

• Renaissance artists used new techniques to produce paintings that showed people in an emotional and realistic way. *(page 623)*

• Renaissance ideas and art spread from Italy to northern Europe. *(page 625)*

Locating Places
Flanders (FLAN•duhrz)

Meeting People
Dante Alighieri (DAHN•tay A•luh•GYEHR•ee)

Johannes Gutenberg (yoh•HAHN•uhs GOO•tuhn•BUHRG)

Leonardo da Vinci (LEE•uh•NAHR•doh duh VIHN•chee)

Michelangelo Buonarroti (MY•kuh•LAN•juh•LOH BWAW•nahr•RAW•tee)

William Shakespeare (SHAYK•SPIHR)

Building Your Vocabulary
humanism (HYOO•muh•NIH•zuhm)

vernacular (vuhr•NA•kyuh•luhr)

Reading Strategy

Organizing Information Create a diagram to show features of Renaissance art.

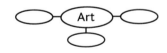

NATIONAL GEOGRAPHIC

When & Who?

1400

1500

1600

c. 1455 Johannes Gutenberg uses printing press to print the Bible

1494 Leonardo begins painting *The Last Supper*

1512 Michelangelo finishes painting Sistine Chapel's ceiling

1601 Shakespeare writes *Hamlet*

Renaissance Humanism

Main Idea Humanists studied the Greeks and Romans, and the development of the printing press helped spread their ideas.

Reading Focus Have you ever tried to draw a copy of a painting you like? Is it harder to copy what other people have done or to come up with new ideas for your own pictures? Read to learn how Renaissance writers borrowed ideas from the past but tried to be original too.

In the 1300s, a new way of understanding the world developed in medieval Europe. This new approach was called **humanism** (HYOO•muh•NIH•zuhm). It was based on the values of the ancient Greeks and Romans. Humanists believed that the individual and human society were important. Humanists did not turn away from religious faith, but they wanted a balance between faith and reason. Their new ideas encouraged men to be active in their cities and achieve great things.

Ancient Works Become Popular
In the 1300s, Italians began to study early Roman and Greek works. For most of the Middle Ages, Western Europeans knew little about ancient Greek and Roman writings. When they went on the Crusades, however, they opened trade with the Middle East and began to get information from the Arabs. Arab scholars knew classic Greek and Roman works very well. In addition, when the Turks conquered Constantinople in 1453, many Byzantine scholars left and moved to Venice or Florence.

One famous scholar of the ancient works was Petrarch (PEH•TRAHRK). Francesco Petrarch was a poet and scholar who lived in the 1300s. He studied Roman writers like Cicero and wrote biographies of famous Romans.

Petrarch encouraged Europeans to search for Latin manuscripts in monasteries all over Europe. In time, his efforts paid off and new libraries were built to keep the manuscripts. The largest was the Vatican Library in Rome.

Italians studied more than ancient books. They studied the old buildings and statues all around them. All over Rome, one could see workers cleaning the dirt and rubble from broken columns and statues. Italian artists eagerly studied the proportions of the ancient works. If they knew how long a statue's arms were compared to its height, they would be able to understand why it looked so perfect.

Ancient Greek manuscript on Archimedes ▼

◄ **Francesco Petrarch has been called the father of Italian Renaissance humanism.** *How did Petrarch contribute to the preservation of Roman knowledge?*

HISTORY MAKERS

Movable Type c. 1450

Johannes Gutenberg, a German goldsmith, built a printing press modeled after a winepress. Once the press was completed, Gutenberg spent two years printing his first book. For each page, he set metal letters in a frame, rolled ink over the frame, and pressed the frame against paper. Around 1455, he completed printing what is now known as the Gutenberg Bible, or the 42 Line Bible. This was the first book printed using movable metal type, sparking a revolution in publishing and reading.

▼ **Gutenberg Bible**

Changes in Literature During the Renaissance, educated people wrote in "pure" Latin, the Latin used in ancient Rome. Petrarch thought classical Latin was the best way to write, but when he wanted to write poems to the woman he loved, he wrote in the **vernacular** (vuhr•NA•kyuh•luhr). The vernacular is the everyday language people speak in a region—Italian, French, or German, for example. When authors began writing in the vernacular, many more people could read their work.

In the early 1300s, **Dante Alighieri** (DAHN•tay A•luh•GYEHR•ee), a poet of Florence, wrote one of the world's greatest poems in the vernacular. It is called *The Divine Comedy*. As a young man, Dante was active in politics, but when noble families began fighting over power, he had to leave Florence. That was when he wrote his long poem—more than 14,000 lines. *The Divine Comedy* tells the gripping tale of the main character's journey from hell to heaven. The horrible punishments for different sins were vividly described.

Another important writer who used the vernacular was Chaucer. Chaucer wrote in English. In his famous book, *The Canterbury Tales*, he describes 29 pilgrims on their journey to the city of Canterbury. *The Canterbury Tales* describes the levels of English society, from the nobles at the top to the poor at the bottom. The English Chaucer used in his writing is the ancestor of the English we speak today.

The Printing Press Spreads Ideas

The printing press was a key to the spread of humanist ideas throughout Europe. In the early 1450s, **Johannes Gutenberg** (yoh•HAHN•uhs GOO•tuhn•BUHRG) developed a printing press that used movable metal type. This type of printing press made it possible to print many books much more quickly. With more books available, more people learned to read. Scholars could read one another's works and debate their ideas in letters.

Ideas grew and spread more quickly than ever before in Europe.

The Chinese had already invented movable type, but it did not work well with their large alphabet of characters. For Europeans, the printing press was a big improvement. It was easy to use with linen paper, another Chinese invention.

Gutenberg's Bible, printed in the 1450s, was the first European book produced on the new press. Soon books flooded Europe. About 40,000 books were published by 1500. Half of these were religious works like the Bible or prayer books.

How Did Humanism Affect Society?

Humanist scholars studied the Greeks and Romans to increase their knowledge of many different topics. They were curious about everything, including plants and animals, human anatomy and medicine, and the stars and planets. Their study of mathematics helped them in many subjects.

One of the best Renaissance scientists was also a great artist, **Leonardo da Vinci** (LEE•uh•NAHR•doh duh VIHN•chee). Leonardo dissected corpses to learn anatomy and studied fossils to understand the world's history. He was also an inventor and an engineer.

Most of what we know about Leonardo comes from his notebooks. Leonardo filled their pages with sketches of his scientific and artistic ideas. Centuries before the airplane was invented, Leonardo drew sketches of a glider, a helicopter, and a parachute. Other sketches show a version of a military tank and a scuba diving suit.

✓ **Reading Check** **Explain** What was the benefit of writing in the vernacular?

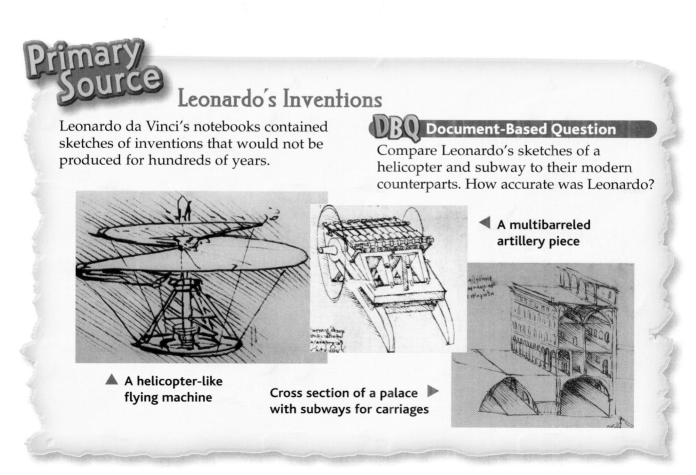

Primary Source

Leonardo's Inventions

Leonardo da Vinci's notebooks contained sketches of inventions that would not be produced for hundreds of years.

DBQ **Document-Based Question**

Compare Leonardo's sketches of a helicopter and subway to their modern counterparts. How accurate was Leonardo?

◀ **A multibarreled artillery piece**

▲ **A helicopter-like flying machine**

Cross section of a palace ▶ **with subways for carriages**

Biography

LEONARDO DA VINCI
1452–1519

Leonardo was born in Vinci, Italy, to a peasant woman named Caterina. Shortly after Leonardo's birth, she left the boy in the care of his father. By the time Leonardo was 15 years old, his father knew his son had artistic talent. He arranged for Leonardo to become an apprentice to the famous painter Andrea del Verrocchio.

By 1472, Leonardo had become a master in the painters' guild of Florence. He worked in Florence until 1481, and then he went to the city of Milan. There he kept a large workshop and employed many apprentices. During this time, Leonardo began keeping small pads of paper tucked in his belt for sketching. Later he organized the drawings by theme and assembled the pages into notebooks.

Seventeen years later, Leonardo returned to Florence, where he was welcomed with great honor. During this time, Leonardo painted some of his masterpieces. He also made scientific studies, including dissections, observations of the flight of birds, and research on the movement of water currents.

In 1516 Leonardo accepted an invitation to live in France. The king admired Leonardo and gave him freedom to pursue his interests. During the last three years of his life, Leonardo lived in a small house near the king's summer palace. He spent most of his time sketching and working on his scientific studies.

▲ Leonardo da Vinci

> "Nothing can be loved or hated unless it is first known."
>
> –Leonardo da Vinci

▲ The *Mona Lisa* by Leonardo da Vinci

Then and Now

Leonardo's curiosity fueled his creativity and interest in science. What invention created in the last 100 years do you think would impress Leonardo the most? Why?

Artists in Renaissance Italy

Main Idea Renaissance artists used new techniques to produce paintings that showed people in an emotional and realistic way.

Reading Focus Have you ever had trouble making your drawings look real and three-dimensional? Read to learn how Renaissance artists learned to make their art look natural and real.

During the Renaissance, wealthy Italian families and church leaders paid artists to create paintings, sculptures, and buildings for display throughout their cities. The pope himself funded many works of art to decorate the Vatican. Renaissance artists followed the models of the ancient Romans and Greeks but expressed humanist ideas.

What Was New About Renaissance Art?

If you compare medieval and Renaissance paintings, you will see major differences in their styles. Renaissance art tries to show people as they would appear in real life. It also tries to show people's emotions. When a medieval artist depicted the birth of Jesus, he wanted to remind Christians about their belief that Jesus was born to save the world. A Renaissance artist painting the same scene might try to show how tender Mary looked with her tiny baby.

Renaissance painters also used new techniques. The most important was perspective (puhr•SPEHK•tihv), a method that makes a drawing or painting look three-dimensional. Artists had tried to use perspective before, but Renaissance artists perfected it. Using perspective, objects in a scene appear to be at different distances from the viewer. The result is a more realistic image.

To make their paintings more realistic, Renaissance artists also used a technique called chiaroscuro (kee•AHR•uh•SKYUR•oh).

▲ The sculpture, *La Pieta*, by Michelangelo shows Mary holding the body of Jesus after his death. *What did Renaissance artists try to portray in their works?*

Chiaroscuro softened edges by using light and shadows instead of stiff outlines to separate objects. In Italian, *chiaro* means "clear or light," and *oscuro* means "dark." Chiaroscuro created more drama and emotion in a painting.

The Peak of the Renaissance The artistic Renaissance lasted from about 1350 to 1550, but it hit its peak between 1490 and 1520. At that time, three great artists were producing their masterpieces—Leonardo da Vinci, Raphael Sanzio, and **Michelangelo Buonarroti** (MY•kuh•LAN•juh•LOH BWAW•nahr•RAW•tee).

Although Leonardo also became a great scientist and inventor, he trained as an artist. Born in 1452, he began his training in Florence at a young age. Training in workshops was an old tradition, but during the Renaissance, individual artists began to do something no medieval artist had done— they signed their own work.

One of Leonardo's most famous works is *The Last Supper*, which he began painting in 1494 on a wall behind a church altar. He painted on wet plaster with watercolor paint. A painting done this way is called a

The Way It Was

Focus on Everyday Life

The Life of a Renaissance Artist

If a young boy in Renaissance Italy wanted to be an artist, he would become an apprentice at a workshop run by an established artist. The main job of apprentices was preparing materials for the master artist and his assistants. Apprentices used minerals, spices, egg yolk, and other everyday materials to mix paints. They readied wax and clay for sculpture modeling. Eventually, apprentices became assistants. Talented assistants could become masters of their own workshops.

Master artists could afford to have workshops because of the patronage system in Italy. Patrons—people who pay to support someone else's work—would commission, or hire, an artist to complete a project. That artist was usually helped by his assistants and apprentices. Patrons were usually political and church leaders, organizations, and wealthy bankers and merchants.

▲ Renaissance painter and apprentice

Connecting to the Past

1. What was the main job of apprentices?

2. Does the patronage system or the apprentice system exist today? If so, in what fields?

fresco (FREHS•koh), which in Italian means "fresh." Frescoes were painted in churches all over Italy.

One of Leonardo's great artistic skills is visible in *The Last Supper*. In this painting of Jesus and his disciples, Leonardo was able to show human emotions through small differences in how each apostle held his head or the apostle's position in relation to Jesus. Leonardo showed this skill again in the *Mona Lisa*. People still argue about what the woman in the portrait is thinking—what is the mystery behind her smile?

Although Raphael worked at the same time as Leonardo, he was much younger. Even as a young man, Raphael worked with ease and grace and became known as one of Italy's best painters. Italians especially loved the gentle Madonnas he painted. He also painted many frescoes in the Vatican Palace. Perhaps his best-known painting is the *School of Athens*, which depicts a number of Greek philosophers.

The third great Renaissance artist was Michelangelo. Like many other artists of the time, Michelangelo painted, sculpted, and designed buildings. He painted one of the best-known Renaissance works—the ceiling of the Sistine Chapel in Rome.

Although he painted many outstanding works, Michelangelo was a sculptor at heart. He believed his talents were inspired by God. He carved his statues to show perfect versions of human beings as a symbol of God's beauty and perfection. Michelangelo's best-known sculpture is the 13-foot-tall statue *David*. The sculptor made David seem calm, yet ready for action. Also impressive is Michelangelo's statue of the biblical Moses. The huge figure appears both wise and powerful.

Reading Check **Compare and Contrast**
What were some of the differences between medieval and Renaissance artists?

The Renaissance Spreads

Main Idea Renaissance ideas and art spread from Italy to northern Europe.

Reading Focus If you were a Canadian artist, would your painting look different than if you lived in Arizona? Read to learn how the Renaissance changed as it moved into northern Europe.

In the late 1400s, the Renaissance spread to northern Europe and later to England. The printing press helped humanist ideas to spread, as did people who traveled.

What Is the Northern Renaissance?

The Northern Renaissance refers to the culture in places we know today as Belgium, Luxembourg, Germany, and the Netherlands. Like Italian artists, northern artists wanted their works to have greater realism, but they used different methods. One important method they developed was oil painting. First developed in **Flanders** (FLAN•duhrz)—a region that is in northern Belgium today—oils let artists paint intricate details and surface textures, like the gold braid on a gown.

Jan van Eyck was a master of oil painting. In one of his best-known paintings, a newly married couple stands side by side in a formal bedroom. Van Eyck showed every fold in their rich gowns and every detail of the chandelier above their heads.

Albrecht Dürer (AHL•brehkt DUR•uhr) is perhaps one of the greatest artists of the Northern Renaissance. Dürer was able to master both perspective and fine detail. He is best known for his engravings. An engraving is made from an image carved on metal, wood, or stone. Ink is applied to the surface, and then the image is printed on paper.

Dürer's *Four Horsemen of the Apocalypse* is an outstanding example of a woodcut, a print made from carved wood. In it, four fierce horsemen ride to announce the end of the world.

Globe Theater

William Shakespeare's plays were performed at the Globe Theater in London. It could hold about 3,000 people. Plays were performed every day of the week except Sunday. Performances occurred during the day, since the theater had no lights. *When did the Renaissance spread to northern Europe and England?*

Flags announced the type of play. White flags meant comedies, black flags meant tragedies, and red flags stood for history plays.

Wealthy and important people sat beneath the covered section.

Poor commoners, called groundlings, stood on the ground for the show. They often brought fruit and vegetables to throw at actors they did not like.

Who Was William Shakespeare? In England, the Renaissance took place in writing and theater more than in art. The Renaissance began in England in the later 1500s, during the rule of Elizabeth I.

Theater was popular in England in the 1500s. Admission was only one or two cents, so even the poor could attend. English playwrights, or writers who create plays, wrote about people's strengths, weaknesses, and emotions.

The greatest English writer of that era was **William Shakespeare** (SHAYK•SPIHR). He wrote tragedies, comedies, and historical plays. Some of his great tragedies include *Hamlet, Macbeth,* and *Romeo and Juliet.* In each tragedy, the characters' flaws cause their downfall. Among his most famous comedies are *A Midsummer Night's Dream, Twelfth Night,* and *Much Ado About Nothing.* His best-known historical plays include

▲ Dürer's *Four Horsemen of the Apocalypse*

Henry V and *Richard III.* Shakespeare's plays are still performed today and remain very popular.

 **Compare** How did the northern Renaissance differ from the Italian Renaissance?

> **History Online**
> **Study Central**™ Need help with the material in this section? Visit jat.glencoe.com

Section 2 Review

Reading Summary

Review the Main Ideas

- During the Renaissance, scholars examined the ancient works of the Greeks and Romans, began to write in the vernacular, and explored many scientific fields.

- Italian Renaissance artists employed new techniques and created masterpieces of painting and sculpture.

- As the Renaissance spread to northern Europe and England, artists and writers, such as Dürer and Shakespeare, created great works.

What Did You Learn?

1. Explain the beliefs of humanists during the Renaissance.

2. Explain the artistic technique of perspective.

Critical Thinking

3. **Summarizing Information** Draw a chart like the one below. Use it to describe the artistic work and techniques of each artist listed.

Leonardo da Vinci	
Michelangelo	
Jan van Eyck	
Shakespeare	

4. **Evaluate** What was the importance of the printing press on Renaissance society?

5. **Science Link** Describe the scientific efforts and contributions of Leonardo da Vinci.

6. **Explain** How were the ideals of the Renaissance expressed in England? Provide examples in your answer.

7. **Expository Writing** Choose a painting or sculpture shown in this section. In a short essay, describe the work and explain how it demonstrates Renaissance techniques or characteristics.

A MIDSUMMER NIGHT'S DREAM

**By William Shakespeare,
Adapted by E. Nesbit**

Before You Read

The Scene: This story takes place in Athens, Greece, in a legendary time when magical creatures lived among humans.

The Characters: Hermia and Lysander are in love. Demetrius loves Hermia, and Helena loves Demetrius. Oberon and Titania are the King and Queen of the Fairies.

The Plot: Hermia and Lysander run away to be married. Demetrius follows them because he loves Hermia. Helena follows Demetrius because she loves him. The fairies they encounter try to use magic to help the four humans.

Vocabulary Preview

betrayed: gave to an enemy

mortal: human

quarrel: argument

glade: grassy open space in a forest

suitor: one who wants to marry another

bade: asked

scheme: plan

Have you ever tried to help someone but made the situation worse? In this story, fairies attempt to help four young people traveling through the woods, but their efforts do not go as planned.

As You Read

Keep in mind that William Shakespeare wrote this story as a play. E. Nesbit rewrote the story in paragraph form to make it shorter and easier to read.

Hermia and Lysander were [in love]; but Hermia's father wished her to marry another man, named Demetrius.

Now in Athens, where they lived, there was a wicked law, by which any girl who refused to marry according to her father's wishes, might be put to death. . . .

Lysander of course was nearly mad with grief, and the best thing to do seemed to him for Hermia to run away to his aunt's house at a place beyond the reach of that cruel law; and there he would come to her and marry her. But before she started, she told her friend, Helena, what she was going to do.

Helena had been Demetrius' sweetheart long before his marriage with Hermia had been thought of, and being very silly, like all jealous people, she could not see that it was not poor Hermia's fault that Demetrius wished to marry her instead of his own lady, Helena. She knew that if she told Demetrius that Hermia was going, as she was, to the wood outside Athens, he would follow her, "and I can follow him, and at least I shall see him," she said to herself. So she went to him, and betrayed her friend's secret.

Now this wood where Lysander was to meet Hermia, and where the other two had decided to follow them, was full of fairies,[1] as most woods are, if one only had the eyes to see them, and in this wood on this night were the King and Queen of the fairies, Oberon and Titania. Now fairies are very wise people, but now and then they can be quite as foolish as mortal folk. Oberon and Titania, who might have been as happy as the days were long, had thrown away all their joy in a foolish quarrel. . . .

So, instead of keeping one happy Court and dancing all night through in the moonlight, as is fairies' use, the King with his attendants wandered through one part of the wood, while the Queen with hers kept state in another. And the cause of all

---

[1]**fairies:** imaginary beings, usually having small human form and magic powers

this trouble was a little Indian boy whom Titania had taken to be one of her followers. Oberon wanted the child to follow him and be one of his fairy knights; but the Queen would not give him up.

On this night, in a glossy moonlight glade, the King and Queen of the fairies met.

"Ill² met by moonlight, proud Titania," said the King.

"What! jealous, Oberon?" answered the Queen. "You spoil everything with your quarreling. Come, fairies, let us leave him. I am not friends with him now."

"It rests with you to make up the quarrel," said the King. "Give me that little Indian boy, and I will again be your humble servant and suitor."

"Set your mind at rest," said the Queen. "Your whole fairy kingdom buys not that boy from me. Come fairies."

And she and her train rode off down the moonbeams.³

"Well, go your ways," said Oberon. "But I'll be even with you before you leave this wood."

Then Oberon called his favorite fairy, Puck. Puck was the spirit of mischief. . . .

"Now," said Oberon to this little sprite,⁴ "fetch me the flower called Love-in-idleness. The juice of that little purple flower laid on the eyes of those who sleep will make them when they wake to love the first thing they see. I will put some of the juice of that flower on my Titania's eyes, and when she wakes, she will love the first thing she sees, were it lion, bear, or wolf, or bull, or meddling monkey, or a busy ape."

---

²**ill:** causing suffering or distress
³**moonbeams:** rays of light from the moon
⁴**sprite:** fairy

While Puck was gone, Demetrius passed through the glade followed by poor Helena, and still she told him how she loved him and reminded him of all his promises, and still he told her that he did not and could not love her, and that his promises were nothing. Oberon was sorry for poor Helena, and when Puck returned with the flower, he bade him follow Demetrius and put some of the juice on his eyes, so that he might love Helena when he woke and looked on her, as much as she loved him. So Puck set off, and wandering through the wood found, not Demetrius, but Lysander, on whose eyes he put the juice; but when Lysander woke, he saw not his own Hermia, but Helena, who was walking through the wood looking for the cruel Demetrius; and directly he saw her he loved her and left his own lady, under the spell of the crimson flower.

When Hermia woke she found Lysander gone, and wandered about the wood trying to find him. Puck went back and told Oberon what he had done, and Oberon soon found that he had made a mistake, and set about looking for Demetrius, and having found him, put some of the juice on his eyes. And the first thing Demetrius saw when he woke was also Helena. So now Demetrius and Lysander were both following her through the wood, and it was Hermia's turn to follow her lover as Helena had done before. The end of it was that Helena and Hermia began to quarrel, and Demetrius and Lysander went off to fight. Oberon was

he cut 6x u Im Amerin
hand 6x w
he's how place he cut 6x w

enameled[5] skin of a snake. Oberon stooped over her and laid the juice on her eyes. . . .

Now, it happened that when Titania woke the first thing she saw was a stupid clown, one of a party of players who had come out into the wood to rehearse their play. This clown had met with Puck, who had clapped[6] [a donkey's] head on his shoulders so that it looked as if it grew there. Directly Titania woke and saw this dreadful monster, she said, "What angel is this? Are you as wise as you are beautiful?"

"If I am wise enough to find my way out of this wood, that's enough for me," said the foolish clown.

"Do not desire to go out of the wood," said Titania. The spell of the love-juice was on her, and to her the clown seemed the most beautiful and delightful creature on all the earth. "I love you," she went on. "Come with me, and I will give you fairies to attend on you."

So she called four fairies, whose names were Peaseblossom, Cobweb, Moth, and Mustardseed.

"You must attend this gentleman," said the Queen. "Feed him with apricots, and dewberries, purple grapes, green figs, and mulberries. Steal honey-bags for him from the humble-bees, and with the wings of painted butterflies fan the moonbeams from his sleeping eyes." . . .

"Would you like anything to eat?" said the fairy Queen.

very sorry to see his kind scheme to help these lovers turn out so badly. So he said to Puck:

"These two young men are going to fight. You must overhang the night with drooping fog, and lead them so astray, that one will never find the other. When they are tired out, they will fall asleep. Then drop this other herb on Lysander's eyes. That will give him his old sight and his old love. Then each man will have the lady who loves him, and they will all think that this has been only a Midsummer Night's Dream. Then when this is done all will be well with them."

So Puck went and did as he was told, and when the two had fallen asleep without meeting each other, Puck poured the juice on Lysander's eyes. . . .

Meanwhile Oberon found Titania asleep on a bank. . . .There Titania always slept a part of the night, wrapped in the

---

[5]**enameled:** coated with a glassy substance
[6]**clapped:** forcefully put

"I should like some good dry oats," said the clown—for his donkey's head made him desire donkey's food—"and some hay to follow."

"Shall some of my fairies fetch you new nuts from the squirrel's house?" asked the Queen.

"I'd rather have a handful or two of good dried peas," said the clown. "But please don't let any of your people disturb me, I am going to sleep."

Then said the Queen, "And I will wind thee in my arms."

And so when Oberon came along he found his beautiful Queen lavishing kisses and endearments on a clown with a donkey's head. And before he released her from the enchantment, he persuaded her to give him the little Indian boy he so much desired to have. Then he took pity on her, and threw some juice of the disenchanting flower on her pretty eyes; and then in a moment she saw plainly the donkey-headed clown she had been loving, and knew how foolish she had been.

Oberon took off the [donkey's] head from the clown, and left him to finish his sleep with his own silly head lying on the thyme and violets.

Thus all was made plain and straight again. Oberon and Titania loved each other more than ever. Demetrius thought of no one but Helena, and Helena had never had any thought of anyone but Demetrius. As for Hermia and Lysander, they were as loving a couple as you could meet in a day's march, even through a fairy-wood. So the four [mortals] went back to Athens and were married; and the fairy King and Queen live happily together in that very wood at this very day.

Responding to the Reading

1. How did Demetrius and Lysander fall in love with Helena?
2. How did the story get its title, *A Midsummer Night's Dream?*
3. **Cause and Effect** Why were Lysander and Demetrius preparing to fight?
4. **Predict** What do you think might have happened if Oberon had not interfered with the conflict among the four young people?
5. **Reading** **Read to Write** Reread the last paragraph in the story, then write another ending to the story that could replace that paragraph.

The Reformation Begins

Get Ready to Read!

What's the Connection?

During the Middle Ages, all of Western Europe's Christians were Catholic. The movement called the Reformation, however, questioned Catholic beliefs and power.

Focusing on the Main Ideas

* The reforms of Martin Luther led to the creation of new Christian churches. *(page 634)*

* Political leaders often supported Protestantism because they wanted more power. *(page 639)*

* John Calvin's Protestant teachings spread across Europe and into North America. *(page 640)*

Locating Places

Wittenberg (WIH•tuhn•BUHRG)
Geneva (juh•NEE•vuh)

Meeting People

Martin Luther
Desiderius Erasmus (DEHS•ih•DIHR•ee•uhs ih•RAZ•muhs)
John Calvin

Building Your Vocabulary

Reformation (REH•fuhr•MAY•shuhn)
indulgence (ihn•DUHL•juhns)
denomination (dih•NAH•muh•NAY•shuhn)
theology (thee•AH•luh•jee)
predestination (pree•DEHS•tuh•NAY•shuhn)

Reading Strategy

Cause and Effect Create a diagram to show some of the reasons for the Reformation.

Reasons for the Reformation

NATIONAL GEOGRAPHIC **When & Where?**

1500	1530	1560

1517 Martin Luther writes Ninety-Five Theses

1519 Charles V becomes Holy Roman Emperor

1555 Peace of Augsburg signed

London
Wittenberg
Paris
Geneva
Rome

Calls for Church Reform

Main Idea The reforms of Martin Luther led to the creation of new Christian churches.

Reading Focus Can you think of any reformers in the United States? Read to learn how some Europeans set out to reform the Catholic Church and ended up starting a new church instead.

In 1517 a young monk named **Martin Luther** challenged the Roman Catholic Church. He publicly argued that the pope could not decide what a person had to do to get into heaven. Eventually, his challenge to the pope's authority led to the creation of new churches in Western Europe.

At first, Luther only wanted to reform the Catholic Church. This is why we call these events the **Reformation** (REH•fuhr•MAY•shuhn). The Reformation, however, became the beginning of a movement in Christianity known as Protestantism. By the end of the Reformation, many new Christian churches had appeared in Europe. The religious unity the Catholic Church had created in Western Europe, and which had lasted for hundreds of years, had been broken.

What Ideas Led to the Reformation?

In the last section, you read about humanism. When humanism spread to northern Europe, it led to a new movement in Christianity called Christian humanism. Its best-known leader was a scholar and clergyman named **Desiderius Erasmus** (DEHS•ih•DIHR•ee•uhs ih•RAZ•muhs).

Erasmus wrote that human beings could use their reason to become better Christians and thereby improve the Church. He studied ancient Christian works for inspiration.

One of Erasmus's goals was to translate the Bible into the vernacular. He wanted a farmer working in the fields to be able to stop and read the Bible. Erasmus also wrote that what mattered was that people be good in their everyday lives. It was not enough to participate in religious activities, like going to church on Sunday.

The Church Upsets Reformers

By the 1300s, many people believed that the Church had problems. It taxed people heavily, and some bishops behaved like they were kings. They built palaces, spent money on fine art, and made sure that their relatives had good jobs. In many villages, priests could barely read or give a good sermon.

Many Catholics became angry at the Church's focus on money. One Church practice that especially angered them was the selling of indulgences. An **indulgence** (ihn•DUHL•juhns) was a pardon from the Church for a person's sins. The Church had given out indulgences before, but it did not usually sell them. In the 1500s, however, the

▲ Desiderius Erasmus, the most famous Christian humanist, criticized the wealth and power of Catholic leaders. *What change did Erasmus want to make to the Bible?*

pope needed money to repair the church of St. Peter's in Rome. To get that money, he decided to sell indulgences in northern Germany.

The sale of indulgences outraged Martin Luther. Luther had looked in the Bible and found nothing that said an indulgence could pardon sin. The whole idea of selling God's forgiveness seemed unholy to him.

Martin Luther was not the first person to question the pope's power. As early as the 1370s, an English priest named John Wycliffe (WIH•KLIHF) had opposed Church policies. He preached that Christians needed only to recognize Jesus Christ as a power above them, not the pope.

Wycliffe and Luther both challenged the pope's power, but they had something else in common—their respect for the Bible. Wycliffe wanted everyone to read the Bible. After Wycliffe died, his followers translated the Bible into English for the first time.

▲ **This painting shows indulgences being sold in a village marketplace.** *Why was the Church selling indulgences?*

▲ **Indulgence box**

Who Was Martin Luther?
Martin Luther became one of the most famous men in history. His break with the Catholic Church led to a revolution in Christianity. Why would a religious man disagree with his faith? First of all, Luther was angered by the behavior of Church leaders. Secondly, he was worried about his own soul.

Luther was born in 1483 in a small German village. A bright and sensitive boy, he grew up in a disciplined family. His father wanted him to study law, but Luther often thought about serving the Church. One day, he was out riding when a bolt of lightning knocked him to the ground. According to legend, Luther made up his mind to be a monk at that moment.

When Luther went to Rome on a pilgrimage, he was shocked at the behavior of the Roman clergy. Back home in Germany, he taught at a university in the town of **Wittenberg** (WIH•tuhn•BUHRG). He worried about the Church's problems and also about his own soul. With the plague killing people all around him, it is not surprising that Luther worried about whether he would go to heaven when he died.

The Church said that Luther would be saved and would go to heaven if he performed good works and received the sacraments. Still Luther worried that this was not true. He prayed and fasted long hours as he searched for answers to his

▲ Martin Luther began the Reformation when he made public his Ninety-Five Theses. *How did the Catholic Church react to Luther's actions?*

questions. He prayed so long that sometimes he fell unconscious on the cold church floor.

Luther found his answers by studying the Bible. He concluded that only faith, not good works, brought salvation. He believed that salvation was a gift from God, not something earned by doing good works.

In 1517, when the Church began selling indulgences, Luther was astonished. How could the Church tell peasants that buying an indulgence would save them? He angrily prepared a list of 95 arguments against indulgences and sent them to his bishop. Some accounts say that Luther also nailed them to the door of Wittenberg

History Online

Web Activity Visit jat.glencoe.com and click on *Chapter 17—Student Web Activity* to learn more about the Reformation.

Cathedral for everyone to read. The list became known as the Ninety-Five Theses. Thousands of copies were printed and read all across the German kingdoms.

Revolt Leads to New Churches At first the Church did not take Luther very seriously. Soon, though, Church leaders saw that Luther was dangerous. If people believed Luther, they would rely on the Bible, not priests. Who would need priests if the sacraments were not needed to get to heaven?

The pope and Luther argued for several years, but Luther refused to change his position. Finally, the pope excommunicated Luther. This meant Luther was no longer a member of the Church and could no longer receive the sacraments. He was also no longer considered a monk.

In the following years, Luther's ideas led to the creation of a new **denomination** (dih•NAH•muh•NAY•shuhn), or organized branch of Christianity. It was known as Lutheranism and was the first Protestant denomination.

Lutheranism has three main ideas. The first is that faith in Jesus, not good works, brings salvation. The second is that the Bible is the final source for truth about God, not a church or its ministers. Finally, Lutheranism said that the church was made up of all its believers, not just the clergy.

Peasant Revolts Luther's debate with the pope was so famous that even peasants in the countryside had heard about it. They liked what they heard about Luther.

The life of a peasant had always been hard, but in the 1520s, it was terrible. The crops had been poor for several years. On top of that, noble landowners increased the taxes that peasants had to pay.

Because of their suffering, Luther's ideas stirred the peasants to revolt. If

Luther had a right to rebel against an unjust pope, then the peasants must have a right to stand up to greedy nobles.

The peasants began by listing their demands. Like Luther, they based their ideas on the Bible. One leader said the peasants would no longer work for the nobles, "unless it should be shown us from the Gospel that we are serfs."

When the nobles did not give in, huge revolts broke out. It was not long, however, before the peasants were defeated. The nobles had better weapons and horses and won easily, killing thousands of peasants.

At first Luther sympathized with the peasants, but he soon changed his mind. He was afraid of what might happen without a strong government. Luther used his powerful sermons to tell peasants that God had set the government above them and they must obey it.

Reading Check **Cause and Effect** What was the result of the Church's decision to sell indulgences in 1517?

Linking Past & Present

The Anabaptists, Amish, and Mennonites

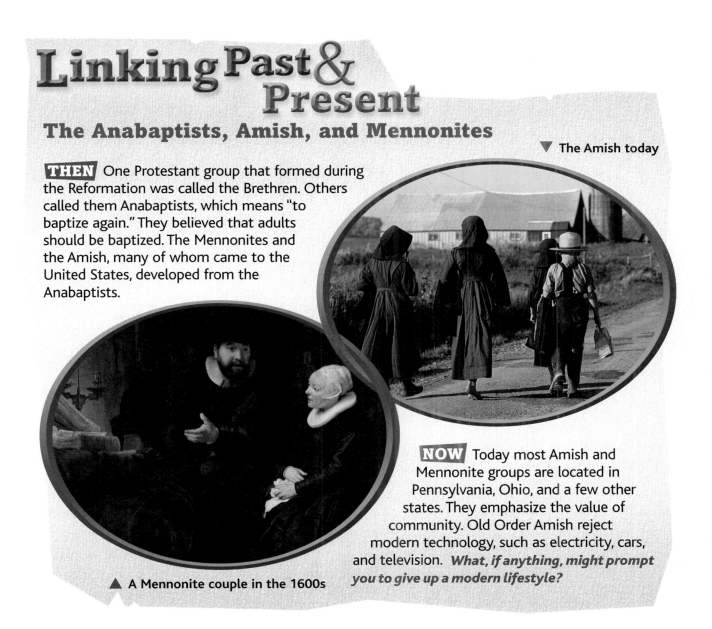

▼ The Amish today

THEN One Protestant group that formed during the Reformation was called the Brethren. Others called them Anabaptists, which means "to baptize again." They believed that adults should be baptized. The Mennonites and the Amish, many of whom came to the United States, developed from the Anabaptists.

NOW Today most Amish and Mennonite groups are located in Pennsylvania, Ohio, and a few other states. They emphasize the value of community. Old Order Amish reject modern technology, such as electricity, cars, and television. *What, if anything, might prompt you to give up a modern lifestyle?*

▲ A Mennonite couple in the 1600s

Biography

MARTIN LUTHER
1483–1546

▲ Martin Luther

Long before Martin Luther struggled with the Catholic Church, he faced difficult issues. Luther was born in Eisleben, Germany, in 1483 to a family of miners. Both his parents beat Luther as a child. Martin Luther and his father had terrible tempers. Luther later said his father's beatings caused him to feel bitter and hateful toward his family.

To avoid his abusive home life, Luther focused on his education. He was a student at the Latin School in Mansfield in 1488. As a teenager he went to two other schools away from home. At his father's urging, he considered studying law but instead earned a bachelor's degree in philosophy in 1502.

Later, Luther entered a monastery to separate himself from his abusive past. In 1505 he traveled to Erfurt and became a monk. He then went to Wittenberg in 1508 and stayed with a group of Augustinian hermits. There he continued his study of theology.

Luther was a determined young man. Although he was a priest, he began to question the practices of the Catholic Church. His reforms resulted in a break with the Church. In 1525 he married a former nun named Katharine von Bora. They had six children and lived in a former monastery.

> **"He who gives to a poor man, or lends to a needy man, does better than if he bought pardons."**
>
> –Martin Luther,
> "The Ninety-five Theses (1517)"

Although known for his hot temper—which cost him many friendships—Luther and his wife cared for as many as 20 orphans whose parents died from the plague. In his later years, Luther enjoyed gardening and music, and continued his lifelong love of writing. He died in 1546, probably of a heart attack.

▲ Wittenberg today

Then and Now

Martin Luther was willing to stand up for his beliefs, even if that meant offending people. Can you think of anyone in the news who has shown that same willingness?

Politics and Lutheranism

Main Idea Political leaders often supported Protestantism because they wanted more power.

Reading Focus Under the United States Constitution, the government cannot favor any one religion. Read to learn what happened in Europe during the Reformation when kings decided what faith people had to follow.

In the past, there had been thinkers who challenged Catholic beliefs, but the Church had always remained in control. What had changed in the 1500s that allowed Protestantism to take hold? One reason Protestantism succeeded is that some of Europe's kings realized they could increase their power by supporting Lutheranism against the Catholic Church.

You read earlier about the Holy Roman Empire, which covered much of central Europe. The heart of the empire was made up of about 300 small German kingdoms. In 1519 Charles V became the Holy Roman Emperor. His empire included the lands of the Holy Roman Empire, as well as all of Spain, the Netherlands, parts of Italy, and territories in the Americas.

The local rulers and nobles of the Holy Roman Empire were concerned about Charles V's power. They did not want a strong central ruler. They wanted to keep ruling their own little kingdoms.

Many German rulers decided to become Lutherans for religious and political reasons. By doing so, their kingdom also became Lutheran. After breaking with the Catholic Church, these rulers seized lands owned by Catholic monasteries in their kingdoms. Now they, and not the Church, would earn income from those lands.

At the same time, when the Catholic Church left a kingdom, it meant that church taxes no longer flowed out of the kingdom.

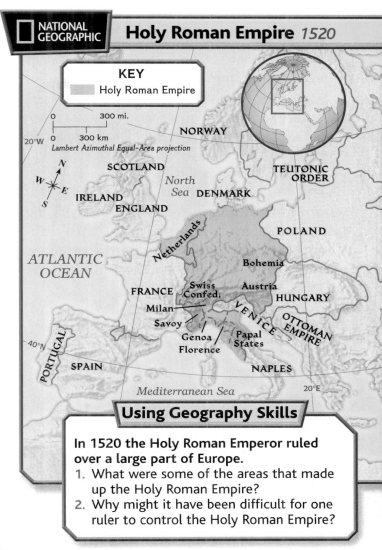

NATIONAL GEOGRAPHIC

Holy Roman Empire 1520

KEY
Holy Roman Empire

Lambert Azimuthal Equal-Area projection

Using Geography Skills

In 1520 the Holy Roman Emperor ruled over a large part of Europe.
1. What were some of the areas that made up the Holy Roman Empire?
2. Why might it have been difficult for one ruler to control the Holy Roman Empire?

Rulers could impose their own church taxes and keep the money for themselves. This made rulers who became Protestants stronger and the Church weaker.

Charles V eventually went to war with the German rulers who converted to Lutheranism, but he was unable to defeat them. In 1555 the fighting ended with the Peace of Augsburg. This agreement let each German ruler decide whether his kingdom would be Lutheran or Catholic. As a result most of northern Germany became Protestant, while the south stayed Catholic.

Reading Check **Explain** Why did many German princes support Martin Luther's ideas?

Calvin and Calvinism

Main Idea John Calvin's Protestant teachings spread across Europe and into North America.

Reading Focus Are there some things you are sure are true? Read to learn how some Protestants developed a faith where everyone agreed that some people were going to heaven and others were not.

Who Was John Calvin?

John Calvin was born in France in the early 1500s. Everyone in his hometown expected that such a dutiful and intelligent boy would become a priest. When he reached the right age, he went off to Paris to study **theology** (thee•AH•luh•jee). Theology is the study of questions about God.

Calvin was very interested in religion. He got up early to read books on theology. During the day, he debated ideas with other students and then went home to read late into the night.

Although Calvin lived in France, he began to hear about the ideas of Martin Luther. Secretly, Calvin began to read about Luther at his college. He and the other students were careful to whisper when they discussed Luther's ideas. The more Calvin read, the more he was convinced by Luther's new ideas.

Eventually, Calvin had to leave Paris because it became too dangerous to talk about Lutheranism. Sometimes he hid out at friends' houses. Once he dared to return to his hometown, but he was arrested and spent months in a damp jail. Calvin finally found safety in **Geneva** (juh•NEE•vuh), Switzerland, a Protestant city. There his powerful preaching convinced many people to follow him.

What Is Calvinism?

Calvin agreed with Luther that faith was more important than good works, but he added other ideas too. Calvinism became the basis of many Protestant churches, including the churches of Puritans and Presbyterians in England and Scotland.

Calvin's main idea was that God's will is absolute and decides everything in the world in advance. God has decided who will go to heaven and who will not. This belief is called **predestination** (pree•DEHS•tuh•NAY•shuhn), meaning that no matter what people do, the outcome of their life is already planned.

Primary Source

Knowledge of God

John Calvin's writings helped Europeans accept Protestantism.

"What help is it . . . to know a God with whom we have nothing to do? Rather, our knowledge should serve first to teach us fear and reverence [respect]; secondly, with it as our guide and teacher, we should learn to seek every good from him, and having received it, to credit it to his account. . . . Again, you cannot behold him clearly unless you acknowledge him to be the fountainhead [source of life] and source of every good."

—John Calvin, *Institutes of the Christian Religion*

▲ John Calvin

DBQ Document-Based Question

According to Calvin, what is needed for believers to understand God clearly?

Some people could say that if their life's outcome were already determined, then why would it matter if they were good or bad? However, most people decided that they were probably among the saved. To prove it, they worked hard, behaved well, and obeyed the laws of their towns. In this way, Calvinism became a powerful tool in society. It encouraged people to work hard at their business and to behave themselves.

Another important idea of Calvinism is that neither kings nor bishops should control the Church. Calvinists believed that congregations should choose their own elders and ministers to run the church for them.

This idea had a strong impact on England and on many of the English settlers in America. The idea that a congregation should be allowed to choose its own

▲ In this picture, John Calvin is shown speaking before leaders in Geneva. *Which Protestant churches were based on Calvinism?*

leaders helped support the idea that the people should also be allowed to elect their own political leaders.

✓ Reading Check **Compare** How did Calvin's ideas differ from those of Luther?

History Online

Study Central™ Need help with the material in this section? Visit jat.glencoe.com

Section 3 Review

Reading Summary

Review the Main Ideas

- Many Christians, including Martin Luther, believed the Catholic Church was becoming corrupt. This led people to leave the Church and create new Christian churches.

- Many European rulers and nobles supported Luther's reforms for political as well as religious reasons.

- John Calvin's Protestant teachings inspired his followers to work hard and live good lives.

What Did You Learn?

1. What were indulgences, and why did they become controversial?

2. What were John Calvin's basic beliefs about God's will?

Critical Thinking

3. **Organizing Information** Draw a diagram to list the three main ideas of Lutheranism.

```
       Lutheranism
   ┌───────┬───────┐
 [   ]   [   ]   [   ]
```

4. **Explain** What were the Ninety-Five Theses?

5. **Cause and Effect** Who was Erasmus, and how were his ideas about Christianity affected by humanism?

6. **Analyze** How did Germany's peasants react to Luther's teachings, and what was Luther's response?

7. **Creative Writing** Write a script for a play about an imaginary meeting between Martin Luther and John Calvin. Think about what the two men may have discussed concerning their beliefs and how they differed.

Catholics and Protestants

Get Ready to Read!

What's the Connection?

In the last section, you learned about the rise of Protestantism. In this section, you will read about the Catholic Church's attempts at reform and the struggle between Europe's Protestants and Catholics.

Focusing on the Main Ideas

• Catholics and Protestants fought religious wars across Europe. *(page 643)*

• Henry VIII created the Anglican Church in England. *(page 648)*

• As part of the Counter-Reformation, Catholic kingdoms began sending missionaries overseas to convert people to Christianity. *(page 650)*

Locating Places

Trent
Navarre (nuh•VAHR)
Paris
London

Meeting People

Ignatius of Loyola (ihg•NAY•shuhs uhv loy•OH•luh)
Henry of Navarre
Henry VIII
Mary I
Elizabeth I

Building Your Vocabulary

seminary (SEH•muh•NEHR•ee)
heresy (HEHR•uh•see)
annul (uh•NUHL)

Reading Strategy

Cause and Effect Create a diagram to show the results of the Catholic Church's attempts at reform.

| Reform |
| Results | Results |

NATIONAL GEOGRAPHIC

When & Where?

1550   1600   1650

London
Paris
Trent
Rome

1545 Pope Paul III opens the Council of Trent

1593 Henry of Navarre becomes Catholic to win French throne

1648 The Thirty Years' War ends

Counter-Reformation

Main Idea Catholics and Protestants fought religious wars across Europe.

Reading Focus Have you visited Protestant and Catholic churches? Could you see any differences? Read to learn the reasons for those differences.

In the 1500s and 1600s, the Catholic Church set out to defeat Protestantism and convince people to return to the Church. This effort came to be called the Counter-Reformation. As you learned earlier, the Reformation also triggered a series of bloody wars in Europe between Catholic and Protestant rulers. When the last wars ended in 1648, Europe was divided into Catholic and Protestant areas.

The Church Tries to Reform Itself The Catholic Church waged a war against Protestantism, but it knew it needed to reform itself. Pope Paul III understood this need. After becoming pope, Paul called a church council at **Trent,** near Rome. The council held meetings for 20 years, from the 1540s to the 1560s.

The Council of Trent made Catholic beliefs clear. It also set up strict rules for how bishops and priests should behave. The Catholic clergy were told to work even harder at instructing people in the faith. To train new priests, seminaries were set up. A **seminary** (SEH•muh•NEHR•ee) is a special school for training and educating priests.

In 1540 Pope Paul III took another important step. He recognized a new order of priests, the Society of Jesus, known as the Jesuits. Jesuits were the pope's agents in Europe. They taught, preached, and fought **heresy** (HEHR•uh•see). A heresy is a religious belief that contradicts what the Church says is true.

▲ The Council of Trent is believed to be the basis for the Catholic Counter-Reformation. *What did the Council of Trent accomplish?*

Ignatius and Christianity

Ignatius of Loyola became devoted to the Christian religion while recovering from an injury.

"In everything else he was healthy except that he could not stand easily on his leg and had to stay in bed. As he was much given to reading . . . when he felt better he asked to be given some of them [books] to pass the time. But in that house none of those that he usually read could be found, so they gave him a Life of Christ and a book of the lives of the saints in Spanish. As he read them over many times, he became rather fond of what he found written there."

—*The Autobiography of St. Ignatius Loyola,* Joseph F. O'Callaghan, trans.

▲ **Ignatius of Loyola**

DBQ Document-Based Question

Why do you think Ignatius read the religious books even though they were not the type of book he usually read?

The man who founded the Jesuits was a Spaniard, **Ignatius of Loyola** (ihg•NAY•shuhs uhv loy•OH•luh). He was a daring soldier, but his life changed when he was wounded in battle. While recuperating, he read about Christian saints who performed brave deeds to defend their faith. Ignatius decided he would be a soldier for Jesus Christ.

The Religious Wars in France

John Calvin was originally from France, and many French people became interested in his ideas. As Calvinism spread in France, French Protestants became known as Huguenots.

Only about seven percent of the French people became Protestants, but almost half of France's nobles did, including the Bourbon family. The Bourbons were the second most powerful family in France. They ruled a kingdom in southern France called **Navarre** (nuh•VAHR) and were also in line for the throne of France.

Many French nobles wanted to weaken the king. The Huguenot nobles especially wanted the king weak so they could practice their religion freely. At the same time, France's king, Henry II, wanted to build a strong central government.

Henry II died in 1559, and his son Francis II died the following year. This meant that Francis's brother Charles, a 10-year-old boy, was now king. Since Charles was too young to rule, his mother ran the government for him. His mother was Catherine de' Medici—the daughter of Lorenzo de' Medici, the powerful Italian leader of Florence.

Catherine was determined to keep the French kingdom strong for her son. She believed the Huguenots were a threat to the king's power and refused to compromise with them. In 1562 a civil war that would last more than 30 years began in France between Protestants and Catholics.

In 1589 **Henry of Navarre,** the leader of Huguenot forces and head of the Bourbon family, became King Henry IV of France. For the next few years, the war continued because Catholic nobles would not accept a Protestant as king. Henry won most of his battles but was unable to capture **Paris.**

Henry IV then made a famous deal. He knew most French people were Catholic and that they demanded a Catholic king. Henry agreed to become a Catholic so the French people would accept him as king.

In 1593 Henry went to Paris and put on white satin for the Catholic ceremony. As he passed through the church doors, he smiled and, according to tradition, said that Paris was "worth a mass." He meant it was worth becoming a Catholic to rule all of France.

Henry IV did not forget his Huguenot followers, however. He issued an edict, or order, while visiting the city of Nantes in 1598. The Edict of Nantes said Catholicism was France's official religion, but it also gave Huguenots the right to worship freely.

What Was the Thirty Years' War? The worst religious war of the Reformation era was fought in the Holy Roman Empire in the 1600s. The war began in Bohemia—today known as the Czech Republic. Protestant nobles in Bohemia rebelled against their Catholic king. Other Protestant kings in Germany decided to help the rebels, and the war expanded throughout the empire.

The war lasted 30 years, from 1618 to 1648, and quickly became a war of kingdoms. France, Sweden, Denmark, England, and the Netherlands sent troops to help the

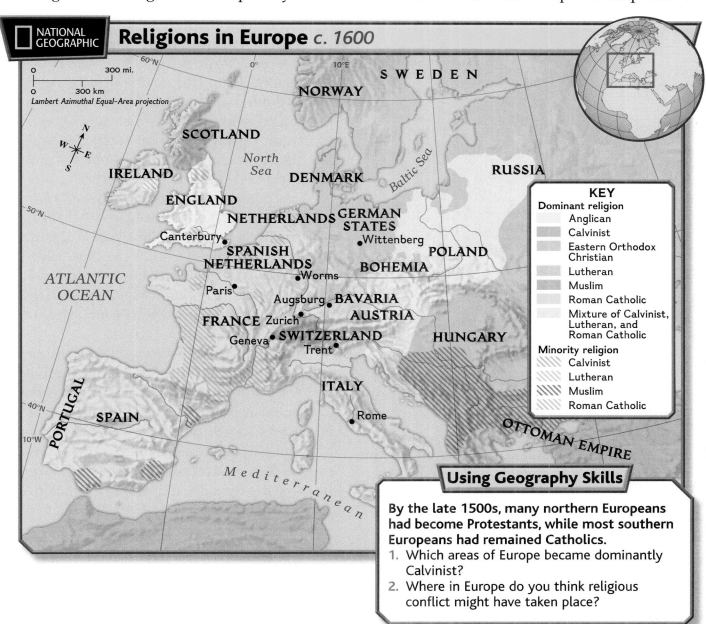

NATIONAL GEOGRAPHIC

Religions in Europe c. 1600

0 — 300 mi.
0 — 300 km
Lambert Azimuthal Equal-Area projection

KEY

Dominant religion
- Anglican
- Calvinist
- Eastern Orthodox Christian
- Lutheran
- Muslim
- Roman Catholic
- Mixture of Calvinist, Lutheran, and Roman Catholic

Minority religion
- Calvinist
- Lutheran
- Muslim
- Roman Catholic

Using Geography Skills

By the late 1500s, many northern Europeans had become Protestants, while most southern Europeans had remained Catholics.
1. Which areas of Europe became dominantly Calvinist?
2. Where in Europe do you think religious conflict might have taken place?

▲ This photo shows the Alhambra, a Muslim palace and fortress in Granada, Spain. *What happened to Spanish Muslims after Ferdinand and Isabella took power?*

Maimonides ▶

Protestants, while Spain and the Holy Roman Empire backed the Catholics.

Town fought against town, and roving troops murdered peasants on the roads. When it was over, only wolves were found wandering where some towns used to be. The war weakened Spain and helped make France one of Europe's most powerful countries.

The Reformation in Spain
The ideas of Luther and Calvin never became very popular in Spain. Still, when Protestants began fighting in Europe, it affected Spain. Spanish rulers became suspicious of Protestant countries and of anyone in Spain who was not Catholic.

When the Reformation began in the 1500s, Spain was a young nation. It had been founded in 1469 when King Ferdinand and Queen Isabella married and joined their two kingdoms. These monarchs wanted a strong nation. They felt that all their subjects should be Catholic, because that would keep Spain's citizens loyal and united.

When Ferdinand and Isabella began to rule, many Muslims still lived in Spain. As you read in earlier chapters, Muslims ruled Spain from about A.D. 700 to 1200. During those years, people of different religions lived together in relative harmony.

The Muslims made non-Muslims pay special taxes and limited their rights, but they did not seek to kill or expel nonbelievers. Jews, for example, found life in Muslim Spain better than other places in Europe. As you read in earlier chapters, Jews were persecuted throughout Europe during the Middle Ages.

Muslim Spain during the Middle Ages was a golden age for Jewish thinkers and poets. The most famous Jewish scholar was Maimonides (my•MAH•nuh•DEEZ). He was born in Spain and his books on religion and medicine earned him great respect.

This golden age ended when Catholics took control of Spain. Jews and Muslims were no longer welcome. In 1492 Ferdinand and Isabella ordered all Jews and Muslims to convert to Catholicism or leave the country. To ensure religious unity, they also set up the Spanish Inquisition to investigate people's beliefs.

The Spanish Inquisition was a Catholic court, similar to the one the Catholic Church had set up in Europe to investigate heresy. The Spanish Inquisition was much crueler, however. Charges of heresy were made just to eliminate enemies. Horrible tortures were invented to force confessions of guilt. The head of the Spanish Inquisition, Tomás de Torquemada (TAWR•kuh•MAH•duh), executed some 2,000 Spaniards. Even the pope in Rome could not stop him.

✓ **Reading Check** **Identify** What deal earned Henry of Navarre the French throne?

Biography

CATHERINE DE' MEDICI
1519–1589

▲ Catherine de' Medici

Catherine de' Medici was an Italian woman who played an important role in French history. She was born in Florence to Lorenzo de' Medici and Madeleine de la Tour d' Auvergne. Catherine was orphaned as a baby and was raised by relatives. At age 14, Catherine was married to Henry, a French prince. Catherine took Italian artists, musicians, writers, and dancers with her to the French court. She was never fully accepted in France, however, because she was Italian and was not from a royal family.

In 1547 Catherine's husband became King Henry II. After he died in a jousting accident in 1559, their three oldest sons—Francis II, Charles IX, and Henry III—succeeded each other as king. Although Catherine was no longer queen, she still had much influence over her sons.

Catherine is blamed for many of the conflicts between French Catholics and French Protestants, called Huguenots. In 1568 she outlawed freedom of worship. In 1572 Catherine arranged the murder of a Huguenot adviser. His death sparked the Saint Bartholomew's Massacre, which resulted in the deaths of about 6,000 Huguenots. Catherine was not always opposed to Huguenots. In fact, she arranged the marriage of her daughter Margaret to Henry of Navarre, a former Protestant Huguenot who became King Henry IV of France.

Views on Catherine's accomplishments are mixed. Some blame her entirely for the French religious wars. Others remember her efforts to protect her sons. Still others remember her as a Renaissance woman because she supported the arts, added to the royal library, and sponsored a dance and theater pageant that is considered to be the first ballet. Catherine died in 1589 of pneumonia.

> **"God and the world will have reason to be satisfied with me."**
>
> –Catherine de' Medici, *Biography of a Family*

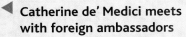
◄ **Catherine de' Medici meets with foreign ambassadors**

Then and Now

If Catherine de' Medici were running for political office today, do you think she would be a popular candidate? Why or why not?

The English Reformation

Main Idea Henry VIII created the Anglican Church in England.

Reading Focus You have probably heard about the Pilgrims. Do you know why the Pilgrims left England to come here? Read to learn how the Reformation came to England and why some Protestants decided to leave England and go to America.

Because England is an island, ideas from Europe sometimes took longer to get there. Surprisingly, though, England broke away from the Catholic Church earlier than the rest of Europe. That change was based on a political decision by the English king. Later, however, the English people strongly debated Reformation ideas.

Henry VIII Starts His Own Church In the history of England, no king is more famous than **Henry VIII.** He ruled England from 1509 to 1547. He was stubborn, impatient, and cruel. Henry married six queens, divorced two, and beheaded two more. He imprisoned bishops and nobles in the Tower of **London** (LUHN•duhn) for disagreeing with him. They also were eventually beheaded.

◀ In his attempt to divorce his wife and marry another woman, Henry VIII broke away from the Catholic Church and created the Church of England. *Why did the pope refuse to annul Henry VIII's marriage?*

Henry and his father were members of the Tudor family. In the 1400s, before the Tudors came to the throne, England's nobles had been at war with each other. Henry was determined to keep the peace and to keep the Tudors on the throne.

To do this he needed a son to succeed him, but Henry had no son. His wife Catherine had given birth only to one surviving daughter. Henry asked the pope to **annul** (uh•NUHL), or cancel, his marriage to Catherine.

An annulment is not the same as a divorce. If the pope annulled the marriage, it would be as if the marriage had never happened. It would mean that Henry could find a new wife to give birth to sons. Those sons would be heirs to the throne, not the daughter Catherine had given him.

Popes had annulled marriages before, but this time the pope refused. Catherine was the daughter of Ferdinand and Isabella of Spain. Her nephew was the Holy Roman Emperor. Spain was the strongest Catholic kingdom at that time, and the pope did not want to make Catherine's family angry.

Henry had the archbishop of Canterbury—the highest bishop in England—annul the marriage. In response, the pope excommunicated Henry from the Church. Henry then declared that the king, not the pope, was the head of the Church in England.

Henry ordered all the priests and bishops in England to accept him as the new head of their church. Some refused and were killed. The most famous was Sir Thomas More, who was executed in 1535. Henry then seized the Catholic Church's land in England and gave some of it to his nobles. This kept the nobles loyal to the king and to the Church of England. If they ever let the Catholic Church regain power in England, they would have to give up their land.

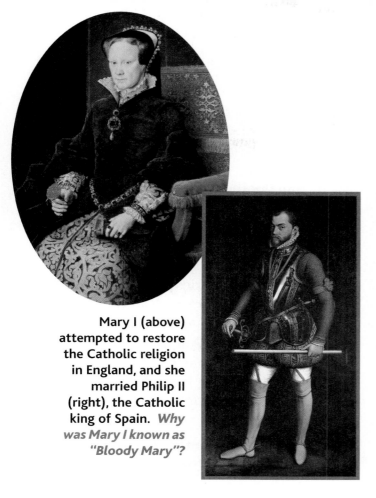

Mary I (above) attempted to restore the Catholic religion in England, and she married Philip II (right), the Catholic king of Spain. *Why was Mary I known as "Bloody Mary"?*

Who Was Bloody Mary? The Church of England came to be known as the Anglican Church. It kept most of the rituals and sacraments of the Catholic Church. However, many English Catholics were not satisfied. They wanted to stay Catholic. They backed Henry and Catherine's daughter Mary when she became Queen **Mary I** in 1553. Mary had been raised Catholic and wanted to make England a Catholic kingdom again.

Mary restored the Catholic Church in England and arrested Protestants who opposed her. In her struggle to make England Catholic again, Mary burned 300 people at the stake. The English were horrified and called her "Bloody Mary."

Mary ruled about five years, then died. Her half-sister Elizabeth took over the throne, becoming Queen **Elizabeth I.** Elizabeth was a Protestant. She restored the Anglican Church and went on to become one of the greatest rulers in English history.

How Did Calvinism Affect England?

Although the Catholics were defeated, the religious battles were not over. A new fight began to make the Anglican Church more Protestant in its beliefs and rituals.

By the late 1500s, the ideas of John Calvin had reached England. Many educated people read Calvin's works and became convinced that he was right. They began to demand that the Anglican Church give up its Catholic ways of doing things. These reformers became known as Puritans because they wanted to purify the Anglican Church of Catholic ideas.

Puritans began to form their own congregations. These congregations were independent. They made their own decisions about what their congregations should and should not do. They did not report to a bishop of the Anglican Church, and they chose their own ministers.

Queen Elizabeth I tolerated the Puritans, but when James I became king in 1603, the Puritans faced harder times. James refused to allow anyone to disagree with the Anglican Church. The king headed the Anglican Church and appointed its leaders. The leaders, in turn, chose the priests for the congregations. James believed that by choosing their own ministers, the Puritans were challenging the king's power.

James I and the king who came after him, Charles I, persecuted the Puritans. They shut down Puritan churches and jailed Puritan leaders. Many Puritans decided to move to America to practice their religion freely. There they founded colonies that eventually became the states of Massachusetts, Connecticut, New Hampshire, and Rhode Island.

✓ **Reading Check** **Cause and Effect** Why did Henry VIII create the Anglican Church?

Missionaries Go Overseas

Main Idea As part of the Counter-Reformation, Catholic kingdoms began sending missionaries overseas to convert people to Christianity.

Reading Focus Do you think spreading democracy is important? Read to learn how Catholic missionaries tried to spread their religion to other people in the world.

When the Counter-Reformation began, many Catholics became committed to spreading their faith. As part of this new energy and determination, Catholic kingdoms began sending missionaries overseas to America and Asia.

The Jesuits were active missionaries in the 1500s and 1600s. French and Spanish Jesuits headed to America and Asia. In America, the Native Americans called them the "Black Robes."

The first Jesuit missionary to Japan, Francis Xavier, arrived in 1549. The Japanese at first welcomed the Jesuits. By 1600, the Jesuits had converted thousands of Japanese to Christianity.

Eventually the Jesuits clashed with people who believed in Buddhism and Shintoism. The Japanese Shogun, or military ruler, banned Christianity in Japan and expelled all missionaries.

Spanish missionaries had much greater success in the Philippine Islands. Most of the people there eventually became Catholic. Today the Philippines are the only Asian country with a Catholic majority. French missionaries tried to convert the people of Vietnam but were expelled by Vietnam's emperor.

Reading Check **Identify** In what parts of the world did Catholic missionaries teach?

Section 4 Review

History Online

Study Central™ Need help with the material in this section? Visit jat.glencoe.com

Reading Summary

Review the Main Ideas

- Across Europe, religious wars between Catholics and Protestants were fought in the 1500s and 1600s, while the Spanish monarchs tried to make Spain an exclusively Catholic country.

- In England, Henry VIII broke with the Catholic Church and created the Anglican Church. Puritans later tried to reform the Anglican Church and then fled to America.

- Catholic missionaries tried to spread their religion to Asia and America.

What Did You Learn?

1. What was the Council of Trent, and what did it accomplish?

2. Why was the Edict of Nantes important?

Critical Thinking

3. **Organizing Information** Draw a chart like the one below. Fill in details about the steps the Catholic Church took to counter the Reformation.

Church's Efforts to Stop Protestantism

4. **Analyze** Why did Henry VIII form the Anglican Church?

5. **Explain** Who were the Puritans, and what were their beliefs and practices?

6. **Predict** How do you think conflicts over religion affected the world outside of Europe?

7. **Expository Writing** Write a short essay summarizing the history of Catholicism in Spain in the 1400s and 1500s.

Section 1 The Renaissance Begins

Vocabulary
Renaissance
secular
diplomacy

Focusing on the Main Ideas
- The wealthy urban society of the Italian city-states brought a rebirth of learning and art to Europe. *(page 609)*
- Italy's location helped its city-states grow wealthy from trade and banking, but many of the cities fell under the control of strong rulers. *(page 611)*
- Unlike medieval nobles, the nobles of the Italian city-states lived in cities and were active in trade, banking, and public life. *(page 614)*

Section 2 New Ideas and Art

Vocabulary
humanism
vernacular

Focusing on the Main Ideas
- Humanists studied the Greeks and Romans, and the development of the printing press helped spread their ideas. *(page 619)*
- Renaissance artists used new techniques to produce paintings that showed people in an emotional and realistic way. *(page 623)*
- Renaissance ideas and art spread from Italy to northern Europe. *(page 625)*

Section 3 The Reformation Begins

Vocabulary
Reformation
indulgence
denomination
theology
predestination

Focusing on the Main Ideas
- The reforms of Martin Luther led to the creation of new Christian churches. *(page 634)*
- Political leaders often supported Protestantism because they wanted more power. *(page 639)*
- John Calvin's Protestant teachings spread across Europe and into North America. *(page 640)*

▲ Gutenberg Bible

Section 4 Catholics and Protestants

Vocabulary
seminary
heresy
annul

Focusing on the Main Ideas
- Catholics and Protestants fought religious wars across Europe. *(page 643)*
- Henry VIII created the Anglican Church in England. *(page 648)*
- As part of the Counter-Reformation, Catholic kingdoms began sending missionaries overseas to convert people to Christianity. *(page 650)*

Review Vocabulary

Write **True** beside each true statement. Replace the word in italics to make false statements true.

___ 1. *Diplomacy* is the art of negotiating.

___ 2. When the pope needed money in the 1500s, he sold *indulgences.*

___ 3. The Renaissance belief that the individual and human society were important was known as *theology.*

___ 4. A *heresy* is a special school for training and educating priests.

___ 5. *Predestination* encouraged Calvinists to prove they were among the saved.

___ 6. Writers began to write in the *secular,* the everyday language of a region.

Review Main Ideas

Section 1 • The Renaissance Begins

7. What set the stage for the Renaissance in Italy?

8. What made nobles of the Renaissance different from nobles of previous times?

Section 2 • New Ideas and Art

9. What did the humanists believe?

10. How did Renaissance art differ from the art of the Middle Ages?

Section 3 • The Reformation Begins

11. What happened when Martin Luther tried to reform the Catholic Church?

12. Describe John Calvin's teachings.

Section 4 • Catholics and Protestants

13. Where and why did the Thirty Years' War begin?

14. What changed England from a Catholic to a Protestant country?

Critical Thinking

15. **Analyze** Do you think banking played a role in the wealth and art of the Italian city-states? Explain.

16. **Conclude** Some Puritans moved to North America to practice their religion without interference from European leaders. How was that desire for religious freedom reflected in the U.S. Constitution?

Review Reading Skill — Analyze and Clarify — Go Beyond the Words

17. Read this passage about the importance of the printing press. Then answer the questions at the right to help you analyze and clarify how the printing press affected Europe.

In the early 1450s, Johannes Gutenberg developed a printing press that used movable metal type. This type of printing press made it possible to print many books much more quickly. With more books available, more people learned to read. Scholars could read one another's work and debate their ideas in letters. Ideas grew and spread more quickly than ever before in Europe.

Who? _____   Where? _____

What? _____   Why? _____

When? _____

To review this skill, see pages 606–607.

Geography Skills

Study the map below and answer the following questions.

18. **Location** What geographical advantage does Venice have over Milan?

19. **Human/Environment Interaction** Why might Mantua have been at a disadvantage in terms of trade?

20. **Movement** If you traveled from the city of Florence to the city of Venice, in what direction would you be going?

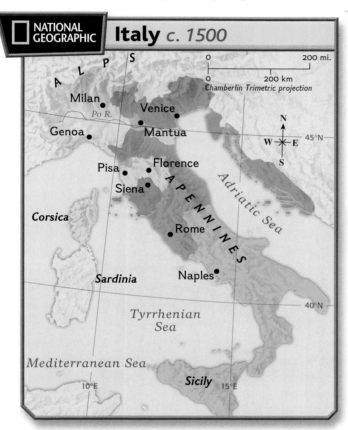

NATIONAL GEOGRAPHIC **Italy** c. 1500

Read to Write

21. **Expository Writing** Research the life of Renaissance nobles, merchants, shopkeepers, or peasants. Then write an essay describing the lifestyle and position of the group you chose.

22. **Using Your FOLDABLES** Use information in your completed foldable to create a poster about one of the changes that occurred during the Renaissance and Reformation. Draw pictures, write captions, create titles, and so on. Present your poster to the class.

Using Technology

23. **Researching** The Renaissance revived the Greek idea that a well-rounded person took part in a variety of activities, including sports. Use the Internet and your local library to research one of the following sports of the Renaissance: javelin hurling, tennis, archery, fencing, boxing, or hunting. Present your findings to your classmates. Discuss who participated and any resemblances to modern-day sports.

Linking Past and Present

24. **Inferring** Renaissance artists, architects, and writers were greatly influenced by ancient Greek and Roman culture. Do you think people in those professions today are equally influenced by artists and writers of the past? Why or why not?

Primary Source Analyze

These are two of Luther's Ninety-Five Theses.

"37. Every true Christian, whether living or dead, has a share in all the benefits of Christ and of the Church, . . . even without letters of pardon. . . .

45. Christians should be taught that he who sees any one in need, and, passing him by, gives money for pardons, is not purchasing for himself the indulgences of the Pope but the anger of God. . . ."
— Martin Luther, "Ninety-five Theses"

DBQ Document-Based Questions

25. According to Luther, is the buying of indulgences necessary?

26. What does Luther say is a use for money that will please God?

Chapter 18

Enlightenment and Revolution

◀ A statue of Louis XIV on horseback outside of the palace of Versailles in France

NATIONAL GEOGRAPHIC — When & Where?

1500	1600	1700	1800
1492 Columbus reaches the Americas	**1543** Copernicus supports idea of sun-centered universe	**1690** John Locke writes about government	**1776** Declaration of Independence is signed

Chapter Preview

By the end of the Renaissance, Europe and the rest of the world were entering a time of rapid change. Read this chapter to find out how voyages of exploration and scientific discoveries affected people in different parts of the world.

 View the Chapter 18 video in the *World History: Journey Across Time* Video Program.

History **O**nline
Chapter Overview Visit jat.glencoe.com **for a preview of Chapter 18.**

 Section 1

The Age of Exploration

In the 1400s, Europeans began to explore overseas and build empires. Trade increased and goods, technology, and ideas were exchanged around the world.

 Section 2

The Scientific Revolution

Scientific ideas and discoveries gave Europeans a new way to understand the universe.

 Section 3

The Enlightenment

During the 1700s, many Europeans believed that reason could be used to make government and society better.

 Section 4

The American Revolution

Britain and France established colonies in North America. Britain's American colonies eventually rebelled against Britain and formed a new nation, the United States.

 **FOLDABLES™ Study Organizer**

Summarizing Information *Make this foldable to help you organize and summarize information about the Enlightenment and era of revolutions.*

Step 1 *Mark the midpoint of a side edge of one sheet of paper. Then fold the outside edges in to touch the midpoint.*

Step 2 *Fold the paper in half again from side to side.*

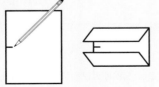

Step 3 *Open the paper and cut along the inside fold lines to form four tabs.*

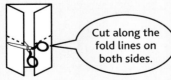

 Cut along the fold lines on both sides.

Step 4 *Label as shown.*

Reading and Writing *As you read the chapter, write information under each appropriate tab. Be sure to summarize the information you find by writing only main ideas and supporting details.*

Reading Social Studies

1 Learn It!

Your Reading Strengths

Different people read differently. Some people read and understand something quickly, while other people may need to read something several times to comprehend it fully. It is important to identify your own strengths and weaknesses as a reader.

Read the following paragraph describing the story of how Newton discovered gravity:

> **According to tradition, Newton was sitting in his garden one day when he watched an apple fall to the ground. The apple's fall led him to the idea of gravity, or the pull of the earth and other bodies on objects at or near their surfaces.**
>
> *—from pages 675–676*

Reading Tip

Depending upon what you are reading, you may need to slow down or speed up. When you study, read more slowly. When you read for pleasure, you can read more quickly.

- Can you visualize this scene in your mind, almost like a movie?
- Are there any words you do not know?
- What questions do you have about this passage?
- What does this scene make you think of based on what you have previously read, seen, or experienced?
- Do you need to reread it?

2 Practice It!

Improve Your Reading

The paragraph below appears in Section 3. Read the passage and answer the questions that follow.

> During the 1600s and 1700s, many European thinkers favored limits on government power. However, powerful kings and queens ruled most of Europe. This system was known as **absolutism.** In this system, monarchs held absolute, or total, power. They claimed to rule by divine right, or by the will of God. This meant that rulers did not answer to their people, but rather to God alone.
>
> —*from page 686*

- What words or sentences made you slow down as you read?
- Did you have to reread any parts?
- What questions do you still have after reading this passage?

Read to Write

Choose one explorer, philosopher, or scientist that you were introduced to in this chapter. Write a list of questions that a modern talk-show host might ask if he or she interviewed this person.

▼ Catherine the Great

◀ Peter the Great

3 Apply It!

As you read the chapter, identify one paragraph in each section that is difficult to understand. Discuss each paragraph with a partner to improve your understanding.

Section 1

The Age of Exploration

Get Ready to Read!

What's the Connection?
You have learned how Italy's cities grew rich from trade. In the 1400s, other European states began exploring the world in search of wealth.

Focusing on the Main Ideas
- In the 1400s, trade, technology, and the rise of strong kingdoms led to a new era of exploration. *(page 659)*
- While the Portuguese explored Africa, the Spanish, English, and French explored America. *(page 661)*
- To increase trade, Europeans set up colonies and created joint-stock companies. *(page 666)*
- Exploration and trade led to a worldwide exchange of products, people, and ideas. *(page 668)*

Locating Places
Strait of Magellan (muh•JEH•luhn)
Netherlands (NEH•thuhr•luhnz)
Moluccas (muh•LUH•kuhz)

Meeting People
Vasco da Gama
Christopher Columbus
Magellan (muh•JEH•luhn)
John Cabot (KA•buht)
Jacques Cartier (ZHAHK kahr•TYAY)

Building Your Vocabulary
mercantilism (MUHR•kuhn•TUH•LIH•zuhm)
export (EHK•SPOHRT)
import (IHM•POHRT)
colony (KAH•luh•nee)
commerce (KAH•muhrs)
invest (ihn•VEHST)

Reading Strategy
Cause and Effect Complete a diagram like the one below showing why Europeans began to explore.

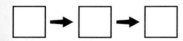

When & Where?

NATIONAL GEOGRAPHIC

NORTH AMERICA
EUROPE
CHINA
AFRICA INDIA
SOUTH AMERICA

1400

1500

1600

1420
Portugal begins mapping Africa's coast

1492
Columbus reaches the Americas

1520
Magellan's crew sails around the world

1588
England defeats the Armada

Europe Gets Ready to Explore

Main Idea In the 1400s, trade, technology, and the rise of strong kingdoms led to a new era of exploration.

Reading Focus Do you like traveling to places that you have never been? Read to see why Western Europeans set off to explore the world.

In the 1400s and 1500s, nations in Western Europe began exploring the world. They soon gained control of the Americas and parts of India and Southeast Asia as well. Why did they begin exploring in the 1400s? Many events came together to create just the right conditions for exploration.

Trade With Asia As you have read, in the Middle Ages, Europeans began buying vast amounts of spices, silks, and other goods from Asia. In the 1400s, however, it became harder to get those goods.

First of all, the Mongol Empire had collapsed. The Mongols had kept the Silk Road running smoothly. When their empire collapsed, local rulers along the Silk Road imposed new taxes on merchants. This made Asian goods more expensive.

Next, the Ottoman Turks conquered the Byzantine Empire and blocked Italian merchants from entering the Black Sea. The Italians had trading posts on the coast of the Black Sea where they bought goods from Asia. Now, they could no longer reach them. They had to trade with the Turks instead, and this drove prices even higher.

Europeans still wanted the spices and silks of East Asia. Anyone who could find a way to get them cheaply would make a lot of money. Merchants began looking for a route to East Asia that bypassed the Middle East. If they could not get there by land, maybe they could get there by sea.

◀ Early compass

▲ European explorers and traders began to use smaller, faster ships called caravels in the 1400s. *What advantage did triangular sails offer a ship?*

Astrolabe ▲

New Technology Even though the Europeans wanted to go exploring, they could not do it without the right technology. The Atlantic Ocean was too dangerous and difficult to navigate.

By the 1400s, they had the technology they needed. From the Arabs, Europeans learned about the astrolabe and the compass. The astrolabe was an ancient Greek device that could be used to find latitude. The compass, invented by the Chinese, helped navigators find magnetic north.

Even with these new tools, the Europeans needed better ships. In the 1400s, they began using triangular sails developed by the Arabs. These sails let a ship zigzag into the wind.

▲ Prince Henry's school for navigation helped make possible the discovery of new water routes and new lands. Here, Prince Henry is shown watching for the return of his ships. *What types of professionals did Prince Henry invite to his research center?*

They also began building ships with many masts and smaller sails to make their ships go faster. A new type of rudder made steering easier. In the 1400s, these inventions came together in a Portuguese ship called the caravel. With ships like the caravel, Europeans could begin exploring the world.

The Rise of Strong Nations Even with

new technology, exploration was still expensive and dangerous. For most of the Middle Ages, Europe's kingdoms were weak and could not afford to explore. This situation began to change in the 1400s.

The rise of towns and trade helped make governments stronger. Kings and queens could tax the trade in their kingdom and then use the money to build armies and navies. Using their new power, they were able to build strong central governments.

By the end of the 1400s, four strong kingdoms—Portugal, Spain, France, and England—had developed in Europe. They had harbors on the Atlantic Ocean and were anxious to find a sea route to Asia. The question was where to go.

Did Maps Encourage Exploration? By the

1400s, most educated people in Europe knew the world was round, but they only had maps of Europe and the Mediterranean. When the Renaissance began, however, people began to study ancient maps as well as books written by Arab scholars.

Twelve hundred years earlier, a Greek-educated Egyptian geographer named Claudius Ptolemy had drawn maps of the world. His book *Geography* was discovered by Europeans in 1406 and printed in 1475.

With the invention of the printing press, books like Ptolemy's could be printed and sold all over Europe. Ptolemy's ideas about cartography, or the science of mapmaking, were very influential. His basic system of longitude and latitude is still used today.

European cartographers also began reading a book written by al-Idrisi, an Arab geographer. Al-Idrisi had published a book in 1154 showing the parts of the world known to Muslims. By studying the works of al-Idrisi and Ptolemy, Europeans learned the geography of East Africa and the Indian Ocean. If they could find a way around Africa, they could get to Asia.

✓ **Reading Check** **Summarize** What were the main reasons the Europeans began exploring the world in the 1400s?

Exploring the World

Main Idea While the Portuguese explored Africa, the Spanish, English, and French explored America.

Reading Focus Have you ever done something daring or tried something new not knowing how it would turn out? Read to learn how European explorers took chances and went places no Europeans had ever been before.

By the early 1400s, Europeans were ready to explore. England and France were still fighting each other, however, and Spain was still fighting the Muslims. This gave Portugal the chance to explore first.

Who Was Henry the Navigator?
In 1419 Prince Henry of Portugal, known as "Henry the Navigator," set up a research center in southern Portugal. He invited sailors, cartographers, and shipbuilders to come and help him explore the world.

In 1420 Portugal began mapping Africa's coastline and trading with Africa's kingdoms. It also seized the Azores (AY•ZOHRZ), Madeira (muh•DIHR•uh), and Cape Verde islands. Soon after, the Portuguese discovered sugarcane would grow on the islands.

Sugar was very valuable in Europe. To work their sugarcane fields, the Portuguese began bringing enslaved Africans to the islands. This was the beginning of a slave trade that would eventually bring millions of enslaved people to the Americas as well.

In 1488 the Portuguese explorer Bartolomeu Dias reached the southern tip of Africa. Nine years later, **Vasco da Gama** (VAS•koh dah GA•muh) rounded the tip of Africa, raced across the Indian Ocean, and landed on India's coast. A water route to East Asia had at last been found.

Santa María

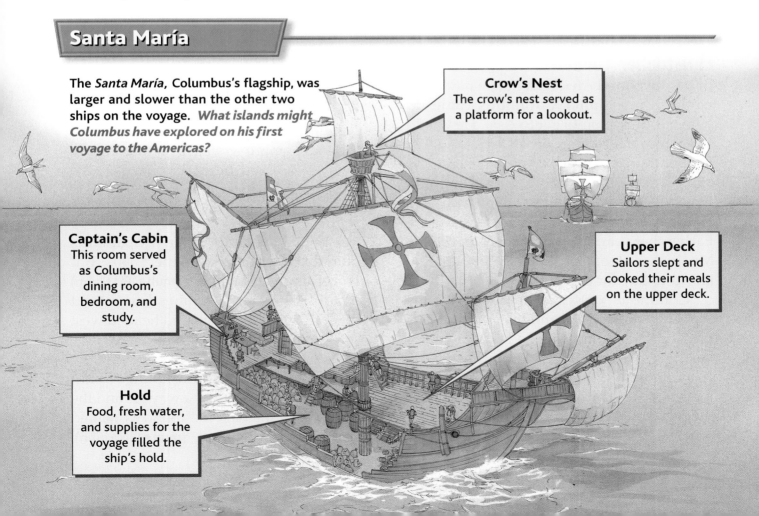

The *Santa María*, Columbus's flagship, was larger and slower than the other two ships on the voyage. *What islands might Columbus have explored on his first voyage to the Americas?*

Crow's Nest
The crow's nest served as a platform for a lookout.

Captain's Cabin
This room served as Columbus's dining room, bedroom, and study.

Upper Deck
Sailors slept and cooked their meals on the upper deck.

Hold
Food, fresh water, and supplies for the voyage filled the ship's hold.

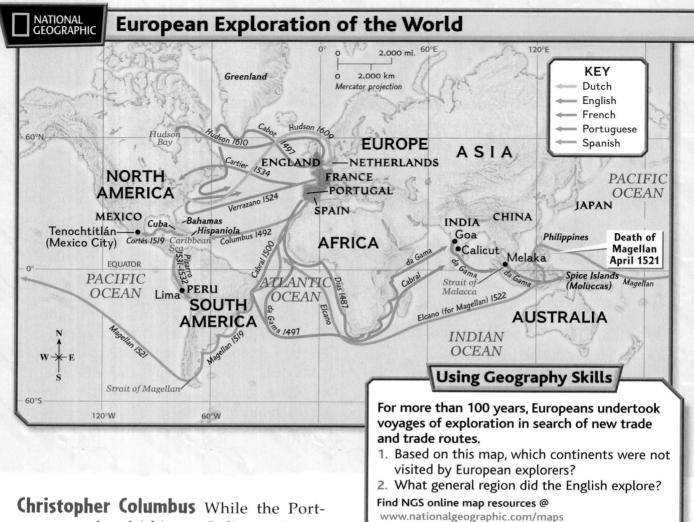

KEY
→ Dutch
← English
← French
← Portuguese
→ Spanish

Death of Magellan April 1521

Using Geography Skills

For more than 100 years, Europeans undertook voyages of exploration in search of new trade and trade routes.

1. Based on this map, which continents were not visited by European explorers?
2. What general region did the English explore?

Find NGS online map resources @
www.nationalgeographic.com/maps

Christopher Columbus While the Portuguese explored Africa, an Italian navigator named **Christopher Columbus** came up with a daring plan to get to Asia. He would sail across the Atlantic Ocean.

Columbus needed money to make the trip. The rulers of Portugal, England, and France all turned him down. Finally in 1492 Ferdinand and Isabella of Spain said yes. Earlier that year, they had finally driven the Muslims out of Spain. They could now afford to pay for exploration.

Columbus outfitted three ships: the *Santa María*, the *Niña*, and the *Pinta*. In 1492 they left Spain and headed west. As the weeks passed, the crew grew desperate. Finally they sighted land, probably the island of San Salvador. Columbus claimed the land for Spain and then explored the nearby islands of Cuba and Hispaniola.

Columbus thought he was in Asia. He made three more voyages to the region but never realized he had arrived in the Americas. Eventually, Europeans realized they had reached two huge continents.

Who Was Magellan? Many Spaniards explored the Americas in the 1500s, but only Ferdinand **Magellan** (muh•JEH•luhn) tried to finish what Columbus had set out to do. In 1520 he left Spain and headed west to sail around the Americas and then all the way to Asia.

Magellan sailed south along South America. Finally, he found a way around the continent. The passage he found is named the **Strait of Magellan** (muh•JEH•luhn).

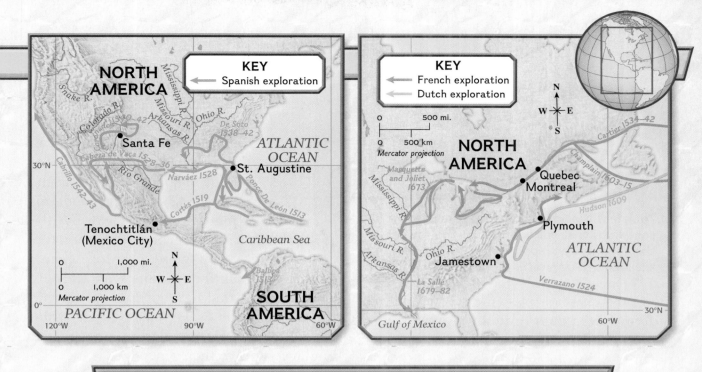

NORTH AMERICA

KEY
← Spanish exploration

Snake R.
Colorado R.
Mississippi R.
Missouri R.
Arkansas R.
Ohio R.
Coronado 1540–42
De Soto 1538–42
• Santa Fe
ATLANTIC OCEAN
Cabeza de Vaca 1528–36
30°N
Cabrillo 1542–43
Rio Grande
Narváez 1528
• St. Augustine
Ponce De León 1513
Cortés 1519
Tenochtitlán (Mexico City) •
Caribbean Sea
Balboa 1513
0   1,000 mi.
0   1,000 km
Mercator projection
N W E S
SOUTH AMERICA
0°
PACIFIC OCEAN
120°W   90°W   60°W

KEY
← French exploration
← Dutch exploration

0   500 mi.
0   500 km
Mercator projection

NORTH AMERICA

N W E S

Cartier 1534–42
Champlain 1603–15
Marquette and Joliet 1673
Mississippi R.
Missouri R.
Ohio R.
Arkansas R.
• Quebec
Montreal •
Hudson 1609
• Plymouth
• Jamestown
ATLANTIC OCEAN
La Salle 1679–82
Verrazano 1524
30°N
Gulf of Mexico   60°W

Important European Explorers

Christopher Columbus

Voyages: 1492, 1493, 1498, 1502

First European to sail west searching for a water route to Asia

Vasco da Gama

Voyage: 1497–1499

First European to sail around the south of Africa and reach India

Ferdinand Magellan

Voyage: 1519–1522

Led the first expedition to sail completely around the world

Jacques Cartier

Voyages: 1534, 1535, 1541

Explored the St. Lawrence River

Henry Hudson

Voyages: 1607, 1608, 1609, 1610

Explored the Hudson River and Hudson Bay

After passing through the stormy strait, his ship entered a vast sea. It was so peaceful, or pacific, that he named the sea the Pacific Ocean.

Magellan then headed west. His sailors nearly starved and had to eat leather, sawdust, and rats. Finally, after four months at sea, they reached the Philippines. After local people killed Magellan, his crew continued west across the Indian Ocean, around Africa, and back to Spain. They became the first known people to circumnavigate (suhr•kuhm•NA•vuh•GAYT), or sail around, the world.

The First English and French Explorers

As the news spread about Columbus's journey, England decided to search for a northern route to Asia. In 1497 an English ship commanded by **John Cabot** (KA•buht) headed across the Atlantic.

Cabot arrived at a large island he named Newfoundland. He then traveled south

▲ **To defeat the Spanish Armada, the English sent ships that had been set on fire toward the Spanish warships.** *Why was the defeat of the Spanish Armada important?*

along the coast of present-day Canada but did not find a path through to Asia. Cabot disappeared on his second trip and was never heard from again.

In 1524 France sent Giovanni da Verrazano to map America's coast and find a route through to Asia. Verrazano mapped from what is today North Carolina north to Newfoundland but found no path to Asia.

Ten years later, the French tried again. This time they sent **Jacques Cartier** (ZHAHK kahr•TYAY). Cartier sailed past Newfoundland and entered the St. Lawrence River. Hoping he had found a passage to Asia, Cartier made two more trips to map the St. Lawrence River. After these trips, France stopped exploring. By the mid-1500s, French Protestants and Catholics were fighting a civil war. There was no more exploring until it was settled.

Spain Fights England After Columbus, the Spanish went on to build a vast empire in America. They forced enslaved Native Americans to grow sugarcane and mine gold and silver. Later they brought enslaved Africans to the region to work on their farms.

Spanish nobles called conquistadors traveled to America in the hopes of becoming rich. Hernán Cortés conquered the Aztec, and Francisco Pizarro conquered the Inca. Soon after their victories, vast amounts of gold and silver began to flow to

Europe from Spain's empire in America.

Meanwhile, England had become Spain's enemy. As you have read, in 1534 King Henry VIII of England broke from the Catholic Church and made his kingdom Protestant. By the 1560s, the Dutch had become Protestant, too, even though they were part of Spain's empire at that time. Spain was strongly Catholic and tried to stop Protestantism in the **Netherlands** (NEH•thuhr•luhnz). When the Dutch people rebelled against Spain, England came to their aid.

To help the Dutch, Queen Elizabeth I of England let English privateers attack Spanish ships. Privateers are privately owned ships that have a license from the government to attack ships of other countries. People nicknamed the English privateers "sea dogs." They raided the Spanish treasure ships that were bringing gold back from America.

England's raids frustrated Philip II, the king of Spain. In 1588 he sent a huge fleet known as the Spanish Armada to invade England. In July 1588, the Armada headed into the English Channel—the narrow body of water between England and Europe. The Spanish ships were large and had many guns, but they were hard to steer. The smaller English ships moved much more quickly. Their attacks forced the Armada to retreat north. There a great storm arose and broke up the Armada.

The defeat of the Spanish Armada was an important event. The Spanish were still strong, but England now had the power to stand up to them. This encouraged the English and Dutch to begin exploring both North America and Asia.

Reading Check **Identify** Who was the first European to sail to India? Whose crew was first to sail around the world?

Biography

ELIZABETH I
1533–1603

Elizabeth I is one of the most popular British rulers—but she was more loved by the people of England than by her father, King Henry VIII. Elizabeth's young life was filled with change and sadness. She was born to Henry VIII and his second wife, Anne Boleyn. The king was upset when Elizabeth was born, because he wanted a boy to inherit the throne.

When Elizabeth became queen, she surrounded herself with intelligent advisers. Together they turned England into a strong, prosperous country. Elizabeth supported Protestantism in England and in the rest of Europe. She sent aid to the French Huguenots and Protestants in Scotland and the Netherlands. She worked well with Parliament but called few sessions during her reign. She was a skilled writer and speaker and won the love and support of the English people.

Elizabeth never married, which was unusual at that time. Many men were interested in marrying her, but she turned down their proposals. One reason Elizabeth probably remained single was to maintain control of the government at a time when most rulers were men. She also used her status to the advantage of England. Many prominent men wanted to marry her, and she sometimes threatened to marry someone's enemy in order to get him to do what she wanted.

Elizabeth's personality also influenced England's society. She loved horse riding, dances, parties, and plays. Her support of the arts resulted in the development of new English literature and music. Elizabeth was so popular by the time of her death that the date she became queen was celebrated as a national holiday for 200 years.

▲ Queen Elizabeth I

"I have the heart and stomach of a king and of a king of England, too."

–Elizabeth I, "Armada Speech"

Then and Now

Even though Queen Elizabeth I had an unhappy childhood, she overcame it to become one of England's most popular leaders. Today England's Queen Elizabeth II has also faced sad situations. Research her life and write a short essay comparing her life to the life of Elizabeth I.

The Commercial Revolution

Main Idea To increase trade, Europeans set up colonies and created joint-stock companies.

Reading Focus Do you know anyone who works at home? Read to learn how merchants in the 1600s gave people jobs at home and changed the world trade system.

▲ **These ships sailed for the Dutch East India Company, which carried out trade in Asia.** *Which European nation did the Dutch replace in the spice trade?*

While Spain built its empire in America, Portugal began building a trading empire in Asia. In 1500, shortly after Vasco da Gama's trip, the Portuguese sent 13 ships back to India. Led by Pedro Alvares Cabral (PAY•throo AHL•vahr•ihs kuh•BRAHL), the Portuguese fought a war against the Muslim merchants in the Indian Ocean.

After defeating the Arab fleet, the Portuguese built trading posts in India, China, Japan, the Persian Gulf, and in the **Moluccas** (muh•LUH•kuhz), or Spice Islands of Southeast Asia. From these bases, they controlled most of southern Asia's sea trade.

What Is Mercantilism?

As Europeans watched Spain and Portugal grow wealthy from their empires, they tried to figure out how they had become rich. They came up with the idea of **mercantilism** (MUHR•kuhn•TUH•LIH•zuhm). Mercantilism is the idea that a country gains power by building up its supply of gold and silver. Mercantilists believe the best way to do this is to **export** (EHK•SPOHRT), or sell to other countries, more goods than you **import** (IHM•POHRT), or buy from them. If you export more than you import, more gold and silver flows in from other countries than goes out.

Mercantilists also thought countries should set up colonies. A **colony** (KAH•luh•nee) is a settlement of people living in a new territory controlled by their home country. Colonists are supposed to produce goods their country does not have at home. That way, the home country will not have to import those goods from other countries.

Trade Empires in Asia

Mercantilism encouraged Europeans to set up trading posts and colonies in Asia and North America. By the end of the 1500s, Spain had set up a colony in the Philippines. The Spanish shipped silver to the Philippines from America and then used it to buy Asian spices and silk for sale in Europe.

In the 1600s, English and French merchants landed in India and began trading with the people there. In 1619 the Dutch built a fort on the island of Java, in what is now Indonesia. They slowly pushed the Portuguese out of the spice trade.

What Are Joint-Stock Companies?

Trading overseas was very expensive. In the 1600s, however, new ways of doing business developed in Europe. Historians call this the "commercial revolution." **Commerce** (KAH•muhrs) is the buying and selling of goods in large amounts over long distances.

To trade goods long distance, merchants needed a lot of money. They had to buy many goods, store them in warehouses, and ship them over land and sea. They had to know what people in distant lands wanted to buy and what prices were like there.

This new business created a new type of businessperson called an entrepreneur. Entrepreneurs **invest** (ihn•VEHST), or put money into a project. Their goal is to make even more money when the project is done.

Many projects were so large that a group of entrepreneurs had to come together and form a joint-stock company. A joint-stock company is a business that people can invest in by buying a share of the company. These shares are called stocks.

What Is the Cottage Industry?
To trade over a long distance, merchants need a large supply of goods. They also have to buy goods at low prices so they can make money selling them at higher prices elsewhere.

By the 1600s, merchants had become frustrated by artisans and guilds. They charged too much and could not make goods fast enough. So merchants began asking peasants to make goods for them. In particular, they asked the peasants to make wool cloth. The peasants were happy to make extra money and glad to find work they could do in their homes.

This system was called the "putting out" system. Merchants would buy wool and put it out to the peasants. This system is also sometimes called the "cottage industry," because the small houses where peasants lived were called cottages.

✓ **Reading Check** Explain How did merchants raise the money for overseas trade?

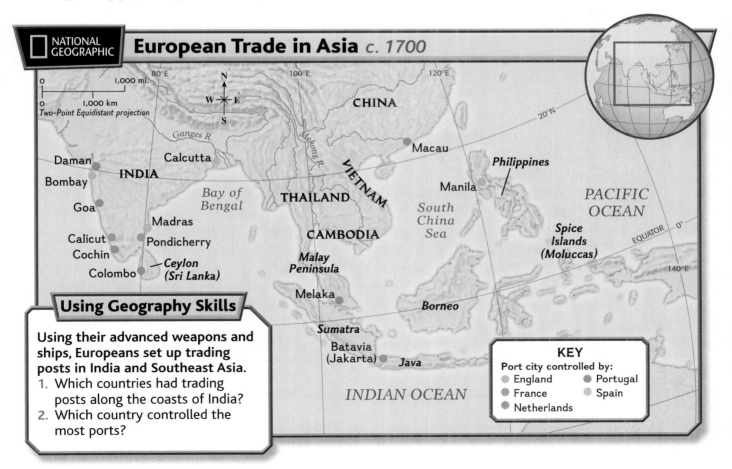

NATIONAL GEOGRAPHIC
European Trade in Asia *c. 1700*

Using Geography Skills

Using their advanced weapons and ships, Europeans set up trading posts in India and Southeast Asia.
1. Which countries had trading posts along the coasts of India?
2. Which country controlled the most ports?

KEY
Port city controlled by:
- England
- France
- Netherlands
- Portugal
- Spain

A Global Exchange

Main Idea Exploration and trade led to a worldwide exchange of products, people, and ideas.

Reading Focus Have you heard about insects from other countries that hurt American crops? Read to learn how the movement of goods and people between America and the rest of the world caused great changes.

After the Age of Exploration, the economies of Europe, Africa, Asia, and America changed. As Europe traded with the world, a global exchange of people, goods, technology, ideas, and even diseases began. We call this transfer the Columbian Exchange, after Christopher Columbus.

Two important foods—corn and potatoes—were taken to Europe from North America. Corn was used to feed animals. Larger, healthier animals resulted in more meat, leather, and wool. The potato was also important. Europeans discovered that if they planted potatoes instead of grain, about four times as many people could live off the same amount of land.

Other American foods, such as squash, beans, and tomatoes, also made their way to Europe. Tomatoes greatly changed cooking in Italy, where tomato sauces became very popular. Chocolate was a popular food from Central America. By mixing it with milk and sugar, Europeans created a sweet that is still popular today.

Some American foods, such as chili peppers and peanuts, were taken to Europe, but they also made their way to Asia and Africa where they became popular. Both Europeans and Asians also began smoking tobacco, an American plant.

Many European and Asian grains, such as wheat, oats, barley, rye, and rice, were planted in the Americas. Coffee and tropical fruits, such as bananas, were brought to America as well. Eventually, coffee and

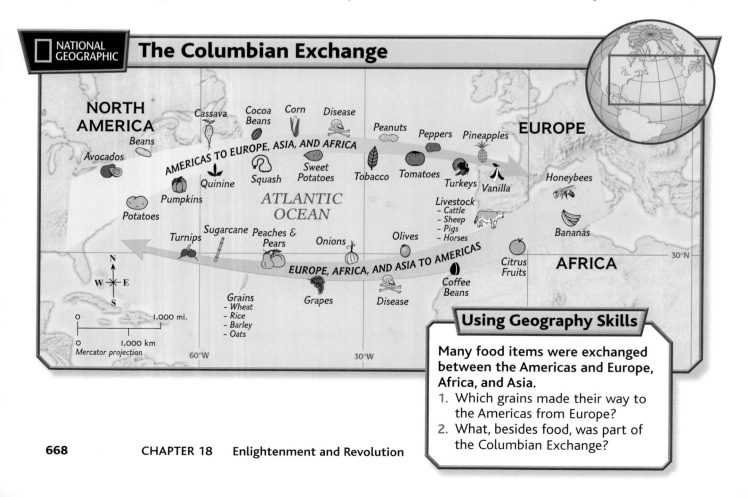

NATIONAL GEOGRAPHIC

The Columbian Exchange

NORTH AMERICA — Cassava — Cocoa Beans — Corn — Disease — Peanuts — Peppers — Pineapples — EUROPE

Beans — Avocados — AMERICAS TO EUROPE, ASIA, AND AFRICA — Quinine — Squash — Sweet Potatoes — Tobacco — Tomatoes — Turkeys — Vanilla — Honeybees

Pumpkins — ATLANTIC OCEAN — Livestock - Cattle - Sheep - Pigs - Horses — Bananas

Potatoes — Turnips — Sugarcane — Peaches & Pears — Onions — Olives — Citrus Fruits — AFRICA

EUROPE, AFRICA, AND ASIA TO AMERICAS

Grains - Wheat - Rice - Barley - Oats — Grapes — Disease — Coffee Beans

1,000 mi. — 1,000 km — Mercator projection — 60°W — 30°W — 30°N

Using Geography Skills

Many food items were exchanged between the Americas and Europe, Africa, and Asia.

1. Which grains made their way to the Americas from Europe?
2. What, besides food, was part of the Columbian Exchange?

banana farms employed thousands of workers in Central and South America.

New animals such as pigs, sheep, cattle, chickens, and horses were also brought to America. Chickens changed the diet of many people in Central and South America, while horses changed the lives of Native Americans on the Great Plains. Horses provided a faster way to move from place to place. As a result, Native Americans began hunting buffalo as their main food source.

A huge movement of people also took place after Europeans obtained sugarcane from Asia and began growing it in the Caribbean. To plant and harvest the sugarcane, they enslaved millions of Africans and moved them to the Americas.

Europeans also changed Asian society. With their guns and powerful ships, the Europeans easily defeated Arab fleets and Indian princes. Across Asia, the Europeans forced local rulers to let them set up trading posts. Within a short time, the East India Company of England had built an empire in India, and the Dutch East India Company had built an empire in Indonesia.

The arrival of the Europeans in Japan also changed that society. Using guns and cannons imported from Europe, a new shogun was finally able to defeat the feudal lords, the daimyo, and reunite Japan.

Not everything exchanged between Europe and America was good. When Europeans arrived in America, they were carrying germs that could kill Native Americans. Many diseases, including smallpox, measles, and malaria, swept across the Americas killing millions of people.

✓ **Reading Check** **Describe** Describe the Columbian Exchange.

Section 1 Review

History Online
Study Central™ Need help with the material in this section? Visit jat.glencoe.com

Reading Summary
Review the Main Ideas

- Rising prices of Asian goods, strong central governments, and new sailing technology led to European exploration of the world.

- Portugal found a route to India while Spain, England, and France explored America.

- Europeans used joint-stock companies to build colonies and trading posts in Asia following the ideas of mercantilism.

- European exploration and trade brought about a global exchange of goods, technology, and disease.

What Did You Learn?

1. What was a caravel, and why was it important?

2. Describe the accomplishments of Ferdinand Magellan.

Critical Thinking

3. **Organize Information** Draw a chart like the one below. Use it to name the explorers discussed in this section, the country they sailed for, and the places they explored.

Explorer	Country Sailed for	Area Explored

4. **Summarize** Describe the development of the African slave trade.

5. **Understand Cause and Effect** Why did merchants create joint-stock companies and use cottage industries?

6. **Analyze** How did foods imported from the Americas benefit Europe? Identify some of those foods.

7. **Reading** **Monitor and Adjust** Write a 10-question multiple choice test to help you review the important information in this section. Exchange tests with a classmate.

Section 2

The Scientific Revolution

Get Ready to Read!

What's the Connection?
One result of the Renaissance was a new interest in science. During the 1600s, people began to observe, experiment, and reason to find new knowledge.

Focusing on the Main Ideas
- The thinkers of the ancient world developed early forms of science and passed this knowledge to later civilizations. *(page 671)*

- European interest in astronomy led to new discoveries and ideas about the universe and Earth's place in it. *(page 673)*

- The Scientific Revolution led to new discoveries in physics, medicine, and chemistry. *(page 675)*

- Using the scientific method, Europeans of the 1600s and 1700s developed new ideas about society based on reason. *(page 678)*

Meeting People
Ptolemy (TAH•luh•mee)
Copernicus (koh•PUHR•nih•kuhs)
Kepler (KEH•pluhr)
Galileo (GA•luh•LEE•oh)
Newton (NOO•tuhn)
Descartes (day•KAHRT)

Building Your Vocabulary
theory (THEE•uh•ree)
rationalism (RASH•nuh•LIH•zuhm)
scientific method
hypothesis (hy•PAH•thuh•suhs)

Reading Strategy
Compare and Contrast Use a diagram like the one below to show the similarities and differences in the views of Ptolemy and Copernicus.

Ptolemy — Copernicus

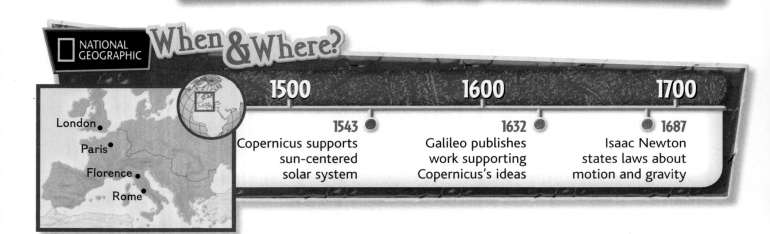

NATIONAL GEOGRAPHIC When & Where?

London
Paris
Florence
Rome

1500 — 1600 — 1700

1543 Copernicus supports sun-centered solar system

1632 Galileo publishes work supporting Copernicus's ideas

1687 Isaac Newton states laws about motion and gravity

The Scientific Revolution

Main Idea The thinkers of the ancient world developed early forms of science and passed this knowledge to later civilizations.

Reading Focus Have you ever taught a skill or passed on an idea to a younger brother or sister? Read in this chapter how the scientific ideas of early thinkers were passed on to later generations.

From earliest times, people have been curious about the world around them. Thousands of years ago, people began to use numbers, study the stars and planets, and watch the growth of plants and animals. These activities were the beginnings of science. Science is any organized study of the natural world and how it works.

Early Scientists

Early civilizations developed different kinds of science to solve practical problems. Among the first sciences were mathematics, astronomy, and medicine. Mathematics was used for record keeping and building projects. Astronomy helped people keep time and figure out when to plant and harvest crops. Early civilizations also developed medical practices, such as surgery, acupuncture, and the use of herbs, for treating illnesses.

The ancient Greeks left behind a large amount of scientific knowledge. They believed that reason was the only way to understand nature. As they studied the world, they developed theories. A **theory** (THEE•uh•ree) is an explanation of how or why something happens. A theory is based on what you can observe about something. It may not be correct, but it seems to fit the facts.

In Ancient Greece, the Greek philosopher Aristotle observed nature and collected vast amounts of information about plants and animals. He then took the facts

▲ This model shows the universe according to the ideas of the Polish astronomer Nicolaus Copernicus, with the sun at the universe's center. *What did Ptolemy's geocentric theory state?*

he gathered and classified, or arranged them into groups, based on their similarities and differences.

The Greeks made many important scientific advances, but their approach to science had some problems. For example, they did not experiment, or test, new ideas to see if they were true. Many of their conclusions were false because they were based on "common sense" instead of experiments.

For example, in the A.D. 100s, the Egyptian-born astronomer **Ptolemy** (TAH•luh•mee) stated that the sun and the planets moved around the earth in circular paths. After all, it did seem like the earth was the center of the universe. Astronomers in Europe accepted Ptolemy's geocentric, or earth-centered, theory for more than 1,400 years.

Science During the Middle Ages

Under Roman rule, most thinkers continued to accept the scientific knowledge of the Greeks. After the fall of Rome, during the Middle Ages, most people were more interested in theology, the study of God, than in the study of nature. For scientific knowledge, they relied on Greek and Roman writings and saw no need to check their facts or to make their own observations. Many of these ancient works, however, were either lost or poorly preserved. In the writings that survived, errors were added as copies were made.

Meanwhile, Arabs and Jews in the Islamic Empire preserved much of the science of the Greeks and Romans. They carefully copied many Greek and Roman works into the Arabic language. They also came into contact with the science of the Persians and the Indian system of mathematics.

Arabic and Jewish scientists made advances of their own in areas such as mathematics, astronomy, and medicine. However, in spite of these achievements, scientists in the Islamic world did not experiment or develop the instruments necessary to advance their scientific knowledge.

During the 1100s, European thinkers became interested in science again as a result of their contacts with the Islamic world. Major Islamic scientific works were brought to Europe and translated into Latin. The Hindu-Arabic system of numbers also spread to Europe, where it eventually replaced Roman numerals. Christian thinkers, such as Thomas Aquinas, tried to show that Christianity and reason could go together. During the 1100s, Europeans began building new universities. They

A New View of the Universe

Ptolemaic Universe

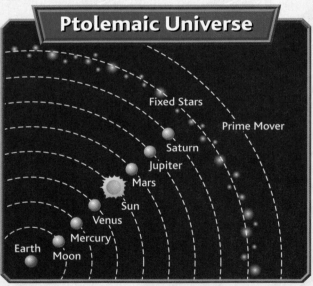

Fixed Stars

Prime Mover

Saturn

Jupiter

Mars

Sun

Venus

Mercury

Earth

Moon

The astronomical theory of Ptolemy (left) placed Earth at the center of the universe (above). His theory was accepted for more than a thousand years. *According to the diagram, how many planets besides Earth were known at the time of Ptolemy?*

would play an important role in the growth of science.

Beginning in the 1400s, voyages of exploration further added to Europe's scientific knowledge. Better charts, maps, and navigational instruments helped voyagers reach different parts of the world. Through exploration, the size of oceans and continents became better known. Scientists gathered and classified new knowledge about plants, animals, and diseases in different parts of the world.

As scientific knowledge grew, the stage was set for a new understanding of the natural world that would shake Europe to its foundations.

Reading Check **Describe** Describe scientific knowledge during the Middle Ages.

A Revolution in Astronomy

Main Idea European interest in astronomy led to new discoveries and ideas about the universe and Earth's place in it.

Reading Focus What would people on Earth think if life were discovered on other planets? Read to see how Europeans reacted to new discoveries about the universe.

During the 1500s, European thinkers began to break with the old scientific ideas. They increasingly understood that advances in science could only come through mathematics and experimentation. This new way of thinking led to a revolution, or sweeping change, in the way Europeans understood science and the search for knowledge. Astronomy was the first science affected by

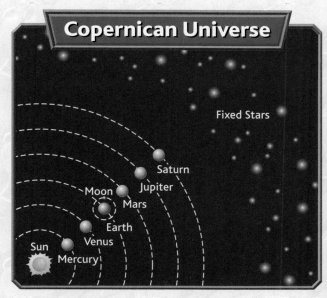

Copernican Universe

Fixed Stars

Saturn
Jupiter
Moon
Mars
Earth
Venus
Sun
Mercury

NICOLAS COPERNICVS

Nicolaus Copernicus (right), a Polish mathematician, believed that the sun was at the center of the universe. His model (above) placed Earth and the other planets in orbits around the sun. *Why did Europeans again become interested in science in the 1100s?*

the Scientific Revolution. New discoveries brought changes in the way Europeans saw the universe. They challenged traditional thinking that God had made the earth as the center of the universe.

Who Was Copernicus? Leading the Scientific Revolution was a Polish mathematician named Nicolaus **Copernicus** (koh•PUHR•nih•kuhs). In 1543 Copernicus wrote a book called *On the Revolutions of the Heavenly Spheres.* He disagreed with Ptolemy's view that the earth was the center of the universe. Copernicus believed that Ptolemy's theory was too complicated. Instead, he developed a simpler heliocentric, or sun-centered, theory of the universe. Copernicus's theory stated that the Sun, not Earth, was the center of the universe. The planets moved in circular paths around the Sun.

Kepler's Revolution The next step in the march of science was taken by a German astronomer named Johannes **Kepler** (KEH•pluhr). He supported Copernicus's theory but also made corrections to it. Kepler added the idea that the planets move in ellipses (ih•LIHP•SEEZ), or oval paths, rather than circular

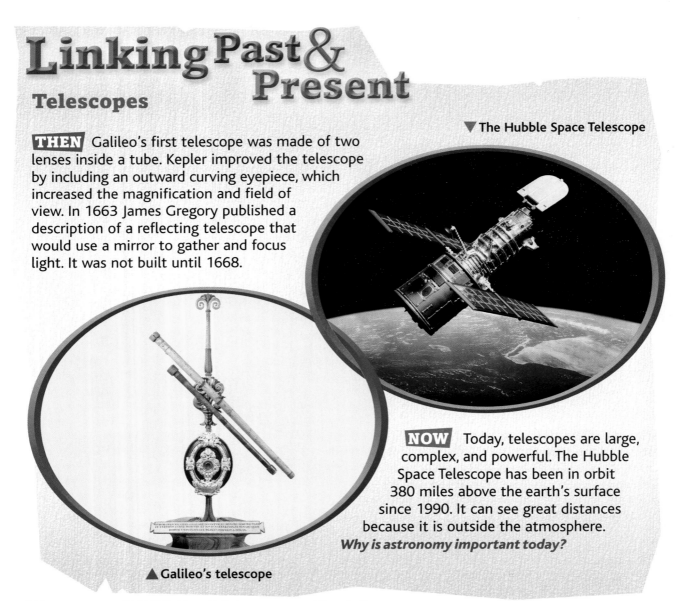

Linking Past & Present

Telescopes

THEN Galileo's first telescope was made of two lenses inside a tube. Kepler improved the telescope by including an outward curving eyepiece, which increased the magnification and field of view. In 1663 James Gregory published a description of a reflecting telescope that would use a mirror to gather and focus light. It was not built until 1668.

▼ **The Hubble Space Telescope**

NOW Today, telescopes are large, complex, and powerful. The Hubble Space Telescope has been in orbit 380 miles above the earth's surface since 1990. It can see great distances because it is outside the atmosphere.
Why is astronomy important today?

▲ Galileo's telescope

ones. His theory made it easier to explain the movements of the planets. It also marked the beginning of modern astronomy.

Who Was Galileo? An Italian scientist named Galileo Galilei made the third great breakthrough in the Scientific Revolution. **Galileo** (GA•luh•LEE•oh) believed that new knowledge could come through experiments that were carefully carried out. For example, Galileo challenged Aristotle's idea that the heavier the object is, the faster it falls to the ground. Galileo's experiments proved that Aristotle was wrong. Objects fall at the same speed regardless of their weight.

Galileo also realized that scientific instruments could help humans better explore the natural world. He improved instruments, such as the clock and telescope. With the telescope, Galileo found clear evidence supporting Copernicus's view that Earth revolves around the Sun.

Galileo also played an important role in the development of new scientific instruments. In 1593 he invented a water thermometer that, for the first time, allowed temperature changes to be measured. Galileo's assistant, Evangelista Torricelli, then used the element called mercury to build the first barometer, an instrument that measures air pressure.

When Galileo published his ideas in 1632, his work was condemned by the Roman Catholic Church. The Catholic Church held to the geocentric, or earth-centered, view of the universe, believing that it was taught in the Bible. The pope ordered Galileo to come to Rome to be tried for heresy. Church threats finally forced Galileo to withdraw many of his statements. Even so, Galileo's ideas spread throughout Europe and changed people's views about the universe.

✓ **Reading Check** **Explain** How did Galileo prove Copernicus's theory?

New Scientific Discoveries

Main Idea The Scientific Revolution led to new discoveries in physics, medicine, and chemistry.

Reading Focus Think about all the facts you know about medicine. For example, you know your heart pumps blood, your lungs breathe air, and your body is made of cells. Read to learn how scientists of the 1600s and 1700s made discoveries we often take for granted today.

Throughout the 1600s and 1700s, the Scientific Revolution continued to spread. Many new discoveries were made in physics, medicine, and chemistry.

Who Is Isaac Newton? Despite continuing scientific breakthroughs, the ideas of Copernicus, Kepler, and Galileo needed to be brought together as one system. This feat was accomplished by an English mathematician named Isaac **Newton** (NOO•tuhn).

According to tradition, Newton was sitting in his garden one day when he watched an apple fall to the ground. The

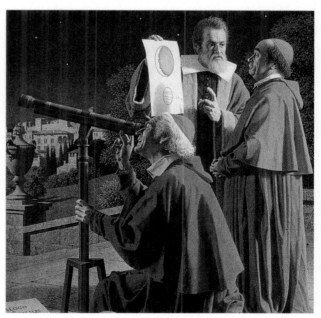

▲ In this painting, Galileo presents his astronomical findings to the Catholic clergy. *How did Galileo respond to the Church's condemnation of his work in astronomy?*

apple's fall led him to the idea of gravity, or the pull of the earth and other bodies on objects at or near their surfaces.

In a book called *Principia,* published in 1687, Newton stated his laws, or well-tested theories, about the motion of objects in space and on Earth. The most important was the universal law of gravitation. It explains that the force of gravity holds the entire solar system together by keeping the sun and the planets in their orbits. Newton's ideas led to the rise of modern physics, or the study of physical properties such as matter and energy.

Medicine and Chemistry Sweeping changes were made in medicine in the 1500s and 1600s. Since Roman times, European doctors had relied on the teachings of the Greek

History Online

Web Activity Visit jat.glencoe.com and click on *Chapter 18—Student Web Activity* to learn more about early scientific discoveries.

physician Galen. Galen wanted to study the human body, but he was only allowed to dissect, or cut open, animals.

In the 1500s, however, a Flemish doctor named Andreas Vesalius began dissecting dead human bodies for research. In 1543 Vesalius published *On the Structure of the Human Body.* In this work, Vesalius presented a detailed account of the human body that replaced many of Galen's ideas.

Other breakthroughs in medicine took place. In the early 1600s, William Harvey, an English doctor, proved that blood flowed through the human body. In the mid-1600s, an English scientist named Robert Hooke began using a microscope, and he soon discovered cells, the smallest structures of living material.

Beginning in the 1600s, European scientists developed new ideas in chemistry. Chemistry is the study of natural substances and how they change. In the mid-1600s, Robert Boyle, an Irish scientist, proved that all substances are made up of basic elements that cannot be broken down.

European scientists of the 1700s also developed ways to study gases. They discovered hydrogen, carbon dioxide, and oxygen. By 1777, Antoine Lavoisier (AN•twahn luhv•WAH•zee•AY) of France had proven that materials need oxygen to burn. Marie Lavoisier, also a scientist, contributed to her husband's work.

Reading Check **Identify** According to Newton, what force held the planets in orbit?

The Scientific Revolution

Scientist	Nation	Discoveries
Nicolaus Copernicus (1473–1543)	Poland	Earth orbits the Sun; Earth rotates on its axis
Galileo Galilei (1564–1642)	Italy	other planets have moons
Johannes Kepler (1571–1630)	Germany	planets have elliptical orbits
William Harvey (1578–1657)	England	heart pumps blood
Robert Hooke (1635–1703)	England	cells
Robert Boyle (1627–1691)	Ireland	air is made of gases
Isaac Newton (1642–1727)	England	gravity; laws of motion; calculus
Antoine Lavoisier (1743–1794)	France	how materials burn

Understanding Charts

During the Scientific Revolution, scientists made discoveries in many fields, such as astronomy and medicine.
1. What did William Harvey discover?
2. **Identify** Which scientists' discoveries dealt with chemistry?

Biography

SIR ISAAC NEWTON
1642–1727

Isaac Newton was born into a farming family on December 25, 1642, in Woolsthorpe, England. His father died before Newton was born. His mother remarried when he was three years old. His new stepfather did not want the boy to live with them, so Newton was raised by his grandmother.

Newton earned a degree from Trinity College, part of Cambridge University, in 1664. He planned to work for the university, but from 1664 to 1666, it closed because of the plague. Newton spent the next two years in his hometown. While there, he made some of his most important discoveries. He developed his theory of gravity, invented a new kind of mathematics called calculus, and discovered that white light is made up of all of the different colors of light.

Newton returned to Cambridge, earned a master's degree, and was appointed to several positions there. His life was very stressful because many scientists questioned his calculations. These criticisms made Newton reluctant to publish his discoveries, but eventually he did. His book *Principia* is considered one of the greatest scientific books ever written. In it Newton describes his three laws of motion and his ideas about gravity.

▲ Newton analyzing light rays

"If I have seen farther, it is by standing upon the shoulders of giants."
–Isaac Newton, in a letter to Robert Hooke

During his life, Newton won many awards for his discoveries. In 1705 he became the first scientist ever to be knighted by the English king.

▲ Trinity College today

Then and Now

Newton's findings were criticized by some scientists of his time. Do research to find a scientific discovery made in the last 50 years that others have questioned or criticized. Describe your findings to the class.

The Triumph of Reason

Main Idea Using the scientific method, Europeans of the 1600s and 1700s developed new ideas about society based on reason.

Reading Focus What do modern scientists do in their laboratories? Read to understand how methods of scientific research changed Europeans' understanding of human society in the 1600s and 1700s.

As scientists made new discoveries, European thinkers began to apply science to society. For these thinkers, science had proven that the physical universe followed natural laws. By using their reason, people could learn how the universe worked. Using this knowledge, people also could solve existing human problems and make life better.

Descartes and Reason One of the most important scientific thinkers was the Frenchman René **Descartes** (day•KAHRT). In 1637 he wrote a book called *Discourse on Method.* In this book, Descartes began with the problem of knowing what is true. To find truth, he decided to put aside everything that he had learned and make a fresh start. To Descartes, one fact seemed to be beyond doubt—his own existence. Descartes summarized this idea by the phrase, "I think, therefore I am."

In his work, Descartes claimed that mathematics was the source of all scientific truth. In mathematics, he said, the answers were always true. This was because mathematics began with simple, obvious principles and then used logic to move gradually to other truths. Today, Descartes is viewed as the founder of modern **rationalism** (RASH•nuh•LIH•zuhm). This is the belief that reason is the chief source of knowledge.

What Is the Scientific Method?

Scientific thought was also influenced by English thinker Francis Bacon, who lived from 1561 to 1626. Bacon believed that

The Microscope

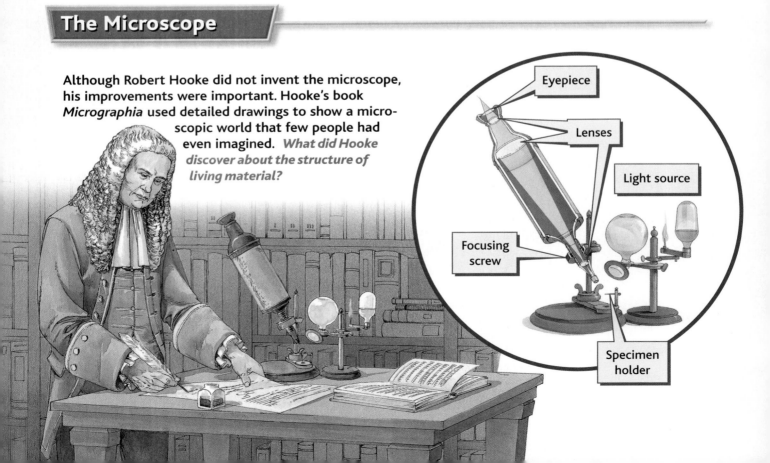

Although Robert Hooke did not invent the microscope, his improvements were important. Hooke's book *Micrographia* used detailed drawings to show a microscopic world that few people had even imagined. *What did Hooke discover about the structure of living material?*

Eyepiece

Lenses

Light source

Focusing screw

Specimen holder

ideas based on tradition should be put aside. He developed the **scientific method,** an orderly way of collecting and analyzing evidence. It is still the process used in scientific research today.

The scientific method is made up of several steps. First a scientist begins with careful observation of facts and then tries to find a **hypothesis** (hy•PAH•thuh•suhs), or explanation of the facts. Through experiments, the scientist tests the hypothesis under all possible conditions to see if it is true. Finally, if repeated, experiments show that the hypothesis is true, and then it is considered a scientific law.

Francis Bacon ▲

✓ **Reading Check** **Explain** What is the scientific method?

The Scientific Method

Observe some aspect of the universe.

↓

Hypothesize about what you observed.

↓

Predict something based on your hypothesis.

↓

Test your predictions through experiments and observation.

↓

Modify hypothesis in light of results.

Understanding Charts

The scientific method is still important today.
1. What is the next step after predictions are tested through experiments and observation?
2. **Conclude** Why is the scientific method necessary to create scientific law?

History Online

Study Central™ Need help with the material in this section? Visit jat.glencoe.com

Section ② Review

Reading Summary

Review the Main Ideas

- The thinkers of the ancient world developed early forms of science and passed this knowledge to later generations.
- European interest in science led to new discoveries and ideas about the universe and Earth's place in it.
- The Scientific Revolution led to new discoveries in physics, medicine, and chemistry.
- Descartes invented rationalism, and Bacon developed the scientific method.

What Did You Learn?

1. Who was Copernicus, and what was the heliocentric theory?

2. Describe Francis Bacon's beliefs about scientific reasoning.

Critical Thinking

3. **Summarize** Draw a diagram like the one below. Add details to show some of the new ideas developed during the Scientific Revolution.

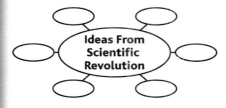

Ideas From Scientific Revolution

4. **Drawing Conclusions** What do you think Descartes meant when he said, "I think, therefore I am"?

5. **Science Link** Explain Kepler's view of the solar system.

6. **Analyze** Why did the Church condemn Galileo's astronomical findings?

7. **Writing Questions** Imagine that you could interview Galileo about his work and his life. Write five questions you would like to ask him. Include possible answers with your questions.

Section 3

The Enlightenment

Get Ready to Read!

What's the Connection?
As you have read, the Scientific Revolution led to new discoveries. At the same time, it also led to many new ideas about government and society.

Focusing on the Main Ideas
• During the 1700s, many Europeans believed that reason could be used to make government and society better. *(page 681)*

• The Enlightenment was centered in France, where thinkers wrote about changing their society and met to discuss their ideas. *(page 684)*

• Many of Europe's monarchs, who claimed to rule by the will of God, tried to model their countries on Enlightenment ideas. *(page 686)*

Locating Places
Prussia (PRUH•shuh)
Austria (AWS•tree•uh)
St. Petersburg (PEE•tuhrz•BUHRG)

Meeting People
Thomas Hobbes (HAHBZ)
John Locke
Montesquieu (MAHN•tuhs•KYOO)
Voltaire (vohl•TAR)

Building Your Vocabulary
natural law
social contract
separation of powers
deism (DEE•IH•zuhm)
absolutism (AB•suh•LOO•TIH•zuhm)

Reading Strategy
Summarizing Information Complete a table like the one below showing the major ideas of Enlightenment thinkers.

Thinkers	Ideas

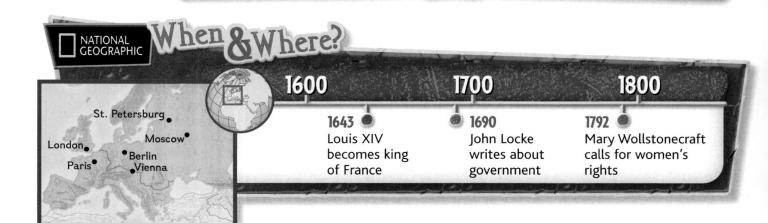

When & Where?

1643 Louis XIV becomes king of France

1690 John Locke writes about government

1792 Mary Wollstonecraft calls for women's rights

New Ideas About Politics

Main Idea During the 1700s, many Europeans believe that reason could be used to make government and society better.

Reading Focus What makes people get along with each other? Do they need rules, a strong leader, or to learn to work together? Read to learn how thinkers in Europe answered these questions.

During the 1700s, European thinkers were impressed by scientific discoveries in the natural world. They believed that reason could also uncover the scientific laws that governed human life. Once these laws were known, thinkers said, people could use the laws to make society better.

As the Scientific Revolution advanced, many educated Europeans came to believe that reason was a much better guide than faith or tradition. To them, reason was a "light" that revealed error and showed the way to truth. As result, the 1700s became known as the Age of Enlightenment.

During the Enlightenment, political thinkers tried to apply reason and scientific ideas to government. They claimed that there was a **natural law,** or a law that applied to everyone and could be understood by reason. This law was the key to understanding government. As early as the 1600s, two English thinkers—Thomas Hobbes and John Locke—used natural law to develop very different ideas about how government should work.

Who Was Thomas Hobbes?

Thomas Hobbes (HAHBZ) wrote about English government and society. During his life, England was torn apart by civil war. Supporters of King Charles I fought those who backed Parliament. Charles I wanted to have absolute, or total, power as king. Parliament claimed to represent the people

▲ This illustration is from the title page of Hobbes's *Leviathan.* *What sort of government did Hobbes support in* **Leviathan?**

and demanded a greater voice in running England. The fighting finally led to Charles's execution. This event shocked Thomas Hobbes, who was a strong supporter of the monarchy.

In 1651 Hobbes wrote a book called *Leviathan.* In this work, Hobbes argued that natural law made absolute monarchy the best form of government.

According to Hobbes, humans were naturally selfish and violent. They could not be trusted to make decisions on their own. Left to themselves, people would make life "nasty, brutish, and short." Therefore, Hobbes said, they needed to obey a government that had the power of a leviathan, or sea monster. To Hobbes, this meant the rule of a king, because only a strong ruler could give people direction.

Why Is John Locke Important?

Another English thinker **John Locke** thought differently. He used natural law to affirm citizens' rights and to make government answerable to the people.

The Law of Nations

Montesquieu's beliefs about government are still influential today.

"Again, there is no liberty, if the judiciary power be not separated from the legislative and executive. Were it joined with the legislative, the life and liberty of the subject would be exposed to arbitrary control; for the judge would be then the legislator. Were it joined to the executive power, the judge might behave with violence and oppression."

▲ Montesquieu

—Montesquieu,
The Spirit of Laws

DBQ Document-Based Question

According to Montesquieu, why should judges be independent?

During Locke's life, another English king, James II, wanted to set up an absolute monarchy against Parliament's wishes. In 1688 war threatened, and James fled the country. Parliament then asked Mary, James's daughter, and her husband, William, to take the throne. This event came to be called the "Glorious Revolution."

In return for the English throne, William and Mary agreed to a Bill of Rights. In this document, they agreed to obey Parliament's laws. The document also guaranteed all English people basic rights, like those the Magna Carta had given to the nobles. For example, people had the right to a fair trial by jury and to freedom from cruel punishment for a crime.

In 1690 John Locke explained many of the ideas of the Glorious Revolution in a book called *Two Treatises of Government*. Locke stated that government should be based on natural law. This law, said Locke, gave all people from their birth certain natural rights. Among them were the right to life, the right to liberty, and the right to own property.

Locke believed that the purpose of government is to protect these rights. All governments, he said, were based on a **social contract**, or an agreement between rulers and the people. If a ruler took away people's natural rights, the people had a right to revolt and set up a new government.

Who Was Montesquieu? England's government after the Glorious Revolution was admired by thinkers in France. They liked it better than their own absolute monarchy. In 1748 Baron **Montesquieu** (MAHN•tuhs•KYOO), a French thinker, published a book called *The Spirit of Laws*.

In this book, Montesquieu said that England's government was the best because it had a separation of powers. **Separation of powers** means that power should be equally divided among the branches of government: executive, legislative, and judicial. The legislative branch would make the laws while the executive branch would enforce them. The judicial branch would interpret the laws and judge when they were broken. By separating these powers, government could not become too powerful and threaten people's rights.

✓ **Reading Check** **Explain** According to Montesquieu, how should government be organized?

Biography

JOHN LOCKE
1632–1704

John Locke was born in Somerset, England. His father was a lawyer but also served as a cavalry soldier. Using his military connections, he arranged for his son John to get a good education. Locke studied classical languages, grammar, philosophy, and geometry at Oxford University. To Locke, the courses were not exciting, so he turned to his true interests—science and medicine.

After graduating, Locke went to work for governments in Europe. He continued to study science and philosophy. He particularly liked the work of Descartes. In 1671 Locke began recording his own ideas about how people know things. Nineteen years later, he published his ideas in *An Essay Concerning Human Understanding*. In this book, Locke argued that people's minds are blank when they are born and that society shapes what people think and believe. This idea meant that if people could make society better, it would also make people better.

▲ John Locke

> **"Law is not to abolish or restrain, but to preserve and enlarge freedom."**
>
> —John Locke, *Two Treatises of Government*

In 1683 Locke fled to Holland after the English government began to think his political ideas were dangerous. During that time, he was declared a traitor and was not able to return until after the Glorious Revolution of 1688. It was at that time that he wrote his famous *Two Treatises of Government*. Soon afterward, Locke retired to Essex. There he enjoyed frequent visits from Sir Isaac Newton and other friends until his death in 1704.

▲ William and Mary being crowned following the Glorious Revolution

Then and Now

Give examples of how Locke's ideas have influenced our lives and ideas.

The French Philosophes

Main Idea The Enlightenment was centered in France, where thinkers wrote about changing their society and met to discuss their ideas.

Reading Focus What role do writers play in the United States today? Read on to find out what effect writers had on Europe during the Enlightenment.

During the 1700s, France became the major center of the Enlightenment. As the Enlightenment spread, thinkers in France and elsewhere became known by the French name *philosophe* (FEE•luh•ZAWF), which means "philosopher." Most philosophes were writers, teachers, journalists, and observers of society.

The philosophes wanted to use reason to change society. They attacked superstition, or unreasoned beliefs. They also disagreed with Church leaders who opposed new scientific discoveries. The philosophes believed in both freedom of speech and the individual's right to liberty. They used their skills as writers to spread their ideas across Europe.

Who Was Voltaire? The greatest thinker of the Enlightenment was François-Marie Arouet, known simply as **Voltaire** (vohl•TAR). Born in a middle-class family, Voltaire wrote many novels, plays, letters, and essays that brought him fame and wealth.

Voltaire became known for his strong dislike of the Roman Catholic Church. He blamed Church leaders for keeping

◀ Voltaire

▲ During the Enlightenment, upper-class nobles held gatherings of writers, artists, government officials, and other nobles in their homes to discuss and debate new ideas. *How did the philosophes spread their ideas?*

knowledge from people in order to maintain the Church's power. Voltaire also opposed the government supporting one religion and forbidding others. He thought people should be free to choose their own beliefs.

Throughout his life, Voltaire was a supporter of **deism** (DEE•IH•zuhm), a religious belief based on reason. According to the followers of deism, God created the world and set it in motion. He then allowed it to run itself by natural law.

Who Was Diderot?

Denis Diderot was the French philosophe who did the most to spread Enlightenment ideas. With the help of friends, Diderot published a large, 28-volume encyclopedia. His project, which began in the 1750s, took about 20 years to complete.

The *Encyclopedia* included a wide range of topics, such as science, religion, government, and the arts. It became an important weapon in the philosophes' fight against traditional ways. Many articles attacked superstition and supported freedom of religion. Others called for changes that would make society more just and caring.

The Enlightenment and Women

The Enlightenment raised questions about the role of women in society. Previously, many male thinkers claimed that women were less important than men and had to be controlled and protected. By the 1700s, however, women thinkers began calling for women's rights. The most powerful supporter of women's rights was the English writer Mary Wollstonecraft. Many people today see her as the founder of the modern movement for women's rights.

Primary Source: Natural Rights of Women

Mary Wollstonecraft argued that the natural rights of the Enlightenment should extend to women as well as men.

▲ Mary Wollstonecraft

"In short, in whatever light I view the subject, reason and experience convince me that the only method of leading women to fulfill their peculiar [specific] duties is to free them from all restraint by allowing them to participate in the inherent rights of mankind. Make them free, and they will quickly become wise and virtuous, as men become more so, for the improvement must be mutual."

—Mary Wollstonecraft,
A Vindication of the Rights of Woman: With Strictures on Political and Moral Subjects

DBQ Document-Based Question

What did Wollstonecraft believe would happen if women were allowed rights?

In 1792 Mary Wollstonecraft wrote a book called *A Vindication of the Rights of Woman*. In this work, she claimed that all humans have reason. Because women have reason, they should have the same rights as men. Women, Wollstonecraft said, should have equal rights in education, the workplace, and in political life.

Rousseau's Social Contract

By the late 1700s, some European thinkers were starting to criticize Enlightenment ideas. One of these thinkers was Jean-Jacques Rousseau (zhahn zhahk ru•SOH).

Rousseau claimed that supporters of the Enlightenment relied too much on reason. Instead, people should pay more attention to their feelings. According to Rousseau, human beings were naturally good, but civilized life corrupted them. To improve themselves, he thought people should live simpler lives closer to nature.

In 1762 Rousseau published a book called *The Social Contract.* In this work, Rousseau presented his political ideas. A workable government, he said, should be based on a social contract. This is an agreement in which everyone in a society agrees to be governed by the general will, or what society as a whole wants.

✓ Reading Check **Describe** Who were the philosophes?

The Age of Absolutism

Main Idea Many of Europe's monarchs, who claimed to rule by the will of God, tried to model their countries on Enlightenment ideas.

Reading Focus If you were given the chance to be a leader, how would you treat the people you ruled? As you read, think about the power of Europe's kings and queens during the 1600s and 1700s.

During the 1600s and 1700s, many European thinkers favored limits on government power. However, powerful kings and queens ruled most of Europe. This system was known as **absolutism** (AB•suh•LOO•TIH•zuhm). In this system, monarchs held absolute, or total, power. They claimed to rule by divine right, or by the will of God. This meant that rulers did not answer to their people, but rather to God alone.

The Way It Was

Focus on Everyday Life

Music of the Enlightenment The 1700s was one of the greatest musical periods in history. Before this time, almost all music was religious in nature and was limited to church performances. During the Enlightenment, music was played in theaters for the first time, and some of the new pieces were not religious.

▲ A string quartet

Many types of music existed in the 1700s. Sonatas were performed with one instrument and a piano, and string quartets were played with four instruments. Concertos and symphonies were longer and involved an orchestra. Operas were full-scale theatrical performances using vocal and instrumental music.

Baroque music emphasized drama and emotion. Johann Sebastian Bach and George Frederick Handel composed baroque music. Bach composed

However, as the Enlightenment spread, many of Europe's absolute rulers turned to philosophes for help in making their governments work better. At the same time, however, they did not want to lose any of their power. Historians used to call these rulers enlightened despots. Despots are rulers who hold total power.

Louis XIV: France's Sun King

During the 1600s, France was one of Europe's strongest nations. In 1643 Louis XIV came to the throne. As king, Louis XIV was the most celebrated absolute monarch. His reign of 72 years—the longest in European history—set the style for Europe's kings and queens. Louis was known as the Sun King, the source of light for his people and for Europe's nobles and rulers.

Louis relied on a bureaucracy, but he was the source of all political authority in France. He is said to have boasted, "I am the State."

Louis's army fought and won wars to expand France's territory, but these conflicts were costly in money and soldiers to France. The king's constant wars and excessive spending weakened France and the monarchy.

Frederick the Great

During the 1600s and 1700s, Germany was a collection of over 300 separate states. Of these states, two—**Prussia** (PRUH•shuh) and **Austria** (AWS•tree•uh)—became great European powers.

The most famous Prussian ruler was Frederick II, also called Frederick the Great. He ruled from 1740 to 1786. As Prussia's king, Frederick strengthened the army and fought wars to gain new territory for Prussia. He also tried to be an "enlightened ruler." He supported the arts and learning and tried to carry out enlightened reforms. He permitted his people to speak and publish more freely. He also allowed greater religious toleration.

---

many pieces of music that are still popular today. Handel wrote many operas, but he is best known for *Messiah,* an oratorio, or religious composition that mixes voices, orchestra, and organ.

Classical music emerged in the mid-1700s. Classical composers, inspired by the ancient Greeks and Romans, emphasized balance, harmony, and stability. Franz Joseph Haydn and Wolfgang Amadeus Mozart wrote classical music. Haydn's use of instruments made the symphony more popular. Mozart composed a large number of musical pieces that remain popular today.

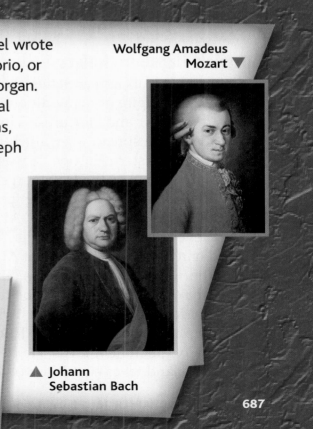

Wolfgang Amadeus Mozart ▼

▲ Johann Sebastian Bach

Connecting to the Past
1. What is the difference in tone between baroque and classical music?
2. What factors allowed music to thrive during the 1700s?

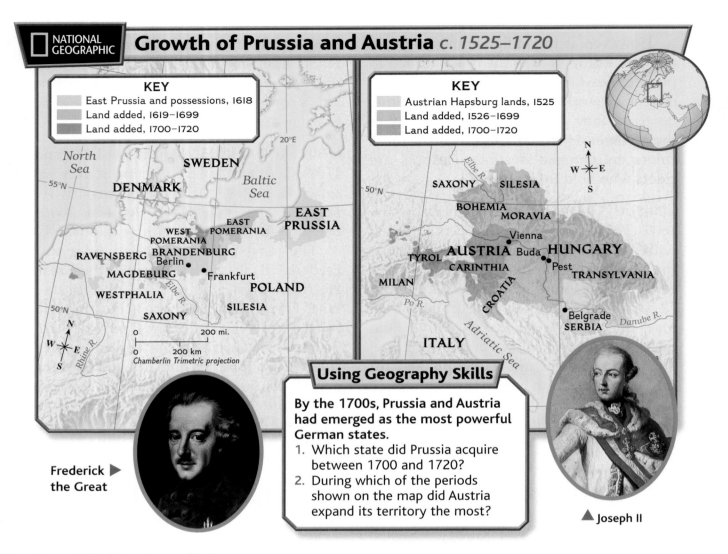

Growth of Prussia and Austria c. 1525–1720

KEY
- East Prussia and possessions, 1618
- Land added, 1619–1699
- Land added, 1700–1720

KEY
- Austrian Hapsburg lands, 1525
- Land added, 1526–1699
- Land added, 1700–1720

Frederick ▶ the Great

Using Geography Skills

By the 1700s, Prussia and Austria had emerged as the most powerful German states.
1. Which state did Prussia acquire between 1700 and 1720?
2. During which of the periods shown on the map did Austria expand its territory the most?

▲ Joseph II

Austria's Hapsburg Rulers By the 1700s, the other powerful German state—Austria—ruled a large empire of many different peoples, languages, and cultures. This vast Austrian empire spread over much of central and southeastern Europe. It was ruled by a family known as the Hapsburgs.

In 1740 a young Hapsburg princess named Maria Theresa became Austria's ruler. Clever and talented, Maria Theresa worked hard to improve the lot of Austria's serfs, who worked for the nobles. She also tried to make government work better.

After Maria Theresa died in 1780, her son, Joseph II, became ruler. Joseph II admired Enlightenment ideas. He freed the serfs, made land taxes equal for nobles and

farmers, and allowed books to be published freely. Most of Joseph's reforms failed, however. The nobles opposed Joseph's changes, and he was forced to back down. However, the former serfs, now farmers, were allowed to keep their freedom.

Russia's Peter I and Catherine II To the east of Austria stretched the vast empire of Russia. As you read previously, Russia was ruled by all-powerful rulers known as czars. One of the most powerful czars was Peter I, also known as Peter the Great. During his reign from 1689 to 1725, Peter tried to make Russia into a strong and up-to-date European power. He began reforms to make the government work more smoothly.

Peter also improved Russia's military and expanded Russia's territory westward to the Baltic Sea. In 1703 he founded a city called **St. Petersburg** (PEE•tuhrz•BUHRG) in this area. A few years later, Russia's capital was moved to St. Petersburg from Moscow.

After Peter died, conflict erupted among Russia's nobles. Then, in 1762 a German princess named Catherine came to the throne of Russia. Early in her reign, Catherine was devoted to Enlightenment ideas. She studied about and wrote letters to the philosophes. She even thought about freeing the serfs, but a serf uprising changed her mind. In the end, she allowed the nobles to treat the serfs as they pleased.

Under Catherine, Russia gained even more land and increased its power in Europe. As a result, Catherine became known as "the Great." However, by 1796,

Russia grew more powerful ▶ during the reigns of Peter the Great (above) and Catherine the Great (right). *How did Peter try to make Russia a European power?*

the year Catherine died, the ideas of liberty and equality had spread across Europe. These ideas seriously threatened the rule of powerful kings and queens.

Reading Check **Explain** How did the ideas of absolute monarchs conflict with the ideas of Enlightenment thinkers?

History Online

Study Central™ Need help with the material in this section? Visit jat.glencoe.com

Section 3 Review

Reading Summary

Review the Main Ideas

- In the 1700s, many Europeans thought reason could make government and society better. Hobbes, Locke, and Montesquieu developed ideas about how to improve government.

- Enlightenment thinkers, such as Voltaire, Diderot, and Rousseau, described ways to make society better.

- By the 1700s, most of Europe's rulers were absolute monarchs. Some, however, tried to create governments based on Enlightenment ideas.

What Did You Learn?

1. Who were the French philosophes?

2. What was the *Encyclopedia*, and what message did it attempt to deliver to its readers?

Critical Thinking

3. **Organizing Information** Draw a chart to list the rulers of the Enlightenment, their countries, and their accomplishments.

Ruler	Country	Accomplishments

4. **Cause and Effect** How did civil war in England affect Hobbes?

5. **Explain** Do you think enlightened despots were really enlightened?

6. **Conclude** Which of the Enlightenment thinkers discussed in this section do you think had the most impact on modern society? Explain your answer.

7. **Civics Link** Describe how beliefs about people and government during the Enlightenment are reflected in our government today.

The American Revolution

Get Ready to Read!

What's the Connection?

Between the 1500s and 1700s, Europeans set up colonies in North America. In the British colonies, English traditions and the Enlightenment gave colonists a strong sense of their rights.

Focusing on the Main Ideas

- European colonies in North America developed differently from each other and from Europe. *(page 691)*

- Great Britain faced problems in North America, because the American colonists objected to new British laws. *(page 695)*

- The American colonies formed a new nation, the United States of America. *(page 698)*

Locating Places

Quebec (kwih•BEHK)
Jamestown
Boston
Philadelphia

Meeting People

Pilgrim
George Washington
Tom Paine
Thomas Jefferson

Building Your Vocabulary

representative government
constitution
popular sovereignty
   (SAH•vuh•ruhn•tee)
limited government

Reading Strategy

Cause and Effect Complete a cause-and-effect diagram showing why the British colonies declared independence.

NATIONAL GEOGRAPHIC When & Where?

Saratoga • Boston
New York
Philadelphia
Yorktown
Charles Town

1600 **1700** **1800**

1620
Pilgrims found colony in Massachusetts

1776
Declaration of Independence is signed

1789
U.S. Constitution is adopted

Settling North America

Main Idea European colonies in North America developed differently from each other and from Europe.

Reading Focus What would make you want to move to a new place? In this chapter, you will learn why Europeans settled in North America from the 1500s to the 1700s.

Previously, you learned that Spain and Portugal built colonies in the Americas in the 1500s. Beginning in the 1600s, the French, English, and other Europeans began setting up their own colonies in the Americas. While most of Spain's colonies were in the Caribbean, Mexico, and South America, most of France and England's colonies were in North America.

The Spanish in North America The Spanish did not ignore the lands north of Mexico and the Caribbean. In the 1500s, Spanish conquistadors explored the southeastern corner of North America and the lands north of Mexico. They had hoped to find wealthy empires like those of the Aztec and Inca. Instead, they found only small villages of Native Americans. As a result, Spain remained much more interested in its colonies in Mexico, Peru, and the Caribbean, because they provided large amounts of silver and gold.

The Spanish did not completely ignore the rest of North America. They built settlements and forts along the northern edge of their territory. These settlements, such as St. Augustine in Florida and Santa Fe in New Mexico, were intended to keep other Europeans out of Spanish territory.

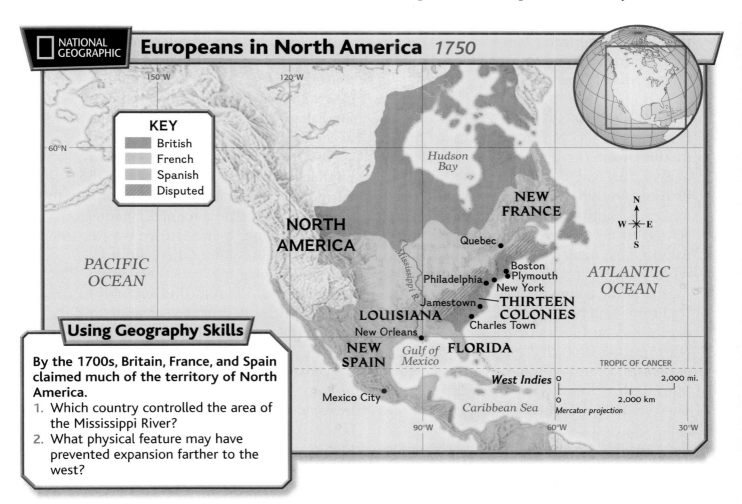

NATIONAL GEOGRAPHIC

Europeans in North America *1750*

KEY
- British
- French
- Spanish
- Disputed

Using Geography Skills

By the 1700s, Britain, France, and Spain claimed much of the territory of North America.

1. Which country controlled the area of the Mississippi River?
2. What physical feature may have prevented expansion farther to the west?

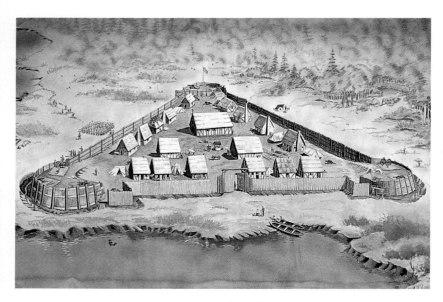

▲ This painting shows what the original settlement at Jamestown may have looked like in 1607. *What prevented the Jamestown settlement from collapsing?*

Spanish priests also headed north. They set up missions, or religious communities, to teach Christianity and European ways to the Native Americans. Missions were set up in California, New Mexico, Florida, and other areas of North America.

France Settles North America
The French came to North America to make money from fur trading. By the 1600s, beaver fur had become very popular in Europe. In 1608 French merchants hired explorer Samuel de Champlain (sham•PLAYN) to help them. Champlain set up a trading post named **Quebec** (kwih•BEHK) in what is now Canada. Quebec became the capital of the colony of New France.

From Quebec, French fur trappers, explorers, and missionaries moved into other parts of North America. In 1673 the explorers Louis Joliet and Jacques Marquette found the Mississippi River. Then in 1682 a French explorer named La Salle followed the Mississippi all the way to the Gulf of Mexico. He named the region

Louisiana in honor of King Louis XIV. The French settlers in southern Louisiana also began bringing in enslaved Africans to grow sugarcane, rice, and tobacco.

The English Settle in America
English settlers came to North America for many reasons. While merchants set up some English colonies to make money, others were set up by people who wanted religious freedom. England's colonies grew rapidly because of economic problems in England. Many people in England wanted to move to America because their landlords had evicted them from their farms. In America, they had a chance to own land for themselves. Still others came because they were unemployed and needed work.

By 1600, England's rulers had accepted the ideas of mercantilism. Colonies and trading posts in Asia and America were making Europe's kingdoms wealthy. The English government believed colonies were needed to keep England strong.

In 1607 the Virginia Company, an English joint-stock company, set up the first permanent English settlement in North America. The settlers named it **Jamestown** after King James I. Jamestown was the first town of a new colony called Virginia.

Life in Virginia was very hard. The colonists could barely find enough to eat. Many settlers died from starvation and the cold winters, and others were killed in clashes with Native Americans.

During those first years, the colony made no money for the merchants who had invested in it. It might have collapsed had not one of the settlers, John Rolfe, discovered that tobacco could grow in Virginia's soil.

Tobacco was popular in Europe in the 1600s. Soon the colonists in Virginia were growing it in large amounts and selling it for a lot of money. Tobacco became the first cash crop of the English colonies. A cash crop is grown in large quantities to sell for profit.

Eventually, tobacco was grown on large farms called plantations. Because plantations need many workers, the English began bringing in enslaved Africans to work the land. The success of Virginia encouraged the English government to set up more colonies in America to grow cash crops. The colony of South Carolina, for example, began growing rice and indigo. The English also began setting up colonies in the Caribbean to grow sugarcane.

Not all English settlers came to North America in search of wealth. Some came to find religious freedom. As you read in the last chapter, many Protestants in England were Puritans. Puritans wanted to rid the Anglican Church of Catholic rituals and allow each congregation to choose its own leaders. King James I and his son King Charles I both believed Puritans were a threat to their authority and persecuted them.

In 1620 a group of Puritans known as the **Pilgrims** decided to go to America so that they could worship freely. In 1620 they boarded a ship called the *Mayflower* and set out for North America. They landed just north of Cape Cod in what is today the state of Massachusetts. They named their settlement Plymouth.

The success of the Pilgrims encouraged other Puritans to begin leaving England for America. Led by John Winthrop, a group of Puritans landed in America and founded the colony of Massachusetts. Others soon followed. By 1643, more than 20,000 Puritans had moved to America. They founded Rhode Island, Connecticut, and New Hampshire.

Primary Source

The Mayflower Compact

The Pilgrims governed themselves according to this document.

"Having undertaken for the Glory of God, and Advancement of the Christian Faith, and the Honour of our King and Country, a Voyage to plant the first colony in the northern Parts of Virginia; Do . . . covenant [agree] and combine ourselves together into a civil Body Politick [political group], for our better Ordering and Preservation. . . . And by Virtue hereof do enact, constitute, and frame, such just and equal Laws, . . . and Offices, from time to time, as shall be thought most meet and convenient for the general Good of the Colony; unto which we promise all due Submission and Obedience."

—Mayflower Compact, November 21, 1620

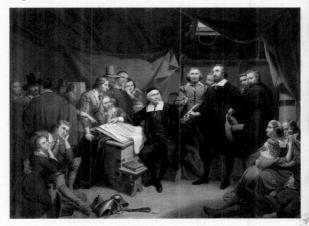

▲ The Pilgrims sign the Mayflower Compact.

 **Document-Based Question**

To what do the Pilgrims promise submission and obedience?

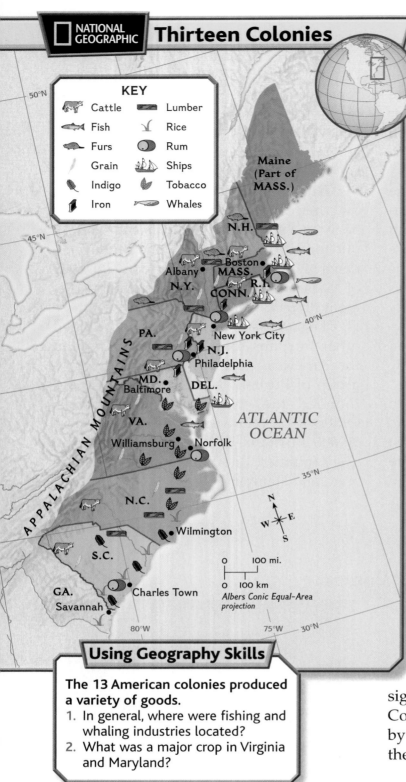

NATIONAL GEOGRAPHIC Thirteen Colonies

KEY

- 🐄 Cattle
- 🐟 Fish
- 🦫 Furs
- Grain
- Indigo
- Iron
- Lumber
- Rice
- Rum
- Ships
- Tobacco
- Whales

Maine (Part of MASS.)

N.H.
Albany · Boston MASS.
N.Y. CONN. R.I.
New York City
PA.
N.J. Philadelphia
MD. DEL.
Baltimore
VA.
Williamsburg · Norfolk
N.C.
· Wilmington
S.C.
GA. Charles Town
Savannah

APPALACHIAN MOUNTAINS

ATLANTIC OCEAN

N W E S

0   100 mi.
0   100 km
Albers Conic Equal-Area projection

50°N
45°N
40°N
35°N
30°N
80°W   75°W

Using Geography Skills

The 13 American colonies produced a variety of goods.
1. In general, where were fishing and whaling industries located?
2. What was a major crop in Virginia and Maryland?

Other people seeking religious freedom set up colonies as well. English Catholics founded Maryland in 1634. The Quakers, another religious group that had been persecuted in England, founded Pennsylvania in 1680.

By the early 1700s, the English had created 13 colonies along the coast of North America. These colonies had different economies and societies, but they had one thing in common: they wanted to govern themselves.

Self-Government in America The tradition of self-government began early in the English colonies. To attract more settlers, the head of the Virginia Company gave the colonists in Virginia the right to elect burgesses, or representatives, from among the men who owned land. The first House of Burgesses met in 1619. It was patterned after the English Parliament and voted on laws for the Virginia colony.

The House of Burgesses set an example for **representative government,** or a government in which people elect representatives to make laws and conduct government. It was not long before other colonies set up their own legislatures as well.

A year after the Virginia House of Burgesses met, the Pilgrims arrived in North America and began their own tradition of self-government. Before going ashore, the Pilgrims signed an agreement called the Mayflower Compact. They agreed to rule themselves by choosing their own leaders and making their own laws.

Over the years, most of the English colonies began drawing up **constitutions,** or written plans of government. These documents let the colonists elect assemblies and protected their rights.

✓ **Reading Check** Compare and Contrast
How was the founding of Jamestown different from the founding of Plymouth?

Trouble in the Colonies

Main Idea Great Britain faced problems in North America, because the American colonists objected to new British laws.

Reading Focus Do you like to make your own decisions, without someone else telling you what to do? Read to find out why the American colonies wanted to make decisions without British interference.

During the early 1700s, there were many changes in England and its overseas colonies. In 1707 England united with Scotland and became the United Kingdom of Great Britain. The term *British* came to mean both the English and the Scots.

By 1750, Great Britain had become the world's most powerful trading empire. It had 13 prosperous colonies along the Atlantic coast of America and others in India and the Caribbean. For years, Britain and its American colonies seemed to get along well. This relationship changed, however, when the British tried to control trade and impose taxes on the colonies. These efforts angered colonists.

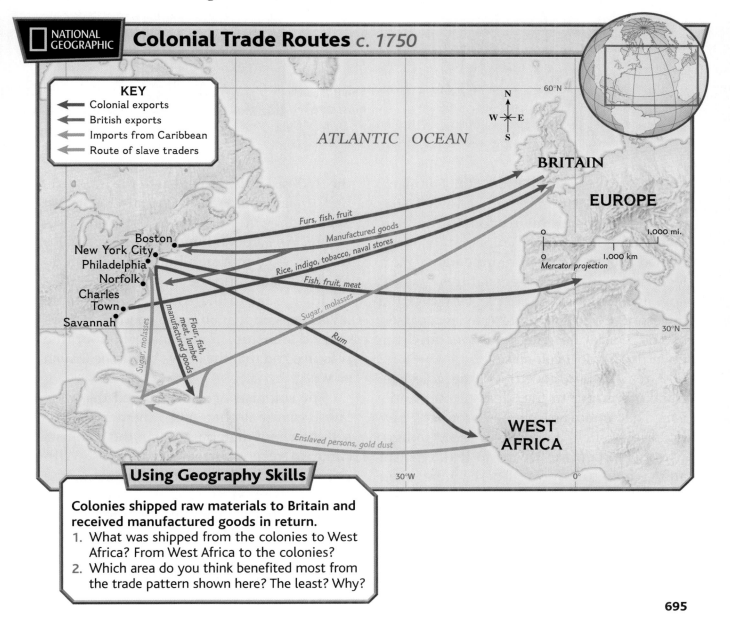

NATIONAL GEOGRAPHIC

Colonial Trade Routes c. 1750

KEY
- Colonial exports
- British exports
- Imports from Caribbean
- Route of slave traders

Using Geography Skills

Colonies shipped raw materials to Britain and received manufactured goods in return.

1. What was shipped from the colonies to West Africa? From West Africa to the colonies?
2. Which area do you think benefited most from the trade pattern shown here? The least? Why?

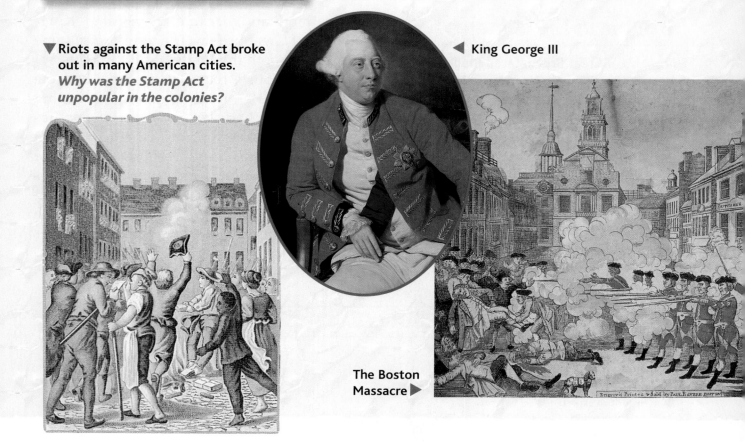

▼ Riots against the Stamp Act broke out in many American cities. *Why was the Stamp Act unpopular in the colonies?*

◄ King George III

The Boston Massacre ▶

Colonial Government and Trade

For many years, Great Britain had allowed the American colonies the freedom to run their local affairs. In each colony, men who owned property elected representatives to a legislature. Colonial legislatures passed laws and could tax the people. However, the governor of a colony could veto laws passed by the legislature. The king appointed the governor in most colonies.

Great Britain controlled the colonies' trade according to the ideas of mercantilism. The American colonies produced raw materials, such as tobacco, rice, indigo, wheat, lumber, fur, deerskin leather, fish, and whale products. These were then shipped to Great Britain and traded for manufactured goods such as clothing, furniture, and goods from Asia, such as tea or spices.

To control this trade, Britain passed a series of laws called the Navigation Acts in the 1600s. Under these laws the colonists had to sell their raw materials to Britain even if they could get a better price elsewhere. Any goods bought by the colonies from other countries in Europe had to go to England first and be taxed before they could be sent to the Americas. The trade laws also said that all trade goods had to be carried on ships built in Britain or the colonies and that the crews had to be British as well.

The colonists at first accepted the trade laws because it guaranteed them a place to sell their raw materials. Later, the colonists came to resent British restrictions. With population in the colonies growing, the colonists wanted to make their own manufactured goods. They also wanted to sell their products elsewhere if they could get higher prices. Many colonial merchants began smuggling, or shipping goods in and

▲ During the Boston Tea Party, a group of colonists, some dressed as Native Americans, dumped chests of tea into Boston Harbor. Many more colonists cheered them on from shore. *What was Britain's response to this event?*

out of the country without paying taxes or getting government permission.

Why Did the British Tax the Colonies?

Between 1756 and 1763, the French and British fought for control of North America. The British won, gaining nearly all of France's North American empire. The war was very costly, however, and left the British government deep in debt. Desperate for money, the British made plans to tax the colonists and tighten trade rules.

In 1765 Parliament passed the Stamp Act, which taxed newspapers and other printed material. All of these items had to bear a stamp showing that the tax was paid. The colonists were outraged. They responded by boycotting, or refusing to buy, British goods.

Finally, delegates from nine colonies met in New York to discuss the Stamp Act. They sent a letter to the British government

stating that the colonies could not be taxed except by their own assemblies. The British backed down for a while, but they still needed money. In 1767 Parliament placed taxes on glass, lead, paper, paint, and tea.

Tax Protests Lead to Revolt The American colonists grumbled about the new taxes. They bullied the tax collectors, and journalists drew ugly cartoons of King George III. Worried, the British sent more troops to **Boston,** Massachusetts, where the largest protests had taken place.

In March 1770, violence broke out. A crowd of colonists began insulting British soldiers and throwing snowballs at them. The soldiers fired into the crowd. Five people were killed. This event came to be called the Boston Massacre. Shortly thereafter, all of the taxes were repealed, or canceled, except the one on tea.

In 1773 Parliament passed the Tea Act. It allowed a British trading company to ship tea to the colonies without paying the taxes colonial tea merchants had to pay. This allowed the company to sell its tea very cheaply and threatened to drive the colonial tea merchants out of business.

In Massachusetts, angry colonists decided to take action. A group of protesters dressed as Native Americans boarded several British ships in Boston Harbor and dumped their cargoes of tea into the water. This event is known as the Boston Tea Party.

To punish the colonists, Parliament in 1774 passed laws that closed down Boston Harbor and put the government of Massachusetts under military rule. It also said that British troops should be quartered, or given a place to live, in colonists' homes. The colonists called these laws the Intolerable Acts, or laws they could not bear.

The Intolerable Acts made the colonists more determined to fight for their liberties.

In September 1774, delegates from 12 colonies met in Philadelphia. They called themselves the First Continental Congress. The Congress spoke out against the Intolerable Acts and called for their repeal.

Colonial leaders, however, were divided about what to do. Some, like George Washington of Virginia, hoped to settle the differences with Great Britain. Others, like Samuel Adams of Massachusetts and Patrick Henry of Virginia, wanted the colonies to become independent.

✓ **Reading Check** **Identify** What was the Boston Tea Party?

The War of Independence

Main Idea The American colonies formed a new nation, the United States of America.

Reading Focus What causes people to go to war? Read to find out how the war between Great Britain and the Americans shaped the course of world history.

Before the colonists could decide what to do, fighting broke out in Massachusetts. The British set out to destroy a store of weapons at Concord. On April 19, 1775, they met colonial troops at Lexington and fought the first battle of the American Revolution.

Primary Source

The Declaration of Independence

On July 4, 1776, Congress approved the Declaration of Independence. The preamble—the first part of the document—explains Congress's reason for issuing the declaration:

"When in the Course of human events, it becomes necessary for one people to dissolve the political bands which have connected them with another. . . . they should declare the causes which impel them to the separation."

The document also explained that people have certain basic rights:

"We hold these truths to be self-evident, that all men are created equal, that they are endowed by their Creator with certain unalienable Rights, that among these are Life, Liberty and the pursuit of Happiness."

—Declaration of Independence, July 4, 1776

DBQ **Document-Based Question**

Why do you think the Congress thought they had to issue a written declaration of independence?

▲ Benjamin Franklin, John Adams, and Thomas Jefferson, shown left to right, worked together to write the Declaration of Independence.

▲ The American leaders who met in Philadelphia in 1787 and wrote the United States Constitution were some of the nation's greatest political minds.
What sort of system of government did the Constitution create?

In May 1775, the Second Continental Congress met in **Philadelphia. George Washington** was named head of a new colonial army. The Congress then tried again to settle their differences with Great Britain. They appealed to King George III, who refused to listen.

More and more Americans began to think that independence was the only answer. In January 1776, a writer named **Tom Paine** made up many minds when he wrote a pamphlet called *Common Sense.* Paine used strong words to condemn the king and urged the colonists to separate from Great Britain.

The Declaration of Independence On July 4, 1776, the Congress issued the Declaration of Independence. Written by **Thomas Jefferson** of Virginia, the Declaration stated that the colonies were separating from Great Britain and forming a new nation, the United States of America.

In the Declaration, Jefferson explained why the colonists were founding a new nation. To do this, Jefferson borrowed the ideas of John Locke. In Section 3, you learned about Locke's idea that people have the right to overthrow governments that violate their rights. The Declaration stated that "all men are created equal" and have certain God-given rights. It said that King George III had violated colonists' rights, and so they had the right to rebel.

The Declaration also drew from earlier English documents, such as the Magna Carta and the English Bill of Rights. Both documents established the idea that governments are not all-powerful and that rulers had to obey the laws and treat citizens fairly.

How Did the Americans Win the War?
After the Declaration was made, the war between the British and Americans dragged on. The first important American victory came in 1777 at the Battle of Saratoga in New York. This battle marked a turning point in the war. France, Great Britain's old enemy, realized that the United States might actually win. In 1778 France agreed to help the Americans.

The French were very important in the final victory. This came in 1781 at the Battle of Yorktown on the coast of Virginia. The French navy blocked the British from escaping by sea, while American and French forces surrounded and trapped the British inside Yorktown. Realizing they could not win, the British laid down their weapons. Peace negotiations began, and two years later, the Treaty of Paris ended the war.

The United States Constitution In 1783
Great Britain recognized American

independence. At first the United States was a confederation, or a loose union of independent states. Its plan of government was a document called the Articles of Confederation. The Articles created a national government, but the states held most powers. It soon became clear that the Articles were too weak to deal with the new nation's problems.

In 1787, 55 delegates met in Philadelphia to change the Articles. Instead, they decided to write a constitution for an entirely new national government. The new United States Constitution set up a federal system, in which powers were divided between the national government and the states. Following the ideas of Montesquieu, power in the national government was divided between executive, legislative, and judicial branches. A system called checks and balances enabled each branch to limit the powers of the other branches.

Under the Constitution, the United States was a republic with an elected president instead of a king. Elections held in 1789 made George Washington the first president of the United States. That same year, a Bill of Rights was added to the U.S. Constitution. The Bill of Rights set out certain rights the government could not violate. These rights included freedom of religion, speech, and press, and the right to trial by jury.

The U.S. Constitution was also shaped by Enlightenment principles. One of these is **popular sovereignty** (SAH•vuh•ruhn•tee), or the idea that government receives its powers from the people. Another is **limited government,** or the idea that a government may use only those powers given to it by the people.

 **Reading Check** **Explain** Why did the colonists decide to separate from Great Britain and create a new nation?

History Online
Study Central™ Need help with the material in this section? Visit jat.glencoe.com

Section 4 Review

Reading Summary

Review the Main Ideas

- In North America, the French settled in Canada and along the Mississippi River, while the British settled along the Atlantic coast.

- Americans protested when the British government attempted to impose more control and more taxes on the colonies.

- The Americans defeated the British in the American Revolution and set up a republican form of government with powers divided among three branches.

What Did You Learn?

1. When and where was the first battle of the American Revolution fought?

2. What is the Bill of Rights?

Critical Thinking

3. **Sequence Information** Draw a time line like the one below. Fill in events related to the American Revolution.

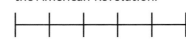

4. **Analyze** Why did England's colonies in America grow quickly?

5. **Civics Link** Which of John Locke's ideas appeared in the Declaration of Independence?

6. **Explain** How did the search for religious freedom affect the founding of colonies in America?

7. **Persuasive Writing** Write two letters to the editor at a colonial newspaper. One should support British involvement in its American colonies. The other should support the colonists' arguments for independence.

Section 1 — The Age of Exploration

Vocabulary
mercantilism
export
import
colony
commerce
invest

Focusing on the Main Ideas
- In the 1400s, trade, technology, and the rise of strong kingdoms led to a new era of exploration. *(page 659)*
- While the Portuguese explored Africa, the Spanish, English, and French explored America. *(page 661)*
- To increase trade, Europeans set up colonies and created joint-stock companies. *(page 666)*
- Exploration and trade led to a worldwide exchange of products, people, and ideas. *(page 668)*

Early astrolabe ▼

Section 2 — The Scientific Revolution

Vocabulary
theory
rationalism
scientific method
hypothesis

Focusing on the Main Ideas
- The thinkers of the ancient world developed early forms of science and passed this knowledge to later civilizations. *(page 671)*
- European interest in astronomy led to new discoveries and ideas about the universe and Earth's place in it. *(page 673)*
- The Scientific Revolution led to new discoveries in physics, medicine, and chemistry. *(page 675)*
- Using the scientific method, Europeans of the 1600s and 1700s developed new ideas about society based on reason. *(page 678)*

Section 3 — The Enlightenment

Vocabulary
natural law
social contract
separation of powers
deism
absolutism

Focusing on the Main Ideas
- During the 1700s, many Europeans believed that reason could be used to make government and society better. *(page 681)*
- The Enlightenment was centered in France, where thinkers wrote about changing their society and met to discuss their ideas. *(page 684)*
- Many of Europe's monarchs, who claimed to rule by the will of God, tried to model their countries on Enlightenment ideas. *(page 686)*

Section 4 — The American Revolution

Vocabulary
representative government
constitution
popular sovereignty
limited government

Focusing on the Main Ideas
- European colonies in North America developed differently from each other and from Europe. *(page 691)*
- Great Britain faced problems in North America, because the American colonists objected to new British laws. *(page 695)*
- The American colonies formed a new nation, the United States of America. *(page 698)*

Review Vocabulary

Write the key term that completes each sentence.

a. constitution
b. scientific method
c. separation of powers
d. mercantilism
e. commerce
f. absolutism

1. According to the idea of ___, a country gains power by gathering gold and setting up colonies.
2. A(n) ___ is a written plan for government.
3. Francis Bacon developed the ___.
4. The system in which monarchs held total power was called ___.
5. Montesquieu believed that a(n) ___ was needed for good government.
6. The buying and selling of goods in large amounts over long distances is called ___.

Review Main Ideas

Section 1 • The Age of Exploration
7. What led to the European era of exploration?

8. How were joint-stock companies related to overseas trade?

Section 2 • The Scientific Revolution
9. Describe the scientific discoveries of Newton and Galileo.
10. What was the importance of the scientific method?

Section 3 • The Enlightenment
11. How did the Enlightenment affect Europe's rulers?
12. How did the ideas of Thomas Hobbes and John Locke about government differ?

Section 4 • The American Revolution
13. Why did the American colonists want independence from Britain?
14. How did the new government of America reflect ideas developed during the Enlightenment?

Critical Thinking

15. **Economics Link** How are the ideas of mercantilism reflected in our economy today?

Review

Reading Skill — Monitor and Adjust — Your Reading Strengths

16. Write five questions you would ask to help you better understand the information in the following paragraph.

To help the Dutch, Queen Elizabeth I of England let English privateers attack Spanish ships. Privateers are privately owned ships that have a license from the government to attack ships of other countries. People nicknamed the English privateers "sea dogs." They raided the Spanish treasure ships bringing gold back from America.

To review this skill, see pages 656–657.

Geography Skills

Study the map below and answer the following questions.

17. **Place** Which city in Europe was the first to receive the potato as part of the Columbian Exchange?

18. **Movement** Why do you think so much time passed before the potato was introduced in Sweden and Finland?

19. **Movement** Does it appear from the map that trade between nations followed a strict pattern?

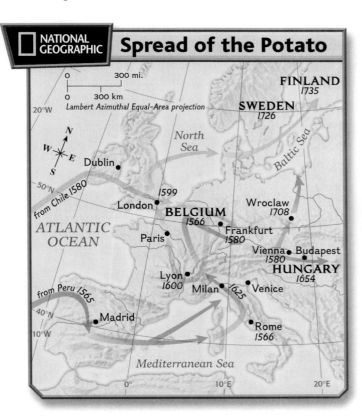

NATIONAL GEOGRAPHIC

Spread of the Potato

0   300 mi.
0   300 km
20°W   Lambert Azimuthal Equal–Area projection

FINLAND
1735

SWEDEN
1726

North Sea

Baltic Sea

N
W   E
S

Dublin

50°N

from Chile 1580

1599

London

BELGIUM
1566

Paris

ATLANTIC OCEAN

Wroclaw
1708

Frankfurt
1580

Vienna   Budapest
1580

HUNGARY
1654

Lyon
1600

Milan   1625   Venice

from Peru 1565

40°N

10°W

Madrid

Rome
1566

Mediterranean Sea

0°   10°E   20°E

Read to Write

20. **Descriptive Writing** Write a brief essay describing Montesquieu's beliefs about government and explaining how they are reflected in the U.S. Constitution.

21. **Using Your FOLDABLES** Work with a few classmates to create a question and answer game using the information in your foldables. Questions should cover the Scientific Revolution, Enlightenment, Age of Exploration, and American Revolution. Switch groups to play the games.

Using Technology

22. **Researching** Use the Internet and your local library to research present-day exploration in space and in the depths of the ocean. Find out about the technologies used, how these explorations are funded, and their impact on our knowledge of the universe. Write a report on how present-day explorers and their voyages are similar to and different from those of Europe in the Age of Exploration.

Linking Past and Present

23. **Analyzing** The music, art, and literature of the Enlightenment reflected people's views during that time. Write a description of how present-day music, art, and literature reflect how people currently feel about society. Give examples to support your opinion.

Primary Source **Analyze**

Portuguese official Duarte Barbosa described the way his country dealt with African kingdoms.

"The king of this city [Mombasa] refused to obey the commands of the King our Lord, and through this arrogance he lost it, and our Portuguese took it from him by force. He fled away, and they slew [killed] many of his people and also took captive many, both men and women, in such sort that it was left ruined and plundered and burned."

—Duarte Barbosa, "The East Coast of Africa"

DBQ **Document-Based Questions**

24. What did the king of Mombasa do that angered the Portuguese?
25. How did the Portuguese handle the conflict?

Comparing Early Modern Civilizations

Compare early modern civilizations by reviewing the information below. Can you see how the people of these civilizations had lives that were very much like yours?

Where in the World?

NATIONAL GEOGRAPHIC

- Chapter 16
- Chapter 17
- Chapter 18

	The Americas Chapter 16	Renaissance and Reformation Chapter 17	Enlightenment and Revolution Chapter 18
Where did these civilizations develop?	• North America • Central America • Caribbean islands • South America	• Europe	• Western Europe • North America • Africa • South Asia • Southeast Asia
Who were some important people in these civilizations?	• Pachacuti, ruled A.D. 1438–1471 • Montezuma II, ruled A.D. 1502–1520 • Atahualpa, ruled A.D. 1525–1533	• Leonardo da Vinci A.D. 1452–1519 • Martin Luther A.D. 1483–1546 • Queen Isabella (Spain), ruled A.D. 1474–1504	• Christopher Columbus A.D. 1451–1506 • Queen Elizabeth I (England), ruled A.D. 1558–1603 • Galileo Galilei A.D. 1564–1642
Where did most of the people live?	• Hunter-gatherers • Farming villages • Cities (Tenochtitlán and Cuzco)	• City-states (Italy) • Commercial cities (London, Paris) • Farming villages	• Port cities (Lisbon, Amsterdam) • Overseas settlements and plantations
What were these people's beliefs?	• Traditional Native American religions	• Northern Europe: Protestant • Southern Europe: Roman Catholic • Jewish communities	• Europeans spread Christianity overseas • Rise of Deism in Europe and America

	The Americas Chapter 16	Renaissance and Reformation Chapter 17	Enlightenment and Revolution Chapter 18
What was their government like?	• Local groups ruled by chiefs and councils • Powerful emperors or kings (Maya, Aztec, and Inca) 	• Italian city-states ruled by wealthy families • Most European areas ruled by kings, princes, and nobles 	• English king's powers are limited, representative government spreads • United States founded as a republic 
What was their language and writing like?	• Native Americans spoke hundreds of languages • Mayan and Aztec languages written in hieroglyphics • Inca had no written language	• Printed books helped spread knowledge • Vernacular used in Protestant worship • Latin remains language of Catholic Church 	• Meeting of cultures meant spread of knowledge about languages • European languages brought by settlers to overseas colonies
What contributions did they make?	• Developed trade networks and methods of farming and building 	• Furthered education • Created lifelike art • Different religions existed side by side	• Reason seen as a way to truth • General rules developed for scientific study • Beginning of modern democracy
How do these changes affect me? *Can you add any?*	• Native Americans passed on foods (corn, chocolate, potatoes) • Many place names in the Americas are based on Native American words (Chicago, Mississippi)	• Renaissance and Reformation Europeans passed on practice of printing books • School subjects (history, language) are rooted in Renaissance learning	• Supported rights (free speech, religion, press) that we enjoy today • Scientific tools (microscope, telescope) and vaccines for disease developed

Modern Times

Why It's Important

Each civilization that you will study in this unit made important contributions to history.

- Western countries built new societies based on industry.
- Western rivalries over land and resources sparked World War I, the first global conflict.
- World War II made the United States and the Soviet Union world leaders.
- By 2000, advances in technology brought peoples of the world closer together. Conflicts, however, developed among different groups.

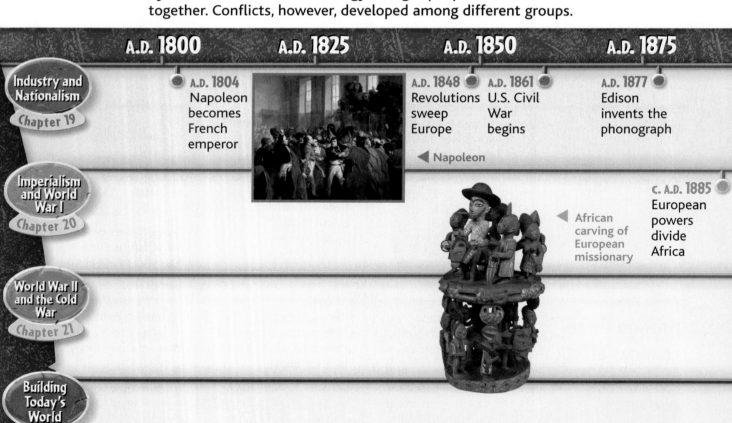

| A.D. 1800 | A.D. 1825 | A.D. 1850 | A.D. 1875 |

Industry and Nationalism
Chapter 19

A.D. 1804
Napoleon becomes French emperor

A.D. 1848
Revolutions sweep Europe

A.D. 1861
U.S. Civil War begins

A.D. 1877
Edison invents the phonograph

◀ Napoleon

Imperialism and World War I
Chapter 20

◀ African carving of European missionary

C. A.D. 1885
European powers divide Africa

World War II and the Cold War
Chapter 21

Building Today's World
Chapter 22

NATIONAL GEOGRAPHIC
Where in the World?

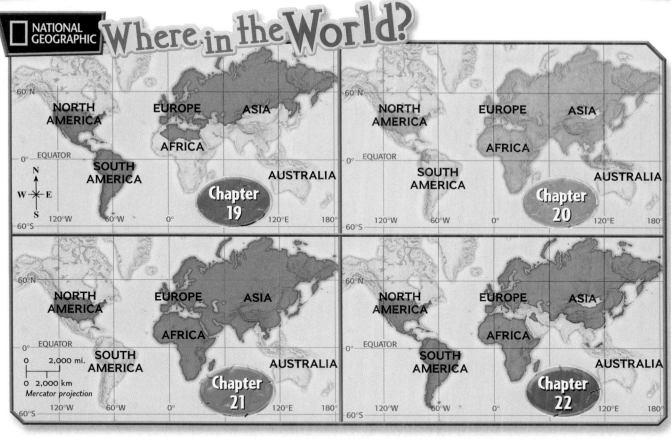

Chapter 19

Chapter 20

Chapter 21

Chapter 22

A.D. 1900   A.D. 1925   A.D. 1950   A.D. 1975   A.D. 2000

◄ Woman factory worker

◄ Houses of Parliament, London

A.D. 1898
United States declares war on Spain

C. A.D. 1900
Japan becomes a power in Asia

A.D. 1917
World War I ends

BE A U.S. MARINE!

◄ World War I poster

A.D. 1933
Hitler leads Germany

A.D. 1941
U.S. enters World War II

A.D. 1949
Communists rule in China

C. A.D. 1957
African independence begins

◄ Nigerians celebrate independence

A.D. 1948
Israel becomes a nation

A.D. 1979
Islamic revolution in Iran

A.D. 1989
Communism ends in Eastern Europe

A.D. 2001
Terrorist attacks on U.S.

Israel's Flag ▶

◄ Ayatollah Khomeini

Unit

Places to Locate

1 Arc de Triomphe

See Industry and Nationalism Chapter 19

2 British Parliament

See Imperialism and World War I Chapter 20

NORTH AMERICA

Atlantic Ocean

Pacific Ocean

SOUTH AMERICA

People to Meet

Napoleon Bonaparte

1769–1821
French leader
Chapter 19, page 721

Simón Bolívar

1783–1830
South American military and political leader
Chapter 19, page 750

Marie Curie

1867–1934
Polish-born French scientist
Chapter 19, page 740

Mohandas Gandhi

1869–1948
Indian leader
Chapter 21, page 844

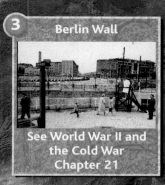

3 Berlin Wall

See World War II and
the Cold War
Chapter 21

4 Sarajevo, Bosnia

See Building Today's
World
Chapter 22

5 Cape Town, South Africa

See Building Today's
World
Chapter 22

EUROPE

ASIA

*Mediterranean
Sea*

*Red
Sea*

*Persian
Gulf*

AFRICA

*Indian
Ocean*

**Vladimir
Lenin**

1870–1924
Communist leader
Chapter 20, page 795

**Franklin
Roosevelt**

1882–1945
U.S. president
Chapter 21, page 817

Golda Meir

1898–1978
Israeli prime minister
Chapter 22, page 877

**Nelson
Mandela**

1918–present
South African president
Chapter 22, page 873

Chapter 19

Industry and Nationalism

Steel plant on the Tees River in Middlebough, England ▶

NATIONAL GEOGRAPHIC When & Where?

1750	1800	1850	1900
1769 Watt improves steam engine	**1799** Napoleon comes to power	**1848** Karl Marx writes *Communist Manifesto*	**1871** Germany is united

Chapter Preview

In the late 1700s, the French Revolution and the Industrial Revolution brought great changes to Europe and the United States. Read this chapter to find out how the rise of factories and the spread of nationalism changed how people lived their lives.

 View the Chapter 19 video in the *World History: Journey Across Time* Video Program.

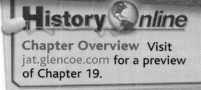
Chapter Overview Visit jat.glencoe.com for a preview of Chapter 19.

The French Revolution and Napoleon

In 1789 the French overthrew their king and tried to build a republic. A few years later, however, Napoleon seized power and built a new French empire.

The Industrial Revolution

During the 1800s, Europe and North America began using machines to produce large quantities of goods. During this time, new inventions improved life for many people.

Society and Industry

The growth of industry led to the growth of cities and new social groups, as well as many new problems and new ideas.

Nationalism and Nation-States

Nationalism and liberalism led to new nations and the emergence of democracy in Europe and the Americas.

Organizing Information *Make this foldable to help you organize and analyze information by asking yourself questions about industry and nationalism.*

Step 1 *Fold four sheets of paper in half from top to bottom.*

Step 2 *On each folded paper, make a cut 1 inch from the side on the top flap.*

Cut 1 inch from the edge through the top flap only.

Step 3 *Place the folded papers one on top of the other. Staple the four sections together and label the top four tabs: The French Revolution and Napoleon, The Industrial Revolution, Society and Industry, Nationalism and Nation-States.*

Staple here.

The French Revolution and Napoleon

Reading and Writing *As you read the chapter, write the main ideas for each section under the appropriate tabs of your foldable. Then write one statement for each tab that summarizes all of the main ideas in that tab.*

Chapter 19 Reading Social Studies

Reading Skill

Understanding Concepts

1 Learn It!

Reading for Meaning

Sometimes, you can define a word but still not clearly understand what it means. It often takes a while to learn the full meaning of a word, especially if the word describes a concept or idea. Thinking about a word or asking yourself questions about it may help you to understand a concept more clearly.

For example, in the following paragraph from page 720, it is easy to see that the word *nationalism* means "the desire of a people for self-rule," but what does that definition really mean?

Nationalism is a complex concept made up of many ideas.

> Two forces helped to bring Napoleon's empire to an end. One was **nationalism,** or the desire of a people for self-rule. The nations of Europe rejected Napoleon's rule and the French customs he forced on them.
>
> *—from page 720*

Definitions help you understand a word, but they do not always fully explain concepts.

Reading Tip

When you discover a new word in your reading, watch for multiple meanings of the word in books, movies, television, and conversations.

Ask yourself questions to increase your understanding of the word *nationalism*. Here are some questions you might ask:

- How is nationalism different from patriotism?
- How do we show nationalism in the United States?
- Is there such as thing as regional nationalism in a country, such as "southern-ism"?
- What color or music comes to mind when you think of nationalism? Why?

2 Practice It!

Ask Questions

Choose one word that you do not understand fully from each section of Chapter 19. For each word, try to understand the meaning by asking the following questions:

1) **Who might use the word? When would he or she use it?**

2) **What else do you want to know about this word?**

3) **How would you illustrate the word?**

4) **What actions go along with this word?**

Read to Write ·······
Choose any word from Chapter 19 that represents a concept, such as *bourgeoisie, industrialism, socialism,* or *guerilla warfare.* Write about the word for several minutes, noting anything that comes to mind when you read the word. Then, search the word online to expand your interpretation of the word.

3 Apply It!

Choose a word from the chapter that is familiar to most people. Ask five people how they define the word. How did their answers help you to understand the word?

The French Revolution and Napoleon

Get Ready to Read!

What's the Connection?

Many ideas of the American Revolution also affected Europe. In France, the people started a revolution and overthrew the king. The French Revolution then led to the rise of Napoleon.

Focusing on the Main Ideas

- The French Revolution began because the people were treated unfairly and because their country had serious economic problems. *(page 715)*

- French radicals used terror to enforce their reforms. *(page 717)*

- Napoleon Bonaparte used his military success to take control of the French government. *(page 719)*

- Through military conquests, Napoleon built a huge, but short-lived, empire in Europe. *(page 720)*

Locating Places

Versailles (VUHR•SY)
Waterloo (WAW•tuhr•LOO)

Meeting People

King Louis XVI (LOO•ee)
Maximilien Robespierre (mak•see•meel•ya   ROHBZ•PYEHR)
Napoleon Bonaparte (nuh•POH•lee•uhn   BOH•nuh•PAHRT)

Building Your Vocabulary

estates
bourgeoisie (BURZH•WAH•ZEE)
coup d'etat (KOO day•TAH)

Reading Strategy

Cause and Effect Use a diagram like the one below to explain the causes of the French Revolution.

Cause:	
	The French Revolution
Cause:	

NATIONAL GEOGRAPHIC When & Where?

1780   1800   1820

1789 The Bastille falls

1799 Napoleon comes to power

1812 Napoleon invades Russia

1814 Congress of Vienna meets

London
Paris
Madrid
Moscow
Vienna
Rome

The French Revolution Begins

Main Idea The French Revolution began because the people were treated unfairly and because their country had serious economic problems.

Reading Focus During the French Revolution, people tried to create a new society and government. If you could change our society today, what changes would you make?

Previously you learned about the American Revolution. The example of the American Revolution influenced many people in France. They, too, wanted political change based on the ideas of freedom and equality. The French Revolution, which began in 1789, changed France and all of Europe.

What Caused the French Revolution?

In the 1700s, France was one of Europe's most powerful countries. French kings ruled it with absolute power. Nobles had many privileges and lived in great wealth. Most people, however, were poor, had little education, and struggled to make a living.

The French people were divided into three **estates**, or classes. The First Estate was the Catholic clergy, or church officials. They did not pay taxes, and they received money from church lands. The Second Estate was the nobles. They filled the highest posts in government and the military. Like the clergy, the nobles were free from taxes. They lived in luxury at the king's court or in their country houses surrounded by large areas of land.

Everyone else in France belonged to the Third Estate. At the top of this group was the **bourgeoisie** (BURZH • WAH • ZEE), or the middle classes. They included merchants, bankers, doctors, lawyers, and teachers. Next were the city workers—artisans, day laborers, and servants. At the bottom were the peasants, who made up more than 80 percent of the French people.

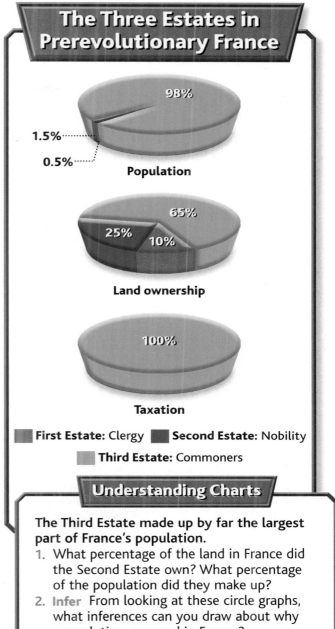

The Three Estates in Prerevolutionary France

Population
- 98%
- 1.5%
- 0.5%

Land ownership
- 65%
- 25%
- 10%

Taxation
- 100%

■ **First Estate:** Clergy ■ **Second Estate:** Nobility
■ **Third Estate:** Commoners

Understanding Charts

The Third Estate made up by far the largest part of France's population.
1. What percentage of the land in France did the Second Estate own? What percentage of the population did they make up?
2. **Infer** From looking at these circle graphs, what inferences can you draw about why a revolution occurred in France?

Members of the Third Estate had no voice in the government, but they paid the country's taxes. As Enlightenment ideas about freedom and equality spread, the middle class came to resent more and more the privileges of the nobles and clergy.

The French King Is Overthrown

In 1788 food shortages and rising prices caused great discontent throughout the country. At the same time, the French government was almost bankrupt because of costly wars and increasing expenses for the king's court. After French banks decided they could no longer afford to loan the government money, **King Louis XVI** (LOO•ee) asked the nobles and clergy to pay taxes, but they refused. Louis then called a meeting of the country's legislative body, the Estates-General, at his palace at **Versailles** (VUHR•SY). It was the only way he could impose new taxes. The Estates-General was made up of representatives from all three estates.

In the Estates-General, the nobles and clergy refused to give up their privileges. Frustrated, the delegates of the Third Estate decided to meet separately. They declared themselves to be the National Assembly and began work on a new constitution for France.

The people celebrated this victory, but they began to worry. News came that the king was gathering troops at Versailles. The people of Paris got ready to fight. Early on July 14, 1789, a large crowd stormed a hated royal fortress and prison called the Bastille (ba•STEEL).

News of the Bastille's fall spread to the countryside, where the peasants rose against the nobles. To calm the people, the National Assembly passed new laws that ended the privileges of the clergy and nobles. It also issued the Declaration of the Rights of Man and the Citizen. The Declaration said that the powers of government came from the people, not the king.

In 1791 the National Assembly made France a constitutional monarchy. France was to be ruled by an elected assembly, and the king's power was limited. Louis, however, would not accept these changes. In June 1791, he and his wife Marie Antoinette tried to flee to Austria. They did not get far. At a town east of Paris, soldiers arrested the king and queen and returned them to Paris.

Worried that Austria's ruler would send troops to aid Louis, the National Assembly declared war on Austria in 1792. Soon after, Prussia joined Austria in fighting France. The war did not go well for France. Angry about France's defeats, radicals—or people wanting far-reaching changes—took over Paris and helped set up a new government called the National Convention.

Primary Source

Declaration of the Rights of Man and the Citizen

On August 26, 1789, the French National Assembly approved 17 articles that stated their basic freedoms. Four of the articles are listed below.

2. The aim of every political association is the preservation of the natural . . . rights of man. These rights are liberty, property, security, and resistance to oppression [hardship].

9. Every man being presumed innocent until he has been proven guilty, . . .

▲ Declaration of the Rights of Man and the Citizen

11. The free communication of ideas and opinions is one of the most precious of the rights of man; every citizen can then freely speak, write, and print. . . .

—Declaration of the Rights of Man and the Citizen (August 1789)

 **Document-Based Question**

Which freedoms do Articles 2, 9, and 11 protect?

Reading Check **Identify** Who belonged to the three estates in France?

The Reign of Terror

Main Idea French radicals used terror to enforce their reforms.

Reading Focus Have you ever heard the phrase "The end justifies the means"? In other words, if your goal is right, is it okay to do anything, even break the law or hurt people, to reach that goal? What do you think?

Many of the radicals who formed the National Convention—France's new government—belonged to the Jacobin club. This was a large network of political groups in France. They were called Jacobins (JA•kuh•buhnz) because they held meetings at the Jacobin monastery in Paris. Once in power, the Jacobins divided into two groups.

The Struggle for Power In the Convention, delegates argued about the revolution's future. One group of the Jacobins was the Girondists (juh•RAHN•dihsts), who came from the Gironde, a region in southwest France. The Girondists believed that the revolution had gone far enough. They wanted to protect the interests of the middle class.

Across the aisle was the group of Jacobins that favored still more changes. Its members were known as the Mountain, because they sat on high benches at the rear of the hall. Leaders of this group, such as Georges-Jacques Danton and Jean-Paul Marat, saw themselves as the voice of the people and defenders of the revolution.

▲ When the Bastille was attacked on July 14, 1789, it was defended by a little more than 100 soldiers, and it held only 7 prisoners. *Why did the people of Paris storm the Bastille?*

The Mountain soon controlled the Convention. They used their power to get rid of the former king. In late 1792, Louis was tried and found guilty of helping France's enemies. A month later, Louis was beheaded on the guillotine—a new machine designed to quickly execute people. Louis's execution scared other European rulers. In early 1793, Britain, Spain, the Netherlands, and Sardinia joined Austria and Prussia in their war against France.

Who Was Robespierre?

Soon after the king's execution, the National Convention set up the Committee of Public Safety to run the country. This new body quickly came under the control of a lawyer named **Maximilien Robespierre** (mak•see•meel• ya ROHBZ•PYEHR).

The Committee took harsh steps to end growing unrest in France. Revolutionary courts sentenced to death by guillotine anyone believed to be disloyal to the revolution. This included Girondists, clergy, nobles, and even women and children. In all, about 40,000 people died, including Queen Marie Antoinette. This period became known as the Reign of Terror.

During this time, Robespierre tried to create a "Republic of Virtue." He thought the revolution should inspire people to be good citizens. Under Robespierre's lead, the Committee opened new schools, had new farming skills taught to the peasants, and worked to keep prices under control. Robespierre even created a new religion that worshiped a "Supreme Being." This attempt to replace France's traditional Catholic faith, however, did not last.

With France under threat from abroad, the Committee decided to raise a new army. All single men between the ages of 18 and 25

The French Revolution

Marie Antoinette is led to her execution. *Why was the guillotine adopted for executions?* ▼

▼ Model of a guillotine

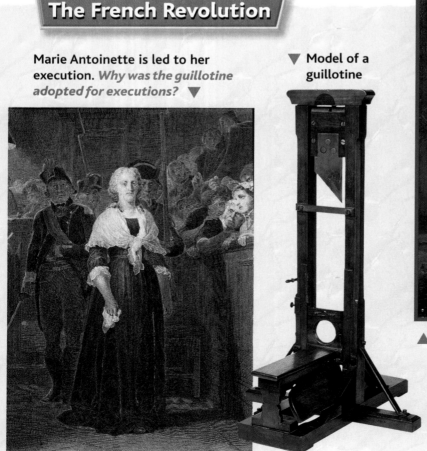

▲ This painting shows a supporter of the revolution known as a sans-cullote, which means "without breeches." Sans-cullotes were shopkeepers, artisans, and workers who got their name because they wore long pants, rather than the knee-length breeches of the upper class.

were conscripted, or required to join up. With this new force of almost a million soldiers, France was able to throw back the foreign invaders. Military victories gave revolutionary generals great confidence. They soon became important in French politics.

As the fear of foreign invasions lessened, people in France grew tired of all the killings and wanted to end the Reign of Terror. When Robespierre refused, government leaders had him executed. After Robespierre's fall, moderate middle-class leaders created a new government led by a five-man council. This council, called the Directory, spent its time trying to handle food shortages, rising prices, government bankruptcy, and attacks by other countries. By 1799, the Directory had lost much support. The French people began to look for a strong leader who could restore order.

Reading Check **Contrast** How did the Girondists differ from the Mountain?

The Rise of Napoleon

Main Idea Napoleon Bonaparte used his military success to take control of the French government.

Reading Focus What qualities make a great leader? As you read about Napoleon, ask yourself which of his qualities won him the confidence of the French people.

While the Directory lost support in France, the French army was winning great victories in neighboring lands. One young general, battling Austrian armies in Italy, especially captured the French people's imagination. His name was **Napoleon Bonaparte** (nuh•POH•lee•uhn BOH•nuh•PAHRT).

Napoleon Bonaparte was born on the Mediterranean island of Corsica in 1769. He went to military school and became an officer. Napoleon supported the revolution. His military talent helped him rise to the rank of general by the time he was 24 years old.

Periods of Revolution and Empire in France, 1789–1815

1785	1790	1795	1800	1805	1810	1815

May 1789 Estates-General

June 1789 National Assembly

1791 Legislative Assembly

1792 National Convention

1795 The Directory

1799 Consulate of Napoleon

1804 Empire of Napoleon

1815 Defeat of Napoleon

Understanding Charts

1. How many years did the Directory stay in power?
2. **Compare** Which period lasted the longest?

◀ This painting shows Napoleon Bonaparte (center) seizing control of the French government in 1799. *At what age did Napoleon become a general in the French army?*

▲ The Arc de Triomphe in Paris, a monument to French military victories, was begun by Napoleon in 1806 and finally finished in 1836. *What territories were included in Napoleon's empire?*

After his successes in Italy, Napoleon attacked the British in Egypt in 1799. While in Egypt, he heard of the worsening political troubles back home. He immediately returned to France. There, he took part in a **coup d'etat** (KOO day•TAH). This is when the top government leaders are suddenly replaced by force by a new group of leaders. Napoleon became the most powerful man in the country, with the title of First Consul. France had the strong leader many believed it needed.

Napoleon moved quickly to strengthen his control. He reorganized the government, created many new schools, and appointed local officials. He reorganized the country's finances and tax system. He created a new legal system. Known as the Napoleonic Code, it was based on Enlightenment ideas. Napoleon also made peace with the Catholic Church, which had opposed the revolution.

Napoleon did not remain true to all of the ideas of the French Revolution. People were equal under the law, but freedom of speech and the press was limited. A new group of nobles, based on ability rather than wealth or family ties, was created. Then, in 1804, Napoleon crowned himself emperor, and France became an empire.

✓ **Reading Check** **Explain** After becoming consul, how did Napoleon strengthen his control?

Napoleon's Empire

Main Idea Through military conquests, Napoleon built a huge, but short-lived, empire in Europe.

Reading Focus Many talented people use their abilities to rise high. Some, however, try to do too much and fall. Read to learn how Napoleon finally lost his power and his empire.

Being emperor of France was not enough for Napoleon. He wanted to build a great empire. Beginning in 1803, Napoleon won a number of victories that helped him reach his goal. By 1807, Napoleon had an empire that stretched across Europe from the Atlantic Ocean to Russia.

Napoleon's empire included many different territories. Napoleon directly ruled France and parts of Germany and Italy. His relatives, however, governed other lands, such as Spain and the Netherlands. Outside the empire, independent countries, such as Prussia, Austria, and Sweden, were forced to become France's allies.

Napoleon Fights Britain Two forces helped to bring Napoleon's empire to an end. One was nationalism, or the desire of a people for self-rule. The nations of Europe rejected Napoleon's rule and the French customs he forced on them. The other force was the combined might of Britain and Russia.

Only Britain and Russia remained undefeated by Napoleon. The French emperor hoped to invade Britain. However, in 1805, the British admiral Lord Horatio Nelson destroyed the French fleet at the Battle of Trafalgar off Spain's coast. After that, Napoleon tried to obtain victory in a different way. He forbade the countries in his empire to trade with Britain. His plan, called the Continental System, was hard to enforce, and it proved unsuccessful.

Biography

Napoleon Bonaparte
1769–1821

Even though Napoleon Bonaparte's first battle was a snowball fight, he took the game seriously. At the time, Napoleon was a young cadet at the Brienne military academy in northeastern France. A surprise snowfall had given the boys a break from their schoolwork. Instead of throwing random snowballs at his classmates, Napoleon showed his leadership skills by forming a full-scale attack. He gave the boys on his team duties and places to stand. They easily beat the other team because of his warlike strategies.

Before the other cadets realized his abilities, Napoleon was picked on by his classmates because of his short height, unusual name, and Italian-sounding accent. Napoleon did not care for his fellow cadets because they were from wealthy families and were French. Napoleon's father was a lawyer, but Napoleon was one of eight children and the family was not wealthy. In fact, Napoleon often sent money home. Napoleon resented the French in general because they invaded his homeland, the Mediterranean island of Corsica, in 1768. Historians say that one year later—on the day he was born—Napoleon's homeland was forced to celebrate the anniversary of the French takeover.

Napoleon's teachers found him to be smart and capable, especially in mathematics, but a poor speller. He earned a scholarship to a Paris military academy and tested well enough to become a second lieutenant in the army at age 16. Little did anyone know that someday he would become a military leader and emperor of France.

▲ Napoleon Bonaparte

"I have sacrificed all of my interests to those of the country."
–Napoleon Bonaparte, "Farewell to the Old Guard"

Then and Now

What skills would prepare someone to be a good military leader today?

Napoleon Invades Russia Napoleon next decided to take on Russia. He organized a large force of about 600,000 soldiers called the Grand Army. In the summer of 1812, the Grand Army invaded Russia. Except for one battle, the Russians refused to fight. Instead, they drew Napoleon's army deeper into Russia. When Russia's harsh winter arrived, Napoleon's forces were unprepared and helpless. Their retreat was a disaster. Fewer than 100,000 men returned alive.

France's enemies then captured Napoleon and exiled him to the Mediterranean island of Elba. He escaped to the French mainland in the spring of 1815. His troops flocked to their old commander. Napoleon returned to Paris in triumph. At **Waterloo** (WAW•tuhr•LOO) in Belgium, an international force led by Britain's Duke of Wellington finally defeated Napoleon. This time, Napoleon was sent to the island of St. Helena in the southern Atlantic Ocean, where he died in 1821.

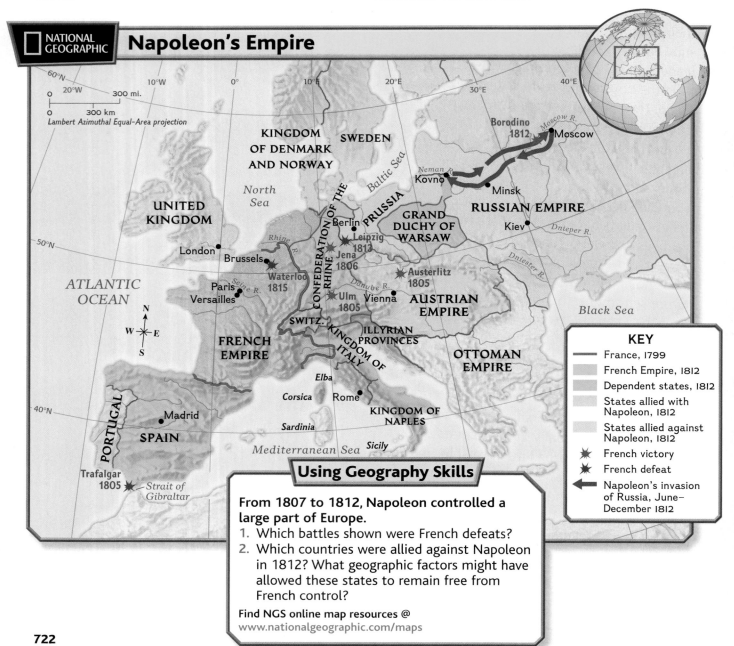

NATIONAL GEOGRAPHIC   Napoleon's Empire

KEY
— France, 1799
French Empire, 1812
Dependent states, 1812
States allied with Napoleon, 1812
States allied against Napoleon, 1812
✴ French victory
✸ French defeat
← Napoleon's invasion of Russia, June–December 1812

Using Geography Skills

From 1807 to 1812, Napoleon controlled a large part of Europe.

1. Which battles shown were French defeats?
2. Which countries were allied against Napoleon in 1812? What geographic factors might have allowed these states to remain free from French control?

Find NGS online map resources @ www.nationalgeographic.com/maps

The Congress of Vienna In September 1814, European leaders met in the Austrian capital of Vienna. Their goal was to return Europe to the way it was before the French Revolution. The leader of the conference, known as the Congress of Vienna, was Austria's foreign minister Klemens von Metternich (MEH•tuhr•nihk). Like the other leaders, Metternich was a conservative. Conservatives at that time believed in traditional values, orderly ways, and a strong role for religion. They rejected calls for individual rights and self-rule. American conservatives today believe in traditional values, but they also support individual political rights and self-rule.

At the Congress of Vienna, Metternich and the other leaders wanted to create a balance of power, or equal strength among countries. They hoped that a balance of

◀ Klemens von Metternich

power would prevent any single nation, such as France, from controlling Europe.

The European leaders at Vienna were against individual rights and nationalism. Hoping to crush revolutionary ideas, they brought back to power the royal families who had ruled in Europe before Napoleon. To keep the peace, the leaders also agreed to meet from time to time at conferences. These meetings were called the Concert of Europe.

✓ **Reading Check** **Analyze** How did nationalism help defeat Napoleon?

History Online

Study Central™ Need help with the material in this section? Visit jat.glencoe.com

Section 1 Review

Reading Summary

Review the Main Ideas

- Rising prices, food shortages, and unemployment in France led the Third Estate to rebel, creating a new elected assembly.

- French radicals known as Jacobins gained control of the government and executed thousands of people who opposed their reforms.

- As political troubles in France worsened, Napoleon Bonaparte took control of the country.

- After creating a large empire, Napoleon was finally defeated. European leaders attempted to restore a balance of power.

What Did You Learn?

1. What was the main idea of the Declaration of the Rights of Man and the Citizen?

2. What were the goals of the Congress of Vienna?

Critical Thinking

3. **Organize Information** Draw a chart like the one below. Use it to describe the divisions in French society.

First Estate	
Second Estate	
Third Estate	

4. **Summarize** What were some of the achievements of the Committee of Public Safety?

5. **Compare and Contrast** Compare the goals of the French and American Revolutions.

6. **Sequence Information** What events led to Napoleon's defeat and the fall of the French Empire?

7. **Reading** **Understanding Concepts** Make a recruiting poster for the French army, either in the revolutionary period or under Napoleon. Use language and illustrations that convey the ideals, emotions, and events of the time.

Section 2

The Industrial Revolution

Get Ready to Read!

What's the Connection?
While France and other nations were undergoing political changes, the Industrial Revolution was changing the way people worked and lived.

Focusing on the Main Ideas
- The Industrial Revolution began in Great Britain because of the enclosure movement, Britain's natural resources, and new British inventions. *(page 725)*

- The Industrial Revolution spread beyond Great Britain's shores to Europe and the United States. *(page 729)*

Meeting People
James Hargreaves (HAHR•GREEVZ)
Richard Arkwright (AHRK•RYT)
Edmund Cartwright (KAHRT•RYT)
James Watt
Robert Fulton

Michael Faraday (FAR•uh•DAY)
Thomas Edison

Building Your Vocabulary
industrialism (ihn•DUHS•tree•uh•LIH•zuhm)
textile (TEHK•STYL)
capital
partnership
corporation (KAWR•puh•RAY•shuhn)

Reading Strategy
Organizing Information Use a diagram like the one below to show four of the major inventions and their inventors that helped start the Industrial Revolution.

The Industrial Revolution

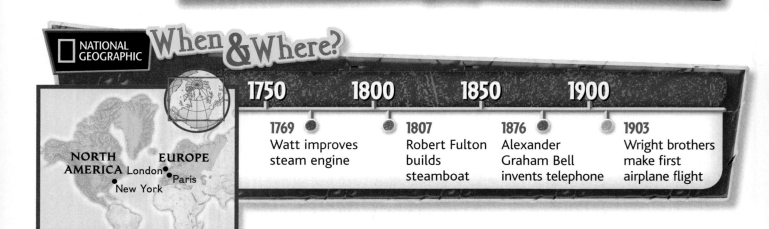

NATIONAL GEOGRAPHIC **When & Where?**

NORTH AMERICA   EUROPE
London• •Paris
•New York

1750	1800	1850	1900

1769
Watt improves steam engine

1807
Robert Fulton builds steamboat

1876
Alexander Graham Bell invents telephone

1903
Wright brothers make first airplane flight

Industrialism Begins

Main Idea The Industrial Revolution began in Britain because of the enclosure movement, Britain's natural resources, and new British inventions.

Reading Focus How would your life be different if you did not have cars, telephones, or electricity? All of these things came from the Industrial Revolution. Read to learn how industry began.

While political revolution swept through Europe, a new economic system known as **industrialism** (ihn•DUHS•tree•uh•LIH•zuhm) began in Britain. There, people began to rely on the use of machinery, rather than on animal or human power. Over the next 200 years, industrialism would spread from Britain to dramatically change life in other parts of the world. Industry changed life so much that historians call these changes the Industrial Revolution.

Before the rise of industrialism, most people lived in small farming villages. They raised their own food and made their own goods. In Britain during the early 1700s, cloth was made in villages. As you read previously, this system was known as cottage industry. Under this system, most

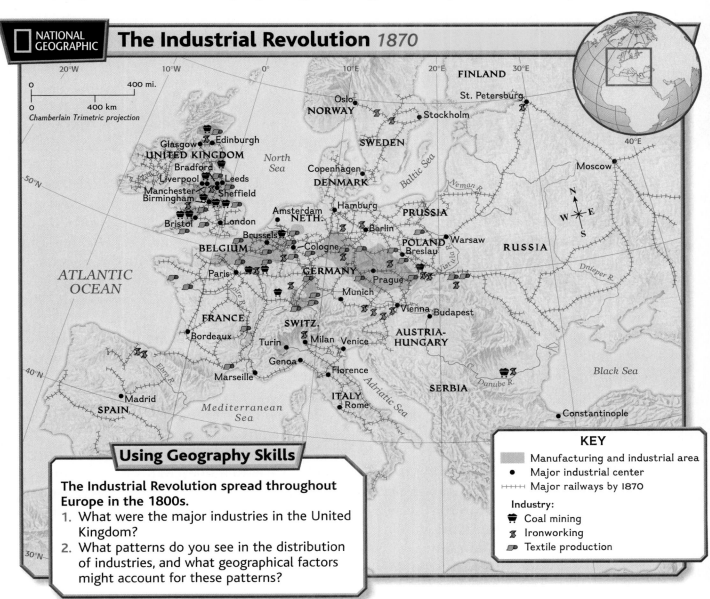

NATIONAL GEOGRAPHIC

The Industrial Revolution 1870

Using Geography Skills

The Industrial Revolution spread throughout Europe in the 1800s.
1. What were the major industries in the United Kingdom?
2. What patterns do you see in the distribution of industries, and what geographical factors might account for these patterns?

KEY

▨ Manufacturing and industrial area
• Major industrial center
├┼┼┼┤ Major railways by 1870

Industry:
⛏ Coal mining
⚒ Ironworking
🧶 Textile production

The Way It Was

Focus on Everyday Life

Traveling by Early Railroad In the 1700s and early 1800s, the best way to travel in England was on horseback or by stagecoach. By the late 1840s, however, stagecoach companies were being forced out of business with a new invention: the steam locomotive. The locomotive was invented in England in the early 1800s. It was first used to move coal and iron ore from mines to factories. Then passengers started riding the trains.

Boarding and riding a grand locomotive, nicknamed the "iron horse," was an exciting trip. The wealthy bought tickets for first-class seats in fancy, enclosed passenger cars. These customers sat on plush cloth and leather benches with wood and brass handrails. The seats were located behind the locomotive

▲ Early English train from the 1840s

work was done in workers' cottages, where families worked together.

Merchants went from cottage to cottage, bringing the workers raw wool and cotton. Using hand-powered spinning wheels and looms, the workers would spin the thread and weave it into wool and cotton cloth. The merchants then picked up the finished cloth to sell. The Industrial Revolution began in the woven cloth, or **textile** (TEHK•STYL), industry. Merchants could make so much money from textiles that they began to look for ways to make cloth better and faster. By the 1700s, changes in Britain made this possible.

What Caused the Industrial Revolution?

The Industrial Revolution began in Britain for many reasons. One important cause of Britain's Industrial Revolution was a change in how Britain's landowners used their land. In the 1700s the enclosure

movement began. Britain's Parliament passed new laws that allowed landowners to fence off their land. For hundreds of years, local villagers had rented the land from landowners and divided it into small strips, each worked by a family. Now the villagers were told they could not use the land the way they wanted.

Enclosure allowed landowners to make more money. Whole areas could grow the same crop, which meant larger harvests and greater profits. Often the land was turned into pasture for sheep whose wool was used by the textile industry.

Successful farming provided landowners with extra money. Many chose to invest, or put money, into new businesses. Money invested in businesses is called **capital.** A growing middle class joined wealthy landowners and merchants in investing capital in new industries.

where the smoke would rise above the train's front section and not bother the riders.

People who bought cheaper tickets sat in the second-class section. Second-class railway cars were open to the air, and passengers had to wait their turn for a bench seat to become available. Third-class passengers could buy very cheap tickets and stand in train cars with open sides. Some had benches. The smoke from the coal-powered steam engines often dirtied the riders' clothes. They ignored this discomfort because riding a train was faster and cheaper than traveling in uncomfortable stagecoaches.

▲ Interior of a railway car

Connecting to the Past

1. What accommodations were provided for first-class passengers?
2. Why did third-class passengers prefer to travel by train than by stagecoach?

Still another cause was the large number of people available to work in industry. The enclosure movement forced many peasants off the land. They then moved to the cities and became workers in new industries.

In the 1700s, Britain's population grew rapidly. More and better food meant that people were healthier, lived longer, and had larger families. This increase in population also provided workers for the new factories.

Finally, Britain's natural resources and geography also helped in the rise of industry. The British had large supplies of coal and iron. Coal replaced wood as the fuel for running machines. Iron was used in building and in making machines. The country had many fine harbors and rivers for transporting goods. Rivers also provided power for the earliest cotton mills.

New Inventions Britain also had a number of talented inventors. Their inventions made the Industrial Revolution possible. Many of these first inventions were developed in the late 1700s for the textile industry. **James Hargreaves** (HAHR•GREEVZ) invented a spinning jenny that could spin cotton into thread very quickly. **Richard Arkwright** (AHRK•RYT) developed a way to power a spinning machine with water, and **Edmund Cartwright** (KAHRT•RYT) created a new powered loom. This machine could weave the thread into cloth as fast as the new spinning machines produced it.

In 1769 **James Watt** designed a steam engine that could power the new machines. Steam soon replaced water as the major source of power.

As the need for machines grew, iron was needed to make machine parts. In 1753 Henry Cort found a way to use coal to turn iron ore into pure iron. As a result, iron became cheaper, production grew, and coal mining became a major industry. In 1856 Henry Bessemer invented an inexpensive way to make large amounts of iron into steel, which was harder and stronger than iron. Soon mining towns and steel centers grew in areas with supplies of iron ore and coal.

The Rise of Factories and Railroads

Factories were the major centers of the Industrial Revolution. Why did they develop? Machines became too large and expensive for home use. Factories brought workers and machines together in one place under managers.

As the Industrial Revolution began, business owners reorganized their companies to raise the money they needed to buy machines and build factories. One way to do this was to form a **partnership** where two or more people owned the business and pooled their own money. Another way was to create a **corporation** (KAWR•puh•RAY•shuhn). A corporation raises money by selling shares in the company to investors. Creating a corporation allowed business leaders to build large factories with hundreds of workers.

New forms of transportation also led to industrial growth. In 1807 **Robert Fulton,** an American inventor, developed a boat powered by a steam engine. The biggest improvement in land transportation was the railroad. By the mid-1800s, steam-powered locomotives carried raw materials, finished goods, and people faster and cheaper than any other kind of transportation.

✓ Reading Check **Explain** How did enclosure help to bring about the Industrial Revolution?

Steam Engine

In a locomotive, coal is burned in the engine's firebox. The hot gases from the fire travel through tubes and empty into the smokebox, after heating water in the boiler and creating steam. The throttle releases steam into the steam chest, where a valve controls the movement of the steam into the cylinder. In the cylinder, the steam pushes the piston, which is connected to a drive rod that turns the locomotive's wheels. *How did railroads affect industry?*

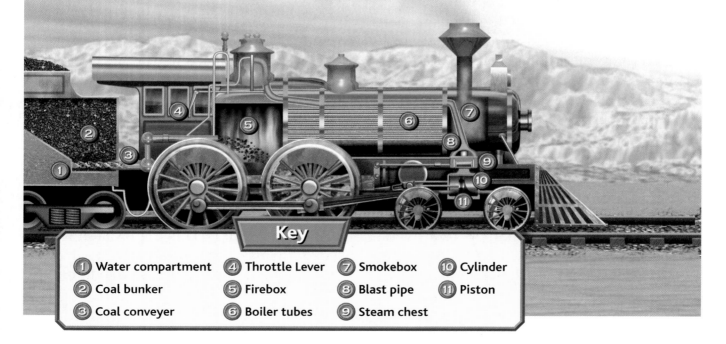

Key

① Water compartment	④ Throttle Lever	⑦ Smokebox	⑩ Cylinder
② Coal bunker	⑤ Firebox	⑧ Blast pipe	⑪ Piston
③ Coal conveyer	⑥ Boiler tubes	⑨ Steam chest	

The Spread of Industry

Main Idea The Industrial Revolution spread beyond Great Britain's shores to Europe and the United States.

Reading Focus Important inventions fueled the spread of the Industrial Revolution. What inventions of your lifetime do you feel have had the greatest impact on your life today?

Britain's advances in industrial technology gave it an advantage over other countries. To protect that advantage, Britain's Parliament passed laws keeping ideas, inventions, and skilled workers from leaving the country. In spite of these laws, however, the Industrial Revolution soon spread to other areas.

Industry in Europe and America From Britain the Industrial Revolution spread to France, Belgium, Germany, and the United States. European governments encouraged the rise of industries. They helped build factories, railroads, canals, and roads. By the 1820s, British business owners and investors had made so much money from industry that they began to invest in factories and railroads in Europe. Their investments helped the Industrial Revolution get started in other countries.

The Industrial Revolution also took hold in the United States. British investors and American engineers built factories for making textiles and shoes. Workers, including women and children, left rural areas to work in cities.

Like Britain, the United States had many natural resources. Americans quickly built roads and canals to move goods and people across the vast nation. Fulton's steamboat improved transportation on inland waterways, and railroads soon crisscrossed the country.

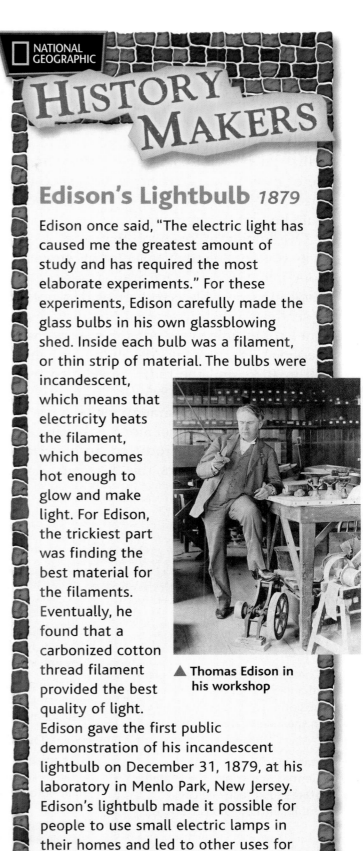

NATIONAL GEOGRAPHIC

HISTORY MAKERS

Edison's Lightbulb 1879

Edison once said, "The electric light has caused me the greatest amount of study and has required the most elaborate experiments." For these experiments, Edison carefully made the glass bulbs in his own glassblowing shed. Inside each bulb was a filament, or thin strip of material. The bulbs were incandescent, which means that electricity heats the filament, which becomes hot enough to glow and make light. For Edison, the trickiest part was finding the best material for the filaments. Eventually, he found that a carbonized cotton thread filament provided the best quality of light.

▲ Thomas Edison in his workshop

Edison gave the first public demonstration of his incandescent lightbulb on December 31, 1879, at his laboratory in Menlo Park, New Jersey. Edison's lightbulb made it possible for people to use small electric lamps in their homes and led to other uses for electricity.

New Scientific Discoveries As the 1800s continued, many scientific discoveries helped to keep the Industrial Revolution going. Iron was replaced by steel. Starting in the 1870s, steel became the leading industrial metal. Other inventions made use of electricity. Electricity could be converted easily to heat, light, or motion, and could be sent through wires.

One important invention that used electricity was the telegraph, invented by Samuel Morse in the 1830s. The telegraph made communication possible across great distances by sending coded messages through wires. Other communications advances were the telephone, invented by Alexander Graham Bell in 1876, and the radio, developed by Guglielmo Marconi in 1895.

In 1831 **Michael Faraday** (FAR•uh•DAY) discovered that a magnet moving through a coil of copper wire produced an electric current. Within 40 years, this discovery led to the invention of electric generators. **Thomas Edison** developed the lightbulb, which used electricity to create light. As demand for electricity rose, investors in Europe and the United States funded the first power plants. These were powered by coal or oil.

Major breakthroughs also took place in transportation. In the 1880s Germany's Rudolf Diesel and Gottlieb Daimler invented internal combustion engines that produced a lot of power by burning oil-based fuels. Within a few decades, internal combustion engines powered boats. They also made possible two other new kinds of transportation: the car and the airplane. In 1903 two American inventors, Orville and Wilbur Wright, successfully tested the world's first powered airplane.

Reading Check **Cause and Effect** Which key inventions resulted from the development of electricity?

History Online

Study Central™ Need help with the material in this section? Visit jat.glencoe.com

Section ❷ Review

Reading Summary

Review the Main Ideas

- Changes in agriculture and plentiful deposits of iron and coal helped Great Britain lead the way in the Industrial Revolution.

- France, Belgium, northern German states, and the United States soon followed Great Britain into the Industrial Age.

What Did You Learn?

1. What natural resources and features helped industries develop in Great Britain?

2. What important inventions were created following the development of electricity?

Critical Thinking

3. **Organize Information** Create a table like the one below. Fill in inventors' names and inventions.

Inventor	Invention

4. **Economics Link** Describe the difference between a partnership and a corporation.

5. **Describe** Describe the inventions that changed how people communicate.

6. **Analyze** What did Rudolf Diesel and Gottlieb Daimler invent, and why was it important?

7. **Expository Writing** Choose the invention or development from the chapter that you believe has had the greatest impact on the world. Write an essay explaining your choice.

Section 3

Society and Industry

Get Ready to Read!

What's the Connection?

In the last section, you read about the causes of the Industrial Revolution. In this section, you will learn how industry changed society.

Focusing on the (Main Ideas)

- The Industrial Revolution caused cities to grow bigger and changed how people lived and worked. *(page 732)*

- The Industrial Revolution led to new ideas about politics, society, and the economy. *(page 734)*

- Artists, writers, and composers reflected the changes that industrialism brought to society. *(page 736)*

- Important scientific discoveries during the Industrial Revolution changed the way people lived and how they understood the world. *(page 738)*

Meeting People

Adam Smith

Karl Marx

Louis Pasteur (LOO•ee   pas•TUHR)

Albert Einstein (EYEN•STYN)

Charles Darwin (DAHR•wuhn)

Building Your Vocabulary

urbanization (UHR•buh•nuh•ZAY•shuhn)

liberalism (LIH•buh•ruh•LIH•zuhm)

socialism (SOH•shuh•LIH•zuhm)

labor union

Reading Strategy

Contrasting Use a table like the one below to compare major ideas of the industrial era.

	Main Ideas
liberalism	
socialism	

When & Where?

NATIONAL GEOGRAPHIC

NORTH AMERICA • London • Paris • New York EUROPE

1800 — 1850 — 1900

c. 1780 Romanticism begins in the arts

1848 Karl Marx writes *Communist Manifesto*

1859 Charles Darwin presents theory of evolution

c. 1870 Impressionism begins in France

Industry Changes Society

Main Idea The Industrial Revolution caused cities to grow bigger and changed how people lived and worked.

Reading Focus How is life in the country different from life in the city today? How is it similar? Read to learn about the new way of life rural people faced when they moved to the city during the Industrial Revolution.

The Industrial Revolution brought changes in many areas of life. These changes took place in Europe, North America, and elsewhere by the 1860s. Industrial growth still changes the way people live today.

Cities Grow in Size One important change was the rapid growth in the size of cities. **Urbanization** (UHR•buh•nuh•ZAY•shuhn) is the movement of people from rural areas to cities. A nation is urbanized when most of its people live in cities. Britain was the first country to become urbanized. City popula-

tions also grew in the other parts of Europe and in the United States.

Why did cities grow so quickly? As farms used more machines, fewer workers were needed. To find jobs, many rural workers headed to nearby cities hoping to find work in the new factories.

What Was Industrial Life Like? Before the rise of industry, a person's place in society was set by birth. Few were able to rise to higher positions. The growth of industry, however, brought new opportunities.

In Europe, wealthy factory owners were able to live like nobles. They had several homes and many servants to wait on them. Less wealthy people such as managers, lawyers, doctors, and engineers formed the industrial middle class. Some of them also could afford servants and fine homes.

The growth of industry and cities also created a large working class. The working class was made up of people who toiled in the factories and mines. Their lives were

▼ This photograph from the late 1800s shows housing conditions in England. *Why did cities grow so rapidly during the Industrial Revolution?*

▲ This scene shows workers in a steel mill in France.

much harder than those of the upper or middle classes.

Entire working-class families—children as well as adults—had to work to make enough money to live. Working conditions varied from barely acceptable to dreadful. Hours were long—up to 16 hours a day, 6 days a week. Injuries were common in hot, dirty, and unhealthy factories and mines. Many children lost fingers or limbs. Death and injury occurred often.

Living conditions in the cities were often wretched. However, workers still flocked to cities to fill factory jobs because they could not find work on the farms. Despite the low pay and long hours, most workers had better lives and more money than when they lived in the country. They found that city life had many benefits. Cities offered many leisure-time opportunities. These included parks, education for adults and children, concerts, libraries, museums, and sports. Women discovered a new independence.

As time passed, working conditions did improve. Some reformers, including many religious people, were able to better the lives of workers. Hours were reduced for female and young workers. Living conditions in the cities remained very unhealthy, but some improvements did occur. New laws were passed that made factories safer and reduced pollution and unclean food and water in the cities.

Life Changes for Women

The Industrial Revolution greatly changed women's lives. At first, it was believed that a woman's place was in the home. Her job was to raise children and do household tasks. Women had fewer legal rights than men. During the 1800s, women worked to change their position and find new roles.

The Way It Was

Young People In...

Working Conditions in Mills

For children working in mills and factories, the workday began early, often before dawn. A regular shift began at 5 in the morning. Children who arrived late for work usually did so in tears. They knew that their wages would be cut and that they would be severely punished.

Children arrived for work hungry, but breakfast was not allowed until 8 or 9 o' clock in the morning. Breakfast usually consisted of an oatcake and cans of boiled milk and water. Children ate their breakfast standing up, still working at their stations. Once a year, they were served cheese and brown bread for a special dinner. Because the children were tired and hungry, they often became drowsy while working. When this happened, the overseer woke them up by dunking them headfirst into a vat of cold water.

Many children developed breathing problems and became sick with an illness known as "mill fever." The air that children breathed was contaminated with dust, grease, oil, and gas.

▲ Child coal miners in England

Connecting to the Past

1. Why were children afraid to arrive late for work?
2. What was the cause of "mill fever"?

The workplace played a major role in changing the position of women. Women found jobs in both industry and government service. There were also more opportunities for education. A drop in family size during the 1800s helped to change the lives of women as well.

During the 1800s, women began to demand equal rights with men. In the United States, Britain, and other countries, women challenged long-standing ideas. They especially demanded the right to vote.

Reading Check **Identify** What developed in cities as people began to work fewer hours?

New Political Ideas

Main Idea **The Industrial Revolution led to new ideas about politics, society, and the economy.**

Reading Focus What does the word *liberal* mean to you? Read to find out how a new philosophy with this name affected society in the 1800s.

The Industrial Revolution brought many changes, both good and bad. Starting in the early 1800s, people looked for ways to understand issues and solve the problems that industry had created. A number of different ideas developed to address these concerns.

Linking Past & Present

Women in the Workforce

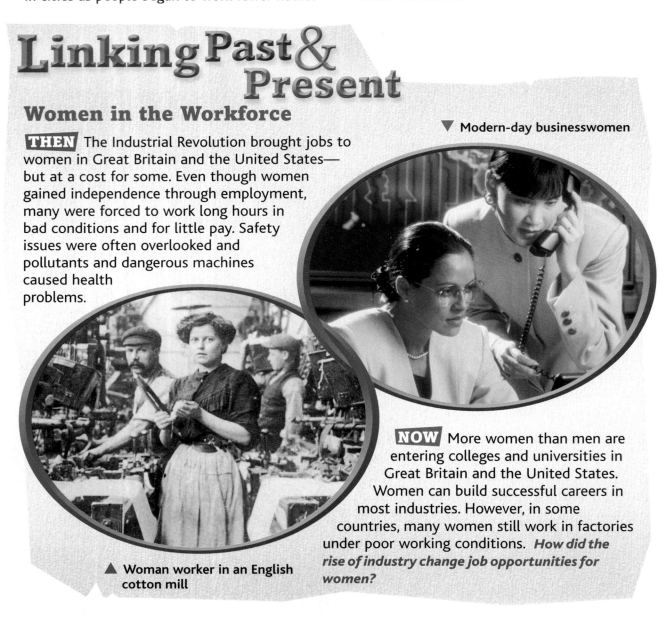

THEN The Industrial Revolution brought jobs to women in Great Britain and the United States—but at a cost for some. Even though women gained independence through employment, many were forced to work long hours in bad conditions and for little pay. Safety issues were often overlooked and pollutants and dangerous machines caused health problems.

▼ **Modern-day businesswomen**

NOW More women than men are entering colleges and universities in Great Britain and the United States. Women can build successful careers in most industries. However, in some countries, many women still work in factories under poor working conditions. *How did the rise of industry change job opportunities for women?*

▲ **Woman worker in an English cotton mill**

What Is Liberalism? One of these new ideas was **liberalism** (LIH•buh•ruh•LIH•zuhm). Liberalism is a political philosophy based on the ideas of the Enlightenment. The word *liberal* had a different meaning in the 1800s than it does today in the United States. Liberals today agree with liberals of the 1800s about some ideas but disagree on others. Earlier, you read about conservatives in the 1800s and how they too believed different things than conservatives do today.

Liberals in the 1800s believed that all people have basic rights. These include equality before the law and freedom of speech and the press. Many liberals wanted freedom of religion. Liberals also believed that the power of governments should be limited by written constitutions and that elected assemblies should make laws. Liberals did not believe that everyone should be allowed to vote. Most thought that this right should be restricted to men who owned property.

Liberalism was popular among the new middle class. Middle-class businesspeople believed that government should not interfere with business or society. British economist **Adam Smith** defended this idea. He argued that if government stayed out of the economy and let businesses compete, it would lead to more prosperity and a better society. This idea became known as "laissez-faire," a French word meaning "to let be."

Two British thinkers, however, wanted to use government to help make society better. Jeremy Bentham (BEHN•thuhm) and

History Online

Web Activity Visit jat.glencoe.com and click on *Chapter 19—Student Web Activity* to learn more about the rise of industry.

Primary Source *The Communist Manifesto*

In outlining their plan for society, Karl Marx and his friend Friedrich Engels urged the working class to unite.

"In short, the Communists everywhere support every revolutionary movement against the existing social and political order of things. . . .

The Communists disdain [refuse] to conceal their views and aims. They openly declare that their ends can be attained only by the forcible overthrow of all existing social conditions. Let the ruling class tremble at a communist revolution. The proletarians have nothing to lose but their chains. They have a world to win.

Working men of all countries, unite!"

—Karl Marx and Friedrich Engels, *The Communist Manifesto*

▲ Karl Marx

DBQ **Document-Based Question**

What do Marx and Engels mean when they say that there is nothing to lose but chains?

John Stuart Mill were utilitarians. They believed society should promote the greatest happiness for the most people. Utilitarianism (yoo•TIH•luh•TEHR•ee•uh•NIH•zuhm) endorsed ideas like full rights for women, better education, and improved health services.

What Is Marxism? Another new idea of the 1800s was **socialism** (SOH•shuh•LIH•zuhm). Socialists believe that factories, land, capital, and raw materials—what they called the means of production—should be

▲ **This painting shows men, women, and children working in an early factory.** *Why did labor unions develop?*

owned and controlled by society, through the government. Many people developed the ideas of socialism, but the most important person was a German writer named **Karl Marx.**

Marx was a German thinker who lived during the 1800s. Marx believed that competition among social classes harmed society. He predicted that, over time, the working class, which he called the proletariat (PROH•luh•TEHR•ee•uht), would rise up and create a communist society. Under communism, social classes would end and people would live in a classless society.

Marx's ideas, later called Marxism, were very influential. His ideas were the basic ideas of socialist political parties in Germany, Britain, Scandinavia, and other countries. These socialist parties favored government control of industry.

Another response to the horrors of factory life was the growth of labor unions. A **labor union** is an association of workers who unite to improve wages and working conditions. Strikes, or work stoppages, often forced owners to bargain with union leaders. In many European countries, unions supported socialist political parties.

✓ **Reading Check** **Describe** What did Jeremy Bentham and John Stuart Mill believe?

New Art and Literature

Main Idea Artists, writers, and composers reflected the changes that industrialism brought to society.

Reading Focus Art, music, and literature are often shaped by the society in which they are created. How do today's music, books, and movies reflect today's society?

The rise of industry changed how people lived and worked. It also led to new movements in art, literature, and music. The often ugly face of the new industrialized world caused some artists to turn away from it. Others, however, chose to portray it.

Romanticism and Realism In the late 1700s, artists and writers known as the romantics began to react against the Enlightenment. Instead of reason, their movement called romanticism valued feelings and the imagination as the best way to find the truth.

Poets, such as Britain's William Wordsworth and Germany's Johann von Goethe (yoh•HAHN fawn GUH•tuh), looked to nature, the past, and the unusual as their subjects. In their works, these writers tried to express their inner feelings about life. Romantic painters, such as Eugène Delacroix (yoo•JEEN DEH•luh•KWAH) of France, also chose strange and unusual subjects. The first great romantic musician was Ludwig van Beethoven (LOOD•wihg vahn BAY•TOH•vuhn). This German composer's music expressed strong emotion and intense drama.

By the mid-1800s, another movement—realism—took hold. Some artists turned away from the romantic emphasis on feelings. These writers and painters, known as realists, tried to show life as it truly was.

Novelists like Charles Dickens of Great Britain, Honoré de Balzac (AHN•uh•RAY day BAWL•ZAK) of France, and Leo Tolstoy (tohl•stoy) of Russia focused on ordinary people in ordinary settings. They used details to create a picture of everyday life. Painters like France's Gustave Courbet (GUS•TAHV kur•BAY) also showed figures and scenes from ordinary life. While romantics tried to escape from industrialized society, realists chose to examine it closely.

Modernism and Impressionism

Two other movements appeared later in the 1800s. One was modernism. An important part of modernism was the study of social problems. Novelists such as Émile Zola of France, and Theodore Dreiser of the United States, and dramatist Henrik Ibsen of Norway explored social issues of the day. Subjects included crime, alcoholism, and women's rights. Other modernists took a different approach. Symbolist poets believed that the outer world was only a reflection of an individual's inner reality. They studied dreams and symbols for meaning and used them in their works.

A modernist movement in painting was called impressionism. Beginning in the 1870s, impressionists were especially interested in the effect of light on different outdoor objects and surfaces. The most famous impressionists were French. They included Claude Monet (moh•NAY), Pierre-Auguste Renoir, and Edgar Degas (duh•gah). Mary Cassatt of the United States was also a famous impressionist painter. Composers, led by France's Claude Debussy (DEH•byu•SEE), even translated impressionist ideas into dreamy, shimmering music.

✔ **Reading Check** **Describe** What element was most important to modernists?

▼ *The Stonebreakers* by Gustave Courbet, 1849

▲ *Nympheas* by Claude Monet, 1907

Courbet painted scenes from everyday life, while Monet focused on the beauty of nature. *Which artist rejected the artistic movement of romanticism?*

Science and Medicine

Main Idea **Important scientific discoveries during the Industrial Revolution changed the way people lived and how they understood the world.**

Reading Focus Do you know why children often look like their birth parents? Read to find out who discovered how characteristics are passed from one generation to another.

During the 1800s, scientists took many important steps forward. Their work brought many practical benefits to society in the fields of medicine and health. It also enabled people to better understand the world.

Why Was Pasteur Important? One of the first important medical advances was the discovery of vaccines to ward off disease. In 1796 the English doctor Edward Jenner noticed that dairy workers who caught cowpox did not get the deadly smallpox. Jenner believed that vaccinating or injecting people with cowpox would make them immune to smallpox. Jenner's theory proved correct.

It took a while, however, before the vaccination process could be explained. Finally, in 1868, French chemist **Louis Pasteur** (LOO•ee pas•TUHR) discovered bacteria, or germs. He also proved that they cause disease. Pasteur showed that killing bacteria would prevent many diseases.

Early surgery was a gruesome process. The discovery of anesthesia, or pain-deadening drugs such as ether, was a great step forward. So were the methods developed by Englishman Joseph Lister to sterilize medical equipment. Before Lister, many patients died after surgery due to infection.

An Austrian monk named Gregor Mendel was responsible for a key scientific breakthrough. In the 1860s his work with pea plants finally solved an ancient mystery: to predict which characteristics or traits get passed to the next generation. Based on his observations, Mendel developed a system of rules that could predict whether a living organism would inherit traits from its parents. Mendel's ideas became very influential, and he is known today as the father of the science called genetics.

Einstein and Physics By the end of the 1800s, new ideas in the physical sciences, or physics, changed the way people understand the world. Atomic theory is the idea that everything is made up of tiny particles called atoms. Scientists gradually learned more about atoms, including the composition of different elements and the qualities of X rays and electricity. They learned

▲ Among his discoveries, Louis Pasteur developed a vaccine against rabies. *How did Pasteur's discovery of bacteria lead to the prevention of disease?*

Major Scientific Discoveries

Year	Scientist	Discovery	Impact
1803	John Dalton	elements are composed of atoms	provided proof to support the atomic theory
1820s	Mary Anning	fossils of dinosaurs, including the plesiosaur	helped scientists learn more about the Jurassic period of history
1850s	Louis Pasteur	disease-causing bacteria	allowed for doctors to fight disease more easily
1859	Charles Darwin	all living things evolve as their environment changes	questioned whether mankind originated from God or nature
1890s	Wilhelm K. Roentgen	X rays	allowed doctors to see a person's bones from the inside
1890s	Ivan Pavlov	actions are unconscious reactions	determined that, through training, any action could be learned
1898	Marie and Pierre Curie	the element radium within atoms	proved that atoms were active
1900	Max Planck	energy is not continuous	influenced the study of the atom
1905	Albert Einstein	theory of relativity	led to the development of the atomic bomb
1905	Nettie Stevens	X and Y chromosomes determine gender	led to the advanced study of human genetic material

Understanding Charts

In the late 1800s and early 1900s, scientists and inventors made tremendous advances that would affect the world for years to come.
1. During what years did important advancements in the understanding of atoms take place?
2. Which two scientists had the greatest impact on medicine?

that atoms are composed of even smaller individual particles. A Polish scientist, Marie Sklodowska Curie (kyu•REE), and her French husband, Pierre Curie, discovered the element radium in 1898. Radium is radioactive, which means it gives off energy.

Within a few years, a German scientist named **Albert Einstein** (AL•buhrt EYEN•STYN) caused a revolution in people's thinking about the universe. Previously, you learned that people during the 1600s came to believe that the universe was a well-run machine that obeyed natural laws. In 1905, however, Albert Einstein overturned these long-held ideas about time, space, mass, and motion. His theory of relativity stated that space and time were relative and

changing, rather than permanent and unchanging. As a result of Einstein's theory, people were able to imagine a more fluid, unstructured view of reality.

Einstein also developed a famous equation—$E=Mc^2$—where E is energy, M is mass, and c is the speed of light. The equation shows that all physical things contain vast amounts of energy. Using this idea, scientists eventually created the atomic bomb and nuclear reactors.

Biography

ALBERT EINSTEIN
1879–1955
MARIE SKLODOWSKA CURIE
1867–1934

In the late 1800s and early 1900s, both Albert Einstein and Marie Curie helped to advance science.

Albert Einstein was born on March 14, 1879, in Württemberg, Germany. He grew up in Munich in a Jewish family. Einstein became a teacher and then worked in a patent office in Switzerland. Einstein earned many awards for his scientific theories, including the Nobel Prize in physics. Einstein fled Nazi Germany and moved to the United States in 1933. Although his famous equation $E = Mc^2$ helped to advance scientific knowledge, he was bothered by the fact that it also made the atomic bomb possible. Late in his life, he began urging nations to give up nuclear weapons. He died on April 18, 1955, in Princeton, New Jersey.

Marie Curie was born Maria Sklodowska in Warsaw, Poland, in 1867. She graduated from high school at age 15, then attended classes at the Floating University, an illegal night school forbidden by Poland's Russian rulers. When Maria enrolled at the Sorbonne University in Paris in 1891, she became known as Marie. There she met Pierre Curie. They were married in 1895 and had two daughters. She earned her doctorate in 1903, and when Pierre died in an accident in 1906, Marie took his position teaching and researching at the Sorbonne. During World War I, she used X-ray units to help doctors treat wounds. She also helped create the Curie Foundation in 1920 to advance science and medicine. Twice she was awarded the Nobel Prize in physics. Marie died on July 4, 1934, in France.

▲ Albert Einstein

> "Imagination is more important than knowledge."
> –Albert Einstein

▲ Marie Curie

Then and Now

Both Einstein and Curie wanted their discoveries to better society. Identify and describe a topic or subject you would like to study because you think advances in that area could help people live better lives.

Who Was Charles Darwin? Like many others, **Charles Darwin** (DAHR•wuhn) wondered why there were so many different kinds of life in the world. His research led him to a conclusion: plants and animals change very slowly over time. The ones that survive do so because they are better adapted to their environment. They win the "battle" for survival and produce offspring. The offspring have the same characteristics that helped their parents adapt.

Darwin also believed that humans developed from animal species. His ideas were—and remain—controversial. Some religious people believed that his theories contradicted the biblical story of creation. Others believed it opened the door to a world without morals. Many people, however, came to accept Darwin's theory.

▲ Charles Darwin

Some people believed that Darwin's ideas about competition between species applied to society as well. This idea, called Social Darwinism, was popular with those who supported laissez-faire economics. Why? They believed that different individuals, companies, and countries engaged in economic competition, just like species. Weaker ones would fail, while stronger ones would prosper.

 **Reading Check** **Compare** How was the work of Edward Jenner similar to that of Louis Pasteur?

Section 3 Review

History Online
Study Central™ Need help with the material in this section? Visit jat.glencoe.com

Reading Summary
Review the Main Ideas

- The Industrial Revolution led to the growth of cities and the creation of the industrial working class.

- New political and economic philosophies, such as liberalism and socialism, developed during the Industrial Revolution.

- A number of different artistic movements arose during the Industrial Age, including romanticism, realism, modernism, and impressionism.

- Important scientific advances took place in the fields of medicine, biology, and physics during the 1800s.

What Did You Learn?

1. Describe the working conditions in Industrial Age factories.

2. How did the artistic movement known as realism approach life in the Industrial Age?

Critical Thinking

3. **Cause and Effect** Draw a diagram like the one below. Fill in causes that led to the growth of cities during the Industrial Age.

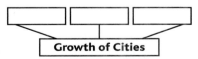

Growth of Cities

4. **Economics Link** Describe the economic philosophy of Adam Smith. Which members of British society agreed with his ideas?

5. **Summarize** What is a labor union, why did they become popular, and how did they force businesses to negotiate?

6. **Analyze** How were Darwin's scientific theories applied to society?

7. **Writing Questions** Imagine you are a newspaper writer interviewing Karl Marx. Write three or four questions you might ask him about his beliefs. Include possible answers.

You Decide ...

The Industrial Revolution: Benefits vs. Problems

Benefits

Many people, particularly factory owners, landowners, and financial investors, believed that the changes brought about by the Industrial Revolution benefited people of all classes. Lower-class men, women, and children worked in factories. Men of the middle class often served as managers. Men of the upper class were often factory owners.

Many debated the issue of child labor. One journalist published the following report:

"[T]he industry of the young not only contributes to the increase of our national wealth, but also to their own advantage.

In many factories they are not only usefully employed, but, at the same time, are trained up in those habits of morality and good feeling which are most likely to ensure their own lasting happiness and to make them valuable members of society."
—*from* The Penny Magazine, *November 16, 1833*

Benefits of the Industrial Revolution included the following:
- new inventions and technology, such as lightbulbs, refrigerators, electric ovens, and medicine
- factories made goods at low cost, which made food and goods affordable for more people
- development of new forms of transportation and communication, such as railroads, steamships, automobiles, airplanes, and telephones
- growth of the middle class
- rapid growth of cities
- greater job opportunities
- greater independence for women
- greater opportunities for education

▲ Rolls Royce Silver Ghost, an early automobile from 1906

▲ **Workers at a mine in England**

Problems

Other people, such as social reformers, doctors, and the lower-class factory workers themselves, believed that the Industrial Revolution not only created many problems, but that it seriously harmed those who worked in factories day after day. A young boy who started working in a textile factory at the age of six wrote this account:

"I have frequently worked at the frame till I could scarcely get home, and in this state have been stopped by people in the streets who noticed me shuffling along, and advised me to work no more in the factories; but I was not my own master. During the day, I frequently counted the clock, and calculated how many hours I had still to remain at work; my evenings were spent in preparing for the following day—in rubbing my knees, ankles, elbows, and wrists with oil, etc. I went to bed, to cry myself to sleep, and pray that the Lord would take me to himself before morning."

Problems created by the Industrial Revolution included the following:

- dangerous factory machinery caused serious accidents and deaths
- people worked in cramped, hot, and dimly lit factories
- long working hours—up to 16 hours a day, 6 days a week
- low pay
- unhealthy living conditions in crowded cities
- pollution from factories dirtied the air and rivers
- rise of cities broke up traditional small village communities
- people had to spend much more time traveling to and from work
- families did not work together all day on a farm; instead each family member had to go to separate jobs

You Be the Historian

Checking for Understanding
1. What were two benefits of the Industrial Revolution? What were two problems?
2. What problems caused by the Industrial Revolution are still problems today?
3. Do you think the benefits created by the Industrial Revolution outweighed the problems? Write a brief essay that explains your view. Be sure to use facts to support your position.

Section 4

Nationalism and Nation-States

Get-Ready to Read!

What's the Connection?

The French Revolution and the Industrial Revolution led to increased feelings of nationalism. That desire for self-rule led to reforms and revolutions in many parts of the world.

Focusing on the Main Ideas

• Two powerful ideas, nationalism and reform, helped reshape Europe politically during the mid-1800s. *(page 745)*

• In the mid-1800s, two new countries, Italy and Germany, were created. *(page 747)*

• In the early 1800s, the people of Latin America rebelled and gained their independence. *(page 749)*

• Nationalism in the United States led the country to expand its borders, but differences between the North and South led to a bloody civil war. *(page 751)*

Meeting People

William Gladstone

Giuseppe Garibaldi (joo•ZEHP•pay GAR•uh•BAWL•dee)

Otto von Bismarck (AHT•oh fawn BIHZ•MAHRK)

Simón Bolívar (see•MAWN boh•LEE•VAHR)

Building Your Vocabulary

kaiser (KY•zuhr)

caudillo (kow•THEE•yoh)

abolitionism (A•buh•LIH•shuhn•IH•zuhm)

Reading Strategy

Organizing Information Use a table like the one below to list Latin American leaders and their achievements.

Leader	Achievements

NATIONAL GEOGRAPHIC When & Where?

1800

1835

1870

1803 U.S. buys Louisiana Territory

1821 Mexico gains independence

1832 British middle-class men gain the vote

1871 Germany is united

NORTH AMERICA
Washington, D.C.
SOUTH AMERICA
EUROPE
Berlin
Rome

Nationalism and Reform

Main Idea Two powerful ideas, nationalism and reform, helped reshape Europe politically during the mid-1800s.

Reading Focus What does the term *self-rule* mean to you? What does it include? Who should have it?

Nationalism is the desire of people with the same history, language, and customs for self-rule. During the 1800s, nationalism, along with demands for political reform, led to dramatic and important changes in Europe and the Americas.

Democracy in Great Britain While war and revolt raged in most of Europe, change came peacefully to Britain. In the early 1800s, nobles ran Britain's government, and the middle and working classes could not vote. This situation soon changed. In 1832 a liberal British government passed a law that gave voting rights to most middle-class men. New industrial cities gained more seats in Parliament. Industrial workers, however, still did not have the vote. In the 1840s their supporters, known as Chartists, demanded the vote for all men and the use of secret ballots.

The Chartists failed to get the government to agree to their demands. Britain's political parties continued to make reforms, however, especially after **William Gladstone** became prime minister in 1868. Gladstone

The British Parliament

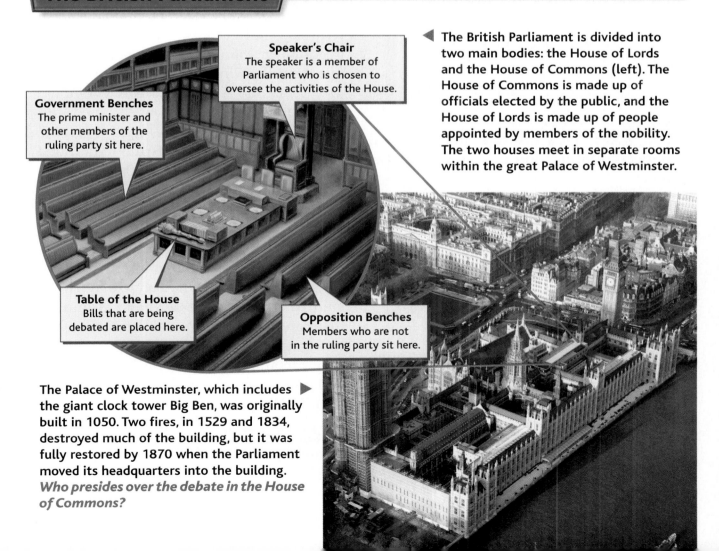

Speaker's Chair
The speaker is a member of Parliament who is chosen to oversee the activities of the House.

Government Benches
The prime minister and other members of the ruling party sit here.

Table of the House
Bills that are being debated are placed here.

Opposition Benches
Members who are not in the ruling party sit here.

◀ The British Parliament is divided into two main bodies: the House of Lords and the House of Commons (left). The House of Commons is made up of officials elected by the public, and the House of Lords is made up of people appointed by members of the nobility. The two houses meet in separate rooms within the great Palace of Westminster.

The Palace of Westminster, which includes ▶ the giant clock tower Big Ben, was originally built in 1050. Two fires, in 1529 and 1834, destroyed much of the building, but it was fully restored by 1870 when the Parliament moved its headquarters into the building.
Who presides over the debate in the House of Commons?

led the Liberal Party, which was backed by many middle-class voters. He served four terms as British prime minister, or political leader. Gladstone's reforms allowed voters to cast their ballots in secret and reorganized electoral districts to give more equal representation.

Gladstone's great political rival was Benjamin Disraeli, leader of the Conservative Party. Disraeli served two terms as prime minister. In 1867 his government gave the vote to many workers. In 1900 a new political party was created. Claiming to represent the working class, this party was known as the Labour Party. It eventually replaced the Liberals as the main rival of the Conservatives.

In the early 1900s, British women known as suffragettes pushed for women to have the right to vote. They staged demonstrations and hunger strikes. In 1918 Parliament gave all women over 30 the right to vote.

The Revolutions of 1848
In 1848 revolutions swept across Europe. Their starting point was France. Protests in support of political reforms erupted in Paris. The French king Louis-Philippe was driven from his throne, and France became a republic.

Events in France sparked revolts in other parts of Europe. Seeking self-rule, Hungarians, Italians, and Germans all rebelled against their monarchs. These revolts failed, but the ideas of nationalism and political reform remained strong among Europe's middle and working classes.

In France, Napoleon's nephew, Louis Napoleon, was elected president and later emperor. Under Napoleon III, France enjoyed economic advances, but the government was not democratic.

In 1870 Napoleon III declared war on Prussia. The powerful German state won an easy victory, and Napoleon III's government fell. The defeat stirred unrest in France. Workers seized control of Paris and set up a socialist government known as the Commune. A bloody civil war broke out. Troops supported by the upper-class government crushed the workers. In 1875 France became a republic once again. Distrust between its upper and working classes remained strong, however.

Reform in Austria and Russia
During the late 1800s, rulers in Austria and Russia tried to prevent political reform and weaken nationalist movements. Humiliating defeats in war, however, forced both Austria and Russia to make some changes.

In Austria, the government made a deal with the Hungarians, who wanted their freedom. In 1867 Hungary became a separate kingdom linked to Austria. Together they ruled the Austro-Hungarian Empire. The Hungarians were now satisfied, but other groups in Austria-Hungary were not. Their demands for self-rule continued throughout the rest of the 1800s.

In Russia, military defeat made the government realize that the country was far behind industrialized Europe. Czar Alexander II decided to create new industries and improve farming. In 1861 he freed the serfs—peasants who had to stay on the land where they were born and farm it for their landlords. Not enough land was given to the newly freed peasants, however, and they remained dissatisfied. Many writers and philosophers opposed to the czar's rule began calling for revolution.

Reading Check **Explain** How did political change in Britain differ from political change in other parts of Europe?

The Rise of Italy and Germany

Main Idea In the mid-1800s, two new countries, Italy and Germany, were created.

Reading Focus Which do you think is more important for a nation: democracy or a strong economy where everyone has a job? Why? Read to find out about how two newly united countries answered this question.

In the early 1800s, the countries we know today as Italy and Germany did not yet exist. Instead, these areas were divided into many small, independent states. By the 1850s, the rise of nationalism in Europe strengthened the desire of many Italians and Germans to create united countries.

How Did Italy Become a Country? In 1848 most of Italy's states were dominated by Austria. Piedmont, in northern Italy, was independent, and it was ruled by King Victor Emmanuel and the prime minister, Camillo di Cavour (kah•MEEL•loh dee kuh•VUR).

Both of these men wanted to unite Italy. After Piedmont helped Britain and France in a war with Russia, France agreed to help Piedmont drive Austria out of Italy. In 1859, with France's help, Piedmont won a war against Austria. This victory was the first step toward uniting Italy. Soon, people in other northern Italian states revolted against their rulers and united with Piedmont.

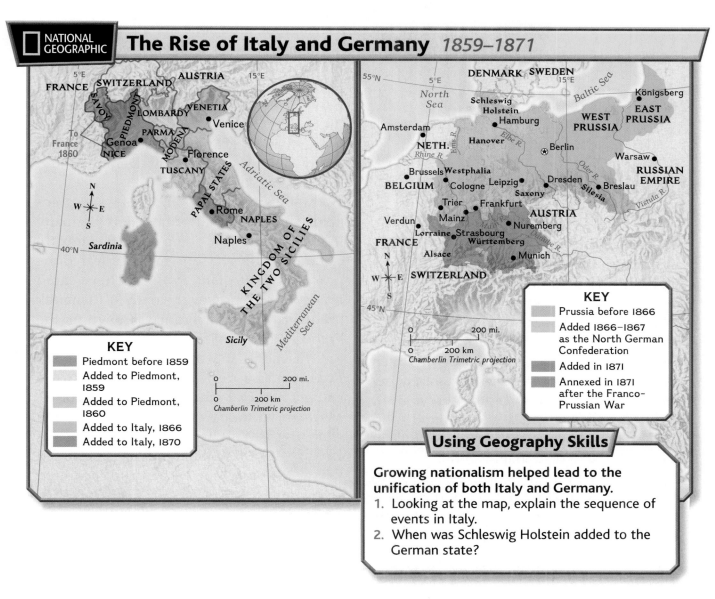

NATIONAL GEOGRAPHIC

The Rise of Italy and Germany 1859–1871

KEY
- Piedmont before 1859
- Added to Piedmont, 1859
- Added to Piedmont, 1860
- Added to Italy, 1866
- Added to Italy, 1870

KEY
- Prussia before 1866
- Added 1866–1867 as the North German Confederation
- Added in 1871
- Annexed in 1871 after the Franco-Prussian War

Using Geography Skills

Growing nationalism helped lead to the unification of both Italy and Germany.

1. Looking at the map, explain the sequence of events in Italy.
2. When was Schleswig Holstein added to the German state?

▲ King Victor Emmanuel (left) ruled a united Kingdom of Italy. Otto von Bismarck (right) served as prime minister under William I of Prussia and helped unite the German states.
What did Bismarck mean when he said he would unite Germany by "blood and iron"?

At the same time, nationalists led revolts in southern Italy. Their leader was **Giuseppe Garibaldi** (joo•ZEHP•pay   GAR•uh•BAWL•dee). This revolutionary leader gained control of the island of Sicily in 1860. Garibaldi was a master of guerrilla warfare (guh•RIH•luh   WAWR•FEHR), a form of war in which soldiers make surprise attacks on the enemy and then go back into hiding. Garibaldi's army landed on Italy's mainland and gained control over more territory. People in the south then voted to join a united Italy.

In 1861 the Kingdom of Italy was set up as a constitutional monarchy under Victor Emmanuel. Two areas remained outside Italy. One was Rome, which was under the pope's control. The other was an area of northeast Italy, which remained Austrian. By 1870, wars had brought both areas into the new Italian kingdom, and the unity of the country was complete.

Bismarck Unites Germany Nationalism was also strong in the German states. Many of these states' rulers were not willing to give up their political power though. Nationalists, however, had strong support from the northern German state of Prussia, which had grown powerful and prosperous. Prussia was ruled by William I, who dreamed of uniting all German states under his leadership. In 1862 he appointed **Otto von Bismarck** (AHT•oh   fawn   BIHZ•MAHRK) as his prime minister.

Bismarck was a deeply conservative Junker (YUNG•kuhr), or wealthy landowner. He vowed to govern Prussia by "blood and iron" rather than by votes and speeches. Bismarck quickly raised money and strengthened the army. He used the army to easily defeat neighboring Denmark and Austria in two short wars.

As Bismarck hoped, these successes helped him unite all of northern Germany in Prussia's new empire. The mostly Catholic southern German states feared the power of Protestant Prussia. They feared France more, however. In 1870 Bismarck fought a war with France, known as the Franco-Prussian War.

This conflict was a great success for Prussia and a disaster for France. Prussia gained two of France's border territories. More importantly, the southern German states agreed to unite with Prussia. On January 18, 1871, William was proclaimed **kaiser** (KY•zuhr), or emperor, of a united Germany.

✓ **Reading Check** **Explain** What role did King Victor Emmanuel play in the unification of Italy?

Nationalism in Latin America

Main Idea In the early 1800s, the people of Latin America rebelled and gained their independence.

Reading Focus Do you want to be independent? What does that word mean to you? Read to learn what happened when people in Latin America fought for their independence.

While nationalism advanced in Europe, the European-ruled colonies of Latin America were moving toward independence. The American and French Revolutions stirred the people of Latin America to action. Everywhere, colonists tried to take charge of their own affairs.

New Nations in Latin America

The first successful revolt against European rule took place in Haiti, an island territory in the Caribbean Sea. There, François-Dominique Toussaint-Louverture led enslaved Africans in a revolt that eventually threw off French rule in 1804.

In Spanish and Portuguese Latin America, the fight for freedom increased in the next decade. In Mexico, two Catholic priests, Miguel Hidalgo and José María Morelos, urged poorer Mexicans to fight for freedom. Both men were defeated and executed.

Despite many battles, Mexicans did not gain their independence until 1821. After a short period of rule under an emperor, Mexico became a republic in 1823. Soon after, many people in Central America broke free from Mexican rule and began to form their own countries.

In the northern part of South America, **Simón Bolívar** (see•MAWN boh•LEE•VAHR), a wealthy military leader, led the fight for freedom. Between 1819 and 1825, forces under Bolívar's command defeated the Spanish and won independence for the present-day countries of Venezuela, Colombia, Panama, Ecuador, and Bolivia.

While Bolívar fought for freedom in the north, a soldier named José de San Martín (hoh•SAY day SAN•mahr•TEEN) was fighting for freedom in the south. In 1817 San Martín led his army from Argentina across the Andes mountain ranges and into Chile, taking the Spanish forces by surprise. A few years later, San Martín and Bolívar jointly defeated the Spanish in the Pacific coastal country of Peru.

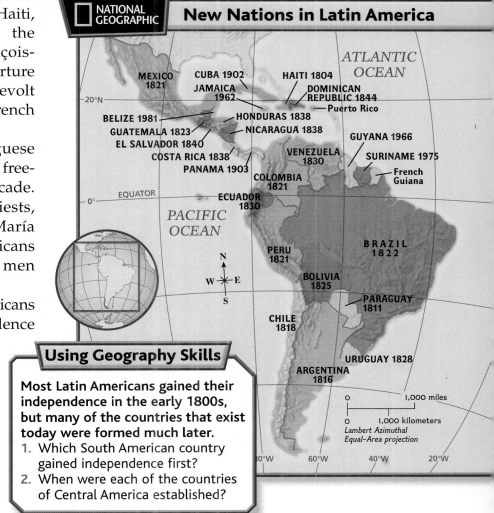

NATIONAL GEOGRAPHIC

New Nations in Latin America

ATLANTIC OCEAN

MEXICO 1821
CUBA 1902
JAMAICA 1962
HAITI 1804
DOMINICAN REPUBLIC 1844
Puerto Rico
BELIZE 1981
HONDURAS 1838
GUATEMALA 1823
NICARAGUA 1838
EL SALVADOR 1840
GUYANA 1966
COSTA RICA 1838
VENEZUELA 1830
SURINAME 1975
PANAMA 1903
French Guiana
COLOMBIA 1821
ECUADOR 1830
PACIFIC OCEAN
PERU 1821
BRAZIL 1822
BOLIVIA 1825
PARAGUAY 1811
CHILE 1818
URUGUAY 1828
ARGENTINA 1816

20°N
EQUATOR 0°

N W E S

0   1,000 miles
0   1,000 kilometers
Lambert Azimuthal Equal-Area projection

80°W   60°W   40°W   20°W

Using Geography Skills

Most Latin Americans gained their independence in the early 1800s, but many of the countries that exist today were formed much later.
1. Which South American country gained independence first?
2. When were each of the countries of Central America established?

Biography

SIMÓN BOLÍVAR
1783–1830

Simón Bolívar was born July 24, 1783, in Venezuela. Although many people who lived in the area were poor, the Bolívars were rich and owned land. By age nine Simón's parents had died. His uncle hired tutors for him, but the young boy became bored and began to misbehave. When Bolívar was 11 years old, a man named Simón Rodríguez became his teacher and lifelong friend. Rodríguez introduced Bolívar to the ideas of European thinkers who believed in equality and freedom.

The two Simóns stayed together for many years, until Rodríguez left Venezuela in 1797. When Bolívar was 16, he visited his teacher and the two traveled across Europe. When he was 18, Bolívar married a young Spanish woman named María Teresa, and they moved back to Venezuela. She died eight months later, and Bolívar never married again.

Bolívar went to Paris and watched as Napoleon Bonaparte was crowned emperor. As Bolívar saw thousands cheering Napoleon, he realized he could earn the respect of the Venezuelan people if he freed them from Spain's harsh government. Bolívar traveled to Rome and on top of Monte Sacro, he pledged:

> "I swear before you, I swear before the god of my fathers . . . that I shall not rest until I have broken the chains that oppress us [keep us down]."

He led many battles throughout South America before his goal to liberate his homeland came true. He became known among them as "El Libertador," which means "The Liberator."

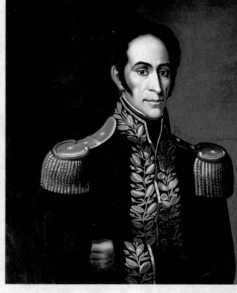

▲ Simón Bolívar

"We have already seen the light, and it is not our desire to be thrust back into darkness."
—Simón Bolívar, The Jamaica Letter

▲ Statue of Simón Bolívar in Caracas, Venezuela

Then and Now

Identify other leaders who freed a territory or group of people. Why did they get involved?

What Problems Did Latin America Face?

By the end of the 1820s, most of Spain's colonies in Latin America had won their independence. During the 1820s, Brazil also broke away from Portugal without bloodshed. Brazil was a monarchy before becoming a republic in 1889.

After Latin America won its independence, the United States made it known that it would protect the region. In 1823, United States president James Monroe warned the European powers not to interfere in the countries of Latin America. His statement, called the Monroe Doctrine, guided U.S. actions toward Latin America in the years ahead.

After gaining independence, most Latin Americans hoped their countries would become democratic and prosperous. These goals, however, were difficult to reach.

One major problem was frequent political conflict. Latin Americans quarreled over the role of religion in their society. Individual countries fought over boundary lines. Tensions developed between the rich and the poor.

At the same time, a series of strong leaders made it difficult for democracy and prosperity to develop. These were known as **caudillos** (kow•THEE•yohs). Caudillos were usually rich men, supported by the upper class. They often ruled as dictators. Some built roads, schools, and new cities. Many, however, favored the wealthy over the poor. Wealthy Latin Americans owned almost all of the land. The caudillos did nothing to help workers in the countryside, who remained landless and struggled to make a living. The wide divide between rich and poor is still a major problem in parts of Latin America today.

Reading Check **Identify** Who were the caudillos?

Nationalism in the U.S.

Main Idea Nationalism in the United States led the country to expand its borders, but differences between the North and South led to a bloody civil war.

Reading Focus Do you feel a spirit of nationalism? How do you express it? Find out how Americans of an earlier time expressed their nationalism.

Nationalism also helped shape the United States during the 1800s and led to a steady growth in the size of the country. Many Americans believed expansion would make the young country richer and more powerful. However, nationalism also led to conflicting ideas about the nation's future.

The United States Expands West During the 1800s, the United States gradually expanded its borders westward. In 1803 the country doubled in size by buying the Louisiana Territory from France. During the first 50 years of the 1800s, the United States also gained Florida from Spain and the Oregon Territory from Britain. Many

▲ During the mid-1800s, many American settlers headed west to lands in the Oregon Territory. *What was Manifest Destiny?*

Americans came to believe in the "Manifest Destiny" of the United States, or the idea that the United States should stretch from the Atlantic Ocean to the Pacific Ocean.

In 1845, the United States annexed Texas, which had previously declared independence from Mexico. This greatly angered Mexico. A dispute over the Texas-Mexico border caused more trouble. By the following year, Mexico and the United States were at war. The United States defeated Mexico. In 1848 the peace treaty ending the war gave the United States the area that today includes California and several other western states.

Westward expansion brought new opportunities to settlers. They set up communities and built states in the new lands. The expansion also brought suffering—loss of land, culture, and often life—to Native Americans who had lived in the American West for centuries.

The American Civil War As the United States expanded westward, different ways of life developed in the Northern and Southern states. By the mid-1800s, these differences had begun to threaten national unity. The South was rural. Its agricultural economy depended on raising cotton.

Growth of the United States

◀ African American soldiers prepare for battle during the Civil War

▲ In the United States, slavery in the South helped cause the American Civil War. *What crop in the South depended on the use of enslaved workers?*

▲ Female suffragists marching for the right to vote

◀ Immigrants arriving in the United States at Ellis Island

Cotton growing, in turn, depended on millions of enslaved African American workers. On the other hand, the North was building more and more industries. People, including new immigrants, or arrivals from overseas, were flocking to the growing cities. Some Northerners believed in **abolitionism** (A•buh•LIH•shuhn•IH•zuhm), a movement to end slavery.

The disagreement over slavery grew more and more heated. By 1860, the United States consisted of both free, or non-slave, states and slave states. That year, Abraham Lincoln, an opponent of slavery, was elected president. Fearing that Lincoln would try to end slavery, 11 states by early 1861 had seceded, or left, the United States. They formed a new nation: the Confederate States of America. Fighting erupted in April, and the American Civil War began.

The North had a much larger population and more factories and railroads than the South. In spite of this huge advantage, the Confederate States won most of the early battles. Gradually, however, the North's many resources gave it the upper hand. The war ended after four years of bloody fighting. More than 600,000 Americans died.

The war had other effects as well. The North's victory united the country. Millions

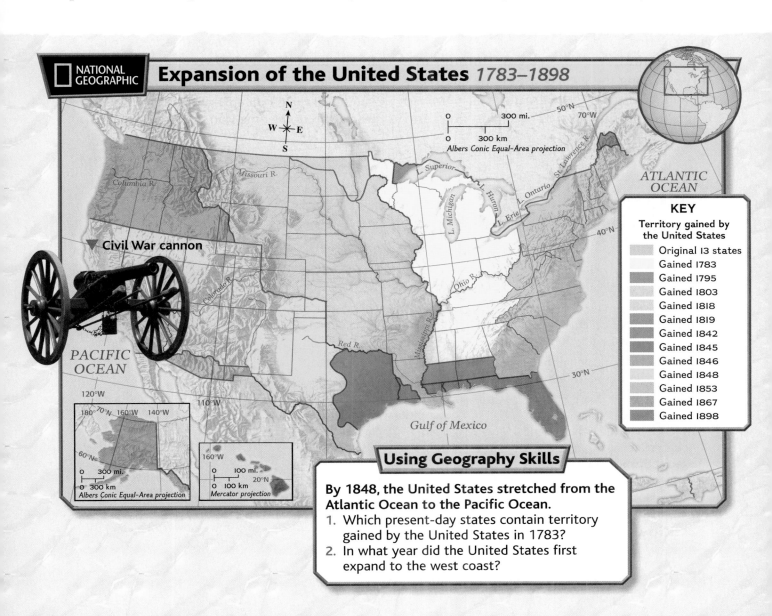

NATIONAL GEOGRAPHIC

Expansion of the United States *1783–1898*

Civil War cannon

KEY

Territory gained by the United States

- Original 13 states
- Gained 1783
- Gained 1795
- Gained 1803
- Gained 1818
- Gained 1819
- Gained 1842
- Gained 1845
- Gained 1846
- Gained 1848
- Gained 1853
- Gained 1867
- Gained 1898

Using Geography Skills

By 1848, the United States stretched from the Atlantic Ocean to the Pacific Ocean.

1. Which present-day states contain territory gained by the United States in 1783?
2. In what year did the United States first expand to the west coast?

of African Americans were freed from slavery. The federal government was strengthened. Also, new factories, railroads, and cities were built at an ever-increasing speed.

A New Society
As industry grew, so did the United States's population. Between 1870 and 1900, the number of Americans doubled.

Immigrants contributed greatly to this growth. Before the Civil War, most immigrants came from northern Europe, mainly the British Isles, Germany, and Scandinavia. Then, during the late 1800s, immigration from southern and eastern Europe increased. After landing at Ellis Island in New York, most of these immigrants headed to the cities to find work.

Communities of Asian immigrants thrived along the west coast by the late 1800s as well. Chinese immigrants first came to California in the late 1840s to find gold and stayed to work in the mines and build railroads. By 1900, immigrants from Japan also arrived in the country.

Political Rights
During the 1800s, the United States, like countries in Europe, became more democratic. The election of Andrew Jackson as U.S. president in 1828 was seen as a victory for the "common people." Jackson's election was made possible by the spread of voting rights to almost all adult white males.

As the 1800s moved forward, women also began to demand political equality. Women suffragists fought hard for women's right to vote. Finally, in 1920, the Nineteenth Amendment to the Constitution was ratified, or approved. This guaranteed women in all states the right to vote.

✔ Reading Check **Contrast** How were the South and the North different during the period leading up to the American Civil War?

History Online

Study Central™ Need help with the material in this section? Visit jat.glencoe.com

Section 4 Review

Review the Main Ideas
- The idea of nationalism and the need for reform led to uprisings, wars, and political changes in Europe in the mid-1800s.
- Leaders like Garibaldi in Italy and Bismarck in Germany helped unite their respective countries.
- Colonies in Central and South America became independent countries following revolts against Spanish rule.
- The United States expanded to the Pacific coast, and then fought a terrible civil war over the issue of slavery.

What Did You Learn?
1. How did Bismarck unite the German states?
2. What were caudillos and how did they affect society in Latin America?

Critical Thinking
3. **Summarize** Draw a diagram like the one below. Fill in the outer ovals with territories gained by the United States during the 1800s.

United States Expansion

4. **Describe** Describe the reform attempted in Russia in the 1800s, why it occurred, and whether it was a success.
5. **Citizenship** Which of the countries discussed in the chapter became more democratic in the 1800s?
6. **Compare and Contrast** Compare the Northern and Southern states before the Civil War.
7. **Expository Writing** In a short essay, define *nationalism* and tell whether you think it is still a powerful idea in the world today.

Section 1 The French Revolution and Napoleon

Vocabulary
estates
bourgeoisie
coup d'etat

Focusing on the Main Ideas

- The French Revolution began because the people were treated unfairly and because their country had serious economic problems. *(page 715)*
- French radicals used terror to enforce their reforms. *(page 717)*
- Napoleon Bonaparte used his military success to take control of the French government. *(page 719)*
- Through military conquests, Napoleon built a huge, but short-lived, empire in Europe. *(page 720)*

Section 2 The Industrial Revolution

Vocabulary
industrialism
textile
capital
partnership
corporation

Focusing on the Main Ideas

- The Industrial Revolution began in Great Britain because of the enclosure movement, Britain's natural resources, and new British inventions. *(page 725)*
- The Industrial Revolution spread beyond Great Britain's shores to Europe and the United States. *(page 729)*

Section 3 Society and Industry

Vocabulary
urbanization
liberalism
socialism
labor union

Focusing on the Main Ideas

- The Industrial Revolution caused cities to grow bigger and changed how people lived and worked. *(page 732)*
- The Industrial Revolution led to new ideas about politics, society, and the economy. *(page 734)*
- Artists, writers, and composers reflected the changes that industrialism brought to society. *(page 736)*
- Important scientific discoveries during the Industrial Revolution changed the way people lived and how they understood the world. *(page 738)*

Section 4 Nationalism and Nation-States

Vocabulary
kaiser
caudillo
abolitionism

Focusing on the Main Ideas

- Two powerful ideas, nationalism and reform, helped reshape Europe politically during the mid-1800s. *(page 745)*
- In the mid-1800s, two new countries, Italy and Germany, were created. *(page 747)*
- In the early 1800s, the people of Latin America rebelled and gained their independence. *(page 749)*
- Nationalism in the United States led the country to expand its borders, but differences between the North and South led to a bloody civil war. *(page 751)*

Review Vocabulary

Match the word in the first column with its definition in the second column.

___ 1. capital   **a.** way of life based on machinery and factories

___ 2. labor union   **b.** money invested in businesses

___ 3. coup d'etat   **c.** association of united workers

___ 4. bourgeoisie   **d.** German emperor

___ 5. kaiser   **e.** sudden government takeover

___ 6. urbanization   **f.** French middle class

___ 7. industrialism   **g.** movement from rural areas to cities

Review Main Ideas

Section 1 • The French Revolution and Napoleon

8. What caused the unrest among the French people that led to revolution?

9. What was the result of Napoleon Bonaparte's military successes?

Section 2 • The Industrial Revolution

10. In which country did the Industrial Revolution begin?

11. Which other areas were affected by the Industrial Revolution?

Section 3 • Society and Industry

12. How was industrialism reflected by artists, writers, and composers?

13. What was the result of important scientific discoveries during this time period?

Section 4 • Nationalism and Nation-States

14. Identify two ideas that reshaped Europe during the mid-1800s.

15. How did nationalism affect Italy and Germany?

Critical Thinking

16. **Explain** Why did French leaders decide to execute Robespierre?

17. **Cause and Effect** What new ideas resulted from the factory system?

18. **Contrast** How were the ideas of romanticism different from those of the Enlightenment?

Review Reading Skill — Understanding Concepts — Reading for Meaning

19. Read the following sentences from pages 718–719. Based on the information, write a paragraph defining what Robespierre might have meant when he called for a "Republic of Virtue."

During this time, Robespierre tried to create a "Republic of Virtue." He thought the revolution should inspire people to be good citizens. Under Robespierre's lead, the Committee opened new schools, had new farming skills taught to the peasants, and worked to keep prices under control.

To review this skill, see pages 712–713.

Geography Skills

Study the map below and answer the following questions.

20. **Region** What resources gave England an advantage in developing industries?

21. **Location** Which two industrial centers are located near both coal and iron ore fields?

22. **Analyze** Why do you think there were no railroads in northern Scotland and Ireland?

NATIONAL GEOGRAPHIC

Industrialization in Britain

KEY
- Iron ore fields
- Coal fields
- Railways, 1850
- □ Industrial centers

SCOTLAND

Glasgow

North Sea

Belfast

IRELAND

Dublin

Liverpool   Leeds
Manchester

WALES

Birmingham

ENGLAND   London

ATLANTIC OCEAN

0   100 mi.
0   100 km
Chamberlain Trimetric projection

Read to Write

23. **Expository Writing** Write an essay comparing the events and results of the rules of Bismarck and Napoleon III (Louis Napoleon). What personal characteristics did each man have that contributed to his accomplishments?

24. **Using Your FOLDABLES** Work in a small group to create a poster or other visual aid using the information written on one of your foldable tabs. For example, your group may choose to reflect Society and Industry by showing pieces of art and literature that resulted from each social movement.

Using Technology

25. **Research** Unity is still a goal of many Europeans. Use the Internet and your local library to research efforts to unify Europe. Share your findings with the class.

Linking Past and Present

26. **Compare** How are the Declaration of the Rights of Man and the Citizen and the U.S. Constitution similar?

Primary Source Analyze

Captain Kincaid was a member of the Duke of Wellington's Rifle Brigade. He described this moment near the end of the battle at Waterloo.

"Presently a cheer which we knew to be British commenced far to the right, and made everyone prick up his ears; it was Lord Wellington's long-wished-for orders to advance.... Lord Wellington galloped up to us at the instant, and our men began to cheer him; but he called out, 'No cheering, my lads, but forward, and complete our victory!'"

—Captain J. Kincaid, "Waterloo, 18 June 1815: The Finale"

DBQ Document-Based Questions

27. Why did Wellington tell the soldiers not to cheer for him?

28. Why do you think the soldiers were eagerly waiting for the orders to advance?

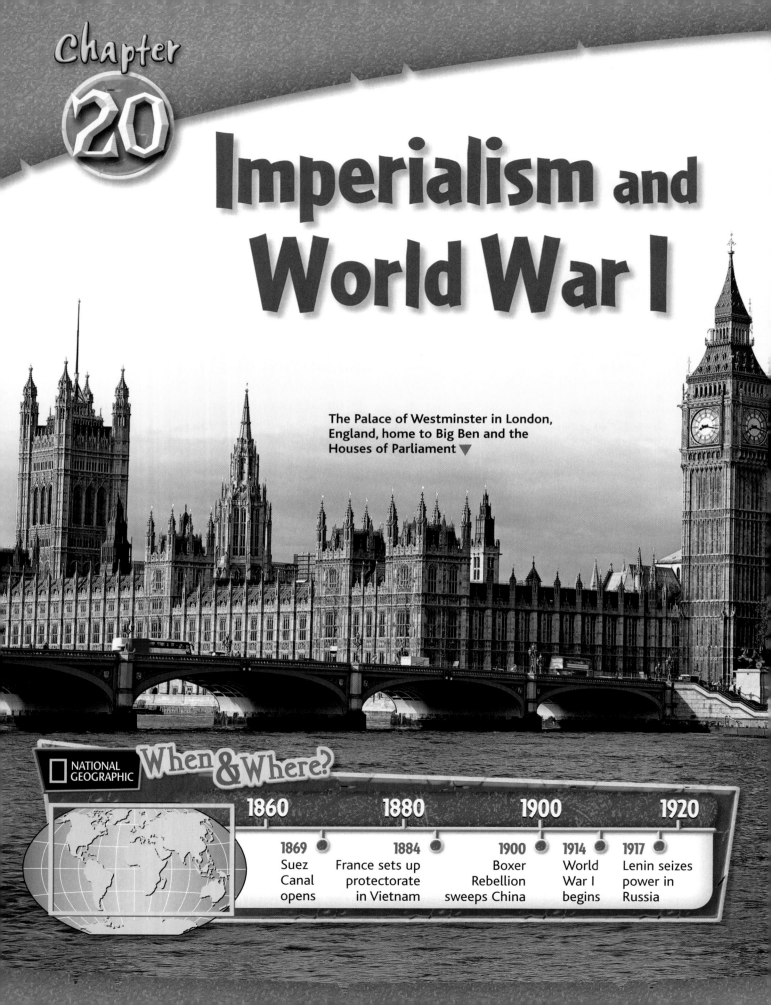

Chapter 20

Imperialism and World War I

The Palace of Westminster in London, England, home to Big Ben and the Houses of Parliament ▼

NATIONAL GEOGRAPHIC When & Where?

1860	1880	1900	1920
1869 Suez Canal opens	**1884** France sets up protectorate in Vietnam	**1900** Boxer Rebellion sweeps China	**1914** World War I begins **1917** Lenin seizes power in Russia

Chapter Preview

The early 1900s was a period of conflict in much of the world. Read this chapter to find out how a war in Europe became a world war that affected millions of people.

 View the Chapter 20 video in the *World History: Journey Across Time* Video Program.

History Online
Chapter Overview Visit jat.glencoe.com **for a preview of Chapter 20.**

The New Imperialism

By 1900, many industrial nations, including Britain, France, Germany, Spain, and the United States, had expanded their trade and built empires in different parts of the world.

Nationalism in China and Japan

During the 1800s, Chinese and Japanese societies were influenced by Europeans and Americans.

World War I Begins

Growing tension between European powers eventually led to World War I.

World War I Changes the World

World War I led to the fall of empires, a revolution in Russia, and the creation of new nations and governments.

Identifying *Make this foldable to help you identify and learn key terms.*

Step 1 *Stack four sheets of paper, one on top of the other. On the top sheet of paper, draw a large circle.*

Step 2 *With the papers still stacked, cut out all four circles at the same time.*

Step 3 *Staple the paper circles together at one point around the edge.*

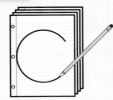

Staple here.

This makes a circular booklet.

Step 4 *Label the front circle as shown and take notes on the pages that open to the right.*

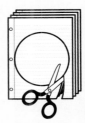

Chapter 20 Key Terms

Reading and Writing *As you read the chapter, write the terms from* Locating Places, Meeting People, *and* Building Your Vocabulary *in your foldable. Write a definition for each term. Then turn your foldable over (upside down) to write a short sentence using each term.*

Reading Social Studies

Reading Skill
Prioritizing

1 Learn It!

What's Important?

As you study history, it may seem impossible to keep all the facts in your head. Once you understand that the author does not expect you to remember every word of the text, you can begin to focus on what is truly important or prioritize. Prioritize means "to list in order of importance." Prioritizing will help you read more critically and do better on tests.

Read the sentences below.

> **World War I, also called the Great War, was different from any earlier war. Both sides developed new, more powerful weapons to help them break through enemy lines.** Machine guns fired bullets one after the other at a rapid speed. Huge artillery guns fired shells more than 75 miles (120 km). Poison gases were used for the first time, and tanks and flamethrowers were introduced.

The words in blue show the ideas that the author intended to be most important.

The other sentences act as supporting details.

Reading Tip

Use the two-column note-taking method when you read. Record the most important points in one column and the supporting ideas in the other column.

2 Practice It!

Read this paragraph from Section 4, page 791. Discuss the questions that follow with a learning partner to practice prioritizing.

In January 1919, peace talks began at Versailles (vuhr•SY) outside Paris. The principal figures at the talks were U.S. president Woodrow Wilson, British prime minister David Lloyd George, French premier Georges Clemenceau, and Italian prime minister Vittorio Orlando.

Read to Write · · · · · · ·

Choose any three topics from Chapter 20 with interesting headings. Write a "study sheet" for each topic, noting the most important fact, sentence, or concept. Then explain why your statement reflects the most important part of the topic.

1. Is it important to remember the date of the peace talks?
2. Is it important to remember where the peace talks occurred?
3. Is it important to remember the principal figures at the talks?
4. If you had to remember only one of the principal figures, who would it be?
5. Is it important to read further to find out more about the peace talks?

3 Apply It!

Read the first page of Section 2 on page 772. What do you think is the most important idea on that page? Support your answer.

Section 1

The New Imperialism

Get Ready to Read!

What's the Connection?
In past chapters, you learned how the Industrial Revolution changed the lives of Europeans. By the 1800s, industry had also changed Europe's relationship with the world.

Focusing on the Main Ideas
- European nations built empires to help their economy and to spread their ideas. *(page 763)*

- Control of India passed from the East India Company to the British. *(page 764)*

- European nations ruled almost all of Africa by 1914. *(page 766)*

- The United States became an imperial nation after defeating Spain and taking control of the Philippines and Puerto Rico. *(page 769)*

Locating Places
Singapore (SIHNG•uh•POHR)
Cuba (KYOO•buh)
Philippines (FIH•luh•PEENZ)
Panama (PA•nuh•MAH)

Meeting People
Robert Clive
Leopold II
William McKinley

Building Your Vocabulary
imperialism
   (ihm•PIHR•ee•uh•LIH•zuhm)
colony
protectorate
   (pruh•TEHK•tuh•ruht)
sphere of influence
sepoy (SEE•POY)

Reading Strategy
Organizing Information Use a chart like the one below to show the colonies that each imperialist nation controlled.

Imperialist Nation	Colonies

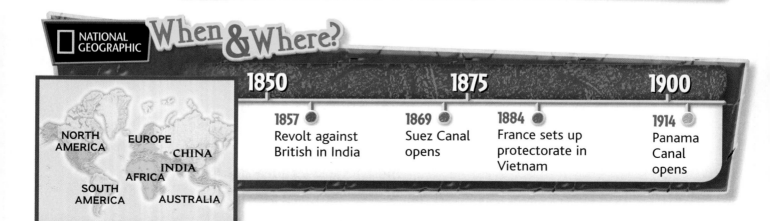

NATIONAL GEOGRAPHIC **When & Where?**

NORTH AMERICA EUROPE CHINA INDIA AFRICA SOUTH AMERICA AUSTRALIA

1850　　　　　　　**1875**　　　　　　　**1900**

1857 Revolt against British in India

1869 Suez Canal opens

1884 France sets up protectorate in Vietnam

1914 Panama Canal opens

The Rise of Imperialism

Main Idea European nations built empires to help their economy and to spread their ideas.

Reading Focus A store owner with too many goods on the shelves must find new customers or he or she will lose money. Read on to find out how Europeans solved a similar problem on a grander scale.

▲ **French military officers with peasants in the Tonkin region of Vietnam**

As nationalism spread, the industrial countries of Europe looked abroad for raw materials and new markets. In the 1800s, they rushed to take over lands in Asia and Africa where these markets and goods were found. As a result, the world entered the Age of Imperialism. **Imperialism** (ihm•PIHR•ee•uh•LIH•zuhm) is a type of relationship between countries in which one nation directly or indirectly controls the government or the economy of another nation.

Building Empires

Europeans wanted new lands for more than just trade and profit. They believed that ruling foreign peoples would add to a country's power. They also believed that imposing their ideas and practices on others would improve the lives of foreign peoples.

Imperial nations ruled other people in many different ways. Sometimes they created a **colony,** which they ruled directly. Sometimes they set up a **protectorate** (pruh•TEHK•tuh•ruht). There the local people had their own government, but the imperial government controlled the military and could tell the local rulers what to do. In other cases they set up a **sphere of influence,** a region where only one imperial power had the right to invest or to trade.

The First Empires: Southeast Asia

As early as the 1500s, Europeans were drawn to Southeast Asia for its spices. They took control of many island groups, including the Philippines and the East Indies. During the 1800s, Europeans began taking over Southeast Asia's mainland. There they grew crops, such as coffee and tea. They also began to use the area's raw materials, such as petroleum, rubber, and tin.

In 1819 a British official named Thomas Stamford Raffles founded a colony on a small island at the tip of the Malay Peninsula. Known as **Singapore** (SIHNG•uh•POHR), or "the city of the lion," it became an important port for ships going to and from China.

The French followed the British to mainland Southeast Asia. Both countries soon competed for territory. The British took control of the rest of the Malay Peninsula and Burma to the north. Meanwhile, French Catholic missionaries entered nearby Vietnam. Fearing the British would move into Vietnam, the French sent in troops, and in 1884 Vietnam became a French protectorate. In all of Southeast Asia, only Siam—today known as Thailand—kept its freedom.

Reading Check **Contrast** What is the difference between a colony and a protectorate?

Britain's Empire in India

Main Idea Control of India passed from the East India Company to the British.

Reading Focus Has a new business ever moved into your neighborhood? What things did it make better or worse? As you read, ask how Britain made things better and worse in India.

Earlier you learned that the Moguls ruled India in the early 1600s. As time went on, their power weakened. Rulers spent too much money on wars and palaces, and Indian people began to resent this waste. At the same time, Hindus did not like the Moguls trying to make them Muslims. Rising discontent made it easy for Europeans to take over India.

What Was the East India Company? In 1600 British traders from the East India Company arrived in India. Over the next 50 years, they built a string of trading forts along India's coasts. The East India Company set up an army and supported local Indian rulers who agreed to work with them. The company's army also fought the French, Britain's main rival in India.

One of the most energetic East India Company officials was **Robert Clive.** He led British and Indian soldiers against French forts. By 1757, Clive and his army had pushed the French out of most of India. The French were left with only one fort and a few coastal holdings.

During the next 100 years, Britain's East India Company took over much of India and

Imperialism in Asia

▲ Troops traveling through India

▲ This photo shows an upper-class Indian family during the time of British rule.

These native workers are shown on a plantation in Ceylon. ▶

What year did British traders arrive in India?

grew wealthy. It brought many European ideas and practices to the Indian people. Many Indians, however, felt that the British were trying to change their culture.

In 1857 **sepoys** (SEE•POYZ), or Indian soldiers in the company's army, rebelled against their British officers. The revolt then spread rapidly across northern India. Britain quickly sent more soldiers to India and put down the rebellion. Afterward, there were bitter feelings between the British and the Indians.

British Rule in India Soon after the uprising, Britain took direct control of India from the company. A viceroy, an official standing in for Britain's Queen Victoria, arrived to head the Raj (RAHJ), as British India's government was now called. The viceroy's government both helped and hurt the Indian people.

The British brought order to India. The government was run well, and schools were founded. In addition, the British introduced railroads, the telegraph, and a postal service throughout India.

British rule, however, brought great hardships as well. Cheap British textiles flooded India and destroyed the local textile industry. The British also forced many farmers to grow cotton instead of food. Soon India did not produce enough food to feed its people. In the 1800s, millions of Indians died from starvation.

✓ **Reading Check** **Cause and Effect** Why did the Indians rebel against the British?

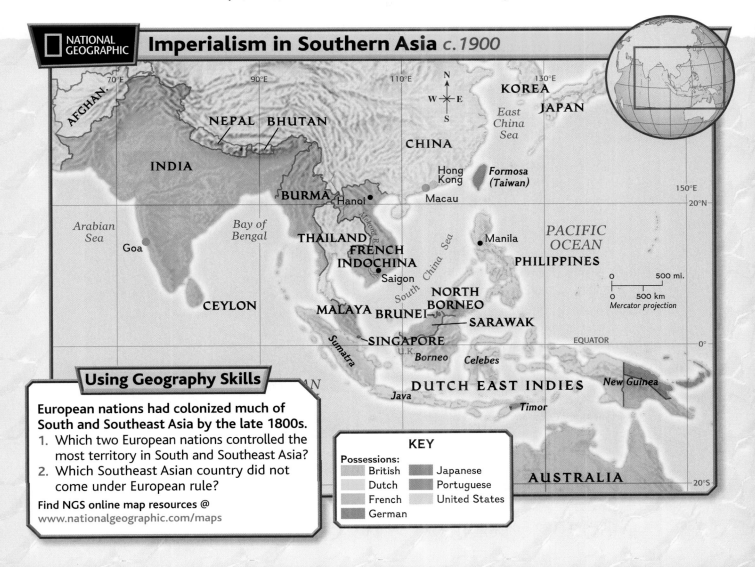

NATIONAL GEOGRAPHIC

Imperialism in Southern Asia c. 1900

KEY

Possessions:
- British
- Dutch
- French
- German
- Japanese
- Portuguese
- United States

Using Geography Skills

European nations had colonized much of South and Southeast Asia by the late 1800s.

1. Which two European nations controlled the most territory in South and Southeast Asia?
2. Which Southeast Asian country did not come under European rule?

Find NGS online map resources @
www.nationalgeographic.com/maps

Europe Divides Africa

Main Idea European nations ruled almost all of Africa by 1914.

Reading Focus Have you ever bought something just because everyone else had it? Read to learn why Europeans competed to take over Africa.

Africa was the last populated continent to be colonized by Europeans. In previous chapters, you learned that Europeans in the 1500s built trading stations along Africa's west coast. In the 1800s, European missionaries and explorers finally opened up Africa's inland areas to European control.

The Struggle for North Africa

The first part of Africa to be conquered by Europe was also the closest. In the early 1800s, Europeans crossed the Mediterranean and took control of North Africa. French soldiers seized control of the territories that are today the countries of Algeria and Tunisia. The last territory France claimed in North Africa was Morocco, which it divided with Spain in 1904.

At the eastern end of North Africa, European businesses began operating in Egypt. In 1869 they opened the Suez Canal. Built by Egyptian workers and paid for with French funds, it linked the Mediterranean and Red Seas. The Suez Canal provided a shorter water route to India and East Asia. In 1875 the British took control of the Suez Canal. After Egyptians rebelled, the British made Egypt a protectorate.

By 1900, only Tripoli, today known as Libya, remained free from European control. Then, in 1911, Italy defeated the Ottoman empire in a brief war and was given control of Tripoli.

Primary Source

"Standard Treaty"

The British Royal Niger Company presented this fill-in-the-blank treaty to many African leaders.

"We, the undersigned Chiefs of _____, with the view to the bettering of the condition of our country and people, do this day cede [give] to the Royal Niger Company, for ever, the whole of our territory extending from _____. . . .

The said Royal Niger Company agree to pay native owners of land a reasonable amount for any portion they may require.

The said Royal Niger Company bind themselves to protect the said Chiefs from the attacks of any neighboring aggressive tribes."

—Royal Niger Company, "Standard Treaty"

▼ British colonists in Nigeria

DBQ Document-Based Questions

What does the Royal Niger Company offer to the Africans in exchange for their land?

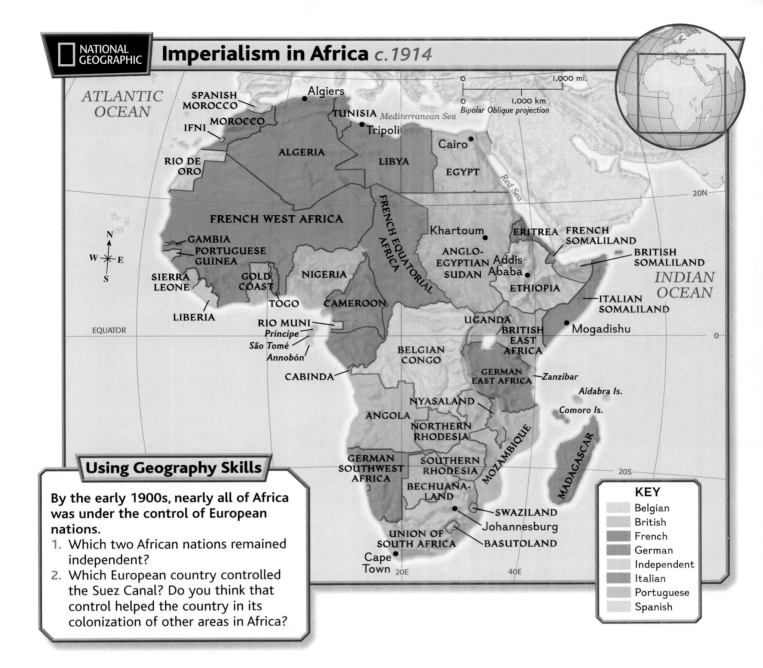

Imperialism in Africa c.1914

NATIONAL GEOGRAPHIC

ATLANTIC OCEAN

SPANISH MOROCCO
MOROCCO
IFNI
RIO DE ORO

Algiers
TUNISIA
Mediterranean Sea
Tripoli

1,000 mi.
1,000 km
Bipolar Oblique projection

ALGERIA
LIBYA

Cairo
EGYPT

Red Sea

20N

FRENCH WEST AFRICA

FRENCH EQUATORIAL AFRICA

Khartoum

ANGLO-EGYPTIAN SUDAN

Addis Ababa

ERITREA FRENCH SOMALILAND
BRITISH SOMALILAND

GAMBIA
PORTUGUESE GUINEA
SIERRA LEONE
LIBERIA

GOLD COAST
TOGO

NIGERIA
CAMEROON

ETHIOPIA

ITALIAN SOMALILAND

INDIAN OCEAN

N
W—E
S

EQUATOR

RIO MUNI
Príncipe
São Tomé
Annobón

CABINDA

BELGIAN CONGO

UGANDA
BRITISH EAST AFRICA

Mogadishu

0

ANGOLA

NYASALAND
NORTHERN RHODESIA

GERMAN EAST AFRICA

Zanzibar
Aldabra Is.
Comoro Is.

MOZAMBIQUE

MADAGASCAR

20S

GERMAN SOUTHWEST AFRICA

SOUTHERN RHODESIA
BECHUANA-LAND

SWAZILAND
Johannesburg
BASUTOLAND

UNION OF SOUTH AFRICA
Cape Town

20E
40E

KEY
Belgian
British
French
German
Independent
Italian
Portuguese
Spanish

Using Geography Skills

By the early 1900s, nearly all of Africa was under the control of European nations.
1. Which two African nations remained independent?
2. Which European country controlled the Suez Canal? Do you think that control helped the country in its colonization of other areas in Africa?

West and Central Africa During the 1800s, most of West and Central Africa also came under European rule. For hundreds of years, Europeans had been involved in trading enslaved West Africans. By the early 1800s, however, many Europeans had decided slavery was wrong and should be stopped. When Britain declared the slave trade illegal, other European nations soon followed its lead.

Europeans then sought out West Africa's gold, timber, hides, and palm oil. To control this trade, Britain, France, and Germany took over areas along Africa's Atlantic coast. Eventually, they moved inland. Meanwhile, the only place in West Africa where non-Europeans ruled was Liberia. There, African Americans freed from slavery had founded the republic of Liberia in 1847.

In Central Africa, European control began when King **Leopold II** of Belgium decided to conquer the region. The king spoke often about improving the lives of Central Africa's people. His main concern, however, was making money by selling rubber grown on plantations in the Congo.

▲ These African workers are shown on a rubber plantation in French Equatorial Africa. The pails are full of liquid rubber tapped from rubber trees. *Which European country was the first to conquer territory in Central Africa?*

In the 1600s, Dutch settlers arrived on Africa's southwestern coast. There they founded the port of Cape Town. The Dutch settlers became known as Afrikaners or Boers. In the early 1800s, Britain seized the Dutch territory and renamed it Cape Colony. The Boers resented British rule. So they moved inland and settled areas that they named the Orange Free State and the Transvaal.

As the Boers moved into these areas, they fought African groups that were already living there. One group known as the Zulu had created a large empire in the 1800s. The Zulu often fought with the Boers. By the late 1800s, the Zulu were also fighting the British, who eventually destroyed the Zulu Empire.

Leopold ordered his soldiers to force Africans to collect rubber for him. Anyone who resisted was shot. After missionaries and other Europeans protested, however, the king turned over the Congo to Belgium's government. The government did away with forced labor.

Leopold's move into the Congo spurred other European powers into action. Over the next few years, they divided the rest of the African continent among themselves. By 1914, Liberia and Ethiopia were the only independent African countries.

What Was the Boer War?

The European race for the African continent led to a war in South Africa. This conflict became known as the Boer War. It was fought between the British and the Boers. How did this war begin?

Tensions grew between the British and Boers when British settlers discovered gold and diamonds in the Transvaal. Britain's Cecil Rhodes—Cape Colony's prime minister and the owner of several gold and diamond companies—decided to take the Transvaal from the Boers. War erupted in 1899 and ended with the Boers' defeat three years later.

In 1910 Britain united the Boer republics, the Cape Colony, and one other British colony into the Union of South Africa. This new country became self-governing within the British Empire. The Boers and British ran the government, keeping out South Africa's much larger nonwhite population.

Reading Check Identify What territories in Africa had rubber plantations?

The War of 1898

Main Idea The United States became an imperial nation after defeating Spain and taking control of the Philippines and Puerto Rico.

Reading Focus Did you know Puerto Rico is part of the United States? Read to learn how the United States built its early empire.

In the late 1800s, the United States joined European powers in the race for colonies. By that time, the United States had become an industrial nation. As its economic power rose, many Americans in business and government came to believe that their country needed raw materials and new markets overseas to keep the economy growing.

America Defeats Spain In its search for markets and raw materials, the United States looked to Latin America and islands in the Pacific. In the late 1800s, Spain still ruled the Caribbean islands of **Cuba** (KYOO•buh) and Puerto Rico. However, in 1895 Cuba rebelled against Spain.

American newspapers printed vivid stories of killing and cruelty in Cuba. As a result, U.S. president **William McKinley** sent the U.S. battleship *Maine* to protect Americans who lived and worked there. While anchored in the harbor of Havana, Cuba's capital, the ship exploded.

American newspapers blamed Spain and pressured the president to take action. In April 1898, McKinley asked Congress to declare war. Four months later, the United States had won the war. Spain lost much of its remaining empire. Cuba became a republic under American protection. Puerto Rico and the Pacific islands of Guam and the **Philippines** (FIH•luh•PEENZ) became American territories.

Panama Canal

The Panama Canal, completed in 1914, enables ships to pass from the Atlantic to the Pacific Ocean without traveling all the way around South America. The canal is made up of three main locks. These locks raise and lower ships from oceans to lakes and back again. The Gatun Lock, the largest in the canal, is pictured here. It contains three gates that hold ships in the water before they are raised or lowered to the next gate. Going through the Gatun Lock, a ship will be raised or lowered by over 85 feet. Passage through the 50 mile long canal takes 8 days!

How did the building of the canal affect trade in North and South America?

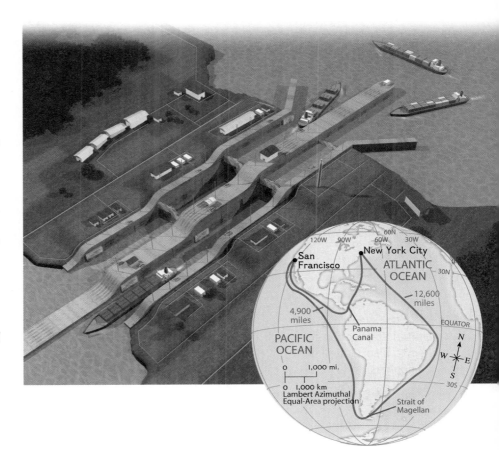

The Philippines, however, rejected American rule. Led by Emilio Aguinaldo (ah•MEEL•yoh AH•gee•NAHL•doh), the Filipinos rebelled against the U.S. and attacked American troops. By 1903, the Americans had crushed their uprising.

In 1898 Hawaii also came under American control. American settlers in Hawaii had overthrown the Hawaiian queen Liliuokalani (lih•LEE•uh•woh•kuh•LAH•nee) in 1893. However, it was not until after the War of 1898 that Congress approved American control of Hawaii.

Imperialism in Latin America

The War of 1898 had shown how important it was for the United States to be able to move its navy quickly between the east and west coasts. The trip around South America took a long time. It also slowed down trade between the coasts. As a result, U.S. president Theodore Roosevelt decided to build a canal across **Panama** (PA•nuh•MAH) to connect the Atlantic and Pacific Oceans. At that time, Panama was part of the country of Colombia.

Because Colombia was unwilling to give up its land, in 1903 Americans helped Panamanians rebel against Colombia. After winning independence, Panama signed a treaty allowing the United States to build the canal. The Panama Canal opened in 1914, greatly shortening the route between the Atlantic and Pacific Oceans.

 **Reading Check** **Analyze** How did control of the Philippines help the U.S. economy?

Section 1 Review

History Online

Study Central™ Need help with the material in this section? Visit jat.glencoe.com

Reading Summary

Review the **Main Ideas**

- Following the Industrial Revolution, European nations began building empires in Asia and Africa.

- The East India Company built Britain's empire in India.

- Nearly all of Africa came under foreign rule as the Europeans sought resources.

- After the War of 1898, the United States took control of Puerto Rico, Guam, the Philippines, and Hawaii.

What Did You Learn?

1. Besides economics, what reasons did European countries have for building empires?

2. What was the Boer War and why was it fought?

Critical Thinking

3. **Summarizing Information** Draw a diagram like the one below. Fill in the ovals with the names of areas under British control in the 1800s.

British Possessions

4. **Explain** Why were European nations interested in the countries of Southeast Asia?

5. **Compare and Contrast** How did British rule both help and hurt India?

6. **Analyze** Describe the actions taken by the United States in Panama in the early 1900s. Why was the United States interested in Panama?

7. **Descriptive Writing** Imagine you are a native of India in the late 1800s. Write a letter to a friend describing how you feel about British rule.

8. **Reading** **Prioritizing** Look back on the rise of imperialism. Determine what the most important reasons were for countries to take control of other nations.

Section 2

Nationalism in China and Japan

Get Ready to Read!

What's the Connection?
European imperialism changed the shape of the world in the late 1800s. However, Chinese nationalism and Japanese imperialism also made their mark on global affairs.

Focusing on the Main Ideas
- The arrival of Europeans greatly changed Chinese society. *(page 772)*

- Sun Yat-sen introduced ideas that helped cause the collapse of the Qing dynasty. *(page 774)*

- After Americans visited Japan, the Japanese reorganized their society and economy and began building an empire. *(page 777)*

Locating Places
Hong Kong (HAHNG   KAHNG)
Edo (EH•doh)
Port Arthur

Meeting People
Sun Yat-sen (SUN   YAHT•SEHN)
Yuan Shigai (yu•AHN   SHIHR•KY)
Oda Nobunaga
   (ohd•ah   noh•bun•ah•gah)
Tokugawa Ieyasu (toh•kug•ah•wah
   ee•eh•yahs•u)
Matthew Perry
Mutsuhito (MOOT•suh•HEE•toh)

Building Your Vocabulary
extraterritoriality (EHK•struh•TEHR•
   uh•TOHR•ee•A•luh•tee)
daimyo (DY•mee•OH)

Reading Strategy
Summarizing Information Use a chart like the one below to summarize the work of three Asian leaders.

Leader	Accomplishments

NATIONAL GEOGRAPHIC When & Where?

Beijing · Tokyo (Edo) · Shanghai · Hong Kong

1850   **1875**   **1900**

1842
The Opium War ends

1868
Meiji era begins in Japan

1900
Boxer Rebellion erupts in China

1905
Japan defeats Russia

China and the West

Main Idea The arrival of Europeans greatly changed Chinese society.

Reading Focus Have you ever played sports where everyone on the team gets a chance to play? Read to learn how the Open Door policy applied the same idea to China.

During the Age of Imperialism, China was ruled by the Qing dynasty. The Qing came to power in 1644. Qin rulers were descended from the Manchus, warriors who lived to the northeast of China. The Qing dynasty ruled China until 1911.

Under Qing rule, the Chinese followed their traditional way of life until the 1800s. Then came the Industrial Revolution in Europe. European businesses and merchants wanted to increase their trade with China.

What Was the Opium War?

By 1800, the Chinese already were trading with many Europeans, including the British. Chinese demand for British goods, however, was low. On the other hand, British demand for Chinese goods, especially tea, was high. As a result, the British had to trade more valuable goods, such as silver, for Chinese products.

The British then tried to get the Chinese to buy more cotton from India. When that failed, the British started selling opium to the Chinese. Opium is an addictive drug, so demand shot up in southern China. Silver began flowing into, rather than out of, British pockets.

The Chinese emperor warned the British to stop trading opium. When the British refused, war broke out in 1839. Chinese troops surrounded the port at Guangzhou. They demanded that traders surrender their opium. British warships responded by destroying forts on China's coasts and rivers. The Chinese emperor surrendered, and the Opium War ended in 1842.

After the war, the Chinese agreed to open five ports to British ships, limit taxes on British goods, and pay for the costs of the war. They also gave the British the island of **Hong Kong** (HAHNG KAHNG), which in time became one of the world's busiest ports. Europeans who lived in China were subject to their own laws but not Chinese laws. This legal practice is called **extraterritoriality** (EHK•struh•TEHR•uh•TOHR•ee•A•luh•tee).

▼ Britain's navy was important to the spread of British power around the world. Here a British warship attacks Chinese naval forces. *What did the British gain by their victory in the Opium War?*

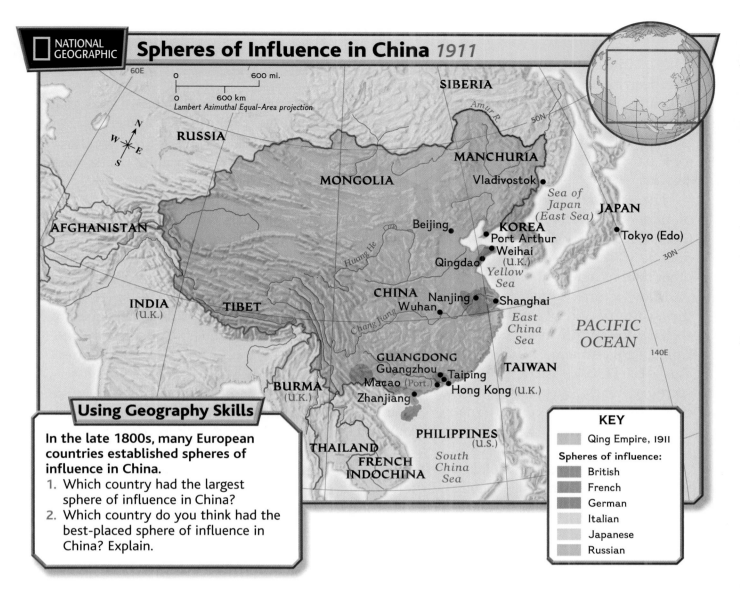

Spheres of Influence in China 1911

NATIONAL GEOGRAPHIC

Using Geography Skills

In the late 1800s, many European countries established spheres of influence in China.

1. Which country had the largest sphere of influence in China?
2. Which country do you think had the best-placed sphere of influence in China? Explain.

KEY

Qing Empire, 1911

Spheres of influence:
- British
- French
- German
- Italian
- Japanese
- Russian

China Tries to Reform During the 1850s, Chinese peasants were subject to high taxes and suffered from harsh weather. Crops failed, and many Chinese starved to death. As a result, peasant unrest spread across China.

In 1851 a religious leader named Hong Xiuquan (HAHNG ZHOO•GWAHN) organized a huge rebellion. He convinced many Chinese peasants that the time had come to overthrow the emperor and build a "Heavenly Kingdom" in China where life would be much better. The words Tai Ping mean "Heavenly Kingdom," so this rebellion became known as the Tai Ping Rebellion. It lasted for 13 years. The rebels captured many cities and controlled much of southern China. Eventually, Europeans helped the Chinese government destroy the rebel army. About 20 million people lost their lives in the Tai Ping Rebellion.

Reform-minded Chinese officials convinced the emperor that Western technology could help stop uprisings and foreign takeovers. As a result, the Chinese built railroads, weapons factories, and shipyards. Despite these changes, Europeans continued to chip away at the emperor's power.

European Spheres of Influence After the Tai Ping Rebellion, powerful leaders arose in China's heartland. They sold the right to trade, build, and mine in their area to European nations. In this way, different parts of China became spheres of influence under the control of Russia, Britain, France, and Germany. Even Japan, now a rising power, took part of China—the offshore island of Taiwan.

The United States did not claim a sphere of influence in China. Instead, it called for an Open Door policy under which China was open to trade with all countries. In 1899 the other nations agreed to this policy.

Many Chinese hated the foreigners in their country and began to organize secret societies to drive them out. Some members of China's government, including the Empress Tzu Hsi (TSOO SHEE), supported these secret societies. Europeans and Americans called them Boxers, because the name of their secret society meant "righteous and harmonious fists."

In 1900 the Boxers attacked foreigners and Chinese Christians in Beijing. Britain, France, Germany, Russia, Japan, and the U.S. sent in troops and crushed the Boxer Rebellion.

Reading Check **Describe** What did Great Britain gain from winning the Opium War?

▲ Members of the secret society known as the Boxers are rounded up after the failed rebellion. *Why did the Boxer Rebellion fail?*

The Revolution of 1911

Main Idea Sun Yat-sen introduced ideas that helped cause the collapse of the Qing dynasty.

Reading Focus If you could, how would you change the government? Read to find out what Chinese rebels did when they had the chance to make changes.

Chinese leaders tried to hold on to their power by making more changes. For example, they replaced China's civil service examination system with a European-style educational system. They also set up regional assemblies and a national assembly.

Middle-class Chinese considered these changes to be too little too late. They grew angry when they learned that the assemblies could not pass laws but only give advice to the emperor. Furthermore, peasants, artisans, and miners continued to resent the high taxes the government had imposed to pay its debts to foreign nations.

In 1905 a young medical doctor named **Sun Yat-sen** (SUN YAHT • SEHN) founded a movement of revolutionaries that later became known as the Nationalist Party. Its members believed the Qing dynasty could no longer rule the country. Unless China was united under a strong government, it would be at the mercy of other countries. Sun developed a three-stage plan to change China: (1) take over the government, (2) prepare the people for self-rule, and (3) establish a constitution and a democracy.

In 1911 Sun's followers staged an uprising, and the Qing dynasty fell. Sun's Nationalists did not have the military or political backing to set up a government, however. As a result, they turned to the head of the Chinese army, General **Yuan Shigai** (yu•AHN SHIHR•KY).

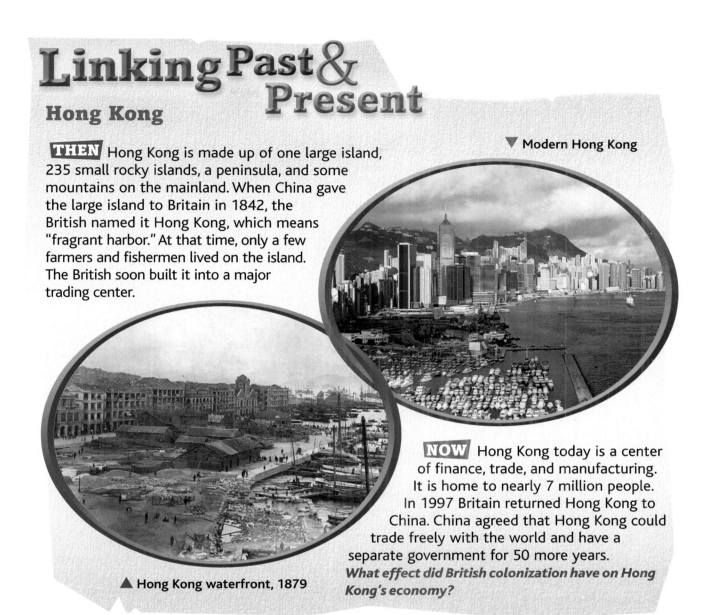

Linking Past & Present

Hong Kong

THEN Hong Kong is made up of one large island, 235 small rocky islands, a peninsula, and some mountains on the mainland. When China gave the large island to Britain in 1842, the British named it Hong Kong, which means "fragrant harbor." At that time, only a few farmers and fishermen lived on the island. The British soon built it into a major trading center.

▼ Modern Hong Kong

▲ Hong Kong waterfront, 1879

NOW Hong Kong today is a center of finance, trade, and manufacturing. It is home to nearly 7 million people. In 1997 Britain returned Hong Kong to China. China agreed that Hong Kong could trade freely with the world and have a separate government for 50 more years.
What effect did British colonization have on Hong Kong's economy?

General Yuan agreed to serve as president of a new Chinese republic. However, Yuan understood little about democracy and freedom. He ruled in a traditional way and refused to listen to those who called for democracy. When Yuan put an end to the new parliament, the Nationalist Party launched a revolt. The rebellion failed, and Sun Yat-sen fled to Japan.

Yuan died in 1916. One of his officers succeeded him, but the central government started to fall apart. Warlords, or local military leaders, seized power in the provinces and fought one another. Their soldiers caused widespread destruction.

Sun Yat-sen returned to China in 1917 and worked to rebuild the Nationalist Party. In the early 1920s, he decided to create a Nationalist army with the help of Chiang Kai-shek, a young Chinese officer. Sun died in 1925, but three years later Chiang led the army to victory and reunited China under a Nationalist government.

Reading Check **Identify** What was Sun Yat-sen's three-stage plan to change China?

Biography

SUN YAT-SEN
1866–1925

Sun Yat-sen was born in 1866 to a farming family from the small Chinese village known as Cuiheng. From a young age, he wanted a life different from what his society offered. He did not want to be a farmer, although he did help in the fields and raised chickens and ducks. Nor did he want to enter the Chinese civil service. He begged his parents to let him travel to other lands with his older brother, Sun Mei. At first they refused because of his young age, but once Sun Yat-sen turned 12, they agreed to let him go to Honolulu, Hawaii. There he attended an Anglican boys' school, where he was introduced to Christianity.

Because his brother became a wealthy and respected businessman in Hawaii, Sun Yat-sen did not have to become a laborer, as did most other Chinese who migrated to the West. Instead, Sun Yat-sen concentrated on his studies. He studied the English language and European and American political ideas. He became convinced that China needed a revolution. He attended Oahu College and announced that he wanted to become a Christian. This upset his brother, who sent him back to China.

In China, Sun Yat-sen and some of his friends purposely damaged a wooden statue of the Northern God, a patron god of Cuiheng. His rebellious behavior shocked his family and the villagers. He was sent to Hong Kong, where he earned a medical degree and became involved in politics.

▲ Sun Yat-sen

> **"[N]ationalism does not mean discriminating against people of different nationality."**
> —Sun Yat-sen

▲ Pagoda at the tomb of Sun Yat-sen

Then and Now

How did Sun Yat-sen's education prepare him for his role as a Chinese leader? Do research to find how our current president's education prepared him for his leadership role.

The Rise of Imperial Japan

Main Idea After Americans visited Japan, the Japanese reorganized their society and economy and began building an empire.

Reading Focus Have you ever watched what someone else did and then changed how you did things to match what they did? Read to learn how the Japanese changed their society to be more like Europeans and Americans.

Like China, Japan felt pressures from Europe and the United States. Previously you learned that Japan was in chaos at the end of the 1400s. The shogun, or the country's military ruler, no longer controlled the country. **Daimyo** (DY•mee•oh), or heads of noble families, ruled their own lands and waged war on their neighbors.

During the 1500s, three powerful leaders restored strong central government to Japan. The first was **Oda Nobunaga** (ohd•ah noh•bun•ah•gah). He seized Kyoto, the capital, and placed the shogun under his control. Then, he spread his rule over Japan's central plains. After Nobunaga, another strong military leader named Toyotomi Hideyoshi (toh•yoh•toh•mee hee•dee•yoh•shee) ruled Japan. Hideyoshi was, in turn, followed by the powerful daimyo **Tokugawa Ieyasu** (toh•kug•ah•wah ee•eh•yahs•u), who became shogun in 1603. Ieyasu's descendants remained in power until 1868. The Tokugawa family's long rule was known as the "Great Peace."

Europeans in Japan

Meanwhile, Europeans were starting to trade with Japan. In fact, Hideyoshi and Ieyasu used European firearms to help unify Japan. Jesuit missionaries arrived soon after the traders and converted thousands of Japanese to Christianity by the late 1500s.

The Jesuits angered Hideyoshi by destroying Japanese shrines. As a result, he

▲ This Japanese painting shows Commodore Perry's arrival in Edo Bay in 1853. *Before Perry arrived in Japan, who were the only Europeans allowed to trade there?*

banned Christian activities, expelled all missionaries, and persecuted Japanese Christians. European merchants were the next to go. Ieyasu allowed only the Dutch to remain in Japan at the port of Nagasaki.

Tokugawa rulers oversaw major changes in Japan. The samurai gradually ceased to be a warrior class. Many became managers on the lands of the daimyo. Trade and industry spread, especially in cities such as **Edo** (known today as Tokyo), Kyoto, and Osaka. The class system became rigid. It excluded *eta,* or outcasts, who worked in trades thought to be impure, such as killing animals and tanning hides. Laws stated where the *eta* lived, how they dressed, and even how they wore their hair. Women also led very restricted lives.

Perry Arrives in Japan

In 1853 Commodore **Matthew Perry** and four American warships arrived in Edo Bay (now Tokyo Bay). Perry presented a letter from U.S. president Millard Fillmore to the shogun. The letter invited

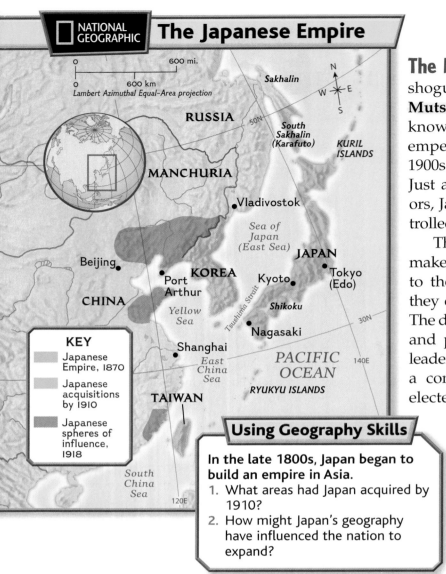

NATIONAL GEOGRAPHIC The Japanese Empire

0 — 600 mi.
0 — 600 km
Lambert Azimuthal Equal-Area projection

RUSSIA

Sakhalin

South Sakhalin (Karafuto)

KURIL ISLANDS

MANCHURIA

Vladivostok

Sea of Japan (East Sea)

Beijing

KOREA

JAPAN

Port Arthur

Kyoto

Tokyo (Edo)

CHINA

Yellow Sea

Shikoku

Nagasaki

Shanghai

East China Sea

PACIFIC OCEAN

TAIWAN

RYUKYU ISLANDS

South China Sea

KEY

Japanese Empire, 1870

Japanese acquisitions by 1910

Japanese spheres of influence, 1918

Using Geography Skills

In the late 1800s, Japan began to build an empire in Asia.
1. What areas had Japan acquired by 1910?
2. How might Japan's geography have influenced the nation to expand?

The Meiji Restoration

At the time the shogun was overthrown, Emperor **Mutsuhito** (MOOT•suh•HEE•toh) was known as the Meiji, or "Enlightened," emperor. Thus, the late 1800s and early 1900s is known in Japan as the Meiji era. Just as shoguns controlled earlier emperors, Japan's new ruling samurai now controlled Mutsuhito.

The Meiji leaders were determined to make Japan a great power able to stand up to the Europeans and Americans. First, they did away with the old social system. The daimyo lost much of their land, power, and privileges. Then, in 1889, Japanese leaders wrote a new constitution to set up a constitutional monarchy. The people elected lawmakers to the legislature.

Power, however, was held by the Meiji leaders, who acted on behalf of the emperor. They chose the prime minister and his advisers.

Japan's new government set up a modern army and navy. All Japanese men were expected to serve for a certain amount of time in the armed forces. Meiji leaders also made major changes in Japan's society. They improved roads and opened public schools. Education was required for all, including women.

Above all, the Meiji pushed for Japan to industrialize. They helped build new factories and gave certain privileges to the rich and powerful families who ran them. Japan's new industrial society also had a dark side though. Mill workers often worked 20-hour days, and miners were shot when they refused to work in extreme heat.

Japan to have trade and diplomatic relations with the United States.

Within six months, Perry and an even larger fleet returned to Japan for an answer to the president's letter. Fearing an American attack, the Japanese agreed to open ports to U.S. trade and to exchange ambassadors. Japan soon made similar agreements with European nations.

Many Japanese were unhappy with the treaties and considered them unfair. They feared the treaties would keep Japan weak. In 1868 a group of samurai attacked the shogun's palace in Kyoto and took power in the emperor's name.

Japan Builds an Empire

As they watched European nations and the United States rise in power and wealth, Japanese leaders came to believe a nation needed an empire to be strong. Colonies would supply Japan with raw materials, cheap labor, and markets for manufactured goods.

As the first step toward building an empire, in 1876 the Japanese navy forced Korea to open its ports to Japanese trade. The Chinese had controlled Korea for a long time and resented Japan's presence there.

In 1894 China and Japan went to war. The Japanese destroyed China's fleet and captured the Manchurian city of **Port Arthur.** In the peace treaty that followed, China agreed to give Taiwan to Japan and independence to Korea.

Russia also wanted to trade with Korea. As a result, Japan and Russia competed for markets there. In 1904 Japan attacked a Russian naval base at Port Arthur, which Russia had seized from China in 1898. The Japanese army then marched into Manchuria. Russian troops in the area tried to stop them but were driven back.

▲ Japan's modern naval fleet easily defeated Russia's forces. *Why did Japan come into conflict with Russia?*

Meanwhile, Russia sent its main fleet all the way around the world to attack Japan. When it arrived, Japan's new modern navy quickly sank the Russian ships. In 1905 Russia agreed to give up Port Arthur and part of Sakhalin (SA•kuh•LEEN), an island north of Japan. The whole world now recognized Japan as a major power.

 **Explain** Why did the samurai attack and replace the shogun?

History Online

Study Central™ Need help with the material in this section? Visit jat.glencoe.com

Section 2 Review

Reading Summary

Review the Main Ideas

- In the 1800s, European powers created spheres of influence and controlled trade within China.

- A revolution overthrew the Qing dynasty in 1911 but failed to create a democratic government for China.

- The Meiji Restoration changed Japan's society and economy and made Japan into a major world power.

What Did You Learn?

1. What were the causes of the Boxer Rebellion?

2. Why did Admiral Perry sail to Japan? What was the result of his mission?

Critical Thinking

3. **Sequencing Information** Draw a time line like the one below. Fill in dates and events related to changes in China in the 1800s and 1900s.

1842   1916

4. **Cause and Effect** How did trade between Britain and China lead to the Opium War?

5. **Compare and Contrast** What was the Open Door policy, and how was it different from European policies?

6. **Summarize** Describe Japan's rise to power in the in the late 1800s and early 1900s.

7. **Persuasive Writing** Write an editorial for a newspaper in China presenting your views on China's treatment by the European powers.

World War I Begins

Get Ready to Read!

What's the Connection?

You have seen how imperialism contributed to tensions among Europeans. Eventually, these tensions led to a worldwide conflict.

Focusing on the Main Idea

- Alliances, militarism, and nationalism led to a crisis in Europe. *(page 781)*

- The assassination of Archduke Franz Ferdinand sparked World War I. *(page 784)*

- Americans supported the Allies because of pro-British feelings and business links. *(page 786)*

Locating Places
Balkans (BAWL•kuhnz)
Serbia (SUHR•bee•uh)

Meeting People
Franz Ferdinand
(FRANZ   FUHR•duhn•AND)
Woodrow Wilson

Building Your Vocabulary
militarism
(MIH•luh•tuh•RIH•zuhm)
conscription (kuhn•SKRIHP•shuhn)
entente (ahn•TAHNT)
mobilization
(MOH•buh•luh•ZAY•shuhn)
rationing
propaganda (PRAH•puh•GAN•duh)
blockade

Reading Strategy
Contrasting Use a Venn diagram like the one below to show the major countries that made up the Allies and the Central Powers.

Allies — WWI Alliances — Central Powers

NATIONAL GEOGRAPHIC **When & Where?**

BRITAIN
London
Paris
GERMANY   RUSSIA
Berlin
FRANCE AUSTRIA-HUNGARY
Rome

1910   **1915**   **1920**

1908
Austria-Hungary takes over Bosnia

1914
World War I begins

1915
German submarine sinks the *Lusitania*

1917
U.S. enters World War I

The Causes of World War I

Main Idea Alliances, militarism, and nationalism led to a crisis in Europe.

Reading Focus Do you cheer for the American team during the Olympics and feel proud of your nation? Read to learn how national pride and feelings of independence led Europe to the brink of war.

After Napoleon was defeated, it would be almost 100 years before another major war erupted in Europe involving all the countries. In the early 1900s, however, tension was growing among the European powers.

Nationalism
Nationalism, a feeling of intense loyalty to one's country, caused much of the tension in Europe. As you read in earlier chapters, nationalism led to the birth of new nations, such as Italy and Germany. The actions of Germany soon challenged the position of older nations such as Britain and France. At the same time, the spread of nationalism threatened to break apart other countries in Europe. Some groups of people, such as those in the Austro-Hungarian Empire, demanded independent nations of their own.

The Race for Empires
Tensions in Europe also grew out of the desire of nations to enlarge their empires. As you read earlier, European nations competed for colonies in Africa, Asia, and other parts of the world. These not only created new markets and

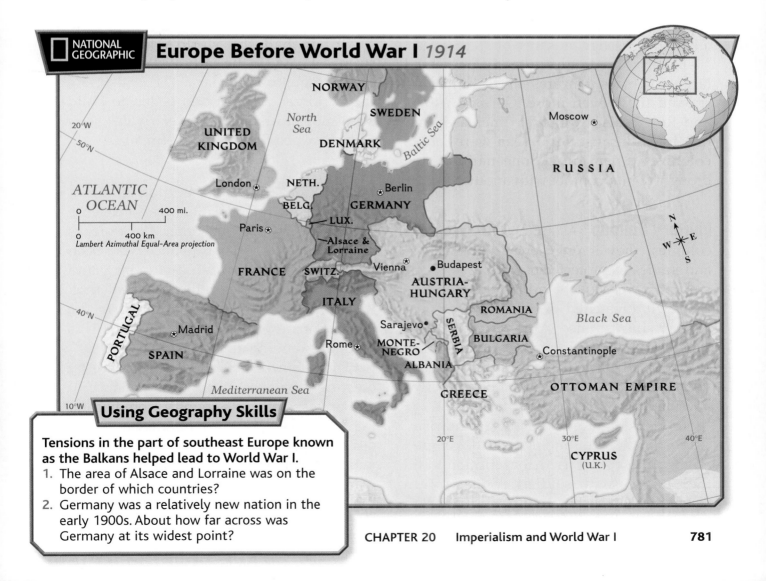

NATIONAL GEOGRAPHIC

Europe Before World War I *1914*

Using Geography Skills

Tensions in the part of southeast Europe known as the Balkans helped lead to World War I.

1. The area of Alsace and Lorraine was on the border of which countries?
2. Germany was a relatively new nation in the early 1900s. About how far across was Germany at its widest point?

▲ The competition for colonies led to a focus on military strength. This photo shows British troops on parade. *Which European countries used conscription to build large armies?*

▲ Prior to World War I, Germany built up its navy, including these battleships anchored in the harbor at Kiel, Germany. *Which country had the world's largest and strongest navy around 1900?*

supplied raw materials, they also added to a nation's prestige, or sense of greatness.

Britain and France already possessed large overseas empires and wanted to expand them even more. Germany, Italy, and Russia also wanted to increase their holdings. Because few areas were left to colonize, expansion by one nation often brought it into conflict with another.

Military Buildup

As nations competed for colonies, they strengthened their armies and navies to protect their interests. If one nation increased its military might, its rivals felt threatened and built up their own military in response. As a result of these buildups, Europeans were caught up in a spirit of **militarism** (MIH•luh•tuh•RIH•zuhm). This term refers to a fascination with war and the military.

In this atmosphere of militarism, Germany, France, and Russia developed huge armies. They used conscription to fill their armies with soldiers. **Conscription** (kuhn•SKRIHP•shuhn) requires citizens to serve in the military for a certain period of time. In the United States, people refer to conscription as "the draft."

Britain had the world's largest and strongest navy. In the early 1900s, Germany began to build up its navy. The British saw this action as a threat and began to build even more warships. A bitter rivalry soon grew between Britain and Germany.

Forming Alliances

As militarism grew, nations began to make alliances, or defense agreements to help each other if war breaks out. By 1914 two major alliances had been formed. Germany, Austria-Hungary, and Italy banded together in the Triple Alliance. Britain, France, and Russia joined in the Triple Entente. An **entente** (ahn•TAHNT) is an understanding among nations.

The alliances helped to keep peace by creating a balance of power. A balance of power keeps any one country from becoming too strong. Yet Europe's alliances actually created a great danger. An attack on one nation was all that was needed to trigger a war involving many countries. Europe was like a barrel of gunpowder. Only a spark was needed to set it off. It seemed likely that the spark would be lit in Europe's Balkan Peninsula.

The Balkan Crises In the early 1900s, the Balkan Peninsula in southeastern Europe was a hotbed of nationalist rivalries. For hundreds of years, the Ottoman and the Austro-Hungarian Empires had ruled the **Balkans** (BAWL•kuhnz). As nationalism spread, groups within these empires demanded independence.

Among these nationalist groups were the South Slavs. They included the Serbs, Bosnians, Croats, and Slovenes. The Serbs were the first to win their freedom. They formed a state called **Serbia** (SUHR•bee•uh) and believed their mission was to unite the South Slavs.

The Russians, who were Slavs as well, backed Serbia. Austria-Hungary, fearing the South Slavs in their empire would want to break away, tried to limit Serbia's growth. In 1908 Austria-Hungary took over Serbia's neighbor, Bosnia, from the Ottomans. The Serbs were furious. They wanted Bosnia to be part of their country.

With Russian support, the Serbs prepared for war. Then Emperor William II of Germany demanded that Russia accept Austria-Hungary's takeover of Bosnia or face war with Germany. Russia backed down. However, it was determined not to be humiliated by Germany again.

In 1912 the Balkan League—Bulgaria, Greece, Montenegro, and Serbia—declared war on the Ottoman empire. As a result, the Turks lost nearly all their European territory. However, the Balkan League soon fell apart.

Greeks and Serbs demanded land that Bulgaria had won in the war, so Bulgaria attacked the Greeks and Serbs. The Turks saw their chance to win back land and attacked Bulgaria. The Treaty of Bucharest ended the fighting, but Europeans expected the Balkan region to go to war again soon.

Reading Check **Identify** What was the danger created by forming alliances?

NATIONAL GEOGRAPHIC

HISTORY MAKERS

Assassination of an Archduke *June 28, 1914*

Archduke Franz Ferdinand of Austria-Hungary visited Sarajevo in June of 1914 with his wife Sophie. Sarajevo was a city in the Austro-Hungarian Empire. Some people who lived in that part of the empire wanted to be free from Austria-Hungary. Those people were especially angry because the archduke and his wife arrived on the anniversary of a battle in which Serbia lost its independence. A terrorist organization made plans to kill the archduke and his wife during their visit. On June 28, a terrorist named Gavrilo Princip shot them while they were riding in a motorcade. A month later, Austria-Hungary declared war on Serbia. Each nation received help from its allies. The result was World War I.

Archduke Ferdinand and his wife in their car in Sarajevo ▶

The War Begins

Main Idea The assassination of Archduke Franz Ferdinand sparked World War I.

Reading Focus Remember how the terrorist attack on 9/11 led to a war? The same thing happened in 1914. A single terrorist helped set off World War I.

The spark that finally set off a major war was lit in Sarajevo (SAR•uh•YAY•voh), a small town in Bosnia. There, in June 1914, a man named Gavrilo Princip shot and killed Archduke **Franz Ferdinand** (FRANZ FUHR•duhn•AND), heir to the throne of Austria-Hungary. Princip was a member of a secret nationalist group called the Black Hand. This group wanted the Bosnian Serbs, ruled by Austria-Hungary, to be ruled by Serbia.

Austria-Hungary blamed the Serbian government for the archduke's death.

It declared war on Serbia. Russia, Serbia's ally, began **mobilization** (MOH•buh•luh•ZAY•shuhn), or assembly and movement of troops. By mobilizing, Russia showed that it was ready to go to war to protect Serbia. Germany then showed its support of Austria-Hungary by declaring war on Russia. Shortly after, France entered the war on the side of Russia. Germany's plan for attacking France required German troops to go through Belgium. Britain had promised to help Belgium stay neutral, so when Germany invaded Belgium, Britain declared war on Germany too.

When the war broke out in 1914, France, Russia, and Great Britain became known as the Allies. Later, in 1915, Italy joined them. Austria-Hungary, Germany, the Ottoman empire, and Bulgaria were known as the Central Powers.

Trenches of World War I

The more powerful, longer-range weapons of World War I led to the development of complex systems of trenches. Frontline troops lived in the trenches between attacks. Soldiers stationed in forward listening posts gave advance warning of enemy offensives. Attacks were made in "no-man's land": the open ground between the trenches. Shell craters and barbed wire slowed down attackers, leading to their slaughter by machine guns and artillery. Communications trenches allowed reserves to be brought up to the front lines safely. *How did the trenches help protect soldiers during battle?*

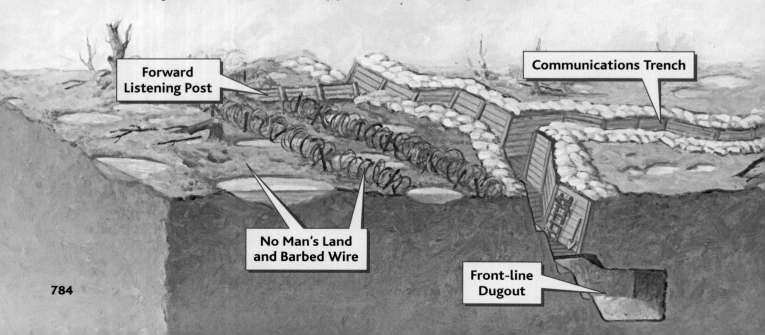

Forward Listening Post

Communications Trench

No Man's Land and Barbed Wire

Front-line Dugout

No Quick Victory Much of the fighting in World War I took place on the Western Front, the battle zone between France and Germany. There, the French and the British stopped the German advance in September 1914. However, the battle line barely moved for three years.

Troops on both sides dug themselves into the ground in trenches protected by barbed wire. This kind of fighting is called trench warfare. To get at the enemy, soldiers on each side had to climb out of trenches and cross open land while machine guns and artillery—modern versions of cannons—fired at them. In major battles, several hundred thousand soldiers were killed or wounded.

A New Kind of War World War I, also called the Great War, was different from any earlier war. Both sides developed new, more powerful weapons to help them break through enemy lines. Machine guns fired bullets one after the other at a rapid speed. Huge artillery guns fired shells more than 75 miles (120 km). Poison gases were used for the first time, and tanks and flamethrowers were introduced. Newly developed submarines attacked ships at sea, while early versions of airplanes battled in the sky.

World War I was also the first war in which civilians, or people who are not soldiers, were important to winning the war. As the war dragged on, it became a total war. This means governments made use of all their resources and people. Total war affected the lives of all citizens, not just soldiers.

Supplies had to be made and bought for millions of soldiers. To do this, governments decided what civilians could buy and sell.

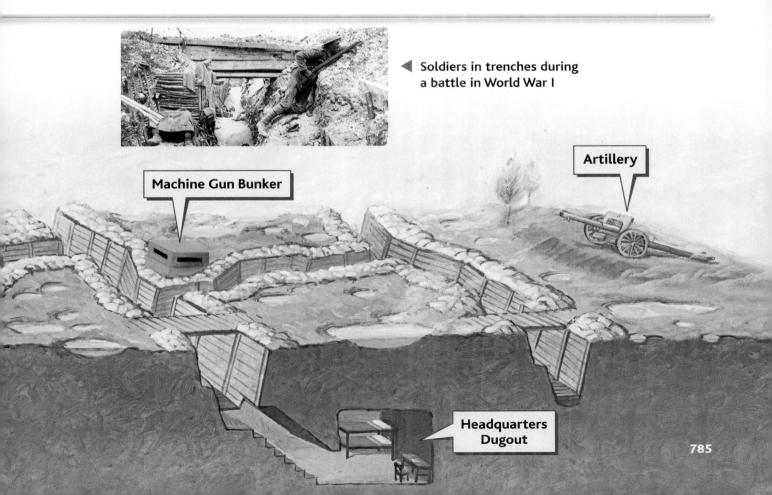

◀ Soldiers in trenches during a battle in World War I

Artillery

Machine Gun Bunker

Headquarters Dugout

They used **rationing,** or a system of limiting the amount of foods and materials in use. They controlled trade and took over industries and railroads.

Total war also led to government control of public opinion. Wartime governments used **propaganda** (PRAH•puh•GAN•duh), or biased government-controlled information, to shape what people thought about the war. The government also controlled what was printed in newspapers and sometimes even stopped their publication.

✓ **Reading Check** **Describe** Why did so many soldiers die in World War I?

America Enters the War

Main Idea Americans supported the Allies because of pro-British feelings and business links.

Reading Focus Have you ever had to choose sides in an argument? How do you decide who to support? Read to learn why America chose sides in World War I.

When World War I began, U.S. president **Woodrow Wilson** declared that the United States was not supporting either side. "We must be impartial [not involved] in thought as well as in action." Despite the president's plea, many Americans took sides.

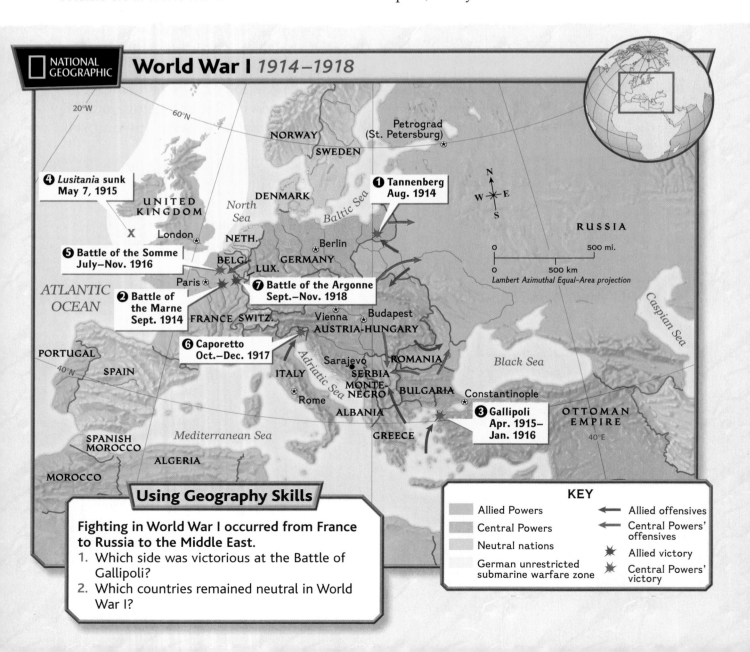

NATIONAL GEOGRAPHIC

World War I *1914–1918*

❹ *Lusitania* sunk
May 7, 1915

❶ Tannenberg
Aug. 1914

❺ Battle of the Somme
July–Nov. 1916

❷ Battle of the Marne
Sept. 1914

❼ Battle of the Argonne
Sept.–Nov. 1918

❻ Caporetto
Oct.–Dec. 1917

❸ Gallipoli
Apr. 1915–
Jan. 1916

Lambert Azimuthal Equal-Area projection

KEY

- Allied Powers
- Central Powers
- Neutral nations
- German unrestricted submarine warfare zone
- ← Allied offensives
- ← Central Powers' offensives
- ✳ Allied victory
- ✳ Central Powers' victory

Using Geography Skills

Fighting in World War I occurred from France to Russia to the Middle East.
1. Which side was victorious at the Battle of Gallipoli?
2. Which countries remained neutral in World War I?

Submarine Warfare Many of Wilson's advisers backed Britain. They believed that an Allied victory was the only way to keep a balance of power in the world. American loans to Germany were limited. In contrast, American loans to the Allies skyrocketed. By 1917, the Allies owed American banks more than $2 billion.

In addition to loans, the Allies received food, equipment, and other supplies from the United States. The British imposed a **blockade** on Germany. That is, they used their warships to stop goods from leaving or entering German ports. To fight back, the

History Online
Web Activity Visit jat.glencoe.com and click on *Chapter 20—Student Web Activity* to learn more about World War I.

Germans began using the world's first oceangoing submarines. The Germans called them U-boats. In February 1915, the Germans warned that U-boats would sink any ship sailing the waters around Britain.

Despite the warning, the British passenger liner *Lusitania* entered the war zone. A German submarine fired on the ship, killing nearly 1,200 passengers—including 128 Americans. Many Americans were

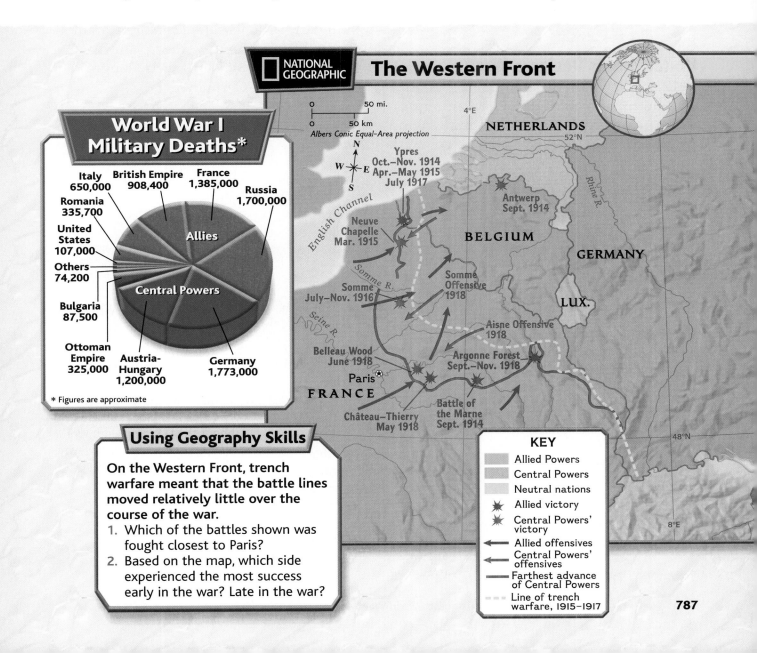

NATIONAL GEOGRAPHIC

The Western Front

0   50 mi.
0   50 km
Albers Conic Equal-Area projection

World War I Military Deaths*

Italy 650,000
British Empire 908,400
France 1,385,000
Russia 1,700,000
Romania 335,700
United States 107,000
Others 74,200
Bulgaria 87,500
Ottoman Empire 325,000
Austria-Hungary 1,200,000
Germany 1,773,000

Allies

Central Powers

* Figures are approximate

NETHERLANDS
Ypres Oct.–Nov. 1914 Apr.–May 1915 July 1917
Antwerp Sept. 1914
Rhine R.
Neuve Chapelle Mar. 1915
BELGIUM
GERMANY
English Channel
Somme R.
Somme Offensive 1918
LUX.
Somme July–Nov. 1916
Seine R.
Aisne Offensive 1918
Belleau Wood June 1918
Argonne Forest Sept.–Nov. 1918
Paris
FRANCE
Château–Thierry May 1918
Battle of the Marne Sept. 1914

Using Geography Skills

On the Western Front, trench warfare meant that the battle lines moved relatively little over the course of the war.
1. Which of the battles shown was fought closest to Paris?
2. Based on the map, which side experienced the most success early in the war? Late in the war?

KEY

Allied Powers
Central Powers
Neutral nations
* Allied victory
* Central Powers' victory
← Allied offensives
← Central Powers' offensives
— Farthest advance of Central Powers
--- Line of trench warfare, 1915–1917

▲ American soldiers helped turn the tide of the war against Germany. *Why did the United States decide to enter World War I?*

outraged, but the U-boats kept sinking ships. By 1916, however, German leaders had grown worried that the United States might enter the war. They promised to give ships warning before sinking them, so people could get off safely.

United States Declares War In January 1917, a German official named Arthur Zimmermann cabled the German ambassador in Mexico. In the cable, Zimmermann proposed that Mexico ally itself with Germany if war broke out between Germany and the United States. In return, Mexico would regain "lost territory in Texas, New Mexico, and Arizona" after the war. The British intercepted the Zimmermann telegram and gave it to American newspapers. Outraged Americans began demanding war with Germany.

In February, German submarines began sinking ships again without warning. German leaders knew the attacks might draw the United States into the war. However, they did not believe that Americans could mobilize quickly enough to save the Allies. Between February 3 and March 21, U-boats sank six American merchant ships without warning. On April 6, 1917, President Wilson asked Congress to declare war on Germany.

✓ **Reading Check** **Explain** Why did the United States favor Britain over Germany in World War I?

History Online

Study Central™ Need help with the material in this section? Visit jat.glencoe.com

Section ③ Review

Reading Summary

Review the Main Ideas

- In the early 1900s, nations of Europe formed alliances and built up their military forces.

- The assassination of an Austro-Hungarian archduke led to declarations of war across Europe.

- German submarine attacks against American ships eventually brought the United States into the war on the side of the Allies.

What Did You Learn?

1. What happened in Sarajevo in 1914, and why was it important?

2. Name three things that led to World War I.

Critical Thinking

3. **Organizing Information** Use a chart like the one below to list the countries that fought in World War I.

Allies	
Central Powers	

4. **Explain** What is militarism and what problems did it cause in Europe?

5. **Cause and Effect** Why did the soldiers decide to use trench warfare?

6. **Analyze** Why was World War I a "total war"?

7. **Expository Writing** Write a headline and a brief article about the U.S. entry into World War I. Discuss the reasons why the United States finally entered the war.

Section 4

World War I Changes the World

Get Ready to Read!

What's the Connection?

As you read, by 1917 neither side was gaining ground in World War I. The arrival of American troops would mark a turning point in the war.

Focusing on the Main Ideas

• With American help, the Allies stopped the German advance. *(page 790)*

• The Bolsheviks rose to power as a result of the czar's poor leadership. *(page 793)*

Locating Places

Argonne Forest

Versailles (vuhr•SY)

Meeting People

David Lloyd George

Georges Clemenceau (zhawrzh KLEH•muhn•SOH)

Vittorio Orlando (veet•TAWR•yoh awr•LAN•doh)

Atatürk (AT•uh•TUHRK)

Vladimir Lenin (VLAD•uh•MIHR LEH•nuhn)

Building Your Vocabulary

armistice (AHR•muh•stuhs)

reparation (REH•puh•RAY•shuhn)

mandate (MAN•DAYT)

duma (DOO•muh)

soviet (SOH•vee•EHT)

Reading Strategy

Organizing Information Use a diagram like the one below to show the new territories created from the Ottoman empire.

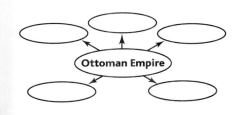

When & Where?

NATIONAL GEOGRAPHIC

BRITAIN
GERMANY • Berlin
FRANCE
ITALY TURKEY
SOVIET UNION

1916 — 1920 — 1924

1917 Lenin seizes power in Russia

1918 World War I ends

1921 Communists win Russian Civil War

1923 Turkey becomes a republic

The War Ends

Main Idea With American help, the Allies stopped the German advance.

Reading Focus Have you ever heard the expression "the cavalry to the rescue"? As you read, decide which group represented the cavalry during World War I.

In late 1917, troopships carried wave after wave of American soldiers to Europe. Allied hopes soared. They would soon get the help they needed to win the war.

In November 1917, the Russians pulled out of the war. German troops on the Eastern Front were sent west. There, they strengthened Germany's army as it advanced toward Paris in 1918. On June 1, American and French troops blocked the advance at the town of Château-Thierry. Four months later, Americans launched their own massive attack in the Battle of the **Argonne Forest.** The Americans suffered major losses but shattered the German defenses.

Meanwhile, the Austro-Hungarian Empire was in chaos, and the Ottoman Turks surrendered. Faced with a mutiny in the navy and a popular revolt in Berlin, the German emperor stepped down. On November 11, 1918, Germany signed an **armistice** (AHR•muh•stuhs), or cease-fire, that ended the war.

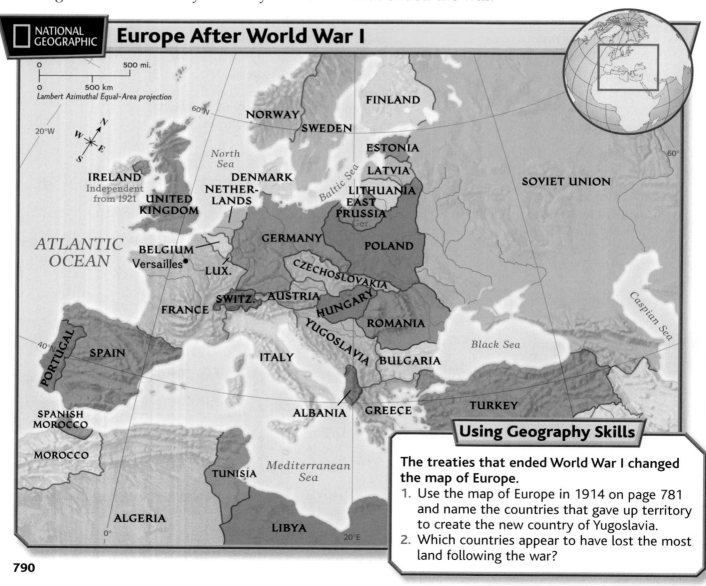

NATIONAL GEOGRAPHIC

Europe After World War I

Using Geography Skills

The treaties that ended World War I changed the map of Europe.

1. Use the map of Europe in 1914 on page 781 and name the countries that gave up territory to create the new country of Yugoslavia.
2. Which countries appear to have lost the most land following the war?

The Treaty of Versailles In January 1919, peace talks began at **Versailles** (vuhr•SY) outside Paris. The principal figures at the talks were U.S. president Woodrow Wilson, British prime minister **David Lloyd George,** French premier **Georges Clemenceau** (zhawrzh KLEH•muhn•SOH), and Italian prime minister **Vittorio Orlando** (veet•TAWR•yoh awr•LAN•doh).

Wilson presented a plan called the Fourteen Points. The plan stated that national groups in Europe should form their own countries. It also called for a League of Nations, an organization in which member nations would cooperate to keep the peace.

The Treaty of Versailles stripped Germany of most of its armed forces and required the Germans to pay **reparations** (REH•puh•RAY•shuhnz), or war damages, of $33 billion to the Allies. The treaty also called for the creation of a League of Nations.

President Wilson returned to the United States to win approval for the treaty. Some senators argued that the League might force the United States to fight in more foreign wars. Twice the Senate voted on the treaty and twice rejected it. As a result, the League of Nations was formed without the United States.

New Nations in Europe
The war and the treaties that followed redrew the map of Europe. Both the German and Russian empires lost territory in southeastern Europe. The Austro-Hungarian Empire disappeared completely.

The lands from these three empires became nation-states: Finland, Latvia, Estonia, Poland, Lithuania, Czechoslovakia, Austria, and Hungary. In addition, Romania gained territory from Russia, Hungary, and Bulgaria. Serbia became the center of a new state called Yugoslavia, which combined Serbs, Croats, and Slovenes.

▲ The four most important leaders at the Versailles conference were (left to right) Vittorio Orlando, David Lloyd George, Georges Clemenceau, and Woodrow Wilson. *How did the peace terms at Versailles affect Germany?*

The idea that peoples had a right to rule themselves shaped many of the decisions at the peace talks. However, different groups in Eastern Europe were mixed together. The treaties were not able to draw national borders neatly so that all people of a single ethnic group could be within one country. As a result, almost every new Eastern European country had a dominant group and many smaller groups. As time went on, friction between the different groups made these countries very unstable.

What Happened to the Ottoman Empire?
In making peace, the Allies also looked at the Middle East. Their major concern was what to do with the Ottoman empire, which had been defeated along with the other Central Powers.

The Allies decided to break up the Ottoman empire. The only area left to the Ottomans was the area of present-day Turkey. In 1919 Greece invaded Turkey and seized the western parts of the Anatolian Peninsula. In response, Turkish general Mustafa Kemal rallied forces to his country's defense. Turkish armies under Kemal finally drove out the Greeks. The Turkish victory led to the end of the Ottoman sultan's rule. In 1923 Turkey became a republic.

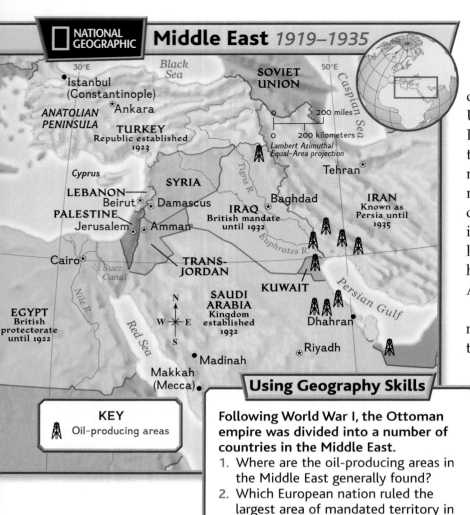

30°E

•Istanbul
(Constantinople)

ANATOLIAN
PENINSULA ⊛Ankara

*Black
Sea*

50°E

**SOVIET
UNION**

TURKEY
Republic established
1923

Caspian Sea

0 — 200 miles
0 — 200 kilometers
*Lambert Azimuthal
Equal-Area projection*

Cyprus

SYRIA

LEBANON—
Beirut⊛ ⊛Damascus
PALESTINE
Jerusalem⊛ ⊛Amman

IRAQ
British mandate
until 1932

Baghdad

Tigris R.

Tehran⊛

IRAN
Known as
Persia until
1935

Euphrates R.

Cairo⊛ *Suez
Canal*

**TRANS-
JORDAN**

KUWAIT

Persian Gulf

N
W—E
S

EGYPT
British
protectorate
until 1922

Nile R.

Red Sea

**SAUDI
ARABIA**
Kingdom
established
1932

Dhahran•

•Riyadh

•Madinah

Makkah
(Mecca)•

KEY
⛏ Oil-producing areas

Using Geography Skills

Following World War I, the Ottoman empire was divided into a number of countries in the Middle East.

1. Where are the oil-producing areas in the Middle East generally found?
2. Which European nation ruled the largest area of mandated territory in the Middle East? Which countries did it rule?

These new territories were called **mandates** (MAN•DAYTZ). Under the mandate system, the League of Nations governed each territory but allowed a member nation to run it. Because these mandated territories were largely created by outsiders, most people in the Middle East did not feel loyal to them. The Arabs did, however, share a strong sense of Arab nationalism.

In the 1920s, a local leader named Ibn Saud united Arabs on the Arabian Peninsula. In 1932 he created the kingdom of Saudi Arabia. At first the new country was desperately poor. Then American businesses struck oil at Dhahran on the Persian Gulf and the kingdom grew wealthy.

Meanwhile, in Palestine—a mandate run by the British—nationalism caused

Kemal, whom the people called **Atatürk** (AT•uh•TUHRK), became president of Turkey. Atatürk introduced many social and political changes to modernize the country. Turkey began to consider itself European as well as Asian. For example, all Arabic features were erased from the Turkish language, and Turkish citizens had to adopt last names, like Europeans. Atatürk also tried to reduce the influence of Islamic religious leaders on the government.

New Countries in the Middle East
After the war, the Allies divided up the Arab regions of the Ottoman empire. France took control of Lebanon and Syria. Britain acquired Iraq, Jordan, and Palestine.

new problems. In the late 1800s, nationalism began to affect Jews living in Europe. Jewish nationalists, known as Zionists, wanted to create a Jewish homeland in Palestine where the ancient Jewish city of Jerusalem was located. Zionist settlers began moving to the Middle East in the 1890s. During World War I Britain issued the Balfour Declaration promising Jews a nation in Palestine. Angry Arabs wondered how the Jews could establish a national home where the people were 80 percent Muslim. However, by 1939, more than 400,000 Jews lived in Palestine. To satisfy the Arabs, the British tried to limit the flow of Jewish settlers into the territory.

✓ **Reading Check** **Analyze** Why did the United States not join the League of Nations?

The Russian Revolution

(Main Idea) **The Bolsheviks rose to power as a result of the czar's poor leadership.**

Reading Focus Have you ever seen a protest march? Do you think protest can change things? Read to learn how protests led to a revolution in Russia.

During World War I, Russia fought alongside Britain and France. However, the war only worsened Russia's problems at home. Russia's ruler, Czar Nicholas II, was unable to solve these problems. His rigid rule no longer fit the times. As a result, the Russian people turned against him when he failed to meet Russia's new challenges.

Problems in Russia During the early 1900s, most Russians were very discontent. Peasants paid high taxes. Groups that were not Russian were often mistreated, and middle-class reformers wanted a voice in the government. Urban workers were perhaps the most dissatisfied. They toiled long hours in dirty, airless factories and received little pay.

In 1904 a war between Russia and Japan made matters worse. The war cost Russia land and money. As a result, food prices went up and wages went down. Peasants, urban workers, and middle-class students blamed the czar for the poor economy.

In 1905 an uprising took place. It began when thousands of workers appeared in the square before the czar's palace in St. Petersburg. They carried petitions asking for a national assembly, freedom of speech and religion, and better conditions for workers and peasants. Government soldiers fired on the crowd, killing hundreds of unarmed people. Workers in the city responded by going on strike. Finally, Czar Nicholas II agreed to some of the workers' demands. A **duma** (DOO•muh), or national

▲ This 1913 photo shows Czar Nicholas II and his family, all of whom were killed during the revolution. *How did World War I help cause the Russian Revolution?*

assembly, was created, but it had only limited powers. The czar, however, closed down the duma when it tried to act independently.

The Czar Is Overthrown World War I brought still more hardships to the Russian people. The country did not have enough factories to produce weapons or enough railroads to carry supplies to the front. As a result, Russia suffered higher casualties than any other country. Nearly 8 million soldiers were killed or wounded in battle. Civilians suffered from a lack of food and fuel.

The Russian people could stand no more. In March 1917, they revolted. Striking workers, led by women textile workers, jammed the streets of St. Petersburg. They demanded bread and peace. The workers were soon joined by soldiers stationed in the city. Finally, the czar gave up his throne, and the 300-year-old Romanov dynasty came to an end.

Ten Days That Shook the World

John Reed was an American journalist who witnessed the Russian Revolution. The events described in this passage took place on November 8, 1917.

"It was just 8:40 when a thundering wave of cheers announced the entrance of the presidium [committee], with Lenin—great Lenin— among them. . . .

▲ John Reed

Now Lenin, . . . stood there waiting, apparently oblivious to the long-rolling ovation, which lasted several minutes. When it finished, he said simply, 'We shall now proceed to construct the Socialist order!' Again that overwhelming human roar. . . .

'The revolution of 6 and 7 November,' he ended, 'has opened the era of the Social Revolution. . . . The labour movement, in the name of peace and Socialism, shall win, and fulfil its destiny. . . .'"

—John Reed, *Ten Days That Shook the World*

DBQ Document-Based Question

Does John Reed agree or disagree with Lenin? How do you know?

Members of the duma then formed a provisional, or temporary, government. Alexander Kerensky served as its leader. Despite the suffering caused by the war, the provisional government did not withdraw Russian troops from the front. In fact, the provisional government became preoccupied with the war. As a result, it did not carry out reforms at home and lost the support of the people.

Who Is Lenin? Many workers, soldiers, and peasants believed that the provisional government was too middle class. They formed **soviets** (SOH • vee • EHTS), or committees, to represent their interests. Soon the soviets and the provisional government became locked in a bitter struggle for control of Russia.

Members of the soviets were workers and peasants from different socialist groups. As you read in earlier chapters, socialists wanted workers to overthrow capitalism and build a society in which all could share equally in the wealth. The most radical of these groups was the Bolsheviks. They believed that a small party of revolutionaries could use force to bring about this ideal society. Their leader was **Vladimir Lenin** (VLAD • uh • MIHR   LEH • nuhn).

Under Lenin, the Bolsheviks promised to take Russia out of the war and to give all land to the peasants. They vowed to give the factories to the workers and the government to the soviets. Three slogans summed up the Bolshevik program: "Peace, Land, Bread," "Worker Control of Production," and "All Power to the Soviets."

The Bolsheviks Seize Power In October 1917, Bolsheviks controlled the soviets in Russia's two largest cities: St. Petersburg and Moscow. As a result, the Bolsheviks were in a good position to take over Russia's government.

In November 1917, the Bolsheviks seized the Winter Palace in St. Petersburg. This was the location of the provisional government. The government collapsed with little bloodshed. Lenin became the head of the new government.

Biography

VLADIMIR LENIN
1870–1924

▶ Vladimir Lenin

Vladimir Lenin, the founder of the Bolshevik Party and the first leader of the Soviet Union, grew up as Vladimir Ilyich Ulyanov in a happy, close-knit family. Ulyanov developed a great passion for learning early in his childhood. Both of his parents were educated. His father was a teacher and school inspector. His mother was the daughter of a landowning physician.

In school, young Ulyanov excelled in his studies, particularly in Latin and Greek. He graduated first in his class from high school and seemed destined to become a scholar. However, two tragic events affected the direction of his life. First, in 1886, his father suddenly died from a brain hemorrhage. Then, the next year, his oldest brother, Alexander, was hanged for involvement with a revolutionary group. Because of his brother's revolutionary activities, Ulyanov was denied many academic opportunities. In response, he renounced religion and Russia's political system. In January 1889, he became a Marxist.

Ulyanov's high school principal helped him get into law school, and he graduated in 1891, once again first in his class. Two years later, he moved to St. Petersburg, where he worked as a lawyer and developed an underground Marxist movement. Ulyanov became more involved in revolutionary propaganda efforts, and in 1895 he was arrested and exiled to Siberia for three years.

After exile, Ulyanov and his wife moved to Munich, Germany, where they published a newspaper that attempted to unite Marxist groups throughout the world. In 1901 Ulyanov adopted the pseudonym "Lenin"—a reference to Russia's Lena River, which is longer than the mighty Volga and flows in the opposite direction.

> **"We shall now proceed to construct the Socialist order!"**
> –Vladimir Lenin, as quoted in *Ten Days That Shook the World*

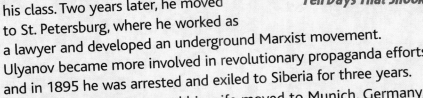

◀ Parade in Moscow honoring Marx, Engels, and Lenin in 1988

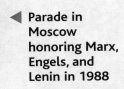

Then and Now

Lenin was arrested and sent to Siberia for three years for his protests. Do research to find an example of a modern political or social leader who has been exiled for his or her political beliefs.

The Russian Civil War Soon after, Lenin signed a peace treaty with Germany. A price was attached, however. In exchange for peace, the Bolsheviks had to give up large areas of land that had once been part of Russia's empire. Although the treaty ended Russia's involvement in World War I, it did not solve Russia's troubles at home.

Several groups—the czar's supporters, liberals, and moderate socialists—opposed Lenin's government. In 1918 these groups took up arms against the Bolsheviks—now known as Communists. In the war that followed, the Communists were called Reds because they flew a red revolutionary flag. Leon Trotsky organized the Red Army. He used force and education to make his soldiers loyal to the Communist cause.

The Communists' enemies became known as Whites. They promised to defeat

◀ Leon Trotsky used the draft to fill the Red Army and created a strong military force based on strict discipline. *Why did the Whites eventually lose the Civil War?*

the Reds quickly and get Russia back into World War I. As a result, the Allies and the United States sent them aid.

The Reds and Whites fought for three grim years. Both sides burned villages and killed civilians. Meanwhile, workers and peasants were starving. The Whites were disorganized, outnumbered, and poorly equipped. In 1921 they finally gave up. Lenin and the Communists now controlled the entire country.

✓ **Reading Check** **Identify** Why did the provisional government lose support?

Section 4 Review

History Online

Study Central™ Need help with the material in this section? Visit jat.glencoe.com

Reading Summary

Review the **Main Ideas**

• With American help, the Germans were defeated, ending the war. A number of new nations in Europe and the Middle East were created following the war.

• In Russia, the czar was overthrown, and the Bolsheviks, or Communists, took power.

What Did You Learn?

1. What were the Fourteen Points and why were they important?

2. What changes did Atatürk make after becoming president of Turkey?

Critical Thinking

3. **Organizing Information** Draw a diagram similar to the one below. In the outer ovals, fill in the names of new countries created after World War I.

New Nations

4. **Analyze** Were the attempts to create countries along ethnic lines following World War I successful? Why or why not?

5. **Sequencing Information** Describe the major events leading to the fall of the Russian czar.

6. **Analyze** How were Lenin and the Bolsheviks able to come to power in Russia?

7. **Writing Questions** Imagine you are a reporter in the era of World War I. Write a series of four or five questions that you would like to ask the leaders of Europe. Include possible answers to your questions.

Chapter 20 Reading Review

Section 1 The New Imperialism

Vocabulary

imperialism
colony
protectorate
sphere of influence
sepoy

Focusing on the Main Ideas

- European nations built empires to help their economy and to spread their ideas. *(page 763)*
- Control of India passed from the East India Company to the British. *(page 764)*
- European nations ruled almost all of Africa by 1914. *(page 766)*
- The United States became an imperial nation after defeating Spain and taking control of the Philippines and Puerto Rico. *(page 769)*

Section 2 Nationalism in China and Japan

Vocabulary

extraterritoriality
daimyo

Focusing on the Main Ideas

- The arrival of Europeans greatly changed Chinese society. *(page 772)*
- Sun Yat-sen introduced ideas that helped cause the collapse of the Qing dynasty. *(page 774)*
- After Americans visited Japan, the Japanese reorganized their society and economy and began building an empire. *(page 777)*

Section 3 World War I Begins

Vocabulary

militarism
conscription
entente
mobilization
rationing
propaganda
blockade

Focusing on the Main Ideas

- Alliances, militarism, and nationalism led to a crisis in Europe. *(page 781)*
- The assassination of Archduke Franz Ferdinand sparked World War I. *(page 784)*
- Americans supported the Allies because of pro-British feelings and business links. *(page 786)*

Section 4 World War I Changes the World

Vocabulary

armistice
reparation
mandate
duma
soviet

Focusing on the Main Ideas

- With American help, the Allies stopped the German advance. *(page 790)*
- The Bolsheviks rose to power as a result of the czar's poor leadership. *(page 793)*

Review Vocabulary

Write the vocabulary word that completes each sentence.

a. soviets   e. reparations

b. conscription   f. colony

c. armistice   g. daimyo

d. protectorate   h. entente

1. Heads of noble families in Japanese society were called ___.

2. Russian workers formed ___ to voice their concerns.

3. The government of a(n) ___ is guided by a foreign power.

4. A cease-fire is also called a(n) ___.

5. ___ requires citizens to join the military.

6. A(n) ___ was directly ruled by an imperial nation.

7. Germany paid war damages, or ___, to the Allies.

8. An understanding among nations is called a(n) ___.

Review Main Ideas

Section 1 • The New Imperialism

9. Why did European nations establish empires?

10. Why were European nations interested in Africa?

Section 2 • Nationalism in China and Japan

11. How did the arrival of the Europeans change Chinese society?

12. How did Sun Yat-sen's ideas lead to the collapse of the Qing dynasty?

Section 3 • World War I Begins

13. Explain the causes of World War I.

14. Why did Americans support the Allies?

Section 4 • World War I Changes the World

15. What resulted from the German advance on the Allies?

16. Why were the Bolsheviks able to rise to power in Russia?

Review

Reading Skill | Prioritizing

What's Important?

Read the passage below from page 784.

The spark that finally set off a major war was lit in Sarajevo, a small town in Bosnia. There, in June 1914, a man named Gavrilo Princip shot and killed Archduke Franz Ferdinand, heir to the throne of Austria-Hungary.

17. If you had to answer the question "What event started World War I?", which information in this passage would be most important?

18. If you had to answer the question "When did the war begin?", which information would be most important?

To review this skill, see pages 760–761.

Critical Thinking

19. **Cause and Effect** What caused the Boer War?

20. **Analyze** Instead of importing opium to China, what else might the British have done to restore the balance of trade?

21. **Explain** How did the assassination of Ferdinand lead to war?

22. **Analyze** Do you think the Treaty of Versailles asked too much of Germany? Why or why not?

Geography Skills

Study the map below and answer the following questions.

23. **Place** Which nation in the Middle East remained neutral during World War I?

24. **Movement** Why were Allied troops moving into the Ottoman empire?

25. **Analyze** Which group won most of the battles fought in the Ottoman empire?

History Online

Self-Check Quiz To help you prepare for the Chapter Test, visit jat.glencoe.com

Read to Write

26. **Expository Writing** Write a brief essay comparing and contrasting the causes of the revolutions in America, France, and Russia.

27. **Using Your FOLDABLES** Create a crossword puzzle using the terms on your foldable. Use the terms' definitions as the crossword clues. Be sure to provide an answer key.

Using Technology

28. **Researching** Use the Internet and your local library to research the total costs of World War I. On a computer, create a table or graph that shows the costs and number of deaths during the war.

Linking Past and Present

29. **Expository Writing** Choose one nation in Africa and research its history from the colonial era to the present. Write a short essay about your chosen country's history.

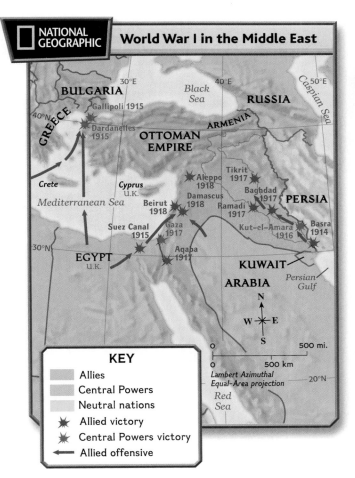

NATIONAL GEOGRAPHIC

World War I in the Middle East

KEY
- Allies
- Central Powers
- Neutral nations
- ✳ Allied victory
- ✳ Central Powers victory
- ← Allied offensive

Primary Source

Analyze

Journalist Henry Stanley located explorer and missionary David Livingstone in Africa in 1871:

"We have at last entered the town. There are hundreds of people around me.... It is a grand triumphal procession....

... [A]s I come nearer I see the white face of an old man among them.... I am shaking hands with him. We raise our hats, and I say:

'Dr. Livingstone, I presume?'"

—H.M. Stanley, "Stanley Finds Livingstone, 10 November 1871"

DBQ Document-Based Question

Why do you think the Africans held a "grand triumphal procession" for Mr. Stanley?

Chapter 21

World War II and the Cold War

World War II dive-bomber in flight ▼

NATIONAL GEOGRAPHIC When & Where?

1925	1935	1945	1955
1929 The Great Depression begins	**1939** Germany invades Poland	**1945** Atomic bombs are dropped on Japan	**1950** The Korean War begins **1954** The French leave Vietnam

Chapter Preview

Read this chapter to learn about World War II and the Cold War, two very different conflicts that shaped the lives of your grandparents and parents.

 View the Chapter 21 video in the *World History: Journey Across Time* **Video Program.**

 ## The Rise of Dictators

The Great Depression led to the New Deal in the United States, but in Europe and Japan dictators and military leaders came to power.

 ## World War II Begins

Britain and France tried to appease Hitler in the 1930s, but in 1939 he invaded Poland and World War II began. Two years later, Japan attacked Pearl Harbor, and the United States entered the war as well.

 ## The Allies Win the War

From 1943 to 1945, the Allies pushed the Germans out of Italy, France, and Russia, and then invaded Germany. Meanwhile, American troops pushed back the Japanese in the Pacific, then dropped the atomic bomb on Japan.

 ## The Cold War

Soon after World War II, a conflict began between the United States and the Soviet Union. It was known as the Cold War.

 ## The End of Empire

In the decades following World War II, nations in Asia and Africa began to demand independence.

 **FOLDABLES™**
Study Organizer

Sequencing Information *Make this foldable to help you sequence important events that occurred during World War II and the Cold War.*

Step 1 *Fold two sheets of paper in half from top to bottom. Cut each in half.*

Cut along the fold lines.

Step 2 *Turn and fold the four pieces in half from top to bottom.*

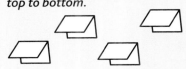

Reading and Writing
As you read the chapter, write the important events and dates that occurred during World War II and the Cold War on each section of your time line.

Step 3 *Tape the ends of the pieces together (overlapping the edges slightly) to make an accordion time line.*

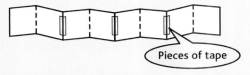

Pieces of tape

Reading Social Studies

Reading Skill

Discussion Questions

1 Learn It!

Building Discussion Skills

Discussing what you read is one way to gain a better understanding of a subject. In addition to your own knowledge and opinions, you gain the knowledge and opinions of others. In the passage below, the author asks questions to help you think about important decisions made in World War II. How would you answer the questions? What knowledge could you gain by listening to others answer these questions? What other questions could you ask to start a group discussion on this topic?

> In April 1945, Franklin Roosevelt died, and Harry S Truman became president. Truman faced a difficult decision. Should he risk American lives by invading Japan, or should he use the newly developed atomic bomb to end the war?
>
> —from page 829

Reading Tip

To have a good discussion requires listening carefully to what other people are saying. You might even want to jot down what they say so you can respond to their comments.

2 Practice It!

Read to Discuss

Read the passage below. As you read, write five questions that would help you launch a discussion with others and help you to gain a better understanding of the information in this passage. Share your questions in a discussion with a group of classmates.

Read to Write ·······
During a class discussion, write down notes about things others say. After the discussion, do a quickwrite. Write everything you would like to say that you did not get a chance to say out loud.

Reading the Bhagavad Gita proved to be one of the greatest influences on Gandhi's life. It returned him to the Hindu religion. It also exposed him to two ideas that he would come to live by in his life and work. One idea was that material goods kept a person from pursuing a spiritual life. The other idea was to be peaceful and even-tempered in all situations.

—from page 844

3 Apply It!

As you read Chapter 21, keep a list of questions, comments, or statements from the text that you would like to talk about later.

Section 1

The Rise of Dictators

Get Ready to Read!

What's the Connection?
The outcome of World War I and serious economic problems led to the rise of dictators in several countries.

Focusing on the Main Ideas
- New economic problems led to the Great Depression. *(page 805)*
- The Great Depression encouraged the rise of European dictators. *(page 808)*
- After Lenin's death, Stalin established a brutal regime in the USSR. *(page 810)*
- Economic problems led to militarism in Japan. *(page 811)*

Locating Places
Ruhr Valley (RUR VA•lee)
Manchuria (man•CHUR•ee•uh)

Meeting People
Benito Mussolini (buh•NEE•toh MOO•suh•LEE•nee)
Adolf Hitler
Joseph Stalin

Building Your Vocabulary
inflation
depression
totalitarian state (toh•TA•luh•TEHR•ee•uhn)
collectivization (kuh•LEHK•tih•vuh•ZAY•shuhn)

Reading Strategy
Organizing Information Complete a diagram like the one below identifying the policies of three dictators.

Dictator	Policy

NATIONAL GEOGRAPHIC **When & Where?**

NORTH AMERICA EUROPE ASIA

1921   **1929**   **1937**

1922 Mussolini becomes Italy's leader

1928 Stalin starts Five-Year Plans

1929 The Great Depression begins

1933 Hitler becomes dictator of Germany

Postwar Economic Problems

Main Idea New economic problems led to the Great Depression.

Reading Focus Have you ever wondered why people accept paper money? After all, it is just paper, not anything valuable. Read to learn what happened in Germany when paper money became worthless.

The end of World War I left many nations unhappy. Defeated peoples, such as the Germans, felt humiliated. They resented losing territory and making war payments. Even people in winning nations, such as Italy and Japan, felt that they did not get enough land for the sacrifices they had made. When economic troubles came, frustration and fear added to this anger.

▲ Following World War I, Germany's economy was weak, and the German people faced hard times. In the photo above, German women search for scraps of food in a garbage pile.

At right, a woman uses worthless German paper money to start a fire in her kitchen stove. *What did France do when Germany could not pay the reparations it owed?* ▶

A Troubled Germany You read earlier that the Treaty of Versailles blamed Germany for causing the war. As a result, the Germans owed the Allies a huge sum in reparations, or payments for war damages. Germany's new democratic government made the first payment in 1921. The next year, however, it claimed that it could not afford to pay any more.

France had hoped to use its share of reparations to rebuild its economy after the war. When Germany could not pay, France sent troops into the **Ruhr Valley** (RUR VA•lee), a rich industrial area in western Germany. The French wanted to take the wealth from the valley's mines and factories to make up for the unpaid reparations.

Angry German workers resisted the French takeover by going on strike. To pay

Focus on Everyday Life

The Great Depression The Great Depression brought misery to millions of people. Begging for food on the streets became widespread.

More and more people became homeless. One person in Germany reported that: "An almost unbroken chain of homeless men extends the whole length of the great Hamburg-Berlin highway . . .— whole families had piled all their goods into baby carriages and wheelbarrows that they were pushing along as they plodded forward in dumb despair."

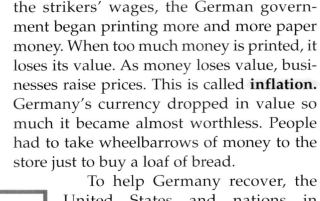

▲ Workers protest economic conditions.

Some of the unemployed staged hunger marches to get attention. In many countries, desperate people began to vote for political parties that offered extreme solutions. Across Europe, Fascist Parties and Communist Parties won more and more votes.

Connecting to the Past
1. What did some people in Europe do after they lost their jobs during the Great Depression?
2. How did people try to change their society during the Great Depression?

the strikers' wages, the German government began printing more and more paper money. When too much money is printed, it loses its value. As money loses value, businesses raise prices. This is called **inflation.** Germany's currency dropped in value so much it became almost worthless. People had to take wheelbarrows of money to the store just to buy a loaf of bread.

To help Germany recover, the United States and nations in Western Europe created the Dawes Plan in 1924. Developed by Charles Dawes, an American banker, the Dawes Plan reduced the amount Germany owed and set payments that its government could handle. The plan also arranged for American banks to loan $200 million to Germany. Good times followed, but they were short-lived.

What Caused the Great Depression?
During the 1930s, the world's industrialized countries were hit by an economic depression. A **depression** is a period of low economic activity when many people lose their jobs. The 1930s depression was so severe that it became known as the Great Depression. During this time, factories closed and millions of people lost their jobs.

One major cause of the Great Depression was the crash of the U.S. stock market. Before the depression struck, American companies were producing much of the world's manufactured goods. People saw their chance to make a fortune by investing in these companies. As a result, the U.S. stock market boomed.

Many investors bought stock on margin. In other words, they paid only a small amount of the stock price and borrowed the rest of the money. As long as stock prices kept rising, buying on margin was safe. Investors would sell their stock when the price increased, repay their loan, and keep the difference as a profit.

Meanwhile, factories began having trouble selling everything they produced. Workers were not paid high enough wages to buy all the goods being made. This overproduction forced factory owners to slow production. They then cut back the number of workers they employed.

In October 1929, fears about the economy grew. People were pressured to pay back their loans. When they failed to pay, panic struck. Stock prices tumbled and wiped out the fortunes of many investors. Banks collapsed, and when they did many people lost all of their savings.

▲ President Franklin D. Roosevelt often attempted to ease the concerns of the American public by addressing them over the radio. *What effect did Roosevelt's New Deal have?*

The Depression Spreads Frightened American investors withdrew money from Germany and other European markets. These withdrawals caused the collapse of European banks as well. By 1931, trade was slow and jobs were scarce in both North America and Europe.

The worst year of the depression was 1932. By that time, one out of four Americans and British and two out of five Germans were out of work. People who had been put out of their homes lived in shacks built out of cardboard or tin.

FDR and the New Deal In the United States, President Franklin D. Roosevelt set up a program known as the New Deal. To provide people with money to buy food and housing and to put them back to work, the federal government set up several different agencies. One of these, the Civilian

Conservation Corps (CCC), gave jobs mostly to young people. They planted trees and built facilities in the nation's parks. The Works Progress Administration (WPA) paid jobless workers to build dams, roads, bridges, and hospitals. It also gave work to artists and writers. Other new government agencies tried to help farmers, business leaders, and home owners.

The federal government also carried out reforms. In 1935 Roosevelt convinced Congress to pass the Social Security Act. This program gave pensions, or payments, to citizens after they turned 65 and retired. It also provided Americans with unemployment insurance. If someone lost their job, they received money from the government until they found a new one. Roosevelt's New Deal failed to restore the economy completely, but it did give Americans hope about the future.

✓ **Reading Check** **Describe** How did the Dawes Plan affect Germany?

The Rise of Fascism and Nazism

Main Idea The Great Depression encouraged the rise of European dictators.

Reading Focus If you were penniless and homeless, would you vote for someone who promised to make your life better? Read to find out why Italians and Germans supported ruthless dictators.

The Great Depression brought fear to many people. Despite facing hard times, the people in the United States, Britain, and France held on to democracy. In many other countries, such as Italy and Germany, people had less loyalty to democratic values. They looked to strong leaders for help. These leaders became dictators—rulers who control their countries by force.

Under these dictators, a new form of government called totalitarianism developed. In a **totalitarian state** (toh•TA•luh•TEHR•ee•uhn), political leaders try to *totally* control the way citizens think and live. During the 1930s, totalitarian leaders used books, newspapers, the arts, and schools to influence their people. New technology, such as films and the radio, was also used to spread the government's point of view. People who disagreed or voiced other ideas were harshly punished.

Mussolini Takes Power The first country to become a totalitarian state was Italy. After World War I, Italy had a huge debt to pay off and many people did not have jobs. Workers went on strike for higher wages. Some hoped for a communist revolution similar to what was happening in Russia.

With the country in chaos, a man named **Benito Mussolini** (buh•NEE•toh MOO•suh•LEE•nee) created the Fascist Party and promised to restore order, fix Italy's economy, and make Italy a great nation. His followers wore black shirts and beat up people who opposed them. In 1922 Mussolini's followers staged a huge march on Rome. To prevent violence, Italy's king agreed to appoint Mussolini as head of the government.

Mussolini was known as *Il Duce* (eel DOO•chay), or "The Leader." He quickly put an end to democratic rule in Italy. Within a few years, Mussolini had banned all political parties except his Fascist Party. Personal freedoms and a free press no longer existed. Boys and girls of all ages had to join groups that taught them loyalty to the Fascist government. Mussolini built up Italy's military and promised to regain the glory of the ancient Romans.

▲ To gain control of Italy, Benito Mussolini used violence and political pressure to destroy his opponents. *What political changes did Mussolini bring to Italy?*

The Rise of Adolf Hitler

The Great Depression led to the rise of a totalitarian state in Germany. During the early 1930s, millions of Germans lost their jobs, and many businesses failed. Voters in large numbers supported a political leader named **Adolf Hitler.** In his speeches, Hitler appealed to people's fear about the economy and their bitterness about the Treaty of Versailles.

Hitler was leader of the National Socialist German Workers' Party, or the Nazi Party. Hitler and the Nazis portrayed the German people as better than all others. Germany, they believed, had a right to expand its territory. The Nazis were known for their anti-Semitism, or hatred of the Jews. They blamed the Jews for Germany's problems. Hitler presented these ideas in a book called *Mein Kampf,* or "My Struggle."

Many Germans, worried about the economy, began to vote for the Nazis. By 1932, the Nazi Party had become the largest party in the German parliament. A year later, Hitler was named Germany's chancellor, or prime minister. Next, the German parliament handed all power to Hitler while he dealt with the country's problems. In this way, Hitler became dictator of Germany.

Once in power, Hitler did away with all political parties except the Nazis. He had books about democracy burned. He took over the courts and set up a secret police.

▲ To gather support for the Nazi Party, Hitler often addressed the German people at large rallies and used other propaganda techniques. *What were some of the basic beliefs of the Nazi Party?*

He took over radio and newspapers and broke up unions. The Nazis also set up large prisons called concentration camps. There, they sent people who disagreed with Nazi ideas.

The Nazi government reflected Hitler's strong anti-Semitism. The Nazis took away the Jews' businesses and jobs. Jews could not go to school or get medical care.

Nazis also tried to restrict women's rights. According to the Nazis, women were meant to be wives and mothers, not leaders. So the government discouraged women from becoming lawyers, doctors, or professors. Instead, posters urged women to "Get a hold of pots and pans . . .".

✓ Reading Check **Analyze** Why do you think the king of Italy let Mussolini take control of Italy?

Stalin and the Soviet Union

Main Idea After Lenin's death, Stalin established a brutal regime in the USSR.

Reading Focus If you ran the government, how would you fix the problems in your community? Do you think government ever causes problems by trying to fix things? Read to learn how Stalin's government caused great hardship when trying to change the USSR.

Harsh rule also came to Russia. Previously, you learned about Lenin, the Russian Revolution, and the civil war that followed. By 1922, Lenin's government was securely in power. In that year, Russia's Communist leaders formed the Union of Soviet Socialist Republics (USSR), or the Soviet Union. This vast territory included Russia and most of the conquered lands of the old Russian Empire.

Stalin Takes Power

After a series of strokes, Lenin died in 1924. After Lenin died, a struggle for power took place in the Soviet Union. By the late 1920s, **Joseph Stalin** had become the ruler of the Soviet Union. Under Lenin, Stalin's job had been to appoint party officials. When the power struggle began, the thousands of officials Stalin had appointed supported him. Their support helped him seize power.

Government Plans the Economy

Stalin wanted the Soviet Union to become an industrial power as soon as possible. Beginning in 1928, he introduced a series of Five-Year Plans. These were programs that set economic goals for a five-year period. Under the Five-Year Plans, steel mills, power plants, and oil refineries were built and kept under government control. Factory managers had to produce a certain amount of goods.

Under Stalin's orders, the government also took control of all farming. Stalin's plans called for **collectivization** (kuh•LEHK•tih•vuh•ZAY•shuhn). This meant combining small farms into large, factory-like farms run by the government.

Many peasants, however, wanted to keep working on their own farms. They resisted collectivization by destroying their houses, cows, and pigs. This resistance did not last long. Peasants who refused to cooperate with the government were either shot or sent to prison.

In Ukraine, a region south of Russia, Stalin caused a famine to control the people. He had officials seize the grain supplies. As a result, millions of peasants in Ukraine starved to death.

By 1939, the Soviet Union had become a major industrial power. The people, however, paid a high price for swift industrial growth. Workers labored long hours for low wages. Consumer goods, such as clothes and household goods, were poorly made

▲ Joseph Stalin (right) took power in the Soviet Union after the death of Vladimir Lenin (left). *Why did Stalin set up the Five-Year Plans?*

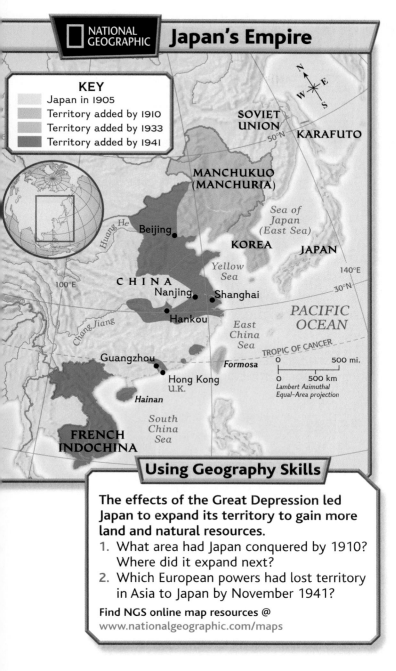

Japan's Empire

KEY

Japan in 1905

Territory added by 1910

Territory added by 1933

Territory added by 1941

SOVIET UNION

KARAFUTO

50°N

MANCHUKUO (MANCHURIA)

Sea of Japan (East Sea)

Huang He

Beijing

KOREA

JAPAN

Yellow Sea

140°E

100°E

CHINA

Nanjing

Shanghai

30°N

Hankou

East China Sea

PACIFIC OCEAN

Chang Jiang

TROPIC OF CANCER

Guangzhou

Formosa

0   500 mi.

Hong Kong U.K.

0   500 km

Hainan

Lambert Azimuthal Equal-Area projection

South China Sea

FRENCH INDOCHINA

Using Geography Skills

The effects of the Great Depression led Japan to expand its territory to gain more land and natural resources.

1. What area had Japan conquered by 1910? Where did it expand next?
2. Which European powers had lost territory in Asia to Japan by November 1941?

Find NGS online map resources @ www.nationalgeographic.com/maps

and hard to find, and housing shortages were common.

Above all, millions of farmers, workers, and government officials suffered under Stalin. Those people who opposed Stalin's actions were killed or sent to remote prison camps deep in the vast forests of icy Siberia.

Reading Check **Explain** What did Stalin's Five-Year Plans achieve? What problems did they cause?

The Military Rules Japan

Main Idea Economic problems led to militarism in Japan.

Reading Focus Is it ever okay for people to steal something if they need it? Read to learn how Japanese leaders used that argument to justify invading another country.

About the same time that the Soviet Union fell under Stalin's strict control, Japan's military gained control of Japan's government. As you read earlier, Japan had become an industrial power by the early 1900s. As Japan's economy grew, so too did its population. Between 1872 and 1925, the number of people in Japan rose from 35 million to 60 million.

What Problems Did Japan Face? Japan's government hoped that new factories and new markets would create jobs for the larger population. So its leaders stressed manufacturing and foreign trade. Japan's industry grew rapidly, and Japanese factory-made goods were sold worldwide.

The Japanese government helped develop large private companies called *zaibatsu*. By the late 1930s, these companies controlled much of Japan's economy. While factory managers and rural landowners grew wealthy, factory workers and farmers were poorly paid and housed. Often there was not enough food to feed Japan's growing population. Food prices rose rapidly and often led to food riots. When the Great Depression reached Japan, workers and farmers suffered most.

Japan Invades Manchuria The Great Depression caused a worldwide fall in prices. This brought disaster to Japan's factories. Millions of workers lost their jobs. Some began to starve.

Starving workers and farmers blamed Japan's politicians for their problems. The leaders of Japan's military claimed that Japan's problems were caused by European and American ideas. They said that Japan should return to its old warrior traditions. Their ideas began to influence all areas of Japanese life.

As Japan's trade declined, Japan's military leaders argued that Japan needed more land and natural resources to make its economy stronger. Without government approval, army leaders in 1931 invaded **Manchuria** (man•CHUR•ee•uh), the northeast region of China. When Japan's prime minister tried to stop the war, the military killed him. From then on, Japan's government did what the military wanted. Over the next few years, several Japanese mili-

▲ In the 1930s, the Japanese military became more aggressive. This photo shows Japanese cavalry in China. *What area did Japan invade in 1931?*

tary officers were chosen to serve as prime minister. Under their leadership, Japan began making plans to build an empire in Asia even if it meant war with other countries.

 **Explain** How did *zaibatsu* affect the social structure in Japan?

History **O**nline
Study Central™ Need help with the material in this section? Visit jat.glencoe.com

Section ❶ Review

Reading Summary

Review the Main Ideas

- The crash of the stock market led to the Great Depression. In the United States, Franklin Roosevelt introduced programs to help the economy.

- In Europe, Benito Mussolini became dictator of Italy and Adolf Hitler became dictator of Germany.

- In the Soviet Union, Joseph Stalin took power and placed all farms and factories under government control.

- Japan's economic problems enabled the military to take control of the government.

What Did You Learn?

1. What was the New Deal and why was it proposed?

2. What ideas did Adolf Hitler reveal in *Mein Kampf?*

Critical Thinking

3. **Compare and Contrast** Draw a chart like the one below. Fill in details about leaders and events in the 1920s and 1930s.

United States	Italy	Germany	Soviet Union	Japan

4. **Summarize** What was a totalitarian state, and how did totalitarian states gain the support of the country's citizens?

5. **Analyze** Were Stalin's economic plans for the Soviet Union, both industrial and agricultural, successful? Explain.

6. **Expository Writing** Imagine you are living in the U.S. in the 1930s. Write a letter to a pen pal in another country describing the actions the president is taking to help Americans during the Great Depression and whether or not you agree with those actions.

7. **Reading** Discussion Questions Write five questions that would help you launch a discussion about why Hitler and the Nazis were able to take power in Germany.

Section 2

World War II Begins

Get Ready to Read!

What's the Connection?

You have read how economic hard times paved the way for dictatorships in Europe. The goals of these dictators soon led to a new world war.

Focusing on the Main Ideas

- Other European nations stood by as Germany expanded its territory. **(page 814)**

- World War II began when Germany invaded Poland in September 1939, leading France and Britain to declare war. **(page 815)**

Locating Places

Rhineland
Sudetenland (soo•DAY•tuhn•LAND)
Munich (MYOO•nihk)
Nanjing (NAHN•JIHNG)
Pearl Harbor

Meeting People

Neville Chamberlain
(NEHV•uhl   CHAYM•buhr•luhn)

Winston Churchill
(WIHN•stuhn   CHUHRCH•HIHL)

Building Your Vocabulary

appeasement (uh•PEEZ•muhnt)

Reading Strategy

Sequencing Information Create a diagram like the one below to track the areas invaded by Germany.

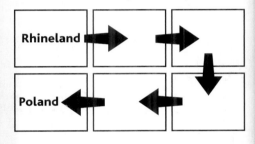

When & Where?

1934	1938	1942

1935 Hitler begins expanding Germany's army

1936 Spanish Civil War begins

1939 Germany invades Poland

1941 Japanese planes bomb Pearl Harbor

Appeasement Fails

Main Idea Other European nations stood by as Germany expanded its territory.

Reading Focus How do you deal with bullies? Is it better to stand up to them or give them what they want? Read on to find out how Europe's leaders dealt with Adolf Hitler's demands.

One reason Adolf Hitler was popular in Germany was because he criticized the Treaty of Versailles. Many Germans believed the treaty was unfair. Hitler promised in his speeches that he would no longer obey the treaty.

The Treaty of Versailles kept Germany's military forces small. Hitler, however, insisted that this was unfair. In March 1935, he stated that Germany would build a new air force and increase the size of its army. The Treaty of Versailles had also declared that no German troops could be in the **Rhineland,** a German territory west of the Rhine River along the French border. In 1936 Hitler ordered troops into the Rhineland.

France wanted to expel the German troops from the Rhineland, but the French government would not act without British help. Britain did not want to use force against Germany. Instead, British leaders chose a policy of **appeasement** (uh•PEEZ•muhnt). Appeasement is the idea that if you meet another government's demands, you can avoid war.

Hitler gained a close ally in Italy's Benito Mussolini. In 1935 Mussolini sent Italian forces to invade the African nation of Ethiopia. Britain and France opposed

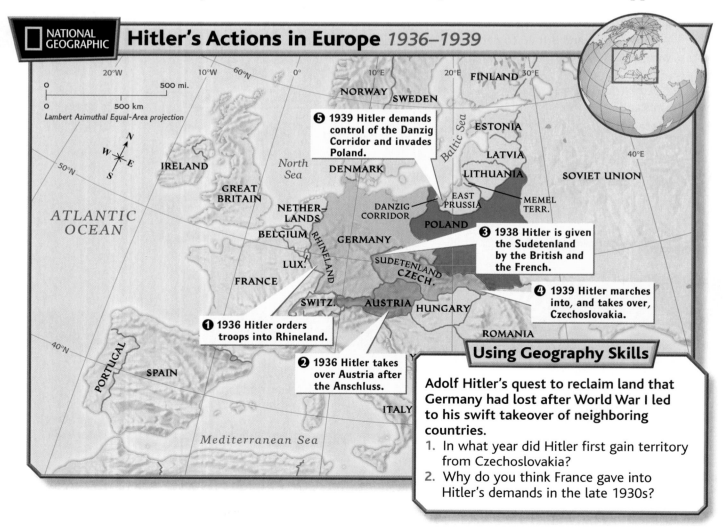

NATIONAL GEOGRAPHIC

Hitler's Actions in Europe *1936–1939*

500 mi.

500 km

Lambert Azimuthal Equal-Area projection

❺ 1939 Hitler demands control of the Danzig Corridor and invades Poland.

❸ 1938 Hitler is given the Sudetenland by the British and the French.

❹ 1939 Hitler marches into, and takes over, Czechoslovakia.

❶ 1936 Hitler orders troops into Rhineland.

❷ 1936 Hitler takes over Austria after the Anschluss.

Using Geography Skills

Adolf Hitler's quest to reclaim land that Germany had lost after World War I led to his swift takeover of neighboring countries.

1. In what year did Hitler first gain territory from Czechoslovakia?
2. Why do you think France gave into Hitler's demands in the late 1930s?

the invasion but took no military action to stop it. Hitler, however, threw his support to Mussolini.

Next, the two dictators intervened in Spain. From 1936 to 1939, a civil war divided that country. Germany and Italy helped a Spanish military leader, General Francisco Franco, overthrow Spain's new republic. Soon after, Italy and Germany formed an alliance.

Next, Hitler turned to Austria. He insisted that Austria, a German-speaking country, should be part of Germany. In March 1938, he sent troops into Austria and took it over.

Hitler then turned to Austria's neighbor, Czechoslovakia, and demanded that the Czechs give Germany the **Sudetenland** (soo•DAY•tuhn•LAND), an area in western Czechoslovakia where many Germans lived. Czechoslovakia was ready to fight to keep the Sudetenland, but Britain and France preferred to negotiate. In September 1938, European leaders met in the German city of **Munich** (MYOO•nihk).

At the Munich Conference, Britain and France agreed to give the Sudetenland to Germany. Hitler, in turn, promised not to expand Germany's territory further. The British prime minister, **Neville Chamberlain** (NEHV•uhl CHAYM•buhr•luhn), returned home and declared that there would be "peace in our time."

Hopes for peace were smashed the following year. In March 1939, German forces took over western Czechoslovakia and set up a Nazi-friendly state in the eastern part. Hitler then demanded control of Danzig, a German city inside Polish territory. In response, Britain promised to support Poland if the Germans invaded.

Reading Check **Analyze** Why did British and French leaders appease Hitler?

The War Begins

Main Idea World War II began when Germany invaded Poland in September 1939, leading France and Britain to declare war.

Reading Focus Have you ever had to do something really difficult? What helped you to do it? Read to learn how the British endured defeats and German bombings.

In the summer of 1939, Hitler prepared to invade Poland. He worried, however, that such an attack would anger Stalin because Poland bordered the Soviet Union. Though bitter enemies, Hitler and Stalin signed a treaty in August 1939 in which they promised not to attack each other. They also agreed to divide Poland between them. This agreement freed Hitler to attack Poland.

▲ This photo shows a Czech woman weeping as she salutes invading German troops. *What happened after Britain and France gave the Sudetenland to Germany?*

▲ During the Battle of Britain, German planes bombed British cities, hoping to break the will of the British people. *What advantage did the Royal Air Force have during the Battle of Britain?*

Poland and France Fall

On September 1, 1939, Hitler sent his armies into Poland. Two days later, Britain and France declared war on Germany. The German attack on Poland was quick and fierce. In less than a month, the conquered country was split in half by Hitler and Stalin.

In April 1940, the Germans attacked Denmark and Norway. In May, they invaded the Netherlands and Belgium. German troops and tanks then smashed through French defenses and raced across northern

History Online

Web Activity Visit jat.glencoe.com and click on *Chapter 21—Student Web Activity* to learn more about World War II.

France. A few weeks later, on June 22, 1940, France surrendered to Germany. At this time, Italy joined the war on Germany's side.

What Was the Battle of Britain?

Hitler expected the British to ask for peace. Instead, the new prime minister of Great Britain, **Winston Churchill** (WIHN•stuhn CHUHRCH•HIHL), declared, "We shall never surrender."

In August the German air force began an all-out effort to destroy Britain's Royal Air Force and clear the way for a German invasion of Britian. This air battle became known as the Battle of Britain.

The Royal Air Force also had a new technology called radar. Radar stations along the coast detected incoming German airplanes and directed British fighter planes to stop them. On October 12, 1940, Hitler cancelled his plans to invade Britain. Great Britain escaped invasion thanks to a few hundred pilots. Churchill told the British Parliament: "Never . . . was so much owed by so many to so few."

America Stays Neutral

The United States remained neutral during the early years of the war. In the 1930s, Congress had passed several laws making it illegal to help other countries in a war if the U.S. was neutral. President Roosevelt, however, believed that Germany was a threat to the United States. He convinced Congress to approve a cash-and-carry policy. This law let Britain buy goods from American businesses as long as they paid cash and carried the goods to Britain in their own ships. A year later, he asked Congress to pass the Lend-Lease Act. This law allowed the U.S. to lend weapons to Britain. Roosevelt also ordered the American navy to protect the British ships from German submarines when they were close to the United States.

Biography

WINSTON CHURCHILL
1874–1965
FRANKLIN D. ROOSEVELT
1882–1945

Winston Churchill grew up in Blenheim Palace, England, raised by a beloved nanny. His father, Lord Randolph Churchill, was a member of the British Parliament. Churchill attended private schools where he struggled with his studies. When Churchill switched to the Royal Military Academy, he began doing well. He studied military tactics, mapmaking, and military law. Later he joined the cavalry and fought in India and Africa. Afterward, he became a journalist and found fame reporting on the Boer War.

Franklin Delano Roosevelt was born in Hyde Park, New York, to a wealthy family. Roosevelt was educated at home by a governess until he turned 14. Then he was sent to a school near Boston. Like Churchill, Roosevelt did not do well in school. Because President Theodore Roosevelt was his cousin, Roosevelt wanted to work in government. He went to Harvard University and Columbia Law School.

▲ Winston Churchill

At age 26, Churchill won election to the British Parliament. This was the beginning of his political career that led eventually to him becoming prime minister of England. At age 28, Roosevelt won election to the New York State senate, but then came down with polio and lost much of the use of his legs. Refusing to allow his disability to end his career, he went on to become governor of New York and then president.

▲ Franklin D. Roosevelt

"Together we cannot fail."
–Franklin D. Roosevelt, *Fireside Chats*

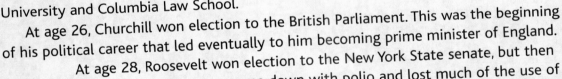

Then and Now

Both Churchill and Roosevelt came from families already involved in politics. How do you think this affected their decision to pursue that type of career? Identify a few present-day families that are active in politics.

Hitler Invades the Soviet Union Unable to defeat the British, Hitler decided that Germany needed the resources of the Soviet Union. He also believed that the Soviets' vast land area could provide "living space" for Germans in the future. In June 1941, German forces attacked the Soviet Union. They destroyed most of the Soviets' warplanes, disabled thousands of Soviet tanks, and captured half a million Soviet soldiers.

As the Germans advanced, Stalin ordered a scorched-earth policy. Soviet troops and civilians burned cities, destroyed their own crops, and blew up dams that produced electric power.

These actions made it harder for the Germans to supply their troops and keep moving forward. Then the rainy season began, turning the roads to mud and trapping German wagons and trucks. Soon afterward the harsh Russian winter set in, catching the German army unprepared.

Despite loss of soldiers and equipment, German troops reached the outskirts of Moscow on December 2, 1941. That was as far as they got. The Soviets refused to surrender, and the Germans were unable to break into the city.

Japan Attacks Pearl Harbor While Hitler and Mussolini waged war in Europe, the Japanese launched new attacks in East Asia. In Section 1, you learned about Japan's takeover of Manchuria in 1931. During the 1930s, the Japanese moved steadily southward into China. In December 1937, they

The Attack on Pearl Harbor

On December 7, 1941, Japan carried out its plan to attack the United States and bring them into World War II. Early that morning, a group of Japanese warplanes flew over the military base in Pearl Harbor, Hawaii. Without warning, they dropped bombs on the men and women below and destroyed countless ships as they sat in their docks unprotected. The attack cost many thousands of American lives and prompted the U.S. to enter the war. *Why do you think the Japanese chose to attack a base in Hawaii?*

seized **Nanjing** (NAHN•JIHNG), the Chinese capital. China's leader, Chiang Kai-shek, refused to surrender, and the government moved into China's interior.

Japan next moved into Southeast Asia. After the fall of France in 1940, Japanese forces sized the French colony of Indochina. Japan also planned to take the Dutch East Indies, British Malaya, and the American territory of the Philippines. The Japanese goal was to gain badly needed rubber, oil, and food supplies.

President Roosevelt wanted Britain to defeat Germany. He worried that Britain would also have to fight Japan if Japan attacked the British Empire in Asia. So Roosevelt tried to stop Japan by using economic pressure. When Japan invaded Indochina, President Roosevelt prevented the Japanese from withdrawing money they had in American banks. He also stopped the sale of oil, gasoline, and other natural resources that Japan lacked.

Angered by American actions, the Japanese decided to go to war against the United States. On December 7, 1941, Japanese warplanes carried out a surprise attack on the American fleet at **Pearl Harbor,** Hawaii. The attack destroyed many battleships and planes. More than 2,300 soldiers, sailors, and civilians were killed.

The next day, President Roosevelt asked Congress to declare war on Japan. He called December 7 "a date which will live in infamy [disgrace]." Congress quickly declared war on Japan. Three days later, Germany and Italy declared war on the United States.

✓ **Reading Check** **Identify** What was the United States's cash-and-carry policy?

Study Central™ Need help with the material in this section? Visit jat.glencoe.com

Section 2 Review

What Did You Learn?

1. Describe what happened at the Battle of Britain.

2. Describe how the United States aided Britain before Pearl Harbor was attacked.

Critical Thinking

3. **Sequencing Information** Draw a time line like the one below. Fill in details about German aggressions in Europe beginning with the occupation of the Rhineland and ending with the invasion of Russia.

March 1936 ——————————— June 1941

4. **Analyze** Describe the British policy of appeasement. Why do you think such a policy did not work with Hitler?

5. **Evaluate** What was the importance of the Battle of Britain?

6. **Cause and Effect** What American actions caused Japan to carry out their attack on Pearl Harbor?

7. **Expository Writing** Choose an event from the section and write a newspaper article about it. Include a headline, details about the event, and why the event was important.

Reading Summary

Review the Main Ideas

• In the mid-1930s, Germany began to rearm and seize surrounding territories, while Britain and France followed a policy of appeasement.

• The German invasion of Poland in 1939 began World War II. In 1941, Japan attacked Pearl Harbor, bringing the United States into the war.

The Unexpected Treasure

Adapted by Gary Schmidt

Before You Read

The Scene: This story takes place in Kraków, Poland, shortly before World War II.

The Characters: Eisik is a poor Jewish boy living in Kraków with his family.

The Plot: Eisik's family is very poor. He has three dreams in which a man tells him to go to a particular place to find treasure. Eisik must decide whether or not to follow the dreams' directions.

Vocabulary Preview

embankment: raised structure that holds back water

flourished: waved boldly

slate: rock used as a construction material

sprinted: ran as fast as possible

Have you ever had a dream and wanted it to be true? In this story, a boy dreams about a solution to his family's problems and then tries to make the dream come true.

As You Read

This story is a mixture of fact and fiction. It is based on a story about Rabbi Eisik, a man born in Kraków who found a great treasure and used it to build a House of Prayer in his neighborhood.

Eisik, the youngest boy in his family, believed that his must be one of the poorest families in all of Poland. Poorer than poor. When their Rabbi spoke of poverty, Eisik knew, he was speaking of Eisik's family. Even his hunger was hungry, and his jacket was more patch than jacket. He had seen plucked plump chickens hanging in the butcher's shop, but his mother had never, as far as Eisik knew, even been inside such a shop. He had never tasted a candy, and he wondered what one might taste like. He wondered if a house could ever be too warm. He knew that it could be too cold.

Eisik's family was very poor.

One night, Eisik dreamed that a man came to him and pointed to a bridge in Kraków.[1] "Look by the arch of the bridge,"[2] he said, "and you will find a great treasure." Eisik woke up that morning smiling, but he knew better than to believe in a silly dream, and he soon forgot about it.

The next night the dream came again. The same man pointed to the bridge. "Look by the arch of the bridge, and you will find a great treasure." Again, Eisik woke in the morning smiling, but he knew that it was just a silly dream. He soon forgot about it.

On the third night, the man came again into his dreams, and now he was angry. "Do I come all the way into the

---

[1]**Kraków:** a city in southern Poland
[2]**arch of the bridge:** curved pieces that connect the main structure to the banks on either side and support the weight of the bridge

World of Confusion[3] for nothing every night?" he demanded. "Now, boy, look by the arch of the bridge, and you will find a great treasure."

When Eisik woke, he was trembling. He went to his mother and asked if she believed that dreams can come true. She leaned down and kissed him on the forehead. "Of course they can come true. Weren't you born to us?"

Eisik packed some food and set off for Kraków.

It was a long walk, and the sun was well on its way to rest before Eisik reached the city and found the bridge. He scrambled down the embankment and onto a slate walk. It was slimy with the damp of the water, so he crept slowly, looking into all the shadows, testing the bricks to see if they might give and the treasure be hidden behind them. But there was nothing at all. Tired and wet, he climbed back up to the bridge.

"You there! What are you doing?" A swastikaed[4] guard. Eisik froze.

"What are you doing, creeping about the bridge like that?"

And Eisik, scared and ashamed, could only say, "It was a dream. A dream told me I should do it."

"A dream? A dream?" The guard laughed. "Don't you know better than to believe in a silly dream? Don't you know that dreams mean nothing? Why, these last three nights, I've had the same dream again and again: A man comes and tells me that there is a great treasure hidden under the stove in the house of a poor family with a boy named Eisik.

---

[3]**World of Confusion:** the characters' name for their way of life during a time of restrictions and fear
[4]**swastikaed:** wearing a swastika, a Nazi symbol

Do you see me running off, looking into every Jewish house with a boy named Eisik and digging under their stove? Do you?"

Eisik shook his head, but his heart stopped.

The guard flourished his rifle at him. "Off now, and don't trouble me with dreams."

Eisik sprinted from the bridge and ran out of Kraków all the way home, where his father and mother and brothers and sisters were waiting for him. They threw their arms around him, and his mother wept, and even his father. "We thought . . ." they began, and could not go on. They feared to say aloud what they had thought in the World of Confusion where anything at all might happen.

And when they had all gone inside, Eisik and his father moved their iron stove. They pried up a layer of bricks, and beneath it they found a box filled with gold and silver coins. It was enough, said Papa, to get all of them, even Grandpapa and Tante,[5] out of Poland. Maybe even to America.

And Eisik hoped that that dream would come true as well.

---

[5]**Tante:** French for *aunt*

Responding to the Reading

1. How does Eisik find treasure by looking by the arch of the bridge?

2. When Eisik talks with his mother about dreams, each of them is referring to a different type of dream. What are the two meanings of *dream* used in that conversation?

3. **Analyze** Why do you think Eisik did not tell his family where he was going and that he would arrive home late?

4. **Compare** How do Eisik and the guard react differently to their dreams?

5. **Reading** **Read to Write** Eisik and his family had dreams of a future in which they were safe and had enough money for food and heat. What types of dreams do you have? Write a brief essay in which you identify three of your goals and explain what you need to do to make those dreams come true.

823

Section 3

The Allies Win the War

Get-Ready to Read!

What's the Connection?

You have read about how dictators expanding their power and territory led to World War II. In this section, you will learn how the Allies defeated Germany, Japan, and Italy, and won World War II.

Focusing on the Main Ideas

- The Allies fought for four long years in Europe and in the Pacific. *(page 825)*

- The Nazis murdered millions of people in an attempt to destroy Jews and other European ethnic groups. *(page 827)*

- The successful invasion on D-Day was the beginning of the end of World War II. *(page 828)*

Locating Places

Auschwitz (OWSH•VIHTS)

Meeting People

Douglas MacArthur (muh•KAHR• thuhr)

Dwight D. Eisenhower (EYE•zuhn• HOWR)

Harry S Truman (TROO•muhn)

Building Your Vocabulary

genocide (JEH•nuh•SYD)

D-Day

Reading Strategy

Sequencing Complete a table like the one below showing two events that occurred in each year.

Year	Event	Event
1942		
1943		
1944		
1945		

NATIONAL GEOGRAPHIC When & Where?

NORTH AMERICA   EUROPE   ASIA

1941

1943

1945

1942 Battle of Midway stops Japanese advance

1943 Italy surrenders to Allies

1944 Allies land in France on D-Day

1945 Atomic bombs are dropped on Japan

The Great Struggle

Main Idea The Allies fought for four long years in Europe and in the Pacific.

Reading Focus Have you ever had to follow a step-by-step plan to finish a project? Read to learn how step-by-step, the Allies pushed back the Axis powers.

World War II was a huge war. On one side were the Allies—the United States, Great Britain, the Soviet Union, and China. On the other side were the Axis powers— Germany, Italy, and Japan. It was fought on two fronts—in Europe and in the Pacific. Winning battles required outstanding leaders and hundreds of thousands of troops. At home, civilians worked hard to provide resources and goods for the war effort.

Stopping Japan's Advance By mid-1942, Japan had driven the Americans out of the Philippines and seized many islands in the Pacific. The United States set out to stop the Japanese advance. In June 1942,

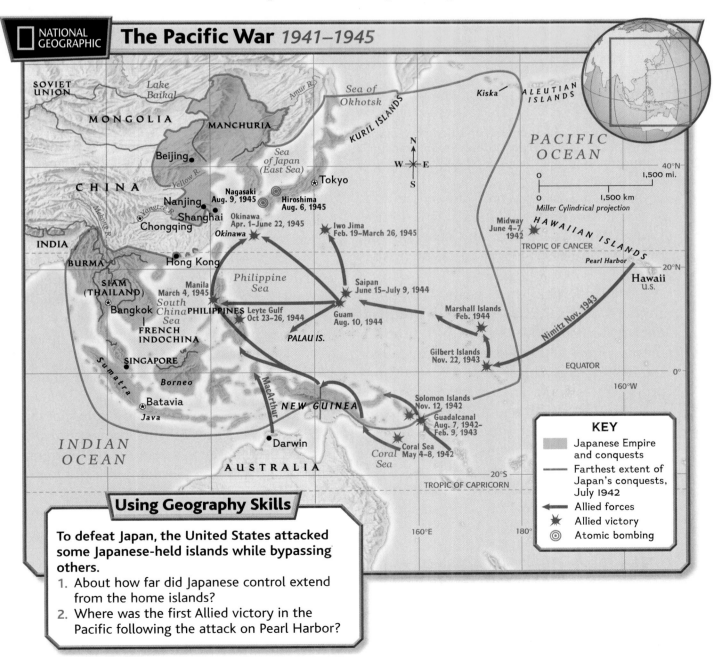

NATIONAL GEOGRAPHIC

The Pacific War *1941–1945*

Using Geography Skills

To defeat Japan, the United States attacked some Japanese-held islands while bypassing others.

1. About how far did Japanese control extend from the home islands?
2. Where was the first Allied victory in the Pacific following the attack on Pearl Harbor?

KEY
- Japanese Empire and conquests
- Farthest extent of Japan's conquests, July 1942
- Allied forces
- Allied victory
- Atomic bombing

▲ The leaders of the three major Allied powers met at Tehran in 1943. Shown are (left to right) Joseph Stalin, Franklin D. Roosevelt, and Winston Churchill. *What did the Allies agree to at Tehran?*

advances in North Africa, British forces in 1942 defeated the Germans in Egypt. Later that year, British and American forces landed in Morocco and Algeria. Moving swiftly eastward, they drove the Germans out of North Africa in May 1943.

Allied troops then moved into southern Europe. They took the island of Sicily in the summer of 1943 and landed on Italy's mainland in September. U.S. general **Dwight D. Eisenhower** (EYE•zuhn•HOWR) directed the overall invasion. Another American general, George Patton, and British general Bernard Montgomery actually led the troops.

the American forces won a major sea and air battle at Midway Island. This battle stopped Japan's advance and changed the course of the Pacific war in favor of the Allies.

During the next three years, U.S. commanders in the Pacific—General **Douglas MacArthur** (muh•KAHR•thuhr) and Admiral Chester Nimitz—carried out a plan called island-hopping. This called for attacking certain key islands. The United States then used these islands for jumping forward to others, moving closer and closer to Japan.

By 1945, the Americans had recaptured the Philippines and destroyed much of Japan's air force and navy. The Japanese, however, fought fiercely as American forces closed in on Japan itself.

Driving Back the Germans Meanwhile,
the war raged on in Africa, the Soviet Union, and Europe. After early German

As the Allies advanced, the Italians overthrew Mussolini and surrendered. German forces in Italy fought on but failed to stop the Allied move into central Italy. In June 1944, the Allies finally took Rome, Italy's capital.

Meanwhile, Allied leaders made plans for the world after the war was over. In late 1943 Roosevelt, Churchill, and Stalin met in the Middle East at Tehran, the capital of Iran. At this Tehran Conference, the leaders agreed to divide up Germany after defeating Hitler. Stalin also agreed to help the United States defeat Japan and to join an international organization for keeping peace after the war.

✓ **Reading Check** **Contrast** How was the war in the Pacific different from the war in Europe?

The Holocaust

Main Idea The Nazis murdered millions of people in an attempt to destroy Jews and other European ethnic groups.

Reading Focus Today many people use the word *Nazi* to mean "someone very evil." The main reason is the Holocaust. Read on to learn about this dark chapter in human history.

During World War II, the Nazis began a program of **genocide** (JEH•nuh•SYD), or the killing of an entire group of people. Hitler wanted to destroy all of Europe's Jews. As many as 6 million Jews were killed in what has become known as the Holocaust. Millions of others, including Slavs and Roma, or Gypsies, were also ruthlessly killed.

In Section 1, you learned that the Nazis passed laws against the Jews during the 1930s. These laws declared that Jews were no longer German citizens. By the end of the decade, Nazi actions became more violent.

On the night of November 9, 1938, the Nazis burned synagogues, destroyed Jewish shops, and killed many Jews. About 30,000 Jewish men were sent to concentration camps, large prison camps used to hold people for political reasons. This event became known as *Kristallnacht,* or the "night of shattered glass," because of the Jewish shop windows that were broken by Nazi mobs.

During World War II, the Nazis mistreated the Jews in the lands they conquered. They forced Jews to wear a yellow, six-pointed star on their clothing.

The Nazis began the mass killing of Jews when the German army invaded the Soviet Union in 1941. Special Nazi forces accompanied the army. They captured and shot any Jews they found and dumped them in mass graves.

In January 1942, German leaders agreed on what they called "the final solution." Nazis rounded up millions of Jews and hundreds of thousands of other innocent people in the areas they controlled. Then the prisoners traveled in trains and trucks to death camps, such as **Auschwitz** (OWSH•VIHTS) in Poland. At the camps, many people died in poison gas chambers. Others died of starvation. Still others were victims of cruel experiments carried out by Nazi doctors. Later, as Allied forces moved into Nazi-held areas, they saw firsthand the unspeakable horrors of the death camps. People around the world were stunned by this terrible result of Nazi brutality.

Reading Check **Identify** What is genocide, and how did the Nazis attempt to carry it out?

▲ Toward the end of the war, Allied troops liberated a number of concentration camps. The survivors at the camps were often near starvation. *What was the "final solution"?*

The Allies Win

Main Idea The successful invasion on D-Day was the beginning of the end of World War II.

Reading Focus Can you recall important days in your life? For Europeans who lived through World War II, June 6, 1944, stands out in their memory. Read on to find out why.

By 1944, the Germans and Japanese were falling back everywhere. No longer on the defensive, the Allies were preparing to invade Germany and Japan.

What Was D-Day? For months, Allied forces under General Eisenhower had been preparing for the invasion of occupied France. On June 6, 1944, or **D-Day**—the day of the invasions—ships carried troops and equipment across the English Channel to the French province of Normandy. As battleship guns pounded German positions, Allied soldiers moved onto the beaches.

From their Normandy foothold, the Allies launched an attack against the Germans. By early August, General Patton and his tanks were racing across northern France while General Montgomery and his British troops advanced along the coast into Belgium. At the same time, the people of Paris rose up against the Germans. On August 25, the Germans retreated, and Allied troops entered Paris.

On December 16, 1944, the Germans counterattacked. As their troops advanced, they pushed back the Allied lines, creating a bulge. The attack later became known as the Battle of the Bulge. After weeks of fighting, the Americans won the battle and then headed into Germany.

By late 1944, the Soviets had driven the Germans from Russia and back across Poland. By February 1945, Soviet troops were just outside Berlin. On April 30, 1945, Hitler committed suicide in Berlin. On May 7, 1945, the Germans surrendered.

Primary Source

D-Day

On D-Day, June 6, 1944, American troops landed in Normandy, France. Lieutenant John Bentz Carroll describes the invasion:

"Two hundred yards out, we took a direct hit. . . .

. . . Somehow or other, the ramp door opened up . . . Everyone started to jump off into the water. They were being hit as they jumped, the machine gun fire was so heavy.

. . . The tide was moving us so rapidly. . . . We would grab out at some of those underwater obstructions and mines built on telephone poles and girders, and hang on. We'd take cover, then make a dash through the surf. . . .

The men would line up behind those poles. They'd say, 'You go—you go—you go,' and then it got so bad everyone just had to go anyway."

—quoted in *D-Day: Piercing the Atlantic Wall*

▲ **American soldiers in a landing craft on D-Day**

DBQ **Document-Based Question**

What made D-Day so dangerous for troops landing on the beaches?

Dropping the Atomic Bomb In October 1944, General McArthur invaded the Philippines with more than 160,000 troops and 700 ships. The Americans captured the islands about five months later. Meanwhile, other Americans continued island-hopping toward Japan. They finally came within reach of Japan in 1945.

On March 9, American bombers began dropping firebombs on Japan's cities. These bombs used jellied gasoline to start fires. During the firebombing of Tokyo, strong winds fanned the flames, creating an intense firestorm. The fire killed more than 80,000 Japanese and destroyed 250,000 buildings. Still, the Japanese would not surrender.

In April 1945, Franklin Roosevelt died, and **Harry S Truman** (TROO•muhn) became president. Truman faced a difficult decision. Should he risk American lives by invading Japan, or should he use the newly developed atomic bomb to end the war?

Since 1941, Americans had been building an atomic bomb. A team of engineers and scientists carried on their research at a secret laboratory in Los Alamos, New Mexico. Their program was called the Manhattan Project. On July 16, 1945, the first atomic bomb went off in a test near Alamogordo, New Mexico.

Truman's advisers disagreed about using the bomb. Admiral William Leahy opposed its use because it would kill thousands of civilians. He argued that an economic blockade and ordinary bombing would persuade the Japanese to surrender. Secretary of War Henry Stimson wanted to warn the Japanese about the bomb and at the same time offer to let them keep their emperor if they agreed to surrender.

Truman followed neither course. He threatened Japan with "prompt and utter destruction" if they did not surrender unconditionally. The Japanese failed to reply.

NATIONAL GEOGRAPHIC

HISTORY MAKERS

The Atomic Bomb 1945

In 1939, American scientists began racing to develop an atomic bomb before the Germans. By 1943, British, Canadian, and American scientists were working together on this project under the direction of J. Robert Oppenheimer. Most of the research was conducted in Los Alamos, New Mexico, and was code-named the "Manhattan Project."

On July 16, 1945, scientists in Alamogordo, New Mexico, tested the first atomic bomb. The explosion sent a great shock wave through the valley and was so hot that the desert sand turned into glass.

On August 6, 1945, one month after the first test, the United States dropped an atomic bomb on Hiroshima, Japan. The attack showed that war had changed. It was now possible to destroy an entire city with one bomb.

▲ Hiroshima after the atomic bomb hit

On August 6, 1945, a plane named the *Enola Gay* dropped an atomic bomb on the Japanese city of Hiroshima. Between 80,000 and 120,000 people were killed instantly. Thousands more died slowly from burns and radiation sickness.

Three days later, an American plane dropped another bomb on the city of Nagasaki. It killed between 35,000 and 74,000 people. On August 15, 1945, the Japanese surrendered.

Rebuilding the World About 55 million people died in World War II. These included 22 million Soviets, 8 million Germans, 2 million Japanese, and 300,000 Americans. Also included were millions killed in campaigns of genocide, or mass murders of ethnic groups.

Even before the war ended, the Allies had started an organization to keep the peace. In April 1945, representatives from 50 countries drew up a charter for the United Nations (UN). The UN General Assembly would vote on issues and choose members of the Security Council. The Security Council would investigate international problems and propose settlements. It had five permanent members—the United States, the USSR, Britain, France, and China—as well as other elected members.

After the war, the Allies tried Nazi leaders at Nuremberg, Germany, for "pursuing aggressive war" and for committing "crimes against humanity." Similar war trials took place in Japan. The war crimes trials punished many of the people responsible for World War II and the Holocaust. They also served notice that the world would not allow these crimes to be repeated.

 **Reading Check** **Cause and Effect** What were the results of the atomic bombs dropped on Hiroshima and Nagasaki?

History Online
Study Central™ Need help with the material in this section? Visit jat.glencoe.com

Section 3 Review

Reading Summary
Review the Main Ideas

- In the Pacific, the Americans fought the Japanese island by island. In Europe, American and Allied troops invaded North Africa and Italy.

- During the Holocaust, the Germans murdered millions of people, including Jews and other minorities.

- The Allied invasion of France in June 1944, led to the fall of Germany. The United States's use of two atomic bombs on Japanese cities caused Japan to surrender.

What Did You Learn?

1. Describe the U.S. plan for defeating Japan in the war.

2. What was D-Day?

Critical Thinking

3. **Sequencing Information** Draw a time line like the one below. Fill in events related to the war against Germany beginning with the landings of Allied troops in North Africa and ending with D-Day.

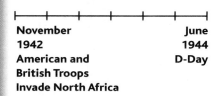

November 1942
American and British Troops Invade North Africa

June 1944
D-Day

4. **Evaluate** Do you think it would have been more important to defeat the Germans or the Japanese first during the war? Explain your answer.

5. **Summarize** Describe the German persecution of Jews leading up to the Holocaust.

6. **Describe** Describe the organization and purpose of the United Nations.

7. **Creative Writing** Write the dialogue for a conversation that might have occurred between the Allied leaders— Roosevelt, Churchill, and Stalin—at the Tehran Conference in 1943.

Get Ready to Read!

What's the Connection?
In the last section, you learned that World War II devastated Europe and Asia. This section discusses a new international conflict that shaped the next 40 years.

Focusing on the Main Ideas
- Soviet efforts to spread communism led to conflict with the United States, which wanted to contain communism. *(page 832)*

- The Cold War spread to Asia after China's communist revolution and the outbreak of the Korean War. *(page 837)*

- People in the postwar world experienced prosperity, change, and conflict. *(page 839)*

Locating Places
Berlin
Taiwan (TY•WAHN)

Meeting People
Nikita Khrushchev
  (nuh•KEE•tuh   krush•CHAWF)
John F. Kennedy
Chiang Kai-shek
  (jee•AHNG   KY•SHEHK)
Mao Zedong (MOW   ZUH•DUNG)
Martin Luther King, Jr.

Building Your Vocabulary
containment
Truman Doctrine
Marshall Plan
racial segregation
  (SEH•grih•GAY•shuhn)

Reading Strategy
Organizing Information Complete a diagram like the one below to show the causes of the Cold War.

Cold War Begins

NATIONAL GEOGRAPHIC When & Where?

NORTH AMERICA
EUROPE
•Berlin
ASIA
KOREA
CUBA

1945   1955   1965

1947 The Truman Doctrine is announced

1950 The Korean War begins

1955 The Soviets create the Warsaw Pact

1962 The Cuban missile crisis erupts

The Cold War Begins

Main Idea **Soviet efforts to spread communism led to conflict with the United States, which wanted to contain communism.**

Reading Focus Have you ever wanted to stop someone from doing something without having a fight? Read to learn how the United States tried to stop communism without going to war.

During World War II, the United States and the Soviet Union had set aside their differences. As they moved toward victory in 1945, these two powerful nations began to disagree about what the world was to be like after the war.

For Americans, economic growth was the key to world peace. They wanted to promote growth through world trade. They also wanted to spread democracy and free enterprise. Free enterprise, you remember, is the system in which businesses compete freely for profits with few government controls.

In contrast, Soviet leaders wanted to spread communism. As the war ended, Soviet armies had pushed back German armies in Eastern Europe and set up Communist governments in the region. The Soviets feared that one day Germany might try again to attack them. Having communist states in Eastern Europe would make a German invasion harder to do.

The deep differences between the Americans and the Soviets made them mistrust each other, and they began to compete for world leadership. This rivalry lasted from 1945 to 1990 and became known as the Cold War.

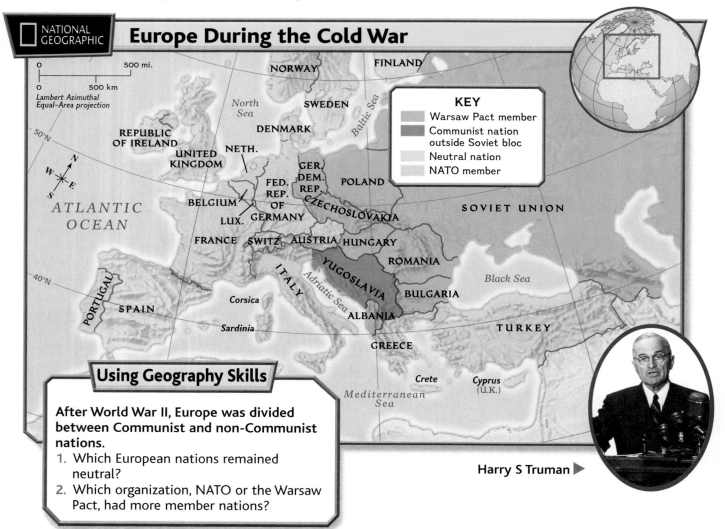

NATIONAL GEOGRAPHIC

Europe During the Cold War

500 mi.

500 km

Lambert Azimuthal
Equal-Area projection

KEY
- Warsaw Pact member
- Communist nation outside Soviet bloc
- Neutral nation
- NATO member

NORWAY FINLAND SWEDEN North Sea Baltic Sea DENMARK REPUBLIC OF IRELAND UNITED KINGDOM NETH. GER. DEM. REP. POLAND FED. REP. OF GERMANY BELGIUM LUX. CZECHOSLOVAKIA SOVIET UNION ATLANTIC OCEAN FRANCE SWITZ. AUSTRIA HUNGARY ROMANIA ITALY YUGOSLAVIA Adriatic Sea Black Sea PORTUGAL SPAIN Corsica BULGARIA ALBANIA Sardinia GREECE TURKEY Crete Cyprus (U.K.) Mediterranean Sea

Using Geography Skills

After World War II, Europe was divided between Communist and non-Communist nations.
1. Which European nations remained neutral?
2. Which organization, NATO or the Warsaw Pact, had more member nations?

Harry S Truman ▶

Yalta and Potsdam In February 1945, the "Big Three" Allied leaders—Roosevelt, Churchill, and Stalin—met at Yalta, a Soviet port on the Black Sea. They discussed, among other things, the fate of newly freed Europe. Their disagreements over Europe helped cause the Cold War.

Germany presented a special problem. The leaders finally agreed to divide Germany into four zones, or parts, until elections could be held to determine its future. The Soviet Union was to control the eastern part of Germany. The United States, Great Britain, and France were to divide the western part. The German capital of **Berlin** was also to be split among the four nations. At Yalta, the three leaders also agreed that other countries released from Nazi rule should have free elections.

In April 1945, U.S. president Roosevelt died. Vice President Harry S Truman then became president. The next month, American, Soviet, and British leaders met at Potsdam, Germany. At Potsdam, Stalin demanded that the Germans pay high reparations for damaging the Soviet Union. Truman firmly opposed this demand and angrily told the Soviets to keep their promises.

The Soviets soon broke their promises made at Yalta. Stalin did not hold free elections in Eastern Europe. Instead, the Soviets set up Communist governments there, and Soviet forces remained in the region.

What Was Containment?
The British leader Winston Churchill was concerned about Soviet control in Eastern Europe. In 1946, in a speech in Fulton, Missouri, he warned that the Soviets might try to expand their control beyond Eastern Europe.

Like Churchill, President Truman and other U.S. government leaders worried

The Iron Curtain

In 1946, while visiting Fulton, Missouri, Winston Churchill gave a speech titled "The Sinews of Peace." In the speech, he tried to explain what was happening in Eastern Europe:

"From Stettin in the Baltic to Trieste in the Adriatic, an iron curtain has descended across the Continent [Europe]. Behind that line lie all the capitals of the ancient states of Central and Eastern Europe. Warsaw, Berlin, Prague, Vienna, Budapest, Belgrade, Bucharest and Sofia, all these famous cities and the populations around them lie in what I must call the Soviet sphere, . . . The Communist parties, which were very small in all these Eastern States of Europe, have been raised to preeminence and power far beyond their numbers and are

▲ **Winston Churchill**

seeking everywhere to obtain totalitarian control. Police governments are prevailing in nearly every case."

—Winston Churchill,
The "Iron Curtain" Speech

DBQ Document-Based Question

What does the "iron curtain" divide?

about the growing Soviet threat. How were they to stop the Soviets?

For an answer, they turned to the ideas of George F. Kennan, an American diplomat and expert on Soviet affairs. Kennan claimed that the United States and the Soviet Union could not cooperate. He believed, however, that war could be avoided. He argued that the Soviet Union had many internal economic problems, and he believed it would collapse if the United States could stop it from spreading communism. Kennan's ideas led to a new U.S. foreign policy known as **containment.** This policy held that the United States would try to "contain," or hold back the spread of communism.

Germany Divided

EAST GERMANY

FRENCH SECTOR
EAST BERLIN
BRITISH SECTOR
SOVIET SECTOR
WEST BERLIN
AMERICAN SECTOR

EAST GERMANY

DENMARK

N
W — E
S

5°E
0   100 mi.
0   100 km
Chamberlin Trimetric projection

0   10 mi.
0   10 km
Lambert Azimuthal Equal-Area projection

55°N

Hamburg

British Zone

Hannover

Braunschweig

WEST GERMANY (FEDERAL REPUBLIC OF GERMANY)

Berlin

POLAND

EAST GERMANY (GERMAN DEMOCRATIC REPUBLIC)

10°E   15°E

French Zone   Frankfurt

American Zone

50°N

FRANCE

45°N

KEY

Allied occupation zone

Soviet occupation zone

Routes of the Berlin Airlift, 1948–1949

Division of Allied zone

Using Geography Skills

Following World War II, the Allied and Soviet sections of Germany formed two separate countries.
1. Which three nations occupied West Germany?
2. Which West German city on the route of the Berlin Airlift was closest to Berlin? How far away was it?

The policy of containment soon went into effect. Civil war was raging in Greece. There, Communist rebels were trying to overthrow the Greek government. At the same time, the Soviets put enormous pressure on Turkey to give them naval bases on the Dardanelles straits leading to the Mediterranean Sea.

On March 12, 1947, Truman asked Congress for money to help Greece and Turkey. His speech outlined a plan that was later named the **Truman Doctrine.** Its immediate effects were to give aid to the Greeks and the Turks. In the long run, the doctrine pledged the United States to fight the spread of communism worldwide.

In June 1947, Secretary of State George C. Marshall proposed that the United States give aid to Western European countries as well. Their economies were in ruins, and the people were starving. The **Marshall Plan** pumped $13 billion worth of supplies, machinery, and food into Western Europe. The economic recovery that followed weakened the appeal of communism.

Germany Meanwhile, the western Allies and the Soviet Union disagreed on the future of Germany. President Truman believed that a reunited, prosperous Germany was important for Europe. Stalin, however, feared that a reunited Germany would attack the Soviet Union.

In June 1948, the United States, Britain, and France announced that they were uniting their zones to form a new West German republic. Each nation's section of Berlin would be included in the new republic as well, even though the city lay within Soviet-held eastern Germany.

In response, Soviet troops moved into position around West Berlin. They imposed a blockade, stopping all traffic on road, railroad, and water routes through eastern

Germany to West Berlin. As a result, the city was cut off from needed supplies. The Soviets hoped this blockade would force the Americans, British, and French to reconsider their plan.

President Truman refused to give in to the Soviets. He ordered a massive airlift to save West Berlin. For almost a year, cargo planes carried food, medicine, fuel, and other supplies into the city. In May 1949, Stalin finally ended the blockade.

Despite the airlift's success, Berlin and Germany remained divided. By the end of 1949, there were two German states—West Germany, a democracy allied with the United States, and East Germany, a communist state tied to the Soviet Union.

To stop communism, the United States, Canada, and 10 West European countries formed the North Atlantic Treaty Organization (NATO) in 1949. Member nations agreed to aid any member who was attacked. Six years later, West Germany was allowed to form an army and to join NATO. In response, the Soviets in 1955 set up a military alliance with the Communist governments of Eastern Europe. It was known as the Warsaw Pact.

After Stalin died in 1953, **Nikita Khrushchev** (nuh•KEE•tuh krush•CHAWF) emerged as the new Soviet leader. In 1961 Khrushchev demanded that the Western powers withdraw from Berlin. U.S. president **John F. Kennedy** refused. Meanwhile, many East Germans fled to West Germany. The Soviets then built a wall that separated Communist East Berlin from the rest of the city. Guards on the wall shot anyone who tried to escape East Berlin. For nearly 30 years, the Berlin Wall was an important symbol of the Cold War struggle.

NATIONAL GEOGRAPHIC The Way It Was

Focus on Everyday Life

Life in Divided Berlin

When the Berlin Wall was first built, stretches of it consisted of only knee-high barbwire, so friends, neighbors, and families could still greet each other. Soon after, the barbwire was replaced with guard towers and cement blocks that divided the city.

If a person's home lay on one side of the Wall and his or her office on the other, that person could not go to work. West Berliners used raised platforms to see what was happening on the other side of the Wall. At night, the streets of West Berlin sparkled with lights, but in East Berlin, all was dark except for the guard towers. Anyone who tried to escape over the Wall to West Berlin was shot. West Berliners built a memorial of crosses dedicated to those who died trying to cross the Wall.

◀ Residents of West Berlin look over the Berlin Wall into East Berlin.

Connecting to the Past

1. Why do you think many East Germans risked their lives to cross over the Wall?

2. How would your life change if a wall were built in the center of your city?

Nuclear Arms During the 1950s and 1960s, nuclear weapons played an important role in the Cold War. By the early 1950s, the Soviets had their own nuclear weapons. International tensions rose as the United States and the Soviet Union built up their missiles and bombers. By the 1960s, they were also using their rockets to send people into space. The Russians put the first man in space, but the Americans landed the first men on the moon.

The Cold War also spread to areas outside of Europe. In fact, the most dangerous Cold War dispute took place in Cuba, a small Caribbean island close to the United States—only 90 miles (144 km) south of Florida. There, in 1959, a new government came to power under a leader named Fidel Castro.

In October 1962, President Kennedy learned that the Soviets had placed long-range missiles in Cuba. Immediately, the president ordered the navy to blockade, or close off, Cuba until the Soviets removed the missiles. Kennedy also warned that the United States would launch a nuclear attack on the Soviets if they fired any of their Cuban missiles on the United States.

As the two superpowers neared the edge of nuclear war, people all over the world waited anxiously. After five difficult days, Soviet ships turned away from the blockade. Soviet leaders also agreed to withdraw their missiles from Cuba. The United States agreed not to invade Cuba. Nuclear war had been avoided.

✓ **Reading Check** **Explain** What was containment, and why was it used?

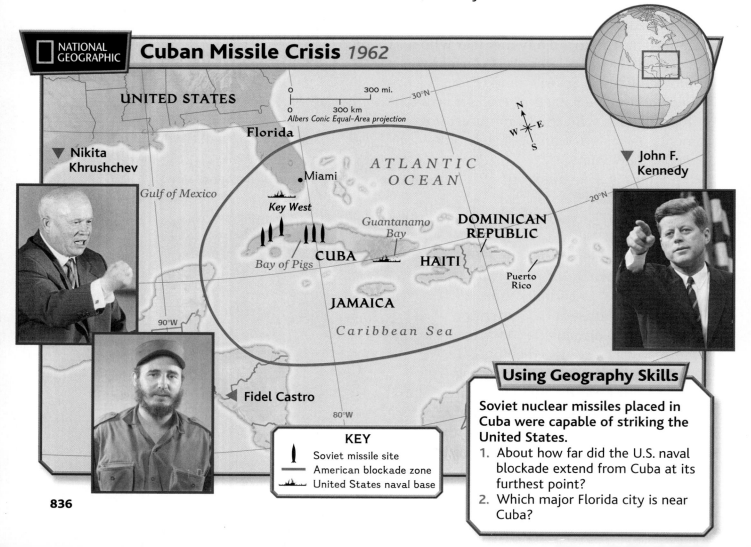

NATIONAL GEOGRAPHIC

Cuban Missile Crisis 1962

UNITED STATES

0   300 mi.
0   300 km
Albers Conic Equal-Area projection

30°N

Florida

▼ Nikita Khrushchev

Gulf of Mexico

ATLANTIC OCEAN

•Miami

Key West

▼ John F. Kennedy

20°N

Guantanamo Bay

DOMINICAN REPUBLIC

Bay of Pigs   CUBA   HAITI

Puerto Rico

JAMAICA

90°W

Caribbean Sea

▼ Fidel Castro

80°W

KEY

▮ Soviet missile site
— American blockade zone
⚓ United States naval base

Using Geography Skills

Soviet nuclear missiles placed in Cuba were capable of striking the United States.

1. About how far did the U.S. naval blockade extend from Cuba at its furthest point?
2. Which major Florida city is near Cuba?

The Cold War Spreads to Asia

Main Idea The Cold War spread to Asia after China's communist revolution and the outbreak of the Korean War.

Reading Focus Have you ever had a friend become your enemy or an enemy end up your friend? Read on to learn about the changing relationships among the United States and countries in Asia.

The Cold War also spread to Asia. In the late 1940s, Communist governments came to power in China and part of Korea. These Communist governments created challenges for the U.S. policy of containment.

Communist Revolution in China

Previously, you learned that **Chiang Kai-shek** (jee•AHNG KY•SHEHK) became leader of China in the mid-1920s. He tried to unite China and wipe out the Communists. However, in 1927, the Chinese Communists began a movement to gain control of the country. Their leader was **Mao Zedong** (MOW ZUH•DUNG).

During the 1930s, Chiang's Nationalist forces and Mao's Communist troops stopped fighting each other. They joined together to fight the Japanese, who had invaded China. After World War II, the struggle between the Nationalists and Communists continued. Despite American aid, Chiang Kai-shek lost the people's support.

In 1949 Mao's Communists forced the Nationalists to leave the Chinese mainland and go to the island of **Taiwan** (TY•WAHN). There, Chiang set up a Nationalist government, claiming it ruled all of China. The Communists set up their own government on mainland China headed by Mao Zedong. They called it the People's Republic of China.

Mao's main goal was to make China a strong, modern country. In the 1950s, Mao's

▲ Mao Zedong became the leader of China following the Communist defeat of Chiang Kai-shek's forces. *How did Mao attempt to make China into a strong, modern nation?*

government took over China's industries and businesses. It also created large, government-run farms from the small plots of land worked by peasants. Instead of food production increasing, it declined as a result of bad weather and the people's resistance. Famine soon struck, killing almost 15 million people. As result, the government was forced to back down from its more extreme policies.

War in Korea

At the end of World War II, the Americans and Soviets divided Korea at the 38th parallel. The Communists set up a government in the north, and an American-backed government took over the south. On June 25, 1950, North Korean troops invaded South Korea in an attempt to take over that country.

U.S. president Harry Truman saw the invasion as a test of the containment policy. He persuaded the United Nations to send troops. Most of these UN troops were

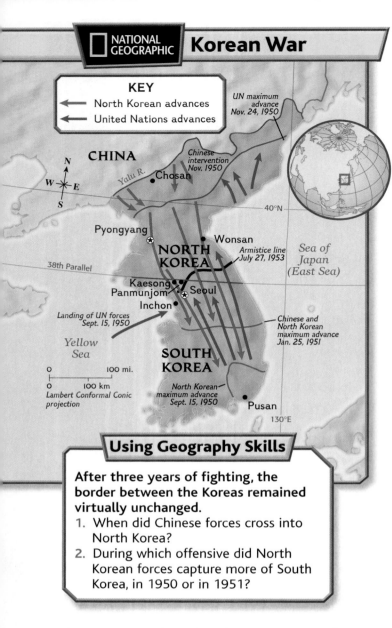

KEY

← North Korean advances

← United Nations advances

CHINA

Yalu R.
• Chosan

Chinese intervention Nov. 1950

UN maximum advance Nov. 24, 1950

40°N

Pyongyang
⊛

NORTH KOREA

• Wonsan

38th Parallel

Armistice line July 27, 1953

Sea of Japan (East Sea)

Kaesong
Panmunjom
Inchon •

⊛ Seoul

Landing of UN forces Sept. 15, 1950

Yellow Sea

Chinese and North Korean maximum advance Jan. 25, 1951

SOUTH KOREA

0   100 mi.

0   100 km
Lambert Conformal Conic projection

North Korean maximum advance Sept. 15, 1950

• Pusan

130°E

Using Geography Skills

After three years of fighting, the border between the Koreas remained virtually unchanged.

1. When did Chinese forces cross into North Korea?
2. During which offensive did North Korean forces capture more of South Korea, in 1950 or in 1951?

American and under the command of U.S. general Douglas MacArthur.

General MacArthur and the UN forces pushed the North Koreans back across the 38th parallel and then advanced toward the Chinese border. The Chinese Communists saw the advancing troops as a threat. Hundreds of thousands of Chinese crossed the border and drove the UN forces back to South Korea.

MacArthur suggested that dropping atomic bombs on Chinese bases and supply lines would gain a quick victory. President Truman, however, refused and fired MacArthur for disagreeing with him. He

did not want the Korean War to turn into a world war. By mid-1951, each army was dug in along a line near the 38th parallel. Both sides realized there was no chance for further gains. In 1953 North Korea and South Korea signed a truce. The two Koreas remain divided along a border near the 38th parallel.

Japan Recovers From 1945 to 1952, Japan was an occupied country. Allied military forces under General Douglas MacArthur controlled the country. This American-led government greatly reduced Japan's military so that Japan could no longer threaten its neighbors. It also introduced reforms. Japan received a democratic constitution. Japanese women and workers gained more rights. Small farmers also were given more land.

In 1952 Japan regained its independence. The Korean War, however, kept Japan's ties to the United States very close. American troops needed all kinds of war supplies, from medicines to trucks. To have a source of supplies nearby, the United States poured $3.5 billion into Japan's factories. Japanese shipbuilders, manufacturers, and electronics industries all benefited from American aid.

Help from the United States created an economic boom in Japan. The Japanese government worked closely with business leaders to plan the country's industrial growth. For example, in the late 1950s, government and industry agreed to invest heavily in the research and development of electronics products for the home. By the early 1970s, Japanese radios, televisions, stereos, and other items were competing with similar American products in the world market.

✓ **Reading Check** **Analyze** How did the Korean War help Japan's economy?

The Cold War Era

[Main Idea] **People in the postwar world experienced prosperity, change, and conflict.**

Reading Focus Can you recall hard times and good times in your life? Read on to learn which nations might consider the postwar years hard times and which might recall them as good times.

After World War II, the Soviet Union rebuilt its heavy industry and boosted its military might. In Soviet-controlled Eastern Europe, governments copied the Soviet system. Factories began producing more machinery and fewer consumer goods.

Life Behind the Iron Curtain
Most Soviets and East Europeans fared poorly as a result of this push for heavy industry. Food, clothing, and housing were in short supply. The average family lived in a one-room apartment. In addition, people feared being punished if they disagreed with the communist system.

East Europeans also disliked Soviet control of their countries. In October 1956, unrest swept Hungary. Students and workers staged street protests in Budapest, Hungary's capital, for changes in the government. Strikes and riots spread. A new government came to power and demanded an end to Soviet controls. In early November, Soviet tanks and troops poured into Hungary and crushed the revolt.

In January 1968, Czechoslovakia's leader Alexander Dubček also tried to make changes. He loosened controls on the press and travel abroad. Dubček's program was called "socialism with a human face." The program was short-lived, however. In

Space Exploration

In the 1960s, the Soviet Union and the United States competed with one another to be the first to conquer space travel. This competition, called the Space Race, led to the advancement of technology and the further study of space. *During what period of history did the Space Race occur?*

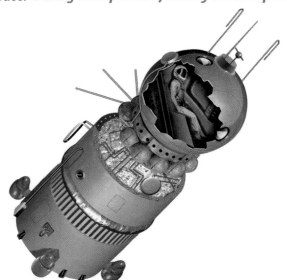

▲ In 1961 Russia sent the spacecraft *Vostok* into orbit. Inside was Yuri Gagarin, the first human being ever to travel into space.

▲ The lunar module was used by NASA in 1969 to land two men safely on the moon. U.S. astronaut Neil Armstrong was the first human being ever to set foot on the moon.

▲ To maintain control over its East European allies, the Soviet Union sometimes resorted to force. Here, Soviet tanks are shown on the streets of Czechoslovakia. *Why did the Soviets invade Czechoslovakia?*

August 1968, Soviet troops invaded Czechoslovakia and installed a strict Communist government.

Western Europe Rebuilds

The Marshall Plan helped Europe rebuild quickly from the ruins of World War II. West Germany's recovery was called an "economic miracle." By the 1960s, West Germany had Europe's strongest economy.

In France, war hero General Charles de Gaulle was president for part of the 1950s and most of the 1960s. During his presidency, France enjoyed a stable government. It became a major producer of aircraft, weapons, and cars. As a result, the French economy grew at a fast rate—even faster than the American economy.

Meanwhile, in Great Britain the Labour Party defeated Churchill's Conservative Party. The new government worked to improve the lives of the British people. Insurance was provided for the aged, sick, and jobless. A national health care service gave medical care to everyone.

In 1957 France, West Germany, Belgium, the Netherlands, Luxembourg, and Italy set up the European Economic Community (EEC). EEC members agreed to end all trade barriers among them. This meant that businesses could sell their goods in other member nations without paying taxes to cross the border. The EEC was seen as the first step in building a united Europe.

Life in the United States

During the 1950s, Americans earned higher wages and purchased more consumer goods than ever before. As a result, factory production soared. The postwar "baby boom," or increased birthrate, promised even more economic growth in the future.

A new civil rights movement also began in the 1950s. In 1954 the U.S. Supreme Court ruled against **racial segregation** (SEH• grih•GAY•shuhn), or separation of the races, in public schools. In the 1950s, President Dwight D. Eisenhower used federal agencies to make sure that states ended segregation in their schools. This was an important victory for African Americans, who had been working hard to gain civil rights throughout the 1940s and 1950s.

Led by Baptist minister **Martin Luther King, Jr.,** the civil rights movement next focused attention on discrimination, or unfair treatment, of African Americans in housing, voting, and public places. News coverage of King's speeches and marches convinced many Americans that discrimination against African Americans was wrong.

President John F. Kennedy expressed support for African Americans before he was assassinated in 1963. However, his successor, Lyndon Johnson, was the one who pushed a new Civil Rights Act and a Voting Rights Act through Congress. President Johnson also introduced many new programs designed to end poverty, improve education, and provide medical care to the poor and elderly. His programs came to be called the Great Society.

Meanwhile, women were demanding equality in the workplace. After World War II, more and more women became lawyers, doctors, and government leaders. Yet, women received lower pay than men for the same work.

In the early 1900s, the women's rights movement had been a strong force. The movement declined, however, after the passage of the Nineteenth Amendment giving women the right to vote. Concern over inequality in the workplace united women again in the 1960s. In 1963 supporters of women's rights won passage of the Equal

▲ President Lyndon Johnson (left) and Martin Luther King, Jr. (right) worked to end discrimination against African Americans. *What were Johnson's Great Society programs intended to do?*

Pay Act, which outlawed paying men more than women for the same job.

 **Reading Check** **Compare** How did the Soviets react to reforms in Hungary and in Czechoslovakia?

History Online

Study Central™ Need help with the material in this section? Visit jat.glencoe.com

Section 4 Review

Reading Summary

Review the Main Ideas

• During the Cold War, the United States and the Soviet Union competed for power in Europe, leading to the creation of NATO and the Warsaw Pact.

• In Asia, Communists took control of mainland China, and U.S. aid helped rebuild Japan.

• In the U.S. and Western Europe, economies grew strong. In Eastern Europe and the Soviet Union, people faced shortages, and some countries tried to overthrow Communist rule.

What Did You Learn?

1. What was the Marshall Plan, and why was it important?

2. Who were the original members of the EEC, and what was its purpose?

Critical Thinking

3. **Organizing Information** Draw a chart like the one below. Fill in details about issues facing the United States during the 1950s and 1960s.

Life in the United States During the 1950s and 1960s

4. **Summarize** How were the Truman Doctrine, the Marshall Plan, and the Berlin Airlift significant in the U.S. fight against communism?

5. **Cause and Effect** How did conflict in Asia following World War II affect Japan's economic recovery?

6. **Analyze** Why was life harsh for ordinary citizens in the Soviet Union and Eastern European nations in the 1950s?

7. **Persuasive Writing** Write a letter to the editor describing your views on a policy or event from the Cold War.

Section 5

The End of Empire

Get Ready to Read!

What's the Connection?

In past sections, you read about nationalism, communism, and the Cold War. This section explains how all three contributed to the collapse of European empires between 1945 and the present.

Focusing on the Main Ideas

- Led by Gandhi, India gained independence from Britain. **(page 843)**

- Nationalist movements led to independence for many Southeast Asian nations. **(page 846)**

- Most African colonies gained independence in the 1950s and 1960s. **(page 850)**

Locating Places

Pakistan (PA•kih•STAN)
Kashmir (KASH•MIHR)
Bangladesh (BAHNG•gluh•DEHSH)

Meeting People

Mohandas K. Gandhi
(MOH•huhn•DAHS   GAHN•dee)
Jawaharlal Nehru
(juh•WAH•huhr•LAHL   NEHR•oo)
Ho Chi Minh (HOH•CHEE•MIHN)
Nelson Mandela

Building Your Vocabulary

civil disobedience
Pan-Africanism
apartheid (uh•PAHR•TAYT)

Reading Strategy

Summarizing Information Complete a diagram like the one below to show the challenges India faced after becoming independent.

Challenges Since Independence

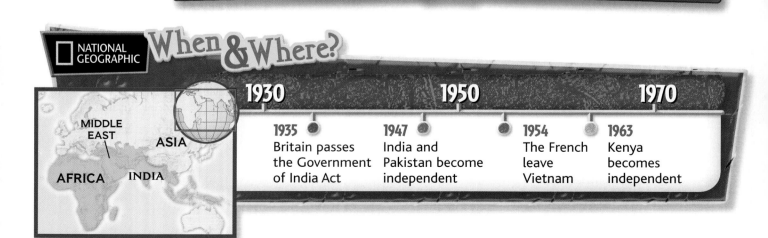

1930		1950		1970
1935 Britain passes the Government of India Act	**1947** India and Pakistan become independent		**1954** The French leave Vietnam	**1963** Kenya becomes independent

MIDDLE EAST
ASIA
AFRICA
INDIA

India Becomes Independent

Main Idea Led by Gandhi, India gained independence from Britain.

Reading Focus Have you ever tried hard to win someone over to your point of view? Read to learn how Indians finally convinced the British to leave their country.

▲ Mohandas Gandhi (right) worked for an independent India along with Jahawarlal Nehru (left), who became India's first prime minister. *How did Gandhi protest British rule?*

Previously, you learned that India came under British rule in the 1700s. The British built railroads, bridges, and ports in India. They did little, however, for India's people, who faced famine and other hardships. By the late 1800s, a movement for freedom began to take root and spread across the country.

The Indians who first called for independence were upper class and British-educated. Many lived in cities, such as Bombay (now Mumbai), Calcutta (now Kolkata), and Madras (now Chennai). Some were trained in British law and held government posts.

India's nationalists wanted reform and not revolution. The British, however, were slow in making changes. In 1885 a group of Indian leaders met in Mumbai to form the Indian National Congress (INC). The INC did not ask for independence right away. They did demand a role in ruling India.

Who Was Gandhi?
In 1919 a crowd of 10,000 Indians gathered for a political meeting at a walled garden in the city of Amritsar. Without warning, British troops blocked the exit from the garden and opened fire. They killed hundreds of people and wounded over a thousand. This Amritsar massacre made Indians more determined than ever to end British rule.

The most popular Indian leader was **Mohandas K. Gandhi** (MOH•huhn•DAHS GAHN•dee). He opposed violence in all forms. Instead, he protested British rule using nonviolent **civil disobedience**—the refusal to obey unjust laws.

In 1930 Gandhi led Indians in protesting the salt tax. The British taxed every grain of salt sold. They also made it illegal for Indians to collect salt on their own. Gandhi and his followers openly defied the British ban. The salt tax protests resulted in 60,000 arrests, including Gandhi's.

Pressured by protests, the British Parliament passed the Government of India Act in 1935. This law allowed Indians to run India's provinces, or regions. The British, however, kept control of India's national affairs.

Some Indians rejected the act. Others accepted it as a step toward full independence. The INC began running candidates for offices in regional governments. In 1937 candidates who were Hindu in religion won in 7 of the 11 provinces. As a result, India's Muslims began to worry how the much larger Hindu population might treat them in an independent India.

Biography

MOHANDAS GANDHI

1869–1948

When Mohandas Gandhi was arrested in 1922 and charged with rebellion, he defended himself by saying, "Nonviolence is the first article of my faith." Gandhi's strong belief in nonviolence developed early in his childhood. His mother, Putlibai, who was a devout Hindu, taught the principles of peace and tolerance to Mohandas and his older siblings.

Gandhi grew up in Porbandar, the capital of a small territory in western India. He did not do well in school. In one school report, he was described as "good at English, fair in Arithmetic and weak in Geography; conduct very good, bad handwriting." At home, Gandhi helped his mother with chores and helped take care of his dying father. In his free time, he took long walks by himself.

Gandhi's family wanted him to follow in his father's footsteps and study law. So in 1888 Gandhi sailed to England and entered one of London's law colleges. While living in London, he read for the first time an English translation of the Bhagavad Gita. Reading the Bhagavad Gita proved to be one of the greatest influences on Gandhi's life. It returned him to the Hindu religion. It also exposed him to two ideas that he would come to live by in his life and work. One idea was that material goods kept a person from pursuing a spiritual life. The other idea was to be peaceful and even-tempered in all situations.

In his work as a lawyer, Gandhi found that his true calling was mediation, or helping opposing groups resolve conflicts. In his later role as a political and spiritual leader, his talent for mediation helped him tackle enormous conflicts involving colonialism, racism, and violence.

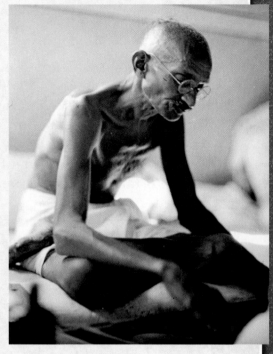

▲ Mohandas Gandhi

> "The force of love is the same as the force of the soul or truth."
>
> —Mohandas Gandhi, "Indian Home Rule"

Then and Now

Why do you think that Gandhi's approach to conflict resolution remains important and necessary in society today?

British India Is Divided After World War II, India's Hindus and Muslims were bitterly divided. The British realized that India would have to be split into a Hindu country and a Muslim country. **Pakistan** (PA•kih•STAN)—the Muslim country—would be made up of two regions separated by India—the Hindu country. West Pakistan was northwest of India, and East Pakistan was to the northeast.

On August 15, 1947, India and Pakistan became independent. Many Hindus in Pakistan fled to India, while many Muslims in India fled to Pakistan. Fighting erupted during this mass movement, and more than 1 million people were killed.

Tensions With Pakistan When British India ended, local states ruled by princes had to decide their future. Most became part of India. Others went with Pakistan.

The state of Kashmir joined neither India nor Pakistan. Most people in **Kashmir** (KASH•MIHR) were Muslims, but the ruler was Hindu. Pakistan invaded Kashmir, and its ruler turned to India for help. The result was a war between Pakistan and India. In 1949 the war ended, with most of Kashmir controlled by India.

In addition to conflicts with India, Pakistan faced conflicts within. Military leaders took over the elected government and ruled from 1958 until 1971. Also in 1971, East Pakistan declared its independence. After a brief civil war, it became a new nation named **Bangladesh** (BAHNG•gluh•DEHSH).

India and Pakistan continued to clash. More wars were fought over Kashmir, and both nations built nuclear weapons. In December 2001, Kashmir terrorists killed

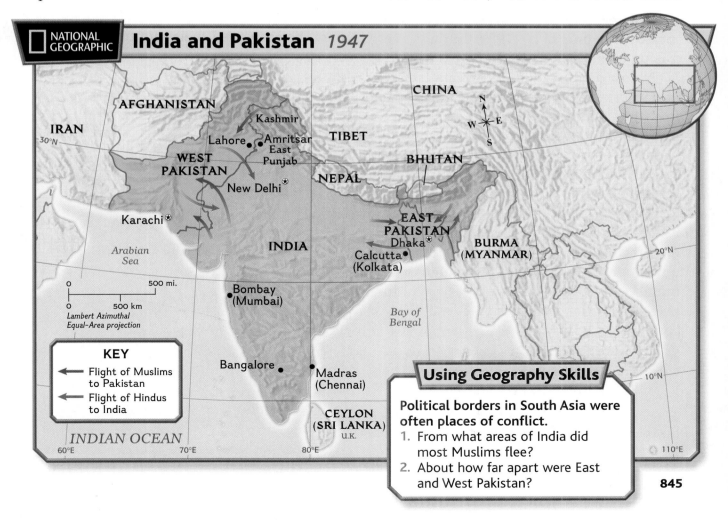

NATIONAL GEOGRAPHIC

India and Pakistan *1947*

AFGHANISTAN
IRAN
30°N
Kashmir
Lahore
Amritsar
East Punjab
WEST PAKISTAN
New Delhi
Karachi
Arabian Sea
INDIA
CHINA
TIBET
NEPAL
BHUTAN
EAST PAKISTAN
Dhaka
Calcutta (Kolkata)
BURMA (MYANMAR)
20°N
Bombay (Mumbai)
Bay of Bengal
Bangalore
Madras (Chennai)
CEYLON (SRI LANKA) U.K.
10°N
INDIAN OCEAN
60°E   70°E   80°E   110°E

0   500 mi.
0   500 km
Lambert Azimuthal Equal-Area projection

KEY
← Flight of Muslims to Pakistan
← Flight of Hindus to India

Using Geography Skills

Political borders in South Asia were often places of conflict.
1. From what areas of India did most Muslims flee?
2. About how far apart were East and West Pakistan?

nine people at India's Parliament building. The Indian government blamed Pakistan, but Pakistan denied responsibility. Five months later, terrorists attacked an Indian army base in Kashmir. This time, India and Pakistan almost went to war but pulled back after successful talks.

India Tries to Modernize

After independence, the Indian National Congress, renamed the Congress Party, began to rule India. The party's leader and India's first prime minister was **Jawaharlal Nehru** (juh•WAH•huhr•LAHL NEHR•oo). A British-educated lawyer, Nehru had helped lead India's freedom movement. In 1948 Nehru lost a close ally when Gandhi was assassinated.

Nehru tried to raise the standard of living in India through Five-Year Plans. He placed industry under government control. He also expanded farmlands, which set the stage for India's Green Revolution, or rapid increase in crops. By 1979, Indians were raising enough crops to feed all of India.

Nehru died in 1964. Two years later, his daughter, Indira Gandhi, became prime minister. Gandhi continued her father's policies but was assassinated in 1984. Gandhi's son, Rajiv Gandhi, served as prime minister from 1984 to 1989. He, too, was killed while campaigning.

While India struggled politically, reforms in the 1990s helped shift the country toward a free enterprise economy. The government now encourages foreign investments. One of the fastest-growing industries in India today is the making of computer products.

✓ **Reading Check** Cause and Effect What was the result of the massacre at Amritsar?

Achmed Sukarno was Indonesia's first leader after ▶ the country gained independence. *Why did the Dutch give Indonesia independence?*

Empire Ends in Southeast Asia

Main Idea Nationalist movements led to independence for many Southeast Asian nations.

Reading Focus How old is the United States? Did you know that most countries in the world are less than 100 years old? Read to learn why so many new countries have appeared so recently.

Nationalism also erupted in Southeast Asia. After World War II, many Southeast Asian nations gained their freedom. Some countries reached this goal more easily than others did. For example, the United States granted independence to the Philippines in 1946, but the Netherlands was less willing to give up its control of the Dutch East Indies.

The Dutch Leave Indonesia

After World War II, Achmed Sukarno and his nationalists declared the East Indies to be independent. They renamed their country Indonesia.

The Dutch at first opposed this move. Then, Indonesia's Communists revolted. Fearing a Communist takeover, the Dutch in 1949 accepted Sukarno's government.

In 1965 Indonesia's Communists tried again to seize power. Indonesia's army killed about 300,000 people believed to be Communist supporters. Then, the army's commander, General Suharto, replaced Sukarno as ruler.

In 1975 Suharto's troops seized the nearby Portuguese colony of East Timor. Suharto was a harsh leader, and East Timor's people fought his rule. Finally, in August 1999, Indonesia's government allowed East Timor to vote on independence. After the election, Indonesia's soldiers in East Timor staged attacks. The UN sent troops to stop the violence. With UN help, East Timor became independent in 2002.

The British Leave Myanmar and Malaysia

Burma, now Myanmar, had been under British rule for many years. In 1948 it became independent. Communists and ethnic groups within Burma soon rose up against the government. To restore order, military leaders seized control in 1962.

Burma's military leaders ran the economy and cracked down on opponents. The people of Burma protested. Finally, the military leaders agreed to hold elections in 1990. Before the voting took place, they arrested Aung San Suu Kyi (AWNG SAN SOO CHEE)—the key democratic leader. She won the election, but Burma's military leaders rejected the results. After her release in 1995, Aung San Suu Kyi continued to work for democracy.

Independence also came to British colonies on the Malay Peninsula and the island of Borneo. After defeating Communist guerrillas, the British granted freedom to these territories. In 1963 the territories united to form the independent Federation of Malaysia.

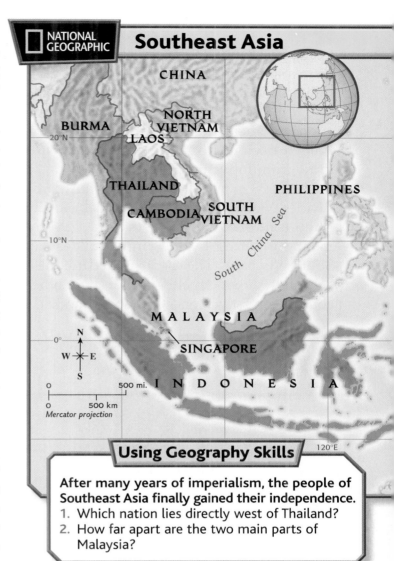

NATIONAL GEOGRAPHIC Southeast Asia

Using Geography Skills

After many years of imperialism, the people of Southeast Asia finally gained their independence.
1. Which nation lies directly west of Thailand?
2. How far apart are the two main parts of Malaysia?

The French Fight in Vietnam During World War II, the Japanese seized Indochina from the French. A Communist named **Ho Chi Minh** (HOH•CHEE•MIHN) formed a group called the Vietminh to drive out the Japanese. Soon afterward, the United States began sending military aid to the Vietminh.

When Japan gave up control of Indochina, Ho Chi Minh declared Vietnam independent. France, however, wanted to get back Vietnam and the rest of Indochina. French troops returned to Vietnam in 1946 and drove the Vietminh into hiding.

The Vietminh fought the French and slowly won control of the country-side. Worried that Ho Chi Minh was a

Communist and determined to stop communism's spread in Asia, the United States gave military aid to French forces in Vietnam.

Despite American help, the French could not beat the Vietminh. In 1954 the French decided to make peace and withdraw from Indochina.

An agreement called the Geneva Accords divided Vietnam at the 17th parallel. Ho Chi Minh controlled North Vietnam. A government supported by the United States ran South Vietnam. The Geneva Accords also accepted the independence of two other countries in Indochina—Cambodia and Laos.

Americans Fight in Vietnam The Geneva Accords called for elections to unite Vietnam, but South Vietnam's leader refused to hold them. He feared the elections in the Communist north would not be fair and worried that southern Vietnamese might vote for Ho Chi Minh. After South Vietnam refused to hold elections, Ho Chi Minh decided to unite Vietnam through force. He set up a guerrilla army in South Vietnam known as the Vietcong. To help South Vietnam's government fight the Vietcong, U.S. president Dwight D. Eisenhower sent aid and military advisers to South Vietnam.

The Vietnam War

◀ French soldiers wait in their trenches during a break in fighting in Dien Bien Phu, Vietnam. *In what year did the French troops withdraw from Vietnam?*

U.S. infantrymen leap from a military helicopter on their way to a mission in Vietnam. ▼

▲ Ho Chi Minh became the leader of North Vietnam following Japan's retreat from the country in World War II.

During the 1960s, the United States was drawn deeper into the fight for Vietnam. In 1964 U.S. president Lyndon Johnson reported that North Vietnam had attacked American ships in the Gulf of Tonkin. In early August, Congress passed the Gulf of Tonkin Resolution giving Johnson permission to fight a war in Vietnam. In 1965 Johnson sent the first American combat troops to fight the Vietcong.

By the late 1960s, many Americans opposed the war. Finally, in 1973 U.S. president Richard Nixon withdrew American forces from Vietnam. At least 2 million people, including 58,000 Americans, died in the war.

About 10 million South Vietnamese became refugees. Many were called "boat people" because they fled the country in boats. Twenty years later, some boat people were still living in refugee camps far from home.

In 1975 North Vietnam's army reunited Vietnam and imposed a Communist government on the south. Faced with a failing economy, Vietnam's leaders began to allow privately owned businesses in the late 1980s. In 1995 Vietnam improved its relations and trade with the United States.

✓ **Reading Check** **Explain** Why did the U.S. decide to help the French in Vietnam?

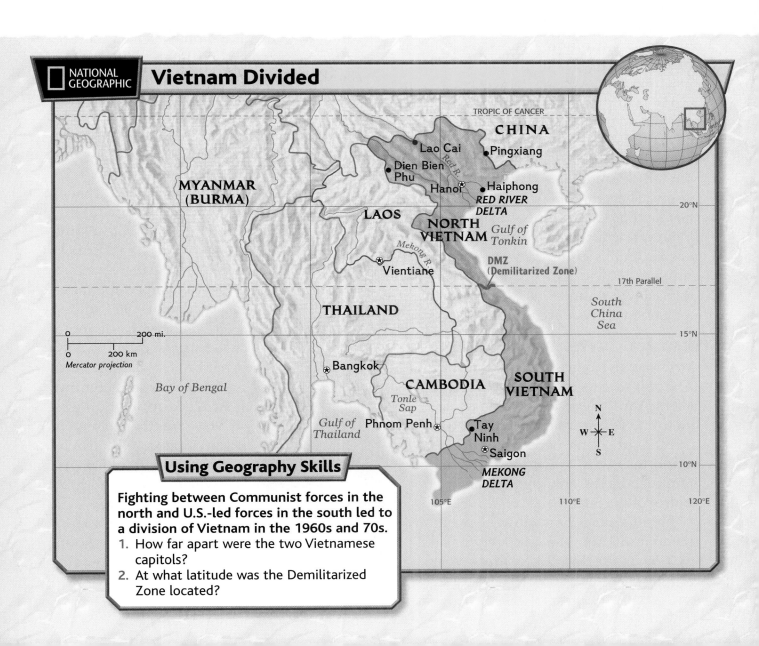

NATIONAL GEOGRAPHIC

Vietnam Divided

TROPIC OF CANCER

CHINA

Lao Cai • Pingxiang

Dien Bien Phu

MYANMAR (BURMA)

Hanoi ⊛ • Haiphong

RED RIVER DELTA

20°N

LAOS

NORTH VIETNAM

Gulf of Tonkin

Mekong R.

⊛ Vientiane

DMZ (Demilitarized Zone)

17th Parallel

THAILAND

South China Sea

15°N

0   200 mi.
0   200 km
Mercator projection

Bay of Bengal

• Bangkok

CAMBODIA

Tonle Sap

Gulf of Thailand

Phnom Penh ⊛

• Tay Ninh

⊛ Saigon

SOUTH VIETNAM

N
W—E
S

10°N

MEKONG DELTA

105°E   110°E   120°E

Using Geography Skills

Fighting between Communist forces in the north and U.S.-led forces in the south led to a division of Vietnam in the 1960s and 70s.

1. How far apart were the two Vietnamese capitols?
2. At what latitude was the Demilitarized Zone located?

Africa Becomes Independent

Main Idea Most African colonies gained independence in the 1950s and 1960s.

Reading Focus What do you do if you think you are not being treated fairly? Do you speak out? Read on to learn how Africans sought better treatment and independence from European rulers.

Black Africans fought in World War I with British and French forces. Many hoped they would be rewarded with independence. Instead, Britain and France further increased the size of their empires.

After the war, Africans became more politically active and staged protests. European governments responded with force and arrests. But they also began to make reforms. Africans, however, were not happy with these halfway steps. They wanted independence.

Nationalism was strong among European-educated Africans. Most of them worked in colonial government and businesses. They saw the striking gap between the way Europeans supported democracy at home yet denied it to colonial peoples overseas. From this group came the leaders who convinced Africans to demand their freedom. However, most of Africa would not gain independence until the 1960s.

New Arab States in North Africa

African movements for freedom had their first success in North Africa. After World War II, Egyptian nationalists set out to end British influence in Egypt. In 1952 Egypt's king, whom the British supported, was overthrown. British troops left Egypt, although Britain kept control of the Suez Canal until 1956.

Egypt's neighbor, Libya, won its freedom in 1951. The discovery of oil in 1959 made Libya's leaders very wealthy. The people of Libya, however, remained poor. In 1969 a military officer named Muammar al-Qaddafi overthrew Libya's king and set up a socialist government. Its goal was to spread Libya's oil revenue more equally among the people.

France began letting go of its North African empire in 1956. At this time, the French gave full independence to Morocco and Tunisia. Because many French people lived in Algeria, France decided to keep control there. Algerian Arabs, however, fought back to free their homeland. Algeria finally won independence in 1962.

Africa South of the Sahara
Freedom also came to African colonies south of the Sahara. Kwame Nkrumah (KWAHM•eh ehn•KROO•muh) led a nationalist movement in Britain's colony of the Gold Coast in West Africa. In 1950 Nkrumah led workers in a strike that put pressure on British officials. The British jailed Nkrumah but soon freed him as protests continued. In 1957 the Gold Coast, now renamed Ghana, became independent under Nkrumah.

Nigeria, Britain's largest African colony, won its freedom in 1960. Other British colonies in Africa followed. After a violent uprising in the 1950s, Kenya became independent in 1963 under the leadership of Jomo Kenyatta. The new nations of Zambia and Malawi arose in central Africa during the mid-1960s. Another colony in the region, Rhodesia, broke away from Britain. However, a small but powerful group of Europeans remained in control. This group refused to allow the

▲ Jomo Kenyatta

▲ Ghana, led by Kwame Nkrumah, shown here speaking, was the first former British colony to gain independence in Africa. *What was Britain's largest African colony and when did it gain freedom?*

much larger black population to rule. After a long struggle, the African population finally won control. In 1980 Rhodesia became the independent nation of Zimbabwe.

France wanted to avoid conflicts in its colonies south of the Sahara. In 1958 the French gave their colonies a choice. They could have limited self-rule with French aid, or they could become totally independent with no help from France.

Guinea's nationalist leader, Ahmed Sékou Touré (ah•MEHD SEH•koo TOO•ray), chose full independence. France withdrew its officials from Guinea and vowed not to help the new nation. Then Guinea accepted aid from the Soviet Union. France did not want its other African colonies to follow this same path, so it gave them both full independence and aid.

In the Belgian Congo, nationalist leaders demanded independence during the 1950s. Belgium reacted by arresting the leaders. As riots mounted, the Belgians finally gave the Congo its freedom in 1960. Ten years later, the country was renamed Zaire. Today it is known as the Democratic Republic of Congo.

Portugal ruled its colonies of Angola and Mozambique with an iron hand. During the 1960s, rebels attacked the Portuguese, but Portuguese troops kept the rebels in check until the 1970s. Then a revolution in Portugal unseated that country's dictator. Portugal's new democratic government freed Angola and Mozambique in 1975.

Some African leaders believed in **Pan-Africanism**—the unity of all black Africans. In 1963 thirty-two African states founded the Organization of African Unity (OAU). The OAU was the first step toward joining all the new countries in a broader community. Today, the OAU has been replaced by an even more closely united organization known as the African Union (AU).

Apartheid in South Africa Previously, you learned that Boer and British territories united in 1910 to form South Africa. Most of South Africa's people were black Africans, but the smaller European population ran the government. Black South Africans founded the African National Congress (ANC) in 1912 in hopes of gaining power.

In the 1940s, white South Africans strengthened their rule through a system known as apartheid, or "apartness."

Apartheid (uh•PAHR•TAYT) was carried out through laws that separated racial and ethnic groups and limited the rights of blacks. For example, black South Africans had to live in separate areas called "homelands." People of non-European background were not even allowed to vote. Blacks protested the laws, and the white government responded by cracking down on the protesters.

In 1960 police opened fire on a peaceful march in the town of Sharpeville. They killed 69 people. Two thirds of them were shot in the back while running away. In 1962 police arrested **Nelson Mandela,** the leader of the ANC. The arrest did not end the protests against apartheid, but it would be nearly 30 years before South Africa abolished the apartheid system.

✓ **Reading Check** **Explain** Why did France eventually give its African colonies aid and independence?

History Online
Study Central™ Need help with the material in this section? Visit jat.glencoe.com

Section 5 Review

Reading Summary

Review the Main Ideas
- India gained independence from Britain, struggled to modernize, then began building a free enterprise economy.
- Nationalist movements led many Southeast Asian colonies to independence. Communist and democratic nations fought to influence and control these new nations.
- Nationalist movements developed in Africa in the 1950s and 1960s. Many African colonies soon gained independence.

What Did You Learn?

1. What was the Gulf of Tonkin Resolution, and why was it important?

2. What was the INC, and what role did the INC play in India's independence movement?

Critical Thinking

3. **Sequencing Information** Draw a time line like the one shown. Fill in events related to the war in Vietnam.

Japanese leave Vietnam, 1945 — North Vietnam defeats South Vietnam, 1975

4. **Contrast** What were the differences between the independence movements in Algeria and Kenya?

5. **Cause and Effect** What was the result of Nehru's Five-Year Plans?

6. **Identify** Which groups were fighting for control of Indonesia after World War II?

7. **Creative Writing** Suppose you are the leader of a newly independent nation. Write five goals for your country and explain how the country will work toward those goals.

Section The Rise of Dictators

Vocabulary
inflation
depression
totalitarian state
collectivization

Focusing on the Main Ideas
- New economic problems led to the Great Depression. *(page 805)*
- The Great Depression encouraged the rise of European dictators. *(page 808)*
- After Lenin's death, Stalin established a brutal regime in the USSR. *(page 810)*
- Economic problems led to militarism in Japan. *(page 811)*

Section World War II Begins

Vocabulary
appeasement

Focusing on the Main Ideas
- Other European nations stood by as Germany expanded its territory. *(page 814)*
- World War II began when Germany invaded Poland in September 1939, leading France and Britain to declare war. *(page 815)*

Section The Allies Win the War

Vocabulary
genocide
D-Day

Focusing on the Main Ideas
- The Allies fought for four long years in Europe and in the Pacific. *(page 825)*
- The Nazis murdered millions of people in an attempt to destroy Jews and other European ethnic groups. *(page 827)*
- The successful invasion on D-Day was the beginning of the end of World War II. *(page 828)*

Section The Cold War

Vocabulary
containment
Truman Doctrine
Marshall Plan
racial segregation

Focusing on the Main Ideas
- Soviet efforts to spread communism led to conflict with the United States, which wanted to contain communism. *(page 832)*
- The Cold War spread to Asia after China's communist revolution and the outbreak of the Korean War. *(page 837)*
- People in the postwar world experienced prosperity, change, and conflict. *(page 839)*

Section The End of Empire

Vocabulary
civil disobedience
Pan-Africanism
apartheid

Focusing on the Main Ideas
- Led by Gandhi, India gained independence from Britain. *(page 843)*
- Nationalist movements led to independence for many Southeast Asian nations. *(page 846)*
- Most African colonies gained independence in the 1950s and 1960s. *(page 850)*

Chapter 21 Assessment and Activities

Review Vocabulary

Write **True** for each true statement. Replace the word in italics to make false statements true.

____ 1. Printing extra German money added to *depression* and caused prices to rise.

____ 2. Britain's *appeasement* policy led them to accept Germany's demands.

____ 3. The U.S. Supreme Court ruled against *Pan-Africanism*.

____ 4. The Nazis began a program of *apartheid* during World War II.

____ 5. Ghandi used *civil disobedience* to protest British rule.

____ 6. *Containment* means that a government takes over farmland.

Review Main Ideas

Section 1 • The Rise of Dictators

7. How did the Great Depression encourage the rise of European dictators?

8. What happened in the USSR after Lenin's death?

Section 2 • World War II Begins

9. Why did European nations stand by as Germany expanded its territory?

10. When did World War II begin?

Section 3 • The Allies Win the War

11. Why did the Nazis murder millions of people unconnected to their war with the Allies?

12. Which event is considered the beginning of the end of World War II?

Section 4 • The Cold War

13. Which two nations most shaped the postwar world?

14. Which nation became the chief American ally in Asia?

Section 5 • The End of Empire

15. What led to independence for many Southeast Asian countries?

16. During which decades did most African colonies gain independence?

Review Reading Skill ‹ Discussion Questions

17. Read the excerpt below from page 809. Write five questions that you could ask about this topic to launch a discussion.

> Once in power, Hitler did away with all political parties except the Nazis. He had books about democracy burned. He took over the courts and set up a secret police. He took over radio and newspapers and broke up unions.

To review this skill, see pages 802–803.

Critical Thinking

18. **Identify** What is fascism and where did it originate?

19. **Analyze** Why do you think Hitler invaded Poland even though Britain had promised to support Poland?

20. **Explain** What was gained by U.S. involvement in the Korean War?

Geography Skills

Study the map below and answer the following questions.

21. **Place** Which nations had army headquarters in Berlin after World War II?

22. **Location** Which river ran through both East and West Berlin?

23. **Movement** Which nation controlled the largest area in Berlin?

NATIONAL GEOGRAPHIC

Berlin *1945–1949*

KEY
— Berlin Wall
∴ Army HQ 1945–1949
— Main roads

0   10 mi.
0   10 km
Lambert Azimuthal Equal-Area projection

French HQ
FRENCH
BRITISH
British HQ
SOVIET
Spree R.
Soviet HQ
American HQ
AMERICAN

EAST GERMANY

Read to Write

24. **Creative Writing** Suppose you are living in West Berlin when the Wall is built and you can no longer even see your friends and family members in East Berlin. Write four diary entries explaining how the Wall is affecting your everyday life.

25. **Using Your FOLDABLES** Have students use posterboard to expand the dates and events on their foldables into an illustrated time line. Students should use sketches and images from magazines or the Internet with each entry on the time line.

Using Technology

26. **Internet Research** Use the Internet and your local library to research the Holocaust and another, more recent, genocide in the African nation Rwanda. How are the two tragedies similar? How are they different? Discuss both genocides as a class and possible ways to prevent future genocides.

Linking Past and Present

27. **Analyzing** Is containment an important issue in U.S. foreign policy today? Explain your reasoning.

Primary Source Analyze

A journalist with the Vietcong near Hanoi recorded the events of December 10, 1965.

"Then the sun goes down and everything starts to move.

. . . The engines are started and the convoys grind away through the darkness behind the pinpoints of masked headlamps. There are miles of them, heavy Russian-built trucks, anti-aircraft batteries, all deeply buried under piles of branches and leaves; processions of huge green haystacks. North Vietnam by day is abandoned; by night it thuds and grinds with movement."

—James Cameron, "The Vietnam War: A Reporter with the Vietcong, near Hanoi, 10 December 1965"

DBQ Document-Based Questions

28. When does all the movement of Vietcong supplies and machines take place?

29. What does "processions of huge green haystacks" refer to?

Building Today's World

A U.S. astronaut approaches ▶ the *Westar VI* satellite during a mission in space.

NATIONAL GEOGRAPHIC When & Where?

1960	1975	1990	2005
1959 Fidel Castro takes power in Cuba	**1979** Revolution in Iran over-throws shah	**1991** Soviet Union breaks up	**2003** Iraq war begins

Chapter Preview

After the fall of communism, people looked forward to a new era of peace. Nations and ethnic groups, however, soon clashed around the world. Read this chapter to find out how the world community tries to solve these and other problems.

 View the Chapter 22 video in the *World History: Journey Across Time* Video Program.

Section 1 Challenges in Latin America

Many countries in Latin America face economic problems, but they are making efforts to build stable democracies.

Section 2 Africa and the Middle East

Apartheid in South Africa ends, but African nations still face many challenges. Conflict in the Middle East continues as Arab and Israeli leaders search for solutions.

Section 3 The Cold War Ends

Revolutions in Eastern Europe and the collapse of the Soviet Union bring about the end of the Cold War in Europe.

Section 4 The World Enters a New Century

As globalism and technology bring the world's people closer together, terrorism and war continue to be problems.

FOLDABLES™ Study Organizer

Organizing Information *Make the following foldable to help you organize information about today's world.*

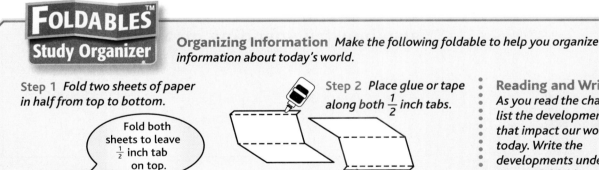

Step 1 *Fold two sheets of paper in half from top to bottom.*

Fold both sheets to leave ½ inch tab on top.

Step 2 *Place glue or tape along both ½ inch tabs.*

Step 3 *Fit both sheets of paper together to make a cube as shown.*

Step 4 *Turn the cube and label the foldable as shown.*

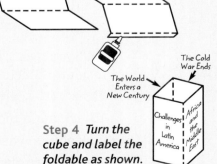

The Cold War Ends
The World Enters a New Century
Challenges in Latin America
Africa and the Middle East

Reading and Writing *As you read the chapter, list the developments that impact our world today. Write the developments under the correct foldable category.*

Reading Social Studies

Reading Skill

Extending the Text

1 Learn It!

Reading Beyond the Text

It is impossible for textbooks to have all of the information on a subject. If a topic interests you, it is important to know how and where to get more information. Reading beyond the text increases your own knowledge and satisfies your curiosity. It will also help you become a better student. Read the following text from Section 4:

> During the 1980s and 1990s, conservative policies gained support in the United States. President Ronald Reagan lowered taxes, cut government rules, and decreased spending on social welfare. He also boosted spending on the military.
>
> —*from page 892*

Reading Tip

Keep your reading skills sharp by reading something every day!

If you were interested in learning more about President Reagan's policies or his life, you could:

- Do a Web search for Ronald Reagan.
- Check out a biography from a library.
- Ask adults what they remember about Reagan.
- Read news magazines, especially from June 2004 after Reagan died.

2 Practice It!
What Interests You?

The following paragraph refers to two other recent presidents, Bill Clinton and George W. Bush. Choose a topic from the paragraph that you would like to know more about, such as *Democrats, Republicans, welfare, Bill Clinton,* or *George W. Bush.* With a partner, think of three ways you could find out more about your chosen topic.

Read to Write ·······
Writing a letter can help you to find out more about something that interests you. Write a letter to your state representative or senator asking him or her to answer questions you have about state politics.

Clinton, a moderate Democrat, favored some conservative policies. Under Clinton, the budget was balanced, and the welfare system was changed. Then, in 2000, Republican George W. Bush was elected president. A conservative, Bush convinced Congress to pass large tax cuts and an education reform law.

—*from page 892*

3 Apply It!

As you read about the **War on Terror** on pages 892–894, write down any word, phrase, or fact that interests you. Make a list of ways you could find more information.

Challenges in Latin America

Get Ready to Read!

What's the Connection?

Nationalism in Asia and Africa led to independence for many colonies. Read how the already independent nations of Latin America struggled to become successful and democratic.

Focusing on the Main Ideas

- Latin America's economy has depended on exports and foreign investment. *(page 861)*

- In Central America, repressive governments, social conflict, and civil wars made progress difficult. *(page 863)*

- During the twentieth century, Mexico struggled to overcome economic, social, and political challenges. *(page 864)*

- Most South American countries have struggled to create fragile democracies and improve their economies. *(page 866)*

Locating Places

Mexico
Cuba
Argentina

Meeting People

Fidel Castro
Jean-Bertrand Aristide
Lázaro Cárdenas (KAHR•duhn•AHS)
Juan Perón (pay•ROHN)

Building Your Vocabulary

export
embargo (ihm•BAHR•goh)
nationalize (NASH•nuh•LYZ)

Reading Strategy

Summarizing Information Create a table to show the reforms put in place by Latin American leaders.

Leaders	Reforms

NATIONAL GEOGRAPHIC When & Where?

CUBA
MEXICO
BRAZIL
ARGENTINA

1920   **1960**   **2000**

1933 Good Neighbor Policy begins

1959 Fidel Castro takes power in Cuba

1994 U.S., Mexico, and Canada sign NAFTA

Latin America's Economy

Main Idea Latin America's economy has depended on exports and foreign investment.

Reading Focus What does it mean to be a good neighbor? Read to find out how a change in U.S. policy was aimed at building better relations with its neighbors.

Previously, you learned that countries in Latin America gained their independence in the 1800s. Latin Americans soon found out that it was easier to set up republics than to make them work. While the rich controlled social and political life, the poor had little, if any, power.

Exporting Raw Materials

Latin America's economy depended on agriculture and mining. During the late 1800s, industrial countries demanded more of Latin America's food products and minerals. Businesspeople from these countries set up companies in Latin America. These companies **exported,** or sold abroad, Latin American products, such as bananas, sugar, coffee, copper, and oil.

As the number of exports rose, some Latin American countries grew only one or two key products. For example, Honduras raised bananas, and Colombia grew coffee. Prices and profits increased because of these exports, but any decline in demand had serious effects. Prices dropped, followed by severe losses in income and jobs.

Despite the problems it caused, Latin America's dependence on exports also brought benefits. Foreign investors built ports, roads, and railroads. Cities increased in size and population, and a middle class of lawyers, teachers, and businesspeople grew. Much, however, had not changed. The wealthy still held the power, and most Latin Americans struggled to make a living.

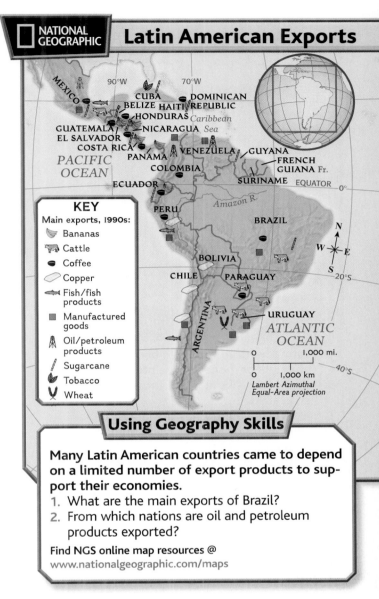

NATIONAL GEOGRAPHIC

Latin American Exports

KEY

Main exports, 1990s:

- Bananas
- Cattle
- Coffee
- Copper
- Fish/fish products
- Manufactured goods
- Oil/petroleum products
- Sugarcane
- Tobacco
- Wheat

Using Geography Skills

Many Latin American countries came to depend on a limited number of export products to support their economies.

1. What are the main exports of Brazil?
2. From which nations are oil and petroleum products exported?

Find NGS online map resources @ www.nationalgeographic.com/maps

The United States and Latin America

During the 1900s, the United States increased its influence in Latin America. Previously, you learned about the American victory in the Spanish-American War of 1898. One result of the war was that the United States gained control of the Caribbean island of Puerto Rico.

Five years later, the United States helped Panama win its independence from Colombia. In return, Panama gave the United States control of the area where the

Debt in Latin America

Country	Total Amount Owed (in U.S. dollars)
Brazil	$242 billion
Mexico	$155 billion
Argentina	$140 billion
Chile	$42 billion
Venezuela	$37 billion
Colombia	$36 billion
Peru	$30 billion
Ecuador	$18 billion
Uruguay	$11 billion
Panama	$10 billion
El Salvador	$6 billion
Dominican Republic	$6 billion

Source: World Bank, 2002

Understanding Charts

Latin American countries borrowed large amounts of money to maintain their weak economies, but many of those economies still failed.

1. Which country has the largest debt? How much larger is that country's debt than that of the Dominican Republic?
2. **Conclude** Why does a high debt hurt a country's economy?

Panama Canal was built. Over the next 25 years, the United States sent troops to Haiti, Nicaragua, and the Dominican Republic to protect U.S. interests.

Meanwhile, American businesspeople increased their holdings in Latin America. One of the most powerful American firms in Latin America was the United Fruit Company. It owned land, railroads, and fruit-packing plants in many nations of Central America. American companies also controlled copper mines in Chile and Peru, as well as oil wells in **Mexico,** Peru, and Bolivia.

Many Latin Americans distrusted the United States because of its great wealth and power. To improve relations, U.S. president Franklin D. Roosevelt in 1933 announced the Good Neighbor Policy toward Latin America.

He promised that the United States would not intervene militarily in Latin America. He pledged a greater respect for the rights of the United States's southern neighbors.

Debt and Trade The Great Depression of the 1930s brought hardships to Latin America. Exports declined, and Latin Americans had less money to buy factory-made goods from abroad. They began to develop their own industries. Some of these industries were foreign-owned. Others were run by Latin American governments.

After World War II, agriculture was still important, but industries continued to grow in Latin America. Some of the money for new industries came from large, multinational corporations. Multinational corporations are companies that invest and do business in more than one country.

To encourage economic growth, Latin American leaders also borrowed heavily from banks in the United States and other countries. As a result, Latin America owed large sums of money to other parts of the world. This mounting debt seriously weakened Latin American economies. Prices rose, wages fell, and people lost jobs.

Difficult reforms in the 1980s helped strengthen many Latin American economies. The harshness of these changes, however, turned Latin Americans against their dictators. During the 1990s, democratic movements succeeded in several countries.

Today, Latin America's democratic governments face many challenges. Population is growing rapidly, but resources are limited. Differences between rich and poor still create social tensions. In addition, growing trade in drugs has increased crime and corruption in parts of Latin America.

Reading Check **Cause and Effect** What was the result of Latin American debt to foreigners in the 1980s?

Problems in Central America

Main Idea In Central America, repressive governments, social conflict, and civil wars made progress difficult.

Reading Focus What would it be like to live in a country where a civil war was raging? What difficult choices might you have to make?

In the 1900s, a few people held most of the wealth and power in Central America and the Caribbean. Rebels fought for changes that they thought would better the lives of poorer Latin Americans.

The Cuban Revolution Previously, you learned that **Cuba** won its freedom from Spain in 1898. During most of the 1900s, military dictators ruled Cuba. American companies controlled most of the country's wealth, which was based on sugar and mining. In 1959 a young lawyer named **Fidel Castro** led a revolution and took control of the government.

Castro promised democracy. Instead, he set up a communist state and accepted aid from the Soviet Union. When he seized American-owned property, relations with the United States became even worse. In 1961 the United States tried to overthrow Castro. A small force of Cubans who had fled the revolution were trained and armed by the American government. They were then sent to invade Cuba, but after landing at the Bay of Pigs in Cuba, they were quickly defeated by Castro's forces.

In 1962 the United States put in place an **embargo** (ihm•BAHR•goh), or ban on trade, against Cuba. Poor harvests, loss of trade, and bad government planning brought disaster to Cuba's economy. The country remained very poor, and Cubans continued to flee to the United States. Most of these Cubans settled in Florida.

▲ While fighting to overthrow Cuba's government, the guerrilla forces of Fidel Castro (standing, center) often hid in the island's jungles. *Why did Castro's new government come into conflict with the United States?*

Dictators and Rebels Castro wanted to spread communism in Latin America. The United States was just as determined to prevent it. The Cold War contributed to conflicts in many Central American nations in the 1970s and 1980s. In El Salvador, fighters supported by Castro battled government troops armed by the United States. Thousands of people died before a settlement ended the fighting in 1992.

In Nicaragua, rebels called Sandinistas overthrew the brutal dictator Anastasio Somoza in 1979. Nicaragua's new government turned to Cuba and the Soviet Union for aid.

People in Nicaragua who opposed the Sandinistas formed groups known as the contras, from the Spanish word meaning "against." With U.S. help, the contras fought Sandinista forces. This conflict finally ended in the early 1990s, when free elections were held and the Sandinistas lost power.

Another war took place in Guatemala. There, American-backed government forces fought rebel groups from 1960 to 1996. About 150,000 people died, and the civil war severely weakened the economy.

Because of income from the Panama Canal, Panama enjoyed some prosperity. In 1983 General Manuel Noriega, backed by the United States, took power. His harsh rule and drug dealing, however, soon cost him American support. In 1989 the United States invaded Panama and overthrew him.

In the Caribbean republic of Haiti, a family of cruel dictators called the Duvaliers (doo•VAL•yayz) ruled from 1957 to 1986. In 1990 a reformer named **Jean-Bertrand Aristide** (AR•ih•STEED) was elected president. Military officers forced Aristide out a year later. With U.S. help, he returned to power in 1994 but was overthrown again in 2004. Haiti's economy remains poor, and its people face many hardships.

✓ **Reading Check** **Explain** How did the Cold War affect events in Cuba and Central America?

Mexico Pushes to Modernize

Main Idea During the twentieth century, Mexico struggled to overcome economic, social, and political challenges.

Reading Focus What challenges in your life have forced you to make changes? Read to find out how Mexican leaders have made changes to improve their country.

Mexico is the United States's nearest southern neighbor. Since World War II, Mexico has developed many new industries and worked to better the lives of its people.

The Revolution of 1911 In the early 1900s, dictator Porfirio Díaz (pawr•FEER•yoh DEE•AHS) ruled Mexico. He encouraged foreigners to invest in Mexico's oil wells and other businesses. Wealthy Mexicans prospered, but peasants and workers faced increasing hardships.

The Mexican Revolution

◄ As president of Mexico, Lázaro Cárdenas distributed 44 million acres of land to Mexican peasants.

Mexican dictator ► Porfirio Díaz ruled from 1877 to 1911.

▲ During the Mexican Revolution, armed bands of rebels fought government forces and seized the property of wealthy landowners. *Why was Porfirio Díaz overthrown?*

In 1911 liberal reformers overthrew Diaz. A dictator, however, seized power two years later. U.S. president Woodrow Wilson opposed the takeover. He ordered U.S. troops to take the Mexican port of Veracruz. This show of force ended the general's rule, and American troops withdrew.

Meanwhile, revolution swept Mexico. Regional leaders competed for power. Armies of farmers, workers, and ranchers fought each other. Fleeing the violence, many Mexicans moved to the United States.

By the early 1920s, Mexico had a stable government. However, only one political party ruled. It was called the Institutional Revolutionary Party. For the rest of the 1900s, most of Mexico's elected officials came from this party.

In the 1930s, Mexico entered a time of reform. President **Lázaro Cárdenas** (KAHR•duhn•AHS) gave land to landless peasants. He also worked to free Mexico's industries from foreign control. In 1938 he **nationalized** (NASH•nuh•LYZD), or had the government take over, foreign-owned oil wells. Owners of American and European oil companies were furious, but most Mexicans saw it as a positive change. Mexico later paid the oil companies for the takeover. A national company called PEMEX was set up to run the oil wells.

Slow but Steady Growth Thanks to its oil industry, Mexico made economic gains after World War II. The government, however, still had to borrow money from abroad to build new industries. When world oil prices fell in the 1980s, Mexico faced economic hardships.

To save money, the government cut services and jobs. It also sold off many government-owned businesses to private owners. Mexico's economic troubles made people turn away from the Institutional

▲ The passage of NAFTA has led to even more traffic along the U.S.-Mexico border, as well as the creation of foreign-owned factories, or maquiladoras, near the border. *What three countries signed NAFTA?*

Revolutionary Party. In 2000 the newly elected president of Mexico, Vicente Fox, came from a different political party—for the first time in 70 years.

Meanwhile, Mexico moved to break down barriers to trade with other countries. In 1994 Mexico, the United States, and Canada signed the North American Free Trade Agreement (NAFTA). Mexico's leaders hoped that free trade would encourage companies to open factories and create more jobs.

As a result of NAFTA, Mexico has built new industries and boosted living standards. Along Mexico's border, many companies from the United States and elsewhere have built maquiladoras (muh•KEE•luh•DOHR•uhs), or factories that assemble parts made in other countries. These factories have given jobs to thousands of Mexican workers.

✓ **Reading Check** **Explain** How did government reforms help to improve Mexico's economy?

Reform in South America

Main Idea Most South American countries have struggled to create fragile democracies and improve their economies.

Reading Focus Which is more important to people, democracy or prosperity? Read to find out how the desire for both affected the history of South America.

During most of the 1900s, South America was a region of great contrasts. Its cities grew rapidly, with both poor and wealthy neighborhoods. New industries developed, but old ways of farming were still practiced. Dictators ran governments with the support of a small group of wealthy landowners and businesspeople. Despite some progress, many South Americans remained poor.

Argentina In the early 1900s, the economy of **Argentina** faltered, and military leaders took over. One of these military leaders, **Juan Perón** (pay•ROHN), came to power in the 1940s. With his popular wife Evita at his side, Perón tried to improve the economy and help workers. His crackdown on basic freedoms made people unhappy, however. In 1955 a revolt drove Perón from power, and democracy returned.

Military officers again took control of Argentina in the 1970s. They ruled harshly, and their use of force resulted in the deaths of many people. In 1982 Argentina lost a war with Britain over the Falkland Islands. The Falklands, also known as the Malvinas, lie in the Atlantic Ocean near Argentina. Argentina's loss weakened the military, and the country returned to democracy.

Brazil Like Argentina, Brazil had difficulty building a democracy. During the 1930s, dictator Getúlio Vargas (zhuh•TOOL•yoo VAHR•guhs) set up new government-run industries. He raised wages, cut working hours, and allowed labor unions. Vargas, however, used the army to stay in power until 1945.

During the mid-1960s, Brazil was a democracy. Fear of a Communist takeover, however, led the military to take power in 1964. The new leaders encouraged foreign investment to create industries. Progress was made, but workers gained few benefits.

In the 1980s, Brazil's people demanded change. The military gradually returned the country to democracy. In recent years, Brazil's government has tried to cut spending and improve its economy.

Primary Source

"Cuba Appears"

Pablo Neruda was a Chilean poet who won the Nobel Prize for Literature in 1971. Much of his poetry is about politics. This poem praises Fidel Castro's revolution in Cuba.

▲ Pablo Neruda

"everything falls in the dust of the dead

when the people set their violins

and looking forward interrupt and sing,

interrupt the hatred of shadows and watchdogs,

sing and wake the stars with their song

and pierce the darkness with guns.

And so Fidel came forth cutting shadows

so that the jasmine tree could dawn."

—Pablo Neruda, "Cuba Appears"

DBQ Document-Based Question

What did Neruda mean by saying "interrupt the hatred"?

Linking Past & Present

Coffee Cultivation in Brazil

THEN Coffee growing in Brazil began in the mid-1700s. The first coffee growers used large knives, called machetes, to clear land in the rain forest. As the demand for coffee grew, planters became wealthy owners of huge estates, or *fazendas.* Planters brought hundreds of thousands of enslaved Africans to Brazil to work on the plantations.

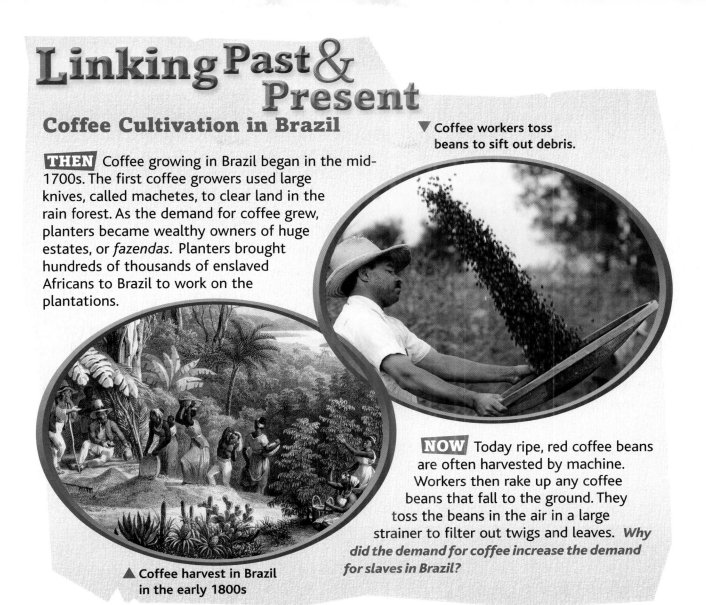

▼ Coffee workers toss beans to sift out debris.

▲ Coffee harvest in Brazil in the early 1800s

NOW Today ripe, red coffee beans are often harvested by machine. Workers then rake up any coffee beans that fall to the ground. They toss the beans in the air in a large strainer to filter out twigs and leaves. *Why did the demand for coffee increase the demand for slaves in Brazil?*

Chile During most of the 1900s, Chile was South America's most stable democracy. Then, in 1970, Salvador Allende (ah•YAYN•day) was elected president. He was the first Marxist in the Americas to win office in a free election. Allende nationalized industries, boosted wages, and gave land to the poor.

Allende's reforms angered Chile's military and business groups. The military overthrew Allende in 1973. A general named Augusto Pinochet (PEE•noh•CHEHT) became Chile's new ruler.

Pinochet proved to be a ruthless dictator. He jailed Marxists and others opposed to his government and violated citizens' rights. Many people were tortured and killed. In 1990 public opposition and international pressure finally forced Pinochet to leave office. Chile returned to democracy. In 2004, Chile signed a free trade agreement with the United States that continued to boost the country's economic growth.

Venezuela Like much of Latin America, Venezuela went back and forth from democracy to military rule. Oil was its major source of wealth. As rising oil prices brought more money to the country, the middle class grew, and many people prospered.

In the 1990s, oil prices fell, and Venezuela suffered. The government could no longer help the poor and jobless. In 1998 Venezuelans, angry at the government, elected a former military leader, Hugo Chavez, as president.

Chavez promised changes in the country's government and economy. His plans to increase his power, however, caused divisions among Venezuela's people. Chavez held on to power but faced much opposition to his rule.

Colombia Colombia, Venezuela's neighbor, was also marked by violence and civil war. From the late 1940s to the mid-1960s, fighting took place between rival political parties. About 300,000 people died. Then, in the mid-1960s, groups of rebels in the countryside began fighting the government. They demanded more land and rights for poor farmers.

By the 1980s, drug dealers had become a major force in Colombia. Dealers paid poor farmers more to grow coca leaves than the farmers could earn growing coffee. Coca leaves are used to make the drug cocaine. Drug dealers used their profits to build private armies. With help from the United States, Colombia's government has tried to break the power of the drug dealers but with little success.

✓ **Reading Check** **Explain** Why did Argentina's and Chile's military dictators give up power?

History Online

Study Central™ Need help with the material in this section? Visit jat.glencoe.com

Section 1 Review

Reading Summary

Review the Main Ideas

- Latin America's dependence on exports kept the region poor and made it difficult for democracy to succeed.

- Since the Mexican Revolution, Mexico has had a democratic government and has made economic progress.

- Poverty and social conflict have led to a number of violent revolutions and civil wars in the countries of Central America.

- For many years, dictators controlled the countries of South America. Recent attempts at democracy have not always been successful.

What Did You Learn?

1. How have multinational corporations affected Latin American countries?

2. How did Cárdenas change Mexico's economy?

Critical Thinking

3. **Summarizing Information** Draw a chart and list the changes that occurred in each South American country's government in the 1900s.

Country	Changes in Government

4. **Cause and Effect** What effects did the increased export of Latin American food products and raw materials in the late 1800s and early 1900s have on the region?

5. **Sequence** Describe the development of democracy in Mexico.

6. **Persuasive Writing** Create a poster encouraging citizens of a Latin American country to adopt a democratic system.

7. **Reading** **Extending the Text** Besides this textbook, list five places where you could find information about the challenges that Latin American countries face today.

Section 2

Africa and the Middle East

Get Ready to Read!

What's the Connection?

While Latin American nations were struggling for stability, nations in Africa and the Middle East also faced challenges and conflicts.

Focusing on the (Main Ideas)

- The countries of Africa south of the Sahara faced many challenges in the late twentieth century. *(page 870)*

- Black South Africans won their freedom after years of hardship and struggle. *(page 872)*

- The creation of Israel in 1948 sparked a conflict that still exists today. *(page 874)*

- Political and social conflicts continue to keep the Middle East in turmoil. *(page 876)*

Locating Places

Israel (IHZ•ree•uhl)
Egypt (EE•jihpt)
Iran (ih•RAHN)
Iraq (ih•RAHK)

Meeting People

Nelson Mandela
Yasir Arafat (ahr•uh•FAHT)
Anwar el-Sadat
Ruhollah Khomeini
   (ru•HAWL•la   koh•MAY•nee)
Saddam Hussein (hoo•SAYN)

Building Your Vocabulary

refugee (REH•fyu•JEE)
apartheid (uh•PAHR•TAYT)
intifada

Reading Strategy

Organizing Information Complete a diagram like the one below to show the challenges facing African nations.

When & Where?

1950	1975	2000
1956 Egypt takes over Suez Canal	**1979** Revolution in Iran overthrows shah	**1994** Nelson Mandela becomes South Africa's president

ISRAEL
IRAQ
SOUTH AFRICA

African Challenges

Main Idea The countries of Africa south of the Sahara faced many challenges in the late twentieth century.

Reading Focus What would it be like to be forced from your home? Read to find out how conflict has left many Africans homeless.

Africa south of the Sahara was politically unstable and was struggling with its economy during the late 1900s. War, drought, and famine blocked efforts to build modern societies.

Civil Wars Since the 1960s, many African countries have suffered from civil war. Previously, you learned that European nations in the 1800s divided Africa into colonies. In doing so, they tore apart once-united regions and threw together ethnic and religious groups that did not get along.

After independence, many countries kept the old colonial boundaries. Within each new country, different groups began fighting each other. In recent years, ethnic conflicts have divided people in Nigeria, Ivory Coast, Liberia, Somalia, Sudan, Rwanda, Burundi, and the Democratic Republic of Congo.

In these wars, many people have died or have become **refugees** (REH•fyu•JEEZ), people who flee to another country to escape persecution or disaster. Unrest in one country often has spilled over into neighboring countries. In some cases, United Nations (UN) peacekeeping troops have been called in to maintain peace.

African Economies African nations have faced economic difficulties, too. Africa south of the Sahara is rich in mineral resources, such as oil, gold, and diamonds. These resources, however, are not evenly distributed. Some countries are rich, while others are poor.

Industry plays only a small role in Africa's economies. In the past, colonial rulers used Africa as a source of raw materials and left the continent largely undeveloped. Today

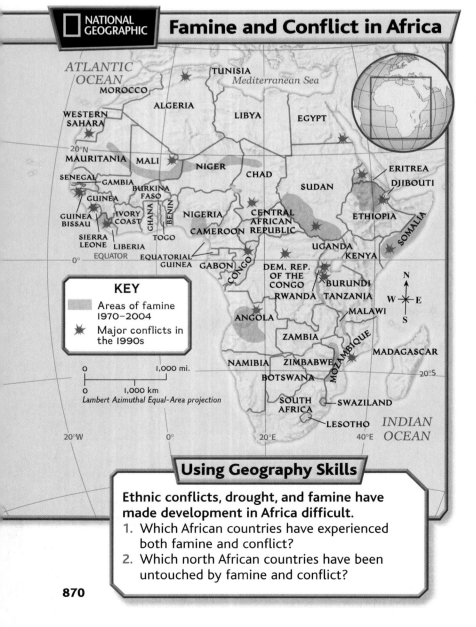

NATIONAL GEOGRAPHIC **Famine and Conflict in Africa**

KEY

Areas of famine 1970–2004

Major conflicts in the 1990s

0 1,000 mi.
0 1,000 km
Lambert Azimuthal Equal-Area projection

Using Geography Skills

Ethnic conflicts, drought, and famine have made development in Africa difficult.
1. Which African countries have experienced both famine and conflict?
2. Which north African countries have been untouched by famine and conflict?

African nations south of the Sahara are struggling to build factories and businesses.

Most people in Africa still depend on farming or livestock herding. They usually are able to grow only enough food to feed their families. Some farmers work on large, company-run farms that grow cash crops to send overseas. These crops include coffee, cacao, cotton, tea, peanuts, and bananas.

Like Latin America, many African economies rely on a single export crop to earn money. When prices for these crops drop, incomes fall and jobs are lost.

Drought and famine are constant problems for Africa. These disasters have led to many deaths in countries such as Ethiopia, Niger, Sudan, and Mali. Many African countries must buy food from other countries. Often this food is expensive and not plentiful. African governments are now teaching people better ways to farm, but much remains to be done to increase food production.

▲ As African populations continue to rise quickly, more and more people move to the cities, and shantytowns like this one in Cape Town, South Africa, continue to grow. *Why have many Africans left the countryside for cities?*

Ways of Life Independence has led to change in many African countries. Most Africans still live in villages, but cities have grown rapidly. In recent years, many Africans have left the countryside and moved to cities in search of jobs and better education. Governments find it difficult to provide shelter, water, and electricity for so many new city dwellers.

Health care is also an issue in Africa. Millions of people have been infected with the virus that causes AIDS. People who have AIDS often cannot work to support their families, and many children have been orphaned by the disease. Governments are trying to deal with this emergency, but providing good health care is very expensive.

✔ **Reading Check** **Identify** List three things that contribute to economic difficulties in Africa.

The End to Apartheid

Main Idea Black South Africans won their freedom after years of hardship and struggle.

Reading Focus What guarantees that you have the same rights as the person sitting next to you? Read to find how South Africans struggled to get the same guarantee.

Previously, you learned that South Africa was ruled by whites who denied basic rights to the much larger non-European population. This South African system of treating different groups separately and unequally was called **apartheid** (uh•PAHR•TAYT). From the 1950s to the 1980s, people inside and outside South Africa protested against apartheid.

Struggle for Freedom
Within South Africa, blacks and other non-Europeans organized to bring about change. In the early 1960s, one of the largest groups, the African National Congress (ANC), called for an armed uprising. Soon South African government forces were battling guerrilla groups backed by the ANC.

Meanwhile, many black South Africans, such as ANC leader **Nelson Mandela,** were jailed for resisting apartheid. Others, such as church leader Desmond Tutu, worked for peaceful change. The United Nations condemned apartheid, and many countries cut off trade with South Africa.

A New South Africa
Because of this pressure, the white-run government began to end apartheid in the late 1980s. Then, in 1990, the government released Nelson Mandela from prison. Over the next few years, talks led to the end of the remaining apartheid laws. All South Africans, regardless of race, were declared equal under the law.

In 1994 South Africa held its first democratic election that allowed people of different races to vote. South Africans elected Nelson Mandela to be their nation's first black president. He worked to unite and rebuild the country. Mandela served as president until 1999. His successor, Thabo Mbeki, carried on Mandela's policies.

Reading Check **Identify** Who is Nelson Mandela, and why is he important?

◄ These people are waiting in line to vote in South Africa's first democratic election in 1994. *Why did the white-run government in South Africa begin to end apartheid in the late 1980s?*

Biography

NELSON MANDELA

1918–

▲ Nelson Mandela

In 1990, a crowd of 50,000 people gathered at the city hall in Cape Town, South Africa, to welcome Nelson Mandela home from prison. While Mandela was imprisoned, his reputation had grown steadily. He had become a powerful symbol of the anti-apartheid movement. Free at last, Mandela immediately resumed his life's work to achieve a democratic, free, and equal society in South Africa.

Nelson Rolihlahla Mandela was born in the village of Qunu in Transkei, South Africa. Mandela's father, Henry Mgadia Mandela, served as the main adviser to the Paramount Chief of the Tembu Tribe. After his father's death, the Paramount Chief was young Mandela's guardian. Listening to cases that came before the Chief's court, Mandela decided that he wanted to become a lawyer. He was educated at University College of Fort Hare and the University of Witwatersrand. In 1952 Mandela and his longtime friend, Oliver Tambo, opened the first black law practice in South Africa. But not even their professional status as lawyers spared them from apartheid.

By the end of 1952, Mandela was deputy president of the African National Congress. The government responded to the ANC's strikes, boycotts, and civil disobedience—peaceful methods of resistance to apartheid—with force and violence. With Mandela as its commander-in-chief, a military wing of the ANC was formed to engage in violent forms of political struggle. In 1964 Mandela was sentenced to life imprisonment for plotting to overthrow the government.

While in prison, Mandela maintained a strict schedule of exercise and work and became a source of strength for other prisoners. The simple pleasure of sunlight was denied to him for nearly 30 years. Today, watching the sun set is one of Mandela's greatest pleasures.

> "I greet you in the name of peace, democracy and freedom for all."
>
> —Nelson Mandela, upon his release from prison as quoted in *Millennium Year by Year*

Then and Now

Nelson Mandela said, "The struggle is my life." In what way are these words significant not only to Mandela, but to the people of South Africa as well?

The Arab-Israeli Conflict

Main Idea The creation of Israel in 1948 sparked a conflict that still exists today.

Reading Focus Do you think that people of very different backgrounds can live together peacefully? Read to see how this issue affects the Middle East.

After World War II, many changes came to the Middle East. One was the founding of **Israel** (IHZ•ree•uhl). This new nation met the desire of many Jews for a homeland in Palestine. Israel also provided shelter for Jews who had survived the Holocaust. Its birth, however, sparked a bitter conflict with the Arabs that continues today.

Palestine Is Divided The horrors of the Holocaust brought the world's attention to the Jews. In 1947 the UN divided Palestine into a Jewish state and an Arab state. Arabs in Palestine and in neighboring countries opposed this decision. In 1948 the Jews set up Israel in their part of Palestine. David Ben-Gurion (BEHN•gur•YAWN) was Israel's first prime minister.

War soon broke out between Israel and its Arab neighbors. The war ended with Israel's victory and brought many changes. The fighting forced many Palestinian Arabs to flee to Arab countries. There, they settled in refugee camps, hoping to return home someday. Also, many Jews from Europe, Asia, and Africa began settling in Israel.

The Suez Crisis After Israel was formed, many Arabs united around President Gamal Abdel Nasser of **Egypt** (EE•jihpt). Nasser wanted to make Egypt strong and modern. He hoped that a new Egypt would lead the Arab world to greatness.

Oil in the Middle East

Many nations earn their wealth through oil, which is drawn from large fields. In order to get the natural oil reserves out of the ground, tall pumping towers are built. Before these towers can be put in place, however, a hole must first be drilled into the ground with an oil rig. The tall metal frame, or derrick, supports all of the equipment on the rig. A large and powerful drill is placed in the ground and digs its way to the oil beneath the surface. The drill bit is surrounded by a metal casing, which acts as a vacuum hose and removes mud, rock, and debris that the drill cuts through. The blades cut into the earth, leaving behind a hole from which the pumping towers can extract the oil. *Why are oil and oil products so important to the Middle East?*

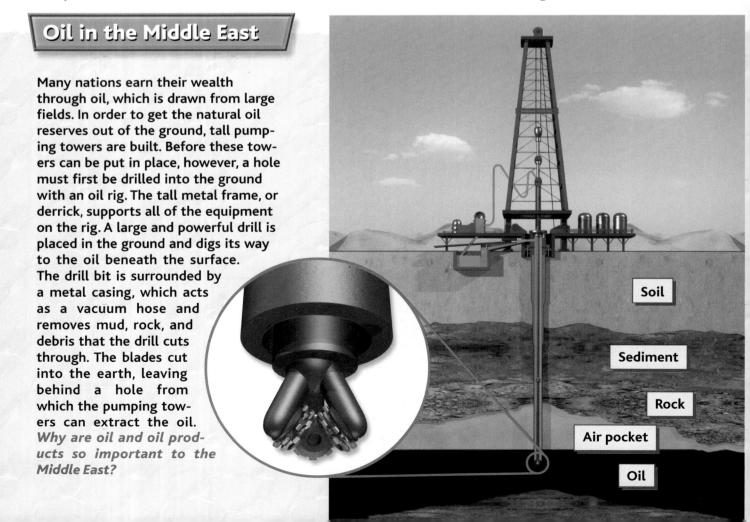

Soil

Sediment

Rock

Air pocket

Oil

Nasser also set out to reduce Europe's influence in the Middle East. In 1956 he seized the Suez Canal from its European owners. Britain and France then joined Israel in invading Egypt. Britain and France hoped to get rid of Nasser and take back the canal. Israel wanted to end Egypt's military threat.

The United States and the Soviet Union both opposed the invasion. Worried that the invasion would make Egypt a Soviet ally, U.S. president Dwight Eisenhower pressured Britain, France, and Israel into withdrawing. Egypt kept the canal and began accepting Soviet aid. Nasser became even more popular in the Arab world.

The Six-Day War Tensions remained high between Israel and the Arabs. In 1967 another war broke out. Fearing an attack from Egypt, Israel bombed Egyptian airfields on June 5. Within six days, Israel had wiped out the air forces of its Arab neighbors. Israeli troops moved west into the Gaza Strip and Egypt's Sinai Peninsula and north into the Golan Heights, which were part of Syria. Israel also captured the old city of Jerusalem and the West Bank, the part of Jordan that was west of the Jordan River.

When the fighting ended, the UN asked Israel to leave the captured areas. It asked the Arab nations to accept Israel. Both sides refused. Israel's victory in 1967 has shaped events in the Middle East up to the present. About one million Palestinians came under Israeli rule. Israeli settlers also began building towns in the West Bank and Gaza Strip.

In 1964 **Yasir Arafat** (ahr•uh•FAHT) became the leader of the new Palestine Liberation Organization, or PLO. The PLO's goal was to destroy Israel and take its land for Palestinians. PLO members seized passenger planes and carried out

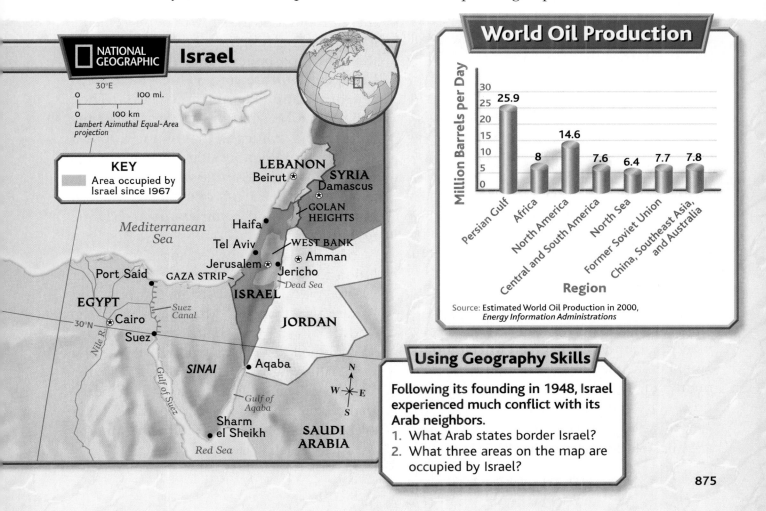

NATIONAL GEOGRAPHIC

Israel

30°E

0   100 mi.

0   100 km

Lambert Azimuthal Equal-Area projection

KEY

Area occupied by Israel since 1967

Mediterranean Sea

LEBANON
Beirut ⊛
SYRIA
Damascus ⊛
GOLAN HEIGHTS
Haifa
Tel Aviv
WEST BANK
Jerusalem ⊛   ⊛ Amman
Port Said   GAZA STRIP   Jericho
EGYPT   *Dead Sea*
ISRAEL
Suez Canal
30°N ⊛ Cairo
JORDAN
Suez
Nile R.
SINAI   • Aqaba
Gulf of Suez   *Gulf of Aqaba*
Sharm el Sheikh   SAUDI ARABIA
Red Sea

N W—E S

World Oil Production

Million Barrels per Day

Region	Million Barrels per Day
Persian Gulf	25.9
Africa	8
North America	14.6
Central and South America	7.6
North Sea	6.4
Former Soviet Union	7.7
China, Southeast Asia, and Australia	7.8

Region

Source: Estimated World Oil Production in 2000, *Energy Information Administrations*

Using Geography Skills

Following its founding in 1948, Israel experienced much conflict with its Arab neighbors.
1. What Arab states border Israel?
2. What three areas on the map are occupied by Israel?

acts of terrorism against Israel's people. Terrorism is the use of violence against civilians to achieve a political goal.

What Is OPEC?
In 1973 Egypt's president, **Anwar el-Sadat**, ordered his military to attack Israel. Sadat hoped to recapture the Sinai Peninsula. Egypt's forces smashed through Israel's defenses, but eventually Israel, led by Prime Minister Golda Meir (meh•IHR), pushed them back. A cease-fire ended the fighting.

Many Arab countries belong to the Organization of Petroleum Exporting Countries, or OPEC. Formed in 1960, OPEC includes most of the world's major oil-producing countries. Its purpose is to control world oil prices by regulating how much oil OPEC members produce.

In the middle of the war between Egypt and Israel, the Arab members of OPEC announced that they would no longer sell oil to countries that supported Israel. They also convinced OPEC to make oil prices four times higher than they currently were. This caused an energy crisis and high inflation in the U.S. and Europe. Even after Arab states agreed to sell oil to the U.S. again in 1974, prices stayed high.

By the late 1970s, Egypt wanted both peace and American aid. President Sadat decided to reach out to Israel. In 1978 he and Israeli leader Menachem Begin (BAY•gihn) met with U.S. president Jimmy Carter at Camp David in Maryland. The talks led to the Camp David Accords. In this historic treaty, Egypt agreed to recognize Israel, and Israel agreed to give up the Sinai Peninsula. The Israeli-Egyptian agreement marked the beginning of a peace process that continues today.

✔ Reading Check **Identify** What is the PLO, and what role did it play in the Middle East?

War in the Middle East

Main Idea Political and social conflicts continue to keep the Middle East in turmoil.

Reading Focus How do you keep yourself from getting discouraged after you fail at something? Read to find out how repeated failures affected the search for peace in the Middle East.

The conflict between Israel and the Palestinians is one of many challenges in the Middle East. As in other parts of the world, a few people are rich, while many are poor. Some countries prosper because of oil. Others lack resources. The number of people in the Middle East is growing rapidly, placing more demands on limited resources. One resource, water, is in short supply.

Iran's Islamic Revolution One response to these problems is the growth of movements based on the religion of Islam. Many of these groups believe that American and European culture and values have kept Muslim nations poor and weak. They believe that Muslims must return to Islamic culture and values if they want to build strong, prosperous societies. To achieve this goal, some of these groups try to use terrorism and violence to overthrow Muslim governments and bring about an Islamic revolution.

The first country where an Islamic revolution took place was **Iran** (ih•RAHN). After World War II, Iran became Europe and America's strongest Muslim ally in the Middle East. Its shah, or king, was Mohammed Reza Pahlavi (rih•ZAH PA•luh•vee). With American and European help, the shah began to turn Iran into a modern industrial country. Many Iranian Muslims, however, disliked the shah's harsh ways and the changes in their society.

Biography

GOLDA MEIR
1898–1978

Golda Meir overcame many hardships to help establish a Jewish homeland. She also became Israel's first female foreign minister and the first female prime minister of a Middle Eastern country. Meir accomplished goals that were unbelievable for a woman in the mid-1900s, but her journey was not easy.

During the early 1900s, Jewish families in Russia were persecuted. The Russian government passed hundreds of laws that restricted Russian Jews, including laws saying when they could marry and where they could live. Many Jews were forced to stay inside a fenced area called the Jewish Pale. Czar Nicholas blamed the Jews for economic problems. Many Jews were beaten to death.

Golda Meir lived in the Russian Ukraine with her parents Moshe and Blume Mabovits, and her siblings. Because her father was a carpenter, her family was allowed to leave the Jewish Pale and live in the city of Kiev, but many times Moshe did not get paid for his work because he was a Jew.

Meir and her family moved to the United States. She was a good student, loved politics, and was determined to help the Jewish people. She joined a Jewish movement in Colorado, collected money to help Jews in Poland and the Ukraine, and traveled to Palestine to see the new Jewish nation being built.

Meir later married Morris Meyerson and had children. But she remained active in politics. After World War II, she aided Jews rescued from German concentration camps. Once the Jewish state of Israel was created, Meir was active in its government. She served as prime minister from 1969 to 1974. Over time Golda Meir became one of the most influential leaders of Israel.

▲ Golda Meir

"Would it not be better for all to build a future for the Middle East based on cooperation?"

—Golda Meir, "Appeals for Reconciliation"

Then and Now

Read Meir's quote above. Give an example of how cooperation has been used to solve a problem in your own community.

The Ayatollah Khomeini (left) brought back traditional Islamic ideas to Iranian society following the overthrow of Shah Mohammad Reza Pahlavi (above). *What is an Islamic republic?*

Revolution in Iran Angry with the shah, many Iranians looked to their religious leaders to guide them. The most powerful Iranian ayatollah, or clergyman, lived in exile in France. His name was **Ruhollah Khomeini** (ru•HAWL•la koh•MAY•nee). Khomeini organized protests against the shah's government. In 1979, as protests mounted, the shah fled the country. Khomeini then returned to Iran and became the nation's new ruler. He and the other religious leaders made Iran an Islamic republic and enforced the strict laws of a traditional Muslim society.

Many people in Iran hated the United States because it had supported the shah. In late 1979, student militants, or people with strong views, attacked the U.S. embassy and took 52 Americans as hostages, or captives, for more than a year.

Iran also clashed with **Iraq** (ih•RAHK). Iraq was led by a dictator named **Saddam Hussein** (hoo•SAYN). In the 1980s, Iran and Iraq fought a war that cost thousands of lives.

The Persian Gulf War Iraq was nearly broke after its long war with Iran. It decided to seize its oil-rich Persian Gulf neighbor, Kuwait. In 1990 Saddam Hussein sent his army to take over Kuwait.

In response, the United States joined other nations in a coalition, or a group united for action. In 1991 coalition forces pushed the Iraqis out of Kuwait. They also destroyed much of Iraq's army. Many wanted Saddam Hussein overthrown, but he stayed in power.

After this Persian Gulf War, the coalition wanted to keep Hussein from making chemical and biological weapons, such as poison gas and deadly germs. A UN team was sent to keep watch over Iraqi military programs.

A Fragile Peace During the 1980s, Palestinian Arabs in the West Bank and Gaza Strip grew increasingly angry at being under Israeli control. In 1987 their anger finally exploded in an *intifada,* or uprising. Workers went on strike, and street protesters hurled stones at Israeli soldiers.

History Online

Web Activity Visit jat.glencoe.com and click on *Chapter 22—Student Web Activity* to learn more about the Middle East.

In the early 1990s, the United States set up peace talks between Israel and the Palestinians. In 1993 Israel agreed to give the Palestinians self-rule in certain areas. In return, the Palestinians accepted Israel's right to exist. A government known as the Palestinian Authority was created to rule in the Palestinian areas. During the 1990s, Israel also signed a peace treaty with Jordan.

Many Israelis and Palestinians supported the peace efforts. Some, however, did not. In the late 1990s and early 2000s, Palestinian militants began setting off bombs in Israel.

In response, Israel seized or killed many Palestinian leaders. In 2002, Israel moved with force in the West Bank to crush militant groups. To keep out attackers, Israel also began building a wall along its border with the Palestinian areas.

◀ A long-time Palestinian leader, Yasir Arafat, became the head of the Palestinian Authority when it was created in the 1990s. *How did Israel respond to the wave of Palestinian attacks in the late 1990s?*

As a step toward freeing themselves of the Palestinian issue, the Israelis made plans in 2004 to pull out of the Gaza Strip. Meanwhile, Palestinians began to demand better government from the Palestinian Authority.

✓ **Reading Check** **Explain** What happened when Iraqi troops invaded Kuwait in 1990?

History Online

Study Central™ Need help with the material in this section? Visit jat.glencoe.com

Section 2 Review

Reading Summary

Review the Main Ideas

- In the late 1900s, many countries in Africa south of the Sahara faced civil war, famine, disease, and political unrest as they attempted to modernize.

- The creation of an Israeli state in 1948 angered many Arabs and led to a number of wars and other conflicts in the region.

- The Israeli and Palestinian conflict, along with conflicts between Muslim groups and countries, has kept the Middle East in turmoil.

What Did You Learn?

1. What was apartheid, and what brought about its end?

2. What was the oil embargo of the early 1970s? Why was it put in place?

Critical Thinking

3. **Organizing Information** Draw a diagram like the one below. Use the outer ovals to list challenges faced by Africa south of the Sahara today.

Challenges

4. **Cause and Effect** What were the results of the Six-Day War? How did they affect Arab-Israeli relations at that time?

5. **Explain** How was Israel founded? Why did this cause problems?

6. **Analyze** What role has the United States played in the Middle East?

7. **Expository Writing** Write an essay discussing the problems facing the Middle East today and what might be done to ease tensions there in the future.

Section 3

The Cold War Ends

Get Ready to Read!

What's the Connection?
In Chapter 21 you read about the Cold War. Read to find out how nations changed during the final decades of the Cold War.

Focusing on the Main Ideas
- After nearly 50 years of bitter rivalry with the United States, in the 1990s the Soviet Union and its Eastern European empire fell apart. *(page 881)*
- The fall of communism unleashed deadly ethnic hatreds in the Balkan nation of Yugoslavia. *(page 884)*
- China moved toward a free-market economy, but its leaders still opposed democratic reforms. *(page 885)*

Locating Places
Russia

Yugoslavia

Meeting People
Mikhail Gorbachev (GAWR•buh•CHAWF)

Boris Yeltsin

Josip Broz Tito

Slobodan Milosevic (SLOH•buh• DAHN muh•LOH•suh•VIHCH)

Deng Xiaoping (DUHNG SYOW•PING)

Building Your Vocabulary
détente (day•TAHNT)

glasnost (GLAZ•nohst)

perestroika (PEHR•uh•STROY•kuh)

ethnic cleansing

Reading Strategy
Compare and Contrast Complete a Venn diagram to show the characteristics of glasnost and perestroika.

Glasnost — Perestroika

NATIONAL GEOGRAPHIC When & Where?

NORTH AMERICA EUROPE RUSSIA CHINA

1965   1985   2005

1966 Cultural Revolution begins in China

1991 Soviet Union breaks up

1995 Dayton talks settle Bosnian conflict

The Fall of the Soviet Union

Main Idea After nearly 50 years of bitter rivalry with the United States, in the 1990s the Soviet Union and its Eastern European empire fell apart.

Reading Focus Why do things change in the world? Do you think people make a difference, or are big developments in economics and technology responsible? Read to learn why the Soviet Union collapsed.

Previously, you learned about the Cold War. In the 1970s, relations between the U.S. and the two Communist giants—the Soviet Union and China—began to improve.

What Was Détente?

In the 1970s, the United States introduced a new policy called détente. **Détente** (day•TAHNT) comes from a French word that means "a relaxation of tensions." How did détente begin?

In 1972 U.S. president Richard Nixon made a historic trip to China. There, Nixon and China's Communist leaders agreed to have diplomatic relations and to promote trade. Nixon's visit was carefully watched by the Soviets. The alliance between China and the Soviet Union had ended in the 1960s, and the Soviets no longer trusted China. The Soviets feared that closer U.S.-Chinese ties would be bad for them. So they began to reach out to the United States.

Later, in 1972, U.S. president Nixon and Soviet leader Leonid Brezhnev held talks and signed several agreements. One agreement was SALT, or the Strategic Arms Limitation Treaty. It put limits on the nuclear weapons of both superpowers.

Despite high hopes, détente did not last. In 1979 the Soviets invaded Afghanistan. There, Soviet forces fought to keep a Communist government in power. The United States opposed the invasion, and President Jimmy Carter reduced trade.

▲ The period of détente negotiated by Soviet leader Leonid Brezhnev (left) and President Richard Nixon (right) lasted seven years. *What ended the détente of the 1970s?*

Reagan Pressures the Soviets

In 1981 Ronald Reagan became president of the United States. Reagan was strongly anti-communist. Calling the Soviet Union an "evil empire," Reagan started a military buildup. In doing so, he challenged the Soviets to an arms race. The Soviet economy was already having problems, and the arms race weakened it further. The Soviet economic crisis helped bring to power Soviet leaders willing to reform their system.

Reagan also gave American support to groups trying to overthrow Communist governments. For example, the United States helped forces in Central America and Africa opposed to the spread of communism. It also backed Islamic groups fighting the Soviets in Afghanistan.

Who Was Gorbachev?

In 1985 **Mikhail Gorbachev** (GAWR•buh•CHAWF) became the Soviet leader. He swiftly began to transform the Soviet Union. Under the policy of

"Tear Down This Wall"

On June 12, 1987, Ronald Reagan delivered a speech to the people of West Berlin while standing at a gate along the Berlin Wall.

"Behind me stands a wall that encircles the free sectors of this city. . . .

. . . We hear much from Moscow about a new policy of reform and openness. . . .

Are these the beginnings of profound changes in the Soviet state? Or are they token gestures, intended to raise false hopes in the West, or to strengthen the Soviet system without changing it? . . .

General Secretary Gorbachev, if you seek peace, if you seek prosperity for the Soviet Union and Eastern Europe, if you seek liberalization: Come here to this gate! Mr. Gorbachev, open this gate! Mr. Gorbachev, tear down this wall!"

—Ronald Reagan, "Remarks at the Brandenburg Gate"

▲ President Ronald Reagan speaking at the Berlin Wall

DBQ Document-Based Question

What two possibilities does Reagan see in the Soviet policies of reform and openness?

glasnost (GLAZ•nohst), or "openness," Soviet citizens could say and write what they thought without fear of being punished. Another policy, known as **perestroika** (PEHR•uh•STROY•kuh), or "rebuilding," aimed at boosting the Soviet economy. It gave factory managers more freedom and called for small, privately owned businesses. Gorbachev encouraged East European Communist leaders to follow his reforms.

The Berlin Wall Falls

In 1987 U.S. president Ronald Reagan visited West Berlin. Standing at the Berlin Wall that divided the city, he said, "[I]f you seek peace, . . . Mr. Gorbachev, tear down this wall!"

Like the Soviet Union, the communist lands of Eastern Europe had weak economies. Their people began to push for democratic change. The first step was in Poland, where the labor union Solidarity called for reforms. East Europeans wondered if Gorbachev would act to stop reforms. Gorbachev, however, said he would not interfere.

Without Soviet support, the governments in Eastern Europe crumbled one by one. In 1989 revolutions took place in Poland, Hungary, Czechoslovakia, Romania, and Bulgaria. Free elections were held. East Europeans who opposed communism, such as Lech Walesa (lehk vah•LEHN•suh) in Poland and Vaclav Havel (VAHT•SLAHF HAH•vehl) in Czechoslovakia, were elected to lead the new governments.

Finally, it was Germany's turn. On November 9, 1989, East Germany's Communist leaders bowed to pressure. They threw open the main gate in the Berlin Wall. The next day, soldiers and civilians began knocking down the wall. Less than a year later, the two parts of Germany were reunited after more than 40 years of division.

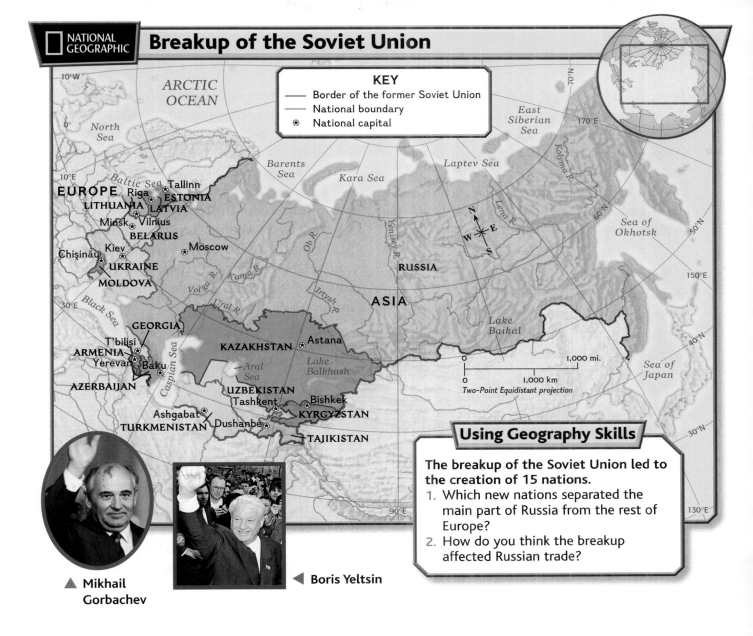

Breakup of the Soviet Union

NATIONAL GEOGRAPHIC

KEY
- Border of the former Soviet Union
- National boundary
- ⊛ National capital

ARCTIC OCEAN

North Sea

Baltic Sea

EUROPE

Barents Sea

Kara Sea

Laptev Sea

East Siberian Sea

ESTONIA Tallinn
Riga **LATVIA**
LITHUANIA Vilnius
Minsk
BELARUS
Kiev Moscow
Chişinău **UKRAINE**
MOLDOVA

RUSSIA

Sea of Okhotsk

GEORGIA
T'bilisi
ARMENIA Baku
Yerevan
AZERBAIJAN

ASIA

KAZAKHSTAN Astana

Lake Balkhash

Aral Sea

Lake Baikal

Sea of Japan

UZBEKISTAN
Tashkent Bishkek
KYRGYZSTAN
Ashgabat Dushanbe
TURKMENISTAN **TAJIKISTAN**

0   1,000 mi.
0   1,000 km
Two-Point Equidistant projection

Using Geography Skills

The breakup of the Soviet Union led to the creation of 15 nations.
1. Which new nations separated the main part of Russia from the rest of Europe?
2. How do you think the breakup affected Russian trade?

▲ Mikhail Gorbachev

◀ Boris Yeltsin

The Soviet Union Collapses As communism ended in Eastern Europe, the Soviet Union faced growing unrest among its ethnic groups. Gorbachev was criticized by both hard-liners and reformers. Hard-liners wanted to stop changes, while reformers felt that Gorbachev was not moving fast enough. The reformers were led by a rising leader named **Boris Yeltsin.** He became president of Russia, the largest Soviet republic.

In August 1991, hard-line Communists tried to use the military to take over the government. Boris Yeltsin called on the people to resist. When the military backed down, the hard-liners were forced to give up. Their fall marked the beginning of the end of the Soviet Union. Within a few months, **Russia** and all of the other Soviet republics declared independence. By the end of 1991, one of history's largest empires had disappeared.

In Russia, President Yeltsin and his successor Vladimir Putin struggled to improve the country's economy. Free-enterprise reforms have had some success. The growth of crime and violence, however, has alarmed many Russians. A bloody war also has raged in the southern area of Chechnya, which has tried to break away from Russia.

✓ **Reading Check** **Explain** What caused the collapse of the Soviet Union?

The Breakup of Yugoslavia

Main Idea The fall of communism unleashed deadly ethnic hatreds in the Balkan nation of Yugoslavia.

Reading Focus What are some roles you think the United Nations can play? Read to find out one role the UN played in southeastern Europe.

In Eastern Europe, the fall of communism created a new wave of nationalism. Soon national and ethnic groups began opposing each other. These rivalries exploded, with horrifying results, in the country of **Yugoslavia.**

A Balkan Flashpoint

Yugoslavia was a war-torn area located in Europe's Balkan Peninsula. Its problems began in 1980, the year Communist leader **Josip Broz Tito** died. Since World War II, Tito's strong dictatorship had held Yugoslavia's six republics together. When Tito died, however, different ethnic groups struggled for power.

In the early 1990s, four republics declared their independence. They were Slovenia, Croatia, Bosnia-Herzegovina, and Macedonia. The republic of Serbia, however, wanted to keep Yugoslavia together and to keep all Serbs within Yugoslavia. Its leader, **Slobodan Milosevic** (SLOH•buh•DAHN muh•LOH•suh•VIHCH), used force to keep some of the land in the other republics under Yugoslavia's control.

What Is Ethnic Cleansing?

The heaviest fighting took place in Bosnia-Herzegovina. There, Serbs aided by Milosevic fought Croats and Muslims. The Bosnian Serbs carried out **ethnic cleansing**—using force to remove an entire ethnic group from an area. Many people died or became refugees.

The United States pushed for peace talks. In 1995 the leaders of Bosnia-Herzegovina, Serbia, and Croatia met in Dayton, Ohio. They signed a peace agreement that divided Bosnia into Croat-Muslim and Serb regions. NATO troops then entered Bosnia as peacekeepers.

Kosovo

The Serbs next tried to remove Albanian Muslims from Kosovo. Kosovo had been a self-governing province of Yugoslavia. Albanians there wanted independence. As many refugees left Kosovo in 1999, NATO countries led by the United States bombed Serb military targets. The Serbs finally allowed a NATO peacekeeping force to enter Kosovo.

In 2000, Milosevic was overthrown, and a democratic government replaced him. Milosevic was arrested and brought to trial before an international court.

Reading Check Explain What was the goal of Serbia's foreign policy?

▲ A refugee walks past a war-damaged building in the city of Sarajevo, in what was formerly the country of Yugoslavia. *Which four republics of Yugoslavia declared their independence in the 1990s?*

Revolution and Reform in China

Main Idea China moved toward a free-market economy, but its leaders still opposed democratic reforms.

Reading Focus Do you think people who own their own businesses work harder than other people? Why or why not? Read to learn how private ownership of business changed China.

Previously, you learned that China became Communist in 1949. China's Communist leaders set out to make China a modern country. By the mid-1960s, China still had a long way to go. At this time, Chinese leaders tried new ways to move the country forward.

The Cultural Revolution
Communist leader Mao Zedong feared China was losing its revolutionary spirit. In 1966 he began the Cultural Revolution. "Undesirables" were driven from the Communist Party, and thinkers who favored more freedom were arrested. Meanwhile, students called Red Guards attacked political leaders, teachers, and others and accused them of not supporting communism.

The Cultural Revolution disrupted daily life. People stopped working, and factory production slumped. Battles broke out between Red Guards and other citizens. The Chinese army finally was called out to stop the Cultural Revolution.

China Reforms Its Economy
When Mao Zedong died in 1976, **Deng Xiaoping** (DUHNG SYOW•PING) became China's new leader. He cared more about economic growth than about revolutionary spirit. Deng supported a plan—the Four Modernizations—that called for changes in four areas: industry, culture, science and technology, and defense.

Focus on Everyday Life

Cultural Revolution in China During the Cultural Revolution, millions of Red Guards embraced Mao Zedong's slogan: "It is right to rebel." Mao encouraged the Red Guards to rid China of all traces of its traditional values. During the Cultural Revolution, those values were called the Four Olds: old ideology, old culture, old customs, and old habits.

Relationships between people began to break down as individuals were encouraged to turn each other in for breaking even the most absurd rules. Students attacked their teachers. Children accused their parents. Brothers and sisters turned against one another. Husbands and wives suffered severe punishment, even torture and death, if they refused to inform on their spouses.

▲ Members of the Red Guard in front of a portrait of Mao Zedong

Connecting to the Past
1. What did Mao want to get rid of in China during the Cultural Revolution?
2. What impact did the Cultural Revolution have on relationships in society, such as ties among family members?

Under Deng, the government relaxed its control over factories and farms. Factory managers could decide what goods to produce and what prices to charge. Farmers could keep some of the profits from the food they grew. Deng also encouraged foreigners to set up and run businesses in special areas of China known as economic zones.

Deng's reforms made China's economy grow. More goods were produced, and many Chinese enjoyed a better standard of living. For the first time, China's people were able to buy consumer goods, such as televisions and appliances.

Demands for Democracy Despite economic change, many Chinese were unhappy under Communist rule. They wanted to have free elections and basic rights, such as freedom of speech, religion, and the press.

In the spring of 1989, hundreds of thousands of people, mostly students, gathered in Tiananmen (TEE•EHN•AH•MEHN) Square in the heart of Beijing. They demanded that China become a democracy.

The protests were peaceful, but they frightened the government. So Deng sent soldiers and tanks into Tiananmen Square to break up the gatherings. Between 500 and 1,000 civilians were killed. Countries around the world protested China's harsh treatment of its citizens.

During the 1990s, China gained back territories lost in the 1800s to Europeans. China took control of Hong Kong from Britain in 1997. It gained the port of Macau from Portugal two years later. Both cities are centers of manufacturing, trade, and finance.

✔ **Reading Check** **Explain** What was the purpose of the demonstration in Tiananmen Square in 1989?

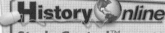
History Online
Study Central™ Need help with the material in this section? Visit jat.glencoe.com

Section 3 Review

Reading Summary
Review the Main Ideas

- The Cold War between the United States and the Soviet Union came to an end in the 1990s. Communism fell in the USSR and in its Eastern European empire.

- When Communist governments fell, old ethnic hatreds arose in Yugoslavia and led to the breakup of that nation.

- Throughout the twentieth century, the Chinese people were denied democratic freedoms. However, leaders like Deng Xiaoping modernized the Chinese economy.

What Did You Learn?

1. Who were the Red Guards? What role did they play in the Cultural Revolution?

2. How did Ronald Reagan try to weaken the Soviet Union?

Critical Thinking

3. **Organizing Information** Complete a diagram like the one below to show the Four Modernizations of Deng Xiaoping.

Four Modernizations

4. **Explain** What problems arose in Russia after the Soviet Union was dissolved?

5. **Analyze** Why do you think the people living in communist nations of Eastern Europe felt it was safe to rebel in 1989?

6. **Explain** Why did President Nixon go to China in 1972?

7. **Creative Writing** Do you think Mikhail Gorbachev was the most important leader in the 1900s? Write a brief essay giving your opinion and supporting it with historical facts.

Section 4

The World Enters a New Century

Get Ready to Read!

What's the Connection?

Read to find out how the changes in the 1990s continued into the 2000s.

Focusing on the Main Ideas

- Advances in technology have brought the world closer together economically, politically, and culturally. *(page 888)*

- Political and economic changes continued to affect key regions of the world at the close of the twentieth century. *(page 890)*

- A devastating attack on September 11, 2001, focused the world's attention on terrorism. *(page 892)*

Locating Places

Iraq

Afghanistan (af•GA•nuh•STAN)

Meeting People

Bill Gates

Bill Clinton

George W. Bush

Osama bin Laden
(oh•SAHM•uh bihn LAHD•uhn)

Building Your Vocabulary

globalism (GLOH•buh•LIH•zuhm)

euro (YUR•oh)

deforestation

nuclear proliferation (NOO•klee•uhr pruh•LIH•fuh•RAY•shuhn)

terrorism

weapons of mass destruction

Reading Strategy

Identifying Information Complete a table like the one below to show the name and purpose of each regional trade organization.

Organization Name	Purpose

NATIONAL GEOGRAPHIC **When & Where?**

NORTH AMERICA EUROPE ASIA AFRICA SOUTH AMERICA AUSTRALIA

1990 — 1998 — 2006

1993 European Union (EU) is formed

1995 WTO is created

2001 Terrorists attack the United States

2003 Iraq War begins

The New Global Economy

Main Idea Advances in technology have brought the world closer together economically, politically, and culturally.

Reading Focus Describe something you know about the way people live in India, China, or South Africa. How do you know what you know? Read to find out why the world has become more connected during the last 30 years.

In recent years, the nations of the world have developed a global economy. This means that they depend on one another for raw materials, to make goods, and for markets in which to sell goods. Think of the many ways you use products from other countries. These are examples of how all the people on our planet are now closely linked together. What has made all of this possible?

The Technology Revolution One reason is the technology revolution. Today we take for granted computers, cell phones, cable television, and compact discs. Back in 1970, these things had either not been invented yet or were not widely available.

The invention that has driven the technology revolution is the computer. In the 1960s, scientists developed the integrated circuit, a small electronic device. A decade later, even more powerful circuits called microprocessors appeared. They made it possible to make smaller, much faster computers that could store a lot of information.

The Computer

The invention of the computer has opened up whole new avenues of communication across the world. Its conception, in the 1960s, helped make way for new technology. Computers are used by people every day to organize information, write documents, create images, and for countless other activities. The computer has become an essential tool for most of the world.
How do people use the computer for communication?

Power Supply · CD/DVD ROM Drive · Disk Drive · Fan · CPU (Central Processing Unit) · Monitor · Video Card · Sound Card · Mouse · Motherboard · Keyboard

In 1976 Stephen Wozniak and Steven Jobs built the first small computer for personal use. In the 1980s, **Bill Gates** developed software that tells computers how to do specific tasks. Soon an affordable personal computer was available.

Through their personal computers, people are now able to go on the Internet. This is a huge web of linked computer networks. The Internet has made global communications almost instant.

What Is Globalism?

The technology revolution has tied together people and nations more closely then before. It has contributed to the rise of **globalism** (GLOH•buh•LIH•zuhm). This is the idea that the world's economy and politics are all part of one big system. People and nations cannot stay separate from each other anymore.

Today, few nations can fully meet all the needs of their people without global trade. To encourage global trade, nations have created a number of organizations. After World War II, the United States and other nations set up the World Bank and the International Monetary Fund (IMF). These organizations made it easier for businesses to invest in other countries. Over the years, many nations also participated in talks to make trade between countries free and easy. These talks led to GATT treaties—General Agreement on Trade and Tariffs.

In 1995 the nations that had signed the GATT treaties over the years agreed to create the World Trade Organization (WTO). Made up of more than 140 member nations, the WTO arranges trade agreements and settles trade disputes.

In different world regions, nations have joined together to form trading groups. For example, nations in Europe formed the European Union (EU) in 1993. One of the EU's goals is to unite Europe politically and

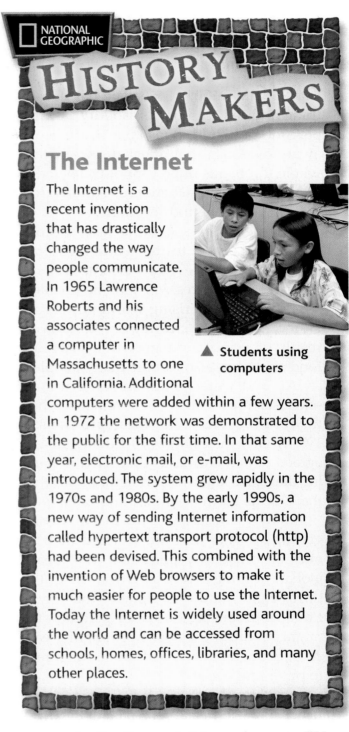

HISTORY MAKERS

The Internet

The Internet is a recent invention that has drastically changed the way people communicate. In 1965 Lawrence Roberts and his associates connected a computer in Massachusetts to one in California. Additional computers were added within a few years. In 1972 the network was demonstrated to the public for the first time. In that same year, electronic mail, or e-mail, was introduced. The system grew rapidly in the 1970s and 1980s. By the early 1990s, a new way of sending Internet information called hypertext transport protocol (http) had been devised. This combined with the invention of Web browsers to make it much easier for people to use the Internet. Today the Internet is widely used around the world and can be accessed from schools, homes, offices, libraries, and many other places.

▲ **Students using computers**

economically. Toward this end, some EU members in 2002 began using a common currency called the **euro** (YUR•oh).

Elsewhere, the North American Free Trade Agreement (NAFTA) created a free-trade area for Canada, the United States, and Mexico. The Asia Pacific Economic

Cooperation (APEC) agreement has tried to do the same among nations that border the Pacific Ocean.

Global Challenges Globalism has boosted trade and led to more prosperity in many parts of the world. It also has made people aware of issues that affect the world as a whole. Problems often cannot be solved by one nation alone. Therefore, nations must work together to find solutions.

In recent years, people have become aware of dangers to the world's environment. For example, many people fear that the earth's resources will soon be unable to support a rapidly rising world population. **Deforestation,** the clearing of forests, is one result of population growth. Water and food shortages also trouble many people.

Air and water pollution concern many scientists. Most experts believe nations have to work together to fix these problems. In 1987 twenty-three nations, including the U.S., agreed to ban chemicals suspected of harming the ozone layer—a part of the atmosphere that shields Earth from the Sun's radiation.

Many scientists also think that the earth is getting warmer and are worried that this may be caused by pollution. The idea of global warming is very controversial. In 1997 thirty-eight nations signed the Kyoto Protocol promising to reduce pollution that might be causing global warming. By early 2005, enough nations had ratified the treaty to put it into effect.

Another global problem is **nuclear proliferation** (NOO•klee•uhr pruh•LIH•fuh•RAY•shuhn), or the spread of nuclear weapons. Nuclear weapons programs in countries such as **Iraq,** North Korea, Libya, Iran, India, and Pakistan have been the focus of world concern.

✓ **Reading Check** **Describe** How did computers change between the 1940s and the 1980s?

A Changing World

(Main Idea) Political and economic changes continued to affect key regions of the world at the close of the twentieth century.

Reading Focus What are some things you own that were made in Asia? Read to find out how several East Asian countries became economic powers.

As a global economy has spread, many political changes have taken place. East Asia's countries now play a growing role in world affairs, and the nations of Europe are moving toward unity. In the United States, a conservative political movement has shaped the role of government.

The Rise of East Asia Today, a group of nations and territories in East Asia have been nicknamed the "Asian Tigers." They include South Korea, Taiwan, Singapore, and the Chinese port of Hong Kong. Why are they called this name? Following Japan's example, these four "Tigers" have built strong, modern economies.

While economically successful, some of the "Asian Tigers" are crowded and polluted. Many people, like those pictured below in Taipei, Taiwan, wear masks to protect themselves from pollution. *What are some products manufactured in Taiwan?* ▼

In the 1990s, South Korea moved from military rule to democracy. Its high technology and manufacturing industries have grown tremendously. South Korea now exports ships, cars, computers, and electronic appliances.

The island of Taiwan lies off China's coast. Taiwan is still a part of China, but it has a different government. Many Taiwanese would like Taiwan to be independent, but China's Communist leaders want Taiwan to be under their rule. Now a democracy, Taiwan has a booming economy that produces computers, radios, televisions, and telephones.

The port of Hong Kong is also part of China. Despite Communist rule, Hong Kong has been allowed to keep its strong, free-enterprise economy. Another prosperous port is Singapore at the tip of the Malay Peninsula. Although small in size, Singapore has a highly productive economy.

The European Union

Europe today ranks as one of the major economic and cultural centers of the world. In forming the European Union, some European countries want to make their continent an economic superpower like the United States.

Britain, once ruler of a global empire, has struggled with economic problems. During the 1980s, Conservative Party rule under Margaret Thatcher led to economic reforms. Since the 1990s, Britain's economy has done much better. Under the Labour Party, headed by Tony Blair, the government has given more power to regions such as Scotland and Wales.

France chose a Socialist, François Mitterand, as its president in 1981. Under Mitterand, the government ran some industries and passed laws to help workers. Since then, the French have twice voted for a

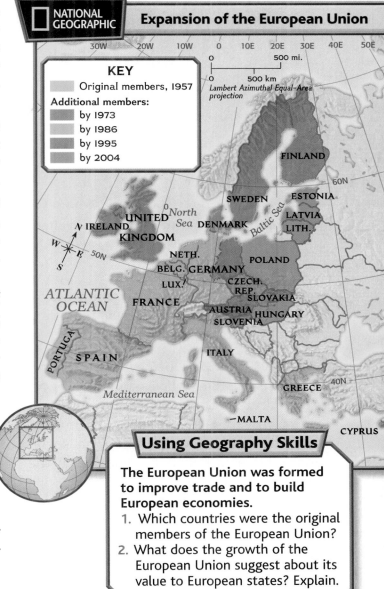

NATIONAL GEOGRAPHIC

Expansion of the European Union

KEY
Original members, 1957
Additional members:
by 1973
by 1986
by 1995
by 2004

500 mi.
500 km
Lambert Azimuthal Equal-Area projection

Using Geography Skills

The European Union was formed to improve trade and to build European economies.
1. Which countries were the original members of the European Union?
2. What does the growth of the European Union suggest about its value to European states? Explain.

conservative leader, Jacques Chirac, to deal with economic problems.

Germany enjoys a healthy economy, but has had difficulty in joining its western and eastern parts under one government. One challenge has been to close the gap between the prosperous west and less well-off east.

Europe's Mediterranean countries also have undergone many changes. In Italy, political power has changed hands many times. Also, rivalry between the wealthy north and the poorer south has caused

▲ New York City's World Trade Center soon after terrorists crashed airliners into the buildings

political tensions. Elsewhere, Spain, Portugal, and Greece are now democracies. Once isolated from Europe, they are taking active roles in European affairs.

The United States

During the 1980s and 1990s, conservative policies gained support in the United States. President Ronald Reagan lowered taxes, cut government rules, and decreased spending on social welfare. He also boosted spending on the military.

To pay for the spending, the federal government had to borrow money, and as a result, the federal debt—or the money the government owed to banks—greatly increased. George Bush, who followed Reagan as president, faced an economic downturn. He was defeated by Democrat **Bill Clinton** in 1992.

Clinton, a moderate Democrat, favored some conservative policies. Under Clinton, the budget was balanced, and the welfare system was changed. Then, in 2000, Republican **George W. Bush** was elected president. A conservative, Bush convinced Congress to pass large tax cuts and an education reform law.

✔ **Reading Check** **Identify** What are the "Asian Tigers"?

The War on Terror

Main Idea A devastating attack on September 11, 2001, focused the world's attention on terrorism.

Reading Focus Where were you when you heard about the attacks of 9/11? What did you think and feel? Read to learn how these attacks caused change all over the world.

In recent years, the world has seen the growth of terrorism. **Terrorism** is the use of violence against civilians to reach a political goal. Terrorists—either as individuals or groups—act on their own and are usually not part of a government. Their goal includes changing governments, and their attacks are aimed at civilians as well as soldiers.

Since World War II, many terrorist groups have operated worldwide. For example, the Irish Republican Army (IRA) has used terrorism in an attempt to force Britain to give up control of Northern Ireland. Italy's Red Brigades killed political leaders whom they blamed for an unjust society. State-sponsored terrorism is terrorism that is led or aided by national governments. Governments in countries such as Iraq, Iran, Syria, Cuba, **Afghanistan** (af•GA•nuh•stan), and North Korea have helped terrorist groups.

Today, most terrorist acts against Americans have been carried out by groups from the Middle East. Strong feelings against the United States are based in part on American support for Israel. Many Muslims also feel that American and European cultures undermine Islamic values.

What Happened on 9/11?

On September 11, 2001, the world saw a horrifying act of terrorism. Terrorists seized four American passenger planes. Two planes were deliberately crashed into New York City's World Trade Center. A third plane was flown into the Pentagon, the U.S. military headquarters. A fourth plane was seized, but the passengers heroically fought back. This plane crashed in Pennsylvania. The attacks killed nearly 3,000 people.

The terrorists were later found to be part of al-Qaeda (al•KY•duh), a terrorist group created by a Saudi Arabian named **Osama bin Laden** (oh•SAHM•uh bihn LAHD•uhn).

Who Is Osama bin Laden?
Al-Qaeda grew out of the Muslim struggle against the Soviets in Afghanistan. Osama bin Laden was one of the fighters there. Using his family's wealth, bin Laden formed al-Qaeda to recruit new fighters.

When the Soviets left Afghanistan, bin Laden decided that all Americans and Europeans should be pushed out of the Muslim world. Bin Laden then turned al-Qaeda into a terrorist group. His followers set off bombs at U.S. embassies in Kenya and Tanzania in 1998. They also attacked a U.S. Navy ship in Yemen in 2000.

After the 9/11 attacks, the United States declared war on terrorism. It first focused at Afghanistan. There, bin Laden and al-Qaeda hid out with the help of the militant Muslim government called the Taliban. The Taliban was defeated, and the United States helped set up a new Afghan government.

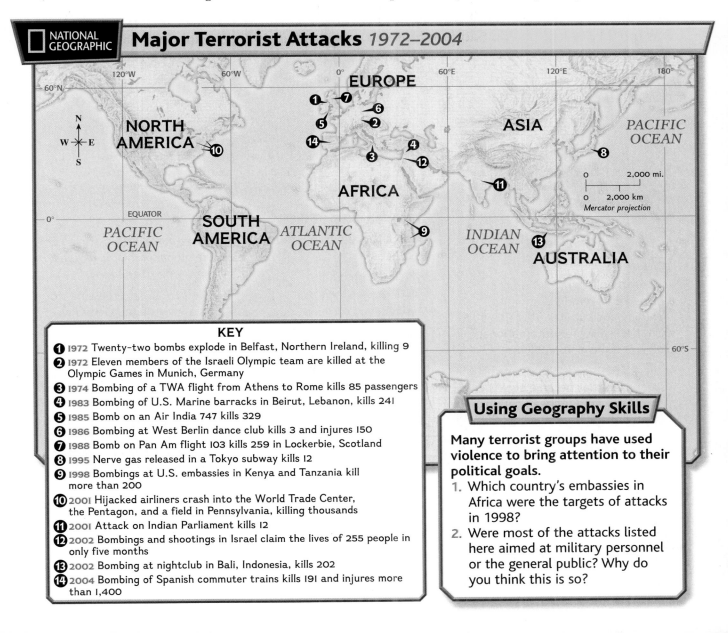

NATIONAL GEOGRAPHIC

Major Terrorist Attacks 1972–2004

KEY

1. 1972 Twenty-two bombs explode in Belfast, Northern Ireland, killing 9
2. 1972 Eleven members of the Israeli Olympic team are killed at the Olympic Games in Munich, Germany
3. 1974 Bombing of a TWA flight from Athens to Rome kills 85 passengers
4. 1983 Bombing of U.S. Marine barracks in Beirut, Lebanon, kills 241
5. 1985 Bomb on an Air India 747 kills 329
6. 1986 Bombing at West Berlin dance club kills 3 and injures 150
7. 1988 Bomb on Pan Am flight 103 kills 259 in Lockerbie, Scotland
8. 1995 Nerve gas released in a Tokyo subway kills 12
9. 1998 Bombings at U.S. embassies in Kenya and Tanzania kill more than 200
10. 2001 Hijacked airliners crash into the World Trade Center, the Pentagon, and a field in Pennsylvania, killing thousands
11. 2001 Attack on Indian Parliament kills 12
12. 2002 Bombings and shootings in Israel claim the lives of 255 people in only five months
13. 2002 Bombing at nightclub in Bali, Indonesia, kills 202
14. 2004 Bombing of Spanish commuter trains kills 191 and injures more than 1,400

Using Geography Skills

Many terrorist groups have used violence to bring attention to their political goals.

1. Which country's embassies in Africa were the targets of attacks in 1998?
2. Were most of the attacks listed here aimed at military personnel or the general public? Why do you think this is so?

The Invasion of Iraq In 2002, President George W. Bush turned his attention to countries that supported terrorism. He was also concerned about these countries producing **weapons of mass destruction** (WMD). These weapons include nuclear, chemical, and biological weapons that can kill tens of thousands of people at a time. The president feared these countries might give these weapons to terrorists.

Bush and some other world leaders believed that as long as Saddam Hussein stayed in power, Iraq would develop deadly weapons and support terrorists. In 2003, a coalition of countries led by the United States invaded Iraq. The Iraqi army was quickly defeated, and Saddam Hussein was captured.

For the United States and its partners, rebuilding Iraq was more difficult than defeating the Iraqi army. Saddam Hussein's supporters, foreign terrorists, and Islamic militants all battled coalition forces. These groups tried to defeat American efforts to rebuild Iraq's economy and create a democracy. In June 2004, the United States handed control of Iraq to a temporary Iraqi government. The new government began preparing Iraq for free elections.

To make it harder for terrorists to recruit followers, President Bush also announced plans to work for democracy in the Middle East. He also called for an independent Palestinian state in the region.

 **Explain** What was the connection between Afghanistan and al-Qaeda?

Section 4 Review

History Online

Study Central™ Need help with the material in this section? Visit jat.glencoe.com

Reading Summary

Review the Main Ideas

- The technology revolution has helped unite world economies, politics, and cultures. This globalism has led to new international organizations and problems.

- In the 1980s and 1990s, several Asian countries became economic powers, European nations created the EU, and the United States experienced changes in leadership and policy.

- A devastating act of terrorism occurred on September 11, 2001, in the United States and led to a worldwide war on terrorism.

What Did You Learn?

1. What are weapons of mass destruction?

2. Which nation did the "Asian Tigers" use as their economic model?

Critical Thinking

3. **Sequencing Information** Complete a diagram like the one below to show the events that occurred after the 9/11 terrorism attack.

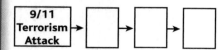

4. **Identify** What are some of the global problems nations are trying to address?

5. **Explain** What problems did the newly united Germany face?

6. **Analyze** Why is Taiwan's future uncertain?

7. **Expository Writing** Interview an adult to find out what technology was available when he or she was in school. Write an essay comparing technology back then to the technology available to your class today.

Chapter 22 Reading Review

Section 1 Challenges in Latin America

Vocabulary
export
embargo
nationalize

Focusing on the Main Ideas
- Latin America's economy has depended on exports and foreign investment. *(page 861)*
- In Central America, repressive governments, social conflict, and civil wars made progress difficult. *(page 863)*
- During the twentieth century, Mexico struggled to overcome economic, social, and political challenges. *(page 864)*
- Most South American countries have struggled to create fragile democracies and improve their economies. *(page 866)*

Section 2 Africa and the Middle East

Vocabulary
refugee
apartheid
intifada

Focusing on the Main Ideas
- The countries of Africa south of the Sahara faced many challenges in the late twentieth century. *(page 870)*
- Black South Africans won their freedom after years of hardship and struggle. *(page 872)*
- The creation of Israel in 1948 sparked a conflict that still exists today. *(page 874)*
- Political and social conflicts continue to keep the Middle East in turmoil. *(page 876)*

Section 3 The Cold War Ends

Vocabulary
détente
glasnost
perestroika
ethnic cleansing

Focusing on the Main Ideas
- After nearly 50 years of bitter rivalry with the United States, in the 1990s the Soviet Union and its Eastern European empire fell apart. *(page 881)*
- The fall of communism unleashed deadly ethnic hatreds in the Balkan nation of Yugoslavia. *(page 884)*
- China moved toward a free-market economy, but its leaders still opposed democratic reforms. *(page 885)*

Section 4 The World Enters a New Century

Vocabulary
globalism
euro
deforestation
nuclear proliferation
terrorism
weapons of mass destruction

Focusing on the Main Ideas
- Advances in technology have brought the world closer together economically, politically, and culturally. *(page 888)*
- Political and economic changes continued to affect key regions of the world at the close of the twentieth century. *(page 890)*
- A devastating attack on September 11, 2001, focused the world's attention on terrorism. *(page 892)*

Review Vocabulary

Match the word in the first column with its definition in the second column.

___ 1. nationalize   **a.** forced removal of an ethnic group

___ 2. embargo   **b.** government prevention of trade

___ 3. ethnic cleansing   **c.** violence against civilians to achieve a goal

___ 4. détente   **d.** to put under government control

___ 5. terrorism   **e.** relaxation of tensions

Review Main Ideas

Section 1 • Challenges in Latin America

6. Which nation influenced the development of Latin America in the 1900s?

7. What prevented economic progress in Central America?

Section 2 • Africa and the Middle East

8. What challenged the countries of Africa south of the Sahara in the late 1900s?

9. Why is the Middle East one of the world's most dangerous regions?

Section 3 • The Cold War Ends

10. What was unique about China's progress in the late 1900s?

11. When and how did the Cold War end?

Section 4 • The World Enters a New Century

12. In what ways has technology brought the world closer together?

13. What event focused the world's attention on terrorism?

Critical Thinking

14. **Identify** How and when were West and East Germany reunited?

15. **Contrast** How were the policies of and support for Mexican leaders Porfirio Díaz and Lázaro Cárdenas different?

16. **Explain** What happened during the Six-Day War?

Review

Reading Skill — Extending the Text

Reading Beyond the Text

17. The Internet is a good source of information if you know how to narrow your search. List five guide words that you would use to search for more information about each of the topics listed below.

    a. the leader of China in 1950

    b. the role of apartheid in South African history

    c. the invention of the first computer

    d. the number of people who died in the Persian Gulf War compared to the number of people who died in the Vietnam War

To review this skill, see pages 858–859.

Geography Skills

Study the map below and answer the following questions.

18. **Place** List the countries that formed after the breakup of Yugoslavia.

19. **Location** Which country has the most access to the Adriatic Sea?

20. **Movement** Why do you think that three of the capitals of former Yugoslavian countries are located on rivers?

NATIONAL GEOGRAPHIC

Breakup of Yugoslavia

KEY
— Boundary of former Yugoslavia, 1991

Read to Write

21. **Descriptive Writing** Select three of the many challenges facing the world today. Write a brief essay about how these three challenges could affect your life and how you could help resolve these challenges.

22. **Using Your FOLDABLES** Work with a partner to create an outline map of the world on poster board. Indicate on your map the locations of each event and the development you recorded in your foldable.

Using Technology

23. **Create a Display** Use the Internet and other media to find information about the latest technological advances. Create a bulletin board using the information you found. Label and describe the new technology.

History Online

Self-Check Quiz To help you prepare for the Chapter Test, visit jat.glencoe.com

Linking Past and Present

24. **Evaluate** In 1994 power passed peacefully from the white minority government of South Africa to a multiracial government that includes black South Africans. How might that process serve as a model for solving problems in other countries?

Building Citizenship Skills

25. **Analyze** During the 1970s and 1980s, many Latin American nations were affected by civil war and internal conflicts. These wars were often in response to an unfair and unjust government. The United States supported many movements within these nations in order to overthrow dictators who had wrongfully taken power. It was necessary for the United States to aid those fighting against their governments in order to maintain or establish strong democratic values in the country. In what ways do people in the United States fight for what is right and protect democracy?

Primary Source Analyze

Czech leader Václav Havel spoke at the 1993 Council of Europe Summit about European unity.

"I think that all of us . . . can agree that the common basis of any effort to integrate Europe should be the wealth of values and ideals we share. Among them are respect for the uniqueness and the freedom of each human being, for a democratic . . . political system, for a market economy, and for the principles of civil society and the rule of law."

—Václav Havel, "The Council of Europe Summit: Vienna, October 8, 1993"

DBQ Document-Based Questions

26. What does Havel identify as the common basis for European unity?

27. What do you think Havel means by "principles of civil society"?

Comparing Modern Civilizations

Compare modern civilizations by reviewing the information below. Can you see how the people of these civilizations had lives that were very much like yours?

	Industry and Nationalism **Chapter 19**	Imperialism and World War I **Chapter 20**	World War II and the Cold War **Chapter 21**	Building Today's World **Chapter 22**
Where did these events take place?	• Europe (including Russia) • North America • South America	• Europe • Asia/Pacific • Africa • North America • South America	• Europe • Asia/Pacific • Africa • North America • South America	• Europe • Asia/Pacific • North America • South America
Who were some important people during these events?	• Napoleon Bonaparte (1769–1821) • Queen Victoria ruled (1837–1901) • Otto von Bismarck (1815–1898)	• Theodore Roosevelt (1858–1919) • Vladimir Ilyich Lenin (1870–1924)	• Adolf Hitler (1889–1945) • Joseph Stalin (1879–1953) • Franklin D. Roosevelt (1882–1945)	• Mikhail Gorbachev (1931–present) • Ronald Reagan (1911–2004)
Where did most of the people live who experienced these events?	• Industrial cities arose in Europe and North America	• Trade increased city growth throughout the world	• Cities and industries developed worldwide	• Cities grow significantly in Asia, Africa, and Latin America

	Industry and Nationalism Chapter 19	Imperialism and World War I Chapter 20	World War II and the Cold War Chapter 21	Building Today's World Chapter 22
What were people's beliefs at this time?	• Scientific ideas challenged religious traditions	• Western missionaries spread Christianity	• Islam, Hinduism, and Buddhism influenced new nations	• Christianity remains strong in the Americas • Islam, Hinduism, and Buddhism influence the West
What were governments like at this time?	• Republics largely in the Americas • Monarchies in the rest of the world	• Western powers set up colonies in Africa and Asia • World War I: republics replaced monarchies	• World War II: democracies and Communist USSR fought Fascist dictators • Cold War: struggle between democracy and communism	• Communism ended in Europe • Democracy spreads, but dictators continue to rule in many places
What were world languages like during these events?	• Language was linked to pride in one's nation or group	• European languages spread to overseas colonies	• English became a major global language	• Global culture—different languages mix and borrow from each other
What changes took place during this time?	• Constitutional governments are formed • Variety of machine-made goods appeared	• Ideas, goods, and people moved from place to place	• Vote given to women and other groups	• Respect for human rights increases • Living standards improve
How do these changes affect me? *Can you add any?*	• Public-supported schools are founded • Organized sports developed • Automobiles and telephones are invented	• U.S. becomes active in world affairs • Airplane invented	• Radio, movies, and television introduced • U.S. highway network built	• Internet, personal computers, and cellular phones are widely used

Appendix

What Is an Appendix?

An appendix is the additional material you often find at the end of books. The following information will help you learn how to use the Appendix in **Journey Across Time.**

SkillBuilder Handbook

The **SkillBuilder Handbook** offers you information and practice using critical thinking and social studies skills. Mastering these skills will help you in all your courses.

Standardized Test Preparation

The skills you need to do well on standardized tests are practiced in the **Standardized Test Practice** section of this Appendix.

Primary Sources Library

The **Primary Sources Library** provides additional first-person accounts of historical events. Primary sources are often narratives by a person who actually experienced what is being described.

Suggested Readings

The **Suggested Readings** list suggests the titles of fiction and non-fiction books you might be interested in reading. These books deal with the same topics that are covered in each chapter.

Glossary

The **Glossary** is a list of important or difficult terms found in a textbook. Since words sometimes have other meanings, you may wish to consult a dictionary to find other uses for the term. The glossary gives a definition of each term as it is used in the book. The glossary also includes page numbers telling you where in the textbook the term is used.

The Spanish Glossary

The **Spanish Glossary** contains everything that an English glossary does, but it is written in Spanish. A Spanish glossary is especially important to bilingual students, or those Spanish-speaking students who are learning the English language.

Gazetteer

The **Gazetteer** (GA•zuh•TIHR) is a geographical dictionary. It lists some of the world's largest countries, cities, and several important geographic features. Each entry also includes a page number telling where this place is talked about in your textbook.

Index

The **Index** is an alphabetical listing that includes the subjects of the book and the page numbers where those subjects can be found. The index in this book also lets you know that certain pages contain maps, graphs, photos, or paintings about the subject.

Acknowledgements and Photo Credits

This section lists photo credits and/or literary credits for the book. You can look at this section to find out where the publisher obtained the permission to use a photograph or to use excerpts from other books.

Test Yourself

Find the answers to these questions by using the Appendix on the following pages.

1. **What does *dynasty* mean?**
2. **What is the topic of the first Unit 3 Primary Source reading?**
3. **On what page can I find out about Julius Caesar?**
4. **Where exactly is Rome located?**
5. **What is one of the Suggested Readings for Unit 3?**

SkillBuilder Handbook

Contents

Finding the Main Idea

Why Learn This Skill?

Understanding the main idea allows you to grasp the whole picture and get an overall understanding of what you are reading. Historical details, such as names, dates, and events, are easier to remember when they are connected to a main idea.

1 Learning the Skill

Follow these steps when trying to find the main idea:

- Read the material and ask, "Why was this written? What is its purpose?"

- Read the first sentence of the first paragraph. The main idea of a paragraph is often found in the topic sentence. The main idea of a large section of text is often found in a topic paragraph.

- Identify details that support the main ideas.

- Keep the main idea clearly in your mind as you read.

Cultural diffusion has increased as a result of technology. Cultural diffusion is the process by which a culture spreads its knowledge and skills from one area to another. Years ago, trade—the way people shared goods and ideas—resulted in cultural diffusion. Today communication technology, such as television and the Internet, links people throughout the world.

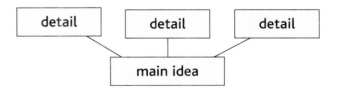

1. What is the main idea of this paragraph?
2. What are some details that support that main idea?
3. Do you agree or disagree with the main idea presented above? Explain.
4. Practice the skill by reading three paragraphs in your textbook and identifying their main ideas.

2 Practicing the Skill

Read the paragraph at the top of the next column that describes how the culture of the world is changing. Answer the questions, and then complete the activity that follows. If you have trouble, use the graphic organizer to help you.

3 Applying the Skill

Bring a newspaper or magazine to class. With a partner, identify the main ideas in three different articles. Then describe how other sentences or paragraphs in the article support the main idea.

Taking Notes and Outlining

Why Learn This Skill?

If you asked someone for his or her phone number or e-mail address, how would you best remember it? Most people would write it down. Making a note of it helps you remember. The same is true for remembering what you read in a textbook.

1 Learning the Skill

Taking notes as you read your textbook will help you remember the information. As you read, identify and summarize the main ideas and details and write them in your notes. Do not copy material directly from the text.

Using note cards—that you can reorder later—can also help. First write the main topic or main idea at the top of the note card. Then write the details that support or describe that topic. Number the cards to help you keep them in order.

Schools in the Middle Ages ③
• Catholic church set up cathedral schools.

• Only sons of nobles could go to these schools.

You also may find it helpful to use an outline when writing notes. Outlining can help you organize your notes in a clear and orderly way.

First read the material to identify the main ideas. In this textbook, section headings and subheadings provide clues to the main ideas. Supporting details can then be placed under each heading. Each level of an outline must contain at least two items. The basic pattern for outlines is as follows:

Main Topic
  I. First idea or item
  II. Second idea or item
    A. first detail
    B. second detail
      1. subdetail
      2. subdetail
  III. Third idea or item
    A. first detail
    B. second detail

2 Practicing the Skill

Look back at Chapter 2, Section 1. Outline the main ideas of the section as shown above.

3 Applying the Skill

Use the outline that you created in step 2 to write a paragraph with a main idea and at least three supporting details.

Reading a Time Line

Why Learn This Skill?

Have you ever had to remember events and their dates in the order in which they happened? A time line is an easy way to make sense of the flow of dates and events. It is a simple diagram that shows how dates and events relate to one another. On most time lines, years are evenly spaced. Events on time lines are placed beside the date they occurred.

1 Learning the Skill

To read a time line, follow these steps:

- Find the dates on the opposite ends of the time line. They show the period of time that the time line covers.

- Note the equal spacing between dates on the time line.

- Study the order of events.

- Look to see how the events relate to each other.

2 Practicing the Skill

Examine the time line below. It shows major events in the history of early Egypt. Then answer the questions and complete the activity that follows.

1. When does the time line begin? When does it end?

2. What major event happened around 1550 B.C.?

3. How long did the Hyksos rule Egypt?

4. What happened to Egypt around 1670 B.C.?

3 Applying the Skill

List 10 key events found in Unit 1 and the dates on which these events took place. Write the events in the order in which they occurred on a time line.

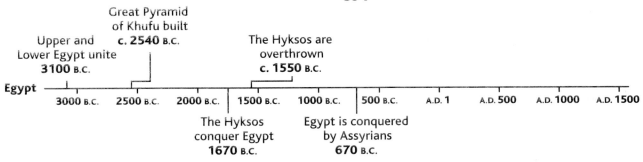

Ancient Egypt

Sequencing and Categorizing Information

Why Learn This Skill?

Sequencing means placing facts in the order in which they happened. *Categorizing* means organizing information into groups of related facts and ideas. Both actions help you deal with large quantities of information in an understandable way.

1 Learning the Skill

Follow these steps to learn sequencing and categorizing skills:

- Look for dates or clue words that provide you with a chronological order: *in 2004, the late 1990s, first, then, finally, after the Great Depression,* and so on.

- Sequencing can be seen in unit and chapter time lines or on graphs where information covers several years.

- If the sequence of events is not important, you may want to categorize the information instead. To categorize information, look for topics and facts that are grouped together or have similar characteristics. If the information is about farming, one category might be *tools of farming.*

- List these categories, or characteristics, as the headings on a chart.

- As you read, look for details. Fill in these details under the proper categories on the chart.

2 Practicing the Skill

Read the paragraph below and then answer the questions that follow.

Buddhism started in India about 500 B.C. but was mostly driven out by 300 B.C. The religion of Islam also influenced India's history. In the A.D. 700s, Muslims from southwest Asia brought Islam to India. In the 1500s, they founded the Mogul empire and ruled India for the next 200 years.

1. What information can be organized by sequencing?

2. What categories can you use to organize the information? What facts could be placed under each category?

3 Applying the Skill

Look at the Geographic Dictionary on pages GH14 and GH15. Record any terms that would fit into the category "bodies of water." Also, find two newspaper or magazine articles about an important local issue. Sequence or categorize the information on note cards or in a chart.

Recognizing Point of View

Why Learn This Skill?

If you say, "Cats make better pets than dogs," you are expressing a point of view. You are giving your personal opinion. Knowing when someone is giving his or her personal point of view can help you judge the truth of what is being said.

1 Learning the Skill

Most people have feelings and ideas that affect their point of view. A person's point of view is often influenced by his or her age, background, or position in a situation.

To recognize point of view, follow these steps:

- Identify the speaker or writer and examine his or her views on an issue. Think about his or her position in life and relationship to the issue.

- Look for language that shows an emotion or an opinion. Look for words such as *all, never, best, worst, might,* or *should.*

- Examine the speech or writing for imbalances. Does it have only one viewpoint? Does it fail to provide equal coverage of other viewpoints?

- Identify statements of fact. Factual statements usually answer the *Who? What? When?* and *Where?* questions.

- Determine how the person's point of view is reflected in his or her statements or writing.

2 Practicing the Skill

Read the following statement about wildlife in Africa, and answer the questions below.

Mountain gorillas live in the misty mountain forests of East Africa. Logging and mining, however, are destroying the forests. Unless the forests are protected, all of the gorillas will lose their homes and disappear forever. As a concerned African naturalist, I must emphasize that this will be one of the worst events in Africa's history.

1. What problem is the speaker addressing?
2. What reasons does the speaker give for the loss of the forests?
3. What is the speaker's point of view about the problem facing the gorillas in East Africa?

3 Applying the Skill

Choose a "Letter to the Editor" from a newspaper. Summarize the issue being discussed and the writer's point of view about that issue. State what an opposing point of view to the issue might be. Describe who might hold this other viewpoint in terms of their age, occupation, and background.

Distinguishing Fact From Opinion

Why Learn This Skill?

Suppose a friend says, "Our school's basketball team is awesome. That's a fact." Actually, it is not a fact; it is an opinion. Knowing how to tell the difference between a fact and an opinion can help you analyze the accuracy of political claims, advertisements, and many other kinds of statements.

1 Learning the Skill

A **fact** answers a specific question such as: What happened? Who did it? When and where did it happen? Why did it happen? Statements of fact can be checked for accuracy and proven.

An **opinion,** on the other hand, expresses beliefs, feelings, and judgments. It may reflect someone's thoughts, but it cannot be proven. An opinion often begins with a phrase such as *I believe, I think, probably, it seems to me,* or *in my opinion.*

To distinguish between facts and opinions, ask yourself these questions:

- Does this statement give specific information about an event?

- Can I check the accuracy of this statement?

- Does this statement express someone's feelings, beliefs, or judgment?

- Does it include phrases such as *I believe,* superlatives, or judgment words?

2 Practicing the Skill

Read each statement below. Tell whether each is a fact or an opinion, and explain how you arrived at your answer.

(1) The Han dynasty ruled China from 202 B.C. to A.D. 220.

(2) The Han dynasty was a much better dynasty than the Qin dynasty.

(3) The Han divided the country into districts to be better able to manage such a large area.

(4) The government should not have encouraged support for arts and inventions.

(5) The Han kept very good records of everything they did, which helps historians today learn about them.

(6) Han rulers chose government officials on the basis of merit rather than birth.

(7) No other ruling family in the world can compare with the Han dynasty of China.

(8) Han rulers should have defended the poor farmers against the harsh actions of wealthy landowners.

3 Applying the Skill

Read one newspaper article that describes a political event. Find three statements of fact and three opinions expressed in the article.

Analyzing Library and Research Resources

Why Learn This Skill?

Imagine that your teacher has sent you to the library to write a report on the history of ancient Rome. Knowing how to choose good sources for your research will help you save time in the library and write a better report.

1 Learning the Skill

Not all sources will be useful for your report on Rome. Even some sources that involve topics about Rome will not always provide the information you want. In analyzing sources for your research project, choose items that are nonfiction and that contain the most information about your topic.

When choosing research resources ask these questions:

- Is the information up-to-date?

- Does the index have several pages listed for the topic?

- Is the resource written in a way that is easy to understand?

- Are there helpful illustrations and photos?

2 Practicing the Skill

Look at the following list of sources. Which would be most helpful in writing a report on the history of ancient Rome? Explain your choices.

(1) A travel guide to Italy today

(2) A guide to early Roman art and architecture

(3) A children's storybook about ancient Europe

(4) A history of ancient Greece

(5) A study of the rise and fall of the Roman Empire

(6) A book on modern republican ideas

(7) A biographical dictionary of ancient rulers of the world

(8) An atlas of the world

3 Applying the Skill

Go to your local library or use the Internet to create a bibliography of sources you might use to write a report on the history of ancient Rome. List at least five sources.

▲ Roman mosaic showing gladiators in battle

Analyzing Primary Source Documents

Why Learn This Skill?

Historians determine what happened in the past by combing through bits of evidence to reconstruct events. These types of evidence—both written and illustrated—are called primary sources. Examining primary sources can help you understand history.

1 Learning the Skill

Primary sources are sources that were created in the historical era being studied. They can include letters, diaries, photographs and pictures, news articles, legal documents, stories, literature, and artwork.

To analyze primary sources, ask yourself the following questions:

- What is the item?
- Who created it?
- Where did it come from?
- When was it created?
- What does it reveal about the topic I am studying?

2 Practicing the Skill

The primary source that follows comes from *Stories of Rome* by Livy. Livy was a Roman historian who lived from 59 B.C. to A.D. 17. Here he has written a story with a moral, or lesson to be learned. Read the story, and then answer the questions that follow.

Once upon a time, the different parts of the human body were not all in agreement. . . . And it seemed very unfair to the other parts of the body that they should worry and sweat away to look after the belly. After all, the belly just sat there . . . doing nothing, enjoying all the nice things that came along. So they hatched a plot. The hands weren't going to take food to the mouth; even if they did, the mouth wasn't going to accept it. . . . They went into a sulk and waited for the belly to cry for help. But while they waited, one by one all the parts of the body got weaker and weaker. The moral of this story? The belly too has its job to do. It has to be fed, but it also does feeding of its own.

Excerpt from *Stories of Rome*,
Livy, c. 20 B.C.

1. What is the main topic?
2. Who did the hands and mouth think was lazy?
3. What did the hands and mouth do about it?
4. What was the moral—or lesson—of the story?

3 Applying the Skill

Find a primary source from your past—a photo or newspaper clipping. Explain to the class what it shows about that time in your life.

Building a Database

Why Learn This Skill?

A database is a collection of information stored in a computer or on diskette files. It runs on software that organizes large amounts of information in a way that makes it easy to search and make any changes. It often takes the form of a chart or table. You might build databases to store information related to a class at school or your weekly schedule.

1 Learning the Skill

To create a database using word-processing software, follow these steps:

- Enter a title identifying the type of information in your document and file names.

- Determine the set of specific points of information you wish to include. As the database example on this page shows, you might want to record data on the imports and exports of specific countries.

- Enter the information categories along with country names as headings in a columned chart. Each column makes up a *field*, which is the basic unit for information stored in a database.

- Enter data you have collected into the *cells*, or individual spaces, on your chart.

- Use your computer's sorting feature to organize the data. For example, you might alphabetize by country name.

- Add, delete, or update information as needed. Database software automatically adjusts the cells in the chart.

2 Practicing the Skill

On a separate sheet of paper, answer the following questions referring to the database on this page.

1. What type of information does the database contain?

2. What related fields of information does it show?

3. The author learns that Canada also exports clothing, beverages, and art to the United States. Is it necessary to create a new database? Explain.

3 Applying the Skill

Build a database to help you keep track of your school assignments. Work with four fields: Subject, Assignment Description, Due Date, and Completed Assignments. Be sure to keep your database up-to-date.

U.S. International Commerce

Country	Japan	United Kingdom	Canada
Exports to U.S.	Engines, rubber goods, cars, trucks, buses	Dairy products, beverages, petroleum products, art	Wheat, minerals, paper, mining machines
Value of Exports to U.S.	$128 billion	$35.2 billion	$232.6 billion
Imports from U.S.	Meat, fish, sugar, tobacco, coffee	Fruit, tobacco, electrical equipment	Fish, sugar, metals, clothing
Value of Imports from U.S.	$67.3 billion	$42.8 billion	$199.6 billion

Summarizing

Why Learn This Skill?

Imagine you have been assigned a long chapter to read. How can you remember the important information? Summarizing information—reducing large amounts of information to a few key phrases—can help you remember the main ideas and important facts.

1 Learning the Skill

To summarize information, follow these guidelines when you read:

- Separate the main ideas from the supporting details. Use the main ideas in a summary.

- Use your own words to describe the main ideas. Do not copy the selection word for word.

- If the summary is almost as long as the reading selection, you are including too much information. The summary should be very short.

2 Practicing the Skill

To practice the skill, read the paragraph below. Then answer the questions that follow.

The Ming dynasty that followed the Mongols tried to rid the country of Mongol influence. The Ming leaders believed that China could become a great empire. They expanded Chinese control over parts of East Asia, including Korea, Vietnam, and Myanmar (Burma). To re-establish the importance of Chinese culture, they encouraged the practices of older Chinese traditions, especially in the arts. Chinese literature during the Ming era followed the styles of ancient Chinese writers. Some of the finest Chinese paintings and pottery were created during this period. Ming rulers also built the Forbidden City.

1. What are the main ideas of this paragraph?
2. What are the supporting details?
3. Write a brief summary of two or three sentences that will help you remember what the paragraph is about.

3 Applying the Skill

Read a newspaper or short magazine article. Summarize the article in one or two sentences.

Evaluating a Web Site

Why Learn This Skill?

The Internet has grown to become a necessary household and business tool as more people use it. With so many Web sites available, how do you know which one will be the most helpful to you? You must look at the details, so you do not waste valuable time in Web searches.

1 Learning the Skill

The Internet is a valuable research tool. It is easy to use, and it often provides fast, up-to-date information. The most common use of the Internet by students is in doing research. However, some Web site information is not really accurate or reliable.

When using the Internet to do research, you must evaluate the information very carefully. When evaluating the Web site, ask yourself the following questions:

• Do the facts on the site seem accurate?

• Who is the author or sponsor of the site, and what is that person's or organiza-
  . tion's reason for maintaining it?

• Does the site information explore a subject in-depth?

• Does the site contain links to other useful resources?

• Is the information easy to read and access?

2 Practicing the Skill

To practice the skill, find three Web sites on the shoguns or samurai of Japan. Follow these steps and write your explanation.

1. Evaluate how useful these sites would be if you were writing a report on the topic.

2. Choose which one is the most helpful.

3. Explain why you chose that site.

3 Applying the Skill

If your school had a Web site, what kind of information would be on it? Write a paragraph describing this site.

A Japanese samurai warrior ▶

Understanding Cause and Effect

Why Learn This Skill?

You know if you watch television instead of completing your homework, you probably will not get a good grade. The cause—not doing homework—leads to the effect—not getting a good grade.

1 Learning the Skill

A *cause* is any person, event, or condition that makes something happen. What happens as a result is known as an *effect*.

These guidelines will help you identify cause and effect.

- Identify two or more events.

- Ask questions about why events occur.

- Look for "clue words" that alert you to cause and effect, such as *because, led to, brought about, produced,* and *therefore.*

- Identify the outcome of events.

2 Practicing the Skill

As you read the following passage, record cause-and-effect connections in a chart or graphic organizer.

Around 200 B.C., Mesopotamians were among the first in the world to blend copper and tin to make bronze.

Bronze brought many changes to life in Mesopotamia. For one thing, bronze was much harder than the copper products that were used until that time. Because it was harder, bronze made better tools and sharper weapons. This improvement in technology was a help to farmers, craftworkers, and soldiers alike.

Molten [melted] bronze was also easier to pour than the metals used earlier. Craftworkers were able to make finer arrows, ax-heads, statues, bowls, and other objects.

3 Applying the Skill

Look again at the chapter you are currently reading. Choose a major event that is described and list its causes.

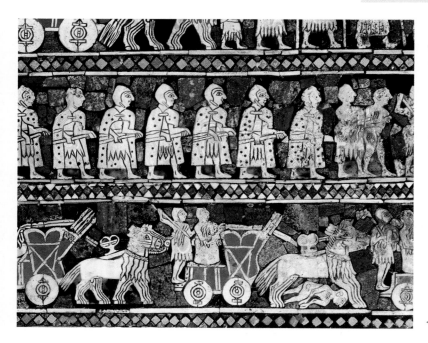

◀ The Royal Banner of Ur

Making Comparisons

Why Learn This Skill?

Suppose you want to buy a portable CD player, and you must choose among three models. To make this decision, you would probably compare various features of the three models, such as price, sound quality, size, and so on. By making comparisons, you will figure out which model is best for you. In the study of world history, you often compare people or events from one time period with those from a different time period.

1 Learning the Skill

When making comparisons, you examine and identify two or more groups, situations, events, or documents. Then you identify any similarities (ways they are alike) and differences (ways they are different). For example, the chart on this page compares the characteristics of two ancient civilizations.

When making comparisons, apply the following steps:

- Decide what items will be compared. Clue words such as *also, as well as, like, same as,* and *similar to* can help you identify things that are being compared.

- Determine which characteristics you will use to compare them.

- Identify similarities and differences in these characteristics.

2 Practicing the Skill

To practice the skill, analyze the information on the chart at the bottom of this page. Then answer these questions.

1. What items are being compared?

2. What characteristics are being used to compare them?

3. In what ways were the Phoenicians and Israelites similar? In what ways were they different?

4. Suppose you wanted to compare the two peoples in more detail. What are some of the characteristics you might use?

3 Applying the Skill

Think about two sports that are played at your school. Make a chart comparing such things as: where the games are played, who plays them, what equipment is used, and other details.

Phoenician and Israelite Civilizations

Cultural Characteristic	Phoenicians	Israelites
Homeland	Canaan	Canaan
Political Organization	city-states	12 tribes; later, kingdom
Method of Rule	kings/merchant councils	kings/council of elders
Main Occupations	artisans, traders, shippers	herders, farmers, traders
Religion	belief in many gods and goddesses	belief in one, all-powerful god
Main Contribution	spread of an alphabet	principles of social justice

Making Predictions

Why Learn This Skill?

In history you read about people making difficult decisions based on what they think *might* happen. By making predictions yourself, you can get a better understanding of the choices people make.

1 Learning the Skill

As you read a paragraph or section in your book, think about what might come next. What you think will happen is your *prediction.* A prediction does not have a correct or incorrect answer. Making predictions helps you to carefully consider what you are reading.

To make a prediction, ask yourself:

• What happened in this paragraph or section?

• What prior knowledge do I have about the events in the text?

• What similar situations do I know of?

• What do I think might happen next?

• Test your prediction: read further to see if you were correct.

◄ Aztec shield

2 Practicing the Skill

To practice the skill, read the following paragraph about the Aztec Empire. Then answer the questions.

The Aztec of ancient Mexico built the strongest empire of any Native American group. They mined gold, silver, and other goods for trade. In building their empire, they conquered many other Native American groups. The Aztec fought their enemies using wooden weapons with stone blades.

In the 1500s, a Spanish army seeking gold heard about the Aztec and their riches. Led by Hernán Cortés, the Spaniards were helped by enemies of the Aztec. Armed with steel swords, muskets, and cannons, the Spaniards moved towards the Aztec capital.

1. Choose the outcome below that is most likely to occur between the Aztec and Spaniards.

   a. The Spaniards will avoid the Aztec altogether.

   b. The two groups will become friends.

   c. The Spaniards will conquer the Aztec.

   d. The Aztec will conquer the Spaniards.

2. Explain why you chose the answer you did.

3 Applying the Skill

Watch a television show or a movie. Halfway through the show, write your prediction of how it will end on a piece of paper. At the end of the show, check your prediction.

Drawing Inferences and Conclusions

Why Learn This Skill?

Suppose your teacher brought an artifact to class and a classmate exclaimed, "That came from Greece, didn't it?" You might infer that your classmate had an interest in Greece.

1 Learning the Skill

To *infer* means to evaluate information and arrive at a *conclusion*. Social studies writers do not always spell out everything in the text. When you make inferences you "read between the lines." You must then use the available facts and your own knowledge of social studies to draw a conclusion.

Use the following steps to help draw inferences and make conclusions:

- Read carefully for stated facts and ideas.
- Summarize the information and list the important facts.
- Apply related information that you may already know to make inferences.
- Use your knowledge and insight to develop some conclusions about these facts.

2 Practicing the Skill

Read the passage below and answer the questions.

Many Greek temples were decorated with sculpture. Greek sculpture, like Greek architecture, was used to express Greek ideas. The favorite subject of Greek artists was the human body. Greek sculptors did not copy their subjects exactly, flaws and all. Instead, they tried to show their ideal version of perfection and beauty.

1. What topic is the writer describing?
2. What facts are given?
3. What can you infer about Greek cities from the information?
4. What conclusions can you draw about how the Greeks felt about sculptures?

3 Applying the Skill

Read one of the biographies in this text. What can you infer about the life of the person described? Draw a conclusion about whether or not you would like to meet this person.

◄ Ancient Greek sculptures of Socrates (far left), Plato (middle), and Aristotle (left)

Recognizing Economic Indicators

Why Learn This Skill?

Every day, business and government leaders are faced with the challenge of trying to predict what will happen to the economy in the coming months and years. To help these leaders in making decisions, economists, or scientists who study the economy, have developed ways to measure an economy's performance. These ways are called economic indicators.

1 Learning the Skill

Economic indicators are statistics, or numbers, that tell how well the economy is doing and how well the economy is going to do in the future. They include the number of jobless, the rate at which prices rise over a period of time, and the amount of goods and services that are produced and sold. Each month, the U.S. Department of Commerce gathers data for 78 economic indicators covering all aspects of the state of the United States economy. The chart below lists some common terms for economic indicators that you may read about.

▲ Prices on the stock market often rise or fall based on changes in economic indicators.

2 Practicing the Skill

Start an Economics Handbook. Using a dictionary, look up each economic term listed on this chart. Write a definition for each term in your Economics Handbook.

3 Applying the Skill

Think about one of the countries you have read about in this text that has grown to be wealthy. Using the terms that you just defined, write a paragraph describing that country's wealth.

Economic Indicators

Term	Definition
Saving	
Income	
Expenditure	
Consumption	
Inflation	
Debt	
Gross Domestic Product (GDP)	
Interest Rates	
Credit	
Export	
Import	

Interpreting Political Cartoons

Why Learn This Skill?

Political cartoonists use art to express political opinions. Their work appears in newspapers, magazines, books, and on the Internet. Political cartoons are drawings that express an opinion. They usually focus on public figures, political events, or economic or social conditions. A political cartoon can give you a summary of an event or circumstance and the artist's opinion in a quick and entertaining manner.

1 Learning the Skill

To interpret a political cartoon, follow these steps:

- Read the title, caption, or conversation balloons. Most cartoons will carry at least one of these elements. They help you identify the subject of the cartoon.

- Identify the characters or people shown. They may be caricatures, or unrealistic drawings that exaggerate the characters' physical features.

- Identify any symbols shown. Symbols are things that stand for something else. An example is the American flag that is a symbol of our country. Commonly recognized symbols may not be labeled. Unusual symbolism will be labeled.

- Examine the actions in the cartoon—what is happening and why?

- Identify the cartoonist's purpose. What statement or idea is he or she trying to get across? Decide if the cartoonist wants to persuade, criticize, or just make people think.

2 Practicing the Skill

On a separate sheet of paper, answer these questions about the political cartoon below.

1. What is the subject of the cartoon?
2. What words give clues as to the meaning of the cartoon?
3. What item seems out of place?
4. What message do you think the cartoonist is trying to send?

3 Applying the Skill

Bring a news magazine to class. With a partner, analyze the message in each political cartoon that you find.

Standardized Test Practice

Standardized tests are one way educators measure what you have learned. This handbook is designed to help you prepare for standardized tests in social studies. On the pages that follow, you will find a review of the major social studies critical thinking skills that you will need to master to be successful when taking tests.

Contents

Interpreting a Map

Before 1492, people living in Europe in the Eastern Hemisphere had no idea that the continents of North America and South America in the Western Hemisphere existed. That was the year Christopher Columbus first reached the Americas. His voyage of exploration paved the way for other European voyages to the Western Hemisphere. The voyages of the early explorers brought together two worlds. Previously these parts of the globe had no contact with each other. Trade between the hemispheres changed life for people on both sides of the Atlantic Ocean. The trade between the peoples of the Eastern Hemisphere and the Western Hemisphere is referred to as the Columbian Exchange.

Skills Practice

Although globes are the best, most accurate way to show places on the round earth, people can more easily use maps to represent places. A map is made by taking data from a round globe and placing it on a flat surface. To read a map, first read the title to determine the subject of the map. Then read the map key or the labels on the map to find out what the colors and symbols on the map mean. Use the compass rose to identify the four cardinal directions of north, south, east, and west. Study the map of the Columbian Exchange and answer the questions that follow on a separate sheet of paper.

1. What is the subject of the map?

2. What do the arrows represent?

3. What continents are shown on the map?

4. What foods did Europeans acquire from the Americas?

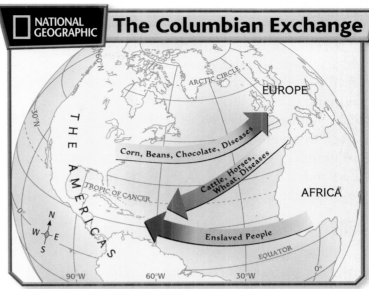

NATIONAL GEOGRAPHIC The Columbian Exchange

Corn, Beans, Chocolate, Diseases

Cattle, Horses, Wheat, Diseases

Enslaved People

5. What did the Americas acquire from Europe?

6. What people were brought from Africa to the Americas?

7. In what direction is Europe from the Americas?

Standardized Test Practice

DIRECTIONS: Use the map and your knowledge of social studies to answer the following question on a separate sheet of paper.

1. Which of the following statements about the Columbian Exchange is true?

   A Food products were traded only between Africa and the Americas.

   B Europeans acquired cattle from the Americas.

   C Europeans introduced corn, tomatoes, and beans to Native Americans.

   D Enslaved Africans were brought to the Americas.

Interpreting a Political Map

By 1750, or the middle of the eighteenth century, there were 13 British colonies in North America. A colony is a group of people living in one place who are governed by rulers in another place. The British colonists in America were ruled by the monarchy and Parliament of Great Britain. That meant that rulers living 3,000 miles away made laws for the American colonists.

Skills Practice

Political maps illustrate divisions between territories such as nations, states, colonies, or other political units. These divisions are called boundaries. Lines represent the boundaries between political areas. To interpret a political map, read the map title to determine what geographic area and time period it covers. Identify the colonies or other political units on the map. Look at the map key for additional information. Study the map on this page and answer the questions that follow on a separate sheet of paper.

1. List the New England Colonies.

2. Which were the Middle Colonies?

3. Which Middle Colony bordered Pennsylvania to the north?

4. Which was the southernmost early British colony?

5. Name the body of water that formed the eastern border of the colonies.

6. Where was Charles Town located?

NATIONAL GEOGRAPHIC

The Thirteen Colonies *1750*

Lake Ontario
ME. (part of Mass.)
N.H.
Salem
Boston • Plymouth
N.Y.
Hartford •
New Haven •
R.I.
CONN.
MASS.
40°N
Lake Erie
PA.
New York City
Philadelphia •
N.J.
0   200 miles
0   200 kilometers
Lambert Equal-Area projection
DEL.
St. Mary's •
MD.
ATLANTIC OCEAN
VA.
Jamestown
N
W   E
S
N.C.
70°W
S.C.
Charles Town
GA.
Savannah
60°W   30°N

• Town or City
New England Colonies
Middle Colonies
Southern Colonies

Standardized Test Practice

DIRECTIONS: Use the map and your knowledge of social studies to answer the following questions on a separate sheet of paper.

1. The New England Colony that covered the largest land area was
   A Virginia.
   B Pennsylvania.
   C Massachusetts.
   D New Hampshire.

2. The northernmost Middle Colony is the present-day state of
   F Maryland.
   G New York.
   H Massachusetts.
   J Pennsylvania.

3. The settlement of Plymouth was located
   A near Jamestown.
   B in Massachusetts.
   C in the Southern Colonies.
   D in Virginia.

Interpreting Charts

Government is a necessary part of every nation. It gives citizens stability and provides services that many of us take for granted. However, governments can sometimes have too much power.

The United States was founded on the principle of limited government. Limited governments require all people to follow the laws. Even the rulers must obey rules set for the society. A democracy is a form of limited government. Not all forms of government have limits. In unlimited governments, power belongs to the ruler. No laws exist to limit what the ruler may do. A dictatorship is an example of an unlimited government.

Limited Governments

Representative Democracy	Constitutional Monarchy
People elect leaders to rule	King or queen's power is limited
Individual rights important	Individual rights important
More than one political party	More than one political party
People give consent to be governed	People elect governing body

Unlimited Governments

Dictatorship	Absolute Monarchy
One person or small group rules	King or queen inherits power
Few personal freedoms	Usually some freedoms
Rule by force, often military	Officials are appointed by king or queen
Ruler does not have to obey rules	Monarch has complete authority

Skills Practice

Charts are visual graphics that categorize information. When reading a chart, be sure to look at all the headings and labels. Study the charts on this page and answer the questions that follow on a separate sheet of paper.

1. What do the charts compare?

2. Which political systems are forms of limited government?

3. Which form of government often uses military rule?

4. In which political system does the king or queen have complete power?

Standardized Test Practice

DIRECTIONS: Use the charts and your knowledge of social studies to answer the following questions on a separate sheet of paper.

1. Information found in the charts shows that the most restrictive form of government is a

   A dictatorship.

   B representative democracy.

   C absolute monarchy.

   D constitutional monarchy.

2. Under which type of government do citizens have the most power?

   F unlimited government

   G limited government

   H absolute monarchy

   J dictatorship

3. An example of an unlimited government is

   A the United States in the 1960s.

   B Libya in the 1970s.

   C the United Kingdom in the 1980s.

   D Mexico in the 1990s.

Making Comparisons

The roots of representative democracy in the United States can be traced back to colonial times. In 1607 English settlers founded the colony of Jamestown in present-day Virginia. As the colony developed, problems arose. Later, colonists formed the House of Burgesses to deal with these problems. Citizens of Virginia were chosen as representatives to the House of Burgesses. This became the first legislature, or lawmaking body, in America.

Today citizens of the United States elect representatives to Congress. The major function of Congress is to make laws for the nation. There are two houses, or chambers, of the U.S. Congress. Legislative bodies with two houses are said to be bicameral. The bicameral Congress of the United States includes the Senate and the House of Representatives. Article I of the U.S. Constitution describes how each house will be organized and how its members will be chosen.

Skills Practice

When you make a comparison, you identify and examine two or more groups, situations, events, or documents. Then you identify any similarities and differences between the items. Study the information presented on the chart on this page and answer the questions that follow on a separate sheet of paper.

1. What two things does the chart compare?

2. How are the qualifications for each house of the U.S. Congress similar?

3. The members of which house are probably more experienced? Why?

The U.S. Congress

House of Representatives	Senate
Qualifications: Must be 25 years old; Must be U.S. citizen for 7+ years; Must live in the state they represent	**Qualifications:** Must be 30 years old; Must be U.S. citizen for 9+ years; Must live in the state they represent
Number of Representatives: 435 total representatives; number of representatives per state is based on state population	**Number of Representatives:** 100 total senators; two senators elected from each state regardless of state population
Terms of Office: Two-year terms	**Terms of Office:** Six-year terms

Standardized Test Practice

DIRECTIONS: Use the chart and your knowledge of social studies to answer the following questions on a separate sheet of paper.

1. Which of the following statements best reflects information shown in the chart?

   A The Senate has more members than the House of Representatives.

   B Representatives to the House are elected to two-year terms.

   C House members must be residents of their states for at least 9 years.

   D A state's population determines its number of senators.

2. One inference that can be made from information shown on the chart is that

   F Texas elects more senators than Rhode Island.

   G Texas elects more House members than Rhode Island.

   H Texas elects fewer senators than Rhode Island.

   J Texas elects fewer House members than Rhode Island.

Interpreting Primary Sources

When Thomas Jefferson wrote the Declaration of Independence, he used the term "unalienable rights." Jefferson was referring to the natural rights that belong to humans. He and the other Founders of our nation believed that government could not take away the rights of the people.

Skills Practice

Primary sources are records of events made by the people who witnessed them. A historical document such as the Declaration of Independence is an example of a primary source. Read the passage below and answer the questions that follow on a separate sheet of paper.

> "We hold these truths to be self-evident, that all men are created equal, that they are endowed by their Creator with certain unalienable Rights, that among these are Life, Liberty, and the pursuit of Happiness . . ."
>
> —Declaration of Independence, July 4, 1776

1. What does the document say about the equality of men?

2. List the three natural, or unalienable, rights to which the document refers.

After gaining independence, American leaders wrote the U.S. Constitution in 1787. The Bill of Rights includes the first 10 amendments, or additions, to the Constitution. The First Amendment protects five basic rights of all American citizens. Study the chart on this page and answer the questions that follow.

1. Which right allows Americans to express themselves without fear of punishment by the government?

2. Which right allows people to worship as they please?

3. Which right allows citizens to publish a pamphlet that is critical of the president?

4. What is the Bill of Rights?

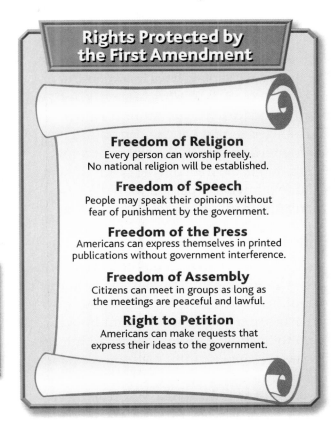

Rights Protected by the First Amendment

Freedom of Religion
Every person can worship freely. No national religion will be established.

Freedom of Speech
People may speak their opinions without fear of punishment by the government.

Freedom of the Press
Americans can express themselves in printed publications without government interference.

Freedom of Assembly
Citizens can meet in groups as long as the meetings are peaceful and lawful.

Right to Petition
Americans can make requests that express their ideas to the government.

Standardized Test Practice

DIRECTIONS: Use the chart and your knowledge of social studies to answer the following question on a separate sheet of paper.

1. Which First Amendment right protects citizens who are staging a protest outside a government building?

   A freedom of speech

   B freedom of the press

   C freedom of assembly

   D freedom of religion

Interpreting a Political Cartoon

Just as the government of the United States is limited in its powers, freedoms extended to Americans also have limits. The First Amendment was not intended to allow Americans to do whatever they please without regard to others. Limits on freedoms are necessary to keep order in a society of so many people. The government can establish laws to limit certain rights to protect the health, safety, security, or moral standards of a community. Rights can be restricted to prevent one person's rights from interfering with the rights of another. For example, the freedom of speech does not include allowing a person to make false statements that hurt another's reputation.

Skills Practice

The artists who create political cartoons often use humor to express their opinions on political issues. Sometimes these cartoonists are trying to inform and influence the public about a certain topic. To interpret a political cartoon, look for symbols, labels, and captions that provide clues about the message of the cartoonist. Analyze these

elements and draw some conclusions. Study the political cartoon on this page and answer the questions that follow on a separate sheet of paper.

1. What is the subject of the cartoon?

2. What words provide clues as to the meaning of the cartoon?

3. Whom does the person in the cartoon represent?

4. What is the person doing?

5. What do the subject's thoughts suggest about the task faced by those involved in planning the new nation's government?

6. What limits are placed on First Amendment rights? Why are these rights limited?

Standardized Test Practice

DIRECTIONS: Use the political cartoon and your knowledge of social studies to answer the following questions on a separate sheet of paper.

1. The most appropriate title for the cartoon is

   A Limits on Government.

   B Parliament at Work.

   C Limiting Rights.

   D Unlimited Government.

2. The sources of our rights as citizens of the United States come from which of the following?

   F the Declaration of Independence and the U.S. Constitution

   G the will of the president

   H unwritten customs and traditions

   J the United Nations charter

Interpreting a Circle Graph

"E pluribus unum" is a Latin phrase found on United States coins. It means "Out of many, one." The United States is sometimes called a "nation of immigrants." Unless you are a Native American, your ancestors came to America within the last 500 years.

Groups of people who share a common culture, language, or history are referred to as ethnic groups. American neighborhoods include many different ethnic groups. The circle graph on this page shows the major ethnic groups in the United States.

Skills Practice

A circle graph shows percentages of a total quantity. Each part, or slice, of the graph represents a part of the total quantity. To read a circle graph, first read the title. Then study the labels to find out what each part represents. Compare the sizes of the circle slices. Study the circle graph and answer the questions that follow on a separate sheet of paper.

1. What information does this circle graph present?

2. Which ethnic group includes the largest percentage of Americans?

3. Which groups represent less than 1 percent of the people in the United States?

4. What percentage of the United States population is represented by African Americans?

5. The smallest ethnic group has lived in the United States the longest. What is this ethnic group?

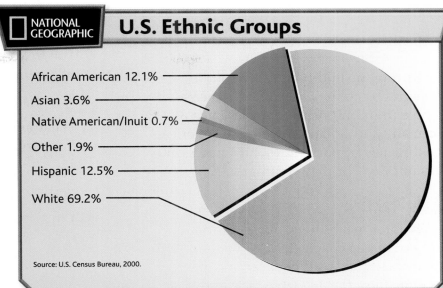

NATIONAL GEOGRAPHIC

U.S. Ethnic Groups

African American 12.1%
Asian 3.6%
Native American/Inuit 0.7%
Other 1.9%
Hispanic 12.5%
White 69.2%

Source: U.S. Census Bureau, 2000.

Standardized Test Practice

DIRECTIONS: Use the graph and your knowledge of social studies to answer the following questions on a separate sheet of paper.

1. Which group's population is about three times greater than the number of Asians?

   A African American

   B White

   C Native American/Inuit

   D Other

2. How does the Hispanic population compare to the African American population of the United States?

   F It is greater than the African American population.

   G It is the smallest segment of the United States population.

   H It is less than half the size of the African American population.

   J It is slightly less than the African American population.

Drawing Inferences and Conclusions

During the mid-nineteenth century, immigration to the United States increased. People from European countries such as Germany and Ireland traveled to America seeking new opportunities. Life, however, was not easy for these immigrants.

Skills Practice

To infer means to evaluate information and arrive at a conclusion. When you make inferences, you "read between the lines." You must use the available facts and your own knowledge of social studies to form a judgment or opinion about the material.

Line graphs are a way of showing numbers visually. They are often used to compare changes over time. Sometimes a graph has more than one line. The lines show different quantities of a related topic. To analyze a line graph read the title and the information on the horizontal and vertical axes. Use this information to draw conclusions. Study the graph on this page and answer the questions that follow on a separate sheet of paper.

1. What is the subject of the line graph?

2. What information is shown on the horizontal axis?

3. What information is shown on the vertical axis?

4. Why do you think these immigrants came to the United States?

Standardized Test Practice

DIRECTIONS: Use the line graph and your knowledge of social studies to answer the following questions on a separate sheet of paper.

1. The country that provided the most immigrants to the United States between the years 1820 and 1860 was

    A Great Britain.

    B Ireland.

    C Germany.

    D France.

2. In about what year did the number of German immigrants to the United States reach a peak?

    F 1845

    G 1852

    H 1855

    J 1860

3. Irish migration to the United States increased in the mid-1800s because of

    A a terrible potato famine in Ireland.

    B the failure of a German revolution in 1848.

    C the nativist movement.

    D the availability of low-paying factory jobs.

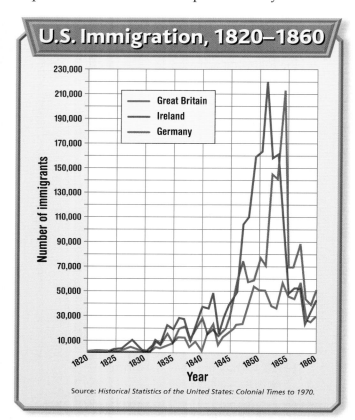

U.S. Immigration, 1820–1860

Number of immigrants

Great Britain
Ireland
Germany

Source: *Historical Statistics of the United States: Colonial Times to 1970.*

Comparing Data

The world's earliest civilizations developed more than 6,000 years ago. The discovery of farming led to the rise of ancient cities in Mesopotamia and the Nile River valley. These early cities shared one important characteristic—they each arose near waterways. Since water was the easiest way to transport goods, the settlements became centers of trade.

Since then cities have grown all over the world. Every 10 years, the United States Census Bureau collects data to determine the population of the United States. (A census is an official count of people living in an area.) The first census was conducted in 1790. At that time, there were 3.9 million people in the 13 original states. The most recent census occurred in 2000. The results of that census showed that more than 280 million people reside in the 50 states that make up our nation.

Skills Practice

The charts on this page show populations of the five most populous cities in the United States during different time periods. When comparing information on charts be sure to read the titles and headings to define the data being compared. Study the charts and answer the questions below on a separate sheet of paper.

1. Which U.S. city had the greatest population in 1790?

2. Which U.S. city had the greatest population in 2000?

3. What was the population of Philadelphia in 1790?

4. What was Philadelphia's population in 2000?

5. Which cities are on both lists?

Population of Five Largest U.S. Cities, 1790

City	Number of People
New York City	33,131
Philadelphia	28,522
Boston	18,320
Charleston	16,359
Baltimore	13,503

Population of Five Largest U.S. Cities, 2000*

City	Number of People
New York City	8,008,278
Los Angeles	3,694,820
Chicago	2,896,016
Houston	1,953,631
Philadelphia	1,517,550

*Numbers do not include metropolitan areas.

Standardized Test Practice

DIRECTIONS: Use the charts and your knowledge of social studies to answer the following questions on a separate sheet of paper.

1. One inference that can be made from the charts is that the most populous cities in the United States

   A have good weather.

   B were founded early in our nation's history.

   C are port cities.

   D are in the eastern United States.

2. In 1790 the major cities of the United States were all

   F larger than 20,000 people.

   G located in the East.

   H Northern cities.

   J founded for religious reasons.

Primary Sources Library

Working With Primary Sources

Suppose that you have been asked to write a report on changes in your community over the past 25 years. Where would you get the information you need to begin writing? You would draw upon two types of information—primary sources and secondary sources.

Definitions

Primary sources are often first-person accounts by someone who actually saw or lived through what is being described. In other words, if you see a fire or live through a great storm and then write about your experiences, you are creating a primary source. Diaries, journals, photographs, and eyewitness reports are examples of primary sources. **Secondary sources** are second-hand accounts. For instance, if your friend experiences the fire or storm and tells you about it, or if you read about the fire or storm in the newspaper, and then you write about it, you are creating a secondary source. Textbooks, biographies, and histories are secondary sources.

Checking Your Sources

When you read primary or secondary sources, you should analyze them to figure out if they are dependable or reliable. Historians usually prefer primary sources to secondary sources, but both can be reliable or unreliable, depending on the following factors.

Time Span

With primary sources, it is important to consider how long after the event occurred the primary source was written. Chances are the longer the time span between the event and the account, the less reliable the account is. As time passes, people often forget details and fill in gaps with events that never took place. Although we like to think we remember things exactly as they happened, the fact is we often remember them as we wanted them to occur.

Reliability

Another factor to consider when evaluating a primary source is the writer's background and reliability. First, try to determine how this person knows about what he or she is writing. How much does he or she know? Is the writer being truthful? Is the account convincing?

Opinions

When evaluating a primary source, you should also decide whether the account has been influenced by emotion, opinion, or exaggeration. Writers can have reasons to distort the truth to

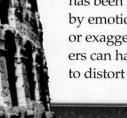

The Roman Colosseum

suit their personal purposes. Ask yourself: Why did the person write the account? Do any key words or expressions reveal the author's emotions or opinions? Compare the account with one written by another witness to the event. If they differ, ask yourself why they differ and which is more accurate.

Interpreting Primary Sources

To help you analyze a primary source, use the following steps:

- **Examine the origins of the document.**
  You need to determine if it is a primary source.

- **Find the main ideas.**
  Read the document and summarize the main ideas in your own words. These ideas may be fairly easy to identify in newspapers and journals, for example, but are much more difficult to find in poetry.

- **Reread the document.**
  Difficult ideas are not always easily understood on the first reading.

- **Use a variety of resources.**
  Form the habit of using the dictionary, the encyclopedia, and maps. These resources are tools to help you discover new ideas and knowledge and double-check other sources.

King Tut's Mask

Classifying Primary Sources

Primary sources fall into different categories:

 **Printed Publications**

Printed publications include books such as autobiographies. Printed publications also include newspapers and magazines.

 **Songs & Poems**

Songs and poems include works that express the personal thoughts and feelings or political or religious beliefs of the writer, often using rhyming and rhythmic language.

 **Visual Materials**

Visual materials include a wide range of forms: original paintings, drawings, sculptures, photographs, film, and maps.

 **Oral Histories**

Oral histories are chronicles, memoirs, myths, and legends that are passed along from one generation to another by word of mouth. Interviews are another form of oral history.

 **Personal Records**

Personal records are accounts of events kept by an individual who is a participant in, or witness to, these events. Personal records include diaries, journals, and letters.

 **Artifacts**

Artifacts are objects such as tools or ornaments. Artifacts present information about a particular culture or a stage of technological development.

For use with Unit 1

Early Civilizations

The people of early civilizations formed societies. These societies had a sense of justice and sets of values. As today, the family was the basic unit of society where values and justice were learned.

Reader's Dictionary

Bull of Heaven: mythical creature sent by the gods to kill Gilgamesh and Enkidu

Humbaba: evil spirit who guards the cedar forest through which Gilgamesh and Enkidu travel

steppe: wide, rolling, grassy plain

reproach: fault

Canaan: an ancient land that lay along the Syrian Desert

This Sumerian tablet is covered with cuneiform writing, the language in which the Epic of Gilgamesh *was written.*

The *Epic of Gilgamesh*

 **Printed Publications**

The Epic of Gilgamesh—*written c. 2500 B.C.—is one of the most well-known ancient tales. In this passage, Gilgamesh describes his adventures and journeys with his best friend, Enkidu.*

We overcame everything: climbed the mountain,
captured the **Bull of Heaven** and killed him,
brought **Humbaba** to grief, who lives in the
    cedar forest;
entering the mountain gates we slew lions;
my friend whom I love dearly underwent with
    me all hardships.
The fate of mankind overtook him.
Six days and seven nights I wept over him
until a worm fell out of his nose.
Then I was afraid.
In fear of death I roam the wilderness. The case of
    my friend lies heavy in me.
On a remote path I roam the wilderness. The case
    of my friend Enkidu lies heavy in me.
On a long journey I wander the **steppe.**
How can I keep still? How can I be silent?
The friend I loved has turned to clay. Enkidu, the
    friend I love, has turned to clay.
Me, shall I not lie down like him,
never again to move?

An Egyptian Father's Advice to His Son

 **Personal Records**

Upper-class Egyptians enjoyed collecting wise sayings to provide guidance for leading an upright and successful life. This excerpt of instructions from Vizier Ptah-hotep dates from around 2450 B.C.

If you have, as leader, to decide on the conduct of a great number of men, seek the most perfect manner of doing so that your own conduct may be without **reproach.** Justice is great, invariable, and assured; it has not been disturbed since the age of Ptah. . . .

If you are a wise man, bring up a son who shall be pleasing to Ptah. If he conforms his conduct to your way and occupies himself with your affairs as is right, do to him all the good you can; he is your son, a person attached to you whom your own self has begotten. Separate not your heart from him. . . .

If you are powerful, respect knowledge and calmness of language. Command only to direct; to be absolute is to run into evil. Let not your heart be haughty, neither let it be mean. . . .

Ancient Israelites

 **Printed Publications**

Much of the history of the ancient Israelites is recorded in the Bible. The Bible tells about a man named Abraham and his wife Sarah:

The Lord said to [Abraham], 'Leave your own country, your kin, and your father's house, and go to a country that I will show you. I shall make you into a great nation; I shall bless you. . . .'
[Abraham] . . . set out as the Lord had bidden him. . . . He took his wife [Sarah], his brother's son Lot, and all the possessions they had gathered . . . and they departed for **Canaan.**

When Abraham arrived in Canaan, the Bible says that God made a covenant, or special agreement, with him. It is considered by the Jewish people to be the beginning of their history.

When they arrived there, [Abraham] went on as far as the sanctuary. . . . When the Lord appeared to him and said, 'I am giving this land to your descendants,' [Abraham] built an altar there to the Lord who had appeared to him.

An ancient scroll from the Jewish Torah

Document Based Questions

1. What happened to the friend of Gilgamesh?
2. What is shown on the Sumerian tablet?
3. Does any part of the Egyptian father's advice have value today for sons or daughters? Be specific and support your answer.
4. According to the Bible, what did the Lord tell Abraham to do, and why?

The Ancient World

Primary Sources Library

Some of the greatest thoughts in modern civilization came from the ancient world. Important philosophers and religious leaders formed ideas we still express today. These ideas are timeless.

Reader's Dictionary

refinements: improvements

regulations: rules

nurture: upbringing

immortal: never dying

palpable: obvious

The *Analects* of Confucius

Printed Publications

An *analect is a selected thought or saying. The sayings below were written by the Chinese philosopher Confucius in c. 400 B.C.*

"If you make a mistake and do not correct it, this is called a mistake."

"Be dutiful at home, brotherly in public; be discreet and trustworthy, love all people, and draw near to humanity. If you have extra energy as you do that, then study literature."

"If leaders are courteous, their people will not dare to be disrespectful. If leaders are just, people will not dare to be [ungovernable]. If leaders are trustworthy, people will not dare to be dishonest."

A certain pupil asked Confucius about government: "What qualifies one to participate in government?"

Confucius said, "Honor five **refinements**. . . . Then you can participate in government."

The pupil asked, "What are the five refinements?"

Confucius said, "Good people are generous without being wasteful; they are hard working without being resentful; they desire without being greedy; they are at ease without being [proud]; they are dignified without being fierce."

Statue of Confucius

The Rights of Women

*I*n the Republic, *Plato presents his ideas on a just society in the form of dialogues, or imaginary conversations, between Socrates and his students. In this dialogue, Socrates has just finished questioning his student about the type of men who might make the best "watchdogs" of Athenian government. He surprises his student by turning to the subject of women.*

Let us further suppose the birth and education of our women to be subject to similar or nearly similar **regulations** [as men]; . . .

What do you mean?

What I mean may be put into the form of a question, I said: Are dogs divided into hes and shes, or do they both share equally in hunting and in keeping watch and in the other duties of dogs? [O]r do we entrust to the males the entire and exclusive care of the flocks, while we leave the females at home, under the idea that the bearing and [feeding of] their puppies is labour enough for them?

No, he said, they share alike; the only difference between them is that the males are stronger and the females weaker.

But can you use different animals for the same purpose, unless they are [raised] in the same way?

You cannot.

Then, if women are to have the same duties as men, they must have the same **nurture** and education?

Yes.

The *Rig Veda*

*T*he Vedas, written in ancient India, are the oldest writings of the Hindu religion. This song was written c. 1100 B.C.*

The goddess Night has drawn near, looking about on many sides with her eyes. She has put on all her glories.

The **immortal** goddess has filled the wide space, the depths and the heights. She stems the tide of darkness with her light.

The goddess has drawn near, pushing aside her sister the twilight. Darkness, too, will give way.

As you came near to us today, we turned homeward to rest, as birds go to their home in a tree.

People who live in villages have gone home to rest, and animals with feet, and animals with wings, even the ever-searching hawks.

Ward off the she-wolf and the wolf; ward off the thief. O night full of waves, be easy for us to cross over.

Darkness—**palpable,** black, and painted—has come upon me. O Dawn, banish it like a debt.

A representation of the Hindu god Siva

Document Based Questions

1. What are the five refinements according to Confucius?
2. What does Plato think will help make men and women more equal?
3. Who is the sister to the goddess Night in the last reading?
4. What does the song say Dawn should do about Darkness?

New Empires and New Faiths

With the growth of new empires came great change. Events occurred that gave people the chance to be great leaders and heroes. New faiths continued to form new ideas.

Reader's Dictionary

cognizant: aware

trifling: insignificant

posterity: future time

allay: calm

incurred: brought upon oneself

Incense burner from the Byzantine Empire in the shape of a church

A Woman on the Throne

Printed Publications

*I*n 1081 an able general named Alexius Commenus *captured Constantinople. As Emperor Alexius I, he defended the Byzantine Empire against attacks from invaders. His daughter, Anna Comnena, retold the story of his reign in a book called* The Alexiad (uh•lehk•see•uhd). *She begins her account by describing Alexius's decision to turn the government over to his mother Anna Dalassena.*

He really longed that his mother rather than himself should take the helm of the state, but so far he had concealed this design [plan] from her, fearing that if she became **cognizant** of it, she might actually leave the palace [for a convent]. . . . Therefore in all daily business he did nothing, not even a **trifling** thing, without her advice . . . and made her a partner in the administration of affairs, sometimes too he would say openly that without her brain and judgement the Empire would go to pieces.

. . . she was perhaps more devoted to her son than most women. And so she wished to help her son. . . . She ruled . . . with the Emperor, her son, and at times even took the reins alone and drove the chariot of Empire without harm or mishap. For besides being clever she had in very truth a kingly mind, capable of governing a kingdom.

A Heroic Rescue Attempt

Personal Records

Pliny the Elder—a Roman admiral and well-known author and scientist—died attempting to rescue people trapped at the foot of Mt. Vesuvius when it erupted. His nephew, Pliny the Younger, recorded his uncle's death in a letter written to a Roman historian named Tacitus. The letter forms an eyewitness account of the eruption and expresses Roman views of courage and duty.

Thank you for asking me to send you a description of my uncle's death so that you can leave an accurate account of it for **posterity**; . . .

As he was leaving the house he was handed a message from Rectina, . . . whose house was at the foot of the mountain, so that escape was impossible except by boat. She was terrified by the danger threatening her and implored him to rescue her. . . . Ashes were already falling, hotter and thicker as the ships drew near. . . . For a moment my uncle wondered whether to turn back, but when the helmsman advised this he refused, telling him that Fortune stood by the courageous. . . . This wind was . . . in my uncle's favour, and he was able to bring his ship in.

Meanwhile on Mount Vesuvius broad sheets of fire and leaping flames blazed at several points. . . . My uncle tried to **allay** the fears of his companions. . . . They debated whether to stay indoors or take their chance in the open, for the buildings were now shaking with violent shocks, and seemed to be swaying. . . .

. . . A sheet was spread on the ground for him [uncle] to lie down, and he repeatedly asked for cold water to drink. Then the flames and smell of sulphur which gave warning of the approaching fire drove the others to take flight. . . . He stood . . . and then suddenly collapsed, I imagine because the dense fumes choked his breathing. . . . When daylight returned on the 26th—two days after the last day he had seen—his body was found. . . .

The Quran

Printed Publications

The Quran is the holy book of Islam. The verses below come from Chapter 1, verses 2–7.

Praise be to Allah, the Lord of the Worlds,
The Compassionate, the Merciful,
Master of the Day of Judgement,
Only You do we worship, and only You
do we implore for help.
Lead us to the right path,
The path of those You have favoured
Not those who have **incurred** Your wrath or
have gone astray.

Document Based Questions

1. Why did Alexius conceal his plans to turn the government over to his mother?
2. Why did Pliny the Elder sail to Mt. Vesuvius?
3. Does Pliny the Younger consider his uncle a hero? Why or why not?
4. Who is the quote from the Quran praising?

The Middle Ages

During the Middle Ages, civilizations began to develop to be more as we know them in modern times. There were still strong leaders—some good, some bad. But it became a time when the common people began to demand their rights. Women especially started to have a voice in their status and how they would live.

Reader's Dictionary

ebony: a hard, heavy wood

score: twenty

mitqal: an ancient unit of measure

heirs: descendants

abject: low

Drawing of Mansa Musa

The Sultan of Mali

Personal Records

An Arab scholar named Ibn Fadl Allah al Omari describes the West African court and army of Mansa Musa in the 1330s. He refers to Mansa Musa as sultan, *the Arab word for "king."*

The sultan of this kingdom presides in his palace on a great balcony called *bembe* where he has a seat of **ebony** that is like a throne fit for a large and tall person: on either side it is flanked by elephant tusks turned towards each other. His arms stand near him, being all of gold, saber, lance, quiver, bow and arrows. He wears wide trousers made of about twenty pieces [of stuff] of a kind which he alone may wear. Behind him there stand about a **score** of Turkish or other pages which are bought for him in Cairo. . . . His officers are seated in a circle about him, in two rows, one to the right and one to the left; beyond them sit the chief commanders of his cavalry. . . . Others dance before their sovereign, who enjoys this, and make him laugh. Two banners are spread behind him. Before him they keep two saddled and bridled horses in case he should wish to ride.

Arab horses are brought for sale to the kings of this country, who spend considerable sums in this way. Their army numbers one hundred thousand men of whom there are about ten thousand horse-mounted cavalry: the others are infantry having neither horses nor any other mounts. . . .

The officers of this king, his soldiers and his guard receive gifts of land and presents. Some among the greatest of them receive as much as fifty thousand *mitqals* of gold a year, besides which the king provides them with horses and clothing. He is much concerned with giving them fine garments and making his cities into capitals.

The Magna Carta

 Printed Publications

The Magna Carta, signed in England in 1215, for the first time gave common people some freedoms and protections. It also limited the power of King John.

To all free men of our kingdom we have also granted, for us and our **heirs** for ever, all the liberties written out below. . . .

No widow shall be compelled [forced] to marry, so long as she wishes to remain without a husband. . . .

For a trivial offence, a free man shall be fined only in proportion to the degree of his offence. . . .

No sheriff, royal official, or other person shall take horses or carts for transport from any free man, without his consent. . . .

No free man shall be seized or imprisoned . . . or outlawed or exiled . . . except by the lawful judgement of his equals or by the law of the land.

To no one will we sell, to no one deny or delay right or justice.

All merchants may enter or leave England unharmed and without fear, and may stay or travel within it, by land or water, for purposes of trade. . . .

All these customs and liberties that we have granted shall be observed in our kingdom.

The Tale of Genji

 Personal Records

The Tale of Genji is the story of a young man searching for the meaning of life. It was written by Murasaki Shikibu in A.D. 1010. Genji's friend described three classes of women: those of high rank and birth whose weak points are concealed; those of the middle class; and those of the lower class. This is part of Genji's reply.

[Genji said] "It will not always be so easy to know into which of the three classes a woman ought to be put. For sometimes people of high rank sink to the most **abject** positions; while others of common birth rise to . . . think themselves as good as anyone. How are we to deal with such cases?"

Murasaki Shikibu

Document Based Questions

1. What conclusions can you draw about Mansa Musa's power?
2. Why do you think Mansa Musa treated his soldiers so well?
3. According to the Magna Carta, when can a man be imprisoned?
4. What does Genji seem to realize about the social classes that his friend does not?

A Changing World

World exploration expanded as countries looked for new lands to conquer. There was great competition among European countries to claim undiscovered riches. This exploration did not always benefit the people already living in explored lands, however.

Reader's Dictionary

finery: fancier clothes and jewelry

installed: placed in

plunder: stolen goods, usually during war

stench: a very bad smell

scorn: anger

Aztec and Spanish soldiers in battle

Arrival of the Spaniards

Aztec accounts of the Spanish conquest of Mexico in 1519 are recorded in The Broken Spears, edited and translated by Miguel Leon-Portilla. This selection describes the meeting of Montezuma and Cortés.

The Spaniards arrived . . . near the entrance to Tenochititlan. That was the end of their march, for they had reached their goal.

[Montezuma] now arrayed himself in his **finery,** preparing to go out to meet them. . . .

. . . Then he hung the gold necklaces around their necks and gave them presents of every sort as gifts of welcome.

When [Montezuma] had given necklaces to each one, Cortés asked him: "Are you [Montezuma]? Are you the king? . . ."

And the king said: "Yes, I am [Montezuma]." Then he stood up to welcome Cortés; he came forward, bowed his head low and addressed him in these words: "Our lord, you are weary. The journey has tired you, but now you have arrived on the earth. You have come to your city, Mexico. You have come here to sit on your throne. . . ."

When the Spaniards were **installed** in the palace, they asked [Montezuma] about the city's resources. . . . They questioned him closely and then demanded gold.

[Montezuma] guided them to it. . . .

. . . When they entered the hall of treasures, it was as if they had arrived in Paradise. . . . All of [Montezuma's] possessions were brought out: fine bracelets, necklaces with large stones, ankle rings with little gold bells, the royal crowns and all the royal finery—everything that belonged to the king. . . . They seized these treasures as if they were their own, as if this **plunder** were merely a stroke of good luck.

The Life of Olaudah Equiano

Printed Publications

Olaudah Equiano was kidnapped from West Africa and brought to America as a slave. In 1789 he wrote an account of this frightening journey. Here he describes the first part of that trip.

The first thing I saw was a vast ocean, and a ship, riding at anchor, waiting for its cargo. The ocean and the ship filled me with astonishment that soon turned to fear. I was taken to the ship and carried on board! . . .

The crew took me down below decks, into the ship's stinking hold. With the horribleness of the **stench** and my crying I was so sick and low that I couldn't eat. I wanted to die. . . .

That first day, among the poor chained men in the hold, I found some people of Benin.

"What are they going to do to us?" I asked.

"They are taking us away to work for them," a man from Benin explained.

"And do they only live here," I asked, "in this hollow place, the ship?"

"They have a white people's country," the man explained, "but it is far away."

"How can it be," I asked, "that in our whole country nobody ever heard of them?"

"They live *very* far away," another man explained.

Queen Elizabeth's Speech To Her Troops

Oral Histories

In 1588, a Spanish fleet, known as the Spanish Armada, was sent to invade England. Queen Elizabeth I spoke to her troops before the battle.

Let tyrants fear: I have so behaved myself that under God I have placed my chiefest strength and safeguard in the loyal hearts and goodwill of my subjects. Wherefore I am come . . . to live and die amongst you all, to lay down for my God and for my kingdom and for my people mine honor and my blood even in the dust. I know I have the body but of a weak and feeble woman, but I have the heart and stomach of a king and a king of England too—and take foul **scorn** that . . . any prince of Europe should dare to invade the borders of my realm.

Queen Elizabeth I

Drawing of a slave ship

Document Based Questions

1. What gifts did Montezuma give to Cortés?
2. Why do you think Montezuma took Cortés to see his personal treasury?
3. How did Equiano travel from Africa to the Americas?
4. In her speech, is Queen Elizabeth I encouraging or discouraging her troops? Explain.

For use with Unit 6

Modern Times

One of the major ideas of the world's modern times is the theme of justice and equality for all people. All over the world—in India, the United States, and Africa—this theme has been supported by great leaders.

Reader's Dictionary

doctrine: a principle or belief

Gentile: a person who is not Jewish

dichotomy: having two sides

oppression: cruel use of authority or power

Mohandas K. Gandhi

Peaceful Noncooperation

 **Printed Publications**

Mohandas K. Gandhi, the great Indian nationalistic leader, spoke to over 500,000 people in 1920. He addressed them about his philosophy of peaceful rebellion against and noncooperation with the rule of Great Britain over India.

I have been told that non-cooperation is unconstitutional. I venture to deny that it is unconstitutional. On the contrary, I hold that non-cooperation is a just and religious **doctrine;** it is the inherent [natural] right of every human being and it is perfectly constitutional. . . . I do not claim any constitutionality for a rebellion successful or otherwise, so long as that rebellion means in the ordinary sense of the term, what it does mean, namely, wresting justice by violent means. On the contrary, I have said it repeatedly to my countrymen that violence, whatever end it may serve in Europe, will never serve us in India.

. . . I am asking India to follow this non-violent non-cooperation. . . . As soon as India adopts the doctrine of the sword, my life as an Indian is finished. It is because I believe in a mission special to India and it is because I believe the ancients of India after centuries of experience have found out that the one true thing for any human being on earth is not justice based on violence but justice based on sacrifice of self. . . . I cling to that doctrine and I shall cling to it forever. . . .

I Have a Dream

In 1963 civil rights leader Dr. Martin Luther King, Jr., spoke to more than 200,000 people in a peace march on Washington, D.C. He spoke about his dreams for the future of African Americans and the United States.

I say to you today, my friends, that in spite of the difficulties and frustrations of the moment I still have a dream. . . . I have a dream that one day this nation will rise up and live out the true meaning of its creed: "We hold these truths to be self-evident, that all men are created equal."

I have a dream that one day on the red hills of Georgia the sons of former slaves and the sons of former slaveowners will be able to sit down together at the table of brotherhood. . . .

I have a dream that my four little children will one day live in a nation where they will not be judged by the color of their skin but by the content of their character. . . .

. . . When we let freedom ring, when we let it ring from every village and every hamlet, from every state and every city, we will be able to speed up that day when all of God's children, black men and white men, Jews and **Gentiles,** Protestants and Catholics, will be able to join hands and sing the words of the old Negro spiritual: "Free at last! Free at last! Thank God Almighty, we are free at last!"

Dr. King speaking

Nobel Peace Prize Winner

In 1993 Nelson Mandela of South Africa accepted the Nobel Peace Prize for his efforts to end the unequal treatment of the black citizens of South Africa.

I extend my heartfelt thanks to the Norwegian Nobel Committee for elevating us to the status of a Nobel Peace Prize winner. . . .

We speak here of the challenge of the **dichotomies** of war and peace, violence and non-violence, racism and human dignity, oppression and repression and liberty and human rights, poverty and freedom from want.

We stand here today as nothing more than a representative of the millions of our people who dared to rise up against a social system whose very essence is war, violence, racism, **oppression,** repression and the impoverishment of an entire people.

I am also here today as a representative of the millions of people across the globe, the anti-apartheid movement, the governments and organizations that joined us, not to fight against South Africa . . . but to oppose an inhuman system. . . .

Because of their courage and persistence . . . we can, today, even set the dates when all humanity will join together to celebrate one of the outstanding human victories of our century.

Document Based Questions

1. What does Gandhi believe about violent rebellion in India?
2. What does Dr. King say is America's most important creed?
3. Nelson Mandela fought to end unequal treatment for what people in what country?
4. What is one belief each of these leaders seem to share? Explain.

Suggested Readings

If you are interested in reading more about people and events in world history, the following list will help you. The book titles listed for each unit are fiction and nonfiction books you can read to learn more about that time period.

Unit 1:

Arnold, Caroline. *Stone Age Farmers Beside the Sea.* Clarion Books, 1997. A photo-essay describing the prehistoric village of Skara Brae.

Bunting, Eve. *I Am the Mummy Heb-Nefert.* Harcourt Brace, 1997. Fictional story of a mummy recalling her past life as the wife of the pharaoh's brother.

Courlander, Harold. *The King's Drum, and Other African Tales.* Harcourt, 1962. Folktales taken from Africa south of the Sahara.

Deem, James M. *Bodies from the Bog.* Houghton Mifflin, 1998. A photo-essay that looks at information from the well-preserved bodies found in a Danish bog.

Gregory, Kristiana. *Cleopatra VII: Daughter of the Nile.* Scholastic Inc., 1999. A fictional diary written by Cleopatra.

Herrmann, Siegfried. *A History of Israel in Old Testament Times.* Fortress Press, 1975. The Old Testament as a history of early Israel, with evidence from sources other than the Bible.

Lattimore, Deborah Nourse. *Winged Cat: A Tale of Ancient Egypt.* HarperCollins, 1995. A tale of a servant girl and a High Priest using the Book of the Dead to investigate the death of the girl's sacred cat.

Maltz, Fran. *Keeping Faith in the Dust.* Alef Design Group, 1998. Fictional account of a 16-year-old girl whose family is forced to flee their home near the Dead Sea to the fortress of Masada, where Roman forces are held off by the Jews for seven years.

Morley, Jacquelin. Mark Bergin, and John James. *An Egyptian Pyramid.* Peter Bedrick, 1991. Explains how the pyramids were built and their purpose.

Perl, Lila. *Mummies, Tombs, and Treasure: Secrets of Ancient Egypt.* Clarion Books, 1990. An account of what ancient Egyptians believed about death and the afterlife.

Travis, Lucille. *Tirzah.* Herald Press, 1991. Fictional story of a 12-year-old boy who flees from Egypt with Moses during the Exodus.

Trumble, Kelly. *Cat Mummies.* Clarion Books, 1996. Reasons and background examining why ancient Egyptians mummified thousands and thousands of cats.

Wetwood, Jennifer. *Gilgamesh, and Other Babylonian Tales.* Coward, McCann & Geoghegan, 1970. Retells ancient tales of Sumer and Babylon.

Unit 2:

Chang, Richard F. *Chinese Mythical Stories.* Yale Far Eastern Publications, 1990. Legends and myths of China.

Craft, Charlotte. *King Midas and the Golden Touch.* Morrow, 1999. The myth of King Midas and his greed for gold.

Evslin, Bernard. *Heroes and Monsters of Greek Myth.* Scholastic, 1988. A collection of Greek myths.

Fleischman, Paul. *Dateline: Troy.* Candlewick Press, 1996. Author uses modern wars (Persian Gulf, Vietnam) to better understand the Trojan War.

Ganeri, Anita. *Buddhism.* NTC Publishing Group, 1997. Overview of Buddhist history and beliefs.

Ganeri, Anita. *Hinduism.* NTC Publishing Group, 1996. Overview of Hindu history and beliefs.

Hamilton, Edith. *The Greek Way.* Norton, 1983. The story of the Greek spirit and mind told by great writers.

Harris, Nathaniel. *Alexander the Great and the Greeks.* Bookwright Press, 1986. Contributions Alexander made to the Greeks.

Homer and Geraldine McCaughrean. *The Odyssey.* Oxford, 1999. Illustrated retelling of *The Odyssey* using modern language.

Ross, Stewart. *The Original Olympic Games.* NTC Publishing Group, 1999. A history of the Olympics.

Theule, Frederic. *Alexander and His Times.* Henry Holt and Co., 1996. A pictorial and historic account of the life of Alexander the Great.

Unit 3:

Boyd, Anne. *Life in a 15th-Century Monastery (A Cambridge Topic Book).* Lerner Publications, 1979. An account of the daily life of monks in the monastery at Durham, England.

Browning, Robert. *The Byzantine Empire.* Charles Scribner's Sons, 1980. The Byzantine world from A.D. 500 to fall of Constantinople in 1453.

Burrell, Roy. *The Romans: Rebuilding the Past.* Oxford University Press, 1991. A historical outline of ancient Rome.

Comte, Fernand. *Sacred Writings of World Religions.* Chambers, 1992. The history, beliefs, and major figures of more than 20 religions, among them Judaism, Islam, and Christianity.

Dillon, Eilis. *Rome Under the Emperors.* Tomas Nelson, 1975. Views of Roman society and family life in the time of Trajan, as seen by young people of four different families and social classes.

Powell, Anton. *The Rise of Islam.* Warwick Press, 1980. An overview of Islamic culture.

Tingay, Graham. *Julius Caesar.* Cambridge University Press, 1991. An account of the life and achievements of Julius Caesar.

Unit 4:

Giles, Frances and Joseph. *Life in a Medieval Village.* Harper Perennial, 1990. An illustrated look at the way most medieval people passed their lives.

Haugaard, Erik Christian. *The Revenge of the Forty-Seven Samurai.* Houghton Mifflin, 1995. The tale of Jiro, a young boy who must aid 47 samurai who are attempting to avenge the unjust death of their lord. This historical novel provides a detailed look at Japanese feudal society.

Heer, Friedrich. *Charlemagne and His World.* Macmillan, 1975. Large, lavishly illustrated description of the period.

McKendrick, Meveena. *Ferdinand and Isabella.* American Heritage, 1968. Photographs and contemporary paintings help re-create the period.

Sanders, Tao Tao Liu. *Dragons, Gods, and Spirits from Chinese Mythology.* NTC, 1997. Collection of myths, legends, and folktales providing insight into the culture and historic development of China.

Scott, Sir Walter. *Ivanhoe.* Longmans, Green, and Co., 1897. A twelfth-century story of hidden identity, intrigue, and romance among the English nobility.

Wisniewski, David. *Sundiata: Lion King of Mali.* Houghton Mifflin, 1999. Story about the ancient king of Mali and how he defeated his enemies to become the ruler.

Unit 5:

Cowie, Leonard W. *Martin Luther: Leader of the Reformation (A Pathfinder Biography).* Frederick Praeger, 1969. A detailed biography of Luther.

Davis, Burke. *Black Heroes of the American Revolution.* Harcourt, Brace and Jovanovich, 1991. Highlights achievements of African Americans during the Revolution.

Hibbard, Howard. *Michelangelo.* Westview Press, 1985. Biography of Michelangelo told through his paintings, poems, and personal letters.

Hooks, William H. *The Legend of White Doe.* Macmillan, 1998. Tale about Virginia Dare, the first child of English settlers born in the Americas.

Lomask, Milton. *Exploration: Great Lives.* Scribners, 1988. Biographies of explorers.

Mee, Charles L. *Daily Life in the Renaissance.* American Heritage, 1975. Works of art showing people in their daily lives.

O'Dell, Scott. *The Hawk that Dare Not Hunt by Day.* Houghton Mifflin, 1975. Novel about a boy who helps the reformer Tyndale smuggle his translation of the Bible into England.

Stuart, Gene S. *America's Ancient Cities.* National Geographic Society, 1988. An illustrated collection of essays on cultures of North America and Mesoamerica.

Unit 6

Alvarez, Julia. *Before We Were Free.* Knopf Books for Young Readers, 2002. This story tells of a young girl and her family trying to flee the dictatorship of the Dominican Republic in the 1960s.

Ambrose, Stephen E. *The Good Fight: How World War II Was Won.* Atheneum Books for Young Readers, 2001. This book gives an account of World War II based on personal anecdotes from soldiers.

Blumberg, Rhoda. *What's the Deal? Jefferson, Napoleon, and the Louisiana Purchase.* National Geographic Society, 1998. This piece explores the Louisiana Purchase as something more than a simple business deal.

Chang, Jung. *Wild Swans: Three Daughters of China.* Doubleday, 1991. This fictional biography traces three generations of Chinese women as they live through Chinese warlords, Mao and Communism, and the Tiananmen Square massacre of 1989.

Connell, Kate. *They Shall Be Heard: Susan B. Anthony and Elizabeth Cady Stanton.* Steck-Vaughn, 1993. This book discusses the work of Anthony and Stanton during the early years of the struggle for woman suffrage.

Falstein, Mark. *Nelson Mandela.* Globe Fearon, 1994. This book tells the story of Mandela's life, from being in prison for 27 years to becoming president of South Africa in 1994.

Holliday, Laurel. *Children of Israel, Children of Palestine: Our Own True Stories.* Pocket Books, 1998. This book contains the stories of 36 men, women, and children of Israeli and Palestinian descent who reflect on their feelings on growing up during such a turbulent time.

Lewington, Anna. *Mexico: A Study of an Economically Developing Country.* Raintree Steck-Vaughn Publishers, 1996. This book explores the history, geography, economy, and people of Mexico in the modern world.

Marrin, Albert. *Napoleon and the Napoleonic Wars.* Viking Penguin, 1991. This is a biography of Napoleon Bonaparte, highlighting his military genius and goals for conquest.

Marrin, Albert. *Stalin: Russia's Man of Steel.* Viking Penguin, Inc., 1988. This book tells how Joseph Stalin used terror and an iron fist to transform Russia from a backward country into a major world superpower in the first half of the 1900s.

Moscow, Henry. *Russia Under the Czars.* American Heritage Publishing Co., Inc., 1962. This story tells how the Russian czars withstood external invasion, only to fall to the revolutionaries led by Lenin.

Murphy, Jim. *The Boys War: Confederate and Union Soldiers Talk About the Civil War.* Houghton Mifflin, 1993. This book uses primary sources to detail the role of juvenile soldiers in the Civil War, as well as the effects that their experiences had in shaping the rest of their lives.

Nordhoff, Charles and James N. Hall. *Falcons of France.* Little, Brown and Co., 1957. This novel tells of the Lafayette Flying Corps, an expert team of French fighter pilots in World War I.

Rosenberg, Tina. *The Haunted Land: Facing Europe's Ghosts After Communism.* Random House, 1995. This book tells of countries that broke from communism in the 1900s and built democracies.

Savage, Katharine. *The Story of the United Nations.* Henry Z. Walck, Inc., 1970. This book details the creation of the UN and its early history.

Severance, John B. *Gandhi: Great Soul.* Clarion Books, 1997. This book details the life of Mohandas Gandhi and highlights his nonviolent campaign for the independence of India.

Sommer, Robin Langley. *Nien Cheng: Prisoner in China.* Blackbirch Press, Inc., 1992. This book tells the story of Nien Cheng, a Chinese woman who spent six years in solitary confinement during the rule of Mao Zedong in China.

Stowe, Harriet Beecher. *Uncle Tom's Cabin.* Bantam Classics, 1983. This famous novel gives a fictional account of the evils of slavery in the United States in the mid-1800s.

Veciana-Suarez, Ana. *Flight to Freedom.* Scholastic, 2004. This fictional biography tells the story of thirteen-year-old Yara and how her life changes as she leaves Communist Cuba for a new life and new challenges in Florida.

Zeinert, Karen. *Those Incredible Women of World War II.* The Milbrook Press, 1994. This book focuses on the contributions of women during World War II.

A

 (A marker)

abolitionism movement to end slavery (p. 753)

absolutism system of rule in which monarchs held total power and claimed to rule by the will of God (p. 686)

acupuncture Chinese practice of easing pain by sticking thin needles into patients' skin (p. 246)

adobe sun-dried mud brick (p. 591)

agora in early Greek city-states, an open area that served as both a market and a meeting place (p. 122)

alphabet group of letters that stand for sounds (p. 85)

anatomy the study of body structure (p. 305)

animism belief that all natural things are alive and have their own spirits (p. 490)

annul to cancel (p. 648)

anthropologist scientist who studies the physical characteristics and cultures of humans and their ancestors (p. 9)

anti-Semitism hatred of Jews (p. 548)

apartheid policy of racial segregation in the Republic of South Africa from 1948–1991; Afrikaans for "apartness" or "separateness" (pp. 852, 872)

apostle early Christian leader who helped set up churches and spread the message of Jesus (p. 348)

appeasement idea that by meeting another government's demands, war can be avoided (p. 814)

aqueduct human-made channel built to carry water (p. 291)

archaeologist scientist who learns about past human life by studying fossils and artifacts (p. 9)

aristocrat noble whose wealth came from land ownership (p. 227)

armistice agreement to end fighting; cease-fire (p. 790)

artifact weapon, tool, or other item made by humans (p. 9)

artisan skilled craftsperson (p. 20)

astronomer person who studies stars, planets, and other heavenly bodies (pp. 30, 185)

B

barbarian uncivilized person (p. 435)

barter to exchange goods without using money (p. 319)

bazaar marketplace (p. 389)

blockade use of warships to stop goods and people from leaving or entering an area (p. 787)

bourgeoisie middle classes of society, including merchants, bankers, doctors, lawyers, teachers, and other professional people (p. 715)

Brahman in Hinduism, the universal spirit of which all gods and goddesses are different parts (p. 203)

Buddhism religion founded by Siddhartha Gautama, the Buddha; taught that the way to find truth was to give up all desires (p. 205)

bureaucracy a group of appointed officials who are responsible for different areas of government (p. 229)

C

caliph important Muslim political and religious leader (p. 380)

calligraphy beautiful handwriting (p. 421); the art of producing beautiful handwriting (p. 501)

capital money available for investment in business (p. 726)

caravan group of traveling merchants and animals (pp. 30, 373)

caste social group that a person is born into and cannot change (p. 199)

cataract steep rapids formed by cliffs and boulders in a river (p. 39)

caudillos strong leaders who mainly ruled by military force, usually with the support of the rich and upper class (p. 751)

census a count of the number of people (p. 432)

city-state independent state made up of a city and the surrounding land and villages (p. 19)

civil disobedience refusal to obey unjust laws of a government (p. 843)

Glossary

civilization complex society with cities, organized government, art, religion, class divisions, and a writing system (p. 17)

clan group of families related by blood or marriage (pp. 461, 487)

clergy religious officials, such as priests, given authority to conduct religious services (pp. 355, 538)

collectivization system of combining small farms into large, factory-like farms run by the government (p. 810)

colony settlement in a new territory that keeps close ties with its homeland (pp. 121, 666, 763)

comedy form of drama in which the story has a happy ending (p. 161)

commerce the buying and selling of goods in large amounts over long distances (p. 666)

concordat agreement between the pope and the ruler of a country (p. 521)

confederation a loose union of several groups or states (p. 592)

Confucianism system of beliefs introduced by the Chinese thinker Confucius; taught that people needed to have a sense of duty to their family and community in order to bring peace to society (p. 236)

conquistador Spanish conqueror or soldier in the Americas (p. 595)

conscription enrollment into military service by force; military draft (p. 782)

constitution written plan of government (pp. 488, 694)

consul one of the two top government officials in ancient Rome (p. 269)

containment U.S. policies that intended to prevent the spread of communism (p. 834)

corporation business organization that is allowed to own property and sell shares to investors in order to raise money (p. 728)

coup d'etat forced replacement of top government leaders by a new group of leaders (p. 720)

covenant agreement (p. 82)

crier announcer who calls Muslim believers to prayer five times a day (p. 394)

cuneiform Sumerian system of writing made up of wedge-shaped markings (p. 20)

currency system of money (p. 294)

daimyo powerful military lord in feudal Japan (pp. 496, 777)

Dao the proper way Chinese kings were expected to rule under the Mandate of Heaven (p. 230)

Daoism Chinese philosophy based on the teachings of Laozi; taught that people should turn to nature and give up their worldly concerns (p. 238)

D-Day June 6, 1944; the day in World War II when Allied forces invaded Normandy, France (p. 828)

deforestation clearing of forests (p. 890)

deism religious belief based on reason (p. 685)

deity god or goddess (p. 49)

delta area of fertile soil at the mouth of a river (p. 39)

democracy government in which all citizens share in running the government (p. 126)

denomination an organized branch of Christianity (p. 636)

depression a period of low economic activity when many people lose their jobs (p. 806)

détente policy promoting a relaxation of tensions between nations (p. 881)

dharma in Hinduism, the divine law that requires people to perform the duties of their caste (p. 204)

dhow an Arab sailboat (p. 452)

Diaspora refers to the scattering of communities of Jews outside their homeland after the Babylonian captivity (p. 96)

dictator in ancient Rome, a person who ruled with complete power temporarily during emergencies (p. 271)

diplomacy the art of negotiating with other countries (p. 615)

direct democracy system of government in which people gather at mass meetings to decide on government matters (p. 139)

disciple close follower of Jesus (p. 344)

doctrine official church teaching (p. 355)

domesticate to tame animals and plants for human use (p. 13)

drama story told by actors who pretend to be characters in the story (p. 160)

Glossary

duma Russian national assembly of elected lawmakers (p. 793)

dynasty line of rulers from the same family (pp. 44, 210, 226)

economy organized way in which people produce, sell, and buy goods and services (p. 410)

embalming process developed by the ancient Egyptians of preserving a person's body after death (p. 49)

embargo order that bans or restricts trade with another country (p. 863)

empire group of territories or nations under a single ruler or government (pp. 23, 89)

entente understanding among nations that provides for a common course of action (p. 782)

epic long poem that tells about legendary or heroic deeds (p. 157)

Epicureanism philosophy founded by Epicurus in Hellenistic Athens; taught that happiness through the pursuit of pleasure was the goal of life (p. 184)

estates classes into which French people were divided before the French Revolution: the Catholic clergy (First Estate), the nobles (Second Estate), and the townspeople (Third Estate) (p. 715)

ethnic cleansing using force to remove an entire ethnic group from an area (p. 884)

euro common currency shared by countries of the European Union since 1999 (p. 889)

excommunicate to declare that a person or group no longer belongs to a church (pp. 361, 521)

exile period of forced absence from one's country or home (p. 94)

export to sell to another country (pp. 666, 861)

extended family family group including several generations as well as other relatives (p. 469)

extraterritoriality legal practice of foreigners living in a country but not subject to the host country's laws (p. 772)

fable short tale that teaches a lesson (p. 158)

feudalism political system based on bonds of loyalty between lords and vassals (pp. 497, 523)

fief under feudalism, the land a lord granted to a vassal in exchange for military service and loyalty (p. 524)

filial piety children's respect for their parents and older relatives, an important part of Confucian beliefs (p. 234)

fjord steep-sided valley that is an inlet of the sea (p. 518)

Forum open space in Rome that served as a marketplace and public square (p. 306)

fossil the trace or imprint of a plant or animal that has been preserved in rock (p. 9)

genocide the deliberate killing of a racial, political, or cultural group (p. 827)

glacier huge sheet of ice (p. 573)

gladiator in ancient Rome, person who fought animals and other people as public entertainment (p. 306)

glasnost Mikhail Gorbachev's Soviet policy that permitted open discussion of political and social ideas (p. 882)

globalism idea that every nation's economy and politics are part of one worldwide system (p. 889)

gospel ("good news") one of the four accounts of Jesus' life, teachings, and resurrection (p. 355)

grand jury group that decides whether there is enough evidence to accuse a person of a crime (p. 537)

griot storyteller (p. 449)

guild medieval business group formed by craftspeople and merchants (pp. 503, 530)

guru religious teacher and spiritual guide in Hinduism (p. 201)

Hellenistic Era period when the Greek language and Greek ideas spread to the non-Greek peoples of southwest Asia (p. 178)

helot person who was conquered and enslaved by the ancient Spartans (p. 126)

Glossary

heresy belief that differs from or contradicts the accepted teachings of a religion (pp. 547, 643)

hierarchy organization with different levels of authority (p. 355)

hieroglyphics system of writing made up of thousands of picture symbols developed by the ancient Egyptians (p. 42)

Hinduism system of religion that grew out of the religion of the Aryans in ancient India (p. 203)

historian person who studies and writes about the human past (p. 9)

humanism Renaissance movement based on the values of the ancient Greeks and Romans, such as that individuals and human society were important (p. 619)

hypothesis proposed explanation of the facts (p. 679)

icon Christian religious image or picture (p. 359)

iconoclast person who opposed the use of icons in Byzantine churches, saying that icons encouraged the worship of idols (p. 360)

ideograph a character that joins two or more pictographs to represent an idea (p. 228)

igloo dome-shaped home built by the Inuit (p. 590)

imperialism a nation's direct or indirect control over the government or economy of other usually smaller or weaker nations (p. 763)

import to buy from another country (p. 666)

incense material burned for its pleasant smell (p. 62)

indulgence pardon from the Church for a person's sins (p. 634)

industrialism economic system in which people rely more on the use of machinery and technology than on animal or human power (p. 725)

inflation period of rapidly increasing prices (pp. 319, 806)

intifada armed uprising of Palestinians against Israeli occupation of the West Bank and Gaza Strip (p. 878)

invest to put money into a project (p. 667)

irrigation method of bringing water to a field from another place to water crops (p. 18)

kaiser German for "emperor" (p. 748)

karma in Hinduism, the good or bad energy a person builds up based upon whether he or she lives a good or bad life (p. 204)

knight in the Middle Ages, a noble warrior who fought on horseback (p. 524)

labor union association of workers who unite to improve worker rights, wages, benefits, and working conditions (p. 736)

laity church members who are not clergy (p. 355)

latifundia large farming estates in ancient Rome (p. 278)

legacy what a person leaves behind when he or she dies (p. 178)

Legalism Chinese philosophy developed by Hanfeizi; taught that humans are naturally evil and therefore need to be ruled by harsh laws (p. 239)

legion smaller unit of the Roman army made up of about 6,000 soldiers (p. 266)

liberalism political belief based on the ideas of the Enlightenment, which stress progress, the essential goodness of humankind, and individual freedom (p. 735)

limited government idea that a government may only use the powers given to it by the people (p. 700)

mandate formal order (pp. 230, 792)

Marshall Plan U.S.-sponsored program to provide economic aid to European countries after World War II, from 1948–51; named after U.S. Secretary of State George Marshall who proposed it to Congress (p. 834)

martial arts sports, such as judo and karate, that involve combat and self-defense (p. 499)

martyr person willing to die rather than give up his or her beliefs (p. 353)

mass Catholic worship service (p. 546)

matrilineal refers to a group that traces descent through mothers rather than fathers (p. 469)

meditation practice of quiet reflection to clear the mind and find inner peace (p. 499)

mercantilism the idea that a country gains power by building up its supply of gold and silver (p. 666)

messiah in Judaism, a deliverer sent by God (pp. 101, 344)

militarism fascination with war and the military (p. 782)

minaret tower of a mosque from which the crier calls believers to prayer five times a day (p. 394)

missionary person who travels to carry the ideas of a religion to others (pp. 363, 520)

mobilization assembly and movement of troops in order to prepare for action (p. 784)

monastery religious community where monks live and work (pp. 362, 413)

monopoly control of all (or almost all) trade or production of a certain good (p. 576)

monotheism the belief in one god (p. 81)

monsoon in South Asia, a strong wind that blows one direction in winter and the opposite direction in summer (p. 195)

mosaic picture made from many bits of colored glass, tile, or stone (p. 333)

mosque Muslim house of worship (p. 389)

mummy body that has been embalmed and wrapped in linen (p. 50)

myth traditional story describing gods or heroes or explaining natural events (p. 155)

nationalize remove from private ownership and place under government control (p. 865)

natural law law that applies to everyone and can be understood by reason (p. 681)

nirvana in Buddhism, a state of wisdom and freedom from the cycle of rebirth (p. 205)

nomad person who regularly moves from place to place (p. 10)

novel long fictional story (p. 432)

nuclear proliferation spread of nuclear weapons (p. 890)

oasis green area in a desert fed by underground water (p. 373)

ode poem that expresses strong emotions about life (p. 304)

oligarchy government in which a small group of people holds power (p. 126)

oracle sacred shrine where a priest or priestess spoke for a god or goddess (p. 156)

oral history the stories passed down from generation to generation (p. 470)

Pan-Africanism movement to unite black Africans throughout the world and to establish independence for African nations (p. 852)

papyrus reed plant of the Nile Valley, used to make a form of paper (p. 42)

parable story that used events from everyday life to express spiritual ideas (p. 345)

partnership business owned by two or more people who agree to share the profits and losses (p. 728)

paterfamilias ("father of the family") name for the father as head of the household in ancient Rome (p. 307)

patrician wealthy landowner and member of the ruling class in ancient Rome (p. 269)

Pax Romana ("Roman Peace") long era of peace and safety in the Roman Empire (p. 287)

peninsula body of land with water on three sides (p. 117)

perestroika Mikhail Gorbachev's plan to rebuild the Soviet Union's government and economy (p. 882)

persecute to mistreat a person because of his or her beliefs (p. 353)

pharaoh all-powerful king in ancient Egypt (p. 48)

philosopher thinker who seeks wisdom and ponders questions about life (pp. 140, 169)

philosophy study of the nature and meaning of life; comes from the Greek word for "love of wisdom" (p. 169)

pictograph a character that stands for an object (p. 228)

Glossary

Glossary

pilgrim person who travels to go to a religious shrine or site (p. 213)

plague disease that spreads quickly and kills many people (pp. 319, 554)

plane geometry branch of mathematics that shows how points, lines, angles, and surfaces relate to one another (p. 185)

plateau area of high flat land (p. 446)

plebeian member of the common people in ancient Rome (p. 269)

polis the early Greek city-state, made up of a city and the surrounding countryside and run like an independent country (p. 122)

pope the bishop of Rome, later the head of the Roman Catholic Church (p. 356)

popular sovereignty idea that a government receives its power from the people (p. 700)

porcelain type of ceramic ware that is made of fine clay and baked at high temperatures (p. 418)

praetor important government official in ancient Rome (p. 270)

predestination belief that no matter what a person does, the outcome of his or her life is already planned by God (p. 640)

propaganda controlled spread of biased information to influence what people think (p. 786)

prophet person who claims to be instructed by God to share God's words (p. 87)

protectorate small country ruled by and/or protected by a larger one (p. 763)

proverb wise saying (p. 89)

province political district (p. 28)

pyramid huge stone structure built by the ancient Egyptians to serve as a tomb (p. 50)

Q

quipu rope with knotted cords of different lengths and colors (p. 588)

Quran holy book of Islam (p. 377)

R

rabbi Jewish leader and teacher of the Torah (p. 101)

racial segregation separation or isolation of people to specific residential areas, organizations, or institutions based upon their race (p. 840)

raja prince who led an Aryan tribe in India (p. 199)

rationalism the belief that reason is the chief source of knowledge (p. 678)

rationing system of limiting the amounts of food and materials in use (p. 786)

Reconquista ("reconquest") Christian struggle to take back the Iberian Peninsula from the Muslims (p. 558)

reform change that tries to bring about an improvement (pp. 320, 411)

Reformation movement to reform the Catholic Church; led to the creation of Protestantism (p. 634)

refugee person who flees to another country to escape persecution or disaster (p. 870)

regent person who acts as a temporary ruler (p. 334)

reincarnation rebirth of the soul or spirit in different bodies over time (p. 204)

Renaissance ("rebirth") period of renewed interest in art and learning in Europe (p. 609)

reparation payments made to the winner of a war by a losing country to pay for damages; war damages (p. 791)

representative democracy system of government in which citizens choose a smaller group to make laws and governmental decisions on their behalf (p. 139)

representative government system of government in which people elect leaders to make laws (p. 694)

republic form of government in which the leader is not a king or queen but a person elected by citizens (p. 265)

resurrection the act of rising from the dead (p. 347)

rhetoric public speaking (p. 307)

S

Sabbath weekly day of worship and rest for Jews (p. 94)

saint Christian holy person (p. 333)

salvation the act of being saved from sin and allowed to enter heaven (p. 350)

samurai class of warriors in feudal Japan who pledged loyalty to a noble in return for land (p. 494)

Sanskrit written language developed by the Aryans (p. 199)

satire work that pokes fun at human weaknesses (p. 304)

satrap official who ruled a state in the Persian Empire under Darius (p. 133)

satrapies the 20 states into which Darius divided the Persian Empire (p. 133)

savanna grassy plain (p. 69)

schism separation (p. 361)

scholasticism medieval way of thinking that tried to bring together reason and faith in studies of religion (p. 550)

scientific method orderly way of collecting and analyzing evidence (p. 679)

scribe record keeper (p. 20)

sect a smaller group with distinct beliefs within a larger religious group (p. 499)

secular interested in worldly rather than religious matters (p. 609)

seminary school for training and educating priests and ministers (p. 643)

separation of powers equal division of power among the branches of government (p. 682)

sepoy Indian soldier hired by the British East India Company to protect the company's interests in the region (p. 765)

serf peasant laborer bound by law to the lands of a noble (p. 524)

sheikh leader of an Arab tribe (p. 373)

Shiite Muslim group that accepts only the descendants of Muhammad's son-in-law Ali as rightful rulers of Muslims (p. 382)

shogun military ruler of feudal Japan (p. 495)

shrine holy place (p. 490)

social class group of people who share a similar position in society (p. 233)

social contract agreement between rulers and the people upon which a government is based (p. 682)

socialism social system based on shared or governmental ownership of businesses, factories, land, and raw materials (p. 735)

Socratic method way of teaching developed by Socrates that used a question-and-answer format to force students to use their reason to see things for themselves (p. 170)

solid geometry branch of mathematics that studies spheres and cylinders (p. 186)

Sophist professional teacher in ancient Greece; believed that people should use knowledge to improve themselves and developed the art of public speaking and debate (p. 169)

soviet Russian committee or council made up of representatives from the workers, soldiers, and peasants (p. 794)

specialization the development of different kinds of jobs (p. 15)

sphere of influence area in which an imperial or foreign power has exclusive rights and privileges (p. 763)

steppe wide, rolling, grassy plain (p. 424)

Stoicism philosophy founded by Zeno in Hellenistic Athens; taught that happiness came not from following emotions, but from following reason and doing one's duty (p. 184)

stupa Buddhist shrine that is shaped like a dome or mound (p. 211)

subcontinent large landmass that is part of a continent but distinct from it (p. 195)

sultan military and political leader with absolute authority over a Muslim country (pp. 383, 467)

Sunni Muslim group that accepts descendants of the Umayyads as rightful rulers of Muslims (p. 382)

Swahili refers to the culture and language of East Africa (p. 467)

synagogue Jewish house of worship (p. 94)

tanka Japan's oldest form of poetry; an unrhymed poem of five lines (p. 501)

technology tools and methods used to help humans perform tasks (p. 11)

terror violent actions that are meant to scare people into surrendering (p. 426)

terrorism use of violence against citizens to achieve political goals (p. 892)

textile woven or knit cloth (p. 726)

theocracy government headed by religious leaders (p. 208)

theology the study of religion and God (pp. 550, 640)

theory an explanation of how or why something happens (p. 671)

Torah the laws that, according to the Bible, Moses received from God on Mount Sinai; these laws later became the first part of the Hebrew Bible (p. 82)

totalitarian state political state in which the government tries to totally control the way citizens think and live (p. 808)

tragedy form of drama in which a person struggles to overcome difficulties but meets an unhappy end (p. 160)

treason disloyalty to the government (pp. 431, 599)

trial jury group that decided whether an accused person was innocent or guilty (p. 537)

tribe group of related families (pp. 81, 424)

tribute payment made by one group or nation to another to show obedience or to obtain peace or protection (pp. 60, 89)

triumvirate in ancient Rome, a three-person ruling group (p. 280)

Truman Doctrine U.S. policy to provide economic aid to Greece and Turkey after World War II; named after U.S. President Harry S Truman who created the plan (p. 834)

tyrant person who takes power by force and rules with total authority (p. 125)

urbanization movement of people from rural areas to cities (p. 732)

vassal in feudalism, a noble who held land from and served a higher-ranking lord, and in return was given protection (pp. 496, 523)

vault curved structure of stone or concrete forming a ceiling or roof (p. 303)

vernacular everyday language used in a country or region (pp. 552, 620)

veto to reject (p. 270)

warlord military leader who runs a government (p. 409)

weapons of mass destruction nuclear, chemical, or biological weapons that can kill or destroy on a very large scale (p. 894)

Zoroastrianism Persian religion founded by Zoroaster; taught that humans had the freedom to choose between right and wrong, and that goodness would triumph in the end (p. 133)

Glossary

Spanish Glossary

A

abolitionism / abolicionismo movimiento para terminar con la esclavitud (pág. 753)

absolutism / absolutismo sistema de gobierno en que los monarcas tiene poder absoluto y alegan gobernar según decreto divino (pág. 686)

acupuncture / acupuntura práctica china para aliviar el dolor clavando la piel de los pacientes con agujas delgadas (pág. 246)

adobe / adobe ladrillo de barro secado al sol (pág. 591)

agora / ágora en las primeras ciudades-estado griegas, un área abierta que servía tanto de mercado como de lugar de reunión (pág. 122)

alphabet / alfabeto grupo de letras que representan sonidos (pág. 85)

anatomy / anatomía estudio de la estructura corporal (pág. 305)

animism / animismo creencia de que todas las cosas naturales están vivas y tienen sus propios espíritus (pág. 490)

annul / anular el acto de invalidar (pág. 648)

anthropologist / antropólogo científico que estudia las características físicas y las culturas de los seres humanos y sus antepasados (pág. 9)

anti-Semitism / antisemitismo odio hacia los judíos (pág. 548)

apartheid / apartheid política de segregación racial establecida en Sudáfrica, que se aplicó de 1948 a 1991. Palabra en lengua afrikaans que significa separación (págs. 806, 872)

apostle / apóstol nombre dado a líderes cristianos que ayudaban a establecer iglesias y a difundir el mensaje de Jesucristo (pág. 348)

appeasement / conciliación evitar la guerra mediante la satisfacción de las demandas de un gobierno extranjero (pág. 814)

aqueduct / acueducto canal construido por el hombre para transportar agua (pág. 291)

archaeologist / arqueólogo científico que aprende acerca de la vida humana en el pasado estudiando fósiles y artefactos (pág. 9)

aristocrat / aristócrata noble cuya riqueza provenía de la propiedad de la tierra (pág. 227)

armistice / armisticio acuerdo para terminar las hostilidades; cese al fuego (pág. 790)

artifact / artefacto arma, herramienta u otro artículo hecho por humanos (pág. 9)

artisan / artesano persona hábil artísticamente (pág. 20)

astronomer / astrónomo persona que estudia las estrellas, a los planetas y a otros cuerpos celestiales (págs. 30, 185)

B

barbarian / bárbaro persona incivilizada (pág. 435)

barter / trueque intercambiar bienes sin utilizar dinero (pág. 319)

bazaar / bazar mercado (pág. 389)

blockade / bloqueo uso de embarcaciones de guerra para detener la entrada o salida de bienes y personas de un área (pág. 787)

bourgeoisie / burguesía clase media de la sociedad. Incluye comerciantes, banqueros, médicos, abogados, maestros y otros profesionales (pág. 715)

Brahman / Brahman en el hinduismo, el espíritu universal del que todos los dioses y diosas son partes diferentes (pág. 203)

Buddhism / budismo religión fundada por Siddhartha Gautama, Buda; enseñó que la manera de hallar la verdad era renunciar a todo deseo (pág. 205)

bureaucracy / burocracia grupo de funcionarios designados que son responsables de diferentes áreas del gobierno (pág. 229)

C

caliph / califa importante líder político y religioso musulmán (pág. 380)

calligraphy / caligrafía hermosa escritura a mano (pág. 421); el arte de producir tal hermosa escritura (pág. 501)

capital / capital dinero disponible para invertir en negocios (pág. 726)

caravan / caravana grupo itinerante de mercaderes y animales (págs. 30, 373)

caste / casta grupo social en el que una persona nace y que no puede cambiar (pág. 199)

cataract / catarata rápidos empinados formados por precipicios y rocas erosionadas en un río (pág. 39)

caudillos / caudillos líderes fuertes que gobernaron mediante el uso de la fuerza militar. Generalmente contaban con el apoyo de los ricos y la clase alta (pág. 751)

census / censo conteo del número de personas (pág. 432)

city-state / ciudad-estado estado independiente compuesto por una ciudad y la tierra y aldeas circundantes (pág. 19)

civil disobedience / desobediencia civil rehusarse a obedecer leyes injustas de un gobierno (pág. 843)

civilization / civilización sociedad compleja, con ciudades, un gobierno organizado, arte, religión, divisiones de clase y un sistema de escritura (pág. 17)

clan / clan grupo de familias relacionadas por sangre o casamiento (págs. 461, 487)

clergy / clero funcionarios religiosos, como los sacerdotes, con autoridad concedida para llevar a cabo servicios religiosos (págs. 355, 538)

collectivization / colectivización sistema en el que se unen numerosas parcelas, para formar grandes campos agrícolas que funcionan como fábricas y son controladas por el estado (pág. 810)

colony / colonia asentamiento en un territorio nuevo que mantiene lazos cercanos con su tierra natal (págs. 121, 666, 763)

comedy / comedia forma de drama en el que la historia tiene un final feliz (pág. 161)

commerce / comercio compra y venta de bienes en cantidades grandes y a través de largas distancias (pág. 666)

concordat / concordato acuerdo entre el Papa y el gobernante de un país (pág. 521)

confederation / confederación unión libre de varios grupos o estados (pág. 592)

Confucianism / confucianismo sistema de creencias introducidas por el pensador chino Confucio; enseñó que las personas necesitaban tener un sentido del deber hacia su familia y la comunidad para llevar paz a la sociedad (pág. 236)

conquistador / conquistador soldado español en las Américas (pág. 595)

conscription / conscripción reclutamiento forzoso en el servicio militar; servicio militar (pág. 782)

constitution / constitución plan de gobierno (págs. 488, 694)

consul / cónsul uno de los dos altos funcionarios en la Roma antigua (pág. 269)

containment / contención políticas de los Estados Unidos diseñadas para evitar el avance del comunismo (pág. 834)

corporation / corporación organización empresarial, comercial o mercantil que puede poseer propiedades, así como obtener fondos mediante la venta de acciones a inversionistas (pág. 728)

coup d'etat / golpe de estado sustitución forzada de los dirigentes de gobierno por otros dirigentes (pág. 720)

covenant / pacto acuerdo (pág. 82)

crier / almuecín anunciador que llama a los creyentes musulmanes a orar cinco veces al día (pág. 394)

cuneiform / cuneiforme sistema sumerio de escritura compuesto de símbolos con forma de cuña (pág. 20)

currency / moneda sistema monetario (pág. 294)

daimyo / daimyo poderoso señor militar en el Japón feudal (págs. 496, 777)

Dao / Dao manera apropiada en que se esperaba que los reyes chinos gobernaran bajo el Mandato del Cielo (pág. 230)

Daoism / Daoism filosofía china basada en las enseñanzas de Laozi; enseñó que las personas debían volverse a la naturaleza y renunciar a sus preocupaciones terrenales (pág. 238)

D-day / Día D 6 de junio de 1944. Día en que las fuerzas aliadas invadieron Normandía, Francia, durante la Segunda Guerra Mundial (pág. 828)

deforestation / deforestación tala de los bosques (pág. 890)

deism / deísmo doctrina religiosa basada en la razón (pág. 685)

deity / deidad dios o diosa (pág. 49)

delta / delta área de tierra fértil en la boca de un río (pág. 39)

democracy / democracia forma de gobierno en la que todos los ciudadanos participan en la administración del gobierno (pág. 126)

denomination / denominación rama organizada del cristianismo (pág. 636)

depression / depresión periodo de baja actividad económica en el que muchas personas quedan desempleadas (pág. 806)

détente / detente política que promueve el aliviamiento de las tensiones entre países (pág. 881)

dharma / dharma en el hinduismo, la ley divina que llama a las personas a realizar los deberes de su casta (pág. 204)

dhow / dhow velero árabe (pág. 452)

Diaspora / diáspora se refiere al esparcimiento de las comunidades de judíos fuera de su tierra natal después del cautiverio babilónico (pág. 96)

dictator / dictador en la Roma antigua, una persona que gobernaba temporalmente con poder absoluto durante emergencias (pág. 271)

diplomacy / diplomacia el arte de negociar con otros países (pág. 615)

direct democracy / democracia directa sistema de gobierno en el que las personas se congregan en reuniones masivas para decidir sobre asuntos de gobierno (pág. 139)

disciple / discípulo seguidor de Jesucristo (pág. 344)

doctrine / doctrina enseñanza oficial de la iglesia (pág. 355)

domesticate / domesticar domar animales y plantas para uso humano (pág. 13)

drama / drama historia contada por actores que pretenden ser personajes en la misma (pág. 160)

duma / duma asamblea nacional rusa conformada por legisladores electos (pág. 793)

dynasty / dinastía línea de gobernantes de la misma familia (págs. 44, 210, 226)

E

economy / economía manera organizada en la que las personas producen, venden y compran bienes y servicios (pág. 410)

embalming / embalsamado proceso desarrollado por los antiguos egipcios para la conservación del cuerpo de una persona después de muerta (pág. 49)

embargo / embargo ley que prohibe o limita el intercambio comercial con otro país (pág. 863)

empire / imperio grupo de territorios o naciones bajo un mismo mandatario o gobierno (págs. 23, 89)

entente / pacto acuerdo entre naciones que permite realizar acciones comunes (pág. 782)

epic / epopeya poema largo que cuenta acerca de actos legendarios o heroicos (pág. 157)

Epicureanism / epicureísmo filosofía fundada por Epicuro en la Atenas helenista; enseñó que la felicidad a través de la persecución del placer era la meta de la vida (pág. 184)

estates / estados clases en las cuales se dividían los habitantes de Francia, antes de la Revolución: el clero católico (Primer estado), la nobleza (Segundo estado) y los ciudadanos (Tercer estado) (pág. 715)

ethnic cleansing / limpieza étnica uso de la fuerza para eliminar a un grupo étnico de una región determinada (pág. 884)

euro / euro moneda común de los países de la Unión Europea desde 1999 (pág. 889)

excommunicate / excomulgar declarar que una persona o grupo no pertenece más a la iglesia (págs. 361, 521)

exile / exilio período de ausencia forzada de una persona de su país u hogar (pág. 94)

export / exportar vender a otro país (págs. 666, 861)

extended family / familia extendida grupo familiar que incluye a varias generaciones así como a otros parientes (pág. 469)

extraterritoriality / extraterritorialidad práctica legal que se aplica a extranjeros que habitan en un país, pero no son sujetos de sus leyes (pág. 773)

F

fable / fábula cuento corto que enseña una lección (pág. 158)

Spanish Glossary

Spanish Glossary

feudalism / feudalismo sistema político basado en lazos de lealtad entre señores y vasallos (págs. 497, 523)

fief / feudo bajo el feudalismo, la tierra que un señor otorgaba a un vasallo a cambio de su servicio militar y lealtad (pág. 524)

filial piety / piedad filial el respeto de los niños para sus padres y parientes mayores, una parte importante de las creencias confucianas (pág. 234)

fjord / fiordo valle de paredes abruptas que es una bahía del mar (pág. 518)

Forum / Foro espacio abierto en Roma que servía como mercado y plaza pública (pág. 306)

fossil / fósil huella o impresión de una planta o animal que se ha conservado en piedra (pág. 9)

genocide / genocidio asesinato deliberado de un grupo étnico, político o cultural (pág. 827)

glacier / glaciar masa inmensa de hielo (pág. 573)

gladiator / gladiador en la Roma antigua, persona que peleaba contra animales y otras personas como entretenimiento público (pág. 306)

glasnost / glasnost política establecida por Mikhail Gorbachev en la Unión Soviética, que permitió la discusión abierta de ideas políticas y sociales (pág. 882)

globalism / globalismo noción de que la economía y las políticas de todos los países forman parte de un sistema mundial único (pág. 889)

gospel / evangelio ("buena nueva") uno de los cuatro relatos sobre la vida, enseñanzas y resurrección de Jesucristo (pág. 355)

grand jury / gran jurado grupo que decide si hay suficiente evidencia para acusar a una persona de un delito (pág. 537)

griot / griot narrador en poblados africanos (pág. 449)

guild / gremio grupo medieval de negocios formado por artesanos y mercaderes (págs. 503, 530)

guru / gurú maestro religioso y guía espiritual en el hinduismo (pág. 201)

Hellenistic Era / Era helenista período cuando el idioma y las ideas griegas se esparcieron a los habitantes no griegos del suroeste de Asia (pág. 178)

helot / ilota persona conquistada y esclavizada por los espartanos antiguos (pág. 126)

heresy / herejía creencia que difiere de las enseñanzas aceptadas de una religión o que las contradice (págs. 547, 643)

hierarchy / jerarquía organización con diferentes niveles de autoridad (pág. 355)

hieroglyphics / jeroglíficos sistema de escritura compuesto por miles de símbolos gráficos desarrollados por los antiguos egipcios (pág. 42)

Hinduism / hinduismo sistema religioso que se originó a partir de la religión de los arios en la antigua India (pág. 203)

historian / historiador persona que estudia y escribe acerca del pasado humano (pág. 9)

humanism / humanismo movimiento del renacimiento basado en las ideas y los valores de los antiguos romanos y griegos, de tal manera que los individuos y la sociedad humana eran importantes (pág. 619)

hypothesis / hipótesis explicación que se propone de los hechos (pág. 679)

icon / icono imagen o retrato religioso cristiano (pág. 359)

iconoclast / iconoclasta persona que se oponía al uso de ídolos en las iglesias bizantinas, aludiendo que los iconos alentaban el culto de ídolos (pág. 360)

ideograph / ideógrafo un carácter que une dos o más pictografías para representar una idea (pág. 228)

igloo / iglú casa con forma de domo construida por los inuitas (pág. 590)

imperialism / imperialismo ocurre cuando una nación controla el gobierno o la economía de otras naciones más pequeñas o más débiles (pág. 763)

import / importar comprar de otro país (pág. 666)

incense / incienso material que al quemarse despide un olor agradable (pág. 62)

indulgence / indulgencia perdonar la iglesia los pecados de una persona (pág. 634)

Industrialism / industrialismo sistema económico en el cual las personas dependen más del uso de maquinaria y tecnología, que del uso de fuerza animal o humana (pág. 725)

inflation / inflación período de incremento rápido de precios (págs. 319, 806)

intifada / intifada levantamiento armado de los palestinos contra la ocupación israelí de la Franja de Gaza y la Ribera Occidental (pág. 878)

invest / invertir poner dinero en un proyecto (pág. 667)

irrigation / irrigación método para llevar agua de otro lugar a un campo para regar las cosechas (pág. 18)

kaiser / káiser palabra alemana que significa emperador (pág. 748)

karma / karma en el hinduismo, la energía buena o mala que una persona desarrolla según si vive una vida buena o mala (pág. 204)

knight / caballero en la Edad Media, un guerrero noble que peleaba a caballo (pág. 524)

labor union / sindicato asociación de trabajadores que se unen para mejorar los derechos, los salarios, las prestaciones y las condiciones laborales de los trabajadores (pág. 736)

laity / laicado miembros de iglesia que no constituyen el clero (pág. 355)

latifundia / latifundios grandes propiedades agrícolas en la Roma antigua (pág. 278)

legacy / legado lo que una persona deja cuando muere (pág. 178)

Legalism / legalismo filosofía china desarrollada por Hanfeizi; enseñó que los humanos son naturalmente malos y por lo tanto necesitaban ser gobernados por leyes duras (pág. 239)

legion / legión unidad más pequeña del ejército romano, compuesta por aproximadamente 6,000 soldados (pág. 266)

liberalism / liberalismo corriente política basada en las ideas de la Ilustración, las cuales hacen énfasis en el progreso, la bondad intrínseca del ser humano y las libertades individuales (pág. 735)

limited government / gobierno limitado idea de que un gobierno sólo puede usar los poderes cedidos por los ciudadanos (pág. 700)

mandate / mandato orden formal (págs. 230, 792)

Marshall Plan / Plan Marshall programa patrocinado por los Estados Unidos para proporcionar ayuda a los países europeos después de la Segunda Guerra Mundial, de 1948 a 1951. Fue nombrada así en honor a George Marshall, entonces secretario de estado de los Estados Unidos, y quien la propuso al Congreso (pág. 834)

martial arts / artes marciales deportes, como el judo y el karate, que involucran combate y defensa personal (pág. 499)

martyr / mártir persona dispuesta a morir antes que renunciar a sus creencias (pág. 353)

mass / misa servicio de culto Católico (pág. 546)

matrilineal / matrilineal se refiere a un grupo de personas que busca su ascendencia a través de las madres más que de los padres (pág. 469)

meditation / meditación práctica de reflexión silenciosa para aclarar la mente y encontrar la paz interior (pág. 499)

mercantilism / mercantilismo doctrina según la cual un país obtiene poder al amasar un abastecimiento de oro y plata (pág. 666)

messiah / mesías en el judaísmo, un salvador mandado por Dios (págs. 101, 344)

militarism / militarismo fascinación con la guerra y los asuntos militares (pág. 782)

minaret / minarete torre de una mezquita desde donde el almuecín llama a los creyentes a la oración cinco veces al día (pág. 394)

missionary / misionero persona que viaja para llevar las ideas de una religión a otros (págs. 363, 520)

mobilization / movilización disposición y movimiento de tropas que se preparan para realizar acciones militares (pág. 784)

Spanish Glossary

monastery / monasterio comunidad religiosa donde los monjes viven y trabajan (págs. 362, 413)

monopoly / monopolio el control de todo (o casi todo) el comercio o la producción de ciertos bienes (pág. 576)

monotheism / monoteísmo la creencia en un solo dios (pág. 81)

monsoon / monzón en la Asia del sur, un viento fuerte que sopla en una dirección en el invierno y en la dirección opuesta en el verano (pág. 195)

mosaic / mosaico figura hecha con muchos trozos de vidrios de colores, azulejo o piedra (pág. 333)

mosque / mezquita casa de culto musulmana (pág. 389)

mummy / momia cuerpo que se ha embalsamado y envuelto en lino (pág. 50)

myth / mito cuento tradicional que describe dioses o a héroes o explica eventos naturales (pág. 155)

nationalize / nacionalizar eliminar la propiedad privada de bienes o de capital, para sustituirla por el control del gobierno (pág. 865)

natural law / ley natural ley que se aplica a todos y la cual puede entenderse por razonamiento (pág. 681)

nirvana / nirvana en el budismo, un estado de sabiduría y libertad del ciclo del renacimiento (pág. 205)

nomad / nómada persona que regularmente se mueve de un lugar a otro (pág. 10)

novel / novela historia ficticia larga (pág. 432)

nuclear proliferation / proliferación nuclear aumento del número de armas nucleares (pág. 890)

oasis / oasis área verde en un desierto, alimentada por agua subterránea (pág. 373)

ode / oda poema que expresa emociones fuertes acerca de la vida (pág. 304)

oligarchy / oligarquía gobierno en el que un grupo pequeño de personas mantiene el poder (pág. 126)

oracle / oráculo templo sagrado en donde un sacerdote o sacerdotisa hablaban a nombre de un dios o diosa (pág. 156)

oral history / historia oral historias transmitidas de generación en generación (pág. 470)

Pan-Africanism / Panafricanismo movimiento para unir a los africanos de piel negra de todo el mundo, con el fin de lograr la independencia de las naciones africanas (pág. 852)

papyrus / papiro planta de juncos del Valle de Nilo, empleada para hacer un tipo de papel (pág. 42)

parable / parábola historia que usa acontecimientos de la vida diaria para expresar ideas espirituales (pág. 345)

partnership / sociedad compañía que es propiedad de dos o más personas, quienes acuerdan compartir las ganancias y las pérdidas (pág. 728)

paterfamilias / paterfamilias ("padre de la familia") nombre dado al padre como cabeza de la casa en la Roma antigua (pág. 307)

patrician / patricio hacendado poderoso y miembro de la clase gobernante en la Roma antigua (pág. 269)

Pax Romana / Paz Romana era prolongada de paz y seguridad en el Imperio Romano (pág. 287)

peninsula / península extensión territorial rodeada de agua en tres lados (pág. 117)

perestroika / perestroika plan establecido por Mikhail Gorbachev para reconstruir el gobierno y la economía de la Unión Soviética (pág. 882)

persecute / perseguir maltratar una persona a causa de sus creencias (pág. 353)

pharaoh / faraón rey todopoderoso en el antiguo Egipto (pág. 48)

philosopher / filósofo pensador que busca la sabiduría y formula preguntas acerca de la vida (págs. 140, 169)

philosophy / filosofía estudio de la naturaleza y significando de la vida; viene de la palabra griega que significa "amor a la sabiduría" (pág. 169)

pictograph / pictógrafo carácter que representa a un objeto (pág. 228)

pilgrim / peregrino persona que viaja para ir a un relicario o sitio religioso (pág. 213)

plague / peste enfermedad que se esparce rápidamente y mata a muchas personas (págs. 319, 554)

plane geometry / geometría plana rama de las matemáticas que muestra cómo se relacionan los puntos, las líneas, los ángulos y las superficies (pág. 185)

plateau / meseta área de tierra alta y plana (pág. 446)

plebeian / plebeyo miembro de las personas comunes en la Roma antigua (pág. 269)

polis / polis antigua ciudad-estado griega, compuesta de una ciudad y las áreas circundantes y gobernada como un país independiente (pág. 122)

pope / Papa el obispo de Roma, posteriormente, la cabeza de la iglesia católica romana (pág. 356)

popular sovereignty / soberanía popular idea de que un gobierno recibe su poder de los ciudadanos (pág. 700)

porcelain / porcelana tipo de artículo de cerámica hecho de arcilla fina y horneado a altas temperaturas (pág. 418)

praetor / pretor importante funcionario de gobierno en la Roma antigua (pág. 270)

predestination / predestinación creencia de que sea lo que sea que haga una persona, el resultado de su vida ya ha sido planificado por Dios (pág. 640)

propaganda / propaganda diseminación controlada de información sesgada, para influir en las ideas de las personas sobre algún asunto determinado (pág. 786)

prophet / profeta persona que declara estar instruido por Dios para compartir Sus palabras (pág. 87)

protectorate / protectorado país pequeño que es protegido o que está bajo el dominio de un país más grande (pág. 763)

proverb / proverbio dicho sabio (pág. 89)

province / provincia distrito político (pág. 28)

pyramid / pirámide inmensa estructura de piedra construida por los antiguos egipcios para utilizarse como una tumba (pág. 50)

quipu / quipu lazo con cuerdas anudadas de longitudes y colores diferentes (pág. 588)

Quran / Corán libro sagrado del Islam (pág. 377)

rabbi / rabino líder judío y maestro del Torá (pág. 101)

racial segregation / segregación racial separación o aislamiento de personas en áreas habitacionales, organizaciones e instituciones específicas, según su etnicidad (pág. 840)

raja / rajá príncipe que dirigió a una tribu aria en la India (pág. 199)

rationalism / racionalismo la creencia de que la razón es la fuente principal del conocimiento (pág. 678)

rationing / racionamiento limitación de la cantidad de alimentos y materiales disponibles (pág. 785)

Reconquista ("reconquest") / *reconquista* lucha cristiana para recuperar la península Ibérica de los musulmanes (pág. 558)

reform / reforma cambio que intenta producir una mejora (págs. 320, 411)

Reformation / reforma movimiento para reformar la iglesia católica; condujo a la creación del protestantismo (pág. 634)

refugee / refugiado persona que huye hacia otro país para escapar de desastres o persecución (pág. 870)

regent / regente persona que opera como un gobernante temporal (pág. 334)

reincarnation / reencarnación renacimiento del alma o el espíritu en cuerpos diferentes a través del tiempo (pág. 204)

Renaissance / renacimiento ("nacer de nuevo") período en que se renovó el interés en las artes y el conocimiento en Europa (pág. 609)

reparation / gastos de reparación pagos que el país derrotado en una guerra se compromete a realizar, para resarcir al país victorioso de los daños sufridos; daños colaterales de la guerra (pág. 791)

representative democracy / democracia representativa sistema de gobierno en el que los ciudadanos escogen a un grupo más pequeño para promulgar leyes y tomar decisiones gubernamentales en su nombre (pág. 139)

representative government / gobierno representativo sistema de gobierno en que los ciudadanos eligen a sus líderes para promulgar leyes (pág. 694)

republic / república forma de gobierno en la que el líder no es un rey ni una reina sino una persona elegida por los ciudadanos (pág. 265)

resurrection / resurrección acto de volver a la vida (pág. 347)

rhetoric / retórica hablar en público (pág. 307)

Sabbath / sabbat día semanal de culto y descanso para los judíos (pág. 94)

saint / santo persona cristiana santificada (pág. 333)

salvation / salvación acto de ser salvado del pecado y aceptado para entrar al cielo (pág. 350)

samurai / samurai clase de guerreros en el Japón feudal que prometía lealtad a un noble a cambio de tierra (pág. 494)

Sanskrit / Sánscrito idioma escrito desarrollado por los arios (pág. 199)

satire / sátira obra que hace burla de las debilidades humanas (pág. 304)

satrap / sátrapa funcionario que gobernaba un estado en el Imperio pérsico durante la época de Darío (pág. 133)

satrapies / satrapies los 20 estados en los cuales Darío dividió al Imperio pérsico (pág. 133)

savanna / sabana llanura cubierta de hierba (pág. 69)

schism / cisma separación (pág. 361)

scholasticism / escolástica forma de pensamiento medieval que trató de unir a la razón y a la fe en estudios religiosos (pág. 550)

scientific method / método científico manera organizada de recoger y analizar pruebas (pág. 679)

scribe / escriba conservador de registros (pág. 20)

sect / secta un grupo más pequeño con creencias distintas dentro de un grupo religioso más grande (pág. 499)

secular / secular que se interesa en bienes materiales en lugar de asuntos religiosos (pág. 609)

seminary / seminario escuela en donde se entrenan y se educan a los sacerdotes y los ministros (pág. 643)

separation of powers / separación de poderes división equitativa de los poderes entre las ramas del gobierno (pág. 682)

sepoy / cipayo soldado indio contratado por la Compañía Británica del Oriente de la India (British East India Company) para proteger los intereses de la compañía en la región (pág. 765)

serf / siervo trabajador campesino atado por ley a las tierras de un noble (pág. 524)

sheikh / jeque líder de una tribu árabe (pág. 373)

Shiite / chiíta grupo musulmán que acepta sólo a los descendientes de Ali, el hijo político de Mahoma, como auténticos líderes de los musulmanes (pág. 382)

shogun / shogun gobernante militar del Japón feudal (pág. 495)

shrine / relicario lugar sagrado (pág. 490)

social class / clase social grupo de personas que comparten una posición semejante en la sociedad (pág. 233)

social contract / contrato social acuerdo entre mandatarios y ciudadanos sobre el cual se basa un gobierno (pág. 682)

socialism / socialismo sistema social basado en la propiedad compartida de empresas, fábricas, tierras y materias primas (pág. 735)

Socratic method / método socrático método de enseñanza desarrollado por Sócrates que emplea un formato de pregunta y respuesta para forzar a los estudiantes a utilizar su raciocinio para ver las cosas por sí mismos (pág. 170)

solid geometry / geometría sólida rama de las matemáticas que estudia a las esferas y los cilindros (pág. 186)

Sophist / Sofista maestro profesional en Grecia antigua; creían que las personas deben utilizar el conocimiento para mejorarse a sí mismas y desarrollaron el arte de hablar en público y el debate (pág. 169)

soviet / soviet consejo o comité ruso formado por representantes de los trabajadores, soldados y campesinos (pág. 794)

specialization / especialización desarrollo de diferentes tipos de trabajos (pág. 15)

sphere of influence / esfera de influencia área sobre la cual una potencia extranjera o imperial tiene derechos y privilegios exclusivos (pág. 763)

steppe / estepa ancha planicie ondeada cubierta de hierba (pág. 424)

Stoicism / estoicismo filosofía fundada por Zeno en la Atenas Helenista; enseñaba que la felicidad provenía no de seguir a las emociones, sino a la razón y de cumplir con nuestro deber (pág. 184)

stupa / estupa templo budista con forma de cúpula o montículo (pág. 211)

subcontinent / subcontinente gran masa de tierra que forma parte de un continente pero está separada de él (pág. 195)

sultan / sultán líder político y militar con autoridad absoluta sobre un país musulmán (págs. 383, 467)

Sunni / sunní grupo musulmán que sólo acepta a descendientes de los Omeyas como auténticos gobernantes de los musulmanes (pág. 382)

Swahili / suajili se refiere a la cultura e idioma de Africa del Este (pág. 467)

synagogue / sinagoga casa de culto judía (pág. 94)

tanka / tanka forma más antigua de poesía en Japón; poema sin rima de cinco líneas (pág. 501)

technology / tecnología instrumentos y métodos utilizados para ayudar a los humanos a realizar tareas (pág. 11)

terror / terror acciones violentas para atemorizar personas para que rendirse (pág. 426)

terrorism / terrorismo uso de la violencia contra los ciudadanos para lograr obejtivos políticos (pág. 892)

textile / textil ropa tejida o fabricada (pág. 726)

theocracy / teocracia gobierno dirigido por líderes religiosos (pág. 208)

theology / teología el estudio de la religión y de Dios (págs. 550, 640)

theory / teoría explicación de cómo o por qué ocurre algo (pág. 671)

Torah / Torá las leyes que, según la Biblia, Moisés recibió de Dios en el monte Sinaí; estas leyes se convirtieron después en la primera parte de la Biblia hebrea (pág. 82)

totalitarian state / estado totalitario estado en el que el gobierno trata de controlar por completo la manera en que las personas viven y piensan (pág. 808)

tragedy / tragedia forma de drama en la que una persona se esfuerza para vencer dificultades pero encuentra un final infeliz (pág. 160)

treason / traición deslealtad al gobierno (págs. 431, 599)

trial jury / jurado grupo que decide si una persona acusada es inocente o culpable (pág. 537)

tribe / tribu grupo de familias relacionadas (págs. 81, 424)

tribute / tributo pago realizado por un grupo o nación a otra para mostrar obediencia o para obtener paz o protección (págs. 60, 89)

triumvirate / triunvirato en la Roma antigua, un grupo gobernante de tres personas (pág. 280)

Truman Doctrine / Doctrina Truman política de los Estados Unidos diseñada para ayudar económicamente a Grecia y a Turquía, después de la Segunda Guerra Mundial. Recibió este nombre en honor a su creador, Harry S Truman, entonces presidente de los Estados Unidos (pág. 834)

tyrant / tirano persona que toma el poder por la fuerza y gobierna con autoridad total (pág. 125)

urbanization / urbanización migración de habitantes de áreas rurales hacia la ciudad (pág. 732)

vassal / vasallo en el feudalismo, un noble que ocupaba la tierra de un señor de más alto rango y lo servía, y a cambio le daba protección (págs. 496, 523)

vault / cámara estructura curva de piedra o cemento que forma un techo (pág. 303)

vernacular / vernáculo idioma cotidiano empleado en un país o región (págs. 552, 620)

veto / veta rechazar (pág. 270)

warlord / caudillo líder militar que dirige un gobierno (pág. 409)

weapons of mass destruction / armas de destrucción masiva armas químicas, biológicas o nucleares que pueden matar a gran cantidad de gente o causar grave destrucción (pág. 894)

Zoroastrianism / zoroastrismo religión persa fundada por Zoroastro; enseñaba que los humanos tenían la libertad de escoger entre lo correcto y lo incorrecto, y que la bondad triunfaría al final (pág. 133)

Gazetteer

A Gazetteer (GA•zuh•TIHR) is a geographic index or dictionary. It shows latitude and longitude for cities and certain other places. Latitude and longitude are shown in this way: 48°N 2°E, or 48 degrees north latitude and two degrees east longitude. This Gazetteer lists most of the world's largest independent countries, their capitals, and several important geographic features. The page numbers tell where each entry can be found on a map in this book. As an aid to pronunciation, most entries are spelled phonetically.

A

Aachen [AH•kuhn] City in Germany near the Belgian and Dutch borders; capital of Charlemagne's Frankish empire. 50°N 6°E (pp. 512, 516)

Actium [AK•shee•uhm] Cape on the western coast of Greece. 37°N 23°E (p. 297)

Aden [ay•dehn] Port city of the Red Sea in southern Yemen. 12°N 45°E (p. 433)

Aden, Gulf of Western arm of the Arabian Sea, between Yemen, Somalia, and Djibouti. 11°N 45°E (p. 445)

Adrianople [AY•dree•uh•NOH•puhl] Ancient city in northwestern Turkey, now called Edirne. 41°N 26°E (p. 323)

Adriatic [AY•dree•A•tihk] **Sea** Arm of Mediterranean Sea between Italy and the Balkan Peninsula. 44°N 14°E (pp. 144, 263, 269, 274, 293, 516, 548, 609, 653, 688, 725, 747, 786, 832, 897)

Aegean [ih•JEE•uhn] **Sea** Gulf of the Mediterranean Sea between Greece and Asia Minor, north of Crete. 39°N 24°E (pp. 117, 134, 144, 149, 176, 548)

Afghanistan [af•GA•nuh•STAN] Central Asian country west of Pakistan. 33°N 63°E (pp. R3, R19, 176, 198, 765, 773, 845)

Africa [AF•rih•kah] Second-largest continent, south of Europe between the Atlantic and Indian Oceans. 10°N 22°E (pp. R2, R3, R4, R5, R20, R21, 33, 109, 262, 263, 269, 274, 293, 297, 352, 358, 361, 367, 380, 385, 433, 444, 446, 449, 460, 463, 468, 469, 473, 479, 518, 554, 565, 573, 658, 662, 668, 707, 709, 762, 767, 842, 870, 893)

Agincourt [A•juhn•KOHRT] Village in northern France. 52°N 6°E (pp. 557, 561)

Agra [AH•gruh] City in India, site of the Taj Mahal. 27°N 78°E (pp. 394, 845)

Ahaggar [uh•HAH•guhr] **Mountains** Arid, rocky, upland region in southern Algeria in the center of the Sahara. 25°N 6°E (p. 445)

Albania [al•BAY•nee•uh] Country on the Adriatic Sea, south of Yugoslavia. 42°N 20°E (pp. R3, 781, 786, 790, 832, 897)

Albany Capital city of New York. 42°N 73°W (p. 694)

Aleppo [uh•LEH•poh] City of northwest Syria near the Turkish border. 36°N 37°E (p. 799)

Alexandria [A•lihg•ZAN•dree•uh] City and major seaport in northern Egypt in the Nile River delta. 31°N 29°E (pp. 176, 179, 182, 189, 246, 293, 323, 329, 352, 361, 367, 374)

Algeria [al•JIHR•ee•uh] Country in North Africa. 29°N 1°E (pp. R2, R3, 767, 790, 870)

Algiers [al•JIHRZ] Capital city of Algeria, largest Mediterranean port of northwestern Africa. 36°N 2°E (pp. R3, 385, 767)

Alps [ALPS] Mountain system of south central Europe. 46°N 9°E (pp. 263, 269, 274, 513, 514, 609, 653)

Alsace [al•SAS] Region of France. 48°N 7°E (pp. 747, 781)

Altay Mountains Mountain range in Asia. 49°N 87°E (pp. R5, 225)

Altun Mountains Range of mountains that are a part of the Kunlun Shan in China. 35°N 83°E (p. 225)

Amazon [A•muh•ZAHN] **River** River in northern South America, second-longest river in the world. 2°S 53°W (pp. R2, R4, 473, 565, 577)

Amman [a•MAHN] Capital of Jordan. 32°N 36°E (pp. 792, 875)

Amsterdam [AHM•stuhr•dahm] Capital of the Netherlands. 52°N 4°E (pp. 548, 725)

Amur River River of northeast Asia flowing along the border between China and Russia. 52°N 141°E (pp. 773, 825)

Andes [AN•deez] Mountain range along the western edge of South America. 13°S 75°W (pp. R4, R15, 577)

Angola [ang•GOH•luh] Southern African country north of Namibia. 14°S 16°E (pp. R3, 767, 870)

Ankara [AHNG•kuh•ruh] Capital of Turkey. 40°N 33°E (p. 792)

Antioch [AN•tee•AHK] Ancient capital of Syria, now a city in southern Turkey. 36°N 36°E (pp. 246, 352, 361, 367, 542)

Antwerp [ANT•WUHRP] City in northern Belgium. 51°N 4°E (pp. 548, 787)

Anyang [AHN•YAHNG] City in northern China, was China's first capital. 36°N 114°E (pp. 224, 226, 251)

Apennines [A•puh•NYNZ] Mountain range that runs through Italy. 43°N 11°E (pp. 263, 269, 609, 653)

Appalachian Mountains Mountain system of eastern North America. 38°N 82°W (pp. R4, R11, 590, 694)

Aqaba [AH•kuh•buh] Port city in Jordan. 29°N 35°E (pp. 799, 875)

Arabia [uh•RAY•bee•uh] Desert peninsula of southwestern Asia across the Red Sea to Africa. 27°N 32°E (pp. R18, R19, 17, 70, 109, 246, 329, 380, 385, 425, 433, 554, 799)

Arabian [uh•RAY•bee•uhn] **Desert** Arid region in eastern Egypt; also called the Eastern Desert. 22°N 45°E (pp. R18, R19, 17, 28, 39, 75)

Arabian [uh•RAY•bee•uhn] **Peninsula** Great desert peninsula in extreme southwestern Asia. 28°N 40°E (pp. R5, R18, R19, 374, 445, 448, 452)

Arabian [uh•RAY•bee•uhn] **Sea** Portion of the Indian Ocean between the Arabian Peninsula and India. 16°N 65°E (pp. R3, R5, R19, 109, 176, 193, 195, 198, 210, 213, 219, 246, 374, 380, 409, 425, 433, 452, 554, 565, 765, 845)

Aragon Region and former kingdom in northeastern Spain. 42°N 1°W (p. 538)

Aral [AR•uhl] **Sea** Large inland sea in central Asia. 45°N 60°E (pp. R3, R5, 132, 198, 246, 380, 383, 397, 424, 425, 554)

Arctic Ocean Smallest of the four oceans. 85°N 170°E (pp. R2, R3, 573, 590)

Argentina [AHR•juhn•TEE•nuh] South American country east of Chile. 36°S 67°W (pp. R2, R14, 749, 860, 861)

Argonne [AHR•gawn] Wooded region of France. 49°N 5°E (pp. 786, 787)

Arkansas River River in the western United States. 38°N 100°W (pp. R11, 663)

Armenia [ahr•MEE•nee•uh] Southeastern European country between the Black and Caspian seas. 40°N 45°E (p. 883)

Asia Largest of the seven continents. 50°N 100°E (pp. R22, R23, 13, 17, 33, 409, 424, 439, 518, 565, 573, 662, 707, 709, 804, 813, 824, 831, 883, 893)

Asia Minor Region of the ancient world, roughly corresponding to present-day Turkey. 38°N 31°E (pp. R22, 17, 28, 117, 121, 132, 176, 179, 189, 269, 274, 277, 292, 293, 297, 323, 327, 329, 342, 352, 358, 361, 367, 374, 380, 385, 542)

Assyria [uh•SIHR•ee•uh] Ancient country in Asia that included the Tigris River valley in Mesopotamia. 35°N 42°E (p. 28)

Athens [A•thuhnz] Capital of Greece. 38°N 23°E (pp. 117, 121, 124, 125, 134, 138, 144, 149, 154, 176, 182, 293)

Atlantic Ocean Second-largest body of water in the world. 5°S 25°W (pp. R2–9, R11, R13–16, R20–22, 13, 121, 293, 329, 352, 361, 463, 473, 513, 516, 538, 555, 561, 573, 590, 645, 663, 691, 725, 769, 790, 832, 893)

Atlas [AT•luhs] **Mountains** Mountain range in northwestern Africa on the northern edge of the Sahara. 31°N 5°W (pp. R20, R21, 445)

Austerlitz Town in the southeast Czech Republic. 49°N 16°E (p. 722)

Australia [aw•STRAYL•yuh] Island continent southeast of Asia. 25°S 135°W (pp. R3, R5, 13, 33, 662, 707, 762, 825, 893)

Austria [AWS•tree•uh] Country in central Europe. 47°N 12°E (pp. R3, R16, 385, 548, 639, 688, 722, 747, 790, 814, 832, 891)

Austria-Hungary [AWS•tree•uh HUHNG•guh•ree] Nation in central Europe from 1867 to 1918 that included what are now Austria, Hungary, Slovakia, and the Czech Republic, as well as parts of present-day Poland, Romania, Italy, Slovenia, Croatia, Bosnia and Herzegovina, and Serbia and Montenegro. 20°E 47°N (pp. 780, 781, 786)

Axum [AHK•soom] Ancient kingdom in northeastern Africa. 14°N 38°E (p. 451)

Azerbaijan [A•zuhr•by•JAHN] European-Asian country on the Caspian Sea. 40°N 47°E (p. 883)

Azores [AY•zohrz] Group of nine islands in the North Atlantic Ocean. 37°N 29°W (pp. R2, R4, R20, R21)

Babylon [BA•buh•luhn] Ancient city, on the banks of the Euphrates River in northern Mesopotamia. 32°N 45°E (pp. 16, 17, 26, 28, 86, 93, 132, 174, 176)

Baghdad [BAG•DAD] Capital city of Iraq. 33°N 44°E (pp. R3, 374, 379, 380, 383, 385, 397, 423, 425, 452, 554, 792, 799)

Bahamas [buh•HAH•muhz] Country made up of many islands between Cuba and the United States. 23°N 74°W (pp. R2, R4, R13, 662)

Balkan [BAWL•kuhn] **Peninsula** Peninsula in southeastern Europe bounded by the Black, Aegean, Mediterranean, Adriatic and Ionian seas. 42°N 20°E (pp. 117, 327, 329)

Balkans [BAWL•kuhnz] Countries on the Balkan Peninsula, which include Slovenia, Croatia, Bosnia and Herzegovina, the Former Yugoslav Republic of Macedonia, Serbia and Montenegro, Albania, Greece, Romania, Bulgaria, and European Turkey. 23°E 44°N (pp. 781, 786)

Baltic [BAWL•tihk] **Sea** Sea in northern Europe connected to the North Sea. 55°N 17°E (pp. R3, R5, R16, R17, 513, 518, 538, 548, 555, 645, 688, 703, 722, 725, 781, 786, 790, 814, 832, 883)

Baltimore [BAWL•tuh•MOHR] City in northern Maryland in the United States. 39°N 77°W (p. 694)

Bangkok [BANG•KAHK] Capital of Thailand. 14°N 100°E (pp. R3, 433, 825, 849)

Bangladesh [BAHNG•gluh•DEHSH] South Asian country bounded by Myanmar and India. 24°N 90°E (pp. R3, 198, 845)

Barcelona [BAHR•suh•LOH•nuh] City in northeastern Spain. 41°N 2°E (p. 555)

Basutoland [buh•SOO•toh•luhnd] Country in southern Africa, now called Lesotho. 29°S 28°E (p. 767)

Bay of Bengal [BEHN•gawl] Arm of the Indian Ocean between India and the Malay Peninsula. 17°N 87°E (pp. R3, R5, R22, R23, 109, 193, 195, 210, 213, 246, 409, 411, 425, 433, 439, 565, 667, 765, 845)

Bay of Pigs Small inlet of the Caribbean Sea on the southern coast of western Cuba. 22°N 81°W (p. 836)

Bechuanaland [behch•WAH•nuh•luhnd] Region in south central Africa, now the nation of Botswana. 22°S 23°E (p. 767)

Beijing [BAY•JIHNG] Capital of China. 40°N 116°E (pp. R3, 409, 411, 423, 424, 425, 430, 431, 439, 554, 771, 773, 778, 811, 825)

Beirut [bay•ROOT] Capital of Lebanon. 34°N 36°E (pp. 792, 799, 875)

Belarus [BEH•luh•ROOS] Eastern European country west of Russia. 54°N 28°E (p. 883)

Belfast [BEHL•fast] Capital of Northern Ireland. 54°N 5°W (p. 757)

Belgium [BEHL•juhm] Country in northwestern Europe. 51°N 5°E (pp. R3, R16, 703, 725, 747, 781, 787, 790, 814, 832, 891)

Belgrade [BEHL•GRAYD] Capital of Yugoslavia. 45°N 21°E (pp. 548, 555, 688, 897)

Belize [buh•LEEZ] Central American country east of Guatemala. 18°N 89°W (pp. R2, R13, 583, 749, 861)

Benin [buh•NEEN] West African country west of Nigeria. 8°N 2°E (p. 870)

Bering Sea Part of the North Pacific Ocean between the Aleutian Islands and the Bering Strait. 55°N 175°E (pp. R2, R3, R4, R5, R23, 573, 825)

Berlin [behr•LIHN] Capital of Germany. 53°N 13°E (pp. 722, 725, 744, 747, 780, 781, 786, 789, 831, 834, 855)

Bhutan [boo•TAHN] South Asian country northeast of India. 27°N 91°E (pp. R3, R22, R23, 198, 765, 845)

Birmingham City in central England. 52°N 1°W (pp. 725, 757)

Black Sea Inland sea between southeastern Europe and Asia Minor. 43°N 32°E (pp. R3, R5, R17, R18, 109, 121, 132, 144, 176, 179, 189, 246, 255, 269, 274, 292, 293, 297, 323, 329, 352, 361, 367, 374, 380, 383, 385, 397, 425, 513, 518, 538, 542, 554, 565, 639, 722, 725, 781, 786, 790, 792, 832, 883)

Bohemia [boh•HEE•mee•uh] Historical region and former kingdom in what is now the Czech Republic. 49°N 13°E (pp. 639, 645, 688)

Bolivia [buh•LIHV•ee•uh] Country in South America. 17°S 64°W (pp. 749, 861)

Bombay City in western India, now called Mumbai. 18°N 72°E (pp. 667, 845)

Bordeaux [bawr•DOH] City in southwestern France. 44°N 0°W (pp. 557, 561, 725)

Borneo [BAWR•nee•oh] Island in the Malay Archipelago in southeastern Asia. 0°N 112°E (pp. R3, 246, 425, 433, 554, 667, 765, 825)

Bosnia-Herzegovina [BAHZ•nee•uh HEHRT•seh•GAW•vee•nuh] Country in southeastern Europe between Croatia and Serbia-Montenegro. 44°N 18°E (p. 897)

Boston [bahs•tuhn] Capital of Massachusetts. 42°N 71°W (pp. 691, 694, 695)

Botswana [bawt•SWAH•nah] Southern African country north of the Republic of South Africa. 22°S 23°E (p. 870)

Brazil [bruh•ZIHL] Largest country in South America. 9°S 53°W (pp. R2, 473, 749, 860, 861)

Breslau [BREHS•low] City in southwest Poland. 51°N 17°E (pp. 725, 747)

Bristol [BRIHS•tuhl] City in southwest England. 51°N 2°W (p. 725)

Britain Largest island in the British Isles. 54°N 4°W (pp. R2–3, R4–5, R16, 286, 293, 297, 302, 317, 323, 352, 358, 361, 695, 757, 780)

British East Africa Former group of British colonial possessions in East Africa, consisting of Kenya, Uganda, Zanzibar, and Tanganyika. 3°S 35°E (p. 767)

Bruges [BROOZH] City in northwestern Belgium. 51°N 3°E (p. 522)

Brunei [bru•NY] Southwest Asian country on the northern coast of the island of Borneo. 5°N 114°E (p. 765)

Brussels [BRUH•suhlz] Capital of Belgium. 51°N 4°E (pp. 722, 725, 747)

Gazetteer

Buda [BOO•duh] Town in Hungary that combined with Pest and Óbuda to form Budapest. 47°N 19°E (p. 688)

Budapest [BOO•duh•PEHST] Capital of Hungary. 47°N 19°E (pp. 703, 725, 781, 786)

Bulgaria [BUHL•GAR•ee•uh] Country in southeastern Europe on the Balkan Peninsula. 42°N 24°E (pp. R3, R17, 176, 781, 786, 790, 799, 832, 897)

Burkina Faso [buhr•KEE•nuh FAH•soh] West African country. 12°N 3°E (p. 870)

Burma [BUHR•muh] Country in southeast Asia, now known as Myanmar. 16°N 96°E (pp. 765, 773, 825, 845, 847)

Burundi [bu•ROON•dee] Country in East Africa. 3°S 30°E (p. 870)

Byblos [BIH•bluhs] Ancient city of Phoenicia on the Mediterranean Sea, near present-day Beirut, Lebanon. 34°N 35°E (pp. 17, 90, 105, 132)

Byzantine [BIH•zuhn•TEEN] **Empire** Eastern part of the Roman Empire that survived after the breakup of the western part of the empire in the A.D. 400s; Constantinople was its capital. 41°N 29°E (pp. 383, 518, 538, 542)

Byzantium [buh•ZAN•tee•uhm] Ancient city that became the capital of the Eastern Roman Empire; was later renamed Constantinople and is now called Istanbul. 41°N 29°E (p. 293)

C

Cahokia [kuh•HOH•kee•uh] City in southwestern Illinois on the Mississippi River near St. Louis; largest city of the Mississippian Mound Builders. 38°N 90°W (p. 572)

Cairo [KY•roh] Capital of Egypt. 31°N 32°E (pp. R3, 380, 385, 452, 479, 767, 792, 875)

Calcutta [kal•KUHT•uh] City in eastern India, now known as Kolkata. 22°N 88°E (pp. R3, 845)

Calicut [KAL•ih•KUHT] Seaport in southwestern India, now called Kozhikode. 11°N 75°E (pp. 433, 662, 667)

California State in the western United States. 36°N 120°W (pp. R6, R8)

Cambodia [kam•BOH•dee•uh] Southeast Asian country south of Thailand and Laos. 12°N 104°E (p. 849)

Cameroon [ka•muh•ROON] Central African country. 6°N 11°E (p. 870)

Campania [kam•PAY•nyuh] Region in southern Italy on the Tyrrhenian Sea. 41°N 14°E (p. 263)

Canada [KA•nuh•duh] Country in North America north of the United States. 50°N 100°W (pp. R2, R6, R7)

Cannae [KA•nee] Ancient town in southern Italy. 41°N 16°E (p. 274)

Canterbury [KAN•tuhr•BEHR•ee] City in Kent in southeastern England. 51°N 1°E (p. 645)

Cape Town Legislative capital of the Republic of South Africa. 34°S 18°E (p. 767)

Caporetto Village in northwestern Slovenia. 46°N 13°E (p. 786)

Caribbean [KAR•uh•BEE•uhn] **Sea** Part of the Atlantic Ocean bordered by the West Indies, South America, and Central America. 15°N 76°W (pp. R2, R4, 473, 565, 590, 662, 663, 691, 836, 861)

Carpathian [kahr•PAY•thee•uhn] **Mountains** Mountain system in central and Eastern Europe. 49°N 20°E (p. 513)

Carthage [KAHR•thihj] Ancient city on the northern coast of Africa. 37°N 10°E (pp. 263, 268, 269, 274, 292, 293, 297, 329, 337, 367, 514)

Caspian [KAS•pee•uhn] **Sea** Saltwater lake in southeastern Europe and southwestern Asia, the largest inland body of water in the world. 40°N 52°E (pp. R3, R5, R17, 17, 109, 132, 176, 179, 198, 246, 255, 293, 297, 329, 361, 374, 380, 383, 385, 397, 424, 425, 513, 518, 542, 554, 565, 709, 786, 790, 792, 799, 883)

Castile [kas•TEEL] Former kingdom in Spain. 39°N 3°E (p. 538)

Çatal Hüyük [chah•TAHL hoo•YOOK] Early Neolithic community in present-day Turkey. 38°N 35°E (p. 8)

Caucasus [KAW•kuh•suhs] **Mountains** Range of mountains between the Caspian and Black seas. 43°N 42°E (pp. R17, 374)

Central African Republic African country south of Chad. 8°N 21°E (p. 870)

Central America Area of North America between Mexico and South America. 11°N 86°W (pp. 749, 861)

Ceylon [sih•LAHN] Country in the Indian Ocean, now called Sri Lanka. 8°N 82°E (pp. R22, 433, 667, 765, 845)

Chaco Canyon [CHAH•koh] Center of Anasazi civilization in present-day New Mexico. 36°N 108°W (p. 578)

Chad African country west of Sudan. 18°N 19°E (p. 870)

Chaeronea [KEHR•uh•NEE•uh] Ancient town in Greece near Thebes. 38°N 22°E (p. 176)

Changan [CHAHNG•AHN] Capital of China during the Tang dynasty, now called Xian. 34°N 108°E (pp. 240, 241, 246, 408, 409, 411, 416, 439)

Chang Jiang [CHAHNG JYAHNG] River in China, formerly called the Yangtze River. 30°N 117°E (pp. 225, 226, 230, 241, 246, 409, 411, 424, 425, 431, 439, 811)

Charles Town City in southeastern South Carolina, now called Charleston. 33°N 80°W (pp. 694, 695)

Chernigov [chehr•NEE•guhf] Principality in the Kievan Rus. 51°N 31°E (p. 548)

Chichén Itzá [chee•CHEHN eet•SAH] Most important city of the Mayans, located in the northern part of the Yucatán Peninsula. 20°N 88°W (p. 575)

Chile [CHEE•lay] Country in South America. 35°S 72°W (pp. 749, 861)

China [CHY•nuh] Country in East Asia, world's largest by population; now called the People's Republic of China. 37°N 93°E (pp. R3, R5, R22–23, 109, 198, 225, 226, 230, 241, 246, 409, 411, 416, 424, 425, 431, 433, 439, 554, 658, 662, 667, 762, 765, 773, 778, 811, 825, 838, 845, 847, 849)

Chittagong [CHIH•tuh•GAHNG] Port city in Bangladesh. 22°N 90°E (pp. 433, 554)

Chongqing [chung•CHING] City in south-central China on the Chang Jiang. 29°N 106°E (pp. 811, 825)

Clermont City in central France. 45°N 3°E (pp. 534, 542, 544)

Cologne [kuh•LOHN] City in west central Germany on the Rhine River. 50°N 6°E (pp. 542, 725, 747)

Colombia [kuh•LUHM•bee•uh] Country in South America west of Venezuela. 4°N 73°W (pp. 749, 861)

Congo [KAHNG•goh] Central African country. 3°S 14°E (p. 870)

Congo [KAHNG•goh] **River** River in Central Africa. 2°S 17°E (p. 469)

Connecticut A state in the northeastern United States. 41°N 73°W (p. 694)

Constantinople [KAHN•STAN•tuhn•OH•puhl] City built on the site of Byzantium, now known as Istanbul in present-day Turkey. 41°N 29°E (pp. 246, 302, 317, 323, 327, 329, 337, 351, 352, 358, 361, 367, 374, 379, 380, 425, 518, 542, 555, 725, 781, 786, 792)

Copan [koh•PAHN] Ancient city of the Mayan people, in northwestern Honduras. 14°N 89°W (p. 575)

Coral Sea Arm of the southwest Pacific Ocean bounded by Australia, Papua New Guinea, the Solomon Islands, and Vanuatu. 20°S 155°E (p. 825)

Cordoba [KAWR•duh•buh] City in southern Spain. 37°N 4°W (pp. 379, 380, 555)

Corinth City of ancient Greece, southwest of the modern city of Corinth. 37°N 22°E (pp. 117, 144, 269, 274)

Corsica [KOHR•sih•kuh] Island in the Mediterranean Sea. 42°N 8°E (pp. R5, R16, 121, 263, 269, 274, 293, 329, 337, 538, 555, 609, 653, 722, 832)

Costa Rica [KAWS•tah REE•kah] Central American country south of Nicaragua. 11°N 85°W (pp. R2, 749, 861)

Crécy [kray•SEE] Site in France of battle in which England defeated France in 1346. 50°N 48°E (pp. 557, 561)

Crete [KREET] Greek island southeast of mainland in the southern Aegean Sea. 35°N 24°E (pp. R17, 116, 117, 121, 132, 134, 149, 179, 189, 269, 274, 293, 329, 337, 385, 542, 548, 555, 799, 832)

Crimea [kry•MEE•uh] Peninsula in southeastern Ukraine. 45°N 33°E (p. 548)

Croatia [kroh•AY•shuh] Southeastern European country on the Adriatic Sea. 46°N 16°E (p. 897)

Cuba [KYOO•buh] Island country in the West Indies. 22°N 79°W (pp. R2, R4, 662, 749, 836, 860, 861)

Cuzco [KOOS•koh] City in southern Peru. 13°S 71°W (pp. 572, 577, 582, 593, 603)

Cyprus [SY•pruhs] Island country in the eastern Mediterranean Sea, south of Turkey. 35°N 31°E (pp. R3, R5, R17, 62, 90, 121, 132, 179, 189, 269, 274, 293, 329, 385, 542, 781, 792, 799, 832, 891)

Czechoslovakia [CHEHK•oh•sloh•VAH•kee•ah] Former country of central Europe; now called Czech Republic and Slovakia. 49°N 18°E (pp. 790, 814, 832, 891)

Damascus [duh•MAS•kuhs] Capital of Syria. 34°N 36°E (pp. 90, 105, 246, 352, 361, 374, 380, 383, 385, 397, 792, 799, 875)

Danube [DAN•yoob] **River** Second-longest river in Europe. 43°N 24°E (pp. R5, 176, 269, 274, 293, 297, 323, 329, 337, 383, 385, 397, 425, 513, 514, 516, 538, 555, 725)

Danzig City in northern Poland. 54°N 18°E (pp. 555, 814)

Dardanelles [dahr•dehn•EHLZ] Strait between the Aegean Sea and the Sea of Marmara that separates European Turkey from Asian Turkey. 40°N 26°E (p. 799)

Dead Sea Salt lake in southwestern Asia. 31°N 35°E (pp. R5, 17, 39, 75, 90, 105, 875)

Deccan [DEHK•uhn] **Plateau** Region in India. 19°N 76°E (pp. R5, 195, 198)

Delhi [DEH•lee] City in northern India. 28°N 76°E (pp. R3, 379)

Delos [DEE•LAHS] Greek island in the southern Aegean Sea. 37°N 25°E (pp. 138, 144)

Delphi [DEHL•FY] Ancient Greek town and site of Temple of Apollo. 38°N 22°E (p. 117)

Denmark [DEHN•MAHRK] Scandinavian country in northwestern Europe. 56°N 8°E (pp. R3, 639, 645, 688, 722, 725, 781, 786, 790, 814, 832, 834, 891)

Djibouti [jih•BOO•tee] East African country. 12°N 43°E (p. 870)

Dominican [duh•MIH•nih•kuhn] **Republic** Country in the West Indies. 19°N 71°W (pp. 749, 836, 861)

Dresden [DREHZ•duhn] A city of east-central Germany on the Elbe River. 51°N 13°E (p. 747)

Dublin [DUH•blihn] Capital of Ireland. 53°N 6°W (p. 757)

Dutch East Indies Islands of Southeast Asia now known as Indonesia. 40°S 118°E (p. 765)

East Africa Region in east Central Africa comprised of Burundi, Kenya, Rwanda, Somalia, Tanzania, and Uganda. 5°N 35°E (pp. R3, R5, R20, R21, 246)

East China Sea Arm of the Pacific Ocean between China and the Ryukyu Islands. 30°N 125°E (pp. R5, 225, 226, 230, 241, 251, 409, 411, 425, 439, 765, 773, 778, 811)

Eastern Desert Arid region in eastern Egypt, also called the Arabian Desert. 22°N 45°E (pp. 39, 75)

East Germany Officially called the German Democratic Republic. 53°N 13°E (pp. 832, 834)

East Prussia [PRUH•shuh] Historical region and former province of Prussia on the Baltic Sea in present-day Poland and Russia. 54°N 20°E (p. 814)

East Sea Arm of the Pacific Ocean, lying between Japan and the Asian mainland; also called the Sea of Japan. 40°N 132°E (pp. R5, 225, 485, 778)

Ebro River River in northeastern Spain, emptying into the Mediterranean Sea. 42°N 2°W (pp. 516, 725)

Ecuador [EH•kwuh•DAWR] South American country southwest of Colombia. 1°S 79°W (pp. 749, 861)

Edinburgh Capital city of Scotland. 55°N 3°W (pp. 555, 725)

Edo [EH•doh] Village in Japan where the Sumida River joins Tokyo Bay, site of present-day Tokyo. 35°N 140°E (pp. 485, 507, 771, 773, 778)

Egypt [EE•jihpt] Country in North Africa on the Mediterranean Sea. 26°N 27°E (pp. R3, 17, 28, 39, 62, 70, 75, 121, 132, 176, 246, 286, 293, 297, 302, 317, 327, 329, 352, 361, 367, 374, 380, 383, 385, 397, 448, 452, 479, 767, 792, 799, 870, 875)

Elba [EHL•buh] An island of Italy in the Tyrrhenian Sea. 42°N 10°E (p. 722)

El Salvador [ehl SAL•vuh•DAWR] Central American country southwest of Honduras. 14°N 89°W (pp. 749, 861)

England Part of the island of Great Britain lying east of Wales and south of Scotland. 51°N 1°W (pp. R2–3, R4–5, R16, 518, 522, 534, 538, 542, 544, 639, 645, 662, 757)

English Channel Narrow sea separating France and Great Britain. 49°N 3°W (pp. 557, 787)

Equator An imaginary circle that divides the earth into the Northern Hemisphere and the Southern Hemisphere. (pp. R2, R3, R4, R5, 33, 425, 433, 445, 452, 463, 469, 479, 554, 565, 577, 667, 707, 749, 765, 767, 769)

Equitorial Guinea [ee•kwuh•TOHR•ee•uhl GIH•nee] Central African country. 2°N 8°E (p. 870)

Eridu [EHR•ih•DOO] Ancient settlement in Mesopotamia. 31°N 46°E (p. 17)

Eritrea [EHR•uh•TREE•uh] East African country north of Ethiopia. (pp. 767, 870)

Estonia [eh•STOH•nee•uh] Republic in northeastern Europe, one of the Baltic states. 59°N 25°E (pp. 548, 790, 814, 883, 891)

Ethiopia [EE•thee•OH•pee•uh] East African country. 8°N 38°E (pp. 452, 479, 767, 870)

Etruria [ih•TRUR•ee•uh] Ancient region on the Italian peninsula that was home to the Etruscans; area is now called Tuscany. 30°N 46°E (p. 263)

Euphrates [yu•FRAY•TEEZ] **River** River in southwestern Asia that joins the Tigris River near the Persian Gulf. 36°N 40°E (pp. 17, 109, 121, 132, 176, 179, 189, 246, 255, 293, 297, 329, 374, 380, 383, 397)

Europe One of the world's seven continents, sharing a landmass with Asia. 50°N 15°E (pp. R3, R5, R16–17, 13, 28, 33, 109, 255, 473, 565, 573, 658, 662, 668, 695, 707, 724, 744, 762, 780, 781, 786, 790, 804, 813, 814, 824, 831, 832, 891, 893)

Federal Republic of Germany Formerly West Germany. 51°N 8°E (pp. 832, 834)

Gazetteer

Fertile Crescent Region in the Middle East that reaches from Israel to the Persian Gulf, including the Tigris and Euphrates Rivers. 34°N 45°E (p. 17)

Finland [FIHN•luhnd] Northern European country east of Sweden. 63°N 26°E (pp. 790, 814, 832, 891)

Florence [FLOHR•uhnz] City in the Tuscany region of central Italy at the foot of the Apennines. 43°N 11°E (pp. 555, 608, 609, 639, 653, 670, 725, 747)

Florida State in the southeastern United States. 30°N 84°W (pp. 691, 836)

Formigny [FAWR•mee•NYUH] Site in northern France of a French victory during the Hundred Years' War. 49°N 0°W (pp. 557, 561)

Formosa [fawr•MOH•suh] An island in southeastern Asia off the coast of China, now known as Taiwan. 24°N 122°E (pp. 765, 811)

France [FRANS] Third-largest country in Europe, located south of Great Britain. 47°N 1°E (pp. R2–3, R4–5, R16, 380, 385, 518, 522, 534, 538, 542, 544, 548, 639, 645, 662, 722, 725, 747, 780, 781, 786, 787, 789, 790, 814, 832, 834, 891)

Frankfurt Port city in west central Germany on the Main River. 50°N 8°E (pp. 555, 688, 703, 747, 834)

French Equatorial Africa Former French colonial possession in western and central Africa, encompassing the present-day republics of Chad, the Central African Republic, the Republic of the Congo, and Gabon. 0°N 20°E (p. 767)

French Guiana [gee•A•nuh] French-owned territory in northern South America. 5°N 53°W (pp. 749, 861)

French Indochina [IHN•doh•CHY•nuh] Peninsula between India and China comprised of Cambodia, Laos, and Vietnam. 16°N 107°E (pp. 765, 773, 811, 825)

French West Africa Former French colonial unit comprised of the following eight modern countries: Senegal, Guinea, Côte d'Ivoire, Benin, Mauritania, Mali, Burkina Faso, and Niger. (p. 767)

Gabon [ga•BOHN] Central African country. 0° 12°E (p. 870)

Galilee [GA•luh•LEE] Region of ancient Palestine, now part of northern Israel, between the Jordan River and the Sea of Galilee. 32°N 35°E (pp. 352, 361, 367)

Gallipoli [guh•lih•PUH•lee] City and narrow peninsula of northwest Turkey. 40°N 26°E (pp. 786, 799)

Gambia [GAM•bee•uh] West African country along the Gambia River. 13°N 16°W (pp. 767, 870)

Ganges [GAN•JEEZ] **Plain** Flat, fertile area around the Ganges River. 24°N 89°E (pp. 195, 198)

Ganges [GAN•JEEZ] **River** River in India that flows from the Himalaya to the Bay of Bengal. 24°N 89°E (pp. R3, R5, R22, 193, 195, 198, 210, 213, 219, 246, 409, 424, 667)

Gaugamela [GAW•guh•MEE•luh] Area near Babylon and the Tigris River. 36°N 44°E (pp. 174, 176)

Gaul [GAWL] Ancient Roman name for the area now known as France. 45°N 3°E (pp. 274, 277, 286, 293, 297, 302, 317, 323, 352, 358, 361)

Gaza [GAH•zuh] **Strip** Coastal area along the Mediterranean Sea bordering Israel and Egypt. 31°N 34°E (p. 875)

Geneva [juh•NEE•vuh] City in western Switzerland. 46°N 6°E (p. 633)

Genoa [geh•NOH•uh] City in northwestern Italy. 44°N 9°E (pp. 542, 548, 555, 608, 609, 639, 653, 725, 747)

Georgia [JAWR•juh] Asian-European country bordering the Black Sea south of Russia. 42°N 43°E (p. 883)

German Democratic Republic Formerly East Germany. 53°N 13°E (pp. 832, 834)

Germany [JUHR•muh•nee] Western European country south of Denmark. 51°N 10°E (pp. R3, 518, 725, 747, 780, 781, 786, 787, 789, 790, 814, 834, 891)

Ghana [GAH•nuh] Country in West Africa on the Gulf of Guinea. 8°N 2°W (pp. R2, 448, 451, 870)

Giza [GEE•zuh] City in northern Egypt and site of the Great Pyramid. 29°N 31°E (pp. 17, 39, 47, 62, 75)

Glasgow [GLAHZ•goh] Largest city in Scotland. 55°N 4°W (pp. 725, 757)

Gobi [GOH•bee] Vast desert covering parts of Mongolia and China. 43°N 103°E (pp. R5, 109, 225, 246, 409, 411, 425, 431, 439)

Golan [GOH•lahn] **Heights** Region between northeast Israel and southwest Syria. 33°N 35°E (p. 875)

Gold Coast Former British colony, now the nation of Ghana in West Africa. 3°N 1°W (p. 767)

Gomel [GOH•muhl] Port city in southeastern Belarus. 52°N 31°E (p. 548)

Granada [gruh•NAH•duh] Province on the southern coast of Spain. 37°N 3°W (pp. 380, 394, 553)

Great Britain Island off the western coast of Europe comprising England, Scotland, and Wales. 54°N 2°W (pp. 814, 832)

Great Rift Valley Depression extending from Syria to Mozambique. 5°S 35°E (p. 445)

Great Wall Wall built in the 200s B.C. to protect China's northern border. 338°N 109°E (p. 431)

Greece [GREES] Country in southeastern Europe on the Balkan Peninsula. 39°N 21°E (pp. R3, R5, R17, 117, 121, 124, 132, 134, 138, 149, 154, 176, 263, 268, 269, 274, 277, 286, 292, 293, 297, 302, 317, 323, 351, 352, 358, 361, 367, 385, 781, 786, 790, 799, 832, 891, 897)

Guadalcanal [GWAHD•uhl•kuh•NAL] Largest of the Solomon Islands in the western Pacific Ocean. 9°S 160°E (p. 825)

Guam [GWAHM] U.S. possession in the Pacific Ocean. 14°N 143°E (p. 825)

Guangdong [GWAHNG•DUHNG] Province of southeast China on the South China Sea. 23°N 113°E (p. 773)

Guangzhou [GWAHNG•JOH] Port city in southern China on the Chang Jiang. 23°N 113°W (pp. R3, 246, 409, 411, 425, 431, 439, 773, 811)

Guantanamo [gwahn•TAH•nuh•MOH] **Bay** Inlet of the Caribbean Sea near Cuba. 20°N 75°W (p. 836)

Guatemala [GWAH•tay•MAH•lah] Central American country south of Mexico. 16°N 92°W (pp. 749, 861)

Guinea [GIH•nee] West African country. 11°N 12°W (p. 870)

Guinea-Bissau [GIH•nee bih•SOW] West African country. 12°N 20°W (p. 870)

Gulf of Mexico [MEHK•sih•KOH] Gulf on part of the southern coast of the United States. 25°N 94°W (pp. R2, R4, 565, 575, 590, 663, 691, 753)

Gulf of Tonkin [TAWN•kihn] Arm of the South China Sea off the coast of Vietnam. 20°N 108°E (p. 849)

Guyana [gy•AH•nuh] South American country between Venezuela and Suriname. 8°N 59°W (pp. 749, 861)

Hadrian's Wall Ancient Roman stone wall built to protect the northern boundary of Roman Britain. 55°N 3°W (pp. 293, 297)

Hainan [HY•NAHN] Province in southeastern China and island in the South China Sea. 32°N 120°E (pp. R5, 225, 811)

Haiphong [HY•FAWNG] City in northeast Vietnam on the Red River delta near the Gulf of Tonkin. 20°N 106°E (p. 849)

Haiti [HAY•tee] Country in the West Indies. 19°N 72°W (pp. 749, 836, 861)

Hamburg City in north central Germany. 53°N 10°E (pp. 548, 725, 747, 834)

Han [HAHN] Chinese state along Huang He and Chang Jiang. 33°N 112°E (p. 241)

Hangzhou [HAHNG•JOH] City in southeastern China. 30°N 120°E (pp. 246, 408, 409, 411, 416, 424, 425, 439, 554)

Hanoi [ha•NOY] Capital of Vietnam. 21°N 106°E (pp. 765, 849)

Hanover City in northwest Germany. 52°N 9°E (pp. 747, 834)

Harappa [huh•RA•puh] Ancient city in the Indus River valley in present-day Pakistan. (pp. 194, 198, 219)

Hawaii [huh•WY•ee] State of the United States in the central Pacific Ocean comprising the Hawaiian Islands. 20°N 157°W (p. 825)

Heian [HAY•ahn] Ancient capital city of Japan, now called Kyoto. 35°N 135°E (pp. 485, 491, 498, 507)

Himalaya [HIH•muh•LAY•uh] Mountain system forming a barrier between India and the rest of Asia. 29°N 85°E (pp. R5, R22–23, 193, 195, 198, 213, 219, 246, 409, 424, 425, 439)

Hindu Kush Major mountain system in central Asia. 35°N 68°E (pp. 109, 198, 213, 219)

Hiroshima [hee•roh•SHEE•mah] City in southern Japan. 34°N 132°E (p. 825)

Hispaniola [HIHS•puh•NYOH•luh] Island in the West Indies. 19°N 72°W (pp. R4, 662)

Hokkaido [hah•KY•doh] Second-largest island of Japan. 43°N 142°E (pp. R3, R5, 484, 485, 507)

Holstein [HOHL•steen] Region and former duchy of northern Germany. 54°N 10°E (p. 747)

Holy Roman Empire Lands in western and central Europe, empire founded by Charlemagne. 52°N 15°E (pp. 512, 522, 534, 538, 542, 544, 639)

Honduras [hahn•DUR•uhs] Central American country on the Caribbean Sea. 15°N 88°W (pp. 749, 861)

Hong Kong [HAWNG KAWNG] Port and industrial center in southern China. 22°N 115°E (pp. 765, 771, 773, 811, 825)

Honshu [HAHN•shoo] Largest island of Japan, called the mainland. 36°N 138°E (pp. R3, R5, 484, 485, 507)

Huang He [HWAHNG HUH] Second-longest river in China, formerly called the Yellow River. 35°N 113°E (pp. 225, 226, 230, 241, 246, 409, 411, 424, 425, 439, 811)

Hudson Bay Inland sea in Canada. 60°N 85°W (pp. R2, R4, 565, 590, 662, 691)

Hungary [HUHNG•guh•ree] Eastern European country south of Slovakia. 46°N 17°E (pp. R3, R16, 518, 538, 548, 639, 688, 703, 790, 814, 832, 891, 897)

Ifni [EEF•nee] Former Spanish possession, now part of Morocco. 29°N 8°W (p. 767)

India [IHN•dee•uh] South Asian country south of China and Nepal. 23°N 77°E (pp. R3, R5, R22, 109, 193, 194, 195, 198, 210, 213, 219, 246, 380, 383, 409, 425, 433, 435, 554, 662, 658, 667, 762, 765, 773, 825, 842, 845)

Indian Ocean Third-largest ocean. 10°S 70°E (pp. R3, R5, 13, 109, 195, 198, 210, 213, 425, 433, 452, 463, 469, 479, 554, 565, 662, 765, 767, 825, 845, 893)

Indonesia [IHN•duh•NEE•zhuh] Island republic in Southeast Asia, consisting of most of the Malay Archipelago. 40°S 118°E (pp. R3, R5, R23, 847)

Indus [IHN•duhs] **River** River in Asia that begins in Tibet and flows through Pakistan to the Arabian Sea. 27°N 68°E (pp. R3, R5, 109, 176, 193, 195, 198, 210, 213, 219, 246, 380, 383, 409, 424, 425, 565)

Ionian [eye•OH•nee•uhn] **Sea** Arm of the Mediterranean Sea. 38°N 18°E (pp. 117, 144, 149, 263)

Iran [EYE•ran] Southwest Asian country on the eastern shore of the Persian Gulf, formerly called Persia. 31°N 53°E (pp. R3, R19, 176, 198, 792)

Iraq [EYE•rak] Country in southwestern Asia near the Persian Gulf. 32°N 42°E (pp. R3, R18–19, R22, 176, 792, 869)

Ireland Island west of Great Britain occupied by the Republic of Ireland and Northern Ireland. 54°N 8°W (pp. R2, R4, R16, 518, 538, 645, 757, 790, 814, 832, 891)

Israel [IHZ•ree•uhl] Southwest Asian country south of Lebanon. 32°N 34°E (pp. R3, R18, 1, 90, 105, 176, 869, 875)

Issus [IHS•uhs] Ancient town of Asia Minor located north of the Syrian border. 37°N 36°E (p. 176)

Istanbul [ihs•tan•BUHL] Largest city in Turkey; formerly called Byzantium and Constantinople. 41°N 28°E (p. 792)

Italy Southern European country south of Switzerland and east of France. 43°N 11°E (pp. R3, R5, R16, 121, 262, 263, 268, 269, 274, 277, 286, 292, 293, 297, 302, 317, 323, 327, 329, 337, 342, 351,

352, 358, 361, 367, 385, 516, 518, 522, 542, 609, 645, 653, 688, 722, 725, 747, 781, 786, 789, 790, 814, 832, 891)

Ivory Coast Section of coastal western Africa. 7°N 6°W (p. 870)

Iwo Jima [EE•wuh JEE•muh] Largest of the Volcano Islands of Japan in the northwest Pacific Ocean east of Taiwan. 24°N 141°E (p. 825)

Jamaica [juh•MAY•kuh] Island country in the West Indies. 18°N 78°W (pp. 749, 836)

Jamestown Settlement in southeast Virginia. 37°N 77°W (p. 691)

Japan [juh•PAN] Chain of islands in the northern Pacific Ocean. 36°N 133°E (pp. R3, R5, R23, 225, 409, 425, 484, 485, 491, 498, 507, 662, 765, 773, 778, 811)

Java [JAH•vuh] Island in southern Indonesia. 8°S 111°E (pp. R3, R5, R23, R24, 425, 554, 765, 825)

Jeddah [JEHD•uh] City in western Saudi Arabia. 21°N 39°E (p. 433)

Jena [YAY•nuh] City in central Germany. 50°N 11°E (p. 722)

Jericho [JEHR•ih•KOH] Oldest Neolithic community, in the West Bank between Israel and Jordan. 25°N 27°E (pp. 8, 875)

Jerusalem [juh•ROO•suh•luhm] Capital of Israel and a holy city for Christians, Jews, and Muslims. 31°N 35°E (pp. 17, 28, 80, 86, 90, 93, 105, 132, 329, 342, 351, 352, 358, 361, 367, 374, 380, 383, 385, 397, 534, 542, 544, 792, 875)

Jordan [JAWRD•uhn] Southwest Asian country south of Syria. 30°N 38°E (p. 875)

Jordan [JAWRD•uhn] **River** River flowing from Lebanon and Syria to the Dead Sea. 30°N 38°E (pp. 17, 90, 105)

Judaea [ju•DEE•uh] Territory in southwest Asia and a region of historic Palestine. 31°N 35°E (pp. 342, 352, 361, 367)

Judah [JOO•duh] Southern kingdom of ancient Hebrews in Canaan, renamed Palestine. 25°N 49°E (pp. 90, 105)

Kamakura [kah•MAH•kuh•RAH] City in Japan, former location of the Shogun military government. 35°N 139°E (pp. 485, 491)

Karakorum [KAR•uh•KOHR•uhm] Capital of the Mongol Empire during most of the 1200s. 47°N 102°E (pp. 423, 424, 425)

Kashmir [KASH•mihr] Historical region of northwest India and northeast Pakistan. 33°N 77°E (p. 845)

Gazetteer

Kathmandu [KAT•MAN•DOO] Capital of Nepal. 27°N 85°E (pp. 210, 845)

Kazakhstan [kuh•ZAHK•STAHN] Large Asian country south of Russia. 48°N 59°E (p. 883)

Kenya [KEHN•yuh] East African country. 1°N 37°E (p. 870)

Key West Island off the southern coast of Florida. 24°N 81°W (p. 836)

Khanbaliq [KAHN•buh•LEEK] Capital of Kublai Khan's Mongol Empire, now called Beijing. 40°N 116°E (pp. 423, 425)

Khartoum [kahr•TOOM] Capital of Sudan. 16°N 33°E (p. 767)

Khyber Pass Mountain pass in western Asia connecting Afghanistan and Pakistan. 34°N 71°E (p. 194)

Kiev [KEE•EHF] Capital of Ukraine, on the Dnieper River. 50°N 30°E (pp. R3, 425, 534, 548, 555, 722, 883)

Kievan Rus State made of small territories around Kiev, destroyed by Mongols in 1240. 50°N 30°E (p. 538)

Knossos [NAH•suhs] Ancient city on Crete. 35°N 24°E (pp. 116, 117, 149)

Korea Peninsula in eastern Asia, divided into the Democratic People's Republic of Korea (North Korea) and the Republic of Korea. 38°N 127°E (pp. R3, R5, R23, 225, 409, 411, 484, 491, 498, 765, 773, 778, 811, 831)

Kosovo [KOH•suh•voh] Province of southern Yugoslavia in the Serbian republic. 42°N 21°E. (p. 897)

Kunlun Shan [KOON•LOON shuhn] Major mountain system in western China. 35°N 83°E (p. 225)

Kush [KUHSH] Ancient region in present-day Sudan, formerly called Nubia. 21°N 33°E (p. 70)

Kut-el-Amara Town in southeastern Iraq on the Tigris River; also called Al Kut. 32°N 45°E (p. 799)

Kuwait [ku•WAYT] Country on the Persian Gulf between Saudi Arabia and Iraq. 29°N 48°E (pp. 792, 799)

Kyoto [kee•OH•toh] Ancient capital of Japan, formerly called Heian. 35°N 135°E (pp. 485, 491, 498, 507, 778)

Kyrgyzstan [KIHR•gih•STAN] Central Asian country on China's western border. 41°N 75°E (p. 883)

Kyushu [kee•OO•shoo] One of the four major islands of Japan. 33°N 131°E (pp. R3, 484, 485, 507)

Laos [LOWS] Southeast Asian country south of China and west of Vietnam. 20°N 102°E (pp. 847, 849)

Latin America [LA•tihn uh•MEHR•ee•kuh] Countries of the Western Hemisphere south of the United States, especially those countries that developed from the colonies of Spain, Portugal, and France. 5°S 65°W (p. 861)

Latium [LAY•shee•uhm] Region in west central Italy. 42°N 12°E (p. 263)

Latvia [LAT•vee•uh] Eastern European country west of Russia on the Baltic Sea. 57°N 25°E (pp. 790, 814, 883, 891)

Lebanon [LEH•buh•nuhn] Southwest Asian country on the eastern coast of the Mediterranean Sea. 34°N 34°E (pp. R3, 176, 792, 875)

Leeds City in north-central England. 53°N 1°W (pp. 725, 757)

Leipzig [LIHP•sihg] City in southeastern Germany. 51°N 12°E (pp. 722, 747)

Leon [lay•OHN] Historic region and former kingdom in Spain. 41°N 5°W (p. 538)

Lesotho [luh•SOH•TOH] Southern African country within the Republic of South Africa. 30°S 28°E (p. 870)

Liberia [ly•BIHR•ee•uh] West African country. 7°N 10°W (pp. 767, 870)

Libya [LIH•bee•uh] North African country west of Egypt. 28°N 15°E (pp. R3, 176, 767, 790, 870)

Lisbon [LIHZ•buhn] Capital of Portugal. 39°N 9°W (p. 555)

Lithuania [LIH•thuh•WAY•nee•uh] Eastern European country northwest of Belarus. 56°N 24°E (pp. 790, 814, 883, 891)

Liverpool City in northwestern England. 53°N 3°W (pp. 725, 757)

Lombardy [LAWM•buhr•dee] Region of northern Italy. 45°N 9°E (p. 747)

London [LUHN•duhn] Capital of the United Kingdom, on the Thames River. 52°N 0° (pp. R2, 518, 542, 553, 555, 557, 561, 633, 642, 670, 680, 703, 714, 722, 724, 725, 757, 780, 781, 786)

Lorraine [loh•RAYN] Historical region and former province of northeast France. 49°N 6°E (pp. 747, 781)

Luoyang [luh•WOH•YAHNG] City in northern China on the Huang He. 34°N 112°E (pp. 224, 230, 246, 251, 409, 439)

Luxembourg [LUHK•suhm•BUHRG] Small European country between France, Belgium, and Germany. 50°N 7°E (pp. 781, 786, 787, 790, 814, 832, 834, 891)

Macau [muh•KOW] Region on the southeastern coast of China. 22°N 113°E (pp. 430, 667, 765, 773)

Macedonia [MA•suh•DOH•nee•uh] Country in southeastern Europe on the Balkan Peninsula. 41°N 22°E (pp. 117, 174, 176, 269, 274, 897)

Machu Picchu [MAH•choo PEE•choo] Incan settlement in the Andes northwest of Cuzco, Peru. 13°S 72°W (p. 577)

Madagascar [MA•duh•GAS•kuhr] Island in the Indian Ocean off the southeastern coast of Africa. 18°S 43°E (pp. R3, R5, R21, 445, 479, 767, 870)

Madinah [mah•DEE•nuh] Holy Muslim city in western Saudi Arabia. 24°N 39°E (pp. 372, 380, 383, 385, 397, 792)

Madras [MAHD•ruhs] City in India, also called Chennai. 13°N 80°E (p. 845)

Madrid [muh•DRIHD] Capital of Spain. 41°N 4°W (pp. 714, 722, 725, 781)

Makkah [MAH•kuh] Holy city of Muslims, also known as Mecca, in western Saudi Arabia. 21°N 39°E (pp. 372, 374, 380, 383, 385, 397, 425, 433, 448, 452, 554, 792)

Malawi [mah•LAH•wee] Southern African country. 11°S 34°E (p. 870)

Malaya [muh•LAY•uh] Peninsula of Asia. 6°N 102°E (p. 765)

Malaysia [muh•LAY•zhuh] Southeast Asian country with land on the Malay Peninsula and on the island of Borneo. 4°N 101°E (p. 847)

Mali [MAH•lee] Republic in northwestern Africa. 15°N 0°W (pp. 451, 870)

Manchester City in northwest England. 53°N 2°W (pp. 725, 757)

Manchuria [man•choo•REE•uh] Region of northeast China comprising the provinces of Heilongjiang, Jilin, and Liaoning. 49°N 117°E (pp. 773, 778, 811, 825)

Manila [muh•NIH•luh] Capital of the Philippines. 15°N 121°E (pp. 765, 825)

Marathon [MAHR•uh•THAHN] Village of ancient Greece northeast of Athens. (p. 134)

Marne River in northeast France that flows into the Seine River. 49°N 3°E (p. 786)

Marseille [mahr•SAY] City in southern France. 43°N 5°E (pp. 542, 555, 725)

Massachusetts State in the northeastern United States. 42°N 72°W (p. 694)

Massalia [muh•SAH•lee•uh] Ancient Greek colony on the site of present-day Marseille. 44°N 3°E (p. 293)

Mauritania [mawr•uh•TAY•nee•uh] West African country. 20°N 14°W (p. 870)

Mediterranean [MEHD•ih•tuh•RAY•nee•uhn] **Sea** Inland sea of Europe, Asia, and Africa. 36°N 13°E (pp. R3, R5, 17, 28, 39, 62, 70, 75, 90, 105, 109, 117, 121, 132, 144, 149,

Gazetteer

176, 179, 189, 263, 269, 274, 292, 293, 297, 323, 329, 337, 352, 361, 367, 374, 380, 383, 385, 397, 425, 445, 452, 463, 479, 513, 514, 518, 538, 542, 548, 555, 609, 639, 645, 653, 703, 709, 722, 725, 747, 767, 781, 786, 790, 832, 875)

Mekong [MAY•KAWNG] River River in southeastern Asia. 18°N 104°E (pp. 246, 409, 411, 424, 439, 667, 849)

Memel Territory [MAY•muhl] Former German territory, now part of Lithuania. 40°N 20°E (p. 814)

Memphis Ancient capital of Egypt. 29°N 31°E (pp. 38, 39, 47, 59, 62, 70, 75, 80)

Meroë [MEHR•oh•ee] Capital city of Kush. 7°N 93°E (pp. 68, 70, 452)

Mesa Verde National park in southwestern Colorado containing artifacts and cliff dwellings from the Anasazi. 37°N 108°W (p. 578)

Mesoamerica [MEH•zoh•uh•MEHR•ih•kuh] Ancient region including present-day Mexico and most of Central America. 10°N 92°W (p. 575)

Mesopotamia [MEH•suh•puh•TAY•mee•uh] Early center of civilization, in the area of modern Iraq and eastern Syria between the Tigris and Euphrates Rivers. 34°N 13°E (pp. 17, 28, 132, 380)

Mexico [MEHK•sih•KOH] North American country south of the United States. 24°N 104°W (pp. R2, 575, 662, 749 860, 861)

Mexico City Capital of Mexico. 19°N 99°W (pp. R2, 658, 662, 663)

Miami [my•AM•ee] City in southeast Florida. 25°N 80°W (p. 836)

Midway [MIHD•way] Islands Atoll in the North Pacific Ocean, about one-third of the way from Honolulu to Tokyo. 28°N 177°W (p. 825)

Milan [mih•LAHN] City in northern Italy. 45°N 9°E (pp. 548, 555, 609, 639, 653, 688, 703, 725)

Minsk [MIHNSK] Capital of Belarus. 54°N 28°E (p. 722)

Mississippi [MIHS•ih•SIHP•ee] River Large river system in the United States. 32°N 92°W (pp. R2, R4, 590, 663)

Modena [MOH•deh•nah] City in northern Italy. 44°N 10°E (p. 747)

Mogadishu [MAH•guh•DIH•shoo] Capital of Somalia. 2°N 45°E (pp. R3, 433, 452, 460, 479, 767)

Mohenjo-Daro [moh•HEHN•joh DAHR•oh] Ancient settlement in the Indus Valley. 27°N 68°E (pp. 198, 219)

Moldova [mawl•DAW•vuh] Small European country between Ukraine and Romania. 48°N 28°E (p. 883)

Moluccas [muh•LUH•kuhz] Group of islands in Indonesia, formerly called the Spice Islands. 2°S 128°E (pp. R5, 662, 667)

Mombasa [mawm•BAHS•uh] City and seaport of Kenya. 4°S 39°E (pp. 433, 452)

Mongolia [mahn•GOH•lee•uh] Country in Asia between Russia and China. 46°N 100°E (pp. R3, 225, 409, 425, 431, 439, 773, 825)

Monrovia [muhn•ROH•vee•uh] Capital of Liberia. 6°N 11°W (p. 767)

Montenegro [MAWN•tuh•NEHG•roh] Republic of Yugoslavia, in the southwest part of the country, bordering on the Adriatic Sea. 42°N 19°E (pp. 781, 786, 897)

Morocco [muh•RAH•koh] North African country. 32°N 7°W (pp. R20, R21, 380, 473, 479, 767, 786, 790, 870)

Moscow [MAHS•koh] Capital of Russia. 55°N 37°E (pp. R3, 425, 540, 714, 722, 725, 781, 883)

Mount Everest [EHV•ruhst] Highest mountain in the world, located in the Himalaya between Nepal and Tibet. 28°N 86°E (pp. 193, 195)

Mount Fuji [FOO•jee] Highest mountain in Japan. 35°N 138°E (pp. 485, 507)

Mount Olympus [uh•LIHM•puhs] Highest mountain in Greece on the border between Thessaly and Macedonia. 41°N 23°E (p. 117)

Mount Sinai [SY•NY] Part of a rocky mass on the Sinai Peninsula of northeastern Egypt. 29°N 33°E (p. 90)

Mozambique [moh•zahm•BEEK] Southern African country south of Tanzania. 20°S 34°E (pp. 767, 870)

Munich [MYOO•nihk] City in southeastern Germany. 48°N 11°E (p. 725)

Myanmar [MYAHN•MAHR] Southeast Asian country formerly called Burma. 21°N 95°E (p. 845)

Mycenae [MY•SEE•nee] Ancient city in Greece. 37°N 22°E (pp. 116, 117, 149)

Nagasaki [nah•gah•SAH•kee] City in Japan. 32°N 129°E (pp. 778, 825)

Namibia [nuh•MIH•bee•uh] Southern African country. 20°S 16°E (p. 870)

Nanjing [NAHN•JIHNG] City in eastern China, capital during the Ming dynasty. 32°N 118°E (pp. 430, 431, 433, 811, 825)

Napata [NA•puh•tuh] Ancient capital of Kush. 18°N 32°E (pp. 68, 70)

Naples [NAY•puhlz] City in Italy. 40°N 14°E (pp. 555, 609, 639, 653, 722, 747)

Nara [NAH•ruh] First permanent capital of Japan. 34°N 135°E (pp. 485, 491, 507)

Navarre [nuh•VAHR] Former kingdom in southern France and northern Spain. 42°N 1°W (p. 538)

Nazareth [NA•zuh•ruhth] Ancient town near Galilee, now in northern Israel. 32°N 35°E (pp. 352, 361, 367)

Nepal [nuh•PAWL] Mountain country between India and China. 28°N 83°E (pp. R3, 198, 202, 765, 845)

Netherlands [NEH•thuhr•luhnz] Country in northwestern Europe. 53°N 3°E (pp. R2–3, R4–5, R16, 639, 645, 662, 725, 747, 781, 786, 787, 790, 814, 832, 891)

New Carthage [KAHR•thihj] City in Spain, also called Cartagena. 38°N 1°W (pp. 269, 274)

New Delhi [NOO DEH•lee] Capital of India. 29°N 77°E (p. 845)

New Guinea [GIHN•ee] Island in the western Pacific Ocean, north of Australia. 5°S 140°E (pp. 765, 825)

New York State in northeastern United States. 43°N 78°W (p. 724)

New York City City in southeastern New York state at the mouth of the Hudson River. 41°N 74°W (p. 769)

Nicaragua [nih•kuh•RAH•gwuh] Central American country south of Honduras. 13°N 86°W (pp. 749, 861)

Niger [NY•juhr] West African country. 18°N 9°E (p. 870)

Nigeria [ny•JIHR•ee•uh] West African country. 9°N 7°E (pp. 767, 870)

Nile [nyl] River World's longest river flowing north from the heart of Africa to the Mediterranean Sea. 27°N 31°E (pp. R3, R5, R20, R21, 38, 39, 47, 59, 62, 68, 70, 75, 109, 121, 132, 176, 179, 189, 246, 269, 293, 297, 329, 374, 383, 385, 397, 425, 445, 452, 875)

Nineveh [NIH•nuh•vuh] Ancient capital of Assyria, on the Tigris River. 26°N 43°E (pp. 17, 26, 132)

Ningxia [NIHNG•shee•AH] Region in northwestern China. 37°N 106°E (p. 424)

Normandy [NAWR•muhn•dee] Region and former province of France. 49°N 2°E (p. 518)

North America Continent in the northern part of the Western Hemisphere between the Atlantic and Pacific Oceans. 45°N 100°W (pp. R2, R4, R6–11, 13, 565, 573, 590, 658, 662, 663, 668, 691, 707, 724, 744, 762, 813, 824, 831, 893)

North Korea [kuh•REE•uh] East Asian country in the northernmost part of the Korean Peninsula. 40°N 127°E (p. 838)

North Sea Arm of the Atlantic Ocean between Europe and Great Britain. 56°N 3°E (pp. R16, 293, 513, 514, 518, 538, 542, 548, 555, 639, 645, 722, 725, 757, 781, 786, 790, 814, 832)

Norway [NAWR•WAY] Northern European country on the Scandinavian peninsula. 63°N 11°E (pp. R3, R16, 538, 639, 645, 722, 725, 781, 786, 790, 814, 832)

Novgorod [NAHV•guh•RAHD] City in western Russia. 58°N 31°E (p. 540)

Nubia [NOO•bee•uh] Region in present-day Sudan on the Nile River, later known as Kush. 21°N 33°E (p. 39)

Nuremburg City in south central Germany. 49°N 11°E (pp. 555, 747)

Nyasaland [ny•ahs•uh•luhnd] Country in southeastern Africa, now called Malawi. 13°S 34°E (p. 767)

Oder River [OH•duhr] River in north central Europe, emptying into the Baltic Sea. 52°N 14°E (p. 513)

Okinawa [oh•keh•NAH•wuh] Island group of the central Ryukyu Islands in the western Pacific Ocean (p. 825)

Olympia [ohz•LIHM•pee•uh] Site of the ancient Olympic Games in Greece. 38°N 22°E (pp. 125, 154)

Oman [oh•MAHN] Country on the Arabian Sea and the Gulf of Oman. 20°N 57°E (pp. R3, R5, R19, 198)

Orléans [AWR•lay•AHN] City in north central France. 47°N 1°E (pp. 553, 557, 561)

Osaka [oh•SAH•kuh] City and port in Japan. 34°N 135°E (pp. R3, 507)

Oslo [AHZ•loh] Capital of Norway. 60°N 11°E (p. 725)

Ostia [AHS•tee•uh] Ancient city of Italy in Latium at the mouth of the Tiber River. 44°N 10°E (p. 293)

Ottoman Empire Turkish empire from the late 1200s in Asia Minor throughout the Middle East. 45°N 25°E (pp. 639, 645, 722, 781, 786, 799)

Pacific Ocean The largest and deepest of the world's four oceans, covering more than a third of the earth's surface. 0° 170°W (pp. R2–3, R4–5, R6–10, R12, R15, 13, 225, 409, 425, 426, 433, 485, 749, 765, 769, 773, 811, 825, 893)

Pakistan [PA•kih•STAN] Officially the Islamic Republic of Pakistan, a republic in South Asia, marking the area where

South Asia converges with southwest Asia. 28°N 67°E (pp. R3, 176, 198, 845)

Palestine [PAL•ih•styn] Historic region, situated on the eastern coast of the Mediterranean Sea. 31°N 35°E (pp. 286, 293, 297, 302, 327, 383, 397, 534, 542, 792)

Panama [PA•nuh•MAH] Central American country on the Isthmus of Panama. 9°N 81°W (pp. 749, 861)

Panama [PA•nuh•MAH] **Canal** Ship canal crossing the Isthmus of Panama and connecting the Caribbean Sea with the Pacific Ocean. 9°N 79°W (p. 769)

Papal [PAY•puhl] **States** Territory in Italy formerly under direct temporal rule of the pope. 43°N 13°E (pp. 538, 639, 747)

Paraguay [PAR•uh•GWY] South American country northeast of Argentina. 24°S 57°W (pp. 749, 861)

Paris [PAR•uhs] Capital of France. 49°N 2°E (pp. 516, 518, 542, 555, 557, 633, 642, 714, 722, 724, 725, 780, 781, 786, 787)

Parma [PAHR-mah] City in north-central Italy. 44°N 10°E (p. 747)

Pataliputra [PAH•tuh•lih•POO•truh] Capital of Maurya. 24°N 86°E (pp. 209, 210, 246)

Pearl Harbor Inlet of the Pacific Ocean on the southern coast of Oahu, Hawaii. 21°N 157°W (p. 825)

Peloponnesus [PEH•luh•puh•NEE•suhs] A peninsula in southern Greece. 37°N 22°E (pp. 117, 124, 125, 144)

Pergamum [PUHR•guh•muhm] An ancient city of northwest Asia Minor in Mysia, now Turkey. 39°N 28°E (pp. 179, 189)

Persepolis [puhr•sei•puh•LEES] Ancient capital of Persian empire, now in ruins. 30°N 53°E (pp. 132, 176, 374)

Persia [PUHR•zhuh] The conventional European designation of the country now known as Iran. 32°N 55°E (pp. 132, 144, 176, 246, 374, 380, 383, 385, 397, 425, 554, 799)

Persian [PUHR•zhuhn] **Gulf** An arm of the Arabian Sea in southwestern Asia, between the Arabian Peninsula on the southwest and Iran on the northeast. 27°N 50°E (pp. R19, 17, 109, 132, 176, 374, 380, 383, 385, 397, 448, 452, 554, 565, 709, 792, 799)

Peru [puh•ROO] South American country south of Ecuador and Colombia. 10°S 75°W (pp. 749, 861)

Petrograd [PEH•troh•grad] City in Russia, now St. Petersburg. 59°N 30°E (p. 786)

Philadelphia [FIL•uh•DEHL•fee•uh] City in eastern Pennsylvania on the Delaware River. 40°N 75°W (pp. 690, 691, 694, 695)

Philippines [FIH•luh•PEENZ] Island country in the Pacific Ocean southeast of China. 14°N 125°E (pp. R3, R5, 662, 667, 765, 773, 825, 847)

Piedmont [PEED•mahnt] Region in northwest Italy bordering France and Switzerland. 45°N 8°E (p. 747)

Pisa [PEE•sah] City in central Italy. 43°N 10°E (pp. 542, 609, 653)

Plataea [pluh•TEE•uh] Ancient city of Greece. 39°N 22°E (p. 134)

Plateau of Tibet [tuh•BEHT] World's highest plateau region, bordered by the Himalaya, Pamirs, and Karakoram mountain ranges. (p. 225)

Plymouth [PLI•muhth] Town in eastern Massachusetts, first successful English colony in New England. 42°N 71°W (pp. 663, 691)

Poland [POH•luhnd] Country in central Europe. 52°N 17°E (pp. R3, R16–17, 538, 639, 645, 688, 725, 790, 814, 832, 834, 891)

Po River River in northern Italy, the longest in the country. 45°N 11°E (pp. 263, 274, 513, 514, 653, 688)

Port Arthur City in northeastern China, now called Lüshun. 38°N 121°E (pp. 773, 778)

Portugal [POHR•chih•guhl] A long narrow country on Atlantic Ocean, sharing the Iberian Peninsula with Spain. 38°N 8°W (pp. R2, 639, 645, 662, 722, 781, 786, 790, 814, 832, 891)

Portuguese Guinea [GIH•nee] Country in northwestern Africa, now called Guinea-Bissau. 11°N 14°W (p. 767)

Posen City in western Poland. 52°N 17°E (p. 548)

Prayagal City in central India, part of the Mauryan empire, 321 B.C. 26°N 81°E (p. 210)

Principe [prin•SEEP•e] Island of Africa in the Gulf of Guinea. 1°N 7°E (p. 767)

Prussia [PRUH•shuh] Former kingdom and state of Germany. (pp. 538, 722, 725, 747)

Puerto Rico [PWEHR•toh REE•koh] Island in the Caribbean Sea; U.S. Commonwealth. 19°N 67°W (pp. 749, 836)

Puteoli [pyu•TEE•uh•LY] Port city on the Bay of Naples. 42°N 14°E (p. 293)

Pyrenees [PIR•uh•nees] Mountain range in southwestern Europe, extending from the Bay of Biscay to the Mediterranean Sea. 43°N 0°E (pp. 269, 274, 513, 514, 516)

Qin [CHIHN] Chinese state along Huang He and Chang Jiang. 33°N 112°E (p. 241)

Qingdao [CHING•DOW] City of eastern China on the Yellow Sea north of Shanghai. 36°N 120°E (p. 773)

Quanzhou [chuh•WAHN•JOH] City in southeastern China. 25°N 111°E (pp. 431, 433)

Quebec [kih•BEHK] City in Canada. 47°N 71°W (pp. 663, 691)

Ramadi [ruh•MAH•dee] Town in central Iraq. 33°N 43°E (p. 799)

Red Sea Narrow, inland sea, separating the Arabian Peninsula, western Asia, from northeastern Africa. 23°N 37°E (pp. R3, R5, R18–19, R20, R21, 28, 70, 121, 132, 179, 246, 293, 329, 352, 361, 367, 374, 383, 385, 397, 425, 433, 445, 448, 554, 709, 792, 799, 875)

Rhineland [RYN•luhnd] Region along the Rhine River in western Germany. 38°N 91°W (p. 814)

Rhine [RYN] **River** One of the principal rivers of Europe. 50°N 7°E (pp. 293, 513, 514, 538, 542, 688, 722)

Rhodes [RODZ] Island in the Aegean Sea. 36°N 28°E (pp. 269, 274)

Rhodesia [roh•DEE•shuh] Region of south-central Africa south of Congo and comprising modern-day Zambia and Zimbabwe. 19°S 29°E (p. 767)

Rhone [RON] **River** River of southeastern France. 44°N 4°E (pp. 557, 561)

Rio de Oro [REE•o dai O•ro] Historical region in the southern section of the Western Sahara on the northwestern coast of Africa. 24°N 14°W (p. 767)

Rio Grande [REE•oh GRAND] River that forms part of the boundary between the United States and Mexico. 30°N 103°W (pp. R2, R4, 590, 663)

Rocky Mountains Mountain system in western North America. 50°N 114°W (pp. R4, 590)

Romania [ru•MAY•nee•uh] Eastern European country east of Hungary. 46°N 23°E (pp. 781, 786, 790, 814, 832, 897)

Rome [ROHM] Capital of Italy. 41°N 12°E (pp. R3, 262, 263, 268, 269, 274, 277, 286, 292, 293, 297, 302, 317, 323, 327, 329, 337, 342, 351, 352, 358, 361, 367, 514, 516, 518, 522, 534, 542, 548, 555, 608, 609, 633, 642, 645, 653, 670, 703, 714, 722, 725, 744, 747, 780, 781, 786)

Russia [RUH•shuh] Independent republic in Eastern Europe and northern Asia, the world's largest country by area. 61°N 60°E (pp. R3, R17, 645, 722, 725, 747, 773, 778, 781, 786, 883)

Rwanda [ruh•WAHN•duh] East African country. 2°S 30°E (p. 870)

Ryukyu [RYUK•yoo] **Islands** Island group of southwest Japan between Kyushu and Taiwan. 26°N 128°E (p. 778)

Sahara [suh•HAR•uh] Desert region in northern Africa that is the largest hot desert in the world. 23°N 1°W (pp. R5, R20, R21, 70, 374, 445, 448, 449, 479)

Saigon [sy•GAWN] City in Vietnam, now called Ho Chi Minh City. 10°N 106°E (pp. 765, 849)

St. Augustine [AW•gus•steen] City in northeastern Florida on the Atlantic coast; oldest permanent existing European settlement in North America. 30°N 81°W (p. 663)

St. Petersburg Second-largest city and largest seaport in Russia, located in the northwestern part of the country. 59°N 30°E (pp. R3, 725, 786)

Sakhalin [sahk-HAH-lin] Island of southeast Russia in the Sea of Okhotsk; also called Karafuto. 51°N 143°E (p. 778)

Salamis [SA•luh•muhs] Island in eastern Greece in the Gulf of Saronikós. 37°N 23°E (p. 134)

Salonica City and port in northeastern Greece. 40°N 23°E (p. 548)

Samarkand [sah•mahr•KAHNT] City in southern Uzbekistan. 39°N 67°E (pp. 424, 425, 554)

Samaria [suh•MAHR•ee•uh] Ancient city and state in Palestine, located north of present-day Jerusalem east of the Mediterranean Sea. 32°N 35°E (pp. 86, 90, 105)

San Francisco City in northern California on the Pacific coast. 38°N 122°W (p. 769)

Santa Fe [SAN•tuh FAY] Capital of New Mexico located in the north central part of the state. 36°N 106°W (p. 663)

São Tomé [SAH•o TO•mai] Capital city and island in the Gulf of Guinea off western Africa. 1°N 7°E (p. 767)

Sarajevo [SAR•uh•YAY•voh] Capital of Bosnia and Herzegovina. 43°N 18°E (pp. 781, 786, 897)

Sardinia [sahr•DIN•ee•uh] Island off western Italy, in the Mediterranean Sea. 40°N 9°E (pp. R5, 263, 269, 274, 293, 329, 337, 538, 555, 609, 653, 722, 747, 832)

Sardis [SAWR•dihs] Ancient city of Asia Minor, now in Turkey. 38°N 28°E (pp. 132, 134)

Saudi Arabia [SOW•dee uh•RAY•bee•uh] Southwest Asian country, occupying most of the Arabian Peninsula. 22°N 46°E (pp. R3, R18–19, 176, 792, 875)

Savoy [sah•VO•yuh] Former duchy lying between Italy and France. 43°N 21°E (pp. 639, 747)

Saxony [SAHK•suh•nee] Historical region of northern Germany. 51°N 13°E (p. 747)

Scandinavia [SKAND•i•NAI•vee•ah] Region in northern Europe consisting of Norway, Sweden, and Denmark. 62°N 14°E (pp. 512, 544)

Schleswig [SHLEHS•wihg] Historical region and former duchy of northern Germany and southern Denmark. 54°N 9°E (p. 747)

Scotland One of the four countries that make up the United Kingdom in the northern part of Great Britain. 57°N 5°W (pp. R16, 518, 538, 639, 645, 757)

Sea of Japan Arm of the Pacific Ocean lying between Japan and the Asian mainland. 40°N 132°E (pp. R5, R23, 225, 485, 773, 778, 811, 825, 838)

Seine [SAYN] **River** River in northern France. 48°N 4°E (pp. 513, 514, 516, 518, 557, 561)

Seleucia [suh•LOO•shee•uh] Kingdom extending eastward from Asia Minor into what is now Pakistan. 36°N 36°E (pp. 179, 189)

Senegal [seh•nih•GAWL] West African country. 15°N 14°W (p. 870)

Seoul [SOHL] Capital of South Korea. 38°N 127°E (p. 838)

Serbia [SUHR•bee•uh] Republic in southeastern Europe. 44°N 21°E (pp. 725, 781, 786, 897)

Shanghai [SHANG•hy] City of eastern China at the mouth of the Chang Jiang. 31°N 121°E (pp. 771, 773, 778, 811, 825)

Sheffield City in north-central England. 53°N 1°W (p. 725)

Shikoku [shih•KOH•koo] One of the four largest islands of Japan. 33°N 133°E (pp. 484, 485, 507, 778)

Siam [sy•AM] Country of southeastern Asia, now called Thailand. 17°N 101°E (p. 825)

Siberia [sei•BIR•ree•yuh] Large region consisting of the Asian portion of Russia as well as northern Kazakhstan. 57°N 97°E (pp. R5, R23, 425)

Sichuan [SEHCH•WAHN] Province of south-central China. 30°N 103°E (p. 811)

Sicily [SIH•suh•lee] Largest island in the Mediterranean Sea off the coast of southern Italy. 37°N 13°E (pp. R5, 121, 262, 263, 269, 274, 293, 329, 337, 352, 361, 367, 538, 542, 553, 555, 609, 653, 722, 747)

Gazetteer

Sidon [SEI•duhn] City in southwestern Lebanon on the Mediterranean Sea. 33°N 35°E (pp. 17, 90, 105, 293)

Sierra Leone [see•EHR•uh lee•OHN] West African country south of Guinea. 8°N 12°W (pp. 767, 870)

Silesia [sy•LEE•zhuh] Region of central Europe, once part of Prussia but now largely in Poland. 51°N 18°E (p. 747)

Silk Road Large network of trade routes stretching from western China to southwest Asia. 34°N 109°E (p. 246)

Sinai [SY•ny] **Peninsula** Land linking southwest Asia with northeast Africa. 29°N 34°E (p. 875)

Singapore [SIHNG•uh•POHR] Southeast Asian island country. 2°N 104°E (pp. 765, 825, 847)

Slovenia [sloh•VEE•nee•uh] Southeastern European country south of Austria. 46°N 15°E (pp. 891, 897)

Solomon Islands Island group of the western Pacific Ocean. 8°S 159°E (p. 825)

Somalia [soh•MAH•lee•uh] East African country. 3°N 45°E (p. 870)

Somaliland [soh•MAH•lee•luhnd] Region of eastern Africa comprising present-day Somalia, Djibouti, and southeast Ethiopia. 8°N 45°E (p. 767)

Somme [SOHM] River in northern France that flows west and northwest to the English Channel. 49°N 2°E (p. 786)

Songhai [SAWNG•HY] Empire located along the Niger River. 13°N 5°E (p. 451)

South Africa [A•frih•kuh] Country at the southern tip of Africa, officially the Republic of South Africa. 28°S 25°E (pp. 767, 869, 870)

South America Continent in the southern part of the Western Hemisphere. 15°S 60°W (pp. R2, R4, R14, R15, 13, 473, 565, 573, 577, 658, 662, 707, 744, 749, 762, 893)

South China Sea Arm of the Pacific Ocean off the eastern and southeastern coasts of Asia. 15°N 114°E (pp. R3, R5, 109, 225, 241, 246, 409, 425, 433, 439, 554, 565, 667, 765, 773, 811, 825, 847, 849)

South Korea [kuhx•REE•uh] East Asian country on the Korean Peninsula. 36°N 128°E (p. 838)

Soviet [SOH•vee•eht] **Union** Former communist country in eastern Europe and northern Asia that included Russia and 14 other soviet socialist republics. 55°N 37°E (pp. 790, 792, 811, 814, 825, 832, 883)

Spain [SPAYN] Country in southwestern Europe. 40°N 4°W (pp. R2–3, R16, 268, 269, 277, 286, 292, 293, 297, 302, 317,

323, 327, 329, 337, 352, 358, 361, 380, 385, 516, 518, 522, 534, 542, 544, 639, 645, 662, 722, 725, 781, 786, 790, 814, 832, 891)

Sparta [SPAHR•tah] City in ancient Greece and capital of Laconia. 37°N 23°E (pp. 117, 121, 124, 125, 134, 138, 144, 149)

Sri Lanka [sree•LAHNG•kuh] Country in the Indian Ocean south of India, formerly called Ceylon. 8°N 82°E (pp. R3, R5, R22, 198, 202, 433, 667, 845)

Stockholm [STAHK•HOHLM] Capital of Sweden. 59°N 18°E (pp. 555, 725)

Strait of Gibraltar [ji•BRAHL•tuhr] Narrow passage connecting the Mediterranean Sea with the Atlantic Ocean. 35°N 5°W (pp. R16, 380, 385)

Strait of Magellan [muh•JEHL•uhn] Channel between the Atlantic and Pacific Oceans on the southern tip of South America. 52°S 68°W (pp. R2, R4, R14, R15, 662, 769)

Strait of Messina [meh•SEE•nuh] Passage separating mainland Italy from the island of Sicily. 38°N 15°E (p. 263)

Strasbourg [STRAHS•boorg] City in eastern France. 48°N 7°E (pp. 548, 747)

Sudan [soo•DAN] East African country. 14°N 28°E (pp. 767, 870)

Sudetenland [soo•DAY•tuhn•LAND] Historical region of northern Czech Republic. 50°N 14°E (p. 814)

Suez Canal [SOO•ehz] Canal in Egypt connecting the Mediterranean and Red seas. 30°N 32°E (pp. 767, 799, 875)

Sumatra [soo•MAH•trah] Island in western Indonesia. 2°N 99°E (pp. R3, R5, R23, 425, 433, 554, 667, 765, 825)

Suriname [SUR•uh•NAH•muh] South American country between Guyana and French Guiana. 4°N 56°W (pp. 749, 861)

Susa [soo•SAH] Persian capital, in the region of southern Mesopotamia. 34°N 48°E (pp. 17, 132, 176)

Swaziland [SWAH•zee•LAND] Southern African country west of Mozambique, almost entirely within the Republic of South Africa. 27°S 32°E (pp. 767, 870)

Sweden [SWEED•uhn] Northern European country on the eastern side of the Scandinavian peninsula. 60°N 14°E (pp. R3, R16, R17, 538, 688, 703, 722, 725, 781, 786, 790, 814, 832, 891)

Switzerland [SWIHT•suhr•luhnd] European country south of Germany. 47°N 8°E (pp. 725, 747, 781, 786, 790, 814)

Syracuse [SIHR•uh•KYOOS] City in Sicily. 37°N 15°E (p. 182)

Syria [SIHR•ee•uh] Southwestern Asian country on the east side of the

Mediterranean Sea. 35°N 37°E (pp. R3, R18–19, 62, 176, 177, 274, 286, 293, 329, 352, 374, 380, 383, 385, 792, 875)

Syrian [SIHR•ee•uhn] **Desert** Desert of the northern Arabian Peninsula, including northern Saudi Arabia, northeastern Jordan, southeastern Syria, and western Iraq. 32°N 40°E (pp. R18–19, 17, 90, 105)

Taiwan [TY•WAHN] Island country off the southeast coast of China; seat of the Chinese Nationalist government. 23°N 122°E (pp. R3, R5, R23, 225, 765, 773)

Tajikistan [tah•JIH•kih•STAN] Central Asian country. 39°N 70°E (p. 883)

Taklimakan [TAH•kluh•muh•KAHN] **Desert** Desert in northwestern China. 40°N 83°E (p. 225)

Tannenberg Village in northeast Poland. 53°N 20°E (p. 786)

Tanzania [TAN•zuh•NEE•uh] East African country. 7°S 34°E (p. 870)

Tarsus [TAHR•suhs] City in southern Turkey. 37°N 34°E (pp. 352, 361, 367)

Tenochtitlán [tay•NAWCH•teet•LAHN] Aztec city in the Valley of Mexico. 19°N 99°W (pp. 575, 582, 593, 662, 663)

Teotihuacán [TAY•oh•TEE•wuh•KAHN] Site in central Mexico that in ancient times was one of the largest cities in the world. 19°N 98°W (pp. 572, 575)

Turkmenistan [tuhrk•MEH•nuh•STAN] Central Asian country on the Caspian Sea. 41°N 56°E (p. 883)

Thailand [TY•LAND] Southeast Asian country east of Myanmar. 17°N 101°E (pp. 765, 773, 825, 849)

Thar [TAHR] **Desert** Desert in northwestern India. 25°W 72°E (p. 219)

Thebes [THEEBZ] Ancient city and former capital of Egypt. 25°N 32°E (pp. 28, 39, 59, 62, 70, 75, 132, 479)

Thermopylae [thuhr•MAH•puh•lee] Mountain pass in ancient Greece. 38°N 22°E (p. 134)

Tian [tee•AHN] **Shan** Mountain range in central Asia. 45°N 85°E (p. 225)

Tiber [TY•buhr] **River** River in north Italy. 42°N 12°E (pp. 263, 269, 274)

Tibet [tuh•BEHT] Country in central Asia. 32°N 83°E (pp. 246, 409, 424, 425, 439, 554, 773, 845)

Tigris [TY•gruhs] **River** River in southeastern Turkey and Iraq that merges with the Euphrates River. 34°N 44°E (pp. 17, 121, 132, 176, 179, 189, 246, 255, 293, 297, 329, 374, 380, 383, 397)

Tikrit Town in Iraq. 34°N 43°E (p. 799)

Timbuktu [TIHM•BUHK•TOO] City of Muslim learning in West Africa. 16°N 3°W (pp. 444, 448, 451, 460, 468, 473, 479)

Timor [TEE•mor] Island of southeast Indonesia. 2°S 123°E (p. 765)

Tlaxcala [tlah•SKAH•luh] State in east central Mexico. 19°N 98°W (p. 575)

Togo [TOH•goh] West African country. 8°N 1°E (pp. 767, 870)

Tokyo [TOH•kee•OH] Capital of Japan. 34°N 131°E (pp. R3, 485, 507, 771, 773, 778, 825)

Toledo [to•LAI•do] Historic city in central Spain. 39°N 4°W (p. 555)

Tours [TOOR] City in west central France. 47°N 0°E (p. 516)

Trafalgar [truh•FAL•guhr] Cape off the southwest coast of Spain. 36°N 6°W (p. 722)

Transjordan Southwest Asian country, now called Jordan. 30°N 38°E (p. 792)

Tripoli [TRIH•puh•lee] Capital city of Libya. 32°N 13°E (pp. R3, 385, 448, 479, 767)

Tunis [TOO•nuhs] Capital city of Tunisia. 36°N 10°E (p. 385)

Tunisia [too•NEE•zhuh] North African country on the Mediterrean Sea. 35°N 10°E (pp. 767, 870)

Turkey [TUHR•kee] Country in southeastern Europe and western Asia. 38°N 32°E (pp. R3, R22, 176, 789, 790, 792)

Turkmenistan [tuhrk•MEH•nuh•STAN] Central Asian country on the Caspian Sea. 40°N 56°E (pp. R3, R22, 176)

Tuscany [TUS•kuh•nee] Region of northwest Italy. 43°N 11°E (p. 747)

Tyre [TYR] Town in southern Lebanon on the Mediterranean Sea. 33°N 35°E (pp. 17, 90, 121, 132, 176, 352, 542)

Tyrrhenian [tuh•REE•nee•uhn] Sea Arm of the Mediterranean Sea near Italy. 40°N 12°E (pp. 263, 609, 653)

Uganda [yoo•GAHN•dah] East African country. 2°N 32°E (pp. 767, 870)

Ukraine [yoo•KRAYN] Eastern European country west of Russia on the Black Sea. 49°N 30°E (pp. R3, R17, 548, 883)

Ulm City in southern Germany on the Danube River. 48°N 8°E (p. 722)

United Kingdom Western European island country made up of England, Scotland, Wales, and Northern Ireland. 57°N 2°W (pp. 722, 725, 781, 786, 790, 891, 832)

United States Country in North America made up of 50 states, mostly between Canada and Mexico. 38°N 110°W (pp. 753, 836)

Ur [OOR] Ancient city in Mesopotamia. 32°N 47°E (p. 17)

Ural [YUHR•uhl] **Mountains** Mountain range in Russia. 56°N 58°E (p. R5)

Uruguay [YUR•uh•GWAY] South American country south of Brazil. 33°S 56°W (pp. 749, 861)

Uruk Ancient settlement in Mesopotamia. 33°N 45°E (p. 17)

Uzbekistan [UZ•BEH•kih•STAN] Central Asian country south of Kazakhstan. 42°N 60°E (p. 883)

Venezuela [veh•nuh•ZWAY•luh] South American country on the Caribbean Sea between Colombia and Guyana. 8°N 65°W (pp. 749, 861)

Venice [VEHN•ihs] City in northeastern Italy. 45°N 12°E (pp. 522, 542, 548, 555, 608, 609, 653, 703, 725, 747)

Versailles [vuhr•SY] City in north-central France. 48°N 2°E (pp. 714, 716, 722)

Vienna [vee•EH•nuh] Capital of Austria. 48°N 16°E (pp. 714, 722, 725, 781, 786).

Vietnam [vee•EHT•NAHM] Southeast Asian country east of Laos and Cambodia. 18°N 107°E (pp. 847, 849)

Vistula [vis•TOO•lah] **River** Longest river in Poland. 52°N 20°E (p. 513)

Vladivostok [vluhd•yi•vah•STOK] City of extreme southeast Russia. 43°N 131°E (pp. 773, 778)

Volga [VOL•guh] **River** River in western Russia, longest in Europe. 47°N 46°E (pp. R3, R5, 424, 425, 513, 540)

Wales Principality of the United Kingdom on the western peninsula of the island of Great Britain. 52°N 4°W (p. 757)

Warsaw [WAWR•SAW] Capital of Poland. 52°N 21°E (pp. 725, 747)

Warsaw, Grand Duchy of Political unit created by Napoleon I in 1807 to restore Polish lands seized by Prussia. (p. 722)

Washington, D.C. Capital of the United States, in the District of Columbia. 39°N 77°W (p. 744)

Waterloo [WAW•tuhr•LOO] Town in central Belgium. 51°N 5°E (pp. 714, 722)

Wei He [WAY HUH] River in central China. 34°N 108°E (pp. 225, 226, 230, 241)

West Bank Disputed territory of southwest Asia between Israel and Jordan. 31°N 35°E (p. 875)

Western Sahara [suh•HAR•uh] Country in northwest Africa. 24°N 13°W (p. 870)

West Germany Officially called the Federal Republic of Germany. 51°N 8°E (pp. 832, 834)

West Indies Islands in the Caribbean Sea. 19°N 79°W (p. 473)

Wittenberg [WIH•tuhn•BUHRG] City in east central Germany on the Elbe River. 51°N 12°E (pp. 633, 645)

Xianyang [SHYEHN•YAHNG] City in northern China. 34°N 108°E (p. 241)

Xi Jiang [SHEE•JYAHNG] River in southern China. 24°N 110°E (p. 241)

Yathrib [YA•thruhb] Town in Saudi Arabia, now called Madinah. 24°N 39°E (p. 374)

Yellow Sea Arm of the Pacific Ocean bordered by China, North Korea, and South Korea. 35°N 122°E (pp. R5, R23, 225, 226, 230, 241, 424, 431, 485, 773, 778, 811, 838)

Yugoslavia [YOO•goh•SLAH•vee•uh] Eastern European country south of Hungary; includes Serbia and Montenegro. 44°N 21°E (pp. 790, 832, 897)

Zama [ZAY•muh] Town in northern Africa. 35°N 9°E (p. 274)

Zambia [ZAM•bee•uh] Southern African country. 14°S 24°E (p. 870)

Zanzibar [ZAHN•zuh•bawr] City of Tanzania on Zanzibar Island. 6°S 39°E (p. 767)

Zhanjiang [JAHN•JYAHNG] City of southeast China. 21°N 110°E (p. 773)

Zhou [JOH] Empire in what is now northern China. 34°N 110°E (p. 230)

Zimbabwe [zihm•BAH•bway] Southern African country. 18°S 30°E (p. 870)

Gazetteer

Index

Italicized page numbers refer to illustrations. The following abbreviations are used in the index:
m = map, c = chart, p = photograph or picture, g = graph, crt = cartoon, ptg = painting, q = quote

A

Index

Index

Index

Index

Index

Index

Index

Q

Index

Index

Index

Acknowledgements

Text

33 "The Mesopotamian View of Death" from *Poems of Heaven and Hell From Ancient Mesopotamia,* translated by N.K. Sandars (Penguin Classics, 1971), copyright © N.K. Sandars, 1971. Reprinted by permission of Penguin Group (UK). **53** From *The Prince Who Knew his Fate: an Ancient Egyptian Tale,* translated from hieroglyphs and illustrated by Lise Manniche, copyright © 1982 by Lise Manniche and IBIS. Used by permission of Philomel Books, A Division of Penguin Young Readers Group, A Member of Penguin Group (USA) Inc., 345 Hudson Street, New York, NY 10014. All rights reserved. **239** Excerpt from "Higher Good Is like Water" from *The Essential Tao,* translated and presented by Thomas Cleary. Copyright © 1991 by Thomas Cleary. Reprinted by permission of HarperCollins Inc. **264** Excerpt from *Virgil's Aeneid,* translated by Robert Fitzgerald. Translation copyright © 1981, 1982, 1982 by Robert Fitzgerald. Reprinted by permission of Random House, Inc. **311** "A Wild Goose Chase: The Story of Philemon and Baucis" reprinted with the permission of Margaret K. McElderry Books, an imprint of Simon & Schuster Children's Publishing Division from *Roman Myths* by Geraldine McCaughrean. Text copyright © 1999 by Geraldine McCaughrean. **420** "Seeing a Friend Off" and "Still Night Thoughts" by Li Bo, from *The Columbia Book of Chinese Poetry,* translated by Burton Watson. Copyright © 1984 by Columbia University Press. Reprinted by permission. **421** "Spring Landscape" by Tu Fu, translated by David Hinton, from *The Selected Poems of Tu Fu,* copyright © 1988, 1989 by David Hinton. Reprinted by permission of New Directions Publishing Corp. **454** "Mali-The Madinka Empire: Sundiata: The Hungering Lion" from *African Kingdoms of the Past,* copyright © 1996 by Kenny Mann. Reprinted by permission of the author. **470** "Dignity" by E.A. Babalola, from *Ants Will not Eat Your Fingers: A Selection of Traditional African Poems,* edited by Leonard W. Dobb. Copyright © 1966 by Leonard W. Dobb. Reprinted by permission of Walker and Company. **501** Tanka from the *Kokinshu,* from *From the Country of Eight Islands* by Hiroaki Sato and Burton Watson, copyright © 1981 by Hiroaki Sato and Burton Watson. Used by permission of Doubleday, a division of Random House, Inc. **627** "A Midsummer Night's Dream" from *The Children's Shakespeare* by E. Nesbit. Copyright © 1938 by Random House, Inc. Reprinted by permission. **820** "The Unexpected Treasure," adapted by Gary Schmidt from *Mara's Stories: Glimmers in the Darkness* by Gary Schmidt, © 2001 by Gary Schmidt. Reprinted by permission of Henry Holt and Company LLC. **932** Excerpt from *Gilgamesh* by John Gardner and John Maier, copyright © 1984 by the Estate of John Gardner and John Maier. Used by permission of Alfred A. Knopf, a division of Random House, Inc. **933** Excerpt from Genesis 12 from *The Revised English Bible,* copyright © 1989 Oxford University Press. Reprinted by permission. **934** Excerpts from *The Essential Confucius,* translated and presented by Thomas Cleary. Copyright © 1992 by Thomas Cleary. Reprinted by permission of HarperCollins Inc. **935** "Night" from *The Rig Veda,* translated by Wendy Diniger O'Flaherty (Penguin Classics, 1981), copyright © Wendy Doniger O'Flaherty, 1981. Reprinted by permission of Penguin Group (UK). **938** "Mali in the Fourteenth Century" from *The African Past: Chronicles from Antiquity to Modern Time,* by Basil Davidson. Copyright © 1964 by Basil Davidson. Reprinted by permission of Curtis Brown Ltd. **940** Excerpt from "Epic Description of the Beseiged City" from *The Broken Spears* by Miguel Leon-Portilla. Copyright © 1962, 1990 by Miguel Leon-Portilla. Expanded and updated Edition © 1992 by Miguel Leon-Portilla. Reprinted by permission of Beacon Press, Boston. **941** From *The Kidnapped Prince: The Life of Olaudah Equiano,* by Olaudah Equiano, adapted by Ann Cameron. Copyright © 1995 by Ann Cameron. Reprinted by permission of Alfred A. Knopf, a division of Random House, Inc.

943 From "I Have a Dream" by Dr. Martin Luther King, Jr. Reprinted by arrangement with the Estate of Martin Luther King, Jr., c/o Writers House as agent for the proprietor, New York, NY. Copyright 1963 Martin Luther King, Jr., copyright renewed 1991 Corretta Scott King. **943** From Nelson Mandela's Nobel Peace Prize acceptance speech. Reprinted by permission of The Nobel Institute.

Glencoe would like to acknowledge the artists and agencies who participated in illustrating this program: American Artists Rep., INC.; Mapping Specialists, Inc.; Studio Inklink; WildLife Art Ltd.

Photo Credits

COVER (bkgd)Christie's Images/CORBIS, (tl)Ric Ergenbright/CORBIS, (tr)Paul Hardy/CORBIS, (b)Setboun/CORBIS; **GH1** (t)Dallas and John Heaton/CORBIS, (c)Jamie Harron CORBIS, (b)Owen Franken/CORBIS; **GH2** Getty Images; **GH3** Getty Images; **Tools 0** (t)Ron Sheridan/Ancient Art & Architecture Collection, (bl)AFP Worldwide, (br)James King-Holmes/Photo Researchers, (bkgd)Getty Images; **Tools 1** (t)Scala/Art Resource, NY, (b)Nimatallah/Art Resource, NY; **Tools 2** (t)American Museum of Natural History, (tc)Scala/Art Resource, NY, (bc)Chester Beatty Library, Dublin/Bridgeman Art Library, (b)Reunion des Musees Nationaux/Art Resource, NY; **Tools 3** (t)National Museums of Scotland/Bridgeman Art Library, (c)Borromeo/Art Resource, NY, (b)Asian Art & Archaeology/CORBIS; **Tools 4** (t)Richard T. Nowitz/CORBIS, (b)David Hiser/Getty Images; **Tools 6** (t)Lawrence Manning/CORBIS, (b)Vanni Archive/CORBIS; **Tools 7** (c)Frans Lemmens Getty Images, (t)J. Bertrand/Photo Researchers, (br)Giraudon/Art Resource, NY; **Tools 10** Matthews/Network/CORBIS Saba; **Tools 11** (t)Dan Helms/NewSport/CORBIS, (tc)Tom Lovell/National Geographic Society Image Collection, (bc)Art Resource, NY, (b)CORBIS; **Tools 12** (t)The Art Archive/Bibliothèque Nationale Paris, (tc)Christopher Liu/ChinaStock, (bc)Jean-Leon Huens/National Geographic Society Image Collection, (b)NASA Media Resource Center; **Tools 13** (t)Ed Kashi/CORBIS, (b)Bettmann/CORBIS; **0** (t)Reunion des Musees Nationaux/Art Resource, NY, (c)John Heaton/CORBIS, (b)Tom Lovell/National Geographic Society Image Collection; **1** (tl)Brooklyn Museum of Art, New York/Charles Edwin Wilbour Fund/Bridgeman Art Library, (bl)Erich Lessing/Art Resource, NY, (others)SuperStock; **2-3** ©Worldsat International Inc. 2004, All Rights Reserved; **2** (t)S. Fiore SuperStock, (c)Scala/Art Resource, NY, (bl)Giansanti Gianni/CORBIS Sygma, (bc)Louvre Museum, Paris/Bridgeman Art Library, (br)Metropolitan Museum of Art, Rogers Fund and Edward S. Harkness Gift,1929 (29.3.3); **3** (t to b)Sylvain Grandadam/Getty Images, Timothy Kendall/Museum of Fine Arts, Boston, Gary Cralle/Getty Images, (l to r)O. Louis Mazzatenta/National Geographic Society Image Collection, SuperStock, Bettmann/CORBIS; **4-5** Georg Gerster/Photo Researchers; **10** Michael Holford; **11** American Museum of Natural History; **12** (tr)Giansanti Gianni/CORBIS Sygma, (bl)Kenneth Garrett; **14** (l)Michael Holford, (r)Ron Sheridan/Ancient Art & Architecture Collection; **17** Hirmer Verlag; **18** Scala/Art Resource, NY; **19** (l)Nik Wheeler CORBIS, (r)Michael Holford; **20** Scala/Art Resource, NY; **21** (l)Mesopotamian Iraq Museum, Baghdad, Iraq/Giraudon/Bridgeman Art Library, (r)Will Hart/PhotoEdit; **22** akg-images; **24** Reunion des Musees Nationaux/Art Resource, NY; **25** Louvre, Paris/Bridgeman Art Library; **28** Boltin Picture Library; **29** Gianni Dagli Orti/CORBIS; **30** S. Fiore/SuperStock; **31** Scala/Art Resource, NY; **34-35** Brian Lawrence/Image State; **37** Gianni Dagli Orti CORBIS; **40** John Lawrence/Getty Images; **41** Erich Lessing/Art Resource, NY; **42** (l)Giraudon/Art Resource, NY, (r)Gianni Dagli Orti/CORBIS; **43** (l)Caroline Penn/CORBIS, (r)Kenneth Garrett; **48** Sylvain Grandadam/Getty Images; **50** (t)The British Museum, (b)Musee du Louvre, Paris Explorer/SuperStock;

51 Musee du Louvre, Paris/Explorer SuperStock; 52 John Heaton/CORBIS; 60 Gianni Dagli Orti/CORBIS; 61 (l)Smithsonian Institution, (r)file photo; 63 Metropolitan Museum of Art, Rogers Fund and Edward S. Harkness Gift,1929 (29.3.3); 64 Erich Lessing/Art Resource, NY; 65 (t)Egyptian National Museum, Cairo/SuperStock, (b)Gavin Hellier/Getty Images; 66 (t)Michael Holford, (b)O. Louis Mazzatenta National Geographic Society Image Collection; 69 Egyptian Expedition of The Metropolitan Museum of Art, The Rogers Fund, 1930 (30.4.21)/The Metropolitan Museum of Art; 70 Timothy Kendall/Museum of Fine Arts, Boston; 71 Brooklyn Museum of Art, New York/Charles Edwin Wilbour Fund/Bridgeman Art Library; 72 SuperStock; 73 Egyptian National Museum, Cairo/SuperStock; 76–77 Anthony Pidgeon/Lonely Planet Images; 79 CORBIS; 81 Tom Lovell National Geographic Society Image Collection; 82 (l)North Wind Picture Archives, (r)Leland Bobbe/Getty Images; 83 (t)The Israel Museum, Jerusalem, (c)Stock Montage/SuperStock, (b)Laura Zito/Photo Researchers; 84 (l)Mary Evans Picture Library, (r)Charles & Josette Lenars/CORBIS; 87 Mary Evans Picture Library; 88 (t)Bettmann/CORBIS, (b)Private Collection/Bridgeman Art Library; 89 Stock Montage/SuperStock; 94 (l)Richard T. Nowitz/CORBIS, (c)Bill Aro/PhotoEdit, (r)SuperStock; 95 Walker Art Gallery, Liverpool, Merseyside, UK, National Museums Liverpool/Bridgeman Art Library; 96 CORBIS; 97 (l)Christie's Images Bridgeman Art Library, (r)Nathan Benn CORBIS; 98 Lawrence Migdale Getty Images; 99 SuperStock; 100 Richard T. Nowitz/CORBIS; 101 (t)Dave Bartruff/CORBIS, (c)Gary Cralle/Getty Images, (b)Paul Chesley/Getty Images; 102 Peter Turnley/CORBIS; 103 (t)Stock Montage/SuperStock, (b)SuperStock; 106 (t)Erich Lessing/Art Resource, NY, (b)Louvre Museum, Paris/Bridgeman Art Library; 107 (t)Boltin Picture Library, (tr)Stock Montage/SuperStock, (c)Smithsonian Institution, (b)CORBIS; 108 (t)National Museums of Scotland/Bridgeman Art Library, (c)Borromeo/Art Resource, NY, (b)file photo; 109 (t)Scala/Art Resource, NY, (c)Hugh Sitton/Getty Images, (b)Erich Lessing/Art Resource, NY; 110–111 ©Worldsat International Inc. 2004, All Rights Reserved; 110 (tl)Getty Images, (c)Archives Charmet/Bridgeman Art Library, (bl)Scala/Art Resource, NY, (bcl)Christie's, London/Bridgeman Art Library/SuperStock, (bcr)Vanni/Art Resource, NY, (br)Scala/Art Resource, NY; 111 (t to b)Robert Harding Picture Library, Victoria & Albert Museum, London/Art Resource, NY, Digital Vision, (l to r) Alinari/Art Resource, NY, Sandro Vannini/CORBIS, Hulton/Getty Images, National Geographic Society Image Collection; 112–113 Vanni Archive/CORBIS; 115 Foto Marburg/Art Resource, NY; 117 Steve Vidler SuperStock; 118 (t)Gianni Dagli Orti/CORBIS, (bl)Nimatallah/Art Resource, NY; 119 (t)Alberto Incrocci/Getty Images, (b)Nimatallah/Art Resource, NY; 122 The Art Archive/National Archaeological Museum Athens/Dagli Orti; 123 National Museums of Scotland/Bridgeman Art Library; 125 The Art Archive/E.T. Archive; 126 Foto Marburg/Art Resource, NY; 127 (l)Bettmann CORBIS, (r)Michael Holford; 128 (l)Tom Lovell/National Geographic Society Image Collection, (r)Dan Helms/NewSport/CORBIS; 129 (t)Nimatallah/Art Resource, NY, (b)The Brooklyn Museum, Charles Wilbour Fund; 130 Ronald Sheridan/Ancient Art & Architecture Collection; 131 (l)Mary Evans Picture Library, (c)Bettmann/CORBIS, (r)Roger Wood/CORBIS; 132 SEF/Art Resource, NY; 133 The Art Archive/Dagli Orti; 135 Bettmann/CORBIS; 136 Peter Connolly; 139 Steve Vidler/SuperStock; 141 (t)Scala/Art Resource, NY, (b)Vanni Archive/CORBIS; 142 Smithsonian Institution; 143 Nimatallah/Art Resource, NY; 144 Gianni Dagli Orti/CORBIS; 145 Scala/Art Resource, NY; 147 Nimatallah/Art Resource, NY; 150–151 Roger Wood/CORBIS; 153 Alinari/Art Resource, NY; 155 (cw from top)Bettman/CORBIS, The Art Archive/National Archaeological Museum Athens/Dagli Orti, The Art Archive/Achaeological

Museum Tarquina/Dagli Orti, Lauros/Giraudon Bridgeman Art Library, Lauros/Giraudon/Bridgeman Art Library, The Art Archive/Archaeological Museum Venice/Dagli Orti, Fitzwilliam Museum, University of Cambridge, UK/Bridgeman Art Library, Giraudon/Bridgeman Art Library, Peter Willi/Bridgeman Art Library, Wolfgang Kaehler/CORBIS; 156 Mary Evans Picture Library; 157 James L. Stanfield/National Geographic Society Image Collection; 158 Alinari/Art Resource, NY; 159 Scala/Art Resource, NY; 160 (l)SuperStock, (r)Eric Robert/CORBIS; 161 (t)Erich Lessing/Art Resource, NY, (b)Mary Evans Picture Library; 162 (tl)Joel W. Rogers/CORBIS, (tc)Dave Bartruff/CORBIS, (tr)Vanni Archive/CORBIS, (b)Charles O'Rear/CORBIS; 168 Scala/Art Resource, NY; 169 Scala/Art Resource, NY; 170 (l)Mary Evans Picture Library, (cl)Scala/Art Resource, NY, (cr)Museo Capitolino, Rome/E.T. Archives, London/SuperStock, (r)Reunion des Musees Nationaux/Art Resource, NY; 172 (t)SEF/Art Resource, NY, (b)Scala/Art Resource, NY; 175 file photo; 177 Robert Harding Picture Library; 178 (l)Yan Arthus-Bertrand/CORBIS, (r)Archives Charmet/Bridgeman Art Library; 180 David Lees/CORBIS; 181 Sandro Vannini/CORBIS; 183 Araldo de Luca/CORBIS; 184 Erich Lessing/Art Resource, NY; 185 North Wind Picture Archives; 186 Scala/Art Resource, NY; 187 Sandro Vannini/CORBIS; 190–191 David Cumming/CORBIS; 196 (l)Robert Harding Picture Library, (c)National Museum of India, New Delhi, India/Bridgeman Art Library, (r)Borromeo/Art Resource, NY, (br)Harappan National Museum of Karachi, Karachi, Pakistan/Bridgeman Art Library; 200 (l)Carl Purcell/The Purcell Team, (r)AFP Worldwide; 203 (l)Robert Harding Picture Library, (r)Borromeo Art Resource, NY; 204 (t)SEF/Art Resource, NY, (b)Victoria & Albert Museum, London/Art Resource, NY; 205 Rajesh Bedi/National Geographic Image Collection; 206 Borromeo/Art Resource, NY; 207 (l)Archivo Iconografico, S.A./CORBIS, (r)Christie's Images, London Bridgeman Art Library SuperStock; 208 Sheldan Collins/CORBIS; 211 (l)Robert Harding Picture Library, (r)Hugh Sitton/Getty Images; 212 (l)Ancient Art & Architecture Collection, (r)Hulton Archive/Getty Images News Services; 214 The British Library, London/Bridgeman Art Library; 217 SEF/Art Resource, NY; 220–221 D.E. Cox/Getty Images; 223 file photo; 227 Asian Art & Archaeology CORBIS; 228 Bridgeman/Art Resource, NY; 229 (bl)file photo, (br)The Art Archive/ Musee Cernuschi Paris/Dagli Orti, (others)Asian Art & Archaeology/ CORBIS; 231 file photo; 232 (l)Robert Frerck/Odyssey Productions, (c)ChinaStock, (r)Dennis Cox; 234 Lawrence Manning/CORBIS; 235 (t)Seattle Museum of Art/Laurie Platt Winfrey, (b)Asian Art & Archaeology/CORBIS, (others)Christopher Liu/ChinaStock; 236 Chen Yixin ChinaStock; 237 Vanni/Art Resource, NY; 238 (tl)Robert Frerck/Odyssey Productions, (tc)ChinaStock, (tr)Dennis Cox, (b)Giraudon/Art Resource, NY; 243 (t)ChinaStock, (b)Robert Harding Picture Library; 244 Bibliotheque Nationale, Paris; 245 (l)Ontario Science Centre, (r)Dean Conger/CORBIS; 247 (l)The Art Archive/National Palace Museum Taiwan, (others)The Art Archive/British Library; 249 (t)file photo, (b)Giraudon/Art Resource, NY; 252 (l)Scala/Art Resource, NY, (c)Ancient Art & Architecture Collection, (r)Burstein Collection/CORBIS; 253 (tl)Erich Lessing/Art Resource, NY, (c)Victoria & Albert Museum, London/ Art Resource, NY, (bl)Ronald Sheridan/Ancient Art & Architecture Collection, (br)The British Museum, London/Bridgeman Art Library; 254 (l)Cott Nero DIV f.25v Portrait of St. Matthew/British Library, London/Bridgeman Art Library, (tr)Scala/Art Resource, NY, (br)Ancient Art & Architecture Collection; 255 (t)Pierre Belzeaux/Photo Researchers, (c)Brian Lawrence/SuperStock, (l)Nik Wheeler; 256–257 ©Worldsat International Inc. 2004, All Rights Reserved; 256 (t)Ric Ergenbright, (c)Sean Sexton Collection/CORBIS, (bl)Robert Emmett Bright Photo Researchers, (bcl)Scala/Art Resource, NY, (bcr)Danita Delimont

Ancient Art & Architecture Collection, (br)Werner Forman/Art Resource, NY; **257** (t to b)Brian Lawrence/SuperStock, Richard T. Nowitz CORBIS, Nabeel Turner/Getty Images, (l to r)Scala/Art Resource, NY, Scala/Art Resource, NY, Earl & Nazima Kowall/CORBIS, Bettmann CORBIS; **258–259** Roy Rainford Robert Harding/Getty Images; **261** Ronald Sheridan/ Ancient Art & Architecture Collection; **264** Francis Schroeder SuperStock; **265** (t)file photo, (b)Scala/Art Resource, NY; **266** Stock Montage; **267** Prenestino Museum, Rome/E.T. Archives, London/SuperStock; **269** Michael Holford; **270** Ronald Sheridan/Ancient Art & Architecture Collection; **271** The Art Archive Archeological Museum Beirut/Dagli Orti; **272** North Wind Picture Archives; **273** Alinari/ Art Resource, NY; **278** The Art Archive/Archeological Museum Aquileia/Dagli Orti; **279** Scala/Art Resource, NY; **280** (tl)Archaeological Museum, Venice/E.T. Archives, London/SuperStock, (bl)Louvre, Paris Bridgeman Art Library, (c)Reunion des Musees Nationaux/ Art Resource, NY, (r)Ronald Sheridan/Ancient Art & Architecture Collection; **281** (l)SuperStock, (c)Museo e Gallerie Nazionali di Capodimonte, Naples, Italy/Bridgeman Art Library, (r)Mary Evans Picture Library; **282** Bettmann/CORBIS; **283** North Wind Picture Archive; **284** Nimatallah/Art Resource, NY; **285** Bridgeman Art Library; **287** Victoria & Albert Museum, London/ Bridgeman Art Library; **288** (t)C. Hellier/Ancient Art & Architecture Collection, (tc)Ronald Sheridan Ancient Art & Architecture Collection, (bc)The Art Archive/Museo Capitolino Rome/Dagli Orti, (b)The Art Archive/ Staatliche Glypothek Munich/Dagli Orti; **289** Robert Emmett Bright/Photo Researchers; **290** (l)Seamus Culligan ZUMA/CORBIS, (r)Jonathan Blair/CORBIS; **291** Ric Ergenbright; **292** (l)Roma, Museo Nazion/Art Resource, NY, (cr)Staatliche Glypothek, Munich, Germany/E.T. Archive, London/ SuperStock, (others)Archivo Iconografico, S.A./CORBIS; **294** (tl)B. Wilson/ Ancient Art & Architecture Collection, (tr)Erich Lessing/Art Resource, NY, (others)The Newark Museum/Art Resource, NY; **295** Michael Holford; **298–299** Picture Finders Ltd./eStock; **301** Erich Lessing/Art Resource, NY; **303** Nik Wheeler/CORBIS; **304** Bibliotheque Nationale, Paris, France, Giraudon/Bridgeman Art Library; **306** Pierre Belzeaux/Photo Researchers; **307** (t)Scala/Art Resource, NY, (b)Erich Lessing/Art Resource, NY; **308** Scala/ Art Resource, NY; **309** (l)Stanley Searberg, (r)Giraudon/Art Resource, NY; **310** Reunion des Musees Nationaux/Art Resource, NY; **318** CORBIS; **319** Scala/Art Resource, NY; **320** The Newark Museum/Art Resource, NY; **321** (t)Hagia Sophia, Istanbul, Turkey/E.T. Archives, London/SuperStock, (b)C. Boisvieux/Photo Researchers; **322** Scala/Art Resource, NY; **324** Mary Evans Picture Library; **325** (l)Sean Sexton Collection/CORBIS, (r)Donald Dietz/ Stock Boston PictureQuest; **328** Stapleton Collection, UK/Bridgeman Art Library; **330** Scala/Art Resource, NY; **331** Andre Durenceau/National Geographic Society Image Collection; **332** (l)Giraudon/Art Resource, NY, (c)Brian Lawrence SuperStock, (r)Ronald Sheridan/Ancient Art & Architecture Collection; **333** The Art Archive/Haghia Sophia Istanbul/Dagli Orti; **334** Ancient Art & Architecture Collection; **335** Giraudon/Art Resource, NY; **338–339** Richard T. Nowitz/CORBIS; **341** akg-images/Orsi Battaglini; **343** Nathan Benn CORBIS; **344** (l)Reunion des Musees Nationaux/Art Resource, NY, (r)Scala Art Resource, NY; **345** (l)Erich Lessing/Art Resource, NY, (r)Tate Gallery, London/Art Resource, NY; **346** (t)Elio Ciol/CORBIS, (b)Scala/Art Resource, NY; **347** Louvre, Paris/Bridgeman Art Library; **348** The New York Public Library/Art Resource, NY; **349** (t)Danita Delimont/Ancient Art & Architecture Collection, (b)Victoria & Albert Museum, London/Art Resouce, NY; **350** akg images/Orsi Battaglini; **353** Scala/Art Resource, NY; **356** Cott Nero DIV f.25v Portrait of St. Matthew/British Library, London/Bridgeman Art Library; **357** (t)Scala/Art Resource, NY, (b)Alinari/Art Resource, NY; **359** Scala/Art Resource, NY; **360** (t)Scala/Art

Resource, NY, (b)Michael Holford; **362** (l)Galleria dell' Accademia, Florence, Italy/Bridgeman Art Library, (r)PRAT/CORBIS; **363** C.M. Dixon/Photo Resources; **364** Giraudon/Art Resource, NY; **365** Cott Nero DIV f.25v Portrait of St. Matthew/British Library, London/Bridgeman Art Library; **368–369** Nabeel Turner/Getty Images; **371** Paul Dupuy Museum, Toulouse, France/Lauros-Giraudon, Paris/SuperStock; **373** (l)DiMaggio/Kalish/CORBIS, (r)Kevin Fleming/CORBIS; **375** Bibliotheque Nationale, Paris/Bridgeman Art Library; **376** (t)C. Hellier Ancient Art & Architecture Collection, (b)George Chan/Photo Researchers; **377** (l)AFP/CORBIS, (r)ARAMCO; **380** The Art Archive/Hazem Palace Damascus/Dagli Orti; **381** Burstein Collection/CORBIS; **382** Alison Wright CORBIS; **383** Nik Wheeler; **384** James L. Stanfield/National Geographic Society Image Collection; **385** Bettmann/CORBIS; **386** Chester Beatty Library, Dublin/Bridgeman Art Library; **387** (l)Mary Evans Picture Library, (c)Bettmann/CORBIS; **388** Richard Bickel/CORBIS; **389** (t)Jeff Greenberg Photo Researchers, (b)The Art Archive/Harper Collins Publishers; **390** (l)Stapleton Collection, UK/Bridgeman Art Library, (r)David Turnley CORBIS; **391** (t)R & S Michaud/Woodfin Camp & Assoc., (b)Paul Dupuy Museum, Toulouse, France/Lauros-Giraudon, Paris/Super-Stock; **392** Bettmann/CORBIS; **394** Galen Rowell/CORBIS; **395** ARAMCO; **398** (t)Scala Art Resource, NY, (bl)Smithsonian Institution, (bc)Michael Holford, (br)Giraudon/Art Resource, NY; **399** (tl)Stock Montage, (tr)Michael Holford, (c)Scala/Art Resource, NY, (bl)Roy Rainford/Robert Harding/Getty Images, (br)Bibliotheque Nationale, Paris/Bridgeman Art Library; **400** (tl)The British Museum/Topham-HIP/The Image Works, (c)Angelo Hornak/CORBIS, (bl)Ronald Sheridan/Ancient Art & Architecture Collection, (br)Erich Lessing/Art Resource, NY; **401** (tl)Aldona Sabalis/Photo Researchers, (tc)National Museum of Taipei, (tr)Werner Forman/Art Resource, NY, (c)Ancient Art & Architecture Collection, (bl)Ron Dahlquist/SuperStock, (br)akg-images; **402–403** ©Worldsat International Inc. 2004, All Rights Reserved; **402** (t)Stock Boston, (c)Peter Adams/Getty Images, (bl)Art Resource, NY, (bcl)Ali Meyer/CORBIS, (bcr)Mary Evans Picture Library, (br)Kadokawa/Ancient Art & Architecture Collection; **403** (t to b)Tom Wagner/Odyssey Productions, Greg Gawlowski/Lonley Planet Images, Jim Zuckerman/CORBIS, (l to r)Museum of Fine Arts, Houston, Texas, USA, Robert Lee Memorial Collection, gift of Sarah C. Blaffer/Bridgeman Art Library, Courtesy Museum of Maritimo (Barcelona); Ramon Manent CORBIS, ChinaStock, Christie's Images/CORBIS; **404–405** CORBIS; **407** Kadokawa/Ancient Art & Architecture Collection; **410** (l)The Art Archive Bibliothèque Nationale Paris, (r)Christopher Liu/ChinaStock; **412** Ira Kirschenbaum/Stock Boston; **413** Bettmann/CORBIS; **414** Snark/Art Resource, NY; **415** Michael Freeman/CORBIS; **417** (l)Keren Su/CORBIS, (r)Philadelphia Free Library/ AKG, Berlin SuperStock; **419** Werner Forman Art Resource, NY; **420** The Art Archive/British Library; **421** (l)The Art Archive/National Peace Museum Taiwan, (c)Naomi Duguid/Asia Access, (r)Private Collection/Bridgeman Art Library; **422** (l)The British Museum Topham-HIP/The Image Works, (c)Laurie Platt Winfrey, (r)Seattle Art Museum/CORBIS; **424** (t)National Museum of Taipei, (b)J. Bertrand/Photo Researchers; **425** James L. Stanfield; **426** Werner Forman Art Archive; **427** (t)Kadokawa/Ancient Art & Architecture Collection, (b)Bibliotheque Nationale, Paris, France/Bridgeman Art Library; **428** The Bodleian Library, Oxford, Ms. Bodl. 264, fol.219R; **429** Hulton/Getty Images; **431** Christie's Images/CORBIS; **432** SEF/Art Resource, NY; **433** ChinaStock; **434** ChinaStock; **435** The Art Archive; **436** Bonhams, London, UK/Bridgeman Art Library; **437** Laurie Platt Winfrey; **440–441** Peter Adams/Getty Images; **443** Werner Forman/Art Resource, NY; **445** (t)Christine Osborne/Lonely Planet Images, (tc)Frans Lemmens/Getty Images, (bc)Brand X Pictures, (b)Michael Dwyer Stock Boston/PictureQuest; **449** Volkmar Kurt